C0-ABJ-463

The Handbook of Employee Benefits
Design, Funding, and Administration

The Handbook of Employee Benefits
Design, Funding, and Administration

Edited by
Jerry S. Rosenbloom
Professor of Insurance
Wharton School
University of Pennsylvania

Second Edition

DOW JONES-IRWIN
Homewood, Illinois 60430

This publication is designed to provide accurate and authoritative information in regard to the subject matter covered. It is sold with the understanding that the publisher is not engaged in rendering legal, accounting, or other professional service. If legal advice or other expert assistance is required, the services of a competent professional person should be sought.

From a Declaration of Principles jointly adopted by a Committee of the American Bar Association and a Committee of Publishers.

Project editor: Joan Hopkins
Production manager: Stephen K. Emry
Compositor: Bi-Comp, Inc.
Typeface: 10/12 Times Roman
Printer: R. R. Donnelley & Sons Company

Library of Congress Cataloging-in-Publication Data

The Handbook of employee benefits.

Includes index.
1. Employee fringe benefits—United States.
2. Employee fringe benefits—Law and legislation—United States. 3. Employee fringe benefits—Taxation—Law and legislation—United States. I. Rosenbloom, Jerry S.
HD4928.N62U6353 1989 658.3′25′0973 88–487
ISBN 1-55623-068-0
ISBN 1-55623-175-X (pbk.)

Printed in the United States of America

3 4 5 6 7 8 9 0 DO 6 5 4 3 2 1 0 9

PREFACE

Much has taken place in the employee benefits field since the first edition of *The Handbook of Employee Benefits* was published in 1984. Dramatic changes have been caused by legislation such as the Consolidated Omnibus Budget Reconciliation Act of 1985, Tax Reform Act of 1986, Age Discrimination in Employment Amendments of 1986, Omnibus Budget Reconciliation Acts of 1986 and 1987, and Single Employer Pension Plan Amendments Act of 1986. Moreover, many new employee benefit concepts have been developed and implemented. Yet the basic premise remains that employee benefits can no longer be considered as "fringe benefits" but must be regarded as an integral and extremely important component of an individual's financial security. The most recent U.S. Chamber of Commerce study on employee benefits in the United States indicates that, on average, employee benefits account for nearly 40 percent of a worker's total compensation. In light of the ever-increasing importance of benefit plans, those dealing with them must be well versed in the objectives, design, costing, funding, implementation, and administration of such plans.

While *The Handbook of Employee Benefits* is intended for students in the benefit field and for professionals as a handy reference, it can be a valuable tool for anyone with an interest in the field in general or in a specific employee benefits topic. The *Handbook* can be used either as a reference work for benefit professionals or as a textbook for college courses and professional education and company training programs. Each chapter of the *Handbook* stands alone and is complete in itself. While this produces some overlap in certain of the chapters, it eliminates the need for the reader to "check back" into other chapters, and it provides important reinforcement of difficult concepts.

The chapters of the *Handbook* are structured into 10 parts, each covering a major component of the employee benefit planning process. These are: Part One, Environment of Employee Benefit Plans; Part Two, Designing Employee Benefits—Death Benefits; Part Three, Designing

Employee Benefits—Health-Related Benefits; Part Four, Designing Employee Benefit Plans—Additional Benefits and Services; Part Five, Funding Health and Welfare Benefits; Part Six, Retirement and Capital Accumulation; Part Seven, Accounting, Funding, and Taxation of Retirement and Capital Accumulation Plans; Part Eight, Administration of Employee Benefit Plans; Part Nine, Employee Benefits for Small Business; and Part Ten, Issues of Special Interest in Employee Benefit Planning.

The *Handbook* consists of 55 chapters written by distinguished experts—academics, actuaries, attorneys, consultants, and other benefit professionals—covering all areas of the employee benefits field. Their practical experience and breadth of knowledge provide insightful coverage of the employee benefits mechanism, and the examples presented throughout the *Handbook* illustrate the concepts presented.

The Second Edition of the *Handbook* incorporates the changes in benefit planning caused by the legislative changes mentioned previously. Additionally, new chapters have been added on such topics as the Environment of Employee Benefit Plans, Group Universal Life Insurance, Dependent Care Programs, Employee Benefit Accounting, Retirement Plan Investment Objectives, Taxation of Employee Benefit Plans, Postretirement Issues, Plan Termination Issues, and Employee Benefit Plans for Associations. Other chapters have been consolidated and restructured.

In such a massive project, many people provided invaluable assistance, and it would be impossible to mention them all here. Thanks must be extended, however, to the authors of the individual chapters for the outstanding coverage of their subject areas in a comprehensive and readable manner. Special thanks are due to Mr. Everett T. Allen, Jr., who read the entire manuscript and made many constructive comments and suggestions. I would also like to recognize the many individuals on the Editorial Advisory Board whose work and many contributions on the first edition continue into this edition. I would again like to thank Dr. Davis W. Gregg, the former President of the American College, for his encouragement over the years to undertake such a project. Appreciation also must go to my most able assistant, Diana Krigelman, who spent many hours on all aspects of the manuscript and handled her duties in her usual professional manner.

In a work of this magnitude, it is almost inevitable that some mistakes may have escaped the eyes of the many readers of the manuscript. For these oversights I accept full responsibility and ask the reader's indulgence.

Jerry S. Rosenbloom

CONTRIBUTORS

Bradley J. Allen, Partner, Coopers and Lybrand

Everett T. Allen, Jr., Vice President and Principal, Towers, Perrin, Forster & Crosby, Retired

Burton T. Beam, Jr., CLU, CPCU, Associate Professor of Insurance, The American College

John M. Bernard, Esq., Partner, Ballard, Spahr, Andrews & Ingersoll

Henry Bright, FSA, Vice President, The Wyatt Company

Eugene B. Burroughs, CFA, Senior Advisor, The Prudential Asset Management Company, Inc.

Mary A. Carroll, CPCU, CEBS, ARM, Benefits Consultant

Joseph Casey, University of Central Florida

James A. Clark, Esq., Associate, King & Spalding

Ann Costello, Ph.D., Associate Professor of Insurance, University of Hartford

William E. Decker, Partner, Coopers & Lybrand

Donald J. Doudna, Ph.D., CLU, CPCU, Director of Insurance Development, State of Iowa, and Vice President, Chartered Financial Services

Edmund W. Fitzpatrick, Ph.D., CFP, Associate Professor of Financial Planning, The American College

Arthur C. Folli, Corporate Advisor, Employee Relations Policy and Planning, Arabian American Oil Company

Sharon S. Graham, D.B.A., CFA, Assistant Professor of Finance, University of Central Florida

Mark R. Greene, Ph.D., Distinguished Professor of Risk Management and Insurance, Emeritus, The University of Georgia

Donald S. Grubbs, Jr., J.D., FSA, President, Grubbs and Company, Inc.

Charles P. Hall, Jr., Ph.D., Professor of Health Administration, Insurance and Risk, School of Business Administration, Temple University

G. Victor Hallman III, Ph.D., J.D., CPCU, CLU, Professor of Finance and Insurance, Howard University and Lecturer in Financial and Estate Planning, Wharton School, University of Pennsylvania

Carlton Harker, FSA, EA, CLU, President, ACS Group, a North Carolina Actuarial/Benefit Consulting/TPA

David L. Hewitt, FCA, Partner, Hay/Huggins Company, Inc.

Charles E. Hughes, D.B.A., CLU, CPCU, Associate Professor of Insurance, The American College

Ronald L. Huling, Towers, Perrin, Forster & Crosby

Lloyd S. Kaye, Managing Director, William M. Mercer Meidinger Hansen, Inc.

David R. Klock, Ph.D., CLU, Professor of Finance, University of Central Florida

Phyllis A. Klock, Ph.D., Vice President, American Prepaid Professional Services, Inc.

Harry V. Lamon, Jr., Esq., Partner, Hurt, Richardson, Garner, Todd & Cadenhead

Robert T. LeClair, Ph.D., Associate Professor of Finance, Villanova University

Claude C. Lilly III, Ph.D., CLU, CPCU, Professor of Risk Management and Insurance, Florida State University

Zelda Lipton, Vice President, Columbia Free State Health System

Eric P. Lofgren, FSA, Principal, William M. Mercer Meidinger Hansen, Inc.

Edward E. Mack, Jr., CLU, CPCU, Late Chairman of the Board, Mack and Parker, Inc. and Mass Insurance Consultants and Administrators (MICA), Inc.

Ernest L. Martin, Ph.D., FLMI, Director, Examinations Department, Life Office Management Association

Thomas Martinez, Assistant Professor, Villanova University

Harry McBrierty, Consultant, The Wyatt Company

Dan M. McGill, Ph.D., Frederick H. Ecker Professor of Life Insurance and Chairman, Insurance Department, University of Pennsylvania

Ronald J. Murray, Director, Accounting, Auditing & SEC Consulting, Coopers & Lybrand

Robert J. Myers, LL.D., FSA, Professor Emeritus, Temple University; Chief Actuary, Social Security Administration, 1947-70; Deputy Commissioner, Social Security Administration, 1981-82; and Executive Director, National Commission on Social Security Reform, 1982–83

Robert V. Nally, J.D., CLU, Associate Professor, Villanova University

Robert M. Neiswanger, Secretary, Health Policy, The Travelers Insurance Company

Richard Ostuw, Vice President, Towers, Perrin, Forster & Crosby

Bruce A. Palmer, Ph.D., CLU, Professor of Risk Management and Insurance, Georgia State University

William H. Rabel, Ph.D., FLMI, CLU, Senior Vice President, Life Management Institute, Life Office Management Association (LOMA)

Jerry S. Rosenbloom, Ph.D., CLU, CPCU, Professor of Insurance and Academic Director, Certified Employee Benefit Specialist (CEBS) Program, Wharton School, University of Pennsylvania

Dallas L. Salisbury, President, Employee Benefit Research Institute

Clifford J. Schoner, Esq., Associate Tax Counsel, Sun Company, Inc.

Kathleen Hunter Sloan, Ph.D., Assistant Professor and Chairman, Department of Public Administration, University of Hartford

Robert W. Smiley, Jr., L.L.B., Chairman of the Board, The Benefit Capital Companies, Los Angeles, California

Gary K. Stone, Ph.D., Professor, Michigan State University

Garry N. Teesdale, Vice President, Hay Management Consultants

Richard L. Tewksbury, Jr., Managing Consultant, A. Foster Higgins & Co., Inc.

Jack L. VanDerhei, Ph.D., CEBS, Assistant Professor, University of Pennsylvania

Charles A. Weaver, Late Consultant, Human Resources Development Center; Late Corporate Consultant, Love Care Med Centers, Inc., Indianapolis, Indiana

Bernard L. Webb, Professor, Georgia State University

William G. Williams, Director, Health Care Relations, Provident Mutual Insurance Company of Philadelphia, Retired

Joseph D. Young, Director of Employee Benefits, Joseph E. Seagram & Sons, Incorporated

CONTENTS

PART TWO
Designing Employee Benefits—Death Benefits

PART THREE
Designing Employee Benefits—Health-Related Benefits

PART TEN
Issues of Special Interest in Employee Benefit Planning

CHAPTER 1

THE ENVIRONMENT OF EMPLOYEE BENEFIT PLANS

Jerry S. Rosenbloom

Employee benefits are an extremely important part of almost everyone's financial security. Once considered to be "fringe" benefits because of their relatively small magnitude, today there is no way that employee benefits can be considered as fringe anything. Employee benefits account for almost 40 percent of an individual's total compensation. In many firms, an even higher percentage can apply. To ensure that both employers and employees utilize employee benefit plans in the most effective manner requires a thorough knowledge of all aspects of employee benefit plan design, funding, and administration including benefit communications. This chapter gives the necessary background for the rest of the volume by outlining what employee benefits are, the reasons for their growth, what they are intended to achieve from both the employer and employee perspective, and what makes such plans work.

EMPLOYEE BENEFITS DEFINED

Broad View of Employee Benefits

There are many definitions of employee benefits, ranging from broad to narrow interpretations. In the broad view, employee benefits are virtually any form of compensation other than direct wages paid to employees.[1]

[1] Jerry S. Rosenbloom and G. Victor Hallman, *Employee Benefit Planning,* 2d ed. (Englewood Cliffs, N.J.: Prentice-Hall, 1986), pp. 1–3.

For example, in the annual Chamber of Commerce survey of employee benefits, such benefits are defined broadly to include the following:[2]

1. Employer's share of legally required payments.
2. Employer's share of retirement and savings plan payments.
3. Employer's share of life insurance and death benefits.
4. Employer's share of medical and medically related benefit payments.
5. Payments for nonproduction time while on the job (e.g., paid rest periods, lunch periods, wash-up time, travel time, etc.).
6. Payments for time not worked (e.g., paid sick leave, paid vacations, and holidays).
7. Other items (such as profit-sharing payments, contributions to employee thrift plans, special bonuses and service awards, and employee education expenses).

Table 1–1 illustrates the preceding breakdown of employee benefits for all companies as well as a breakdown by manufacturing and nonmanufacturing companies. As the table indicates, employee benefits are intertwined with almost every facet of an individual's economic and financial security.

A More Limited View of Employee Benefits

The broad view of employee benefits encompasses both legally mandated benefits such as Social Security and other governmental programs and private plans, while the narrow view can be summarized as, "any type of plan sponsored or initiated unilaterally or jointly by employers and employees in providing benefits that stem from the employment relationship that are not underwritten or paid directly by government.[3]

This narrow definition of employee benefits will be the one primarily used in the *Handbook*. That does not mean in any way, however, that legally required benefits are unimportant. Quite the contrary, these benefits are extremely important and must be considered in employee benefit plan design and in integrating private employee benefit plans with the benefits provided by governmental bodies. This interrelationship is stressed throughout the book. In addition to benefits provided through government bodies and those provided through the employment relation-

---

[2] Chamber of Commerce of the United States, *Employee Benefits 1986* (Washington, D.C., 1987).

[3] Martha Remey Yohalem, "Employee Benefit Plans—1975," *Social Security Bulletin* 40, no. 11 (November 1977), p. 19.

ship, benefits provided by an individual for his or her own welfare also are described when appropriate. This so-called tripod of economic security or three-legged stool underlies the foundation of individual and family financial security.

REASONS FOR THE GROWTH OF EMPLOYEE BENEFIT PLANS

The reasons behind the growth of employee benefit plans from fringes to a major component of financial security today are numerous. They arise from external forces as well as the desire of employers and employees to achieve certain goals and objectives.

Business Reasons

A whole host of business reasons explains why employee benefit plans were established and why they have expanded greatly. Employers want to attract and hold capable employees. Having employee benefit plans in place fosters this objective. Also, in many cases an employer's competition has certain benefit plans and therefore it is necessary to have equal or better plans to retain current employees. Moreover, employers hope that corporate efficiency, productivity, and improved employee morale will be the results of good benefit plans. Concern for employees' welfare and social objectives also encouraged the providing of benefits.

Collective Bargaining

Labor unions, through the collective bargaining process, have had a major impact on the growth of employee benefit plans. Perhaps the most notable breakthrough occurred in 1948 when the National Labor Relations Board (NLRB) in *United Steelworkers of America* v. *Inland Steel* ruled that wages also included insurance and fringes such as pension benefits. The decision was appealed, but the original ruling prevailed.[4] Thus, employee benefits became a subject of good-faith collective bargaining and their growth was tremendous after this decision.

The Taft-Hartley Act or Labor Management Relations Act of 1947 was also a landmark case setting forth the rules and regulations under which multiemployer trust funds covering both health and welfare, and retirement-type benefits could operate.

---

[4] See *Inland Steel Company* v. *United Steelworkers of America,* 77NLRB4(1948) and *Inland Steel Company* v. *National Labor Relations Board,* 170 F.(2d) 247, 251 (1949).

TABLE 1–1
Employee Benefits, by Type of Benefit, 1986

Type of Benefit	*Total, All Companies*	*Total, All Manufacturing*	*Total, All Nonmanufacturing*
Total employee benefits as percent of payroll	39.3%	42.0%	36.8%
1. Legally required payments (employer's share only)	8.9	8.7	9.1
a. Old-Age, Survivors, Disability, and Health Insurance (FICA taxes) and Railroad Retirement Tax	6.1	6.6	5.6
b. Unemployment Compensation	1.0	1.3	0.7
c. Workers' Compensation (including estimated cost of self-insured)	1.1	0.8	1.3
d. State sickness benefits insurance	0.8	0.0	1.5
2. Retirement and Savings Plan Payments (employer's share only)	6.7	7.2	6.3
a. Defined benefit pension plan contributions	3.3	4.1	2.5
b. Defined contribution plan payments	1.5	2.0	1.0
c. Money purchase plans	0.1	0.1	0.0
d. Pension plan premiums (net) under insurance and annuity contracts (insured and trusteed)	1.3	0.3	2.2
e. Cost of plan administration	0.1	0.1	0.1
f. Other	0.5	0.6	0.3
3. Life Insurance and Death Benefits (employer's share only)	0.5	0.5	0.5
4. Medical and Medically Related Benefit Payments (employer's share only)	8.3	10.2	6.7
a. Hospital, surgical, medical, and major medical insurance premiums (net)	6.1	6.9	5.4
b. Retiree (payments for retired employees) hospital, surgical, medical, and major medical insurance premiums (net)	0.6	1.0	0.2

c. Short-term disability, sickness or accident insurance (company plan or insured plan)	0.5	0.9	0.2
d. Long-term disability or wage continuation (insured, self-administered, or trust)	0.2	0.2	0.2
e. Dental insurance premiums	0.6	0.8	0.3
f. Other (vision care, physical and mental fitness, benefits for former employees)	0.3	0.3	0.3
5. Paid Rest Periods, Coffee Breaks, Lunch Periods, Wash-Up Time, Travel Time, Clothes-Change Time, Get Ready Time, etc.	3.4	3.3	3.4
6. Payments for Time Not Worked	10.2	10.2	10.1
a. Payments for or in lieu of vacations	5.2	5.2	5.2
b. Payments for or in lieu of holidays	3.1	3.5	2.8
c. Sick leave pay	1.4	0.9	1.8
d. Parental leave (maternity and paternity leave payments)	0.2	0.1	0.2
e. Other	0.3	0.5	0.2
7. Miscellaneous Benefit Payments	1.3	1.9	0.8
a. Discounts on goods and services purchased from company by employees	0.2	0.2	0.3
b. Employee meals furnished by company	0.1	0.1	0.1
c. Employee education expenditures	0.2	0.2	0.1
d. Child Care	0.6	1.1	0.2
e. Other	0.2	0.3	0.1
Total employee benefits as cents per payroll hour	496.2¢	570.7¢	436.2¢
Total employee benefits as dollars per year per employee	10,283	12.035	8,917

Source: Chamber of Commerce of the United States, *Employee Benefits of 1986* (Washington, D.C., 1987), p. 10.

Favorable Tax Legislation

Over the years the tax laws have favored employee benefit plans. Such preferential tax legislation has greatly encouraged the development of employee benefit plans as well as helping to shape their design since many plans seek to maximize the tax treatment or tax consequences of various employee benefit plans. The main tax benefits of employee benefit plans are as follows: (1) most contributions to employee benefit plans by employers are deductible as long as they are reasonable business expenses; (2) contributions from employers within certain limits on behalf of employees are generally not considered income to employees, and (3) on certain types of capital accumulation plans, benefits accumulate tax-free until distributed. Some additional tax benefits may be available when such distributions are made. All in all, favorable tax legislation has had great impact on the development and expansion of employee benefit plans.

Efficiency of the Employee Benefits Approach

The bringing together after the industrial revolution of employees and employers in cities and in business firms really made it possible for the employee benefits concept to flourish by covering many employees under one contract or plan instead of each employee having to go out and purchase an individual insurance contract. The simplicity and convenience of insuring people through their employment seemed to make sense from many standpoints. Employee benefit providers and suppliers, such as insurance companies, banks, or various types of health organizations, all found the marketing of such benefits through the employer to be a cost-effective and administratively efficient channel of distribution.

Other Factors

Many other factors have contributed to the growth of employee benefit plans. One such factor was the imposition during World War II and the Korean conflict of limitations on the size of wage increases granted during these periods. While wages were frozen, employee benefits were not. As a result, compensation of employees could effectively be increased by providing larger benefits. This resulted in a major expansion of employee benefits during these two periods.

Some have argued that various governmental legislation over the years has encouraged employee benefit plans not only through providing favorable tax treatment but by the government's "moral suasion" that if such benefit plans were not established voluntarily by employers and employees, additional governmental programs might result. Allowing employee benefits to be integrated with governmental benefits also has enhanced the private employee benefit approach by taking into consideration benefits provided by governmental plans in benefit plan design.

Development of the group approach to certain employee benefits has also helped expand the employee benefit mechanism. The techniques inherent in the group selection process made possible the providing of benefits that previously could only be provided on an individual basis often requiring medical selection.

GROUP TECHNIQUE

In many types of insurance programs such as group life insurance and group health insurance, the group technique enables these coverages to be written as employee benefit plans.[5] Unlike individual insurance, group insurance is based on a view of the group rather than the individual as a unit. Usually individual insurance eligibility requirements are not required for group insurance written under an employee benefit plan. The concepts that make the group technique work are all designed to prevent "adverse selection." That is to reduce the possibility that less healthy individuals may join a group or be a larger percentage of a group than anticipated because of the availability of insurance or other benefits.

Characteristics of the group technique of providing employee benefits include some or all of the following:[6]

1. *Only certain groups eligible*—While most groups qualify, this requirement is intended to make sure that the obtaining of insurance is incidental to the group seeking coverage. Thus, a group should not be formed solely for the purpose of obtaining insurance.

2. *Steady flow of lives through the group*—The theory behind this concept is that younger individuals should come into the group while older individuals leave the group thus maintaining a fairly constant mortality or morbidity ratio in the group. If the group doesn't maintain this "flow-through the group" and the average age of the group increases substantially, costs could increase dramatically.

3. *Minimum number of persons in the group*—A minimum number of persons, typically ten, must be in the group to be eligible for group

---

[5] See Chapter 5 for an additional discussion of the "group mechanism" to providing employee benefits.

[6] See Rosenbloom and Hallman, *Employee Benefit Planning,* pp. 17–20.

benefits. However, this requirement has been liberalized to the point where two or three individuals in a group may obtain coverage. This minimum number provision is designed to prevent unhealthy lives from being a major part of the group and to spread the expenses of the benefits plan over a larger number of individuals.[7]

4. *A minimum portion of the group must participate*—Typically in group life and health insurance plans if the plan is noncontributory, that is, solely paid for by the employer, 100 percent of eligible employees must be covered. If the plan is contributory, that is, both employer and employee share the cost, 75 percent of the employees must participate. The rationale for this provision is also to reduce adverse selection and spread the expense of administration.[8]

5. *Eligibility requirements*—Frequently eligibility requirements are imposed under group plans for the purpose, once again, of preventing adverse selection. Such provision can include only full-time employees who are actively at work on the date the benefits become effective. A waiting or eligibility period may be used for certain benefits. Also, if employees don't join when eligible and want to enroll at a later date, some form of medical information may be required.

6. *Maximum limits for any one person*—In certain cases, maximum limits on the amount of life or health benefits may be imposed to prevent the possibility of excessive amounts of coverage on any particular unhealthy individual.

7. *Automatic determination of benefits*—To prevent unhealthy lives in a group from obtaining an extremely large amount of a particular benefit or benefits, coverage is determined for all individuals in the group on an automatic basis. This basis may be determined by an employee's salary, service, or position, may be a flat amount for all employees, or may be a combination of these factors.

8. *A central and efficient administrative agency*—To keep expenses to a minimum and to handle the mechanics of the benefit plan, a central and efficient administrative agency is necessary to the successful operation of an employee benefit plan. An employer is an almost ideal unit because he or she maintains the payroll and other employee information needed in meeting appropriate tax and recordkeeping requirements.[9]

---

[7] *Ibid.*, p. 19.

[8] *Ibid.*, p. 20.

[9] *Ibid.*

Over the years many of the requirements just described have been liberalized as providers of employee benefits have gained experience in handling group employee benefits, and because of the competitive environment. Nevertheless, the group selection technique is important in understanding why employee benefits can work on a group basis and how any problems that exist might be corrected.

OVERALL EMPLOYEE BENEFIT CONCERNS

Since employee benefits, as noted previously, provide such an important dimension of financial security in our society, some overall questions need to be asked to evaluate any existing or newly created employee benefit plan. While future chapters in this *Handbook* analyze benefit design, costing, funding, administration, and communication issues, some principles permeate all these areas and need brief mention early in this text.[10]

Employer and Employee Objectives

The design of any employee benefit plan must start with the objectives of the benefits plan from the standpoint of both employer and employee.

What Benefits Should Be Provided?

There should be clearly stated reasons or objectives for the type of benefits to be provided. Benefits provided both under governmental programs and by the individual employees should also be considered.

Who Should Be Covered by the Benefit Plans?

Should only full-time employees be covered? What about retirees or dependents? What about survivors of deceased employees? These and a host of similar questions must be carefully thought through. Of course, some of these issues depend on regulatory and legislative rules and regulations.

---

[10] Some of the ideas presented here are based on Rosenbloom and Hallman, *Employee Benefit Planning,* Chapter 20. For a more detailed analysis, consult this publication.

Should Employees Have Benefit Options?

This is becoming more and more of a crucial question under employee benefit plans. With the growth of flexible or cafeteria benefit plans employee choice is on the increase. Even in nonflexible benefit plan situations, should limited choices be given?

How Should Benefit Plans Be Financed?

Several important questions need to be answered in determining the approach to funding employee benefit plans. Should financing be entirely provided by the employer (a noncontributory approach) or on some shared basis by the employer and employee (contributory approach)? If on a contributory basis, what percentage should each bear?

What funding method should be used? A wide range of possibilities exist, from a total insurance program to total self-funding and a whole range of options between. Even when selecting one of these options, still further questions remain concerning the specific funding instrument to be used.

How Should the Benefit Plan Be Administered?

Should the firm itself administer the plan? Should an insurance carrier or other benefit plan provider do the administration? Should some outside organization such as a third-party administrator (TPA) do this work? Once the decision is made, the specific entity must be selected.

How Should the Benefit Plan Be Communicated?

The best employee benefit plan in existence may not achieve any of its desired objectives if it is improperly communicated to all affected parties. The communication of employee benefit plans has become increasingly important in recent years with increased reporting and disclosure requirements. Effective communication of what benefit plans will and won't do is essential if employees are to rely on such plans to provide part of their financial security at all stages of their life cycles.

Future of Employee Benefits

Many feel that with recent legislation such as the Tax Equity and Fiscal Responsibility Act (TEFRA), Consolidated Omnibus Budget Reconciliation Act (COBRA), Deficit Reduction Act (DEFRA), and Tax Reform Act of 1986 (TRA '86) and the Omnibus Budget Reconciliation Acts of 1986 and 1987 employee benefits are being limited and will be curtailed greatly in the future. While there may be certain limitations and restrictions, employee benefit plans are woven into the fabric of our society in such a way that the basic character or importance of such plans will not be changed. What is happening today in terms of cost-containment, greater efficiencies of the benefits approach, more tailoring to individual needs in the growth of flexible benefits or cafeteria compensation plans, and other refinements will continue to drive the employee benefits mechanism. While it seems certain that employee benefits will not grow as rapidly as they have in the past, the future is rosy and will continue to demand people who are knowledgeable about all aspects of the design, funding, administration, and communication of employee benefits in order to make such plans more effective while helping to provide for the economic security of society at large.

CHAPTER 2

FUNCTIONAL APPROACH TO EMPLOYEE BENEFITS

G. Victor Hallman III

This chapter deals with the functional approach toward analyzing an existing employee benefit program and evaluating the need for new employee benefits. The functional approach can be defined as an organized system for classifying and analyzing the risks and needs of active employees, their dependents, and various other categories of persons into logical categories of exposures to loss and employee needs. These exposures and needs may include: medical expenses, losses resulting from death, losses caused by short- and long-term disabilities, retirement income needs, capital accumulation needs, needs arising out of short- and long-term unemployment, and other employee needs.

THE FUNCTIONAL APPROACH IN CONCEPT

As indicated above, the functional approach essentially is the application of a systematic method of analysis to an employer's total employee benefits program. It analyzes the employer's employee benefits program as a coordinated whole in terms of its ability to meet various employees' (and others') needs and loss exposures within the employer's overall compensation goals and cost parameters. This approach can be useful in overall employee benefit plan design, in evaluating proposals for new or revised benefits, for evaluation of cost-saving proposals, and in effective communication of an employer's total benefits program to its employees.

The functional approach to employee benefits is not really a new concept. In 1967, George C. Foust outlined the functional approach in the American Management Association book entitled *The Total Approach to Employee Benefits*.[1] Similarly, Robert M. McCaffery in his 1972 work on *Managing the Employee Benefits Program* stated:

> The "package" or total approach to employee benefits is simply the purposeful management of an integrated program. Rather than continually reacting to current fads, outside pressures, and salesmen's pitches, the contemporary businessman relies on fundamental principles of management in developing, organizing, directing, and evaluating systems of employee benefits for his organization.[2]

The functional approach represents such systematic management of the employee benefits function.

NEED FOR THE FUNCTIONAL APPROACH

The functional approach is needed in planning, designing, and administering employee benefits for several reasons.

First, in most instances, employee benefits are a very significant element of the total compensation of employees. They have become an important part of the work rewards provided by employers to their employees. Therefore, it is important to employees, and hence their employers, that this increasingly important element of compensation be planned and organized so as to be as effective as possible in meeting employee needs.

Second, employee benefits currently represent a large item of labor cost for employers. Depending on the industry, the particular employer, and how employee benefits are defined, benefits may range from less than 18 percent to over 65 percent of an employer's payroll. Therefore, effective planning and hence avoidance of waste in providing benefits can be an important cost-control measure for employers.

Third, employee benefits, in the past, often were adopted by employers on a piecemeal basis without being coordinated with existing employee benefit programs. Thus, some benefit plans just "grew like

---

[1] George C. Foust, Jr., "The Total Approach Concept," in *The Total Approach to Employee Benefits*, ed., Arthur J. Deric (New York: American Management Association, 1967), chap. 1.

[2] Robert M. McCaffery, *Managing the Employee Benefit Program* (New York: American Management Association, 1972), p. 17.

Topsy." For this reason, it usually is fruitful to apply the functional approach in reviewing existing employee benefit plans to determine where overlapping benefits may exist and costs can be saved, and where gaps in benefits may exist and new benefits or revised benefits may be in order.

Fourth, since new benefits and coverages, changes in the tax laws, changes in the regulatory environment, and other developments in employee benefit planning have come about so rapidly in recent years, it is necessary to have a systematic approach to planning benefits to keep an employer's program in order.

Finally, a given employee benefit or program, such as a pension plan, often provides benefits relating to several separate employee needs or loss exposures. Therefore, an employer's benefit plan needs to be analyzed according to the functional approach so its various benefit programs can be integrated properly with each other.

CONSISTENCY WITH AN EMPLOYER'S TOTAL COMPENSATION PHILOSOPHY

In designing its total compensation package, an employer should seek to balance the various elements of its compensation system, including basic cash wages and salary, current incentive compensation (current cash bonuses and company stock plans), and so-called employee benefits, to help meet the needs and desires of the employees on the one hand and the employer's basic compensation philosophy and objectives on the other. Thus, it is clear the functional approach to planning and designing an employee benefit plan must remain consistent with the employer's total compensation philosophy. A particular employer, therefore, may not cover a particular employee desire for benefits, or may cover it in a rather spartan manner, not because the desire is not recognized but because the employer's total compensation philosophy calls for a relatively low level of employee benefits or, perhaps, benefits oriented in a different direction.

Employers may adopt different business policies regarding the general compensation of their employees. For example, many employers want to compensate their employees at a level about in line with that generally prevailing in their industry or community, or both. They do not wish to be much above or below average compensation levels. The employee benefit programs of such employers also frequently follow this general philosophy. Other employers may follow a high-compensation philosophy (including employee benefits) with the goal of attempting to attract higher levels of management, technical, and general employee talent. This may be particularly true in industries where the need for a highly skilled workforce is relatively great. On the other hand, there may be employers which follow a low-compensation policy, feeling that, for them, the resultant lower payroll costs more than outweigh the resulting higher employee turnover and lower skill level of their workforce. An employer with this kind of philosophy also may want to adopt more modest employee benefit programs.

Type of industry and employer characteristics also will have an impact on an employer's total compensation philosophy and on the design of its employee benefit plan. Figure 2–1 is a grid presented by one employee benefit consulting firm showing the relationship between type of organization, working climate, and compensation mix.

Thus, a larger well-established employer in a mature industry, a financial institution, or a nonprofit organization may take a relatively liberal approach toward meeting the benefits needs and desires of its employees. But developing industrial firms and other growth companies,

FIGURE 2–1
Organizational Style and Compensation Mix

		Reward Management Components			
		Cash		*Noncash*	
Type of Organization	*Working Climate*	*Base Salary*	*Short-Term Incentives*	*Level*	*Characteristics*
Mature Industrial	Balanced	Medium	Medium	Medium	Balanced
Developing Industrial	Growth, Creativity	Medium	High	Low	Short-Term Oriented
Conservative Financial	Security	Low	Low	High	Long-Term, Security-Oriented
Nonprofit	Societal Impact, Personal Fulfillment	Low	None	Low to Medium	Long-Term, Security-Oriented
Sales	Growth, Freedom to Act	Low	High	Low	Short-Term Oriented

Source: Hay-Huggins, member of the Hay Group.

which may have considerable current needs for capital, may seek to rely more heavily on short-term-oriented incentive types of compensation. Further, industries that are highly competitive, subject to cyclical fluctuations, or perhaps in a currently depressed state, may not be willing to add to their relatively fixed labor costs by adopting or liberalizing employee benefits, even if there may be a functional need for them. In fact, such firms may seek to cut back on their employee benefit commitments when possible. However, even in these situations firms should attempt to allocate their available compensation dollars in as consistent and logical a manner as possible to meet the needs and goals of their employees as well as their own corporate compensation objectives. In fact, the functional approach may be even more appropriate in such cases because their resources for compensating employees are relatively scarce.

Another area of employer philosophy that affects the functional approach and how it is actually applied is whether the employer tends to follow a compensation/service-oriented benefit philosophy or a benefit- or needs-oriented philosophy. Employers having a compensation/service-oriented philosophy tend to relate employee benefits primarily to compensation or service, or both, in designing their employee benefit plans. Thus, the level of benefits would tend to be tied in with compensation level, and eligibility for benefits may be conditioned directly or indirectly on salary level. For example, separate benefit plans may be provided for salaried and for hourly rated employees with more generous benefits being made available to the former group. Further, some types of benefits may be available only to certain higher-paid employees or executives. In addition, such employers tend to emphasize service with the employer in determining benefit levels and eligibility for benefits. The theory of this approach is that employee benefits generally should be aimed to reward the longer-service employees who have shown a commitment to the employer. The benefit- or needs-oriented philosophy, on the other hand, tends to focus primarily on the needs of employees and their dependents rather than on compensation and service.

In practice, the design of employee benefit plans tends to be a compromise between these two philosophies. On one side, certain kinds of employee benefits, such as medical expense benefits, tend to be primarily benefit- or needs-oriented. On the other side, benefits like group life insurance and pensions customarily are compensation-oriented, at least for nonunion employees. Thus, this distinction in philosophy really is one of degree. However, the extent to which eligibility for benefits, participation requirements, and levels of employee benefits reflect compensation or service, or both, may affect the extent to which the needs of employees or certain categories of employees will be met by an employee benefit plan.

APPLICATION OF THE FUNCTIONAL APPROACH

While the functional approach to planning employee benefits has been actively discussed since the early 1960s, no clearly developed procedure or technique exists for the application of this approach to individual benefit plans. However, based on the underlying concept and the way it is applied in practice, the following are the logical steps in applying the functional approach to employee benefit plan design, revision, or review. For convenience of presentation, these steps can be listed as follows:

1. Classify employee (and dependent) needs or objectives in logical functional categories.
2. Classify the categories of persons (e.g., employees, some former employees, and dependents) the employer may want to protect, at least to some extent, through its employee benefit plan.
3. Analyze the benefits presently available under the plan in terms of the functional categories of needs or objectives and in terms of the categories of persons the employer may want to benefit.
4. Determine any gaps in benefits or overlapping benefits, or both, provided from *all* sources under the employer's employee benefit plan and from other benefit plans in terms of the functional categories of needs and the persons to be protected.
5. Consider recommendations for changes in the employer's present employee benefit plan to meet any gaps in benefits and to correct any overlapping benefits.
6. Estimate the costs or savings from each of the recommendations made in step 5.
7. Evaluate alternative methods of financing or securing the benefits recommended above, as well as the employee benefit plan's existing benefits.
8. Consider other cost-saving techniques in connection with the recommended benefits or existing benefits.
9. Decide upon the appropriate benefits, methods of financing, and sources of benefits as a result of the preceding analysis.
10. Implement the changes.
11. Communicate benefit changes to employees.
12. Periodically reevaluate the employee benefit plan.

Each of these steps is considered in greater detail below. Naturally, it must be recognized in applying this process to a particular employee benefit plan that some of these steps may be combined with others and some will be taken implicitly. However, each step represents a logical decision-point or consideration in the design or revision of an employee benefit plan.

Classify Employee and Dependent Needs in Functional Categories

The needs and exposures to loss of employees, their dependents, and certain others can be classified in a variety of ways, some being more complete than others. The following classification appears to cover most of the commonly accepted needs and exposures to loss that may be covered under an employee benefit plan:

1. Medical expenses incurred by active employees, by their dependents, by retired (or certain otherwise terminated or suspended) former employees, and by their dependents.
2. Losses due to employees' disability (short-term and long-term).
3. Losses resulting from active employees' deaths, from their dependents' deaths, and from the deaths of retired (or certain otherwise terminated or suspended) former employees.
4. Retirement needs of employees and their dependents.
5. Capital accumulation needs or goals (short-term and long-term).
6. Needs arising from unemployment or from temporary termination or suspension of employment.
7. Needs for financial counseling, retirement counseling, and other counseling services.
8. Losses resulting from property and liability exposures, needs for legal services, and the like.
9. Needs for dependent care assistance (e.g., child-care services).
10. Needs for educational assistance for employees themselves or for employees' dependents, or for both.
11. Other employee benefit needs.

Naturally, a given functional analysis often does not encompass all these needs or loss exposures. The above classification is intended to be more exhaustive than frequently is included in a functional analysis. However, the history of employee benefit planning, particularly since the end of World War II, has been one of continually expanding the areas of employees' (and others') needs for which the employer is providing benefits of various kinds. It seems likely, therefore, that additional categories of needs and loss exposures will be added to the above list from time to time. Also, some of those needs and exposures mentioned only incidentally above may become more important in the future.

Figure 2–2 provides an illustration of the functional approach to employee benefit planning, using the employee benefit plan of a large corporation and the functional categories used by that corporation. Note that the employee needs and exposures to loss are shown on the left-hand margin of the grid while the components of this corporation's employee benefit plan are shown across the top of the grid. This arrangement thus shows how each benefit plan applies to each of these employee needs or loss exposures. Any gaps or duplications in coverage (or need for further information) can be seen more easily through this systematic process of analysis.

Classify by Categories the Persons the Employer May Want to Protect

This step basically involves the issues of who should be protected by an employee benefit plan, for what benefits, for what time period, and under what conditions. These issues have become increasingly important in employee benefit planning as the scope of employee benefit plans has increased not only in terms of the benefits provided but also in terms of continuing to protect employees once the formal employment relationship has ended and of protecting dependents of employees in a variety of circumstances. It is a logical part of the functional approach since the needs and loss exposures of employees imply consideration not only of the kinds of benefits to be provided but also of the persons to be protected and when they will be protected. Thus, in designing its employee benefit plan the employer also should consider how the various functional categories of needs and goals will be met for different categories of persons under a variety of circumstances.

In this type of analysis, the following are among the categories of persons whom the employer may or may not want to protect under its employee benefit plan—under at least some circumstances and benefits:

1. Active full-time employees.
2. Dependents of active full-time employees.
3. Retired former employees.
4. Dependents of retired former employees.
5. Disabled employees and their dependents.
6. Surviving dependents of deceased employees.
7. Terminated employees and their dependents.
8. Employees (and their dependents) who are temporarily separated from the employer's service, such as during layoffs, leaves of absence, strikes, and so forth.

FIGURE 2–2
Illustration of Functional Approach to Employee Benefit Planning

Employee Needs or exposures to Loss	Health Care Plan	Basic Salary Continuation Plan	Extended Salary Continuation Plan	Long Term Disability Plan	Basic Life Insurance Plan	Primary Life Insurance Plan
Medical expenses	Choice among 3 base plans; a major health plan supplements selected base plan. Major health plan provides broad coverage including dental, hearing, vision					
Disability losses	Coverage continues while employee receives disability benefits under company plans	Full salary for up to 30 days of absence each year for illness or injury	After the basic allowance is exhausted, employee's full salary less offsetting benefits is maintained up to a maximum of 25 months depending on length of service	After extended plan ends, 75% of base monthly pay less offsetting benefits for up to 25 months; then, a voluntary, payroll deduction LTD benefit of 50% of salary	Coverage continues while employee receives disability benefits under company plans	Coverage continues while employee receives disability benefits under company plans
In case of death	Dependent coverage continues for 4 months plus an additional period depending upon employee service, at the employer's expense. Thereafter, the plan meets COBRA requirements	Coverage terminates	Coverage terminates	Coverage terminates	Provides beneficiary with a benefit of $3,000	Provides beneficiary with a benefit of 3 times employee's current annual base pay (offset by pension plan's preretirement survivor benefit). Employee also has the option to purchase additional life insurance at favorable group rates, up to 3 times current base pay
Retirement	Major health plan continues for life during retirement after age 65 at the employer's expense	Coverage terminates	Coverage terminates	Coverage terminates	$3,000 coverage continues after retirement for as long as employee lives	Continues after retirement with the amount and duration of coverage depending on the option employee chooses
Capital accumulation						
Dependent care assistance						

Travel Accident Plan	Savings Plan	Employees' Stock Purchase Plan	Pension Plan	Social Security	Workers' Compensation	Supplemental Workers' Compensation	Flexible Spending Accounts (FSAs)
					Pays if illness or injury is job-related under the workers' compensation laws		Allows employees to set aside before-tax up to $3,000 per year for tax-eligible health care expenses
Pays a benefit of up to 3 times employee's annual base pay if disability involves an accidental dismemberment while traveling on company business	Contributions are discontinued when long-term disability benefits begin. Participation may continue unless employee becomes permanently and totally disabled or until formal retirement. Withdrawals are permitted	Employee receiving disability benefits may suspend any payments being made to the plan for a period not to exceed 6 months nor a specified date in the offering	Participation continues while employee receives company disability benefits; service credits accumulate until end of extended disability period or up to 3 months	Pays after 5 months of continuous total disability when approved by Social Security	Pays if disability is job-related under the workers' compensation laws	Increases disability income if employee receives workers' compensation benefits	
Pays beneficiary a lump sum benefit of 3 times employee's annual base pay if death is the result of an accident while traveling on company business	Beneficiary receives the amount credited to employee's account	Payment is made of any amount being accumulated during a "purchase period" with interest	Active employees: preretirement survivors benefit for vested employees' spouses if employees die before retirement; no cost to employee; coordinated with primary life. Retired employees: retiree may elect pension option to provide benefits to beneficiary upon retiree's death; subject to QJSA rules	Pays a lump sum death benefit and monthly survivor income to spouse and children	Pays if death is job-related under the workers' compensation laws	Coverage terminates	
Coverage terminates	Employee may receive the balance in the plan account upon retirement	Stock purchased under plan available at and before retirement; retirees not eligible for future offerings	Defined benefit plan integrated with Social Security pays regular benefit at 65, with alternatives for early and postponed retirement ages before and after 65	Pays regular retirement benefits at age 65 or reduced benefit at 62. Health care expenses may be covered under Medicare	Coverage terminates in accordance with the workers' compensation laws	Coverage terminates	
	Account balance and contributions accumulate; employer contributions and earnings not taxable. Employees may contribute up to 16% of salary or $7,000 (indexed) before-tax per year. Employer matches 50% of contributions, up to 6% of salary. 4 investment options. Withdrawals permitted on termination, or in-service in special cases; loans available	Employees can purchase company stock in amounts based on salary at 85% of stock price at either the beginning or the end of any purchase period; payment in installments					
							Employees may set aside before-tax up to $5,000/yr. for child or other dependent care

9. Other than full-time active employees (e.g., part-time employees, directors, and so forth).

The employer basically must decide how far it wants to extend its employee benefit program, and for what kinds of benefits, to persons who may not be active full-time employees. This represents a significant issue in employee benefit planning both in terms of adequacy of employee protection and of the cost implications for the employer. Some extensions of benefits, such as provision of group term life insurance and medical expense benefits to retirees and perhaps their dependents, can be quite expensive.

The extent to which employers may want to extend coverage of their benefit plans to one or more of these categories of persons varies with employer philosophy, cost constraints, funding considerations, union negotiations, and employee benefit practices in the particular industry and geographic area involved. Such extensions also vary considerably among the different kinds of benefits. For example, medical expense benefits may be extended to active employees, various categories of dependents of active employees, retired former employees, dependents of retired former employees, surviving spouses and other dependents of retired former employees, disabled employees, dependents of disabled employees, and surviving dependents of deceased active employees. Further, medical expense coverage may be provided, and indeed may be required to be provided under the Consolidated Omnibus Budget Reconciliation Act (COBRA), for terminated employees, dependents of terminated employees, dependents of active employees who no longer meet the definition of an eligible dependent under the regular employee benefit plan, dependents of deceased employees, and in certain other situations. Group term life insurance, however, may be provided to active full-time employees, disabled employees who meet the definition of disability under the plan, and retired employees in reduced amounts. Also, some plans provide dependents group life insurance to eligible dependents of active employees. At the other extreme, cash disability income benefits normally are provided only to active full-time employees.

Another factor to consider in this analysis is to what extent and on what contribution basis certain employee benefits will be provided or continued to various categories of persons. Benefits may be provided or continued without contribution by the employee or covered person in full or in a reduced amount. Or, the benefits could be provided or continued with contribution to the cost by the employee or covered person in full or on a reduced basis. Finally, benefits may be provided or continued to covered persons on an elective basis at the covered person's own cost.

Analyze Benefits Presently Available

The next step in the functional approach is to analyze the benefits, terms of coverage, and plan participation by employees in terms of how well the existing or proposed employee benefit plan meets employee needs and desires in the various functional categories for those classes of persons the employer wants to protect or benefit. This step involves measuring the employee benefit plan against the objectives and coverage criteria set up for it under the functional approach outlined above.

Types of Benefits

A common application of the functional approach to employee benefit planning is to outline the different types of benefits under an employee benefit plan that apply to each of the functional categories of employee needs and goals. This may be done in the form of a grid as shown in Figure 2–2. In that figure, for example, employee needs and exposures to loss are shown on the left-hand margin of the grid while the components of the corporation's employee benefit plan are shown across the top of the grid.

Levels of Benefits

In a similar fashion, the levels of benefits under the various components of the employee benefit plan can be determined or shown, or both, for each of the functional categories of needs or goals.

To supplement this analysis, it may be helpful to use benefit illustrations to determine or illustrate the levels of benefits that would be provided under the various components of the employee benefit plan or proposed plan in the event of certain contingencies and using certain assumptions. For example, it might be assumed an employee with certain earnings and using certain salary projections will retire at age 65 with 30 years of service with the employer. This employee's total retirement income then may be estimated from various components of the employer's employee benefit plan as well as from Social Security as of the assumed retirement date. This can be expressed as a percentage of the employee's estimated final pay, which often is referred to as the employee's retirement income "replacement ratio." The employee benefits used in such an analysis may include only the employer's pension plan and Social Security; but it would be more logical to include all potential sources of retirement income available through the employee benefit plan, such as a pension plan, profit-sharing plan, thrift or savings plan, supplemental executive retirement plans, and perhaps other kinds of plans or benefits intended primarily to provide capital accumulation or stock-purchase benefits. Naturally, assumptions must be made for a variety of factors if all these sources of retirement income are considered. Also, different assumptions as to employee earnings, year of retirement, final pay, years of service, and so forth may be used to test the adequacy of retirement income for employees under different conditions.

The same kind of analysis can be made for disability benefits from all sources under the employee benefit plan. When the analysis is made of disability benefits, it may be found that excessive benefits will be paid under certain conditions and for certain durations of disability, while inadequate benefits will be paid under other conditions. Thus, better coordination of disability benefits may be called for in making recommendations for changes in the plan. This approach also may prove fruitful for other employee loss exposures, such as death, medical expenses at various levels and under various conditions, long-term care, and so forth. Finally, the adequacy of benefit levels can be tested for different categories of persons the employer may want to protect.

Another interesting kind of analysis in terms of benefit levels is to estimate the potential for capital accumulation available to employees under the various components of an employee benefit plan designed primarily for this purpose. These may include, for example, profit-sharing plans, thrift or savings plans, stock-purchase plans, stock options, employee stock ownership plans (ESOPs), and so forth. Employees often are pleasantly surprised to learn how much capital can be accumulated under such plans over a period even using relatively conservative investment assumptions.

In evaluating levels of benefits and benefit adequacy, consideration also may be given to optional benefits that may be available to employees under the employee benefit plan. Such options usually involve the opportunity for employees to purchase coverage or additional levels of coverage beyond a basic level of benefits. Through such optional benefits, the employer in effect is giving employees the opportunity at a given cost to themselves to make their total benefits more adequate in certain specific areas. As an example, the life insurance plan shown in Figure 2–2 allows eligible employees to purchase additional life insurance at favorable group rates up to three times their base pay over and above the employer provided benefit of three times annual base pay (subject to certain individual underwriting requirements).

Probationary Periods

In assessing how well an existing employee benefit plan meets the needs and loss exposures of employees and certain other individuals, it also is helpful to analyze the probationary periods required for the various types of benefits contained in the plan. Such probationary periods, or the length of service otherwise eligible employees must have with the employer before they become eligible to participate in the various types of benefits, will have an effect on the plan's protection for employees, their dependents, and possibly others. The longer the probationary period required, the greater is the exposure of employees and others to a loss not covered by the plan. But, many employers believe only employees with certain minimum periods of service, and hence demonstrable connection with the employer, should be eligible for at least certain types of benefits.

Probationary periods by their nature create gaps in coverage for newly hired or newly eligible employees and their dependents. Thus, probationary periods should be analyzed as part of the functional approach to determine whether the resulting gaps in coverage are appropriate and consistent with the employer's objectives and the employees' needs.

It seems desirable that the use of probationary periods in an employee benefit plan should be based on a reasonably consistent employer philosophy. One possible philosophy in this regard is to divide employee benefits into "protection-oriented" benefits and "accumulation-oriented" benefits. *Protection-oriented* benefits would consist of medical expense benefits, life insurance benefits, short- and long-term disability benefits, and so forth. These benefits protect employees and their dependents against serious loss exposures which, if they were to occur, could spell immediate financial disaster for the employees or their dependents, or both. For such benefits, where the need/protection orientation is great, there might be no probationary period, or a relatively short probationary period. The rationale for this would be that the need for immediate coverage would overcome the traditional reasons for using probationary periods or longer probationary periods. *Accumulation-oriented* benefits, such as pension plans, profit-sharing plans, thrift plans, stock-bonus plans, stock-purchase plans, and so forth, could involve relatively long probationary periods if desired by the employer. The theory might be that these kinds of benefits should be a reward for relatively long service with the employer. Also, an employee who stays with the employer would have a relatively long time in which to accumulate such benefits and thus longer probationary periods would not really place the employee at any serious disadvantage or risk.

Eligibility Requirements

Requirements for eligibility for benefits, including definitions of covered persons, obviously affect those who may benefit from or be protected by various employee benefits. In this area, for example, the employer and union—or unions—with whom the employer negotiates should consider such issues as:

1. Which dependents of active employees (and perhaps dependents of retired former employees, disabled employees, and deceased employees—see 2, 3, 4, and 5 below) should or must be covered for medical expense benefits?
2. Should retirees (and perhaps their spouses and other dependents) continue to be covered and, if so, for what benefits?
3. Should survivors of deceased active employees continue to be covered and, if so, for what benefits and for how long?
4. Should survivors of retired former employees continue to be covered and, if so, for what benefits?
5. Should employees or former employees on disability (and perhaps their dependents) continue to be covered and, if so, for what benefits, how long, and under what conditions?
6. Should coverage be extended to employees during layoffs, leaves of absence, strikes, and other temporary interruptions of employment and, if so, for what benefits, how long, and under what conditions?
7. Should coverage be limited only to full-time employees (or employees meeting ERISA requirements) or should coverage or some coverage be extended to part-time employees as well?
8. What coverage should or must be continued or made available to persons after termination of their employment with the employer (or for the dependents of such persons) and on what basis?

The resolution of some of these issues depends in part on statutory or other legal requirements, insurance company underwriting rules, collective bargaining agreements, and similar factors. However, the philosophy or rationale of the employer and union concerning the employee benefit program will have a substantial impact on how some of these coverage and eligibility issues are resolved. At the heart of many of these issues is the basic question of how far an employer (or union) should feel obligated to go, either legally or morally—or possibly can afford to go—in meeting the various needs and loss exposures of its employees, their dependents, and persons who once were employees or dependents of employees but who now have various other relationships with the employer.

Employee Contribution Requirements

If certain employee benefits under an employer's employee benefit plan are contributory (i.e., the employees or possibly their dependents must contribute to the cost of the benefit), this will have an impact on employee participation and hence on how well the plan meets the needs of the employee group as a whole. This really represents a trade-off: between the financing and other advantages of a contributory plan—and the loss of employee participation in the plan, which results from requiring employee contributions, assuming employee participation in the contributory plan is voluntary. Thus, an employer, and union if the plan is negotiated, must decide whether a particular employee benefit will be noncontributory or contributory, and, if it is to be contributory, how much the employees will have to contribute toward the cost of the plan. Further, if the plan is contributory, the employer (and union) will have to decide whether participation will be voluntary or mandatory as a condition of employment. Making a contributory plan mandatory solves the employee participation problem, but it may create serious employee relations problems. Therefore, most employers do not have mandatory contributory plans.

In the context of this cost/employee participation trade-off, one approach toward helping make this decision is to rank employee benefits in terms of the relative degree to which the employer feels that all employees and their dependents should be protected, and hence that the plan should aim for 100 percent participation, compared with plans where such a high level of participation is not deemed essential. This same kind of analysis also might be helpful in determining the level of employee contribution if it is decided to have the plan be contributory. Another factor bearing on this decision is whether other benefits in the employer's overall plan also may be available to meet the same functional need. For example, employee benefit plans frequently contain a number of kinds of benefits intended to help provide retirement income for employees. Still another factor to consider is the extent to which employees or their dependents, or both, may have similar benefits available to them elsewhere. Those employees or dependents who have an alternative source of similar benefits may opt not to participate if the plan is made contributory, thereby helping to avoid duplication of benefits. An example of this is the availability of multiple plans of medical expense benefits when both a husband and wife are employed outside the home.

There seems to be a tendency toward providing employees with alternative benefits or levels of benefits, with varying degrees of employee contributions (if any) required. In any event, as part of its benefit planning system, it will be helpful for an employer to make a benefit-by-benefit analysis, within the context of its overall benefit and compensation philosophy, to evaluate the desirability of any employee (and possibly dependent) contributions to the cost of the various employee benefits or levels of benefits.

Flexibility Available to Employees

The degree to which employees have flexibility in making such choices as whether they will participate in a given employee benefit; the amounts of additional coverage they may wish to purchase; the opportunity to select from among two or more alternative plans of benefits; and even the opportunity to structure their own benefit program, as under a cafeteria compensation approach, for example, clearly has an impact on the extent to which employees may tailor an employee benefit plan to meet their own needs and goals within the functional categories described previously. In fact, it may be argued that the more flexibility employees have, the more likely it is that the benefit program they select will meet their individual needs and goals. It thus can be argued, on the one hand, that flexibility in employee benefit plan design should facilitate the goals of the functional approach to employee benefit planning. On the other hand, it also can be argued that allowing too much employee flexibility in choosing types and amounts of employee benefits may work against the functional approach, because employees may misperceive or not understand their and their families' needs and hence leave some uncovered. This concern often is addressed in employee benefit planning by limiting the choices of employees or by specifying a core of benefits which are not subject to employee choice.

A distinct trend exists toward giving employees more flexibility in the structuring of their own employee benefits. As discussed above, this trend probably buttresses the functional approach, in that it may be presumed that rational employees will opt for those benefits and benefit amounts that will best meet their individual needs and goals.

Actual Employee Participation in Benefit Plans

It was noted above that under the functional approach an employer may analyze the types of benefits provided to employees and their dependents according to the various functional categories. The employer also may estimate or project benefit levels for the benefits in the different categories under certain assumptions and given certain contingencies or events. However, these analyses and estimates of benefits and benefit levels may not completely show how well certain employee benefits actually reach a given employee group. Therefore, an employer also may want to calculate the actual participation ratios of its employees and their dependents for given employee benefit plans. These ratios can be calculated in terms of the employees (and their dependents) actually participating in the plan as a ratio of total full-time employees, as a ratio of total eligible employees, or as both.

A given employee benefit plan may have many good features, and may even be quite liberal in some respects; but if the ratio of employee participation is low, the particular benefit may not be meeting the employer's objectives in terms of its total compensation system.

Of course, if a given employee benefit is noncontributory, and if its eligibility requirements are reasonably liberal, all the eligible employees will be covered and, probably, a reasonably high percentage of total employees also will be covered. However, when employee benefit plans are contributory and/or eligibility requirements are tighter, the participation ratios may drop significantly. When this is the case, an employer may wish to evaluate what steps it might take to improve participation in the particular plan or plans.

Determine Gaps in Benefits and Any Overlapping Benefits

From the preceding steps, it is possible to analyze more effectively any gaps in the employer's present employee benefit plan. These gaps may be in terms of the benefits available from all sources in the plan to meet the various functional categories of employee needs, in terms of the projected levels of benefits for those needs, in terms of the coverage of the various categories of persons the employer may want to protect, and finally in terms of the actual participation of employees in the various components of the employee benefit plan. In a similar fashion, the employer will want to determine any overlapping benefits that presently may be provided from all sources in its employee benefit plan to meet certain categories of needs.

Consider Recommendations for Changes in Present Plan

As a result of the functional approach described above, the employer may consider various recommendations or alternative recommendations for changes in its present employee benefit plan to eliminate gaps in benefits or persons covered and to avoid any overlapping benefits. This step involves the consideration of alternatives which is implicit in any decision-making system.

Estimate Costs (or Savings) for Each Recommendation

This is an important step before any recommendations for improvements, reductions, or changes in an employee benefit plan can be adopted. These cost (or savings) estimates are based upon certain assumptions and may be expressed in terms of ranges of possible cost (or savings) results. An employer normally will have certain overall cost constraints on its employee benefit planning. Therefore, recommended improvements or changes in the plan may have to be assigned certain priorities in terms of which ones the employer can afford to adopt.

Evaluate Alternative Methods of Financing Benefits

This step involves the evaluation of how the recommended changes in benefits for the present plan or existing benefits in the present plan, or both, should be financed or secured. While this may not strictly involve the functional analysis of benefits in relation to needs, it is an essential step in analyzing any employee benefit plan.

Consider Other Cost-Saving Techniques

At this point, the employer also should consider other cost-saving techniques concerning its employee benefits. These may involve changes in benefit plan design, elimination or reduction of certain benefits, use of alternative methods of financing certain benefits, changes in insurers or servicing organizations, changes in investment policies or advisors, the decision to self-fund or retain certain benefits as opposed to seeking insurance coverage, and other similar techniques. Again, while consideration of such techniques may not be directly involved in the functional analysis of an employee benefit plan, it is a logical step in the planning process once such a functional analysis is begun.

Decide upon Appropriate Benefits and Financing Methods

Once the preceding analysis is complete, the employer or union is in a position to decide upon the particular benefit recommendations it wants to adopt or bargain for. The employer also may decide upon appropriate financing methods. This is essentially the selection of the best alternative or alternatives in the decision-making process.

Implement Any Changes

This step involves the implementation of the changes or recommendations decided upon above. It is the implementation phase of the decision-making process.

Communicate Benefit Changes to Employees

The effective communication of employee benefits and changes in such benefits is a vital element in the overall success of any employee benefit plan. It often is a neglected element. An employer may go to a great deal of time, trouble, and expense in making improvements in its employee benefit plan, but all this effort and cost may not be as effective as it could be in terms of good employee relations and meeting the employer's personnel policies if the improvements are not effectively communicated to the employees.

Many employers communicate periodically to employees the current overall status and value of their employee benefits. This frequently is done annually. Such a communication concerning the status and total value of an employee's benefits may be accomplished at least in part by using categories of benefits similar to those classified in the functional approach described above. See Chapter 46 of the *Handbook* for a more detailed discussion of communications.

Periodically Reevaluate the Plan

Employee benefit planning is a task that is never complete. Concepts of employee needs, and the benefits available to meet those needs, are constantly changing. Therefore, the employee benefit plan must be constantly reevaluated and updated.

CHAPTER 3

REGULATORY ENVIRONMENT OF EMPLOYEE BENEFIT PLANS

Dallas L. Salisbury

The regulatory environment of employee benefit plans has changed dramatically over the past 35 years. Major legislation was passed in 1942, 1958, and 1974, with a continuous flow of legislation, regulations, and rulings from then until the recent passage of the Tax Reform Act of 1986. The combined effect of these laws and rules has been to make the administration of employee benefit plans increasingly complex.

This chapter briefly reviews the regulatory environment for private pension and welfare plans; insurance programs; federal, state, and local government pension plans; and disability programs. It is intended to heighten awareness of the complexity of the regulatory environment.

The chapter is not intended to provide legal guidance or to be a guide to compliance. There are several "loose-leaf" services available that should be consulted to keep abreast of the constant changes taking place.

PRIVATE PENSION AND WELFARE PLANS

Pre-ERISA

Before the enactment of the Employee Retirement Income Security Act (ERISA) on Labor Day 1974, only three principal statutes governed private pension plans: the Internal Revenue Code (IRC), the Federal Welfare and Pension Plans Disclosure Act of 1958 (WPPDA), and the Taft-Hartley Act, more formally known as the Labor Management Relations Act of 1947. The latter regulated collectively bargained multiemployer pension plans.

Amendments to the Internal Revenue Code enacted in 1942 established standards for the design and operation of pension plans. The principal purposes were to prevent plans from discriminating or disproportionately benefiting one group of employees over another and to prevent plans from taking excessive or unjustified tax deductions. Until 1974, the Internal Revenue Service was not concerned with the actuarial soundness of plans.

The Federal Welfare and Pension Plans Disclosure Act of 1958 was enacted to protect plan assets against fraudulent behavior by the plan administrator. The act mandated that, upon request, participants concerned with plan malpractice would be provided with information concerning the plan. If misuse or fraud were suspected, it was up to the participant to bring charges against the administrator. A significant amendment to the WPPDA was enacted in 1962. That amendment authorized the Department of Justice to bring appropriate legal action to protect plan participants' interests and authorized the Department of Labor to interpret and enforce the Act. For the first time, the burden of plan asset protection was placed upon the government rather than the individual participants.

Employee Retirement Income Security Act of 1974 (ERISA)

The shift to government protection of participants' rights enacted in 1962 would carry through to ERISA. It reflected a concern for workers, which was confirmed by President John Kennedy in 1962 with appointment of a Committee on Corporate Pension Funds and Other Retirement and Welfare Programs. That committee issued its report in 1965, concluding that private pension plans should continue as a major element in the nation's total retirement security program. The report advocated many changes in the breadth of private plan regulation.

The report received widespread attention and led to the introduction of a number of legislative proposals. Congress concluded that most plans were operated for the benefit of participants on a sound basis, but some were not. To solve this problem, Congress enacted ERISA. ERISA governs every aspect of private pension and welfare plans and requires employers who sponsor plans to operate them in compliance with ERISA standards.

TITLE I: PROTECTION OF EMPLOYEE BENEFIT RIGHTS

Title I of ERISA placed primary jurisdiction over reporting, disclosure, and fiduciary matters in the Department of Labor.The Department of the Treasury is given primary jurisdiction over participation, vesting, and funding. During the first years of ERISA, this "dual-jurisdiction" led to a number of problems which were addressed in 1979 by Reorganization Plan Number 4, discussed in a later part of this chapter. As a result of reorganizations and administrative experience under ERISA, many requirements have been adjusted, resulting in a reduction of regulatory burdens.

Reporting and Disclosure

Plan sponsors are required to provide plan participants with summary plan descriptions and benefit statements. They also are provided access to plan financial information. Documents provided to participants are to be written in "plain English" so they can be easily understood.

Plan sponsors file an annual financial report (Form 5500 series) with the IRS, which is made available to other agencies. In addition, plan sponsors must file amendments when modifications to the plan are made. Taken together, these provisions seek to assure that the government has accurate information on employer-sponsored plans.

Fiduciary Requirements

Plan sponsors are subject to an ERISA fiduciary standard mandating the plan be operated solely for the benefit of plan participants. The fiduciary standard, or "prudent man standard," requires the plan fiduciary perform duties solely in the interest of plan participants with the care a prudent man acting under like circumstances would use. This means any person who exercises discretion in the management and maintenance of the plan or in the investment of the plan assets must do so in the interest of the plan participants and beneficiaries, in accordance with the plan documents, and in a manner that minimizes the risk of loss to the participant. The standard applies to plan sponsors, trustees, and cofiduciaries, and to investment advisors with discretionary authority over the purchase and sale of plan securities. Underlying the standard are prohibitions against business or investment transactions between the plan and fiduciaries or interested parties. Upon violation of the prohibitions, the fiduciary may be held personally liable to the plan for any misuse, fraud, or mismanagement. Exemptions can be applied for when parties feel that actions are not to the detriment of the plan and its participants and should be allowed. Both the IRS and the Department of Labor are responsible for enforcing the fiduciary standards. The Department of Labor may file charges on behalf of the participants if the fiduciary has breached or violated the standards imposed by ERISA. The IRS may fine the employer and revoke the plan's favorable tax treatment. Both civil and criminal actions may arise for violations.

TITLE II: MINIMUM STANDARDS

Title II of ERISA contains minimum standards for participation, vesting, and funding of benefits, which must be satisfied for qualification of a plan. It also contains amendments to the IRC that increase the scope of federal regulation over certain pension plans, whether tax qualified or not.

Participation

Although ERISA (as amended) does not require every employer set up an employer pension or welfare benefit plan, it does impose requirements on those who do. For those employers sponsoring plans, the age of employee eligibility cannot be higher than 21. A maximum of one year of service and 1,000 hours of work also may be required for eligibility.

Vesting

Upon satisfying the participation requirements, further conditions must be met for the participant to become entitled to receive a benefit—that is, to have a vested right to the benefits. There are two alternative vesting requirements contained in ERISA (as amended).

Full vesting after five years of service, with no vesting before the five-year requirement is met.

Graduated vesting from the time the participant completes three years of service (full vesting after seven years):

Benefits

Under ERISA, benefits generally must be earned in a uniform manner while the participant is employed. This does not affect the levels of benefits provided by the plan, only the rate at which the benefits are earned.

Funding

The minimum funding standards attempt to ensure that plans will have sufficient assets to pay benefits. Those employers with plans subject to the standards must establish and maintain a funding standard account. The sponsor must annually contribute the normal cost—the annual cost of future pension benefits and administrative expenses—plus amounts necessary to amortize in equal installments unfunded past service liabilities and any experience losses less experience gains. The amortization period in the former case generally is 30 years, and in the latter case 15 years. The presence of these standards has changed the environment for pension plans, creating greater need for long-range planning.

Tax-Qualified Plans

Requirements for tax qualification of plans has not materially changed since 1942. Meeting these requirements allows the employer to deduct contributions from income and makes investment earnings on plan assets exempt from current taxation.

The structure of tax-qualified plans is determined by ERISA requirements. The terms of the plan must be set forth in a written document. Copies of the plan and related documents must be made available to participants. In addition, a summary of the plan must be made available. The plan sponsor must have created the plan with the intent of permanency.

The provisions of the pension plan also are dictated by the requirements of the IRC.

- As referred to above, the plan must meet minimum participation, vesting, and funding standards and plan assets must be legally segregated from other assets of the sponsor.
- The plan must not benefit only a limited number of favored employees but must benefit employees in general in such a way as to be deemed nondiscriminatory by the IRS. This status must extend to contributions and benefits such that officers, shareholders, or highly compensated employees are not favored when the plan is viewed in its entirety.
- The pension plan must provide definitely determinable benefits.

Overall, the IRC implementing regulations and rulings have had the goal of fostering accrual and preservation of benefits for present and potential plan participants and beneficiaries.

The requirements for a tax-qualified profit-sharing plan are somewhat different in that the plan must cover all employees and the benefit is not determinable.

Fulfillment of all tax qualification requirements entitles the employer to a current deduction from gross income for contributions to the plan. The participating employee recognizes no taxable income until the funds are made available in the form of benefits or are distributed as a lump-sum distribution. When the distribution is made upon termination of service taxes become due unless, in the case of a lump-sum distribution, the funds are rolled over into another plan.

Employees may voluntarily be allowed, or in some cases required, to make contributions to qualified plans. The employee's required contributions are limited to the maximum amount provided in the plan and no tax deduction is allowed.

Nonqualified Plans

Nonqualified employee benefit plans have not been designed to satisfy the IRC requirements and may either be funded or nonfunded. Under the funded plan, the employer agrees to make contributions to the plan for the benefit of the employee. Under an unfunded plan, the employer promises to provide a benefit to the participant at some future time. Most funded plans must satisfy ERISA, while unfunded plans must only meet ERISA's reporting and disclosure provisions.

TITLE IV: PLAN TERMINATION INSURANCE

Title IV of ERISA established the Pension Benefit Guaranty Corporation (PBGC), a governmental body that insures payment of plan benefits under certain circumstances.

Most defined benefit pension plans (those that provide a fixed monthly benefit at retirement) are required to participate in the program and pay premiums to the PBGC.

There are certain restrictions and limitations on the amount of benefits insured, which is adjusted annually to reflect the increasing average wages of the American workforce. The limit applies to all plans under which a participant is covered so that it is not possible to spread coverage under several plans to increase the guaranteed benefit. To be fully insured, the benefit must have been vested before the plan terminated and the benefit level must have been in effect for 60 months or else benefits are proportionately reduced. Further, the guarantee applies only to benefits earned while the plan is eligible for favorable tax treatment.

In an effort to protect against employers establishing plans without intending to continue them, ERISA introduced the concept of contingent employer liability in the event of plan termination for single-employer plans and for multi-employer plans in the event of employer withdrawal or insolvency. Additional complex requirements that apply to multiemployer plans also were established by Congress in 1980.

The PBGC has served to change substantially the environment in which plans operate. For present sponsors, and for those thinking of establishing new defined benefit plans, Title IV should be carefuly reviewed to assure its implications are fully understood.

LEGISLATION OF THE 1980s

The 1980s saw a series of legislative measures with common themes enacted into law. The laws included the Economic Recovery Tax Act of 1981 (ERTA), the Tax Equity and Fiscal Responsibility Act of 1982 (TEFRA), the Retirement Equity Act of 1984 (REA), the Deficit Reduction Act of 1984 (DEFRA), the Consolidated Budget and Reconciliation Act of 1985 (COBRA), the Tax Reform Act of 1986 (TRA '86) and the Omnibus Reconciliation Act of 1987 (OBRA). The themes included:

- Employee benefit tax incentives should be limited to those benefits that offer a clear social purpose and provide protection against some risk.
- Coverage and nondiscrimination rules should be designed to assure that low- and middle-income employees actually benefit from plans.
- Benefits provided to the highly compensated on a tax-favored basis should be restricted to those provided to other employees (in the case of health and welfare plans) and by both dollar and percentage limits (in the case of retirement programs), and those with a top-heavy workforce must pay a minimum benefit to all workers.
- Tax deductions for programs that are not subject to coverage and nondiscrimination rules, such as individual retirement accounts (IRAs), should not be available to high income taxpayers with pension coverage.
- Defined benefit and defined contribution programs should have a common primary purpose of delivering income at or near normal retirement ages and should not serve the purpose of short-term savings or an overriding purpose of encouraging early retirement.

- Defined benefit and defined contribution plans should always be a supplement to Social Security, and there should be absolute limits on the total amount of tax-favored retirement income that can be received from tax-favored plans.
- Defined benefit and defined contribution benefit values should be treated as common property, and survivor benefits should generally be available, decisions on benefit forms being common decisions.

COBRA established rules to assure that individuals would have access to continued group health insurance upon job termination, and Congress can be expected to expand this concept to one of assured access for all Americans.

OBRA of 1987 significantly tightened funding standards for defined benefit plans, further restricted plan terminations, and moved the PBGC to a much higher and variable premium. Legislation consistent with the themes just noted will continue to be considered and enacted with emphasis on the larger theme that employers should be responsible for keeping promises once made *regardless of the financial implications for the business*.

ADDITIONAL REGULATORY AGENCIES

Labor Laws

A number of laws, from both statutory and case law, give the Department of Labor authority to monitor and regulate employee benefit plans.

Among them is the National Labor Relations Act, which promotes collective bargaining between employers and employees' representatives. The Taft-Hartley Act contains specific provisions similar to ERISA and the IRC relating to plan structure and content.The landmark case of *Inland Steel Company* v. *the National Labor Relations Board* prohibits an employer from refusing to bargain with employees upon a properly presented demand to bargain regarding employee benefit plans.

Equal Employment Opportunity Commission (EEOC)

The EEOC's interest in employee benefit plans stems from various acts that prohibit discriminatory plan practices. The Civil Rights Act of 1964, Title VII, is interpreted by the EEOC as defining discrimination between men and women with regard to fringe benefits as an unlawful employment practice. The Equal Pay Act of 1963 makes employer discrimination between the sexes in the payment of wages for equal work unlawful. Benefits under employee benefit plans are a form of wages and must be free from discrimination, held one EEOC decision. The Age Discrimination in Employment Act of 1967 and its 1975 and 1979 amendments clearly prohibit discrimination on the basis of age.

Securities and Exchange Commission (SEC)

Under the Securities Act of 1933, information concerning securities publicly offered and sold in interstate commerce or through the mails is required to be disclosed to the SEC. At first blush, the act does not seem to apply to employee benefit plans. However, a security is defined by the act as including participation in any profit-sharing agreement. The Securities Act of 1934 affects the administration of plans by imposing disclosure and registration requirements and antifraud provisions. The SEC has not actively enforced requirements, but the scope of legal SEC jurisdiction has been debated and litigated.

The Investment Company Act of 1940 regulates reporting and disclosure, structure, content, and administration of investment companies. A pension benefit plan could be subject to this act if it fits the definition of an investment company. An investment company, as defined by the act, is one engaged in the business of holding, trading, investing, or owning securities.

Other Acts and Agencies

The Small Business Administration (SBA) receives complaints from small businesses regarding the relationship of small business to agencies of the federal government.

Banking laws also apply. The National Bank Act permits national banks to act as trustees in a fiduciary capacity in which state banks or trust companies are permitted to act under the laws of the state where the national bank is located. This affects private employee benefit plans because banks act as fiduciaries. The Federal Reserve Act and the Federal Reserve System can affect pension and welfare plans, since plans may either be borrowers or lenders. Because there is regulation of interest payable on deposits in banks that are members of the Federal Reserve System, IRA and Keogh plans are affected in terms of possible rates of return. The Federal Deposit Insurance Act also affects these plans that are not covered by the PBGC since funds held by an insured bank, in its capacity as fiduciary, will be insured up to $100,000.

The Commerce Department is concerned with ERISA's impact on the health of the economy. The Department of Health and Human Services (HHS) tries to keep track of individuals with deferred vested benefit plans as well as administering Social Security and other public programs that have a substantial impact on private plan design.

THE REGULATION OF INSURANCE

Both the individual state governments and the federal government regulate insurance. The states regulate rates, financial examination, formation of the company, qualification of officers, licensing, and taxing. The federal government provides for regulation as noted above in addition to the activity of the Federal Insurance Administrator, the Interstate Commerce Commission, and the Federal Trade Commission.

A growing concern exists over which level of government is the most appropriate for the regulation of insurance. It is felt by many that there should be greater federal involvement. Advocates of federal regulation argue that state regulation lacks uniformity and that multiple state regulation is more costly than federal regulation, that the state insurance commissioners are unqualified, and that the states cannot effectively regulate interstate companies. Those who favor state regulation feel the states are more responsive to local conditions and needs, that state regulation encourages innovation and experimentation, and that the decentralization of power is advantageous.

At present there exists an ongoing disagreement between the states and the federal government over the extent of preemption of state laws by ERISA. The federal government believes it could move towards greater regulation without legal difficulty. This is based upon the federal ability to regulate interstate commerce, to provide for the general welfare, and to tax. Section 514(a) of ERISA states that it shall supersede any and all state laws insofar as they may now or later relate to any employee benefit plan. The preemption does not apply to any state law that regulates insurance. But, to what extent does ERISA preempt laws enacted under the insurance codes of the states, when such laws are designed specifically to apply to the insurance-type functions of employee benefit plans?

The Department of Labor advocated a broad interpretation of Section 514, which would preempt most state statutes even if the laws deal with areas not explicitly covered by ERISA, such as the content of health benefit plans. The federal courts have not been so consistent in their interpretation of the statute. In one case, *Fleck* v. *Spannaus,* the court decided ERISA does not preempt causes of action occurring before January 1, 1975. But in another case, *Azzaro* v. *Harnett,* the court held that Congress intended absolute preemption in the field of employee benefits.

Even the insurance exception found in section 514 is subject to limitations: "No employee benefit plan shall be deemed to be an insurance company or engaged in the business of insurance for the purpose of any law of any state purporting to regulate an insurance company."

In general, the courts have tended to preempt state regulation which relates to employee pension and retirement plans. This stems from the broad-based protections incorporated in ERISA for pension plan participants. The courts are less inclined to preempt state laws which apply to employee health and insurance plans. ERISA has had a more limited application to welfare plans and a more narrow view of the preemptive effect in the health and welfare plan area. When health insurance benefits are mandated in traditional insurance contracts, rather than through comprehensive health care legislation, claims of federal preemption will not hold. However, when an employer's prepaid health care plan satisfies the ERISA definition, state regulation is preempted.

Where the line eventually will be drawn between state and federal regulation of health and welfare plans is very uncertain. The debate will most likely center on the degree to which arrangements have insurance versus noninsurance characteristics. Ultimately, the courts can be expected to be heavily involved.

FEDERAL, STATE, AND LOCAL GOVERNMENT PENSION PLANS

Public plans represent a substantial level of retirement income promises for federal, state, and local employees. Benefit levels promised in public plans exceed those of the private sector. Public plans exist free of federal regulatory controls like those imposed by ERISA. For practical purposes there is only a limited "regulatory environment."

Public employee pension programs are receiving a considerable amount of attention today because of the sharp increases in current appropriations necessary to support retirement programs. Federal regulation of private plans has given rise to a Congressional commitment to the study of public plans and to an assessment of whether a public plan version of ERISA should be enacted.

Research has revealed that large cities with their own pension plans are likely to provide some of the most generous benefits available in the public sector. Public employees generally have more liberal early retirement provisions in their pension plans than private employees, and public plans usually include a provision for automatic increases in retirees' benefits when the cost of living increases.

State and local plans are viewed by many as being substantially underfunded. Actuarial, financial, auditing, and disclosure requirements are viewed as deficient. Many charge that fiduciary standards are seriously breached. Other characteristics of public plans have led to criticisms, including:

- Their retirement benefits replace a substantial percentage of final pay after only 20 to 25 years of service.
- Their normal retirement ages are set well ahead of the end of productive working lifetimes.
- They are generous in granting a high proportion of early disability retirements in "high risk" professions (police, firemen, and the like), rather than retaining the workforce in less hazardous positions.

Substantial concern also is generated because some federal, state, and local employees currently are not covered by the Social Security program. Because of noninclusion, or lack of integration when both programs are involved, there is a belief that public employees obtain "windfall" benefits or unnecessarily large benefits, or both. For example, a recent government study indicated that income replacement ratios for public employees serving 30 years at average wages received more than 100 percent of salary in 53 percent of all cases, and 125 percent of salary in more than 10 percent of all cases.

These and other issues have led to the development of state commissions to advise state legislators on pension issues. The threat of an impending federal intervention (in the form of PERISA—the Public Employee Retirement Income Security Act) has stimulated efforts in many states to monitor state and local pension funds more closely and to improve reporting and disclosure practices.

DISABILITY PROGRAMS

In 1975, cash disability payments equaled 25 percent of all cash payments to retirees, survivors, and the disabled. Disability programs resemble pension programs in that their purposes are similar (both, generally, are intended to maintain the income of workers and their dependents or survivors when they are unable to work), program finances are intertwined, and disability programs are sometimes used to substitute for retirement programs.

Disability program trends indicate that cash disability programs have grown rapidly and that the federal role in disability programs has increased. Analyses indicate workers of all ages are being awarded disability benefits more frequently than in previous years. Per capita benefits generally have grown more rapidly than earnings and the difference in growth rates has been larger since 1970.

Social factors also add to the increase in disability payouts. Society is doing more to support the disabled. More and more people identify themselves as disabled. It is indicated that disability programs may be repeating the welfare crisis of the 1960s, the dramatic increase in beneficiaries largely representing a growing percentage of eligible persons claiming benefits.

Social Security Disability Benefits

To qualify for Social Security disability benefits, the wage earner must be unable to engage in any substantial activity by reason of medically determined physical or mental impairment that can be expected to result in death or to last for a continuous period. Total disability exists if the claimant's disability equals or exceeds the standards as established and is documented by a medical report using the language required by the regulations. The Social Security Act considers age, education, and previous work experience when applying the disability standard. The wage earner also must meet special earnings requirements to be covered. The wage earner must have performed 20 quarters of employment in the 40 quarters immediately prior to the alleged onset of disability. The benefit payout begins on the sixth month of disability.

CONCLUSION

The regulatory environment of employee benefit programs is far-reaching and complex. It involves all levels of government in at least some areas, and numerous different agencies at each level, all with the purpose of protecting the potential recipient and adding security to the benefit promise.

The degree to which the environment is refined is constantly changing. There has been no rest from discussion of new legislative proposals or new regulatory initiatives. Some proposals aim at reducing regulation, others at increasing it. Frequently the short-term effect is the same: creation of uncertainty which inhibits the growth and development of employee benefit programs.

The challenge for the practitioner is to understand the environment, to understand how it affects particular situations, and to affect it when the opportunity arises.

CHAPTER 4

SOCIAL SECURITY AND MEDICARE

Robert J. Myers

Economic security for retired workers, disabled workers, and survivors of deceased workers in the United States is, in the vast majority of cases, provided through the multiple means of Social Security, private pensions, and individual savings. This is sometimes referred to as a "three-legged stool" or the three pillars of economic-security protection. Still others look upon the situation as Social Security providing the floor of protection, with private sector activities building on top of it and public assistance programs, such as Supplemental Security Income (SSI) providing a net of protection for those whose total retirement income does not attain certain levels or meet minimum subsistence needs.

Although some people may view the Social Security program as one that should provide complete protection, over the years it generally has been agreed that it should only be the foundation of protection.

As described elsewhere in this book, private pension plans have, to a significant extent, been developed to supplement Social Security. This is done in a number of ways, both directly and indirectly. The net result, however, is a broad network of retirement protection.

This chapter discusses in detail the retirement, disability, and survivor provisions of the Social Security program, not only their historical development and present structure but also a summary of the financial crises of the late 1970s and early 1980s (and what was done to solve them) and possible future changes. Following this, the Medicare program is described. Also, descriptions of the two public assistance programs (Supplemental Security Income and Medicaid) that supplement Old Age, Survivors and Disability Insurance (OASDI) and Medicare are given.

The term *Social Security* as used here is the meaning generally accepted in the United States, namely, the cash benefits provisions of the OASDI program. International usage of the term *social security* is much broader than this and includes all other types of programs protecting individuals against the economic risks of a modern industrial system, such as unemployment, short-term sickness, work-connected accidents and diseases, and medical care costs.

OLD-AGE, SURVIVORS, AND DISABILITY INSURANCE PROGRAM

Persons Covered Under OASDI

OASDI coverage—for both taxes and earnings credits toward benefit rights—currently applies to somewhat more than 90 percent of the total work force of the United States. About half of those not covered have protection through a special employee retirement system, while the remaining half are either very low-paid intermittent workers or unpaid family workers.

The vast majority of persons covered under OASDI are so affected on a mandatory, or compulsory, basis. Several categories, however, have optional or semioptional coverage. It is important to note that OASDI coverage applies not only to employees, both salaried and wage earner, but also to self-employed persons. Some individuals who are essentially employees are nonetheless classified as self-employed for the sake of convenience in applying coverage.

Compulsory coverage is applicable to all employees in commerce and industry, interpreting these classifications very broadly, except railroad workers, who are covered under a separate program, the Railroad Retirement system. Actually, however, financial and other coordinating provisions exist between these two programs, so that, in reality, railroad workers are really covered under OASDI. Members of the armed forces are covered compulsorily, as are federal civilian employees hired after 1983. Compulsory coverage also applies to lay employees of churches (with certain minor exceptions), to employees of nonprofit charitable and educational institutions, and to American citizens who work abroad for American corporations. Self-employed persons of all types (except ministers) also are covered compulsorily unless their earnings are minimal (i.e., less than $400 a year).

From a geographical standpoint, OASDI applies not only in the 50 states and the District of Columbia but also in all outlying areas (American Samoa, Guam, Puerto Rico, and the Virgin Islands).

Elective coverage applies to a number of categories. Employees of state and local governments can have coverage at the option of the employing entity, and, in the case where a retirement system exists at the time of election, only when the current employees vote in favor of coverage. Similar provisions are available for American employees of foreign subsidiaries of American corporations, the latter having the right to opt for coverage. Once that coverage has been elected by a state or local government, it cannot be terminated. Approximately 70 percent of state and local government employees are now covered as a result of this election basis.

Because of the principle of separation of church and state, ministers are covered on the self-employed basis, regardless of their actual status. Furthermore, they have the right to opt out of the system within a limited time after ordination on grounds of religious principles or conscience. Americans employed in the United States by a foreign government or by an international organization are covered compulsorily on the self-employed basis.

Historical Development of Retirement Provisions

When what is now the OASDI program was developed in 1934–35, it was confined entirely to retirement benefits plus lump-sum refund payments to represent the difference, if any, between employee taxes paid, plus an allowance for interest, and retirement benefits received. It was not until the 1939 act that auxiliary (or dependents) and survivors benefits were added, and not until the 1956 act that disability benefits were made available. It is likely that only retirement benefits were instituted initially because such type of protection was the most familiar to the general public, especially in light of the relatively few private pension plans then in existence.

The "normal retirement age" (NRA) was originally established at 65. This figure was selected in a purely empirical manner, because it was a middle figure. Age 70 seemed too high, because of the common belief that relatively so few people reached that age, while age 60 seemed too low, because of the large costs that would be involved if that age had been selected. Many of the existing private pension plans at that time had a retirement age of 65, although some in the railroad industry used age 70. Furthermore, labor-force participation data showed that a relatively high proportion of workers continued in employment after age 60. A widely quoted reason why age 65 was selected is that Bismarck chose this age when he established the German national pension program in the 1880s; this, however is not so, because the age actually used originally in Germany was 70. The 1983 Act provided for the NRA to increase from age 65 to age 67 in a deferred, gradual manner. Specifically, the NRA is 65 for those attaining this age before 2003 and first becomes 67 for those attaining this age in 2027.

The original program applied only to workers in commerce and industry. It was not until the 1950s that coverage was extended to additional categories of workers. Now, almost all are covered, including the self-employed.

The initial legislation passed by the House of Representatives did not require eligible persons to retire when age 65 or over in order to receive benefits, although it was recognized that the retirement requirement would be essential to include in the final legislation. The Senate inserted a requirement of a general nature that benefits would be payable only upon retirement, and this was included in the final legislation. Over the years, this retirement test, or work clause, has been the subject of much controversy, and it has been considerably liberalized and made more flexible over the years.

Beginning in the 1950s, pressure developed to provide early-retirement benefits, first for spouses and then for insured workers themselves. The minimum early-retirement age was set at 62, again a pragmatic political compromise, rather than being based on any completely logical reason. The three-year differential, however, did represent about the average difference in age between men and their wives but, of course, as with any averages, the difference actually is larger in many cases. The benefit amounts are reduced when claimed before the NRA, and are increased, although to not as great an extent, for delaying retirement beyond the NRA. As the NRA increases beyond age 65, the reduction for claiming benefits at age 62 becomes larger.

Eligibility Conditions for Retirement Benefits

To be eligible for OASDI retirement benefits, individuals must have a certain amount of covered employment. In general, these conditions were designed to be relatively easy to meet in the early years of operation, thus bringing the program into effectiveness quickly. Eligibility for retirement benefits—termed *fully insured status*—depends upon having a certain number of "quarters of coverage" (QC), varying with the year of birth or, expressed in another manner, depending upon the year of an individual's attainment of age 62.

Before 1978, a QC was defined simply as a calendar quarter during which the individual was paid $50 or more in wages from covered employment; the self-employed ordinarily received four QCs for each year of coverage at $400 or more of earnings. Beginning in 1978, the number of QCs acquired for each year depends upon the total earnings in the year. For 1978, each full unit of $250 of earnings produced a QC, up to a maximum of four QCs for the year. In subsequent years the requirement has increased, and will continue to increase in the future, in accordance with changes in the general wage level; for 1988, it is $470.

The number of QCs required for fully insured status is determined from the number of years in the period beginning in 1951, or with the year of attainment of age 22, if later, and the year before the year of attainment of age 62, with a minimum requirement of six. As a result, an individual who attained age 62 before 1958 needed only six QCs to be fully insured. A person attaining age 62 in 1987 has a requirement of 36 QCs, while a person attaining age 65 in 1987 needs 33 QCs. The maximum number of QCs that will ever be required for fully insured status is 40, applicable to persons attaining age 62 after 1990. It is important to note that, although the requirement for the number of QCs is determined from 1951, or attainment of age 22, and before attainment of age 62, the QCs to meet the requirement can be obtained at any time (e.g., before 1951, before age 22, and after age 61).

Beneficiary Categories for Retirement Benefits

Insured workers can receive unreduced retirement benefits in the amount of the Primary Insurance Amount (or PIA), the derivation of which will be discussed next, beginning at the NRA, or actuarially reduced benefits beginning at earlier ages, down to age 62. For retirement at age 62 currently (and until 1999), the benefit is 80 percent of the PIA. As the NRA increases beyond 65, the reduction will become larger (eventually being 30 percent).

Retired workers also can receive supplementary payments for spouses and eligible children. The spouse receives a benefit at the rate of 50 percent of the PIA if claim is first made at the NRA or over, and at a reduced rate if claimed at ages down to 62 (currently, a 25 percent reduction at age 62—i.e., to 37.5 percent of the PIA); as the NRA increases beyond 65, the reduction for age 62 will be larger, eventually being 35 percent. However, if a child under age 16 or a child aged 16 or over who was disabled before age 22 is present, the spouse receives benefits regardless of age, in an unreduced amount. Divorced spouses, when the marriage had lasted at least 10 years, are eligible for benefits under the same conditions as undivorced spouses.

Children under age 18 (and children aged 18 or over and disabled before age 22, plus children attending high school full-time at age 18 also are eligible for benefits, at a rate of 50 percent of the PIA; prior to legislation in 1981, post-secondary school students aged 18–21 were eligible for benefits, and spouses with children in their care could receive benefits as long as a child under age 18 was present. Grandchildren and great-grandchildren can qualify as "children" if they are dependent on the individual *and* if both parents of the child are disabled or deceased.

An overall maximum on total family benefits is applicable as is discussed later. If a person is eligible for more than one type of benefit (e.g., both as a worker and as a spouse), in essence only the largest benefit is payable.

Computation and Indexing Procedures for Retirement Benefits

As indicated in the previous section, OASDI benefits are based on the PIA. The method of computing the PIA is quite complicated, especially because several different methods are available. The only method dealt with here in any detail is that generally applicable to people who reach age 65 after 1981.

Persons who attained age 65 before 1982 use a method based on the average monthly wage (AMW). This is based essentially on a career average, involving the consideration of all earnings back through 1951. To take into account the general inflation in earnings that has occurred in the last three decades, automatic-adjustment procedures are involved in the benefit computations. However, these turned out to be faulty, because they did not—and would not in the future—produce stable benefit results when comparing initial benefits with final earnings. Accordingly, in the 1977 amendments, a new procedure applicable to those attaining age 62 after 1978 was adopted, but the old procedure was retained for earlier attainments of age 62. The result has been to give unusually and inequitably large benefits to those who attained age 62 before 1979, thus creating a "notch" situation.

Persons who attain age 62 in 1979–83 can use an alternative method somewhat similar to the AMW method, but with it having certain restrictions, if this produces a larger PIA than the new, permanent method. In actual practice, however, this modified-AMW method generally produces more favorable results only for persons attaining age 62 in 1979–81 and not continuing in employment after that age.

Still another method is available for all individuals who have earnings before 1951. In the vast majority of such cases, however, the new-start methods based on earnings after 1950 produce more favorable results.

The first step in the ongoing permanent method of computing the PIA applicable to persons attaining age 65 in 1982 or after, is to calculate the Average Indexed Monthly Earnings (AIME). The AIME is a career-average earnings formula, but it is determined in such a manner as to closely approximate a final average formula. In a national social insurance plan, it would be inadvisable to use solely an average of the last few years of employment, because that could involve serious manipulation through the cooperation of both the employee and the employer, whereas in a private pension plan, the employer has a close financial interest not to do so. Furthermore, as described later, OASDI benefit computation is not proportionate to years of coverage or proportion of worklife in covered employment, as is the case for private pension plans generally.

The first step in computing the AIME is to determine the number of years over which it must be computed. On the whole, such number depends solely on the year in which the individual attains age 62. The general rule is that the computation period equals the number of years beginning with 1951, or the year of attaining age 22, if later, up through the year before attainment of age 62, minus the so-called five dropout years. The latter is provided so that the very lowest five years of earnings can be eliminated. Also, years of high earnings in or after the year of attaining age 62 can be substituted for earlier, lower years.

As an example, persons attaining age 62 in 1987 have a computation period of 31 years (the 36 years in 1951–86, minus 5). The maximum period will be 35 years for those attaining age 62 after 1990. For the infrequent case of an individual who had qualified for OASDI disability benefits and who recovered from the disability, the number of computation years for the AIME for retirement benefits is reduced by the number of full years after age 21 and before age 62 during any part of which the person was under a disability.

The AIME is not computed from the actual covered earnings, but after indexing them, to make them more current as compared with the wage level at the time of retirement. Specifically, covered earnings for each year before attainment of age 60 are indexed to that age, while all subsequent covered earnings are used in their actual amount. No earnings before 1951 can be utilized, but all earnings subsequently, either before age 22 or after age 61, are considered.

The indexing of the earnings record is accomplished by multiplying the actual earnings of each year before the year that age 60 was attained by the increase in earnings from the particular year to the age-60 year. For example, for persons attaining age 62 in 1987 (i.e., age 60 in 1985), any earnings in 1951 would be converted to indexed earnings by multiplying them by 6.00984, which is the ratio of the nationwide average wage in 1985 to that in 1951. Similarly, the multiplying factor for 1952 earnings is 5.65782, and so on. Once the earnings record for each year in the past has been indexed, the earnings for the number of years required to be averaged are selected to include the highest ones possible; if there are not sufficient years with earnings, then zeroes must be used. Then, the AIME is obtained by dividing the total indexed earnings for such years by 12 times such number of years.

Now, having obtained the AIME, the PIA is computed from a benefit formula. There is a different formula for each annual cohort of persons attaining age 62. For example, for those who reached age 62 in 1979, the formula was 90 percent of the first $180 of AIME, plus 32 percent of the next $905 of AIME, plus 15 percent of the AIME in excess of $1,085. For the 1980 cohort, the corresponding dollar bands are $194, $977, and $1,171, while those for the 1988 cohort are $319, $1,603, and $1,922. These bands are adjusted automatically according to changes in nationwide average wages.

A different method of computing the PIA for retirement benefits (and also for disability benefits, but not for survivor benefits) is applicable for certain persons who receive pensions based in whole or in part on earnings from employment not covered by OASDI or Railroad Retirement (in the past or in the future, and in other countries as well as in the U.S.). This is done to eliminate the windfall benefits (due to the weighted nature of the benefit formula) that would otherwise arise. Excluded from this provision are the following categories: (1) persons who attain age 62 before 1986; (2) persons who were *eligible* for such pension before 1986; (3) disabled-worker beneficiaries who became disabled before 1986 (and were entitled to such benefits in at least one month in the year before attaining age 62); (4) persons who have at least 30 years of coverage (as defined hereafter); (5) persons who were employed by the federal government on January 1, 1984, and were then brought into coverage by the 1983 Amendments; and (6) persons who were employed on January 1, 1984, by a nonprofit organization which was not covered on December 31, 1983, and had not been so covered at any time in the past.

Under this method of computation of the PIA, ultimately the percentage factor applicable to the lowest band of earnings will be 40 percent, instead of 90 percent. As a transitional measure, those who become first eligible for OASDI benefits in 1986 have an 80 percent factor, while it is 70 percent for the 1987 cohort, 60 percent for the 1988 cohort, and 50 percent for the 1989 cohort.

For persons who have 26–29 "years of coverage" (as defined hereafter), an alternative phase-in procedure is used (if it produces a larger PIA). The percentage factor applicable to the lowest band of earnings in the PIA formula is 80 percent for 29 years of coverage, 70 percent for 28 years, 60 percent for 27 years, and 50 percent for 26 years.

In any event, under any of the foregoing procedures, the PIA as computed in the regular manner will never be reduced by more than 50 percent of the pension based on noncovered employment (or the pro rata portion thereof based on noncovered employment after 1956 if it is based on both covered and noncovered employment).

Prior to legislation in 1981, if the PIA benefit formula produced a smaller amount than $122 in the initial benefit computation, then this amount was nonetheless payable. However, for persons first becoming eligible after 1981, no such minimum is applicable.

A special minimum applies to the PIA for individuals who have a long period of covered work, but with low earnings. As of December 1987, this minimum is approximately $20.10 times the "years of coverage" in excess of 10, but not in excess of 30; thus, for 30 or more years of coverage, the minimum benefit is $402.00. A "year of coverage" is defined as a year in which earnings are at least 25 percent of the maximum taxable earnings base; for 1979 and after, this base is taken to be what would have prevailed if the ad hoc increases in the base provided by the 1977 act had not been applicable, and, instead, the automatic increases had occurred. Thus, for this purpose, the 1988 base is taken as $33,600, instead of the actual one of $45,000.

The resulting PIAs then are increased for any automatic adjustments applicable because of annual increases in the consumer price index (CPI)—or, when the balance of the OASDI Trust Funds is relatively low, by the annual increase in nationwide wages if this is less than the CPI rise—that occur in or after the year of attaining age 62, even though actual retirement is much later. These automatic adjustments are made for benefits for each December. Such CPI increases in the recent past have been 9.9 percent for 1979, 14.3 percent for 1980, 11.2 percent for 1981, 7.4 percent for 1982, 3.5 percent for 1983 and 1984, 3.1 percent for 1985, 1.3 percent for 1986, and 4.2 percent for 1987.

The resulting PIA then is reduced, in the manner described previously, for those who first claim benefits before the NRA. Conversely, retired workers who do not receive benefits for any months after they attain the NRA, essentially because of the earnings test, which will be described later, receive increases that are termed *delayed-retirement credits* (DRC). Such credits are currently at the rate of 3 percent per year of delay (actually 0.25 percent per month) for the period between ages 65 and 70. For those who attained age 65 before 1982, the DRC is at a rate of only 1 percent per year. For those who attain the NRA after 1989, such credit is gradually increased, until it is 8 percent for those attaining the NRA (then 66) in 2009. The DRC applies only to the worker's benefit and not to that for spouses or children.

A Maximum Family Benefit (MFB) is applicable when there are more than two beneficiaries receiving benefits on the same earnings record (i.e., the retired worker and two or more auxiliary beneficiaries). Not considered within the limit established by the MFB are the additional benefits arising from delayed-retirement credits and the benefits payable to divorced spouses. The MFB is determined prior to any reductions because of claiming benefits before the NRA, but after the effect of the earnings test as it applies to any auxiliary beneficiary (e.g., if the spouse has high earnings, any potential benefit payable to her or him would not be considered for purposes of the MFB of the other spouse).

The MFB is determined from the PIA by a complex formula. This formula varies for each annual cohort of persons attaining age 62. The resulting MFB is adjusted for increases in the CPI in the future (in the same manner as is the PIA). For the 1988 cohort, the MFB formula is: 150 percent of the first $407 of PIA, plus 272 percent of the next $181 of PIA, plus 134 percent of the next $179 of PIA, plus 175 percent of PIA in excess of $767. For future cohorts, the dollar figures are changed according to changes in nationwide average wages. The result of this formula is to produce MFBs that are 150 percent of the PIA for the lowest PIAs, with this proportion rising to a peak of 188 percent for middle-range PIAs, and then falling off to 175 percent—and levelling there—for higher PIAs.

Earnings Test and Other Restrictions on Retirement Benefits

From the inception of the OASDI program, there has been some form of restriction on the payment of benefits to persons who have substantial earnings from employment. This provision is referred to as the "earnings or retirement test." It does not apply to nonearned income, such as from investments or pensions. The general underlying principle of this test is that retirement benefits should be paid only to persons who are substantially retired.

The basic feature of the earnings test is that an annual exempt amount applies, so that full benefits are paid if earnings, including those from both covered and noncovered employment, are not in excess thereof. Then, for each $2 of excess earnings, $1 in benefits is withheld; beginning in 1990, the reduction will be on a "$1 for $3" basis for those at and above the NRA. For persons aged 65 or over (at any time in the year), the annual exempt amount is $8,400 for 1988, with the amounts for persons at and above the NRA for subsequent years being automatically determined by the increases in nationwide wages. Beginning with the month of attainment of age 70, the test no longer applies. For persons under age 65, the exempt amount is $6,120 in 1988, with automatic adjustment thereafter.

An alternative test applies for the initial year of retirement, or claim, if it results in more benefits being payable. Under this, full benefits are payable for all months in which the individual did not have substantial services in self-employment and had wages of 1/12 of the annual exempt amount or less. This provision properly takes care of the situation where an individual fully retires during a year, but had sizable earnings in the first part of the year, and thus would have most or all of the benefits withheld if only the annual test had been applicable.

Earnings of the "retired" worker affect, under the earnings test, the total family benefits payable. However, if an auxiliary beneficiary (spouse or child) has earnings, and these are sizable enough to affect the earnings test, any reduction in benefits is applicable only to such individual's benefits.

If an individual receives a pension from service under a government-employee pension plan under which the members were not covered under OASDI on the last day of her or his employment, the OASDI spouse benefit is reduced by two thirds of the amount of such pension. This provision, however, is not applicable to women—or to men who are dependent on their wives—who become eligible for such a pension before December 1982, while for December 1982 through June 1983, the provision applies only to those (both men and women) who cannot prove dependency on their spouse. This general provision results in the same treatment as occurs when both spouses have OASDI benefits based on their own earnings records; and then each receives such benefit, plus the excess, if any, of the spouse's benefit arising from the other spouse's earnings over the benefit based on their own earnings, rather than the full amount of the spouse's benefit.

Historical Development of Disability Provisions

It was not until the 1956 Act that monthly disability benefits were added to the OASDI program, although the "disability-freeze" provision (in essence, a waiver-of-premium provision), described later, was added in the 1952 Act.[1] It may well be said that long-term disability is merely premature old-age retirement.

---

[1] Actually, it was so written in that legislation as to be inoperative, but then was reenacted in 1954 to be on a permanent, ongoing basis.

The monthly disability benefits initially were available only at ages 50 and over, that is, deferred to that age for those disabled earlier, with no auxiliary benefits for the spouse and dependent children. These limitations were quickly removed, by the 1958 and 1960 acts.

Eligibility Conditions for Disability Benefits

To be eligible for disability benefits, individuals must be both fully insured and disability insured.[2] Disability status requires 20 QC earned in the 40-quarter period ending with the quarter of disability, except that persons disabled before age 31 also can qualify if they have QC in half of the quarters after age 21.[3] The definition of disability is relatively strict. The disability must be so severe that the individual is unable to engage in any substantial gainful activity, and the impairment must be a medically determinable physical or mental condition that is expected to continue for at least 12 months or to result in prior death. Benefits are first payable after completion of six full calendar months of disability.

Beneficiary Categories for Disability Benefits

In addition to the disabled worker, the same categories of dependents can receive monthly benefits as in the case of old-age retirement benefits.

Benefit Computation Procedures for Disability Benefits

In all cases, the benefits are based on the Primary Insurance Amount (PIA), computed in the same manner as retirement benefits, except that fewer dropout years than five are allowed in the computation of the Averaged Indexed Monthly Earnings (AIME) for persons disabled before age 47. The disabled worker receives a benefit equal to 100 percent of the PIA, and the auxiliary beneficiaries each receive 50 percent of the PIA, subject to the Maximum Family Benefit.

An overall maximum on total family benefits is applicable, which is lower than that for survivor and retirement benefits—namely, no more than the smaller of (1) 150 percent of the PIA or (2) 85 percent of AIME (but not less than the PIA). If a person is eligible for more than one type of benefit (e.g., both as a worker and as a surviving spouse), in essence only the largest benefit is payable.

---

[2] Blind persons need be only fully insured.

[3] For those disabled before age 24, the requirement is six QC in the last 12 quarters.

Eligibility Test for Disability Benefits and Other Restrictions on Benefits

The earnings or retirement test applies to the auxiliary beneficiaries of disabled workers, but *not* to the disabled worker beneficiary. However, the earnings of one beneficiary (e.g., the spouse of the disabled worker) do not affect the benefits of the other beneficiaries in the family (e.g., the disabled worker or the children). The test does not apply to disabled worker beneficiaries, because any earnings are considered in connection with whether recovery has occurred, except those during trial work periods (which may possibly lead to recovery later).

OASDI disability benefits are coordinated with disability benefits payable under other governmental programs (including those of state and local governments), except for needs-tested ones, benefits payable by the Veterans Administration, and government employee plans coordinated with OASDI. The most important of such coordinations is with Workers' Compensation (WC) programs, whose benefits are taken into account in determining the amount of the OASDI disability benefit (except for a few states that provide for their WC benefits to be reduced when OASDI disability benefits are payable—possible only for states that did this before February 19, 1981). The total of the OASDI disability benefit (including any auxiliary benefits payable) and the other disability benefit recognized cannot exceed 80 percent of "average current earnings" (generally based on the highest year of earnings in covered employment in the last six years, but indexed for changes in wage levels following the worker's disablement).

Disability Freeze

In the event that a disability beneficiary recovers, the so-called disability-freeze provision applies. Under this, the period of disability is "blanked out" in the computation of insured status and benefit amounts for subsequent retirement and survivor benefits.

Historical Development of Survivor Provisions

When what is now the OASDI program was developed in 1934–35, it was confined entirely to retirement benefits (plus lump-sum refund payments to represent the difference, if any, between employee taxes paid, plus an allowance for interest, and retirement benefits received). It was not until the 1939 act that monthly survivor benefits were added with respect to deaths of both active workers and retirees, in lieu of the refund benefit.

The term "widow" is used here to include also widowers. Until recently, the latter did not receive OASDI benefits on the same basis as widows, either being required to prove dependence on the deceased female worker or not being eligible at all. Now, because of legislative changes and court decisions, complete equality of treatment by sex prevails for OASDI survivor benefits.

The minimum eligibility age for aged widows was initially established at age 65. This figure was selected in a purely empirical manner, because it was a round figure (see the earlier discussion about retirement benefits as to why this was selected as the minimum retirement age).

Beginning in the 1950s, pressure developed to provide early-retirement benefits, first for widows and spouses and then for insured workers themselves. The minimum early-retirement age was set at 62, again a pragmatic political compromise, rather than a completely logical choice. The three-year differential, however, did represent about the average difference in age between men and their wives (but, of course, as with any averages, in many cases the actual difference is larger). The benefit amounts were not reduced for widows when they claimed before age 65 under the original amendatory legislation, but this is no longer the case.

Eligibility Conditions for Survivor Benefits

To be eligible for OASDI survivor benefits, individuals must have either *fully insured status* or *currently insured status*. The latter requires only 6 QC earned in the 13-quarter period ending with the quarter of death.

Survivor Beneficiary Categories

Two general categories of survivors of insured workers can receive monthly benefits. Aged survivors are widows aged 60 or over (or at ages 50–59 if disabled) and dependent parents aged 62 or over. Young survivors are children under age 18 (or at any age if disabled before age 22), children aged 18 who are full-time students in elementary or secondary educational institutions (i.e., defined just the same as in the case of retirement and disability beneficiaries), and the widowed parent of such children who are under age 16 or disabled. In addition, a death benefit of $255 is payable to widows or, in the absence of a widow, to children eligible for immediate monthly benefits.

The disabled widow receives a benefit at the rate of 71.5 percent of the deceased worker's PIA if claim is first made at ages 50–59. The benefit rate for other widows grades up from 71.5 percent of the PIA if claimed at age 60 to 100 percent if claimed at the Normal Retirement Age, which is age 65 for those attaining age 60 before 2000, grading up to 67 for those attaining age 60 in 2022 and after. Any Delayed-Retirement Credits the deceased worker had earned also are applicable to the widow's benefit. Widows, regardless of age, caring for an eligible child (under age 16 or disabled) have a benefit of 75 percent of the PIA. Divorced spouses, when the marriage lasted at least 10 years, are eligible for benefits under the same conditions as undivorced spouses.

The benefit rate for eligible children is 75 percent of the PIA. The benefit rate for dependent parents is 82½ percent of the PIA, unless two parents are eligible, in which case it is 75 percent for each one.

The same overall maximum on total family benefits is applicable as is the case for retirement benefits. If a person is eligible for more than one type of benefit, e.g., both as a worker and as a surviving spouse, in essence only the largest benefit is payable.

Benefit Computation Procedures for Survivor Benefits

In all cases, the monthly survivor benefits are based on the PIA, and then are adjusted to reflect the Maximum Family Benefit, both of which are computed in essentially the same manner as is the case for retirement benefits.[4]

Eligibility Test for Survivor Benefits and Other Restrictions

Marriage (or remarriage) of the survivor beneficiary generally terminates benefit rights. The only exceptions are remarriage of widows after age 60 (or after age 50 for disabled widows) and marriage to another OASDI beneficiary (other than one who is under age 18).

From the inception of the OASDI program, there has been some form of restriction on the payment of benefits to persons who have substantial earnings from employment, the earnings or retirement test. The same test applies to survivor beneficiaries as to retirement benefits. However, the earnings of one beneficiary (e.g., the widowed mother) do not affect the benefits of the other beneficiaries in the family (e.g., the orphaned children).

---

[4] For individuals who die before age 62, the computation is made as though the individual had attained age 62 in the year of death. In addition, for deferred widow's benefits, an alternative computation based on indexing the deceased's earnings record up to the earlier of age 60 of the worker or age 60 of the widow is used if this produces a more favorable result.

If a widow receives a pension from service under a government-employee pension plan under which the members were not covered under OASDI on the last day of her employment, the OASDI widow's benefit is reduced by two-thirds of the amount of such pension. This provision, however, is not applicable to women (or men who were dependent on their wives) who became eligible for such a pension before December 1982 or to individuals who became first so eligible from December 1982 through June 1983 and who were dependent on their spouses.

Financing Provisions of OASDI Program

From its inception until the 1983 Act, the OASDI program has been financed entirely by payroll taxes (and interest earnings on the assets of the trust funds), with only minor exceptions, such as the special benefits at a subminimum level for certain persons without insured status who attained age 72 before 1972. Thus, on a permanent ongoing basis, no payments from general revenues were available to the OASDI system; the payments for covered federal civilian employees and members of the armed forces are properly considered as "employer" taxes.

The 1983 Act introduced two instances of general-revenues financing of the OASDI program. As a one-time matter, the tax rate in 1984 was increased to what had been previously scheduled for 1985 (i.e., for both the employer and employee, from 5.4 percent to 5.7 percent), but the increase for employees was, in essence, rescinded, and the General Fund of the Treasury made up the difference to the OASDI Trust Funds. On an ongoing basis, the General Fund passes on to the trust funds the proceeds of the income taxation of OASDI benefits (first effective for 1984), and, in fact, does so somewhat in advance of actual receipt of such monies.

The payroll taxes for the retirement and survivors benefits go into the OASI Trust Fund, and all benefit payments and administrative expenses for these provisions are paid therefrom. The balances in the trust fund are invested in federal government obligations of various types, with interest rates at the current market values. The federal government does not guarantee the payments of benefits. If the trust fund were to be depleted, it could not obtain grants, or even loans, from the general treasury. However, a temporary provision (effective only in 1982) permitted the OASI Trust Fund to borrow, repayable with interest, from the DI and HI Trust Fund. A total of $17.5 billion was borrowed ($12.4 billion from HI). The last of such loans were repaid in 1986.

Payroll taxes are levied on earnings up to only a certain annual limit, which is termed the *earnings base*. This base is applicable to the earnings of an individual from each employer in the year, but the person can obtain a refund (on the income tax form) for all employee taxes paid in excess of those on the earnings base. The self-employed pay taxes on their self-employment income on no more than the excess of the earnings base over any wages which they may have had.

Since 1975, the earnings base has been determined by the automatic-adjustment procedure, on the basis of increases in the nationwide average wage. However, for 1979–81, ad hoc increases of a higher amount were legislated; the 1981 base was established at $29,700. The 1982 and subsequent bases were determined under the automatic-adjustment provision. The 1987 base was $43,800, while that for 1988 is $45,000.

The payroll tax rate is a combined one for OASI, Disability Insurance (DI), and Hospital Insurance (HI), but it is allocated among the three trust funds. The employer and employee rates are equal. The self-employed pay the combined employer-employee rate, but in 1984–89 they have an allowance for the reduction in income taxes if half of the OASDI-HI tax were to be considered as a business expense (as it is for incorporated employers); such allowance is a uniform reduction in the tax rate—2.7 percentage points in 1984, 2.2 percentage points in 1985, and 2.0 percentage points in 1986–89. After 1989, the direct procedure of considering half of the OASDI-HI taxes as a deduction from income is to be done.

The employer and employee rates were 1 percent each in 1937–49, but have gradually increased over the years, until being 7.15 percent in 1986–87 (the latter subdivided 5.2 percent for OASI, 0.5 percent for DI, and 1.45 percent for HI). These rates increased to 7.51 percent in 1988, and are scheduled to increase to 7.65 percent in 1990 (and after), the latter being subdivided 5.6 percent for OASI, 0.6 percent for DI, and 1.45 percent for HI.

Past Financing Crises of OASDI Program

In the mid-1970s, the OASI and DI Trust Funds were projected to have serious financing problems over both the long range and the short range. This was thought to be remedied as to the short range by the 1977 Act, which raised taxes (both the rates and the earnings bases). At the same time, the long-range problem was partially solved by phased-in significant benefit reductions, by lowering the general benefit level, by freezing the minimum benefit, and by the "spouse government pension" offset, although an estimated deficit situation was still present for the period beginning after about 30 years.

As experience showed, the short-range problem was not really solved. The actuarial cost estimates assumed that earnings would rise at a somewhat more rapid rate than prices in the short range, but the reverse occurred—and to a significant extent—in 1979–81. Because increases in tax income depend on earnings and because increases in benefit outgo depend on prices, the financial result for the OASI Trust Fund was catastrophic. It would have been exhausted in late 1982 if it had not been for legislation enacted in 1981. The DI Trust Fund did not have this problem, because the disability experience, which had worsened significantly in 1970–76, turned around and became relatively favorable—more than offsetting the unfavorable economic experience.

The 1981 Act significantly reduced benefit outgo in the short range by the following actions:

1. The regular minimum benefit (an initial PIA of $122) was eliminated for all new eligibles after 1981, except covered members of religious orders under a vow of poverty.
2. Child school attendance benefits at ages 18–21 were eliminated by a gradual phase-out, except for high school students age 18.
3. Mother's and father's benefits with respect to nondisabled children terminate when the youngest child is age 16 (formerly age 18).
4. Lump-sum death payments were eliminated, except when a surviving spouse who was living with the deceased worker is present, or when a spouse or child is eligible for immediate monthly benefits.
5. Sick pay in the first six months of illness is considered to be covered wages.
6. Lowering of the exempt age under the earnings test to age 70 in 1982 was delayed until 1983.
7. The Workers' Compensation offset against disability benefits was extended to several other types of governmental disability benefits.
8. Interfund borrowing among the OASI, DI, and HI Trust Funds was permitted, but only until December 31, 1982, and then no more than sufficient to allow payments of OASI benefits through June 1983.

Further action beyond the 1981 Amendments was essential to restore both the short-range and long-range solvency of the OASDI program. Because of the difficult political situation, President Reagan established the National Commission on Social Security Reform—a bipartisan group whose members were appointed both by President Reagan and the Congressional leadership—to study the problem and make recommendations for its solution. Such recommendations were adopted almost in their entirety in the 1983 Act.

This legislation made the following significant changes in the OASDI program (as well as some in the HI program as well):

1. OASDI and HI Coverage Provisions
   a. OASDI-HI coverage of new federal employees and current political appointees, elected officials, and judges. (HI coverage of all federal civilian employees was effective in 1983 under previous law.)
   b. Coverage of all nonprofit employees.
   c. State and local employees now covered prohibited from withdrawing.
   d. Employee contributions to cash-or-deferred arrangements (Sec. 401 [k]) and under nonqualified deferred-compensation plans when no substantial risk of forfeiture is present are covered.
2. OASDI Benefit Provisions
   a. Cost-of-living adjustments are deferred for six months (i.e., will always be in checks for December payable in early January).
   b. The indexing of benefits in payment status is changed from being based only on the CPI to the lower of CPI or wage increases when the trust funds are relatively low.
   c. Gradual increases will be made in the normal retirement age from the present 65, beginning with those attaining age 62 in 2000—so that it will be 66 for those attaining such age in 2009–20, then rising to 67 for those attaining such age in 2027 and after. Age 62 is retained as the early-retirement age, but with appropriate, larger actuarial reductions.
   d. Gradual increases will be made in the credit for postponing claiming (or not receiving) benefits beyond the normal retirement age from 3 percent per year for persons attaining age 65 in 1982–89 to 8 percent for persons attaining normal retirement age in 2009 and after.
   e. The retirement earnings test for persons at the normal retirement age up to age 70 is liberalized, beginning in 1990, by changing the "$1 for $2" reduction in benefits for earnings above the annual exempt amount to a "$1 for $3" basis.
   f. Several minor changes are made to liberalize benefits which primarily affect women (e.g., indexing deferred widow(er)'s benefits by whichever is more favorable, prices or wages, and increasing the benefit rate for disabled widow(er)s aged 50–59 from 50–71.5 percent depending upon age at entitlement to a uniform 71.5 percent.)
   g. The situation as to windfall benefits for retired and disabled workers who have pensions from noncovered employment and OASDI benefits based on a short period of covered employment is alleviated.

h. The offset of government employee pensions based on employment not covered by OASDI against OASDI spouse and widow(er) benefits is reduced from a full offset to a two-thirds offset.
i. Restrictions are placed on the payment of benefits to prisoners receiving retirement and survivor benefits (previous law related essentially to disability beneficiaries).
j. Restrictions are placed on the payment of benefits to aliens residing abroad who have, in general, not had at least five years of residence in the United States.

3. Revenue Provisions, OASDI and HI
a. OASDI tax rate scheduled for 1985 is moved to 1984 for employers, but not employees. Trust funds receive, from general revenues, additional amount of taxes as if employee rate had been increased.
b. Self-employed will pay the combined OASDI-HI employer-employee rate, minus (for 1984–89) a credit (in lieu of a business expense deduction for such taxes). The trust funds receive, from general revenues, the additional amount of taxes as if the full employer-employee rate had been paid.
c. About 72 percent of the OASDI tax rate increase scheduled for 1990 will be moved forward to 1988.
d. Part of OASDI benefits (but not more than 50 percent) will be subject to income tax for persons with high incomes, with the proceeds going into the OASDI Trust Funds.
e. A lump-sum transfer of general revenues will be made to meet the cost of certain gratuitous military-service wage credits (which, under previous law, would have been paid for in future years).
f. Interfund borrowing (which, under previous law, was permitted only in 1982) will be allowed in 1983–87, with specific repayment provisions (before 1990 at the latest) and with prohibitions against borrowing from a fund which is relatively low.
g. Operations of OASDI and HI Trust Funds will be removed from Unified Budget after FY 1992.
h. Two public members will be added to the Boards of Trustees.

4. HI Reimbursement Provisions
a. A new method of reimbursement of providers of services will be gradually phased in. This will be done on the basis of uniform amounts (but varying as among nine geographical areas and as between rural and urban facilities) for each of 467 Diagnosis Related Groups.
b. No change is made in the minimum eligibility age for HI benefits for the aged (i.e., it remains at 65).

5. SMI Provisions
   a. The enrollee premium rate will be changed to a calendar-year basis (to correspond with the OASDI COLAs). The rate for July 1982 through June 1983 will continue through December 1983.
   b. No change is made in the minimum eligibility age for SMI benefits for the aged (i.e., it remains at 65).

Possible Future OASDI Developments

Advisory groups have, over the years, urged that there should be so-called universal coverage. Following the 1983 Amendments, relatively little remains to be done in this area, except perhaps to cover compulsorily all new hires in state and local government employment (as was done in the federal area).

The minimum retirement age at which unreduced benefits are payable was increased from the present 65 to age 67, phased in over a period of years, by the 1983 Act. This was done in recognition of the significant increase in life expectancy that has occurred in the last 40 years, as well as the likely future increases. If life expectancy increases even more rapidly than currently projected, a further increase in such age would reduce the long-range future cost of the program resulting from such improvement.

The earnings test has always been subject to criticism by many persons, who argue that it is a disincentive to continued employment and that "the benefits have been bought and paid for, and therefore should be available at age 65." The 1983 Act, by increasing ultimately (beginning with those who attain age 66 in 2009) the size of the delayed retirement credits (to 8 percent per year) to approximately the actuarial-equivalent level, virtually eliminated the earnings test insofar as the cost aspects thereof are concerned. In other words, when the DRC is at an 8 percent level, the individual receives benefits for delayed retirement having approximately the same value as if benefits were paid without regard to the earnings beginning at the Normal Retirement Age. Some persons have advocated that the DRC should be at the 8 percent rate as soon as possible.

As to disability benefits, the definition might be tightened, such as by using "medical only" factors (and not vocational ones). Conversely, the definition could be liberalized so as to be on an occupational basis at age 50 and over. Also, the five-month waiting period could be shortened.

The general benefit level was significantly increased in 1969–72 (by about 23 percent in real terms), but financial problems caused this to be partially reversed in subsequent legislation (1974 and 1977). Nonetheless, there will be efforts by many persons to reverse the situation and expand the benefit level.

Over the years, the composition of the OASDI benefit structure—between individual-equity aspects and social-adequacy ones—tended to shift more toward social adequacy. The 1981 Amendments, however, moved in the other direction (e.g., by phasing out student benefits and the minimum-benefit provision). There may well be efforts in the future to inject more social adequacy into the program—or, conversely, more individual equity.

It frequently has been advocated that people should be allowed to opt out of the OASDI system and provide their own economic security through private-sector mechanisms, using both their own taxes and those of their employer. Although this approach has certain appealing aspects, it has some significant drawbacks. First, it is not possible to duplicate to any close extent the various features of OASDI, most importantly the automatic adjustment of benefits for increases in the CPI.

Second, because the low-cost individuals (young, high-earnings ones) would be the most likely to opt out, there is the question of where the resulting financing shortfalls of the OASDI program would come from, with respect to the high-cost persons remaining in it. Those who make such proposals (or even the more extreme ones, which involve terminating OASDI for all except those currently covered who are near retirement age) do not answer this question. The only source of financing would be from general revenues, and this means more general taxes, which would be paid to a considerable extent by those who have opted out!

Many proposals have been made in the past that part of the cost of OASDI should be met from general revenues. At times, this has been advocated to be done in an indirect manner, such as by moving part of the HI tax rate to OASDI and then partially financing HI from general revenues. The difficulty with this procedure is that no general-revenues monies are available; instead, the General Fund of the Treasury has large deficits. In turn, this would mean either that additional taxes of other types would have to be raised or that the budget deficit would become larger, and inflation would be fueled. Those opposed to general-revenues financing of OASDI, and of HI as well, believe that the financing, instead, should be entirely from direct, visible payroll taxes. Nonetheless, it is likely that there will continue to be pressure for general-revenues financing of OASDI.

SUPPLEMENTAL SECURITY INCOME PROGRAM

The SSI program replaced the federal/state public assistance programs of aid to the aged, blind, and disabled, except in Guam, Puerto Rico, and the Virgin Islands. Persons must be at least age 65 or be blind or disabled to qualify for the SSI payments.

The basic payment amount, before reduction for other income, for 1988 is $354 per month for one recipient and 50 percent more for an eligible couple. An automatic-adjustment provision closely paralleling that used under OASDI is applicable.

A number of "income disregards" are present. The most important is the disregard of $20 of income per month per family from such sources as OASDI, other pensions, earnings, and investments. The first $65 per month of earned income is disregarded, plus 50 percent of the remainder.

SSI has certain resource exemptions. In order to receive SSI, for 1987, resources cannot exceed $1,800 for an individual and $2,700 for a couple ($1,900/$2,850 for 1988 and $2,000/$3,000 for 1989 and after). However, in determining resources, certain items are excluded—the home, household goods and personal effects (depending on value), an automobile with value of $4,500 or less, burial plots, and property needed for self-support—if these are found to be reasonable. Also, if life insurance policies have a face amount of $1,500 or less for an individual, their cash values are not counted as assets.

Some states pay supplements to SSI.

In addition to SSI, there is a public assistance program that provides payments for widowed mothers (and fathers) with children. This is on a state-by state basis, with part of the cost borne by the federal government.

MEDICARE PROGRAM

Health (or medical care) benefits for active and retired workers and their dependents in the United States is, in the vast majority of cases, provided through the multiple means of the Medicare portion of Social Security for persons aged 65 and over and for long-term disabled persons, private employer-sponsored plans, and individual savings. As mentioned earlier, this is sometimes referred to as a "three-legged stool" or the three pillars of economic security protection. Still others look upon the situation for persons aged 65 and over and for long-term disabled persons as Medicare providing the floor of protection for certain categories, or, in other cases, providing the basic protection, with public assistance programs, such as

Medicaid, providing a net of protection for those whose income is not sufficient to purchase the needed medical care not provided through some form of prepaid insurance.

Private health benefit plans supplement Medicare to some extent. In other instances—essentially for active workers and their families—health benefit protection is provided by the private sector. The net result, however, is a broad network of health benefit protection.

Historical Development of Provisions

Beginning in the early 1950s, efforts were made to provide medical care benefits (primarily for hospitalization) for beneficiaries under the OASDI program. In 1965, such efforts succeeded, and the resulting program is called Medicare.

Initially, Medicare applied only to persons age 65 and over. In 1972, disabled Social Security beneficiaries who had been on the benefit rolls for at least two years were made eligible, as were virtually all persons in the country who have end-stage renal disease (i.e., chronic kidney disease). Since 1972, relatively few changes in the coverage or benefit provisions have been made.

Medicare is really two separate programs. One part, Hospital Insurance (HI),[5] is financed primarily from payroll taxes on workers covered under OASDI, including those under the Railroad Retirement system. Beginning in 1983, all civilian employees of the Federal Government were covered under HI, even though, in general, not covered by OASDI. Also, beginning in April 1986, all newly hired state and local government employees are covered compulsorily (and, at the election of the governmental entity, all employees in service on March 31, 1986 who were not covered under OASDI can be covered for HI). The other part, Supplementary Medical Insurance (SMI), is on an individual voluntary basis and is financed partially by enrollee premiums, with the remainder, currently slightly more than 75 percent, coming from general revenues.

Persons Protected by HI

All individuals aged 65 and over who are eligible for monthly benefits under OASDI or the Railroad Retirement program also are eligible for HI benefits (as are federal employees and state and local employees who have sufficient earnings credits from their special HI coverage). Persons

---

[5] Sometimes referred to as Part A. Supplementary Medical Insurance is Part B.

are "eligible" for OASDI benefits if they could receive them when the person on whose earnings record they are eligible is deceased or receiving disability or retirement benefits, or could be receiving retirement benefits except for having had substantial earnings. Thus, the HI eligibles include not only insured workers, but also spouses, disabled children (in the rare cases where they are at least age 65), and survivors, such as widowed spouses and dependent parents. As a specific illustration, HI protection is available for an insured worker and spouse, both at least age 65, even though the worker has such high earnings that OASDI cash benefits are not currently payable.

In addition, HI eligibility is available for disabled beneficiaries who have been on the benefit roll for at least two years (beyond a 5-month waiting period). Such disabled eligibles include not only insured workers, but also disabled child beneficiaries aged 18 and over but disabled before age 22, and disabled widowed spouses, age 50–64.

Further, persons under age 65 with end-stage renal disease (ESRD) who require dialysis or renal transplant are eligible for HI benefits if they meet one of a number of requirements. Such requirements for ESRD benefits include being fully or currently insured, being a spouse or a dependent child of an insured worker or of a monthly beneficiary, or being a monthly beneficiary.

Individuals aged 65 and over who are not eligible for HI as a result of their own or some other person's earnings can elect coverage, and then must make premium payments, whereas OASDI eligibles do not. The standard monthly premium rate is $235 for 1988.

Benefits Provided under HI

The principal benefit provided by the HI program is for hospital services. The full cost for all such services, other than luxury items, is paid by HI during a so-called spell of illness, after an initial deductible has been paid and with daily coinsurance for all hospital days after the 60th one, but with an upper limit on the number of days covered. A spell of illness is a period beginning with the first day of hospitalization and ending when the individual has been out of both hospitals and skilled nursing facilities for 60 consecutive days. The initial deductible is $540 in 1988. The daily coinsurance is $135 for the 61st to 90th days of hospitalization. A nonrenewable lifetime reserve of 60 days is available after the regular 90 days have been used; these lifetime reserve days are subject to daily coinsurance of $270 in 1988. The deductible and coinsurance amounts are adjusted automatically each year after 1988 to reflect past changes in hospital costs.

Benefits also are available for care provided in skilled nursing facilities, following at least three days of hospitalization. Such care is provided only when it is for convalescent or recuperative care, and not for custodial care. The first 20 days of such care in a spell of illness are provided without cost to the individual. The next 80 days, however, are subject to a daily coinsurance payment, which is $67.50 in 1988, and it will be adjusted automatically in the future in the same manner as the hospital cost-sharing amounts. No benefits are available after 100 days of care in a skilled nursing facility for a particular spell of illness.

In addition, an unlimited number of home health service benefits are provided by HI without any payment being required from the beneficiary. Also, hospice care for terminally ill persons is covered if all Medicare benefits other than physician services are waived; certain cost restrictions and coinsurance requirements apply with respect to prescription drugs.

HI benefit protection is provided only within the United States, with the exception of certain emergency services available when in or near Canada. Not covered by HI are those cases where services are performed in a Veterans Administration hospital or where the person is eligible for medical services under a workers' compensation program. Furthermore, Medicare is the secondary payor in cases when: (a) medical care is payable under any liability policy, especially automobile ones; (b) during the first 12 months of treatment for ESRD cases when private group health insurance provides coverage; (c) for persons aged 65 and over (employees and spouses) who are under employer-sponsored group health insurance plans (which is required for all plans of employers with at least 20 employees) unless the employee opts out of it; and (d) for disability beneficiaries under the plan of an employer with at least 100 employees when the beneficiary is either an "active individual" or a family member of an employee.

Financing of HI

With the exception of the small group of persons who voluntarily elect coverage, the HI program is financed by payroll taxes on workers in employment covered by OASDI. This payroll tax rate is combined with that for OASDI and is subject to the same maximum taxable earnings base. The HI tax rate is the same for employers and employees; self-employed persons pay the combined employer-employee tax rate, but have an offset to allow for the effect of business expenses on income taxes (as described earlier in connection with OASDI taxes). Such HI tax rate for employees is 1.45 percent in 1987 and all future years. It should be noted that long-range actuarial cost estimates indicate that this rate will not provide adequate financing after about a decade from now (or perhaps even sooner).

The vast majority of persons who attained age 65 before 1968, and who were not eligible for HI benefit protection on the basis of an earnings record, were nonetheless given full eligibility for benefits without any charge. The cost for this closed blanketed-in group is met from general revenues rather than from HI payroll taxes.

The HI Trust Fund receives the income of the program from the various sources and makes the required disbursements for benefits and administrative expenses. The assets are invested and earn interest in the same manner as the OASDI Trust Funds.

Although the federal government is responsible for the administration of the HI program, the actual dealing with the various medical facilities is through fiscal intermediaries, such as Blue Cross and insurance companies, which are reimbursed for their expenses on a cost basis. Beginning in 1988, reimbursement for inpatient hospital services is based on uniform sums for each case for 470 diagnosis-related groups.

Persons Protected under Supplementary Medical Insurance

Individuals aged 65 or over can elect coverage on an individual basis regardless of whether they have OASDI insured status. In addition, disabled OASDI beneficiaries eligible for HI and persons with ESRD eligible under HI can elect SMI coverage. In general, coverage election must be made at about the time of initial eligibility, that is, attainment of age 65 or at the end of the disability-benefit waiting period. Subsequent election during general enrollment periods is possible but with higher premium rates being applicable. Similarly, individuals can terminate coverage and cease premium payment of their own volition.

Benefits Provided under SMI

The principal SMI benefit is partial reimbursement for the cost of physician services, although other medical services, such as diagnostic tests, ambulance services, prosthetic devices, physical therapy, medical equipment, and drugs not self-administerable, are covered. Not covered are out-of-hospital drugs, most dental services, most chiropractic services, routine physical and eye examinations, eyeglasses and hearing aids, and services outside of the United States, except those in connection with HI services that are covered in Canada. Just as for HI, there are limits on SMI coverage in Workers' Compensation cases, medical care under liability policies, private group health insurance applicable to ESRD, and employer-sponsored group health insurance for employees and their spouses.

SMI pays 80 percent of "recognized" charges, under a complicated determination basis that usually produces a lower charge than the reasonable and prevailing one, after the individual has paid a calendar-year deductible of $75. Special limits apply on out-of-hospital mental health care costs and on the services of independent physical and occupational therapists. The cost-sharing payments ($75 deductible and 20 percent coinsurance) are waived for certain services—e.g., home health services, pneumococcal vaccine, certain clinical diagnostic laboratory tests, and certain second opinions for surgical procedures.

Financing of SMI

The standard monthly premium rate is $24.80 for 1988. The premium is higher for those who fail to enroll as early as they possibly can, with an increase of 10 percent for each full 12 months of delay. The premium is deducted from the OASDI benefits of persons currently receiving them, or is paid by direct submittal in other cases.

The remainder of the cost of the program is met by general revenues. In the aggregate, persons aged 65 and over pay only 25 percent of the cost, while for disabled persons such proportion is only about 22 percent. As a result, enrollment in SMI is very attractive, and about 95 percent of those eligible to do so actually enroll.

The enrollee premium rate is changed every year, effective for January. In practice, the rate of increase in the premium rate is determined by the percentage rise in the level of OASDI cash benefits in the previous year under the automatic adjustment provisions, although for the premium years 1984–88, the premium rate is set at 25 percent of the cost for persons aged 65 or over.

The SMI Trust Fund was established to receive the enrollee premiums and the payments from general revenues. From this fund are paid the benefits and the accompanying administrative expenses. Although the program is under the general supervision of the federal government, most of the administration is accomplished through so-called "carriers", such as Blue Shield or insurance companies, on an actual cost basis for their administrative expenses.

Possible Future Development of Medicare

Over the years, numerous proposals have been made to modify the Medicare program. Some of these would expand it significantly, while others would curtail it to some extent.

Among the proposals that would expand the program are those to establish some type of national health insurance program, having very comprehensive coverage of medical services applicable to the entire population. Somewhat less broadly, other proposals would extend Medicare coverage to additional categories of OASDI beneficiaries beyond old-age beneficiaries aged 65 and over and disabled beneficiaries on the roll for at least two years—such as to early-retirement cases at ages 62–64 and to all disability beneficiaries.

In another direction, liberalizing proposals have been made to add further services, such as out-of-hospital drugs, physical examinations, and dental services. Still other proposals have been made in the direction of reducing the extent of cost-sharing on the part of the beneficiary by lowering or eliminating the deductible and coinsurance provisions and by eliminating the duration-of-stay limits on HI benefit eligibility.

Proposals have been made to reduce the cost of the Medicare program by increasing the cost-sharing payments made by the beneficiary. For example, the cost-sharing in the first 60 days of hospitalization could be changed from a one-time payment of the initial deductible to some type of daily coinsurance that would foster the incentive to shorten hospital stays. Another proposal is to adjust automatically, from year to year, the SMI annual deductible, which, unlike the HI cost-sharing payments, is a fixed amount, although it has been increased by ad hoc changes from the initial $50 in 1966 to $75 in 1982 and after.

In early 1987, the Reagan Administration proposed that the Medicare program should be expanded to cover better the costs of catastrophic acute illness, defined as out-of-pocket expenses in excess of $2,000 annually (to be adjusted for inflation in the future). The additional cost would be met by a premium payment from the enrollees of about $5 per month initially. This proposal met with widespread approval by members of Congress—although not as to all details, especially the method of financing. As a result, both the House and Senate passed catastrophic Medicare bills in 1987, but the differences between the two bills (which were not great) were not reconciled by year-end—although they almost certainly will be in 1988. These bills differ from the administration proposal in being somewhat more liberal (such as providing a catastrophic out-of-hospital drug benefit) and in using financing from premiums that vary with income (a drastic change in basic principle).

A major risk for persons aged 65 and over that is not covered by Medicare is the cost of long-term custodial nursing-home care. Although many persons recognize the serious nature of this problem, it is currently being met only on a means-test basis by the Medicaid program. Some people believe that the problem should be met on an "insurance" basis under a new Part C of Medicare, but others think that it is not an "insurable'' risk and must be handled on a means-test basis (possibly liberalized somewhat).

Proposals have also been made recently to cover compulsorily under HI all state and local government employees (and not merely new hires after March 1986)—as has been done for federal employees.

As to financing aspects, proposals have been made to eliminate the enrollee premiums under SMI and to replace them by complete financing from general revenues or by partial financing from payroll taxes, while at the same time reducing the HI tax rates and making up for this by partial general revenue financing of HI. It also has been proposed that the HI program should be financed partially, or even completely, by general revenues.

Proposals concerning the reimbursement of physicians under SMI have been made to discourage or prevent them from charging the beneficiaries more than the allowable charges. Similarly, various proposals have been made to lower the cost of the HI program as far as reimbursement of hospitals and skilled nursing facilities is concerned, although this would have no effect on the Medicare beneficiary directly.

MEDICAID

Over the years, the cost of medical care for recipients of public assistance and for other low-income persons has been met in a variety of ways. Some years ago, these provisions were rather haphazard, and the medical care costs were met by inclusion with the public assistance payments. In 1960, a separate public assistance program in this area was enacted—namely, Medical Assistance for the Aged (MAA), which applied to persons age 65 and over, both those receiving Old-Age Assistance and other persons not having sufficient resources to meet large medical expenses.

Then in 1965, the MAA program and the federal matching for medical vendor payments for public assistance categories other than MAA were combined into the Medicaid program. This new program covered not only public assistance recipients, but also persons of similar demographic characteristics who were medically indigent.

The Medicaid program is operated by the several states, with significant federal financing being available. Only one state, Arizona, does not have a Medicaid program. Some states cover only public assistance recipients.

Medicaid programs are required to furnish certain services, to receive federal financial participation. These services include those for physicians, hospitals (both inpatient and outpatient), laboratory and X-ray tests, home health visits, and nursing home care. Most other medical services, such as drugs, dental care, and eyeglasses, can be included at the option of the state, and then federal matching will be made available. Also, states can pay the SMI premiums for their Medicaid recipients eligible for that program, and thus the states can have the advantage of the relatively large general revenues financing in that program.

The federal government pays a proportion of the total cost of the Medicaid expenditures for medical care that varies inversely with the average per capita income of the state. This proportion is 55 percent for a state with the same average per capita income as the nation as a whole. States with above-average income have a lower matching proportion, but never less than 50 percent. Conversely, states with below-average income have a higher federal matching percentage, which can be as much as 83 percent. The federal government also pays part of the administrative costs of the Medicaid programs; generally, this is 50 percent, although for certain types of expenses which are expected to control costs, the federal percentage is higher.

CHAPTER 5

GROUP LIFE INSURANCE: TERM AND PERMANENT

William H. Rabel
Jerry S. Rosenbloom

INTRODUCTION

Death benefits are a nearly universal employee benefit in the United States. Almost all employers, regardless of size, provide as an integral part of their employee benefit program some form of death benefits for their employees. Death benefits may be provided through public sector programs, such as workers' compensation and Social Security, as well as through private programs, such as pension plans and group life insurance.

Traditionally, group life insurance has covered employees against death during their working years. The protection provided usually is one-year renewable group term life insurance, with no cash surrender value or paid-up insurance benefits. However, a relatively small amount of permanent group life insurance (less than 1 percent of the total) is in force. Furthermore, with the growth of retirement plans other forms of death benefits have developed, such as arrangements for the payment of a lifetime pension to the spouse of a career employee who dies before retirement.

In some cases, life insurance also is provided for dependents of employees, typically in small amounts such as $1,000 or $2,000. Moreover, employee benefit plans may continue a reduced amount of death benefits on retired employees.

Survivor income death benefits (SIBs) also have become a part of employee benefit plans in recent years. These plans differ from traditional employer-sponsored death benefit plans since a benefit is payable only to certain specified surviving dependents of the employee and is payable only in installments. Mandated survivor benefits to spouses are available under certain conditions under the Employee Retirement Income Security Act of 1974 (ERISA). The enactment of the Tax Equity and Fiscal Responsibility Act of 1982 (TEFRA) also has implications for the design of death benefit plans, as did the Retirement Equity Act of 1985 (REA) which provided a preretirement survivor annuity under pension plans for surviving spouses of vested employees who die in active service and who were not yet eligible for early retirement. More recently, the Tax Reform Act of 1986 (TRA 86) has many implications for the design of death benefit plans and will be discussed throughout the chapter.

THE GROUP MECHANISM

While it is not within the province of this chapter to discuss fully the intricacies of the group mechanism, it will be helpful to understand some basics, in order to understand where it can be used. Five essential features of group insurance should be understood.

First, unlike individual insurance, in which the risk associated with each life is appraised, group insurance makes use of group selection. In other words, an entire group is insured without medical examination or other evidence of individual insurability. For many years, state regulation and prudent practice have mandated stringent underwriting rules concerning the minimum number of individuals in a group, the minimum proportion to be insured, etc. However, in recent years, these rules were relaxed somewhat under competitive pressure and decades of experience with the group underwriting process. TRA 86 created a new section in the Internal Revenue Code (IRC), Section 89, which mandates noncontributory group life plans to establish eligibility and nondiscrimination rules. The rules are effective during 1988 plan years unless written regulations are not ready by 1988 in which case the rules will become effective January 1, 1989.

A second feature of group insurance is that premiums on a plan are usually subject to experience rating. The larger the group, the greater the degree to which its cost of insurance reflects its own loss experience. Normally, if experience has been favorable an experience credit (sometimes called a dividend) may be paid at the end of the year.

Another feature of the group mechanism calls for economies of administration. The plan is administered by an employer, a union, or some other agency that is positioned to obtain administrative efficiencies through payroll deductions and/or other centralized functions.

Group insurance makes use of a master contract, which contains all conditions concerning the coverage. Individual insureds receive a group certificate which provides proof that they are covered, shows the amount of coverage, and the coverages provided. Often insureds receive a booklet known as a summary plan description that describes the plan in easy-to-read language. The master contract leads to a fifth feature, which is that the plan may last long beyond the lifetime (or participation in the group) of any one individual.

GROUP TERM LIFE INSURANCE

The importance of group term life insurance in employee benefit plans is shown by data in Table 5–1. This table reveals that at the end of 1985, group life insurance in force in the United States totaled $2,561.6 billion. It is interesting to note that while the amount of group insurance in force continued to increase during the decade of the eighties, the increase in master policies has slowed and group has decreased as a percentage of life insurance sold. This suggests that the market is beginning to reach maturity.

Table 5–2 shows that while only 76.2 percent of group life insurance master policies in force at year-end 1985 covered employer-employee groups, they accounted for 88.1 percent of the total amount of group life insurance in force. The average amount of coverage per employee was $24,738. Survivor income and dependent coverages accounted for $111.7 billion, as shown in Table 5–3. These coverages combined accounted for less than .05 percent of group life in force.

Benefits

Group term life insurance benefit amounts should be based on a plan designed to avoid or minimize possible adverse selection either by the employees or the employer. Factors to consider in the selection of a benefit schedule include (1) the employees' needs, (2) the overall cost of the plan, (3) the nondiscrimination requirements of the law, and (4) the employees' ability to pay if the plan is contributory. The interrelationship

TABLE 5–1

Group Life Insurance in Force in the United States (selected years: 1940–1985)

						Purchases		
Years	*Number of Master Policies*	*Number of Certificates*	*Average Amount per Certificate*	*Amount in Force (millions)*	*Percent of Total Insurance in Force*	*Number of Certificates*	*Amount*	*Percent of Total Insurance Purchases*
1940	23,000	8,800,000	1,700	$ 14,938	12.9%	285,000	691	6.4%
1950	56,000	19,288,000	2,480	47,793	20.4	2,631,000	6,068	21.1
1960	169,000	43,602,000	4,030	175,903	30.0	3,731,000	14,615	19.7
1965	234,000	60,930,000	5,060	308,078	34.2	7,007,000	23,585	20.6
1970	304,000	79,844,000	6,910	551,357	39.3	5,219,000	46,590	26.5
1975	378,000	96,693,000	9,360	904,695	42.3	8,146,000	93,490	32.4
1980	586,000	117,762,000	13,410	1,579,355	44.6	11,373,000	183,432	31.2
1981	631,000	121,611,000	15,510	1,888,612	46.4	11,923,000	216,702	31.9
1982	636,000	124,279,000	16,630	2,066,361	46.1	11,930,000	250,532	29.1
1983	635,000	126,628,000	17,530	2,219,573	44.7	13,450,000	271,609	26.5
1984	634,000	127,405,000	18,780	2,392,358	43.5	14,605,000	293,521	26.3
1985	642,000	129,904,000	19,720	2,561,595	42.3	16,243,000	319,503	26.0

Source: *Life Insurance Fact Book.*

TABLE 5–2

Group Life Insurance in Force by Type and by Size Of Insured Group in the United States 1985

	Number of Master Units	% of Total	Number of Members (000 omitted)	% of Total	Insurance in Force		Average Amount of Insurance Per Member
					Amount (000,000 omitted)	% of Amount	
Type of group							
Related to employment or occupation							
Employer-employee	483,810	76.2	62,092	56.3	$1,634,942	88.1	$26,331
Union and joint employer-union	4,360	0.7	4,967	4.5	39,504	2.1	7,953
Multiple employer trusts	110,600	17.4	2,335	3.1	39,271	2.1	16,818
Professional society	780	0.1	678	0.0	28,047	1.5	41,367
Employee association	1,130	0.2	1,364	1.2	32,141	1.7	23,564
Other—related to employee benefit program	860	0.1	419	0.4	3,963	0.2	9,458
Other—not related to employee benefit program	120	*	15	*	52	*	3,467
Total	601,660		71,870		$1,777.920	95.7	24,738

Not related to employment or occupation							
Fraternal society	210	*	151	.1	2,115	0.1	14,007
Savings or investment group	25,070	9.9	35,823	32.5	28,796	1.6	804
Credit card holders	70	*	102	.1	1,328	0.1	13,020
Mortgage insurance	5,640	.8	1,990	1.8	39,845	2.2	20,023
Other	2,330	.4	370	.3	4,842	0.3	13,086
Total	33,320		38,436		$ 76,926		2,001
Total all groups	634,980	100.1	110,306	100.0	$1,854,846	100.0	16,815
Size of group							
Fewer than 10 members	N.A.	N.A.	2,349	2.1	$ 26,434	1.4	11,253
10–24 members	N.A.	N.A.	3,805	3.5	42,670	2.3	11,214
25–99 members	N.A.	N.A.	9,598	8.7	124,809	6.7	13,004
100–499 members	N.A.	N.A.	12,293	11.1	175,006	9.5	14,236
500 or more members	N.A.	N.A.	82,261	74.6	1,485,927	80.1	18,064
Total all groups	634,980		110,306	100.0	$1,854,846	100.0	16,815

Note: Data exclude dependent coverage Federal Employees Group Life Insurance, and Servicemen's Group Life Insurance. Group credit life insurance on loans of over 10 years duration is included.

* Less than .05% N.A. = Not available

Source: American Council of Life Insurance.

TABLE 5–3
Employee and Dependent Coverage Under Group Life Insurance in the United States 1985

	Number of Master Policies	*Amount*
Purchased during year		
Primary coverage, employee and other	186,170	$ 297,148,000,000
Survivor benefit coverage	N.A.	1,418,000,000
Dependent coverage	7,120*	9,812,000,000
Mortgage insurance issued through a lending agency	900	11,125,000,000
Total	187,070	$ 319,503,000,000
In force at end of year		
Primary coverage, employee and other	635,680	$2,405,900,000,000
Survivor benefit coverage	N.A.	38,312,000,000
Dependent coverage	41,770*	73,430,000,000
Mortgage insurance issued through a lending agency	5,980	43,953,000,000
Total	641,660	$2,561,595,000,000

* These policies cover employees as well as dependents and are also included with employee master policies.
N.A.—Not available.

Source: American Council of Life Insurance.

of factors has resulted in the development of group term life insurance benefit schedules related to earnings, occupation or position, or a flat benefit amount for everyone covered, and length of service. Benefit schedules also exist which are a combination of two or more of the types of benefit schedules mentioned above.[1]

The most common benefit schedule bases the amount of insurance on the employee's earnings. An illustration of such a schedule in Table 5–4 follows:

---

[1] See Davis W. Gregg, "Fundamental Characteristics of Group Insurance," in *Life and Health Insurance Handbook,* 3d ed., eds. Davis W. Gregg and Vane B. Lucas (Homewood, Ill.: Richard D. Irwin, 1973), pp. 357–58.

TABLE 5–4
Sample Schedule Basing Benefits on Amount of Employee Earnings

Monthly Earnings	*Group Term Life Insurance*
Less than $1,500	$20,000
More than $1,500 but less than $2,000	25,000
More than $2,000 but less than $2,500	30,000
More than $2,500 but less than $3,000	40,000
More than $3,000	50,000

Such a schedule would be held not to discriminate in favor of key employees (including executives), thus making the plan eligible for favorable tax treatment if other conditions are met.

Financing

Any employee benefit program, including group term life insurance, may be financed on either a noncontributory basis (where the employer pays the total amount for the insurance) or a contributory basis (where the employees share the cost with the employer). A number of advantages are claimed for each approach. The advantages claimed for the *noncontributory approach* follow.[2]

All Employees Insured. All eligible employees who have completed the probationary period and are actively at work have coverage. Thus, the plan has maximum participation and minimizes adverse selection.

Tax Advantages. Under conditions described later in this chapter, employer premium costs are deductible as an ordinary business expense for federal income tax purposes, whereas employee contributions under a contributory plan are not unless under an IRC Section 125 plan up to a maximum of $50,000 of life insurance.

Simplicity of Administration. Records for individual employees are easier to maintain than under contributory plans primarily because no payroll deduction procedures are necessary.

---

[2] Ibid., pp. 358–60.

Economy of Installation. Since all employees are covered, it is not necessary to solicit plan membership among individual employees.

Greater Control of Plan. The employer may have more control over changes in benefits under noncontributory plans because, in the absence of collective bargaining, unilateral action may be more feasible when employees are not sharing in the cost of the plan.

The *contributory approach* to financing group term life insurance also has certain claimed advantages.[3]

Larger Benefits Possible. More liberal benefits are possible if employees also contribute.

Better use of Employer's Contributions. A contributory plan, provided enough individuals participate under the nondiscrimination requirements, may permit the employer to direct group term life insurance funds to the employees with the greatest needs. Employees who elect not to contribute, and hence are not covered, tend to be young, single individuals who may have few life insurance needs and among whom employee turnover also may be high. Therefore, if such is the case, a contributory plan allows employer funds to be used most effectively by sharing the cost of benefits for the employees who have greater needs and who also are most likely to be long-service employees.

Employees May Have More Control. The contributory plan may afford employees a greater voice in the benefits since they are paying part of the cost.

Greater Employee Interest. Employees may have a greater interest in plans in which they are making a contribution.

Important Group Term Life Insurance Provisions[4]

Beneficiary Designation

Under group term life insurance, an employee may name and change his or her beneficiary as desired. The only restriction is that the insurance

---

[3] Ibid.

[4] See William G. Williams, "Group Life Insurance," in *Life and Health Insurance Handbook,* 3d ed., eds. Davis W. Gregg and Vane B. Lucas (Homewood, Ill.: Richard D. Irwin, 1973), pp. 373–77.

must benefit someone other than the employer. If, at the death of the employee, no beneficiary is named, or if a beneficiary is named but does not survive the employee, the proceeds may be payable at the insurer's option to any one or more of the following surviving relatives of the employee: wife, husband, mother, father, child or children, or to the executor or administrator of the estate of the deceased employee. If any beneficiary is a minor or otherwise incapable of giving a valid release, the insurer is able to pay the proceeds under a "facility of payment" clause, subject to certain limits.

Settlement Options

The covered employee or the beneficiary may elect to receive the face amount of the group term life insurance on an installment basis rather than in a lump sum. The installments are paid according to tables listed in the group master policy. An insurer generally offers optional modes of settlement based on life contingencies. But the basis is seldom mentioned or guaranteed in the contract, and insurance company practices at the time of death govern.[5]

Assignment

Group term life insurance generally may be assigned if the master policy and state law both permit. Assignment of group term life insurance is important as a means for an employee to remove the group life insurance proceeds from his or her gross estate for federal estate tax purposes by absolutely assigning all incidents of ownership in the group term life insurance to another person or to an irrevocable trust. This was an important estate-planning technique for some employees whose estates potentially were subject to federal estate taxation. However since *ERTA* allows unlimited estate tax marital deduction, the attractiveness of assigning proceeds has decreased.

Conversion Privilege

If an employee's life insurance ceases because of termination of employment, termination of membership in a classification(s) eligible for coverage, or retirement, he or she may convert the group term insurance to an individual permanent life insurance policy. The employee must apply to the insurer in writing within 30 days of termination and pay the premium for his or her attained age, the type of insurance, and the class or risk involved; however, medical evidence of insurability is not necessary.

---

[5] Ibid., p. 376.

Under the law, employers must notify employees of their conversion rights within fifteen days after they take effect.

A more restricted conversion privilege may be provided for an employee if the group master policy is terminated or amended so as to terminate the insurance in force on the employee's particular classification. The employee may not convert more than $2,000 worth of coverage. The reason for such a limitation is to avoid the situation where an employer purchases group life insurance and quickly terminates the plan to allow individually uninsurable individuals to convert large amounts of individual life coverage.

Thirty-One-Day Continuation of Protection. This provision gives a terminated employee an additional 31 days of protection while evaluating the conversion privilege or awaiting coverage under the group life insurance plan of a new employer.

Continuation of Insurance

The employer can elect to continue the employee's group term life insurance in force for a limited period, such as three months, on a basis that precludes adverse selection during temporary interruptions of continuous, active, full-time employment. Upon expiration of the continuation period, premium payments are discontinued, and the employee's insurance is terminated. However, in this event, the insurance, as well as the right to exercise the conversion privilege, is still extended for 31 days after termination of the insurance.

Waiver of Premium Provision

Because employees may become disabled, group life insurance policies generally contain a waiver-of-premium provision. Under a typical waiver-of-premium provision, the life insurance remains in force if: (1) the employee is under a specified age, such as 60 or 65, at the date of commencement of total disability; (2) total disability commences while the person is covered; (3) total disability is continuous until the date of death; and (4) proof of total and continuous disability is presented at least once every 12 months.[6]

The waiver-of-premium provision is one of three types of disability benefit provisions used for group life plans. The second, the maturity value benefit, pays the face amount of the group term life insurance in a

---

[6] Ibid., pp. 374–75.

lump sum, or monthly installments when an employee becomes totally and permanently disabled. A third type of disability provision, the extended death benefit, pays group life insurance death claims incurred within one year after termination of employment. It requires the employee be continuously and totally disabled from the date of termination of employment until death occurs.

Dependent Coverage

The growth of dependents' group life insurance has been relatively slow, partly because of the taxation of amounts greater than $2,000. When provided, a typical schedule of benefits might give the dependent spouse life insurance equal to 50 percent of the employee's coverage but not more than $2,000. Typical benefits for dependent children often are graded from $100 between the child's age of 14 days to six months up to, for example, $1,000 or $1,500 between ages 5 and 19 years.

The death benefit normally is payable automatically in one lump sum to the insured employee or, in the event of the prior death of the employee, either to the employee's estate or, at the option of the insurer, to one of certain specified classes of "order-of-preference" beneficiaries.

Coverage of Employees after Retirement[7]

Retired Employees

Upon retirement, a former employee's group term life insurance often is discontinued and the high cost of conversion at the retiree's advanced age usually makes use of the conversion privilege impractical. Therefore, many employers are continuing reduced amounts of group term life insurance on retired employees under various types of reduction formulas. One formula reduces the insurance by 50 percent at retirement. Another uses a graded percentage system decreasing the amount of coverage each year after retirement age until a certain minimum benefit is reached; for example, 10 percent per year until 50 percent of the amount in force immediately prior to retirement is attained. Taxation of the postretirement benefits is the same as for active employees. Because continuing group life insurance on retired lives is costly, employers may consider funding coverage for retired employees through some other means such

---

[7] See Jerry S. Rosenbloom and G. Victor Hallman, *Employee Benefit Planning*, 2d ed. (Englewood Cliffs, N.J.: Prentice-Hall, 1986), pp. 47–52.

as group paid-up, group ordinary, or a separate "side fund" to pay the premiums at retirement.

Active Employees

Coverage requirements for active employees after age 40 are strongly influenced by the Age Discrimination in Employment Act of 1967 (ADEA), as amended in 1978 and HR 4154 which became effective on January 1, 1987. This latest amendment to ADEA eliminated the age 70 ceiling on active employment. Essentially, employees age 40 and above are considered the protected group. Plans may be "cut back," but individual plans have to be actuarially analyzed to determine cost justified reductions.

Until new regulations under ADEA are issued, it appears an employer (1) may reduce life insurance coverage each year starting at age 65 by 8 to 9 percent of the declining balance of the life insurance benefit, or (2) make a one-time reduction in life insurance benefits at age 65 of from 35 to 40 percent and maintain that reduced amount in force until retirement. The 8 to 9 percent annual reduction is justified by mortality statistics showing that, on the average, for example, the probability of death increases by that amount each year for the age 60 to 70 group. The one-time 35 to 40 percent reduction is justified by the difference in mortality expected, for example, by employees in the age 65 through age 69 bracket, compared to the mortality expected in the age 60 through age 64 bracket. An employer also may be able to cost justify greater reductions in group term life insurance benefits on the basis of its *own* demonstrably higher cost experience in providing group term life insurance to its employees over a representative period of years.

ADEA also permits use of a "benefit package" approach for making cost comparisons for certain benefits under ADEA. This benefit package approach offers greater flexibility than a benefit-by-benefit analysis as long as the overall result is no lesser cost to the employer and is no less favorable in terms of the overall benefits provided to employees.

Advantages and Disadvantages of Group Term Life Insurance

In summary, employers and employees are interested in evaluating the relative advantages and limitations of group term life insurance as an employee benefit.[8]

---

[8] See W. G. Williams, *Group Life Insurance,* pp. 377–78.

Advantages to the Employer

From the employer's perspective the following might be considered advantages of including a well-designed group term life insurance program as one of its employee benefits.

- Employee morale and productivity may be enhanced by offering this element of financial security.
- The coverage is necessary for competitive reasons, since most employers offer this form of protection.
- The life insurance protection is an aid to attaining good public and employer-employee relations.

Advantages to Employees

Group term life insurance dovetails into an employee's financial security planning.

- It adds a layer of low-cost protection to personal savings, individual life insurance, and Social Security Benefits.
- It helps reduce the anxieties about the consequences of the employee's possible premature death.
- If the plan does not favor "key" employees, the employer's contributions are not reportable as taxable to the insured employee for federal income tax purposes unless the total amount of group insurance from all sources exceeds $50,000; then the employee is only taxed on the value of amounts in excess of $50,000, as determined by a table in the Internal Revenue Code, less any contributions the employee made to the plan. However, if the plan discriminates in favor of key employees, the actual cost of all coverage (or the amount of its value as determined in the code, whichever is greater) will be taxable to the employee. In other words, the employee loses the $50,000 worth of tax-free life insurance, and may end up paying a higher rate on amounts in excess of $50,000. However, even if the plan is discriminatory, "rank and file" employees will not suffer adverse tax consequences. A group term life insurance plan may be considered to discriminate in favor of key employees unless the plan benefits at least 70 percent of all employees, at least 85 percent of the participants are not key employees, the plan is part of a cafeteria type, or the plan complies with a reasonable classification system found by the Internal Revenue Service (IRS) to be nondiscriminatory. In applying these IRS rules, part time and seasonal workers as well as those with fewer than three years of service do not have to be considered. Employees covered by a collective bar-

gaining agreement where group term life insurance has been bargained for also may be excluded.

- If employees are contributing toward the cost, their contributions are automatically withheld from their paychecks, making it convenient and also reducing the possibility of lapse of insurance.
- The conversion privilege enables terminated employees to convert their group term life insurance to individual permanent policies without individual evidence of insurability.
- Liberal underwriting standards provide coverage for those who might be uninsurable or only able to get insurance at substandard rates.

Disadvantages

Despite its many advantages, group term life insurance has some disadvantages. First, the employee usually has no assurance the employer will continue the group policy in force from one year to the next. Group life insurance plans seldom are discontinued, but business failures can and do occur, and the conversion privilege upon termination of a group life policy may be of limited value to the employees because of the high cost of conversion on an attained-age basis.

Another limitation exists when employees change employers, because group term life insurance is not "portable." Only about one out of every hundred terminating employees uses the conversion privilege. In practice, however, most employees changing jobs expect to be insured for the same or a higher amount of group life insurance with their new employers. Group term life insurance provides "protection only," while employee needs, at least partially, may dictate some other form of life insurance that has a savings or cash value feature. Also, with salary-related plans, coverage may be lowest when it is most needed (e.g., for a young employee with dependents). The next section looks at permanent forms of group life insurance, and other methods of funding death benefits under employee benefit plans are examined in later chapters.

PERMANENT FORMS OF GROUP LIFE INSURANCE

Given the expense of providing retired employees with group term life insurance, it is not surprising that permanent forms of group life have engendered some degree of interest over the years. After all, even though most retired workers do not have dependent children, many of them have dependents, most often spouses, and some have problems of estate liquidity. Furthermore, a lifetime of work may not be sufficient to provide the legacy hoped for by many retirees, and their financial goals are made particularly elusive by the high level of inflation that has plagued most countries since World War II. Therefore, the thought of obtaining permanent insurance through the relatively low-cost group mechanism has a certain amount of appeal.

Several forms of group permanent life insurance have been developed over the years, mostly in response to policies which have provided favorable tax treatment to group term life insurance. Among those to be examined here are group paid-up insurance and various forms of continuous premium coverage, including level-premium group, supplemental group (including group universal life), and group ordinary life insurance.

GROUP PAID-UP LIFE INSURANCE

First written in 1941, group paid-up life insurance allows all or part of an employee's scheduled group coverage to be so written that it will be fully paid up when the employee retires. During his or her working life, the employee makes a regular contribution that is used to purchase paid-up increments of whole life insurance. Each purchase increases the total amount of paid-up insurance owned. Figure 5–1 illustrates how units of paid-up insurance accumulate.

For tax reasons, discussed in the next section, employers do not purchase permanent insurance for their employees under this plan. Rather, they supplement the employees' purchases of permanent insurance with decreasing amounts of term insurance. After each contribution, the amount of term insurance decreases by exactly the amount that the paid-up insurance increases. Thus, the combined amount of both types of insurance remains constant at the amount set by the benefits schedule. Figure 5–1 illustrates the combination of coverages in this product.

Contributions

Employee contributions generally are designed to be level throughout the employee's working life. Naturally, because of actuarial considerations, the amount purchased with each contribution decreases as the employee gets older. Furthermore, costs are higher for individuals who enter the plan at older ages because they have fewer years in which to accumulate paid-up coverage. Therefore, in theory, a schedule of contributions should be graded for age of entry into the plan and anticipated length of service, and this is a common practice.

To provide certain minimum benefits for all employees and to encourage a high level of participation (particularly among older employees), some employers have set a single contribution rate for all employ-

FIGURE 5–1
Interrelationship between Increasing Increments of Paid-Up Group Life Insurance and Decreasing Increments of Group Term Life Insurance

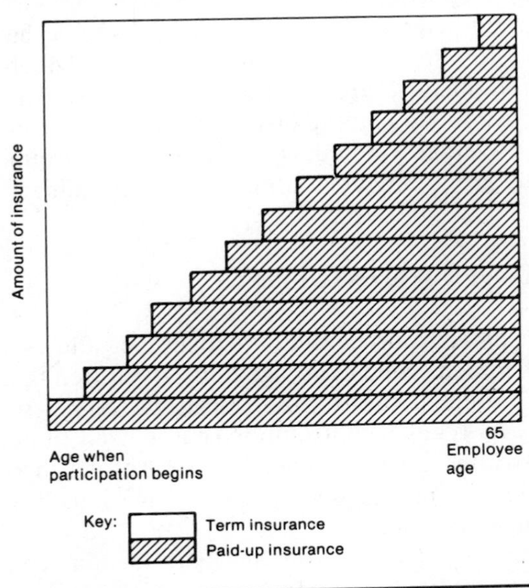

ees. The rates are attractively low, frequently \$1.00 to \$1.30 per month per \$1,000 of coverage. Table 5–5 illustrates the amounts of paid-up insurance that can be accumulated by workers at various ages with a monthly contribution of \$1. When the flat contribution results in inadequate coverage for older employees, the employer may supplement the paid-up insurance by continuing the necessary amount of term insurance after the employee retires. Sometimes a flat contribution schedule is limited to those who are with a firm for a minimum time when the coverage starts, while new employees pay according to an age-graded schedule. All such arrangements should be carefully reviewed to ensure that they do not run afoul of the nondiscrimination prohibitions in the tax laws.

Plan Provisions

As is normal for group insurance, benefits are determined by a schedule. In general, the provisions found in group term contracts also apply to the term portion of the paid-up plan as well. These include conversion and disability benefits (such as waiver of premium).

TABLE 5–5
Accumulated Amounts of Paid-Up Insurance Based on $1 Monthly Contribution

Entry Age	*Number of Years in Plan* 5	15	25	35	45
20	$229	$609	$905	$1,139	$1,329
30	178	474	708	899	—
40	139	373	563	—	—
50	110	301	—	—	—
60	91	—	—	—	—

Source: Robert W. Batten et al., *Group Life Insurance* (Atlanta, Georgia: Life Office Management Association, 1979), p. 111.

The employee-owned paid-up segment of the policy develops cash values, which are the greater of (1) the employee's contributions without interest, or (2) the standard nonforfeiture values as shown in the policy. In contrast to individual life policies, however, cash values are available only when the worker's employment terminates. Except in the case of termination, most plans do not permit surrender of the policy, and contracts do not contain a loan privilege.

The justifications for the constraints on loans and surrenders are that the cost of administering these benefits would offset some of the savings made possible through the use of the group technique, and access to cash values could lead to an undermining of the goal of the plan—to provide post-retirement protection. Finally, it sometimes is maintained that access to policy values could subject insurers to adverse financial selection on a line of coverage for which contingency margins have not explicitly been added.

Under the provisions of most plans, the life company may delay paying surrender values for a set period of time after employment is terminated. This is to prevent employees from quitting temporarily and then resuming their jobs just to obtain the policy surrender values. Obviously, there may be a great temptation to do so during a strike, layoff, or other period of economic stress for the worker. This restrictive provision is not applied when employees terminate with small amounts of coverage (e.g., less than $1,000). In such cases, policies are surrendered automatically for purposes of administrative simplicity.

It is important to note that coverage is not surrendered, and cash values are not available, if the master contract terminates. Paid-up coverage remains intact as long as employment is not terminated.

Although the reasons for not including a policy loan provision in traditional group paid-up policies still seem valid, limitations on the availability of surrender values seem less justifiable in light of contemporary consumer standards. It seems likely that those still in force will be phased out in the face of competitive pressures.

Premium Rates and Experience Rating

Group term policyowners (usually an employer) normally receive a dividend or "experience credit" each year if plan experience has been favorable. As a result of revenue rulings beginning in 1971, the term account may not subsidize the permanent account, or vice versa. In other words, each account must stand on its own feet. Thus, favorable experience credits must be allocated to the account from which they originate, whether it is the term or the paid-up account. Favorable experience may be passed on to the paid-up account in the form of a dividend to insureds, or as reduced rates for future purchases.

All normal or customary practices in experience rating are subject to change under the pressure of competition. When competition is intense, insurers may expand their tendency to pool the underwriting experience of different coverages or even different lines (e.g., group term and group permanent, or group life and group health). Pooling may lead to changes in the experience-rating practices.

Uses of Group Paid-Up Insurance

Group paid-up tends to appeal to firms with fewer than 500 employees. Furthermore, it generally is underwritten only for groups that display certain characteristics. As a first requirement, only those employers that provide stable employment can purchase group paid-up. Since strikes and layoffs interrupt employee contributions, and therefore interfere with the accumulation of paid-up coverage, they must be most unusual for the industry in which the policyowner operates. Furthermore, some carriers will not underwrite a case until the firm has been in business for a minimum period (e.g., three years).

Insurers also require that turnover be very low for the employer. To a degree, the turnover problem can be controlled by a long probationary period. However, the underwriting rules of some carriers exclude employers that have an annual turnover rate in excess of 5 percent. In addition, some establish minimum age requirements for participation (e.g., age 30–35).

Advantages of Group Paid-Up Life Insurance

Adherents of group paid-up life insurance claim it provides several advantages to employers or employees, or both. First and foremost, as contrasted with group term, it does provide permanent protection. Related to this is the advantage of cash value accumulations by the insured that can be made available when employment terminates. Both of these features are related to a third, which is that group paid-up provides a scientific way to fund postretirement coverage over the working life of the employee.

Group paid-up plans facilitate the conversion by long-service employees of any term coverage remaining at age 65, because it usually is a relatively small proportion of the scheduled amount, and because converted coverage is purchased at net rates. Thus, for these two reasons, retirees may end up being able to afford even more permanent coverage than they anticipate.

A sixth advantage to group paid-up is that employers electing to continue all or part of the coverage on retirees find the scheduled amount of term reduced well below the amount needed in the absence of paid-up insurance. This smaller financial burden may be easier for a business to justify.

A seventh advantage, when compared with other forms of permanent group coverage (discussed below), is that the status of these plans is well established with the Internal Revenue Service. They are a known commodity, and no serious modification of existing plans has been required by tax rulings to date. Therefore, it is highly unlikely that they will be subject to unfavorable rulings in the future. Another important tax factor is that the employer-purchased term coverage receives the favorable tax treatment accorded to all group term coverage.[9]

The group paid-up system provides still other advantages. Being contributory, the plan encourages participation only by those who need insurance. At the same time, in contrast to group term plans, employees may be more willing to contribute to the cost of group paid-up because they can see a permanent benefit growing out of their premiums.[10]

It is worth noting that insurers may be willing to offer higher limits on

---

[9] See: William H. Rabel and Charles E. Hughes, "Taxation of Group Life Insurance," *Journal of Accounting, Auditing, and Finance* 1, no. 2, p. 177, for a thorough discussion of this topic.

[10] For a discussion of the advantages of contributory group life plans, see Robert Batten et al., *Group Life and Health Insurance* (Atlanta, Georgia: Life Office Management Association, 1979), p. 42.

group plans containing permanent coverage than on term alone. The amount at risk for each individual continually diminishes throughout his or her working life. Furthermore, margins in interest earnings on reserves may support a more liberal benefit schedule.

Disadvantages of Group Paid-Up Life Insurance

Among the greatest disadvantages of group paid-up insurance is that the type of employer that can use it is limited, as explained above. Another limitation relates to the relatively high cost of administering the plan, when compared with term insurance. More professional advice is needed in designing, installing, and administering the plan. Furthermore, changes in benefits, eligibility status, and the like often require more record changes than would be required for term. A third disadvantage is that employer costs are higher in the early years of the plan than they would be for group term. Thus, the employer may delay the plan until it can be afforded. The high cost in the early years is due to start-up costs, as well as to the need to fund coverage for employees approaching retirement. In some cases, the employer may decide not to purchase a term plan to provide temporary protection with the result that there is no protection at all.

Finally, the principal advantage of group paid-up is also its principal weakness. Employee contributions purchase permanent coverage, and therefore afford less current protection for each premium dollar.

LEVEL PREMIUM GROUP PERMANENT LIFE INSURANCE

In exploring various approaches to providing postretirement coverage through the group mechanism, it was only a matter of time before someone suggested taking standard, level-premium, whole life insurance and writing it on a group basis. The idea was to have the employer pay all or part of the premium and to have the employee pay any amount not paid by the employer. However, before this approach could develop much of a following, the Treasury Department quashed it for all practical purposes in a 1950 tax ruling (Mimeograph 6477). The ruling required employees to include as current taxable income any employer contribution toward the cost of permanent insurance, unless the insurance is nonvested and forfeitable in the case employment is terminated. As a result of this ruling, the use of traditional level premium group life has been limited principally to qualified pension plans or to forfeitable group life plans. However, recently an adaptation of the concept has begun to emerge in the form of supplemental group life.

GROUP ORDINARY LIFE INSURANCE

In the mid-1960s a new type of permanent coverage was introduced that purported to allow employers to contribute to permanent policies due to some newly introduced standards in the tax law. Over the years these products have varied widely in design, but are known collectively as "group ordinary" or "Section 79" plans.

In concept, group ordinary allows employees to elect to take all or a part of their term insurance as permanent coverage. In effect, the contract is divided into protection and savings elements. Employer contributions are used to pay only for the term insurance component of the permanent contract, while employee contributions are credited to cash values. The plan can be limited payment (e.g., life paid up at 65) or ordinary whole life. Had plans been limited to this simple design, the taxation of group life insurance would be less complex than it is today.

However, inherent in the group ordinary concept is the fact that premium contributions will vary from year to year, as the amount at risk under the policy and the insured's death rate vary. The variability of premium limited the attractiveness of the product, and companies began to seek ways of smoothing or leveling the premium. Of course, such designs fly in the face of the tax rules providing that payments can be used to purchase term insurance only; premium-leveling by its very nature creates a reserve. Furthermore, the IRS suspected that some products were designed so that employers were paying more than their fair share of expenses under the contract. (This practice had been common under group paid-up, and was never brought into question until the IRS began to scrutinize group ordinary.) As a result, during the 1960s and 1970s a tug-of-war developed in which the IRS would write regulations and carriers would try to design plans that would comply while still being attractive in the marketplace. The final result is that today all group permanent insurance issued must meet stringent, complex rules which ensure that (1) employer contributions are not used to purchase permanent insurance and (2) employee-owned benefits are self-supporting. A few group ordinary plans remain in force under these circumstances, but the coverage is not widely marketed.

FUTURE OF PERMANENT GROUP LIFE INSURANCE

In 1974 permanent forms of group insurance constituted eight tenths of one percent of the total amount of group insurance outstanding. As Table 5–6 indicates, by 1981 it had shrunk to one half of one percent, and was only three tenths of one percent in 1985. Although group paid-up continues to attract a low but steady level of interest, other forms of group permanent business continue to shrink.

Supplemental group life insurance, the part of the market that seems to have the most promise, appears to be giving way to "mass marketed" or "wholesale" life insurance. This approach involves the issue of individual insurance through the endorsement (and sometimes the administrative support) of a third party. Over $27 billion of mass marketed insurance is now in force, including over $5 billion which has been issued through employers. It seems likely that much of this coverage would have been sold as supplemental group, if the mass marketed coverage were not available.

As the foregoing discussion suggests, the group insurance business is a dynamic, ever-changing arena. Large purchasers are highly sophisticated, and are constantly seeking better products and services for their money. By the same token, carriers compete fiercely for the business and are always innovative in their products and administrative procedures. As time passes, the distinctions among various product lines will continue to blur, and it appears likely that, in the near future, scholars and practitioners will have to begin developing an entirely new taxonomy for describing the group life insurance business.

Retired Lives Reserve

Another approach used to fund life insurance benefits for retired employees is a retired lives reserve plan. A retired lives reserve arrangement can be set up as a separate account through a life insurance company or through a trust arrangement for providing group term life insurance for retired employees. Such an approach provides for the funding of retiree life insurance over the employees' active employment period.

Retired lives reserve plans were once a popular mechanism for providing life insurance for retired employees because of very favorable tax implications for the employer. Recent restrictions imposed by DEFRA have limited the previous favorable tax aspects of retired lives reserve plans, for both employers and employees, and such plans have decreased in importance.

TABLE 5–6
Group Life Insurance In Force in the United States

	1981			1985		
Plan of Insurance	*Number of Policies* (000 omitted)*	*Amount (000.000 omitted)*	*Percent of Amount*	*Number of Policies* (000 omitted)*	*Amount (000.000 omitted)*	*Percent of Amount*
Term						
Decreasing	2,300	$ 54,500	2.9	2,200	$ 58,100	2.3
Other	118,600	1,824,900	96.6	126,600	2,494,600	97.4
Permanent						
Whole Life						
Premium paying	1,100	7,500	0.4	500	6,400	0.2
Paid-up	600	1,400	0.1	600	2,000	0.1
Endowment	†	100	††	†	200	††
Retirement income	†	200	††	†	300	††
Total group	122,600	$1,888,600	100.0	129,900	$2,561,600	100.0

Note: "Group" include credit life insurance on loans of more than 10 years duration. "Credit" is limited to life insurance on loans of 10 years or less duration.

* Includes group certificates. † Less than 50,000. †† Less than .05%.

Source: American Council of Life Insurance.

Accidental Death and Dismemberment Insurance

In addition to providing group term life insurance or some form of group insurance with cash values, employers typically also provide accidental death and dismemberment insurance (AD&D). The AD&D benefit usually is some multiple of the amount of group term life insurance provided the employee under the plan's benefit formula. AD&D insurance is payable only if the employee's death is a result of accident. Percentages of the AD&D coverage amount are payable in the event of certain dismemberments enumerated in the contract or employee booklet.

SUPPLEMENTAL GROUP LIFE INSURANCE

In the past few years, interest has been kindled in an employee-pay-all approach to providing permanent insurance, which has some features of both group and individual insurance. Sometimes called supplemental insurance, it may be provided under a master policy with a certificate being issued to each employee. Alternatively, sometimes individual policies are issued when the coverage is written. Premiums are paid through payroll deduction, and do not receive favored tax treatment. Depending on competitive factors and amounts available, coverage may be purchased with minimal individual underwriting. Since the employee owns the coverage, it goes with him or her if employment is terminated.

GROUP UNIVERSAL LIFE

Interest in supplemental protection has been substantially increased through the addition of group universal life (GUL) in the mid-1980s. At least a dozen companies that are very active in the group market are offering this coverage.

GUL is a permanent form of insurance that (like individual universal life) has two separate parts: (1) pure term protection, and (2) an accumulation fund. Periodically the employee contributes to the fund, which is credited with interest at a competitive rate. Each month the carrier deducts the cost of pure term protection for the amount at risk under the policy and the cost of administering the policy. The insured may elect to increase the face amount of the policy, provided that certain requirements are met. Like other insurance products, reserves accumulate on a tax-deferred basis and are tax free if paid as a death benefit. Since GUL is becoming such an important form of benefit for many employees, the next chapter covers this subject in detail.

CHAPTER 6

GROUP UNIVERSAL LIFE PROGRAMS*

Everett T. Allen, Jr.

BACKGROUND

To understand group universal life insurance programs (GULP), it is helpful to begin with a look at its direct forebear—individual policy Universal Life (UL). This form of permanent life insurance has come on the market only in the last ten years, yet it already is a major product line for almost all life insurers (accounting for more than 50 percent of some insurers' newly issued individual policy business).

The hallmark of UL is flexibility. Among its distinguishing characteristics are the following:

- Policyholders decide on the amount and timing of premium payments. They can, for example, fund the policy up front with a single premium and make additional payments at irregular intervals and in irregular amounts. They can also arrange premium "holidays" for any payments scheduled at a specific time.
- Premiums—minus mortality charges and expenses—create policy cash values that are credited with interest, typically at current rates for new investments with some applicable guaranteed floor amount (e.g., 4 percent). This interest accumulates tax-free (as it does with

* This chapter is reprinted herein with the permission of TPF&C, a Towers Perrin company.

most forms of permanent life insurance) and can totally escape income taxes if ultimately paid out as a death benefit.

- Policyholders can usually choose between a *level death benefit* (i.e., the policy's cash value plus whatever amount of term insurance is required to provide the level benefit selected) or an *increasing death benefit* (i.e., a level amount of term insurance plus the policy's cash value). They may also be able to increase their amount of term insurance—subject to some controls to prevent adverse selection.
- Policyholders can withdraw or borrow against cash values, or use the money to purchase paid-up life insurance. If they do not pay future term premiums, both mortality charges and administrative expenses (including premium taxes) are withdrawn from the cash values. If cash values are used up for any reason, leaving nothing to cover term premiums due, the policy is terminated.

In essence, UL offers individuals the chance to "buy term and invest the difference." GULP provides the same opportunity, but with a key difference: coverage is available on a group basis in a form similar to the coverage available under an employee benefit plan. Thus, GULP can be written as a supplement to, or replacement for, an existing group term life insurance plan. In addition, GULP may well have other important applications for employers. These include:

Funding ERISA excess and top-hat plans (both defined benefit and defined contribution).

Replacing coverage lost under discriminatory post-retirement life insurance plans.

Serving as an alternative to the so-called Clifford Trust.

Although GULP works much the same way that individual UL does, there are some differences:

- Because GULP is underwritten on a group basis, mortality charges may or may not be based on the underlying experience of the group. In addition, coverage amounts are guaranteed up to some limit without evidence of insurability. These limits vary from plan to plan, depending on plan provisions, the size of the participating group and the insurer's underwriting standards.
- Rates are set on a prospective basis (although the experience of the group may be used for this purpose) and the contracts are generally *nonparticipating*.
- Group underwriting requirements are used to avoid adverse selec-

tion and may limit GULP's flexibility to some extent. Actively-at-work requirements, for example, generally apply and some formula is used to determine amounts of coverage available (e.g., one or two times pay). Health statements or other proof of insurability may also be required in some situations—for example, if participation falls below some predetermined level. In addition, while an individual UL policyholder may be able to choose between a level or increasing death benefit, a GULP purchaser may be limited to one of these choices. But despite such constraints, overall plan design remains significantly more flexible than that available through a traditional, supplemental group insurance contract.

- GULP is not typically sold by insurance agents and is therefore available on a no-commission basis. (Individual UL policies, by contrast, are sold by agents who receive commissions for their sales and service efforts, even in cases where an employer permits "mass marketing" of such policies to employees.)
- Charges for any administrative services provided by the carrier should be lower for GULP than for individual coverage.

Finally, note that GULP is written on an employee-pay-all basis. Introducing employer contributions could eliminate most of its advantages, particularly its status under Sections 79 and 89 of the Internal Revenue Code.

SPECIFIC GULP FEATURES

Coverage Options

Under GULP, the purchase of term insurance can be separated from the savings or cash value element. Thus, employees can buy only term insurance or whatever combination of term insurance and savings best meets both their death-benefit and capital-accumulation objectives.

Employees select an amount of term insurance from the choices available—either a flat amount or a multiple of pay. In the latter case, the plan could provide for coverage to increase automatically in relation to pay. Although some plans limit coverage to employee life insurance, it is possible to include accidental death and dismemberment insurance and dependent coverage for spouses and children. Typically, children are covered only for term insurance, but spouses may be able to accumulate cash values. It is also possible to add waiver of premium coverage (payable in the event of an employee's disability) to the term insurance.

Payment Arrangements

Employee contributions for both the cost of the term insurance and administrative expenses are automatically withheld from aftertax pay. Employees who wish to add a savings element authorize an additional amount to be deducted from pay as well. In theory, these latter contributions can be variable, but in practice, design and administrative considerations may require regular savings. Even so, employees might be able to change their rate of savings, suspend savings contributions from time to time or contribute lump sum amounts (called "drop-ins"). In many respects, given these features, GULP more closely resembles a defined contribution plan than a traditional life insurance "product."

Insurance Rates

Premium rates for term insurance are negotiated based on the experience and characteristics of the participating group and can be quite attractive. (Table 6–1 illustrates the rates used for one existing plan.) Generally, they are guaranteed anywhere from one up to three or five years, with higher rates presumably applicable for coverage with extended guarantees.

While rates (even though guaranteed) can be designed to increase each year by age, linking rates to five-year age brackets is possible. Premi-

TABLE 6–1
Illustrative Term Insurance Rates (Per $1,000)

Age	*Monthly Rate*
Under 30	$ .069
30–34	.089
35–39	.099
40–44	.152
45–49	.259
50–54	.428
55–59	.669
60–64	1.040

ums can also be lower for nonsmokers than for smokers. Or nonsmokers might be given additional term insurance (e.g., 20 percent more) for the standard premium.

Cash Values

The interest credited to cash values varies depending upon current rates for new investments and insurer practices. At present, declared rates range between 8 percent and 9 percent—somewhat higher than those now available from many money market funds. Once a rate is declared, moreover, it may apply for a limited period such as one year. A permanent guaranteed floor rate of interest (e.g., 4 percent) is also set for purposes of state insurance and Federal tax laws.

Table 6–2 illustrates the buildup in cash values over a ten-year period for a 25-year-old employee with level term insurance of $70,000 plus a savings contribution of ten times the term premium. The illustration is based on sample rates and expense charges furnished by a major insurer. A credited interest rate of 9.5 percent is assumed.

As noted earlier, participating employees may withdraw cash values at any time and may replace them later with supplemental contributions. Employees may also be able to borrow from the insurer, using their cash values as collateral security. The interest charged for such loans exceeds the rate being credited to cash values—possibly by 1.5 percent or 2 percent. In addition, a withdrawal or loan transaction may trigger a transaction charge (e.g., $10 or $20) against the cash value.

Benefit Portability

An attractive feature of GULP is that individual coverage may be portable when insured employees terminate employment or retire. Specifically, some insurers would permit employees to continue coverage on a premium-paying basis—making payments directly to the insurance company—for the full duration of the mortality table (e.g., to age 100). In such a case, different mortality costs and expense charges may apply to continued coverage because all non-active insureds are "lumped" for experience purposes. In any event, if coverage is continued, it is important to clarify whether the subsequent experience of former employees will be charged back to the employer group and reflected in future premium levels.

As the previous discussion illustrates, GULP is not a product. Rather, it is a highly flexible type of coverage that involves many of the

TABLE 6–2
Illustration of Cash Value Buildup*

End of Year	*Attained Age*	*Term Contribution*	*Fund Contribution*	*Expenses*	*Deposit*	*Interest*	*Fund Balance*	*Total Death Benefit*
1	26	$ 84	$ 840	$ 37	$ 803	$ 41	$ 844	$70,844
2	27	168	1,680	74	1,606	162	1,768	71,768
3	28	252	2,520	112	2,408	371	2,779	72,779
4	29	336	3,360	149	3,211	676	3,887	73,887
5	30	420	4,200	186	4,014	996	5,010	75,010
10	35	841	8,410	372	8,038	5,086	13,124	83,124

* *Assumptions:*
1. $70,000 of term insurance.
2. fund contribution of ten times term premium.
3. interest at 9.5 percent.

design and financial issues applicable to other employee benefit plans. Some of these issues are:

Selecting eligibility requirements.

Establishing insurance schedules.

Fixing contribution schedules.

Obtaining competitive bids and negotiating contract provisions.

Clearly, given these considerations, the insurance "product" ultimately used is not "off the shelf," but rather the result of a careful design and negotiation process. Moreover, an insurer's underwriting and administrative requirements can influence design or become a factor in carrier selection.

TAX AND LEGAL ISSUES

Internal Revenue Code Section 79

It is generally advantageous for broad-based life insurance plans to be covered under IRC Section 79, which governs the tax treatment of group term life insurance provided to employees. This is not, however, true for GULP. One reason is that Section 79(d) nondiscrimination requirements do not apply if GULP falls outside the purview of Section 79. Equally important, imputed income problems can be avoided.

To illustrate the effect of Section 79's imputed income requirements, consider a traditional, supplemental group life program, set up on an employee-pay-all basis, where the term insurance cost for a 60-year-old executive is $.85 per month per $1,000 of coverage. The executive has $500,000 of coverage costing $5,100 per year. The imputed cost for this coverage (based on Table I rates) is $7,020. Assuming basic coverage of at least $50,000, this executive faces $1,920 of imputed income *even though* he has paid the full cost of the insurance. If, however, the plan were not subject to Section 79, he would have no additional imputed income.

Compounding the above problem in the case of permanent life insurance is the manner in which the IRS determines the cost of permanent benefits provided. Although common sense would suggest that this cost equal the yearly side fund contribution, the prescribed formula is:

$$\text{Cost} = NSP_B * (CV_E/NSP_E - CV_B/NSP_B)$$

where NSP is the net single premium, CV is the policy cash value and B and E represent beginning- and end-of-year values.

The following example, based on typical values provided by a large insurer, points up the impact of this formula:

Term Cost:	$ 125	
Side Fund Contribution:	375	
Side Fund Interest:	125	
CV_B:	1,000	
CV_E:	1,500	
NSP_B (50):		.42334
NSP_E (51):		.43558

Cost = .42334 (1,500/.43558 − 1,000/.42334) or $457.85

In this case, because the total employee contribution is $500, only $42.15 would be allocated to group term life insurance and available as an offset to Table I imputed income. And this is true even though the actual term cost is $125!

Clearly, there are sound reasons for removing GULP from the scope of Section 79. The next question is: how can it be done?

Section 1.79-1(a) of the Income Tax Regulations provides, in part, that life insurance is not group term life insurance for purposes of Section 79 unless:

1. It provides a general death benefit that is excludable from gross income under Section 101(a).
2. It is provided to a group of employees.
3. It is provided under a policy carried directly or indirectly by the employer.
4. The amount of insurance provided to each employee is computed under a formula that precludes individual selection.

Since GULP meets conditions 1, 2, and 4, to escape Section 79 treatment, it must *not* be "carried directly or indirectly by the employer." What would this entail? Under Section 1.79-0 of the Regulations, a life insurance policy is carried directly or indirectly by an employer if:

(a) The employer pays any part of the cost of the life insurance directly or through another person; or
(b) The employer or two or more employers arrange for payment of the cost of the life insurance by their employees and charge at least one employee less than the cost of his or her insurance, as determined under Table I of Section 1.79-3(d)(2), and at least one other employee more than the cost of his or her insurance, determined in the same way.

The first requirement can be met by setting GULP up on an employee-pay-all basis. The second requirement can be met in one of two ways. One is to ensure that term premiums are always greater or less than Table I rates at all ages. The other is to write GULP through an independent trust arrangement established by an insurer or other third party (e.g., a consulting or brokerage firm), thereby ensuring that the employer has no part in arranging for the coverage.

Under this latter approach, the trustee becomes the policyholder and fees and/or commissions are paid by the trust or the insurer. The fact that the employer withholds and remits employee contributions and permits descriptive materials to be given to employees does not bring the program within Section 79. However, the employer could not participate in the insurer selection process or in the development of premium rates.

The question of paying for the cost of life insurance is very important. It would seem that amounts paid directly by an employer to a third party for items such as communication and enrollment would *not* invoke Section 79 treatment. In preparing specifications, it may be prudent to specify the third party's role and to isolate the insurer's expense load for any services included in the insurer's expense level. These charges should then be removed or paid directly to the third party by the carrier on a fee-for-service basis. Presumably, fees paid by the employer in excess of the expense load would be permissible since they are not part of the cost of insurance.

Internal Revenue Code Section 89

The Tax Reform Act of 1986 establishes a comprehensive set of nondiscrimination requirements for group term life and accident or health plans. Employee-pay-all plans, however, are not subject to these requirements. Thus, if GULP is established with only employee contributions and with no employer-provided benefits, the requirements of Section 89 should not apply.

Deficit Reduction Act of 1984 (DEFRA)

DEFRA poses a problem that does affect GULP's design and operation—taxation on the buildup of cash values. To avoid such taxation, a life insurance product must meet the definition of life insurance as specified in Section 7702(a) of the Code. In general, life insurance contracts must meet one of two tests, the cash value accumulation test (7702(a)(1)) or the guideline premium requirement test (7702(a)(2)).

Under the cash value accumulation test, the cash surrender value may not at any time exceed the net single premium required to fund future benefits under the contract. To meet this test, therefore, insurers using it have to stipulate that when the cash value limit is reached, all or part of the cash value will either be used to purchase paid-up insurance or refunded to the employee.

TABLE 6–3
IRS Guideline Premiums

	Annual Guideline Premiums (Per $1,000)	
Issue Age	*Level Benefit*	*Increasing Benefit*
35	$13.43	$ 32.63
40	16.82	40.01
45	21.21	49.16
50	27.00	60.56
55	34.76	74.84
60	45.22	92.77
65	59.70	115.50

Under the guideline premium requirement test, the accumulated premiums paid cannot exceed the IRS guideline premium limitation (see Table 6–3).

Accumulated premiums paid must also meet the cash value corridor test of Section 7702(a)(2)(B), which states that the death benefit must never be less than the applicable percentage of the cash surrender value. The "applicable percentage" is 250 percent, but it is reduced, after the insured reaches age 40, in accordance with the following table:

In the case of an insured with an attained age, as of the beginning of the contract year, of:		*The applicable percentage decreases by a ratable portion for each full year:*	
More than	*But not more than*	*From*	*To*
40	45	250%	215%
45	50	215	185
50	55	185	150
55	60	150	130
60	65	130	120
65	70	120	115
70	75	115	105
75	90	105	100
90	95		

Typically, insurers using this test automatically increase the amount of term insurance to comply with the cash value corridor requirement. They will also return premiums to employees to avoid violating the guideline premium limitation. In addition, insurers are likely to impose some overall maximum on the amount an employee can contribute to build cash values, thereby avoiding IRS limitations for a considerable time period. Plan design should recognize this issue.

The insurer must be relied on to make certain that the contract can be classified as life insurance. Thus, it is important to understand the differences between these two approaches and ensure that the carrier's administrative system is capable of "warning" employees before an automatic purchase of additional insurance (term or paid-up) is made or cash values or premiums are refunded.

Employee Retirement Income Security Act of 1974 (ERISA)

Although neither a Section 89 nor an employer-sponsored plan, GULP seems to fall within the broad definition of welfare plans under Title I of ERISA and would be subject to this law's reporting, disclosure and fiduciary requirements. If, as is likely, GULP replaces an existing group term life plan, this administrative burden will be no more onerous than under the conventional approach. But there may be additional fiduciary implications because of the "investment" aspects of the program.

Taxation of Withdrawals and Loans

If an employee withdraws cash values without changing the face amount of his or her coverage, the amount withdrawn is not subject to tax until it exceeds the employee's cost basis or investment in the contract (i.e., the sum of all term insurance premiums, all net additions to the side fund and administrative costs). Thereafter, the withdrawal is taxable as ordinary income.

Loan proceeds are not subject to income tax unless and until cash values are used to repay the loan. At that time, the transaction is treated as a withdrawal. (Interest on such loans will not be deductible after 1990.)

Taxation of Death Benefits

The full amount of the proceeds payable at death (term insurance and cash values) is considered life insurance and therefore not subject to income tax. However, the proceeds are includable for estate tax purposes unless the employee's incidents of ownership have been assigned at least three years prior to death, or if it can be proved that assignments within three years of death were not made in contemplation of death.

ADVANTAGES AND DISADVANTAGES

GULP offers a number of advantages to employers. Specifically:

- A successfully implemented plan may relieve pressure on the employer to provide postretirement life insurance coverage.
- GULP is a low-cost "benefit improvement," much like an unmatched 401(k) plan.
- GULP offers a way to move away from an existing subsidized flat-rate plan.
- Significant benefits are available for key employees.
- Because GULP is generally sold on a group basis, there is no need for individual insurance agents to solicit employees.
- If an employee continues coverage after termination of employment, the employer will not face conversion charges.

GULP also offers many advantages to employees. Among them:

- Employees can consolidate all coverages for themselves and their dependents under one contract.
- Upon termination of employment, the coverage may be portable.
- Premiums are flexible in amount and timing.
- Investment income is on a tax-deferred or tax-free basis and, at least currently, may be higher than that available from money market funds.
- GULP appears to be the least costly way to purchase term or permanent life insurance.
- GULP is a convenient way to purchase insurance; premium payments are made on a payroll deduction basis.
- Guaranteed issue amounts are available at levels sufficiently high to cover most employee needs.
- Cash values offer a source of funds for emergencies. This may be very attractive since withdrawals from qualified defined contribution plans are subject to an early distribution tax.
- Employees receive periodic reports and are kept up-to-date on the status of their life insurance program.
- Upon retirement, employees can use their cash value to purchase paid-up insurance.

The appeal and versatility of GULP notwithstanding, employers should be aware of certain potential disadvantages before adopting such a program for any reason. Among the major issues to consider:

- Employees may view GULP as a more attractive savings vehicle than an employer-sponsored 401(k) plan. If that occurs and precipitates a drop in 401(k) participation, the 401(k) plan could have trouble meeting ADP and ACP tests for participation by higher-paid employees.
- GULP cannot be funded with before-tax employee contributions if it is to remain outside the scope of Section 89. Thus, it cannot be part of a flexible benefit program.
- Although employers are not technically involved in operating a GULP, they may well bear the brunt of employee dissatisfaction if servicing problems arise.
- To preclude financial selection, insurers may move toward short-term interest guarantees. In such a case, the interest credited to individual accounts will probably depend on when the monies are invested. Although the yields on current investments are likely to be as good as, or better than, those available from other investment vehicles, there is no guarantee that the total cash value will enjoy similar results, especially in a period of rising inflation.
- Changes in the law, regulations and rulings could bring GULP within the purview of Section 89 or make taxable the buildup of cash values.
- As with any form of permanent life insurance, participants could face adverse financial results if coverage is surrendered early.
- Low GULP participation may saddle employers with administrative burdens and no offsetting advantages.
- The feasibility and consequences of terminating the master policy and/or obtaining coverage with another insurer remain unclear. For example, can individual units of coverage continue after termination of the master policy? If so, will there be any change in the structure of premiums, cash values, interest credits and other policy provisions? Can reserves be transferred to another insurer and, if so, would this be a taxable transaction?

COMMUNICATING GULP TO EMPLOYEES

GULP's very flexibility necessitates careful employee communication. After all, employees are being offered an opportunity to participate in a program with many choices—generally without the benefit of face-to-face explanations and enrollment by insurance agents or insurance company personnel. Although insurance carriers will undoubtedly provide communication assistance (at no additional specified cost), bear in mind they want to sell the product. Generally, therefore, it will be up to employers to ensure their employees receive a balanced presentation and understand both the advantages and disadvantages of participation.

Pretesting the concept with employees in focus groups can help employers determine the magnitude of the communication challenge. Based on this information, employers can then prepare appropriate written and audiovisual communication materials to explain how the program works and the various options available to employees. Trained employer personnel should also be available to answer questions and help employees make appropriate choices. Although strategies and techniques will be much the same as those used for other employee benefit plans (particularly savings or 401(k) plans), employers may have to place extra emphasis on communicating initial and ongoing choices and their implications. Employers who wish to encourage participation for a specific reason (e.g., to replace postretirement life insurance) may also have to use specific "selling" techniques.

ADMINISTRATION/DESIGN CHECKLIST

Administration

Administration of GULP can be complicated, combining the record-keeping and systems requirements of both group insurance and defined contribution plans. This is, in fact, one of the main reasons that some carriers may not be in a position to offer GULP. It also points up the importance of evaluating administrative capability in selecting a carrier.

Administrative requirements include the following:

- Linking with payroll systems to accommodate withholding
- Establishing coverage amounts and contribution levels and allocating these amounts to term and savings elements
- Collecting and remitting contributions to the carrier with appropriate allocations between savings and term insurance coverage
- Maintaining individual account balances (including charges and credits)
- Processing such transactions as:
  Changes in beneficiary, coverage amounts, contribution levels and address/location.

Contribution suspensions.

Addition or deletion of participating employees.

Loans, withdrawals and claims.

Transferring administration for terminating and retiring employees.

Producing annual reports.

In addition, plan administration encompasses the experience-rating process, the resolution of underwriting questions and the preparation and filing of tax reports (e.g., Form 1099) and financial reports to the employer and employees (e.g., Form 5500 and SARs).

Although third parties are likely to offer GULP administrative services, this development may be inappropriate for several reasons:

- Insurers are developing their own administrative capability and are not receptive to the idea of using an outside administrator.
- The costs would be redundant and therefore unattractive.
- It does not appear that any third-party "system" would be distinguishable from, or superior to, the ones developed by insurers.
- Significant interaction with individual policyholders would be required; an unnecessary and costly role for any third party.

Design

What follows is a list of the issues involved in designing GULP—many of which have to be negotiated with the insurer and must be included in the competitive bidding process. Key considerations include:

1. Eligibility requirements (age, service, minimum pay level, employment classification).
2. Coverage to be included.
   a. Term only.
   b. Term plus savings.
   c. Accidental death and dismemberment.
   d. Declared interest rate.
   e. Policy loan interest rate.
   f. Regular administrative charges.
   g. Transaction fees.
   h. Reserve basis for paid-up insurance.
3. Underwriting.
   a. Guaranteed issue amount.
   b. Evidence of insurability requirements.
   c. Open enrollment availability.

  d. Dependent coverage.
  e. Waiver of premium.
4. Term coverage amounts to be included.
  a. Number of choices.
  b. Flat amounts.
  c. Multiples of pay.
    (1) Initially frozen.
    (2) Automatically increased with pay.
5. Savings provisions.
  a. Number of choices.
  b. Maximum contribution level.
  c. Regular contributions.
  d. Variable contributions.
  e. Floor rate of interest.
  f. Declared rate of interest.
6. Other provisions.
  a. Withdrawals.
  b. Policy loans.
  c. Paid-up insurance options.
  d. Portability.
7. Premiums and other financial considerations.
  a. Level.
  b. Guarantees.
  c. Renewal rating process.
  d. Floor interest rate.

CHAPTER 7

DESIGNING MEDICAL CARE EXPENSE PLANS

Charles P. Hall, Jr.

BACKGROUND

"The severe and continuing escalation of health care costs over the past decade is a matter of growing concern to virtually all segments of our society. It has caused great financial stress to both public and private sponsors of health benefits plans, with the private sponsors being especially hard hit. Yet despite much rhetoric, there is little evidence of lasting solutions being developed." That opening statement from Chapter 8 of the first edition of this book (1984) is equally true today, despite enormous changes that have taken place in the delivery, financing, and organization of health care over the past half decade.

Indeed, the issue of cost containment continues to occupy center stage at both the public policy and corporate policy levels. While some of the recent benefit innovations that were described in the first edition have now become traditional in their own right, others have virtually disappeared, and a whole new lexicon of terms has emerged to describe yet another generation of "recent" innovations. Moreover, despite the reduction in the overall inflation rate from the levels of the early 1980s, it is painfully clear that, in relative terms, health care costs are more out of control than ever before. In 1986, when the overall consumer price index rose by only 1.1 percent, the health care index rose over 7 percent—the largest differential ever recorded. By late 1987 there were widespread predictions that the annual inflation rate in benefit plan costs would again soar well into the double-digit range for the year.

It remains true that there are only a few basic approaches to the effective control of the cost of medical care expense benefit plans. It can be accomplished either by controlling the factors that affect the costs of these plans (e.g., the ordering and providing of care and services by doctors, hospitals, and other care givers; the shifting of costs from (or to) other sectors to private medical expense plans; inflation and changes in technology; and changes in the demand for and resulting utilization of health care services) or by designing the benefit or plan to minimize the impact of changes in the various cost factors.

This chapter will identify some of the major factors that must be taken into account in the design of employee health benefit plans if there is to be any hope for meaningful cost containment.

PUBLIC POLICY ISSUES

It indeed would be foolish for anyone responsible for the design of employee health plans not to pay very close attention to public policy issues relating to health care. This has been a politically charged arena for decades, and there have been widespread shifts in government policy, with enormous impact on the private sector. Often, the changes have been both arbitrary and capricious in their impact. Employers have found that cost containment from the point of view of the government frequently translates into cost shifting to the private sector, as a means of saving on the costs of public programs such as Medicare and Medicaid, while at the same time avoiding either tax increases or added pressure on the mounting federal deficit.

When Congress changed the ground rules for Medicare reimbursement from a retrospective, cost-related basis to a prospective system based on diagnostic related groups (DRGs) in 1983, it had a profound and lasting effect, not only on the financing of care, but also on the organization and delivery of medical services. There is no question that this action gave rise to redoubled efforts on the part of employers to search for ways to protect themselves against federal cost shifts and to discover meaningful cost control measures of their own.

For the prudent benefits planner or manager, then, it makes sense to keep a close watch on emerging issues. With luck, it may be possible to anticipate changes and design plans that will minimize any undesirable impact on the firm or its employees. It may also be possible to successfully lobby either for or against proposals that are of direct concern. There are, at present, several such issues.

The Uninsured

From a public policy perspective, mounting concern about the growing number of Americans who are uninsured for health care costs and continued pressure from the huge federal deficit have resulted in government policies that have extended employee benefits, involuntarily in most instances. Whereas employers formerly utilized "carve-out" provisions designed to make their group benefits responsible only for those items not covered by Medicare for over-65 workers, Congressional action has now made the employee benefit primary for all active workers, regardless of age.

In other action, Congress made it mandatory, effective July 1, 1987, that companies with at least 20 employees make medical benefits available at group rates for up to 18 months after a worker leaves employment, regardless of whether the worker left voluntarily, retired, or was dismissed. Furthermore, family members may be entitled to continued coverage even if the worker dies or gets divorced, and that right may be extended for up to three years.

At this writing, consideration is being given to bills that would mandate all employers to provide certain health benefits. It has been estimated that the most prescriptive of these bills, S-1265, proposed by Senator Edward Kennedy (D-Mass.), could result in "an immediate increase in group medical plan expenditures of anywhere from 24 percent to 70 percent (or higher) within the initial year of its proposed adoption;" one study found that "Not one of 70 companies surveyed has a health benefit program in place that meets the requirements" of this proposal.[1]

Retiree Coverage

The most ominous development, from the viewpoint of the employer, has been the recent tendency of the courts to find that certain postretirement health benefits that companies had extended to their workers—often as a gesture of goodwill—are now fully guaranteed as vested contractual rights, with no residual right on the part of the employer to reduce them either by increasing retirees' contributions via premium, deductible, or coinsurance modifications, or by eliminating previously covered benefits. Apparently, Congress can make such changes in Medicare provisions at will, but the courts are holding private employers to a higher standard.

---

[1] *Medical Benefits*, September 30, 1987, pp. 1, 2.

With continued rapid growth in the over-65 population, growing life expectancy, and increasingly costly medical technology for dealing with the diseases of the elderly, many firms now find themselves faced with potentially catastrophic unfunded liabilities in this area. There are sure to be dramatic changes—most likely, cutbacks—in the future level of employer coverage for retired workers, at least with respect to acute care services, as a result of these developments. At the very least, retiree benefits will be described in very careful contract language that will protect the employer from unanticipated and unwanted commitments. This response, however, might generate further Congressional mandates.

Catastrophic Coverage

Note, too, that Congress has continued to vacillate in its own efforts to enact acceptable catastrophic coverage for the elderly. The administration's proposal continues to focus on acute medical services, while the prevailing view of most health economists and the elderly themselves is that the most pressing need is for an acceptable form of long-term care insurance that provides adequate protection for nursing home and home health services as well as some basic social services that, presumably, would cost less and enable the elderly to maintain some semblance of independence.

There has been a surge of interest in long-term care insurance by the private sector in the past year, and while the development is still in its infancy, it may well be the next frontier of employee benefits, either by choice or by mandate. If, as has been stated in the past, a major underlying purpose for employee benefit plans is satisfaction of employee needs, then surely this is an area that is ripe for development. The need is not likely to be met adequately by individuals acting on their own, and deficit politics will not permit the government to create major new programs at this time. But Congress could direct employers to provide at least some benefits.

Other Current and Emerging Issues

Some of the other areas relating to health benefits in which Congress has shown recent interest suggest that the field will remain controversial for years. For example, the Congressional Office of Technology Assessment (OTA) has been looking into the possible impact on insurance and employment of rapid technological development in genetic testing. At issue is whether Congress should establish regulations dealing with the use of such tests for either insurance underwriting and rating, or employment decisions. Concern has been expressed that insurers might require genetic tests and refuse coverage where the results suggest either the certainty of or a predisposition for such diseases as Tay Sachs, sickle cell anemia, and certain forms of heart disease. These tests as part of a pre-employment physical could result in refusal to employ as a means of avoiding higher benefit costs.

In the current frenzy over Acquired Immune Deficiency Syndrome (AIDS), laws have been proposed to either mandate coverage or prohibit preinsurance testing designed to exclude coverage. Some such laws have already been passed at lower levels of government. This is like forcing a fire insurance company to sell a policy to someone whose house is already burning.

OTA has also been investigating the cost of providing infertility benefits. The focus here has been on the cost of providing such services to veterans and their families. However, Congresswoman Pat Schroeder recently introduced legislation not limited to veterans that would not only provide benefits for infertility services, but would also help finance adoptions.

There is also widespread interest in both public and private circles in the provision of more extensive mental health benefits. Concern ranges from conditions that strike primarily among the elderly, such as senile dementia and Alzheimer's disease, to problems with alcohol and drug abuse, which seem to have their most severe impact among youth and young adults.

Occasionally, there are initiatives in Washington that save employers money on their benefit plans. One such example, so far unsuccessful, is the effort by the Reagan administration to abolish the provision in the federal Health Maintenance Organization Act that requires employers to pay at least as much toward the cost of an employee's HMO benefits as is paid for the traditional plan under the dual choice mandate.

State Level Issues

Aside from these activities at the federal level, public policy action at the state level has also occurred. While the trend toward enactment of state-mandated health benefits peaked in the late 1970s, special interest groups continue to lobby for this type of legislation. Recent court decisions that have found such laws not in conflict with provisions of the Employee Retirement Income Security Act (ERISA) may result in renewed activity. In general, employers have fought these mandates, though not always successfully.

Some states, in an effort to either curb or at least rationalize these efforts, while at the same time trying to control the escalation of health care costs, have established various commissions and review panels to provide legislative guidance. In Pennsylvania, for example, the creation of a Health Care Cost Containment Commission in 1986 carried with it the creation of a Mandated Benefits Review Panel that is charged with responsibility for reviewing all proposed mandated benefits in accordance with very explicit criteria spelled out in the law. The panel, composed of experts from the fields of biostatistics, health economics, and health research, reports to the commission, which also obtains input from the insurance commissioner and the secretary of health. The commission then makes a recommendation to the legislature as to the desirability of specific proposals. Several other states are studying similar proposals.

In summary, "Washington watching" and "state capitol watching" will continue to be very important in the design of medical care expense plans.

ENVIRONMENTAL FACTORS

Despite one of the most extended periods of peacetime prosperity in the nation's history, concerns about renewed inflation, rising interest rates, growing federal deficits, persistent foreign trade imbalances, and fluctuations in the value of the dollar have combined to produce a good deal of economic uncertainty. Dramatic fluctuations in the stock market at the time of this writing have done little to increase confidence.

The Work Force

There have been major changes in the American work force over the past decade, and some of these changes have had an important impact on employee benefits There has been a sharp increase in the total number of employed workers, but this has been accompanied by a marked shift in the nature of American industry. The traditional smokestack industries that were so dominant in the years after World War II have dramatically declined in importance, at least in relative terms, as the pressure of foreign competition and the rapid shift of American industry from a manufacturing to a service orientation has progressed.

This is of enormous importance from the standpoint of medical care expense plans for several reasons. The traditional manufacturing giants were, typically, large employers with a heavily unionized work force. While they never accounted for a majority of the labor market, the negotiated benefits they obtained often became the pattern for other firms to emulate. The majority of the workers were blue collar, and most were from single-income families. Over the past decade, changes in the workplace have been characterized by a shift from manufacturing to service industries, from large to small firms, from heavily unionized blue-collar to minimally organized white-collar positions, and from a male-dominated to an almost equally gender-balanced work force. More importantly, a larger proportion of the work force now comes from multiple income households, and a significant proportion of workers are employed on a part-time basis.

One result of all this is that a very significant portion of the uninsured in America are actually employed, whereas historically the uninsured were concentrated among the unemployed.

Demographics and Technology

The graying of America continues, with both average life expectancy and the average age of the population increasing as the baby boom generation matures. Furthermore, there has been a noticeable increase in the birthrate as women who had previously postponed motherhood began having children.

The first and last six months of life continue to be the most expensive, from a medical point of view. Increasingly sophisticated medical technology now makes it possible to preserve the life of babies who only a few years ago would have had no chance for survival. At the other extreme, the ability to extend life, though not necessarily to improve its quality, has become both a societal blessing and a curse. This applies, as well, to the vast majority of the population not at the extremes of age.

The technology in question is both extraordinarily expensive and controversial. It is clear that our ability to develop acceptable ethical, legal, and moral standards by which to determine the appropriate use of the new technology has lagged far behind our scientific progress. Nevertheless, those who design and sponsor medical plans must face hard decisions as to the criteria they will establish for coverage. Should everyone be eligible for organ transplants? Intensive care? Experimental treatment? These questions continue to be addressed on an ad hoc basis under many benefit plans, while others have established formal policies.

Third Party and Medical Care Organization

Neither the pace nor the nature of the changes that have occurred in third party reimbursement during the decade of the 1980s could have been predicted. At the beginning of the decade, over 90 percent of all benefit plans were covered under either traditional commercial health insurance or Blue Cross/Blue Shield plans. While it was expected that Health Maintenance Organizations (HMOs) would eventually capture a larger share of the market, most people at that time were thinking in terms of group model HMOs. All HMOs combined for only 4 percent of health plan enrollments in 1980.

Although there were self-insured benefit plans and third party administrators (TPAs) in the market, they were not a major force. Preferred provider organizations (PPOs) had not even been invented, and the concept of managed care was largely confined to theoretical discussions. There was also a great deal of talk about consumer choice and competition in health care plans, though no one really seemed to understand fully what the implications of such a development might be. Again, much of the discussion was theoretical, led by Dr. Alain Enthoven of Stanford University.

By mid-decade, it was being estimated by some that traditional plans would account for no more than 5 percent of total plan enrollments by 1990, with managed care (25 percent), PPOs (40 percent), and HMOs (30 percent) (independent practice association [IPA] [22 percent] and group model [8 percent] accounting for the rest).[2] While these estimates were seen by some as exaggerated, it was generally conceded by late 1987 that over half of all benefit plans had already left the traditional fold.

But this only begins to tell the story. As noted earlier, the federal HMO Act originally created a mandate for employers to offer a dual option to their employees if a federally qualified HMO was available; they also had to contribute at least as much toward the cost of the HMO option as they did for the original plan. Despite the dual choice mandate, however, HMO growth lagged during the 1970s, probably because the amount of coverage required for qualification pushed their cost out of a competitive range. Moreover, there was continued provider aversion to the group model HMO. In recent years, however, HMO growth has increased dramatically, with most of it concentrated among Independent Practice Association plans, which are more widely accepted by physicians.

Three other factors may also account for this more rapid growth. First, HMOs now have been around long enough for the public to understand them better, and there has been time enough for a new generation of families to emerge who did not have preexisting relationships with physicians that would have to be broken, as was often the case with their parents. Furthermore, one of the early limitations of HMOs, especially with the highly mobile U.S. population, was their limited, usually local, service area. By the end of 1986, however, the proportion of HMOs affiliated with national HMO firms was nearing 50 percent, up from less

[2] Sanford C. Bernstein & Co., Interstudy, Minneapolis, Minn., 1985.

than 40 percent only 18 months earlier. Finally, the emergence of a new category of sponsorship, joint hospital-insurer companies, undoubtedly has had a salutory impact on marketing results.

With the advent of PPOs, many employers began to offer triple option plans to their workers—either the traditional indemnity or Blue Cross/Blue Shield coverage, an HMO, or a PPO.

PPOs caught on quickly with employers, and their growth was almost exponential in the five years after their origination in California. One of the attractions of the PPO model has been the flexibility it affords. Unlike HMOs, which have a clear legal definition as well as both federal and (frequently) state published guidelines for qualification, PPOs remained virtually unregulated until recently, when some states began to set guidelines for risk-bearing PPOs.

Another attraction is that the PPO actually has provided large employers an opportunity to do some cost shifting of their own, after being the recipients of unwanted federal cost shifts for years. This short-run attraction, however, could become the long-run Achilles' heel of PPOs. By negotiating for discounted fees or charges, utilization review and quality assurance in exchange for control of a significant market share, large employers can exert considerable pressure on health care providers. Depending on the specifics of particular markets, this could result in providers trying to make up some of the discounts by charging smaller and weaker consumers more for similar services—precisely the complaint that industry lodged against government in the past. Should this in fact happen, it is not unreasonable to anticipate that at some point there will emerge political pressure for legislation to protect the "little guy." Until then, however, PPOs will continue to flourish, and their form and sponsorship will continue to evolve.

Indeed, the pace of change had become so rapid by 1987 that virtually no one could provide either an accurate count or description of all the existing marketplace options. The distinctions between and among the various plans continue to blur, as various hybrids evolve. New forms, such as open-ended HMOs, which allow enrollees to use out-of-plan providers and still receive indemnity coverage, and the even more recent point-of-service plans, which permit the insured to select either indemnity, HMO, or PPO coverage *at the time service is being rendered* (which differentiates it from the usual triple option arrangement), appear on a regular basis. Another recent development, the Social HMO (SHMO) is an emerging concept designed to address the needs of the frail elderly by integrating community services in a manner that will permit them to live independently in their own homes for as long as possible.

The medical care delivery system also continues to change. The enormous success of proprietary hospital chains such as the Hospital Corporation of America during the late 1970s and early 1980s led many to predict, as recently as two years ago, that the hospital field literally would be taken over by a handful of similar corporations by the end of the century. One of the anticipated developments had these superhospital corporations not only controlling the delivery of hospital services but also taking over the insurance of health care benefits through their own captive subsidiaries.

There has been a dramatic change in those forecasts, however, as some of the proprietary hospital groups suddenly encountered hard times, and most of them abandoned or cut back on their insurance plans. Not only was the demise of the independent, nonprofit community hospital greatly exaggerated, but analysts failed to foresee the emergence of several new varieties of affiliation between nonprofit hospitals on both local, regional, and national lines.

Virtually every community has seen the emergence of new medical delivery facilities in recent years. These include hospital-based short procedure units (SPUs), ambulatory surgicenters, free-standing diagnostic imaging centers, trauma centers, and various kinds of either specialized or generalized medical clinics, to name just a few. Services delivered at these sites are routinely covered under most health benefit plans.

Competition for customers (patients) will continue to escalate in the months and years ahead, as will the quest for truly effective cost containment. The resulting pressures will undoubtedly keep the world of health care delivery and financing every bit as volatile as it has been over the past decade. It will also continue to challenge the ingenuity of those responsible for the design of benefit plans.

Health Care Coalitions

Health care coalitions, which initially emerged in the mid-1970s, have continued to grow in strength and influence during the 1980s. While corporate employers continue to dominate most such groups, membership has broadened to include representatives of providers, unions, insurers, and others. They concern themselves with virtually the entire spectrum of health-related issues, and they have become increasingly sophisticated in their understanding of those issues. While cost of care remains a dominant concern, especially on the part of employer members, quality of care is also a primary goal. Many of the coalitions are actively involved in the design of employee health benefits, legislative analysis, and legislative advocacy. Many are involved directly in the development or analysis of health data such as cost evaluation and utilization patterns. They are often able to provide valuable assistance in the design of effective benefits.

BENEFIT PROVISIONS

Some significant changes in benefit plan provisions have occurred in recent years. Most of those changes have been triggered by a response to the many public policy and environmental issues that have been discussed. While relatively few totally new provisions have been introduced since the first edition of this handbook was published, there have been some major adjustments in existing provisions.

Alternatives to Inpatient Care

Preadmission testing (PAT) was a relatively new concept just a few years ago; it is now not only available but mandatory under most medical benefit plans. There is a general consensus that a well-administered plan does effectively reduce the average length of stay (LOS) for patients, and physicians seem more comfortable with the concept than they were when it was first introduced.

Ambulatory surgical benefits have by now achieved almost universal recognition as both an effective and safe way to reduce benefit costs. Indeed, there is a growing tendency for benefit plans to identify an extensive list of surgical procedures that will be compensated *only* if performed on an outpatient or ambulatory basis. This surgery may be performed in a hospital SPU, a surgi-center that may or may not be directly tied to a hospital, or sometimes even in a physician's office. There is some variability among plans as to which locations will be covered, but there is little disagreement on the fact that ambulatory surgery lowers costs.

The growth of HMOs, PPOs, and other forms of managed care arrangements has led to more widespread coverage of a range of outpatient services that have often not been covered in the past. Because these plans have resulted in much closer association between plan managers and health care providers, a relationship of trust seems to be emerging. It has been widely noted that employers, insurers, and providers recognize themselves to be more interdependent than in the past. Providers, at a time of projected physician surplus and declining utilization of inpatient facilities, are very much interested in capturing a guaranteed market share. Employers and insurers are able to do that, but they are demanding provider cooperation in terms of quality and utilization controls as well as, in most cases, cost/charge concessions.

Note, however, that serious controversies loom on the expanding horizon of alternatives to inpatient care. They will lead to both legislative and court battles. The most recent entry, Nursing Service Organizations (NSOs), results from efforts by the American Nursing Association "to secure an independent . . . , influential role for nurses in delivery of health care in institutions, in the community, and in home care" (Report:00 [A-87] of The Board of Trustees, American Medical Association, December, 1987).

According to the AMA report, all NSO models have five things in common: nurse domination—physician referrals are not required and nurses decide when physician consultation is needed; direct fee-for-service payments to nurse practitioners or payment through fiscal intermediaries for nursing services; provision for community or institutional care; nurses substitute for more costly physician care, especially in the community and home; and all emphasize health maintenance as well as care for the sick.

Not surprisingly, the AMA opposes this development and is working hard to defeat Congressional efforts (HB 5457) to amend Title XVIII of the Social Security Act to sanction NSOs as an HMO for Part B Medicare minus physicians' services. Both NSOs and other nurse practitioner models will confront the notion of two tiered medical systems and may require changes in existing medical practice and licensure laws. While various health care professionals do battle, consumers, employers and insurers could get caught in the middle.

In contrast to the "front-end" ambulatory services discussed above, home health services offer an opportunity for early discharge and the possible savings that can accrue because of the substantial cost differential between inpatient and home health services. It may be necessary to educate the consuming public as to the desirability and efficacy of such services. Since most Americans have a perception of hospital services as the "best" services, they might be reluctant to accept the substitution—especially since, for many, there were virtually no point-of-service payments required to obtain the hospital care. Many providers and patients still underestimate the quality of available home health services, and there remain some benefit plans that do not reimburse for them. Nevertheless, there has been some expansion of coverage, and modifications to many deductible and coinsurance provisions for inpatient services have generated more interest in the alternative treatment.

The issues remain complex and often produce puzzling results. A major insurer recently refused to allow substitution of 24-hour home nursing services for continued hospitalization, despite potential savings of $45,000 per month. Apparently fear of setting a precedent regarding coverage of an unlisted benefit outweighed the desire to save on the immediate case.[3]

Inpatient Alternatives to Acute Care

There have been no dramatic changes in the level or type of coverage for skilled nursing home (SNF) services in recent years. It remains as a supplement to hospitalization benefits, usually on a two-for-one basis in terms of days of protection. Most plans continue to have a requirement of at least three days of prior hospitalization as a prerequisite to eligibility.

As has been noted earlier in this chapter, one of the emerging areas of potential catastrophic exposure, particularly for the elderly, is long-term nonacute care. This may involve a minimum of medical services. The coverage in question has not traditionally been provided through either private benefit plans or Medicare, except to a very limited degree. This may be the next frontier for employee benefit plans. Congress has struggled, without success, to deal with the problem, and several politicians have called for private sector solutions. It has recently been reported that long-term care insurance is now available commercially in all 50 states, though the plans vary widely and have not been extensively promoted to date. Individual purchases are not likely to accomplish much, because of the potential for adverse selection and the resulting high costs. There is likely to be growing interest over the next decade, as the graying of America continues and more people find themselves in need of this coverage.

There has been little progress in the provision of hospice benefits in recent years. It remains limited and experimental coverage, with no good data currently available. It is possible that the soaring cost of dying that accompanies our high-tech medical interventions will generate a sharp upsurge in interest for hospice care—especially if we can come to terms with some of the ethical, legal, and moral dilemmas of caring for the dying.

Other Provisions

Second surgical opinions are now a standard benefit in most plans. Though there is still some question as to the exact payoff, the "sentinel effect" is judged to be worthwhile by most benefits managers. Whether such specific benefits as dental, vision, prescription drug, preventive

---

[3] Richard Burke, "Going Home: A Question of Policy," *The Philadelphia Inquirer,* (January 23, 1988), p. 1A.

care, mental health, and substance abuse treatment are included is determined by the specific needs and demands of individual worker groups, the biases of the employer, the cost of benefits as they relate to the resources available, and the location. The latter is important because of the large number of states that have enacted mandated benefits laws for one or more of the listed benefits.

COST SHARING PROVISIONS

There have been major adjustments in the cost-sharing provisions under most health benefit plans in the last five years. After a decade or more of expanding benefits to more comprehensive levels, during which time there were strong incentives under the tax law to have noncontributory health plans, employers have changed their approach. They discovered that many workers were so insulated from the cost of health care that they not only failed to appreciate the benefits, but they tended to abuse them, or at the very least, not use them wisely.

There has been a marked swing back to contributory plans, accompanied by a sharp increase in deductibles under most plans. These deductibles, along with various coinsurance provisions, are increasingly being used in conjunction with PPOs to shape the utilization of services by the insureds. The waiver of a deductible provision can be used as a positive incentive to direct patients to cost-effective and high-quality practitioners and facilities.

SUMMARY

Medical care expense plans exist in an extremely volatile and rapidly changing arena, over which benefit managers exercise little effective control. Benefit managers are forced to react to environmental and political factors that shape the nature of treatment, the cost of care, and our perceptions about both. Despite new delivery and financing mechanisms and a multitude of specific benefit provisions, there is little evidence that significant cost containment or control in the health care sector has yet been achieved, after years of trying.

By some measures, costs are more out of control than ever before. This poses a monumental challenge for the future. It is interesting to speculate where costs would be if the cost containment initiatives of the past decade had not been developed. Would it have made a difference?

CHAPTER 8

HOSPITAL PLANS

Charles P. Hall, Jr.

INTRODUCTION

It was, until recently, an easy task to describe group health insurance products by using the traditional and relatively straightforward classifications of hospital, surgical, medical, major medical, and comprehensive policies. The lines of demarcation between the different products were generally quite clear, although there was some blurring in the area of comprehensive coverage. For better or worse, this is no longer the case. The dramatic changes that were described in Chapter 7, "Designing Medical Care Expense Plans," have led to similarly sharp product modifications, and while many traditional products still exist, they are likely to account for a rapidly diminishing share of the market in years to come.

It is, however, useful to trace the historical development of group hospitalization coverage in order to understand how the present stage was achieved. Group hospitalization insurance was the first of the now diverse health related employee benefits to appear in the United States. Though there were a few isolated earlier examples, it is customary to identify the modern origin of health insurance with the Baylor University Hospital prepayment plan, which emerged in the late 1920s and ultimately gave birth to Blue Cross.

In general, commercial insurance companies were not active in medical care expense insurance until about a decade later. Beginning in the 1940s, growth accelerated, spurred by such factors as the wage and price stabilization programs of World War II and the identification of these benefits as appropriate matters for collective bargaining just after the war.

Because of their pioneering role, the early Blue Cross plans had a profound and lasting impact on the nature of hospitalization benefits. Aside from insisting on distinguishing their "prepayment" method from traditional commercial insurance, they were philosophically wedded to the concepts of service benefits, first-dollar coverage, and community rates.

SERVICE BENEFITS

Service benefits were possible because of the special relationship that Blue Cross plans had (and have) with hospitals. Blue Cross operated through contracts with both subscribers and hospitals. Typically, the hospital fixed the price for its services in its contract with Blue Cross; this enabled Blue Cross to compute an appropriate subscription fee (premium) for its members, while defining benefits in terms of days of coverage. Note that not all Blue Cross–hospital contracts were the same. In some cases, they were based on actual hospital costs, while in others they were based on hospital charges. There was often a considerable difference between the two. The determining factors included the strength of the Blue Cross plan vis à vis the local hospitals, which was determined in large part by the market share of Blue Cross subscribers, and the philosophy of local Blue Cross leadership. In general, cost-based contracts were more common in the northeastern and upper midwestern states, where labor unions were strongest and Blue Cross penetration was greatest. Blue Cross plans also usually enjoyed some discount allowance on the strength of their presumed role as a "quasi-social insurance plan" that offered open enrollment periods each year, thus allegedly lowering the hospitals' level of bad debts by making insurance more readily available to all comers.

Commercial insurers, lacking direct contracts with hospitals, typically promised their insureds, instead, a certain fixed number of dollars per day up to a specified number of days. These were known as indemnity plans. The clear result of this disparity was that Blue Cross subscribers always knew exactly how many days of hospitalization were available to them without cost, while commercial insureds knew only how many days they would be eligible to collect up to some stated number of dollars. They had no assurance that the number of dollars available would be adequate to pay the hospital in full. As a result, commercially insured patients always carried a residual financial risk avoided by Blue Cross subscribers—at least until the latter had exhausted the total days of coverage provided in their contract.

Not surprisingly, many consumers preferred the relative certainty of full-service contracts, and by the end of the 1970s, many commercial insurers offered a service benefit in the form of full coverage for the cost of semiprivate room accommodations, up to some maximum dollar limit. This still entailed some pricing problems, but they could be handled by the insurer under experience-rated programs, though at considerable risk to the employer, who typically paid the bulk of the premiums.

When Medicare was introduced in the mid 1960s, the basic benefit to the elderly was in the form of a service benefit for 60 days of hospitalization, but it was modified with some indemnity principles in the form of an initial deductible and a coinsurance arrangement for stays in excess of 60 days. Most importantly for later developments, however, the government, like Blue Cross before it, had two separate commitments—the promised benefits to beneficiaries, and a reimbursement arrangement with the hospitals. The latter was tied to a retrospective cost-based formula.

Rapidly escalating health care costs, a growing number of elderly, and sharp increases in the utilization of health care services, especially among the elderly, all combined to send government expenditures for the Medicare program far beyond even the most generous predictions of actuaries. At the same time, both the federal and state treasuries were facing additional strain from the mounting costs of the massive Medicaid programs. In efforts to control these costs, ''allowable costs'' to hospitals were progressively redefined (reduced) by Congress. Not surprisingly, many Blue Cross plans tried to redefine the costs they were responsible for to match the Medicare definition, since in many cases Blue Cross was the administrative agency for Medicare.

As the proportion of patients covered by cost-based contracts grew, so did the financial problems of hospitals. Clearly, no organization can stay in business indefinitely even with full-cost reimbursement, unless it can find ways to replace its physical plant and keep up with technological change. Hospitals, however, found themselves with increasing numbers of their patients under less-than-full-cost-coverage. To remain solvent, they had to make up the shortfall from charge-based (e.g., primarily commercially insured) patients. As the number of cost-based patients increased, of course, the proportion of charge-based patients from which the hospitals were able to recover dwindled, and the differential between costs and charges got out of hand, in some cases exceeding $100 per day for identical services.

This had a devastating impact on the ability of commercial health insurers to compete in the marketplace. The aggregate Medicare/Medicaid shortfall (underpayment to hospitals) had reached nearly $6 billion in fiscal year 1982. Though this constituted cost saving for the government programs, it was only cost shifting for society and represented an enormous hidden tax on parts of the private sector.

In 1983, sensing that costs were still escalating at an unacceptable pace, Medicare switched to a prospective reimbursement system based on "diagnostic related groups" (DRGs). Hospitals are now reimbursed a fixed amount, based on the allowable length of stay for the patient's principal diagnosis. If the patient leaves the hospital in less than the allowable time, the hospital benefits, but if the patient overstays that time, the hospital is at risk for the additional costs. From the beneficiary's point of view, however, Medicare still provides, basically, a service benefit.

For years, commercial insurers and self-insured employers remained quite passive in the face of the increasing cost shifting described above; though they were not hesitant to voice their complaints, they did little else to fend off the added burden. There were several reasons for their passivity. They had neither the geographic monopolies enjoyed by the Blue Cross plans nor the "clout" inherent in government programs. While there were a few exceptions, for example, in "company town" situations where they were able to negotiate discounts, they were reluctant to push for concessions for the same reason that they avoided collective action against hospitals—fear of antitrust prosecution.

Much of that fear dissolved with the introduction of the preferred provider organization (PPO) concept in California in 1982. Specific legislation in California authorized this concept of contracting with health care providers for preferred status in terms of price, utilization review, and quality control. The concept was an outgrowth of the pro-competition school of thought, and was initially proposed as a means for the state to gain control over its wildly escalating Medicaid costs, by contracting with low-cost providers to service the poor. When the legislature specifically authorized private sector payers to do the same, it opened the floodgates to some of the most dramatic changes ever seen in the financing of health care in this country. While the PPO movement will be described in more detail later in this chapter, it should be noted here that one of the strong incentives that have made PPOs popular with insureds is that they often promise full-service benefits to those who use the designated providers.

FIRST-DOLLAR BENEFITS

Initially, Blue Cross plans were at least as interested in assuring hospital solvency as they were in protecting patients from financial strain. This suggested full coverage for all charges. Furthermore, the plans tried to distinguish their operation from traditional insurance by emphasizing that they were prepayment plans, providing service benefits from the first moment of hospitalization. Their direct contractual relationship with hospitals helped make this feasible.

Initially, commercial insurers followed rather blindly the same pattern of first-dollar benefits. Later, it was the commercial insurers who introduced some of the traditional trappings of the insurance trade, such as deductibles and coinsurance. Nevertheless, the pattern of first-dollar coverage had been established and, perhaps because of the incorporation of these benefits in many of the early union-negotiated contracts, the pattern persisted on a wide front. By the early 1980s, there were increasing allegations that, though originally well intentioned, such benefits were uneconomical and also promoted overuse (misuse) of benefits. By removing any point-of-service financial responsibility from patients, it was claimed that they neither knew nor cared about the increasing costs of medical care, and providers were spared any pressure from their patients to hold costs down.

The economic slowdown of the early 1980s resulted in a historical first—massive union "give-backs" of benefits under their health care coverage. These included reintroduction and/or increases in deductibles, changes in coinsurance provisions, and, in some cases, a return to contributory rather than noncontributory premium plans. Despite the fact that the economy rebounded, data reported by the Health Insurance Association of America (HIAA) in recent issues of its regularly published *Source Book of Health Insurance Data* and its *Update* as well as in its publications on *New Group Health Insurance* all show significant increases in deductibles since the early 1980s. Furthermore, it has been widely claimed that these changes have been perceived to be among the most effective cost-containment techniques available to insurers. Indeed, even many Blue Cross plans began to make wider use of various cost-sharing provisions, in a departure from their earlier commitment to first-dollar benefits.

In the crazy, mixed-up world of employee benefits, however, many insurers, as noted above, were, at the same time that they nominally increased their cost-sharing provisions, offering to waive them altogether if the insureds used providers designated as PPOs. Among other things, this reflects the clash of traditional insurance techniques with the rapidly emerging concept of managed care. Under managed care programs, the major thrust is to control cost through the use of efficient providers who deliver high-quality care and may offer additional discounts, but who also closely monitor utilization, so that the savings on unit costs are not offset by more frequent visits or unnecessarily intensive treatment. Other aspects of managed care will be discussed later in this chapter.

COMMUNITY RATING

Community rating, a uniform rate for all subscribers or insureds in a given area, though still the philosophical favorite of many, especially in Blue Cross ranks, has long since become insignificant in the group insurance market. The competitive pressures from corporate insurance buyers and unions to obtain rates commensurate with their real or perceived "preferred risk" status were simply too great to be resisted in most cases. Most Blue Cross plans still use community rates for their individual subscribers, and some also may use them for small groups, but all have some form of experience rating available to large group customers. Under the federal Health Maintenance Organization Act, HMOs must, in order to be qualified, adhere to specific rules regarding community rating, too, but there are ways to avoid this restriction.

OTHER HEALTH INSURANCE

After the initial breakthrough in hospital insurance, a series of "named peril" health insurance coverages followed—first surgical benefits, and then nonsurgical medical benefits, both in and out of hospital settings. Blue Shield emerged in these areas as the prepayment counterpart to Blue Cross. In the late 1940s a few companies also introduced "dread disease" policies, with quite high limits of protection for a very narrow range of conditions—often only one disease (e.g., polio).

By the early 1950s, commercial health insurers introduced the major medical concept, characterized by a comprehensive range of coverage with high dollar limits after some initial deductible and, usually, a coinsurance or percentage participation clause. Originally designed primarily as supplements to one or more of the basic coverages described previously, these policies soon evolved into yet another form, so-called comprehensive major medical plans, which actually eliminated the need for any separate basic policies.

With the exception of a few special areas such as dental insurance and, more recently, separate plans for prescription drugs, vision care, and substance abuse or other psychiatric services, most of the changes in medical expense reimbursement coverages since the late 1950s have merely been refinements reflecting pressure for broader coverage brought on as a result of some combination of the rapid escalation of health care costs, changes in medical technology, or changes in consumer demand.

Even in the special areas mentioned, where separate plans frequently emerged as the result of special interest advocacy groups, sometimes aided by support from providers of the specialized services, the benefits were often simply included in expanded basic plans. In some cases, notably mental health benefits, special restrictions in the form of larger coinsurance or more stringent limits on the days of coverage became commonplace. Expanded mental health benefits were frequently included in the basic plan as the result of state legislation mandating the coverage. Other obvious exceptions have resulted from federal policy actions, such as the emergence of so-called Medigap policies after the enactment of Medicare.

One other type of hospital insurance has acquired fairly wide acceptance. It is the so-called hospital indemnity policy. Patterned somewhat after disability income policies, these are not really indemnity policies at all. They could more appropriately be called "status" policies. They pay stated dollar amounts on either a daily, weekly, or monthly basis for people confined in a hospital (in some cases, skilled nursing facilities are also covered). They pay the predetermined amount without regard to actual charges incurred or income lost and, perhaps more important to many buyers, without regard to any other insurance holdings. Some of the popularity of these policies undoubtedly can be attributed to consumers' fears about the continued rapid escalation of health care costs. They see these policies as providing an added buffer, in case their medical expense reimbursement coverages fall short.

As a result of the continued graying of America and growing recognition that Medicare does not adequately address the full range of health care needs of the elderly, a private market for long-term care insurance has begun to emerge since the mid-1980s. By early 1987 a report in *Business Insurance* noted that private policies were available in all 50 states, though the range of benefits differs greatly, and no significant market penetration has been achieved by any product. Many insurers are understandably reluctant to enter this arena, since so little is known about it and the long-term risks appear to be substantial.

However, given the continuing deficit problems of the federal government, public solutions are not likely to be offered in the immediate future, a prediction that is fortified by the terms of the catastrophic health insurance bill that was just passed by the Senate at the time of this writing, and that will now go to a conference committee for reconciliation with a similar bill passed earlier by the House. It continued the focus on acute health care services that has characterized Medicare since its inception. With encouragement from legislators at both the state and federal level, the private sector has been stepping up its efforts to develop products that will address this need. Some home health services have already been added to existing policies.

For a variety of reasons, it is unlikely that individual policies will ever be able to address adequately this growing need for the long-term, nonacute health needs of the elderly. As a result, there are many who believe that this will represent the next major frontier for the development of employee benefits. Whether this happens through a formal insurance program or through sponsorship of some form of elder day care is yet to be determined. The day-care approach could either be linked with the growing network of child day-care centers that have developed to meet the changing needs of the American work force in an era when both parents often work outside the home, or they could be set up as independent units dealing strictly with the elderly.

EXTENT OF PRIVATE HOSPITAL INSURANCE

In part because it was the earliest form of health insurance and in part because the hospital continues to be the most costly setting in which to be treated, hospital insurance continues to be the most widely held form of health insurance protection in the country, although for statistical purposes it will no longer be possible to track discrepancies among hospital, surgical, and basic medical policies. In the 1986 *Update* to its *Source Book of Health Insurance Data* (announced as the last in this series), the Health Insurance Association of America (HIAA), for the first time since it started recording the data in 1940, dropped the separate classifications of surgical and physicians' expense insurance from the report. They now have been combined into a "Medical other than hospital expense" category. Major medical and dental expense plans are still recorded separately.

The 1986 *Update,* the latest available, with data through 1984, showed just over 188 million Americans with hospital expense insurance, down from an all-time high of 191 million in 1982. The medical-other-than-hospital category was very close, with over 187 million insureds. Major medical expense insurance continued to expand rapidly, and the number insured rose from 85 to 91.5 percent of those covered for basic hospitalization from 1983 to 1984, when over 172 million were reported with this benefit. Dental expense plans, which were not even reported before 1967, covered nearly 107 million people by 1984.

Successive declines in the number covered for hospital insurance in 1983 and 1984, as well as preliminary indications of the same trend continuing in 1985 and 1986, are considered matters of grave concern by some, especially policymakers in Washington, and increase the pressure for some form of national health insurance (NHI) or, alternatively, mandatory health insurance to be provided by all employers. The only other time since 1940 that there was a year-to-year decline in the number insured was in 1976.

Factors contributing to the decline include, but are not limited to: continuing cost increases that have caused some small firms and individuals to drop their coverage; the changing composition of American industry, with a relative decline in the large, heavily unionized smokestack industries that typically had extensive health insurance benefits; and a rapid growth in the service sector, which is characterized by relatively small, nonunion firms dominated by white-collar workers. Indeed, the dramatic increases in new jobs and employment that have marked the Reagan years have been concentrated in small firms.

But for the federal budget deficit and the growing trade deficit, both of which have scuttled most proposals for expanded social programs in recent years, the growing number of uninsureds would probably have sparked renewed interest in NHI. Instead, Congress is now considering bills, such as one proposed by Senator Edward Kennedy (D-Mass.), that would require virtually all employers to provide health insurance as an employee benefit. Such a bill, however, would only address a part of the problem, since a large number of unemployed uninsureds also exist.

Over 14.5 million persons over age 65 still purchase private hospital insurance in addition to Medicare, the majority in the form of some brand of Medigap policy designed to supplement Medicare Part A. Over half of this senior coverage is provided by Blue Cross and Blue Shield Associations, and other plans, including HMOs, have also become increasingly involved in the market in recent years. There is considerable duplication of coverage under Medigap policies, and many of the elderly continue to purchase them out of fear and ignorance, while others cannot afford coverage, do not want extra protection, or mistakenly believe that Medicare coverage is complete. It is difficult to predict with certainty what impact the recent enactment of catastrophic coverage for Medicare will have, if signed into law by President Reagan, but it is certainly possible that it will reduce the attractiveness of Medigap policies and will produce an overall decline in the number of those over 65 who purchase private hospital insurance.

HIAA data show that commercial insurers cover over five times as many people under group as opposed to individual hospital insurance policies. Most of these group policies are part of an employee benefit plan and provide more generous benefits than are available under individual policies. The majority of Blue Cross and Blue Shield coverage is also in the form of group contracts, and the same is true for HMOs and other plans.

RECENT MARKET TRENDS

In *New Group Health Insurance* (1986), the HIAA provides some insights on the latest market trends. Of the 137,239 employees in employee groups of 25–499[1] who were covered by new group insurance plans in the first three months of 1986, over 92,000 were under comprehensive major medical expense plans, which include basic hospital benefits, while fewer than 16,000 were under basic hospital expense plans. Nearly 24,000 others were covered by supplementary major medical plans that, of course, include hospital benefits beyond those in the basic plan being supplemented.

But these figures alone reveal very little about some of the fundamental changes that have taken place in the market. They reflect neither the dramatic trend toward self-insurance and third party administrator plans nor the exponential growth in managed care and PPO arrangements that are often integrated with traditional group benefits. Indeed, the HIAA has not made any concerted effort to date to report on these recent developments, beyond noting that it includes in its group insurance statistics those self-insured plans for which an insurer provides the administrative services. PPOs are not even mentioned by footnote in their 1986 *Update*, and they get a total of 10 lines in the 1986 *New Group Health Insurance* publication. This is not too surprising when it is realized that even the two trade groups that purport to speak for PPO plans cannot agree on the number in existence at any given point in time. With HMOs also growing rapidly in number, and new combinations and permutations of the various concepts emerging almost daily, it will be some time before the market stabilizes and accurate counts and descriptions will again be available. For that reason, it may be worthwhile to attempt to describe the scope of hospital expense benefits as they currently exist under the more or less traditional contracts before addressing the most recent developments.

Scope of Hospital Expense Benefits

Under the new basic hospital plans in 1986, 75 percent paid in full for semiprivate accommodations (down from 88 percent in 1981), and 79 percent were fully insured for miscellaneous hospital expenses of $1,000

---

[1] This size group was considered to be representative because it accounted for over 76 percent of the new groups, though only about 46 percent of the newly covered employees.

or more, for example, for laboratory fees, drugs, dressings, and X rays, plus a whole range of services and supplies ranging from special dietary services, use of operating, delivery, recovery, and other special treatment rooms, to the provision of special equipment and medications. Among the 25 percent of the plans that did not pay in full for semiprivate rooms, about half allowed a daily rate of $100 or more. Despite the decline in full coverage of daily charges, however, there was a marked increase in the duration of hospital benefits, from only 6.9 percent of covered workers with an unlimited number of days of coverage in 1981 to 24.6 percent with such coverage in 1986.

Blue Cross plans continue to provide full service benefits in semiprivate accommodations for most hospital stays. Depending on the area and plan involved, Blue Cross might pay either costs or charges to the hospital, but in either case, most Blues still are granted some discount compared to commercial insurers or self-paying patients. The duration of the hospital coverage also varies by plan and group contract, with some plans relating their benefit to the diagnostic related group (DRG) formula now operating under Medicare and others still relying on a stated number of days as a maximum limit. Blue Cross plans continue to offer much more limited benefits to subscribers who are confined in nonmember hospitals. In both Blue Cross and commercial health insurance contracts, the bed and board coverage includes general nursing service and all other regular daily services and supplies furnished by the hospital. Blue Cross plans normally provide no coverage for diagnostic admissions unless performed in a member hospital.

Some covered benefits under basic plans today were formerly covered only under major medical plans. Examples include nursing home and home health services plus a whole range of outpatient procedures, many of which are now viewed as cost-saving procedures. Use of laboratory, diagnostic imaging, and other special services, including short procedure units and free-standing surgical centers are also covered routinely by most policies today. Ambulance service may also be provided. Even some fairly sophisticated services such as radiation therapy, certain forms of chemotherapy, and physical and inhalation therapy following an inpatient stay are included. In many cases, these extended services are seen as cost containment features, since they tend to offer service at lower unit cost than would be encountered by inpatients. In times past, they were often excluded because they were seen as add-on costs that were not as rigidly controlled as were hospital admissions. Advances in technology also played a major role in making some of these extras feasible, especially in the case of outpatient surgery.

Among the new comprehensive major medical expense plans in 1986, 28 percent had a single deductible of $200 or more, and an additional 5 percent had a similar deductible that did not apply to hospital or surgical expenses. For the supplementary major medical plans, 85 percent had a single deductible of $100 or more. Between 95–99 percent of all major medical plans had maximum benefits of $100,000 or more, and 90 percent of them had limits of $1 million or more in 1986, compared to only 84 percent in 1981. Over 60 percent of the plans had out-of-pocket limits of $1,000 or less for insureds, and 95 percent had benefits for treatment of nervous and mental disorders.

Among the new groups in 1986, 118,000 employees had specific coverage for intensive care in the hospital, 64,000 had some nursing home or extended care facility coverage, and 80,000 were covered for home health care expenses in lieu of hospitalization or confinement in an extended care facility. HIAA did not report on the breakdown of these added benefits between basic hospital and major medical policies, but they can be found under both types of contracts. Note that between 1981 and 1986 the maximum daily benefit under nursing home coverage, which is almost exclusively provided as an extension of hospitalization benefits, increased marginally; during the same period there was a modest decline in the number of contracts providing fewer than 60 days of coverage, a slight increase in contracts providing for durations of from 60–359 days, and a sharp drop in the provision of 360 or more days of coverage.

As noted at the beginning of this chapter, it is increasingly difficult to describe group health benefits under the traditional policy classifications. As can be deduced from the *New Group Health Insurance* statistics cited above, the pressure for comprehensive coverage under group health programs is so strong that only a very small proportion of the new policies are issued as basic hospital plans anymore, and even those contain many benefits that used to be restricted to major medical contracts. Furthermore, they are almost always marketed in combination with a major medical supplement.

Exclusions

Even with the changing circumstances of the past few years, most of the old standard exclusions continue to appear under most hospital expense insurance policies. Among them are: occupational illness or injury eligible for benefits under workers' compensation laws; convalescent or rest cures, custodial or domiciliary care; services not ordered by a physician or not reasonably necessary for diagnosis and treatment; procurement or use of special appliances or equipment; services a patient is entitled to receive under the laws or regulations of any government or its agencies; and war or service-connected injuries or diseases. These examples are not exhaustive, and the specific list of exclusions, of course, must be checked in the case of each individual policy.

General Provisions

All group insurance contracts contain a range of general provisions, many of which are almost universal, whether by law or by custom. Examples include the 31-day grace period for payment of premiums, a clause on incontestability, an entire contract clause that also specifies how valid changes may be accomplished, and a provision to adjust benefits automatically whenever and wherever they conflict with statutes. Another whole set of provisions has to do with claims submission and payment procedures. These provisions often apply equally to a whole set of employee benefits, from life insurance to health insurance.

Provisions specific to hospital insurance that deserve mention are those dealing with the definition of a benefit period of confinement and coordination of benefits. The latter is a cost-containment mechanism to prevent duplication of benefits. A single benefit period under hospitalization insurance typically is considered to be any one or more periods of confinement of the insured, unless separated by a return to full-time employment for at least one week, or unless subsequent confinement is due entirely to causes unrelated to the previous confinement. For dependents, unless the causes are unrelated, a subsequent confinement in less than three months generally is considered a continuation of the previous hospital stay. Some insurers apply the harsher three-month rule to primary employee insureds as well.

An important provision to check is the definition of *dependent*. The term normally encompasses the spouse and all unmarried children, including those who may have been legally adopted, until age 19. An extension of coverage usually is granted until age 24 or 25 for children who are full-time students. Naturally, the specific ages may vary by company policy.

Commercial Insurers Respond to Changing Markets

As has been noted, dramatic changes in the health insurance market have taken place over the past half decade. Perhaps the two most important triggers to these changes have been the evolution of PPOs and related managed care concepts and the change in Medicare reimbursement from a retrospective, cost-based mechanism to a prospective payment system based on DRGs. When the first edition of this *Handbook* was published in 1984, the commercial insurance industry and its clients were really suffering under the twin burdens of federal cost shifting from the Medicare program and Blue Cross discounts. As was stated:

> In certain parts of the country, notably the northeast, sale of basic group hospital expense benefits has been virtually abandoned to Blue Cross by commercial insurers, who now compete largely in the arena of so-called wraparound (supplementary) major medical on top of basic Blue Cross programs. This rather strange phenomenon is explained in terms of the often enormous disparity that exists between costs and charges in the delivery of hospital services.
>
> In regions where Blue Cross market penetration is substantial, where Blue Cross has negotiated cost-reimbursement or other discount contracts with its member hospitals, and where a large elderly population is covered under another cost-based program, Medicare, commercially insured patients, and self-paying patients must bear the brunt of attempts by hospitals to remain fiscally viable. Charges billed to those patients may be as much as 15 to 20 percent higher than the charges to Blue Cross and Medicare patients receiving identical services.
>
> . . . When added to another competitive advantage, exemption from premium tax, which is afforded to Blue Cross in many states, it is not surprising commercial insurers sometimes find it difficult to compete. The impact of the premium tax exemption becomes even greater as costs rise, since it is a flat percentage tax.
>
> Insurers, especially in areas where their market share is modest, find their premiums to group subscribers must rise even more sharply than the already disproportionate increase in the medical price index. As hospitals try to shift their losses arising from narrowly defined cost definitions issued by the government under Medicare and negotiated by Blue Cross from its dominant market position, the "paying customers" with commercial insurance get caught in the middle. (p. 143)

By the summer of 1987, several large commercial insurance companies were aggressively back in the basic hospital expense insurance market. The Philadelphia director of group marketing for The Prudential Insurance Company of America, Lloyd McGinley, stated in an interview that, "We no longer abandon the basic hospital contract. Prudential is now entering into arrangements with local hospitals that are very similar to those negotiated by Blue Cross. We already have contracts with 20 hospitals in the Philadelphia area under our PruCare Plus program, and we are wrapping basic hospital plans in with this program whenever possible, providing coverage from the ground up." More than 1,500 physicians who are affiliated with these hospitals have also signed up with the program.

Prudential is the largest private commercial health insurer in the country, with over 20 million insureds, and it now offers a full range of health insurance options to its clients. It has, of course, always had traditional indemnity benefits. It has offered its PruCare HMO option for the last 13 years, and now has 38 HMOs nationwide with 650,000 members. It first offered its PruCare Plus PPO option just under two years ago in Cincinnati, and it has already achieved 90 percent utilization within its network in that market. There are now over 200,000 individuals enrolled in the PruCare Plus program in several market areas, and the plan is to have at least one of its managed care systems in each of the nation's 90 largest metropolitan markets by 1990.

In addition to being able to offer "triple option" services—"a completely integrated health care package through which the employer offers employees a full selection all from the same source"—Prudential also offers an Administrative Services Only (ASO) option with stop-loss protection to clients who wish to self-insure.

As McGinley noted, though traditional basic hospitalization benefits will still be available, they are not likely to be very attractive except in markets where PruCare Plus and PruCare HMO are not available. All of the various Prudential plans utilize most of the now-standard cost-containment features such as deductibles, coinsurance, mandatory second opinions on surgery, preadmission testing, and preadmission and concurrent review for hospitalization. The specific advantages of PruCare Plus are that it preserves complete freedom of choice for patients in choosing their provider, while offering incentives to use the participating providers through differential deductibles and/or coinsurance provisions. Participating providers are chosen for their credentials in terms of quality of care and their commitment to cost containment and utilization review.

Since the PruCare Plus plan is, essentially, a comprehensive insurance package that includes medical, surgical, and other benefits as well as hospitalization, it is clear that if it succeeds to the degree that is anticipated, the traditional separate classification of hospital expense insurance will become quite meaningless except in small markets. Currently, Prudential markets its hospitalization policies primarily to groups of 250 or more employees, and it can offer benefits that largely parallel those of Blue Cross, for example, 120 days in a semiprivate room with unlimited extras, or it can make a straight indemnity or per diem coverage available. Generally, the policy will contain at least a $100 deductible with an 80/20 coinsurance provision, plus 100 percent coverage after $2,000–$2,500. It provides standard conversion benefits based on state statutes and minimum required benefits and has standard preexisting condition exclusions. Prudential also offers the usual Medicare supplement as a retirement benefit, and it currently services over 2 million senior citizens under its agreement with the American Association of Retired Persons (AARP).

Most of Prudential's large commercial insurance competitors have also developed one or more alternatives to their traditional hospital expense insurance products. The Metropolitan, for example, has its Met-Elect PPO. The Met's approach to the PPO market has been somewhat more selective, in that it generally contracts with a very small number of hospitals in a given geographic area, preferring to single out just a few that pass its fairly rigorous statistical analysis as to quality of care and efficiency of operation. In their promotional literature they stress the benefits to all parties from their program. Their stated objective is "to help control health care costs by encouraging the use of cost-effective, efficient providers of services." They "recognize that there are often significant differences in both the level of efficiency with which hospitals provide services and the prices charged by various hospitals for their services," and they encourage insured employees to obtain services from hospitals and physicians who provide a "quality product at a reasonable price." Providers find the Met-Elect PPO a way to increase their market share of patients and to increase the loyalty of existing patients. Employers not only get reduced unit costs, but also more cost-effective use of services by their employees. Employees get assurance of high-quality, comprehensive services, usually at lower cost, while retaining freedom of choice of provider. The distinctive part of Met-Elect is its reliance on the detailed statistical analysis provided by Corporate Health Strategies (CHS), a subsidiary that specializes in the statistical analysis of health care claim data. The medical department also assesses the credentials and service characteristics of each hospital. Physicians are recruited only from the staffs of participating hospitals, and utilization review and benefit plan design options are similar to those used by Prudential and other insurers.

The Travelers, like Prudential, currently offers a triple option, including traditional coverage, an HMO affiliation—Travelers' Health Plan—and Travelers Preferred, a PPO. Travelers Preferred introduces the concept of a patient advocate, whose role is to help employees better understand their options and to offer guidance and advice in the use of health care benefits. The patient advocate program is staffed with registered nurses who employees can call with their questions. By providing better and more complete information to employees, they are aided in making more cost-effective treatment choices. A related program, Taking Care, provides employees with health care information that focuses on the importance of self-care and lifestyle modification, both of which are viewed as being important in the ongoing battle to contain health care costs. The information is provided in the form of a basic book plus monthly newsletters.

Other insurers, such as Aetna Life & Casualty, have linked up with national hospital organizations, in their case the Voluntary Hospitals of America (VHA), and formed Partners National Health Plans, a national network of HMOs.

Perhaps a brief comment is in order about insurer attitudes toward the coverage of new and costly medical technologies such as organ transplants, open heart surgery, and infertility services, (for example, in vitro fertilization). No blanket statement can be made with great certainty. Most policies will not cover procedures that are still considered experimental, but there is no one, universally accepted definition of when a procedure changes from an experimental to an accepted procedure.

More than likely, cases at the margin will be discussed with the insured employer before a decision is made, because it is often true that the political or public relations cost of refusing a claim will be far greater than the economic cost of providing the benefit. Since these at-the-margin decisions often deal with life and death issues, it may at times be prudent to pay the claim even if it is not technically covered by the contract. Again, the decision is sometimes taken out of the insurer's or employer's hands, as when the state decides to mandate certain benefits. It has already been mentioned that many states (over 30) have mandated mental health benefits, and at least one state currently mandates coverage of in vitro fertilization.

At the time of this writing, one of the most controversial issues in the health insurance arena is what to do about covering Acquired Immune Deficiency Syndrome (AIDS). As a recently discovered disease, that has, at present, no cure and a 100 percent fatality rate within only a few years, it presents several dilemmas to both insurers and government policymakers. Some reactions have been almost hysterical. In Washington, D.C., for example, a law was passed prohibiting insurers from testing applicants for AIDS as a precondition for coverage. The reaction of several companies was to withdraw from the Washington market. It doesn't seem reasonable to prohibit companies from using what has always before been considered a legitimate underwriting tool. They have never been prohibited from checking for heart trouble or cancer before issuing policies. On the other hand, individual underwriting has typically not been used in group insurance. Should it be allowed for AIDS? Note that many companies are currently paying benefits to AIDS victims without any questions. Will this be a viable path if it becomes as widespread an epidemic as some have predicted?

Blue Cross Response to Changing Markets

Despite their national linkage through the Blue Cross and Blue Shield Association in Chicago, there are many variations among the various Blue Cross plans across the country. The importance of the historical role of Blue Cross has already been described. More recently, they have also been battered by the increasingly competitive forces in the marketplace. As noted earlier, there are still some plans, mostly in the south and west, that contract to pay hospitals charges, much like commercial insurers. In the northeast and upper midwest, the Blues were more likely to have cost-based contracts with their hospitals. Under both circumstances, however, they provided primarily service benefits to their subscribers.

As a group, many individual Blue Cross plans got involved quite early in the movement toward HMOs, and there are currently over 100 Blue Cross–related HMOs in the country. But not all plans were equally enthusiastic about this development, and some are still not involved. Since Medicare changed to DRG-based reimbursement, however, the pace of change has quickened. Not only have many plans moved to prospective reimbursement arrangements with their member hospitals, but they have also accelerated their development of HMO, PPO, and other managed care plans. Indeed, there are now quite a few Blue Cross/Blue Shield plans that are capable of offering the same triple option choices that were discussed for commercial insurers. Blue Cross of Greater Philadelphia is a relative newcomer to the triple option ranks, having purchased the Delaware Valley HMO in January 1987, shortly after launching Personal Choice, its PPO option that is jointly sponsored by Pennsylvania Blue Shield. But Blue Cross had been involved in some aspects of managed care even before these recent initiatives, through other elements of their contracts with hospitals.

Like some commercial insurers, for several years Blue Cross had been designating certain surgical procedures as reimbursable only if performed on an outpatient basis. Indeed, they were one of the first to introduce this concept in the early 1980s. They had also stopped automatic payment for large "batch" laboratory tests on admission unless the tests were individually ordered by the admitting physician, with appropriate justification. They also have used most of the other cost-containment techniques that were described in the section on commercial insurers, including preadmission testing and mandatory second surgical opinions. In 1985, the Philadelphia Blue Cross plan introduced both a prospective payment plan to its hospital contract and a Quality Care Admission Review program, which depends on the expertise of professional nurses trained in managed care working in cooperation with over 100 board certified physician consultants. In 1986, they added a special unit for the management of psychiatric and substance abuse utilization. Blue Cross also uses a postprocedure validation of "emergency" procedures.

The prospective case payment plan in use by Philadelphia Blue Cross is of interest as a contrast to the DRG system that is used by Medicare and many other Blues and insurers around the country. The plan is based on a flat payment per admission, which does not vary by diagnosis or length of stay. The original agreement was based on data from fiscal year 1985. Total costs for the year divided by the number of Blue Cross cases provided the base cost per case for the next year. Blue Cross used a 4.4 percent inflator plus a 1 percent allowance for new medical technology. They also provided a 5.5 percent community services allowance as their contribution to free care, bad debts, wellness, and health promotion programs. This was done for all member acute care hospitals. Specific costs, for example, capital, malpractice premiums, and medical education costs were considered pass-throughs and were paid on the basis of audited costs. This innovative approach seems to have been working quite well, though there will undoubtedly be some conflicts when the time comes to renegotiate the cost per case because of changes in a hospital's case mix index. Outpatient care is still reimbursed on an audited cost basis, since no one has yet come up with a workable prospective calculation for these services.

Blue Cross continues to community rate in Philadelphia for its public enrollees, but it uses experience rates for most groups. Like many of its commercial insurance competitors, it also offers its services under ASO contracts. It also continues to enjoy about a 20 percent discount from area hospitals, though it notes that New York Blue Cross recently lost most of its discount. Even New Jersey, with its all-payer system, still allows Blue Cross a small discount. This is usually justified partially on the grounds of providing an available market for nongroup enrollees, thus saving hospitals some bad debt expense.

At the present time, Personal Choice, the Blue Cross sponsored PPO, is being marketed most aggressively. Under the terms of this agreement, hospitals are given additional financial incentives for holding inpatient utilization lower than the average for the community. Again, there is reason to believe that the PPO plan will become dominant vis à vis the traditional Blue Cross plan in the not too distant future.

The Surge in Self-Insurance

It was noted earlier that there have been enormous changes in the health insurance market. One of the most important changes has been in the rapid growth of self-insured health benefits in the past five years. While there is no single published source of data on this matter, there is little doubt that growth has been substantial. There are many possible explanations, but the major reasons are probably related to concern with the continued rapid escalation of costs. As health benefit costs go ever higher, savings on premium taxes alone provide some incentive to self insure. More importantly, the fact that PPOs and other managed care arrangements can be set up independent of an insurer—especially if a firm has a large concentration of workers in a given market—may have encouraged some employers to try their hand at holding the cost line. In some cases they must have believed that it would be difficult not to improve on the record of their insurer. Another factor may be the increased number of third party administrators, which has made the market more competitive than ever before. Finally, as employers have awakened to the fact that there are possible ways to effectively manage health care costs, they may feel that their own management skills are up to the task, after many years of virtually abdicating any responsibility in this regard.

MANAGED CARE AND HOSPITAL COVERAGE

What, exactly, are the objectives of managed care, and why has its emergence had such a profound impact on hospital expense insurance? There are three major objectives that most people could agree on. They are to: (1) assist the patient in achieving his or her full potential for restored health; (2) provide coordination and continuity of medically necessary health services to the patient; and (3) ensure access to medically needed care in the most appropriate and cost-effective manner.

In fact, managed care is a process, the primary components of which include preadmission certification or admission review, concurrent review and discharge planning while in the hospital, and posthospital or long-term needs assessment. In the preadmission stage, it is important to evaluate the level of care that will be needed and develop a treatment plan. In this initial needs assessment it is important to distinguish between the patient who is entering the hospital as a basically healthy person who may be in for elective surgery and will then leave as a healthy person, and the patient who enters with a chronic or catastrophic condition and who will leave either as a permanent invalid, needing an extended period of recuperation, or with severe short-term needs.

The need for in-hospital review should be self-evident, at least with respect to the appropriateness of current treatment. In the past, however, relatively little attention has been paid to planning for posthospital needs. There will, of course, be those who will need no aftercare at all. For the others, a long-term needs assessment as part of the discharge planning process can be very important. Depending on the circumstances, there may be medical, psychosocial, or occupational needs. In addition, there should be an assessment of the benefits available, and an estimate of the total resources that will be required and are available. There is no one formula to define exactly what the components of a well-managed health care plan should contain, but it should be obvious from this brief discussion that the range of possibilities is quite broad. Furthermore, there is mounting evidence that the more comprehensive plans can produce substantial long-term savings. Each employer must determine what is expected from the insurer, the TPA or the employer itself in this regard.

SUMMARY

Group hospitalization insurance, as the earliest and most widely held of the health-oriented employee benefits, was for many years also the easiest to describe. Its provisions were quite straightforward, and almost everyone understood what it was all about. Traumatic changes have occurred over the past decade, however. Remarkable advances in medical technology along with continued rapid inflation of health care costs have been exacerbated by environmental forces including the federal deficit, changes in demographics, and changes in the structure and competitive position of American industry. A hybrid version of group hospitalization insurance has emerged, and a dramatic and revolutionary restructuring of both the medical care delivery system and the health insurance industry has taken place. With diligence and good fortune, perhaps both systems will serve the needs of the people more effectively in the future. For the present, however, it is likely that the turmoil of the past decade has not yet run its course.

CHAPTER 9

SURGICAL AND MEDICAL EXPENSE BENEFITS

Zelda Lipton

INTRODUCTION

Since 1955, the rise in the medical care component of the consumer price index has almost consistently outpaced the rise in prices for all consumer goods and services combined. It has been driven primarily by hospital costs—the largest single item in the delivery of medical care. Although hospital costs therefore offer the greatest opportunity for cost control, design of the remaining benefits in a health insurance plan can influence significantly the utilization of the entire package. Physicians' fees alone represented $82.8 billion dollars or 22.3 percent of the total personal health care dollar spent in 1985. Even more significant, however, physicians themselves are key to the most effective use of the health care system and therefore very directly influence the cost of medical care.

The following two chapters trace the development of surgical and medical expense benefits as well as supplemental major medical and comprehensive plans to meet the need for such protection as it evolved. Although some of the plans described are not commonly in use today, the history sets the stage for the current variations which are referred to here, but described in greater detail in other chapters.

Plans to cover the cost of physicians' services were first introduced in 1920 by county medical societies. Blue Shield plans, which didn't begin until 1939 with the California Medical Association Plan, however, were at the forefront of plan development. They attempted to follow the same full-service philosophy as Blue Cross did for hospital expenses. Physicians contracted with Blue Shield; which paid an agreed-upon level as full payment for services provided to subscribers. However, physicians had long been accustomed to charging patients based on their incomes. As a result, Blue Shield modified its approach to allow a physician to charge patients, with incomes above a stated level, the difference between the Blue Shield reimbursement and the physician's usual fee.

At the same time, private insurance companies were developing indemnity contracts, which reimburse the insured person for services provided by a physician up to the agreed amount in the contract. Physicians would look to the patient, rather than the insurer, for payment. Otherwise patterned after Blue Shield plans, the insurance plans paid first-dollar coverage for a limited number of medical services. Together with hospital benefits, these came to be known as basic benefits. Many insurers have since developed procedures for reimbursing the provider directly, should the buyer prefer that approach.

SURGICAL EXPENSE BENEFITS

The earliest of these basic benefits for physicians' charges covered surgical expenses, because those represented comparatively large expenditures and were believed to be more easily defined and controlled. Surgical expense benefits provide coverage for the cost of surgical procedures required as a result of accident or sickness wherever the surgery is performed.

Surgeons' Fees

Plans are designed to cover surgeons' fees on either a scheduled or reasonable and customary basis.

Dollar-Fee Schedules

Typical early surgical schedules list about 100 procedures in such major categories as abdomen, heart and blood vessels, chest, mouth, and obstetrics.

For each procedure, a specific maximum-dollar payment is allowed. Each maximum depends on the value of that procedure, compared to others, and the overall maximum for multiple procedures by which the schedule is usually identified. The level of overall maximums available has historically ranged from as low as $200 to $1,000 and more. Payment to the insured is the charge made by the surgeon, up to the maximum payment allowed in the schedule for the procedure performed, subject to the multiple procedure provision explained later. For an unlisted procedure, reimbursement is based on its relative difficulty, compared to those listed.

If an employer desired to avoid encouraging escalation of charges, schedules were set to reimburse at a level below the usual charges in an area. Such scheduled plans did contribute toward control of the cost of a plan, since, regardless of inflation, reimbursement for any procedure remained constant. Furthermore, since the patient was directly responsible for the difference between the plan payment and the charge, fees did not escalate as rapidly. However, such a plan very quickly can become outdated in a rising cost environment and result in large out-of-pocket expenses for the insured.

The following are sample allowances in a typical schedule with a $900 overall maximum:

Procedures	*Maximum Payment*
Valvotomy	$900
Extraction of lens for cataract	600
Hysterectomy	540
Cesarean section	450
Appendectomy	330
Herniotomy, single	330
Tonsillectomy	120

Relative Value Schedules

These schedules were developed in the 1950s, with California Medical Services leading the way. The first California Relative Value Schedule was designed in 1956 and revised twice, in 1969 and 1974. It served as a model for many insurance plans. Relative value schedules attach a unit value to a large number of surgical procedures. The relationship of the unit values to each other typically is a function of the relative difficulty of the procedures. The maximum amount payable for a procedure is its unit value multiplied by a dollar amount purchased by the employer; it commonly is referred to as a conversion factor. Payment is subject to the overall schedule maximum and typical multiple procedures provision explained later. A wide range of conversion factors is available; but, as for dollar-fee schedules, the conversion factor should be selected to produce no more than the usual charges in an area.

A relative value schedule permits greater flexibility, particularly for employers with more than one location. Appropriate conversion factors can be applied to the schedule to produce the level of reimbursement reflecting regional differences in cost. Schedules can be kept current by adjusting the conversion factor as costs change.

The following is a sample from a typical relative value schedule. The last column has been added to illustrate the maximum amount payable, subject to the overall maximum and multiple procedure provisions. It assumes a $15 conversion factor had been purchased.

Procedure	*Unit Value*	*Maximum Payment with $15 Conversion Factor*
Valvotomy	140	$2,100
Extraction of lens	80	1,200
Hysterectomy	60	900
Cesarean section	50	750
Appendectomy	40	600
Herniotomy	35	525
Tonsillectomy	20	300

Since the 1974 revision of the California Relative Value Schedule, the Federal Trade Commission has ruled it to be a form of fee setting. As a result, the California Medical Association no longer updates or uses it. Some insurance plans continue to include relative value schedules based on each insurer's own nationwide charge data.

Reasonable and Customary Fees

Alternatively, a surgical plan may be designed to reimburse for a surgeon's fee up to the reasonable and customary charge for the procedure performed, without any identified schedule. "Reasonable and customary" is based on both the charge usually made by the physician for the procedure and the range of charges made by physicians for that same procedure in the locality where performed. Typically, it is set to cover the full charge of 85 or 90 percent of all physicians in a geographical area. Differences arise because of different charge data bases and area designations.

Reasonable and customary surgical plans have the advantage of automatically adjusting to inflation without plan change. For the same reason, they build inflation into the cost of a medical care plan and are accused of encouraging continually increasing charges by surgeons.

Multiple Procedures

Scheduled surgical benefit plans usually limit reimbursement for multiple procedures. The following is one such provision:

> If two or more procedures are performed at the same time in the same operative field, the benefit payable is the largest amount specified for any one of the procedures, and in some plans 50 percent of the others as well.
>
> If two or more procedures are performed at the same time in different operative fields, payment will be made for each, up to the overall schedule maximum.
>
> If two or more procedures are performed as a result of the same or related causes, but not during the course of a single operation, payment will be made for each procedure, but the total amount payable for all such procedures will not exceed the overall schedule maximum, unless they are separated by (1) a return to active, full-time employment in the case of an employee, or (2) typically three or six months in the case of a dependent.

Although reasonable and customary plans often do not include similar language, they may apply similar rationale in evaluating the reasonable charge for multiple procedures.

Associated Benefits

Regardless of the approach to reimbursement of the surgeon, surgical expense benefits plans may cover other physicians' charges associated with surgery.

Assistant Surgeon

Charges for an assistant surgeon sometimes are reimbursed on a scheduled basis. In that case, a dollar amount is identified for each procedure. However, it usually is determined as a percent of the maximum payment provided for the surgeon's fee for the same procedure. Therefore, whether the allowance is expressed as a specific dollar amount or as, in some plans, simply as a percent (e.g., 20 percent) of the surgical allowance, the result is the same. Most relative value plans exclude any assistant surgeon benefit for a surgical procedure with less than 35 units, since such surgery should not require an assistant.

Anesthesiologists

The charge for an anesthetic generally is included in the hospital or outpatient facility charges in connection with a surgical procedure. It is considered part of necessary services and supplies.

However, charges for the administration of anesthetics have been reimbursable in different ways. Some plans consider them part of the hospital benefit, regardless of whether they are billed by a hospital or by a provider who works independently. Another approach offered coverage for administration of an anesthetic by a physician who is not a salaried employee of a hospital under the surgical benefit. In that case, charges may be reimbursed as a percent, such as 20 percent, of the surgical allowance, as a specified unit value that may include a time factor as well or on a reasonable and customary basis.

Pregnancy

Historically, pregnancy expense benefits have been provided, excluded, or limited at the option of the policyholder; because at least normal pregnancies were considered budgetable but represented a relatively high-cost portion of the total health care package. Through the years, several states have mandated coverage for at least complications of pregnancy in all insurance policies.

Complications have been variously defined. A typical definition includes expenses incurred as a result of an extrauterine pregnancy, a pregnancy which terminates by cesarean section or miscarriage, or expenses incurred as a result of sickness caused or contributed to by pregnancy. Some plans use what appears to be broader language, although the intent is the same. They may define complications of pregnancy as pregnancy complicated by concurrent disease or as abnormal conditions significantly affecting usual medical management.

Federal legislation, effective October 31, 1978, changed much of that. It required that, by May 1, 1979, employers with 15 or more employees engaged in interstate commerce (i.e., employers who are, or become, subject to Title VII of the Civil Rights Act of 1964) must provide the same benefits for pregnancy as for any other sickness. The law does not require an employer to provide benefits for abortions "except where the life of the mother would be endangered if the fetus were carried to term or except where medical complications have arisen from an abortion." The burden of compliance rests with the employer and need not be insured even if other benefits are. However, most employers now include equal coverage for pregnancy in their health care insurance plans.

This approach changed the historical treatment of most insured pregnancy benefits. It eliminated the extension of pregnancy coverage for a pregnancy that began while insured and was therefore covered, even if the individual was no longer insured under the plan when the pregnancy terminated. Today, to match the treatment of any other sickness, an insured must be totally disabled as a result of the pregnancy when coverage terminates or the pregnancy is not covered under the extension provisions.

The equal treatment for pregnancy requirement also affects the benefit amount provided to the obstetrician in the surgical schedule of a health insurance plan; it must follow the relativity of the schedule for other procedures. Thus, if surgery is covered on a reasonable and customary basis, pregnancy also must be covered on a similar basis.

Although the law itself left the status of pregnancy benefits for dependents unclear, most consider it impractical in today's environment to provide different pregnancy benefits for employees and dependents. Any potential cost saving is likely to be offset by dissatisfaction among male employees with dependents.

Employers with fewer than 15 employees, or those with 15 or more employees who are not subject to Title VII of the Civil Rights Act of 1964, may continue to exclude or limit pregnancy benefits subject to state law. However, individual state legislation is increasingly following the federal approach.

Special Features

Second Surgical Opinion Programs

Past studies have questioned the necessity for the growing number of surgical procedures being performed throughout the country. As a result, whenever nonemergency surgery is recommended, an individual may wish to obtain a second and even a third opinion to verify the need for the procedure. Many in-force major medical plans consider second surgical opinions as a covered medical expense, and reimburse such charges on a reasonable and customary basis subject to any deductible and coinsurance provisions.

However, to encourage the seeking of a second opinion, insurance plans increasingly are covering the cost of these consultations without any additional cost to the patient. One way is through a predetermined fee payable to consulting surgeons who have agreed to accept the fee as payment in full. Another approach pays 100 percent of reasonable and customary charges of a consulting surgeon, regardless of the rest of the plan design. Sometimes an overall dollar limit is included. In any case, charges for any additional necessary X-rays, laboratory tests, and other diagnostic studies also are covered.

Most plans leave the decision to seek a second opinion up to the insured. Some, however, require a second opinion for elective surgery and/or specified common procedures or payment for the surgery either will be reduced or eliminated. Indications are that savings are greater with a mandatory program.

More recently, verification of the need for recommended surgery has been incorporated into hospital utilization review programs discussed in detail in later chapters. These often require a second opinion if the reviewer determines that one is necessary.

Surgi-Centers

Surgical plans always have covered surgery wherever it was performed, and continue to do so. However, in the interest of further discouraging hospital confinement and its associated high cost, most insurance plans now cover the charges for use of a relatively new type of facility. It is variously referred to as a surgi-center, freestanding or ambulatory surgical facility, or one-day surgical facility. It provides an appropriate setting for certain types of comparatively simple surgical procedures that don't normally require overnight confinement and may or may not be part of a hospital. In either case, the charges for use of the surgi-center generally are covered under the plan's hospital benefits.

To assure quality care, the following are typical requirements that must be met. The facility must:

1. Comply with all legal requirements in the jurisdiction in which located.
2. Be mainly engaged in surgery on its premises, which include operating room(s), recovery room(s), and equipment for emergency care.
3. Have a medical staff, including physicians and graduate registered nurses.
4. Have an agreement with a hospital for immediate acceptance of patients requiring hospital care on an inpatient basis.

Limitations and Exclusions

Normally, surgical expense benefits will not cover the cost of cosmetic surgery. With the growth of separate dental insurance, surgical benefits in a medical care plan also commonly exclude dental surgery unless it is the result of an accident.

PHYSICIANS' VISITS EXPENSE BENEFITS

It was a logical next step, after surgical benefits were added to insurance plans, to address coverage for physicians' charges for other medical services. Thus, physicians' visits coverage was developed and, together with other nonsurgical benefits, often was referred to as basic medical expense insurance. It remained a comparatively limited first-dollar benefit.

Two types of first-dollar physicians' visits plans were offered providing benefits, (1) in the hospital only, or (2) in either the hospital, home, or office.

In-Hospital Visits Only

Following the early direction of medical insurance, physicians' expense benefits plans at first were designed to cover only fees for visits made while the patient is confined in the hospital. Benefits are subject to a specified maximum-dollar amount for each period of hospital confinement and often subject to a maximum per day. The daily amount may vary, depending on the day of confinement on which the visit is made; if so, it is most often higher on the first day, to reflect the greater involvement of the physician at that time.

The benefit period normally coincides with the benefit period for hospital expense benefits. For example, under a 120-day hospital expense insurance plan, with a $20 daily in-hospital physicians' visits benefit, the maximum payment for physicians' visits would be $2,400 (120 × $20). Frequently, too, plans limit payment to the charge for only one visit in any one day.

Hospital, Office, and Home Visits

It wasn't long before plans were expanded to cover physicians' visits in the office or home, as well as in the hospital, but total disability often was required. Such plans, for example, may provide $10 for an office visit, $15 for a home visit, and $15 for a hospital visit. In addition, an overall maximum, such as $600, is established. This limit may be applied to all visits for the care and treatment of any one injury or sickness, or in the case of sickness, all visits in either a calendar year or in 12 consecutive months.

When purchasing a plan to cover physicians' fees in and out of the hospital, the policyholder selects the visit when benefit payments begin, usually any visit from the first to the fourth. If hospital confinement is required, a provision often is added to begin payment with the first visit in the hospital, regardless of when it otherwise would have started. Benefits normally are restricted to only one visit per day.

Compared with hospital-only coverage for physicians' charges, this broader benefit has not been as commonly included on a first-dollar basis. It can result in many small claims, which some believe are covered more appropriately under major medical coverage on a shared basis.

Limitations and Exclusions

Neither of the two types of plans described for physicians' visits expense benefits normally covers charges for a visit after surgery if it is made by a physician connected with the surgical procedure, since a surgeon's charge usually includes post-operative care. Similarly, physicians' visits for pregnancy are not separately covered, because they normally are included in the obstetrician's charge for managing the total pregnancy. In addition, physicians' visits made for dental treatment commonly are excluded from this part of a plan, as are examinations for the prescription or fitting of eyeglasses or hearing aids.

Special Features

Well-Baby Care

The question of whether expenses for normal, healthy babies should be covered from birth under an insurance plan has been debated through the years on much the same grounds as has normal pregnancy. It became even a bigger issue as the pregnancy laws changed and the costs for care of the healthy baby escalated. As coverage for newborns developed, they first were covered only for accident or sickness after 14 days of age. Soon, however, this was extended to include children with specific abnormal conditions at birth. The latter remains true in some plans today. However, it is increasingly common to also cover a defined number of days of nursery charges for the normal child. Before the federal pregnancy legislation, some plans did this only to the extent the mother did not otherwise use her entire pregnancy allowance. With pregnancy no longer specially limited, nursery charges if covered usually are limited to a maximum number of days.

Other charges for a healthy baby, such as a pediatrician's visits, whether the first, usually in the hospital, or subsequently in the office, are under discussion but more commonly are addressed in a preventive care benefit.

Preventive Care

Preventive care has become a buzz word in this era of increasing interest in how it might improve the health of the nation and decrease the cost of medical care for all. In the course of its development, its definition has moved from annual physical examinations for everyone to more sophisticated approaches. New concepts address the cost effectiveness of the procedures recommended, the intervals at which they are performed, and even more basically, methods for changing lifestyles that contribute toward illness. Many approaches are being tried and evaluated.

Health maintenance organizations, which by their nature include more preventive care than most current insurance plans, are studying the effect on health and costs and adjusting their practices to reflect results.

Employers are providing in-house exercise facilities, considering health risk evaluations, and beginning to sponsor programs to foster better health by changing lifestyles, such as smoke-ender and stress-control courses.

Coverage in insurance plans varies greatly. Those that include preventive care at all, typically cover charges for periodic physical examinations up to a maximum-dollar amount, such as $75, for the examination and for any required diagnostic procedures. Other plans are providing routine immunizations and educational materials to insureds to raise awareness of the value of prevention.

The jury is still out, but in the meantime, medical benefit plan designers are involved heavily in how best to provide preventive benefits.

DIAGNOSTIC X-RAY AND LABORATORY EXPENSE BENEFITS

This coverage is designed to complement other first-dollar medical expense benefits already discussed. Without it, X-ray and laboratory analyses normally would be covered as hospital services and supplies, but only if the services are performed when the insured is hospital confined. This benefit, though, provides reimbursement for diagnostic X-ray and laboratory examinations made in a doctor's office, in an independent laboratory, or in an outpatient department of a hospital on an ambulatory basis. As with surgical plans, benefits have been covered on a scheduled or nonscheduled basis.

Scheduled

A scheduled plan is a more controlled approach to first-dollar coverage of diagnostic X-ray and laboratory expenses typical of early designs for each new benefit as it developed. Plans of this type itemize the maximum allowance for each examination—as a dollar amount or as a unit value to be multiplied by a conversion factor. Benefits are provided up to an overall schedule maximum, such as $200 or $250, either for all examinations for any one accident or sickness or for all accidents or sicknesses during any one year. In the past, a two-part schedule sometimes was used. The first part provided coverage for diagnostic X-ray and radioisotope studies, and sometimes was written as a separate coverage. The second part provided payment for diagnostic laboratory services, and generally was written only in conjunction with the first part of the schedule.

Nonscheduled

A nonscheduled plan is a less-restrictive approach since it eliminates maximums for each service. Instead, it provides reimbursement for the actual fee charged for each service, subject to the reasonable and customary test.

As for scheduled plans, overall maximums are set, for example, at $100 or $200, either for all examinations for any one accident or sickness, or for all accidents or sicknesses during any one calendar year. These first-dollar maximums have remained comparatively low because major medical covers expenses that exceed them.

Limitations and Exclusions

Early plans did not cover diagnostic X-ray and laboratory examinations for pregnancy. Since the 1979 Federal Maternity legislation, however, this is no longer true; but the benefit continues to exclude costs for fitting of eyeglasses or of hearing aids or for dental treatment, unless the examination is made to diagnose an injury caused by an accident.

RADIOTHERAPY EXPENSE BENEFITS

Coverage for radiotherapy as a first-dollar benefit developed as the treatment became more prevalent and the cost more significant. However, charges continued to escalate and the first-dollar portion became an ever-smaller part of the total cost. Like diagnostic benefits, the balance was covered under major medical. Many plans, however, have eliminated the first-dollar radiotherapy benefit as it became less meaningful and, instead, cover the cost only under major medical.

If a first-dollar plan is included, it frequently is done through the use of a schedule that assigns a maximum-dollar amount or a unit value to identified services. The cost of covered radiological treatment (e.g., radium or cobalt therapy) includes: (1) administration of the treatment, (2) materials and their preparation, and (3) the use of facilities. The maximum payment for all treatments received during any one day often is limited to the largest payment provided in the schedule for any one of the treatments.

Whether a dollar-amount or unit value schedule is used, the total amount payable for all treatments for the same or related injury or sickness is the overall schedule maximum. Maximums have been available that range from as low as $200 on a dollar-amount schedule to $1,500 or more on a unit value schedule. In some plans this approach is modified to apply the maximum to all treatments for the same or related injury or sickness in a calendar year. The benefit is intended to cover treatment and, therefore, excludes diagnosis.

SUPPLEMENTAL ACCIDENT EXPENSE BENEFITS

This coverage also is variously referred to as additional accident or special accident expense benefits. The concept was first developed to provide an extra limited amount of first-dollar coverage for medical expenses resulting from an accident. Although that was long before the current concern with cost containment, the benefit does address that issue somewhat; it avoids the penalty of the major medical deductible and coinsurance, because treatment for a minor accident is received in a doctor's office and not in a hospital outpatient department.

The coverage usually provides payment toward the cost of the following services as a result of an accidental injury: (1) treatment by a physician, (2) hospital care, (3) registered graduate nursing care (RN), and (4) X-ray and laboratory examinations. Benefits are payable for covered medical expenses that exceed the amount the insured otherwise is entitled to under the rest of the basic medical care plan, up to a maximum for any one accident. The most common maximums are $300 and $500. Most plans require the costs be incurred within 90 days of an accident that happened while the individual was insured.

EXTENSION OF BENEFITS

A key provision of basic benefits from the beginning, which adds significantly to their value to the insured, is the extension of benefits provision. Under its terms, if an individual's insurance terminates, for whatever reason, payment is made for covered services received within three months of termination. But the service must be for an injury or sickness that caused the individual to be totally and continuously disabled from the day his or her insurance terminated until the day the service is rendered.

Thus, disabled persons are not left without coverage for an existing disability because their insurance ended.

CONVERSION PRIVILEGE

Similarly, the conversion privilege offers a way to fill what might otherwise be a gap in coverage for terminating employees. It allows an individual whose insurance terminates after being insured for at least three months to convert to a personal medical care policy without evidence of insurability. Many states require this provision, and even specify the levels of coverage that must be available. Many insurers, however, include it in all plans. The converted policy usually provides more restrictive benefits than those under the terminating group coverage, and experience proves individuals most likely to use the plan take advantage of it. The privilege is not generally available to individuals who terminate coverage for failure to pay premiums, are eligible for Medicare, or become insured under another group medical plan within 31 days of termination. In addition to the conversion privilege, continuation of coverage is now mandated for certain individuals under the Consolidated Omnibus Budget Reconciliation Act.

SUMMARY

The development of basic benefits started with hospital coverage—since it represented the greatest cost of an illness. Additional benefits were developed as other costs increased and as health care plans expanded to satisfy the buyer.

A variety of such benefits have evolved through the years as a result of the continuing demand for fuller coverage. Some, such as the prescription drug benefit, have developed along somewhat different lines, because special administrative issues made the use of participating providers and of a third-party administrator cost-effective. Interest in the vision care benefit has grown, and plans have been written on either a scheduled or participating provider basis. Other benefits, such as home health care and skilled nursing facilities, offer alternatives to hospital confinement and may be covered as either basic or major medical benefits. All are discussed in detail elsewhere in this text.

Furthermore, several limitations not yet mentioned do often apply to basic benefits. These are designed to avoid payment for custodial care, duplicate coverage, illegal or unnecessary charges, etc. Because many also affect major medical benefits, they are treated in the next chapter.

CHAPTER 10

SUPPLEMENTAL MAJOR MEDICAL AND COMPREHENSIVE PLANS

Zelda Lipton

INTRODUCTION

Although the scope of basic medical care benefits has been expanded through the years, it remains primarily hospital oriented and geared toward acute care. Benefits usually are first-dollar, but limited both in the services and charges covered. As medical technology advanced and costs increased, the need for additional coverage for a variety of expenses not covered under the so-called basic benefits and for protection against the financial catastrophe of serious and prolonged illness became increasingly apparent.

In response to that need, major medical insurance plans were introduced in 1949. They grew rapidly, covering over 32 million people by the end of 1960. That number increased to approximately 163 million persons with major medical coverage in some form by the end of 1985.

Major medical provides broad coverage and substantial protection from large, unpredictable, and therefore unbudgetable medical care expenses. As might be expected, with hundreds of companies involved in the development of benefits, many variations in design appeared. Difficult as it is to call anything typical, patterns emerged. From the start, most plans covered a wide range of medical care charges with few internal limits and what was then considered a high per person overall maximum benefit, such as $10,000. Both the range of charges covered and the maximums have increased steadily through the years, but the early requirement that the insured participate to some extent in the cost of care through deductibles and coinsurance remains a conviction for most designers. Although born as a supplement to basic medical care plans, that too has changed—so now two approaches exist to major medical: (1) supplemental major medical over some form of basic benefits, and (2) the stand-alone package, referred to as a comprehensive plan.

APPROACHES DEFINED

Supplemental Major Medical

A supplemental major medical plan pays benefits when the basic benefits are exhausted. The claimant is reimbursed first for any charges covered by specific formulas in the basic plan. Major medical covered expenses not reimbursed under the basic plan are covered under the supplemental major medical, subject to a deductible, payable by the claimant. After satisfaction of this deductible amount, a percentage of the remaining covered expenses are paid up to the supplemental major medical maximum. A commonly included provision caps the claimant's costs by paying 100 percent of major medical covered expenses after the insured has incurred the plan's out-of-pocket maximum.

Depending upon the basic benefits over which it is written, a supplemental major medical plan, or the plan of which it is a part, has come to be designated in several different ways:

1. With the insurer's own basic hospital, surgical, medical benefits, the package is called a base-plus major medical plan.
2. Over another basic plan, such as Blue Cross or Blue Shield, the supplemental major medical more commonly is referred to as superimposed major medical.
3. Over Blue Cross only, the supplemental major medical is known as a wraparound. But even a wraparound can use different design concepts. Traditionally, a wraparound was written to include basic surgical and medical benefits supplemented by major medical. This is much like a base-plus major medical plan except that Blue Cross provides the basic hospital benefits. However, another wraparound design evolved with added simplicity and potential for cost control. It covers all benefits not covered by Blue Cross as part of the major medical subject to a deductible and coinsurance; the Blue Cross hospital benefits are the only basic benefits.

Coverage under the major medical portion of all these approaches differs only to the extent that it must adjust to the basic benefits over which it is written. Whatever its form, the two-part basic and major medical coverage persists for several reasons. It reflects the history of the development of medical insurance, in general, as well as the history of the particular plan—and sometimes the collective bargaining that gave rise to that plan. Over the Blues, the basic Blue Cross plan may have cost advantages in a particular geographical area, because of cost-reimbursement contracts with hospitals, making competition for basic hospital benefits difficult. As a result, the basic Blue Cross plans cover a substantial part of the market in such states as New York, New Jersey, Pennsylvania, Ohio, and Michigan. More attention is being paid to the equity of different hospital charges based on the source of funding, but for now this remains a factor in some locations. Although most Blue Cross/Blue Shield plans working together also offer an extended medical care or master medical plan, patterned after the private insurance industry's supplemental major medical, basic Blues plans with private supplemental major medical continue to be written.

Whatever its form or the reason for using it, a two-part medical care plan with two carriers has some disadvantages. Administration becomes more difficult, since premiums and claims must be submitted to both carriers and benefits must be coordinated. Duplication may exist; however, there may be gaps in coverage caused by such inconsistencies as different definitions, reasonable and customary levels, and preexisting conditions limitations. Furthermore, when two carriers are involved, if the basic plan changes, the liability of the major medical carrier does also. Clear communication between carriers and with the insured is essential. Typical base-plus major medical, superimposed, and wraparound plans are illustrated in Figure 10–1.

Comprehensive

The next step in the logical development of medical care plans was a single integrated program covering both basic and catastrophic costs—a comprehensive plan. The earliest of these were written in 1954. Their growth was slower than supplemental major medical plans at first, but by 1978 almost 37 million of those persons with major medical coverage in some form were covered by comprehensive plans, and the trend continued with 63 million covered at the end of 1985.

A comprehensive plan is simpler to understand and easier to communicate. By applying one overall reimbursement formula to the total covered expenses, without attempting to distinguish between those that

FIGURE 10–1
Typical Supplemental Major Medical Plan Designs

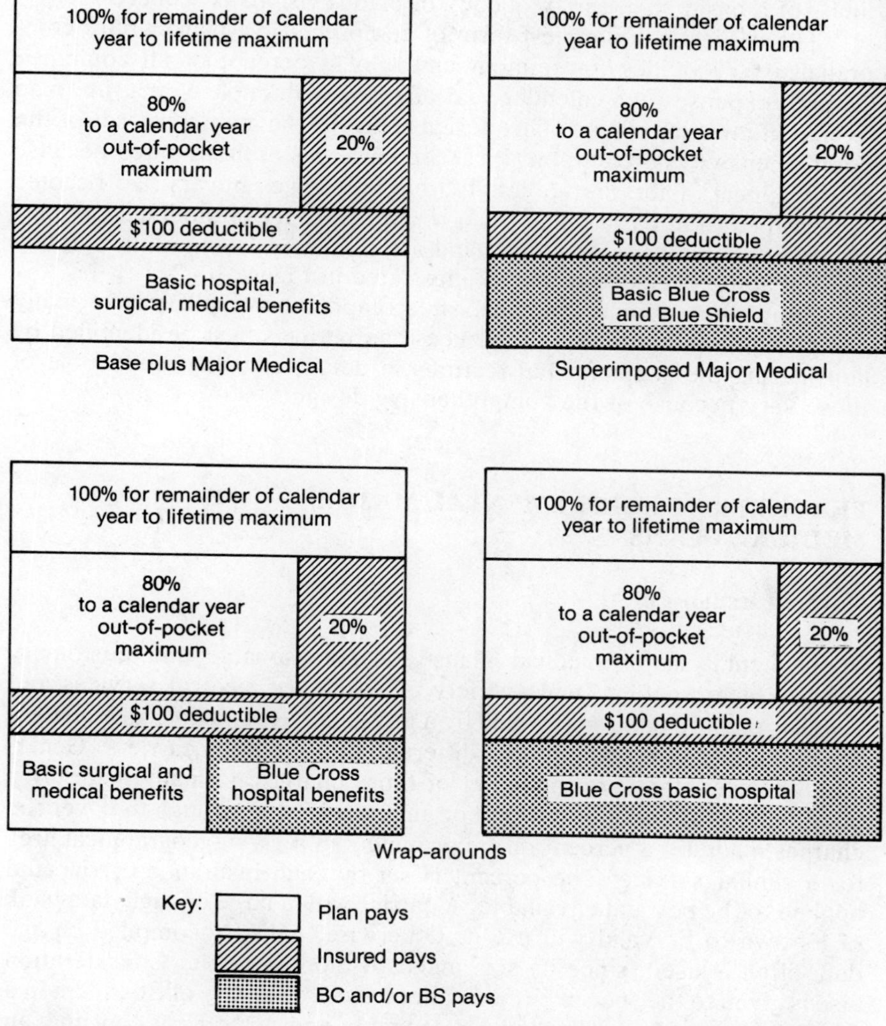

would have been eligible for basic or major medical benefits, it avoids the hazards of both the duplicate coverage and the gaps discussed earlier. Furthermore, since most comprehensive plans have few of the inside limits of a basic plan, the frequency of plan revisions is reduced.

The earliest and simplest form of comprehensive plan, a pure comprehensive, provides for reimbursement of a percent of all combined covered expenses in a calendar year after the deductible is met, up to an overall lifetime maximum. This design achieves the main purposes of the comprehensive approach; but its acceptance was at first limited because of the appeal of the first-dollar, full-pay coverages buyers had become accustomed to in basic plans. As a result, a variety of modified comprehensive designs were developed and are discussed later in this chapter. Typical comprehensive plans are illustrated in Figure 10–2.

Supplemental major medical and comprehensive plans have many common provisions. Their differences can perhaps best be identified by considering the supplemental features in detail, and then how some of those vary because of the comprehensive design.

FEATURES OF SUPPLEMENTAL MAJOR MEDICAL PLANS

Covered Expenses

Supplemental major medical plans cover reasonable and customary charges incurred for a wide variety of necessary medical services and supplies prescribed or performed by a physician. Reasonable and customary charges may be interpreted differently by different carriers. Generally, however, they are the lesser of those charges normally made by a provider for the service rendered or an amount large enough to cover the charges made by a percent of the providers in a given geographical area for a similar service. The percent is set by each insurance carrier and applied to the best data available. A carrier with a large enough data bank of its own to be valid will use it. Otherwise, industry-compiled charge data often is used, since its size makes it more credible. Consideration also is given to the special circumstances and complexity of treatment in a particular case. In applying the reasonable and customary concept, an insurer does not try to set fee levels or interfere with the doctor/patient relationship. Rather, the insurer establishes a contractual liability and the patient assumes the obligation to pay any charges exceeding the benefit maximum that results. Disputes arising out of the determination by the insurer that the reasonable and customary charge is less than the actual

FIGURE 10–2
Typical Comprehensive Plan Designs

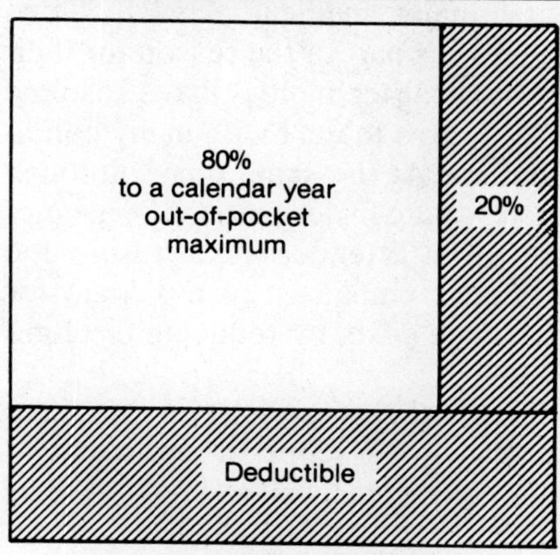

Pure Comprehensive

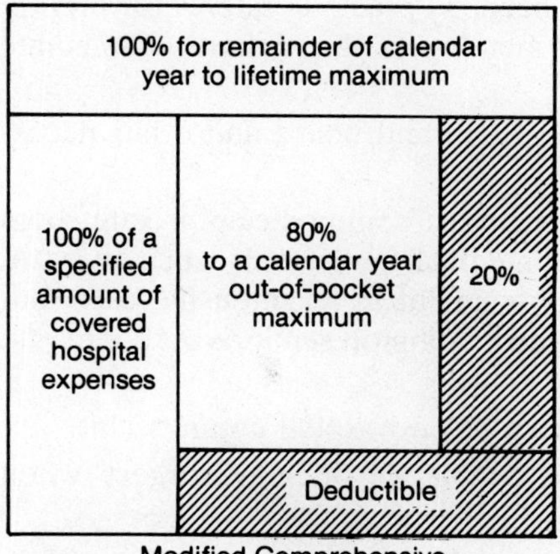

Modified Comprehensive

Key: Plan pays
Insured pays

charge for a service frequently are referred to the appropriate medical society's peer review committee for settlement.

From the beginning, supplemental major medical plans included some out-of-hospital benefits; in fact, that was part of the reason for their development. Continuing advances in medical technology have resulted in new and sophisticated outpatient procedures to deal with many conditions that formerly required hospitalization. At the same time, although all medical care costs have continued to escalate faster than the consumer price index, hospital costs remain the worst offender. As a result, the trend in recent years has put even greater emphasis on coverage for outpatient services in the hope of containing costs by reducing or eliminating hospital stays.

Although specific covered expenses and their descriptions vary from plan to plan, the following illustrates the broad scope of services and facilities for which charges typically are covered as well as some of their limitations and rationale.

Professional services of physicians or surgeons and other recognized medical practitioners, including consulting physicians.

Services of registered nurses or licensed practical nurses for private duty nursing. Neither may be a member of the patient's immediate family.

Hospital charges for semiprivate room and board and other necessary services and supplies.

Private room charges usually at the most common semiprivate room rate to discourage use except if medically necessary, but an extra allowance may be provided. Confinement in an intensive care unit may be at two or three times the most common semiprivate room rate or even the actual charge.

Preadmission testing prior to a scheduled hospital confinement.

Ambulatory surgical facilities to encourage one-day surgery when medically advisable.

Mental illness or alcohol and drug abuse treatment centers for a limited number of days, such as 30 or 60, either per confinement or per calendar year. This is based on the concept that short-term therapy in such facilities is beneficial, but long-term treatment often is custodial in nature and not intended to be covered.

Skilled nursing facilities that meet prescribed requirements. This is limited to a specified number of days, such as 30, per confinement or per calendar year, and usually must follow a hospital stay of at least 3 consecutive days. The intent is to provide for the person who no longer needs acute care in a hospital but does need intermediate care and monitoring. Longer confinement is likely to be custodial.

Home health care for a defined number of visits per calendar year, such as 40 or 80, by physicians, nurses, and home health aides. Care must be under a plan supervised by a home health agency and generally must follow confinement in either a hospital or skilled nursing facility. Home care in lieu of confinement may be covered if services required can be provided more comfortably and less expensively at home.

Anesthetics and their administration.

X-rays and other diagnostic laboratory procedures wherever performed.

X-ray or radium treatments.

Oxygen and other gases and their administration.

Blood transfusions, including the cost of blood if charged.

Prescription drugs.

Professional ambulance service to or from the nearest hospital where care can be provided.

Rental of equipment required for therapeutic use.

Casts, splints, and initial prosthetic appliances, trusses, braces, and crutches.

As explained in the previous chapter, federal legislation now requires certain defined employers to provide the same benefits for pregnancy as for any other illness. The pregnancy benefits need not be insured even if other benefits are. But, if normal pregnancy or only complications are included in the insurance plan, covered expenses described above apply equally to services for the covered pregnancy as to any other illness.

Deductible

The deductible is the amount of covered major medical expenses that must be incurred by the insured before supplemental major medical benefits become payable by the insurer. Its basic purpose is to lower costs by reducing unnecessary utilization and by eliminating small claims and the expense of handling them. It attempts to accomplish this by giving the insured some interest in the up-front cost of medical care.

Levels

Through the years and still today, the most common individual deductible has been $100. Recently, however, some employers have opted for higher deductible amounts, such as $200, $500, $1,000, even $2,000. Some of this reflects an effort toward further control of utilization and, therefore, of premium during a period of rapid inflation. There are employers, though, who choose to self-insure the very high deductibles. For them, some insurance carriers administer all claims and inform the policyholder of the obligation between the insured's $100 and the high $2,000 deductible, for example. The insurance company assumes the risk over and above the $2,000. This approach allows the employer some of the advantages of self-insurance on a small scale with limited risk. It does at the same time, though, defeat the purposes of a high deductible in terms of utilization control.

Some consideration also has been given to relating an insured's deductible amount to income, either as a percent of earnings or by identifying a different deductible amount for various earnings ranges. The premise is that a higher-paid employee can afford to cover a larger part of medical expenses and, unless the deductible is significant enough, it will have little effect on utilization. Earnings related deductibles could become more prevalent in the future in spite of the difficulties with administration of many individual deductible levels on each account which also could change every year.

Type

There are two types of supplemental major medical deductibles: (1) corridor and (2) integrated. The former is by far the more common.

Corridor. This type of deductible is so named because it serves as a corridor between the basic benefits and the supplemental major medical plan. It is applied to covered major medical expenses that exceed amounts covered under the basic plan. Benefits payable under the basic plan are not counted toward satisfaction of the corridor deductible.

Although in wraparound plans the deductible is expressed as benefits paid or payable under the Blue Cross plan plus a specific dollar amount, such as $100, the $100 remains a corridor deductible. This contractual approach is used to allow elimination of any obligation under the major medical portion for expenses which are covered under the basic Blue Cross plan, or would have been except that the insured was for some reason not covered under the Blue Cross portion.

Integrated. An integrated deductible was an early approach to the application of the deductible in a supplemental major medical plan. It is rarely used today. The deductible is the greater of (1) a fairly high amount, such as $1,000, or (2) the basic plan benefits. For example, if the basic plan paid $1,250, a $1,000 deductible would be satisfied and supplemental major medical benefits would be payable for the remaining covered expenses with no further deductible. However, if the basic plan only paid $800, the balance of $200 that is needed to satisfy the deductible would have to be assumed by the insured before supplemental major medical benefits would be payable.

Basis for Application

In conjunction with the deductible, an accumulation period feature is included in one form or another. The accumulation period is that time during which covered medical expenses sufficient to satisfy the deductible must be incurred. It was designed originally as a device to further insure that only relatively substantial claims would be covered. In addition to the length of the accumulation period, the basis for application of the deductible and the benefit period to which it applies vary according to the needs of the policyholder and the underwriting requirements of the insurer.

The following are the two common deductible bases and illustrate how the above features can be combined in a variety of ways.

All-Cause Deductible. Under the all-cause approach, all expenses incurred by an insured, regardless of the number of illnesses or accidents giving rise to the expenses, are considered for purposes of satisfaction of the deductible. Although it is possible to combine the all-cause deductible with various accumulation periods and benefits periods, the calendar year is almost universally used for both (e.g., a $100 deductible applies to each calendar year benefit period and must be satisfied between January 1 and December 31). As a result, this all-cause deductible approach often is referred to as a calendar year deductible.

Its most important advantages are that it is simple to administer, and is considered the easiest for the insured to understand. Benefits are paid, following the satisfaction of the calendar year deductible, for expenses incurred during the remainder of that calendar year. To reduce the seeming inequity between insureds who incur expenses early in the year and those who do so late in the year, a carry-over provision normally is included. This permits expenses incurred in October, November, or December, which are applied toward satisfaction of the deductible for that year, to be used toward satisfying the deductible for the next calendar year.

A policy year or a running 12 months may be substituted for a calendar year. The former is a period beginning with the date each year on which the policy was effective; it is sometimes referred to as the plan year. The latter is any period of 12 months, beginning with the date the first charge is made, counting toward an individual's deductible. This approach is no longer commonly used because of the difficulty of administering a different period for each individual under the plan.

Most plans also have a special deductible modification known as the common-accident provision. It provides that only one deductible will be applied to the total covered expenses incurred when two or more insured persons of the same family sustain injuries in a single accident.

In addition, to reduce the financial effect of the deductible on large families if several members have major expenses in one year, a "family deductible" provision usually is added with an all-cause deductible. This provision can operate in several different ways. The deductible may be waived for any further family members after either any two or any three of them have individually satisfied their deductibles in the same year.

Another approach waives any further deductible for the year when any combination of family members has satisfied a total of two or three times the individual deductible amount. The latter may be modified by requiring that at least one family member satisfies the individual deductible.

Per-Cause Deductible. Under the per-cause approach, all expenses incurred by an insured because of the same or related causes are considered for purposes of satisfaction of the deductible. An accumulation period most often is included, in which case the deductible for each cause must be satisfied within a specified period, typically 60 or 90 days, from the date the first expense is incurred.

In such a plan, the benefit period for each cause starts with the first expense used to satisfy the deductible, and normally ends one or two years after the date it starts or two years from the date the deductible was satisfied. When benefit periods longer than one year are provided, it is common to include an alternate cutoff date that terminates the benefit period. This might be the end of a period of 60 or 90 days, during which less than a certain amount of expenses (such as the deductible amount) is incurred. Once a benefit period ends, the deductible must be satisfied again to start a new one.

The chief advantage of the per-cause approach is that claims for minor, unrelated illnesses can be eliminated. However, an individual may have to satisfy two or more deductibles in any 12-month period. This approach is more difficult to understand and can cause administrative problems since, especially with advancing age, it often is difficult to distinguish among causes of diseases. The per-cause deductible was common in early major medical plans but has not been very popular for some time.

Coinsurance

Coinsurance provides further participation by the insured in part of the cost of medical care. By reimbursing for less than 100 percent of ongoing expenses over the deductible, coinsurance reinforces the objective of retaining the insured's financial interest in the cost of medical services. Thus, it is one more tool in keeping plan costs down.

Levels

By far the largest majority of plans use 80 percent for most reimbursements, but 75 percent to 100 percent are available. However, since even with 80 percent reimbursement the cost of a catastrophic illness can cause financial disaster, many plans eliminate coinsurance and reimburse at 100 percent after a certain dollar amount is reached. This amount has come to be most often expressed as the out-of-pocket maximum (e.g., $1,000) paid by an insured as a result of deductible and coinsurance provisions. Some plans begin to reimburse at 100 percent after an identified amount of covered expenses are incurred. The purpose is the same. In either case, the 100 percent usually applies to the same period used for application of the deductible, most often the remainder of the calendar year. In some plans, however, it applies to the following year as well. For even further protection, a family out-of-pocket maximum equal to two or three times the individual amount often is included.

Mental Illness and Alcohol or Drug Abuse

Although reimbursement for charges for treatment of inpatient mental and nervous disorders or alcohol and drug dependency is at the same coinsurance level as for other inpatient charges, an overwhelming number of plans require greater participation by the insured in the cost of these services on an outpatient basis. They are not only still considered somewhat discretionary but also open-ended as far as control is concerned. A variety of coverage designs and levels are available, but coinsurance for outpatient care is most often set at 50 percent subject to a maximum payment under the plan each calendar year, such as $1,000. This may apply separately to (1) mental illness and to (2) alcohol and drug dependency, or to all combined.

It also is still common, for mental illness and nervous disorders, to limit outpatient coverage to a specific maximum number of visits per year (e.g., 50) and a maximum covered charge per visit (e.g., $50) for even further control. Neither inpatient nor outpatient charges generally are included in out-of-pocket maximums, and they are rarely if ever payable at 100 percent.

Maximum Benefit

Except for specifically identified coverage limitations, reasonable and customary charges for all eligible expenses are covered by the plan provisions up to the overall maximum benefit of the plan. In the 1960s, a $10,000 maximum was common; today $1 million is common, and many plans are written as unlimited. Consistent with the application of the deductible, the overall maximum benefit may be written as either (1) lifetime (all-cause), or (2) per-cause.

Lifetime

Under the lifetime approach, the overall maximum benefit applies to all covered expenses during the entire period of coverage. However, major medical plans, from their beginning, typically included a reinstatement provision to avoid penalizing insureds who have either partially or wholly exhausted their benefits, but who have recovered to the extent of again being acceptable insurance risks. This provision might provide that after a minimum amount of benefits (e.g., $1,000) is used, the maximum may be reinstated to its original level by submitting evidence of insurability satisfactory to the insurance company. In addition, some plans provide a form of "automatic" reinstatement. For example, benefits paid in a calendar year may be reinstated automatically as of January 1 of the following year for amounts from $1,000 to as much as $25,000. Some plans allow continued reinstatement each January 1 until the full amount is restored.

For further control, it is not unusual to include a separate lifetime, nonreinstatable maximum for all mental and nervous disorders, such as $25,000 or $50,000 lifetime. This is in addition to the coinsurance, per-visit and maximum-dollar amount or duration limits discussed earlier.

Per-Cause

Under the per-cause approach, the overall maximum benefit applies to each cause. Thus, if an insured individual is receiving benefits under a per-cause plan for the treatment of both diabetes and a heart condition, a separate overall maximum benefit would be applicable to each illness, as would a separate deductible amount. A typical per-cause reinstatement provision states that, when a covered person has received benefits for any one accidental injury or any one sickness equal to the overall maximum benefit, major medical benefits for that injury or sickness terminate and can only be reinstated if satisfactory evidence of insurability is submitted to the insurance company. Another approach reinstates some or all of the maximum if the insured does not incur medical expenses for the injury or sickness of more than a specified amount, such as $500, during a given period, such as six months.

With the very high maximums being written today, especially on lifetime all-cause plan designs, the maximum benefit reinstatement provisions no longer have the significance they did in the past. Nevertheless, they typically continue to be included unless the maximum benefit is unlimited.

Limitations and Exclusions

The following describes the charges and services most commonly limited or excluded from medical insurance coverages today, with a brief explanation of the reason for each. Those which apply to major medical only are so identified. In addition, such coverages as vision and hearing care are listed, although they are well on their way to being included.

Preexisting Conditions

Because of the potential for selection against the plan, it is common practice to pay major medical benefits for preexisting conditions only after certain requirements are met. A typical preexisting conditions limitation might read:

> A preexisting condition is defined as a condition resulting from an injury or sickness for which expenses were incurred during the three months prior to the effective date of insurance. For such a condition, benefits will be payable only (1) after the completion of a period of three consecutive months ending after insurance becomes effective, and during which the individual received no care or treatment for the condition, or (2) after the individual has been covered for major medical benefits for a period of one year.

Some plans also may cover a preexisting condition of an employee insured for major medical benefits for six months without any interruption in full-time active work. The preexisting conditions provision may be waived either for the group insured on the effective date of the plan only or for all future insureds as well. When this is done, the active service requirements continue to apply, but once an individual is insured under the plan its benefits will be paid for a preexisting condition as for any other condition.

In the case of a plan transferring from one carrier to another, however, many plans universally apply a "no loss—no gain" or "hardship" provision required in some states. It usually provides that an insured will be reimbursed under the new plan at the lesser of the amount which would have been payable under the terminated or the new plan regardless of any preexisting conditions limitations or active service requirements of the new plan.

Duplicate Coverage

In many households today, more than one family member is employed. As a result, a person may be covered under more than one group medical care insurance plan and could profit financially from an illness. Thus, in the interest of cost control for all concerned, a coordination of benefits (COB) provision routinely is included to avoid overinsurance. Until recently it followed the guidelines recommended by a health insurance task force and adopted by the National Association of Insurance Commissioners (NAIC) in 1971. That version of the NAIC Model Group COB Provisions and Guidelines established the order in which carriers were responsible for reimbursement. The provisions allowed a claimant to recover as much of his or her medical care expenses as coverage under each plan permitted, up to 100 percent of charges for expenses allowable under any of the plans. When a plan provides benefits in the form of services rather than cash payments, the reasonable cash value of the services is considered both an "allowable charge" and a benefit paid. To the extent any plan, therefore, did not need to pay its full liability, benefit credits were accumulated and available if they should be needed to cover expenses later in the benefit period. Examples are included on Figure 10–3.

Beginning in June 1984, the NAIC proposed several changes to the 1971 guidelines to adapt to the current environment. First, instead of the father's plan always paying first for a dependent child, the plan of the parent whose birthday falls earliest in the year pays first. Similarly, the plan of an active employee or that employee's dependent pays before the plan of a retiree or an employee on layoff. Since states may or may not adopt the latest NAIC model and do so at varying dates, the guidelines provide that if one plan has the birthday rule and the other does not, the latter determines the order of payment. The retiree/layoff rule is ignored unless both plans include it.

In addition, rather than always covering up to 100 percent of allowable charges under either plan thereby removing any incentive to contain costs, the secondary carrier can retain the deductibles and coinsurance of the most generous plan. Reimbursement from both plans must be at least 50 percent of allowable charges for alcoholism, mental and nervous expenses, or cost-containment features, such as second surgical opinion, and at least 75 percent of all others.

Medical care plans coordinate benefits not only with other group medical insurance plans and health maintenance organizations, but also

FIGURE 10–3
Use of Benefit Credits with Coordination of Benefits

Example 1:

A benefit credit (unused liability) that remains after payment of benefits as secondary carrier may be stored and used at a later date to pay allowable expenses that otherwise would not be paid. For example, the primary carrier may consider certain charges covered under its plan, such as nursing home care, and pay up to its limits. Even though the charges are not covered under the secondary plan, they become allowable expenses under the secondary plan and can be paid with previously accumulated benefit credits (assume $1,500).

Billed for nursing care	$5,000	
Carrier #1 payment at 80 percent	4,000	
Carrier #2 normal liability	0	
Carrier #2 payment from benefit credits	1,000	to pay 100% of charges
Balance due	0	
(Remaining balance in benefit credits $500)		

Example 2:

Carrier #1 has not paid a $20 charge for an office visit since the insured's $100 deductible has not been met.

Carrier #2 has a $50 deductible which has been met previously and some benefit credits have been accumulated from an earlier claim.

Billed	$20	
Carrier #1 payment	0	
Balance due	20	
Carrier #2 liability paid at 80 percent	16	
Carrier #2 payment from benefit credits	4	to pay 100% of charges
Balance	0	

may do so with at least the mandatory benefits under state no-fault automobile laws and Medicare, which until recently had always been primary.

In 1982, the Tax Equity and Fiscal Responsibility Act (TEFRA) amended the Age Discrimination in Employment Act of 1967 (ADEA) to require employers with 20 or more employees to offer active employees age 65 through 69 and their spouses of the same age, the same coverage offered to younger workers. The employee could choose for Medicare to be either primary or secondary.

The Deficit Reduction Act of 1984 extended those provisions to include 65- through 69-year-old dependent spouses of active employees under age 65. The Consolidated Omnibus Budget Reconciliation Act of

1985 (COBRA) further extended the provisions to include active employees and their dependents who are age 70 or older.

For those employees who choose to continue the employer's plan as primary, there is no additional benefit under Medicare. For active employees who choose it, and for any covered retirees, Medicare is secondary and coordination of benefits can be applied.

Another approach is often used in place of coordination of benefits to avoid duplicate coverage particularly in the case of Medicare. Normal liability under the insured plan is determined and directly reduced by the amount paid by Medicare for the same expenses. This is commonly referred to as carve-out. It attempts to provide the individual eligible for Medicare with the same reimbursement under the insured plan and Medicare together as any other insured would receive under the group medical care insurance plan itself. This same approach also may be applied to "no-fault" benefits.

Other variations have been developed to coordinate benefits for the same charges under several plans. For example, in some cases, a plan is designed to specifically fill the gaps in coverage under the primary plan. This was, at first, a common way to supplement Medicare, but is more difficult to keep current. Whatever the variation, all such approaches have the same objective—cost-control by elimination of overinsurance.

Other Limitations and Exclusions

Care Received in Federal or State Hospitals

Experience revealed many of these hospitals furnish free service except when a patient has insurance coverage, in which case some make a charge for services rendered. Since the existence of insurance coverage should not affect the way a hospital's charges are billed, it is the practice of insurers to honor such claims only when an unconditional requirement exists for a person to pay for the services provided, without regard to the existence of insurance. This type of exclusion is very common, although most government hospitals no longer base their charges on the existence of insurance.

Cosmetic Surgery

This is only covered if it is necessary to correct injuries caused by an accident that occurred while insured, or to correct a congenital anomaly in an insured newborn infant. Elective cosmetic surgery is excluded.

Custodial Care

Since the purpose of health insurance is to provide benefits for the treatment of an injury or sickness, various exclusions and limitations are included to terminate benefits when institutionalization of the patient becomes custodial in nature (i.e., there is no longer any medical care being provided).

Dental Care and Treatment

Care or treatment of teeth and gums is usually excluded, except for treatment required because of accidental injury to natural teeth and charges for hospital confinement for dental treatment. With the rapid growth of group dental expense insurance, care must be taken to avoid duplicate coverage.

Elective Items

There are many services, such as television, telephone charges, air conditioners, swimming pools, bath massagers, and trips to different climates, that a patient can elect to use, which can relate to the illness or injury being treated, but which do not contribute materially to the cure of a patient. Charges for many of these might be billed by a medical care provider, such as a hospital or a physician, or secured with a prescription. Because of the questionable relationship of many of these expenses to medical treatment, they usually are excluded.

Routine Health Examinations

Since there is no illness, these budgetable expenses generally have been expected to be paid by the covered person. However, a trend has developed to include preventive care benefits, such as these, either as part of the basic coverage as described or under the major medical plan.

Occupational Accidents and Sicknesses

No benefits are payable for any medical care expenses resulting from an occupational accident, or from sickness covered by any workers' compensation law or similar legislation. Workers' compensation benefits cover the medical care expenses of a worker for job-related accidents and sicknesses. However, in some jurisdictions, owners and partners are not covered for workers' compensation benefits because, by its definition, they are not considered employees. In these cases, insurers may waive this exclusion for owners and partners provided they meet the definition of employee in the insurance plan.

Purchase or Fitting of Eyeglasses or Hearing Aids and Examinations for Them

These services are considered routine care not expected to result in significant expense to the individual, and are not usually reimbursable. No illness in the usual sense is involved in the majority of cases. Nevertheless, in response to demand, plans have been developed covering these services either as basic or major medical benefits.

War

Injuries or illness because of war, whether declared or undeclared, are excluded from coverage because a substantial catastrophic risk is created that is beyond the scope of group health insurance.

Extension of Benefits

As with basic benefits, major medical benefits will be continued after insurance terminates for an injury or sickness that causes the insured to be totally disabled from the date of termination. However, unless the individual is or becomes covered under another group plan for the same injury or sickness, major medical benefits will be extended for one year rather than the three months provided by basic plans. This extension terminates when the individual is no longer totally disabled by the injury or sickness, if that is earlier than one year from termination.

Survivor Coverage

Although not a standard coverage included in all plans, this provision often was available and added considerably to the value of a medical expense benefit plan. It provided for the medical care insurance in effect for dependents on the date of an employee's death to remain in force, usually without payment of premium, for some specified period ranging from six months to two years from the date of the employee's death. Coverage terminated before the end of that period if the surviving spouse remarried, in which case the coverage for all dependents terminated or if any dependent became insured under another group insurance plan, became eligible for Medicare, or no longer qualified as a dependent according to the terms of the contract. Alternatively, some carriers allowed an employer to maintain coverage on dependents of a deceased employee by continuing to pay the required premium.

This survivor coverage, designed to protect surviving dependents from the sudden termination of benefits as a result of the employee's death has been replaced and broadened by the requirements prescribed by COBRA. The law is effective for the ERISA plan year of each employer that begins on or after July 1, 1986. Broadly speaking, an insured or uninsured plan is required to provide the option to continue benefits for employees and dependents who lose group health benefits because of termination, death, or divorce. The cost of continuation can be passed along to eligible participants up to 102 percent of the cost of benefits to the plan for similarly situated active employees. The continuation period varies based on the reason for loss of benefits, but does not exceed 36 months.

Handicapped Children Provision

As early as 1965, states began to require continuation of coverage on handicapped children beyond the age limit provided by the contract. Today, most states have such mandates and most insurers provide the benefits on all plans nationwide. The child must be unmarried, incapable of self-support because of mental or physical handicap, and primarily dependent upon the employee for support. This provision provides a vehicle for coverage of a group of individuals otherwise likely to be uninsurable.

Conversion Privilege

When insurance terminates under previously described circumstances, the right to convert to a personal medical care policy without evidence of insurability generally is available and mandated by some states. Until recently, only limited hospital, surgical, and medical benefits were required to be included in the converted policy. Since 1973, however, a few states have legislated the availability of major medical benefits as well. Insurers are providing the coverage where required, and investigating alternatives to filling the need for broader coverage under converted policies in the most cost-effective way.

COMPREHENSIVE PLAN VARIATIONS AND DIFFERENCES FROM SUPPLEMENTAL MAJOR MEDICAL

Single Formula

As described earlier, a comprehensive plan, in its simplest form, is a medical care benefit design that covers under one formula those expenses earlier considered basic benefits as well as those included in supplemental major medical benefits. In a pure comprehensive, that formula is applied to reasonable and customary charges without the inside limits of basic benefits, such as maximum hospital days or surgical schedules. Although a comprehensive plan can be written on a per-cause or policy year basis, the all-cause calendar year approach is used almost exclusively. The features described as applying to that type of supplemental major medical plan also apply to a calendar year comprehensive plan or their differences are discussed below.

Deductible and Coinsurance

Unlike supplemental major medical, a comprehensive deductible generally is referred to as an ''initial'' deductible rather than integrated or corridor, since at least in the pure comprehensive, the insured must bear expenses up to the deductible amount before the insurance carrier begins to reimburse for any charges. Further participation by the insured through coinsurance until the out-of-pocket maximum is reached applies in a pure comprehensive just as it does in a supplemental major medical plan.

However, to satisfy the market need for a single easy-to-understand design, but with some first-dollar benefits, many other modifications have been made in comprehensive plans concerning the application of the deductible and of coinsurance. The following are some of the variations available, either individually or in combination, depending on the products and underwriting practices of the insurer.

1. The deductible may be waived on all or on some portion of covered hospital expenses, such as the first $2,000, but applied to hospital expenses above that.
2. Coinsurance may be waived for the hospital expenses described above. Together with waiver of the deductible, this creates the commonly called ''full-pay hospital'' area.
3. The deductible may be waived on surgeons' fees.
4. Surgeons' fees may be payable according to a schedule, plus coinsurance for reasonable and customary fees in excess of the schedule with or without a deductible between.
5. The deductible and coinsurance may be waived in other areas—such as $300 of supplemental accident expenses, physicians' hospital visits, or diagnostic tests—to further match the base-plus major medical concept.
6. The deductible may be waived on certain outpatient services—such as ambulatory surgical facilities, preadmission tests, and second surgical opinions—to encourage their use and to avoid high cost hospital confinements if not necessary.
7. The coinsurance percent reimbursement level may be higher than the coinsurance level for the rest of the plan, increased even to 100 percent for some outpatient services to further encourage their use.

Clearly, as some first-dollar (no deductible) and full-pay (no coinsurance) benefits are built into a comprehensive plan, it becomes more like a base-plus major medical and loses some of its simplicity. Its potential for cost containment may be either diminished or increased depending upon the variation and its utilization.

Maximum Benefit

The overall maximum benefit and its reinstatement provisions apply to the entire comprehensive plan, since there is no separate major medical portion. With the rapid escalation of medical care costs, such earlier maximums as $100,000 or $250,000 typically have been increased to $1 million. Many plans even have an unlimited lifetime maximum.

Preexisting Conditions

The preexisting conditions limitation in supplemental major medical plans, from the beginning, has only applied to the major medical portion of the total plan, because benefits under the basic portion were relatively limited. This allowed some reimbursement for a preexisting condition, but up to controlled maximums. Although basic benefits have become so liberal that large amounts can now be paid under that part of the plan for such a condition, the limitation continues to apply only to the major medical.

Application of the same limitation to a comprehensive plan would be much more restrictive, since it would apply to all benefits. A variation on the theme, therefore, has been developed. It defines a preexisting condition in the same way as for a supplemental major medical plan and covers it from the effective date of insurance, but applies a dollar limit, such as $1,000, for the first year of coverage.

Extension of Benefits

The supplemental major medical one-year extension of benefits after termination for a totally disabling injury or sickness applies to the entire comprehensive plan. The confusion of 3 months for basic benefits and 12 for major medical is eliminated.

SUMMARY

The number of persons covered under some form of major medical insurance continues to grow. To the extent paid for with employer funds, the cost of additional services demanded is felt only very indirectly by the insured; but the pressure driving medical costs upward grows relentlessly. As a result of continued cost escalation, renewed interest exists in medical care plan designs aimed at maintaining the insured's concern with the cost of care by requiring that he or she share in it. The comprehensive plan design fits that bill, but more is clearly required.

Comprehensive hospital utilization review programs including preadmission certification, concurrent review, and discharge planning have become commonplace. They are designed to eliminate unnecessary confinements and reduce length of stay. Preferred provider organizations are also proliferating. Designed and managed in a variety of ways with insurers, employers, providers, and administrators in diverse roles, these arrangements often add provider discounts to utilization review to control costs. In the most common design, insureds can receive services from the provider of their choice, but will have less out-of-pocket expense if a preferred provider is used. These more recent benefit designs provide the flexibility to best serve each policyholder's particular interests and are discussed in detail in later chapters.

CHAPTER 11

DENTAL PLAN DESIGN

Ronald L. Huling

INTRODUCTION

In recent years, dental plans have been one of the nation's fastest growing employee benefits. From 1965 to 1985, dental plan participation grew from 3 million individuals to over 100 million. By 1990, enrollment is expected to exceed 100 million.

It is not surprising that dental plans have become so popular. Over half the U.S. population visits a dentist at least once each year. Also, on average, there are 1.8 visits to the dentist per person per year.

The Difference between Medicine and Dentistry

Medicine and dentistry have many differences, and sound dental plan design recognizes these. Two of the more important differences relate to the location and nature of care.

Location

The practice of the typical physician is hospital oriented, while dentists practice almost exclusively in an office setting. Partly because of these practice differences, physicians tend to associate with other physicians with greater frequency than dentists with other dentists. This isolation, along with the inherent differences in the nature of medical and dental care, tends to produce a greater variety of dental care patterns than is the case in medicine. In addition, practicing in isolation does not afford the same opportunities for peer review and general quality control.

Nature of Care

Perhaps contributing more significantly to the differences in medicine and dentistry are the important differences between the nature of medical and dental care. Medical care usually is mandatory, while dental care is often elective. In medicine, the patient typically visits a physician with certain symptoms—often pain or discomfort—and seeks relief. Whether real or imagined, the patient's perception is that delay can mean more pain and, under certain circumstances, even death. Under these circumstances, the physician's charge for treatment traditionally has not been an issue, perhaps from fear of alienating the individual whom the patient has entrusted with his or her care or perhaps in gratitude for the treatment.

Dental treatment, on the other hand, often is elective. Again, unless there is pain or trauma, dental care often is postponed. The patient recognizes that life is not at risk and as a result has few reservations about postponing treatment. In fact, postponement may be preferable to the patient—perhaps because of an aversion to visiting the dentist, which was rooted many years in the past when dental technology was less well developed.

As a result, dentists' charges for major courses of treatment are often discussed in advance of the treatment where there is no pain or trauma and, like any number of other consumer decisions, the patient may opt to defer the treatment to a later time and spend the money elsewhere.

A second difference in the nature of care is that, while medical care is rarely cosmetic, dental care often is requested for cosmetic purposes. A crown, for example, may be necessary to save a tooth, but it also may be used to correct only minor decay because it improves the patient's appearance. Many people place orthodontia into the same category, although evidence exists that failure to obtain needed orthodontic care may result in major gum problems in later life.

A third major difference between the nature of medical and dental care is that dentistry often offers alternative procedures for treating disease and restoring teeth, many of which are equally effective. For example, a molar cavity might be treated by a two-surface gold inlay, which may cost 10 times as much as a simple amalgam filling. In these instances, the choice of the appropriate procedure is influenced by a number of factors including the cost of the alternatives, the condition of the affected tooth and the teeth surrounding it, and the likelihood that a particular approach will be successful.

There are other significant differences in medical care and dentistry that will have an effect on plan design. These include frequency of treatment, the cost of the typical treatment, and the emphasis on prevention.

When dental and medical plans cover the same or similar groups, there will usually be significantly higher utilization of the dental plan than of the medical plan. For any one company, the relative number of claims between the two plans will be heavily influenced by plan design, particularly the deductible provisions.

Another significant difference is that dental expenses generally are lower, more predictable, and budgetable. The average dental claim check is only about $250. Medical claims, on the average, are much higher.

The last difference of significance is the emphasis on prevention. The advantages of preventive dentistry are clearly documented. While certain medical diseases and injuries are self-healing, dental disease, once started, almost always gets progressively worse. Therefore, preventive care probably is more productive in dentistry than medicine.

Providers of Dental Benefits

Providers of dental benefits generally can be separated into three categories: insurance companies; Blue Cross and Blue Shield organizations; and others including state dental association plans (e.g., Delta plans), self-insured, self-administered plans, and group practice or HMO-type plans. Insurance companies cover, by far, the largest share of the population (about 60 percent of those eligible for dental benefits in 1984). Self-administered, self-insured plans, plans employing third party administrators, dental association plans, and HMOs enroll about 39 percent, and Blue Cross/Blue Shield plans another 9 percent.

Insurance company–administered dental benefits and most self-insured, self-administered plan benefits are provided on an indemnity or reimbursement basis. Expenses incurred by eligible individuals are submitted to the administrator, typically an insurer, for payment; and, if the expense is covered, the appropriate payment is calculated according to the provisions of the plan. Payment generally is made directly to the covered employee, unless assigned by the employee to the provider. When benefits are provided on this basis, the plan sponsor normally has substantial latitude in determining who and what is to be covered and at what level.

The dental benefits of both the dental service corporations and the Blue Cross/Blue Shield plans generally are provided on a "service" basis. The major differences between indemnity and service benefits relate to the roles of the provider and the covered individual. Service benefits are payable directly to the provider, generally according to a contract, which fixes the reimbursement level between the dentist and the plan. In some instances, this payment may actually be lower than what would be charged to a direct-pay or indemnity patient. Despite the differences between the indemnity and service approaches, plan design plays an equally important role in both.

Under the group practice or HMO-type arrangement, a prescribed range of dental services is provided to eligible participants, generally in return for a prepaid, fixed, and uniform payment. Services are provided by dentists practicing in group practice clinics, or in individual practice but affiliated for purposes of providing plan benefits to eligible participants. Many of the individuals eligible under these arrangements are covered through collectively bargained self-insurance benefit trusts. In these instances, trust fund payments are used either to reimburse dentists operating in group practice clinics or to pay the prescribed fixed per capita fee. Group practice HMO-type arrangements generally offer little latitude in plan design. As a result, the balance of this chapter, since it is largely devoted to the issue of plan design, may have limited application to these types of arrangements.

Covered Dental Expenses

Virtually all dental problems fall into eight professional treatment categories:

1. *Diagnostic*. Examination to determine the existence of dental disease or to evaluate the condition of the mouth. Included in this category would be such procedures as X-rays and routine oral examinations.
2. *Preventive*. Procedures to preserve and maintain dental health. Included in this category are topical cleaning, space maintainers, and the like.
3. *Restorative*. Procedures for the repair and reconstruction of natural teeth, including the removal of dental decay and installation of fillings and crowns.
4. *Endodontics*. Treatment of dental-pulp disease and therapy within existing teeth. Root canal therapy is an example of this type of procedure.
5. *Periodontics*. Treatment of the gums and other supporting structures of the teeth, primarily for maintenance or improvement of the gums. Quadrant scraping is an example of a periodontic procedure.
6. *Oral Surgery*. Tooth extraction and other surgery of the mouth and jaw.
7. *Prosthodontics*. Replacement of missing teeth and the construction, replacement, and repair of artificial teeth and similar devices. Preparation of bridges and dentures is included in this category.

8. *Orthodontics*. Correction of malocclusion and abnormal tooth position through repositioning of natural teeth.

In addition to the recognition of treatment or services in these eight areas, the typical dental plan also includes provision for palliative treatment (i.e., procedures to minimize pain, including anesthesia), emergency care, and consultation.

These eight different types of procedures usually are categorized into three or four general groupings for purposes of plan design. The first classification often includes both preventive and diagnostic expenses. The second general grouping includes all minor restorative procedures. Charges in the restorative, endodontic, periodontic, and oral surgery areas are included in this classification. The third broad grouping, often combined with the second, includes major restorative work (e.g., prosthodontics). The fourth separate classification covers orthodontic expenses. Later in this chapter plan design is examined in greater detail, with specific differences evaluated in traditional plan design applicable to each of these three or four general groupings.

Types of Plans

Dental plans covering the vast majority of all employees can be divided broadly into two types: scheduled and nonscheduled. Other approaches discussed below are essentially variations of these two basic plan types.

Scheduled Plans

Scheduled plans are categorized by a listing of fixed allowances by procedure. For example, the plan might pay $25 for a cleaning and $100 for root canal therapy. In addition, the scheduled plan may include deductibles and coinsurance (i.e., percentage cost-sharing provisions). Where deductibles are included in scheduled plans, amounts usually are small, or, in some cases, required on a lifetime basis only.

Coinsurance provisions are extremely rare in scheduled plans, since the benefits of coinsurance can be achieved through the construction of the schedule (i.e., the level of reimbursement for each procedure in the schedule can be set for specific reimbursement objectives). For example, if it is preferable to reimburse a higher percentage of the cost of preventive procedures than of other procedures, the schedule can be constructed to accomplish this goal.

There are three major advantages to scheduled plans:

Cost Control. Benefit levels are fixed and, therefore, less susceptible to inflationary increases.

Uniform Payments. In certain instances, it may be important to provide the same benefit regardless of regional cost differences. Collectively bargained plans occasionally may take this approach to ensure the "equal treatment" of all members.

Ease of Understanding. It is clear to both the plan participant and the dentist how much is to be paid for each procedure.

In addition, scheduled plans sometimes are favored for employee relations reasons. As the schedule is updated, improvements can be communicated to employees. If the updating occurs on a regular basis, this will be a periodic reminder to employees of the plan and its merits.

There also are disadvantages to scheduled plans. First, benefit levels, as well as internal relationships, must be examined periodically and changed when necessary to maintain reimbursement objectives. Second, where participants are dispersed geographically, plan reimbursement levels will vary according to the cost of dental care in a particular area, unless multiple schedules are utilized. Third, if scheduled benefits are established at levels that are near the maximum of the reasonable and customary range, dentists who normally charge at below prevailing levels may be influenced to adjust their charges.

Nonscheduled Plans

Sometimes referred to as comprehensive plans, nonscheduled plans are written to cover some percentage of the "reasonable and customary" charges, or the charges most commonly made by dentists in the community. For any single procedure, the usual and customary charge typically is set at the 90th percentile. This means that the usual and customary charge level will cover the full cost of the procedure for 90 percent of the claims submitted in that geographical area.

Nonscheduled plans generally include a deductible, typically a calendar year deductible of $25 or $50, and reimburse at different levels for different classes of procedures. Preventive and diagnostic expenses typically are covered in full or at very high reimbursement levels. Reimbursement levels for other procedures usually are then scaled down from the preventive and diagnostic level, based on design objectives of the employer.

There are two major advantages to nonscheduled plans.

Uniform Reimbursement Level. While the dollar payment may vary by area and dentists, the percent of the total cost reimbursed by the plan is uniform.

Automatically Adjusts for Change. The nonscheduled plan adjusts automatically, not only for inflation but also for variations in the relative value of specific procedures.

This approach also has disadvantages. First, because benefit levels adjust automatically for increases in the cost of care, in periods of rapidly escalating prices cost control can be a problem. Second, once a plan is installed on this basis, the opportunities for modest benefit improvements, made primarily for employee relations purposes, are limited, at least relative to the scheduled approach. Third, except for claims for which predetermination of benefits is appropriate, it rarely is clear in advance what the specific payment for a particular service will be, either to patient or dentist.

Other approaches are, for the most part, merely variations of the two basic plans. Included in this list are combination plans, incentive plans, and dental combined with major medical plans.

Combination Plan

This is simply a plan in which certain procedures are reimbursed on a scheduled basis, while others are reimbursed on a nonscheduled basis. In other words, it is a hybrid. While many variations exist, a common design in combination plans is to provide preventive and diagnostic coverage on a nonscheduled basis (i.e., a percentage of usual and customary, normally without a deductible). Other procedures than preventive and diagnostic are provided on a scheduled basis.

The principal advantage of a combination plan is that it provides a balance between (1) the need to emphasize preventive care, and (2) cost control. Procedures that are traditionally the most expensive are covered on a scheduled basis, and, except where benefit levels are established by a collective bargaining agreement, the timing of schedule improvements is at the employer's discretion. Preventive and diagnostic expenses, however, adjust automatically so the incentive for preventive care does not lose its effectiveness as dental care costs increase.

The combination approach shares many of the same disadvantages as the scheduled and unscheduled plans, at least for certain types of expenses. Benefit levels—for other than preventive and diagnostic expenses—must be evaluated periodically. Scheduled payments do not reimburse at uniform levels for geographically dispersed participants. And dentists may be influenced by the schedule allowances to adjust their charges. Also, actual plan payments for preventive and diagnostic expenses rarely are identified in advance. Finally, it can be said that the combination approach is more complex than either the scheduled or unscheduled alternatives.

Incentive Plan

This type, a second variation, promotes sound dental hygiene through increasing reimbursement levels. Incentive coinsurance provisions generally apply only to preventive and maintenance (i.e., minor restorative) procedures, with other procedures covered on either a scheduled or nonscheduled basis. Incentive plans are designed to encourage individuals to visit the dentist regularly, without the plan sponsor having to absorb the cost of any accumulated neglect. Such plans generally reimburse at one level during the first year, with coinsurance levels typically increasing from year to year only for those who obtained needed treatment in prior years. For example, the initial coinsurance level for preventive and maintenance expenses might be 60 percent, increasing to 70 percent, 80 percent, and, finally 90 percent on an annual basis as long as needed care is obtained. If, in any one year, there is a failure to obtain the required level of care, the coinsurance percentage reverts back to its original level.

The incentive portion of an incentive plan may or may not be characterized by deductibles. When deductibles are included in these plans, it is not unusual for them to apply on a lifetime basis.

The incentive concept, on the one hand, has two major advantages. In theory, the design of the plan encourages regular dental care and reduces the incidence of more serious dental problems in the future. Also, these plans generally have lower first-year costs than most nonscheduled plans.

On the other hand, there are major disadvantages. First, an incentive plan can be complicated to explain and even more complicated to administer. Second, even in parts of the country where this design is more prevalent, little evidence exists to suggest that the incentive approach is effective in promoting sound dental hygiene. Finally, this particular plan is vulnerable to misunderstanding. For example, what happens if the participant's dentist postpones the required treatment until the beginning of the next plan year?

Plans Providing both Medical and Dental Coverages

The last of the variations is the plan that provides both medical and dental coverage. During the infancy of dental benefits, such plans were quite popular.

These plans generally are characterized by a common deductible amount that applies to the sum of both medical and dental expenses. Coinsurance levels may be identical, and, sometimes, the maximum applies to the combination of medical and dental expenses. However, recent design of these plans has made a distinction between dental and medical expenses so each may have its own coinsurance provisions and maximums.

The advantages of this approach are the same as for the nonscheduled plan (i.e., uniform reimbursement levels, automatically adjusts to change, and relatively easy to understand). But this approach fails to recognize the difference between medicine and dentistry, unless special provisions are made for dental benefits. It must be written with a major medical carrier, whether this carrier is competent or not to handle dental protection; it makes it extremely difficult to separate and evaluate dental experience; and it shares the same disadvantages as the nonscheduled approach.

ORTHODONTIC EXPENSES

With possibly a few exceptions, orthodontic benefits never are written without other dental coverage. Nonetheless, orthodontic benefits present a number of design peculiarities that suggest this subject should be treated separately.

Orthodontic services, unlike nonorthodontic procedures, generally are rendered only once in an individual's lifetime; orthodontic problems are highly unlikely to recur. Orthodontic maximums, therefore, typically are expressed on a lifetime basis. Deductibles, which are applicable only to orthodontic services, also are often expressed on a lifetime basis. However, it is quite common for orthodontic benefits to be provided without deductibles, since a major purpose of the deductible—to eliminate small, nuisance-type claims—is of no consequence.

Because adult orthodontia generally is cosmetic, and also because the best time for orthodontic work is during adolescence, many plans limit orthodontic coverage to persons under age 19. However, an increasing number of plans are including adult orthodontics as well, and many participants are taking advantage of this feature.

The coinsurance level for orthodontia expenses is typically 50 percent, but it varies widely depending on the reimbursement levels under other parts of the plan. It is common for the orthodontic reimbursement level to be the same as what applies for major restorative procedures.

Reflecting the nature of orthodontic work, and unlike virtually any other benefit, orthodontic benefits are often paid in installments, instead of at the conclusion of the course of treatment. Because the program of treatment frequently extends over several years, it would be unreasonable to reimburse for the entire course of treatment at the end of the extended time.

FACTORS AFFECTING THE COST OF THE DENTAL PLAN

A number of factors including design of the plan, characteristics of the covered group, and employer's approach to plan implementation affect the cost of the dental plan.

Plan Design

Many issues must be addressed before determining a particular design that is sound and reflects the needs of the plan sponsor. Included in this list are the type of plan, deductibles, coinsurance, plan maximums, treatment of preexisting conditions, whether covered services should be limited, and orthodontic coverage.

An employer's choice between scheduled and nonscheduled benefits requires a look at the employer's objectives. The advantages and disadvantages of scheduled versus nonscheduled, of combination plans, and of others have been described earlier in this chapter.

Deductibles may or may not be included as an integral part of the design of the plan. Deductibles usually are written on a lifetime or calendar year basis, with the calendar year approach by far the more common.

Numerous dental procedures involve very little expense. Therefore, the deductible eliminates frequent payments for small claims that can be readily budgeted. For example, a $50 deductible can eliminate as much as 40 percent of the number of claims. A deductible can effectively control the cost of claim administration.

However, evidence exists that early detection and treatment of dental problems will produce a lower level of claims over the long term. Most insurers feel the best way to promote early detection is to pay virtually all the cost of preventive and diagnostic services. Therefore, these services often are not subject to a deductible.

A few insurance companies are advocates of a lifetime deductible, designed to lessen the impact of accumulated dental neglect. It is particularly effective where the employer is confronted with a choice of (1) not covering preexisting conditions at all; (2) covering these conditions, but being forced otherwise to cut back on the design of the plan; or (3) offering a lifetime deductible, the theory being, "If you'll spend *X* dollars to get your mouth into shape once and for all, we'll take care of a large part of your future dental needs."

Opponents of the lifetime deductible concept claim the following disadvantages:

- A lifetime deductible promotes early overutilization by those anxious to take advantage of the benefits of the plan.
- Once satisfied, lifetime deductibles are of no further value for the presently covered group.
- The lifetime deductible introduces employee turnover as an important cost consideration of the plan.
- If established at a level that will have a significant impact on claim costs and premium rates, a lifetime deductible may result in adverse employee reaction to the plan.

More and more dental plans are being designed, either through construction of the schedule or the use of coinsurance, so that the patient pays a portion of the costs for all but preventive and diagnostic services. The intent is to reduce spending on optional dental care and to provide cost-effective dental practice. Preventive and diagnostic expenses generally are reimbursed at 80 to 100 percent of the usual and customary charges. Full reimbursement is quite common.

The reimbursement level for restorative and replacement procedures generally is lower than that for preventive and diagnostic procedures. Restorations, and in some cases replacements, may be reimbursed at 70 to 85 percent. In other cases, the reimbursement level for replacements is lower than for restorative treatment.

Orthodontics, and occasionally major replacements, have the lowest reimbursement levels of all. In most instances, the plans reimburse no more than 50 to 60 percent of the usual and customary charges for these procedures.

Most dental plans include a plan maximum, written on a calendar year basis, that is applicable to nonorthodontic expenses. Orthodontic expenses generally are subject to a separate lifetime maximum. Also, in some instances, a separate lifetime maximum may apply to nonorthodontic expenses.

Unless established at a fairly low level, a lifetime maximum will have little or no impact on claim liability and only serves to further complicate design of the plan. Calendar year maximums, though, encourage participants to seek less costly care and may help to spread out the impact of accumulated dental neglect over the early years of the plan. The typical calendar year maximum is somewhere between $750 and $1,500.

To put things in perspective: In 1986, only about 14 percent of people visiting a dentist spent from $300 to $999 annually, including insurance company payments, and just 3.5 percent spent over $1,000 or more, including insurance company payments. Most claims are small (60 percent spent $100 or less) and, therefore, the maximum's impact on plan costs is minor.

Another major consideration is the treatment of preexisting conditions. The major concern is the expense associated with the replacement of teeth extracted prior to the date of coverage. Preexisting conditions are treated in a number of ways:

- They may be excluded.
- They may be treated as any other condition.
- They may be covered on a limited basis (perhaps one half of the normal reimbursement level) or subject to a lifetime maximum.

If treated as any other condition, the cost of the plan in the early years (nonorthodontic only) will be increased by about 6 to 10 percent.

Another plan design consideration is the range of procedures to be covered. In addition to orthodontics, other procedures occasionally excluded are surgical periodontics. Although rare, some plans cover only preventive and maintenance expenses. These plans are becoming more common in cafeteria-type plans where employees often may pick a preventive plan or one more comprehensive.

Orthodontic expenses, as noted, may be excluded. However, where these are covered, the plan design may include a separate deductible to discourage "shoppers." The cost of orthodontic diagnosis and models is about $125, whether or not treatment is undertaken. The inclusion of a separate orthodontic deductible eliminates reimbursement for these expenses. Also, orthodontic plan design typically includes both heavy coinsurance and limited maximums to guarantee patient involvement.

An indication of the sensitivity of dental plan costs to some of the plan design features discussed can be seen in the following illustration. Assume a nonscheduled base model plan, which has a $25 calendar year deductible applicable to all expenses other than orthodontics. The reimbursement, or employer coinsurance, levels are:

- Diagnostic and preventive services (Type I): 100 percent.
- Basic services (Type II), including anesthesia, basic restoration, oral surgery, endodontics, and periodontics: 75 percent.
- Major restoration and prosthodontic (Type III): 50 percent.
- Orthodontics (Type IV): 50 percent.

There also is an annual benefit maximum of $750 for Types I, II, and III services, and a lifetime maximum of $750 for orthodontics. Based on this base model plan, Table 11–1 shows the approximate premium sensitivity to changes in plan design. If two or more of the design changes shown in this table are considered together, an approximation of the resulting value

TABLE 11–1
Model Dental Plan

	Relative Value (in percent)
Base model plan	100%
Design changes	
Deductible	
Remove $25 deductible	112
Raise to $50	92
Raise to $100	82
Benefit maximum (annual)	
Lower from $750 to $500	95
Raise to $1,500	107
Coinsurance	
Liberalize percent to: 100–80–60–60*	110
Tighten percent to: 80–70–50–50*	93
Orthodontics	
Exclude	90

* For Types I, II, III, and IV services, respectively.

may be obtained by multiplying the relative values of the respective changes.

The change in deductibles has a significant impact on cost, as much as an 18 percent reduction in cost to increase the deductible from $25 to $100. The change in benefit maximums has some impact, but it is minor. Coinsurance has a definite effect, especially changes for restoration, replacement, and orthodontic portions of the plan, all of which represent about 80 to 85 percent of the typical claim costs. Finally, the inclusion of orthodontics in the base plan is another item of fairly high cost.

Characteristics of the Covered Group

A second factor affecting the cost of the dental plan is the characteristics of the covered group. Important considerations include, but are not limited to, the following:

- Age.
- Gender.
- Location.
- Presence of fluoride in the water supply.
- Income level of the participants.
- Occupation.

The increased incidence of high-cost dental procedures at older ages generally makes coverage of older groups more expensive. Average charges usually increase from about age 30 up to age 75 or so and then decline. One possible explanation for the decline from age 75 is the existence of prosthetic devices at that point and the generally poor dental habits of the current older generation.

Gender is another consideration. Females tend to have higher utilization rates than males. One study showed that females average 1.9 visits to dentists per year, compared with 1.7 for males. These differences probably are attributable to better dental awareness by females, rather than to a higher need.

Charge levels, practice patterns, and the availability of dentists vary considerably by locale. Charge levels range anywhere from 75 to 150 percent of the national average, and differences exist in the frequency of use for certain procedures as well. There is evidence, for example, that more expensive procedures are performed relatively more often in Los Angeles than, say, in Philadelphia.

Interestingly, the presence of fluoride and the time it has been in the water supply also are important. One recent study showed that the prevalence of tooth decay was 40 percent greater in areas with negligible fluoride than in optimal fluoride ones.

Another consideration is income. A recent study shows that dental care expenditures per participant were 6 to 8 percent higher for members of families with incomes of $28,700 or more (in 1984 dollars) than for participants with family incomes below $19,700. In addition, 74.7 percent of the high-income family members were likely to use the plan compared to only about 57.8 percent of the low-income family members.

Essentially four reasons may account for income being a key factor. First, the higher the income level, the greater the likelihood the individual already has an established program of dental hygiene. Second, in many areas there is greater accessibility to dental care in the high-income neighborhoods. Third, a greater tendency exists on the part of higher income individuals to elect higher cost procedures. Last, high-income people tend to use more expensive dentists.

Another important consideration is the occupation of the covered group. While difficult to explain, evidence suggests considerable variation between blue-collar plans and plans covering salaried or mixed groups. One possible explanation is higher awareness and income-level differences. One insurer estimates that blue-collar employees are 15 to 20 percent less expensive to insure than white-collar employees.

Sponsor's Approach to Implementation

The last of the factors affecting plan costs is the sponsor's approach to implementation. Dental work, unlike medical care, lends itself to "sandbagging" (i.e., deferral of needed treatment until after the plan's effective date). Everything else being equal, plans announced well in advance of the effective date tend to have poorer first-year experience than plans announced only shortly before the effective date. Advance knowledge of the deferred effective date easily can increase first-year costs from 25 to 30 percent or even more.

Employee contributions are another consideration. Dental plans, if offered on a contributory basis, may be prone to adverse selection. While there is evidence that the adverse selection is not as great as was once anticipated, most insurers continue to discourage contributory plans. Many insurance companies will still underwrite dental benefits on a contributory basis, provided there are appropriate safeguards. Typical safeguards include:

- Combining dental plan participation and contributions with medical plan participation.
- Limiting enrollment to a single offering, thus preventing subsequent sign-ups or dropouts.
- Requiring dental examinations before joining the plan and limiting or excluding treatment for conditions identified in the exam.

The last item to be addressed, which is dealt with in several chapters later in this book, is claims administration. The nature of dentistry and dental plan design suggests that claims administration is very important. While several years may lapse before an insured has occasion to file a medical claim, rarely does the year pass during which a family will not visit the dentist at least once. Therefore, claims administration capability is an extremely important consideration in selecting a plan carrier—and might very well be the most important consideration.

One key element of claims administration is "predetermination of benefits." This common plan feature requires the dentist to prepare a treatment plan that shows the work and cost before any services begin. This treatment plan generally is required only for nonemergency services and only if the cost is expected to exceed some specified level, such as $200. The carrier processes this information to determine exactly how much the dental plan will pay. Also, selected claims are referred to the carrier's dental consultants to assess the appropriateness of the recommended treatment. If there are any questions, the dental consultant discusses the treatment plan with the dentist prior to performing the services.

Predetermination is very important both in promoting better quality care and in reducing costs. These benefits are accomplished by spotting unnecessary expenses, treatments that cannot be expected to last, instances of coverage duplication, and charges higher than usual and customary before extensive and expensive work begins. Predetermination of benefits can be effective in reducing claim costs by as much as 10 percent. Predetermination also advises the covered individual of the exact amount of reimbursement under the plan prior to commencement of treatment.

CHAPTER 12

VISION CARE PLANS

Robert M. Neiswanger

INTRODUCTION

Programs providing first-dollar benefits for vision care differ in three ways from most of the other services covered by traditional health benefit programs:

1. The individual is buying a product (except for the eye examination). Consequently, the price of the product depends on the provider's "wholesale" cost. While the charge for a medical product includes a professional component, the provider's charge also reflects the ability to buy in volume from manufacturers or wholesalers and to maintain inventories, and these factors cause retail price variations.

2. Providers are in a highly competitive business as to prices, services, and other factors. As a result, some providers of eye glasses are willing to negotiate special pricing arrangements that will result in discounts in exchange for the possibility of an increased patient volume to the provider.

3. Providing first-dollar benefits for glasses means that the insurance company or administrator must deal with a high volume of comparatively low-charge items. Therefore, the organization paying claims must have a specialized program that is highly automated, requires little claim processor manipulation, and will result in administrative costs that do not significantly increase the total price of the item as compared to what could be expected in the absence of insurance.

PROVIDERS OF CARE

Vision care services are provided by ophthalmologists, optometrists, and opticians whose functions generally are as follows:

Ophthalmologists

An ophthalmologist is a doctor of medicine or osteopathy. Basic graduate education is that of a physician or an osteopath with subsequent specialization and training in defects and diseases of the eye. The ophthalmologist may perform surgery and provides medical care and treatment in addition to prescribing corrective lenses.

Some ophthalmologists also dispense glasses, but the majority give the patient a written prescription and the patient then visits an optician for the preparation of the glasses.

In general, ophthalmologists are located in metropolitan areas because, as physicians who perform eye surgery as well as other vision care services, the ophthalmologist is on the staff of a hospital and his or her practice generally is located within the same geographical area as other physicians who use that hospital.

Optometrist

A doctor of optometry also is trained to perform a variety of ocular diagnostic procedures. The extent to which an optometrist may use pharmaceuticals varies, depending on state licensing requirements. Almost all optometrists dispense glasses in addition to their other professional duties.

There are approximately 20,000 optometrists currently practicing in the United States. While the majority of optometrists are in individual or small group practices, a number of large retail outlets have emerged in shopping centers and other areas where the location of the business is selected to be most attractive to the consumer.

Optician

An optician does not perform eye examinations or diagnose problems of the eye. The optician grinds or molds lenses in accordance with a prescription written by an ophthalmologist or optometrist. The lenses then are fitted into the frame and adjusted to fit the face. In general, the independent optician relies on ophthalmologists for patients.

COVERED SERVICES

As mentioned previously, vision care plans cover both a health service—an eye examination—and a product—lenses and frames.

Eye Examination

The plan covers an eye examination that may be performed by an ophthalmologist or optometrist and involves a case history and a series of tests. Most insurance plans limit covered examinations to one every year or, alternatively, one every two years. The length of the examination varies, depending on many factors, including the extent and nature of tests performed by the examiner. In addition to evaluating the structure of the eye and the possible need for corrective lenses, the examination attempts to detect certain eye diseases, such as glaucoma and cataracts, as well as systemic diseases, such as diabetes and hypertension.

Materials

Lenses

A variety of lenses are available and are prepared from a prescription written by an ophthalmologist or an optometrist. It is not the purpose of this chapter to describe the technical preparation of lenses and frames. Many dispensers order total fabrication, including lenses and frames, from a full-service laboratory. Some dispensers of glasses, however, also may perform certain laboratory services.

While lenses perform an essential corrective function, they may be selected by the individual for aesthetic reasons. For example, many individuals prefer contact lenses even though they are not medically necessary. Others want photosensitive lenses or oversized lenses, and these optional selections increase the price of the product. To control the potential cost of the program, some vision care plans provide limitations on certain types of lenses.

Frames

Frames usually are selected more for appearance than utility. There are over 200 foreign and domestic frame manufacturers and thousands of frame styles to choose from. Most dispensers display several hundred frames and change their display to conform with changes in fashion. Charges for frames vary significantly, particularly for "designer" frames and those endorsed by famous personalities. This range in price, and the highly personalized nature of the individual's frame selection, present certain problems in the design of a vision care plan that pays on a non-schedule basis.

FACTORS AFFECTING CHARGES

In general, the charges for an eye examination do not vary significantly among similar providers within a geographic area, provided the tests and length of the examination are similar.

However, a wide range in prices for glasses, including contact lenses, can exist in large metropolitan areas. Such factors as the number of providers, availability of large chain or retail outlets, and the extent of advertising influence local retail prices. Furthermore, competition exists among manufacturers and laboratories, and that type of price and service competition indirectly affects the retail price of the product.

The competitive price of glasses, plus the wide variety of styles in lenses and frames, makes it virtually impossible to develop precise data on all combinations of products. Unlike other health care services, fees in urban areas may be less than in suburban areas.

MARKET POTENTIAL

Scheduled vision care benefits have been available for many years without generating a significant sales market. Within the past few years, certain large unions have bargained for nonscheduled vision care programs, and details of some bargaining agreements require the establishment of participating provider plans (discussed later in this chapter).

The extent to which carriers may wish to develop a variety of standard vision care products that can be offered to small- and medium-size employers depends on an evaluation of the potential sales market. Programs, such as a participating provider plan, generate start-up costs and require claim and computer functions different from other lines of insurance. The commitment of resources and the ability to amortize administrative costs also are a function of market potential.

A perceived need by employees for the benefit is only one reason an employer may purchase a vision care plan. Nevertheless, those who wear glasses know their price and generally respond favorably to this addition to the firm's benefit package. While the number of people with vision deficiencies tends to increase with age, a typical employee group is likely to include between 40 and 60 percent with vision defects.

Addition of a vision care plan also may produce positive results that are difficult to measure. For example, improved worker productivity and a reduction in the number of accidents may occur. Many people do not wear glasses because of lethargy, vanity, or cost, and the availability of a vision care benefit not only defrays part of the cost but gives publicity to the importance of eye care and prompts some people to place a higher priority on this important health service.

Market potential also is limited because the predictable and elective nature of the service may require the carrier to establish underwriting rules to avoid adverse selection, and these rules preclude quotations on certain cases. Employees often are aware of their need for eye examinations and glasses and the approximate cost. Thus, individuals can determine whether any required payroll deduction is likely to exceed the expected charge for the service. Also, those who know that they do not need glasses would be unlikely to enroll in a contributory plan. Therefore, some carriers may not offer vision care without other lines of coverage which are interlocking with vision care, or unless no employee contributions are required and all employees are to be covered.

BENEFIT DESIGN

There are three basic approaches to designing benefits for a vision care plan. These approaches are the schedule plan, the participating provider plan, and reasonable and customary charge plan. Each approach has advantages and disadvantages and, to date, no one pattern has emerged to dominate the marketplace.

Schedule Plans

These plans list the covered vision services and pay the charges of the provider, but not more than the amount listed for the services in the schedule. Figure 12–1 shows an example of a typical schedule plan.

Advantages

This type of basic approach for vision care has four advantages.

1. A schedule plan is likely to encourage economies on the part of individuals in selecting providers and products. In general, a delivery system that maintains the interest of the individual in price is likely to be less expensive for the employer than a program which may encourage more expensive products.

FIGURE 12–1
A Typical Schedule Plan

Procedure	*Maximum Amount*
Eye examination	$ 30
Lenses (pair)*	
Single vision	25
Bifocal	40
Trifocal	50
Lenticular	75
Frames	20
Contact lenses (pair)*	
1. If visual acuity is not correctable to 20/70 in the better eye, except by the use of contact lenses.	150
2. If the patient is being treated for a condition, such as keratoconus or anisometropia, and contact lenses are customarily used as part of the treatment.	150
3. If required following cataract surgery.	150
4. All other contact lenses.	45

* The maximum amount for a single lens is 50 percent of the amount shown for a pair of lenses.

2. Schedule plans provide greater premium stability for employees because benefit payments do not change with inflation.
3. The schedule plans produce lower claim administrative costs because the plans are simpler to administer.
4. Schedule plans are less confusing to employees because the maximum benefit for each item is known in advance. Nonschedule plans do not cover certain items (these options are discussed later in the chapter) and so the individual who selects an option does not know what will be paid.

Disadvantages

There are three:

1. Some employees interpret schedule amounts to represent the amount that should be charged by the provider. Such an interpretation may lead to ill feelings between employees and providers, particularly if scheduled amounts purposely are designed to be modest.

2. Schedule plans can be designed to bear some relationship to average charges. However, inflation can quickly destroy that relationship and may prompt employee pressures to increase the schedule.
3. Several schedules may be necessary to achieve benefit equity in situations where employees are located in different states.

Participating Provider Plans

Participating provider programs for vision care were developed on the premise that they would be successful because (1) that concept was widely used with prescription drugs, and (2) both programs cover not only a "service" but a product that has an acquisition cost and mark-up by the provider.

The vision care insurer or administrator offers all providers in the area a contract that fixes payment to the participating providers, and stipulates that the provider will not charge insured individuals more than the deductible for covered vision care services and products. Those who agree to this contract are called "participating providers."

Payment for covered services is made directly to the participating provider by the insurance company or administrator. Payments under schedule or under reasonable and customary programs may be made to the individual unless an assignment of benefits has been made to the provider. The formula for determining payment to the provider includes two items: first, the acquisition cost of the lenses and frames (material, laboratory charges and the like); second, the formula includes a dispensing fee (this amount may vary by single vision, bifocals, or trifocals, or there may be a single dispensing fee for all conventional glasses). This formula may vary slightly for medically necessary contact lenses. Reimbursement for contact lenses not medically necessary is expressed as a dollar amount, and that amount is known to the individual. Most plans also reimburse for any sales tax and include requirements concerning the quality of lenses and frames.

The participating provider contract and the fixed payment apply to all of the underwriter's policyholders who purchase plans on a participating provider basis and whose employees receive covered services in the area. However, the amount of the deductible, usually $5, $7, or $10, may vary. Some plans provide that the deductible may be satisfied by all covered services, but other programs use a deductible only for lenses and frames. Such items as the frequency of payment made for examinations and glasses (some plans reimburse once every 12 months, other plans provide benefits once every 24 months) and the specifications on the "covered" lenses and frames also may vary among programs.

The insured individual also may obtain an examination and glasses from providers that do not elect to participate in the plan. In this situation, benefits are paid to the employee, not to the provider. The amount of benefit is based on the determination of reasonable and customary charges and, of course, the employee does not know that amount before the expenses for lenses and frames are incurred.

Advantages

There are three for a participating provider plan:

1. Employees know in advance the exact amount (i.e., the deductible amount) they must pay to obtain covered services from a participating provider. Since that amount is minimal, compared to the full retail charge, individuals are encouraged to have regular examinations and correct lenses.
2. Participating provider agreements include quality assurance requirements. For example, the plan specifies minimum standards for lenses and frames. The participating contract may be cancelled if the provider abuses the plan or does not conform to the stipulated quality standards.
3. The vision care provider may increase the dispensing fee for all participating providers, but the ability to control the timing of that increase provides some of the premium stability of a scheduled plan. Of course, part of the payment formula includes "acquisition cost" of the materials; therefore, increases in material and laboratory costs are passed automatically through to the vision care plan.

Disadvantages

There are five:

1. Individuals who select options not covered by the plan may lose the advantage of knowing what they must pay before agreeing to the service. Furthermore, unless the participating provider contract specifies what the provider charges for options, the plan may provide incentives for the provider to sell options to secure full retail price.

   To evaluate this potential disadvantage, it is helpful to understand what material is covered by the plan. Participating provider contracts specify the plan covers all frames under a specific wholesale price. The participating provider is required to display these frames and, while the selection is broad, some individuals prefer frames with a higher wholesale cost than those covered by the plan. The plan also does not cover all types of lenses. For example, it may not cover prescription sunglasses, tinted lenses, or lenses over a certain size.

Obviously, the provider would prefer to charge full retail for these option items. However, some plans limit the charge to acquisition cost, plus a dispensing fee, because the option does not always generate additional expense for the provider. However, in some cases, options may necessitate counseling by the provider, and some participating provider plans recognize a slightly higher dispensing fee if options are selected.

2. Participating providers need specific employee information before providing services for an individual. For example, if the plan limits glasses to once each two years, the participating provider needs to know that the individual is now eligible for another pair of glasses. This information should be available before the glasses are ordered so the provider may discuss the charge with the individual: deductible, if the glasses are covered, or full retail, if the individual is not eligible. Also, the participating provider needs to know the amounts of the deductible, exclusions, and options.

   This information is furnished in various ways, but any method increases the administrative costs of the plan. Furthermore, if the employee is involved in furnishing advance certification, the procedure employees must follow is different and more complicated than for other health insurance benefits.
3. All providers in the area will not enroll as participating providers. Thus, employees may be dissatisfied because their longstanding provider did not join or because it may be necessary to travel an inconvenient distance to locate a participating provider.
4. Monitoring the quality assurance provisions of a participating provider contract are difficult and expensive. Thus, this feature may not be implemented to reduce plan administrative costs.

Reasonable and Customary Charge Plans

The basis for determining benefit payments under this type of plan is the same as used under traditional health lines for nonscheduled benefits. The payment is specified as a percentage—usually 80 percent—of the provider's charge, but not more than an amount established by the underwriter as the maximum for the procedure. The maximum for each procedure is revised periodically. In general, the maximum allowable covers the charge made by almost all providers in the area.

Advantages
There are three advantages.

1. This plan provides benefit equity because, regardless of geographic location, all individuals receive the same percentage benefit.
2. Employees share in inflation. That is the case because, as retail charges increase, the dollar coinsurance amount paid by the individual also increases.
3. The benefit may be similar to all other health benefits provided by the employer. In other words, if other medical expenses are reimbursed based on a percentage of charges, some employers may prefer to continue that method rather than introducing a more complicated certification system, as would be the case with a participating provider plan.

Disadvantages
There are four:

1. Employees have little incentive to price shop.
2. Claim payments increase with inflation. Thus, policyholder budgeting may necessitate covering past losses, because premium levels may have been inadequate.
3. The wide variation in charges because of product differences, and the low level of charges compared to the amount charged by a physician for a surgical procedure, mean it is difficult to establish maximum charge guidelines for use by claim processors. Guidelines set too low generate excessive administrative expenses and create employee dissatisfaction. For example, if on the one hand the guideline is $40 and the provider charges $45, the reduction of $5 may be more than offset by claim administrative expenses. On the other hand, guidelines set too high do nothing to contain costs.
4. It is difficult to provide a different reimbursement level for "options" and this plan could pay considerably more for items, such as designer frames, than either the schedule or the participating provider plan.

EXCLUSIONS AND LIMITATIONS

Vision care programs usually limit the frequency for eye examinations and glasses. For example, the individual may not have a covered exam and glasses until 24 months have elapsed from the time the last exam or glasses or both, were covered by the plan.

Plans do not provide the same reimbursement for medically necessary contact lenses as for contact lenses primarily for aesthetic purposes. The schedule plan illustrates the manner in which "medically necessary" contact lenses may be defined. In general, even under participating provider or reasonable and customary plans, cosmetic contacts are paid at a specified dollar amount.

Nonschedule plans also provide that certain services are optional and not subject to the full provisions of the plan. For example, if the individual wishes oversized lenses, plan reimbursement is intended to be at the same level as would have been provided for standard-size lenses.

Of course, vision care programs exclude eye services covered under the traditional health program. A sample list of other exclusions follows:

1. Lenses that can be obtained without prescription.
2. Orthoptics, vision training or subnormal vision aids.
3. Any service or supply not listed as a covered service or supply.
4. Benefits provided under workers' compensation.

TYPES OF VISION CARE PROVIDERS

Many types of underwriters can make available vision care benefit plans. Two of the more common providers are insurance companies and Blue Cross/Blue Shield organizations.

Alternative mechanisms that administer vision care programs are:

1. Local providers may band together to offer the group purchaser a "closed panel" type of delivery mechanism. These groups may be reimbursed on the traditional fee-for-service, or by acquisition cost plus dispensing fee or capitation system.

2. The employer may contract directly with the same organization that provides safety glasses for plant employees. Employees may obtain lenses and frames and other services either at no cost or at a discount.

3. Specialty companies also have been established that are not closely related to the providers of vision care services. These companies are similar to the specialty organizations that administer prescription drug programs and sell their administrative services. They have recognized there is currently a limited market for service-type participating provider vision care, but that market requires a specialized product and administration. All the traditional insuring and administrative mechanisms may not establish these programs because of start-up and administrative costs. Thus, the specialty company markets its networks and administrative skills to others who may wish to establish vision care programs.

Employer/buyers of group vision care programs should consider more than the traditional competitive factors (rates, retention, service, and the like) in selecting a mechanism for a participating provider program. If reimbursement is to be based on acquisition cost plus dispensing fee, the employer should know who will establish the amount of dispensing fee and how often that fee is to be redetermined. While the dispensing fee must be sufficient to attract a reasonable number of participating providers, it should not be so high as to unnecessarily increase claim payments. It is also important for the employer to know the extent of participating provider networks. Some employers prefer relatively few participating providers, but others want a broad network, including all provider specialties. Furthermore, buyers should be certain the type of lenses and frames covered by the participating agreement offer both quality and style that is pleasing to most employees.

CONCLUSION

Vision care benefits are examples of the expansion of employee benefits to cover high-frequency, low-cost medical services, as opposed to the more traditional concept of insurance as a means of protecting the individual from major financial loss.

It is clear employees are receptive to programs that reimburse for such items as dental expenses, prescription drugs, and glasses. While taken as a single expense, any one of these items is affordable for most people in the employed population; nevertheless, these expenses often are incurred in combination and their total, particularly for individuals with families, can represent a large financial commitment for the employee.

Finally, it is important that claim procedures be as efficient and accurate as possible so the presence of a benefit does not greatly increase the "cost" of the medical service by the addition of significant claim administration costs. In fact, most programs have been successful in that objective.

CHAPTER 13

PRESCRIPTION DRUG PLANS

Robert M. Neiswanger

There are essentially three different methods of reimbursing prescription medications under insurance programs. Of course, medication dispensed while in a hospital is an item included in the institution bill and reimbursed under that portion of the program.

Historically, prescription drugs have always been one of the broad range of medical expenses covered under standard major medical type programs. There may be some minor variations as to prescriptions covered by the program. For example, some carriers may cover any medication that is prescribed by a physician, and other plans limit prescription drugs to those medications that cannot be dispensed without a prescription (sometimes referred to as ''legend'' drugs).

Separating prescription drugs from a major medical program and providing reimbursement as a distinct benefit has become practical because of the development of high speed, automated claim systems. Some insurance companies and specialty administrative organizations have constructed special automated claim systems that can process the high volume of prescription claims. Consequently, prescriptions can be covered in full with deductibles of only $1 or $2 per prescription. This approach is often referred to as a ''card'' system because identification cards are issued in order to provide easy verification of coverage for the pharmacy.

The third major development in reimbursing prescription drugs is to use mail prescription services. Many individuals, particularly those in an older population, require maintenance rather than emergency prescriptions. Insurance companies or special administrators can arrange favorable pricing arrangements with mail prescription services for people who are on maintenance drugs and can wait several days to have their prescription filled.

Each of these three approaches has advantages and disadvantages.

MAJOR MEDICAL PROGRAM

Prescription drugs covered under major medical programs are subject to a deductible and coinsurance and reimbursed with any other expense covered by the program. Advantages of this type of program are:

1. The individual can fill the prescription at any licensed pharmacy.
2. Some employers believe that relatively minor expenses should be paid out of pocket by the individual. The deductibles and coinsurance eliminate small prescription bills, but provide reimbursement to individuals whose total covered medical expense exceeds the deductible.
3. Prescriptions are treated in a consistent manner with other covered medical expenses. Consistency may avoid requests from individuals who incur other types of medical expenses—physician visits or durable medical equipment—that those services be paid on a more liberal basis.

Disadvantages are:

1. Charges for drugs represent full retail price even though some pharmacists might be willing to negotiate in advance with the insurance company for a lower pricing arrangement that would attract more patients to the pharmacy.
2. Applying the reasonable charge cost containment provision is not practical for prescription drugs. Within communities, prices for specific prescriptions can vary significantly because of factors that influence the wholesale cost of the drug to the pharmacist and the pharmacist's pricing and marketing strategies. Furthermore, the charge for an average prescription is so low that claim administrative costs of determining whether the charge is reasonable are likely to be greater than any savings that may result from a reduction in the claim payment.
3. Claim processors may have difficulty in determining whether a pharmacy bill is for a medication that can be dispensed only with a prescription. Consequently, errors may be made in claim payments.

4. If prescription charges are submitted as incurred, the claim processing system is likely to be inefficient since it must evaluate each of the claim submissions in terms of satisfaction of the deductible. In an effort to solve this problem, some carriers ask individuals to submit all prescriptions at specific times or only after they have exceeded the deductible amount.

CARD SYSTEMS

Card system programs are preferred provider arrangements. The insurance company or administrative organization, offers specific pharmacies contracts that prospectively fix the prices of all prescriptions filled by that pharmacy to covered individuals.

The reimbursement agreement usually includes two parts. The first part is the wholesale price of the drug. In some cases, the formula may provide for a wholesale cost at "average wholesale price" because that figure is available in several pharmacy publications and can be checked by the claim system. Some programs may reimburse on "actual wholesale price," but that figure may be more difficult to determine.

The second part of the formula includes a flat dispensing fee that is usually $3 or $4 for each prescription. The amount of that fee is established by the insurance company or administrative organization and may vary geographically.

The program covers drugs that can be dispensed only by a prescription (legend drugs) but also may cover certain specified nonlegend items such as insulin. The plan usually limits the amount dispensed to a 30-day supply or 100 unit dosages. Prescriptions in excess of these amounts are treated as a refill and payable as a separate prescription.

Card systems are possible because of automated claim processing systems that can evaluate and process a large volume of low-charge items. In order to reduce administrative costs, and to provide the participating pharmacy with an immediate method of determining whether the individual is covered by the plan, programs of this nature issue identification cards. The card, which usually contains an expiration date, is presented by the individual, together with the prescription, to a participating pharmacy. The individual is then required to pay a deductible, usually $1 or $2 per prescription, and receives the medication.

The pharmacy submits, usually in bulk, all covered prescriptions to the insurance company at specified periods during the month. These claims are processed and a single check issued to the participating pharmacy for all the claims represented by the submission. Reimbursement for each of these claims is based on the contract formula, less the employee-per-prescription deductible.

Most programs of this nature also provide that the individual can obtain prescriptions from nonparticipating pharmacies. However, the individual is required to pay for the prescription and submit a claim form to the insurance company. Out-of-pocket expenses for employees who use nonparticipating pharmacies are usually greater than they are for participating pharmacies. The financial incentive of the participating provider card program (payment of only a $1 or $2 deductible), and the convenience of the program are such that most people fill prescriptions at participating pharmacies. In the past, carriers and administrators have established contracts with most pharmacies within a community, so access to participating pharmacies has not been a problem for most employees.

In the future, preferred provider prescription card systems may change to exclusive provider arrangements. This would require that the individual obtain prescriptions only from participating providers to receive any reimbursement under the program.

Advantages to the card system are:

1. Reimbursement to participating pharmacies is negotiated in advance by the insurance company or administrator and can be expected to produce some savings for the employer.
2. Individual out-of-pocket expense is negligible (usually $1 or $2), thus the individual is more likely to fill the prescription than under any other type of program. There are some indications that, under conventional plans, some individuals may not fill prescriptions ordered by their physicians. One reason may be the cost of the prescription.
3. Employees react favorably to the program because they are issued an identification card and many people receive some benefit.
4. Specialized claim systems are programmed so as to accurately reimburse only for legend or other drugs covered by the program and to correctly apply reimbursement formulas. Consequently, claim payment errors are reduced.

Disadvantages of the program are:

1. Issuance of ID cards to employees can result in benefits being paid to some terminated individuals. Consequently, most employers with card programs attempt to retrieve prescription drug ID cards at termination of employment. Furthermore, cards contain an expiration date that also provides some protection from abuse.
2. There is a potential for abuse or fraud by unscrupulous pharmacies because all billing is submitted directly to the insurance com-

pany or administrative organization. As a result, some in-store audits should be performed.

3. As with any participating provider program, some individuals must change providers to obtain the financial incentives. In most cases, the insurance company's network of participating pharmacies is broad enough to provide easy access for employees.

Pharmacies also may be part of a health maintenance organization (HMO) network. The pharmacy can be paid on a capitation basis, and people enrolled in the HMO must obtain their medication only from the designated network pharmacy.

MAIL-ORDER PRESCRIPTIONS

A substantial number of prescriptions, particularly for elderly individuals, are for maintenance rather than emergency medication. Arrangements can be made with mail prescription services so that covered individuals may send prescriptions directly to the mail service and receive the filled prescription through the mail.

This arrangement can be implemented either with a traditional major medical program or a card program. However, in order to provide a financial incentive to individuals to use the mail order service, reductions are made in deductibles and/or coinsurance. Care must be taken so that these reductions do not more than offset the potential savings that may result from favorable prospective pricing agreements with mail order services.

Advantages of mail prescription services include:

1. Reimbursement is negotiated in advance between the insurance company or administrative organization and the mail prescription service. Since only one or two outlets will be offered to employees, the mail prescription service can anticipate an increase in volume and that should result in a favorable pricing arrangement.
2. Unless specified otherwise by the physician or patient, the mail prescription service can fill the prescription generically. Often, prices for generic drugs are less than for trade name drugs.
3. The program does not provide limited dosage sizes as is the case in card systems. For example, an individual who is on a maintenance drug under a card system must refill the prescription each 30 days, and the participating pharmacy is paid the wholesale price plus dispensing fee for each refill. For example, if the wholesale price for the drug is $10 and the dispensing fee is $3, the

participating pharmacy will receive $39 if the physician ordered a 90-day supply. If a mail order house fills the prescription for the full 90-day supply, there will be a savings of $6 to the plan (greater savings are possible with lower dispensing fees). Some mail prescription programs include the cost of postage in the reimbursement formula.

4. The prescription is mailed directly to the individual's home, and that may be more convenient for elderly people.

Disadvantages are:

1. The carrier or administrative organization must be convinced that the mail prescription outlet maintains tight quality control over material dispensed in the program.
2. In some cases, an individual may obtain prescriptions for different drugs from more than one doctor. Some prescriptions cause adverse reactions when taken in conjunction with other medication. If all prescriptions are filled by the individual through a single pharmacy, that pharmacist can identify prescriptions that are incompatible with other medication being taken by the individual. That may be more difficult to do with a mail order prescription service.
3. Individuals who obtain a 90- or 180-day supply of a prescription may not use all of the medication. As a result, wastage could actually increase the cost to the employer's program as compared to a plan in which the individual could obtain only a 30-day supply of the medication.

CHAPTER 14

GROUP DISABILITY INCOME BENEFITS

Donald J. Doudna

Losing the ability to work can be devastating to a family's emotional and financial well-being. Yet, the exposure of disability often is neglected by families in their financial planning and not dealt with sufficiently by employee benefit plans. After a brief analysis of the disability exposure, this chapter focuses on issues in providing disability income coverage for employee groups and the various approaches available to meet this loss exposure.

POSSIBILITY OF DISABILITY

The possibility of losing earnings due to an accident or illness is significant. In 1985, 33 million persons, 14 percent of the U.S. civilian noninstitutional population, suffered a limitation of activity because of one or more chronic conditions.[1] It is estimated that one out of four adults between ages 55 and 64 is so severely disabled, they cannot work regularly if at all.[2] Table 14–1 indicates the probability of a disability lasting three months or longer for various age groups.

---

[1] *1986–87 Source Book of Health Insurance Data* (Washington, D.C.: Health Insurance Association of America, 1988) p. 61.

[2] *Transactions, Society of Actuaries,* Report of the Committee to Recommend New Disability Tables for Valuation (individual rate) vol. XXXVII, 1985, p. 574.

TABLE 14–1
Group Long-Term Disability Insurance Crude Rates of Disablement per 1,000 Lives Exposed (Three-Month Elimination Period: Calendar Year of Issue Excluded; Calendar Years of Experience 1976–80)

All Experience Units Combined

Attained Age	*Life Years Exposed*	*Number of Claims*	*Rate of Disablement per 1,000 Lives*
	All Experience, Males, Females, and Sex Unknown		
Under 40	552,098	1,153	2.09
40–44	103,139	390	3.78
45–49	92,824	584	6.29
50–54	83,973	722	8.60
55–59	66,678	970	14.55
60–64	40,471	805	19.89
All ages	939,183	4,624	4.92

Source: *Transactions, Society of Actuaries*, 1982 Reports of Mortality and Morbidity Experiences, 1985, p. 297.

Although results vary among employee groups, it is evident the possibility of disability is an exposure that should be considered thoroughly. This chapter provides some historical perspective on disability insurance, an overview of available disability coverages, an analysis of issues in plan design, and a discussion of administration and cost-saving procedures of the plans.

GROUP COVERAGES AVAILABLE

Historical Perspective

Following the adverse claims experience of the 1930s, insurers were reluctant to provide disability income coverages again until about three decades ago. Some of the adverse claims experience in the early years of disability insurance, of course, can be attributed to the Great Depression. Even if the economy had been stable the probability of negative disability income insurance results was high for several reasons. First, the definitions of disability in the early contracts were extremely liberal, and thus an inordinately high number of cases received benefits. Second, insurers in the disability income market used a flat rate structure. Prices were charged per unit of income replaced, with the same premium sometimes being applied to all ages. Third, insurers neglected to use underwriting safeguards, such as a maximum cutoff age for benefits, and some disability income benefits that should have been terminated earlier, continued for life. These reasons, accompanied by the economic pressures caused by the Depression, encouraged overfiling, and insurers in the 1930s found themselves with inadequate reserves and several years of substantial losses.

Although hospital indemnity policies were revived and became profitable in the early 1950s, disability income protection was not readily available until the 1960s when it became available from two primary sources. The Social Security program initiated a disability income program for disabled workers over the age of 50, and by 1960 an amendment had been passed to provide this protection to workers of all ages. The Social Security disability income program was characterized by a very strict definition of disability and a six-month waiting period. To be eligible for benefits, a claimant had to be incapable of performing any substantial gainful employment, and many persons, though ill or injured, could not meet the "definition-of-disability" or "waiting-period" requirements of this program. When collective bargaining units across the country became aware their disabled members might not be able to collect governmental benefits, they encouraged insurers to make coverage available for the varying needs of their members. Therefore, products were designed to cover a worker who could not perform his or her *own occupation* with benefits that could start after a waiting period of as little as one day and could continue until retirement. Thus began the emergence of short- and long-term disability income coverages as we know them today. The following section describes short- and long-term coverages available today through private insurers or by self-funding.

Short-Term Disability

Short-term disability income benefits apply to cases in which the injured or ill worker is unable to perform the duties of his or her current position. Benefits may be paid for as short a period as one week or may continue for as long as 26 weeks. Although some short-term plans provide income beyond 26 weeks, (some for as long as 52 weeks), 26 weeks normally is considered the break point between short-term and long-term plans. Benefit duration often is dependent upon the length of time an employee has served the employer. Income replacement for short-term disability is available from four major sources: (1) self-funded sick leave plans; (2) insured income replacement plans; (3) state-mandated plans (found in California, Hawaii, New York, New Jersey, Rhode Island, and Puerto Rico); and (4) workers' compensation.

For short periods of disability, say between 1 and 10 days, the employer may continue the worker's entire salary as though the worker had been on the job. This arrangement, called a sick leave plan, normally is self-funded. It is common in such a plan to allow an employee to carry unused benefit days from one year to the next (usually up to some maximum number of days), thereby enabling an employee to "bank" or "save" days to be used in the event of an extended illness or disability. Some sick leave plans provide additional days of sick leave as the length of service with the employer increases. For example, an employer might provide 10 sick leave days the first year and an additional 10 days for each year of service up to a maximum of 180 sick leave days. Unused sick leave days could be carried forward to arrive at the maximum more quickly. Sick leave plans are common for salaried personnel and often are combined with insured long-term disability plans.

Another plan is a group insured or self-insured income replacement plan. To qualify for short-term disability benefits under this group plan, an employee must be unable to work and be off the job, usually for a minimum of five working days because of illness, or one day because of accident. Waiting periods vary, but the general intent is to discourage staying off the job. An attempt is made to assure that the benefit program is not abused because it provides too much income replacement. Income replacement is stated in terms of hundreds of dollars per week or, more commonly, as a percentage of salary. A common benefit agreement replaces 50 to 66.6 percent of gross salary for up to 26 weeks. Newer plans may give a benefit based upon take-home pay or spendable income.

In both insured and self-insured cases payments are considered wages and thus subject to income, social security, and unemployment taxes. Social security and unemployment taxes are not applicable after six months of benefit. However, income tax continues on both short- and long-term insurance benefits for which the employer paid premiums.

Long-term Disability (LTD) Insurance

Long-term disability insurance is characterized by a program that provides income replacement on an insured or formalized self-insured program for a period starting after six months and lasting for the duration of the disability (or until normal retirement age). The definition of disability under the long-term plans usually is broken into two parts. During the first two years of disablement, employees must be disabled to the extent they cannot perform the duties of their own occupations. To quote from a standard contract, "Total disability for the purposes of this policy means the complete inability of the person due to accidental bodily injury or sickness or both during the first 24 months of such disability to perform any and every duty pertaining to his or her own occupation." If the person remains disabled after 24 months, the second part of the definition applies: "Benefits will continue during any continuation of such disability following the first 24 months of disability if the person is unable to engage in any work or occupation for which he or she is reasonably fitted by education, training, or experience."

Most long-term disability programs have either a three-month, six-month, or one-year waiting period. The most common waiting period historically has been six months. After the waiting period, long-term disability plans provide benefits to injured or ill employees until the point they are able to return to work. However, benefit payments for long-term disability usually end at retirement age and cease earlier if the disabled participant should die. Because of amendments to the Age Discrimination in Employment Act (ADEA), coverage for active employees cannot be terminated because of age.

The amount of income replaced by LTD benefits usually is based upon gross salary, with some monthly limitation or maximum. In long-term plans, income is often replaced at a rate of 50–66.6 percent, but can be as much as 75–80 percent of gross income.

ISSUES IN DESIGN

Eligible Groups

Whether a group of employees or labor union members can obtain disability coverage depends upon a number of factors. Key factors in eligibility are group size, sex, age, occupation, and income.

Group Size

Many long-term disability carriers restrict their group disability policies to groups with a minimum of 10 participants. If smaller groups desire coverage, individual underwriting applies, and other lines of coverage often must be purchased to obtain long-term disability for small groups. Although smaller groups may require individual underwriting, claims experience indicates "jumbo" groups with over 5,000 participants also may produce a high incidence of disability. As the group becomes extremely large, there may be a loss of employer control or interest, or both. Thus, groups at both ends of the spectrum may produce a higher incidence of disability and cost the employer more.

Gender

Discussion has arisen over the reason for rate variation based upon the number of females in a group. Table 14–2 demonstrates the statistical difference in incidence of disability for males and females.

As can be seen from Table 14–2, females have a higher incidence of disability than men at younger ages, but a lower incidence at older ages, and their overall morbidity factor is approximately 10 percent greater than for men. Thus, in some organizations with a high percentage of young female workers, disability rates may increase by as much as 25 percent.

TABLE 14–2
Group Long-Term Disability Insurance Rate of Disablement by Gender per 1,000 Lives Exposed (Calendar Years of Experience 1976–1980)

Six-Month Elimination Period	*Male Experience*	*Female Experience*
Under 40	1.02	1.39
40–44	2.02	3.04
45–49	3.56	4.52
50–54	6.33	7.41
55–59	12.20	10.88
60–64	16.63	12.98
All ages	3.78	3.40
Three-Month Elimination Period	*Male Experience*	*Female Experience*
Under 40	1.70	2.83
40–44	3.41	4.84
45–49	5.75	7.67
50–54	8.35	9.50
55–59	15.41	13.30
60–64	21.26	17.63
All ages	4.85	5.24

Source: *Transactions, Society of Actuaries*, 1982 Reports on Mortality and Morbidity, 1985, p. 279.

Some insurers are concerned about the movement toward the unisex mortality and morbidity table. There may be valid reasons for using this table in long-term disability insurance, but these reasons probably do not apply for short-term. Maternity and related illnesses increase group rates for groups that have short waiting periods, but group plans with at least a six-week waiting period are not affected as much by this morbidity factor.

Age

Age is a key factor in the eligibility of a group for both short- and long-term disability coverage, and is even more important in determining the rate to be paid than are group size and gender. The Society of Actuaries *Reports on Mortality and Morbidity Experiences,* show that disabled rates vary significantly from the younger to older ages. See Table 14–3.

The ages of participants in a group affect the number of claims that will occur over the years. Young workers (between ages 20 and 40) have a small probability of disablement and a great capacity for retraining. Young workers have significant incentive to regain their capacity and, therefore, little moral hazard of malingering exists. In most cases, the cost of insuring groups of young employees should be reasonable. However, a large claim reserve may be required to cover the possibility of a young worker becoming seriously disabled.

TABLE 14–3
Group Long-Term Disability Insurance Crude Rates of Disablement per 1,000 Lives Exposed (Six-Month Elimination Period; Calendar Years of Experience 1976–1980)

Attained Age	*Life Years Exposed*	*Number of Claims*	*Rate of Disablement per 1,000 Lives*
	All Experience: Males, Females and Sex Unknown		
Under 40	2,154,087	2,491	1.16
40–44	440,458	1,009	2.29
45–49	427,019	1,620	3.79
50–54	396,023	2,611	6.59
55–59	314,773	3,717	11.81
60–64	177,339	2,708	15.27
All ages	3,909,699	14,156	3.62

Source: *Transactions, Society of Actuaries,* 1982 Reports of Mortality and Morbidity Experiences, 1985, p. 279.

TABLE 14–4
ADEA Option for Benefits

Employee Attained Age at Disablement	*Maximum Months of Income Replacement*
62	42
63	36
64	30
65	24
66	21
67	18
68	15
69	12

Source: Group Contract, The Principal Mutual Life Insurance Company, Des Moines, Iowa.

The probability of sustaining a disability is much greater at older ages. About 80 percent of disabilities in older people are caused by sickness or disease and not by accidental injury. Therefore, if the mean age of the insurance group is high, the probability of disablement caused by sickness is high. Claims tend to last longer among older workers, because of lower educational levels and inability to be trained for other positions.

While the increase in retirement age and the passage of amendments to the Age Discrimination in Employment Act (ADEA) could have a significant impact upon disablement rates, it is too early to know what the exact impact will be. As more workers continue in their jobs after age 65, increased claims may occur. The ADEA, as amended, prohibits forced retirement, but in benefit programs it is still possible to provide for shorter benefit durations without discriminating against an older person. For example, if a working person at age 69 became disabled, the benefits could still be cut off at retirement at age 70.[3] Therefore, the reserve and the cost for that disabling condition would be minimal. If disability occurred between the ages of 62 and 65, a stated number of months of disability income might be provided. Under some plans, if the person becomes disabled prior to age 62, benefits under the disability program are limited to 60 months. In another example, if the person becomes disabled after reaching age 62, the amount of benefit will be based on a sliding schedule as demonstrated in Table 14–4.

---

[3] Under a 1987 ADEA law change disabled employees 70 years of age or older must receive a minimum of 12 months of disability benefits.

In summary, if the group has a high percentage of persons over the age of 60, the potentiality for an increase in disability incidence is present. However, the duration of that disability can be limited by a benefit cutoff age.

Occupation

Claim frequencies vary from one occupation to another, and each class of occupation demonstrates a distinctive accident and sickness frequency. That is, working with steel is more hazardous than working with a computer and thus produces more disabilities. Although workers' compensation provides benefits for occupational injuries, group disability plans may still be affected. In some jurisdictions, workers' compensation income replacement does not begin until after a three to seven-day waiting period, and thus claims could be paid out of a short-term sick leave plan. Additionally, some workers' compensation benefits are inadequate, and the group plan would be needed to supplement income replacement. A long-term disability program may be affected further because of the susceptibility of certain occupations to various chronic conditions. For instance, people employed in mining or chemical industries may develop serious heart or lung conditions, and these ailments may or may not be ruled to have resulted from occupational hazards. If workers' compensation benefits are not awarded, group disability benefits probably will be paid.

Job classification of the employee also may affect disability plans. Historically, hourly paid and lower-paid workers either were declined or rated very heavily. This rating may be attributable to overinsurance problems, discussed later in this chapter. Whether a group is insurable may depend on the percentage of workers in hourly paid or lower-paid positions and the type of job performed. Each insurer has a different underwriting standard, but it is not uncommon, for example, to decline groups involved in agriculture, fishing, chemicals, entertainment, or construction.

Duration

Certain employees may be considered ineligible for coverage because of their age or occupational status. It is common to exclude seasonal or part-time employees from disability plans, as well as persons who have been working for the firm a short time, even if they are employed on a full-time basis. If qualification procedures have been met, there generally is a waiting period before disability income benefits begin. As mentioned previously, waiting periods for short-term disability range from 1 day because of accident, and 7 days because of illness, to 7 days because of accident, and 14 days because of illness. In long-term plans, waiting periods range from one month to one year.

Disability income benefits continue as long as the definition of disability is met and are paid according to the contractual provision until one of several things occurs. First, disability contracts require that the participant be under the care of a physician and that statements to that effect be made on a regular basis. Payments terminate when the participant stops receiving this care. Death of the participant, of course, will terminate disability benefits. In short-term plans, most disability benefits are terminated when the employee has returned to work or has been paid for the maximum number of weeks, and in long-term plans, benefits are terminated when the definition of disability can no longer be met. Because of the two-stage definition of disability discussed earlier, it is normal for an individual to go off benefit status at the end of the 24-month "*own* occupation" definition of disability. If such person continued to be disabled under the "*any* occupation" definition, disability benefits could continue to age 65 or 70 depending on how the benefit package is coordinated with any pension plan that may be in effect. If the pension plan is so set up that retirement income can begin at age 65, disability income stops at that point. If there is no pension plan, disability income should continue until age 70 or until contractual provisions are met. Proper drafting of a disability and pension plan should include some provision for accrual of pension benefits during disablement. If no disability program exists, pension plans often allow early retirement benefits because of disability.

Amount of Benefits

Two perspectives on the amount of income to be replaced by disability income benefits may be valid. Some benefit managers believe disability income should be high enough to allow disabled persons to continue in their normal lifestyle, while others believe disability benefits should be closer to a subsistence level, thereby encouraging employees to return to work. In either case, the goal is to control overall income in a way that discourages malingering. Historically, some firms did not consider that income might be available to participants from several sources, and that participants might collect from various other plans as well as from the employer-provided disability plan. Today, target replacement is in the range of 60 to 70 percent of gross salary, with an offset for benefits received from other sources such as Workers' Compensation and Social Security. Even at this level, overinsurance may result if the disabled party is collecting from several sources. For example, an employee might have an 80 percent replacement of spendable income under workers' compensation and a minimum payment from a disability income plan. This might provide more real income after disability than before. Contributory disability plans should be analyzed carefully, because benefits received as a result of participant premiums are received income-tax free. Thus, the benefit manager faces the task of determining an income replacement level that allows the disabled party to live in a reasonable fashion, but not to the extent that the worker will have so much income that no incentive exists to return to work. The problem is particularly acute for young hourly paid and lower-paid workers because of the amount of income potentially available from Social Security. A high-income replacement percentage from Social Security, combined with a benefit from a disability income plan, may cause an overinsurance problem.

The increase in cost attributable to the overinsurance is not easily quantified. Insurers agree, however, that overinsurance increases both frequency and duration or continuation of claims. Some figures are available concerning cost consequences of increasing the aggregate income level from a 50 percent benefit to a 60 or 70 percent benefit. In a typical group, an increase from 50 to 60 percent of gross income might increase premiums by as much as 50 percent. An increase from 50 to 70 percent could increase premiums by as much as 90 percent. This change of premium reflects an increase in both annuity value and in claims frequency. Careful analysis should be made to assure all offsets are known, and managers need to explicitly state offsets for primary and family Social Security benefits, workers' compensation benefits, and pension and other group insurance benefits. All salary continuation benefits or sick leave plans also should be taken into consideration.

A topic related to the percentage of monthly income to be replaced is the maximum amount of such income to be replaced. In older plans it was common to replace a maximum of $2,000 to $3,000 per month, while newer plans are shifting to $5,000 and $10,000 monthly limits. It is desirable to provide a higher level of income because of inflation, but a reasonable maximum should still be selected. For highly compensated employees, particularly if a plan is contributory, $10,000 per month may cause a problem. On the other hand, if a person were earning $7,000 a month prior to disability, a $2,500 maximum benefit could cause a severe economic strain on the person's family. In cases of highly compensated employees, individual insurance with a higher limit may be purchased or self-insurance may be used to supplement the group plan.

Limitations and Exclusions

Group disability plans have some limitations and exclusions. Some plans have a preexisting clause. That clause could say, "We the insurance company will not pay for disabling conditions that commence within 12 months after the effective date of the person's insurance if the person received treatment or service for such disability during the 3-month period preceding the effective date of his or her insurance." The time periods may vary, but the concept is the same. If a person has been receiving treatment or has been off work because of disabling conditions, or both, he or she may not have group coverage benefits available until the coverage has been in effect for a minimum of 12 months. In addition, a limitation for disability because of intentional or self-inflicted injury is found in most contracts. It also is common to have a limitation or exclusion for disability because of war or any act of war, declared or undeclared.

In the past, disability contracts had two-year benefit limitations for alcoholism, drug addiction, and mental and nervous disorders; but such limitations are being used less frequently now; in many accident and sickness policies, alcoholism is treated as any other illness.

ADMINISTRATIVE AND FINANCIAL ISSUES

Cost Sharing—Contributory versus Noncontributory

As with other employee benefits, it is important to consider whether disability benefits should be paid for on a contributory or noncontributory basis prior to the installation of the plan. The amount of cost sharing affects benefit levels and the taxability of benefits received under disability plans. Benefits attributable to an employee's contributions are received tax free without limit. Therefore, if an employer is asking an employee to contribute a significant portion of the disability insurance premium, the percentage of income replaced must be decreased to take into consideration the tax-free status of benefits received or an overinsurance problem can result.

An additional issue in contributory versus noncontributory plans is the minimum benefit. If an employee is required to contribute, should a minimum benefit be paid from the disability plan even though overinsurance problems might result? In many plans, whether contributory or not, a minimum benefit of $50 per month is provided. As the contribution level rises, employees could reasonably request a higher minimum payout from the plan.

Claims Administration

Claims administration in the group disability area can have a very large impact upon the cost of the program. A variety of claims administration techniques exist, and each technique and form has advantages and disadvantages. The three main types of administration can be characterized as regional, centralized, and combined.

Regionalized Administration

Some large insurers have totally decentralized claims administration and control, in which the claims investigation and claims decision and monitoring take place at a local or regional level. Claims examiners in each state or sales region of the country handle all claims administration for disability in that area. In some cases, when disability income insurance volume is too small to make it efficient to have a claims examiner who specializes in disability claims, a claims examiner may deal in a number of different types of coverages, including disability. It is the responsibility of the claims examiner in the specific region to collect medical data and make a decision on the qualification of a claimant for disability benefits. The claims examiner must have a working knowledge of the various group contract provisions and be able to interpret medical and personal data.

Centralized Administration

The second type of claims administration is the centrally located claims department. In this type, claims work and investigation are performed from a central office. The group policyholder files claims applications directly with the home office. Backup investigations may be performed by independent claims adjusters or by credit bureaus. However, most information about the claim is gained by mail or telephone directly from the policyholder and physicians involved; there usually is no personal interview with the claimant. Generally, the claimant fills out the entire claim form, and payment usually is made directly from the home office, but in some instances it is made by the employer in the interest of better employee relations. Continued monitoring of the data is performed at the central location.

Combined Administration

To obtain the advantages of both the claims contact of regional administration and the cost savings of central administration, certain large insurers have claims systems that use regional claims people but keep the decision process in the home office. Local claims people are used for investigative purposes and to contact the claimant and his or her employer. Employees make claims to the home office, but regional personnel deal with the policyholder. The regional claims people bring together all pertinent claims information and make a personal call on the claimant if it is considered necessary. Compilation of a claims file takes place at the regional outlet. Regional office personnel may make a recommendation on the claim, but approval or denial comes from the central office.

An employee benefit manager must decide what type of claims administration is appropriate for its organization. Because of the delicate nature of disability claims, whether short- or long-term, it seems desirable in most cases that claims administration be handled by a third party and that the third party have a centralized or combined system for adjudicating claims. Claims services may be procured from insurers or specialty firms that monitor and control claims. Then, in the event an employee is dissatisfied, the dissatisfaction is aimed not at the employer but at another entity. In any event, it is important to have quick processing of claims and to have claim investigations started immediately.

Not only should proper claims processing be started for the private coverage, but a system to encourage disabled employees to file for Social Security disability income benefits should be in place. The number of people who receive Social Security disability benefits has changed drastically in the last decade. In the period between 1957 and 1969, it was not uncommon for the percentage of disability claims approved by Social Security to be above 50 percent, and in some years the percentage of claims approved by Social Security for disability benefits was above 60 percent. Because of massive changes in the economy, the percentage of persons who applied for and received Social Security awards dropped drastically in the 1970s. In the period 1970 to 1974, the percentage of applicants approved was less than 50 percent, usually between 40 and 50 percent. In the 1980s, the approval rate for Social Security disability claims has dropped into the 30 percent range. It is important to understand that the increased cost to integrated plans resulting from a lower percentage of Social Security disability claim approvals must be borne by the group policyholder. Thus, for potential cost savings, claims should be followed to their completion. Careful application and possibly reapplication should be made under Social Security if it seems at all possible the claimant could qualify for Social Security disability benefits.

Rehabilitation

Another important part of an employee benefit manager's responsibility in the disability area is to make sure the rehabilitation process gets started as soon as possible. Rehabilitation services may be provided on a local basis or may be provided by an insurance company. The employee benefit manager should aid the insurance company or private rehabilitation firm. Benefit managers can help identify employees who could benefit from rehabilitation and motivate these employees to seek rehabilitative services. Several disability insurers now have trained rehabilitation specialists who will help locate services at the local level. Rehabilitation programs first seek to put the person back in the job he or she was performing prior to the disabling condition. This may be accomplished by restructuring that job or by moving the employee into a slightly different work environment. If restructuring does not work, the next step is retraining for a position in the same company. In each case, early help is most important in getting people back into the production process. The best rehabilitation programs stress existing skills. If it is not possible to go back to the existing workplace, the insurance company involves the claimant in vocational rehabilitation. This is required if a claimant is to receive Social Security benefits. In addition, specific workshops and other education and training can be considered. The employer and the benefit manager must compare the cost of rehabilitation with the cost of keeping the person on the disability rolls. If the insurance carrier is not providing rehabilitation services for people on disability, services should be sought independently. Rehabilitation is a cost-effective device—both in human terms and in dollar terms—and should be part of the plan design.

SUMMARY

This brief overview of the types of coverages available for short- and long-term disability provides background for the more detailed information that follows in Chapter 18. Proper underwriting and claims administration help assure the employee benefit manager that the firm's employees are well protected at an acceptable cost.

CHAPTER 15

HEALTH CARE COST-CONTAINMENT TECHNIQUES

William G. Williams

INTRODUCTION

It is hard to pick up a copy of any general or trade publication these days without seeing some reference to health care cost-containment, which is the effort to control escalating medical care costs. The unprecedented rise in the cost of providing health care is a problem in which we are all both victims and culprits. It is obvious that so intricate a problem is not going to yield to a single, sweeping solution. Frankly, the dilemma is the result of living in a complex society with many conflicting objectives. For example, we want everyone to have the best medical care, *and we want cost-containment*. We want everyone to have the freedom to choose who will provide them with health care, and to go to that provider as often as they want, *and we want cost-containment*. We want every community, neighborhood, and religious group to have their own hospital, *and we want cost-containment*. We want every hospital, nursing home, and doctor's office to be equipped in the most modern fashion, and *we want cost-containment*. We want every citizen to have access to care without money being a barrier to receiving that care, and *we want cost-containment*.

Anyone who has ever served on a hospital board or worked with a cost-containment coalition is aware of these conflicting objectives and of the difficulties involved in resolving them. Problems are easy to identify;

workable solutions are not. Nevertheless, growing concern with the substantial increase in the money spent for health care has focused the attention of employers, the public, government, and the providers of medical care services on finding ways to solve the cost problem.

Health care cost-containment techniques involve a set of interrelated components that produce cost savings for the employer. Included among the components are benefit plan design ideas, claims review, external cost control systems, and health education and promotion. It is unlikely that any one health care cost-containment technique will produce large savings for a plan. However, when a number of these techniques are put into effect together, then meaningful cost reductions can be achieved.

BENEFIT PLAN DESIGN IDEAS

Today, changes in health benefit plans are taking place because of legislative mandates, changes in medical care institutions, emergence of new types of providers, development of new methods of medical care and treatment, and continuing health care cost increases. These changes affect the overall costs of health benefit plans, and if the changes cannot be controlled, plans must be designed to minimize their effect. Such benefit plan design ideas as deductibles, coinsurance, cost-sharing, coordination of benefits, subrogation, preadmission testing, emergency room treatment, weekend admissions, incentives for outpatient surgery, medical necessity language, skilled nursing care, home health care, preventive care, second surgical opinions, hospice care, and birthing centers serve this function.

Deductibles

A deductible, which is the cost of medical care expenses a covered person must incur and pay before medical care benefits become payable under a plan, may be expressed as a dollar amount ($100, $200, $500, $1,000), a percentage of the insured employee's income (1 percent), or both. Traditionally, they have been expressed in fixed-dollar amounts; however, there recently has developed a tendency to adopt or to consider income-related deductibles, because such deductibles adjust automatically to inflationary trends and may serve as a health care cost-containment technique.

Deductibles eliminate the high costs of investigating and paying for small claims; they lower employer costs for a medical care expense plan and employee costs for a contributory plan; and they contribute to controlling misuse of medical care, because the user's financial involvement encourages questioning the amount and type of treatment received. However, the use of deductibles may pose a financial impediment to treatment, and the costs of care may increase if treatment is postponed. Employees may be dissatisfied with insurance plans including deductibles and opt for alternative plans, such as health maintenance organizations (HMOs) and preferred provider organizations (PPOs), which usually do not use deductibles. The combination of a deductible and other cost-sharing features (such as coinsurance, copayment, or inside limits) also may impose a financial hardship on insured persons. Modifications of the deductible principle that have evolved in response to these concerns include benefit designs that involve separate deductibles, maximum family deductibles, common accident deductible provisions, and deductible carry-over provisions.

To encourage insureds to seek less expensive alternatives, deductibles can be waived for preadmission testing, outpatient surgery, and second surgical opinions.

Ultimately, the impact of deductibles applied to inpatient care is likely to be limited to discouraging frivolous admissions. When applied to outpatient care, however, this technique may discourage prompt diagnosis and treatment of legitimate illnesses, with a result that the higher cost of later treatment may outweigh the savings accrued through the intended avoidance of nuisance claims.

Coinsurance

Another way to assure that an individual participates in sharing a risk is to require that his or her participation in the payment of covered medical care expenses be a continuing one. A coinsurance provision typically indicates the insurance plan will pay a specified percentage (usually 80 percent) of all or of certain covered medical care expenses in excess of any applicable deductible. The remaining percentage (20 percent) is borne by the insured. In many plans today, a coinsurance limit or ''cap'' eliminates the coinsurance factor for the balance of the calendar year, after the insured has paid a fixed amount in expenses (e.g., $1,000, $1,500, $2,500).

Variable coinsurance percentages are found in many major medical expense insurance plans. In one plan, for example, inpatient and outpatient benefits are payable at 80 percent of all covered medical care expenses incurred during any one calendar year, in excess of any deductible, until the out-of-pocket maximum is reached; thereafter, 100 percent of all additional covered expenses for the balance of the year are paid. These features (where permissible) do not apply to the expenses incurred for outpatient treatment of alcoholism, drug addiction, and mental and nervous disorders, which are payable at 50 percent of the charges incurred and limited to a total maximum amount each calendar year (e.g., $1,000).

In order to influence insureds to obtain medical care on an outpatient basis, (i.e., ambulatory surgery and ambulatory care), reimbursement could be 100 percent of usual, customary, and reasonable (UCR) charges instead of 80 percent. Also, to discourage elective hospital admissions on Fridays and Saturdays, coinsurance factors can be increased, (e.g., from 20 to 50 or 60 percent).

Those who favor the use of deductibles and coinsurance say:

1. They may lead to a reduction in the use of health services and, hence, reduction of costs.
2. They reduce premiums because, for a given set of benefits, the insurance company pays less of the bill. Savings are eventually passed on to the employer and employee, although the effect is really to shift some of the cost burden from the employer to the employee.
3. They are equitable in the sense that the amount insured persons pay is related to the health services they use.

But those who oppose their use argue that:

1. They may not reduce utilization of health services because physicians, not consumers, make such decisions.
2. To the extent that they do decrease utilization, they may discourage needed preventive care.
3. For some employees they may present a financial barrier to receiving necessary care.

The use of deductibles and coinsurance as disincentives to overutilization and unnecessary care will probably increase, resulting in an immediate containment of premium costs. However, there does not seem to be any optimum deductible amount or coinsurance rate in which excessive utilization is reduced but people are not discouraged from getting necessary care. Whatever the amount or percentage, there must always be some trade-off in the efforts to balance the two competing objectives of coverage adequacy and cost control.

Cost Sharing

Cost sharing which is a key issue in medical benefits design, usually takes four different forms:

1. Deductibles.
2. Coinsurance.

3. Copayment (i.e., a specified dollar amount per day of inpatient care or per unit of service).
4. Premium contributions by employees.

Although cost sharing reduces health care expenditures many experts believe employees who share in health care costs should do so at the point of service (i.e., by utilizing deductibles, coinsurance, and copayment) rather than through increased premium contributions by employees which lower the employer's health insurance premiums, but do not affect the overall cost of health care.

Coordination of Benefits (COB)

Very simply defined, coordination of benefits (COB) is: A process by which two or more insurers, insuring the same person for the same or similar group health insurance benefits, limit the aggregate benefits he or she receives to an amount not exceeding the actual amount of loss, that is, not more than 100 percent[1] of allowable expenses.

Coordination of benefits was developed as a health care cost-containment technique because of the rapid growth of overinsurance. Overinsurance occurs when a person is insured under two or more insurance policies and is eligible to collect an aggregate of benefits that exceeds his or her actual loss. The main sources of overinsurance are:

1. Both husband and wife employed and eligible for group health insurance benefits.
2. Persons employed in two jobs, both of which provide group health insurance benefits.
3. Association group plans, especially among salaried and professional people who usually already have group health insurance benefits through their employers.

Since COB is an arrangement among several group insurance plans to predetermine responsibility for coverage so the total of all "coordinated" benefits paid will not exceed 100 percent of allowable expenses, it is necessary to determine which insurer is to pay any claim first. If only one group insurance plan has a COB provision, the group insurance plan

---

[1] Since June 1984, the National Association of Insurance Commissioners (NAIC) rules permit an option for plans to coordinate at less than 100 percent of allowable expenses, provided that the percent of allowable expenses for COB purposes is never less than 80 percent.

without the COB provision pays its benefits first and the group insurance plan with a COB provision pays second, that is, it coordinates its benefits based on the benefits paid by the primary group insurance plan. However, when both group insurance plans have a COB provision, both have the right to reduce their benefits based on the benefits paid by the other group insurance plan. To prevent the possibility of an insured being caught in the middle of a dispute between two insurers, and to provide a consistent and simple order of benefit determination (i.e., who pays first), the COB provisions set out the following system:

1. The plan covering the patient as an employee pays before the plan covering the patient as a dependent.

2. If the patient is a dependent child of parents who are *not* separated or divorced: The plan covering the parent whose birthday falls earlier in the year pays before the plan covering the parent whose birthday falls later in the year. If both parents have the same birthday, the plan which covered the parent longer pays before the plan which covered the other parent for a shorter time. However, if one coordinating plan uses this "birthday" rule and the other uses the old "male/female" rule, both plans will follow the "male/female" rule. (The benefits of a plan which covers the person on whose expenses claim is based as a dependent of a male person shall be determined before the benefits of a plan which covers such person as a dependent of a female person.) This fallback provision avoids the possibility that under different rules, both plans will be primary or both plans will be secondary.

3. If the patient is a dependent child of parents who *are* separated or divorced:

a. The plan or the parent with custody pays first,
b. The plan of the spouse of the parent with custody (the stepparent) pays next, and
c. The plan of the parent without custody pays last.

If the specific terms of a court decree state that one of the parents is responsible for the child's health care expenses, and the entity obliged to pay or provide the benefits of that parent's plan has actual knowledge of those terms, that plan pays first. If any benefits are actually paid or provided before that entity has actual knowledge, this "court decree" rule is not applicable.

4. A plan which covers the patient as an active employee, that is, one who is not laid off or retired, or that employee's dependent, pays before the plan which covers that person as a laid off or retired employee or that employee's dependent. If both plans do not have this rule, and if, as a result the plans do not agree on the order of benefits, this rule is ignored.

5. If none of the above rules determine the order of benefits, the plan which covered the patient longer pays before the plan which covered that person for the shorter period of time.

The following claim example illustrates what occurs in the absence, and the presence, of a COB provision:

> Mrs. Jones has filed a claim for $600 with both company A and company B. Company A insures Mrs. Jones as a female employee under a plan covering 80 percent of eligible expenses after a $25 deductible is satisfied. Company B insures her as a dependent spouse under a plan providing 75 percent of eligible expenses after a $100 deductible is met. In the absence of COB both companies would have to pay Mrs. Jones as follows:

Company A		*Company B*	
Allowable expenses	$600	Allowable expenses	$600
Less deductible	25	Less deductible	100
	$575		$500
× 80% coinsurance	.80	× 75% coinsurance	.75
Benefit payable	$460	Benefit payable	$375

In the absence of a COB provision, both insurers would pay the full benefits payable under the plans which in this example totals $835. In this case the insured, Mrs. Jones, would have made money to the extent of $235 as a result of her medical care expenses.

Using our example again, here is how the payments would be calculated with the presence of a COB provision in both plans:

Company A		*Company B*	
Allowable expenses	$600	Allowable expenses	$600
Less deductible	25	Less Company "A"s benefit	460
	$575	Company B pays	$140
× 80% coinsurance	.80		
Company A pays	$460		

Thus under COB, company B paid only $140, producing a benefit saving of $235. This amount is credited to Mrs. Jones, to be applied to any future claims she might have against company B during the claim determination period, generally a calendar year. This credit can be used to provide benefits that would not have otherwise been paid. If, for example, the policy with company B provides psychiatric outpatient benefits, but only to a maximum of $500 in a claim determination period, and Mrs. Jones incurs $750 of psychiatric outpatient expenses in that same claim determination period, then the $235 credit could be used to extend benefits beyond the $500 maximum. The effect of COB in Mrs. Jones's case, then, is that, between the two insurers, she received reimbursement of the full $600 of expenses and has a $235 credit with company B.

Coordination of benefits is a necessary health care cost-containment technique used to minimize duplicate payments for covered services and thereby limit the potential of a net financial gain to the person seeking medical care. It is estimated the use of COB saves approximately 4 to 8 percent in claim payments that would otherwise have been made.

Subrogation

In general, subrogation means the substitution of another party, in this case the employer or the insurer, in place of a party (the employee or a dependent) who has a legal claim against a third party. Thus an employee benefit plan which included subrogation would provide the employer or insurer with rights with respect to claims that a covered employee or dependent might have against third parties, such as negligent tortfeasors in automobile accidents, and the employer's insurer would receive reimbursement if the employee or the dependent received a liability recovery from a third party. Insurers may be reluctant to include specific subrogation provisions in group insurance contracts because of the time delays involved in settling claims.

Preadmission Testing (PAT)

The purpose of preadmission testing is to help contain hospital costs by reducing the number of in-hospital patient days through having the necessary X-rays, laboratory tests and examinations conducted on an outpatient basis, prior to a scheduled hospital admission, and reimbursed as if on an inpatient basis. It is important to note PAT is not an outpatient diagnostic benefit program, but is offered as an inpatient reimbursement alternative to a longer hospital confinement or, in some cases, to an unnecessary hospital confinement.

Advantages to Patients

The advantage for the patient who is being admitted for medical care is that treatment can begin immediately. This is far better than admitting the patient a day or two ahead of time to have tests run and then waiting for the results before treatment is begun.

It reduces the possibility of patients being admitted on weekends for routine or elective surgery and necessary tests scheduled for the following week. It allows the patient to become familiar with the hospital before admission, and means an alleviation of anxiety as well as less time away from home and job.

Advantages to Physicians

Getting test results early—especially in cases where there is a history of heart disease, diabetes, and the like—is a great advantage to the patient's physician. It helps the provider get a jump on planning the course of treatment. Should there be negative test results, the admission can be canceled before the patient comes to the hospital.

The physician who is able to confirm a diagnosis and develop a plan of treatment before the patient is admitted is also able to begin treatment promptly upon the patient's arrival. Once the test results are available and the physician is sure of the admission, all the admitting department has to do is type the bed assignment and date of admission on the admission form and wait for the patient to show up. Because all the paperwork can be prepared in advance, the admissions process is effectuated promptly and smoothly.

The tests also are available for the anesthesiologist's evaluation prior to the patient's arrival for surgery. This enables the anesthesiologist to determine the proper type and amount of anesthesia in an unharried atmosphere.

How PAT Works

In general, this is how preadmission testing works:

1. After the diagnosis has been established, the procedure scheduled and the patient's room reserved by the hospital, the attending physician orders those tests and examinations which he or she considers to be necessary before the procedure can be performed.
2. The patient is instructed to report at a scheduled time and specified place in the hospital where the tests are to be completed. The results of the tests are reported to the attending physician and are made a part of the patient's hospital chart at the time of admission.
3. Charges for the tests are billed by the hospital to the insurer as a part of the bill for in-hospital care, according to the benefit provisions of the patient's insurance plan.
4. The time period prior to admission, during which the tests and

examinations are to be made, is determined by the medical judgment of the attending physician. Most tests will be made as close to the admission date as practicable so the test results may be completely dependable and acceptable.

5. When the admission must be cancelled or postponed for any reason outside the patient's control, the insurer will still make payment for the tests, and when the admission is rescheduled will make the same benefits available again.
6. The above procedures apply to elective surgical admissions and medical confinements.

How Is PAT's Cost-Containment Potential Compromised?

It is compromised in the following ways:

1. By the pattern of medical practice in the community. For example, providers in a fee-for-service setting lack the financial incentive to use PAT. In addition, some providers admit their patients several days prior to surgery to allow for their adjustment to hospitalization.
2. By the often-mistaken assumptions of the patient, doctor, or hospital that the patient's insurer provides more comprehensive coverage for inpatient care.
3. By the desire of hospitals to keep their beds filled. Hospitals with low occupancy, on the one hand, have strong financial incentives to fill beds and to render all possible services on an inpatient basis. On the other hand, hospitals with high occupancy have strong incentives to reduce the length of hospital stays and make beds available.
4. By the physician's time involvement in the scheduling of tests.
5. By the matter of convenience to both physician and patient. For example, some patients find it difficult to go back and forth to the hospital on an outpatient basis; other patients are very sick or elderly and cannot go back and forth to the hospital.
6. By the mistaken notion of the patient that testing on an inpatient basis is more thorough.
7. By the lack of coordination in the scheduling of tests and the availability of beds and operating rooms. Inefficient scheduling of all elements in this process leads to delays, which offset any PAT savings.
8. By the reluctance of hospitals and physicians to participate because of the spectre of malpractice suits. This attitude is probably

the result of concern about any testing done in facilities outside the hospital, such as an ambulatory care center, independent clinical laboratory, or physician's office. In addition, in many cases hospital-based laboratories are contracted out to a physician or group of physicians. Since their reimbursement formula often is dependent upon utilization, it would not be in their interest to encourage the use of "outside" facilities.

Conclusions

PAT benefit programs, which are relatively easy to add to existing benefit plans, are provided at no additional cost to employers or employees. Effectively utilized, they can generate cost savings. PAT programs alone can help to reduce hospital lengths of stay. When combined with a hospital utilization review program evaluating the necessity of a hospital admission, the quality of care, and the length of stay for a given diagnosis, PAT has considerable potential to encourage hospitals to improve their admission and presurgical testing procedures. Ultimately, it usually is the physician who decides whether to use PAT, but the decision can be influenced by the patient concerned about the escalating cost of medical care who asks, "Can't my presurgical or medical tests be done on an outpatient basis?"

PAT programs offer the potential for reducing both the cost per hospital admission and the time lost from work. At the same time, PAT can help reduce the need for more hospital bed construction.

Emergency Room Treatment

To discourage the unnecessary use of hospital emergency rooms (i.e., in lieu of a doctor's office), a deductible can be utilized (e.g., $50) or the coinsurance could be 50–50 rather than 80–20 percent. Usually a physician can advise whether an individual should utilize the services of a hospital emergency room.

Weekend Admissions

Hospitals, like many businesses, reduce their activities on weekends. In many cases a patient admitted on a Friday or Saturday and another person admitted the following Monday receive the same treatment and both leave the hospital on the same day. Because of unnecessary elective (nonemergency) admissions to hospitals on Fridays or Saturdays, insurers are either not providing benefits, requiring a substantial deductible (e.g., $250, $500), or 50–50 or 60–40 coinsurance. Necessary weekend admissions (e.g., childbirth, a life-threatening or potentially disabling emergency) would be reimbursed like any other days and no disincentives would be applied.

Incentives For Outpatient Surgery

Insureds are provided with incentives to utilize outpatient surgery, when it's medically feasible. The deductible is waived and the surgery is reimbursed at 100 percent instead of 80–20 percent. Outpatient surgery is being performed at hospital outpatient facilities, free-standing surgical centers, or in a doctor's office. Utilization review programs review medical information and evaluate it against medical criteria to determine medical necessity and appropriateness of inpatient admission and the proposed treatment plan. For example, could the proposed treatment be delivered in a more cost-effective setting without any sacrifice in quality of treatment or the anticipated result?

Medical Necessity Language

Medical care and treatment is "medically necessary" if it meets all of the following conditions:

1. The care and treatment is appropriate given the symptoms, and is consistent with the diagnosis, if any. "Appropriate" means that the type, level, and length of service, and setting are needed to provide safe and adequate care and treatment;
2. It is rendered in accordance with generally accepted medical practice and professionally recognized standards;
3. It is not treatment that is generally regarded as experimental, educational, or unproven; and
4. It is specifically allowed by the licensing statutes which apply to the provider who renders the service.

With respect to confinement in a hospital "medically necessary" further means that the medical condition requires confinement and that safe and effective treatment cannot be provided as an outpatient.

Skilled Nursing Care

Skilled nursing care refers to care that is usually furnished in a skilled nursing facility (SNF) and can only be performed by, or under the supervision of, licensed nursing personnel. The care in an SNF includes room and board charges, registered nursing services, physical therapy, drugs, supplies, and equipment. Intermediate care and respite care may or may not be covered, and custodial care is generally not covered.

The shift in emphasis today to out-of-hospital care (i.e., insurers providing less costly alternatives to hospitalization without sacrificing the quality of the care) has resulted in development of a concept sometimes referred to as progressive care. In this environment, a patient proceeds through various levels of care, as dictated by his or her health condition, not necessarily beginning with a hospital confinement. For example, these levels could include intensive care, normal acute inpatient hospital care, confinement in a skilled nursing facility requiring limited medical attention, and home health care.

It is well recognized that the latter days of a hospital confinement require a lesser level of care than that provided in a general acute care hospital. Accordingly, if a plan includes skilled nursing care and home health care, the patient with the concurrence of the attending physician could be prevailed upon to transfer to a lesser level of care. The obvious cost savings relative to these levels of care is the greatly reduced per diem charge, compared to a hospital's room and board charge.

Home Health Care

Like skilled nursing care (care in an extended care facility, nursing home, or convalescent home), home health care is an alternative to costly inpatient hospital care. A comprehensive range of health care services (e.g., part-time or intermittent nursing care provided under the supervision of a registered nurse, physical therapy, occupational therapy, medications and laboratory services, and part-time or intermittent services of a home health aide) can be provided to a patient at home. Decisions to use home health care benefits are based on such factors as family capabilities and patient desires. Home health care programs are appropriate for chronically ill or disabled persons as well as for patients who require only monitoring during rehabilitation or maintenance care.

Home health care provides supportive care at costs considerably less than hospital confinement, and in an atmosphere often far more restful to the patient.

Preventive Care

Traditionally, medical care has focused on treatment rather than on prevention of illness. However, many health experts today believe the incidence and/or severity of illnesses, such as heart disease, stroke, and cancer, can be greatly reduced through proper preventive care and early diagnosis.

Preventive care can take many forms, some of them being periodic physical examinations to minimize complications through early detection, well-baby care (under two years; including immunizations), well-child care (2–15 years; including immunizations), and patient counseling by physicians for non-illnesses (e.g., smoking cessation, weight control, diet counseling, physical fitness, nutrition). Insurers are increasingly involved in examining the value of all of these forms to determine which preventive measures are health and cost effective. For example, some differences of opinion exist, even within the medical profession itself, concerning the value of annual physical examinations versus cost and the most effective use of physicians' time. Those who approve the concept of preventive physical examinations lean toward providing specific tests periodically, the frequency being based on age and sex. Ultimately, say the experts, preventive care may reduce a company's health care costs, though results are difficult to measure.

Second Surgical Opinions

"Second opinion" has been defined as a prospective screening process that relies on a consulting physician's or surgeon's evaluation of the need for surgery that another surgeon has recommended. Thus, anyone for whom elective, nonemergency surgery is recommended is well advised to obtain a second opinion before proceeding. For example, while one doctor may recommend surgery, another may recommend medication or postponing an operation. A second opinion encourages doctors to review the necessity and advisability of surgery, instills patient confidence by reducing anxieties, and discloses alternatives that may avoid or postpone surgery. The decision whether to accept surgery or alternative treatment is still the patient's.

What Kinds of Surgery Are Suitable for Second Opinions?

The following are typical procedures often suitable for a second surgical opinion:

Dilatation and curettage (D and C).
Surgery of the thyroid, tonsils, or adenoids.
Surgery of the back, hip, or knee joint.
Surgery of the colon, duodenum, or stomach.
Surgery of the gallbladder or prostate.
Surgery for hernia.

Hysterectomy.

Surgery of the breast.

Surgery for hemorrhoids.

Surgery of the heart, veins, or arteries.

This is a partial list, because many observers say that almost 90 percent of all surgery can be categorized as elective and nonemergency. It is important to remember second surgical opinion programs do not cover second opinions for the following:

Normal pregnancies.

Elective abortions.

Occupational accidents or diseases.

Surgery involving local infiltration anesthesia.

Second opinions rendered while confined in hospital.

Surgery that may be performed in a doctor's office, such as incision and drainage of an abscess.

Cosmetic surgery.

Dental surgery.

Sterilizations.

How Are Second Opinions Reimbursed?

In specifically designed second surgical opinion programs, the manner of reimbursement may be as follows:

1. One hundred percent of the first $100 of such charges and 80 percent of the balance of such charges are payable. No cash deductible applies.
2. A fixed fee (e.g., $50) is payable to the consulting surgeon if he or she agrees to accept the fee as payment in full. Charges for necessary X-rays and laboratory tests, up to a fixed limit (e.g., $75) will be reimbursed in addition to the fixed fee payable to the consulting surgeon. No deductible or coinsurance provisions are applicable to this benefit.
3. One hundred percent of usual, customary and reasonable charges incurred in seeking a second (and third) opinion from a consulting surgeon, prior to being hospitalized for the proposed elective surgery. This surgical consultation benefit also includes any charges for additional necessary X-rays, laboratory tests, and other diagnostic studies. No deductible or coinsurance provisions are applicable to this benefit.

Voluntary versus Mandatory Second Surgical Opinion Programs

A second surgical opinion program is instituted either on a voluntary or a mandatory basis. The major problem with the voluntary program is underutilization. Indeed, many employees do not understand the second surgical opinion option. The degree to which voluntary programs are used often hinges directly on the enthusiasm of management in promoting the concept and the inclusion of an incentive. For example, surgery without a second opinion is reimbursed at 50 percent, whereas surgery following a second, or even a third opinion, is reimbursed at 100 percent.

Mandatory programs, which require patients to seek a second opinion before insurance will pay for the surgery, have been subject to many objections. They concern the denial of payment if second opinions are not obtained; payment of a reduced benefit if the claimant has surgery without getting a second opinion or after receiving a nonconfirming second opinion; regimentation that takes away the patient's right of free choice; and, possible adverse effects on the physician/patient relationship. Enforcement is a problem for mandatory programs, as well as denial of payment, which can cause employee dissatisfaction. Despite the objections and concerns, mandatory second surgical opinion programs show promise as an effective cost-containment technique.

Under either type of program, and regardless of the consulting surgeon's opinion, the final decision whether to go ahead with the operation lies with the patient. The potential for cost savings in a second surgical opinion program lie primarily in the following areas:

Surgeries not confirmed and not performed.

Surgeries performed on an ambulatory rather than an inpatient basis, as initially recommended.

General reduction in surgical claims because of physician awareness of the program. This is known as the "sentinel" effect.

Hospice Care

Hospice care is a mode of care aimed at providing terminally ill patients (i.e., patients whose prognosis for life expectancy is six months or less) with an alternative to traditional modes of treatment. The hospice concept gradually emphasizes palliative care (medical relief of pain) rather than curative care for patients for whom there is no chance of a cure. While there is no standard definition of a hospice, there are four basic principles that distinguish hospices from the traditional health care system:

1. Patient and family, not the patient alone, are considered the unit of care.
2. A multidisciplinary team, which may include a physician, nurse, home health aide, social worker, psychiatrist, psychologist, clergy, and trained volunteers as well as family members, is used to assess the physical, psychological, and spiritual needs of the patient and family, develop an overall plan of care, and provide coordinated care.
3. Pain and collateral symptoms associated with the terminal illness are controlled, but no heroic efforts are made to cure the patient.
4. Bereavement follow-up is provided to the family to help them with the grieving process.

Hospice care is currently delivered through a variety of program models, including

1. The free-standing hospice, with or without direct affiliation with a hospital.
2. The hospice unit within a hospital.
3. The hospice team within a hospital.
4. The hospice unit in a skilled nursing facility.
5. The so-called "hospice without walls" or home health care provider exclusively.
6. The case manager model, which provides home health care services but through existing service providers rather than through its own personnel.

Proponents of hospice care have historically argued that this form of treatment for the terminally ill is less costly than care provided in the typical hospital setting. They acknowledge that hospice care may not be a total substitute for hospital care, in that the terminal patient may at some point need to be admitted to a hospital, but they feel that hospice care has the potential to reduce the overall length of a general hospital stay and thereby reduce costs. Frankly, the selection of hospice care as an alternative may depend on the specific needs of the patient and family, variables which cannot always be controlled by the mere existence of a hospice program.

Birthing Centers

These centers are a popular, cost-effective alternative to acute hospitalization for low-risk deliveries and postpartum newborn care. The centers, which are usually owned and operated by obstetricians or nurse-mid-wives, are close to a full-service hospital which allows easy transport for any complications that may arise during the childbearing process. Because of the popularity of these centers, hospitals have been creating these facilities within the walls of the hospitals.

CLAIMS REVIEW

The usual claims review by carriers is a process in which medical care expense claims are examined before payment. Such analyses of claims do reduce the policyholder's medical care costs by identifying claims that the policyholder is not obligated to pay because of:

- Ineligibility of the employee.
- Ineligibility of a particular service.
- Duplicate reimbursement due to coverage by more than one health plan.
- Discrepancies between the services claimed and the services actually performed.
- Claims which exceed usual, customary, and reasonable charges.

Today, the claims review process generally includes two additional cost containment techniques: utilization review and hospital bill audit programs.

Utilization Review

Utilization Review (UR) is designed to reduce the incidence of unnecessary or inappropriate hospitalization. The procedure, used for both cost and quality control, involves the use of locally determined criteria to establish guidelines for appropriate admissions, hospital lengths of stay, and course of treatment. These criteria are based on age, sex, and diagnosis. The actual review process is either done by independent review organizations or, for a few large insurers, by in-house programs. In addition, some insurers are also utilizing professional review organizations (PROs), which have been established in the states by federal law to monitor the health care services provided by the Medicare and Medicaid programs. A thorough utilization review program involves preadmission certification, concurrent or continued stay review, retrospective review and discharge planning.

Preadmission Certification

This is a process whereby an insured is required to obtain an authorization from the review program in advance (prior to admission) that an elective or non-emergency hospitalization is necessary and will be provided in an appropriate facility. The review and authorization are performed by qualified health care professionals utilizing accepted medical care criteria in order to determine the medical necessity and appropriateness of an inpatient stay and the proposed treatment plan. The result of this review is an assurance that only patients with a medical need for hospitalization are certified for admission, that the proposed treatment is customary for the diagnosis, and that opportunities for treatment to be received in more cost-containing settings (e.g., skilled nursing facilities, outpatient surgical facility, home health care, hospice care) have been identified.

In order for preadmission certification to be effective, participation must be ensured. This is done by providing a benefit design that requires a reduction in benefits for nonparticipation. For example, here is a contractual option which is being utilized:

> If preadmission certification (PAC) is not received, a per admission penalty of $300 will be imposed. This penalty is in addition to any per confinement or other deductible required by the plan and cannot be applied to the out-of-pocket.
>
> If PAC is performed, room and board payment for any days of hospitalization not certified as medically necessary will be reduced by 50 percent.
>
> Payment for any confinement for which outpatient care facilities were recommended will be reduced by 50 percent.

Concurrent or Continued Stay Review

Concurrent Review

This on-site review, takes place when a patient is confined to a hospital. Concurrent review is typically carried out by a nurse coordinator (i.e., a review program employee) who reviews patients' charts within 24 hours of admission, and then at designated intervals until discharge occurs in order to:

- Assess the need for admission to the hospital.
- Assign an initial length of stay and assess the medical need for any extensions.
- Assess the appropriateness of the level of care provided.
- Generally assess the progress and efficiency of the care being given.

- Abstract data for retrospective quality assessment in comparison with medical care criteria.

The nurse coordinator is allowed to authorize care which falls within predetermined explicit quality and length-of-stay guidelines, These guidelines are usually based on common practice and experience. When necessary, the nurse coordinator requests additional information from the attending physician or a decision from a physician who serves as medical advisor (also a review program employee). While the nurse coordinator assigns a diagnosis-specific length of stay, the maximum and any extensions are the purview of the medical advisor consulting with the attending physician. The date representing the minimum length of stay is flagged on the patient's chart; on that date, the patient's length of stay is reviewed and the nurse coordinator, after looking at the patient's chart, may assign a new review date. On that review date, the nurse coordinator may determine that the patient is ready for discharge. Subject to approval by the medical advisor, the nurse coordinator can also recommend that all future reimbursement be canceled; however, the absence of ''medical necessity'' language in an insurer's contract will void this cancellation.

Continued Stay Review

This off-site medical review process is conducted, while the patient is hospitalized, by telephone with the treating physician at designated intervals until discharge occurs. Again using established medical criteria and length-of-stay norms, the review program professionals determine medical necessity and appropriateness of both the treatment plan and the inpatient stay.

Retrospective Review

This is after-the-fact review which applies the same medical criteria as concurrent or continued stay review, but only after the patient is discharged. Obviously, there is more potential for controlling costs while they are occurring, but a retrospective review can still limit costs by identifying medically unnecessary bed days and treatment charges and, where appropriate, isolate unrelated charges.

This type of claims review allows an employer to establish a utilization profile to use in monitoring trends. Included in such a profile would be diagnoses, the kinds and prices of medical services purchased by each employee, where they were provided, and the portion paid by the company. Appropriate action could then be taken in excessively high-cost areas.

Discharge Planning

This process occurs when it is apparent that the patient will be leaving the facility. For patients who have not recovered, arrangements are made for continuing care (e.g., in a skilled nursing facility; for home health care). The attending physician documents and explains the care and treatment needed after discharge.

A basic objective of any utilization review program is to assure that the patient is not located in a care setting that exceeds medical necessity. Far too many beds are filled with patients who should be in a nursing facility, outpatient facility, or at home. Achievement of this objective would result in great cost savings. An important result of an effective UR program is the reduction of "defensive medicine," where physicians tend to overutilize medical services for fear of malpractice suits. Accepted utilization criteria define the necessary tests and services for common diagnoses.

Employer interest in UR (i.e., to scrutinize claims to determine the appropriateness of the care and services rendered, and to determine the costs eligible for coverage) is being expressed individually and through employer coalitions. The potential for implementation of such programs continues to be contingent on the density of insureds in a given geographic area, and on the contractural commitment of an area's hospitals to participate in a private-sector utilization review program. Ultimately, it is the individual physicians who control the resources of a hospital. If any UR system is to have an impact, the behavior of the physicians who have demonstrated consistent patterns of high utilization and excessive lengths of stay by diagnosis must be changed.

Hospital Bill Audit

Hospital Bill Audit programs exist because insurers have long been aware that good medicine and good accounting do not necessarily go hand in hand. To deal with this problem, insurers use independent or internal (sometimes both) auditors to conduct a continuing series of audits of hospital claims most likely to be in error. These include: bills exceeding a certain amount (e.g., $10,000), room and board charges less than 40 percent of the total bill, certain lab tests (e.g., complete blood counts, urinalyses, SMA–12/60s and sodium potassium levels) listed more than once every 24 hours, therapy sessions (physical and occupational) prescribed more than normal, bills that show evidence of treatment for nonrelated conditions, drug charges which are large and frequent, patients who are hospitalized longer than necessary, the number of days confined does not relate to the diagnoses involved, and a high number of charges for whole blood and blood derivatives are shown without any credits being given for donated replacements.

Some of the most prevalent errors are in pharmacy, laboratory, radiology, inhalation therapy, and occupational therapy. Auditors check the doctors' orders, the nurses' notes, pharmacy records, the total charges for therapy divided by the recorded number of hours spent by the therapist, radiology and lab records, as well as the room and board charges and length of stay for a given diagnosis. Insurers have found that every dollar spent on hospital bill audit programs saves almost two dollars in overcharges. It is important to note that hospitals underbill as well as overbill and it is hard to get a hospital to cooperate in an audit if an insurer won't agree to reimburse on underbillings.

EXTERNAL COST CONTROL SYSTEMS

External health care cost-control systems include such elements as ambulatory care facilities, HMOs, PPOs, and large claim management.

A significant portion of the diagnosis and treatment provided hospital inpatients can be rendered more economically on a "walk-in" basis when appropriate facilities and adequately trained personnel are available. Thus, ambulatory care facilities such as ambulatory surgical centers, emergicenters and urgicenters, free-standing diagnostic radiology centers, facilities for the treatment of end stage renal disease, comprehensive outpatient rehabilitation facilities (CORFs), and independent clinical labs serve this purpose.

Ambulatory Surgical Centers

Recognition that many surgeries could be performed on a same-day, outpatient basis (e.g., cataract removal, tonsillectomies, simple hernias, removal of noncancerous cysts, minor gynecological procedures and biopsies of various kinds) led to the development of ambulatory surgical centers. The concept was fostered by the development of new surgical techniques and by the discovery of faster-acting anesthetics that wear off sooner and leave fewer aftereffects.

Two types of ambulatory surgical centers are in operation today: those independent and separate from any hospital—commonly referred to as freestanding ambulatory surgical centers (FASCs) and often called "surgicenters"—and those operating under the auspices of a hospital and known as short-procedure units. In any case, the purpose of these facilities is the performance of surgical procedures considered too demanding for a doctor's office, but not serious enough to warrant an inpatient hospital stay. However, the benefits for ambulatory surgery usually are treated as an extension of inpatient hospital benefits with the same level of coverage as if the surgery had been performed on an inpatient basis.

What Are the Savings in the Ambulatory Surgical Concept?

It is estimated the percentage savings for procedures performed under this concept can range from 15 to 40 percent. Incidentally, the proponents of freestanding (i.e., not hospital-based) surgical facilities point to two reasons for such savings. First, they state they operate more efficiently than do hospitals and thus can handle more patients at lower average cost. Second, they need not provide extensive ancillary and support services, nor 24-hour staffing, and thus are not obliged to redistribute costs for expensive procedures and services to the minor surgical patients.

The counterargument of hospitals is certain services must be provided to the community (e.g., emergency room, open heart, burn treatment, intensive care) and the revenues to fully support these and other expensive services must be obtained by distributing the costs throughout the spectrum of hospital charges. The development of competing, low-cost freestanding surgical facilities therefore is indicated as contributing to higher community costs. Furthermore, some hospital officials assert independent freestanding day surgery services further worsen hospital finances by neglecting to handle a proportionate number of medically indigent patients. In today's world, competition has tempered these hospital arguments as hospitals are erecting free-standing facilities.

It also should be noted in this "savings debate" that some nonsurgical procedures are appropriate in a day surgery setting. For example, among the most frequently performed procedures are chemotherapy and extensive radiological examinations. Finally, it is estimated between 20 and 40 percent of all surgical procedures could be performed on an outpatient basis.

What Are Some of the Advantages of the Ambulatory Surgical Center Concept?

1. Lower cost than inpatient surgery as a patient foregoes a two-to-three day hospitalization by having surgery performed on an outpatient basis.
2. Less time away from home and work, because this type of surgery is less disruptive and permits a patient to return to a regular schedule more quickly.

3. Frees hospital beds for more acutely ill patients.
4. Scheduling is quick and relatively easy, as opposed to the process of securing a hospital bed for inpatient surgery, which may require a wait.
5. Offers great convenience to physicians and patients.
6. The environment is conducive to high patient morale and faster recovery.
7. May obviate the need for the expansion of hospital beds.

By eliminating overnight (or longer) confinement, the cost of a surgical procedure is reduced drastically, while the traumatic effect of hospital confinement on a patient is minimized. Thus, coverage of ambulatory surgery serves to lower a company's health care expenditures in the short-term. However, unless community hospitals respond to the decreased patient load by reducing beds, labor, and assets, hospital rates undoubtedly will rise and effectively negate any savings.

Other Ambulatory Care Facilities

Emergicenters and urgicenters (which provide 24-hour, 7-day-a week service to treat minor conditions such as cuts, bruises, and removal of sutures), free-standing diagnostic radiology centers, facilities for the treatment of end stage renal disease, comprehensive outpatient rehabilitation facilities (CORFs), and independent clinical laboratories have all become more common in recent years. Employers can encourage the utilization of these less costly ambulatory care facilities by waiving plan deductibles and coinsurance.

Health Maintenance Organizations (HMOs)

A much publicized form of alternative health care delivery system is the health maintenance organization, which refers to any public or private organization providing a full range of health services to an enrolled population (i.e., generally through employer-sponsored plans) within a defined geographic area in return for a fixed, prepaid premium for all services provided. The two major types of HMOs are distinguished by the manner in which their physicians are organized and are called individual practice associations (IPAs) and prepaid group practices (PGPs).

Individual Practice Associations

An IPA is composed of a central administrative component (e.g., a foundation sponsored by a medical society, a county medical society, an insurer, or a hospital) and a group of physicians in a community. The participating physicians continue to practice in their own offices and are reimbursed on a fee-for-service basis according to agreed-upon fee schedules. The HMO, however, receives a prepaid premium from its enrollees, and it is thus "at risk" financially for providing the stipulated health care services to its subscribers. The individual physicians are also "at risk" in the sense their fees from the plan may be reduced in the event of poor overall plan experience. Conversely, they may share in any plan profits.

The IPA's greatest strength, physicians practicing in their own offices, is also its greatest weakness because it lacks the peer interaction and physician selection that facilitates control of utilization and costs. IPAs usually do succeed in lowering inpatient hospital utilization rates, but they seldom attain the levels associated with effective prepaid group practices.

Prepaid Group Practices

A PGP may be a medical group model, in which the plan contracts with an existing or forming group practice, or a staff model, in which physicians are hired by the plan and paid a salary. The participating physicians represent the various medical specialties and practice as a team. Primary patient care is provided in multispecialty clinics usually associated with the HMO's own hospital or with participating hospitals. The HMO receives a prepaid premium from its enrollees and is "at risk" for the costs of the covered health care services because it must provide them for the predetermined premiums as well as meet their financial obligations to their closed panel of physicians.

Employers normally want to provide adequate health care benefits to their employees and their dependents in an effective, economical manner. Following are some of the advantages and disadvantages of HMOs for employers and their employees.

Advantages of HMOs

- Broader coverage with emphasis on preventive care.
- Less administrative work.
- Coordinated services at one location (only true for PGPs).
- Lower hospitalization rates, i.e., hospital days per 1,000 insureds.
- Potential for greater cost-effectiveness through incentives to the primary care physicians to constrain health care expenditures.

Disadvantages of HMOs

- Loss of freedom of choice of doctors and hospitals.
- Limitations in choosing specialists as HMO primary care physicians control access.

- Lack of, or inadequate, cost and utilization data collection system.
- Geographically limited.
- Employee misunderstandings (communication problems).
- Out-of-plan area coverage problems.
- Loss of personal physician relationship.
- Location of HMO facilities (transportation, accessibility problems).
- Concern about the fiscal condition of HMOs.
- The expense of offering an HMO option (which can be material).
- Overall savings may not be significant. (This has been experienced by many who have been insured under HMOs.)
- Satisfaction with existing systems of health care delivery by health care consumers.

Despite the disadvantages, HMOs offer a potential solution to problems found in many traditional health care plans. Such problems include

1. Difficulty in finding satisfactory medical care services: an HMO provides access to a team of doctors of all specialties available at most times.
2. The fragmentation of services, e.g., services are at various locations and communication is poor: an HMO team works together at a single location, where patient records and histories are readily available (true for PGPs but not IPAs).
3. The high cost of services.

High inpatient benefits encourage the use of high-cost hospital facilities. The money saved by an HMO in limiting hospital confinements goes, in theory, to provide preventive care and comprehensive outpatient benefits.

Today, with the emphasis of insurers on ''managed health care,'' many of the elements which at one time were unique to HMOs are now included in insurance company health insurance products. For example, insurers are routinely offering preadmission certification, concurrent or continued stay review, retrospective review, and discharge planning. In addition, insurers, are providing increased benefits for the use of preadmission testing, outpatient care and treatment, home health care, and hospice care. Many insurers are now including HMOs as well as PPOs in their product lines. In fact, ''triple options'' (i.e., traditional insured health care plan/an HMO/a PPO) are being offered by many insurance companies, which enables employers to negotiate with one entity rather than three and an influx of employees into the HMO or PPO doesn't distort the demographics or experience of the traditional insured plan.

Preferred Provider Organizations (PPOs)

Simply stated, a PPO is a network of hospitals and/or doctors organized to provide a range of health care services for fees specified in a formal contract and performed according to agreed-upon standards.

This recent type of alternative delivery system came into being because many providers are unwilling to assume the financial risks of HMO participation and many employees are unwilling to limit their choice of providers to HMO participating doctors and hospitals.

Hospitals are organizing PPOs in order to maintain occupancy rates in areas where HMOs and PROs (Private Review Organizations) are reducing hospital utilization. Physicians are affiliating with PPOs in order to maintain patient volume in areas where there are too many physicians and where other health care delivery systems are taking patients away. Employers support PPO development in order to control both inpatient and outpatient utilization in areas where health care costs are escalating out of control.

Participation in a PPO enlarges a provider's patient base (i.e., increased market share) and at the same time creates a minimal financial risk for providers who have agreed to a fee schedule. The PPO option is described and included in an employer's existing medical care benefits plan, but unlike an HMO, no prepayment or capitation amount is paid to the providers. A PPO offers many of the advantages of an HMO, but unlike an HMO it offers freedom of choice for the patient relative to doctors and hospitals. For example, under the most popular type of PPO arrangement known as a "swing plan" the covered person can choose to receive care from either a PPO provider or a non-PPO provider. If a non-PPO provider renders care, the benefits are usually reduced (i.e., a deductible is required; increased coinsurance is required).

PPOs are not an all-purpose remedy for current problems in the health care marketplace; however, all new opportunities for cost-containment should be explored, developed, and utilized if effective from quality and cost standpoints.

Large Claim Management

Traditionally, employers haven't had the opportunity to review catastrophic and high-risk claims from the perspective of total management, that is, addressing the care needs of the patient and family, the health care services provided, and the costs of the care. Today, large claim management programs (also called medical case management) are available to policyholders from independent review organizations or for a few large insurers by in-house programs. The initial stage of a serious illness (e.g., neonatal high risk infant, severe stroke, Lou Gehrig's disease (ALS), multiple sclerosis), or injury (e.g., major head trauma, spinal cord injury, amputations, multiple fractures, severe burns) is the point at which the outcome for better or for worse can be most dramatically changed.

Medical case management firms do a comprehensive assessment of a case, taking into account the patient's needs and treatment plan, committing resources available, and evaluating the work environment and family situation. These case management professionals have the ability to work with medical care providers to implement alternatives if and when they are appropriate. Savings in a large claim management program are generated in three ways:

- Alternate care—movement from a high-cost acute care facility (hospital) to a skilled nursing facility, a rehab facility, or a home health care program.
- Accelerated care—care provided through a specialized facility, additional or intensive therapy, patient and family training, or early home care.
- Reduction of medical complications—complications (e.g., digestive or respiratory problems, skin diseases, or circulatory complications) can often be reduced or prevented through proper care and patient or family education.

Of course the patient and his attending physician always have the last word on the plan of treatment.

HEALTH EDUCATION AND PROMOTION

In today's environment, the support of health education/promotion activities is considered a universal good. Health education/promotion has been defined as "efforts to encourage healthy lifestyles, discourage risk-associated behavior, and educate individuals about health care and the appropriate use of health services." There is a growing belief that healthy lifestyles will improve health status. In this regard, the public has become increasingly cognizant of the impact of lifestyle—smoking or excessive drinking, uncontrolled hypertension, poor diet, lack of exercise, and the like—on the incidence of disease and injury. Individuals have begun to assume more responsibility for their own health, with the understanding that changes in lifestyle can significantly reduce risk factors associated with premature death and disability.

A new philosophy also has emerged regarding the role of the employer in promoting well-being or wellness. There is growing opinion among at least major employers that they have a distinct responsibility to help improve the quality of health of their employees, and company-sponsored programs in health education/promotion offer a promising means to carry out that responsibility.

Health education includes a combination of learning experiences (both informational and educational) that help people to make informed and voluntary decisions about their health and safety, and about the health resources available to them. It provides individuals and families with the knowledge for making their own choices and pursuing their own actions about what is important for health and prepares them to accept the consequences of their decisions just as they would in any form of endeavor.

A health promotion program uses a variety of educational/behavioral strategies (e.g., health risk appraisal, one or more risk-reduction components, health education) to foster changes in daily life habits that could lead to better health. It attempts to integrate the concepts of disease prevention and lifestyle modification with the more traditional practice of treating diseases after they occur. The expectation is that such a program will benefit not only employees and their families but the employer as well by effecting reduced absenteeism and turnover, improved employee morale and productivity and savings on insurance and other employee benefit costs—important objectives of any employer. The program costs might be considered an investment in a company's human resources. The following examples of health promotion programs vary in difficulty to start, in the effort, equipment, and dollars required, and in their benefit:

Smoking cessation.
Hypertension recognition and control.
Stress management.
Weight control.
Employee assistance programs.
Exercise fitness.
Alcohol/drug abuse control.
Cancer risk reduction.
CPR training.
Accident risk reduction.
Self-care.
Emergency medicine.
Glaucoma screening.
Wise utilization of medical care benefits.

This new philosophy is consistent with the mounting intensity of interest in and expectations for health promotion activities. It also coincides with efforts to more effectively contain the escalation in the direct and indirect health, economic, and social costs associated with accidents and illness.

Is There Evidence that Health Education/Promotion Programs Reduce Health Costs?

In all fairness, it is difficult, at this time, to obtain hard data on cost savings, because of the short time these programs have existed. To see the effects of risk factor intervention on morbidity and mortality will take years. However, common sense alone suggests that prevention is preferable to curing, that staying healthy is less expensive than being sick, and that improved lifestyles should improve a person's health and longevity.

CONCLUSIONS

There are no "quick fixes" to the problem of rising health care costs; no magic solutions that lie near at hand. It is self-delusion to believe that major cost-containment results can be achieved in the short-term or middle-term without inflicting unacceptably high levels of discomfort and discontent on the public, the providers, and the payors (Medicare, Medicaid, Health Insurance Companies, Blue Cross/Blue Shield plans, HMOs, self-insureds, and self-pay patients)! Total care costs are essentially a product of volume of service and cost of service. To make significant inroads on either of these factors requires major structural changes in the system, or major behavioral changes on the part of the populace and the providers, or both. There is little sign to date of major behavioral changes, and no established method for producing such changes in large populations.

In the final analysis, the physician continues to be the primary decision-maker in the medical care system. The choice of what needs to be done, how much needs to be done, and where it is to be done is generally under the physician's control; therefore, review by physicians of physicians' practice for propriety, i.e., the provision of services that are medically indicated, may be the best possibility for controlling system-wide health care costs, as the goal of cost containment should be the promotion of an adequate supply of reasonably priced and rationally distributed resources.

All of these health care cost containment techniques are still experimental, and their cost effectiveness has not yet been fully determined. They do however, contribute to cost containment in two ways:

1. They tend to increase the cost consciousness of patients or physicians or both.
2. They tend to foster increased interaction and cooperation among the insured, the insurer, and often the hospital or physician.

It is unlikely that any one health care cost-containment technique will produce large savings for an employer. However, when a number of these techniques are put into effect together, significant cost reductions can be achieved.

CHAPTER 16

DEPENDENT CHILD CARE

Ann Costello
Kathleen Hunter Sloan

INTRODUCTION

The emergence of dependent child care as an employee benefit has been tied to the dramatic increase in the work force of mothers with young children. As a result, child care as an employee benefit has been considered a "women's" benefit. For many years child care in American society was clearly the responsibility of the mother; and, just as clearly, the mother's place was, with few exceptions, in the home. For the past two decades, as more women entered the work force and remained there after having children, the more troubling aspects of working parents and child care have received ever-increasing attention. First, child care represents a considerable expense for the employed parent; second, the desired quality of child care may be difficult to obtain or too costly to be a realistic alternative; and, third, employers desiring to retain working mothers have had to face the issue of either providing or subsidizing child care.

The increased attention paid to the question of employer responsibility for dependent child care stimulated debate over the most appropriate nature and form of child care and brought it forward as an issue of public policy requiring serious legislative deliberation. On a national level, Congress has examined the question of employer responsibility from the aspect of what, if any, direct role the federal government should play in dependent child care, as well as the government's indirect role through providing tax credits to both employer and employee.[1] State legislatures have both debated and enacted legislation to encourage employers to offer child care as an employee benefit. As in any public policy debate, conflicting ideological perspectives have shifted the focus of the debate from the question of the responsibility of employers to provide dependent child care to questions concerning the appropriateness of working mothers, the responsibility of society for children placed in day care, and the issue of whether parental leave from employment is a sounder alternative than day care.[2]

Recent industry studies and observations by employee benefits' experts have identified another major issue, one that has many long-term consequences. Dependent child care is a benefit that meets the employee's need for economic security. It also contributes to employer productivity by enhancing employee performance through the elimination of tensions related to parental concern over child care arrangements. These productivity factors include job stress, high rates of employee turnover, lost concentration on the job, and absenteeism and tardiness related to child care problems; if ignored, they could cost American industry hundreds of millions of dollars each year.[3] Both the needs and productivity requirements relating to dependent child care are of such magnitude that child care has been labeled "the employee benefit of the 1990s." Yet in the late 1980s, of over six million employers, slightly more than 3,000 are reported to offer any form of child care support.[4] The nature of this child care support varies from employer information and referral services to child care subsidies or even employer-owned day-care centers. These variations in the form of employer-sponsored child care have themselves

---

[1] For a review of Congressional action see "Democrats in Congress Open New Push for Child Care Aid," *Congressional Quarterly Weekly Review,* January 11, 1986, pp. 63–67; U.S. House of Representatives Select Committee on Children, Youth and Families, *Improving Child Care Services: What Can Be Done,* Hearings, 98th Congress, 2nd sess., December 1984 (Washington, D.C.: GPO).

[2] For a discussion of the conflicts concerning child care in the differing welfare reform proposals see *Congressional Quarterly Weekly Review,* July 19, 1987, pp. 1587–89. The primary legislative proposals for parental leave introduced in the 100th Congress in 1987 are H.R. 925, introduced by Representative William Clay (D-Mo.) and Representative Patricia Schroeder (D-Colo.), and S-249, introduced by Senator Christopher Dodd (D-Conn.) and Senator Arlen Specter (R-Pa.).

[3] Fern Schumer Chapman, "Executive Guilt: Who's Taking Care of the Children?" *Fortune* 115, no. 4 (February 16, 1987), p. 31.

[4] Cathy Trost, "Child-Care Center at Virginia Firm Boosts Worker Morale and Loyalty," *The Wall Street Journal,* February 12, 1987, p. 27.

contributed to the question of how employers can best design child care benefits for their employees in a way that meets both employee needs and employer objectives.

DEVELOPMENT OF CHILD CARE AS A BENEFIT

Employer concerns over child care as a benefit have, with few exceptions, been related to the increased numbers of mothers of young children who have entered the labor force during the past two decades. Prior to this, the American labor force was predominantly male. Women employees tended to be those without children or at least without preschool children. During the Civil War, World War I, and World War II, the provision of child care facilities such as nurseries or day-care centers permitted women to enter the work force as substitutes for men who had entered military service. During those times, labor shortages disrupted the work force; women with young children were encouraged to serve as temporary replacements for male workers. But when war was over the women were expected to leave these jobs and return home to their children. The "traditional family," in which the husband worked and the wife remained at home with responsibility for caring for the children, was the societal norm.

In recent years, however, social, legal, and demographic factors have contributed to a change in the American family structure. These factors, which include the increased rate of divorce among parents with young children, the increase in single parents with young children, and the increase in families where both parents are employed, have made the traditional family a minority among present workers. Fewer than 25 percent of the population currently live in a traditional family. Moreover, women now have substantially greater choice of whether or not to have children and when to have them. The woman planning a family limited to two children looks on the early childhood years as a limited period of time during which responsibilities for child care must be balanced with work responsibilities. This increase in the number of working mothers of young children has created a labor force comprised of almost equal numbers of men and women, as today's work force has just under 50 percent women.[5]

In the 1950s and 1960s the common practice was for women to work

---

[5] Employee Benefit Research Institute, "Child Care Programs and Developments," issue brief, May 1985, p. 2.

only before they had children and to return to work only after their children were old enough to be relatively self-sufficient within the family.[6] By the 1980s this was no longer the case. After having children, women were no longer leaving employment but were remaining at work.[7] In 1986 more than one half of mothers with children under six were working; in 1987 almost half of mothers with children under one were employed.[8] In 1985 women not currently married comprised 25 percent of working women with dependent children.[9] Today, two-income and single-parent families comprise a major portion of the work force. Moreover, child care is not just a women's issue; many men are single parents because of sole or joint-custody settlements or because they are widowers, and many married men share in child care responsibilities.

There does not appear to be any downward shift in the trends that are causing an increased demand for child care. The divorce rate continues to be high, and there has been increased acceptance of the two-income family. The Population Reference Bureau, in its 1987 major study, has concluded that the demand for child care services will continue to increase in the future.[10] One of the major reasons cited is the generally small number of workers that will be available in the 1990s due to previous low birth rates. Employers will be looking for all available qualified workers, many of whom will have a need for child care in order to be able to work. With the opportunity to delay childbirth, many women will have gained more work experience and may have higher education levels, and, therefore, be more valuable employees. Thus the trade-off in the future will be between higher salaries and staying home to care for children.[11]

Child care costs often run between $50 and $250 a week—or higher—depending on the age of the child, location of care, geographic region, and desired services. The Conference Board estimated that child care is the fourth largest budget item for working parents, after food, housing, and taxes, and that it may represent 30 percent of the family budget.[12] The high cost of child care may keep many low-income women who need work from employment.

---

[6] Martin O'Connell and David E. Bloom, *Juggling Jobs and Babies: America's Child Care Challenge* (Washington, D.C.: Population Research Bureau, 1987), p. 4.

[7] Ibid.

[8] Ibid.

[9] Ibid., p. 2.

[10] Ibid., p. 10.

[11] Ibid., p. 7.

[12] Dana Friedman, "Corporate Financial Assistance for Child Care," *The Conference Board Research Bulletin,* 1985, p. 6.

The development of child care as an employee benefit in many respects has followed the development of other major benefits, particularly health insurance and retirement benefits. Early in the 20th century increasing numbers of employers recognized that the individual employee could not afford to pay the costs of protection from illness and death or did not have the ability to save sufficient income for retirement without the employer's assistance. Viewed in this context, employer inclusion of dependent child care as a part of an employee benefit program further extends that array of employee benefits that are valued by employees because they provide protection from economic insecurity.[13]

Child care is essential if parents of young children are to work outside the home. The high cost of child care, as well as its limited availability, creates a form of economic insecurity for most working parents.[14] If a working mother cannot afford or locate adequate child care, her economic security is threatened by the loss of working income. The additional expenses of child care create a burden of economic insecurity on many young parents, as does the uncertainty of continued employment if the source of child care is lost or if the child is ill and cannot make use of the source.[15]

Since most employers have not yet included dependent child care among their employee benefits, the question arises: Why not? A small, albeit increasing, number of employers offer this benefit currently. Most of them have done so in recognition of both the responsibility of the employer, through the use of benefits, to contribute to employees' economic security and the benefit the employer may receive in the form of improved employee performance and consequent productivity. Some employers, however, may have recognized their responsibility for providing child care services and may also hope that these benefits will enhance productivity, yet they have failed to initiate the benefit because an appropriate form of child care for their employees was not evident. The ability of employers to design child care benefits that meet both employer objectives and employee needs, and that can be easily integrated with existing employee benefit plans, is emerging as the critical next stage in the development of dependent child care as an employee benefit.

---

[13] For more extensive discussion of the economic insecurity aspects on employee benefits see George E. Rejda, *Social Insurance and Economic Policy* (Englewood Cliffs, N.J.: Prentice-Hall, 1976), especially pp. 3–5, 7, and 12–15.

[14] For a comprehensive review of different aspects of the relation of work to child care see U.S. House of Representatives, Select Committee on Children, Youth and Families, *Work in America: Implications for Families,* Hearings, 99th Congress, 2nd sess., April 1986 (Washington, D.C.: GPO).

[15] See "What Working Women Want," Editorial, *The Wall Street Journal,* June 6, 1986.

Productivity and Child Care

Employers have a major interest in providing child care as a benefit if that benefit directly enhances productivity. The relationship between child care and productivity is an important issue, but its exact dimensions have yet to be determined; there persists a basic analytical problem because of the lack of appropriate data. Reasons for tardiness and absenteeism relating to child illness are not accepted as an appropriate excuse by firms; and, therefore, employees often state other reasons for their actions. There are many articles about a particular company's experiences, but aggregate industry data does not exist. Previous studies have concentrated on asking executives or employees for their impressions rather than assembling empirical data. Yet the issue is critical, for it is difficult for employers to act confidently without a clear and substantial basis for benefit design.

Certain recent surveys and studies have attempted to document the effects that problems relating to child care have on reducing productivity. *Fortune* contracted for a nationwide survey of 400 workers with children to examine the conflicts of child care and employment. Its major finding was that "problems with child care are the most significant predictors of absenteeism and unproductive time at work."[16]

In *Child Care and Corporate Productivity,* Fernandez presented the results of a study of 5,000 employees from five large companies. The majority felt that child care problems did cause nonproductivity. Over 70 percent of the employees with children under 18 had used working hours to deal with family concerns. Documentation showed that women bore a larger share than did men of the family duties, and had experienced reduced productivity due to family-related stress. Single male parents showed reactions similar to those of women with children. Overall, Fernandez concluded, "instances of missed days at work, tardiness, leaving work early, and dealing with family issues during working hours were highly positively correlated with employees' difficulties in coping with child care and handling dual family/work roles."[17] Emlen and Koren, in a survey of 8,000 workers in Portland, Oregon, found that workers with children under 18 had higher levels of tardiness and absenteeism than employees with no children under 18.[18]

---

[16] Chapman, "Executive Guilt," p. 31.

[17] John P. Fernandez, *Child Care and Corporate Productivity* (Lexington, Mass.: D. C. Heath, 1986), p. 15.

[18] A. C. Emlen and P. E. Koren, *Hard to Find and Difficult to Manage: The Effects of Child Care on the Workplace* (Portland, Oregon: The Workplace Partnership, 1984), p. 6.

Three separate national surveys asked employers who offered child care services how the company had been affected by the addition of the benefit.[19] The respondents in two of the studies were predominantly employers who sponsored their own day-care centers. The data were of a subjective nature, but did present a positive relationship between corporate child care and improved productivity. Improvements due to the addition of child care were seen in recruitment, employee morale, absenteeism, reduced turnover, and increased employee work satisfaction.

Public Policy for Child Care Benefits

Public attention has been focused mainly on the difficulty that parents have in finding affordable and quality child care. The media has presented the "child care dilemma" in numerous articles and features.[20] The need for child care, in general, and the means to encourage employers to support child care benefits have been on the public policy agendas for both national and state legislatures[21] The number of states enacting legislation that encourages employers to develop day-care facilities is small, and the funds to be used as incentives for employers are quite limited.[22] Federal legislative efforts to establish public policy for child care also have been limited, although during 1987 growing numbers of national political leaders have been lobbying for increased support from employers for child care.

Public policy for child care benefits has been closely linked to tax

---

[19] The three studies that provided the surveys are: Sandra Burud, Pamela R. Aschbacher, and Jacquelyn McCroskey, *Employer Supported Child Care: Investing in Human Resources* (Boston: Auburn House, 1984); Renee Y. Magid, *Child Care Initiatives for Working Parents: Why Employers Get Involved* (New York: American Management Association, 1983); and Kathryn S. Perry, *Employers and Child Care: Establishing Services through the Workplace* (Washington, D.C.: Women's Bureau, U.S. Department of Labor, 1982).

[20] For example, two cover articles: Chapman "Executive Guilt"; and "The Child-Care Dilemma," *Time,* June 22, 1987, pp. 54–63.

[21] For example see "Governor Signs Law Boosting Day Care," *The Hartford Courant,* June 5, 1987, p. B5; "Improvements in Day Care are Only the Beginning," *The Hartford Courant,* May 27, 1986.

[22] Connecticut, one of those states with legislation for child care benefits through enactment of Public Act 83-453, "An Act Increasing Tax Incentives for Industry Sponsored Day Care," has a $250,000 tax-credit program that provides a 50 percent tax credit for businesses that subsidize part or all of their employee day-care costs administered by the Department of Human Resources; a $250,000 low-interest loan program for employers to develop or improve day-care facilities; as well as a tax-credit program for employers who create an employee day-care facility.

policy, as has been the case with other employee benefits.[23] The high costs of child care have brought requests for relief from working parents, although it was not until 1976 that Congress amended the federal tax code to permit the costs of child care to be used as a tax credit. Congress granted the tax-preferred status for child care benefits, as it has to other major employee benefits, by the passage of the Economic Recovery Tax Act of 1981. This legislation made the applicable eligibility requirements for any Dependent Care Assistance Programs maintained by an employer those of Section 129 of the Internal Revenue Code. Such programs must be nondiscriminatory, and the deductible amounts are limited to those expenses eligible for the individual income tax credit for child care, if paid by the employee.[24]

As is the case with other employee benefits, existing public policy encourages diverse means of supporting child care. While the United States has lagged behind other industrial nations in support for child care, there is increasing political pressure for governmental action and for the development of further incentives for employers to offer child care as an employee benefit. While tax policies provide some financial relief to employed parents, and employer tax incentives created by legislative action hope to stimulate more employer support for child care, it is most likely that a mix of private, governmental, and employer-sponsored support will be the outcome of public policy implementation on this subject.

TAX STATUS OF CHILD CARE BENEFITS

Individual Tax Credit

Section 21 of the Internal Revenue Code is the individual federal tax credit available for expenses for dependent care and household services. The eligible expenses are limited to $2,400 for the care of one "qualifying

---

[23] For a review of testimony on tax-preferred status of employee benefits see such Congressional Hearings as U.S. House of Representatives, 98th Congress, 2nd sess., Subcommittee on Select Revenue Measures of the Committee on Ways and Means, *Hearings: Distribution and Economics of Employer Provided Fringe Benefits,* September 1984 (Washington, D.C.: GPO); U.S. Senate, 98th Congress, 2nd sess., Subcommittee on Taxation and Debt Management of the Committee on Finance, *Hearings: Fringe Benefits,* July 1984, (Washington, D.C.: GPO).

[24] See U.S. House of Representatives, 99th Congress, 1st sess., Select Committee on Children, Youth, and Families, Hearings on *Tax Policy: What do Families Need?,* April 1985 (Washington, D.C.: GPO).

individual'' and $4,800 for more than one; further, such expenses cannot exceed the lower of the two incomes of a married couple, or the income of a single person.[25] For a married couple to be eligible, both must be employed. If a working couple has two children and incurs $6,000 of eligible expenses, but one spouse has taxable income of only $1,000 for the year, then $1,000 would be the limit on eligible expenses for computing the tax credit. Special rules apply if a spouse is incapacitated or is a full-time student for at least five months; such an individual with one dependent is assumed to have earned income of $200 per month and for more than one dependent, $400 per month.[26] This applies to only one spouse at a time. Also, a married couple must file a joint return to be eligible for the credit.

To be eligible for tax credits, care and services must be provided for at least one of the following:

1. A child under 15 whom the worker may claim as a tax exemption.
2. A mentally or physically incapacitated dependent or spouse of the taxpayer.[27]

The services may be provided by a babysitter, cook, housekeeper, or maid, so long as they are for the well-being of the dependent individual and are employment related for the worker. Eligible care must be rendered by someone who is not a child (under 19 years old) of the taxpayer and is not claimable as a tax exemption by the worker.[28] If the services are provided outside the home, then those in the second category (mentally or physically incapacitated) must also live at the taxpayer's residence each day for eight hours.[29]

Expenses at a dependent day-care center are allowable if the center meets the state and local governments' regulations and laws.[30] A dependent day-care center is defined as one providing care for more than six individuals, whether profit or nonprofit, and receiving remuneration or services for the care. The tax credit percentage is progressively lowered for every $2,000 increment in adjusted gross income. Starting with $10,000 dollars and below, the percentage is 30 percent; from $10,001–$12,000, it is 29 percent. The decrease continues by 1 percent up to an income of $28,000. At that level and above, the tax credit is 20 percent,

---

[25] I.R.C. Section 21(c)(1, 2).

[26] I.R.C. Section 21(d)(2).

[27] I.R.C. Section 21(b)(1).

[28] I.R.C. Section 21(e)(6).

[29] I.R.C. Section 21(b)(2)(B).

[30] I.R.C. Section 21(b)(2)(C).

subject to the limitations of qualified expenses. The maximum credit available is $720 for the care of one qualifying individual and $1,440 for more than one. If in any tax year the total tax credit is not used, then it is lost and may not be brought forward in future tax years.

In 1986, the dependent tax credit totaled $3 billion. A major discussion of the appropriateness of the tax credit has led to an introduction in Congress of legislation that would modify the current system. Some legislators propose that individuals with incomes over $60,000 or $75,000 not be allowed to use the tax credit, while others try to give more assistance to the lower income worker. The tax credit structure would not help the lower income worker who, because of his or her number of personal exemptions, does not have to pay any federal income taxes.

Employer-Provided Dependent Care

In 1981, the Reagan Administration surprised many by supporting a special tax-free extension to dependent-care assistance provided by employers under the Economic Recovery Tax Act (ERTA). At that time, federal grants to day-care facilities were dramatically cut, the Administration hoping that the private sector would assume some of the responsibility for the cost of the care. The Tax Reform Act of 1986 amended section 129, which concerned qualified Dependent Care Assistance Programs (DCAPs) maintained by employers.

Under the new provisions, payments made in accordance with the tax law are deductible for the employer and excluded from the employee's gross income. The maximum exclusion for a tax year is the lesser of $5,000 or the earned income of the worker or spouse.[31] Eligible expenses and the method for determining the earned income of a spouse who is disabled or is a student are both stated in Section 21 of the Code.

The Tax Reform Act of 1986 imposed uniform nondiscrimination tests on statutory employee benefits; an employer has the option whether or not to include the dependent care program under this classification. If the employer does not do this, then a special nondiscrimination test applies. The average employer-provided benefit for those who are not defined by the Code as highly compensated must be at least 55 percent of the employer-provided benefits to those who are so defined.[32] For those plans that involve the use of a salary reduction, employees with compensation below $25,000 may be disregarded in the calculation.[33] The reasoning for

---

[31] I.R.C. Section 129(a)(2).

[32] I.R.C. Section 129(d)(8)(A).

[33] I.R.C. Section 129(d)(8)(B).

this is that the existence of the tax credit for dependent care would benefit this group of employees more than would a salary reduction. If the plan uses a combination of salary reduction and another method, such as employer subsidy, then the rules will have to be determined by the Secretary of the Treasury.

The tax act mandated certain basic standards that an employee benefit plan must meet in order to protect the employee from having to pay taxes on an employer contribution (preferred tax status). These include:

1. A written plan.
2. Legally enforceable employees' rights under the plan.
3. Reasonable notification to employee of benefits available.
4. Interest of employer to maintain plan indefinitely when established.
5. Maintenance of the plan for exclusive benefit of employees.[34]

Dependent-care programs must comply with these standards and provide, by January 31st of each year, a written statement of expenses incurred for each participant of the plan.[35] Also, the Tax Reform Act of 1986 requires employers to give employees written explanation of Section 21, the tax credit, and explain under what conditions the credit would be more advantageous than the DCAP.[36]

Section 129 does not require that DCAPs be funded, and the employee may not take a tax credit (Section 21) for money excluded under the dependent-care plan. The definitions of "highly compensated employees," "compensation," "excluded employees," and "employer" applicable to statutory employee benefit plans by the Tax Reform Act of 1986 also apply to Dependent Care Assistance Plans.

DESIGN OF CHILD CARE BENEFITS

Employer Objectives

Employers make the decision to offer dependent child care when they find it advantageous in order to meet their objectives. These objectives fall into three major categories:

---

[34] Joint Committee of Taxation, *General Explanation of the Tax Reform Act of 1986* (Chicago: Commerce Clearing House, Inc., 1987), p. 812.

[35] I.R.C. Section 129(d)(7).

[36] Joint Committee on Taxation, *General Explanation*, p. 812.

1. To meet employee needs.
2. To meet employer productivity goals.
3. To improve external relations.

Employee Needs

The employer's objectives in meeting employees' needs is a recognition of the importance of employee benefits as a part of compensation for employment. If the absence of available child care alternatives or the high costs of the child care that is available are creating hardships for employees, then the employer may find it advantageous to offer dependent child care in recognition of employee needs. Personal considerations often dictate whether an individual will accept a particular employer's job offer or another's. Willingness to relocate is not as common as it was in the past; family considerations are much more important. Individuals examine what the employer is willing to provide in total compensation, which includes benefits as a major component.

Employees see the employer's commitment to such a benefit as dependent care as recognition that employees are more than just workers. Many employees are members of two-income families or are single parents; child care is extremely important to them. Assistance in finding quality care or in reducing cost bonds the employee to the company. One of the major outcomes is employee stress reduction; the employee is not constantly worried about problems associated with child care. The design of the actual benefit affects the level of freedom from concern, but almost any form of assistance provides some form of relief. Child care has both emotional and financial costs; employees often have guilt that someone else is taking care of their children and are worried about the short-term and long-term effects on the child. Also, the financial cost of such care may be tremendous. An employee with child care concerns may see the need for and importance of such a benefit as greater than benefits such as a pension or 401(k) plan. The child care problem exists now; the others are something for the future.

Employee Productivity

An employer's addition of child care as an employee benefit to meet employee needs may directly or indirectly improve productivity; however, with increasing health care costs and the passage of more restrictive and demanding employee benefit legislation, employers are very hesitant to add benefits or increase any existing benefit. Firms are not as willing as in the past to implement new programs just to meet employee needs. An employer considering the addition of an employee benefit wants to know how the cost of offering the additional benefits will promote the goals of the employer. If addition of child care will contribute to productivity goals by reducing absenteeism relating to child care problems, by reducing employee turnover and the attendant costs of hiring and training new employees, then the employer may decide potential improvements in productivity outweigh the additional costs of the benefit. Employers have started to realize that if an employee is late, absent, or disturbed because of a child care problem, productivity will be affected. Someone else will have to do the individual's duties, and this creates not only stress for other workers but also scheduling problems. Unforeseen problems, such as a late babysitter or a sick child, may mean that a project is not completed on time. At certain periods of the day, an employee's attention may not be on his or her work, but rather on whether the child has arrived at home after school.

Recent studies suggest a positive relationship between employer-supported dependent care and productivity. Articles about firms that adopted dependent care plans are appearing constantly in the press, and individual firms are noting increased morale, increased employee retention, reduced recruiting costs, and reduced absenteeism as results. All of these appear to have led to increased individual employee productivity. Firms gain from employees who are able to concentrate and commit themselves to their work.

Improvements in External Relations

Besides the productivity gains, an employer may incur additional advantages external to the organization. The installation of new benefits is often announced in the local press and industry publications. The image of a "caring" employer is reinforced; a message is transmitted that the company is progressive and a leader in its human resource management. Other firms may use the plan as a prototype for their benefit package, and the company's name is often repeated as a trendsetter. Positive public relations may be furthered by actual involvement of the company in increasing the quantity and quality of dependent care in the community; this depends, however, on the actual design of the benefit.

ISSUES

While dependent care may offer many advantages to a company, there are major issues that affect its acceptance and are probably causing many firms to hesitate.

Equity

In a conventional employee benefit plan option such as health care, an employee may or may not use the benefit during a given year; but all employees are eligible to use it at any time, and over time all employees may have occasion to rely on it. However, dependent care may only be used by those who have "qualifying individuals" as dependents, and it is estimated that less than 10 percent of the average work force of a large company would use it at any one time.[37] Those employees who do use it will change over time. Employee resentment could arise from those who have no need for such a benefit; compensation funds are being spent for something that does not help them at all. Some employees may feel that they raised their children without any company assistance and question why these employees now should receive such financial help.

Equity is a fundamental issue in employee benefits. Nondiscrimination rules exist to protect against a disproportionate amount of funds for a benefit being spent on top management, owners, and stockholders. Dependent care designed as a conventional benefit may provide assistance to one worker at a particular time, but another employee in a similar job may have no use for it. The equity issue could lead to individual personnel issues; the actual composition of the employee group is important in determining the size of the potential problem.

Upper Management

Decision making concerning dependent care will be made by upper management. Some have argued that senior managers may be older and not really aware of the sociological changes that have affected the demographics of the labor force.[38] Their sensitivity to the issue of child care may not be as acute as is necessary, and they may not be aware of the different options available for plan design.

Firm's Reputation

While there are positive outcomes for the reputation of a company offering dependent care, a risk manager would advise caution when considering the benefit from an external relations perspective. Firms do not want

---

[37] Peter L. Hutchings, "Managing Salary Reduction Dependent Care Benefits," *Benefit News Analysis* 6, no. 9 (October 1984), p. 24.

[38] Phyllis K. Bonfield, "Working Solutions for Working Parents," *Management World*, February 1986, p. 10.

to be involved with any program that may be substandard; the expected gain from such a substandard plan would be more than offset by the problems presented. Personnel complaints and, ultimately, liability suits could severely damage the company's reputation. Recently, several day-care providers were charged with sexual abuse of the children in their care. While this has not been a common occurrence, the risk still exists.[39] In choosing options, a company may decide to deal only with state-licensed or registered providers. As the majority of dependent care in the United States is not licensed, the decision to deal only with licensed providers severely limits the possible use of the benefit by the employees.

As in any business decision, the company must be very careful about the qualifications of any day-care provider with whom it would associate. Attempts to limit liability by having a nonprofit foundation or a professional day-care chain actually control and manage the on-site or off-site facility have been utilized. In plans that simply make referrals, suggestions have often been limited to licensed care; here the purpose is to inform, not to be the provider. Flexible benefits plans and reimbursement accounts merely provide financial aid; choosing the provider, within the requirements of the tax code, is left to the employee. This is similar to the indemnity health plan; the company is not responsible for the medical malpractice of the doctor chosen by the employee. In the same manner, a firm would not be liable for the actions of a dependent-care provider.

Dependent-Care Industry

One of the major obstacles to providing dependent care is the nature of the industry itself. High-quality child care requires dedicated and informed care-providers with both an understanding of child development and the patience to provide the appropriate personal care in stressful situations. The ability to attract and retain qualified workers is difficult, for child-care workers and teachers receive an average pay of only $9,000 and have a turnover rate of 42 percent, the highest of any occupation.[40] Those who have been entrusted with our greatest asset—children—are customarily paid less than garbage workers. Quality of care is hard to maintain with such a high turnover.

There is also a major shortage of available care. Connecticut, which

---

[39] Insurance companies raised premium rates and tightened underwriting requirements during 1986 and 1987 for liability coverage for day-care homes and dependent-care centers. Most policies issued do not cover claims concerning sexual abuse of children.

[40] Jeanne Saddler, "Low Pay, High Turnover Plague Day Care Industry," *The Wall Street Journal,* February 12, 1987, p. 27.

is often cited as being one of the most progressive states for dependent care, still needs care for 40,000 more children.[41] Parents who have to work are forced to look for acceptable alternatives; an "underground" industry exists, whereby payments made to providers are not reported for income tax or Social Security tax purposes. The market for child care is one of high demand and low supply; the seller exercises control because the parent needs the care. Often the parent cannot even legally use the federal tax credit, because the payments are unreported, even though the tax form for Section 21 does not ask to whom the payments were made. Nevertheless, child care is regulated by state agencies, and employers considering offering day-care directly through their own facility must meet state and local regulatory requirements.

EMPLOYER INITIATION OF THE DESIGN PROCESS

The Feasibility Study

When considering the design or redesign of a benefit package, feasibility studies are often conducted to explore the possibilities of a particular benefit.[42] The analysis may be undertaken by management; however, often outside consultants are used for their specific expertise. A benefits administrator may be current in the tax and legal implications of the existing package, but may not be familiar with the implications of a child care benefit. Dependent care is a special type of benefit, and expert assistance may be needed in both the employee benefit field and in the child care field. While this may require the use of more than one consultant, there are specialists who have knowledge of both areas and have access to needed support systems in the legal and tax areas.

The company's overall employee benefit philosophy is the first part of the discussion; the employer's objectives for adding child care should be established. With the objectives clearly designated and the need of the employees and their child care problems identified, those responsible for designing the new benefit may proceed.

The personnel problems that appear to diminish productivity should be reinforced by the benefit design. For example, to meet employer pro-

---

[41] Telephone interview with Jeanne Milstein, Program Manager, Day Care Services, Department of Human Resources, State of Connecticut, July 29, 1987.

[42] Assistance for this section was given by Barbara P. Adolf, Associate Consulting Actuary, Buck Consultants, Harmon Meadows, New Jersey, in a telephone interview on March 13, 1987.

ductivity objectives of reducing training costs, the level of acceptable turnover and the demographic characteristics of employees are important considerations. Some firms, such as Burger King, may accept a high turnover of employees working in their restaurants, while SmithKline and others may spend over $10,000 for recruiting and training per employee and want a very low turnover rate.[43] Some industries such as health care have predominantly female employees in their child-bearing years. The feasibility study should identify and further examine those relevant employee characteristics that suggest that child care would meet the company's objectives. While dependent care may not be useful for all employees, the productivity impact of child care problems on the entire organization may make alleviating those problems a priority.

A firm's ability to afford to spend additional dollars on a new benefit will place constraints on acceptable alternatives. A flexible benefits plan that includes dependent care but also allows the employer more financial control thus may be attractive. Economic projections about future requirements for employees will help management to understand not only the immediate situation but also long-term implications as well. Bio-Polymers, a high technology firm in Hartford, has implemented dependent care because of a tight employment market—both current and projected.[44]

To establish the need for dependent care during the feasibility study and to estimate the possible productivity gains, data from personnel records are an important source of information. Examination of demographics of the employee group will show how many present employees are members of two-income families or are single parents; these data will assist in making projections as to future child care requirements. Comparative data about tardiness, absenteeism, and turnover can be collected for groups of employees with and without children. From this, the company can cost out the possible personnel problems as well as advantages associated with child care programs. Since the collected data are very limited, other techniques may be implemented. Adolf and Rose, in *The Employer's Guide to Child Care*, recommended that the company use informal means and target groups to be effective in the feasibility study.[45] Informa-

---

[43] *The Wall Street Journal,* "A Special News Report on People and their Jobs in Offices, Fields and Factories," June 30, 1987, p. 1.

[44] Susan Howard and Robert Weisman, "Shortage Demands New Ideas," *The Hartford Courant,* November 11, 1986, p. 1.

[45] Barbara Adolf and Karol Rose, *The Employer's Guide to Child Care* (New York: Praeger Publishers, 1985), p. 88.

tion as to whether child care has been mentioned as a problem by employers is gathered from individuals by the personnel department and supervisors.[46] Target groups involve discussions among a small number of specifically selected individuals led by an expert whose purpose is to elicit individual viewpoints concerning child care needs and propose alternative responses to the identified needs. The leader tries to keep the discussion focused on plan design options that would be acceptable to the company.

Management and/or the consultant have the most current cost and tax implications of the different options available. To assist in choosing those that are viable for the firm, information must be available on child care in the local community. In a 1987 study, the Census Bureau stated that working women's children under five years of age were cared for most frequently in another home (37 percent), cared for in the child's home (31 percent), placed in organized child care facilities (23 percent), or cared for at work (8 percent).[47] The employer will try to establish the existing availability of day-care homes and dependent-care facilities. The existence of babysitters may be tied to the employment rate; the lower the rate, then possibly the more individuals who are willing to do this work. The ages of children and appropriate facilities for this age group are important considerations; children may be infants, toddlers, preschoolers, school-age, or those with special needs. Care for infants is the most expensive and often in the shortest supply. Special children may be handicapped or temporarily sick; care of this type may not be available at all. Data are gathered about licensed or registered caretakers, costs, hours of operation, and services provided. If any other local businesses offer dependent-care assistance, their programs are examined.

Company executives should then be able to choose which design options are viable given the overall employee benefit objectives. Besides the obvious factor of cost, the firm must decide what level of involvement should exist in actually providing the dependent care. Low involvement would be a referral system; very high involvement would involve an on-site facility. After analyzing the possible acceptable options, the firm does a formal needs assessment. The firm should be seriously committed before doing this; the employees' expectations may be raised, and negative feelings toward the employer could result if not handled properly. Adolf and Rose state that the questionnaire should cover (1) demographics, (2) attitudes, (3) connection between child care needs and work problems,

---

[46] Ibid.

[47] Census Bureau, "Minding the Kids," *The Wall Street Journal*, May 26, 1987, p. 35.

and (4) special needs.[48] Besides the normal demographics, the first section would also cover the type and operating features of child care currently available. The assessment data will assist the firm in deciding which of the acceptable options would most satisfy employees' needs now and in the future.

EMPLOYER OPTIONS FOR CHILD CARE

On completion of the feasibility study, the employer should have identified the child care needs and associated problems that inclusion of child care as an employee benefit may alleviate, thus meeting the employer's objectives. The limited number of employers offering child care benefits has resulted in a limited number of options in practice. Dana Friedman of the Conference Board, a nationally recognized expert in employer-supported dependent child care, states that the figure is actually much higher than the 3,000, but documentation is not currently available. According to Dr. Friedman, approximately 800 firms offer information and referral services, 800 have dependent care centers, 30 provide vouchers, 300 have employee discounts, 1,500 use dependent-care spending accounts, and 760 provide dependent care in their flexible benefits programs.[49] Employers may offer their employees support for family day care. While employers are free to try innovative new approaches, they may choose those options currently in use by other employers that best fit their objectives.

Information and Referral Service

When no major employee child care problems appear as a result of the feasibility study, the employer may elect a relatively simple form of employer involvement in the use of information and referral services. An employer may join a consortium of other employers or may act alone. Usually a contract is developed with a nonprofit group such as United Way to provide the service. A list of licensed care is compiled, and on-site inspections are made to attempt to control the listing of only high-quality providers. However, the quality is not guaranteed. The option's objective is to match the individual needs of the working parents with the available resources. Some companies have in-house assistance or access to special

---

[48] Adolf and Rose, *The Employer's Guide to Child Care,* p. 91.

[49] Telephone interview with Dr. Dana Friedman, Senior Research Fellow, The Conference Board, on July 21, 1987.

"hotlines." The employers make financial contributions to support the system, which is dependent on already existing child care. The employee does not receive financial assistance from this program unless it is coupled with some other form such as flexible benefits. If an employer is contemplating expanding the dependent-care plan, then the usage of the referral system would be important in estimating the demand for other forms of dependent care.[50]

Family Day-Care Home Support

Employers may have reason to choose the option of support for family day-care homes for their employees. Family day-care homes offer care for up to six children in a home by an individual. This form of care is often cited as preferred for children from one to three years old; also, many homes are willing to accept infants and toddlers. The family day-care home is often more convenient and less expensive than day-care centers and provides a homelike atmosphere.[51] The lower costs, convenience, and neighborhood locations may make this the most attractive option. However, estimates are that since 70 percent or more of the homes are unlicensed, the quality of care may vary greatly.[52] Employers in some localities have provided financial support to cover start-up costs and assisted in the hiring of workers and the development of day-care homes. The homes usually agree to carry the necessary insurance and to act as independent contractors.[53] In some cases, the providers may agree to tuition ceilings on their prices. The employer does not have management or financial control over the homes and is, therefore, not legally liable. The employer may or may not use some form of financial assistance to help employees with the cost of using the homes. (Vouchers, discounts, flexible benefit plans, and reimbursement accounts could be used as well, subject to the Tax Code requirements.)

Workplace Child Care Centers

Analysis of the information gathered in the feasibility study may lead employers to establish a workplace child care center to meet their objectives most advantageously. Child care centers provide for the care of

---

[50] Employee Benefit Research Institute, *Child Care Programs and Developments*, p. 5.

[51] Adolf and Rose, *The Employer's Guide to Child Care*, p. 54.

[52] Friedman, "Corporate Financial Assistance for Child Care," p. 2.

[53] Burud, Aschbacher, and McCrosky, *Employer-Supported Child Care*, p. 189.

more than six children and are usually licensed. Services may be for children from infants through school age. Extensive safety, health, and sanitation requirements are imposed on centers by local and state laws. If there are any educational services such as preschool or kindergarten, then the programs must meet the appropriate educational standards of the community and state. Institutional care is provided, and as many as 100 children, usually from three years and older, may be cared for at one center.

Employers may offer child care in one of the several ways identified by Adolph and Rose. Centers may be:

1. Owned and managed by the company.
2. Owned by the company and operated by an outside group.
3. Contracted out to a nonprofit agency.
4. Contracted with a profit-making service.[54]

A company may act alone or join a consortium of other companies in this endeavor. The consortium concept has been used by companies in locating care in downtown urban areas, but is not very common. Difficulty in trying to meet varying company goals has limited its usage. Another form that is relatively new is the building and operating of centers by developers for their office tenants.[55] The centers are used as a marketing technique to attract employers to lease space.

Employer-supported day-care centers may be at the worksite or nearby. The financial arrangements of the employers may vary. Some firms have supplied the start-up costs and expect the program to be self-sustaining; others have supplied full financial support and subsidized yearly center losses. Major employer concerns are cost, usage, and quality. These programs have high start-up costs, and attendance may fluctuate. In exchange for financial support, employers may want preferential treatment for their employees, reduced rates, or reserved spaces.[56]

The positive aspect of this option care is that the center may be more flexible in providing the types of service required by the company's employees. The center may be open for different shifts of workers and easily accessible in location. Parents, during breaks and lunch, may be able to visit their children. The available resources may permit children to have

---

[54] Adolph and Rose, *The Employer's Guide to Child Care,* p. 37.

[55] See Cathy Trost, "Toddling Trend: Child Care Near the Office," *The Wall Street Journal,* October 6, 1986, p. 33.

[56] Employee Benefit Research Institute, *Fundamentals of Employee Benefit Programs,* 2nd ed. (Washington, D.C.: Employee Benefit Research Institute, 1985), p. 202.

broader experiences than available with a babysitter or day-care home. The employer has the greatest amount of control. Furthermore, the center may enable the employer to recruit new employees from a broader range of the community population, thus fostering a positive image for the firm in the community.

However, there are negative considerations for the company. The employer must be concerned with pricing. The benefit may be provided free to the employee; or, more commonly, the employee will pay part of the cost. The existence of other child care services in the community may be competition for the center; prices may be lower or the location more desirable. If the center is located in an urban location, then the employees may not want to transport their children long distances daily, or on public transportation. Also, the employer may incur extensive administrative and legal problems imposed by providing a center. Liability for the center may become a major issue and liability insurance expensive or unavailable. Some companies set up a 501(c)3 nonprofit corporation to avoid financial loss, but a firm's reputation can be severely damaged by claims of injury to children.

The tax treatment of an employee's use of on-site facility care was provided by the Tax Reform Act of 1986 in Section 129.[57] The utilization and the value of services determine the amount of tax exclusion that is subject to the regular dollar constraints applied to other forms of child care.

Voucher

The employer may find the option of child care vouchers most appropriate in meeting child care objectives. The voucher system provides an employer-financed subsidy applied to any form of child care or some specified form. The dollar amount may be a flat amount or percentage of fixed costs up to a maximum cost.[58] The programs are usually limited to licensed care and are more common in smaller companies, especially in the retail field. Companies are able to assist lower wage workers with the cost. This is attractive to firms that cannot afford or choose not to adopt flexible benefit plans. The employer's costs are fixed, and they do not have any responsibility for providing the care. In programs that are open to any form of licensed or registered care, the employee has complete freedom of choice. The overriding constraint is the availability and quality

---

[57] I.R.C. Section 129(e)(8).

[58] Friedman, "Corporate Financial Assistance for Child Care," p. 12.

of existing child care providers. If there is not enough care available, this program will be of limited use to employees. Equity problems for nonparticipating employees may exist. Section 129 requirements must be followed in the design of the benefit to provide the employee tax-preferred protection on the employer's subsidy.

Discount

In some cases, the employer may decide that the discount option meets the child care objectives. An employer may arrange with local day-care providers for a discount for its employees, the most common discount being 10 percent.[59] The vendor agrees to such a program for marketing reasons to fill unused slots in the program. The cost to the employer is very low, and often an additional 10 percent discount will be subsidized by the company. To provide the tax-preferred status of dependent-care assistance plans, Section 129 requirements must be followed. The discount form of financial assistance allows a program to expand and contract with the changing demand of the working parents.[60]

However, limitations exist for several reasons. The program depends on existing child care programs that may not meet the individual employee needs for care (for example, care for infants).[61] The available care may not be in a desirable location or open at the necessary hours. Employees do not have much choice of care providers, if they wish to participate. The employer has no control over quality of care; if employee dissatisfaction becomes apparent, then the employer has the choice of discontinuing the discount program or trying to negotiate a new plan with other providers. If a subsidy is used, then an equity issue exists for employees with or without children who do not participate in the program.

Flexible Benefit Plans

In 1987, due to rising health care costs and the increasing percentage of the payroll being committed to employee benefits, many firms have shown renewed interest in flexible benefits or "cafeteria" plans (Section 125). In 1981 only 13 companies had adopted the "flex" plans, but by mid-

---

[59] Donna Fenn, "The Kids Are All Right," *Inc.*, January 1985, p. 54.
[60] Friedman, "Corporate Financial Assistance for Child Care," p. 20.
[61] Ibid.

1987 over 800 plans had been established.[62] A cafeteria plan is one where the participants have the option of choosing a qualified benefit or cash.[63] Section 125 of the Tax Code has very tight nondiscrimination rules that affect the actual design of the benefits plan. Most plans are in one of two formats. One provides a core of benefits for all workers, with an additional "cafeteria" portion. In this case, a worker is given a number of credits, usually a flat amount, but possibly with a portion based on salary or length of service; the employee is allowed to choose his or her individual package with the credits. The qualified benefits include any medical expenses, group term life insurance, disability, dependent care, vacation, 410(k), and group legal services. Section 125 also imposes restrictions on the use of certain of the benefits such as group term life insurance and vacation. Not all of the allowable qualified benefits may be offered by a particular employer, and some will provide more than one type of a benefit. For instance, plans may offer more than one type of health care with different deductibles, providers, or coverage. However, employers are very sensitive to the number of benefits provided, since more offerings may mean higher administrative costs.

The second format is totally flexible with no core benefits, and the employee has complete choice among the provided qualified benefits. In both formats, the allowable benefits have tax-preferred status, and the employee is not taxed on the employer's contribution. If the employee wishes to buy more benefits or has to pay part of the cost of the benefit, then this may be done under either format by using pre-tax dollars.

With the changing demographics of the workplace, individual workers increasingly have differing needs; flexible benefits solve many of the problems concerning the types of coverage most appropriate for a particular group. Conventional employee benefits were designed for a traditional family and often may not meet the specific needs of current employees, a majority of whom are single or are in two-income families. Flexible benefits, individually tailored by employees, appear to be more useful for today's more varied work force.

Certain advantages exist for the employer as well; for a flexible benefits program employees must become more aware of the actual benefits and their relative costs in order to be able to make a choice. Since many employers feel that employees do not appreciate or understand the conventional benefits package, this employee involvement in the flexible ben-

---

[62] Assistance for the sections of this chapter on Flexible Benefits and Flexible Spending Accounts was provided by Diane Luedtke, F.S.A., vice president, CIGNA Employee Benefits Services, Inc.

[63] I.R.C. Section 125(c)(1).

efits program is very important, especially considering the high cost of benefits. The employer is also able to use the flexible plan to place a financial control on how much its contribution will be to the total package, rather than having to deal with each individual benefit. In turn, money does not have to be wasted for benefits that an employee may be able to receive from a spouse's employee benefits or simply may not want.

Flexible benefit plans provide an ideal situation for dependent care. Recognizing that only a portion of employees will have a need for such a benefit, the plan allows them to have it without depriving other employees of some portion of compensation cost. The equity issue does not exist; the employee who chooses dependent care elects it instead of some other benefit. Over time the needs of employees will change; some will want dependent care now but not in the future, and for others the reverse will be true.

The cafeteria plan must follow the Dependent Care Assistance Plan rules of Section 129 to be a qualified benefit. The plan may allow for care of children, handicapped dependents, and elderly parents. Reimbursement accounts using salary reduction are under Section 125, and similar requirements for dependent-care administration exist for those plans as well as the flexible benefit programs, both being governed by Section 129. Feasibility studies are often used to decide which qualified benefits should be included and which options should be offered. Often the incorporation of dependent care in a flexible benefit package results from an examination of the whole benefit package, rather than from a consideration of the need for dependent care.

While flexible benefits programs seem to provide the panacea for dependent-care coverage, several factors, such as adequate payroll systems, computer programs, and communications systems, can cause high start-up costs. For a group of 1,000 employees, those costs could easily exceed $100,000. Consultants from specialized firms and certain insurance companies are commonly employed to discuss the desirability and feasibility of such programs. Often the start-up costs may be recovered by savings brought by the new plan in the first two years. Some firms have in-house expertise and facilities to provide much of the computer and communications systems; for them, implementing the program has not been as costly. Others have seen the costs and administrative complexity and have decided simply to offer modified versions that often include reimbursement accounts. Many firms are just beginning to explore the possibility of flexible benefits, realizing that many of the costs will be lower in the future with the advent of better and cheaper technology. Consultants often state that flexible benefits are the way of the future and that their growth will also provide a tremendous increase in dependent-care assistance plans.

Flexible-Spending Accounts

Flexible-spending accounts, commonly referred to as reimbursement accounts, are being used to provide employees with dependent-care benefits. Such an account may be established at a very low or negligible cost to the employer. Employees are allowed to pay for dependent-care expenses with pre-tax dollars by use of a salary-reduction program. Money going into the dependent-care account must be kept separate from the two other possible forms of reimbursement accounts—accident and health, and legal. Employers may contribute to the account, but often do not. The total amount of the dependent-care account is restricted by the requirement of Section 129 of the Code; the total maximum amount that may be in the account is $5,000 for a single person or married couple filing jointly, or $2,500 for a married person filing separately. This is also subject to the earned-income limitation. The employer does not pay Social Security taxes or unemployment taxes on the employee's salary reduction. The employer's savings from such a program are often used to offset the administrative costs of setting up an individual account and reimbursing the employee usually biweekly, monthly, or quarterly for the eligible expenses.

Eligible employment-related expenses provided for qualifying individuals by approved caretakers are governed by the Tax Code's Section 129, Dependent Care Assistance Plan, and Section 22, Tax Credit Allowance for Dependent Care. While the plan may be funded by employee and employer contribution, if any form of salary reduction is used, then the plan is subject to Section 125, cafeteria regulations. The amount of funds that will be committed to the account must be decided in advance and must cover the whole period of the plan. Thus an individual may not choose to participate for only 3 months rather than 12 months in the plan, in order to protect the tax exclusion.

Only a change in family status will allow a change in contribution amount; this could be a change in marital status, addition or loss of dependent, or addition or loss of spousal employment. The plan also requires that any money left in an account at the end of the year is forfeited by the employee; "use it or lose it." The employee is not allowed to shift remaining funds to another reimbursement account or to a 401(k) plan. The employer must use the remaining funds for the exclusive benefit of the employees. The future forfeiture can strongly affect the desirability of such a benefit, and the employee should be conservative in his or her estimate of expenses. Also, it is essential that the employee does a comparison between the benefit of a salary reduction versus the tax credit of Section 21. This is especially true for employees whose combined income of both spouses (or if filing as a single person) is below $25,000.

In compliance with Section 129, the account may be for the care of a child under 15, but also for an adult who resides at the taxpayer's residence for at least eight hours a day and whom the employee can claim as a dependent. This allows for the possibility of adult day care or eldercare, which has vast sociological importance for the future as more parents live longer and may be financially dependent on their children. While this is not very common today, Section 129 provides for this contingency. The definition of dependency is according to the Tax Code and is very restrictive; liberalization in the future is possible and is essential for eldercare to be successful as a benefit.

The discrimination rules and reporting requirements must be strictly adhered to in the plan, and a Section 125 plan document is required for all salary-reduction plans. The mechanics of collecting the appropriate information required by the employer to verify compliance with the requirements of Section 129 concerning employment-related expenses and caretakers is not delineated in the Tax Code. Consultants generally advise that employers require the submission of detailed information from the participating employees. This is essential to fulfill the reporting requirement and to protect the qualified status of the plan.[64] However, many employers do not do this. They do not ascertain, for instance, whether the dependent day-care center is following the laws and regulations of the particular state and local community. Thus some plans may pay for care at an unlicensed center that the state requires to be licensed.

The employer may administer the accounts or may contract with an outside organization, such as a third-party administrator or an insurance company (such as CIGNA), to provide the necessary expertise. Compliance with the Tax Code is essential, and the employer must have a payroll system that is able to handle the different accounts which will affect the calculation of withholding of income and social security taxes for the employee and unemployment and social security taxes for the employer. The timing of the eligible expenses during the year does not have to match the amount of the prefunded dollars in the individual account. For instance, if bills are reimbursed quarterly and there are not enough funds in the account at the time, then the employee is simply reimbursed at the next period when there are sufficient funds.

The reimbursement account does meet the equity issue so often

---

[64] Sylvia M. Burgess, "Cafeteria Plans and Alternative Methods for Providing Taxable Benefits to Employees (Part 1)," *Compensation Planning Journal,* June 1985, p. 184.

raised about dependent care. Those not needing the benefit are not deprived of employer funds that could be used for some more desirable benefit. Also, the employer's costs are usually recovered by the savings generated by the employer not having to pay social security and unemployment taxes on the participating employee's reduction. The employee is, in effect, paying for the cost of such a benefit by trading social security and unemployment earnings credits. Thus, the cost is borne only by those participating in the plan. Typically, less than 10 percent of a company's employees will make use of spending accounts for dependent care.[65] Whether this is due to the individual characteristics of the group (that is, only a small proportion have a need for such a benefit) or a dislike of some characteristic of the plan (such as the need for documentation) or simply a lack of understanding of the benefit is not known.

Sick Child Care

One of the major problems facing parents is the care of their children when they are sick. Most day care centers and many day care homes will not allow sick children; babysitters often are not qualified to care for children who are ill; and home nursing care may be prohibitively expensive. Thus, employers are providing support for child care for illness and designing plans that will provide for specialized temporary care. These programs may involve the care of qualified individuals as babysitters or the use of services of local hospitals with special programs.[66] All of the possible forms of financial assistance for dependent care may be designed to include this, if the services exist. The costs of such programs are far less than the cost of an employee staying home to care for the child and the effects far less disruptive to the work organization.

CONCLUSION

Employers concerned with their responsibility to design benefits which both meet employee needs and contribute to productivity will continue to search for ways to integrate child care into their existing benefit plans.

---

[65] Raymond C. Linstrum, "What to Include in a Flex Program," *Benefit News Analysis* 8, no. 1 (January 1986), p. 4.

[66] For a more thorough discussion of this see Joann S. Lublin, "Corporate Support Gives Boost to Services that Care for Working Parents' Sick Kids," *The Wall Street Journal,* November 13, 1986, p. 35; and Ena Naunton, "Now, Day-Care Centers for Sick Kids," *The Hartford Courant,* February 10, 1986, p. D5.

Employers have gained an increased understanding that parents employed in the labor force who have young children currently comprise, and in the forseeable future will continue to comprise, a substantial portion of the labor force. The high cost of quality child care and problems with its continuing availability can contribute to the economic insecurity of those parents, particularly single parents and those with low incomes. Current evidence indicates that concerns over child care do affect employee performance detrimentally. Responsible employers will seek to improve their ability to analyze the child care needs of their employees and to design benefits that meet employee needs as well as employer objectives, and that are administratively feasible. Any additional federal or state support legislated for child care will complement those employer-sponsored child care benefits.

CHAPTER 17

PROPERTY AND LIABILITY INSURANCE AS AN EMPLOYEE BENEFIT

Bernard L. Webb

INTRODUCTION

While forms of property and liability insurance have been provided as employee benefits for many years, the practice was very limited until the late 1960s. There were reports of automobile insurance benefit plans as early as 1925, but few details are available. Because of the hostility of agent associations and insurance regulatory authorities, the plans were not discussed in public and were sold and serviced in an almost clandestine manner.

The practice received considerable attention at the 1926 meeting of the National Convention of Insurance Commissioners, the predecessor organization of the National Association of Insurance Commissioners.[1] Many commissioners issued regulations at that time prohibiting the practice of insuring employee-owned cars under fleet policies covering company-owned cars. One such ruling was challenged in the courts, but the commissioner's authority to issue it was upheld.[2] Little more was heard of

[1] National Convention of Insurance Commissioners, *Proceedings* (Chicago: National Convention of Insurance Commissioners, 1926), pp. 117–20, 272–76.

[2] *Flat Top Insurance Agency* v. *Sims*, 178 S.E. 518, (W.Va., 1935).

property-liability employee benefit plans for 20 years, though it is clear a few such plans persisted.

Such plans apparently began to spread in the middle 1950s, though progress was slow and not well publicized. The major public manifestation of their growth was the activity of agents' associations in promoting administrative and legislative rules prohibiting the plans.

The first open promotion of property-liability employee benefit plans began in 1965, when the Continental National American Group (CNA) insurance companies announced their entry into the field. Other insurers followed, and plans proliferated until the middle 1970s. Severe underwriting losses at that time caused CNA and a number of other insurers to discontinue such plans. As this is written (1987), several insurers are active selling property-liability employee benefit plans, primarily automobile insurance.

KINDS OF BENEFITS

Virtually all kinds of property-liability insurance for individuals and families have been offered as employee benefits at some time. However, automobile and homeowners insurance (especially the former) have been most common.

Automobile Insurance

Automobile insurance has been the major property-liability insurance employee benefit for two reasons. First, it is compulsory (or virtually compulsory) for car owners in many states. Second, it is the largest single insurance purchase, in terms of premium, for most families.

In most cases, all automobile insurance coverages are offered, including liability, collision, comprehensive, medical payments, towing-cost coverage, and, in the states where applicable, no-fault benefits. The coverages offered under employee benefit plans usually are identical to those offered under policies sold to individuals. In a few cases, the medical payments coverage is modified to coordinate benefits with the employer's medical expense benefit plans. Also, where permitted by state law, a substantial deductible may be provided in the no-fault benefits, applicable only to the employee and family, to coordinate benefits with the employer's medical and income-loss plans.

Employees usually are permitted to select any reasonable limits of liability coverage, and are not restricted to predetermined limits as under group life and health coverage. The same right of selection usually is available for medical payments and no-fault coverage. Physical damage coverages (collision and comprehensive) usually are written for the actual cash value of the vehicle, and employees usually are permitted a selection of deductibles.

In most automobile insurance plans, coverage is provided under individual policies issued to the employees. Some insurers issue master policies to employers with certificates to employees, but the practice is not widespread and is prohibited by law in some states.

Homeowners Insurance

The second most important property-liability insurance employee benefit is homeowners insurance, including tenants coverage for those who do not own a home. It has proved less popular than automobile insurance for two reasons. First, the annual premium for homeowners is likely to be less than automobile insurance premiums for most families. Consequently, the potential savings are smaller. Also, many mortgage lenders require borrowers to pay the premium for homeowners coverage through monthly deposits to an escrow account. This requirement complicates the handling of homeowners policies through employee benefit plans.

Another complication in using homeowners insurance as an employee benefit is the wide variation in the coverages needed, even among families in the same income class. Some families own their homes, while others do not. Some families may need coverage for musical instruments, photographic equipment, golf or other sports equipment, stamp or coin collections, and a wide variety of other special personal property items, while others do not.

Personal Umbrella Liability Coverage

Several insurers offer personal umbrella liability policies under employee benefit programs. These policies offer high limits of liability coverage (usually in multiples of $1 million). The umbrella policy is excess over automobile liability and the liability coverage of the homeowners policy, and does not begin to pay until the limits of those policies have been exhausted.

Personal umbrella policies are especially popular among professional employees, executives, and other highly paid persons. Little variation exists in coverage needs from one person to another, so the administrative burden is much lighter for personal umbrella coverage than for automobile insurance and homeowners policies.

Other Coverages

Several other property-liability coverages have been offered as employee benefits. Boat insurance has been offered by several employers, and at least one airline offers insurance for the personal aircraft owned by its employees. Many employers provide coverage for employees' liability for their on-the-job activities.

KINDS OF PROGRAMS

All the coverages mentioned may be provided under three different kinds of programs. They are distinguished primarily by the relative cost and the amount of underwriting discretion retained by the insurer.

Franchise Plans

The earliest plans were franchise plans, in which the insurer charged the same rates it charged for its individual policies and retained its normal underwriting prerogatives. The principal advantage to the employee was the convenience of installment payment of premiums through payroll deduction. Insurers frequently did not charge interest for the installment payment privilege. In a few cases, the employer paid some or all of the premium, especially for sales personnel or other employees who used their cars for business purposes. Beginning in the late 1960s, franchise plans began to lose ground to mass merchandising plans.

Mass Merchandising Plans

Franchise plans and mass merchandising plans are similar in that the insurer retains the right to underwrite individual employees under both. However, they differ in one important respect because there is a price reduction (in comparison with policies issued individually) under the mass merchandising plans but not under franchise plans.

The extent of the price reduction varies among insurers. It also may vary according to the number of participants in the plan. The amount of expense saving in a particular plan also may affect pricing. The expense savings result primarily from reduction of the agent's commission, but the expense of premium collection and bad debts also may be reduced. Some have suggested better accident prevention measures made possible by mass merchandising may reduce losses, providing another source of premium reduction. However, no statistical evidence of such savings has been made public.

Mass merchandising plans first appeared in substantial numbers around 1970. They still are the dominant form of property-liability employee benefit insurance, but the number of true group plans is increasing.

True Group Plans

Unlike franchise and mass merchandising plans, the insurer under a true group plan agrees to provide coverage for all eligible employees, without the right of individual underwriting. Of course, such an agreement would leave the insurer open to adverse selection in the absence of some method for compelling or enticing low-risk employees to participate in the program.

To avoid adverse selection, insurers that write group property-liability insurance require the employer to pay a part of the premium, a practice not common in franchise or mass merchandising plans. The amount of employer payment required varies among insurers. One insurer requires the employer to pay three or four dollars per week for each employee. Others require the employer to pay at least a specified percentage of the employees' premium, usually from 40 to 60 percent.

For automobile insurance, the insurer may require the employer pay a part of the premium for only one car for each employee. Employees who own more than one car would pay the full premium for the additional vehicles. Without some employer premium payment, the low-risk employees might be able to find insurance outside the plan at a cost equal to or less than the cost within the plan, since the rates within the plan are increased somewhat by the requirement that the insurer provide coverage for all eligible employees. The loss of low-risk employees to competitors, of course, would result in even higher rates for the remaining participants.

ADVANTAGES FOR EMPLOYEES

The advantages realized by the employees vary according to the kind of plan. Quite obviously, a true group plan offers more advantages than a franchise plan.

Lower Cost of Insurance

Both mass merchandising and true group plans offer the advantage of lower cost of insurance to the employee. The difference is especially noticeable under true group plans because the employer usually pays a part of the premium as a requirement of the plan. The magnitude of the premium reduction may vary from a negligible amount to 15 percent or more, not considering any premium payment by the employer. By definition, franchise plans do not offer any reduction in premium.

Greater Availability of Insurance

True group plans make insurance available to some employees who might otherwise be uninsurable. Under franchise and mass merchandising programs, the insurer retains the right to refuse insurance to employees who do not meet its underwriting requirements. However, it appears insurers are more lenient in underwriting individuals under such plans than they are for persons who apply otherwise. Consequently, even franchise and mass merchandising plans probably provide insurance for some people who would find it difficult to obtain in the absence of such plans.

Payroll Deduction

All the plans mentioned usually provide the advantage of installment payment of premium through payroll deduction. In many cases, the insurer does not charge interest or a service fee for the installment payment privilege.

DISADVANTAGES FOR EMPLOYEES

The disadvantages for employees appear to be small. The insurance may terminate when the employment terminates, though some insurers provide some form of conversion privilege. Also, the employees may not have the same flexibility in the selection of coverages that they would have if they purchased their insurance independently. Finally, some employees have expressed concern that their employers may obtain sensitive personal information through the processing of insurance claims or underwriting forms.

ROLE OF EMPLOYER

The role of the employer may vary from plan to plan. In some cases, the employer pays a part of the premium. The employer also may provide advice to employees on the kinds and amounts of insurance they should purchase, However, it is more common for the insurer or agent to provide such advice. It may be illegal in some states for any other person than a licensed insurance agent to provide such advice or to solicit applications for insurance.

In any case, the employer needs to give insurer or agency personnel access to employees for the explanation of the program and the negotiation of applications. The administration of property-liability insurance plans is substantially more complex than the administration of group life and health plans because of (1) the greater variation in the coverage provided, (2) greater frequency of changes, and (3) the complexity of handling claims, especially liability claims. For that reason, most employers prefer not to become involved in the detailed administration of the plan. The details of administration usually are delegated to the insurer or its representatives. Claims administration is seldom if ever performed by the employer, not only because of the complexity of the task but also because many employees would prefer their employer not have access to such detailed information about their off-the-job habits and activities.

In most property-liability insurance plans, the employer's role is limited to (1) selection of the insurer, (2) payment of the premiums from the employer's own funds, through payroll deduction or a combination of the two, (3) mediation of disputes between the insurer and employees. The employer may be involved in notifying the insurer of needed changes in employees' coverage, such as changes of cars or increasing homeowners limits to reflect inflation. However, it is more likely the employees will handle such changes directly with the insurer or its representatives.

FEDERAL INCOME TAX CONSEQUENCES

Property-liability insurance plans do not enjoy the tax advantages that have been granted for pension plans, group life and health insurance, and prepaid legal insurance plans. This lack of tax incentive is a major reason for the slow growth of property-liability insurance plans.

Any property-liability insurance premiums paid by the employer on behalf of an employee are considered taxable income to the employee. It must be reported as income by the employee and the appropriate tax must be paid. Such payments by the employer are deductible expenses for the employer. Several bills have been introduced in Congress to grant property-liability plans the same tax advantage as other employee benefit plans, but none has been passed.

U.S. LABOR CODE

The U.S. Labor Code contains two provisions that may relate to property-liability insurance benefit plans. The first provision prohibits any employee from giving anything of value to any labor organization or an officer or employer thereof if such labor organization represents or could represent the employer's employees.[3] There is a specific exemption for payments into a fund to provide pensions, life insurance, or health benefits for employees. Payments into a fund to provide property-liability insurance for employees are not exempt, and would be illegal. Consequently, such plans could not be administered by labor unions if the employer pays any of the premium.

The second applicable provision of the labor code specifies the factors related to the employment concerning which the employer can be compelled to bargain in good faith with the union. Property-liability insurance plans are not specifically included among the bargainable items, but employers can be required to bargain about ". . . rates of pay, wages, hours of employment, or other conditions of employment."[4]

The National Labor Relations Board (NLRB) held in the *Inland Steel* case that: "The term 'wages' as used in Section 9(a) must be construed to include emoluments of value, like pension and insurance benefits, which may accrue to employees out of their employment relationship."[5] The NLRB's view has been supported by the U.S. courts in at least two circuits.[6] The interpretation adopted by the NLRB and the courts would seem to be sufficiently broad to include property-liability insurance. Consequently, it seems likely an employer can be compelled to bargain for such benefit plans.

STATE REGULATION

The primary responsibility for insurance regulation rests with the states. Historically, state regulation has been hostile to the use of property-liability insurance as an employee benefit. In many cases, regulatory pro-

---

[3] 29 U.S.C. 186.

[4] 29 U.S.C. 158(a), 159(a).

[5] 77 NLRB 4 (1948).

[6] See *United Steel Workers* v. *N.L.R.B.*, 170 F.2d 247 (1948) and *W. W. Cross Co., Inc.* v. *N.L.R.B.*, 174 F.2d 875 (1949).

hibitions have been based on statutory provisions prohibiting unfair discrimination in insurance rating. In some cases, specific statutory prohibitions have been enacted.

Fictitious Group Regulations

Beginning in the 1950s, the insurance commissioners of 17 states adopted fictitious group regulations. The regulations differ somewhat from state to state, but the Florida regulation is reasonably typical:

> The Insurance laws of Florida require that any rate, rating plans or form of fire, casualty or surety insurance covering risks in this state shall not be unfairly discriminatory. Therefore, no insurer, admitted or non-admitted, shall make available through any rating plan or form, fire, casualty or surety insurance to any firm, corporation, or association of individuals, any preferred rate or premiun based upon any fictitious grouping of such firm, corporation, or association of individuals, which fictitious grouping is hereby defined and declared to be any grouping by way of membership, license, franchise, contract, agreement, or any other method or means; provided, however, that the foregoing shall not apply to accident and health insurance.[7]

Unfair discrimination would seem to be a weak basis for such rulings. Group life and health insurance has been accepted as not unfairly discriminatory in all states for many years. No apparent reason exists to treat property-liability insurance differently.

Fictitious Group Statutes

In 1957, Florida replaced its fictitious group regulation with a fictitious group statute. The statute provided:

> (1) No insurer or any person on behalf of any insurer shall make, offer to make, or permit any preference or distinction in property, marine, casualty, or surety insurance as to form of policy, certificate, premium, rate, benefits, or conditions of insurance, based upon membership, nonmembership, employment, of any person or persons by or in any particular group, association, corporation, or organization, and shall not make the foregoing preference or distinction available in any event based upon any fictitious grouping of persons as defined in this code, such fictitious grouping being hereby defined and declared to be any grouping by way of membership, nonmem-

[7] Fla. Ins. Dept., Bulletin No. 211 (1957).

bership, license, franchise, employment, contract, agreement or any other method or means. (2) The restrictions and limitations of this section shall not extend to life and disability insurance.[8]

Effectiveness of Rulings and Statutes

The fictitious group rulings and statutes seemed to be effective for several years after their adoption. However, by the late 1960s, several insurance commissioners had approved filings for franchise and mass merchandising programs in spite of the seeming regulatory and statutory prohibitions. Their actions were challenged in the courts by agent associations, but were generally upheld.[9] Although most of the fictitious group regulations and statutes remained on the books, they became increasingly less effective in controlling property-liability insurance plans for employees.

Enabling Legislation

Beginning in 1969, several states enacted legislation designed specifically to authorize the use of property-liability insurance for employee benefit plans. Minnesota was the first state to adopt such a statute. It reads as follows:

> One rate is unfairly discriminatory in relation to another if it clearly fails to reflect equitably the differences in expected losses, expenses and the degree of risk. Rates are not unfairly discriminatory because different premiums result for policyholders with like loss exposures but different expense factors or like expense factors but different loss exposures, so long as the rates reflect the differences with reasonable accuracy. Rates are not unfairly discriminatory if they attempt to spread risk broadly among persons insured under a group, franchise or blanket policy.[10]

The Minnesota statute was the model for several other states, but Hawaii took a slighily different route. It enacted a rather detailed enabling law specifically for automobile insurance.[11]

---

[8] Fla. Stat., Sec. 626.973 (1972).

[9] See for example, *Georgia Ass'n of Independent Ins. Agents* v. *Travelers Indem. Co.*, 313 F. Supp. 841 (N.D. Ga. 1970); *Independent Ins. Agents* v. *Bolton*, 235 N.E. 2d 273 (Illinois, 1968); and *Independent Ins. Agents* v. *Herrmann*, 486 P. 2d 1068 (Washington, 1971).

[10] Minn. Stat. Ann., Sec. 70A.04(4), (1981).

[11] 24 Hawaii Rev. Stat., Sec. 431-751 et. seq.

At its 1986 annual meeting, the National Association of Insurance Commissioners (NAIC) adopted a model act for group property and liability insurance. The act specifically authorizes the writing of group property and liability insurance under a master policy, with certificates issued to individual participants.[12] However, the NAIC is an advisory body, so the act does not have any legal effect until it is adopted by state legislatures.

Present Status

It appears property-liability insurance can be used as employee benefit plans in all states. However, policy forms, rates, and rating plans must be filed with the insurance commissioner in virtually all states and must be approved before use in over half of the states. In early 1987, one insurer was offering its true group automobile insurance plan to employers in several states. Its plan provided for experience rating of each group, a feature that might complicate approval in some states. Several other insurers were also experimenting with group automobile insurance.

SUMMARY AND CONCLUSIONS

Only a small percentage, probably less than one percent, of personal property-liability insurance is now sold through employee benefit plans. The practice is growing, though at the slow pace that would be expected of an experimental marketing technique.

State regulation, which historically has been hostile to the use of property-liability insurance as an employee benefit, now seems less hostile. However, few states have specific enabling legislation.

Provisions of the federal Internal Revenue Code and the Labor Code place group property-liability insurance at a competitive disadvantage, relative to group life and health insurance and pension plans. Use of property-liability insurance in employee benefit plans is likely to grow slowly unless these federal laws are changed.

---

[12] For the text of the NAIC model act, along with annotations, see Vance C. Gudmundsen, "Group Property and Casualty Insurance: Annotations to the NAIC Model Act," *Journal of Insurance Regulation* 5, no. 2 (December 1986), pp. 224–66.

CHAPTER 18

LEGAL SERVICE PLANS

Claude C. Lilly III

ENVIRONMENT

Legal service plans are not a new development; they have been in effect since the early 1900s. In fact, insurance contracts providing legal benefits were available by 1907. However, legal benefit plans were relegated to a secondary role until the 1970s.

As an employee benefit, prepaid legal service plans have made substantial gains in the 1970s and early 1980s. Legal service plans are not as numerous as most of the traditional benefits. The growth of prepaid service plans has leveled off, and there probably will not be further growth in this area in the short run. Four factors, however, have been primarily responsible for providing an environment conducive to the growth of legal service plans: (1) a change in the public's attitude about using lawyers, (2) a change in federal laws, (3) a change in the attitude of the bar associations, and (4) a change in state laws.

THE PUBLIC'S LEGAL NEEDS

The public has always had a need for lawyers, even if it has not always sought legal help. A study done for the Association of American Law Schools in 1938 found in a sample of 412 families that 315 legal matters arose. However, legal advice was sought for only 35.2 percent of the 315 legal matters.[1] While comparable data are not available today, it is proba-

[1] Charles E. Clark and Emma Corstvet, "The Lawyer and the Public: An A.A.L.S. Survey," 47 *Yale Law Journal* 1276 (1938).

bly safe to assume that the legal needs of Americans have increased. The United States seems caught up in a litigious arena that seems to affect every strata of society. For example, expenditures for legal services grew more rapidly than the national income account during the 1970s and the first half of the 1980s. Even in nonlitigious areas of legal practices (e.g., wills, real estate sales, and taxation), consumers are finding the services of a lawyer are needed more frequently.

FEDERAL LAWS

Three changes in federal laws have affected the growth of legal service plans. First, in 1973, Senators Williams and Javitz introduced S.1423. The bill modified the Labor Management Relations Act of 1947. The bill stated:

> section 302(c) of the Labor Management Relations Act, 1947 is amended . . . by adding immediately before the period . . . or (8) with respect to money or any other thing of value paid by any employer to a trust fund established by such representative for the purpose of defraying the cost of legal services for employees, their families, and dependents.[2]

S.1423 was amended prior to enactment, but the basic provision cited above was not changed. The impact of S.1423 was to introduce prepaid legal service benefits into the area of collective bargaining.

The second federal change was initiated in 1974 by the passage of the Employee Retirement Income Security Act (ERISA). Since prepaid legal plans provided on a group basis are subject to ERISA, state insurance regulation over these plans is limited. Specifically:

> Neither an employee benefit plan described in Section 4(a), which is not exempt under 4(b) (other than a plan established primarily for the purpose of providing death benefits), nor any trust established under such a plan, shall be deemed an insurance company or other insurer.[3]

This allowed prepaid legal plans offered on a group basis (and subject to ERISA) to avoid state insurance regulations unless the group plan is offered by an insurance company.

---

[2] U.S. Congress, Senate, Subcommittee on Labor, "Joint Labor-Management Trust Funds for Legal Services, 1973: Hearings on S.1423," 93rd Congress, 1st session, April 10, 11, and 16, 1973, pp. 2, 3.

[3] Public Law 93-406, Section 514(b)(2)B.

The third, and perhaps the most important federal legislation was passed in 1976. Section 120 of the Internal Revenue Code was so modified that:

> Gross income of an employee, his spouse, or his dependents, does not include—
>
> (1) Amounts contributed by an employer on behalf of an employee, his spouse, or his dependents under a qualified group legal services plan (as defined in subsection (b)), or
>
> (2) The value of legal services, under a qualified group legal services plan (as defined in subsection (b)) to, or with respect to, an employee, his spouse, or his dependents.[4]

Section 120(b) defines a qualified legal service plan as:

> a separate written plan of an employer for the exclusive benefit of his employees or their spouses or dependents to provide such employees, spouses, or dependents with specified benefits through prepayment of, or provision in advance for, legal fees in whole or in part by the employer.[5]

The law further stipulates that contributions can be made only to insurance companies, to qualified trusts, or to legal service providers.

THE AMERICAN BAR ASSOCIATION AND STATE BAR ASSOCIATIONS

Until the 1970s, the bar worked vigorously to block the development of legal service plans. The bar contended legal service plans interfered with the lawyer-client relationship. The American Bar Association Canons of Professional Ethics, under which lawyers functioned until 1969, specifically set forth that lawyers could provide service to associations or groups, but not to the individual members of a group or association.[6] The canons also prohibited a lawyer from letting his or her name or professional services be used to allow the unauthorized practice of law; group plans constituted the unauthorized practice of law.[7] The content of these canons formed the primary weapons for attacking banks, hospital collec-

---

[4] Internal Revenue Code, Chapter 26, Section 120.

[5] Ibid. (This law is set to be eliminated in 1988.)

[6] Special Committee on Evaluation of Ethical Standards, American Bar Association, "Code of Professional Responsibility," preliminary draft, Canon 35 (Chicago: American Bar Association, 1969), pp. 124, 125.

[7] Ibid., Canon 47, p. 127.

tion agencies, unions, and real estate services when any type of legal activity was involved.

The bar's attack on the provision of legal services can be documented easily. As early as 1919, the bar attacked legal service plans offered to retail merchants by merchants' protective associations. Generally, these associations concentrated on collecting overdue accounts.[8] The services offered by these associations were attacked successfully in the courts by the bar as being the unauthorized practice of law.

Automobile clubs in the 1930s offered, as one of their benefits, to provide legal advice and to defend members against legal problems relating to the operation of automobiles. These plans were also attacked successfully by the bar as being the unauthorized practice of law.[9]

The 1930s saw the development of a legal aid department by the Brotherhood of Railroad Trainmen (BRT). The union plan was the first major plan to survive bar attacks. The BRT aided members in settling major injury claims workers had against the railroads. Generally, a member paid no fee for legal advice about how a claim should be handled. If a claim involved litigation, the member was given a list of approved lawyers that could be utilized in fighting a claim. The agreement between a member and a listed lawyer was approved by the BRT, and the contingency fee was established by the BRT with the approved lawyer. The approved lawyers were required to pay a percentage of their contingency fee to the union to continue the operation of the legal program. This system was slowly modified. By 1959, the contingency fee was no longer fixed, and the union stopped receiving any payments from the lawyers.

The bar attacked the BRT plan for many years.[10] But, the attacks were never reviewed by the United States Supreme Court until 1964.

---

[8] See, *State ex rel Lundin* v. *Merchants' Protective Corporation,* 177 P.694 (1919); *People ex rel Lawyers' Institute of San Diego* v. *Merchants' Protective Corporation,* 189 Cal. 531 (1922); and *People ex rel Los Angeles Bar Association* v. *California Protective Corporation,* 76 Cal. App. 354 (1926).

[9] See, *People ex rel Chicago Bar Association* v. *Motorists' Association of Illinois,* 854 Ill. 595 (1933); *People ex rel Chicago Bar Association* v. *Chicago Motor Club,* 199 N.E. 1 (1935); *Seawell* v. *Caroline Motor Club, Inc. et al,* 209 N.C. 624 (1936); *Rhode Island Bar Association* v. *Automobile Service Association,* 100 A.L.R. 226 (1935); *in re Maclub of America Inc.,* 3 N.E. 2d 272 (1936); and *Automobile Club* v. *Hoffmeister,* 338 S.W. 2d 348 (1960).

[10] See, *Ryan* v. *Pennsylvania R.R. Co.,* 268 Ill. App. 372 (1932); *In re O'Neill,* S.F. Supp. 465 (1933); *Hildebrand et al.* v. *State Bar of California,* 225 P.2d 509, 510 (1950); *Atchison, Topeka, and Santa Fe Railway Company* v. *Jackson,* 235F. 2d 392 (1956); and *In re Heinrich,* 140 N.E. 2d 835.

Then a case involving the BRT reached the Supreme Court.[11] It ruled the BRT plan was permitted under the 1st and 14th Amendments to the United States Constitution.

The bar had lost another fight eight months prior to the BRT decision by the Supreme Court. The Virginia legislature had amended the Virginia Code in 1956 to expand the definition of a runner (a person who sought out legal cases) to include "an agent for an individual or organization which retains a lawyer in connection with an action to which it is not a party and in which it has no pecuniary right."[12] The National Association for the Advancement of Colored People (NAACP) in Virginia challenged the law because it blocked the Virginia State Conference of the NAACP from pursuing school desegregation litigation with the use of the conference's staff lawyers. The U.S. Supreme Court ruled the Virginia Code violated the 1st and 14th Amendments.

The BRT and NAACP cases were reinforced in 1967. The United Mine Workers (UMW) Union in Illinois was accused of the unauthorized practice of law because it maintained a staff lawyer who helped members settle workers' compensation claims. The Supreme Court reiterated that vital rights could not be denied and sided with the union.[13]

In spite of the BRT, NAACP, and UMW cases, the American Bar Association maintained its opposition to legal service plans when it developed the Code of Professional Responsibility in 1969 to replace the Canons of Professional Ethics. The new code afforded substantial barriers to legal service plans. The code stipulated specifically that nonprofit legal service plans should be offered only if they met these criteria:

> DR2–103(D) (5) Any other nonprofit organization that recommends, furnishes, or pays for legal services to its members or beneficiaries, but only in those instances and to the extent that controlling constitutional interpretation at the time of the rendition of the services requires the allowance of such legal service activities, and only if the following conditions unless prohibited by such interpretation, are met:
>
> (a) The primary purpose of such organizations does not include the rendition of legal services.
>
> (b) The recommending, furnishing, or paying for legal services to its members is incidental and reasonably related to the primary purposes of such organization.

---

[11] *Brotherhood of Railroad Trainmen* v. *Virginia ex rel Virginia State Bar,* 377 U.S. 1 (1964).

[12] *National Association for the Advancement of Colored People* v. *Button,* 371 U.S. 422 (1963).

[13] *United Mine Workers* v. *Illinois Bar Association,* 389 U.S. 219 (1967).

(c) Such organization does not derive a financial benefit from the rendition of legal services by the lawyer.
(d) The member or beneficiary for whom the legal services are rendered, and not such organization, is recognized as the client of the lawyer in that matter.[14]

While innocuous in appearance, this section, in conjunction with other provisions of the code, was used to block the provision of free legal advice by unions.

The code was attacked in 1971 in the *United Transportation Union* case.[15] The Supreme Court again ruled that unions had the right to group legal services. The court stated:

> the principle here involved cannot be limited to the facts of this case. At issue is the basic right to group legal action, a right first asserted in this Court by an association of Negroes seeking the protection of freedoms guaranteed by the Constitution. The common thread running through our decision in *NAACP* v. *Button, Trainmen,* and *United Mine Workers* is that collective activity undertaken to obtain meaningful access to the courts is a fundamental right.[16]

The American Bar Association has since so modified the code that group legal service plans can be provided. In fact, bar associations have become involved in the development of legal service plans. However, all of the state supreme courts, which are responsible solely or in conjunction with the state bar associations for establishing the rules of conduct for lawyers, have not developed a code of professional responsibility similar to the American Bar Association Code. Technically, some states still have codes of professional responsibility that could impede group legal service plan growth. But, because of the existing case law, it seems unlikely any state code is actually a barrier to the development of group legal service plans.

STATE REGULATION

Until the 1970s, state regulation of legal service plans was minimal. Most regulation was handled through the courts and aimed at obtaining jurisdiction over legal service plans. The first efforts by states to control legal service plans took place during the early 1900s. During this period, the

---

[14] American Bar Association, "Code of Professional Responsibility and Canons of Judicial Ethics," Disciplinary Rule 2-103 (D) (X), p. 8.

[15] *United Transportation Union* v. *State Bar of Michigan,* 401 U.S. 585 (1971).

[16] Ibid., p. 585.

Physician's Defense Company offered legal and defense coverage to doctors. For an annual premium of $15, a doctor could purchase a policy that had an annual aggregate limit of $10,000 and a per case limit of $5,000. Insurance commissioners in some states sought to regulate the company, but the company resisted. Several suits ensued, and the commissioners were generally successful in gaining jurisdiction over the company.[17] As a result, the company finally quit selling its policies. Following these cases, state regulation of legal service plans was fairly dormant until the *United Transportation Union* case in 1971. Following this decision, the states became more interested in legal service plans.

Since 1971, insurance departments have had to deal with several problem areas associated with legal insurance plans. These include:

1. Language to be used (especially in view of the easy-to-read policy movement).
2. Difficulty in ascertaining if rates are appropriate.
3. Possible conflicts with fictitious group laws (this would not apply in all states).
4. Agent's licensing procedures.
5. Premium tax collections.
6. Determination of whether legal insurance plans are life or property and casualty contracts.
7. Determination of whether individual contracts should be written.

The National Association of Insurance Commissioners (NAIC) appointed a subcommittee to examine these and other legal insurance questions. The subcommittee met in 1973 and developed a model act designed to serve as a guideline for the states. The model was adopted by the NAIC in 1974.[18] Most states that have enacted legal insurance plan statutes have followed the NAIC lead.

---

[17] See, *Physicians' Defense Co.* v. *O'Brien,* 111 N.W. 396 (1907) and *Physicians' Defense Co.* v. *Cooper,* 199 F. 576 (1912).

[18] In 1977, Spencer Kimball and Werner Pfennigstorf developed a model legal insurance act. The model act was:

> endorsed by the NAIC Prepaid Legal Expense (D5) Subcommittee prior to the subcommittee's dissolution as "accomplishing its objective of placing before the members of the NAIC alternative methods and approaches to the regulation of prepaid legal services. . . . (NAIC, *Model Laws, Regulations and Guidelines* [Kansas City: NAIC, updated service], pp. 685–91.)

More recently, Kimball and Pfennigstorf have offered additional ideas on model legal insurance laws. See Werner Pfennigstorf and Spencer L. Kimball, "Access Plans for Legal Insurance: How Far Should They Be Regulated?" *Journal of Insurance Regulation* 4, no. 4 (June 1986), p. 57.

The problems cited above were covered in the model legislation; however, some areas were only examined superficially. For example, agent's licensing procedures were glossed over; the model bill stated a commissioner should establish rules and regulations for licensing.

One aspect of the law seems incongruous in view of the regulatory environment. The model bill provides that a commissioner has a responsibility to approve the compensation paid to lawyers and to determine if the rate of compensation is fair. The bill sets what a commissioner should consider in determining if a rate is fair:

(a) The usual and customary fees charged by lawyers, generally in the area where the services are performed.
(b) The services to be provided.
(c) The extent to which participation in the plan guarantees lawyers a steady flow of employment and income.
(d) Any agreement by which a lawyer assumes a part of the risk of operation.[19]

Since commissioners do not approve the fees charged by doctors and hospitals under health contracts, it seems discriminatory that they should approve the fees charged by lawyers. As of 1984, 20 states had passed statutes permitting the writing of legal insurance.[20]

While the regulatory environment at times has been hostile toward the development of legal service plans, the regulatory environment since 1976 has been sufficiently receptive to permit the growth of legal service plans. The growth rate of these plans has been increasing steadily but not spectacularly.

PLANS AND BENEFITS

To understand the types of plans currently being offered, it is necessary to understand the general types of plans and benefits available. The material that follows presents a brief discussion of the types of plans and benefits that have been developed.

---

[19] NIARS Corporation, *Official N.A.I.C. Model Laws, Regulations and Guidelines*, vol. 2 (Minneapolis: NIARS Corporation, 1977), pp. 680–86.

[20] Ibid., pp. 680–13, 680–14, and 680–15.

Types of Plans

Legal Service Plans

Legal service plans refer to any plans designed to offer legal services. They can vary from a very informal plan where a company in-house counsel offers advice, to elaborate plans with a wide range of scheduled benefits.

Prepaid Plans

Legal service plans can be provided either on a fully funded basis (i.e., prepaid) or on a current funding basis where the cost of a plan is handled out of current income. Generally, only employer or union sponsored plans are available on a current basis.

Legal insurance contracts, some labor union plans, and some bar association plans can be classified as prepaid legal plans. One important distinction exists under a trustee plan (e.g., a union or a bar association plan)—benefits may not be guaranteed. If the legal costs exceed the funds in the trust, benefits may be terminated. An insured plan is backed by the surplus of the insurance carrier and, therefore, could offer additional security to those purchasing legal service benefits.

Group versus Individual Plans

Legal service plans may be provided on either a group or an individual basis. (The NAIC model legislation stipulates that coverage can be written on a group or individual basis.) Most coverage has been written on a group basis. There are several reasons. First, it is easier to obtain a spread of risk within a group. Second, administrative costs are held to a minimum. Third, and perhaps most important, the major impetus for legal service plans has come from labor unions for the benefit of their members or employers for the benefit of their employees. Many group plans require a minimum number of participants in each plan or a minimum participation percentage.

Closed versus Open Panel Plans

Union legal service plans, especially in the early stages of their development, tended to be closed panel plans. Under a closed panel arrangement, a group of lawyers and paralegal personnel is hired by the unit providing the legal services. The individuals are paid salaries and are responsible for handling any legal matters set forth in the plan.

Funds are provided by employer contributions or by the union's membership through dues. The funds are invested by the union, and the funds plus the interest earned are used to defray the cost of legal services.

This approach not only can provide quality control but also cost control. Under closed panel plans, the specter of having the legal cost exceed the available funds may be offset since the lawyers are paid salaries. Thus, costs are fixed. (Even if expenses exceed the funds available, the employer or union often is responsible for any deficit.) However, the demands on the closed panel lawyer can become excessive; as a result, in some plans, members may not be provided prompt service.

Another weakness of a closed panel plan is that it may not provide the expertise necessary to handle all of the legal problems that arise. This can be overcome by hiring outside help as needed. The external counsel is paid from the closed panel's funds. When this approach is used, the plan is called a "modified closed panel plan." The term *modified closed panel plan* has been given at least two definitions. In addition to the one just presented, a modified closed panel plan has been defined as a panel where participants can choose between panel attorneys and external attorneys. If participants use an external lawyer, they are directly reimbursed for part or all of their expenses. To illustrate, a plan may sign up half of the attorneys in a city who agree to provide services for set fees. These are called "enrolled lawyers." If a participant does not want to use these enrolled lawyers, he or she can use another attorney. The benefits, however, may be reduced if a nonenrolled attorney is selected. Even if benefits are not reduced, that is, the same hourly rate is paid for a nonenrolled attorney, the amount of coverage may not be enough to pay the legal bill of the nonenrolled attorney. A nonenrolled attorney has not agreed to the set fee schedule, and therefore, his or her rates may be higher than the rates of enrolled attorneys.

Another method is available to handle the problem of not having adequate expertise. Instead of having an in-house closed panel plan, an external closed panel plan can be developed. In this situation, a group of lawyers is retained by a plan. The lawyers agree to work for a flat fee per hour or per case as long as the funds are available. They bill the plan directly for their services. If the funds are not adequate to meet all legal costs, the lawyers still provide services. The lawyers, therefore, become risk bearers; they guarantee services even if they have to work for free. Some lawyers find risk retention unacceptable. So, some plans have formed an external closed panel plan, which provides guaranteed rates; but the lawyers are not required to provide services if the funds are not sufficient to cover the service demands.

Legal service benefits also can be provided under an open panel plan. Under this approach, plan participants are permitted to select any lawyer they wish. The plan pays a schedule of benefits regardless of the cost of a lawyer's services. Benefits may be paid to plan participants or directly to the lawyers. Frequently, these types of plans provide participants with a list of lawyers that provide services for a fixed rate.

Legal Insurance Plans

Contracts affording legal service benefits sold by insurers have several names. The terms most often used are *legal insurance, group legal insurance, prepaid legal insurance,* and *legal expense insurance*. The term used in this chapter to refer to insurance plans is *legal insurance*.

TYPES OF BENEFITS

Schedule of Legal Services

Benefit packages vary significantly. Nearly all plans provide a schedule listing the covered legal areas. For example, a list of covered legal areas might include:

Bankruptcy.
Divorce.
Wills.
Adoption.
Traffic violations.
Felony representation.
Misdemeanors.
Juvenile delinquency actions.
Condemnation.
Real estate.
Debt collection.
Property damage.
Small claims proceedings.
Workers' compensation.
Representation before governmental or administrative boards.

Coverage for Legal Services

Establishing what legal areas are covered is the first step in evaluating benefits. The next step is to ascertain the extent of the benefits in each category. A legal service plan may only provide advice. There may or may not be a charge to the plan participant for each visit or for each occurrence. These are called "limited or access plans." They often provide a referral service, which will recommend lawyers who provide services for reduced fixed fees or hourly rates. In addition to advice, some plans afford services: a will may be drawn up, adoption papers may be processed, or defense advice on civil or criminal charges may be provided. Those plans that provide advice and a group of services (e.g., will preparation, adoptions, and the like) are called "basic plans." The amount of the benefit varies.

Plans that provide a broad range of benefits, including advice, basic services, and legal defense, are called "major plans." Closed panel plans have the ability to offer full coverage for the legal service areas for which benefits are provided, but full coverage is rarely used.

Most open panel plans and some closed panel plans require a plan participant to share in the payment of legal costs, or the plans limit the maximum amount of benefits available in each legal service area. Sharing can be accomplished by:

1. A flat dollar deductible per year—open. (Open or closed indicates the type of plan that normally would use this limitation.)
2. A coinsurance provision—open. (Normally, the plan pays 80 percent; this generally would not apply to closed panel plans unless outside legal talent had to be obtained.)
3. A maximum number of hours of legal service per year or per occurrence—open or closed. (An occurrence could be a visit or a sequence of visits resulting from the same legal problem.)
4. A maximum amount paid for each hour of legal service—open.
5. A maximum number of occurrences per year—open or closed.

Plans also may have waiting periods or internal limits. For example, there may be a six-month waiting period before divorce proceedings are covered or there may be a limit on the number of days of a trial that are covered.

Some plans provide legal checkups in addition to the benefits that have been described. Theoretically, these serve the same purpose an annual physical examination does under health insurance contracts. It may be more difficult to detect potential legal problems than existing health problems.

Exclusions

Most plans exclude some types of legal services. Possible exclusions include:

Criminal charges.
Business ventures.
Collection suits (as a plaintiff).
Charges not made except for existence of a legal service plan.
Class actions.
Tax return preparation.
Contingency fee cases.
Divorce (limited to one spouse per family).
Unreasonable charges.
When fees are paid by another source.
Appeals.
Fines and penalties.
Controversies with the plan.

While still included in many plans, the exclusion for criminal charges is slowly being eliminated. It has been found for many groups that the criminal coverage does not encourage criminal activities, as some early plan administrators had feared it might.

NONINSURANCE PLANS

Union Plans

As indicated earlier, unions have been in the forefront of the legal services plan movement. While the Brotherhood of Railroad Trainmen is important because of its initial efforts, the first modern-day plan to gain national attention was the Shreveport Bar Association plan.

In 1969, Southwestern Administrators, Inc., (SA), agreed to operate a legal service plan for the Shreveport Legal Services Corporation (SLSC). SLSC was formed by the Shreveport Bar Association. The plan developed by SA afforded benefits for:

1. Advice and consultation.
2. Conferences and negotiations.
3. Investigation and research.
4. Document preparation.
5. Litigation costs.
6. Major legal expense benefits.
7. Domestic relations benefits.

SLSC contracted with the Western Louisiana Council of Laborers, AFL-CIO, and one of its members, Local No. 229 of Shreveport, to enter into an open panel prepaid group legal service plan. The plan started operation in 1971.

The purpose of the plan was to gather data. Its results were valuable. The data indicated that contrary to preconceived ideas, low-income individuals did not abuse a legal service plan through excess utilization. The data also showed that an open panel plan was feasible. The plan is still operating.

Many unions established plans following the success of the Shreveport program. The Amalgamated Clothing Workers of America instituted a plan in 1972 that provided benefits for consumer transactions, domestic relations, adoptions, landlord/tenant problems, real estate transactions, and wills.[21] In 1973, District Council 37 of the American Federation of State, County, and Municipal Employees entered into a program that was proposed jointly by the Columbia University School of Law, the Columbia University School of Social Work, and itself. Prior to entering into the pilot plan, the council had a closed panel plan designed to handle only employment rights cases. The council's membership was and is comprised of civil service workers in New York. When the plan was initiated, the membership was (1) 30 percent clerical and administrative, (2) 22 percent technical and professional, (3) 15 percent hospital workers, (4) 18 percent social aides, and (5) 15 percent blue-collar workers. The salaries of the employees ranged from $5,800 to $16,000 (1973 dollars).[22] Other programs for laborers locals, firemen, teamsters, and teachers have been started.

Bar Association Plans

Following the BRT decision described earlier, some bar associations started or attempted to start legal service plans. For example, the Los Angeles County Bar Association attempted to start a plan in 1970 and 1971 with the California Teachers Association, but it was not successful.[23]

---

[21] Amalgamated Clothing Workers of America, Chicago Joint Board, Prepaid Group Legal Service Plan, initiated in Chicago on April 1, 1972.

[22] District Council 37, American Federation of State, County, and Municipal Employees, Columbia University School of Law, Columbia University School of Social Work, "Proposal for Pilot Study of a Legal Services Program for a Working Class Population," mimeographed, 1973, pp. 4, 5.

[23] Marshall A. Caskey, Director of Information, Los Angeles County Bar Association, letter, December 4, 1973.

The Monroe County Bar Association proposed a plan for Rochester, New York.[24] The New Mexico State Bar formed a prepaid group legal services corporation in 1973 to provide legal services.[25] As stated earlier, the Shreveport Bar Association formed the Shreveport Legal Services Corporation. In 1972, the State Bar Association of Texas formed the Texas Legal Protection Plan, Inc. The goal of this nonprofit corporation when it was incorporated was to help the citizens of Texas obtain legal services.[26]

The Arizona Bar Association formed Arizona Legal Services (ALS), which offered what ALS termed a tri-open plan. Under this approach, members of the Arizona Bar Association provided services for ALS for the amounts set forth in the fee schedule. A plan participant selected a lawyer. If the lawyer operated as a member of ALS, he or she provided legal services for the fee agreed to in the plan schedule. If a plan participant elected to use the service of a lawyer who was not enrolled, the benefit payments were less than those for a participating lawyer.[27]

Bar association plans have not grown as rapidly as their union counterparts. The lack of growth is due, in part, to the lack of a captive market. This lack of success has not daunted bar associations, however. The Florida Bar Association sponsored the formation of the Florida Lawyer's Prepaid Legal Services Corporation (FLPLSC). The FLPLSC has joined with Midwest Mutual Insurance Company to offer legal insurance to groups. The sales aspect of the program is controlled by a managing general agent.

Other Plans

Legal service plans have been developed or sold by other organizations. Benefits have been offered to credit card customers. Some universities offer legal services to students, and some plans operate through the mail. Most of these plans have not had a major impact in the more complex areas of legal services. Most of their success has been in offering limited programs.

---

[24] Edwin L. Gasperini and Max Schorr, "Prepaid Group Legal Services—Where We Are," 45 N.Y.S.B. *Journal* 76 (1973).

[25] Claude C. Lilly III, *Legal Services for the Middle Market* (Cincinnati: National Underwriter Company, 1974), p. 97.

[26] Bylaws of Texas Legal Protection Plan, Inc. Article X, pp. 15, 16.

[27] H. Lee Pickering, "Prepaid Legal Insurance—'Justice for All,' " *Management World* 7 no. 10 (1978), p. 18.

INSURANCE PLANS

A review of legal insurance plans proposed in the early 1970s indicates that the insurance industry planned to become deeply involved in the legal services movement. A tremendous gap existed between the initial insurance industry interest and the actual involvement. By 1973, CUMIS Insurance Society, Inc., Federated Insurers of Nashville, Inc., Fireman's Fund Insurance Company, Financial Indemnity Company, Insurance Company of North America, St. Paul Companies, Stonewall Insurance Company, Stuyvesant Insurance Company, and Midwest Mutual Company had designed legal insurance policies or plans, or both. Only Midwest Mutual and CUMIS ever took an active role in offering legal insurance policies.

The reasons for the reduction in the insurance industry's interest can be attributed to several factors. First, loss data were not available. Estimates of plan utilization ranged from 20 to 100 percent. So, insurers who had developed policies were unable to determine an appropriate rate, and were unwilling to gamble.

Second, prepaid legal exposures do not meet all the criteria established by the industry in deciding what is an insurable risk. A loss may not be fortuitous in nature, and it can be difficult to verify. Payments for investigation, research, and trust preparation are examples. Obtaining a large number of homogenous risks also is difficult.

The industry also lacked the ready access to markets that was available to unions. This problem was compounded by the economic decline in the middle of the 1970s and the concomitant high inflation. Employees wanted increased pay, not legal service benefits.

Fourth, the industry encountered opposition from insurance regulators. As indicated earlier, group legal insurance plans probably cannot be written in some states because of the fictitious group statutes. In addition, a few regulators did not seem sure who should sell legal insurance, life companies or property and casualty companies.

Finally, insurers were not sure whether they should offer indemnity plans or service contracts. The latter would have required establishing panels of lawyers to work with the insurers; the former would have limited the degree of cost control.

Currently, some of these obstacles have been eliminated or reduced. Some rating data are now available, and it appears utilization per year will be between 20 and 30 percent. The state regulatory environment has been partially cleared. Employees seem to be more interested in legal services as an employee benefit, and a hybrid between indemnification and service is developing.

Insurance Companies

As mentioned above, CUMIS Insurance Society and Midwest Mutual Insurance Company (Midwest) were involved in the legal insurance area in the early 1970s. CUMIS is part of a financial holding company that specializes in offering coverage to members of credit unions. It eventually dropped its program due to lack of marketability.

Midwest has developed one of the largest pools of insureds for legal insurance. The basic coverage offered by Midwest includes legal advice, legal representation, and major trial coverage. Some of the Midwest plans include maximum-dollar amounts per hour, as well as aggregate-dollar limits. Other plans offer unlimited coverage for certain types of services, for example, preparation of a will, personal bankruptcy cases, and document review.

Midwest has worked closely with unions, employers, and bar associations to establish itself as one of the leaders in the legal insurance area. Some of the union clientele have included teamsters, machinists, retail clerks, and airline pilots. City and county governmental units also have adopted the Midwest plans.

Midwest has worked closely with bar associations. It has offered plans not only in conjunction with the Florida Bar Association, as discussed previously, but also with bar associations in Texas, Rhode Island, Tennessee, Colorado, Idaho, Iowa, Oregon, Kentucky, Maryland, Virginia, Wisconsin, and Arizona.

Under a typical Midwest plan, a participant is encouraged to use the services of an enrolled attorney, since these attorneys have agreed to work for Midwest at fixed rates. If a participant uses a nonenrolled attorney, the participant is reimbursed a fixed amount per hour subject to a limitation per case. For example, a participant might be reimbursed for up to $60 per hour that a nonenrolled attorney charges subject to a maximum per case of $240.

Nonprofit Organizations

Blue Cross and Blue Shield (BC and BS) plans (most of which are nonprofit) were very active in the legal insurance areas. Because BC and BS associations usually are operated on a service basis, they are logical organizations to provide legal insurance on a service basis. In Minnesota, Blue Cross and Blue Shield formed Minnesota Indemnity, Inc. The company marketed coverage to the teachers union in Minnesota. Two plans were available to teachers. One provided limited benefits, bar advice, consultation, office work, and defense; the other provided broad coverage for the same categories.[28] Blue Cross of Indiana also formed a plan.[29] Blue Cross of Western Pennsylvania offered coverage to groups of 10 or more through its wholly owned subsidiary, Consumer Service Casualty Insurance Company.[30]

THE FUTURE OF LEGAL SERVICES AS A FRINGE BENEFIT

> Prepaid legal insurance has now developed to the same point where group health was 50 years ago.[31]

While this quote may be slightly understating the current position of legal services as an employee benefit, it is reasonably accurate. The future of legal services as an employee benefit will be tied both to demand/pull and supply/push.

Demand for legal services will be affected by (1) demographic changes, (2) increasing litigation, (3) union pressures, (4) the economic environment, and (5) the elimination of the tax-exempt status of group prepaid legal service benefits. If the current demographic trends continue, the need for personal legal services will expand. As more women move into the work force in the 1980s, there will be more legal problems.

The litigious nature of our society has been discussed in numerous articles. It is sufficient to state that the existing attitude of the public can only mean the rate of growth of suits will increase.

More than 300 legal service plans currently are being operated by or in conjunction with unions. (Most of these plans are not insured.) This is a small number of plans relative to the potential union membership market. Many unions have brought legal service plans to the bargaining table but have not pushed the plans because other fringe benefits were more impor-

---

28 Personnel Research Associates, *Group Legal Service Plans* (Verona, N.J.: Personnel Research Associates, 1980), p. 16. The program was not successful and was eventually dropped in favor of selling life insurance.

29 Sandy Dement, "A New Bargaining Focus on Legal Services," *AFL-CIO American Federationist* 85, no. 5 (1980), p. 9.

30 Personnel Research Associates, p. 20.

31 Pickering, "Prepaid Legal Insurance," p. 17.

tant or because their membership was more interested in monetary increases.

The elimination of the tax-free status of prepaid legal service plans may hurt the growth of prepaid legal service plans and reduce insurer interest in those plans. It is too early to determine the impact of the tax law change.

CHAPTER 19

FINANCIAL PLANNING

Charles E. Hughes
Robert T. LeClair

INTRODUCTION

Personal financial management is concerned with acquiring and employing funds in a manner consistent with established financial objectives. Since money represents a limited resource that can be spent in an endless variety of ways with widely different results, financial planning plays a critical role in the satisfactory achievement of objectives.

Individuals or families experience problems with debt, current income and expenditures, protection, savings, investments, conflicting objectives, and haphazard or impulsive decisions. Perhaps most important, the individual or family may fail to meet needs and objectives in an economical and satisfactory way. Therefore, advice or consultation on the management of funds becomes a valuable service to those persons.

At one time a common belief existed that only the very wealthy needed to be concerned with personal financial planning. This is no longer the case. Increased income levels, taxation, sophisticated financial markets and instruments, increasing longevity, and the generally higher standard of living have all added to the complexity of managing finances. The growth and change of our economy and social structure have contributed to the widespread acceptance of the need for planning.

The need for and applicability of financial planning is much broader in our society today than most individuals realize. Many people look only at their bank accounts or investment portfolios in determining the extent of their wealth. They fail to consider other assets, including such items as equity in a home, automobiles, furniture, paintings, cash value of life insurance, pension and profit-sharing programs, Social Security benefits, and other hidden assets as part of their financial position. Finally, an individual concentrating on the demands of a career simply doesn't have time to explore all the possibilities for putting money to work and may fail to consider the consequences that can occur if financial planning is neglected.

FINANCIAL PLANNING DEFINED

The management of financial affairs has been changing through the years. There was a time when setting a budget for household expenditures was considered to be adequate financial planning. If it was difficult adhering to that budget, or impossible to carry out that plan, an individual might have sought the advice of a counselor. Such a planner would have reviewed the client's income and expenditures and devised a spending plan that made efficient use of the available income.

As income levels increased, larger amounts of surplus disposable income became available. Individuals and families sought ways of making money work harder for them. Various investments looked interesting, but the complexities of the securities markets appeared to be overwhelming. At this point, the financial planner also was asked to take on the role of an investment adviser. However, investment opportunities were much broader than just securities. The adviser also was expected to be knowledgeable concerning real estate, tax-advantaged investments, and even such "hard" assets as gold or diamonds.

Add to this the client's need for an accountant to prepare tax returns, a lawyer to draft wills and other documents, and an insurance agent to assist in the protection, preservation, and distribution of an estate. Today, the financial planner has become someone who counsels clients in all of these areas, and who serves as an intermediary in all of these functions. From the growing needs of consumers has emerged a new professional, the financial counselor.

The role of the financial counselor is that of providing total financial management for individuals or families to enable these persons to realize the maximum enjoyment of their finances in an efficient and economic manner. The best means of accomplishing the financial objectives of a client is to develop specific plans to direct and control financial activity and progress. The financial counselor must assess the client's current financial position, assist in establishing his or her objectives, consider all constraints and variables that bear on those objectives, and develop realistic projections and plans based on these factors. Financial planning, then, is an ongoing series of interrelated activities. It is a *process*.

PLANNING AS AN EMPLOYEE BENEFIT

The array of programs, plans, and services that have been added to an employee's benefit package has expanded greatly over the past few years. Most benefits, by design, are selected or offered as part of the package for all employees; some are offered only to specific employees or groups of employees.

Financial planning is one benefit that has been limited to key executives or other highly compensated employees. This results partly from the belief that aspects of the program dealing with estate planning apply only to those individuals who will accumulate sufficient wealth to be subject to significant estate taxes.[1] Also, since programs recommended by financial counselors may include forms of tax shelters that contain considerable risk, employees other than top executives might not have sufficient assets or income to justify the amount of risk involved. Finally, from the point of view of the employer, the full financial planning process generally is expensive and this inhibits extension to large numbers of lower-income employees.

Services Provided

Because of the relatively high cost many firms have opted for a partial financial counseling service rather than the full process. These separate services include:

1. Estate planning—disposition at death, insurance arrangements, minimization of taxes, estate liquidity.
2. Tax preparation—federal, state, and local returns; estate and gift tax returns.
3. Investment management—short- and long-term investment programs, tax shelters.

---

[1] The Economic Recovery Tax Act of 1981 made major changes in the law relating to federal estate taxes. The size of estates not subject to tax increased to $600,000 in 1987.

4. Compensation planning—analysis of options available, explanation of benefits.
5. Preparation of wills.

Some of these services may be provided by employees of the firm, while others are contracted for and performed by outside specialists knowledgeable in a particular area. As the number of individual services available expands, the need for full financial counseling becomes more apparent. Many companies are now providing financial planning benefits to their top executives, and some have expanded it to middle managers as well.

Advantages

The major advantages of financial planning as an employee benefit are:

1. Many executives do not have sufficient time to devote to their own financial affairs. Financial counseling as a benefit relieves them of having to spend time in financial planning and permits them to concentrate on business matters.
2. By reducing the likelihood a poor decision will be made on his or her own finances, the executive has greater personal peace of mind.
3. The employer is probably better able to screen and select financial counselors. Thus, the executive is less likely to receive poor advice from unqualified planners.
4. Salaries offered may appear more attractive and competitive since such compensation is being used more efficiently to reach each executive's goals.

Disadvantages

Although financial counseling as an employee benefit would appear to be attractive to both employer and employee, there are several reasons for not providing such services:

1. Financial counseling might be construed as meddling in an employee's personal affairs.
2. There is a feeling the company might be held responsible for bad advice, since it has endorsed the services or employed the counselor.
3. Although the counseling service is considered helpful to highly

compensated employees, many companies are reluctant to provide benefits that are restricted to select groups of employees.
4. The cost of financial counseling.

Cost

The cost of financial planning varies, based on the range of services to be provided and the type of individuals employed to provide them. A financial counselor or counseling firm may operate on a fee-only basis, a commission-only basis, or some combination of commissions and fees. The existence of commissions, which may eliminate or greatly reduce costs to the employer, can be a strong incentive for companies to seek product-oriented purveyors of financial counseling services. It should be understood, however, that insurance or investment advice given to employees could be heavily weighted in favor of products available from the counseling firm. For this reason, employers usually prefer financial counseling on a fee-only basis, since the belief is that this provides the most objective analyses and unbiased recommendations.

Since the financial counseling process often is extremely detailed and complicated, costs of $3,000 to $6,000 or even higher per executive are common for a complete counseling program. Another approach used by some counseling firms involves seminars where the counseling process and available services are explained to groups of eligible employees. Some firms charge a separate fee of $1,000 to $3,500 for the initial data-gathering or fact-finding visit with the employee. In addition, if legal documents or certified financial statements are required, there may be additional legal and accounting fees. Finally, after the initial year of the program, the annual fees for maintaining and updating the program are based on required time and effort, generally averaging $1,000 to $2,000 per employee.

The relatively high cost of financial counseling as an employee benefit has undoubtedly contributed to its limited availability to only highly compensated executives or perhaps to its adoption at all. The cost of financial counseling to the firm can be reduced by offering the benefit to employees on a contributory basis.

The fees paid for financial counseling generally are deductible by the corporation for tax purposes if the total compensation to the employee, including the counseling fee, is not considered unreasonable compensation by the IRS.[2] When this benefit is offered to highly compensated

[2] I.R.C. Section 106.

executives, the fee generally would be small, compared to the executive's total compensation, and it is unlikely that total compensation would be considered unreasonable.

The amount the employer pays to the planning firm for services performed for an employee is considered taxable income to the employee and is subject to withholding tax.[3] However, an offsetting tax benefit may be available to the employee since deductions are allowed for services directed to tax matters or allocable to investment advice.[4] Therefore, it could be possible for the employee to contribute the cost associated with those services allowed as deductions. The counseling firm should indicate clearly the charge for these services as a separate item on its billing.

In addition to the tax aspects, when supplemental legal or accounting fees are necessary, these expenses should be borne by the employee. Overall, contributions by employees could reduce the cost to the employer and make it possible for the firm to offer financial counseling as an employee benefit.

THE FINANCIAL PLANNING PROCESS

It is most important to understand the concept of financial planning not as a product, or as a service, but as a process. Many persons claiming to engage in planning are really selling products and nothing more. A "good plan" is simply one that requires extensive use of their product whatever it may be. Similarly, a view of financial planning as a service provided at one point in time is also inadequate. This concept does not provide for the continuing needs of an individual or family for information, analysis, and review of its program.

Financial planning should be thought of as a series of interrelated activities a person participates in on a continuing basis. It is not something that is completed, even successfully, and then put away or forgotten. This is similar to the modern view of education that embraces learning not only through formal schooling but also throughout one's lifetime. In the same way, financial planning must be done regularly to take account of changes in an individual's circumstances, the availability of new products, and varying financial market conditions.

---

[3] I.R.C. Section 61.

[4] Fees paid for *investment counsel* are deductible only to the extent that all *second tier* miscellaneous itemized deductions cumulatively exceed 2 percent of adjusted gross income.

New tax legislation, fluctuating market interest rates, and the introduction of new or modified investment vehicles are examples of changes that can alter the way people and businesses handle money, as well as the rates of return earned on liquid funds. As new products appear and market conditions change, even the best prepared financial plan will tend to become obsolete. Changes in an individual's personal situation also may require adjustments in the overall plan. Births, deaths, marriage, divorce, or a new business venture can have a great impact on financial as well as personal planning.

The following activities in the process of financial planning must be carried out regularly and, when necessary, should involve qualified, professional advisers:

1. Gather background information.
2. Establish objectives.
3. Develop financial plans.
4. Control and execute plans.
5. Measure performance.

The flowchart shown in Figure 19–1 provides a summary of the individual activities involved in the process and shows the relationships among them.

Background Analysis

Financial planning requires comprehensive data on everyone participating in the program. Such information includes a record of income and expenditures as well as the current financial position of the individual or family. Prior to determining objectives, the counselor needs information regarding the sex, health, age, lifestyle, tastes, and preferences of individual family members. Much of this information is subjective, and attitudes may shift considerably over the years. Such changes make it important that the financial counselor maintain frequent contact with the client to be aware of important changes in these personal and family characteristics.

Another important area of background analysis is the client's attitude toward the degree of risk in the overall financial plan. Feelings about investment risk, personal financial security, and independence are just as important as the client's income statement or net worth. An awareness of risk attitudes permits realistic, acceptable objectives to be established with the individual or family. By ignoring these feelings, the counselor runs the risk of developing a "good plan" that is simply out of touch with the client's personality. Such plans are not likely to be accepted or implemented, and a great deal of time and effort will have been wasted.

FIGURE 19–1
The Financial Planning Process

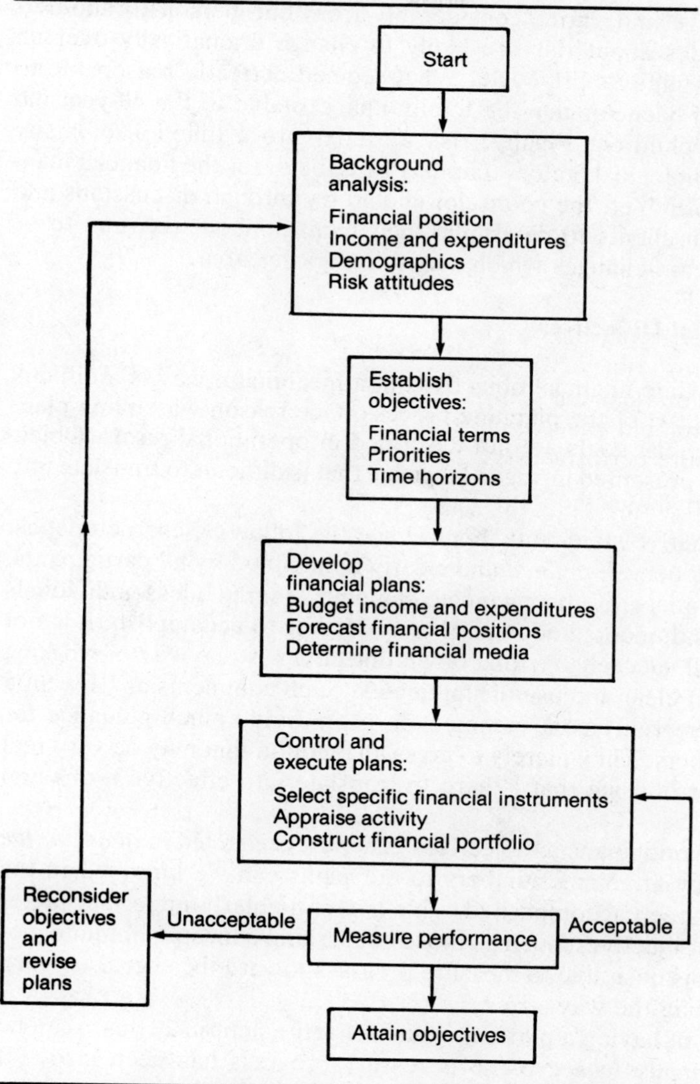

Source: "Introduction to Financial Counseling," *Financial Counseling* (Bryn Mawr: The American College, 1982), p. 133.

Unfortunately, for a number of reasons, attitudes toward risk are very difficult to measure or to judge. First, defining the nature of "risk" is highly subjective and varies considerably from one person to another. Second, attitudes about risk are likely to change dramatically over an individual's or family's life cycle. What seemed perfectly reasonable to the 25-year-old bachelor may be totally unacceptable to the 40-year-old father of four children. Finally, risk attitudes are a function of many personal, psychological factors that may be difficult for the financial manager to deal with. Yet, the counselor should try through discussions and interviews with clients to determine their feelings about risk and to be alert to significant changes which may occur in this area.

Setting Financial Objectives

Stating worthwhile financial objectives in a meaningful way is a difficult but necessary part of the planning process. One reason why many plans fail is that financial goals are not described in operational terms. Objectives often are presented in vague language that is difficult to translate into action.

Each objective statement should have the following characteristics. First, it should be *well-defined* and clearly understood by all participants, including members of the financial planning team. Unless individuals really know and understand what they are trying to accomplish, it is not likely they will succeed. Writing down objectives is one way of working toward a set of clear and useful statements. Such comments as "I want a safe and secure retirement income" do not provide much guidance for financial planners. They merely express an emotion that may be very real to the speaker but one that is hard to translate into effective terms and plans.

Second, good financial objectives generally are stated in *quantitative terms*. Only by attaching numbers to our plans can we know when the objective has been accomplished. This is a particularly important factor for long-term objectives, such as those concerning educational funding or retirement. It is desirable to measure progress toward these goals at various points along the way.

The goal of having a particular sum for retirement in 20 years can be reviewed annually to see if the necessary progress has been made. If earnings have been lower than anticipated, larger contributions may have to be made in succeeding years. If a higher rate of return actually has been realized, future contributions can be reduced. Such fine-tuning is impossible unless numbers are associated with plan objectives. Adding numbers to objectives also helps to make them more understandable to all members of the planning team as well as to participants in the plan.

Finally, each goal or objective should have a *time dimension* attached to it. When will a particular goal be accomplished? How much progress has been made since the last review? How much time remains until the goal is to be accomplished? These questions and similar ones can be answered only if a schedule has been established with objectives listed at particular points in time.

Some aspects of the plan, such as retirement objectives, will have very long timelines associated with them. Others, such as an adjustment to savings, may be accomplished in a few months or a year. Whether long-term or short-term in nature, the timing feature of objective statements is very important. Even long-term goals can be broken down into sub-periods that can coincide with an annual review of the plan.

After the objectives have been stated, they must be put in *priority order*. This ranking process is necessary since different objectives normally compete for limited resources. It is unlikely that a planner will be able to satisfy all of the client's objectives at the same time. Some goals are more important, more urgent, than others. Critical short-term needs may have to be satisfied ahead of longer-range plans.

Once certain goals have been reached, funds may be channeled to other areas. An example would be the funding of children's education. After this goal has been met, resources previously spent on education costs may be allocated to building a retirement fund or some other long-range objective. Unless these and other goals have been assigned specific priorities, it is impossible to organize and carry out an effective plan. Conversely, a set of well-integrated financial objectives can make the actual planning process a relatively easy task.

Individuals and families should have workable objectives in each of the following areas:

1. Standard of Living. Maintaining a particular "lifestyle" normally takes the majority of an individual's financial resources. Setting an objective in this area calls for an analysis of required expenditures, such as food and shelter, as well as discretionary spending on such items as travel, vacations, and entertainment. If almost all income is being spent in this area, it is virtually impossible to accomplish any other objectives.

One widely used rule of thumb states that no more than 80 percent of income should be spent on maintaining a given standard of living. The remaining 20 percent of disposable income should be allocated among the other financial objectives. Obviously, this guideline varies from one person or family to another. But, unless a significant portion of income can be channeled toward the remaining objectives, those goals are not likely to be reached.

2. Savings. Almost everyone recognizes the need for funds that can be used to meet an emergency or other special needs. However, determining the ideal level of savings can be a complex problem. It is influenced by the nature of income received, individual risk attitudes, stability of employment, and other factors, such as the type of health and dental insurance coverage.

It is recommended that savings balances should be equal to at least three months' disposable income. These funds should be maintained in a safe and highly liquid form where rate of return is a secondary consideration. Today, the typical bank money market account or money market mutual fund offers an excellent vehicle for maintaining savings balances. These funds offer a high degree of safety, ready access through the use of checks or telephone redemption of shares, a good rate of return.

3. Protection. This objective incorporates property, liability, disability, life, and medical insurance coverage. It should be designed to provide protection against insurable risks and related losses. Objectives in this area should take account of coverage provided through public programs, such as Social Security, as well as group insurance offered as an employee benefit.

4. Accumulation (Investment). This is possibly the most complex objective in a number of ways. It relates to the buildup of capital for significant financial needs. These needs can be as diverse as a child's college education, a daughter's wedding, or the purchase of a vacation home. The sheer number and variety of such goals makes it difficult to define this objective and to set priorities.

Adding to the difficult nature of this area is the generally long time-horizon for planning that may encompass 20 years or more. Finally, the wide variety of possible investment vehicles that can be used in the planning process adds to the overall complexity. Regardless of the reason for building capital, the critical ingredients in this objective are the ability to quantify the needed amount and to state a target date for its accumulation.

5. Financial Independence. This objective may be thought of as a particularly important subset of the accumulation objective. It concerns the accumulation of assets over a relatively long time in most cases. Such independence may be desired at a particular age and may or may not actually correspond with retirement from employment. Many persons may wish to have complete financial security and independence while continuing to work at a favored occupation or profession.

Since the planning-horizon is such a lengthy one, this objective should be broken down into subgoals that can be evaluated, analyzed, and reworked over the years. More than most others, this area is affected by changes in government programs, such as Social Security, and in benefits paid by employers.

6. Estate Planning. Objectives in this area typically are concerned with the preservation and distribution of wealth after the estate owner's death. However, accomplishing such goals may call for a number of actions to be taken well before that time. Writing a will probably is the most fundamental estate planning objective, and yet thousands of persons die each year without having done so. These people die "intestate" and leave the distribution of their assets to state laws and the courts.

For larger estates, avoidance or minimization of estate taxes is an important consideration. These objectives can be accomplished, but call for careful planning and implementation prior to the owner's death. The use of various trust instruments, distribution of assets through gifts, and proper titling of property all can result in a smaller taxable estate. Carrying out such a program, however, takes time and should be considered as various assets are being acquired. This also is an area where professional guidance generally is necessary. If the financial counselor is not an attorney, one should be consulted in drafting a will or in preparing a trust document.

Developing Financial Plans

Once a realistic, well-defined set of objectives has been established, the financial counselor can begin to develop actual plans. This planning stage includes the budgeting of income and expenditures for the near term, along with a forecast of future activity. A projection of the client's financial position for the next several years also should be made.

These plans should identify the financial instruments that will be included in programs to meet specific objectives. For example, specific savings media should be recommended for those who need more in the way of emergency funds. Should a family increase its regular savings accounts, purchase money market certificates, or buy shares in a money market fund? If an investment program is called for in the plan, recommendations should be made as to the appropriate *types* of investments, such as securities, real estate, or tax shelters.

Executing and Controlling Plans

The next stage of the model calls for the financial counselor to assist in setting the plan in motion. This may involve the purchase or sale of various assets, changes in life insurance protection, additional liability coverage, and other changes. All these activities should be monitored closely and appraised to see that they are effective in accomplishing the stated objectives. The outcome of some actions will be quickly apparent, while others may take a long time to produce results that can be evaluated.

Measuring Performance

The financial counselor is responsible for gathering data on the plan's operations that are used to evaluate his or her performance and the actions of other professionals who may be involved. Such persons may include a banker, an attorney, a life insurance consultant, and an accountant.

This important step determines progress made toward the attainment of objectives. If performance to date is acceptable, no particular corrective action need be taken until the next scheduled review. However, if it is discovered progress to date is unacceptable, several actions may need to be taken. These would include a review of the plans to see if they are still valid, and analysis of the market environment to take note of unanticipated changes.

It also may be necessary to review and alter the original objectives if they are no longer realistic and desirable. When this occurs, the entire plan may have to be recycled through each of the stages described above. This model of financial planning is a dynamic one that is continually repeated as personal, financial, and environmental factors change.

WHO PROVIDES FINANCIAL PLANNING?

Financial planning services are provided by numerous individuals and firms, including banks, insurance companies and agents, investment brokers, benefit consultants, lawyers, accountants, and others. The major firms specializing in financial planning services generally have a staff of professionals who are experts in investments, insurance, tax shelters, and so on, and who work as a team to provide the counseling service. Smaller organizations may concentrate on one area and hire consultants to complete the planning team.

The selection of a counseling firm requires care. It is important that the objectives of the employer are satisfied, and, from the employee's standpoint, that their individual confidences be protected and the advice be in their best interests. Some employers have attempted to provide financial planning services through in-house personnel. This is most effective when the benefit is limited to a single service, such as tax advice. However, problems occur because many executives are hesitant to discuss details of their personal financial affairs with fellow employees.

The selection decision sometimes is simply one of identifying the best fee-only counseling firm available. As indicated earlier, there is a preference for the fee-only basis. However, the objectives of the employer may warrant consideration of product-oriented counselors. For example, if the objective of the counseling benefit is limited to advice on life insurance planning, a competent life insurance agent may be able to satisfy the need. Further, banks, brokerage firms, and life insurance companies have formed financial counseling divisions that provide support services for their personnel. Therefore, although a counselor may be product oriented, he or she has substantial breadth of assistance available to analyze and design broad-based financial plans. In these cases, a fee may be charged even though commissions exist.

Individual professionals call themselves financial counselors, financial planners, or financial advisers. Many of these persons still depend solely on commissions for their income. However, since it is difficult for any single individual to give professional advice in all areas included in a comprehensive plan, the trend is to join together to form firms rich in experience, professionally qualified in all aspects of financial planning, and compensated through fees or a combination of commission and fees. There exist today many quality individuals and firms that provide financial counseling. The most important ingredient, therefore, is to seek the individual or firm that understands financial planning as a process, one that can have important beneficial results for employers and employees alike.

Fiduciary Responsibility

As financial counselors take on a wider range of responsibilities for their clients, a special fiduciary relationship develops between them. This arrangement arises whenever one person places confidence and trust in the integrity and fidelity of another. A fiduciary relationship is characterized by faith and reliance on the part of the client and by a condition of superiority and influence on the part of the counselor.

The existence of a fiduciary responsibility does not depend upon the establishment of any particular legal relationship. Nonlegal relationships can be fiduciary in nature, especially where one person entrusts his or her business affairs to another.

When a fiduciary relationship exists, the fiduciary (counselor) has a duty to act in good faith and in the interests of the other person. A fiduciary is not permitted to use the relationship to benefit his or her own personal interest. Transactions between the client and counselor are subject to close scrutiny by the courts. Especially sensitive are transactions in which the fiduciary profits at the expense of the client. Fiduciaries must subordinate their individual interests to their duty of care, trust, and loyalty to the client.

The Investment Advisers Act of 1940 is particularly important in defining the nature of a fiduciary relationship. One objective of the act is to expose and eliminate all conflicts of interest that could influence an adviser to be other than disinterested. Congress thus empowered the courts to require full and fair disclosure of all material facts surrounding the fiduciary relationship. The adviser must disclose in a meaningful way all material facts that give rise to potential or actual conflicts of interest. For example, an adviser who receives commissions on products sold to clients, such as securities or life insurance, should disclose the amount of sales compensation received on recommended transactions.[5]

CONCLUSION

Financial planning will become an increasingly important employee benefit. This will occur as more firms offer such services and as more employees qualify for eligibility. Another factor contributing to this growth will be the maturity of the financial planning industry itself. While the costs associated with offering financial counseling services as a benefit are not insignificant, clear advantages exist for both the employer and the employee. There also are areas of concern, however, and firms should carefully analyze the nature of their employees and the qualifications of those offering to provide financial planning services for them.

---

[5] Robert W. Cooper and Dale S. Johnson, "The Impact of the Investment Advisers Act of 1940 on CLUs and Other Financial Services Professionals," *CLU Journal,* April 1982, p. 35.

CHAPTER 20

EMPLOYEE ASSISTANCE PROGRAMS

Charles A. Weaver

OVERVIEW

The problem of employees with alcohol or other personal problems has reached alarming proportions in our society. The economic losses to industry associated with such problems are estimated in the billions of dollars annually. The social costs are beyond estimation.

In response to the need to deal with this problem in business and industry, a few companies developed occupational programs in the early 1940s. These early programs, which operated in a vacuum of information and experience, concentrated on alcoholism alone. The result was a program designed to identify the alcoholic in the workplace. Incorporated were traditional attitudes toward alcoholism as a self-inflicted disease denoting moral weakness. These attitudes meant that one was not considered an alcoholic until the final stages of the illness were reached and when stereotypical symptoms like bloodshot eyes, trembling hands, alcohol breath, and lack of cleanliness and personal grooming appeared.

THE CONCEPT

During the 1960s, it was discovered that employees who were not performing their work tasks satisfactorily were much easier to identify than were employees with alcohol problems. An approach evolved reflecting this observation—the employee assistance program (EAP). The concept of EAPs was simple. That is, a predictable number of employees will have declining job performance because of personal problems.

Analysis and follow-up of employees identified because of job performance problems like absenteeism, erratic performance, decreasing productivity, tardiness, poor judgment, and excessive material spoilage indicates that 11.5 percent of any employee population will have personal problems serious enough to affect job performance. Forty-five percent of this total will experience a primary problem with alcohol abuse. Fifty-five percent will experience other problems. Employees whose job performance is affected by alcohol abuse or other problems will be absent from work more often than will employees without job performance problems or employees whose job performance is related to a lack of training or other supervisory deficiencies.

Major causes appear with statistical regularity, as indicated in Table 20–1.

These employees are not "troublemakers." They are "troubled employees," and they often are among the best and hardest working employees an employer has when they work free from the burdens of their personal problems. Troubled employees appear at any level, from the executive suite to the assembly line.

Employee assistance programs should be designed to meet the needs of the individual organization. Personnel policies and management philosophies differ from organization to organization, but EAPs must be an integral part of the organizational structure.

Responsibility for identifying troubled employees in the workplace is a function of supervisors at all levels. It is not the responsibility of super-

TABLE 20–1

Job Performance Problem Source	*Percent of Employee Population*	*Percent of "Troubled" Employee Population*	*Absenteeism Rate*
Alcohol abuse	5.2%	45%	4 × greater
Emotional problems	2.9	25	5 × greater
Family problems	1.5	13	5.7 × greater
Drug abuse	.8	7	5 × greater
Miscellaneous "other"	1.1	10	2 × greater
Total problem employees	11.5 percent of work force.		

Source: From a study of seventeen selected industries by the author, 1978.

visors to *diagnose* or to *counsel* employees, only to deal with poor performance.

A process for supervisors making an EAP recommendation to employees might be as set forth in Figures 20–1 through 20–4.

Before supervisors can confront an employee with a job performance problem, several steps must be taken. These early steps to correcting inappropriate job performance do not mention the EAP as a possible solution. During this phase of problem solving, supervisors are just getting a handle on the scope, magnitude, and changes needed to bring job performance back into line. However, supervisors, as well as the EAP coordinator, should take every opportunity to make EAP information available to employees. EAP information should be given on a continuing basis, but it is not part of solving job performance problems at this point.

The second part of changing job performance is determining how the job performance problem will be resolved. After supervisors have determined what changes are expected, they should decide when this is to occur. Do they expect an employee to change immediately? If absenteeism is a problem, how many days will a supervisor allow an employee to be absent and within what time frame? After they have made some decisions on this and decided that the employee can do the job as expected,

FIGURE 20–1
Step 1 in Supervisor's Process of Making EAP Recommendation to Employees

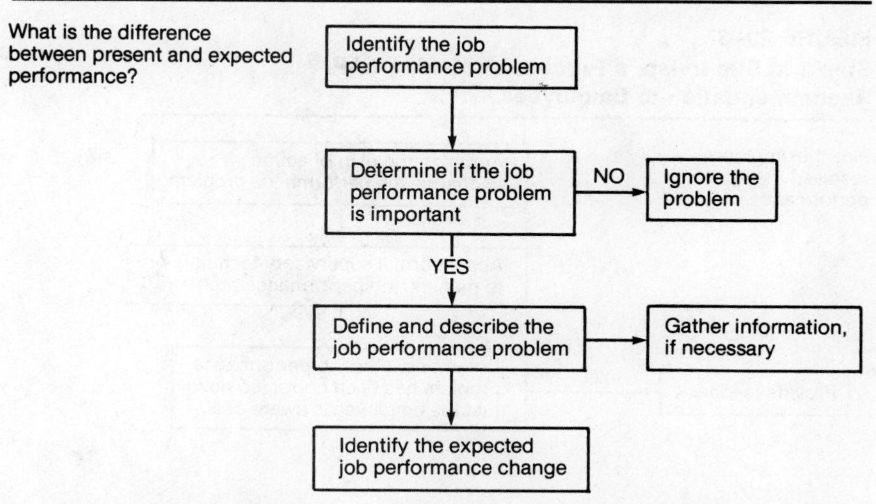

FIGURE 20–2
Step 2 in Supervisor's Process of Making EAP Recommendation to Employees

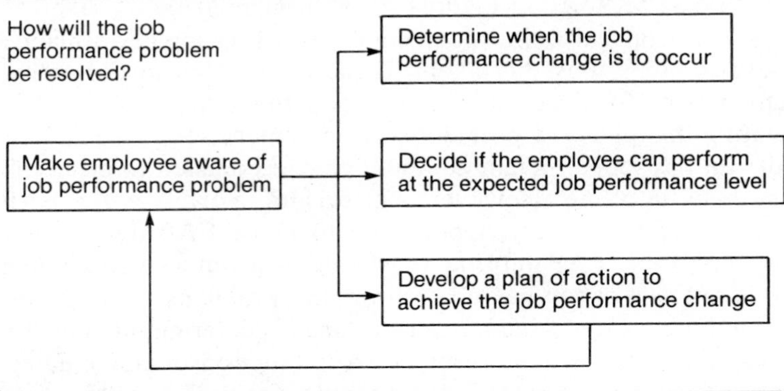

supervisors should develop a plan of action to achieve the job performance change. During this process, supervisors should make the employee aware of the problem, what is expected, and when it is expected. It may be best to jointly develop a plan of action with the employee.

At this point, supervisors are still using normal supervisory techniques, that is, they are doing the same things they have and would be

FIGURE 20–3
Step 3 in Supervisor's Process of Making EAP Recommendation to Employees

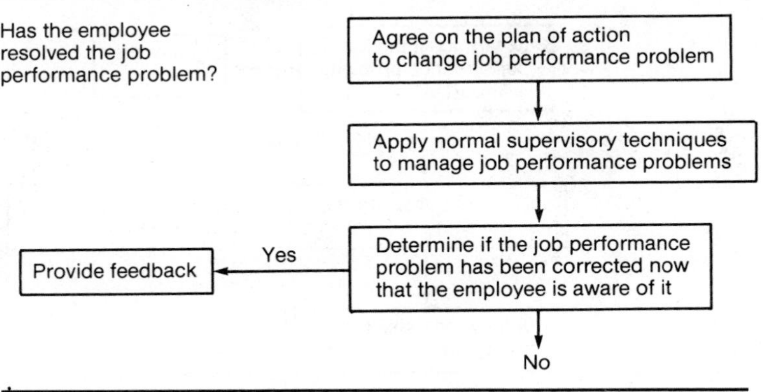

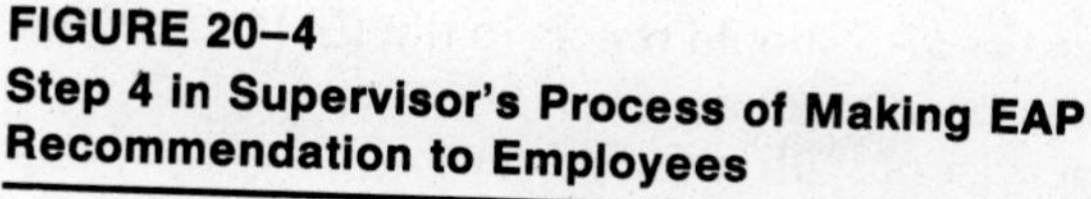

FIGURE 20–4
Step 4 in Supervisor's Process of Making EAP Recommendation to Employees

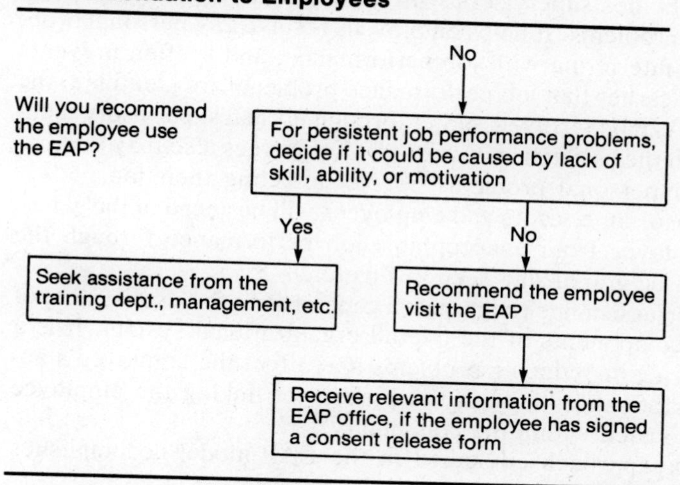

doing without an EAP. Also note that the EAP has not yet been mentioned. At this point, however, supervisors may want to mention the existence of the EAP and provide the employee with additional information on the procedures, what to expect if he or she decides to try the EAP, particularly stressing confidentiality and the voluntary nature of the program.

Once the supervisor and employee have agreed upon a plan of action and are carrying out that plan, the supervisors will want to periodically review the progress the employee is making and determine if further action is warranted. If the job performance has been corrected within the guidelines developed, the supervisor should provide the employee with positive feedback. If the job performance is not being corrected satisfactorily, then supervisors move to step four.

After this plan has failed, and job performance is still unacceptable, it is time to check a few alternatives before the supervisor recommends the EAP. Are there any other explanations for unacceptable job performance? If the supervisor has covered all areas, it is now time to recommend the employee call the EAP coordinator and to urge the employee to use the EAP to resolve any problems that may be affecting his or her job performance. Again, supervisors should spell out confidentiality guidelines, and the voluntary nature of the program. Supervisors should be specific about the consequences of unchanged job performance. This may include termination. Supervisors also should report to the EAP office that a formal recommendation has been made.

The EAP provides supervisors with an additional option to solving job performance problems. It helps employees resolve any personal problem that may be interfering with job performance, and it often prevents termination. The earlier that job performance problems are identified, the sooner problems can be resolved, either through normal supervisory techniques or through the assistance of an EAP. Employees also may want to use the EAP for personal problems not yet affecting their job performance. In this case, supervisors and employees will be ahead of the game. Moving the employee from unacceptable job performance through the EAP system can be graphically seen in Figure 20–5.

An employee assistance program is a general term for a subsystem of interdependent components of the overall organizational system. It is a program for solving or reducing problems that affect the employee's acceptable job performance through the process of linking the employee with resources located within the community.

The systems approach embodied in the EAP model accomplishes four major tasks:

1. It Guarantees Confidentiality. Diagnosis and referral of troubled employees is accomplished by a community professional bound by strict rules of confidentiality. Program referral procedures should be designed to guarantee no one is aware of the employee's problem except the employee, the diagnostic and referral person, and the community resource involved in the treatment program. Supervisors are removed specifically from the task of inquiring into the nature of employees' problems and assisting them in dealing with those problems.

2. It Guarantees Professionalism. The supervisor's role of supervision includes responsibility for monitoring the performance of every individual under his or her supervision and confronting employees with any evidence of unacceptable job performance. In this way, supervisors perform job-oriented tasks: they supervise. If assistance is needed, the supervisor is not involved in rendering such assistance. Rather, trained professionals from the community are utilized to assure proper, efficient, and professional treatment.

3. It Promotes Efficiency. Early intervention is a key to efficient problem solving. Delays in intervention allow problems to grow and intensify. A program that focuses on indicators of problems, while the problems are still relatively minor, promotes efficiency in terms of individual problem solving. In economic terms, it promotes production as a result of a larger work force of nontroubled employees.

4. It Helps Assure Utilization by Avoiding Stigmas. Employee assistance programs offer assistance for all problems. A particular employee's

FIGURE 20–5
Organizational Employee Assistance Program

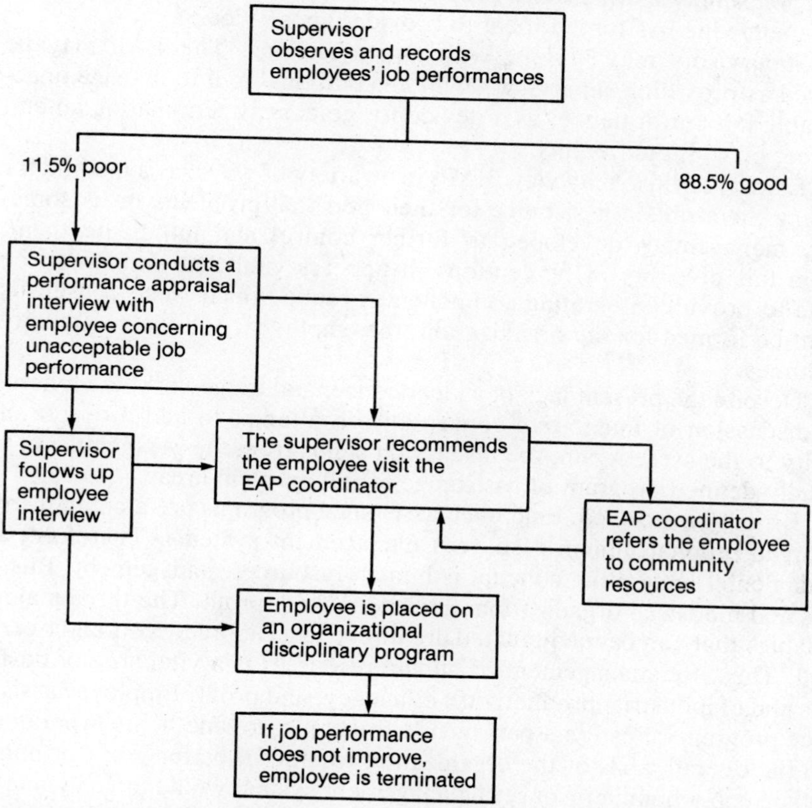

problem is not identified by participation in a specific program, such as an alcohol program. As a result, many of the negative implications of participating in a particular program are avoided.

INTEGRATING COMPONENTS OF EMPLOYEE ASSISTANCE PROGRAMS

There are undoubtedly as many ways to conceptualize an employee assistance program as there are people affected by a program. Top management may see it as a way to save money by maintaining a more efficient work force, as a way of providing an extra benefit to help employees live happier lives with no concrete monetary benefits resulting for management, or simply as one more problem management must deal with because someone has forced them to provide this service.

Supervisors may view it with mixed feelings. The EAP may be viewed as providing supervisors with an additional tool to manage unacceptable job performance, as a device for graciously terminating an employee, or with indifference.

Employees also may view EAPs in a variety of ways: as a method for helping them obtain assistance for their personal problems or as something management developed to further control and intimidate them. Given this diversity of perceptions, it appears vital that an attempt be made to provide integrating components around which some consensus might be formed for the organization, the employee, and the community resources.

Despite the present lack of a clear conceptual framework, the following discussion of integrative concepts is an attempt to add a degree of clarity to the area. Again, the discussion stems from the perspective of a broadly defined program of assistance for all problem areas.

Broadly conceived, employee assistance programs are a component of organizational human resources management systems. Therefore, a fundamental integrative concept is human resources management. Business and industrial organizations exist to make a profit. The three major variables that can be manipulated are direct cost, indirect cost, and overhead. Thus, the management of human resources is a vital area of business and of industrial productivity, efficiency, and profit. Employee assistance programs must be a part of that broad picture and be incorporated into the overall goals of the organization whether it be for profit or nonprofit. Such a human resources management system would include many components in addition to an employee assistance program (e.g., recruiting, training, promotion, wages, benefits, safety, supervisory practices, and so on). However, an EAP might be vital to that system in several ways involving additional integrative concepts.

First, an employee assistance program can reduce losses and inefficiency related to distressed and dysfunctional employees. Ample evidence exists from the behavioral sciences to demonstrate people suffering from emotional distress are less able to concentrate and work efficiently than those who are relaxed and dealing with stress effectively. In the work setting, distress may be manifested by such things as high absenteeism, low productivity, unsatisfactory workmanship, and disruptive interpersonal behavior. To reduce those losses at a cost less than the losses themselves saves an organization money. Cost/benefit, then, is another key to the integrative concept. This concept involves the identification of such employee problems and providing treatment which reduces or eliminates the cause of the dysfunctional behavior.

A second way an EAP might be vital to a human resources management system is in its potential as a problem-prevention tool. Preventive occupational mental health is, therefore, another integrative concept. Employees may be unconcerned with saving their employer's money; therefore, the risk management, cost/benefit model that appeals to employers cannot be presumed to motivate employees to support and participate in an EAP program. However, it generally is accepted that human beings are motivated to reduce painful distress in their lives when they have the means available. The system provided by an employee assistance program supports mental health education and entry into community resources (i.e., community mental health centers, hospitals, and the like), making it easier for employees to gain assistance on a *voluntary* basis. Data indicate a majority of the employees using the system have done so on a voluntary basis, rather than as a result of a supervisor's recommendation related to poor job performance. However, voluntary participation also may lead to savings for the employer and meet the needs of the employee. This savings may be more difficult to measure, especially if large numbers of employees use the system *before* work-dysfunctional behaviors appear, but it would appear to be the ideal result of an effective employee assistance program.

Those concepts previously discussed (i.e., human resources management, cost/benefit, and preventive occupational mental health) are concepts of considerable breadth, under which other key concepts may be subsumed. The most basic of those are briefly discussed below.

1. *Systems* theory is implied in developing employee assistance programs. Systems theory assumes an agency or other social organization consists of an interdependent set of activities composed of subsystems that function within the larger set of parent institution and community. The step-by-step approach to EAP development (e.g., beginning with assessing management commitment and proceeding through implementation to evaluation) represents a systems approach. Each component affects the other components and the overall program affects the organization. The organization, in turn, affects the community. Careful analysis of the key factors affecting the system is essential to employee assistance program development.

2. Gaining stronger commitment and broader-based support within an organization is enhanced by participative management through an employee assistance program advisory committee formed at the outset of the program. *Participation management* is another key concept inherent in the model EAP development. It generally is an accepted organizational development principle that people more strongly support what they help create. Thus, committee involvement in setting policy, establishing goals, planning for employee education, and evaluating program effectiveness is viewed as a vital component of a successful EAP system. To enhance their effectiveness, goal setting and group development skills training should be provided the advisory committee. The committee, as well as the coordinator, must be the driving and organizing forces for the EAP to succeed.

3. *Human relations training for supervisors* is another integral concept in program development models. Supervisors are key members of the problem identification and referral process. Vital to their facilitating worker problem resolution is their ability to listen to troubled employees with a nonjudgmental attitude, convey a sense of compassionate understanding, and, yet, remain sufficiently detached to firmly confront them with job performance inadequacies. These are skills for which many supervisors need training beyond what an organization normally provides. However, skills in human relations are vital to motivating workers to seek assistance rather than avoiding their problems and suffering serious consequences.

4. *Early detection based on job performance* has remained an integrative concept since the inception of EAPs.

5. *Utilization of existing community resources* also has remained an integrative concept and remains central to EAP philosophy. The use of existing community resources is viewed as an alternative far superior to creating internally based programs that duplicate existing resources. The former is both more efficient and cost/beneficial. Effective linkages to a community-based diagnostic/referral source often means bringing accountability to mental health systems and assistance in providing access to those services through the reduction of stigmas.

6. *Integration with personnel management systems*. For the EAP to survive and succeed it must be linked with the way job performance is evaluated, rewards or incentives are provided, health benefits are administered, and labor relations are managed. This is not to say that personnel managers should administer all aspects of EAPs, but that EAPs must be an integral part of all system elements that serve to interact with the organization's human resources. Many organizations may not be able to visualize or adopt EAP concepts because of the limited scope of their human resources management system.

7. *Use of self-help groups*. Although many individuals receive assistance through formal performance management/supervisor referral systems, other organizations that respond to persons in distress out of strictly altruistic motives should not be ignored. Alcoholics Anonymous (A.A.), Alanon, Gamblers Anonymous, and other self-help groups are examples of information-giving nonprofessional means of intervening in crisis situations and of providing emotional support for personal changes. Self-help organizations need to be recognized and legitimized as a means of developing more voluntary modes of participation in EAPs. Self-help organizations should not replace professional diagnosis and treatment, but they are an important ingredient in creating the impetus for an individual to decide to seek help.

THE ROLE OF THE SUPERVISOR

The supervisor's role in employee assistance programs has been the subject of a considerable amount of written material. These materials usually encourage the supervisor to follow several basic steps in productively managing the troubled employee. The first step involves documentation of unacceptable levels of performance to include incidents, behavior patterns, and attendance. A second step is to conduct an interview or series of interviews to confront the employee with the documented performance deficiencies. The employee then is referred to the employee assistance program for help in solving any problems causing the performance deficiencies. The supervisor was not to become involved in solving the employee's personal problems or even attempting a diagnosis. The supervisor's role was to offer the employee a tool for improving his or her job performance.

The matter of supervising a troubled employee is, however, considerably more complex. Three types of barriers provide special problems to the supervisor in working with a troubled employee.

One of the most basic problems for supervisors is the absence of specific production goals or well-defined tasks to be performed by employees. EAPs are founded on the notion that the supervisor should not diagnose the employee's problems but should stick solely to working with job performance. When performance standards are vague or even nonexistent, the supervisor is put in a compromised position. The program must recognize those deficiencies and design training programs to assist the supervisor. *Close coordination is essential with other organizational training efforts.*

Another problem area is that of job stress related to role conflicts, work addiction, job obsolescence, or other work-climate aggravations.

The supervisor needs to learn how to sort out the factors that make work unrewarding. Training in diagnosing the presence of those factors may be necessary in some work settings.

A third area that requires attention is the kind of social sanctions and expectations placed upon the employee about drinking on the job. Many organizations place employees in a role that seems to require drinking on the job or in related social settings. The supervisor needs to be able to recognize those situations where the risks of problem drinking are encouraged by the organization. This is especially difficult for the supervisor. Training in this area may help the supervisor identify organizational roles and expectations that may contribute to performance problems for employees.

Another perspective on the role of the supervisor is that, once a performance problem has been identified, the supervisor must determine whether the problem is caused by inadequate training of the employee or by the lack of potential to perform the job. If the supervisor determines the employee is able to do the job, then another reason must be sought. These "other" reasons assume that the employee could do the job if he or she wished.

The supervisor should check three organizational factors as possible reasons for the performance deficiency:

1. Is the desired performance punishing?
2. Is nonperformance rewarding?
3. Does performing really matter?

If none of those factors is present, then other external variables, such as family, mental health, and alcoholism problems, are likely causes. It is possible that organizational variables and personal/emotional variables are interrelated. When organizational and training factors can be eliminated, an offer of assistance from the employee assistance program is indicated.

Another way of looking at supervisory roles and responses is to deal with the emotional aspects of the supervisor's behavior in managing the troubled employee. The supervisor's behavior can portray a pattern of interaction that parallels that of the spouse of the alcoholic. The pattern typically includes a process of ignoring the problem and hoping for a "miracle," heart-to-heart talks, or reasoning; begging or pleading; and finally bleeding (transfer, fire, retire). The supervisor, in this pattern, feels anger, guilt, fear, and strong ego involvement with the successes and failures of the employee. The supervisor often is unwilling to recognize deviant behavior he or she is not prepared to handle.

What this suggests is that the traditional training done to teach supervisors to identify, confront, motivate, and refer employees is not enough. In traditional training programs, supervisors are given information they will not use in the near future. However, the supervisor needs to develop a connection between the employee's behavior, feelings, and resultant behavior. With such a model, the supervisor is taught to seek out the EAP coordinator at the earliest sign of problems with an employee. Specific procedures are then taught by the EAP coordinator. Excellent interpersonal skills are required of the program coordinator in this model.

The literature on leadership and supervision does not provide many answers to the problem of how to respond to the troubled employee. Leadership is usually defined as a social-influence process. Research has failed to identify any common characteristics shared by leaders across all situations, nor has one style of leadership been shown to produce a desired set of results in all situations.

The question of task-oriented versus person-oriented behavior is one that is situation bound also. The nature of the task, the amount of structure involved, and the kind and amount of power of the leader—and the quality of leader/employee relations—appear to be the most prominent factors involved in determining what supervisory behavior is appropriate.

There is a decision-making process to help supervisors decide what type of leadership style to exercise. Among the questions for the supervisor to ask are: (1) does the problem possess a quality requirement? (2) does he or she (the supervisor) have sufficient information to make a high-quality decision? (3) is the problem structured? (4) is acceptance of the decision by subordinates important for effective implementation? (5) if I were to make the decision by myself, am I reasonably certain that it would be accepted by my subordinates? (6) do subordinates share the organizational goals to be obtained in solving this problem? and (7) is conflict among subordinates likely in preferred solutions? The supervisor in managing the troubled employee may have to ask himself or herself many of these and related questions.

THE EAP COORDINATOR

Most EAPs depend on a small staff or a single person to implement the program. The success of the EAP often depends on the capabilities and support of the coordinator. Current literature on EAPs often provides a rather narrow or limited description of the role of the coordinator and the involvement in program planning. The coordinator's role seems to be deemphasized if the program focuses on alcoholism or substance abuse and has limited commitment from management.

The role of the coordinator includes serving as a point of contact for troubled employees, discussing documentation and ways of handling unacceptable job performance with supervisors, maintaining confidential employee records for evaluation and follow-up purposes, and planning and implementing training programs for supervisors, education programs for employees, and orientation programs for advisory committees.

As part of the program planning process, the number of personnel assigned to the EAP, the amount of staff time allocated to the EAP (i.e., full-time or part-time staff), and whether the EAP is an internally based or externally based program must be determined. These factors, in turn, affect the efficiency of program operation.

The problem is not with specific functions of the EAP coordinator's office but with the perspective of the organization concerning its understanding of the program, its commitment to the concept, and the economic return on invested dollars.

The author supports an externally based program that defines the coordinator's roles as administrator and as referral center to operate from either inside or outside of an organization. While change can occur from inside the organization, an autonomous EAP, such as the consortium model, also can induce change from outside an organization.

The coordinator's role involves stressing the need for change as applied to a particular group (i.e., employees with unacceptable job performance). One of the basic functions of the EAP coordinator is to supply the organization with information to make decisions. In this capacity the coordinator is acting as a catalyst for change. This means demonstrating the need for an EAP in terms of its ability to improve production, reduce absenteeism, protect company assets, and, in general, produce a financial return on money invested in the program. Management also may be sensitive to the humanitarian aspects of EAPs as a secondary concern.

The impact of relevant information may not be immediate. Careful attention to detail and to development seem appropriate for effective program planning. Overnight implementation often meets immediate needs but later undermines the continuing success of an EAP. It is suggested that hurried implementation solves immediate problems but leads to "paper" programs later. Overzealous coordinators should give way to long-term planning that will result in an operating program 5, 10, or 15 years from now. Hence, alliances, timing, and coordinated efforts are important considerations.

The EAP coordinator may induce change by providing the best answer to a problem. In other words, the coordinator can provide part of the solution to job performance problems at the appropriate time (i.e., during the development of an EAP). However, resistance can be generated by attempting to force a solution on reluctant, uninformed management or on community treatment resources. Furthermore, the demands of the coordinator's role often necessitate a full-time person with support staff. However, in many situations the coordinators role is secondary to his or her other responsibilities, such as personnel director, education director, and so on. While certain circumstances may dictate the EAP coordinator perform several functions within the organization, the primary emphasis of the role is of great importance. The success of the program may depend on whether the EAP coordinator is education director first and coordinator second or coordinator first and education director second. Ideally, the EAP coordinator's role is a full-time position with support staff, but a practical solution might be that the position is filled with someone whose primary duties are the EAP with secondary responsibilities.

The establishment of the EAP coordinator as a component of program planning is only part of the development process. The EAP coordinator can assume various role models. For example, a change agent is anyone who seeks to alter or modify the way organizations and people function. Ronald G. Havelock (1973) described four methods of being a change agent. He indicated a change agent may act as a catalyst to initiate change, provide solutions at timely moments, serve as a process helper in problem solving, and link resources with needs.

The roles of a change agent are not mutually exclusive. The EAP coordinator must choose the appropriate emphasis for different circumstances that arise in the development of an EAP. The coordinator will act as a catalyst in starting an employee education program while linking and developing community resources to meet the needs of the EAP, for example. The difficulty lies in the coordinator's ability to select and execute the proper role. A coordinator acting as a change agent can influence a management that does not view employee problems and job performance problems in the same light. To minimize resistance to EAPs as part of the solution to job performance problems, guidelines can be established.

The coordinator's role is a demanding one in terms of the skills required and the level of involvement. According to Havelock (1973) process helpers involve working with the system to recognize and define needs, establish goals and objectives, search for relevent resources, select, create, and match resources with objectives and needs, implement the EAP model, and evaluate the model.

For the program coordinator, process helping skills are necessary to work with the advisory committee, community resources, management structures, and union officials, if applicable. The EAP coordinator should have group facilitation skills to perform this role. A model training program for committees promotes shared leadership, rather than dominance or manipulation by the coordinator.

A key in the process helping role is effective interaction among relevant groups, individuals, and the coordinator. Effective interaction may be viewed as part of the process helping role, while management of information is part of the role of providing solutions. Switching from the providing solutions to the process helper role should occur after corporate commitment has been obtained. As the EAP coordinator becomes a process helper, he or she should develop support for the program, facilitate involvement, and create joint ownership and leadership in the EAP.

For example, the needs and concerns of the organization should be determined prior to offering a solution. The EAP, as part of the solution, must be appropriate for the problem. This may mean determining if absenteeism or production problems are present in the organization, and then determining whether the EAP can assist in solving those problems. The EAP coordinator can assist management in establishing criteria for measuring the effectiveness of the EAP as part of the solution to job performance problems. Management, therefore, can determine if an EAP solves part or all of its job performance problems. The EAP coordinator should build a relationship with management based on trust to discuss problems, manage the adoption process, and promote sharing of knowledge. The coordinator should help establish the EAP in such a manner that the decision makers in the organization have ownership of the solution.

An issue for EAP coordinators is how to utilize their skills and ideas. The EAP coordinator should become a *resource* person for the system, while the advisory committee should discuss, evaluate, and adopt solutions for referral procedures, policy statements, supervisory training, employee education, and the like.

Finally, the EAP coordinator can act in the capacity of linking resources with the needs of the EAP by providing access to community resources for employees. The EAP coordinator should arrange and monitor linkages for employees to community resources. Services available in the community should not be duplicated; however, nonexistent resources should be developed. Often employees do not know that resources exist or how to utilize them; therefore, the coordinator is assuming the role of linking the employee with community resources. This role involves the process of building relationships in which two-way communication is essential.

THE ADVISORY COMMITTEE

The advisory committee operates to give direction and guidance to other components of the EAP. While most advisory committees do not have decision-making authority, the committee can be influential in helping management.

The advisory committee can be given responsibilities that will increase its influence and provide the groundwork for management/labor ownership of the EAP. It is suggested the inclusion of the advisory committee in the planning process increases the probability of a successful EAP. The advisory committee can be assigned to assist in writing policy and procedure statements, for example. Other areas for the advisory committee to provide input include the goals and objectives for the EAP, strategies for implementing the EAP, reviews of proposed supervisory training and employee education programs, development of a strategy for publicizing the program within the organization and community, and monitoring the implementation and evaluation of the program. From the list of tasks given the group, it should be evident the advisory committee is a vital component in the program planning process, and that a committee satisfied with only marginal responsibilities will not be in the best interests of the EAP.

For an EAP to provide long-term benefits for employees, the committee must be committed and have a thorough understanding of its role and responsibilities in the system. Issues and concepts must be discussed, and shared leadership is crucial to its growth. If one element (i.e., labor, management, or program coordinator) dominates the committee, its ability is diminished. Again, the committee should be representative of the major employee groups within the organization. A training program for advisory committee members in effective group decision making is recommended to insure shared leadership and a committee that remains vital.

Although many EAPs have advisory committees, few of them function in an effective manner. The author supports a training program for advisory committees designed to develop group consensus decision-making skills and to provide impetus for continued growth.

The goals of the advisory committee training program are:

1. To provide an understanding of the EAP concept.
2. To develop commitment to the EAP through shared program planning.
3. To teach group consensus decision-making skills.
4. To provide an ongoing group planning structure for future meetings; and
5. To complete important EAP planning tasks (i.e., establish program goals, policies, and procedures).

The design of the advisory committee training should assist participants in becoming effective group members. The design makes use of the *Participation Training* concepts developed by Dr. John McKinley from

Indiana University.[1] The advisory committee learns through the processes of:

1. Volunteering for group roles (i.e., recorder, leader, observer).
2. Determining a topic, goal, and outline for a series of discussion sessions.
3. Obtaining feedback from trained group leaders.
4. Practicing task functions and maintenance roles.
5. Sharing in the evaluating process.
6. Using the group's resources, ideas, and experiences.
7. Developing trust through open communication and responsible risk taking.

The advisory committee training balances process with content in that the participants discuss issues and solve problems while improving their awareness of group decision-making processes.

The trainer's role is to insure participation remains voluntary, to provide process information and group feedback, to serve as a resource person, and to provide guidance for group cohesiveness. Part of the task to be accomplished during the advisory committee training is to develop a policy statement for the EAP congruent with organizational policy statements.

One element found in EAPs is the program policy and procedures statements. Many programs have little depth beyond the policy and procedure statements and can be identified as "paper programs." While the policy and procedure statements do not insure the existence of a program, they are essential to effective programs. Well-designed, publicized statements of policy and procedures can provide momentum for EAPs. The policy statement should outline:

1. The recognized need for the program.
2. Support for the program from both management and labor.
3. The willingness of the organization to commit time and resources to the EAP.
4. Accessible points of contacts for employee assistance and procedures to follow.
5. An acceptable attitude about mental illness, alcoholism, and family/marital problems.
6. A concern by the organization for its employees.

---

[1] John McKinley, *Participant's Manual for Participation Training Institute* (Indianapolis, Ind.: CHR, Inc., 1978).

7. The scope of problems to be covered by the EAP.
8. The target group for the EAP.
9. Job security and promotional opportunities of those participating in the program.
10. Confidentiality of records.
11. Job performance as the basis for supervisory recommendations.
12. The voluntary nature of the program.
13. Sick leave and insurance benefits.
14. The relationship to other personnel and administrative policies.

The explicitness, scope, and tone of the policy must be given careful consideration.

ESTABLISHING LINKAGES WITH COMMUNITY RESOURCES

When EAPs initiate linkages with community resources tension is likely to exist because of uncertainties over roles and expectations. The following are some guidelines for developing productive linkages with community resources which will help overcome tensions caused by distrust, conflict, and inefficiency in the referral system. The guidelines are not absolute but provide direction for both the EAP and the community resource.

1. Understand and know your own organization. Try to clearly identify your organization's goals, values orientation, and contributions to the linkages. Both groups should be able to articulate these elements.
2. Develop a joint agreement on the general purposes of the linkage. Write a broad statement oriented toward the common goals of each organization.
3. Deal openly with issues about power, boundaries, and responsibilities. For the linkage to be effective, all these elements must be negotiated. Shared credit for the formation of the linkage is essential.
4. Establish direct confidential communication systems between the community resources and the EAP office. This communication system will be a key component of the EAP model.
5. Identify facilitators that may assist with the community resource linkages. These persons must not be leaders of the EAP or the community resource. They may be counselors, volunteers, board members, union leaders, A.A. members, or ministers. As

linkage facilitators, they should help to prevent an organization from being dependent on one individual.

6. Identify persons with a variety of skills in such areas as planning, change processes, negotiation, interpersonal communications, and group processes. These persons may include and assist in facilitating understanding between community resources and the EAP. Persons with expertise in specific areas may or may not be outside both systems. Similarly, not all occupational program consultants have these skills.
7. Learning aspects of the linkages should be emphasized. The linkage should create new knowledge, ideas, models, and innovations needed to make the linkage effective.
8. Emphasize program accountability and responsible management of employees flowing into and out of the EAP system. Good recordkeeping is essential, and agreement on referral procedures is necessary.
9. Carry out and use evaluation in the decision-making process. Evaluation models should fit the objectives. The future of an EAP may depend on how well the referral and the diagnosis, treatment, and client progress are documented.
10. Publicize newsworthy and successful activities of the EAP. This may encourage other community resources to participate in the system. Build on successes rather than dwelling on failures. Continually review and revise the system to meet employee needs and correct inadequacies.

The EAP-Community Resource Agreement

This section discusses specific items that may be part of an agreement between the community resources and an EAP. The word agreement is used, rather than contract, since it denotes a more flexible and less authoritarian relationship. An agreement is a vehicle to develop a clear understanding of what each agency expects from the other. The process of negotiating agreements should be done in a pleasant nonthreatening atmosphere where solutions can surface that will allow both participants to have their needs met. Prior to developing agreements, both partners should have their individual needs focused and be able to accurately communicate them to each other. Below are some areas for possible inclusion in an agreement:

1. Specific services offered to the EAP by the community resources.
2. Professional qualifications and roles of individuals to be involved in providing services.

3. Referral procedures to be utilized by the EAP coordinator and employees.
4. Operating schedule and location of the services.
5. Fees for assessment and ongoing treatment.
6. Procedures for handling third-party payments.
7. Procedures for flow of information between the EAP coordinator and community resources and for maintenance of client confidentiality.
8. Follow-up procedures and plans for ongoing support of employees.
9. Treatment modalities to be used.
10. Procedures and criteria for making referrals to other community resources.
11. Plans for evaluating treatment processes.

A key in the EAP model is to establish a clearly focused set of expected behaviors for the EAP and the community resources when referring employees. These expectations should be communicated to all the employees in a general manner and explicitly when an employee seeks assistance through the EAP.

The Referral Process

Referral is a common denominator in many EAPs since few of them can handle all aspects of an employee's problem (i.e., identification, assessment, diagnosis, and treatment). Therefore, referral to community resources is an essential element for EAPs not promoting an internally based program.

A recommendation to the EAP coordinator by the supervisor may be misused unless supportive job performance data are the basis for recommendations. Referral is the process by which the EAP links an employee with the appropriate community resource, as opposed to the recommendation made by the supervisor to visit the EAP coordinator. The linkage resulting from the referral of an employee by the EAP coordinator may include assessment, diagnosis, information, and treatment. Referrals are reserved for persons who have some expertise in determining the cause of problems and in choosing the appropriate community resource for handling the problem. If an EAP coordinator does not have this expertise, he or she would make a recommendation that an employee visit a centralized agency handling all assessments and making the appropriate referrals. Supervisors should *not* make a referral to the EAP, but rather should *recommend* the employee take advantage of the EAP. EAPs are voluntary programs and the supervisor's role should be focused on the job performance of the employee. Referrals should be made by the

EAP coordinator or the person performing the assessment or diagnostic function.

When an employee with a problem contacts the EAP coordinator or the person assigned to be the entry point into the community resource system, a number of actions take place. The employee should be clearly told about the EAP's policy and procedures, especially as they relate to pending disciplinary action. It should be made clear at the outset, that the EAP is a means for employees to seek and to receive assistance for problems affecting job performance and that it is not a shelter from disciplinary action. Making sure that the employee is made responsible for the consequences of his or her job performance actions is an essential element throughout the referral process, both for the EAP and the community resource system. Additionally, it must be clear that utilization of the EAP will in no way affect future job security or advancement. The process of diagnosis, company insurance, and costs should be explained to the employee. Consent forms for authorizing release of information to the EAP coordinator should be available. Protection of confidentiality is essential in all elements of the referral process. Referral to a community resource should be made only after the EAP coordinator or the diagnostic agent has carefully explained the treatment options available to the employee.

To restate, the following should be discussed with the employee at the time of referral:

1. The company's insurance coverage for expenses incurred for services rendered by the treatment resource.
2. The assurance that the employee's promotion opportunities will not be hindered by the use of the EAP or any community resources.
3. Continued employment, pay raises, promotions, or disciplinary action will be based on job performance and not clinical progress.
4. Any type of communication about employee progress in a treatment program will be governed by confidentiality statutes that allow release of certain information only with the consent of the employee.
5. Receiving treatment during working hours will be handled according to the organization's general policy on absences for health reasons or statements on EAP procedures.
6. The process of making the appointment should be outlined. Having a specific person to contact is very helpful to the employee.

Motivating an employee to accept a referral may remain an ongoing problem. An even greater problem is created when the employee denies that a problem exists, even though job performance clearly indicates something is wrong and action required. Dealing with these conditions requires a skilled interviewer who can:

1. Clearly identify with the employee what the consequences will be if behavior is not changed.
2. Identify and help resolve any preconceived barriers to accepting services.
3. Preserve the employee's self-esteem. It is the job performance actions that are unacceptable, not the employee's personality or being.
4. Avoid attaching labels such as psychotic, alcoholic, and so on to employees.
5. Assure the employee that the least restrictive alternative will be used.

Services to Be Provided by Community Resources

One of the first things the EAP coordinator, with the aid of the advisory committee, must do to establish linkages with community resources is to locate them. Many large cities have community service councils or other bodies for coordinating human resources. These organizations frequently publish directories of community resources or have available information. Other excellent sources of information are crisis counseling centers, ministerial associations, police departments, and chambers of commerce. Other EAP or occupational program coordinators may have identified and compiled lists of community resources and should be consulted for advice and sharing of relevant information. Finally, state departments of mental health may offer assistance. They often have directories of public and private facilities.

At least four basic categories of services should be identified.

1. Crisis Intervention. Included in this category are:

a. Twenty-four hour "hotlines" and telephone counseling services.
b. Drop-in centers for immediate service without an appointment.
c. Self-help groups, such as Alcoholics Anonymous.

2. Outpatient Services. These may include assessment, diagnosis, information, education, and ongoing treatment for a variety of problems, such as:

a. Child abuse.
b. Child/adolescent problems.

c. Mental health counseling.
d. Marital counseling.
e. Family counseling.
f. Alcohol/drug dependency.
g. Debt management.
h. Career counseling.
i. Legal counseling.
j. Grief counseling.
k. Family planning/sex education.

Outpatient services may be in the day or evening but are usually focused around a specific problem. Outpatient services will be able to handle many employee problems.

3. Inpatient Services. These services provide intensive care for employees with severe, chronic, and life-threatening problems. A continuum of inpatient services exist, ranging from hospital care to residential treatment. A number of intermediate services, such as half-way houses and day treatment centers, are also available.

4. Self-Help Groups. These groups focus on a specific problem and are operated by persons who have faced and overcome similar situations. The groups are effective in providing aftercare support, education, and crisis assistance. Self-help groups exist in such problem areas as:

a. Alcoholism (A.A. and Alanon).
b. Overeating.
c. Child abuse (Parents Anonymous).
d. Death or dying.
e. Divorce.
f. Single parenting.
g. Gambling and other addictions.
h. Chronic credit management.

Self-help groups are effective for ongoing support. However, they are not a substitute for professional diagnosis and treatment.

Evaluating Community Resources

The emphasis on accountability has spread to all aspects of society, including community resources. The reasons for evaluating community resources are to provide information for making decisions on program operation and to provide the best possible assistance to employees. An evaluation begins with the development of a system to gather data on the flow of employees into and out of community resources. However, there is additional information that should be gathered.

Community resource evaluation should be based on a set of standards, criteria, or principles against which to compare the data gathered. Listed below are some suggested criteria by which to evaluate community resources.

1. The principle of the least-restrictive alternative is followed. For the EAP, this means an emphasis on outpatient care whenever possible, unless it can be demonstrated that inpatient care is essential.
2. Services designed to meet client needs, not agency needs, are incorporated in the community resource principles.
3. A concern for quality of life and a holistic approach for the client is demonstrated.
4. Opportunities for the continuation and integration of normal life experiences are provided.
5. Necessary services are provided to maintain the maximum amount of client stabilization.
6. Overlapping or duplicated services are minimized and program gaps are eliminated.
7. Responsive, timely coordination and referral procedures exist among the community resources.
8. Knowledge and innovations are sought to upgrade the quality of services.
9. Citizen/client participation in planning, implementation, and evaluation of services is present. This is especially crucial for EAP linkages.
10. Regular and thorough evaluations are performed with data being used to improve services.
11. Prevention should be emphasized. Many community resources are willing and able to initiate educational programs for employees on various topics.
12. The needs of special groups should be given attention. These group needs may include the problems of women, minorities, occupational groups such as isolated workers and executives, etc.
13. Client dignity and confidentiality are never compromised.
14. Effective liaison with all types of community resources is maintained whether they are degreed or nondegreed, professional or para-professional, paid or volunteer.
15. Fees are clearly stated and related to well-defined services and the client's ability to pay.

Criteria for determining effectiveness of community resources might include the opinions of certain individuals.[2] For example:

1. Direct users of the community resource both present and past.
2. Indirect users of the community resource, such as:
   a. Families of the user.
   b. Community planning groups.
   c. Interest groups (mental health associations, counselors associations, and the like).
   d. Other community resources.
3. Administrators, board members, and staff of the community agencies.
4. State planning and regulatory agencies (mental health, public health, welfare, education, licensing agencies).

As a general rule, an EAP coordinator should have access to information that does not violate client confidentiality or employee privacy, such as personnel records if the community resource receives public money from the local, state, or federal government. Private community resources are not obligated to disclose information. However, private resources may provide data, since the information will help referral sources make decisions on the use of services.

To summarize, evaluation is a process to be used for judging decision-making alternatives. The evaluation of community resources, therefore, has to be based on clearly stated needs and objectives articulated by the EAP coordinator and the employee. Community resource performance can be measured against the established criteria. Evaluation is not isolated from the community resources, linkages, and referral process but is a key to making good decisions on the appropriate use of community resources for the benefit of the employee.

---

[2] Val D. MacMurray, *Citizen Evaluation of Mental Health Services* (New York: Human Services Press, 1976).

CHAPTER 21

CAFETERIA APPROACHES TO BENEFIT PLANNING

Burton T. Beam, Jr.

INTRODUCTION

Employee benefit plans that provide employees with some choice about the types and amounts of benefits they receive have become quite common. Traditionally, the cost of the optional or supplemental benefits made available under these plans had to be borne by the employee on an after-tax, payroll-deduction basis. Since the early 1970s, however, a steadily growing number of employers have established benefit programs in which all or a large segment of the employees are permitted to design their own benefit package by using a prespecified number of employer dollars to purchase benefits from among a number of available options. The popularity of these plans among employees, as well as favorable tax legislation, has led most benefit consultants to predict that within a few years most employees will be provided benefits in this manner.

While all employee benefit plans offering employee options might be viewed broadly as being cafeteria (or flexible) approaches to benefit planning, this chapter focuses primarily on those cafeteria plans giving employees some choice in selecting the types and levels of benefits that are provided with employer contributions. The chapter will first describe the structure of the cafeteria plans that are available. It will continue by analyzing the reasons for employer interest in these plans, the barriers to their establishment, and the design decisions that must be made by employers.

TYPES OF PLANS

In its purest sense, a cafeteria plan can be defined as any employee benefit plan that allows an employee to have some choice in designing his or her own benefit package by selecting different types or levels of benefits that are funded with employer dollars. At this extreme, a benefit plan that allows an employee to select an HMO as an option to an insured medical expense plan can be classified as a cafeteria plan. However, the more common use of the term *cafeteria plan* denotes something much broader—a plan in which choices can be made among several different types of benefits and possibly cash.

Prior to the addition of Section 125 to the Internal Revenue Code by the Revenue Act of 1978, the use of cafeteria plans had potentially adverse tax consequences for an employee. If an employee had a choice among benefits that were normally nontaxable (such as medical expense insurance or disability income insurance) and benefits that were normally taxable (such as cash or life insurance in excess of $50,000), then the doctrine of constructive receipt would result in an employee's being taxed as if he or she had elected the maximum taxable benefits that could have been obtained under the plan. Therefore, if an employee could elect cash in lieu of being covered under the employer's medical expense plan, an employee who elected to remain in the medical expense plan would have taxable income merely because cash could have been elected. Obviously, this tax environment was not conducive to the use of cafeteria plans unless the only benefits contained in them were normally of a nontaxable nature.

Section 125 provides more favorable tax treatment to a cafeteria plan as defined in that Code section. Such plans are those under which all participants are employees and under which all participants may choose among two or more benefits consisting of cash and qualified benefits. Qualified benefits include most welfare benefits ordinarily resulting in no taxable income to employees if provided outside of a cafeteria plan. There are some exceptions, and the following benefits cannot be provided under a cafeteria plan: scholarships and fellowships, transportation benefits, educational assistance, no-additional-cost services, and employee discounts. However, one normally taxable benefit—group term life insurance in excess of $50,000—can be included. In general, a cafeteria plan cannot include retirement benefits except for a 401(k) plan.

As long as a cafeteria plan meets the Section 125 requirements, the issue of constructive receipt is of no concern. Employees have taxable income only to the extent that they elect normally taxable benefits—cash and group term life insurance in excess of $50,000.

Core Plus Plans

Probably the most common type of cafeteria plan is one that offers a basic core of benefits to all employees, plus a second layer of optional benefits that permits an employee to choose which benefits he or she will add to the basic benefits. These optional benefits can be "purchased" with dollars, or credits, that are given to the employee as part of the benefit package. If these credits are inadequate to purchase the desired benefits, an employee can make additional purchases with aftertax contributions or with before-tax reductions under a flexible spending account.

The following is an example of the plan of one employer. The basic benefits provided to all employees include term life insurance equal to 1½ times salary, travel accident insurance, medical expense coverage for the employee and dependents, and disability income insurance. Employees also are provided with "flexible credits" equal to from 3 to 6 percent of salary, depending on length of service. Each year, an employee is permitted to use his or her flexible credits to purchase benefits from among several options, including additional life insurance equal to one times salary, term life insurance on dependents, dental insurance for the employee and dependents, an annual physical examination for the employee, up to two weeks of additional vacation time, and cash. If an employee's flexible credits are insufficient to purchase the desired benefits, additional amounts can be contributed on a payroll-deduction basis.

A variation of this approach is to have the core plan be an "average" plan for which the employee makes no contribution. The employee then may receive credits if certain benefits are reduced. These credits can be used either to increase other benefits or, if the plan allows, to increase cash compensation.

Predesigned Package Plans

Another type of cafeteria plan is one in which an employee has a choice among several predesigned benefit packages. Typically, at least one of the packages can be selected without any employee cost. If an employee selects a more expensive package, the employee will be required to contribute to the cost of the package. Some employers may also include a bare-bones benefit package, which results in cash being paid to an employee who selects it.

Under some cafeteria plans using this approach (often referred to as a modular approach), the predesigned packages may have significant differences. In comparing two packages, one may be better than others in certain cases, but inferior in other cases. Other employers using this approach have virtually identical packages, with the major difference being in the option selected for the medical expense coverage. For example, the plan of one large bank offers three traditional insured plans, two HMOs, and a preferred provider organization.

Flexible Spending Accounts

Section 125 also allows employees to purchase certain benefits on a before-tax basis through the use of a flexible spending account, or FSA. FSAs, which technically are cafeteria plans, can be used by themselves or incorporated into a more comprehensive cafeteria plan. They are most commonly used alone by small employers who, primarily for cost reasons, are unwilling to establish a broader plan. The cafeteria plans of most large employers contain an FSA as an integral part of the plan.

An FSA allows an employee to fund certain benefits on a before-tax basis by electing to take a salary reduction. The amount of this reduction can then be used to fund the cost of any qualified benefits that are included in the plan. However, they are most commonly used for health insurance premiums, medical expenses not covered by the employer's plan, and dependent care expenses.

The amount of any salary reduction is, in effect, credited to an employee's reimbursement account, and benefits are paid from this account when an employee properly files for such reimbursement. The amount of the salary reduction must be made on a benefit-by-benefit basis prior to the beginning of the plan year. Once made, changes are allowed only under specified circumstances. These include changes in marital status, an increase or decrease in the number of dependents, or a spouse's unemployment or ineligibility to participate in his or her employer's medical expense plan. If the monies in the FSA are not used during the plan year, they are forfeited and belong to the employer. Some employers keep the forfeited money and use it to offset the cost of administering the FSA program. However, almost anything can be done with the money, except giving it back only to the persons who have forfeited it. Some employers give it to charity. Others credit it on a pro rata basis to the accounts of all participants in the FSA program for the following year or use it to reduce future benefit costs (such as contributions to a medical expense plan) for all employees.

An election to participate in an FSA program not only reduces salary for federal income tax purposes, but also lowers the wages on which Social Security taxes are levied. Therefore, those employees who are below the wage base limit after the reduction will pay less in Social

Security taxes, and their future income benefits under Social Security will also be smaller. However, the reduction in benefits will be very small in most cases unless the salary reduction is very large. It should be noted that the employer's share of Social Security tax payments will also decrease. In some cases, the employer's savings may actually be large enough to fully offset the cost of administering the FSA program.

REASONS FOR EMPLOYER INTEREST

The growing interest in cafeteria plans on the part of employers can be traced to a number of factors. Many employers are concerned that employees often do not appreciate the value of the benefits provided under conventional plans. They feel that, by giving an employee a specified total number of dollars to use for purchasing benefits and a list of available benefits with their associated costs, the employee will better perceive not only the total value of the benefits being provided by the employer but also the nature and relative costs of the individual benefits themselves.

The inflexible benefit structure of conventional employee benefit plans does not adequately meet the varying benefit needs of different employees and often leads to employee dissatisfaction. For example, single employees or older employees whose children are grown may see little value in substantial life insurance benefits. Also, the combined benefits of working couples may provide coverage the cost of which could be used for other purposes. Employers view the cafeteria approach to benefit planning as not only a means of more effectively meeting the benefit needs of different employees at a particular time, but also as a way of enabling an individual employee to better meet his or her needs as they change over time. Closely related is the feeling among employers that cafeteria plans are viewed as being less paternalistic than conventional employee benefit programs.

Employers also see the cafeteria approach to benefit planning as providing opportunities to control the escalating benefit levels and costs associated not only with inflation but also with the increasing need to comply with the requirements of newly enacted federal and state legislation. Since a cafeteria plan is essentially a defined contribution plan, rather than a defined benefit plan, it provides a number of opportunities for controlling increases in benefit levels and costs. For example, it may encourage employees to choose medical expense options with larger deductibles to more efficiently use the fixed number of dollars allotted to them under the plan. It also may enable the employer to pass on to the employees any increased benefit costs arising out of compliance with legislation prohibiting age and sex discrimination or mandating additional benefits. In addition, since increases in employer contributions for benefits are not tied directly to increases in benefit costs, the employer has the opportunity to grant percentage increases for benefits that are below the actual overall increase in employee benefit costs.

POTENTIAL BARRIERS

While the majority of employers have shown interest in the cafeteria approach to benefit planning, the failure of many of these employers to actually establish a cafeteria plan stems from the variety of obstacles that must be overcome before a plan can be successfully implemented. These potential barriers to the establishment of cafeteria plans have included, among other things: (1) the tax environment; (2) potential problems associated with unwise benefit selection by employees; (3) negative attitudes on the part of employees, insurers, and unions; (4) adverse selection; and (5) increased implementation and administration costs. However, many of these barriers either have been largely overcome or are less of an obstacle than in the past.

Taxation

Prior to the passage of the Revenue Act of 1978, a federal income tax picture clouded by the issue of constructive receipt probably was the principal barrier to the establishment of cafeteria plans. As previously mentioned, this is no longer an issue. However, the Revenue Act of 1978 did not fully clarify all the tax ramifications of cafeteria plans, but various technical corrections and tax laws since that time have gradually settled many of the unresolved issues. Despite some predictions to the contrary, cafeteria plans were not adversely affected by the Tax Reform Act of 1986. This does not mean that the tax environment surrounding cafeteria plans is simple. Section 125 contains a prohibition against discrimination as to eligibility. A cafeteria plan must be available to a group of employees under a classification set up by the employer that is not found to be discriminatory in favor of highly compensated employees by the secretary of the treasury. If discrimination exists with respect to eligibility, any qualified benefits received by a highly compensated employee will be treated as taxable income for that employee. Highly compensated employees include persons who, during the year or the preceding year, (1) are 5 percent owners of the firm, (2) earn more than $75,000 in annual compensation, and (3) earn more than $50,000 in annual compensation and whose compensation is in the top 20 percent of the firm's employees, and (4) are officers of the firm who earn more than $45,000. (These dollar figures will be indexed annually.)

Each of the benefits under a cafeteria plan is also subject to the nondiscrimination requirements of Section 89 of the Internal Revenue Code. If these requirements are not met, highly compensated employees will be taxed on the discriminatory portion of any benefits received, assuming, of course, that the benefits are not already taxable because of the plan's failure to meet the previously described eligibility requirements.

Section 125 also contains a concentration test for benefits. The test will not be satisfied if the value of the qualified benefits provided to key employees under the plan exceeds 25 percent of the aggregate of the value of the benefits provided to all employees under the plan. If the concentration test is not met, key employees will be taxed on the value of all benefits received under the plan. A key employee is defined as any employee who, during the plan year or any of the preceding four plan years, is (1) an officer of the firm having any annual compensation greater than $45,000, (2) any 1 of the 10 employees having annual compensation from the firm of more than $45,000 and owning the largest interests in the firm, (3) a 5 percent owner of the firm, or (4) a 1 percent owner of the firm having an annual compensation from the firm of more the $150,000.

Unwise Employee Benefit Selection

Often employers are concerned that many employees may not have the expertise to select the proper benefits from among the alternatives offered under a cafeteria plan. Among other things, unwise employee benefit selection may result in inadequate employee protection following a catastrophic loss, in employee dissatisfaction with the plan, and in an increased potential for liability suits against the employer. To avoid, or at least minimize, these problems, employers establishing cafeteria plans must establish effective ongoing communication programs aimed at educating (and perhaps even counseling) employees about the full implications of various benefit choices available to them. However, despite the employer's best efforts, there remains a risk that the communication of incomplete or incorrect information may give rise to increased corporate liability. Moreover, in some cases, a strong conviction on the part of an employer that the organization has a moral obligation to prevent employees from financial injury through faulty decisions may itself be a major barrier to the establishment of a cafeteria plan.

Negative Attitudes

Negative attitudes on the part of employees, insurers, and unions also may serve as obstacles to the institution of a cafeteria plan.

Employees

Negative reactions on the part of employees to an announced proposal to convert from a conventional fixed benefit plan to a cafeteria approach can arise from a variety of sources; for example, suspicion concerning the employer's motivation in making the change, a fear that some important long-standing benefits may be lost, and an apprehension about now having to make choices among benefits of which the individual employee has little knowledge. Since employee support is critical if a cafeteria plan is to be truly successful, the employer must be willing to commit the time and resources necessary to combat these negative attitudes through adequately informing the employees about the reasons for the proposed program, its advantages and disadvantages, and its future implications for them. Moreover, by soliciting the opinions of employees on their perceived benefit needs and incorporating those findings into the decision-making process, the employer will not only help to allay initial employee concerns, but also minimize negative employee attitudes once the cafeteria plan has been instituted.

Insurers

The growth of the cafeteria approach to benefit planning also has been inhibited by the reluctance or inability of some insurance companies to underwrite the optional benefits an employer may wish to include in a cafeteria plan, or to provide meaningful assistance in connection with the implementation and administration of such a plan. While few insurers seem unwilling to experiment with almost any new concept, most have been concerned with the problem of adverse selection because of employee choice. Although the potential for adverse selection is a real problem that must be faced in underwriting a cafeteria plan, insurers are finding it is possible to control the problem at an acceptable level by incorporating certain safeguards in plan design. As a result, the number of insurers willing to underwrite cafeteria plans and provide administrative services for such plans has grown in the last few years.

Unions

Unions generally have had a negative attitude toward employee benefit plans that contain optional benefits. Union management often feels that bargaining over optional benefits is contrary to the practice of bargaining for the best benefit program for all employees. As a result, most cafeteria plans do not apply to union employees.

Adverse Selection

When employees are allowed choice in selecting benefits, the problem of adverse selection arises. This means that those employees who are likely to have claims will tend to pick the benefits that will minimize their out-of-pocket costs. For example, an employee who previously selected a medical expense option with a high deductible might switch to a plan with a lower deductible if medical expenses are ongoing. An employee who previously rejected dental insurance or legal expense benefits is likely to elect these benefits if dental care or legal advice is anticipated in the near future.

It should be noted that adverse selection is a problem whether a plan is insured or self-funded. It also exists outside of cafeteria plans if choice is allowed. However, the degree of choice within a cafeteria plan tends to make the potential costs more severe unless actions are taken to combat the problem.

Several techniques are used to control adverse selection in cafeteria plans. Benefit limitations and restrictions on coverage can be included if a person wishes to add or change coverage at a date later than initial eligibility. This technique has been common in contributory benefit plans for many years. Another technique is to price the options accordingly. If an option is likely to encourage adverse selection, the cost to the employee for that option should be increased above the level that would have been charged if the option had been the only one available. Such pricing has been difficult in the past, but is becoming easier and more accurate as more experience with cafeteria plans develops. The control of adverse selection is also one reason for the use of predesigned package plans. If, for example, the medical expense plan in one option is likely to encourage adverse selection, the option may not include other options for which adverse selection is also a concern (such as dental or legal expense benefits). To further counter increased costs from the medical expense plan, the option may also offer minimal coverage for other types of benefits.

Administrative Costs

Cafeteria plans involve a number of additional developmental, administrative, and benefit costs over and above those associated with conventional employee benefit programs. Because of the greater complexity associated with employee choice, employers establishing cafeteria plans encounter higher initial and continuing administrative costs associated with, among other things, the need for additional employees to administer the program, additional computer time to process employee choices, and a more comprehensive communication program. However, as cafeteria plans have grown in popularity, numerous vendors have developed products that enable employers to carry out these administrative functions in a more cost-effective manner.

In addition to adverse selection, other factors are associated with cafeteria plans that might lead to increased benefit costs. For example, if an employee elected to divert a portion of the employer's contribution from a deferred compensation benefit (such as a profit-sharing plan) to an option involving current benefit payments (such as health insurance), the employer would lose the opportunity to recapture that contribution if the employee were to leave the company before becoming fully vested. Also, the establishment of a cafeteria plan may involve what one benefit consulting firm terms "buy-in" costs for the employer. While conventional employee benefit plans generally require employees to contribute at a uniform rate for group life insurance, cafeteria plans usually charge employees at rates that vary according to age. Since a shift from a conventional benefit plan to a cafeteria plan would increase substantially the cost of group life insurance for older employees, the employer may be required to subsidize that group.

CONSIDERATIONS IN PLAN DESIGN AND ADMINISTRATION

Before committing itself to the establishment of a cafeteria program, an employer must be sure a valid reason exists for converting the company's traditional benefit program to a cafeteria approach. For example, if there is strong employee dissatisfaction with the current benefit program, the solution may lie in clearly identifying the sources of dissatisfaction and making appropriate adjustments in the existing benefit program, rather than making a shift to a cafeteria plan. However, if employee dissatisfaction arises from widely differing benefit needs on the part of the employees, conversion to a cafeteria plan may be quite appropriate. Beyond having a clearly defined purpose for converting from a traditional benefit program to a cafeteria program and being willing to bear the additional administrative costs associated with a cafeteria approach, a number of considerations must be faced by the employer in designing the plan itself and the system for its administration.

Plan Design

Numerous questions arise that must be answered before a cafeteria plan can be designed properly. What benefits should be included in the plan? How should benefits be distributed between the basic and optional portions of the plan? How should an employee's flexible credits be calculated? To what extent should employees be allowed to change their benefit selections?

Benefits to Be Included

Probably the most fundamental decision that must be made in designing a cafeteria plan is determining what benefits should be included. If an employer wants the plan to be viewed as meeting the differing needs of employees, it is important that the employer receive employee inputs concerning the types of benefits perceived as being most desirable. An open dialogue with employees undoubtedly will lead to suggestions that every possible employee benefit be made available. The enthusiasm of many employees for a cafeteria plan will then be dampened when the employer rejects some, and possibly many, of these suggestions for cost, administrative, or psychological reasons. Consequently, it is important that certain ground rules be established regarding the benefits that are acceptable to the employer.

The employer must decide whether the plan should be limited to the types of benefits provided through traditional group insurance arrangements or be expanded to include other welfare benefits, retirement benefits and, possibly, cash. At a minimum, it is important to ensure that an overall employee benefit program provide employees with protection against all major areas of personal risks. This suggests that a benefit program make at least some provision for life insurance, disability income protection, medical expense protection, and retirement benefits. However, it is not necessary that all of these benefits be included in a cafeteria plan. For example, most employers have a retirement plan separate from their cafeteria plan because of Section 125 requirements. Other employers make a certain type of retirement benefit, such as a 401(k) plan, one of the available cafeteria options.

Probably the most controversial issue among employers who have adopted cafeteria plans is whether cash should be an available option. Arguments in favor of a cash option often are based on the rationale that employees should not be forced to purchase optional benefits if they have no need or desire for them. In addition, cash may better fulfill the needs of many employees. For example, a young employee's greatest need may be the necessary down payment for a home, and an older worker's greatest need may be the resources to pay college tuition for children. Some employers may believe the purpose of a cafeteria plan is to provide employee benefits only and not current income. If cash is available, employees will view the plan as a source of increasing their wages or salary rather than as an employee benefit. In plans where cash is an option, the amount that may be withdrawn is sometimes limited. Also, experience has shown that the majority of employees will elect nontaxable benefits in lieu of cash.

In some respects, a cafeteria plan may be an ideal vehicle for providing less traditional types of benefits. Two examples are extra vacation time and child care. Some plans allow an employee to use flexible credits to purchase additional days of vacation. When available, this has proven a popular benefit, particularly among single employees. A problem may arise, however, if the work of vacationing employees must be assumed by nonvacationing employees in addition to their own regularly assigned work. Those not electing extra vacation time may feel resentful of doing the work of someone else who is away longer than the normal vacation period.

In recent years, there has been increasing pressure on employers to provide care for the children of employees. This represents an additional cost if added to a traditional existing benefit program. By including child care benefits in a cafeteria plan, those employees using them can pay for their cost, possibly with dollars from an FSA. However, lower paid employees may be better off financially by paying for child care with out-of-pocket dollars and electing the income tax credit that is available for dependent care expenses.

An important consideration is the number of benefits to be included in a cafeteria plan. The greater the number of benefits, particularly optional benefits, the greater the administrative costs. A wide array of options also may prove to be confusing to many employees and require the need for extra personnel to counsel employees or to answer their questions.

A final concern is the problem of adverse selection. As previously mentioned, this problem can be controlled by proper plan design.

Basic versus Optional Benefits

As mentioned earlier, many cafeteria plans consist of two portions—a minimum level of basic benefits received by all employees, and a second layer of optional benefits that may be purchased by each employee with flexible credits provided by the employer. Once a list of benefits to be included in a cafeteria plan has been determined, it is necessary to decide what benefits should be included as basic benefits and what should be included as optional benefits. At a minimum, the basic benefits should provide a reasonable level of protection against the major sources of personal risk. This suggests that basic benefits should include at least some life insurance, disability income benefits, medical expense benefits, and retirement benefits (unless these are included under a separate retirement plan). Some employers with established cafeteria plans have included additional but less-critical benefits such as travel accident insurance or dependent life insurance in the basic portion of the plan.

The optional layer of the plan may include additional types of benefits not included in the basic plan. It also may include additional amounts of coverage for some of the same types of benefits included in the basic plan, such as additional amounts of life insurance on the employee. In addition, the employee may have the option of electing alternative benefits to some or all of the benefits provided in the basic plan. For example, for an additional cost an employee may elect a medical expense plan with a smaller deductible.

Because of the current provisions of Section 125 of the Internal Revenue Code, cafeteria plans that include both taxable and nontaxable benefits should not include deferred compensation arrangements other than those involving 401(k) plans in the optional benefit layer if the issue of constructive receipt is to be avoided. Also, the plan will be more meaningful to employees if it is so structured that all or most employees will be able to purchase at least some of the optional benefits.

Level of Employer Contributions

An employer has considerable latitude in determining the amount of flexible credits that will be made available to employees to purchase optional benefits under a cafeteria plan. These credits may be a function of one or more of the following factors: salary, age, family status, and length of service.

The major difficulty arises in those situations when the installation of a cafeteria plan is not accompanied by an overall increase in the amount of the employer's contributions to the employee benefit plan. It generally is felt that each employee should be provided with enough flexible credits so that he or she can purchase optional benefits, which, together with basic benefits, are at least equivalent to the benefits provided by the old plan. This probably will lead an employer to determining the amount of flexible credits on some basis so that each employee is provided with an amount of flexible credits comparable to the difference in value between the benefits under the old plan for that employee and the basic benefits under the new cafeteria plan.

Including an FSA Option

An FSA option under a cafeteria plan enables employees to lower their taxes and therefore increase their spendable income. Ignoring any administrative costs, there is probably no reason not to offer this option to employees for benefits such as dependent care. However, salary deductions for medical expenses pose a dilemma. While they save taxes for the employees, they also may result in an employee obtaining nearly 100 percent reimbursement for medical expenses. This may have the effect of negating many of the cost containment features contained in the employer's medical expense plan.

Employees' Ability to Change Benefits

Because the needs of employees change over time, a provision regarding employees' ability to change their benefit options must be incorporated into a cafeteria plan. Since the changing of options results in administrative costs and may result in adverse selection, employees probably should not be permitted to change their benefit selections more frequently than once a year.

Two situations may arise to complicate the issue of the frequency with which benefits may be changed. First, the charges to employees for optional benefits must be adjusted periodically to reflect experience under the plan. If the charges for benefits rise between dates on which employees may change benefit selections, the employer must either absorb these charges or pass them to the employees, probably through increased payroll deductions. Consequently, most cafeteria plans have annual dates on which benefit changes may be made that are the same as the dates when charges for benefits are recalculated. This also usually relates to the date on which any insurance contracts providing benefits under the plan are renewed.

The second situation arises when the amount of the employees' flexible credits are based on their compensation. If an employee receives a pay increase between selection periods, should the employee be granted additional flexible credits to purchase additional benefits at that time? Under most cafeteria plans, the flexible credits available to all employees are calculated only once a year, usually at a date prior to the date by which any annual benefit changes must be made. Any changes in the employee's status during the year will have no effect on an employee's flexible credits until the following year on the date on which a recalculation is made.

Communication

The complexity of a cafeteria plan, compared to a traditional employee benefit plan, requires additional communication between the employer and the employees. Since the concept is new, employees will have many questions. It is doubtful if all these questions can be answered through written information. Group meetings and individual meetings between employees and representatives of the employer probably will be required to explain the operation of the plan. Obviously, the need for these meetings will be greatest when a cafeteria plan is first installed, and for newly hired employees.

Many employees unaccustomed to making choices regarding employee benefits also will seek advice concerning their benefit selections. An employer must make the decision whether to require employees to make their selections with little guidance or to provide extensive counseling services. Either alternative may have legal as well as moral implications. When counseling is provided, it is imperative that it be provided by a qualified and competent staff.

Updating the Plan

Any employee benefit plan will need periodic updating. However, some unique situations exist for cafeteria plans. Since such plans are advertised as better meeting the needs of individual employees, the employer must continually monitor the changing needs and desires of employees. As employee interest increases for benefits not included in the plan, they should be considered for inclusion. If little interest is shown in certain benefits already made available, a decision must be made regarding their continued availability. However, if certain optional benefits are selected by most employees, perhaps they should be incorporated into the basic benefit plan.

The employer is faced with a dilemma if employee benefit costs rise more rapidly than the increases in flexible credits made available to the employees. For example, if the amount of flexible credits are a function of an employee's salary, which is usually the case, an increase of 10 percent in salary results in an increase of 10 percent in flexible credits. However, at the same time, the employee may be faced with an increased cost of 20 percent to retain the optional benefits currently selected under the plan. The employee must either reduce benefits or pay for a portion of the increased cost through additional payroll deductions. Obviously, neither situation is appealing to the employee. In deciding whether to increase flexible credits further, so the employee can choose the same benefits as previously selected, the employer is faced with the difficult task of balancing employee satisfaction with benefit cost control.

CHAPTER 22

ALTERNATIVE INSURANCE COMPANY ARRANGEMENTS

Richard L. Tewksbury, Jr.

The cost of employee group insurance plans has become an increasingly significant part of the corporate budget. Similarly, as these plans have grown in size, the claims experience of an employer's group insurance program has become more predictable. These factors have caused the conventional insurance arrangement to be considered as much a corporate financing vehicle as a direct transfer of the corporate personnel risk.

Responding to these influences, insurance companies have designed a number of alternative arrangements for insuring group insurance programs. This chapter highlights the development of alternative insurance company arrangements and describes each arrangement in detail.

CONVENTIONAL INSURANCE ARRANGEMENT

Alternative insurance arrangements provide an employer ways of potentially reducing the normal costs of a conventional insurance arrangement. It is important to first define a conventional insurance arrangement and its various cost factors so the purpose and advantages of alternative insurance arrangements become apparent.

Definition

In a conventional insurance arrangement, an employer purchases a group insurance contract and agrees to pay premiums to an insurance company. In return, the insurance company agrees to pay specific benefit amounts for such events as death or disability. The employer's annual premium cost is based on the previous financial experience of employers of similar size and characteristics and the actuarial statistics and administrative expenses of the insurance company.

The insurance company uses the premiums paid by all employers to pay all claims incurred under the group insurance plans. The employers whose actual claims costs are less than their premium payments subsidize the employer whose claims costs exceed their premium payments. In a conventional insurance arrangement, there is no reconciliation of an employer's premium payments to its actual claims costs. Instead, any adjustment of premium charges reflects the overall loss experience of all employers.

Premium Cost Factors

The insurance company considers a number of different factors as part of the total cost of insuring a risk.

Paid Claims

This is the total benefits paid to insured employees or their dependents during the policy period.

Reserves

This cost reflects the insurance company's liability to pay benefits in the future for a loss incurred during the policy year. The most common reserve is the incurred but unreported claim reserve established to pay losses incurred during the policy year but not reported for payment until after the policy year has ended. Reserves also are established for special benefit payment liabilities. The most common special reserves are the life insurance waiver of premium reserve and the reserve for future disability benefit payments.

Other Claim Charges

Several additional costs are assumed by the insurance company for providing special benefit coverages, such as extended liability coverage and conversion to an individual insurance policy when a participant terminates employment.

Administrative Charges

Although the terminology and allocation of administrative expenses vary by insurance company, there are six main cost categories:

1. Commissions. This is the payment to a licensed insurance agent or broker for helping the employer obtain the insurance coverage and receive ongoing administrative services. The commission amount normally is determined as a percentage of the premium paid, with the percentage remaining either level or, more often, declining as premium increases.

2. Premium Taxes. A state tax is levied on the premiums received by insurance companies in the resident states of insured employees. This tax expense is passed directly to the employer, normally as a percentage of premium paid. The current tax rate averages about 2 percent of premium, but can vary depending on the state.

3. Risk Charge. Each insured employer contributes to the insurance company's contingency reserve for unexpected, catastrophic amounts of claims in a future period. The risk charge normally is determined by a formula based on the premium amount.

4. Claims Administration Expenses. These are the expenses incurred by the insurance company to investigate claims and calculate and pay the appropriate benefits. These expenses normally are fixed per claim, with the per claim cost varying by the type of benefits paid; e.g., life insurance benefits are relatively simple and quick to administer and have a low administrative cost per claim compared to disability and medical claims that often require medical review and more difficult benefit calculations.

5. Other Administrative Expenses. Charges for actuarial, legal, accounting and other such services, plus overhead expenses are shared by all contractholders. These expenses are determined either as a percentage of the premium amount, a fixed charge, or a variable charge based on the insurance company's actual services provided to the employer.

6. Insurance Company Profit (Stock Company) or Contribution to Surplus (Mutual Company).

ALTERNATIVE INSURANCE ARRANGEMENTS

Definition

An alternative insurance arrangement is a means of financing the transfer of risk that in some way *defers* or *reduces* the premium paid by the employer to the insurance company. Essentially, this is accomplished by varying the normal reserves, claim charges, and administrative costs of the insurance company.

The deferral or reduction of paid premium provides the employer *direct* and *indirect* savings. Direct savings result from the reduction or elimination of specific insurance company charges. Indirect savings are gained through the more efficient and profitable corporate use of money that normally would be held and invested by the insurance company.

The trade-off for these employer savings is the assumption by the employer of certain normal insurance company functions or risk. For example, the employer might assume all or part of the financial liability, i.e., benefit payments to employees, and therefore reduce the necessary premium paid to the insurance company to pay benefit claims. Similarly, the employer might agree to administer all or part of the plan to reduce the insurance company's administrative charges.

Reasons for Alternative Insurance Arrangements

Three main reasons exist for alternatives to the conventional insurance arrangement: the corporate effort to reduce premium charges, the increasing importance of corporate value of money, and the intense competition among insurance companies for the best insurable risks.

Reduce Premium Charges

The employer's main reason for purchasing group insurance is to transfer a personnel risk that has unpredictable occurrence and potential financial loss significantly greater than the insurance company's premium charge. If a significant loss occurs, the insurance is a valuable investment to the employer. But if the losses over a period of time are less than the premium charges, employers begin to further analyze the insured risk and the financial value of the conventional insurance arrangement.

Employers with large insured employee groups have more predictable loss experience. These employers can reasonably project the expected claims costs of their employee groups over time and thereby determine the *expected* annual cost to provide the group insurance benefits. The conventional insurance arrangement then becomes most valuable to protect against the unexpected catastrophic losses.

Because large employers can reasonably project their future benefit costs, they can determine the financial advantages and trade-offs of participating in the financing and assumption of the risk. This participation reduces the premium paid to the insurer and potentially reduces the overall cost to the employer through lesser claim charges, premium tax, risk charge, and other administrative charges. These financial advantages have been the impetus to such alternative insurance arrangements as participating and experience-rated contracts and the many variations of self-insurance by employers.

Corporate Value of Money

The influence of corporate value of money has become increasingly significant with rising premium costs and interest rates. Under the conventional insurance arrangement, the employer periodically pays premiums to the insurance company. To the extent the paid premium exceeds claims costs, the insurance company invests the excess premiums. Similarly, the insurance company earns income from the various claim reserves that it maintains for each group insurance plan. Some of this investment income is credited to the employer, but the total may not equal the rate of return actually earned by the insurance company.

Interest rates have increased to unexpected levels, causing employers to scrutinize the use of corporate money and assure earning the highest available rate of return. If the employer can earn more after taxes in its business than the interest rate credited by the insurance company on surplus premium and claim reserves, it is advantageous to minimize the transfer of funds to the insurer. This influence has encouraged the development of deferred premium arrangements, reduction or waiver of accumulated reserves otherwise held by the insurance company, and various self-insurance arrangements.

Competition

The third reason for alternative insurance arrangements is the intense competition among insurance companies for insuring "good" risks. Under the conventional insurance arrangement, employers share equally in the financing of claims costs through similar premium charges, which means that employers with favorable loss experience, i.e., premiums in excess of plan costs, subsidize employers with unfavorable loss experience, i.e., plan costs in excess of premiums. Employers with favorable loss experience—the "good" risks—will look for alternatives that better reflect their actual costs. The financial advantages and administrative flexibility of alternative insurance arrangements often are the key factors in an employer selecting and continuing with an insurance company.

Also, many employers, especially those with favorable loss experience, have changed to or at least have considered self-insurance of all or part of their group insurance program which minimizes, or even eliminates, the need for an insurance company. For instance, a 1986 study found that 29 percent of surveyed employers self-insured their medical plans in some form in 1978, and by 1986, 67 percent of surveyed employers self-insured all or part of their medical plans.[1]

To attract and maintain insured group insurance plans and to stem the movement toward self-insurance, insurance companies have introduced alternative insurance arrangements that meet the employer's financial needs and offer essentially the same advantages as self-insurance.

BASIC ALTERNATIVE INSURANCE ARRANGEMENTS

Participating Arrangement

A *participating insurance arrangement* differs from the conventional insurance arrangement in that the employer participates in the favorable and unfavorable financial experience during the policy period. If the financial experience is favorable; i.e., the claims and administrative costs are less than the premium paid during the policy period, the employer receives the surplus premium from the insurance company at the end of the policy year. If the financial experience is unfavorable; i.e., the claims and administrative costs are greater than the premium paid during the policy period, the plan is considered to be in a deficit balance equal to the difference between total plan costs and paid premium. In most instances, this deficit balance is carried forward by the insurance company to be recovered in future years of favorable experience.

Therefore, in a participating insurance arrangement the true cost, or *net cost,* of the group insurance plans is the premium paid during the policy year adjusted for the balance remaining at year-end.

Underwriting Factors

Because the insurance company shares with each employer in the actual financial experience of the group insurance plans, there are several underwriting factors included in a participating insurance arrangement that are unnecessary in a conventional insurance arrangement.

Employer Participation

An insurance company will vary the *percentage* of *employer participation* in the actual financial experience depending on two key factors: the "spread" of risk and the predictability of losses.

---

[1] The 1986 Johnson & Higgins Corporate Health Care Benefits Survey.

Spread of risk refers to the ability of the employer's benefit plan to absorb a major, catastrophic loss relative to its paid premium base. The larger the employee group, the easier it becomes to incur a major loss without dramatically affecting the year-end actual financial experience of the plan. This is because the premium charge being paid per insured participant in the plan provides a fund large enough to pay the infrequent major losses as well as the normal benefit costs. Thus, the risk is effectively "spread" across the premium base of the insured employee group. Employee groups of more than 100 employees typically are considered large enough for a participating insurance arrangement, although competition between insurance companies is encouraging participating arrangements for employee groups as small as 50 employees.

Predictability of losses is the second key factor in determining the percentage of participation. Essentially, the more predictable the total losses for each year, the greater the percentage of employer participation. Plans such as medical care, dental, and short-term disability cover risks in which losses normally occur frequently and at relatively low benefit costs per occurrence. The predictability of loss experience for these plans is much better than life insurance and long-term disability plans that cover risks with less frequent losses and normally much higher total benefit costs per loss. For this reason, participating insurance arrangements are more common in medical care, dental, and short-term disability plans.

To limit the employer's percentage of participation in the plan's actual financial experience, the insurance company sets *pooling points*. A pooling point is a dollar limit of annual benefit costs per individual that will be included in the actual financial experience of the participating insurance arrangement. Any individual benefit costs in excess of the pooling point will not be assessed against the plan's financial experience. Instead, this excess amount is included in the insurance company's "pool" of conventional insurance arrangements for the same risk. For example, a group life insurance plan could insure employees with potential benefits of $100,000 or more but have a pooling point of $50,000. This means an individual's benefit claim up to $50,000 is reflected in the plan's actual financial experience and any benefit amounts in excess of $50,000 are assumed by the insurance company.

The employer pays an additional premium charge, called a pooling charge, for the exclusion of benefits in excess of the pooling point. This charge is based on the "pool's" loss experience and reflects the type of risk and expected benefit costs over time that each employer will have in excess of the pooling point. For instance, a life insurance plan pooling charge normally equals the volume of life insurance in excess of the pooling point, multiplied by the insurance company's conventional ar-

TABLE 22–1
Pooling Points

Life Insurance Plan

Volume of Insurance	*Pooling Point*
$ 1 million	$ 20,000
2.5 million	25,000
5 million	35,000
10 million	60,000
25 million	85,000
50 million	135,000

Medical Care Insurance Plan

Annual Premium (000s)	*Annual Benefit Pooling Point*
Less than $200	$ 25,000
$ 200–300	30,000
300–500	40,000
500–750	50,000
750–1,500	75,000
1,500–2,000	100,000
Over 2,000	None

rangement premium charge. The medical care plan pooling charge normally is determined as a percentage of annual premium or paid claims.

Table 22–1 illustrates a typical schedule of pooling point levels for medical care and life insurance plans, which are the most common participating insurance arrangements requiring pooling points.

Underwriting Margin

The premium paid under a participating insurance arrangement includes a charge for the possible fluctuation of actual costs in excess of the expected claims and administrative costs during the policy year. This charge commonly is called the insurance company's *underwriting margin.*

Underwriting margin reflects the normal range of deviation of the plan's actual loss experience in any year to the expected loss experience. The underwiting margin is determined from actuarial studies on the fluctuation of actual claims experience relative to insurance company norms for similar employee groups and types of insurance coverage. In general, the underwriting margin decreases as the predictability of the plan's expected claims experience increases.

TABLE 22–2
Medical Care Insurance Plan

Number of Covered Employees	*Percent of Premium*
Fewer than 250	10–15%
250 to 1,000	7–10
Over 1,000	5–7

The underwriting margin for a basic group life insurance plan varies between 10 percent and 20 percent of premium depending on the size of the employee group and volume of life insurance. Table 22–2 illustrates the typical level of underwriting margins for medical care plans.

Determining the Year-End Balance

The key principle in a participating insurance arrangement is that the employer's final or net cost equals paid premiums adjusted for the year-end balance (surplus or deficit). The year-end balance is determined by the *actual* plan costs in relation to the paid premium.

Basic Formula

The determination of a surplus or deficit year-end balance for group insurance plans is rather straightforward:

Paid premium (−) Claims costs (−) Administrative costs = Balance

Paid premium refers to the employer's total payments to the insurance company during the plan year.

The *claims costs* factor is made up of various charges:

1. *Paid claims:* This total is the actual benefit payments during the policy year.
2. *Reserve charge:* This equals the establishment of or adjustment to claims reserves held for incurred but unreported claims and any other specific pending liabilities, such as waiver of premium life insurance claims and unsettled claims payments at year-end.
3. *Pooling charge:* This is the additional cost for having large individual claims "pooled" in excess of a specific pooling point.
4. *Other claim charges:* The most common charge included in this category is a penalty charge levied against the employer when a terminated employee converts from a group to an individual insurance policy.

The *administrative costs* essentially are the same six expense categories mentioned previously for a conventional insurance arrangement.

Surplus Balance

If the year-end balance is positive, there will be surplus premiums available to be returned to the employer. The following example illustrates how a surplus year-end balance is determined.

Example. During the policy year the employer pays $500,000 of group insurance premiums to the insurance company. Claims paid during the year are $375,000, reserve charges are $10,000, pooling charges are $20,000 and other claim charges $5,000, for a total of $410,000 in claims costs. Total administrative costs equal $60,000. These total costs related to the paid premium result in a year-end balance of $30,000 surplus premium.

Paid premium		$500,000
Less: Claims costs		$410,000
Paid claims	$375,000	
Reserve charges	10,000	
Pooling charges	20,000	
Other charges	5,000	
Less: Administrative costs		$ 60,000
Year-end balance		$ 30,000

Surplus premium that accumulates with the insurance company during the plan year normally is credited with interest earnings that are used to reduce the insurance company's administrative costs. The interest rate credited is usually based on the investment performance of the insurance company's general assets.

The insurance company can return the surplus balance by issuing a *dividend* check equal to the surplus amount. This dividend reduces the year-end employer paid premium total that is tax-deductible as an ordinary business expense under Section 162 of the Internal Revenue Code.

Alternatively, the insurance company could deposit the surplus balance in a special reserve, normally called a *premium stabilization reserve.* The major advantages of a premium stabilization reserve are twofold:

- To avoid a reduction in the tax-deductible paid premium amount at year-end.
- To help stabilize the future budget and cash flow requirements of the plan by supplementing premium rate increases with funds from the special reserve.

A common disadvantage of a premium stabilization reserve is the lower investment earnings credited by the insurance company on the reserve amount compared to what the corporation could earn after tax by internally using the surplus premium. Also, an insurance company may be able to retain and use these funds to pay unexpected plan costs after contract termination.

Another disadvantage of premium stabilization reserves is the potential tax implications if the reserve amount does not meet specific definitions of a "welfare benefit fund." The "fund" definitions were established in the 1984 Deficit Reduction Act (DEFRA) tax reform legislation under Section 419 of the Internal Revenue Code. The principal purpose of this specific legislation is to prevent employers from taking premature deductions for expenses that have not yet been incurred. In essence, a premium stabilization reserve is considered reasonable and deposits to the reserve tax-deductible if there is no guarantee of renewal of the insurance contract and the reserve amount is subject to "significant current risk of economic loss."

Deficit Balance

A negative year-end balance, or *deficit* balance, means the employer's premium paid during the policy year is insufficient to pay the plan's total costs during the year. Such a situation is illustrated in the following example.

Example: The premium and plan costs are the same as the previous example, except paid claims during the year are $425,000 and the total administrative costs are $70,000. The total plan costs now result in a year-end deficit balance of ($30,000) premium.

Paid premium		$500,000
Less: Claims costs		$460,000
Paid claims	$425,000	
Reserve charges	10,000	
Pooling charges	20,000	
Other charges	5,000	
Less: Administrative costs		$ 70,000
Year-end balance		$ (30,000)

The deficit balance is offset during the policy year from the insurance company's corporate surplus to pay all claims and other immediate costs of the plan. In a sense, these insurance company funds act as a "loan" to the employer. In most instances, an employer's deficit balance will be carried forward to future policy years and be repaid through surplus premium balances that may result in future policy years. However, the employer normally is not *contractually* required to repay this insurance company "loan" and can switch insurance companies while a plan deficit is outstanding. This is a risk assumed by the insurance company and is reflected in the risk charge and the underwriting margins of the insurer. While a plan deficit exists, the outstanding balance is charged with an interest expense normally equal to the interest credited on surplus premiums of other policyholders.

Instead of repaying the deficit balance through future surplus premium, the employer could negotiate with the insurance company to repay the "loan" in a lump sum or in installments over a specified period. However, the insurance company interest charge on the outstanding deficit balance normally is less than the interest charge if the employer were to borrow monies from another financial institution. In these instances, it is more cost-effective to repay the outstanding deficit balance through the possible surplus premiums of future policy years.

A third possibility is a participating insurance arrangement in which the insurance company contractually *cannot* recover deficit balances from future employer surplus balances, but still shares annual surplus balances with the employer. This type of arrangement eliminates the insurance company's risk and the enticement for an employer to switch insurance companies before repaying a deficit balance. Also, this type of participating insurance arrangement may be more favorable for the employer because it participates only in years of positive financial results. The trade-off will be a higher annual risk charge or underwriting margin compared to an arrangement that participates in both year-end surplus and deficit balance situations.

Employer Advantages

The potential advantage of a participating insurance arrangement is that the employer pays its "actual" insurance cost and is rewarded for favorable financial experience by the return of year-end surplus premium. During a policy year of favorable experience, cost savings can be gained in several additional ways:

1. *Premium tax* is reduced because it is based on the *net* premium received by an insurance company; i.e., the employer's premium paid during the policy year less the surplus balance returned at year-end.
2. *Administrative costs* are reduced by lower general overhead charges based on net premium paid and by interest income earned on the surplus premium during the policy year, which normally is credited to the plan by reducing the total administrative costs.

The financial trade-off to the employer of a participating insurance arrangement is a higher risk charge and underwriting margin assumed by the insurance company in comparison to a conventional insurance arrangement. Also, the carryover of deficit balances in policy years of unfavorable financial experience will increase the future years' plan costs due to interest charges on the outstanding deficit balance and possibly additional underwriting margins required by the insurance company.

Experience-Rating Arrangement

Whereas a participating insurance arrangement enables the employer to participate in the actual financial experience of each plan year through year-end surplus or deficit balances, an *experience-rating insurance arrangement* enables the actual financial experience of previous policy years to affect the employer's future premium charges. If the employer's actual financial experience has been favorable in the past, the future premium rates will be less than the conventional premium rate of other similar employers. Similarly, if the loss experience has been unfavorable, future premium rates will be increased more than the rates of conventionally insured employers to stabilize the financial condition of this employer's plan.

An experience-rating arrangement can be included with either a participating or a conventional, nonparticipating insurance arrangement. In either case, the actual previous financial experience of the employer's plan is the basis for determining the future plan year's premium rates.

Underwriting Factors

If an employer's actual loss experience has fluctuated significantly in the past, volatile changes can occur in the experience-rated premium charges from year to year. For example, a plan year with favorable loss experience could substantially reduce the next year's premium charges. If unfavorable experience actually occurred during that next year, subsequent premium charges likewise would increase substantially to reflect this unfavorable year. Such yearly swings in premium costs usually disturb employers and hinder their ability to budget future costs and control cash flow needs. Similarly, the insurance company usually finds it more difficult to maintain the loyalty and understanding of the employer when the required premium charges vary significantly from year to year.

To minimize this problem, the insurance company controls the significance of an employer's actual loss experience in determining premium charges. This is done through underwriting factors based on the statistical credibility of the actual paid claims experience and the type of risk.

Statistical Credibility

Statistical credibility refers to the validity of an employee group's actual paid claims experience representing the normal, expected loss experience of such a group. The greater the statistical credibility, the greater the significance given the plan's year-end financial results in determining future premium rates.

Statistical credibility is based on the applicability of the *law of large numbers*. The law of large numbers doctrine states that:

> The larger the number of separate risks of a like nature combined into one group, the less uncertainty there will be as to the relative amount of loss that will be incurred within a given period.[2]

Besides employee group size, statistical credibility also is determined by the number of years of actual paid claims experience that can be analyzed. The statistical credibility of cumulative years of actual experience for a smaller employee group will be similar to that of a much larger employee group for a one-year period. For example, the cumulative five-year life insurance experience of a 350 to 400 employee group has similar statistical credibility to the one-year experience of a 1,750 to 2,000 employee group.

The importance of the *type of risk* is similar to the underwriting of a participating insurance arrangement. Statistical credibility of actual loss experience is greater for risks that occur more frequently and have a lesser average cost per occurrence, such as medical care and short-term disability. Therefore, greater significance can be given to the actual paid claims experience for these types of risks. For instance, one to three years of loss experience normally is necessary to determine the experience-rated premium charges of medical care, dental, and short-term disability coverages.

On the other hand, the insurance company applies statistical credibility to the employer's life insurance and long-term disability loss experience only if three to five years of paid claims experience are available for review. This is due to the volatility of loss experience from year to year for these coverages. By analyzing three to five years' loss experience, individual years of unusually favorable or unfavorable loss experience are melded into a more common overall trend of claims costs.

---

[2] S. S. Huebner and K. Black, *Life Insurance*, 10th ed. (Englewood Cliffs, N.J.: Prentice-Hall, 1982), p. 3.

Credibility Factors

There are several ways an insurance company can control the effect of year-to-year fluctuations of actual loss experience in an experience-rated insurance arrangement. The most common method is to use a weighted average of the employer's actual claims experience and the insurance company's normal loss factors for a similar conventional insurance arrangement. The percentage factor applied to the employer's actual paid claims experience is called the *credibility factor*. The greater the statistical credibility of the risk, the closer the credibility factor is to 100 percent, which implies the employer's prior loss experience is wholly representative of future loss experience.

Table 22–3 shows the common credibility factors applied to life insurance and medical care plans. The life insurance factors are determined by the number of covered employees and the number of available years of actual claims experience. The factors for a medical plan normally are based on the number of employees covered by the plan.

For example if an employer's medical plan covers 200 employees and incurred $250,000 of paid claims last year, a 75 percent credibility factor

TABLE 22–3
Credibility Factors

Life Insurance Plan

Number of Covered Employees	*Number of Years of Experience*		
	1	*3*	*5*
250–500	10%	25%	35%
500–1,000	20	55	75
1,000–2,500	40	65	85
2,500–5,000	65	85	100
5,000–10,000	80	100	100
Over 10,000	100	100	100

Medical Care Insurance Plan

Number of Covered Employees	*Credibility Factors*
50–100	30–50%
100–150	50–65
150–250	65–97
Over 250	100

would be applied to this loss experience. If the insurance company's expected losses for a similar size and type of employee group is $300,000, the expected paid claims for this employee group would be $262,500.

$$\frac{\text{Employer's past year's actual claims}}{\$250{,}000} \times \frac{\text{Credibility factor}}{.75} = \$187{,}500$$

Plus

$$\frac{\text{Insurer's expected losses}}{\$300{,}000} \times \frac{\text{Noncredible factor}}{.25} = \$\ 75{,}000$$

$$\text{Expected claims cost} = \$262{,}500$$

Pooling Points

A second method of controlling loss experience volatility on future premium rates is to establish *pooling points,* as described previously in the section on participating insurance arrangements. By placing dollar maximums on the individual and total plan claim costs that will be included in each plan year's actual financial experience, the volatility of losses in any year is substantially limited. For providing this limitation on the employer's "experience-rated" losses, the insurance company levies a fixed annual charge, or pooling charge.

With a life insurance plan, the pooling charge is added to the average of the prior years' experience-rated paid claims to determine the expected claims costs for the next policy year. For example, if the average experience-rated losses over the last five plan years are $100,000, the life insurance volume in excess of the pooling point is $2,500,000, and the monthly pooling charge is $.60 per $1,000 of life insurance, the expected claims costs for the next policy year are $118,000.

Pooling cost:		
Excess life insurance volume	$2,500,000	
Monthly premium charge	.00060	
Monthly cost	$ 1,500	
	× 12	
Annual pooling cost		$ 18,000
Experience-rated claims cost:		$100,000
Next year's expected claims cost		$118,000

The medical insurance pooling charge normally is stated as a percentage of annual premium or paid claims. For instance, if the paid premium is

$250,000, the pooling point is $30,000 per individual, and the pooling charge is 5 percent of premium, a charge of $15,000 would be included in determining the necessary premium charges for the next year.

Premium Stabilization Reserve

Another alternative for controlling the effect of annual loss fluctuation on premium charges is a *premium stabilization reserve,* previously discussed in the section on participating insurance arrangements. If additional premium is required in the coming plan year to reflect previous years of unfavorable loss experience, a part or all of the necessary premium rate increase is supplemented by premium stabilization reserve funds. For example, assume a premium stabilization reserve of $45,000 exists and additional premium of $40,000 is necessary to equal expected losses for the coming plan year. All or part of this additional premium could come from the premium stabilization reserve.

Determining the Experience-Rated Premium

The exact method for determining the experience-rated premium charges varies by the type of insurance coverage and the insurance company. The explanation below describes the common principles for life insurance and medical care coverages.

Life Insurance

The life insurance premium charge is based on the expected paid claims, underwriting margin, reserve adjustment, pooling charge, and administrative costs.

Expected Paid Claims. Determining the next year's expected paid claims depends on the credibility factor given to the employer's previous actual loss experience. The credibility factor is applied to the average actual paid claims total for a three- to five-year period. This average actual paid claims total should reflect annual changes in the volume of life insurance to provide a meaningful comparison of year-to-year claims experience.

Reserve Adjustment. The incurred but unreported reserve initially is established as a percentage of premium or paid claims and is adjusted each year thereafter to reflect changes in these factors. An estimate of the next year's adjustment is included in the premium charge calculation based on expected paid claims or premium.

Underwriting Margin. This charge normally is stated as a percentage of expected paid claims and reserve adjustments or of total premium. If a participating insurance arrangement is included with the experience-rated arrangement, additional underwriting margin is added.

Pooling Charge. An annual charge based on the volume of "pooled" life insurance and premium rate for the employee group.

Administrative Costs. These normally are determined as a percentage of the experience-rated premium charges.

The sum of these factors cumulatively determines the experience-rated life insurance premium charge for the next policy year. An example of calculating a required premium rate is illustrated in Figure 22–1.

Medical Insurance

The medical insurance premium charge is based on expected paid claims, inflation/utilization trend, underwriting margin, reserve adjustments, pooling charge, and administrative costs. These factors are determined in the same manner as the life insurance premium charges, *except* for the following.

Expected Paid Claims. Much greater credibility is given to the loss experience of the prior plan year, such that developing average loss history over several years normally is unnecessary.

Inflation/Utilization Trend. Rising medical costs (inflation) and plan utilization are distinct economic factors that will increase the next year's paid claims; therefore, the expected paid claims are increased by a trend factor projected for the next policy year.

Pooling Charge. This charge normally is a percentage of paid claims or premium.

FIGURE 22–1
Life Insurance Experience-Rating Calculation

Assumptions:		
	Five-year average actual paid claims	$100,000
	Expected annual losses*	80,000
	Credibility factor	.60
	Underwriting margin	10% of incurred claims
	Reserve adjustment	2,000
	Pooling charges	6,600
	Administrative costs	10,000

Example:

1. Expected paid claims ($100,000 × .6) + ($80,000 × .4)	$ 92,000
2. Reserve adjustment	2,000
3. Incurred claims	94,000
4. Margin: (10% of incurred claims)	9,400
5. Pooling charges	6,600
6. Administrative costs	10,000
Required premium	$120,000

* Based on insurance company's actuarial statistics.

FIGURE 22–2
Medical Care Experience-Rating Calculation

Assumptions:		
	Prior year's paid claims	$250,000
	Expected annual losses*	300,000
	Credibility factor	.75
	Pooling charge	6% of paid claims
	Inflation/utilization trend	12% of expected claims costs
	Underwriting margin	10% of trended losses
	Reserve adjustment	10,000
	Administrative costs	37,000

Calculation:			
1. Expected paid claims:			$262,500
Actual experience factor	($250,000 × .75)	$187,500	
Insurance company factor	($300,000 × .25)	75,000	
2. Pooling charge			15,750
3. Inflation/utilization trend: (1) + (2) × 12%			33,390
4. Trended losses (1) + (2) + (3)			311,640
5. Underwriting margin (4) × 10%			31,164
6. Reserve adjustment			10,000
7. Administrative costs			37,000
Required premium: (4) + (5) + (6) + (7)			$389,804

* Based on insurance company's actuarial statistics.

The sum of these factors cumulatively determines the experience-rated medical premium charge, as illustrated in Figure 22–2.

Employer Advantage

An experience-rated insurance arrangement is much more a method for financing the employer's actual plan costs than a true insurance arrangement in which employers share in the loss experience and have a common premium rate. With the experience-rating arrangement, the primary insurance protection is against the unexpected catastrophic losses in one plan year that might severely affect the ongoing financial condition of the plan. To the employer with favorable and predictable claims experience, this arrangement is a very cost-effective way to share the plan's financial gains without assuming significant financial risks.

ADVANCED ALTERNATIVE INSURANCE ARRANGEMENTS

Advanced alternative insurance arrangements are variations of the basic alternative arrangements. They further increase the financial and administrative flexibility of employer-sponsored group insurance programs.

Realizing the initial savings gained through the basic alternative insurance arrangements, large employers have demanded even greater reliance on their own claims experience to gain potentially significant additional savings. Also, these large employers have become more aware of their own personnel risks and the predictability and severity of losses. With this increased understanding, the need for purchasing insurance has been considered through much the same cost-benefit analysis, based on the corporate value of money, as other major corporate investments.

The employer's goal is to pay only the actual claims costs incurred during the plan year and reasonable administrative costs, without losing the budget stability of a maximum expected plan cost per policy year. To attain this goal, many of the insurance company's specific claim and administrative charges have been reduced or eliminated by the employers assuming the financial liability or administrative function. This reduction, or at least deferral, of premium payments to the insurance company has maximized the cash flow and direct cost savings to the corporation.

Financial Alternatives for the Total Plan

Deferred Premium Arrangement

One to three months' premium payments to the insurance company can be deferred and instead may be used more advantageously by the employer. If and when the insurance contract terminates, the deferred premium payments must be paid to the insurance company.

In essence, this arrangement allows the employer to retain an amount similar to the plan's incurred but unreported reserves until it is actually needed by the insurance company at contract termination. The necessary amount of reserve varies by the type of coverage, with life insurance plan reserves equaling one to two months' premium and disability and medical plan reserves being three to four months' premium. These reserves are part of the insurance company's total corporate assets and normally earn investment income credited against the employer's administrative charges or used to reduce the necessary reserve amount held by the insurer. The interest earned is related to the insurance company's aftertax investment return on its general assets and often is significantly less than an employer's aftertax rate of return earned from funds invested for its own use.

If such a situation exists, the deferred premium arrangement allows an employer to "borrow" the incurred but unreported reserves from the insurance company and invest the funds more effectively to enhance its cash flow and year-end earnings level.

To illustrate this advantage, assume an employer normally pays monthly premiums of $50,000 and has an aftertax corporate value of money of 14 percent. The insurance company currently credits 7 percent interest on incurred but unreported reserves. If the employer and insurer agree to a three-month deferred premium arrangement, the financial advantage would be the annual *additional* investment earnings the employer can earn on the three-month deferred premium amount. In the example below, the employer would earn an additional 7 percent return on each of the $50,000 monthly premium deferrals for the remainder of the policy year, which provides an annual cash flow advantage of $9,625. This is shown in Table 22–4.

The loss of the interest credits from the insurance company would be reflected by an increase in the annual administrative or reserve charges. However, these increases should be offset by the additional employer investment earnings.

Annual Retrospective Premium Arrangement

An annual retrospective premium arrangement reduces the employer's monthly premium payments by a specified percentage with the understanding this percentage of premium will be paid to the insurance company at year-end if the plan's actual claim and administrative costs exceed the paid premium to date. The specific percentage reduction of premium normally relates to the insurance company's underwriting margin. The employer gains a cash flow advantage through the corporate use of this premium amount during the plan year if the corporate value of money exceeds the insurance company's interest credit on surplus premium.

Underwriting margin provides the insurer with premium in excess of

TABLE 22–4
Example of Savings to Employer under a Three-Month Deferred Premium Arrangement

Month	Deferred Premium		Additional Interest Credit		Duration of Policy Year		Savings
1	$50,000	×	7%	×	1 year	=	$3,500
2	50,000	×	7%	×	11/12 year	=	3,208
3	50,000	×	7%	×	10/12 year	=	2,917
					Total	=	$9,625

the premium necessary to pay expected claims and administrative charges, as illustrated below. During the plan year, any surplus premiums held by the insurance company are credited with interest based on the investment return of the insurance company's general corporate assets. In a participating insurance arrangement, this surplus premium is returned to the employer at the end of the plan year.

	Underwriting margin	Retrospective premium
Total premium payable to insurance company	Administrative charges	Premium paid during plan year
	Expected claim charges	

If the insurance company's interest credit is less than the corporate value of money, an annual retrospective premium arrangement is advantageous. By investing during the plan year the premium amount otherwise held by the insurer as underwriting margin, the employer can improve its current cash flow and its year-end earnings level through the additional investment income earned by the corporation.

For example, assume an employer's annual premium cost is $3 million, or $250,000 per month, and the plan's underwriting margin is 10 percent of premium. A 10 percent annual retrospective premium arrangement would reduce the premium payments to $2,700,000 per year and provide $300,000 premium to be invested by the employer during the plan year. The financial advantage is the *additional* investment earnings the employer can earn on the $300,000 reduced premium amount. If the corporate value of money is 14 percent and the insurance company interest credit is 7 percent, the additional investment income to the corporation is approximately $10,500. (This value assumes premiums are paid monthly and the additional investment earnings equal the monthly interest rate times the remaining months of the plan year.)

As part of the annual retrospective premium arrangement, the employer agrees to pay a part or all of the reduced premium amount to the insurance company at the end of the policy year if the actual claims and administrative charges exceed the actual premium paid during the plan year. The insurance company pays charges in excess of paid premium during the year from its capital or surplus accounts. An interest charge is applied to these excess charges which represent the insurance company's lost investment earnings on the funds provided to pay the excess plan costs.

Terminal Retrospective Premium Arrangement

With a terminal retrospective premium arrangement, the employer agrees to pay the outstanding deficit that may exist at the time the insurance contract is terminated with the insurance company. The agreement usually specifies a maximum percentage of premium or dollar amount up to which the employer will indemnify the insurance company at contract termination.

The employer's advantage is that the insurance company substantially reduces the annual risk charge and the underwriting margin factor used in determining the plan's required premium. Both these factors provide the insurance company with additional, contingency premium to be used in case of unexpected, catastrophic claim costs. The terminal retrospective premium arrangement transfers some of this catastrophic risk to the employer; therefore, these charges can be reduced. This reduction is reflected in lower monthly premium costs and gives the employer use of this reduced premium amount for potentially more profitable corporate uses.

Also, this arrangement offers more underwriting flexibility for insuring high benefit limits and special plan design features that pose a potentially greater financial risk to the insurance company. Because some of the risk of underestimating the losses from these special benefit arrangements is transferred to the employer, the insurance company is more apt to underwrite the coverage to satisfy the employer's needs.

Both an annual and terminal retrospective premium arrangement can be included to maximize the reduction of the risk charge and underwriting margin and the potential cash flow savings. However, a terminal retrospective premium arrangement is much less common than an annual arrangement. Insurance companies are less apt to offer a terminal retrospective premium arrangement because its long-term nature makes it difficult to determine a reasonable value to the insurer. Secondly, its attractiveness is limited to the very large employers willing to assume a potential long-term liability and considered a good, long-term credit risk by the insurance company. Therefore, the applicability and current use of this alternative insurance arrangement is rather incidental.

Extended Plan Year Accounting

Some insurance companies will extend the plan year's accounting of claims paid as a means of reducing or eliminating the necessary incurred but unreported claims reserves. These insurers will record the claims incurred before the end of the plan year but paid during the initial months after the plan year as actual paid claims during that plan year. This extended accounting period, which normally is an additional one- or two-month period, allows the actual incurred but unreported claims to be more accurately accounted to the appropriate plan year and substantially reduces or even eliminates the incurred but unreported claims reserves maintained by the insurance company.

For example, if the accounting period for a life insurance plan is extended an additional month, the incurred but unreported reserve, which normally is about 10 percent of premium, often is reduced to 2 to 3 percent of premium. Similarly, extending by two months the plan year accounting for a medical care plan may reduce the incurred but unreported reserve by 50 percent or more.

This financial alternative normally is available only to large employers with fairly consistent and predictable claims experience from month to month. For such employers, this arrangement provides an accurate accounting of incurred but unreported claims. To the extent these actual claims are less than the insurance company's normal reserve factors, the employer can gain a direct savings and cash flow advantage.

ADMINISTRATIVE ALTERNATIVES FOR THE TOTAL PLAN

Besides considering financial alternatives, many employers have implemented administrative options that can provide substantial savings for their group insurance plans. The common and varied uses of computers have made repetitive administrative functions of a group insurance plan relatively easy and inexpensive for an employer to assume. Also, the growing interest in self-insuring group insurance plans has created a substantial market of plan administration firms, called third-party administrators. A recent survey found that almost one fourth of all employers use a third-party administrator and an additional 11 percent of employers self-administer their medical plans.[3] Such firms mainly offer computerized

---

[3] Johnson & Higgins 1986 Corporate Health Care Benefits Survey.

claims payment and data base services of varying sophistication. These services often can be adapted to the employer's needs and are offered at a cost significantly less than the normal administrative costs of a conventional or basic alternative insurance arrangement. In response to these influences, insurance companies offer several administrative alternatives to an employer.

Administrative Services Only Contract

If an employer self-insures all or part of its group insurance plans, the insurance company may provide only the administrative services for these plans through an administrative services only (ASO) contract. This contract is in direct response to the competition of third-party administrators and the employers' need for administering self-insured plans. *No* risk is assumed by the insurance company, and therefore, its administrative charges for this contract differ in several significant ways from an insured arrangement:

1. No premium tax liability is incurred by the insurance company on this type of contract; therefore, no premium taxes are transferred to it and paid by the employer.
2. There is no risk charge because the insurance company assumes no financial liability for the payment of benefits.
3. Normally there are no commission payments made through an ASO contract.
4. General administrative and underwriting activities normally are much less in an ASO contract, which significantly reduces the costs for these activities in comparison to an insured arrangement.

An ASO contract is more effective for self-insured group insurance plans with high claim utilization and greater complexity in the payment of claims. Specifically, self-insured medical care, dental, and short-term disability plans are most often administered through an ASO contract.

There are a number of reasons why an employer might purchase an ASO contract instead of administering the plan itself:

1. The investment in and dedication of computer hardware and storage capacity is quite substantial.
2. Normally, the computer software for a claims payment system must be purchased because the details of such a system are complex and unfamiliar to the employer's computer programmers.
3. The hiring and training of employees to administer the plans can be costly and time-consuming to the employer.

4. There are economies of scale in standard operations performed by the insurance company that cannot be attained by the employer.
5. The insurance company is staffed with legal, medical, and other technical expertise necessary to administer the group insurance plans, especially the complex and unique claims situations that may be disputed, denied, or require extensive professional consultation.
6. The employer maintains a third-party "buffer" in disputing or denying benefit payments.

The insurance company administers the plan and determines the benefit payments under an ASO contract in the same manner as a conventional insurance arrangement. By performing these services, the insurance company accepts the fiduciary responsibilities and powers necessary to administer the plan. However, the insurance company assumes no financial responsibility under this contract. The benefit payment checks are drawn against the employer's cash balances, and the insurance company normally is not identified on these checks.

The services generally provided by the insurance company in an ASO contract are as follows:

Claims processing.

Financial and administrative reports.

Plan descriptions for employees.

Banking arrangements.

Government reporting requirements.

Underwriting services.

Individual conversion policies.

Legal, medical, and other professional services needed to administer the plans.

Selected Administrative Services Arrangement

Many large employers do not want to totally administer their plans but still are interested in assuming some of the group insurance plan administration to reduce an insurer's administrative charges as well as to gain more control over plan administration. Large employers also may be interested in maintaining a unique set of data about plan utilization and costs as a means of analyzing their specific financial trends and determining additional ways of controlling medical care and other plan costs. To meet these needs, some insurance companies are providing selected administrative services through their ASO contracts.

In most cases, the insurance company offers this arrangement only if some group insurance coverage, most often life insurance, is insured with the insurance company. If the employer-administered coverages also are insured, the insurance company normally requires it at least provide the underwriting services for these coverages.

This selected administrative services arrangement is rather new and just beginning to be provided to employers that specifically request it. However, as employers become increasingly involved in the financing and administration of their group insurance plans, this type of arrangement should become more common.

ALTERNATIVES FOR LIFE INSURANCE PLANS

Exclude Waiver of Premium Provision

The waiver of premium provision is common in a group life insurance program. It allows coverage to continue after an employee becomes totally and permanently disabled without continued premium payments by the employer for the employee's coverage. Although such a provision sounds attractive, the additional cost to include it in the life insurance plan often is greater than its actual value, especially for large employers.

It is common for the monthly premium costs to increase 10 to 15 percent because of the increase in incurred but unreported claims reserves and the additional risk of the waiver of premium provision. The additional monthly cost of this provision can be avoided in large part while still providing continued life insurance coverage to a totally disabled employee.

The employer can continue the life insurance coverage by merely continuing to pay monthly premiums for the disabled employees. In most cases, the total cost of these continued premium payments after the disability date will be substantially less than the additional 10 to 15 percent monthly premium charge for *all* employees that an insurance company requires to include the waiver of premium provision.

A disadvantage to excluding the waiver of premium provision potentially could exist if the employer changes insurance companies. There could be a problem in continuing life insurance coverage for previously disabled employees with the new insurer because most contracts only insure employees *actively at work* as of the effective date of the new life insurance coverage. Insurance companies often waive this actively at work provision for large employers but may be more hesitant for smaller employers if the inclusion of disabled employees' coverage could adversely distort the expected loss experience. Therefore, the exclusion of the waiver of premium provision often is suggested only for larger employers.

Claims-Plus Premium Arrangement

A claims-plus premium arrangement bases the employer's monthly life insurance premium on the *actual* loss experience of previous months, plus fixed monthly administrative and reserve charges. To the extent actual monthly loss experience is *less* than the level monthly premium payments normally paid during the plan year, this difference can remain with the employer as additional cash flow. If the employer's corporate value of money is greater than the insurer's interest credit on surplus premium, the employer gains additional investment income on this difference during the plan year.

To limit the risk of the employer having a cash flow loss under this arrangement by incurring benefit claim payments in one or more months higher than the level monthly premium amount, many insurance companies set the maximum monthly employer cost at the level monthly premium amount plus any "surplus" accumulated from prior months. Also, the maximum annual employer cost is limited to the annual premium cost based on the level monthly premium amount. In this way, the employer still is fully insured against unexpected or catastrophic loss experience that may occur during any policy year.

To illustrate how this claims-plus premium arrangement works, assume the employer's normal annual life insurance premium cost is $360,000, or a level monthly premium payment of $30,000. This $30,000 monthly premium payment is based on $27,000 of expected losses per month and a standard monthly administrative and reserve charge of $3,000. Table 22–5 shows the actual monthly premium costs under a claims-plus arrangement given the above assumptions and assumed actual loss experience during the plan year.

The normal administration of the claims-plus arrangement is for the first month's premium payment to equal the level monthly premium payment amount and thereafter the premium payment to equal the actual loss experience of the previous month plus the standard administrative and reserve charge. In the example, the employer pays the normal monthly premium payment of $30,000 in month 1 and from then on pays the actual losses of the previous month plus the standard monthly administrative and reserve charge of $3,000. For instance, the premium payment for month 2 is $23,000, i.e., $20,000 of actual losses in month 1 plus the $3,000 administrative charge. The cumulative balance for month 2 and thereafter

TABLE 22–5
Life Insurance Claims-Plus Arrangement ($ thousands)

	Months												
	1	*2*	*3*	*4*	*5*	*6*	*7*	*8*	*9*	*10*	*11*	*12*	*Total*
Normal premium	$30	$30	$30	$30	$30	$30	$30	$30	$30	$30	$30	$30	$360
Actual losses	20	0	20	50	10	0	0	70	20	50	30	20	290
Administrative/ reserve	3	3	3	3	3	3	3	3	3	3	3	3	36
Actual monthly payment	30	23	3	23	53	13	3	3	73	23	53	26	326
Cumulative balance	—	7	34	41	18	35	62	89	46	53	30	34	34

equals the cumulative difference between actual monthly payments and the normal monthly premium payments. In months 5, 9, and 11, the employer pays substantially more than the normal premium payment, reflecting the previous month's high actual losses. This can occur under this arrangement as long as any monthly premium amount does not exceed the normal premium payment plus the cumulative balance as of that date.

Insurance companies have various trade names for this arrangement, the most common being a "flexible funding" or "minimum premium" arrangement. Normally, such an arrangement is offered only to large employers that have substantial monthly life insurance premiums. Normally, for employers with less than a $12,000 to $15,000 monthly life insurance premium, this arrangement is not advantageous because of the increased internal administration and administrative costs, the volatile fluctuation in monthly claims, and limited potential financial gain.

ALTERNATIVES FOR LONG-TERM DISABILITY PLANS

Long-term disability insurance promises to pay a significant percentage of an employee's income for the duration of his or her total and permanent disability. The number of claims incurred by an employer normally are few, but the total cost per claim normally is quite large because of the expected duration of benefit payments. In the plan year a long-term disability claim is incurred, a reserve is charged to that year's financial experience equal to the expected cost of all future benefit payments. Often, the reserve charge is greater than the premium paid during that year. However, the limited number of claims over a three- to five-year period allows the insurance company to set the premium rate at the expected average annual cost for this time period, thereby keeping it relatively stable and affordable for the employer.

Partial Self-Insurance

The employer can partially self-insure its group long-term disability plan by assuming the financial liability of any claim for a specific duration and transferring the remaining liability to the insurance company. This arrangement reduces the monthly premium payments to the insurance company, provides potential cash flow savings through increased investment earnings on the premium difference, and still provides the employer significant insurance protection against a catastrophic claim situation. Two other financial advantages to a partially self-insured arrangement are (1) the incurred but unreported reserve requirement normally is reduced and (2) the premium tax liability is reduced.

There are two ways this arrangement can be designed. The more common method is for the insurer to assume the benefit payment liability for the first two to five years and the employer to continue benefit payments beyond this specific time period. The advantages of this plan design are several:

1. The average duration for a long-term disability claim is less than two years, so the long-term financial liability and administration assumed by the employer is limited.
2. The insurance company does not establish large reserves for future benefit payments in comparison to a fully insured arrangement, which reduces the required premium payment and offers cash flow savings to the employer.
3. Because an extended period exists before the employer assumes financial liability and begins periodic benefit payments, the employer normally prefunds its liability only from the time the disability actually occurs.

The second plan design option is for the employer to pay the long-term disability benefits for the initial two to five years and the insurance company to assume the risk thereafter. The main employer advantage is that premiums are substantially reduced because the employer is assuming the full liability of the majority of long-term disability claims.

As a general rule, this alternative insurance arrangement is offered only to employers with at least 1,500 to 2,000 employees. For smaller plans, the claim occurrence is too volatile and the potential long-term financial liability normally too large for the employer to effectively self-insure the risk.

ALTERNATIVES FOR MEDICAL AND SHORT-TERM DISABILITY PLANS

Minimum Premium Arrangement

In a minimum premium arrangement, the employer pays the medical care and/or short-term disability benefits directly from a corporate cash account instead of transferring the money to pay benefits through premium payments to the insurance company. The employer essentially self-insures the payment of benefits up to the expected loss level for the plan year, with the insurance company assuming the financial liability for any claims costs in excess of the expected loss level. The only premium paid to the insurer is for the normal administrative, risk, and reserve charges.

A minimum premium arrangement in large part simulates and provides the advantages of a self-insured/ASO arrangement without the employer assuming the financial risk of benefit payments in excess of the annual expected loss level.

The primary advantages of this arrangement are twofold: reduced premium tax liability and potential cash flow savings. The payment of benefits from a corporate cash account is not considered an insurance arrangement in most states,[4] therefore, no premium tax liability is incurred. This offers a direct annual savings on the average equal to 2 percent of the normal premium amount used to pay benefits. Normally, a minimum premium arrangement is suggested only for employers with at least a $250,000 premium. At this minimum level of premium, approximately 85 percent of premium, or $212,500, is used to pay benefits. This implies the annual savings from reduced premium tax liability is approximately $4,250 (2 percent of $212,500). As the premium size increases, the percentage of premium used to pay benefits similarly increases, and the premium tax savings becomes more significant. For instance, an employer paying $5 million in annual medical premium may use 93 percent of the normal premium to pay benefits, or $4,650,000. At this level, the annual premium tax savings would be $93,000.

The second advantage is potential cash flow savings gained from the employer having the corporate use of "surplus" funds during the plan year. Minimum premium arrangements are generally designed so the employer pays benefit claims as they are incurred during the plan year up to the annual expected loss level determined by the insurance company. This limit often is called the employer maximum liability. The employer pays benefits periodically from a separate cash account[5] to meet the plan's claims liability. If the actual claims paid during the initial months of the plan year are less than the proportionate monthly level of expected claims costs, a "surplus" develops in the cash account. To the extent the investment return earned by the corporation on this "surplus" is greater than the insurance company's interest credit on surplus premium, the employer gains additional investment earnings and a cash flow advantage compared to a basic alternative insurance arrangement.

---

[4] Connecticut, Texas, and California assess a premium tax on minimum premium arrangements.

[5] This corporate cash account normally is a direct deposit account of a bank or savings institution, or a 501(c)(9) trust.

By paying benefit claims as they are reported during the plan year, the employer also could have a cash flow *loss* if claims in the initial months are greater than the proportionate level of expected claims costs. To avoid this possibility, a minimum premium arrangement can be designed such that the maximum monthly payment of claims from the cash account equals the proportionate monthly level of expected claims costs, plus any "surplus" funds accumulated during the plan year. If the actual claims costs in a month do exceed this limit, the insurance company pays all excess benefit claims from its funds. If "surplus" funds develop in future months, the insurer immediately uses these "surplus" funds to recoup its payment amount of prior months. The insurance company normally increases its administrative and risk charges to reflect the potential additional monthly liability it assumes in this specific case.

In a minimum premium arrangement, the insurance company administers all claims payments and assumes the risk of claims costs in excess of the annual expected loss level, just as in a conventional or basic alternative insurance arrangement. Figure 22–3 illustrates the flow of a benefit claim from its initial receipt, review, and benefit determination by the insurance company to the issuing and clearing of a corporate check through the corporate account.

The insurance company normally has similar administrative, risk, and reserve charges as in a basic alternative insurance arrangement. The employer pays a monthly premium to the insurer equal to the expected annual cost of these charges. Premium taxes must be paid by the em-

FIGURE 22–3
Claim Flow of Minimum Premium Arrangement

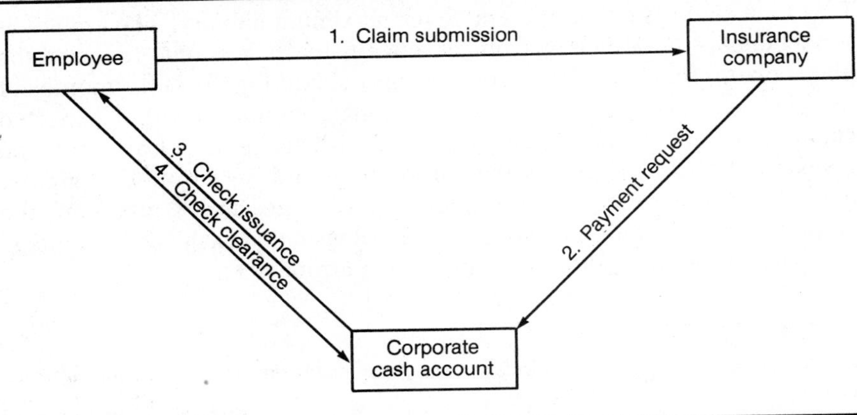

ployer on these monthly premium amounts. In the previous examples where 85 percent and 93 percent of normal premium are deposited into the corporate cash account, the remaining 15 percent and 7 percent of normal premium, respectively, reflect the monthly premium charge for administrative, risk, and reserve costs.

Minimum Premium–No Reserve Arrangement

A significant difference between a minimum premium and self-insured/ASO arrangement is that in the minimum premium arrangement the insurance company still maintains a substantial reserve for incurred but unreported claims. As in other alternative insurance arrangements, the employer potentially can gain a cash flow savings by gaining the corporate use of the reserves. To meet this employer demand, the insurance companies offer a minimum premium–no reserve arrangement.

The employer gains the use of these reserves by the insurance company returning the incurred but unreported reserves it has been holding and reducing the future premium charges paid to the insurance company. This arrangement allows the corporation to use the reserve funds until they are required to pay incurred but unreported claims at the time of plan or contract termination. Because of state insurance regulations, it is generally agreed by insurance companies that they cannot fully release to the employer the financial liability for incurred but unreported claims at termination of its insurance contract with the employer. Therefore, the employer must either repay the reserve amount to the insurer at time of termination or specifically pay the incurred but unreported claims up to the insurer's normal reserve amount for a similar medical and/or short-term disability plan.

The minimum premium–no reserve arrangement essentially offers all the financial advantages of a self-insured/ASO arrangement, with the additional advantage of limiting the employer's liability for benefit payments in excess of the expected annual loss level. The liability for these possible unexpected costs still are assumed by the insurance company. A disadvantage to the minimum premium–no reserve arrangement is that administrative costs will be higher than a normal minimum premium arrangement because the interest credited by the insurance company on reserves, which is applied to reduce the administrative charges, no longer exists. However, the additional investment income gained through the corporate use of these funds significantly offsets this disadvantage.

CHAPTER 23

NONINSURED APPROACHES TO FUNDING HEALTH CARE BENEFITS*

Carlton Harker

This chapter reviews briefly some of the more significant aspects of the self-funding of health care benefits by employers.[1] The most common health care benefits currently being self-funded are medical, dental, disability, and related benefits. Death benefits generally are not self-funded because noninsured benefits of this type in excess of $5,000 are taxable to the beneficiary.[2] (Workers' compensation benefits are excluded because they are not ERISA-covered benefits[3] and also may not be funded by a tax-exempt trust.[4])

The term *employer,* as it is used in this chapter, includes both governmental employers and joint boards of trustees as defined by the Labor Management Relations Act of 1947 (Taft-Hartley Act).[5]

---

* Carlton Harker, *Self-Funding of Health Care Benefits* (Brookfield, Wis.: International Foundation of Employee Benefits Plans, 1988) treats self-funding of health care benefits in a substantially expanded form. This chapter is a condensation of portions of that book.

[1] Employee Retirement Income Security Act of 1974, Section 3(1).

[2] Internal Revenue Code, Section 101. See also *Ross* v. *Odom,* 401 F. 2d 464 5th Cir. (1968) and Internal Revenue Service Technical Advice Memorandum, E.B.P.R. Research Reports, 341.3-21 (1979).

[3] Employee Retirement Income Security Act of 1974, Section 4(b)(3).

[4] Rev. Rul. 74-18, 1974-1 C.B. 139.

[5] Ibid., codified at 29 U.S.C., Section 141-187 (1976).

GENERAL BACKGROUND

Definition of Self-Funding

Self-funding, as used in this chapter, is limited to those arrangements where the total and ultimate responsibility for providing all plan benefits remains with the employer. Since this is the case with excess loss agreements, they are treated as part of self-funding. Where insurers administer self-funded plans under administrative service agreements, such arrangements are self-funded. Modified insured arrangements, such as minimum premium, cost-plus, and retrospective premium agreements, which modify conventional group insurance by amendatory agreements, are not considered. Traditional fully experience-rated group contracts are deemed to have no substantive element of self-funding because of the "upside limit" of risk to the employer and therefore are not covered here.

Dual-Funding

Considerable interest has been shown in recent years in dual-funding. With self-funding, the plan is undivided and wholly the responsibility of the employer. Excess loss coverage, outside the plan, protects the employer from shock losses.

With dual-funding the plan is split into two separate free-standing plans. The employer assumes the responsibility for the portion of the risk up to the attachment point and finances such risk by self-funding. The insurer assumes the responsibility for the portion of the risk over the attachment point and finances such risk by means of high deductible group plans. Some of the advantages with dual-funded plans follow:

- Employer is relieved of the "reimbursement" problem. In self-funding, the employer must pay first and then seek reimbursement with a cancelled check for the excess loss carrier. Dual-funded is indemnity; the insurer must assume responsibility when the attachment point is reached.
- The employer is comforted that the larger claims are controlled by a contract filed with the insurance department, under the jurisdiction of the commissioner and subject to the policy provisions requirements of the state.
- The benefits, provisions, and so forth of the self-funded and the fully insured plan documents need not, nor are they generally, the same.

Extent of Self-Funding

Meaningful data on the nature and extent of self-funding is unavailable, but if we consider only the plans of the larger multistate and government employers and jointly administered (Taft-Hartley) trusts, a substantial percentage of welfare plans are self-funded. Because insurers offer "Administrative Services Only" (ASO) agreements and excess loss coverages to medium and smaller employers, there has been an increasing interest in self-funding among such employers.

Current Interest in Self-Funding

Among the reasons for the current interest in self-funding are:

Economic Considerations

The rapidly increasing cost of providing welfare benefits coupled with high interest rates have encouraged employers to consider self-funding in an attempt to control costs. Some employers wish to control, or reduce, reserves because of the current high value of money, and some believe cash flow is more easily managed with a self-funded program. In addition, certain expenses, such as insurer risk charges and state premium taxes, may be avoided with a self-funded program.

Avoidance of State Mandated Benefits

Since the Employee Retirement Income Security Act of 1974 (ERISA) exempts employee benefit plans from state regulation, the self-funding, multistate employer need not meet the requirements of state-mandated benefits or deal with the effects of the increasing aggressiveness of both the courts and regulators in applying these mandated benefits extraterritorially.

Accepted by Insurers

Many insurers facilitate self-funding by offering ASO agreements under which, as the name implies, the insurer provides only administrative services and does not assume any obligation for claims developing under the contract except at contract termination and for excess loss coverages under which an employer is covered for claims that exceed a specified amount.

Judicial Clarification

In *Farmer* v. *Monsanto* it was held that self-funding would not be construed as *doing an insurance business* if the self-funding was limited to the employees and dependents of the employer and affiliates and the profit motive was absent.[6]

ERISA Preemption

State laws attempting to regulate employee benefit plans generally were preempted by ERISA.[7] This preemption clause of ERISA has been subject to much discussion and litigation and is discussed in more detail later in this chapter.

Elimination of the 85 Percent Income Restriction

The Tax Reform Act of 1969 eliminated the 85 percent income restriction which required that at leat 85 percent of the income to a 501(c)(9) trust be made from employer or employee contributions and which had existed because the interest earnings on asset accumulations were not tax-exempt.

Increasing Popularity of Risk Management

The increase in the practice of risk management techniques by employers with other programs (e.g., state-required disability, workers' compensation) has contributed to employer interest in self-funding of welfare benefits and has facilitated the adoption of such programs.

Potential Limitations of Self-Funding

Many employers carefully consider self-funding and reject the option. There are several reasons why employers may not wish to self-fund. An employer may have a concern over the administrative and financial responsibilities involved, fear an unfavorable employee or union reaction, wish a third-party benefit buffer or wish the protection of the traditional arrangements, e.g., state insurance department protection, ease of providing conversion, or extended coverages. Then, too, some employers look to their insurers as a source of credit or as a carrier for their casualty policies.

When Is Self-Funding Appropriate?

A welfare plan may be fully insured, fully self-funded, or partially self-funded. When an employer has considered the advantages and disadvantages of each, it may decide to take a middle course and adopt partial

---

[6] State ex. rel. *Farmer* v. *Monsanto Co.*, 517 SW. 2d 129 (Mo. Sup. Ct. 1974).

[7] Employee Retirement Income Security Act of 1974, Section 514.

self-funding in order to obtain some advantages of both extremes. In all cases, an employer's individual circumstances should be taken into consideration and a feasibility study done to determine the best approach for each employer.

Legal Issues

A number of legal issues relative to self-funding of welfare benefits should be reviewed. Most, but not all, of these issues are settled.

Doing an Insurance Business

As mentioned earlier, it was held in *Farmer* v. *Monsanto* that self-funding by an employer would not necessarily be deemed *doing an insurance business*. A survey of the 50 state insurance departments conducted by this writer indicated that no state, of the 29 which responded, would question the *Farmer* v. *Monsanto* decision.

ERISA Preemption

While Congress intended that ERISA would preempt those state laws attempting to regulate employee benefit plans, it worded the preemption very cautiously.[8] First, the preemption did not apply to insurance, banking, or securities laws.[9] Second, the Committee of Conference expected the Task Force provided by ERISA to consult closely with the states in its study and report to Congress.[10] Third, the preemption was limited to fiduciary and reporting and disclosure responsibilities.[11] Court decisions and law journal articles resulting from the preemption provisions are too numerous to be cited here, but some observations relating to the preemption provisions are:

1. The preemption issue is far from settled; there is a possibility of future clarifying ERISA amendments.
2. Preemption already has had an impact on several state laws; particularly significant is the preemption of self-funded plans by state laws mandating benefits.
3. Preemption does not apply to providers of health care or to insur-

---

[8] ERISA, Section 514(a).

[9] ERISA, Section 514(b)(2)(A).

[10] ERISA, Section 3022(a)(4) and *II Legislative History of ERISA* (Washington, D.C.: U.S. Government Printing Office, 1974), p. 4650.

[11] See note 1, *supra*.

ers; the question of indirect state regulation of self-funded plans remained unanswered.

4. Significant state regulation of Taft-Hartley welfare funds has been preempted; this preemption may have been both an unanticipated and undesired result of the preemption provision.

State Mandated Benefits

Nearly one half of the states currently have some state-mandated benefits such as required coverage for physical therapy, convalescent home care, and surviving spouse medical expenses. The primary reason for the existence of such benefits is the political influence of special interest groups which is brought about in two ways. First, the groups lobby for special legislation, and second, the groups encourage the regulatory and judicial authorities to administer the laws extraterritorially. By self-funding, state-mandated benefits generally are preempted from state law.[12] Some observers have noted that state-mandated benefits will further encourage self-funding and weaken even more the states' ability to regulate.[13]

Multiple Employer Trusts

Shortly after the enactment of ERISA, a number of multiple employer trusts claimed status as employee benefit plans in order to achieve preemption from state regulation.

Several significant court decisions held that entrepreneur-sponsored multiple employer trusts were not employee benefit plans and therefore were subject to regulation by the state.[14] The courts held that the trusts were not employee benefit plans in cases in which a commonality of employment was lacking and there existed a profit motive by the entrepreneur.

The Department of Labor, in various opinion letters, has ruled that a multiple employer trust is not an employee benefit plan unless it is established and maintained by the employer.[15]

---

[12] ERISA, Section 514; *Wadsworth* v. *Whaland,* 562 F. 2d 70 (1st Cir.) *cert. denied,* 435 U.S. 980 (1978).

[13] R. E. Younger, "Mandated Insurance Coverage—The Achilles Heel of State Regulation?", *Proceedings of the Association of Life Insurance Counsel,* 1978, p. 769.

[14] *Bell* v. *Employee Security Benefit Ass'n,* 437 F Supp. 382 (D. Ken. 1977). *Hamberlin* v. *VIP Ins. Trust,* 434 F. Supp. 1196 (D. Ariz. 1977). *Nat'l Bus. Conf.* v. *Anderson,* 451 Supp. 458 (S.D. Ia. 1977), *Wayne Chem. Inc.* v. *Columbus Agc'y Serv. Corp.,* 426 F. Supp. 316 (N.D. Ind.), *aff'd as modified,* 567 F. 2d 692 (7th Cir. 1977).

[15] Dept. of Labor Op. Ltrs. 79–41A, June 29, 1979; 79–46A, July 19, 1979; 79–49A, July 31, 1979; 79–54A, Aug. 5, 1979 and 79–61A, August 29, 1979.

Multiple Employer Welfare Arrangements (MEWA)

Congress enacted legislation in 1982[16] which provided that self-funded multiple employer trusts were not employee benefit plans automatically eligible for ERISA preemption. MEWAs were to be subject to state regulations as regards financial considerations (reserves, e.g.), but not as regards state-mandated benefits.

Discrimination Issues

The Revenue Act of 1978 and proposed regulations require that self-insured medical reimbursement plans must meet certain nondiscrimination standards in order for the prohibited group to receive favorable tax treatment.[17] The current federal laws and clarifying regulations required that self-funded plans must not discriminate in favor of the prohibited group as to benefits or eligibility, thereto. Insured plans, however, were unaffected and continued to provide fully insured discriminatory plans—often with only a tinge of actual risk shift. The 1986 Tax Reform Act (TRA 86)[18] permits both the fully insured and the self-insured plan to discriminate in favor of the prohibited group—*but* only to a very minor extent.

Self-Funding and Collective Bargaining

Since the National Labor Relations Board ruled in 1973 that the selection of an insurer for welfare plans is a mandatory subject for collective bargaining, collective bargaining negotiations may have a significant impact on self-funding.[19]

Funding

So far as the funding of plan benefits is concerned, self-funded plans may be classified in one of the following ways:

1. *General Asset Plan:* This method uses no trust.
2. *Tax-exempt Trusteed Plan:* This method uses a tax-exempt trust that generally is qualified under Internal Revenue Code Section 501(c)(9).

---

16 Miscellaneous Tax and ERISA Provisions, PL 97–473, *codified* at 96 STAT 2611.

17 Pub. L. No. 95-600, Section 366, *codified at* I.R.C., Section 105(h) and Treas. Reg., Section 1.105-7 (1981).

18 Pub.L. 99–514.

19 Connecticut Light & Power Co., 196 N.L.R.B. No. 149 (1972).

3. *Non-Tax-Exempt Trusteed Plan:* This method would use a non-tax-exempt trust and is rarely seen because of the lack of tax advantages.
4. *Captive Insurer:* By this method the employer uses its own insurer to fund the plan benefits.

General Asset Plan

With a general asset plan, any plan assets are commingled with the general assets of the employer. There usually are no plan assets other than withheld employee contributions because ERISA requires plan assets to be under a trust and contributions to general asset plan liablities usually are not tax deductible by the employer.[20]

Several administrative advantages are gained with a general asset plan. Certain filing requirements are avoided (filing for the tax-exemption of a trust)[21] or simplified (a modified Form 5500 without financial statements or an independent auditor's opinion).[22] Furthermore, no fidelity bond is required, and plan restrictions from the Treasury regulations on the 501(c)(9) trust are avoided.[23]

501(a) Trust

An employer may self-fund medical benefits for certain retired lives as part of a qualified retirement plan.[24] In such circumstances, a pension or profit-sharing trust, qualified under Internal Revenue Code Section 501(a) would be used. More commonly seen is a situation where the tax-exempt trust qualifies under Internal Revenue Code Section 501(c)(9).

501(c)(9) Trust

A special tax-exempt trust is provided by the Internal Revenue Code and Treasury Regulations for a voluntary employees' beneficiary association.[25] When used herein, a 501(c)(9) trust means a vehicle used for self-

---

[20] See note 18 *supra;* Rev. Rul. 79-338, 1979-2 C.B. 212.

[21] I.R.S. Form 1024 (1980) and I.R.S. Form 990 (1980).

[22] Instructions to the Annual Return/Report, Form 5500.

[23] Treas. Reg. Section 1.501(c)(9) (1981).

[24] I.R.C. Section 401(h); Treas. Reg. Section 1.401-14 (1964).

[25] I.R.C. Section 501(c)(9); Treas. Reg. Section 1.501(c)(9) (1980).

funding. A 501(c)(9) trust also may be used as a conduit into which employer contributions may flow and out of which insurance premiums may flow, but the term is not used in that sense in this chapter.

The regulations (*a*) set forth the conditions which a voluntary employees' beneficiary association must meet in order to be a qualifying organization, (*b*) specify the membership requirements, (*c*) enumerate the permitted benefits, (*d*) provide certain guidelines relative to discrimination, and (*e*) set forth other requirements relative to dissolution and record keeping.

Several significant Revenue Rulings have clarified the operation of the 501(c)(9) trust:

1. A 1958 Revenue Ruling determined that the plan and trust are interdependent agreements which together create a voluntary employees' beneficiary association within the contemplation of that term.[26]
2. A 1959 Revenue Ruling determined that membership in a 501(c)(9) trust would exclude such persons as individuals, proprietors, partners, self-employed persons, or trustees designated to administer the funds.[27] This position of the Internal Revenue Service was upheld by the court.[28]
3. A 1969 Revenue Ruling determined that a nonforfeitable contribution to a 501(c)(9) trust with retired lives benefits is deductible as an ordinary and necessary business expense and not as a contribution to a plan of deferred compensation.[29]
4. A 1973 Revenue Ruling determined that a contribution to a 501(c)(9) trust is deductible if it is actuarially determined and legal.[30]
5. A 1974 Revenue Ruling determined that workers' compensation benefits are not acceptable benefits for a 501(c)(9) program.[31]

Recent changes to the Internal Revenue Code[32] gave an employer a safe-harbor basis for determining deductible 501(c)(9) reserves. That is, unless reserves in excess of the statutory limit are claimed. No actuarial

---

[26] Rev. Rul. 58–442, 1958–2 C.B. 194.

[27] Rev. Rul. 59–28, 1959–1 C.B. 120.

[28] *Milwaukee Sign Painters Welfare Fund* v. *U.S.*, 17 A.F.T.R. 2d 264 (E.D. Wisc. 1965).

[29] Rev. Rul. 69–478, 1969–2 C.B. 29; I.R.C. Section 162; I.R.C. Section 404(a).

[30] Rev. Rul. 73–599, 1973–2 C.B. 40.

[31] Rev. Rul. 74–18, 1974–C.B. 139.

[32] 1984 DEFRA, P.L. 98–369, *codified* at 98 STAT 854.

certification is required. Safe-harbor reserves for group health are 35 percent of annual paid benefits.

Non-Tax-Exempt Trusteed Plan

While it is possible to meet the trust requirements of ERISA by using a non-tax-exempt trust, there are no tax advantages in doing so, and therefore such a trust would likely never be used.

Captive Insurer

A captive insurer is formed by a firm for the primary purpose of underwriting some or all of the sponsoring company's risk.[33] ERISA views insuring with a captive insurer as a form of self-dealing but provides an exemption if less than 5 percent of the insurer's premiums are those of the sponsor.[34] This statutory 5 percent limitation was increased to 50 percent by the Department of Labor in 1979.[35]

ADMINISTRATION

When an employer self-funds, the administrative services to the plan may be provided by the employer, by a third-party administrator under a benefit services agreement, or by an insurer under an administrative services only (ASO) agreement. The three most important services from the viewpoint of the employer usually are administration, accounting, and actuarial ones.

Benefit Administration

Benefit administration probably is the single most important administrative consideration in a self-funding arrangement. Some aspects of benefit administration are:

1. Benefit complaint, denial, and litigation.
2. Benefit control activities, such as peer review.
3. Monitoring for duplicate coverage and abuse.

---

[33] See note 18 *supra*.

[34] ERISA Section 406; ERISA Section 408(b)(5).

[35] Prohibited Transaction Exemption 79–41, 44 Fed. Reg. 46,365 (1979).

4. Statistical reports.
5. Coverage interpretation.
6. Determining and processing benefit payments.
7. Cash flow planning.

A third-party buffer to protect the employer from the potential of bad employee relations associated with benefit payment difficulties may be desirable in a self-funding arrangement.

ACCOUNTING

The three accounting considerations connected with a self-funded welfare plan are deduction accounting, plan accounting, and employer accounting.

Deduction Accounting

General Asset Plan

A basic theme supported by statutory, regulatory, and judicial law is that an employer payment to a self-funded reserve maintained in a general asset plan is deductible only when the events establishing the liability have all occurred and the liability is reasonably ascertainable.[36] Deduction for such reserve contribution has not been easily obtained.

Trusteed Tax-Exempt Plan

Contributions to a 501(c)(9) trust generally are deductible as ordinary and necessary business expenses if they are irrevocable and reasonable and actuarially supportable.[37]

Plan Accounting

Plan accounting is the process by which the plan and trust are reflected in the required government reporting and disclosure forms. Table 23–1 sum-

---

[36] I.R.C. Section 461(a). Treas. Reg. Section 1.461–1 (1960); Rev. Rul. 79–338. 1979–2 C.B. 212; Rev. Rul. 70–262, 1970–1 C.B. 122; Rev. Rul. 69–512, 1969–2 C.B. 24; Rev. Rul. 57–485, 1957–2 C.B. 117. *Wien Consol. Airlines* v. *Comm'r of Int. Rev.,* 528 F. 2d 753 (9th Cir. 1976); *Crescent Wharf & Warehouse Co.* v. *Comm'r of Int. Rev.,* 518 F. 2d 772 (9th Cir. 1975); *Thriftmart, Inc.* v. *Comm'r of Int. Rev.,* 59 T.C. 598 (1973).

[37] I.R.C. Section 162(s)(i); Treas. Reg. Section 1.162-10 (1958); Rev. Rul. 56-102 1956-1 C.B. 90; Rev. Rul. 58-128, 1958-1 C.B. 89; Rev. Rul. 69-478, 1969-2 C.B. 29; Rev. Rul. 73-599, 1973-2 C.B. 41; Ltr. Rul. 7828030, April 12, 1978; Ltr. Rul. 7839040, June 28, 1978.

TABLE 23–1
Government Reporting and Disclosure Regulations for Self-Funded Plans

Method of Funding	*Number of Participants*	*Annual Plan Return*	*Annual Trust Return*
General asset	Fewer than 100	No	No
	100 or More	Yes; Mod. Form 5500	No
501(c)(9) trust	Fewer than 100	Yes; Form 5500–C	Yes; Form 990
	100 or More	Yes; Form 5500	Yes; Form 990

marizes the government reporting and disclosure requirements for self-funded plans.

The Internal Revenue Code requires that an annual return be filed for a tax-exempt trust.[38] ERISA requires that an annual return be filed for a welfare plan unless an exemption is provided.[39] A trust return is due 4½ months after the end of a trust year, and a plan return is due seven months after the end of a plan year.[40] A general asset welfare plan with fewer than 100 participants need not file an annual return.[41] A general asset welfare plan with 100 or more participants need only file a modified annual return that has no financial data and need not have an independent auditor's opinion.[42] Late filing penalties accrue with the trust return.[43]

Employer Accounting

Employer accounting is the process by which the plan is reflected in the employer's accounts and in any footnote disclosure. There presently is a lack of clear authority in the employer accounting of self-funded welfare plans. The recent attention has been directed primarily to retirement plans. There is, however, a current study in progress of the employer accounting of self-funded welfare plans.

---

[38] I.R.C. Section 6033. Treas. Reg. Section 1.6033 (1972).

[39] ERISA Section 103.

[40] Instructions to Internal Revenue Service Form 990. Instructions to Annual Return/Report Form 5500.

[41] 29 C.F.R. Section 2550.104-20 (1975).

[42] Id. Section 2550.104-44 (1975).

[43] I.R.C. Section 6033.

The most significant current accounting guides are the American Institute of Certified Public Accountants Audit Guide and the various guides provided by the federal government.[44]

Actuarial Considerations

Regardless of how the benefits are funded, there usually are certain matters to which actuarial attention is, or should be, directed. A feasibility study of self-funding should be made as should a cash-flow study. Levels of contributions and reserves should be reasonable and adequate, management benefit or control-type statistical reports should be prepared, and attachment points with related excess loss coverage should be reasonable. It may be either legally required or prudent to have an actuary provide the following to the Plan:

- Certification of 501(c)(9) reserves.
- Certification of COBRA[45] Continuation Premiums.
- Estimate of future funding levels.
- Estimate of economic values on plan benefits for purposes of meeting discrimination tests.

RECENT DEVELOPMENTS

Cost-Containment

Because of the statutes and regulatory inflexibility of fully insured plans, self-funded plans tend to be selected by employers wishing to adapt cost-containment programs. Examples where self-funded plans would be more serviceable follow:

- Triple funding, where providers must assume some of the upside risk in exchange for being treated as preferred providers.
- Benefit formula reductions for "teaching hospitals" unless such case was medically necessary.
- Subrogation and coordination with automobile medical benefits.

---

[44] Audits of Employee Health and Welfare Funds (N.Y.: A.I.C.P.A., 1972). Medicare Provider Reimbursement Manual (1980); Armed Services Procurement Regulation, 32 C.F.R. Section X. Par. 502 (1976); Cost Accounting Standards Board Regulations, 4 C.F.R. Section 416.50 to 416.80 (1978).

[45] Consolidated Omnibus Budget Reconciliation Act of 1983, Pub.L. 99–272.

- Where minimum plan benefit extension is desired in order to shift the risk from the Plan to a COBRA Continuation Trust as soon as possible.

COBRA Continuation Requirements

As is discussed elsewhere, on employer-sponsored plans, the COBRA legislation mandates the assumption of coverage on certain former participants. Some self-funders have been alarmed at the increase in their potential liability and the endangerment by COBRA to their excess loss arrangements.

Other self-funders reason that their added administrative and cost-containment programs give them sufficient control to overcome any dangers. There are also several risk-transfer devices, by which self-funders can arrange to have COBRA risks transferred, in large part, from their plan to a fully insured plan.

CHAPTER 24

RETIREMENT PLAN DESIGN*

Everett T. Allen, Jr.

Although pension plans vary in terms of specific provisions, they generally fall into one of two categories—they are either *defined benefit* or *defined contribution* in nature. Today, most employees are covered by defined benefit plans; this reflects the fact that large employers and unions historically have favored the defined benefit approach. Since the mid 1970s, however, a significant percentage of all new plans established have utilized the defined contribution approach.

A defined benefit plan provides a fixed amount of pension benefit. The amount of each employee's benefit usually depends on length of service and pay level, for example, a pension of 1 percent of pay for each year of service. In collectively bargained plans, however, pay often is not taken into account; the monthly pension might be a fixed dollar amount (such as $15) for each year of service. In any event, a defined benefit plan promises a fixed level of benefit and the employer contributes whatever is necessary to provide this amount.

By contrast, the defined contribution approach focuses on contribution levels. The employer's contribution may be fixed as a percent of pay or as a flat dollar amount, or it may be based on a variable such as a percent of profits. In some cases, the employer contribution is totally variable and is established each year on a discretionary basis. However it is determined, the contribution (along with any amount contributed by the employee) is accumulated and invested on the employee's behalf. The amount of pension an employee receives will thus vary depending on such

---

* This chapter originally appeared in *Employee Benefits Today; Concepts and Methods* (Homewood, Ill.: International Foundation of Employee Benefits, 1987).

factors as length of plan participation, the level and frequency of contributions, and investment gains and losses.

There are several different types of defined contribution plans. The two most commonly used for pension purposes are the deferred profit-sharing plan and the money purchase pension plan. In a profit-sharing plan, the employer contribution is related to profits or made on a discretionary basis. The money purchase pension plan requires a fixed employer contribution, regardless of profits. Other defined contribution plans (such as savings or Section 401(k) plans) can be used as primary pension vehicles but are usually adopted to supplement basic defined benefit pension plans. Because the focus in this chapter is on pension arrangements, only deferred profit-sharing and money purchase plans are discussed; other defined contribution programs are covered in subsequent chapters.

Regardless of the approach chosen, a pension plan should be designed so that it supports overall employer objectives. This chapter begins with a discussion of these objectives and how they are influenced by the employer's environment and attitudes. Specific design features are then described, with differences between the defined benefit and defined contribution approaches noted, as appropriate. Finally, these two approaches are evaluated from the viewpoint of both employers and employees.

EMPLOYER OBJECTIVES

Business organizations do not exist in a vacuum. They possess individual characteristics and operate in environments that influence what they can and want to accomplish in providing employee benefits. Factors that can affect employee benefit planning and, in particular, the choice between defined benefit and defined contribution programs, include the following:

- *Employer characteristics.* Is the organization incorporated or unincorporated, or is it tax-exempt? Is it mature, or young and growing? Are profits stable or volatile? What growth patterns are anticipated? What are the firm's short- and long-term capital needs? What are its personnel needs, now and in the future?
- *Industry characteristics.* Is the employer part of a clearly defined industry group? Is this industry highly competitive? Does it have a distinct employee benefit pattern? Is it important, from the standpoint of attracting and retaining employees or for cost considerations, to provide benefits or maintain cost levels that are consistent with those of other companies in the same industry?

- *Employee characteristics.* What is the composition of the employee group? How are employees distributed in terms of age, sex, service, and pay? Is this distribution likely to change in the future? How many employees are in the highly paid group?
- *Diversity of operations.* Does the employer operate its business on a diversified basis? If so, should the same or different benefits be provided for employees at each location or in each line of business? How will such factors as profit margins, competitive needs, costs, employee transfer policies, and administrative capabilities affect this decision?
- *Collective bargaining.* Are any employees represented by a collective bargaining unit? Are benefits bargained for on a local basis or is a national pattern followed? Is a multiemployer plan available for some employees and is it an acceptable alternative? How will benefits gained through collective bargaining affect benefits for nonrepresented employees?
- *Community.* Is the employer (or any of its major operating units) located in a large, urban area or is it a dominant employer in a discrete geographic location? What is the role of the employer in the community? What social and civic responsibilities does the employer want to assume? How important is its image in the community? What other employers compete for labor in the local marketplace?

Answers to these questions (and the list is only illustrative) need to be taken into account in setting specific employee benefit plan objectives. The employer's basic compensation philosophy is also important in the objective-setting process, as is its attitude on:

- The role of employee benefits in protecting income in the event of economic insecurity.
- The extent to which employee benefits are considered a form of indirect or deferred compensation.
- Whether employee cost sharing is necessary or desirable.
- Whether employees can or should bear the risks of inflation and investment performance.
- The use of employee benefits in meeting personnel planning needs.
- The amount of choice to be given employees in structuring their own benefits.
- The importance of cost levels, cost controls, and funding flexibility.
- The desirability of integrating plan and statutory benefits.
- The treatment of highly paid employees.

Each employer will have specific and sometimes unique objectives in establishing or modifying an employee benefit plan. And, as noted, these objectives will be influenced by the employer's environment and its attitudes on matters such as those listed above.

Most employers want to attract and retain desirable employees. An adequate benefit program will certainly be of value in achieving this objective. It also seems reasonably clear that the absence of an adequate benefit program will have a negative effect on recruiting and retention efforts. What is not clear, however, is whether a generous benefit program will have an increasingly positive effect in this regard. In the opinion of many employers, money otherwise spent on extra benefits would be more useful in meeting recruitment and retention objectives if it were directed to other elements of compensation.

A competitive benefit program is another common employer objective. This objective must be clarified before it can be implemented. For example, will competitiveness be measured by industry or local standards, or by both? Industry standards might be more relevant for highly skilled employees and executives. For employees whose skills are readily transferable to other industries, however, local practice could be much more important. Once the competitive standard is established, the employer must decide where it wants to rank—as average, above or below average, or among the leaders. It is also important to establish the means by which competitiveness will be measured. The most common technique compares benefits payable at certain times (e.g., at normal retirement) for employees with different pay and service combinations. This approach must be used with caution because it tends to focus on single events and does not consider the value of other plan provisions. More sophisticated techniques, which measure the relative value of plans by provision, in total, and with reference to both employer- and employee-provided benefits, can be used for this purpose.

Cost objectives can have a major impact on plan design. Employers should set specific objectives for liabilities that will be assumed as well as for annual cost accruals. They must also consider the need for contribution flexibility and the control of future costs that are sensitive to inflation and investment risk.

Employer objectives for income replacement levels are critical to the design of pension plans. Most employers seek to provide a pension benefit that, together with primary Social Security benefits, replaces a percentage of the employee's preretirement gross income. In establishing income replacement levels, these factors should be taken into account:

- Employers rarely contemplate full replacement of gross income, primarily because of tax considerations. Most employers also feel that employees should meet some of their own retirement needs through personal savings (many maintain supplemental plans to help employees in this regard). Further, they expect that most employees will have lower living expenses after they retire.

- Income replacement objectives are often set with reference to the employee's pay level during the final year of employment or average pay during the three- or five-year period just prior to retirement.
- The percentage of income replaced is generally higher for lower paid employees than for higher paid employees.
- Income replacement objectives are usually set so that they can be achieved in full only by employees who have completed what the employer considers to be a "career" of employment (usually 25 or 30 years); objectives are proportionately reduced for individuals who have shorter service.

Obviously, income replacement objectives that are set with reference to an employee's final pay and length of service can best be met through a defined benefit plan that bases benefits on final average pay. Achieving such objectives with a career pay defined benefit plan is more difficult, but not impossible. Accrued benefits under a career pay plan can be updated periodically to keep benefits reasonably close to final pay objectives. Although it is almost impossible to establish and meet final pay income replacement objectives with a defined contribution plan, contribution levels can be set so that, under reasonable expectations for pay growth and investment return, final pay objectives might be approximated. As a practical matter, though, actual experience is not likely to coincide with the

TABLE 24–1
Illustrative Income Replacement Objectives
(Employee with 30 Years of Service)

Final Pay	*Retirement Income As a Percentage of Final Pay**
Under $15,000	80–70%
$15,000 to $25,000	75–65
25,000 to 35,000	70–60
35,000 to 50,000	65–55
Over $50,000	60–50

* Including primary Social Security benefits.

assumptions used. Thus, actual benefits will probably be larger or smaller than anticipated, depending on experience. Table 24–1 sets forth a typical set of income replacement objectives.

Many other objectives—for example, the desire to provide employee incentives or to foster employee identification with overall corporate goals through stock ownership—can affect plan design. In any event, once objectives have been established, they should be ranked in order of priority. In some situations, certain objectives can be achieved only at the expense of others. If this is the case, the relative importance of all objectives should be clearly understood.

PLAN PROVISIONS

A pension plan must contain provisions governing which employees are covered, what benefits they will receive, and how and under what conditions these benefits will be paid. Federal tax law plays an important role in this regard because a plan, to be tax-qualified, must meet the requirements of the Internal Revenue Code (IRC) and supporting regulations and interpretations issued by the Internal Revenue Service (IRS) through various public and private rulings.[1]

Employers have no choice with respect to certain mandatory plan provisions (e.g., if an employer wants to change the plan's vesting schedule, employees with at least three years of service must be given the right to elect vesting under the prior provision). Other mandatory provisions give the employer some latitude (e.g., a plan must provide for vesting, but the employer can choose between two permissible schedules). Some provisions are not mandatory but must meet certain requirements if they are included in a plan (e.g., a plan need not require employee contributions, but if it does, the contribution level cannot be burdensome to lower-paid employees). By and large, the requirements of federal tax law revolve around the central concept that a plan cannot discriminate as to coverage, contributions, and benefits—as well as in operation—in favor of highly paid employees.

The discussion that follows covers the major plan features an employer must consider and the approaches most commonly used in estab-

---

[1] A detailed discussion of the requirements of federal tax law are beyond the scope of this chapter, which refers to them only in general terms. For such a discussion, see Everett T. Allen Jr., Joseph J. Melone, Jerry S. Rosenbloom, and Jack L. VanDerhei, *Pension Planning,* 6th ed. (Homewood, Ill.: Richard D. Irwin, 1988).

lishing actual plan provisions. The emphasis is on the practical aspects of design, rather than on legal requirements.

Service Counting

With rare exceptions, an employee's service will be relevant to his or her benefits under the plan. Specifically, service can be used to determine eligibility for: (1) participation in the plan, (2) vested benefits, (3) benefit accruals, (4) early retirement, and (5) ancillary benefits (e.g., spouse or disability benefits). In most plans, service will also be a factor in determining the amount of an employee's benefit.

The law imposes explicit requirements on how service is to be determined for the first three purposes listed above. Generally, service must be measured over a 12-month period (a computation period) that may be a plan, calendar, or employment year. Any such period in which an employee is credited with 1,000 hours of service will be considered a full year of service. The employee's hours of service can be established by counting actual hours worked or by using one of several "equivalency" methods permitted by regulations. Alternatively, an "elapsed time" method can be used to measure service. The law also requires the inclusion of provisions dealing with breaks in service and the conditions under which service before and after such breaks must be aggregated.

For purposes of early retirement and ancillary benefits, service can be determined on any reasonable basis the employer establishes, provided the method does not discriminate in favor of highly paid employees. As a practical matter, however, most employers adopt a uniform method of calculating service for all plan purposes.

Administrative considerations are important in choosing a service-counting method. Actual hours counting, for example, may prove impractical for a plan covering exempt employees who do not maintain detailed records of hours worked. One of the most popular of the available equivalency methods is "monthly" equivalency, which credits an employee with 190 hours for any month in which at least one hour of service is credited. The elapsed time method, which—with the exception of break in service aspects —measures service from date of employment to date of termination, is also popular. However, these methods give part-time employees the equivalent of full-time service. In situations where this could be a problem, different methods of counting service can be used; for example, service for part-time employees could be determined by actual hours counting, and the elapsed time method could be used for full-time employees. The use of different methods is permissible only if it does not result in discrimination.

Eligibility for Participation

A plan may require that an employee complete a minimum period of service and attain a minimum age to be eligible to participate. In general, the maximum permissible service requirement is one year, although up to two years may be used in a pension plan that provides for full and immediate vesting. The highest minimum age that can be used is 21.

These minimum age and service requirements can be useful in plans that necessitate maintenance of individual records for participants—defined contribution plans, contributory plans, or plans funded with individual life insurance or annuity contracts. Some administrative cost and effort is avoided by excluding young or short-service employees from such plans until they are beyond what is considered the high-turnover stage of their employment. By contrast, there is very little (if any) administrative work associated with early terminations under a noncontributory defined benefit plan funded with an arrangement that does not require individual employee allocations—for example, a trusteed plan—and plans of this type often provide for eligiblility immediately upon employment. However, if the plan bases benefits on years of *participation* (rather than years of service), the use of minimum age and service requirements will reduce the period of participation and, as a result, will reduce benefit costs to some extent. Thus, these requirements are sometimes used in noncontributory defined benefit plans.

In the past, maximum age provisions—typically excluding employees hired after age 60—were common in defined benefit plans. (Such provisions cannot be included in defined contribution plans). However, 1986 legislation now prohibits the use of a maximum age provision. Instead, defined benefit plans may provide that the normal retirement age for individuals hired after age 60 will coincide with the completion of five or ten years of participation.

Another type of eligibility requirement relates to employment classifications. A plan may be limited to hourly or to salaried employees, to represented or nonrepresented employees, or to individuals employed at certain locations or in specific lines of business. An employee will have to fall within the designated classification to be eligible to participate. Employers must take care that such plans meet the coverage requirements of the IRC.

Plans that limit eligibility to employees who earn more than a stipulated amount will no longer be permitted because of changes made by the Tax Reform Act of 1986.

Employee Contributions

Some employers prefer that employees contribute toward the cost of their pension benefits. This preference may be philosophical or it may be founded on more pragmatic considerations of cost and benefit levels. Arguments in favor of noncontributory plans seem to have been more persuasive, however. Employee contributions involve additional administrative effort and cost. Further, if a plan is contributory, an employer may face problems with nonparticipating employees who reach retirement age and cannot afford to retire. Another practical consideration is that almost all collectively bargained plans are noncontributory. An employer that has such a plan will find it difficult to require contributions under plans for nonrepresented employees.

The most compelling factor favoring noncontributory plans is federal tax law. Employer contributions to a pension plan are tax deductible; employee contributions are not.[2] Thus, on an aftertax basis, it is more cost-efficient to fund benefits with employer contributions. (This relative efficiency will be diminished somewhat by the lower individual and corporate tax rates effective in 1987, but it will still exist.)

Most defined benefit plans do not, in fact, require employee contributions, nor do deferred profit-sharing plans. Both types of plans may permit voluntary employee contributions—that is, contributions that are not required as a condition of participation. Although many pension plans have such an option, very few employees have taken advantage of the opportunity to make these additional contributions.

Employee contributions are more often required as a condition of participation in money purchase pension plans. In theory, the arguments for and against employee contributions are the same for these plans as they are for other arrangements. However, employers often choose the money purchase approach because of cost constraints; where this is the case, employee contributions may be necessary to bring total contributions to a level that will produce adequate benefits. Further, these plans are often viewed—and communicated to employees—as being similar to

---

[2] Employee contributions can, of course, be made on a before-tax basis under a deferred profit-sharing plan that has a cash or deferred option meeting the requirements of Section 401(k).

savings plans where employee contributions are matched by employer contributions.[3]

If employee contributions are required, they are usually set as a percentage of compensation—typically, from 2 to 6 percent. The contribution rate cannot be so high as to be burdensome for lower paid employees; this is why 6 percent is usually the maximum. If the plan benefit formula is integrated with Social Security by providing a higher accrual rate for pay over a stipulated level, the same pattern is followed with the contribution rate. If the benefit formula is 1 percent of pay up to $10,000 and 1.5 percent on pay over this amount, for example, the contribution rate might be 2 percent of pay up to $10,000 and 3 percent over this amount.

Retirement Ages

Normal Retirement Age

Almost all pension plans specify 65 as normal retirement age. Those plans that have permitted employees to enter after age 60 have usually set the normal retirement age as 65 or, if later, after the completion of a period of participation such as 5 or 10 years. Because the law now prohibits the use of a maximum age for participation, this latter definition of normal retirement age will be used in almost all plans.

It is possible—but relatively uncommon—to specify an age under 65 as the plan's normal retirement age. For one thing, providing full benefits before age 65 can be expensive. For another, provisions of this type can result in a violation of age discrimination laws unless they are carefully designed and operated.

At one time, the concept of a normal retirement age was very significant for defined benefit plans. It was the age at which employees could retire with full, unreduced benefits and without employer consent. Moreover, it was the age at which most employees were expected to retire and the age at which full, unreduced Social Security benefits became available. In most plans, it also marked the point at which pension accruals stopped; continued employment beyond normal retirement usually did not result in increased benefits.

This concept has become diffuse in recent years. Many employers now provide for the payment of full accrued benefits, without reduction,

---

[3] Matching employer contributions under a defined contribution plan as well as after-tax employee contributions will have to satisfy an "actual contribution test" (ACP) beginning in 1989. This test is similar to the "actual deferral percentage" (ADP) test used for elective contributions under a Section 401(k) plan.

on early retirement after the completion of certain age and service requirements. And, in fact, most employees do retire before age 65. Because of changes in age discrimination laws, benefits must accrue for service beyond normal retirement; also, for individuals born after 1937, the Social Security normal retirement age has been raised. For all practical purposes, a plan's normal retirement age remains significant primarily for determining the value of accrued benefits at any point in time and for determining the amount of any reduction for benefits payable in the event of early retirement. The normal retirement age concept has even less significance in defined contribution plans: Once an employee is vested, the value of plan benefits is the same regardless of the reason for the employee's termination (although a retiring employee might have more options as to how the benefit is to be paid).

The distinction between retirement and termination of employment can be important for other employee benefit programs. Some employers, for example, continue employer-supported life insurance and medical expense benefits for retired employees but not for those who terminate employment before qualifying for early retirement. Further, distributions on account of retirement according to plan provisions (and after age 55) will not be subject to the 10 percent additional tax levied on early distributions from a qualified plan.

Early Retirement

Most pension plans permit an employee to retire and receive benefits prior to the plan's normal retirement age. It is customary to require that the employee have attained some minimum age and completed some minimum period of service to qualify for this privilege. The minimum age most frequently used is 55. Minimum service is often set at 10 years, although both shorter and longer periods are used.

The benefit amount payable at early retirement is less than that payable at normal retirement because, in most plans, the employee will not have accrued his or her full benefit. This will not be the case if a defined benefit plan limits service that can be counted in calculating benefits and the employee has already completed the full service period. Even in this situation, however, the benefit could be smaller if it is based on final average pay and the employee loses the advantage of the higher pay base he or she would have achieved if employed until normal retirement age.

Early retirement benefits can be reduced for another reason as well. When benefit payments start before the employee's normal retirement age, they will be paid over a longer period of time; a reduction factor may be applied to recognize these additional payments. This could be a true actuarial factor or, as is more often the case, a simple factor such as one half of 1 percent for each month by which early retirement precedes normal retirement. This type of reduction takes place automatically in a defined contribution plan because the annuity value (in the marketplace) of the employee's account balance will reflect the employee's age and life expectancy.

Many defined benefit plans do not fully reduce the retirement benefit to reflect the early commencement of benefit payments. For example, some plans use a factor of one quarter of 1 percent instead of the one half of 1 percent factor mentioned above. Another common approach is to apply no reduction factor at all if the employee has attained some minimum age (e.g., 60 or 62) and has completed some minimum period of service (e.g., 25 or 30 years), or if the sum of the employee's age and service is a specified number such as 85 or 90.

It is important to understand that there will be additional plan costs when less than a full actuarial reduction (or its equivalent) is used. It is also important to recognize that this type of provision will encourage early retirement and must be considered in the context of the employer's personnel planning needs and objectives.

Deferred Retirement

Prior to the advent of age discrimination laws, it was uncommon for plans to permit deferred retirement solely at the employee's option. If deferred retirement was permitted, it was customary to provide that the benefit payable at actual retirement would be the same as that available at normal retirement—that is, there would be no increase in benefits due to continued employment.

Age discrimination laws, particularly the amendments enacted in 1986, have changed all this. An employee can no longer be discharged for reasons of age; this protection has also been extended to employees over age 70. Further, benefits must continue to accrue under the plan formula for service after the plan's normal retirement age. Thus, as a practical matter, deferred retirement will be permitted under all plans and it will be common for benefits to accrue until the time of actual retirement. However, many plans have or will add a provision that limits the total period of service that can be taken into account for calculating plan benefits; service after this maximum has been reached, whether before or after normal retirement age, will not be taken into account.

Retirement Benefits

Because the defined contribution and defined benefit approaches are totally different in terms of plan provisions for determining retirement benefits, they will be discussed separately in this section. A description of the basic concepts of each of these approaches is followed by brief discussions on Social Security integration, federal tax law limits on contributions and benefits, and the restrictions applicable to ''top heavy'' plans.

Defined Contribution Plans

An employee's retirement benefit under a defined contribution plan—at normal, early, or deferred retirement—is his or her account balance at the time of retirement. This account balance depends on the amounts credited to the employee's account by way of: (1) direct contributions, (2) reallocated forfeitures, and (3) investment gains or losses. The annuity value of this account balance—that is, the amount of pension it will generate—depends on then current interest rates and the employee's age at the time the balance is applied to provide a benefit. If the employee purchases an annuity from an insurance company, the annuity value may also reflect the employee's sex. (Even though laws prevent an employer from discriminating on the basis of sex, insurers are not yet required to use unisex factors in pricing their annuity products.)

The contributions made on an employee's behalf under a money purchase pension plan can be made by the employer or by the employee from aftertax income. These contribution rates are fixed and are stipulated in the plan. Although they can be stated in dollar amounts, they are usually expressed as a percentage of pay. For example, the employer contribution to a noncontributory plan might be set as 6 percent of pay. A contributory plan might require an employee contribution of perhaps 3 percent of pay with a matching employer contribution.[4] Contribution rates are usually established on the basis of projections, using reasonable assumptions for growth in pay and investment results, as to the level of replacement income the contributions will generate for employees retiring after completing a career of employment with the employer. Actual experience is likely to differ from the assumptions employed, with the result that actual benefits will be more or less than those projected.

Contributions under a profit-sharing plan typically are made by the employer only—that is, aftertax employee contributions are not mandatory. These contributions are allocated to employees in proportion to pay. Although allocation can be weighted for service, it rarely is; the IRS takes the position that such an allocation can result in a plan that discriminates in favor of highly paid employees. If the plan has a cash or deferred

---

[4] As noted earlier, matching employer and aftertax employee contributions under a money purchase plan must satisfy an ACP test after 1988.

arrangement, an employee electing to defer is, in a sense, making a contribution; however, the deferred amount is considered to be an employer contribution. In any event, the employer contribution may be determined by formula or, as is often the case, on a discretionary basis from year to year. The contribution amount may be established with a view toward ultimate benefit levels. However, unlike the money purchase pension plan, the profit-sharing plan does not require an employer commitment as to contribution levels and thus provides flexibility as to cost levels and funding.

Both money purchase pension plans and profit-sharing plans may permit employees to augment their account balances by making voluntary or supplemental contributions. These can be made on an aftertax basis or, in the case of a profit-sharing plan (and within permissible limits), through a reduction in pay. Changes in the taxation of distributions and new restrictions on in-service withdrawals from profit-sharing plans may reduce the popularity of this plan feature.[5]

Forfeitures, the second source of credits for an employee's account, arise when employees terminate employment without being fully vested in their account balances. These nonvested amounts can be used to reduce employer contributions or they can be reallocated to employees in the same manner that employer contributions are allocated. Profit-sharing plans often reallocate forfeited amounts. In the past, money purchase plans were required to use forfeitures to reduce employer contributions. Whether this practice will change now that these plans can also reallocate forfeitures remains to be seen.

A third and very important source of credits to an employee's account consists of investment results. Contributions and forfeitures allocated to an employee are invested and the employee's account balance is credited with any investment gains or losses. Some plans invest only in a single fund and all employees share in the aggregate gains and losses. It is more common, however, for employers to offer two or more investment funds and allow employees to choose how their account balances are invested. Available choices might include a fixed income fund (or a guaranteed interest contract with an insurance company) and an equity fund. In the case of a profit-sharing plan, the employee might also be given the choice of investing in an employer stock fund. (In some profit-sharing plans—and many savings plans—a minimum amount must be invested in employer stock.)

---

[5] Presumably, voluntary (unmatched) aftertax employee contributions will also be subject to the ACP test. This, too, could have an adverse effect on the use of this feature.

Defined Benefit Plans

A defined benefit plan is structured to provide a fixed amount of pension benefit at the employee's normal retirement age. The benefit can be a flat dollar amount or flat percentage of pay. It is more common, however, for employees to accrue a unit of benefit for each year of service or participation in the plan. This unit can be a percentage of pay (e.g., 1 percent) or, in the case of some negotiated or hourly employee plans, a dollar amount (e.g., $15).

If a plan provides for a pay-related benefit, the benefit can be determined with reference to the employee's pay each year (a career pay plan) or it can be determined with reference to the employee's pay averaged over a period (such as three or five years) just prior to retirement (a final pay plan). The final pay plan has the advantage of establishing an employee's pension amount on a basis that reflects preretirement inflation, but the employer assumes the cost associated with such inflation. The career pay plan does not protect employees to the same extent, but employers who adopt such plans generally update accrued benefits from time to time to bring actual benefits in line with current compensation. An employer who does this retains some control over the cost of inflation. (A defined contribution plan is, in effect, a career pay plan, but there is no equivalent practice of updating accrued benefits; however, employees might have some degree of inflation protection if the investment return credited to their account balances is higher because of such inflation.) The value of benefits under a nonpay-related plan can also be eroded by inflation. Most of these plans are negotiated, however, and benefits are periodically updated through the collective bargaining process.

The actual formula used in a plan may provide for a full unit of benefit for each year of service or participation, or there may be a maximum period (e.g., 30 years) for which benefits are credited. Some plans provide for a full credit for a specified number of years and a partial credit for years in excess of this number. In any event, the actual design of the formula (including the choice of a career or final pay approach) should reflect the employer's objectives as to income replacement levels.

Integrated Formulas

Most pay-related plans are integrated in some fashion with Social Security benefits. The concept of integration recognizes that Social Security benefits are of relatively greater value to lower paid employees than they are to the highly paid—particularly on an aftertax basis. Thus, integrated formulas are weighted to compensate for this difference. This approach is sanctioned by federal tax law, but stringent rules must be followed to prevent the plan from discriminating in favor of highly paid employees.

There are, in general, two ways for integrating plan and Social Security benefits. The first approach—the "excess" method—provides a contribution or benefit for pay over a stipulated level (the integration level) that is higher than that provided for pay below this level. The second approach—the "offset" method—is used in defined benefit plans and provides that the employee's gross plan benefit is reduced by some amount representing the employer-provided portion of the employee's Social Security benefit.

For defined contribution plans, the contribution rate for pay above the plan's integration level is limited to two times the rate for pay below the integration level. Also, the spread between the two contribution rates cannot exceed the greater of: (1) 5.7 percent, or (2) the Social Security tax for old-age benefits. The integration level for a defined contribution plan may be any amount up to the Social Security taxable wage base at the beginning of the plan year.

For defined benefit excess plans, the accrual rate for pay above the plan's integration level cannot be more than two times the accrual rate for pay below this level. In addition, the spread between these accrual rates cannot exceed a "permitted disparity"—three quarters of 1 percent for each year of participation up to a maximum of 35 years, or a maximum spread of 26¼ percent. The integration level for these plans may be any amount up to the Social Security taxable wage base at the beginning of the plan year. The permitted disparity will be reduced, however, if the plan's integration level exceeds the Social Security covered compensation level—the average of Social Security taxable wage bases for the preceding 35 years. The permitted disparity will also be reduced for plans with a subsidized early retirement benefit.

For defined benefit offset plans, the benefit otherwise accrued cannot be reduced, by the offset, by more than 50 percent. Also, the offset cannot exceed three quarters of 1 percent of final average pay multiplied by years of service up to a maximun of 35 years. For this purpose, final average pay is determined by ignoring pay over the Social Security taxable wage base. The three quarters of 1 percent factor will be reduced, in regulations to be issued for individuals whose final average pay exceeds the Social Security covered compensation level, and for plans with subsidized early retirement benefits.

Limitations

The IRC imposes several limitations on contributions and benefits for highly paid employees. One, which was added by the Tax Reform Act of

1986 and will become effective in 1989, limits the amount of pay that can be taken into account for most qualified plan purposes to $200,000. Another change, effective in 1987, affects profit-sharing plans with a cash or deferred arrangement: The maximum amount that can be deferred each year by an employee on an optional basis will be $7,000.

Under Section 415 of the IRC, a defined benefit plan cannot provide a benefit that exceeds $90,000 or 100 percent of pay, if less, per year. This $90,000 limit is actuarially reduced for retirements before the Social Security retirement age. The annual addition under a defined contribution plan for any employee cannot exceed $30,000 or 25 percent of pay, if less. An overall limit applies to individuals covered under both a defined benefit and a defined contribution plan. In effect, the combined plan dollar limit is 125 percent of the limits considered individually. The combined plan percentage limit is 140 percent. Most employers maintain "excess benefit" plans to restore benefits lost by reason of these limits.

All of the dollar amounts referred to above are indexed to increase with changes in the Consumer Price Index (CPI), generally beginning in 1988. The $30,000 limit for defined contribution plans, however, will not be increased until changes in the CPI have caused the defined benefit plan limit to increase to $120,000.

Top-Heavy Plans

Special rules apply to any plan that is considered top-heavy. In general, this occurs when the value of accrued benefits for key employees is more than 60 percent of the value of all accrued benefits. If this happens:

- The benefit accrual for non-key employees under a defined benefit plan must be at least 2 percent of pay.
- The contributions made for non-key employees under a defined contribution plan must be at least 3 percent of pay.
- The Section 415 limits can be further reduced unless special conditions are met.
- Special and more rapid vesting requirements will apply.

Vesting

A tax-qualified pension or profit-sharing plan must provide that the value of any employee contribution is vested at all times. In addition, an employee must be vested in the accrued benefit attributable to employer contributions at normal retirement and, in any event, after a reasonable length of service. Beginning in 1989, an employer may satisfy this requirement with either of two vesting schedules. The first, and simplest, is five-year "cliff" vesting—all accrued benefits fully vest after five years of service. The second schedule permits graded vesting; 20 percent of accrued benefits vest after three years of service and that percentage increases in 20 percent multiples each year until 100 percent vesting is achieved after seven years. There are two exceptions to these new standards: (1) negotiated multiemployer plans may continue to use 10-year cliff vesting, and (2) top-heavy plans must provide for 100 percent vesting after three years of service or provide for graded vesting with a 100 percent interest achieved in six years.

It should be noted that vesting refers to the right to receive accrued benefits in the form of a retirement benefit. The law does not require an employer-provided death benefit if an employee dies after meeting the plan's vesting requirements; however, the law does require automatic joint and survivor protection if a vested employee dies.

Defined benefit plans usually provide that if an employee terminates employment, his or her vested benefit will be payable at retirement. Defined contribution plans usually pay the employee's vested account balance at termination, although the employee must be given the opportunity to leave the balance in the plan to be paid at a later time. Most plans, including defined benefit plans, have a provision permitting the payment of small benefit amounts (worth less than $3,500) at termination.

Death Benefits

Qualified plans must comply with the joint and survivor requirements of the IRC—whether the vested employee dies before or after retirement. These benefits, however, need not be provided at any cost to the employer.

Even though the inclusion of employer-provided death benefits is fully optional, if they are included the IRS requires that they be incidental to the primary purpose of the plan, which is to provide retirement benefits. This requirement limits the amount of preretirement lump-sum death benefits to 100 times the employee's expected monthly pension or the reserve for this amount, if greater. (An employee's full account balance, of course, can be paid under a defined contribution plan.) Postretirement death benefits provided under an optional form of payment are generally limited so that no more than 50 percent of the value of the employee's pension can be used to continue death benefits to individuals other than the employee's spouse.

Although death benefits are optional, most defined contribution plans provide for a death benefit of the employee's remaining account balance at time of death—whether before or after retirement.

The practice for defined benefit plans varies. If plan benefits are funded with individual life insurance policies, there is likely to be a preretirement death benefit up to 100 times the employee's expected monthly pension. Except for this type of insurance, however, it is unusual for defined benefit plans to pay lump-sum benefits from employer contributions. (If employees have made contributions, these are almost always payable as a death benefit, usually with interest but less any pension payments made to the employee prior to death.) The most common form of employer-provided death benefit under defined benefit plans is a spouse or survivor benefit, under which some part of the employee's accrued benefit is payable, in periodic installments, to the employee's spouse or some other survivor. This benefit is usually payable for life in the case of a spouse or another adult such as a dependent parent; in the case of surviving children, the benefit is usually payable until the child reaches a stipulated age. Although such a benefit could be paid for deaths occurring both before and after retirement, postretirement survivor benefits are provided less frequently because of their higher cost. For the most part, survivor benefits are limited to surviving spouses. As noted, however, some plans will pay benefits to dependent parents or children if there is no surviving spouse.

An employer can provide a survivor benefit indirectly by subsidizing the rates used for joint and survivor protection; that is, by not charging the employee the full actuarial cost of the protection. The customary practice of employers who want to pay for this benefit, however, is simply to do so on a basis that involves no cost to employees.

Disability Benefits

A pension or profit-sharing plan need not provide a disability benefit as such. Of course, if an employee is otherwise vested and terminates employment because of disability, regular benefits payable on termination of employment must be available.

Most employers provide disability income benefits under separate plans. When this is the case, the employer's pension arrangement usually operates to complement the disability income plan by providing for continued benefit accruals or contributions during the period of disability.

Some employers, however, make their pension arrangement the major source of benefits for employees who incur a long-term disability (usually one that lasts for more than six months). Under a defined contribution plan, for example, the employee might be fully vested in his or her account balance, regardless of service, and this amount could be made available in the case of disability—either in a lump sum or in the form of installment payments. A defined benefit plan could treat the disability as an early retirement even though the employee had not satisfied the regular requirements, and might even waive the reduction in benefit that would otherwise occur at early retirement. A defined benefit plan might also provide for a separately stated benefit in the case of disability, possibly with more liberal age and service requirements than those that apply for early retirement. Disability income benefits from defined benefit plans are found more often in negotiated plans than they are in plans covering nonrepresented employees.

From the standpoint of benefit adequacy, employees are usually better off with separate, pay-related disability benefits. Those benefits payable from qualified plans (whether defined contribution or defined benefit) reach reasonable levels only for those employees who have long periods of service or participation.

Other Plan Provisions

Provisions dealing with the following matters must also be included in any pension arrangement:

- The employer's right to amend and terminate the plan.
- Protection of employee rights in the event of plan mergers or the transfer or acquisition of plan assets.
- Treatment of employees on leave of absence (including military leave).
- Rehiring of retirees who are receiving benefits.
- The ability to make benefit payments to a payee who is a minor or otherwise incompetent.
- A prohibition against employees making assignments.
- The rights and obligations of plan fiduciaries, including the right to delegate or allocate responsibilities.

DEFINED CONTRIBUTION VERSUS DEFINED BENEFIT PLANS

A critical decision for any employer who is about to adopt a pension plan is whether to use the defined contribution or defined benefit approach or a combination of the two. As noted at the outset of this chapter, most employees are now covered by defined benefit plans, but the defined contribution approach has grown in popularity since the passage of the Employment Retirement Income Security Act (ERISA). Some of this popularity is attributable to the positive treatment afforded these plans by legislation over the past 10 years; for example, the laws dealing with individual retirement accounts (IRAs), simplified employee pensions (SEPs), 401(k) plans, employee stock ownership plans (ESOPs), and flexible compensation arrangements. Some is also due to legislation that has made it increasingly difficult to design and administer defined benefit plans—changes in the Social Security normal retirement age, joint and survivor requirements, age and sex discrimination laws, provisions relating to qualified domestic relations orders, and the like.

Whatever the reason, more and more employers, including those who maintain defined benefit plans, are examining the defined contribution approach to providing retirement benefits. Thus, it is important to understand and evaluate the basic characteristics of both approaches. The following factors should be considered in deciding which approach is appropriate in a given situation.

1. Most employers have specific income replacement objectives in mind when they establish a retirement plan. A defined benefit plan can be structured to achieve these objectives. The defined contribution approach will probably produce benefits that either fall short of or exceed these objectives for individual employees.
2. By the same token, most employers want to take Social Security benefits into account so that the combined level of benefits from both sources will produce the desired results. Defined contribution plans can be integrated with Social Security benefits to some extent by adjusting contribution levels, but integration can be accomplished more efficiently under defined benefit plans.
3. The defined benefit plan requires an employer commitment to pay the cost of the promised benefits. Thus, the employer must assume any additional costs associated with inflation and adverse investment results. The defined contribution plan transfers these risks to employees and allows the employer to fix its cost.
4. A deferred profit-sharing plan offers an employer the ultimate in contribution and funding flexibility. The money purchase pension plan, however, offers little flexibility because contributions are fixed and must be made each year. Although the defined benefit plan involves an employer commitment as to ultimate cost, there can be significant funding flexibility on a year-to-year basis through the use of various actuarial methods and assumptions, the amortization of liabilities, and the operation of the minimum funding standard account. (There is less flexibility with respect to establishing the annual charge to earnings for

defined benefit plans, however, as a result of new accounting standards.)

5. The other side of the cost issue concerns benefits for employees. A defined benefit plan can protect the employee against the risk of preretirement inflation. In a defined contribution plan, this risk is assumed by the employee, who must rely primarily on investment results to increase the value of benefits during inflationary periods.
6. Employees also assume the risk of investment loss under a defined contribution plan. Many observers feel it is inappropriate for the average employee to assume such a risk with respect to a major component of his or her retirement security.
7. The typical defined contribution plan provides that the employee's account balance is payable in the event of death and, frequently, in case of disability. This, of course, produces additional plan costs or, alternatively, lower retirement benefits if overall costs are held constant. An employer who is interested primarily in providing retirement benefits can use available funds more efficiently for this purpose under a defined benefit plan.
8. Many observers believe that a more equitable allocation of employer contributions occurs under a defined benefit plan because the employee's age, past service, and pay can all be taken into account; the typical defined contribution plan allocates contributions only on the basis of pay. On the other hand, the very nature of a final pay defined benefit plan is that the value of total benefits accrued becomes progressively greater each year as the employee approaches retirement; under a defined contribution plan, a greater value will accrue during the early years of participation. As a result of the greater values accrued in earlier years, defined contribution plans produce higher benefits and costs for terminating employees than do defined benefit plans.
9. Profit-sharing and savings plans offer two potential advantages that are not available under defined benefit and money purchase pension plans. Profit sharing can create employee incentives. These plans can also invest in employer securities, giving employees, as shareholders, the opportunity to identify with overall corporate interests.
10. Younger employees are apt to perceive a defined contribution plan, with its accumulating account values, to be of more value than a defined benefit plan. The reverse is probably true for older employees. Thus, the average age of the group to be covered can be critical.

11. Defined benefit plans are subject to the plan termination provisions of ERISA, thus requiring the employer to pay annual Pension Benefit Guaranty Corporation (PBGC) premiums and exposing the employer's net worth to liability if the plan is terminated with insured but unfunded benefit promises. Defined contribution plans do not have this exposure.

These factors will have different significance for different employers, and a choice that is appropriate for one organization may be inappropriate for another. Many employers will find that a combination of the two approaches is the right answer—a defined benefit plan that provides a basic layer of benefits, along with a defined contribution arrangement that is a source of supplemental benefits.

CHAPTER 25

PROFIT-SHARING PLANS

Bruce A. Palmer

INTRODUCTION

Programs providing retirement income have been the recipients of great attention in recent years. Reasons for this attention are many and varied but most of them relate fundamentally to inflation, other economic problems, and the inability of individuals to provide for their own economic security during their retirement years without assistance from some formal group savings or social program. With the increasing concern expressed about the future viability of the Social Security program and its ability to provide significant benefit levels to most retirees, substantial additional attention has been focused on private employer-sponsored retirement programs.

This chapter continues the discussion of retirement plans that began in Chapter 24 and will extend throughout Part Six of the *Handbook*. Specifically, the chapter focuses on profit-sharing plans as defined in Section 401(a) of the Internal Revenue Code (IRC). Collectively, these plans constitute a major component of the overall retirement benefit structure existing in the private sector.

DEFINITION OF *PROFIT SHARING*

A profit-sharing plan, as the name implies, is a plan or program for sharing company profits with the firm's employees. The contributions to a qualified, deferred profit-sharing plan are accumulated in a tax-sheltered account for the primary purpose of providing income to employees during their retirement years. While the accumulation of income for retirement purposes is their main objective, deferred profit-sharing plans often provide for the distribution of monies on other prescribed occasions to employees or their beneficiaries.

It is important to examine the definition of a profit-sharing plan, as described in federal income-tax regulations:

> A profit-sharing plan is a plan established and maintained by an employer to provide for the participation in his profits by his employees or their beneficiaries. The plan must provide a definite predetermined formula for allocating the contributions made to the plan among the participants and for distributing the funds accumulated under the plan after a fixed number of years, the attainment of a stated age, or upon the prior occurrence of some event such as layoff, illness, disability, retirement, death, or severance of employment.[1]

Under the Employee Retirement Income Security Act of 1974 (ERISA) and the Internal Revenue Code (IRC), profit-sharing plans are treated as defined contribution or individual account plans. Thus, as is true for all defined contribution plans, the employer's financial commitment under a profit-sharing plan relates to the payment of (annual) contributions to the plan. The employer is under no financial obligation to provide a specific dollar amount of retirement benefit in these plans. Further, the employer contributions to defined contribution plans are allocated to individual accounts set up for each plan participant.[2] The contribution amounts in the individual accounts are augmented by each employee's share of any investment earnings on the plan assets and, possibly, further by the proceeds of any forfeitures of accounts created by nonvested (or partially vested) participants who have terminated employment with the firm. As a defined contribution type of plan, the amount of benefit available to the participant at retirement will be solely a function of the amount in the individual account at that time and the level of monthly income which that accumulated amount will purchase. The larger the individual account balance, the greater the amount of monthly income that can be purchased.

---

[1] Reg. 1.401-1(b)(1)(ii).

[2] Federal regulations require that individual accounts be maintained for each plan participant in defined contribution plans.

For purposes of qualifying a plan with the Internal Revenue Service, certain other types of defined contribution or individual account plans generally may be treated the same as, or similar to, profit-sharing plans. These plans include thrift or savings plans, stock-bonus plans, and employee stock-ownership plans (ESOPs). However, since thrift and savings plans (Chapter 27), stock-bonus plans and ESOPs (Chapters 29 and 30) are covered elsewhere in the *Handbook,* these plans will not be described here. Further, while many Keogh (HR-10) plans also involve a profit-sharing-type formula, the discussion presented in this chapter focuses on corporate profit-sharing plans.

The concept of profit sharing, in its broadest sense, encompasses any program under which the firm's profits are shared with its employees. Thus, this concept includes both cash plans and deferred distribution plans. Under cash profit-sharing plans, the share of the profits to be paid to the employees is distributed to them currently as a bonus or a wage/salary supplement (either in the form of cash or employer stock). As a result, these distributions are included in the employees' income in the year of distribution and taxed on top of their other wages, salaries, and other income.[3] Deferred distribution profit-sharing plans are programs in which the profits to be distributed are credited to employee accounts (held under trust) and accumulated for later distribution (e.g., upon retirement, or some other specified event, such as death, disability, or severance of employment, or according to the terms of any plan withdrawal provisions).

In actuality, there are three basic approaches to profit sharing since it is possible for a firm to have a combination cash and deferred profit-sharing plan covering essentially the same group(s) of employees. Under this arrangement, a portion of the profit-sharing allocation is distributed currently to the participant with the remainder deferred. A combination plan can be designed in one of two ways: (1) there may be two separate plans—one cash and the other deferred, or (2) there may be only one plan that possesses both current and deferred features. This latter type of combination plan often is referred to as a cash *or* deferred profit-sharing

---

[3] Payments under cash profit-sharing plans may be made as soon as the respective participants' allocations are determined. Thus, the structure of these plans is much simpler than that of deferred plans since there is no trust fund, no assets to be invested, and so on. Of course, the major disadvantage of these plans is that the payments are currently taxed to the participants.

plan. Many employers have shown a renewed interest in this type of plan since the passage of the Revenue Act of 1978.[4]

While ERISA, under a "grandfather" provision, permitted existing (on June 27, 1974) cash or deferred profit-sharing plans to remain in effect, this law provided no authority for the creation of new plans. The Revenue Act of 1978 added two IRC Sections, 401(k) and 402(a)(8), which together create a basis for the establishment of new qualified cash or deferred plans. IRC Section 401(k) established special additional qualification rules for cash or deferred profit-sharing plans (see Chapter 28). These rules became effective for plan years beginning after December 31, 1979. IRC Section 402(a)(8) relates to the tax treatment accorded these plans. IRC Section 402(a)(8) is particularly important to the continued viability of cash or deferred profit-sharing plans, since under these plans the participant has the right to elect the portion of the total distribution that will be received in the current year (and therefore taxed currently) and the remaining portion that will be deferred. Under this section of the Code, the plan participant can elect annually to receive all or part of the yearly profit-sharing allocation in cash. The portion of each year's allocation that is not received in cash is contributed to the individual participant's account under the deferred portion of the plan, held in trust, and invested until distribution at a later time. The key tax advantage of these plans is that the participant's right to elect cash will not trigger the application of the doctrine of constructive receipt to that portion of the profit-sharing distribution that is actually deferred, thereby preserving its tax-deferred status. However, if the deferred portions of the allocations do not meet the requirements of IRC Section 401(k), all employer contributions (over which the employee held an option to elect) will be considered to have been distributed or made available and, consequently, would be currently taxable to the employee.

When discussing profit-sharing plans in the context of qualified deferred compensation programs (as determined under IRC Section 401), the concept of profit sharing refers to the deferred distribution form or the combination cash/deferred profit-sharing plan. In the subsequent discussion of profit sharing in this chapter, the term *profit-sharing plan* refers to the deferred distribution type of plan, rather than cash profit-sharing, unless otherwise noted. Further, even though combination cash/deferred profit-sharing plans may be qualified with the IRS, future discussion concentrates primarily on the features of the deferred component of these

---

[4] Robert C. Wender, "Renewed Life for Cash or Deferred Profit Sharing Plans," *CLU Journal* 35, no. 4 (October 1981), pp. 18–21.

plans. Although cash distributions of profits are a relatively popular device for sharing profits, this chapter is more concerned with the aspects of plan design, the legal requirements, and the tax aspects surrounding deferred distributions from profit-sharing plans.[5]

Some profit-sharing plans provide for the payment of supplementary contributions (usually voluntary) by the covered employees. However, this chapter does not address any distinctive features that might be attributed to contributory profit-sharing plans nor, as stated earlier, will it focus on thrift or savings plans.[6]

While employer contributions to a profit-sharing plan and plan qualification requirements are described later in much detail, it is worthwhile to make three further observations. First, since employer contributions are keyed to the existence of profits, profit-sharing plans provide maximum contribution flexibility to the employer, because in a low, zero, or negative profit year it is possible the firm does not have to make any contributions at all. There is no fixed minimum level of contribution required by the Internal Revenue Code, as is the case for money purchase and defined benefit pension plans. It also is possible for the firm to provide that no contribution will be made to the plan in any year unless profits exceed a specified level or a predetermined rate of return on stockholder equity. As a result, employer contributions to profit-sharing plans may even be characterized as "voluntary;" however, contributions must be "substantial and recurring" to meet the qualification requirement of plan permanency.

---

[5] Although enjoying significant popularity as an employee benefit, cash (or current distribution) profit-sharing plans are at a considerable disadvantage in terms of their tax treatment when compared with the tax advantages possessed by qualified deferred profit-sharing plans. Further, since these plans provide for a current distribution of profits (and thus are simply a method of providing for the payment of bonuses to all covered employees), they do not constitute retirement plans. This chapter is concerned essentially with profit-sharing plans as a vehicle for providing cash accumulation or retirement income, or both.

[6] The IRS does not have a separation or division of requirements addressing only thrift plans. Thus, many thrift and savings plans qualify with the IRS under the profit-sharing rules and hence would be deemed to be profit-sharing plans. However, the purist would argue that there still exists a fundamental difference between a contributory profit-sharing plan and a thrift or savings plan. In the latter case, employer contributions to the plan are usually fixed at some predetermined percentage "match" (e.g., 25, 50, or 100 percent) of the employee contributions for the purpose of encouraging thrift on the part of the employee. Thus, employer contributions to a thrift plan are dependent primarily on the "level of employee thrift." In contrast, employer contributions to a contributory profit-sharing plan are primarily a function of the "level of profits." Further, in the case of contributory profit-sharing plans where the employee contributions are voluntary, employer contributions to a participant's account often are not made contingent on the payment of contributions by the participant.

Second, Section 404(a)(3) of the IRC permits deductible contributions to a qualified profit-sharing plan to be made out of either current or accumulated profits of the firm.[7]. Thus, if a firm has accumulated profits from previous years of operations, it is possible for the firm to make deductible contributions to the profit-sharing plan that exceed the firm's profit for that year.[8] Finally, when there exist multiple corporations belonging to an "affiliated group" (e.g., a chain of corporations controlled by a common parent) that jointly maintain a profit-sharing plan, IRC Section 404(a)(3)(B) permits those members of the affiliated group that have profits to contribute (and receive a deduction) on behalf of those members that do not have profits.

IMPORTANCE OF PROFIT-SHARING PLANS

While several notable profit-sharing plans had been in existence prior to 1939, that year seems to signal the beginning of the major growth experienced in profit-sharing plans. In 1939 the U.S. Senate's endorsement of the profit-sharing concept, together with subsequent favorable tax legislation, provided the stimulus for the establishment of profit-sharing plans. In the 25 years preceding the enactment of ERISA, the number of deferred profit-sharing plans doubled approximately every 5 years. However, the passage of ERISA, with its reforms and the uncertainties created by its enactment, had a major deterrent effect on the establishment of all types of qualified plans, initially even including profit-sharing plans. The numbers of new profit-sharing plans qualified during 1974 (the year of enactment of ERISA) and during each of the three following years are presented below:[9]

Year	*Number*
1974	24,779
1975	11,162
1976	6,439
1977	9,523

[7] Under prior law, employer contributions to a profit-sharing plan were required to be based on current or accumulated profits. This was repealed under the Tax Reform Act of 1986. An employer now can contribute to a profit-sharing plan even when there are no current or accumulated profits.

[8] Although in practice this event is probably rare, under certain circumstances (presumably related to tax planning) a firm might decide to contribute amounts to the plan which are greater than the firm's profits in a given year.

[9] These figures were obtained from the *Employee Benefit Plan Review Research Reports* (Chicago: Charles D. Spencer & Associates).

The year 1978 became a record-setter—the number of profit-sharing plan approvals exceeded 25,000. Profit-sharing plans continue to remain extremely important in terms of the number of annual new plan approvals.

As indicated above, ERISA had a dramatic reduction effect on the number of new profit-sharing plan approvals for the three years immediately following the year of ERISA's passage. However, the reduction percentage in the number of new pension plan approvals (particularly in the case of defined benefit plans) was even more dramatic.[10] A major reason why deferred profit-sharing plans (and defined contribution plans, in general) assumed a relatively greater role in retirement income planning immediately after the enactment of ERISA in 1974 is that these plans are subject to fewer of ERISA's requirements than are defined benefit pension plans, particularly in the areas of minimum funding and the plan termination insurance and contingent employer liability requirements of the Pension Benefit Guaranty Corporation (PBGC).[11] The popularity of profit-sharing plans also may be due to the increasing recognition of their possible importance as contributors to improved corporate performance. A major study of the 38 largest profit-sharing plans concluded that they seem to have a positive correlation with superior corporate performance.[12] This study further concluded that profit-sharing companies, on average, tend to outperform their competitors who do not have profit-sharing plans, and that a significant reason for the difference in performance is caused by the existence of a profit-sharing plan. The results of this study indicate that the profit-sharing companies outperformed the *Fortune* 500 companies both in terms of the return on sales and the return on equity for the years 1973–76.

The importance of profit-sharing plans is further underscored by the dual purpose that they serve in the overall structure of retirement income planning. Profit-sharing plans often exist as the sole retirement income plan in many firms, particularly in firms of small-to-medium size, where the employers may feel unable to assume the financial commitment associated with a money purchase or defined benefit pension plan.[13] In addi-

---

[10] Ibid.

[11] Later statistics on new plan approvals indicate that the relative growth of profit sharing and other defined contribution plans (when contrasted with defined benefit plan growth) has slowed somewhat in comparison to the 1974–1978 period. *Ibid.*

[12] *Profit Sharing in 38 Large Companies* (Evanston, Ill.: Profit-Sharing Research Foundation, 1978). Collectively, these 38 companies provided coverage to more than 1 million participants.

[13] Profit-sharing plans have become especially popular in those corporations where the ownership is closely held. As with all forms of qualified retirement plans, the profit-sharing

tion, profit-sharing plans many times are formed as a supplement to a pension plan. There are several advantages of this combination approach. Most important, in addition to providing for the possibility of greater total benefits, the pension plan can provide employees with protection against the down-side risk that corporate profits will be low, leading to low levels of contributions to the profit-sharing plan and, ultimately, to the payment of inadequate profit-sharing plan benefits.

EMPLOYER OBJECTIVES IN ESTABLISHING A DEFERRED PROFIT-SHARING PLAN

An employer normally has a number of specific objectives in electing to establish a qualified deferred profit-sharing plan. Certainly, the one objective that comes immediately to mind is that of providing a means or a vehicle, on behalf of covered employees, for the accumulation on a tax-favored basis of substantial amounts of assets that, in turn, would constitute a primary source of income to be distributed at retirement or at other specified occasions. As part of the overall objectives in establishing a qualified plan of any type, the employer is seeking the various tax advantages associated with such a plan. These include the deductibility (within limits) to the firm of employer contributions, the tax-free accumulation of monies held in trust under the plan, the current nontaxability to the employee of employer contributions and investment earnings on plan assets, and special income-tax treatment accorded qualifying lump-sum distributions.[14] In addition to these, however, employers typically have one or

---

plan has the capability to convert a significant portion of the profits that would likely otherwise be paid either in corporate or personal income taxes into a tax-sheltered account where the monies compound with tax-sheltered investment income. The Tax Reform Act of 1986, with its lower maximum tax rates for both individuals and corporations, may lead to a decrease in the popularity of all qualified retirement income plans where tax sheltering has been a primary motivator in their creation. However, it is too early to determine whether closely held businesses will find qualified retirement plans to be unattractive in an era of lower marginal tax rates.

[14] Under prior law, qualifying lump-sum distributions were eligible for the so-called 10-year forward averaging treatment. Capital gains treatment could also be elected for any pre-1974 portion of the distribution. The Tax Reform Act of 1986 repealed the 10-year averaging rules and applied a 6-year phaseout of the capital gains treatment accorded pre-1974 amounts. The new tax treatment provides for five-year forward averaging on a one-time basis, but only for qualifying distributions made after attainment of age 59½. A special election, or transition rule, is available for individuals who attained age 50 before January 1, 1986.

more other important objectives in establishing a profit-sharing plan covering the firm's employees.

As an employee benefit, profit-sharing plans constitute a significant method of compensating employees and of achieving various employer compensation objectives. As such, a profit-sharing plan may be viewed as a compensation device that constitutes a major component of the total compensation approach of those employers who have adopted such plans.

Employers might also desire to establish profit-sharing plans in the hope of improving the productivity and efficiency of the firm.[15] Finding ways to increase productivity has become a major concern in the U.S. today. For many firms, although sales have been increasing over recent years, costs have increased more rapidly and thus have resulted in declining profits. The establishment of new profit-sharing plans might constitute a partial solution to the productivity problem in the United States. Increased productivity might result in one or more of several ways. The establishment of a profit-sharing plan may lead to improved employee morale, and provide a source of motivation to employees to perform in a more productive and efficient manner.[16] Since employer contributions to the plan (and consequently the ultimate level of benefits received by the employee) are tied to the firm's profits, a profit-sharing plan provides the employee with a direct incentive to become more efficient, more productive, resulting in lower costs and higher profits to the firm.[17] To the extent that these anticipated results actually are attained, employees, management, and stockholders alike should all benefit from the establishment of a profit-sharing plan. Also, improved productivity might result in other ways, such as through a reduction in employee turnover rates,[18] through a

---

[15] For an extensive treatment of profit sharing and its effect on productivity, see *Increasing Productivity Through Profit Sharing* (Evanston, Ill.: Profit Sharing Research Foundation, 1981).

[16] See Bert L. Metzger, "How to Motivate With Profit Sharing," *Pension World,* February 1978, pp. 24–28, 32–33.

[17] Major arguments also are presented against this line of reasoning. For example, it is argued that profit-sharing plans reward poor performance equally as well as good performance, thereby questioning whether profit-sharing plans are truly motivational. Further, there is the question about how many employees in a firm can really influence profitability. In summary, the relationships among motivation, increased productivity, and the establishment of deferred profit-sharing plans are still strongly debated issues.

[18] Since the employee is likely aware (*a*) that the vested portion of the funds in his or her individual account will increase with time, and (*b*) that his or her account balance will be further augmented by reallocated forfeitures of other terminating participants who were less than fully vested, an incentive is created for this employee to remain with the firm.

decrease in the absenteeism rate of employees, through an improved ability of the firm to attract higher caliber individuals, and through stimulation of employees to make suggestions for improvement in the "way things are done." All these have the potential to result in a dramatic increase in the productivity and profits of those firms establishing profit-sharing plans. Some firms, in fact, have experienced increased productivity levels of 30 to 40 percent or more after the establishment of a profit-sharing plan. As further support, an important study comparing the profit records of a large number of companies throughout six major industries during the period 1958–77 showed that companies with profit-sharing plans outperformed those companies without such plans by substantial margins.[19] It might be argued that the establishment of a pension plan (either money purchase or defined benefit) also might result in improved productivity to the firm; however, in theory there should exist a more direct relationship between the establishment of a profit-sharing plan and increased productivity than is true for the establishment of a pension plan.

Although both profit-sharing plans and pension plans constitute major approaches to providing asset accumulation and economic security for the covered employees and their dependents, these two approaches provide the employer with substantially different levels of funding flexibility. Under a money purchase or a defined benefit pension plan, the employer has a fixed commitment (not contingent on profit levels) to contribute amounts that meet certain ERISA-prescribed minimum requirements.[20] In most instances, these requirements will result in the employer having to make contributions to the plan during each and every year. Under a profit-sharing plan, it is possible for the firm to not make any contributions to the plan for a given year (or several years). This offers substantially greater contribution flexibility to the employer under the profit-sharing approach than under either the money purchase or defined benefit pension plan approach. The lack of a fixed yearly contribution obligation under profit-sharing plans is especially advantageous for small businesses and for new firms that may be unable to assume the fixed costs required of pension plans. In years of no profits, or when profits fall below a predetermined level, no employer contributions need be made. In contrast, in years of high profits, larger than average contributions might be made to

---

[19] *A Study of the Financial Significance of Profit Sharing—1958 to 1977* (Chicago: Profit-Sharing Council of America, 1980).

[20] For money purchase plans, this entails the payment of a fixed rate of contribution; for defined benefit plans, it requires the payment of contributions at a level necessary to fund the promised benefits. In both cases, it means a specific contribution commitment without regard to the profit levels of the firm.

the profit-sharing plan. In summary, profit-sharing plans possess maximum flexibility with regard to employer contributions.

In establishing any new employee benefit program, most employers will want to take employee desires into account. From the standpoint of the individual employee, in terms of choosing between a profit-sharing plan (or for that matter, any defined contribution plan) and a defined benefit pension plan, the younger and middle-aged employees might prefer the individual account approach inherent in the profit-sharing arrangement over a promised definite level of benefits to be payable many years later at retirement. The defined contribution approach often provides the opportunity to accumulate much greater sums on behalf of younger employees than is true in the case of defined benefit plans. Conversely, older employees generally tend to prefer a defined benefit plan (with its predetermined level of benefits payable in the near future) to either a profit-sharing or a money purchase pension plan. The reason for this preference on the part of older employees is that a profit-sharing or money purchase plan generally will not provide a sufficiently large accumulation of monies to provide adequate retirement benefits for those employees near retirement at the time the plan is established. In choosing between the two approaches, profit-sharing (or money purchase) and defined benefit, the employer should consider the age distribution and the distribution by position within the firm of the employee group to be covered by the plan. In the decision-making process, the employer should also take into consideration the firm's hiring objectives. A defined contribution plan may be preferred if the firm is interested primarily in hiring less experienced, younger employees. In contrast, a defined benefit plan is likely to be more attractive to older executives hired from other firms. Based on these factors, the employer may decide to have a combination profit-sharing and defined benefit plan to appeal to both young and older workers alike.

The employer may be influenced by other objectives in deciding to adopt a profit-sharing plan. For example, as an individual account plan, the employee is provided with the opportunity to share in favorable investment results, which potentially could lead to much higher levels of benefits that can be purchased at retirement.[21] Under defined benefit plans, favorable investment earnings accrue to the benefit of the em-

---

[21] However, the employee also is exposed to the downside risk of low or otherwise unfavorable investment results. This may be a potential source of employee (and possibly employer) dissatisfaction with the plan and, in addition, requires a greater sensitivity on the part of the employer to fiduciary obligations associated with the investment of plan assets. The exposure to potentially increased fiduciary liability constitutes an important disadvantage associated with the adoption of defined contribution plans.

ployer. In addition, in defined contribution plans including profit-sharing, forfeitures of nonvested (and partially vested) terminated participants may be allocated among the remaining participants, thus providing the possibility of even greater benefits to those employees who remain with the firm for long periods.[22] To the extent the employer desires for the employees to share in favorable investment earnings and also share in forfeitures, the profit-sharing approach may be preferred.

Further, the employer may prefer certain other features that may be incorporated into the design of a profit-sharing plan whose incorporation into pension plans is either prohibited or substantially restricted. Specifically, the employer may want to provide the covered employees with the option to make withdrawals from their individual accounts while still actively employed, or the employer may desire that the funds held in the profit-sharing trust be invested in employer stock or other employer securities to a greater extent than permitted under a pension plan. When profit-sharing plan assets are invested in employer securities, the employees have the opportunity to participate to an even greater extent in the success of the company.

Finally, the employer may desire to avoid certain requirements imposed on defined benefit pension plans. These include satisfying specific funding requirements and compliance with the associated minimum funding standards, the payment of plan termination insurance premiums to the Pension Benefit Guaranty Corporation (PBGC), and the exposure to contingent employer liability and the attendent impact on the firm's accounting and financial reports. Further, under profit-sharing plans there should be fewer requirements in the aggregate that must be complied with, less paperwork, and the absence (or substantial reduction) of actuarial cost calculations.

In spite of the many important advantages associated with profit-sharing plans, this discussion would not be complete without identifying some of the important disadvantages associated with the operation of profit-sharing plans, especially since many of these disadvantages are quite significant. One relative disadvantage of profit-sharing plans relates to the difficulty of providing employees with adequate credit for any periods of past service (i.e., service prior to plan inception). Past service credits can be incorporated with relative ease in most defined benefit pension plans. Second, the ultimate benefits payable at retirement under a

---

[22] In the future, the issue of forfeitures and their reallocation may become less important because of the faster vesting requirements imposed by the Tax Reform Act of 1986.

profit-sharing plan (or any other defined contribution plan) may be inadequate for those employees near retirement at the time of plan inception. Third, the profit-sharing amounts contributed to the plan in any year usually are allocated among the individual employee accounts on the basis of the employee's annual compensation. Thus, age and years of service generally are ignored in the profit-sharing allocation formula. Additional disadvantages of profit sharing plans relate to the employee's assumption of the inflation risk, the investment risk (see footnote 21), and the risk of little or no profits to the firm which, collectively, could result in inadequate benefits to the employees.

QUALIFICATION REQUIREMENTS APPLICABLE TO DEFERRED PROFIT-SHARING PLANS

For the most part, the same or similar qualification requirements apply equally to both pension plans and deferred profit-sharing plans. These requirements relate to (1) the plan provisions being contained in a written document (ensuring a formal, enforceable plan), (2) plan permanency, (3) communication of plan provisions to the employees, (4) the plan being established and operated for the exclusive benefit of plan participants or their beneficiaries, (5) minimum participation (eligibility) standards, (6) nondiscrimination in coverage and contributions/benefits, (7) minimum vesting standards, and so forth. Because of the similarity of treatment between pension plans and profit-sharing plans, the discussion of the general legal requirements for plan qualification will be minimized here.

There are, however, a few ways in which profit-sharing plans are treated differently from pension plans for qualification purposes. Additionally, although pension and profit-sharing plans alike are subject to essentially the same eligibility and vesting rules, the eligibility and vesting provisions observed in many profit-sharing plans contain more liberal requirements.

A major way in which the qualification requirements differ between pension plans and profit-sharing plans relates to the investment of plan assets in employer securities. Pension plans (including both defined benefit and money purchase plans) are restricted in terms of their ability to invest plan assets in employer stock. These plans are subject to the ERISA requirement that no more than 10 percent of the fair market value of plan assets can be invested in qualifying employer securities and employer real property. This 10 percent limitation became fully effective after December 31, 1984.[23] ERISA Section 404 limitations do not apply to profit-sharing plans. As a result, profit-sharing plans may invest plan assets in qualifying employer securities and employer real property without restriction on any percentage limitation.[24]

Many employers believe that investment of a portion of profit-sharing plan assets in employer stock provides the employees with additional incentive to improve their performance in job-related activities. The extent to which companies with profit-sharing plans invest a portion of the plan assets in employer stock is likely to be related to several factors, including company size, overall profitability of the firm (including future prospects as regards profitability), marketability of the stock, and others. The Profit Sharing Research Foundation's study on the largest profit-sharing plans in the United States, cited earlier,[25] showed that the investment of profit-sharing plan assets in employer stock is substantially more prevalent among larger companies than among medium-sized firms, and also is more prevalent among companies whose ownership is closely held. Since both advantages and disadvantages are present, great care should be exercised in making decisions concerning the investment of plan assets in employer stock.

As mentioned earlier, profit-sharing plans are not subject to certain provisions of ERISA affecting qualified defined benefit pension plans. These primarily relate to the minimum funding standards and the various plan termination insurance requirements. Further, in defined benefit plans, forfeitures (arising from the termination of one or more participants whose benefits are less than fully vested) must be used to reduce future employer contributions to the plan. In contrast, in profit-sharing plans, forfeitures may be used either to reduce future employer contributions or they may be allocated among the remaining participants in the plan (the usual case), thereby increasing the amounts in their individual accounts.[26]

In addition to those qualification requirements that are distinctive of profit-sharing plans, as described above, other requirements imposed on

---

23 From the covered employee's standpoint, this limitation may not be as important under a defined benefit plan as it is under a money purchase plan. Any appreciation in the employer's stock under the defined benefit plan would serve to reduce future employer contributions, thus resulting in no direct benefit to the employee.

24 Of course, investment of profit-sharing plan assets in employer stock (along with other investment media) must meet the prudent expert standard of ERISA.

25 *Profit Sharing in 38 Large Companies.*

26 From the standpoint of remaining plan participants, the advantage inherent in profit-sharing plans that accrues from reallocation of forfeitures is somewhat mitigated by the presence of more rapid vesting typically found in profit-sharing plans. See *infra.*

qualified profit-sharing plans that are the same as or very similar to those applied to pension plans are still of importance to this section. This is because of their specific application to profit-sharing plans and the way in which these requirements are met (and superseded) in actual plan design. The following discussion will focus on two areas: (1) eligibility (participation) requirements, and (2) vesting requirements.

As regards permissible eligibility requirements, age 21 is the highest minimum age requirement, and one year of service is the longest minimum period of service that may be imposed. (A two-year service requirement is permitted, together with age 21, if the plan provides for full and immediate vesting upon satisfying the plan's eligibility requirements.) These eligibility requirements apply to both profit-sharing and pension plans alike. In addition, the basic coverage rules apply to both profit-sharing and pension plans. Under the Tax Reform Act of 1986, effective for plan years beginning after December 31, 1988, a qualified plan must satisfy one of three alternative coverage tests: (1) at least 70 percent of all (nonexcludable) non–highly compensated employees must be covered; (2) the percentage of non–highly compensated employees covered under the plan must be at least 70 percent of the percentage of highly compensated employees covered by the plan; (3) the previous "fair cross section" test must be satisfied *and* the average benefit for non–highly compensated employees (taking into account all qualified plans maintained by the employer) must be at least 70 percent of the average benefit provided the highly compensated employees.[27] However, for many deferred profit-sharing plans in existence today, the eligibility and coverage provisions tend to be more liberal than what is required as a minimum standard for qualification purposes, and they also tend to be more liberal than those commonly employed in pension plans.

Most profit-sharing plans provide broad coverage of employees although the plans often exclude seasonal and part-time employees (e.g., those who work fewer than 1,000 hours per year). A minimum compensation requirement (for the purpose of integrating the plan with Social Security) is seldom applied in determining eligibility for participation. Some plans make employees eligible on the date of hire. Many others use a minimum service requirement of less than one year. It appears, however, that the majority of plans impose a one-year service requirement. Fur-

---

[27] Employees not meeting the minimum age or service requirements and employees who are members of a collective bargaining unit (where the subject of pension/profit sharing has been bargained in good faith), plus certain nonresident aliens, can be excluded when applying these tests.

ther, there is probably only a limited number of plans that require more than one year of service, in which event the plan must provide full (100 percent) and immediate vesting. Certainly, the use of a maximum age limitation (e.g., age 60) at date of hire is not permitted in profit-sharing plans since these plans are of the defined contribution type. Most profit-sharing plans do not even use a minimum age requirement, despite being permitted to do so under the law. In summary, as regards eligibility and participation, most deferred profit-sharing plans impose only a service eligibility requirement along with the requirement that employees meet a minimum employment test (generally 1,000 hours per year).

Regarding vesting, the Tax Reform Act of 1986 specifies that profit-sharing plans must meet one of two alternative minimum vesting standards: (1) five-year cliff vesting, or (2) seven-year graded vesting. Under the five-year rule, plan participants are not required to have any vested rights in employer-provided benefits until after the completion of five years of service, at which point the participants must be 100 percent vested. Under the seven-year graded vesting rule, participants must be at least 20 percent vested after the completion of three years of service, with the required vesting percentage increasing by 20 percent each year until 100 percent vesting is reached at the end of seven years.[28] An exception to these rules applies to IRC Section 401(k) cash or deferred plans. These plans must provide full and immediate vesting, upon plan participation, in regard to those amounts subject to the cash/deferred election.[29]

A substantial majority of profit-sharing plans provide for more liberal vesting than prescribed under the IRC Section 411(a) alternative minimum standards. A significant percentage of profit-sharing plans provide full and immediate vesting upon plan participation. Some companies provide for full vesting to all plan participants reaching a specified age (e.g., 55) regardless of length of service. Other firms provide full vesting if a

---

[28] These rules are effective for plan years beginning after December 31, 1988. They replaced the original "10-Year Rule," the "5-to-15-Year Rule," and the "Rule of 45" created by ERISA. Collectively bargained multiemployer plans are permitted to continue to comply with the 10-Year Rule. Plans that are classified as "top-heavy" must still comply with additional vesting requirements imposed under the Tax Equity and Fiscal Responsibility Act of 1982 (TEFRA). Specifically, if a plan is "top-heavy," its vesting schedule must comply with one of two rules: (*a*) "three-year cliff vesting," or (*b*) "six-year graded vesting."

[29] Hence, if 40 percent of the distribution may be received in cash or deferred with the other 60 percent required to be deferred, then IRC Section 411 requires nonforfeitability only for the 40 percent subject to the cash/deferred election; vesting for the other 60 percent may be delayed subject to the other minimum vesting standards (e.g., the five-year rule or the seven-year rule).

participant's employment is terminated "through no fault of the employee;" this might occur, for example, at the closing of a plant, department, or smaller organizational unit. Finally, while the law requires that full vesting occur at retirement and upon plan termination, nearly all deferred profit-sharing plans also provide full vesting in the event of the participant's death or total and permanent disability.

The liberal eligibility and vesting requirements typically found in most profit-sharing plans are consistent with an overall employer objective (as regards the establishment of a profit-sharing plan) of providing employees with an incentive to work more efficiently, which, it is hoped, will lead to increased profits for the firm.[30] This objective can be maximized in a deferred profit-sharing plan only through broad participation, through the imposition of few eligibility restrictions, and the providing of liberal vesting.

In conclusion, the employer's reason(s) for establishing a deferred profit-sharing plan, in all likelihood, should have a direct bearing on the specific eligibility and vesting requirements adopted by the plan. That is, an objective of creating employee incentives would indicate short periods for vesting and minimum or no eligibility requirements. Other objectives, such as maximizing the retirement income that may be provided to long-service employees from a specified amount of employer contribution, might indicate longer vesting periods and more stringent eligibility requirements as long as the plan provisions comply with the minimum standards under the law.

---

[30] It also should be noted that the employer's contributions (costs) to a profit-sharing plan are not increased or otherwise affected either by a larger number of participants (through more liberal eligibility requirements) or through more rapid vesting; assuming, of course, that nonvested forfeitures are reallocated among the remaining participants (the typical case) rather than used to reduce future employer contributions. (While this statement is generally true, it is not applicable to those profit-sharing plans that base their contribution on a percentage of compensation subject to a maximum contribution based on profit.) This is in direct contrast to the situation that results in either a money purchase or a defined benefit pension plan. Pension plans that are designed with more liberal eligibility and vesting rules should result in higher costs to the employer. Thus, to reduce total plan costs, pension plans tend to impose more restrictive eligibility rules and less liberal vesting requirements than those used in deferred profit-sharing plans. It is important to note, however, that under profit-sharing plans, the *allocation* of both contributions (profits) and forfeitures among plan participants would be affected by the plan's eligibility and vesting requirements.

CHAPTER 26

PROFIT-SHARING PLANS (continued)

Bruce A. Palmer

CONTRIBUTIONS TO DEFERRED PROFIT-SHARING PLANS

The subject matter pertaining to profit-sharing contributions constitutes a most important topic in regard to the overall design of deferred profit-sharing plans. It is these contribution amounts, together with investment earnings and forfeiture reallocations, that ultimately determine the magnitude of the funds available for distribution to plan participants at retirement or upon other prescribed occasions.

The discussion of profit-sharing contributions is divided into three major subsections. These subsections describe, respectively, the various methods of ascertaining contribution amounts to deferred profit-sharing plans, alternative formulas for allocating the profit-sharing contributions among the plan participants, and the maximum limits imposed under federal tax law on contributions and allocations.

Methods of Determining Profit-Sharing Contributions

A most important concern of profit-sharing plans centers on the question, "How much of the profits should be shared with the employees?" In regard to a specific employer, the portion or percentage of profits that should be contributed is likely to depend on several factors, including (1) the amount and stability of the firm's annual profits; (2) the capital requirements of the firm (e.g., needs for working capital, reserves, and expansion); (3) the level of return to be provided stockholders on their investment in the firm; (4) the presence (or absence) of other capital accumulation or retirement income programs sponsored by the firm; (5) the portion of profits that is to be used in upgrading the (cash) payroll levels of the employees; (6) the maximum limitations under federal tax law applying to annual contributions, deductions, and allocations to participants' accounts; and, of course, (7) the objectives of the plan, particularly the extent to which management believes that the profit-sharing plan serves as a motivator to the covered employees and the extent to which employee behavior can affect, in a significant way, the profit levels of the particular firm in question.[1]

A second area of interest relating to profit-sharing contributions concerns how profits are to be defined. Employers have considerable flexibility in defining "profits" for purposes of their deferred profit-sharing plans, since this term is not defined in great detail under the federal tax laws governing profit-sharing plans. While, traditionally, profits as used in the context of profit-sharing plans relate to current year profits, it is legally permissible for deferred profit-sharing plans to base their profit-sharing contributions on both current profits and profits accumulated from prior years. Further, profits can be defined either in terms of "before-tax profits" or "aftertax profits," with the majority of companies basing their profit-sharing contributions on before-tax profits.[2] Additionally, a significant number of plans provide that only profits in excess of some stipulated minimum dollar amount, or in excess of a minimum return on invested capital, are available for profit sharing.[3] Conditions such

---

[1] One fairly basic concept in this regard is to split profits equally into three shares: (*a*) one third to employees in the form of profit-sharing contributions, (*b*) one third to stockholders in the form of dividends, and (*c*) one third to customers, either through price reductions or expenditures for product improvement. In some instances, element (*c*) is eliminated, with that share going into company surplus and being available for reinvestment in the company's operations. It is important to note that when companies provide as much as a one-third share of profits to employees, it may be that not all of these monies will flow into a deferred profit-sharing arrangement due to limitations on tax deductions and allocations (and possibly for other reasons). Rather, a substantial portion of these profit-sharing monies might be distributed immediately to the employees.

[2] It should be noted that employers are permitted to determine "profits" in accordance with generally accepted accounting principles, rather than in accordance with federal income-tax laws to the extent that these definitions may differ.

[3] Even when a specific provision for a minimum return on capital is not included in a profit-sharing formula, the concept generally is taken into consideration in the profit-sharing deliberations, even though in an indirect way.

as these are commonly referred to as "prior reservations for capital," or simply "prior reservations." Their purpose is to protect the financial interests of the company's shareholders. Employers who incorporate a prior reservation in determining their profit-sharing contributions commonly share a greater percentage of profits, once the reservation has been satisfied, than plans that do not include a prior reservation. The rationale for smaller profit-sharing percentages (often between 5 percent and 10 percent of before-tax profits) in companies not stipulating a prior reservation is that these percentages are applied to all profits, not just those amounts in excess of some stipulated level, as is the case with employers that specify a prior reservation. Prior reservations may be stated in a number of ways including, for example, (1) placing a minimum dollar limitation (e.g., $25,000) on profits, (2) requiring a specified minimum return (e.g., 5 percent) on net worth, or (3) stating a minimum amount (e.g., 30 cents per share) for stockholder dividends before any profit-sharing distributions will be made to the employees.

Another aspect relating to methods of determining profit-sharing contributions centers on the issue of whether to share profits on the basis of a fixed formula, with its terms and conditions communicated in advance to the plan participants, or to permit the company's board of directors annually to determine in a discretionary manner the percentage of profits to be shared. Although the use of a predetermined or fixed-contribution formula is not required under the law (and, consequently, no specific minimum level or rate of contribution is required),[4] profit-sharing contributions must meet two other legal requirements. Specifically, the contributions must be "substantial and recurring"[5] to lend support to the qualification requirement pertaining to plan permanency, and these contributions cannot be applied in any manner (either in amount or time) that would result in discrimination in favor of the highly compensated employees. As long as these general restrictions are complied with, an employer may establish any method or formula for determining the profit-sharing amounts that are to be contributed to the plan.

The major advantage of the discretionary approach, of course, is its tremendous contribution flexibility in the annual determination of contributions. Under this approach, the board of directors has the opportunity of viewing past experience and the firm's current financial position and capital requirements before making the decision on how much or what portion of profits are to be shared in the current year. Contribution rates

---

[4] Reg. 1.401-1(b)(2).

[5] Reg. 1.401-1(b)(2).

may be adjusted upward or downward from previous years' rates based on any number of factors, including the current financial picture of the firm. Under the predetermined formula approach, the plan itself would have to be amended in order to accommodate an employer's desire to adjust the profit-sharing contribution rate. Use of the discretionary method also provides the employer with the assurance that the firm will not have to make contributions to the deferred profit-sharing plan in amounts that might exceed the maximums that may be deducted currently for federal income tax purposes or that these contribution amounts, when taken together with forfeiture reallocations, might violate the "annual additions limit" applicable to additions to the individual participants' accounts.[6] When the discretionary method is used, the plan often stipulates minimum and maximum percentages of profits to be distributed (e.g., 10 percent to 30 percent of profits, or whatever predetermined range that is desired by the employer). These limitations restrict the range within which the board of directors may exercise discretionary authority in regard to contributions to the profit-sharing plan. Other illustrations of discretionary arrangements include "discretionary, but not to be less than 10 percent of before-tax profits," and "discretionary, but approximately 20 percent of before-tax profits." The purpose of such arrangements is to provide some guidelines or constraints to the board of directors as it exercises its discretionary authority. Also, any of these guidelines could include some form of a prior reservation for capital. In conclusion, whether contributions to the plan are discretionary or based on a predetermined formula, the employer's task is simpler than under defined benefit plans since no consideration must be given to actuarial factors such as investment experience, age distribution of employees, and employee turnover in determining the periodic contributions to the plan.

When a firm uses the discretionary method, the general procedure is for the board of directors to make the determination of the dollar amount of profits to be shared shortly before the end of the corporation's taxable year. This is in accordance with the basic rule that, to be deductible, the tax liability must be established prior to the end of the taxable year. With a fixed-formula approach, the formula establishes the liability, and thus the amount of profits to be shared does not have to be ascertained in

---

[6] While these are legitimate concerns when using fixed-contribution formulas, satisfactory results may be obtained through including conditions in the plan specifying that contributions not be in excess of the maximum deductible amount, and that they not be in violation of the "annual additions limit." As a result, these concerns should not be viewed as a deterrent to the use of predetermined or fixed-contribution formulas.

dollar terms until after the end of the tax year for those corporations whose tax is figured on an accrual basis.

At one time, the Internal Revenue Service required that deferred profit-sharing plans include a fixed-contribution formula. However, as a result of several court decisions to the contrary, the IRS rules were liberalized to permit employers to determine the profit-sharing amounts (or percentages) without a predetermined formula. Although approved by the Internal Revenue Service, this method is not without its disadvantages. One of these disadvantages relates to the pressures that the board of directors face in making the decisions pertaining to profit-sharing amounts. If flexibility is a major employer goal, then the firm probably will find the discretionary approach more advantageous; but, at the same time, some type of formula method takes many of the burdens and pressures off the board of directors in making decisions on profit-sharing amounts during periods of economic instability (e.g., when the firm has experienced high profit levels for the current year but the forecast is for a severe economic downturn next year; or, conversely, there are low profits in the current year with much brighter prospects for next year). Previously established guidelines would be helpful to the board of directors when these circumstances arise.

A second disadvantage associated with the discretionary method relates to possible lower employee morale and a weakened sense of financial security. Without a fixed formula, employees may experience feelings of uncertainty about whether they can count on sharing in the profits that they have helped produce. In this context, the argument for using a fixed formula is that the ''ground rules'' are established in advance. At the beginning of the year, the employees have the knowledge that their share of the profits will be determined in accordance with the terms contained in the formula.

A third potential disadvantage is that the Wage-Hour Division of the Department of Labor requires that a company use a definite formula if the firm desires to exclude the profit-sharing contributions from regular pay rates in calculating overtime pay. There are exceptions to this requirement, however. If the profit-sharing contributions are allocated to the participants on a basis that includes overtime pay or the plan provides for full and immediate vesting, contributions determined on a discretionary basis do not have to be included in pay when computing overtime rates.

Finally, the use of the discretionary method may expose the contributions to the potential risk that they will come under any wage (and price) guidelines in effect at the time the contributions are made to the deferred profit-sharing plan. For example, in 1979 the President's Council on Wage and Price Stability released its decision on the treatment of profit-sharing plans. Profit-sharing contributions determined under a discretionary approach were to be treated as incentive pay and, therefore, fall within the wage guidelines. Under the decision, qualified deferred profit-sharing plans that apply a fixed (definite) formula were not to come under the wage guideline calculations to the extent that the formula is not changed.

Despite its flexibility, the aforementioned disadvantages of the discretionary approach are major reasons why many large employers have decided to use a definite predetermined formula. Thirty-six of the 38 companies surveyed in *Profit Sharing in 38 Large Companies* used a predetermined formula for determining annual profit-sharing contributions. Smaller companies (up to 1,000 plan participants) have a greater tendency to determine profit-sharing contributions on a discretionary basis, since they appear to be more concerned with contribution and financing flexibility.

There is an unlimited variety of fixed profit-sharing formulas from which an employer may choose. Most definite predetermined formulas specify fixed percentages or sliding scales (either ascending or descending) of percentages based on before-tax or aftertax profits, with or without prior reservations. Examples of predetermined formulas using a fixed percentage are "10 percent of before-tax profits" and "25 percent of before-tax profits but no more than the amount that is available as a current tax deduction." An illustration of a formula involving a sliding scale (ascending) of percentages used by one large company is: "3.5 percent on the first $100 million of before-tax profits, 5.0 percent on the next $50 million, and 6.0 percent on before-tax profits in excess of $150 million." Because of the obvious disincentive to employee motivation, a formula providing for a scale of decreasing percentages rarely is used. An example of a fixed formula with a prior reservation is "20 percent of before-tax profits in excess of 5 percent of net worth." Certainly, many other examples of predetermined formulas exist.

In addition to its relative inflexibility, a possible disadvantage of a definite predetermined formula is the difficulty, from an employee relations perspective, in amending the formula when the amended formula clearly produces a lesser share of profits for the employees. Thus, careful consideration should be given to the initial decision on the profit-sharing percentage(s) that will be included in the formula. To take advantage of the desirable features of both discretionary and fixed formulas, some employers, especially employers of smaller size, use a combination method whereby the plan uses a definite formula providing a minimum fixed-contribution rate applied to profits and supplements these amounts with additional profit-sharing distributions determined, on a discretionary basis, by the board of directors. The specific approach adopted, whether discretionary, predetermined formula, or combination of these, and the precise details of the method chosen will be reflective of the employer's goals and objectives for the plan and the perceived impact of the plan and its profit-sharing method upon the employee group.

Methods of Allocating Employer Contributions among Plan Participants

Once the amount of profit-sharing contributions has been determined for the year, these monies, in turn, must be allocated to the individual participants' accounts. While qualified deferred profit-sharing plans are not required to use a fixed (or predetermined) formula for determining the level of contributions to the plan, the law does require that a predetermined formula for allocating profit-sharing contributions among employee accounts be specified in the plan. The purpose underlying this requirement is to ensure that the contribution allocation does not discriminate in favor of highly paid employees and officers of the firm. In other words, to ascertain whether a plan meets the qualification requirements, the IRS must be able to examine the allocation formula to determine that allocations will be made in a nondiscriminatory manner.

The employer has a wide range of alternative methods for allocating profit-sharing contributions among individual employee accounts, depending on the nature of the plan and the employer objectives that are sought. The most commonly used approach is based on compensation (with age and years of service ignored); that is, the amounts are allocated according to the ratio of each individual employee's compensation to the total compensation of all covered participants for the year. An allocation method based on compensation usually presents no discrimination problems. To illustrate this method, assume employee A has compensation of $20,000 during the year. If the total covered compensation for the plan participants is $400,000 for the year, employee A would be entitled to 5 percent ($20,000 divided by $400,000) of the total profit-sharing allocation. If the aggregate profit-sharing contributions are $50,000 for the year, employee A's share would be $2,500 (5 percent of $50,000). When using a contribution allocation formula based on compensation, the plan sponsor also must specify the amounts that are to be included in determining compensation. For example, compensation for an individual participant may include all compensation paid the employee during the plan year, even though this individual was a plan participant for only part of the year; or compensation may be defined to include only the amounts earned by the employee for that portion of the year that he or she also was a participant in the plan. Further, compensation must be defined in terms of whether it includes base (or regular) pay only or if it also includes bonuses, overtime, commissions, or other forms of cash compensation.[7] However compensation is defined, it must be determined in a nondiscriminatory manner.

Another type of contribution allocation formula bases the allocation on both compensation and length (years) of service. Formulas incorporating both compensation and service typically allocate profit-sharing contributions on the basis of each participant's number of "points" awarded for the current year in proportion to total credited points of all plan participants for the year. Commonly, one point might be awarded for each $100 of compensation. An additional point, for example, might be given the employee for each of his or her years of service.[8] To illustrate, an employee whose compensation (as defined in the plan) is $25,000 and who has 15 years of service with the employer would be credited with 265 points [($25,000/$100 = 250) + 15] for the current year. The contribution allocation to this employee's account would be determined first by computing the ratio of his or her number of points, 265, divided by the total number of points credited to all plan participants during the year. This ratio (percentage) would then be applied to the current year's profit-sharing contribution to derive the share that is to be allocated to this employee's individual account.

Relatively few deferred profit-sharing plans allocate contributions according to length of service only. Previous rulings indicate that the IRS will closely scrutinize any contribution allocation formula based on length of service (either service-only formulas or compensation-and-service formulas) for the purpose of ascertaining whether the "prohibited discrimination" exists. The discrimination concern relates to the possibility that higher-paid employees and officers also have longer periods of service than do other employees.

---

[7] If the profit-sharing plan does not contain a fixed predetermined contribution formula (i.e., the plan uses a discretionary method), the plan is required under federal labor law (1) to provide for full and immediate vesting, or (2) to include overtime earnings in any definition of compensation on which the allocation of contributions is based; otherwise, the profit-sharing allocations themselves must be added to base pay rates in computing overtime pay. See *supra*.

[8] It is possible that more than one point would be credited to each year of service. Further, units other than $100 might be used in determining the number of points to be awarded for a specific amount of compensation. Considerable flexibility exists in specifying the exact way in which the points are to be awarded, conditioned on the point system not being found by the IRS to be discriminatory.

In summary, the plan's contribution allocation formula is used in determining the participant's share for accounting and recordkeeping purposes. These monies are then allocated to individual employee accounts. However, this does not imply that the contribution dollars are segregated for investment purposes. While the profit-sharing trust may permit each participant's account to be invested in "earmarked" assets (an insurance contract, for example), profit-sharing contributions often are received, administered, and invested by the trustee as commingled assets. In the latter case, the balance in each participant's account at a specific time simply represents his or her current share of the assets (commingled) of the trust. Further, the concept of individual employee accounts does not require that the participant be entitled currently to all or any part of the funds credited to his or her individual account. Rather, this entitlement would depend on the plan's provisions regarding vesting, withdrawals and loans, and other provisions relating to distributions.

Maximum Limits

A number of maximum limits, each of substantial importance, apply to deferred profit-sharing plans. Several of these relate to maximums placed on the amount of profit-sharing contributions that may be deducted, for federal income-tax purposes, by an employer in any one tax year. Other limits, such as the "annual additions limit" and the "Rule of 1.0," relate to maximums imposed on employer-provided contributions/benefits under qualified plans. Collectively, these limits place important constraints on what employers can do for their covered employees through deferred profit-sharing arrangements. All of these limits will be described here.

An overriding consideration in this area is that profit-sharing contributions, when added to all other compensation paid an employee for the year, must be "reasonable" for the services performed by the employee and, in addition, be shown to be an "ordinary and necessary expense" of doing business.[9] If this is not the case, the IRS may deny the tax deduction to the employer for any part or all of the profit-sharing contributions (and, possibly, other compensation amounts as well) made on behalf of the employee.[10]

In the context of specific maximums, probably the single most impor-

---

[9] This statement is not restricted to profit-sharing contributions but is equally true for all forms of compensation.

[10] In most large publicly held firms the question of "unreasonable compensation" arises only on an infrequent basis. When this question is raised, it tends to be in those businesses whose ownership is closely held by a small number of individuals.

tant limit affecting deferred profit-sharing plans is the IRS limit on the maximum amount of contributions that may be deducted by the employer in any one tax year. This limit is set forth in IRC Section 404. For deferred profit-sharing plans, the basic limit on employer contributions is that annual deductible contributions may not exceed "15 percent of compensation otherwise paid or accrued during the taxable year to all employees under the plan."[11] The 15 percent limitation on deductions applies regardless of the manner in which employer contributions are determined (i.e., discretionary versus formula, or type of formula); however, the limit applies only to employer contributions to a deferred profit-sharing arrangement. Employers who provide for both cash and deferred profit sharing, either through an IRC Section 401(k) cash or deferred plan or through separate cash and deferred plans, are subject to the 15 percent deduction limit only on contributions to the deferred portion of the profit-sharing arrangement. Thus, if an employer's profit-sharing arrangement calls for the sharing of 30 percent of the before-tax profits, and if 40 percent of this amount is to be distributed in cash (with the balance deferred), then the limit of IRC Section 404(a)(3) applies only to the 18 percent [30% − (30%) × (40%)] of before-tax profits that is contributed to the deferred plan. Furthermore, the 18 percent of before-tax profits (or a portion thereof) will be deductible as a contribution to the deferred profit-sharing plan to the extent that this amount does not exceed 15 percent of the total compensation of the plan participants.[12]

---

[11] IRC Section 404(a)(3).

[12] Prior to the passage of the Tax Reform Act of 1986, employers were permitted to create "credit carryovers" and "contribution carryovers." A "credit carryover" occurred whenever the employer's contribution for the year was less than the maximum allowable deduction of 15 percent of covered compensation. This credit was carried forward to be available for employer use in any subsequent tax year in which contributions exceeded the 15 percent limit. This enabled employers to take larger tax deductions in later years of higher profits (and larger profit-sharing contributions). A "contribution carryover" was created whenever the employer's contributions for a given year exceeded the maximum allowable deduction for that year. This amount could be carried forward and deducted in a subsequent year in which the employer's contribution that year was less than the otherwise allowable deduction (e.g., 15 percent of covered compensation). This permitted employers to make large contributions in earlier, high-profit years that were in excess of the deductible amount with the excess carried forward and available for deduction in later years of lower profit levels.

Unfortunately, the 1986 tax law repealed the "credit carryover" provisions and applies a 10 percent excise tax penalty to employer contributions exceeding the current allowable deduction. ("Credit carryovers" created and accumulated prior to 1987 can still be used to increase the otherwise available deduction limitations for tax years beginning after December 31, 1986. Since these carryover provisions added greatly to employer contribution flexibility under profit-sharing plans, their restriction may lead to an eventual decrease in the popularity of profit-sharing plans.

Additional limits apply when an employer sponsors both a pension plan and a profit-sharing plan that cover a common group of employees. A 25 percent (of covered compensation) aggregate limit on employer deductions applies when both a profit-sharing plan and a money purchase pension plan exist.

> In the case of a combination profit-sharing plan and defined benefit pension plan, the maximum annual deductible contribution to the combined plans is limited to 25 percent of covered compensation or, if larger, the amount necessary to meet the minimum funding requirements of the defined benefit plan alone. If circumstances are such that the minimum funding rules require the employer to contribute amounts to the defined benefit plan during a year that, by themselves, are in excess of 25 percent of covered compensation, the employer, in effect, is precluded from making a deductible contribution to the profit-sharing plan that year. The separate limit on the deductibility of employer contributions to the profit-sharing plan still applies in combination pension and profit-sharing plans.[13]

Contributions, together with forfeiture reallocations, in deferred profit-sharing plans are subject to the ''annual additions limit'' of IRC Section 415(c). This section of the code prescribes limitations on the amounts of monies that can be added, on an annual basis, to individual participants' accounts under defined contribution plans. Thus, IRC Section 415 applies to both deferred profit-sharing plans and money purchase pension plans. Contributions in excess of the IRC Section 415 limits will result in disqualification of the plan. Thus, the employer must make sure that these limits are complied with. Conceivably, the annual additions limit could reduce the contribution that an employer might otherwise make to the account of an individual participant in a given year.

The term *annual additions* includes (a) employer contributions, (b) forfeiture reallocations, and (c) any employee contributions. For purposes of the annual additions limit, investment earnings allocated to employee's account balances, rollover contributions, and loan repayments are not part of annual additions. Since this chapter is concerned primarily with deferred profit-sharing plans funded exclusively with employer contributions, component (c) of the annual additions limit is of little importance here and therefore will be ignored.

Under IRC Section 415, a qualified defined contribution plan may not provide an annual addition, in any year, to any participant's account which exceeds the lesser of (a) 25 percent of compensation (for that year)

---

[13] IRC Section 404(a)(7).

or (b) a stipulated dollar amount ($30,000 for 1988).[14] To illustrate how the annual additions limit might impose a constraint in the context of a deferred profit-sharing plan, let us consider a simple example. Assume that employer contributions to the profit-sharing plan for the year are equal to the maximum deductible amount of 15 percent of covered compensation. To the extent that forfeitures exist and are reallocated to participants' accounts, the amount of such reallocated forfeitures cannot exceed 10 percent of compensation (applied individually). A possibility exists that for higher-income employees the stipulated dollar maximum (e.g., $30,000) may act as a constraint. This may result in the situation where the annual additions, as a percentage of compensation, for these higher-income employees will be smaller than the annual additions percentage for those employees whose compensation is at such a level (lower) that they are unaffected by the dollar maximum on annual additions. Employers often include specific plan provisions that are designed to avoid this result.

Many employers have combination pension and profit-sharing arrangements that are designed to provide significant amounts of retirement income from the pension plan (although often integrated with Social Security) and to provide for asset or capital accumulation through the establishment of the required individual accounts under the profit-sharing plan. Recently, a number of companies have elected to supplement an existing pension plan through the establishment of a deferred profit-sharing plan. Other companies in recent years have established pension plans to supplement existing profit-sharing arrangements. It is anticipated that this trend will continue, whereby more companies will sponsor both pension and deferred profit-sharing programs to work in tandem in providing employees with greater retirement income security.

In essence, there are two basic ways in which to have a combination plan that includes a deferred profit-sharing arrangement: (1) combination of a money purchase pension plan and a profit-sharing plan; and (2) combination of a defined benefit pension plan and a profit-sharing plan. In the first arrangement, since both plans are of the defined contribution type and assuming the plans cover the same group of employees, the combined plans must comply with the annual additions limit of the lesser of 25 percent of pay or a stated dollar maximum ($30,000 in 1988). In addition, the usual 15 percent annual maximum on the deductibility of employer contributions, in effect, would act as an "internal" limit with regard to the portion of the 25 percent that might be accounted for by the employer

---

[14] In determining (a), only the first $200,000 of compensation can be considered.

contributions to the deferred profit-sharing program. If there are forfeiture reallocations (under either the profit-sharing or money purchase plan), the percentage and dollar amount contributed to the profit-sharing plan may have to be reduced to comply with the annual additions limit, since the money purchase plan specifies a fixed-contribution commitment that must be met by the employer each year.

When a defined benefit pension plan is combined with a deferred profit-sharing plan covering the same employees, the 1.4 (140 percent) rule of IRC Section 415(e) applies. The Tax Equity and Fiscal Responsibility Act of 1982 (TEFRA) revised this rule, currently referred to as the "Rule of 1.0," and also revised the method for calculating defined benefit plan and defined contribution plan fractions.[15] In essence, the revised plan fractions effectively provide an aggregate limit equal to the lesser of 1.25 (as applied to the dollar limits) or 1.4 (as applied to the percentage-of-pay limits).

ALLOCATION OF INVESTMENT EARNINGS AND FORFEITURES

In addition to specifying a contribution allocation formula, deferred profit-sharing plans also must prescribe the methods for allocating investment earnings and forfeitures among the participants' accounts. These latter allocation methods, depending upon the circumstances, may differ from the method applied in allocating employer contributions to participants' accounts under the plan.

Allocation of Investment Earnings

Unless the profit-sharing assets allocated to the participants' individual accounts are "earmarked" for investment purposes (e.g., when life insurance contracts are purchased), these assets will be pooled and invested on an aggregated basis typically by the plan's trustee. As a result, the investment earnings generated from these commingled funds, in turn, must be allocated to the participant's accounts. The most equitable approach is to allocate investment earnings on the basis of the respective sizes of the individual account balances. Presumably, the funds theoretically assigned to each participant's account contribute in a pro rata fashion to the total

[15] It is assumed here that the reader is familiar with the workings of this rule and the IRC Section 415 defined benefit limitations (the lesser of 100 percent of compensation averaged over the highest three consecutive years or a stated dollar amount—1988 limit of $94,023).

investment earnings of the plan, and, therefore, each account should share on a pro rata basis in these earnings. Thus, if a participant's account balance comprises 10 percent of the total of all account balances, that participant's account should be credited with 10 percent of the total investment earnings. Since investment earnings invariably are allocated on the basis of individual account balances, the plan will be applying procedures that will differ between the allocation of investment earnings and the allocation of employer contributions.

Investment earnings on assets held under the profit-sharing trust are measured on a "total return" basis. That is, investment earnings for a given year are defined to include interest and dividends, as well as adjustments in the market value of the underlying assets during the year of measurement. The net result is that the assets of the profit-sharing plan must be valued periodically to determine their market value.[16] In fact, the IRS requires that the accounts of all plan participants be valued in a uniform and consistent manner at least once each year.[17] Many large employers, however, provide for more frequent valuation. It would not be uncommon to find monthly valuations in these plans. Arguments favoring frequent market valuation of plan assets are that the sponsor is provided with greater flexibility in plan administration and that the plan participants are treated more equitably. This latter point is particularly important in the accounting and in the general overall treatment of plan transactions (primarily withdrawals) that occur between valuation dates. Total withdrawals of the participants' shares (represented by their individual account balances) might occur when the employment relationship with the sponsoring firm is terminated or when membership in the plan is terminated due to some other reason(s). Partial withdrawals by active plan participants also might occur if permitted by, and according to, the provisions of the profit-sharing plan document. The issue facing the plan on the occasion of withdrawals, whether partial or total, relates to the values to be placed on the account balances and, consequently, the dollar amounts that are available for distribution. More frequent asset valuations will

---

[16] This does not apply when the entire assets of the plan are invested with a life insurance company through its "general asset account." Rather, in this event, transactions with plan participants (e.g., withdrawals) occur on a book value basis, and interest earnings are credited to participants' account balances according to the life insurance company's own accounting procedures. See Dan M. McGill, *Fundamentals of Private Pensions,* 5th ed. (Homewood, Ill.: Richard D. Irwin, 1984), p. 621, footnote 14.

[17] Certain exceptions exist. For example, an annual valuation is not required when all of the plan assets are invested, immediately, in individual annuity or retirement contracts meeting certain requirements. See Revenue Ruling 73–435, 1973–2 C.B. 126.

assist in achieving a more equitable result (*a*) between individuals making withdrawals and those who do not, and (*b*) among individuals making withdrawals at different points in time. This issue also includes the policy question of whether investment earnings are to be credited to the individual account balances for the period between the last valuation date and the date the funds are withdrawn. If interest is not credited for this period, the amounts (interest) lost to the participants making withdrawals could be substantial unless relatively frequent valuations (e.g., monthly or every two months) are made.

Allocation of Forfeitures

Forfeitures arise under profit-sharing plans when a participant terminates employment and the funds credited to his or her account are less than fully vested. As described earlier, the qualification requirements applicable to deferred profit-sharing plans permit the periodic reallocation of forfeitures among the remaining plan participants. While profit-sharing plans are also permitted to use the forfeitures to reduce future employer contributions, seldom is this the case. The advantage of being able to allocate forfeitures among remaining plan participants is somewhat lessened by the rapid vesting typically found in profit-sharing plans which, in turn, reduces the amounts of forfeitures that otherwise are available for reallocation. Further, any amounts of forfeiture reallocations, together with employer contributions for the year, must comply with the "annual additions limit" contained in IRC Section 415.[18]

All methods of forfeiture reallocation are subject to the principal requirement that they not discriminate in favor of highly paid employees and officers of the firm. Potential discrimination is of particular concern when forfeitures are reallocated on the basis of account balances. The underlying rationale here centers on the premise that officers, shareholder-employees, and highly compensated employees are more likely to have longer periods of service with the firm and, consequently, that they will have much larger account balances than other plan participants. Thus, if account balances constitute the basis for allocating forfeitures, the highly paid key employees may be entitled to substantially larger shares of forfeitures than other employees. The IRS may find this practice to be discriminatory. However, the IRS does not hold that it is "inherently discriminatory," or that the plan will automatically fail to qualify,

[18] See *Supra*.

simply because the plan allocates forfeitures on the basis of account balances.[19] The IRS requires that the allocation (based on account balances) be tested annually to determine whether the plan, in fact, is discriminatory. This is accomplished through submission of all pertinent plan data to the IRS for its determination. Because of the fear of a potential charge of discrimination (and possible loss of the plan's qualified status), "account balances" is a seldom used method in allocating forfeitures. This is particularly true in small plans.

Rather, forfeitures most commonly are reallocated among the individual accounts of remaining participants on the basis of each participant's compensation—the same method that generally is used in allocating employer contributions. Under normal circumstances, a compensation-based method will be considered to result in an equitable allocation among plan participants and thus is not likely to be viewed as discriminatory by the IRS.

WITHDRAWAL AND LOAN PROVISIONS

While the primary objective of many deferred profit-sharing plans is to provide covered employees with the opportunity to accumulate substantial sums of monies to be available at retirement, a number of plans also provide employees with access to these funds on earlier prescribed occasions. This is accomplished by designing the profit-sharing plan to include withdrawal or loan provisions, or both.

Loan Provisions

A substantial number of profit-sharing plans contain loan provisions. These provisions allow participants to borrow up to a specified percentage (e.g., 50 percent) of the vested amounts in their individual accounts. While profit-sharing plans are not legally obligated to include a loan provision, certain regulatory requirements will apply when such a provision is

---

[19] See Revenue Ruling 71–4 and Revenue Ruling 81–10. Revenue Ruling 81–10 basically restates the position of the IRS contained in Revenue Ruling 71–4, but it also provides a permissive formula that can be applied in determining whether forfeiture reallocations based on account balances produce the prohibited discrimination. See also the discussion of this topic in Carmine V. Scudere, "Is It too Risky to Allocate Forfeitures under a P/S Plan on the Basis of Account Balances?" *Journal of Pension Planning and Compliance,* July 1981, pp. 288–93.

incorporated into the plan design.[20] One such requirement is that loans must be made available to all plan participants on a reasonably equivalent basis. Further, loans cannot be made available to officers, shareholder-employees, and highly compensated employees on a basis that is more favorable than that available to other employees. It also is required that the loan be repaid in level payments (made at least quarterly), and that it bear a reasonable rate of interest. As regards any loans not repaid, the Internal Revenue Service may view them as withdrawals, in which case they must meet the conditions described below. As long as the specified terms under the loan provision are properly drawn and prudent, the loans will be exempted from the prohibited transaction provisions under ERISA and also should comply with ERISA's fiduciary standards.

Withdrawal Provisions

In the past, some deferred profit-sharing plans have provided automatic distributions of plan assets to employees (during active employment) after the completion of a stated period of participation or after the lapse of a fixed period of years.[21] Other plans provided employees with the option to withdraw portions of the monies in their individual accounts on "the attainment of a stated age, or upon the prior occurrence of some event such as layoff, illness, disability, retirement, death, or severance of employment." Distributions to participants on these prescribed occasions are permitted under Reg. 1.401–1(b)(1)(ii). Distributions of profit-sharing funds made sooner than the happening of any one of the aforementioned events may lead to the disqualification of the plan.

Obviously, an employee's right to withdraw funds from a deferred profit-sharing plan is dependent on the actual provisions of the plan itself.

---

[20] It is possible that certain loans will be treated as plan distributions and, therefore, subject to current income taxation. Generally, loans will be treated as plan distributions (and subject to taxation) unless two conditions are met:

(1) The employee's total outstanding loan amount does not exceed the *greater* of (*a*) $10,000 or (*b*) one half of the present value of the employee's nonforfeitable benefit. In any event, however, the outstanding loan amount cannot exceed $50,000. Further, the $50,000 limit is reduced by the participant's highest outstanding loan balance during the preceding 12-month period.

(2) The loan (according to its terms and conditions) must be repaid within five years; however, the five-year repayment rule is waived for loans used to purchase a dwelling used as a principal residence of the employee.

[21] The inclusion of such provisions is prohibited in IRC Section 401(k) cash or deferred profit-sharing plans.

The plan is under no regulatory obligation to permit distributions on the occurrence of all the events described above. In fact, some plans do not permit withdrawals prior to the participant's termination of employment. In addition, only vested amounts are available to be withdrawn. When a profit-sharing plan provides for automatic distributions (or permits voluntary withdrawals) after a fixed number of years, IRS regulations require in these situations that only funds that have been deposited for at least two years may be distributed. Thus, if employer contributions have been credited to the participant's account for three years, only amounts equal to the first year's contribution, together with investment income credited that year, are eligible to be withdrawn, but only to the extent the plan permits such withdrawals.[22] Of course, distributions of funds held less than two years may be made in the event of ". . . disability, retirement, death. . ." without affecting qualification. Further, distributions of monies held less than two years also may be made upon the showing of "hardship," if this term is sufficiently defined and consistently applied under the plan. In any event, the actual amounts withdrawn must be included as taxable income by the participant in the year in which the distribution is received. Further, a 10 percent penalty tax will be applied in the future to many types of "premature" distributions from qualified plans. (See *infra*). Thus, the future attractiveness of automatic and other early distributions from profit-sharing plans is likely to be severely diminished.

Relative Advantages and Disadvantages of Withdrawals and Loans

Plan provisions permitting loans or withdrawals, or both, prior to termination of employment provide participants with much added flexibility. Employees may be able to use these funds for down payments on homes, for children's college education expenses, or for other financial needs. An important disadvantage is that these provisions (particularly withdrawal provisions) may prevent the plan from accumulating sufficient funds at retirement.

Loan provisions have certain inherent advantages over withdrawal provisions. Specifically, funds made available through a loan do not cre-

---

[22] After completion of five years of participation in the plan, an employee is legally permitted to withdraw all employer contributions credited to his or her account (assuming the plan so permits), including monies contributed during the two years preceding the date of withdrawal. The completion of five years of participation is an "event" within the meaning of Reg. 1.401-1(b)(1)(ii). As a result, the two-year rule is made inapplicable.

ate taxable income to the borrowing employee. In addition, since loans are likely to be repaid, the retirement income objective of the profit-sharing plan is protected. Some potential disadvantages of loan provisions are:

1. The administrative expense associated with processing loans.
2. An employee objection to being charged interest on his or her "own money."
3. The lower overall investment earnings rate on the total asset portfolio when the loan interest rate is below the earnings rate at which the trustee could otherwise invest the borrowed funds.[23]

Previously, profit-sharing plans containing withdrawal provisions had to be concerned with the "constructive receipt doctrine." The question arose whether the right to withdraw *any* monies from a participant's individual account, whether or not exercised, constituted constructive receipt of *all* (withdrawable) monies allocated to the account. If the constructive receipt doctrine applied, all such amounts available to be withdrawn would be taxable currently to the participant, even though the monies are not actually withdrawn. To avoid application of the constructive receipt doctrine to amounts not withdrawn, plans usually assessed a substantial penalty (e.g., denying participation rights for six months) on employees who made withdrawals. Today, however, the constructive receipt doctrine no longer presents a problem in deferred profit-sharing plans. The Economic Recovery Tax Act of 1981 (ERTA) amended IRC Section 402(a)(1) of the Internal Revenue Code, which deals with the taxation of benefits from a qualified retirement plan. Under the amended provision, distributions from qualified plans are taxed only when actually received by the participant; they are not taxed simply because they are made available to the participant. Thus, the basis for the constructive receipt doctrine has been removed from IRC Section 402(a)(1). This affects the tax treatment of all qualified plans, including profit-sharing plans, and it applies both to distributions at termination of employment and to withdrawals made by active employees. The amended provision became effective for taxable years beginning after December 31, 1981. Today, profit-sharing plans need not contain withdrawal penalties or restrictions simply to avoid constructive receipt issues. However, plan sponsors should determine whether, and to what extent, these penalties

[23] This last disadvantage exists only to the extent that the plan treats participant loans as loans from the entire assets of the trust, rather than treating them as loans from the participants' own individual accounts.

and restrictions are desirable in order to meet plan objectives and to control administrative costs.

Since the passage of the Tax Reform Act of 1986, however, the biggest drawback to including provisions for withdrawals in profit-sharing plans is the 10-percent penalty tax. This additional tax is applied to early distributions from all qualified retirement plans, including profit sharing. An early distribution is one made prior to age 59½, death, or disability. Exemptions are permitted for: (1) periodic annuity benefits, after separation from service, paid over the life (or life expectancy) of the employee or joint lives of the employee and beneficiary; (2) distributions to an employee that are used to pay deductible medical expenses; (3) distributions to a participant, after age 55, who has met the plan's early retirement provisions and has separated from service; (4) lump-sum cash-outs of less than $3,500; and (5) payments to a former spouse or dependent under a qualified domestic relations order.

ADDITIONAL FEATURES OF DEFERRED PROFIT-SHARING PLANS

Certain additional features pertaining to deferred profit-sharing plans are worthy of mention. These plan design features relate to the inclusion of life insurance benefits and integration of the plan with Social Security benefits.

Life Insurance Benefits

There are two important ways in which life insurance benefits may be incorporated into the design of qualified deferred profit-sharing plans.[24] First, life insurance coverage on key personnel in the firm might be purchased by the trust as an investment. The underlying rationale here is that the profit-sharing trust has an insurable interest in the lives of certain employees who are "key" to the successful operation of the firm. These key employees may include officers, stockholder-employees, and certain other employees of the company. Since contributions to the profit-sharing trust are dependent on the continued success and profitability of the firm,

[24] Only a limited discussion is provided here on life insurance in qualified profit-sharing plans. For a more extensive treatment of this topic, see Allen, Melone, and Rosenbloom, *Pension Planning*, 5th ed. (Homewood, Ill.: Richard D. Irwin, 1984), pp. 280–84; and McGill, *Fundamentals of Private Pensions*, pp. 630–34.

and if the future profitability is contingent on the performance of these key employees, then the profit-sharing trust is likely to suffer a substantial reduction in future contribution levels upon the death of one or more of the key employees. This may be particularly true in the case of small-to-medium-size corporations. Under these circumstances, if permitted by the trust agreement, the trustee may desire to protect the profit-sharing trust against potential adverse consequences by purchasing insurance on the lives of the key employees. In such cases, the life insurance contracts are purchased and owned by the trust, with the necessary premiums paid for out of trust assets. While the trust is designated as the beneficiary under such contracts, upon the death of an insured the insurance proceeds are allocated among the individual accounts of the plan participants, typically on the basis of the respective sizes of their account balances.[25]

Second, while deferred profit-sharing plans primarily are plans providing deferred compensation, most plans also provide a benefit payable upon the death of a plan participant. Most profit-sharing plans, at a minimum, pay a death benefit equal to the participant's individual account balance. In addition, however, under Reg. 1.401–1(b)(1)(ii) amounts allocated to participants' accounts may be used to purchase incidental amounts of life insurance coverage. There are several reasons why a participant might desire to have explicit life insurance benefits provided under the profit-sharing plan, including (1) the relatively small accumulation (and, consequently, available death benefits) in the participant's account during the early years of participation, and (2) inadequate amounts of coverage provided under the employer-sponsored group life insurance program.

To the extent that profit-sharing contributions are used to purchase life insurance on plan participants, these contributions must meet certain limitations. However, the limitations are sufficiently liberal that, in many cases, it is possible for plan participants (if desired) to acquire substantial amounts of life insurance coverage. Specifically, if the participant's funds

---

[25] In contrast to the purchase of life insurance on plan participants (see *infra*), the purchase of life insurance on key employees, for the collective benefit of the trust, does not create any current income tax liability for the participants. Furthermore, the tests requiring that purchases of life insurance be incidental in amount do not apply to the types of life insurance purchases described above. However, as a practical matter, the trust is not likely to invest a substantial portion of its assets in such life insurance purchases. Also, under ERISA's fiduciary provisions, the trustee is under the obligation to show that the purchase of life insurance on key personnel is a prudent investment and in the best interests, collectively, of the plan participants.

used to pay life insurance premiums have been accumulated in the participant's account for at least two years, or if the funds are used to purchase either an endowment or a retirement income contract, there are no IRS limits on the amount of life insurance that can be purchased (or the portion of the account balance that may be used to pay premiums). If neither of these requirements is met, the aggregate amount of funds used to pay life insurance premiums must be less than one half of the total contributions and forfeitures allocated to the participant's account; otherwise, the plan may be disqualified. Additional restrictions pertaining to the inclusion of life insurance (on plan participants) in profit-sharing plans are: (1) that the plan must require the trustee to convert the entire value of the life insurance contract at or prior to retirement either to cash or to provide periodic income (in order that no portion of such value is available to continue life insurance protection into the retirement years), or to distribute the insurance contract to the participant; and (2) that the participant must treat the value (P.S. 58 cost) of the pure life insurance protection as taxable income each year.[26]

To maintain its qualified status, a plan must meet the requirements of Reg. 1.401-l(b)(1)(ii); however, life insurance need not be purchased on *all* plan participants to maintain qualification. Rather, the purchase of life insurance can be the decision of individual participants (with some electing the coverage and others not) as long as all participants are offered the same opportunity. To accomplish this, the trust agreement should expressly allow each participant, individually, to direct the trustee to purchase specific investments (e.g., insurance contracts) and "earmark" them for the participant's account. Normally, the trustee is the applicant and owner of any life insurance contracts purchased on the lives of the plan participants. In addition, the trustee pays the premiums on the policies, although these amounts are then charged directly to the individual accounts of those participants electing insurance coverage. Typically, the insured participants designate their own personal beneficiaries, in which

---

[26] The reason for a current tax liability is that the premium for the pure insurance protection is deemed by the IRS to be a current distribution from the trust and therefore currently taxable to the plan participant. The amount that must be included in the participant's gross income each year is determined as follows: [(face amount minus cash value) × (the *lower* of the Table P.S. 58 attained age rate or the insurer's own premium rate for individual one-year term insurance)]. With each succeeding year, the first factor in this formula decreases, providing the face amount is held constant, while the second factor increases. The portion of the premium applied to the buildup of the cash value component of the life insurance contract is considered to be an investment of the profit-sharing trust and, consequently, is not treated as a current distribution nor subject to any current tax liability.

case the proceeds payable upon the death of a participant are paid by the insurer directly to the named beneficiary. If the trustee is named as beneficiary under the insurance contract, the death proceeds are paid to the trustee who, in turn, credits the proceeds to the deceased participant's account.

Integration with Social Security

Deferred profit-sharing plans are seldom integrated with the benefits payable under Social Security (OASDI). A major reason is that any employee incentive factor sought by the employer would tend to be diminished by a plan design that calls for contributions at a lower rate on behalf of employees earning less than a specified minimum.

Because of its defined contribution nature, the integration of profit-sharing plans is accomplished on an excess earnings basis.[27] In this approach, it is necessary to establish an earnings level (known as the integration level) which defines a dollar amount whereby the employer contribution rate differs between earnings above and below this level. Specifically, the employer contribution rate is greater on compensation in excess of the integration level. While lesser dollar amounts are permissible, the integration level often is defined as the current Social Security maximum taxable wage base.

Effective for plan years beginning after December 31, 1988, the integration rules are more restrictive than under prior law. The Tax Reform Act of 1986 requires that the *difference* between the employer contribution rate applied to compensation in excess of the integration level and the contribution rate applied to compensation below the integration level cannot exceed the *lesser* of (1) 5.7 percent (or the tax rate for the old age insurance portion of OASDI, if greater) or (2) the contribution rate applied to compensation below the integration level.[28] To illustrate, if a 3 percent contribution rate is applied to earnings below the integration level, then a maximum of 6 percent can be contributed on excess compensation (i.e., above the integration level). Similarly, if the employer con-

---

[27] The offset approach which reduces plan benefits by a percentage of the benefit payable from Social Security, is not used.

[28] Under prior law, the maximum *difference* between the contribution rates on compensation above and below the integration level was simply restricted to 5.7 percent. Thus, an *excess-only* plan was allowed under which no employer contribution was required on earnings below the integration level so long as the contribution rate applied to excess earnings did not exceed 5.7 percent.

tributes 7 percent on earnings below the integration level, then no more than 12.7 percent can be applied to excess compensation.[29]

Frequently, an employer has established both a pension plan and a deferred profit-sharing plan covering (at least to some extent) the same employees. If both plans are integrated, the regulations will not permit the combined integration under both plans to exceed 100 percent of the integration capability of a single plan. When the employer sponsors two plans covering the same group of employees, and when maximum integration is desired, the simplest approach to integration is to fully integrate one plan and not integrate the other plan at all. Other combinations are permissible, however.

DISTRIBUTIONS

Earlier sections described specific events or occasions leading to distributions under profit-sharing plans. The discussion here is limited to the form and taxation of distributions from qualified deferred profit-sharing plans.

Form

Distributions from profit-sharing plans may take several forms, including lump-sum, installment payments, or a paid-up annuity. Distributions in the form of withdrawals during active employment or distributions to employees who have terminated employment (for reasons other than death, disability, or retirement) generally are made in the form of a lump-sum payment.[30] At death or disability of the plan participant, distributions usually are in the form of a lump-sum payment or installment payments. Finally, at retirement, distributions typically are payable to the participant either as a lump sum, on an installment-payment basis, or as a life annuity provided through an insurance company. To the extent that the

---

[29] For a general rule, let x denote the employer contribution rate applied to compensation below the integration level. Then the maximum contribution rate that can be applied to compensation in excess of the integration level is (a) $2x$, when $x \leq 5.7$ percent and (b) $x + 5.7$, when $x > 5.7$ percent.

[30] As indicated earlier, the applicability of a 10 percent penalty tax on premature distributions may cause employers to limit the availability of in-service withdrawals from profit-sharing plans. Further, when terminating employment prior to age 59½, participants in the future may more frequently choose to roll over the funds into an Individual Retirement Account (IRA) to avoid imposition of the penalty tax.

plan permits an annuity payout form, the plan must satisfy ERISA's rules relating to qualified joint-and-survivor annuities.

Taxation

In general, the tax treatment of distributions from qualified profit-sharing plans is identical to the tax treatment accorded distributions from qualified pension plans.[31] However, the tax treatment accorded distributions consisting of employer securities holds particular importance to profit-sharing plans. Profit-sharing plans are not subject to ERISA's 10 percent limitation on the investment of plan assets in employer securities and tend to invest more heavily in employer securities as a result. When employer securities are distributed as part of a lump-sum distribution under such conditions that otherwise qualify the distribution for favorable tax treatment, IRC Section 402(e)(4)(J) permits the entire net unrealized appreciation on the securities (excess of fair market value over cost basis of securities to the trust) to escape taxation at the time of the distribution. In effect, the only portion taxed to the participant at the time of distribution is the amount of the original employer contributions (i.e., the trust's cost basis). The tax on any unrealized appreciation at date of distribution is deferred until the participant sells the securities at a later date.

---

[31] See the earlier discussions of (1) the five-year averaging rule and (2) the 10 percent penalty tax on premature distributions.

CHAPTER 27

THRIFT AND SAVINGS PLANS

Henry Bright
Harry McBrierty

INTRODUCTION

A thrift plan is the trade name given to an employee benefit plan that promotes savings and thrift among employees by requiring each participant to make periodic contributions to the plan in order to be credited with an employer contribution on his or her behalf. The amount of the employer contribution usually relates, in whole or in part, to the amount the participant contributes. These plans also are referred to as savings plans, thrift incentive plans, savings and investment plans, and by a variety of other names that generally denote an employee savings feature.

With a few exceptions, all thrift plans have been established within the last 30 years. Their prevalence among employers of all sizes has grown continuously. However, their growth in the 1980s has been phenomenal. This, no doubt, is due in large part to the fact that thrift plans are ideally suited for a cash or deferred arrangement whereby the participants' contributions to the thrift plan are on a tax-deferred, salary reduction basis under Section 401(k) of the Internal Revenue Code (IRC). In fact, in recent years, thrift plans are often referred to as "401(k) plans." It should be noted, however, that not all 401(k) plans are thrift plans and not all thrift plans are 401(k) plans.

The popularity of thrift plans is also due to their relatively low cost to the employer and to their enthusiastic acceptance by most employees.

From the employer's viewpoint, a thrift plan is a retirement program that can provide significant benefits, which are financed to a great extent by the contributions of its employees (depending on the ratio of the employees' contributions to its own). From the employees' viewpoint, a thrift plan provides an incentive to save and gives them the opportunity to realize an immediate and substantial return on their own contributions, with the added opportunity of accumulating investment earnings on a deferred tax basis and receiving benefits on a favorable tax basis on retirement or termination. In addition, under 401(k) thrift plans, the employees may make their contributions on a salary reduction basis and thereby reduce the amount of taxes that they have to pay in the year during which they make the contributions.

The influence that the Tax Reform Act of 1986 (TRA' 86) will have on thrift plans is not yet known. Many of the revenue-producing provisions of that Act will make some of the features of thrift plans less attractive. For example, the 10 percent penalty tax on withdrawals before age 59½ will make thrift plans less attractive as a means of accumulating savings for use prior to retirement. Also, the $7,000 cap on elective deferrals and the smaller permissible disparity between the contributions of highly and nonhighly compensated employees under a 401(k) plan will lessen the attractiveness of these plans to higher paid employees. On the other hand, the elimination or reduction in the amount of IRA deductions will make 401(k) thrift plans more attractive to many employees as a means of savings on a tax-deferred basis. Early indications seem to indicate that TRA 86 will not have a significant impact on the popularity of thrift plans, especially those that use a 401(k) cash or deferred arrangement.

This chapter discusses thrift plans in general and does not attempt to describe in detail the specific provisions that apply to plans that utilize the cash or deferred arrangement afforded under IRC Section 401(k). The provisions that apply to 401(k) thrift plans are discussed more thoroughly in Chapter 28 of this *Handbook*.

QUALIFIED STATUS UNDER INTERNAL REVENUE CODE

The Internal Revenue Code includes no specific provisions relating to thrift plans as such. A thrift plan is simply a term used in the industry to describe a contributory defined contribution plan that provides an individual account for each participant with benefits based solely on: (1) the amounts contributed to the participant's account; (2) any income, expenses, gains, and losses; and (3) any forfeitures of accounts of others that may be allocated to the participant's account. This description is the same as that of a profit-sharing plan and of a money purchase pension plan, because thrift plans are qualified under Section 401(a) of the Internal Revenue Code as either profit-sharing plans or money purchase pension plans. Technically, a thrift plan could alternatively be qualified as a stock-bonus plan if it has all of the attributes of a stock-bonus plan.

The provisions of the IRC that govern profit-sharing plans are different in certain respects from those that govern money purchase pension plans. Accordingly, differences exist in the provisions and in the operations of a thrift plan, according to whether it is qualified as a profit-sharing plan or as a money purchase pension plan. Table 27–1 lists some of the principal differences between the two types of thrift plans.

Features common to both types of thrift plan include the following: (1) the plan must provide a definite predetermined formula for allocating contributions among the participants in the plan, and (2) the plan must provide for valuation of plan assets at least once a year.

TABLE 27–1
Principal Differences between Two Types of Thrift Plans

Feature	*Plan Qualified as a Profit-Sharing Plan*	*Plan Qualified as a Money Purchase Pension Plan*
1. Amount of employer contributions	No definite formula required. Usually expressed as a percentage of employee's contributions.	There must be a fixed formula to determine the amount of employer contributions.
2. Source of employer contributions	May provide that they will only be made out of current or accumulated profits.	Are required to be made even if there are no current or accumulated profits.
3. Employer contributions in excess of normal formula	Plan may provide for such excess contributions to be made at the employer's option.	No excess contributions may be made.
4. Withdrawal of employer contributions prior to severance of employment	May be permitted (contributions must have accumulated for at least two years).	No withdrawal of employer contributions is permitted except on severance (or attainment of normal retirement age).

TABLE 27–1 *(continued)*

Feature	*Plan Qualified as a Profit-Sharing Plan*	*Plan Qualified as a Money Purchase Pension Plan*
5. Limit on tax deductions for employer contributions to thrift plan		
a. No other plan maintained	15 percent of covered compensation.	None, but note that Section 415 of the IRC effectively imposes a maximum on contributions of 25 percent of covered compensation.
b. Separate profit-sharing plan maintained	Combined limit of 15 percent of covered compensation.	Combined limit of 25 percent of covered compensation.
c. Separate defined benefit pension plan maintained	Combined limit of 25 percent of covered compensation.	Combined limit of 25 percent of covered compensation or, if greater, the required minimum defined benefit plan contribution.
6. Favorable tax treatment for lump-sum distributions on termination or retirement	Available, provided there is no other profit-sharing plan benefit, or, if there is, provided a lump sum also is received thereunder.	Available, provided there is no other pension plan benefit, or if there is, provided a lump sum also is received thereunder.

PLAN PROVISIONS

Most provisions of thrift plans are similar to those of other employee benefit plans qualified under Section 401(a) of the IRC. The plan must be so structured that, in addition to satisfying the objectives of the employer, it conforms to the requirements of the Internal Revenue Code, the Employee Retirement Income Security Act (ERISA), and other applicable governmental rules and regulations.

Eligibility Requirements

Employees must be eligible to participate on reaching age 21 or on completing one year of service, whichever is later. However, if the plan is not a 401(k) plan and it provides immediate 100 percent vesting, the plan may require as much as two years of service before the employee is eligible. (However, prior to 1989, any thrift plan that provides immediate 100 percent vesting may impose a three-year service requirement). An employee cannot be excluded from participation under a thrift plan because of attainment of a specified maximum age. In practice, most thrift plans permit participation after a year or less.

As with other qualified plans, a thrift plan must cover a sufficient number of employees (after certain permitted exclusions) to satisfy the "percentage test," the "ratio test," or the "average benefits test" of Section 410(b) of the Internal Revenue Code.

The percentage test is satisfied if the plan benefits at least 70 percent of all nonhighly compensated employees. The ratio test is satisfied if the percentage of nonhighly compensated employees that benefit under the plan is at least 70 percent of the percentage of highly compensated employees that benefit. The average benefits test is satisfied if the plan benefits a fair cross-section of employees and the average benefit percentage of the nonhighly compensated employees is at least 70 percent of the average benefit percentage of the highly compensated employees. Since thrift plans require employee contributions and participation is normally not mandatory, the percentage and ratio tests are sometimes difficult to satisfy, and those plans that cannot meet either of those tests need to satisfy the average benefits test if the plan is to achieve and retain a qualified status.

Employee Contributions

The requirement for employee contributions is a distinguishing characteristic of all thrift plans. This is because the amount of the employer's contributions and the predetermined formula for allocating those contributions among the participants are almost always based on the amount that each participant contributes.

Many thrift plans permit the employee contributions to be made on a tax-deferred basis. Under these arrangements, the employee contributions are deducted from the employee's pay and no federal income taxes are due on them until they are paid to the employee or his or her beneficiary. Plans that use this type of arrangement are referred to as 401(k) thrift plans and are subject to special nondiscrimination, withdrawal, and other provisions that do not apply to other thrift plans. These special provisions are discussed very briefly in this chapter but are discussed in more detail in Chapter 28.

All thrift plans require one type of employee contribution, and some thrift plans permit a second type. The first type is that which determines the employee's share of the employer's contribution. The second type is an employee contribution in excess of the maximum employee contribution of the first type. Employee contributions of the second type have no effect whatsoever on the amount of the employer's contribution or on the employee's allocated share of the employer's contribution. For convenience, these types of employee contributions are referred to in this chapter as "basic employee contributions" and as "voluntary employee contributions," respectively.

Basic Employee Contributions

It is not necessary for a thrift plan to require or permit all participants to contribute at the same rate. Most plans permit employees to choose the amount to be contributed, up to the maximum permissible, and some plans have different maximums for different classifications of employees. For example, a plan may permit employees with fewer than a certain number of years of service or participation to contribute within a specified range, while this range may be increased for employees with more years of service or participation. In addition, many plans specify that a minimum contribution, expressed either as a dollar amount or as a percentage of pay, is required. The minimum requirement usually is included for administrative purposes; but, in the past, this minimum was believed to affect the amount of voluntary employee contributions that a plan might permit.

Basic employee contribution requirements must not result in discrimination in favor of highly compensated employees. Such discrimination could arise either because the contributions are burdensome, resulting in inadequate plan coverage for lower paid employees, or because the rates of contribution and benefits are less for lower paid employees under a plan that provides for optional rates of contribution. In comparing benefits for lower paid and higher paid employees, allowance may be made for integration with Social Security benefits, unless the employee also is covered by a separate, fully integrated plan.

Voluntary Employee Contributions

A provision for voluntary employee contributions is an optional feature included in some thrift plans. This provision enables participants to take advantage of the favorable tax treatment afforded the earnings on such contributions. Voluntary employee contributions need to be accounted for separately and may be permitted up to 10 percent of the employee's compensation.

In the past, the maximum total employee contribution to a thrift plan (basic and voluntary combined) was considered to be 10 percent of the employee's compensation plus the minimum basic employee contribution. However, Revenue Ruling 81-234 makes it clear that a voluntary contribution may be as much as 10 percent of compensation and is not affected by either the minimum or the actual basic contribution.

Employer Contributions

The employer's contribution generally is defined in a thrift plan as a fixed percentage of basic employee contributions, although this is not a requirement for a plan qualified as a profit-sharing plan. That percentage also may vary for different classifications of employees as long as the classifications are nondiscriminatory. Some thrift plans qualified as profit-sharing plans provide that the employer, at its discretion, may make contributions in excess of the defined amount of contribution. Thrift plans qualified as money purchase pension plans cannot provide for such additional contributions, since the benefits would no longer be definitely determinable.

The employer's contribution is most often allocated among the participants in direct proportion to the basic employee contribution of each participant. However, other methods of allocation (e.g., a varying percentage based on years of service or participation) may be used, provided such other methods are not discriminatory.

TRA '86 Employee and Employer Matching Contributions Nondiscrimination Test

TRA '86 added a special nondiscrimination test that applies, beginning in 1987, to employee and employer matching contributions under any thrift plan. The purpose of this test is to make sure that the benefits of the highly compensated employees are not significantly higher than those of the other employees. The test is satisfied if the "average contribution percentage" for eligible highly compensated employees does not exceed the greater of (1) 2 times the average contribution percentage for all other eligible employees, subject to a maximum equal to the average contribution percentage for all other eligible employees plus two percentage points, or (2) 1.25 times the average contribution percentage for all other eligible employees. The following schedule illustrates the permissible percentages.

Average Contribution Percentage of Nonhighly Compensated Group of Employees	*Maximum Average Contribution Percentage of Highly Compensated Group of Employees*
1%	2%
2	4
3	5
4	6
5	7
6	8
7	9
8	10
9	11.25
10	12.50
11	13.75
12	15.00

The average contribution percentage for each group of employees is the average of the contribution percentages of all employees in that group. The contribution percentage of each individual is determined by dividing the sum of the employee's own contributions (both basic and voluntary) and the employer's matching contributions made on his or her behalf during the year by the amount of compensation that he or she received during the year.

Forfeitures

When a plan participant incurs a break in service, his or her nonvested benefits may be forfeited and, thereby, become available for other uses. Forfeitures under a thrift plan may be included as part of the employer's contribution (or, stated in another way, used to reduce the amount of the employer's contribution), or may be allocated among the participants in addition to the employer's contribution.

When forfeitures are included as part of the employer's contribution, they are allocated, of course, to the accounts of the participants in the same manner as the rest of the employer's contribution. If the forfeitures are allocated in addition to the employer's regular contribution, they generally are allocated among the participants in the same manner as the employer's contribution, but they may be allocated under other methods. However, if some other method is used, it may be necessary to demonstrate to the IRS that such other method does not discriminate in favor of highly compensated employees. After forfeitures have been allocated to the accounts of the participants, they generally are treated as though they were employer contributions.

Limits on Contributions to Employees' Accounts Each Year

Section 415 of the Internal Revenue Code places a limit on the total amount of employer contributions, forfeitures, and employee contributions that can be credited to the accounts of any participant during a specified year.

This limit, which applies to the aggregate of all defined contribution plans of the employer, requires that the sum of the employer's contributions and forfeitures allocated to an employee's account plus the total of his or her employee contributions (both basic and voluntary) cannot be greater in any year than the smaller of: (*a*) 25 percent of his or her pay; or (*b*) a specified dollar amount that is subject to increase to take into account cost-of-living adjustments. This dollar amount was originally $25,000 in 1974, was increased to $45,475 on January 1, 1982, but was reset by the Tax Equity and Fiscal Responsibility Act (TEFRA) at $30,000 on January 1, 1983. It will remain at $30,000 until the IRC 415 dollar limit for defined benefit plans reaches $120,000, at which time it will increase in tandem with the defined benefit plan limit, with the defined contribution limit being equal to one fourth of the defined benefit limit.

If the employee also is a participant in a defined benefit plan of the employer, an overall limitation exists on the amount of his or her benefits under both types of plans. Consequently, the above limit on the defined contribution plan benefit may have to be reduced, if the required reduction is not made under the defined benefit plan, so that the total benefit from both the defined contribution and defined benefit plans of the employer does not exceed the overall limitation.

The overall limitation is tested by adding the percentage of the maximum limitation computed separately for each type of plan that is being provided for an employee. The resulting sum must not exceed 125 percent for the dollar limitations, or, if less, 140 percent for the percentage limitations.

The overall limitation could be met by reducing benefits under either plan. It usually is preferable to make the reduction in the defined benefit plan, because the precise amount of reduction required cannot be determined until the employee retires, and because the reduction in a defined benefit plan does not become effective until retirement. However, other considerations may make it preferable to reduce the defined contribution plan. A choice should be made and incorporated in the plan document.

Investment of Contributions

Most thrift plans provide for more than one investment fund or type of investment. The participant may specify the percentage of his or her own contributions to be invested each year in each fund. A similar choice may or may not be available to the participant concerning the investment of employer contributions allocated on his or her behalf. Plans that permit the participant to choose investment funds typically provide that the participant may change the specified percentages and may transfer funds credited to his or her account from one investment fund to another on a periodic basis.

Other thrift plans, primarily because of the accounting complexities caused by a multitude of investment options, restrict the options available to employees. Some of those plans, nevertheless, permit participants nearing retirement age to make a one-time election to transfer funds from an equity-type investment fund to either a fixed income or guaranteed income fund, so fluctuations in value may be minimized as participants near retirement.

Among the more common investment funds are employer stock, fixed income funds invested in government bonds or notes, guaranteed return contracts offered by insurance companies, common stock funds, and money market funds, not necessarily in that order. The relative popularity of different investment funds can vary widely at different times; a tendency exists for one or the other type of investment to become extremely popular at certain times, often for very good reasons.

In any case, because both the financial markets and the plan's needs and objectives change over the course of time, it is sound policy to review the available choice of investment funds at regular intervals and to make changes when necessary or appropriate. The plan's wording should be designed to facilitate the making of such changes.

Vesting

Because of their nature and purpose, and as an incentive to encourage broad participation, thrift plans commonly provide for fairly rapid vesting, usually on a graded basis. However, the minimum vesting requirements for thrift plans are the same as for all other qualified pension and profit-sharing plans. In brief, all employer contributions, and funds attributable thereto, must vest at least as rapidly as under one of the following alternatives:

1. After 10 years of service, 100 percent vesting.
2. After 5 years of service, 25 percent vesting, plus an additional 5 percent for each of the next 5 years (50 percent after 10 years of service) plus an additional 10 percent for each of the next 5 years (100 percent after 15 years of service).
3. After 10 years of service or when age plus service (minimum of 5 years) first equals or exceeds 45 years, 50 percent vesting, plus an additional 10 percent for each of the next 5 years of service.

Beginning in 1989 the above alternatives will become obsolete and a plan must provide that a participant will either be 100 percent vested after five years or 20 percent vested after three years with a 20 percent per year increase for each of the next four years (100 percent vesting after seven years of service).

Of course, an employee must always be 100 percent vested in funds attributable to his or her own contributions and be 100 percent vested in the total account on reaching normal retirement age.

Many thrift plans in the past have used what is called ''class year'' vesting. Under these plans, each year's employer contributions (''class'') and the earnings thereon were accounted for separately until they were fully vested, which would be from two to five years after they were made. At that time they would typically be distributed to the employee unless he or she elected to defer receipt until retirement. Under these plans it was possible that an employee would never be 100 percent vested prior to his or her normal retirement age in all of the employer contributions credited to his or her account. Class year vesting was repealed by TRA '86 and will not be allowed after 1988.

Withdrawals while in Service

The in-service withdrawal provisions included in a thrift plan generally are dependent on the objective of the employer in establishing the plan. For the great majority, when the objective of the plan is to provide a means by which the participants can accumulate funds that may be used to meet their financial needs before (as well as after) retirement, the withdrawal provisions are very liberal. However, if the objective of the plan is solely or primarily to provide a source of income after retirement, the withdrawal provisions, if any, will not be as liberal. The 10 percent additional income tax imposed by TRA '86 on taxable withdrawals prior to age 59½ will undoubtedly make in-service withdrawal provisions less attractive.

Withdrawal of Employee Contributions

The in-service withdrawal of all or a portion of an employee's own contributions and interest earned thereon is permitted under many thrift plans. Such a provision must not be such that it can be reasonably expected to result in manipulation of the employer's contribution. Prior to the passage of the Economic Recovery Tax Act of 1981 (ERTA), plans that permitted withdrawal of interest on employees' contributions often provided for restrictions or penalties designed to avoid constructive receipt. While no longer needed for that purpose, many such restrictions may be retained to further discourage manipulation and to encourage savings for retirement.

The potential for the manipulation of employer's contributions arises if the employee is permitted to withdraw all or a portion of basic employee contributions (the employee contributions to which the employer's contribution is geared) without penalty so that he or she could effectively use the same contributions year after year and thereby manipulate the formula allocating the employer's contribution under the plan. The IRS has ruled that plans permitting such manipulations without penalty will not be qualified under Section 401(a) of the Internal Revenue Code. This problem is avoided by providing an appropriate penalty, which is typically the suspension of participation for a specified period such as six months.

The withdrawal of voluntary employee contributions does not present any problems concerning the manipulation of the employer's contributions.

Withdrawal of Employer Contributions

The in-service withdrawal of all or a portion of the employer's contributions in which the participant has a vested interest is permitted in many thrift plans qualified as profit-sharing plans. Such withdrawals are not permissible prior to a participant's normal retirement age under thrift plans that are qualified as money purchase pension plans. The amounts withdrawn normally have to be accumulated in the trust fund for at least two years, although amounts that have not been accumulated for at least two years may be withdrawn by employees with at least five years of participation.

Prior to the enactment of ERTA, some form of penalty was required for withdrawal of employer contributions to avoid constructive receipt.

This might take the form of a penalty of 6 percent of the withdrawal, imposed by reducing future allocations of employer contributions, or by suspending the employee's participation for a specified time. While no longer required, such penalties may be retained, and some controls are still required to avoid the possibility of manipulation by employees.

Some thrift plans permit withdrawal of the total account balance when an employee reaches normal retirement age even if still employed. A thrift plan qualified as a profit-sharing plan may permit such a withdrawal any time after the employee reaches age 59½.

If the thrift plan is qualified as a money purchase pension plan, it cannot incorporate this type of provision, because it is the position of the IRS that pension plans may not provide for any distributions prior to retirement or termination of service. However, a withdrawal can be made from such a plan after the employee attains normal retirement age even though he or she does not separate from service.

401(k) Thrift Plan Withdrawals

In-service withdrawals under 401(k) thrift plans are more restrictive. An employee's salary reduction contributions ("elective deferrals") cannot be withdrawn prior to age 59½ unless it can be demonstrated that the withdrawal is due to hardship. If the employer's contributions are used to satisfy the nondiscrimination tests that apply to cash or deferred arrangements, then these contributions are subject to the same withdrawal restrictions as apply to the employee's own elective deferrals. However, starting in 1989 any such employer contributions, investment earnings on such contributions, and investment earnings on the employee's own elective deferrals may not be withdrawn prior to age 59½ even for hardship reasons.

Loans

Loans to plan participants are permissible under thrift plans if such loans are expressly allowed by the plan on a nondiscriminatory basis, are adequately secured, bear a reasonable rate of interest, and provide for repayment in substantially equal installments, payable not less frequently than quarterly, spread out over a specified period not greater than five years. The amount of a loan cannot exceed the lesser of:

1. $50,000 minus the highest outstanding loan balance of the participant during the preceding 12 months.

2. An amount (inclusive of any existing loans) equal to 50 percent of the participant's vested interest, but this 50 percent limit changes to 100 percent if the loan is for $10,000 or less.

Also, the loan may be for a period longer than five years, if the purpose of the loan is to acquire the principal residence of the participant.

To ensure that loans will not affect the investment performance that could be expected if loans were not permitted, some plans provide that loans will be treated as a directed investment by the participant of the proportion of the account represented by the loan. The investment yield credited to such directed investment then is based solely on the interest payments made in the repayment of the loan.

Distributions on Retirement or Termination

Benefits on the retirement or termination of service of a participant under a thrift plan normally are distributed in a lump-sum payment, by a series of installment payments, or through the purchase of an annuity contract from an insurance company. Lump-sum payments are the most common form of distribution.

Many plans have eliminated the purchase of an annuity as a method of distribution to avoid the complications associated with qualified joint and survivor annuities. Participants who wish to have a life annuity purchased on their behalf may roll over that portion of the distribution exclusive of their own aftertax contributions to an individual retirement account (IRA) sponsored by an insurance company within 60 days after the date they receive their distribution from the thrift plan and use such amount to purchase an annuity. However, the employee's own aftertax contributions cannot be transferred to an individual retirement account. The plan itself could pay the proceeds, including employee contributions, in installments over a fixed period that is not longer than the joint and last survivor life expectancy of the participant and his or her designated joint pensioner.

A thrift plan is required to commence the payment of benefits to a participant not later than the 60th day after the close of the plan year in which the latest of the following events occurs: (1) attaining age 65, or attaining any earlier normal retirement age specified under the plan; (2) 10 years have elapsed from the time participation in the plan commenced; or (3) service with the employer is terminated.

The payment of benefits to the participant may be deferred to a date later than the dates specified above if (1) the plan permits such a deferral and the participant submits to the plan administrator a signed written statement that describes his or her benefit and the date on which the participant elects to have it commence, and (2) the deferral of such payment will not cause the benefits payable on death to be more than "incidental" (which means, essentially, that the participant should be expected under normal life expectancies to receive more than 50 percent of the benefit before his or her death). For example, a participant who retires at age 65 might elect to defer receipt of any benefits until age 70, and then take a percentage of the fund (such as 10 percent) each year thereafter. In practice, benefit payments under a thrift plan typically begin shortly after the date of termination of the participant's service, although some plans provide that payments will not begin until the participant has been gone long enough to incur a forfeiture that is not required to be restored in the event of his or her reemployment.

Starting in 1989, benefit payments will have to begin not later than April 1 of the year following the year in which an employee attains age 70½, even if the participant is still in the service of the employer at that time.

Top-Heavy Provisions of TEFRA

TEFRA imposes restrictions on plans that are "top-heavy." A plan is top-heavy if 60 percent or more of the total of all account balances are for key employees (officers and significant owners).

The principal requirements for top-heavy plans are: (1) vesting at 20 percent after two years service, grading up to 100 percent after six years, or 100 percent vesting after three years service; (2) an employer contribution for each nonkey participant of at least 3 percent of compensation (or, if smaller, the highest percentage received by any key employee); and (3) if the participant is also covered by a defined benefit plan, the overall dollar limitation is based on 100 percent, rather than 125 percent, of the separate dollar limitations, unless additional conditions are met.

TAX ASPECTS OF CONTRIBUTIONS TO THRIFT PLANS

Contributions to qualified thrift plans are afforded the same tax treatment and considerations afforded contributions to other qualified pension, profit-sharing, and stock-bonus plans. Briefly, these include:

1. The employer can take a current deduction for its contributions to the plan (provided the contributions are not in excess of the prescribed deductible limits), and such contributions are not taxable to the employee or his or her beneficiary until actually distributed.

2. Employee elective deferral contributions under a 401(k) thrift plan, up to a certain limit ($7,000 in 1987), are not included in an employee's taxable wages for federal income taxes (they are, however, subject to FICA tax withhholding). All other employee contributions are included in an employee's taxable wages and may not be claimed as a tax deduction.
3. The contributions of both the employer and employees are allowed to earn and compound income on a tax-free basis (to the extent that such income is not deemed to be unrelated business income of the trust), and such earnings are not taxable to the employee or his or her beneficiary until they are actually received.

TAX ASPECTS OF DISTRIBUTIONS FROM THRIFT PLANS

The taxation of distributions from thrift plans varies, of course, in different circumstances. Distributions and withdrawals from qualified thrift plans are taxed in the same manner as distributions and withdrawals from other qualified pension, profit-sharing, and stock-bonus plans. It is not the purpose of this chapter to discuss in detail the taxability of distributions from qualified plans, but some general tax features include the following:

1. Employee contributions that have been made from aftertax dollars are not subject to federal income tax when distributed or withdrawn. However, any withdrawal in respect of employee after-tax contributions is treated as including a prorata portion of investment earnings on those contributions, and that portion is taxable. This prorata rule does not apply to a withdrawal of after-tax contributions contributed prior to January 1, 1987, if the plan—as in effect on May 5, 1986—permitted such a withdrawal.
2. Employee elective deferral contributions under a 401(k) thrift plan, and employer contributions and investment earnings on both the employer and employee contributions are taxable as ordinary income when distributed or withdrawn. In addition, a 10 percent penalty is imposed if the distribution or withdrawal is made before age 59½, unless the distribution is due to early retirement after attaining age 55, is in the form of a level life annuity, or meets certain other specified exceptions. If the distribution is a qualified lump-sum distribution, alternative taxation is available as described in (3) and (4).

3. Special five-year forward averaging tax treatment is available on a one-time basis for qualified lump-sum distributions that are received after age 59½. A transitional rule applies to participants who had attained age 50 before January 1, 1986 that allows them to use pre-1987 lump-sum tax rules on a one-time basis.
4. Alternatively, a qualified lump-sum distribution may be rolled over into an IRA on a tax-free basis. Such a rollover is available if the qualified lump-sum distribution is received before age 59½, as well as after that age.
5. The unrealized appreciation in the value of stock of the employer during the period that it is held in the trust fund is not taxable at the time that it is distributed on behalf of the participant if such stock is distributed as part of a qualified lump-sum distribution or if such stock is attributable to the employee's own contributions.
6. The first $5,000 of any otherwise taxable distribution from the trust fund due to the employee's death is excluded from federal income tax if such death benefit is paid in a lump sum, or if it is forfeitable and paid in installments. All plans of the employer must be combined in applying this exclusion.

In general, the options on form and timing of payment that can be made available under thrift plans are valuable, because they allow for flexibility in an employee's overall tax planning.

ADMINISTRATIVE CONSIDERATIONS

A primary consideration in the design and operation of any thrift plan is the administrative and record-keeping capabilities available to the employer. A thrift plan is required to allocate the contributions to the plan each year among the participants, and must provide for an annual valuation of the trust investments, on a specified date each year, to allocate the investment gains or losses (both realized and unrealized) among the accounts of the participants. While such allocations are required to be performed only once a year, many employers (primarily those with sophisticated record-keeping capabilities) choose to perform either or both allocations more frequently, often on a monthly or quarterly basis.

It is necessary under a thrift plan to be able to determine the benefits to which a participant is entitled. To make such a determination, it is necessary to be able to ascertain the amount of the employee's own contributions (both basic and voluntary), and the funds attributable thereto, and the amount of the employer contributions and forfeitures that have been credited to the participant's account and the funds attributable thereto. In addition, if employer stock is distributed to the participant, it is necessary, for tax purposes, to ascertain the time of acquisition and the cost to the trust fund of each share of stock distributed to the employee.

It is also necessary to be able to ascertain that the plan satisfies the nondiscrimination rules that apply to employee and employer matching contributions and, if a cash or deferred arrangement is involved, to be able to ascertain that the elective deferral contributions of the highly paid employees, as compared to those of the other employees, satisfy the special nondiscrimination tests that apply to 401(k) plans.

Other tasks involved in the administration of a thrift plan include: communicating to each participant the amount of his or her accrued benefits (normally done at least once a year); enrolling the eligible employees as participants in the plan; and obtaining their authorizations for the deduction of the desired employee contributions, their investment fund designations, and their beneficiary designations (and subsequent changes in such authorizations and designations).

While the general operation of a thrift plan is fairly simple and easy to understand, the accounting methods and record-keeping system required to maintain the accounts and to determine the benefits of the participants can be quite complex, depending on the variety of options available to the participants.

CHAPTER 28

CASH OR DEFERRED PLANS*

Jack L. VanDerhei

Conventional deferred profit-sharing plans are discussed in Chapter 25. This chapter deals with a variation of these plans, where the employee is given a choice of receiving an amount in the form of currently taxable compensation (for federal income tax purposes) or of deferring this amount to be taxed at a future time. More specifically, the employee has the choice of receiving an employer contribution in cash or having it deferred under the plan, and/or the choice of making his or her own contribution to a plan from before-tax income, thus avoiding any federal income tax on this amount until it is received in the form of a plan distribution.

Cash or deferred arrangements (CODAs) are not an entirely new concept. They have existed since the 1950s. However, they were beset with legislative and regulatory doubt during the middle 1970s. The Revenue Act of 1978, along with proposed regulations issued by the Internal Revenue Service in 1981, have opened the way for these plans. Their growth, since 1981, has been significant.

This chapter reviews the legislative history of these plans, the technical requirements they must meet, some special considerations that must be taken into account, and their relative advantages and disadvantages, both to employers and employees.

---

* Parts of this chapter are based on material that appeared in Everett T. Allen, Jr., Joseph J. Melone, Jerry S. Rosenbloom, and Jack L. VanDerhei, *Pension Planning*, 6th ed. (Homewood, Ill.: Richard D. Irwin, 1988).

LEGISLATIVE HISTORY OF CODAs

Before 1972, the Internal Revenue Service provided guidelines for qualifying cash option CODAs in a series of revenue rulings. In essence, more than half of the total participation in the plan had to be from the lowest paid two thirds of all eligible employees. If this requirement was met, employees who elected to defer were not considered to be in constructive receipt of the amounts involved even though they had the option to take cash. Salary reduction plans satisfying these requirements were also eligible for the same favorable tax treatment.

In December 1972, the Internal Revenue Service issued proposed regulations that stated that any compensation which an employee could receive as cash would be subject to current taxation even if deferred as a contribution to the employer's qualified plan. Although primarily directed at salary reduction plans, the proposed regulations also applied to cash option profit-sharing plans.

As the gestation period for the Employee Retirement Income Security Act (ERISA) was coming to an end, Congress became increasingly aware of the need to devote additional time to the study of the CODA concept. As a result, ERISA included a section that provided that the existing tax status for CODAs was to be frozen until the end of 1976. Plans in existence on June 27, 1974 were permitted to retain their tax-favored status; however, contributions to CODAs established after that date were to be treated as employee contributions and, as a result, were currently taxable.

Unable to meet its self-imposed deadline, Congress extended the moratorium on CODAs twice; the second time the deadline was extended until the end of 1979.

The Revenue Act of 1978 enacted permanent provisions governing CODAs by adding Section 401(k) to the Internal Revenue Code, effective for plan years beginning after December 31, 1979. In essence, CODAs are now permitted, as long as certain requirements are met.

This legislation, in itself, did not result in any significant activity in the adoption of new CODAs. It was not until 1982, after the Internal Revenue Service issued proposed regulations in late 1981, that employers began to respond to the benefit planning opportunities created by this new legislation. By providing some interpretive guidelines for Section 401(k), and by specifically sanctioning ''salary reduction'' plans, the Service opened the way for the adoption of new plans and for the conversion of existing, conventional plans. For example, many employers converted existing aftertax thrift plans to CODAs to take advantage of the Section 401(k) tax shelter on employee contributions.

The Tax Reform Act of 1984 provided some subtle modifications to Section 401(k). The original specification of the nondiscrimination standards for cash or deferred plans appeared to permit integration with Social Security. This ambiguity was resolved by applying both the general coverage tests and a special actual deferral percentage (ADP) test (both tests are described later in this chapter) to all CODAs. The 1984 legislation also extended cash or deferred treatment to pre-ERISA money purchase plans, although contributions were limited to the levels existing on June 27, 1974.

The changes imposed by the Tax Reform Act of 1986 were much more substantive. In addition to reducing the limit on elective deferrals, this legislation provided a new definition of highly paid employees, restricted the ADP test, modified the list of contingencies on which distributions from CODAs are permitted, and reduced the employer's flexibility in designing eligibility requirements for these arrangements.

At the time this text was prepared, the Service had not issued final regulations. Thus, this chapter is based on the proposed regulations and the statement by the Internal Revenue Service that they can be relied on for plan qualification purposes until final regulations are published.

TECHNICAL REQUIREMENTS

Section 401(k) states that a qualified CODA is any arrangement that:

1. Is part of a profit-sharing or stock-bonus plan, a pre-ERISA money purchase plan, or a rural electric cooperative plan[1] that meets the requirements of Section 401(a) of the Code.
2. Allows covered employees to elect to have the employer make contributions to a trust under the plan on behalf of the employees, or directly to the employees in cash.
3. Subjects amounts held by the trust that are attributable to employer contributions made pursuant to an employee's election to certain specified withdrawal limitations.
4. Provides that accrued benefits derived from such contributions are nonforfeitable.

---

[1] For purposes of IRS Section 401(k), the term *rural electric cooperative plan* means any pension plan that is a defined contribution plan and is established and maintained by a rural electric cooperative or a national association of such cooperatives. For further details see IRC Section 457(d)(9)(B).

5. Does not require, as a condition of participation in the arrangement, that an employee complete a period of service with the employer maintaining the plan in excess of one year.

As a tax-qualified plan, a CODA must meet all of the nondiscriminatory requirements applicable to such plans. The special requirements for CODAs are covered in the following material. Before discussing these requirements, however, it is important to understand the difference between *elective* and *nonelective* contributions. Elective contributions are amounts that an employee could have received in cash but elected to defer. Nonelective contributions are employer contributions that are automatically deferred under the plan.

Type of Plan

As noted, a CODA may be part of a profit-sharing or stock-bonus plan. This, of course, includes thrift and savings plans. The only qualified, defined contribution plan that cannot be established as a CODA is a post-ERISA money purchase or defined contribution pension plan.[2]

As a practical matter, most CODAs fall into one of two categories—either cash or deferred profit-sharing plans, or thrift and savings plans. CODAs can also be subdivided into plans that involve employer contributions only, both employer and employee contributions, and employee contributions only. Plans involving only employee contributions are not expected to be used to a great extent, largely because of the difficulty these plans will experience in satisfying the special tests that are described later.

Individual Limitations

There is a $7,000 limitation on the exclusion of elective deferrals for any taxable year. Any excess amounts (and the earnings on them) are included in the employee's gross income. This limitation applies to the aggregate elective deferral made in a taxable year to all CODAs and simplified employee pensions (described in Chapter 31). The limit is reduced by any employer contributions to a tax deferred annuity (described in Chapter 32) under a salary reduction agreement; however, the limitation is increased (but not to an amount in excess of $9,500) by the amount

[2] CODAs are not available to tax-exempt organizations unless adopted before July 2, 1986, or to states or local government unless adopted before May 6, 1986.

of these employer contributions. This limit is indexed to the Consumer Price Index (CPI) beginning in 1988.

Elective deferrals in excess of the $7,000 annual limit (plus the earnings on such amounts) may be allocated among the plans under which the deferrals were made by March 1st following the close of the taxable year, and the plan may distribute the allocated amount back to the employee by April 15th. Although such a distribution will be includable in the employee's taxable income for the year to which the excess deferral relates, it will not be subject to the 10 percent excise tax that may otherwise apply to distributions prior to age 59½. Any income on the excess deferral will be treated as earned and received in the taxable year in which the excess deferral is made.

Any excess contribution not distributed by this date will remain in the plan, subject to all regular withdrawal restrictions. Moreover, the amount will again be treated as taxable income when it is later distributed.

A second limit, effective in 1989, caps the amount of pay that can be taken into account for most qualified plan purposes, including the determination of contributions and benefits, at $200,000. This limit is also indexed to changes in the CPI.

Nondiscrimination In Coverage

A CODA will not be qualified unless the employees eligible to benefit under the arrangement satisfy the coverage provisions for qualified plans. Beginning in 1989, a plan will have to satisfy any one of the three new tests described below.[3]

1. The *percentage test* is satisfied if the plan benefits at least 70 percent of the sponsoring employer's nonhighly compensated employees.
2. A plan may qualify under the *ratio test* if the percentage of nonhighly compensated employees who benefit under the plan is at least 70 percent of the percentage of highly compensated employees who benefit under the plan.
3. Two conditions must be met for a plan to satisfy the *average benefits test*.
   a. The plan must meet the fair cross-section test applying to plan years beginning before January 1, 1989.
   b. The average employer-provided contributions (including for-

[3] See Chapter 47 for a description of the coverage tests for plan years prior to 1989.

feitures) or benefits for nonhighly compensated employees under all of the employer's qualified plans (including an amount deemed to represent the employer-provided portion of Social Security under rules to be issued) must be, as a percentage of compensation, at least 70 percent of the similar benefit for highly compensated employees.

These tests can be satisfied by combining comparable plans. Further, an exception to the general rule regarding the aggregation of all employees of a controlled group of corporations (see Chapter 47) is permitted under certain circumstances. If an employer has separate lines of business or operating units employing at least 50 employees that are established for bona fide business reasons, and if the plan meets the fair cross-section test applying to plan years beginning before January 1, 1989, any of the tests can also be satisfied separately for each such line of business or unit. The law provides a "safe harbor" test for determining whether a separate facility has been established for bona fide business reasons. To qualify for the safe harbor, the percentage of highly compensated employees at the separate facility may be not less than one half nor more than twice the average percentage of highly compensated employees companywide. Headquarters personnel are not considered a separate line of business.

In addition to meeting one of the basic coverage tests, plans (other than negotiated multiemployer plans) must meet a *minimum coverage test* beginning in 1989. Each plan must meet this test at all times; the test cannot be satisfied by combining comparable plans nor can the test be applied on a line of business or operating unit basis. The minimum coverage test requires that a plan cover the lesser of: (1) 50 employees, or (2) 40 percent of all employees of the employer.

In applying these requirements, it will be permissible to exclude from consideration any employees covered by a collective bargaining agreement if there is evidence that retirement benefits were the subject of good faith bargaining. It is also possible to exclude nonresident aliens who receive no income from the employer from sources within the United States, certain airline pilots, and employees not meeting minimum age and service requirements.

Nondiscrimination in Contributions

A CODA will not be qualified unless the contributions under the plan are deemed to be nondiscriminatory. To satisfy the nondiscrimination in contributions requirement, an actual deferral percentage (ADP) test must be met.

The ADP test is a mathematical test that must be satisfied by the close of each plan year. The first step in applying this test is to determine the actual deferral percentage for each eligible employee. This is done by dividing the amount of contribution deferred at the employee's election by the amount of the employee's compensation. In addition, the employer may elect to include in the numerator any matching or nonelective contributions that satisfy the CODA withdrawal limitations and nonforfeitability requirements (described later in this chapter) and rules to be prescribed by the secretary of the treasury. Excess deferrals must be taken into account in this testing even if they are distributed to comply with the $7,000 cap on elective deferrals.

For purposes of the ADP test, compensation means compensation for service performed for the employer that is currently includable in gross income. An employer may elect to include as compensation any amount that is contributed by the employer to a CODA, tax-sheltered annuity, or simplified employee pension by means of a salary reduction agreement. The secretary of the treasury is directed to prescribe regulations to provide for alternative methods of determining compensation that may be used by an employer, provided that the employer may not use an alternative method if discrimination in favor of highly compensated employees results.

It should be noted that this percentage is determined for all eligible employees, whether or not they are actually participating. Thus, the ADP for a nonparticipating but eligible employee is zero.

The next step is to divide the eligible employees into two groups—the highly compensated employees[4] and all other eligible employees. For

---

[4] A highly compensated employee is defined as one who meets at least one of the following conditions:

1. A 5 percent owner.
2. A person earning over $75,000 a year in either the current or preceding year.
3. A person earning over $50,000 a year in either the current or preceding year and is or was in the top 20 percent of all active employees for such year.
4. An officer earning over 150 percent of the dollar limit for annual additions to a defined contribution plan ($45,000 in 1987) in either the current or preceding year.

In determining who is an officer, no more than 50 individuals (or 10 percent of the employee group, if smaller) need be taken into account. If an employee is a family member (lineal ascendant or descendant and spouse) of a 5 percent owner or one of the top 10 highly paid employees, both will be treated as one person for purposes of the nondiscrimination tests. The $50,000 and $75,000 amounts will be indexed to reflect increases in the Consumer Price Index (CPI) beginning in 1988. If an employee (other than a 5 percent owner) earned less than the test amount in the year before the year he or she entered the prohibited group and was not an officer in that prior year, the employee will not be a member of the prohibited group for the entrance year unless he or she is among the top 100 employees for that year.

each of these groups, the actual deferral percentages are mathematically averaged. If the average ADP for the highly compensated employees does not exceed the average ADP for the nonhighly compensated employees by more than the allowable percentage, the test is satisfied for the year. The allowable percentages are set forth in Table 28–1.

A few examples will help clarify this table.

1. If the ADP for the nonhighly compensated employees is determined to be 1 percent, then the ADP for the highly compensated employees can be as much as 2 percent (1 percent times 2).
2. If the ADP for the nonhighly compensated employees is determined to be 4 percent, then the ADP for the highly compensated employees can be as much as 6 percent (4 percent plus 2 percent).
3. If the ADP for the nonhighly compensated employees is 10 percent, the ADP for the highly compensated employees can be as much as 12.5 percent (10 percent times 1.25).

It should be noted that the ADP test determines a maximum *average* actual deferral percentage for the highly compensated employees. It does not necessarily indicate the maximum deferral percentage for an individual in this group. As long as the average deferral for the highly compensated employees is less than or equal to the maximum allowed, it will be permissible for an individual in this group to defer an amount in excess of that limitation.

If any highly compensated employee is a participant under two or more CODAs of the employer, all such CODAs will be treated as one CODA for purposes of determining the employee's deferral percentage.

The ADP test will also apply separately to aftertax employee contributions and matching contributions on elective deferrals. Elective defer-

TABLE 28–1
Maximum Allowable Average ADPs for Highly Compensated Employees

If Average ADP among Nonhighly Compensated Employees (ADP_{NHC}) Is:	*Then Average ADP among Highly Compensated Employees (ADP_{HC}) May Not Exceed:*
Less than 2 percent	2 times ADP_{NHC}
At least 2 percent but less than 8 percent	ADP_{NHC} plus 2 percent
8 percent or more	1.25 times ADP_{NHC}

TABLE 28–2

Employee	*Compensation*	*Six Percent Nonelective Contribution*	*Two Percent Nonelective Contribution*	*Elective Contribution Elected to be Deferred*
1	$100,000	$6,000	$2,000	$2,000
2	80,000	4,800	1,600	1,600
3	75,000	4,500	1,500	1,500
4	40,000	2,400	800	0
5	30,000	1,800	600	0
6	20,000	1,200	400	0
7	20,000	1,200	400	0
8	10,000	600	200	0
9	5,000	300	100	0

rals and qualified nonelective contributions (those that meet the vesting and withdrawal restrictions for elective contributions) may be taken into account in certain circumstances to be set forth in regulations.[5]

Nondiscrimination Rules for Combined Plans

If a CODA consists of both elective contributions and nonelective contributions, the nonelective portion of the plan must satisfy the general coverage tests and the general nondiscrimination requirements with regard to contributions. Elective deferrals under a CODA may not be taken into account for purposes of determining whether a plan has met these requirements.

Combined plans can satisfy the nondiscrimination requirements by one of two methods. In both cases, the nonelective portion must satisfy the general rules mentioned above; however, the special rules that must be met by all qualified CODAs may be met either by the elective portion of the plan alone or the combined elective and nonelective portions of the plan. The nonelective portion of the plan may be considered in applying the special rules if the contributions satisfy the regulations to be issued by the secretary of the treasury.

Table 28–2, adapted from Proposed Regulation Section 1.401(k)-1, illustrates the application of these rules. An employer with nine employees maintains and contributes to a profit sharing plan the following

[5] See Chapter 27 for more detail.

amounts: 6 percent of each employee's compensation, where such amounts do not satisfy the Section 401(k) nonforfeitability and distribution requirements; 2 percent of each employee's compensation, where such amounts do satisfy the Section 401(k) nonforfeitability and distribution requirements; and up to 2 percent of each employee's compensation, which the employee may elect to receive as a direct cash payment or to contribute to the plan. In 1987, employees 1 through 9 received compensation and deferred contributions as indicated in Table 28–2.

Assuming that none of the employees are 5 percent owners or officers, only employees 1, 2, and 3 are highly compensated employees. The ADP test will not be satisfied if only the elective contributions are measured, since the average ADP for the nonhighly compensated employees is zero and, as can be seen from Table 28–1, the maximum allowable average ADP for the highly compensated employees would also be zero (2 times 0 percent). As a result of the fact that the highly compensated employees generated an average ADP of 2 percent in this example, the combined plan would not satisfy the nondiscrimination tests.

However, the nondiscrimination test may be satisfied if the elective contributions that meet the Section 401(k) nonforfeitability and distribution requirements are allowed to be included in the average ADP determination under the regulations to be issued by the secretary of the treasury. In that case, the average ADP for the nonhighly compensated employees will be 2 percent (0 percent elective plus 2 percent nonelective) and, as can be seen from Table 28–1, this would allow a maximum average ADP for the highly compensated employees of 4 percent (2 percent + 2 percent). The actual average ADP for the highly compensated employees is 4 percent (2 percent elective plus 2 percent nonelective); therefore, the ADP test is not violated.

Note that the plan must also satisfy the coverage requirements described earlier. However, there will be no difficulty satisfying such a test in this example due to the fact that all employees were eligible to benefit under the arrangement.

Methods of Enhancing the Probability that the ADP Test is Met

There are several ways in which an employer can minimize or eliminate the possibility that a plan will not meet the ADP test. The following lists some of the techniques that might be used for this purpose.

1. The plan can be designed so that it is in automatic compliance. For example, the employer might make an automatic 5 percent contribution for all employees that satisfies the CODA withdrawal limi-

tations and nonforfeitability requirements in addition to the requirements to be prescribed by the secretary of the treasury. Employees may then be given the option of contributing up to 1.5 percent of pay by way of salary reduction. The plan will always satisfy the ADP test since the maximum allowable average ADP for the highly compensated employees could be as much as 7 percent (5 percent plus 2 percent) but, in fact, will never exceed 6.5 percent (5 percent nonelective plus 1.5 percent elective).

2. The plan also could be designed to encourage maximum participation from the nonhighly compensated employees. This could be done under a savings plan, for example, by providing for higher levels of employer contributions with respect to lower pay levels.
3. Limits may be placed on the maximum amounts that might be deferred.
4. The plan could include a provision allowing the employer to adjust deferrals (either upward or downward) if the plan is in danger of failing to meet the ADP test.
5. The employer may make additional nonelective contributions at the end of the plan year to the extent necessary to satisfy the test. (Such contributions, of course, would have to satisfy the CODA withdrawal limitations and nonforfeitability requirements and the requirements to be prescribed by the secretary of the treasury.)
6. Contributions for a plan year could be determined in advance of the plan year and, once established on a basis that satisfies the ADP test, could be fixed on an irrevocable basis (except, possibly, that nonhighly compensated employees could be given the option of increasing their contributions).

Curing Discriminatory Deferrals

If, despite the best efforts of the sponsor to prevent discriminatory deferrals, the ADP tests are not satisfied, then the plan must eliminate excess contributions to keep the plan qualified. Excess contributions are defined as the difference between (1) the aggregate amount of employer contributions actually paid over to the trust on behalf of highly compensated employees for such plan year and (2) the maximum allowable contributions for highly compensated employees, based on the average ADP for nonhighly compensated employees as shown in Table 28–1.

A CODA will not be treated as failing to meet the ADP requirements for any plan year if either of the following conditions are met before the close of the *following* plan year:

1. The amount of the excess contributions for such plan year (and any income allocable to such contributions) is distributed.

2. To the extent provided in regulations, the employee elects to treat the amount of the excess contributions as an amount distributed to the employee and then contributed by the employee to the plan.

Excess contributions are distributed by returning contributions made on behalf of highly compensated employees in order of the actual deferral percentages beginning with the highest of such percentages. In other words, the highly compensated employee with the largest ADP would have contributions returned until one of the following occurs:

1. The ADP test is satisfied (i.e., the relationship between ADP_{NHC} and the adjusted ADP_{HC} satisfies the requirements expressed in Table 28–1).
2. The ADP for the highly compensated employee with the largest ADP is reduced to the level of the highly compensated employee with the second largest ADP.

Successive iterations of this procedure are continued until the ADP test is satisfied.

Distributions of excess contributions (and income) may be made without regard to any other provision of law (e.g., qualified domestic relations orders[6] will not be violated). Moreover, although the amounts received are treated as taxable income to the employee the 10 percent penalty tax on early distributions from qualified retirement plans will not apply to any amount required to be distributed under this provision.

Although the plan has until the close of the following plan year to distribute or recharacterize excess contributions to avoid disqualification, an excess contribution may result in a 10 percent penalty tax *for the employer* unless it is distributed (together with any income allocable thereto) before the close of the first 2½ months of the following plan year. Any amount distributed or recharacterized will be treated as received and earned by the recipient in his or her taxable year for which the contribution was made.

Nonforfeitability Requirements

The value of all elective contributions to a CODA must be fully vested at all times. The value of nonelective contributions must vest in accordance with one of ERISA's prescribed vesting standards.[7] It should be noted,

---

[6] See Chapter 41 for a discussion of qualified domestic relations orders.

[7] Beginning in 1989, only two vesting standards will be available (unless the plan is top-heavy). The first standard requires that all accrued benefits must be 100 percent vested after

however, that the vested amount of elective contributions cannot be considered for this purpose. Thus, the vesting of nonelective contributions must be accomplished independently.

As mentioned previously, if nonelective contributions are fully vested from the outset (and if they are subject to the same restrictions on withdrawals as are elective contributions), the secretary of treasury is authorized to prescribe regulations permitting them to be taken into account when applying the ADP test for elective contributions.

Limitations on Withdrawals

A common provision in many profit-sharing and savings plans is one that permits an employee to make a withdrawal of some part of the vested account balance while still actively employed. Sometimes, this withdrawal right is limited to hardship situations; more often than not, however, a withdrawal can be made for any reason, subject to some period of suspension from plan participation.

In the case of a CODA, the ability to make in-service withdrawals is severely limited. The value of elective contributions (and nonelective contributions that are aggregated with elective contributions to meet special CODA nondiscrimination rules) may be distributable only on one of the following conditions:

1. Death.
2. Disability.
3. Separation from service.
4. The termination of the plan (provided no successor plan is established).
5. The sale of substantially all of the assets used by the corporation in a trade or business if the employee continues employment with the corporation acquiring the assets.
6. The sale of a corporation's interest in a subsidiary if the employee continues employment with the subsidiary.

Moreover, in the case of profit-sharing or stock-bonus plans, distributions of elective contributions will be permitted at age 59½, or before 59½ for hardships. However, hardship withdrawals will be limited to the amount of an employee's elective deferrals, without investment income.

---

five years of service. The second standard permits graded vesting, with 20 percent of accrued benefits vesting after three years of service and that percentage increasing in 20 percent multiples each year until 100 percent vesting is achieved after seven years. See Chapter 24 for a discussion of the vesting requirements for plan years prior to 1989.

Limiting the withdrawal of elective contributions to hardship cases only can be of significance to many employers since it could have a negative effect on the participation of lower paid employees, thus creating problems in meeting the ADP test. The proposed regulations define hardship in a very narrow way. Specifically, these regulations require that the hardship be caused by immediate and heavy financial needs of the employee. Further, they require that the withdrawal not exceed the amount required to meet the immediate financial need created by the hardship and not reasonably available from other resources of the employee. Finally, they require that the determination of financial need and the amount of money necessary to meet it must be made in accordance with uniform and nondiscriminatory standards set forth in the plan.

The language of the proposed regulations raises a host of questions about the design and administration of a hardship provision. For example, what is meant by a "heavy financial need"? Will this include the cost of educating children or the purchase of a residence? What is meant by "not reasonably available from other resources of the employee"? Will this require that the employee utilize all available lines of credit before a withdrawal can be made? Of equal importance are questions concerning the employer's role in administering the provision. How deeply must the employer probe into the employee's personal financial situation in order to comply with the regulations? Is such personal involvement desirable from an employee relations viewpoint?

It is hoped that final regulations will liberalize this provision and provide some meaningful rules on which to base hardship withdrawals. In the meantime, some relief might be provided by including a loan provision in the plan.[8] Such a provision would make some monies available to participants during active employment, although it would add to the administrative complexities of the plan.

---

[8] A loan to an employee will be treated as a taxable distribution unless certain requirements are met. These requirements involve the amount of the loan (or accumulated loans) and the time period for repayment. The maximum amounts that can be borrowed without being considered a distribution depend on the amount of the employee's vested interest in his or her account balance. If it is:

1. $10,000 or less, the entire vested interest is available.
2. Between $10,000 and $20,000, $10,000 is available.
3. Between $20,000 and $100,000, 50 percent of the vested interest is available.
4. $100,000 or more, $50,000 is available.

The $50,000 limitation on loans from qualified plans is reduced by the excess of the highest outstanding loan balance during the preceding one-year period over the outstanding balance on the date a new loan is made.

As to the time period for repayment, the loan, by its terms, must be repaid within five

It should be noted that some amounts might still be available for nonhardship, in-service withdrawals. As already noted, nonelective contributions may be withdrawn (unless they are designated to be part of the ADP test). Also, the value of any aftertax employee contributions may be withdrawn, as may the value of any contributions (employer and employee) made to a plan before it became a CODA. Finally, even elective contributions may be withdrawn from a profit-sharing or stock-bonus plan on a nonhardship basis after the employee attains age 59½.

Time When Contributions Credited

For purposes of applying either the general or special CODA discrimination rules, the proposed regulations require that any elective contributions for a plan year actually be made no later than 30 days after the end of the plan year. Nonelective contributions, however, may be made until the due date (including extensions) for the filing of the employer's tax return for the taxable year in which the plan year ends.

Separate Accounting

The proposed regulations state that all amounts held by a plan that has a CODA will be subject to the CODA nonforfeitability and withdrawal requirements unless a separate account is maintained for benefits specifically subject to these requirements. Included are amounts contributed for plan years before 1980, contributions not subject to a deferral election, and contributions made for years when the CODA is not qualified.

OTHER CONSIDERATIONS

The preceding has dealt with the requirements of federal tax law for the qualification of CODAs. There are, however, other issues that must be addressed. The following section discusses the federal income taxation of CODA distributions, the status of elective contributions for purposes of

---

years. However, if the loan is used to acquire a dwelling unit (which is to be used as a principal residence of the participant) and meets the amount limitation, this time limit does not apply.

Also, the loan provision must be available to all participants on a reasonably equivalent basis and must not be made available to the prohibited group in a percentage amount greater than that made available to other employees. The law also requires that the loan bear a reasonable rate of interest, be adequately secured, and be made only by the plan (and not by a third party, such as a bank, with the employee's account balance as security).

Social Security, other employer-sponsored plans, and state and local taxes. It also discusses the express limits of 401(k) contributions, the treatment of excess deferrals, the effect of such contributions on deduction limits, and the Section 415 limitations on contributions and benefits.

Federal Income Taxation of CODA Distributions

CODA distributions arising out of employer contributions (including before-tax employee contributions) or investment income are subject to the same federal income tax treatment as any other qualified plan distribution when the employee has no cost basis. (A detailed discussion of these provisions is provided in Chapter 41.) If aftertax employee contributions were made to the CODA, a portion of the withdrawal will be excluded from federal income tax; otherwise, the entire withdrawal will be taxable. Moreover, with certain limited exceptions, a 10 percent penalty tax will apply to distributions (other than those that are not subject to the regular federal income tax because they are returns of employee contributions) made before the participant's death, disability, or attainment of age 59½.[9]

Social Security

Originally, elective contributions to a CODA were not considered to be wages for purposes of Social Security. Thus, they were not subject to Social Security (FICA) tax, nor were they taken into account when calculating Social Security benefits.

This was changed by the 1983 Social Security amendments. Beginning in 1984, elective contributions will be considered as wages for Social Security (and federal unemployment insurance) purposes. Thus, FICA taxes will be paid on such amounts (if they are under the taxable wage base) and they will be taken into account when calculating an employee's Social Security benefits.

---

[9] Specifically, exceptions are granted if the distributions are:

1. Part of a series of substantially equal periodic payments made for the life (or life expectancy) of the employee or the joint lives (or joint life expectancies) of the employee and his or her beneficiary.
2. Used to pay medical expenses to the extent the expenses exceed 7½ percent of adjusted gross income.
3. Certain distributions made before January 1, 1990 from an ESOP.
4. Payments to alternate payees pursuant to a qualified domestic relations order (QDRO).

Other Employer-Sponsored Plans

A matter of some concern to employers was the question of whether an employee's elective contributions could be considered as part of the compensation base for purposes of other tax-qualified plans. This uncertainty was resolved in 1983 when the Internal Revenue Service ruled that the inclusion (or exclusion) of elective contributions under a CODA as compensation in a defined benefit pension plan does not cause the pension plan to be discriminatory. The Service also noted that the inclusion of nonelective contributions will still be subject to the discrimination standards.

Employers also maintain other pay-related employee benefit plans. These include short- and long-term disability income plans, group term life insurance, survivor income benefits, and in some cases, medical expense benefit plans. There appear to be no legal reasons why pay, for the purpose of these plans, cannot be defined to include elective contributions made under a CODA. If such contributions are to be included, care should be taken to make sure that necessary plan and/or insurance contract amendments are made so that compensation is properly defined.

A CODA will not be qualified if any other benefit provided by the employer is conditioned, either directly or indirectly, on the employee electing to have the employer make or not make contributions under the arrangement in lieu of receiving cash.[10] This does not apply to any matching contribution made by reason of such an election.

State and Local Taxes

Unfortunately, the treatment of elective contributions under state and local tax laws is less than clear. For years, many states followed principles of federal tax law in the treatment of employee benefits. This practice was also followed by many local governments that impose some form of income tax.

With the increased use of IRAs in recent years, and with the publicity

---

[10] This prohibition is subject to a special rule under which a qualified offset arrangement was maintained by the employer on April 16, 1986 and satisfied certain conditions thereafter. For purposes of applying the special participation and discrimination standards described earlier in the chapter, the benefit under the defined benefit plan conditioned on initial elective deferrals may be treated as matching contributions under rules to be prescribed by the secretary of the treasury.

that CODAs have received, there has been growing concern among state and local tax authorities over the potential loss of tax revenue. As a result, the question of state and local taxation of elective contributions has become an important issue.

At this time, the tax treatment of these amounts is uncertain in many jurisdictions. Some state and local authorities have indicated that they will follow federal tax law. However, a few already have announced that elective contributions will be taxable and subject to employer withholding. It seems reasonable to expect that many more state and local authorities will adopt this latter position.

Deduction Limits

Section 404 of the Code imposes limits on the amount an employer can deduct for contributions made to qualified plans. For profit-sharing plans, this limit is expressed as 15 percent of the payroll of the employees covered. If the employer has both a defined benefit plan and a defined contribution plan, the combined limit is 25 percent of the covered payroll.

Elective contributions affect the maximum deduction in two ways. First, they will reduce the amount of the covered payroll to which the percentage limitations apply, thus reducing the dollar amount available as a maximum deduction. Second, they are considered to be employer contributions and thus reduce the amount otherwise available for the employer to contribute and deduct.

As a practical matter, the effect of CODAs on these limits should not be of great concern to most employers. For those who maintain liberal plans, however, the level of elective contributions permitted might have to be limited in order to preserve deductions for regular employer contributions.

Section 415 Limits

Section 415 of the Code imposes limits on the contributions and benefits that might be provided for an employee under qualified plans. These limits are expressed both as a percentage of pay and as a dollar amount. A combined limit applies when an employee participates in both a defined benefit and a defined contribution plan. These limitations should affect only a few, if any, employees in most situations. Nevertheless, it is important that they be observed. A plan will be disqualified if it violates these limitations.

ADVANTAGES AND DISADVANTAGES OF CODAs

The advantages of CODAs are significant, although most of these accrue to employees, rather than employers. Nevertheless, the advantages to employers are important.

From an employer's viewpoint, CODAs have all the advantages normally associated with any employee benefit plan. Thus, they should be of material value in the attraction and retention of employees, in improving employee morale, in achieving a better sense of corporate identification (when employer securities are involved), and so forth. In addition, they can serve specific corporate objectives such as increasing the level of participation in an existing plan that has had conventional aftertax employee contributions. For some employers, converting a conventional savings plan to a CODA, and thus increasing take-home pay for participating employees, could minimize pressures for additional cash compensation.

From the viewpoint of employees, the first and foremost advantage involves taxes. If a conventional savings plan is converted to a CODA, the participating employees can realize an immediate increase in take-home pay. But of more importance is the fact that contributions are accumulating under a tax shelter. This means that an employee can receive investment income on amounts that otherwise would have been paid in taxes. Over a period of years, the cumulative effect of this can be quite substantial. Finally, when amounts are distributed and subject to tax, the actual amount of tax paid might be considerably less than would otherwise have been the case. Installment distributions could be taxed at a lower effective tax rate (due to lower levels of taxable income and indexed tax brackets). And lump-sum distributions also may qualify for favorable five-year averaging tax treatment.

Employees also have the flexibility of determining, on a year-to-year basis, whether to take amounts in cash or to defer these amounts under the plan. Since employee needs and goals change from time to time, this element of flexibility could be quite important.

The disadvantages of CODAs also should be recognized. From the employer's viewpoint, these plans involve complex and costly administration. Also, the employer must be prepared to deal with employee relations and other problems that can occur in any year that the plan fails to satisfy the ADP test. These plans also will involve more communications efforts than are associated with conventional employee benefit plans.

From the viewpoint of employees, the disadvantages of CODAs are not as great. In fact, the only significant disadvantage is that elective contributions are subject to the previously mentioned withdrawal limitations and the possible application of the early distribution tax. This could be of major importance to some employees, particularly those at lower pay levels, and could be a barrier to their participation in the plan.

CHAPTER 29

EMPLOYEE STOCK OWNERSHIP PLANS (ESOPs): THEIR NATURE AND PURPOSE

*Robert W. Smiley, Jr.**

INTRODUCTION AND OVERVIEW

Employee Stock Ownership Plans (ESOPs)

Kelsoism, Two-Factor Economics, and the Results

Louis Kelso started a movement almost 25 years ago that has, through his own efforts and the efforts of many other capable people, resulted in millions of Americans owning part or all of the companies they work for—"a piece of the action." His concept is "universal capitalism," and its thrust is to spread the benefits of capital ownership to all Americans, not just to a few. Simply put, Kelso divides the economic sphere into two factors: labor (the human factor), and capital (the nonhuman factor). Hence the name two-factor economics. He originally proposed that the ownership of productive assets would be represented by shares of stock in corporations that make capital expenditures. These shares would be owned by new capitalists, the employees of the companies making these

---

* This chapter has been reviewed by Gregory K. Brown, a partner in the Chicago law firm of Keck, Mahin & Cate. Mr. Brown specializes in employee benefits and executive compensation and has spoken and written extensively about employee benefit plans, particularly employee stock ownership plans. He received his J.D. from the University of Illinois at Urbana-Champaign in 1975 and a B.S. in Economics from the University of Kentucky in May 1973.

capital expenditures. This shift to new capitalists was to be accomplished through the use of corporate credit and reinvestment into the capital necessary to repay any indebtedness arising from the use of such credit. What Kelso proposed was to have every company set up a tax-qualified employee stock ownership plan and its attendant trust. The trustee would then go to the financial community and borrow money to buy stock in the company the employees work for. The loan would be repaid out of the profits produced by the new plant and equipment that would be purchased with the proceeds of the stock sale. Ultimately, the employees or their beneficiaries at death, on disability, retirement, or other termination of service would receive their shares, and "would live happily ever after" on the dividends. There are now well in excess of 8,000 such plans across the country and more being adopted every day.

Background and Description

The first stock bonus plans were granted tax-exempt status under the Revenue Act of 1921. In 1953, the Internal Revenue Service (IRS) first recognized the use of a qualified employees' plan for debt financing the purchase of employer stock when it published Revenue Ruling 46. In recent years, Congress has encouraged the use of the ESOP financing technique in at least 17 different pieces of legislation.

Employee stock ownership plans (ESOPs) generally can be described as defined contribution, individual account plans similar to stock bonus plans and profit-sharing plans. By relating ESOPs to these familiar employee benefit plans, a base can be established from which these plans can be analyzed and reviewed. As a form of stock bonus plan, ESOPs differ from profit-sharing plans in that an ESOP must make distributions in employer stock, although cash can be distributed—provided the employee is given the option to demand his or her distribution in employer securities or the other special requirements discussed in Chapter 30 are met. It is the ESOP's ability to borrow based on the credit of the company that allows the ESOP to be used as a technique of corporate finance. An ESOP is essentially a stock bonus plan that uses funds that are borrowed to finance the purchase of a company's stock for the firm's employees. The ESOP is a tax-sheltered employee benefit plan on the one hand, and a bona fide technique of corporate finance on the other.

The following example will illustrate the simplest and most basic use of an ESOP.

An Example. Assume that a company in a 40 percent combined federal and state income tax bracket has pre-tax earnings of $150,000, a covered payroll of $600,000, and makes a $90,000 (15 percent of $600,000) contribution to the plan, which then buys stock from the company.

TABLE 29–1
Comparing Plans

	No Qualified Plan	*Profit-Sharing Plan*	*ESOP*
Pre-tax income	$150,000	$150,000	$150,000
Less contribution	0	90,000	90,000
Net taxable income	150,000	60,000	60,000
Income tax (federal and state)	60,000	24,000	24,000
Net aftertax income	$ 90,000	$ 36,000	$ 36,000
Company cash flow	$ 90,000	$ 36,000	$126,000*

* The $90,000 contribution goes to work inside the corporation, as additional equity capital.

Compare this situation with a profit-sharing plan to which the company contributes the same amount. Table 29–1 shows the effect of different plans.

Leveraged ESOPs

An ESOP also may leverage its investments to acquire employer stock, something that a normal pension or profit-sharing plan (except under very limited circumstances) is not permitted to do. This feature makes an ESOP very useful in debt financing. For example, assume the ESOP borrows $500,000 for seven years at a below market annual interest rate of 6.14 percent. (The lender relies on the solvency of the company.) The ESOP then buys $500,000 worth of stock from the company, and the company can use this money as additional working capital in any way it wishes. The company then contributes to the ESOP approximately $90,000 each year, which is used to pay the principal and interest on the $500,000 loan. The company gets a tax deduction for the entire $90,000, even though part of it is used to pay the principal. Assuming a 40 percent corporate tax rate, the company has reduced its ultimate tax bill by $200,000, and the cash flow of the company has been increased by $200,000, the amount of the tax reduction. At the same time, the employees have become beneficial stockholders of the company and, presumably, now have a greater interest in making the company more profitable and in generating the profits necessary to repay the loan.

The Economic Recovery Tax Act of 1981 (ERTA) altered the funding limits applicable to leveraged ESOPs. Whereas prior to ERTA the combination of limits on deductible contributions and maximum allowable annual additions created a practical limit to the size of an ESOP loan, ERTA greatly expanded that limit. After ERTA a plan sponsor may contribute on a deductible basis an amount up to 25 percent of covered payroll to be used solely for principal reduction on an ESOP loan. In addition, the sponsor may contribute on a deductible basis an unlimited amount to service interest on the loan. Relevant adjustments were made to Internal Revenue Code (IRC or Code) Section 415 to allow for the allocation of all released shares (i.e., forfeited and reallocated loan shares need not be considered "annual additions" for purposes of the limitations). Obviously, this allows a much larger block of stock to be purchased than could have been under pre-ERTA law.

For purposes of this chapter, an ESOP means a qualified stock bonus plan, or a combination stock bonus and money purchase pension plan, that meets certain requirements under the Employee Retirement Income Security Act of 1974, as amended (ERISA), and under the Internal Revenue Code of 1986, that allows the plan to borrow from, or on the credit of, the company or its shareholders, for the purpose of investing in the company's securities. The trust gives the lender its note for the money borrowed, which may or may not be secured by a pledge of the stock. Alternatively, the company borrows the money and makes a back-to-back loan to the ESOP on similar terms. The company, shareholders, or both, guarantee the loan. Usually there is an agreement with the lender that the company will make contributions to the trust in sufficient amounts to repay the loan, including interest. As the plan contributions are used to repay the loan, a number of shares are released to be allocated to the employees' individual accounts. As in other qualified plans, benefits usually are paid after employees die, retire, or otherwise leave the corporation.

Alternatives to an ESOP

Compliance with the requirements of the definition of an ESOP is necessary only if the trust forming part of the plan is to be a borrower for the purpose of acquiring stock. If stock is to be acquired without this debt financing, any plan of the eligible individual account variety can be used to accomplish essentially the same purpose. Such plans include profit-sharing plans, stock bonus plans, savings plans, and thrift plans, as well as ESOPs. One of the most attractive stock ownership alternatives was the payroll-based TRASOP (PAYSOP) whereby benefits were funded entirely with what would otherwise be tax dollars. *The PAYSOP was repealed when the ESOP tax credit under Code Section 41 was repealed by the Tax Reform Act of 1986 (TRA '86).* Even though benefits under a

PAYSOP were very small, on an individual participant basis, the fact that they resulted in a tax credit (as contrasted with a deduction) to the company effectively doubled their value from a corporate point of view.

Plans other than an ESOP can aid the company in its financing and also provide employees with the benefits of stock ownership. The most common alternative is a profit-sharing plan (including a 401(k) profit-sharing plan). While trust borrowing with corporate or shareholder guarantees is prohibited, most if not all of the benefits of an ESOP are available to the company and to the employees through a well-designed profit-sharing plan. Distributions may be made to participants in either cash or stock. Contributions may be made in cash or stock; and cash, once contributed, may be used to purchase company stock from the company or the shareholders, as long as certain rules are followed.

The next most common alternative is a stock bonus plan, which is similar to a profit-sharing plan except that benefits are normally distributable in stock of the employer. IRC Section 401(a)(23) now permits a stock bonus plan to distribute cash in lieu of stock, provided the employee has the right to have his or her distribution in employer securities unless the distribution provisions of IRC Section 409(h)(2) apply. The primary purpose of a stock bonus plan is "to give employee-participants an interest in the ownership and growth of the employer's business."[1] This distinction in purpose from pension plans and profit-sharing plans is important in interpreting the fiduciary responsibility provisions of ERISA.

Thrift plans and savings plans[2] were not previously defined in federal income tax law but would encompass the whole gamut of very successful plans that match employee contributions on some basis. Under many thrift and savings plans, especially the larger plans, a very high percentage of the investments are in company stock.

As for these non-ESOP plans being able to repay company debt, the same amount that an ESOP would have borrowed can usually be borrowed by the company directly, and then contributions to the non-ESOP plan can be made in company stock having a value equal to the amount of the amortization payments on the debt. If the stock goes up in value, from the point of view of company costs, it will be less costly for the company to incur the debt than the trust. The reason is that less stock will be contributed by the company if the shares increase in value as the future contributions are made, thereby reducing the repurchase liability for closely held companies because fewer shares of stock have to be re-

---

[1] Rev. Rul. 69-65, 1969-1 C.B. 114.

[2] ERISA Section 407(d)(3).

deemed.[3] Additional stock will not have to be contributed to the ESOP to pay the interest, because the interest already is deductible as an expense by the company.

As discussed earlier, after ERTA a leveraged ESOP can be structured to provide contributions in excess of 15 percent of covered payroll. If a contribution of more than 15 percent of payroll is desired without using a leveraged ESOP, certain pension plans, combined with a profit-sharing plan, may be in order. The pension plan could be a savings plan, and since savings plans generally require the employee to contribute, some assurance of employee contributions can be made by establishing an attractive matching rate, perhaps three to one or better. The two plans combined then would permit a deductible contribution of up to 25 percent of covered payroll.

ESOP as a Financing Vehicle

This subject is covered in greater detail under "Corporate Objectives in Establishing ESOPs," later in this chapter.

Tax Reduction Act Stock Ownership Plans (TRASOPs and PAYSOPs)

Background and Description

When Congress was working on the Tax Reduction Act of 1975, there was strong support to increase the investment tax credit from 7 to 10 percent to spur a lagging economy. Senator Russell B. Long (D) of Louisiana supported the increase, but added a unique twist—the TRASOP. TRASOP stands for tax reduction act stock ownership plan.[4] This provision allowed businesses to take an extra 1 percent investment tax credit if the total additional 1 percent was put into a TRASOP. Let's suppose a company had spent $20 million on new capital outlays in 1980. That corporation would be entitled to $2 million of investment tax credit (usually a direct offset to taxes currently due) under the regular 10 percent investment tax credit. If that company had established a TRASOP, it

---

[3] Robert W. Smiley, Jr., "How to Plan for an ESOP's Repurchase Liability," Prentice-Hall's *Pension and Profit Sharing Service* (Englewood Cliffs, N.J.: Prentice-Hall, April 3, 1980), pp. 1,431–40; and Smiley, "How to Plan for an ESOP's Repurchase Liability," Prentice-Hall's *Pension and Profit Sharing Service* (Englewood Cliffs, N.J.: Prentice-Hall, February 27, 1987), pp. 1,215–29.

[4] Renamed Tax Credit Employee Stock Ownership Plan, Technical Corrections Act of 1979.

would have been eligible for another credit of 1 percent of the $20 million ($200,000). The company would get the additional credit by issuing $200,000 worth of stock (or $200,000 in cash to buy stock) to the plan. The Tax Reform Act of 1976 sweetened the pot by extending the provisions for TRASOPs to 1980 (later extended by the Revenue Act of 1978 through the end of 1983 and finally phased out by ERTA at the end of 1982) and by adding an extra 0.5 percent investment credit contribution by the employer, bringing the total in the example above to 1.5 percent ($300,000). However, another 0.5 percent ($100,000) had to be contributed to the plan by the employees as a matching contribution. The TRASOP provisions permitted a company to elect to take an additional investment credit for acquisition, construction, and other qualifying expenditures made for periods after January 21, 1975, and before January 1, 1983.

As amended by ERTA, and later by the Deficit Reduction Act of 1984 (DEFRA), the TRASOP credit after December 31, 1982, was no longer available based on a company's existing investment tax credit, but instead on its covered payroll, and was called a PAYSOP. After that date, a tax credit was available for contributions equal to 0.5 percent of payroll for calendar years 1983 through 1986. These PAYSOP provisions were scheduled to expire on December 31, 1986. TRA '86 repealed the ESOP tax credit a year earlier than its scheduled expiration. Congress repealed the credit so that it could raise enough money to add the new tax incentives for ESOP financing and to expand the ESOP incentives added by DEFRA.

After the enactment of the Revenue Act of 1978, all TRASOPs were effectively required to be qualified plans under Sections 401 and 409A (later simply IRC Section 409) of the 1954 IRC Code. The TRASOP had to be a new plan, or an existing plan amended to satisfy the TRASOP requirements. With respect to qualified investments made in taxable years beginning prior to January 1, 1979, the plan had to be a profit-sharing plan, a stock bonus plan, or a stock bonus and a money purchase pension plan in combination. For taxable years after December 31, 1978, the TRASOP needed only to be a defined contribution plan. Accordingly, a money purchase pension plan alone could satisfy the requirements.

In addition, the TRASOP had to meet certain rules regarding eligibility, participation, vesting, allocation of employer contributions, benefit and contribution limits, and the kinds of stock that could be held in trust.

The tax credits derived from TRASOPs and PAYSOPs are now history. Several references to historical material are noted in the bibliography at the end of the next chapter.

CORPORATE OBJECTIVES IN ESTABLISHING ESOPs

ESOP as an Employee/Employer Benefit Plan and Technique of Corporate Finance

Advantages of an ESOP to Employer

The principal reasons for the continuing rise in interest in ESOPs are the number of potential advantages of the use of such plans by the employer [and shareholder(s)]. ESOPs are recognized as being able to solve corporate financial needs by the following methods:

1. Financing future growth with pre-tax dollars.
2. Financing future growth at below market interest rates.
3. Refinancing existing debt, repaying both principal and interest with pre-tax dollars and tax-deductible dividends.
4. Increasing cash flow without increasing sales or revenue.
5. Motivating employees to regard the company through the eyes of an owner by letting them share in a "piece of the action" and receive tax-deductible dividends.
6. Creating a friendly base of stockholders (employees) as opposed to disinterested speculators in the public marketplace.
7. Creating a tool to help attract and retain high-quality management and supervisory personnel while cutting down on employee turnover.
8. Encouraging employee ownership of closely held company stock without relinquishing voting control.
9. Improving union relations.
10. Ensuring the future growth of the company through increased employee productivity and increased company profitability.
11. Converting present employee benefit plans from pure expense items and liabilities to vehicles that increase working capital and net worth.
12. Remaining private, while providing an in-house, liquid market for stock.
13. Enabling private shareholder(s) to sell all or part of their holdings at fair market value without the expense and uncertainty of public underwriting, and without paying federal capital gains taxes currently.
14. Creating a financial tool for estate planning that will help maintain the stock's value in an estate and may pay or reduce all or part of a deceased stockholder's federal estate tax liability.

15. Divesting an incompatible subsidiary without the publicity, expense, and uncertainty of finding an outside buyer.
16. Acquiring another company with pre-tax dollars.
17. Providing for the potential recapture of the prior three years' federal income taxes.
18. Being used in conjunction with a takeover defense strategy.
19. Increasing the yields to investors in ESOP companies.

Disadvantages of an ESOP to Employer

As with almost all things, ESOPs have some disadvantages. The value of the company's stock may be independent of company performance. If the company's stock experiences a market decline, or a decline based on appraised values, a substantial risk of employee dissatisfaction may occur. This dissatisfaction may be accentuated if there is leveraging in the ESOP. In most cases, however, the direct link between company performance and trust fund performance will only be a disadvantage if the company stock performs poorly.

Further, since an ESOP may have to make distributions in stock, and since the employee may owe taxes, the company must be certain that the employee has sufficient cash to pay taxes. Otherwise, the stock must be sold to pay taxes, possibly creating a morale problem. The put option provision (described in Chapter 30) usually alleviates this problem.

Dilution is a key disadvantage. When new stock is contributed to the trust, or purchased from the company, the earnings per share on each remaining share may be reduced. A careful analysis must be made to determine whether this potential disadvantage is offset by the increase in working capital and the increased cash flow from the tax savings.

The emerging repurchase liability is another problem that must be dealt with. Again, a careful analysis and the series of solutions available here have to be worked through, scheduled, and acted on.[5]

Voting control may become an issue, unless the ESOP is monitored with considerable forethought. Sometimes, this change of voting control is what is desired; and if it is not, the safeguards that are available should be established in order to avoid a loss of control.

The degree of risk is another factor. The ESOP invests primarily in employer securities and may subject the trust funds to capital risks. The value of the benefit to both the employer and the employee depends on the performance of company stock and the timing of the financing.

---

[5] Smiley, "How to Plan for an ESOP's Repurchase Liability," pp. 1,215–29.

Advantages of an ESOP to Employees

The advantages of an ESOP to employees are obvious: they receive stock in the company that employs them without any cash outlay or financial liability, and without any income tax liability until they receive the stock.

If employees receive company stock in a lump-sum distribution, they can escape current taxation of the unrealized appreciation in the company stock until they sell the stock. They are required to pay tax only on the trust's basis (or fair market value, whichever is lower) in the year a lump-sum distribution is made. This can be quite a benefit if the stock has done well and the employees hold the stock until the tax year in which a sale appears most advantageous to them. In smaller companies, the stock usually is sold immediately, either to the trust or to the company.

Other advantages to employees include:

1. The participant may claim favorable tax treatment on a lump-sum distribution under Code Section 402(e)(4) or may roll over such distribution on a tax-deferred basis under Code Section 402(a)(5).
2. If a lump-sum distribution is made, the participant is not immediately taxed on the unrealized appreciation on the employer's securities distributed; however, an election to be taxed on the unrealized appreciation may be made.
3. Dividends paid on ESOP stock are taxable to the recipient and deductible by the employer when paid or distributed to participants (or their beneficiaries). If the dividends are used to repay ESOP loans, the dividends are not taxable to the recipients, but allocations may be accelerated to participants.

Disadvantages of an ESOP to Employees

The major potential drawback is the "all eggs in one basket" problem, the lack of diversification. If the employer company has financial difficulties, the employee can suffer a double loss; he or she can lose both the ESOP benefits and the job.

Having to sell a block of stock in a closely held corporation can be very difficult. With the put option requirements the problem is easier but an employee could let his or her put option expire and be faced with this problem well into retirement.

Because most distributions are in company stock, ESOPs will place the employees in the position of having to sell the stock they receive, because they usually will not have the cash to pay the taxes due on the amount of the distribution. An individual retirement account rollover, or a rollover to another qualified plan, may eliminate this need for cash to pay taxes at the time of the distribution.

Employees also must face the problem of a liquidity crisis if the employer (or ESOP) does not have sufficient cash on hand to purchase distributed shares. Proper planning by the employer can generally eliminate this problem; however, it must be considered.

Leverage to purchase employer securities is rarely a disadvantage to the employees if the employer is assuming the risk of the loan.

Applications of the ESOP Technique of Corporate Finance

Capital Formation

The primary advantage resulting from the use of ESOP financing techniques is greater cash flow. The basic ESOP model provides for financing new capital formation and corporate growth, with pre-tax dollars being used to repay debt. While conventional loans require repayment of principal with aftertax dollars, ESOP financing enhances the ability of the employer company to meet debt service requirements with pre-tax dollars. (See Table 29–1.)

Borrowing Costs

An independent bank, insurance company, mutual fund, or other qualified commercial corporate lender may exclude from its income 50 percent of the interest received on loans that are directly made to an ESOP, or that are made to an employer that in turn lends the proceeds to its ESOP. The loans must be used to purchase employer securities of the employer corporation. The 50 percent interest exclusion is also available for companies with nonleveraged ESOPs. A loan to an employer will qualify if the employer contributes stock to an ESOP equal in value to the amount of the loan within 30 days of the loan, such stock is allocated to participants within one year, and the term of the loan does not exceed seven years. Financing institutions with a "tax appetite" will pass on part of this tax savings, thereby reducing borrowing costs. The aftertax yields to taxpaying financial institutions on ESOP loans, even after significant rate reductions to borrowers, is still greater than on a conventional loan.

Transfers of Ownership

If stock of a closely held corporation is sold to an ESOP under circumstances where the sale would otherwise qualify as a long-term capital gain, no tax must be paid at the time of the sale provided the following requirements are satisfied. In order to qualify for this very favorable Code Section 1042 treatment, the ESOP must own either (1) at least 30 percent of the value of the outstanding equity of the company after the sale, or (2) at least 30 percent of each class of outstanding stock of the company after the sale, and the proceeds must be reinvested in replacement securities ("qualified replacement property") within a 15-month period that begins three months before and ends 12 months after the sale. The replacement securities must be securities of a domestic operating company and may be public or private securities, giving the seller a virtually unlimited choice. In practice there are very few restrictions. Tax is then deferred until the qualified replacement property is sold, or if the replacement securities become a part of the seller's estate, the capital gains tax is never paid because the replacement securities enjoy the advantage of a step-up-in basis. An excise tax is imposed on the employer for certain dispositions of the stock acquired by the ESOP in the transaction within three years after sale. The stock that is purchased by the ESOP may not be allocated to the seller, members of his or her family (brothers, sisters, spouse, ancestors and lineal descendants and to anyone related to the seller within the meaning of Code Section 267(b) [Code Section 409(n)(1)(A)] or any shareholder who owns more than 25 percent in value or number of any class of outstanding employer stock (or a controlled group member). In determining whether a person owns more than such 25 percent in value or number, the constructive ownership rules of Code Section 318(a) apply taking into account stock held by a qualified plan.

However, individuals who would be ineligible to receive an allocation of qualified securities just because they are lineal descendants of other ineligible individuals may receive an allocation of Code Section 1042 and 2057 securities as long as the total amount of the securities allocated to the lineal descendants is not more than 5 percent of all Code Section 1042 and 2057 securities. In computing this percent amount, all employer securities sold to the ESOP by the seller that are eligible for nonrecognition treatment (including outstanding stock options) are taken into account, according to the TRA '86 Conference Report at pII-852. Existing shareholders may dispose of all or a portion of their shares without the potential dividend treatment that may apply to a corporate redemption under Code Section 302. ESOP financing permits the acquisition of stock from existing shareholders using pre-tax dollars, and the existing shareholders are selling capital assets that can be taxed as long-term capital gains. While TRA '86 repeals the long-term capital gains deduction, the treatment of a sale of securities as a capital gain or loss is still material to the calculation of a taxpayer's tax liability. Normally, for closely held companies, corporate stock redemptions are fraught with potential dividend treatment problems, and require the use of aftertax dollars.

Refinancing Existing Debt

An ESOP may be used to refinance existing corporate debt and to repay it with pre-tax dollars, thereby lowering the borrowing costs. Besides cash contributions, the company could issue new shares of stock to the ESOP equal in value to the amount of debt assumed by the ESOP thus helping cash flow. Sophisticated lenders generally understand that they have greater security with an ESOP since their payment is even before the tax collector's. Dividends are now deductible by the employer if used to repay ESOP debt. In addition, ESOP loans may be refinanced provided certain requirements are met.

Alternative to Going Public

The costs of a public stock offering, SEC registration, and the high expense of operating as a publicly owned company can be avoided through ESOP financing. The shares may be acquired by the ESOP from either the company, or existing shareholders, or both. Since employee shareholders are usually more loyal as shareholders than outsiders, and because an in-house market is usually more stable, the value of the stock may not be subject to the sometimes wild fluctuations found in the public market. In some situations, the ESOP shares will have a higher value than a comparable public company because the ESOP shares may not be subject to a "minority interest discount." A minority interest is usually worth somewhat less than a proportionate share of the total value of the company when the company is valued on an "enterprise (or control) basis." This is because minority shareholders cannot control company policy in many important areas that affect them, such as compensation, dividends, selection of officers, sale or purchase of assets, and other crucial corporate decisions.

Financing of an Acquisition or Divestiture

ESOP financing provides a way for a company to spin off a division or subsidiary to a new company owned by the employees in whole or in part through an ESOP. The new company earnings then would be available to pay off the purchase price, which may have been financed by an installment purchase from the divesting company—or through loans and equity provided from outside lenders, venture capitalists, investor/operators expert in leveraged buyouts or a specialized LBO fund. The success of any leveraged buyout turns on the capacity of the ongoing business to amortize the acquisition debt. The increased aftertax cash flow available through ESOP financing can enhance materially the probability of a successful transaction because repayment of the acquisition indebtedness may be accelerated. In an ESOP leveraged buyout transaction, the employer may effectively amortize both principal and interest payments from pre-tax income. In contrast, only interest is deductible in a conventional leveraged buyout. As a result, ESOP leveraged buyouts are able to support acquisition debt more easily, and the viability of the transaction may not be affected as adversely by fluctuations in interest rates or economic cycles.

The same technique in reverse may be used to finance the acquisition of other companies. The often increased pre-tax earnings of the acquired company, as well as the generally increased (because of the added payroll of the acquired company) employee payroll overall, are variables that may permit accelerated repayment of the debt incurred for financing an acquisition.

Estate Planning

An ESOP may provide a very ready market for the shares of a deceased shareholder. Acquisitions of employer stock from the estate can be debt financed and then repaid with pre-tax dollars. None of the redemption provisions under Code Section 302 and 303 normally apply. Further, a definitive value of the company's stock for estate purposes may be established which is a double-edged sword. Two new incentives have been added by DEFRA and TRA '86. An ESOP may now, with an appropriate administrative prohibited transaction exemption, assume the federal estate tax liability of a deceased shareholder of a closely held company to the extent that the ESOP acquires employer securities from a deceased stockholder or his or her estate. This assumption of estate tax liability is only permitted in the case of an estate that qualifies for the 14-year installment payment of estate taxes under Code Section 6166, where the stock constitutes more than 35 percent of the decedent's adjusted gross estate. The employer is also required to guarantee the ESOP's obligation to pay the tax.

As an added incentive, TRA '86 permits 50 percent of the proceeds from an executor's sale of employer stock to an ESOP to be deducted from the decedent's gross estate for federal estate tax purposes. This provision is effective for sales after October 22, 1986, and prior to January 1, 1992. The estate tax deduction is not available for sales of stock by a shareholder which the shareholder received from a qualified employee plan (e.g., a retirement plan or stock incentive plan), or through the exercise of a statutory stock option; and the stock cannot be allocated to the ESOP accounts of certain relatives of the decedent or any 25 percent or more shareholder of the company under identical rules for prohibited allocation under Code Section 1042 discussed above.

TRA '86 added Code Section 2057, which allows an estate to sell employer securities to an ESOP and receive a 50 percent estate tax deduction for the proceeds from that sale. This provision created substantial interest for ESOPs to purchase employer securities usually at a discount, from the estates of decedents. After enactment of TRA '86, however, it appeared that the statutory provisions contained a number of loopholes, which Congress agreed to close at the next opportunity.

Those loophole-closing provisions were enacted by the Revenue Act of 1987 (" '87 Act"). The '87 Act codified Notice 87-13, 1987-4 I.R.B. 14, but further limits the deduction. In general, the 50 percent estate tax exclusion remains intact except that the maximum estate tax saving is limited to $750,000, the deduction cannot exceed 50 percent of the taxable estate, the employer securities that qualify for the exclusion are restricted to non-publicly-traded securities and the employer securities must have been held by the decedent at his death (longer holding period requirements may apply). The estate tax deduction is also available for sales to PAYSOPs and TRASOPs. To qualify for the deduction the employer securities must be held for one year after purchase and the ESOP must make the purchase with its own funds; i.e., funds accumulated in that plan while it was an ESOP. Excise taxes are imposed on the employer for failure to comply with the holding period and allocation rules.

The rules codifying Notice 87-13 generally are effective as if enacted as part of TRA '86 (for example, the requirement that the decedent must have owned the employer securities at his death). Other limitations are generally effective for sales after February 26, 1987.

Problem Areas in ESOP Financing

Acquisition of Stock. ESOPs may acquire stock from parties in interest if no more than "adequate consideration" is paid. If the purchase price exceeds fair market value, the acquisition from a "party-in-interest" or "disqualified person" would constitute a prohibited transaction subject to penalty taxes and corrective action under Code Section 4975 and ERISA Section 406,would probably violate the fiduciary duty of prudence, and the fiduciaries would have liability for any resulting losses.

Care must be taken, if the stock is not publicly traded, to determine the value of the company stock. Use of an outside appraisal is now mandatory with the addition of the independent appraiser requirement of IRC Section 401(a)(28). The Internal Revenue Service and the Department of Labor are currently closely scrutinizing ESOP acquisitions of employer stock, especially with respect to fair market value.

Debt Financing. ERISA Section 408(b)(3) and IRC Section 4975(d)(3) provide for a prohibited transaction exemption for an ESOP loan primarily for the benefit of participants. The collateral given for a party in interest loan by the ESOP must be limited to employer stock, and the loan must bear no more than a reasonable rate of interest. However, if these conditions are not met, the entire loan may be subject to prohibited transaction penalty taxes, corrective action, and, of course, fiduciary liability.

Usually a loan will be primarily for the benefit of participants if the proceeds are used to acquire company stock on fair terms for the benefit of employees in connection with the financing of corporate capital requirements. Primary security for the loan should be corporate credit, and the company will generally be required to make a commitment to pay sufficient dividends on the company stock, or make sufficient contributions to pay off the debt, or both. Liability of the ESOP for repayment of the loan must be limited to payments received from the company, including dividends, and to any stock remaining in the ESOP that is still used as collateral. The loan, by its nature, must be nonrecourse on other ESOP assets.

The employer contributions required to service debt principal and interest must not exceed the allocation limitations under IRC Section 415; however, since forfeitures of loan shares and dividends used to repay ESOP debt on such shares are not considered annual additions, actual allocations may exceed 25 percent of pay or the then-in-effect dollar limit.

Determination Letter. The usual Internal Revenue Service determination letter issued under Code Section 401(a) offers little protection for the real issues in ESOP financing. While the letter applies to the formal requirements for the tax exemption of the ESOP, it does not apply to issues of operational compliance with the prohibited transaction exemptions under ERISA Section 408(b)(3) and (e) and under Code Section 4975(d)(3) and (13). It is possible to request and to receive a determination letter that the ESOP is qualified under IRC Section 4975. The ERISA Conference Report and the leveraged ESOP regulations direct the Internal Revenue Service and Department of Labor to give *all* aspects of ESOP financing special scrutiny—ostensibly to protect the interests of participants and to prevent abuses of the ESOP technique.

Existing Plan Conversions. If the prudence requirement (discussed later in this chapter) of ERISA is satisfied, the assets of an existing plan may be used to acquire company stock either directly from the company or from existing shareholders by converting the existing plan into an ESOP. The conversion of an existing plan into an ESOP is accomplished by means of an amendment to the plan. This subject is covered in more detail in Chapter 30.

Which Type of ESOP Will Provide What Benefits?

Even though ESOPs are a technique of corporate finance, they are also compensation programs. The company contributions to these plans involve real economic costs incurred in exchange for employee services. As a form of compensation, they have the advantage of making the employees owners of a company. This may, in fact, be their main advantage.

Not all ESOPs, however, are the same. Selecting the proper form depends on the characteristics and goals of the sponsoring company and how the plan is to be used. Careful consideration must be given to how the plans differ. Often, the ESOP leveraging characteristics are not desired and another type of plan may be in order.

Simplicity is a virtue in the benefit field. Stock bonus plans have this major attribute. They are not subject to Code Section 4975(e)(7) regulations. They can use any equity security including nonvoting and/or nonconvertible stock, which may be an important consideration when voting control is a key issue. Stock bonus plans, which do not meet the ESOP requirements, cannot be leveraged if the loan is guaranteed by the company, nor can the stock bonus plan acquire company stock from a shareholder using the popular tax-deferred installment method. Stock bonus plans may now distribute cash in lieu of employer securities, but the employee still has the option to require that his or her distribution be made in employer securities. A profit-sharing plan which invests primarily in company stock is not subject to this demand from employees to distribute company stock.

Leveraged ESOPs enhance immediate transfers of the ownership of companies, subsidiaries, and divisions from the existing owners to the employees. They are, however, subject to the ESOP regulations, including the put option requirements and the "special scrutiny" mandates. The leveraged ESOP is required to invest primarily in common stock or noncallable, convertible preferred stock of the employer.

ESOPs and Corporate Performance

Increased employee productivity often is cited as one advantage of ESOPs. *Productivity* is a term with a decidedly nonspecific meaning. It can be expressed in terms of dollar output per hour of labor, but little, if any, agreement exists among experts on how to increase it—and how to break down the relative contributions of capital and labor. It is almost impossible to prove that giving millions of workers a piece of the action will motivate them to increase productivity. Each company has a group of diverse employees with diverse temperaments, interests, goals, and objectives, and each group may react differently. Some employees are "long-term oriented": they think and talk years ahead. Other employees are much more "short-term oriented." Obviously, there are millions of employees in between. Each company has to analyze its own employee base, make careful and well-thought-out value judgments, and decide which kind of employees it has and wishes to attract.

It is the most fundamental tenet of capitalist theory that economic efficiency is based on individual incentive. The idea that employee-ownership companies would be more efficient than conventionally owned companies follows this common sense conclusion. If an employee's reward is fixed, what reason is there to work harder, smarter, faster, or more creatively? When the rewards are tied directly to productive effort, as they can be in an ESOP company, most employees would be more motivated and productive. Employee attitudes should be *consistent* with their work ethic. Since the late 1970s, researchers have put this reasoning to measurement in several studies.

One study found that employee-ownership companies were 1.5 times more profitable than their comparison companies.[6]

Another study found that employee-ownership companies had an average annual productivity rate 1.5 percent higher than the national average in their industries during the period 1975 to 1979.[7]

One survey of 43 majority-owned employee-ownership companies found that they had an average annual increase in productive employment of almost three times their respective industries.[8]

Another study reviewed the performance of publicly traded companies in which employees own at least 10 percent of the outstanding shares, compared them to their competitors, and found the employee-owned firms outperformed their competitors on measures of sales growth, average operating margins, average return on equity, and the ratio of book value to share growth.[9]

A study sponsored by the National Venture Capital Association

---

[6] Michael Conte and Arnold Tannenbaum, *Employee Ownership,* (Ann Arbor: University of Michigan Survey Research Center, 1980), p. 3.

[7] Thomas R. Marsh and Dale McAllister, "ESOPs Tables," *Journal of Corporation Law* 6, no. 3 (Spring 1981), pp. 614–17.

[8] Corey Rosen and Katherine Klein, "Job Generating Performance of Employee Owned Companies," *Monthly Labor Review,* August 1983, pp. 15–19.

[9] Ira Wagner and Corey Rosen, "Employee Ownership: Its Effect on Corporate Performance," *Employment Relations Today,* Spring 1985, pp. 77–82.

found that companies that shared ownership with employees grew one third faster in terms of sales, but no faster in terms of employment, than companies that did not share ownership. Further, companies that offer ownership to more than 51 percent of their employees had employment growth rates along with increases in net margins two to four times higher than nonemployee-ownership companies, while companies that offer ownership to key employees only had employment growth rates 50 percent lower than companies that offer no employee ownership plan at all.[10]

A 1985 study found that ESOP companies did perform better than the overall U.S. economy in the study period 1972 to 1981.[11]

All of these studies share an underlying assumption that employees work harder and smarter because they are owners. None of them is conclusive that employee ownership is the cause; each study suggests that employee ownership is, in some way, positively related to superior corporate performance.

The most significant study to date, "Employee Ownership and Corporate Performance," by Michael Quarrey, The National Center for Employee Ownership, October 1986, found that ESOP companies in the large sample used were much better performers than their matched comparison companies and their industries in the post-plan period and, unlike the prior studies, did conclude that employee ownership was the cause. Compared to their competitors, ESOP firms grew 3.5 to 3.8 percentage points faster per year after they set up their plans than they had before. Over a 10-year period these figures would represent a 40 percent increase in jobs at ESOP companies and a 40 percent increase in sales. Further, companies that in some positive way changed the roles of employees and managers generally performed better.[12]

There appears to be, at least in manufacturing companies, some correlation between the existence of ESOPs and increases in productivity.[13] The U.S. Senate Finance Committee did a survey of companies using

---

[10] Mathew Trachman, "Employee Ownership and Corporate Growth in High Technology Companies," Report to the National Venture Capital Association, (Arlington, Va.: National Center for Employee Ownership (NCEO), 1985).

[11] Craig Lawrence Boyan, "Employee Stock Ownership Plans: How the Characteristics of an ESOP Affect Its Performance." Undergraduate thesis, Harvard University, 1985.

[12] Corey Rosen, and Michael Quarrey, "How Well is Employee Ownership Working?" *Harvard Business Review* 5, September–October 1987, pp. 126–130.

[13] Randy G. Swad, "ESOPs and Tax Policy: An Empirical Investigation of the Impact of ESOPs on Company Operating Performance." Ph.D. dissertation, Louisiana State University, 1979.

ESOPs. More than 80 companies responded, with statistical results gained from 72 that included complete information. The results provided Senator Russell B. Long, then chairman of the Senate Finance Committee, with vital information to help him show Congress and the regulatory agencies that the pronounced success of ESOP and TRASOP companies is contributing to the economic welfare of the country. The following averages emerged from this important study: at the time of the ESOP installation, which took place three years prior to the study, the typical company had been in business for 24 years. Over the prior three years, an average of 7 percent of the ownership of the company was transferred each year—until the employee stock ownership plan had 20.6 percent of the company stock. During those three years, from pre-ESOP to post-ESOP, annual sales increased from $19,596,000 to $33,780,000, a 72 percent rise. The number of employees increased from 438 to 602, representing an employment jump of 37 percent. The incentive provided by employee stock ownership may have had an effect in significantly raising the productivity from $44,700 sales per employee to $56,000–an increase of 25 percent. The annual profit generated before the ESOP was $794,000, and soared (post-ESOP) to $2,039,000, an increase of 157 percent. In this profile, the company paid taxes, prior to the ESOP, that averaged $312,000 per year. Post-ESOP, that typical ESOP company paid an average of $780,000, an increase in revenue to the government of 150 percent. While the sample was fairly small, other ESOP companies can report similar results.

A nationwide survey indicates that most American adults (over four out of five) believe that workers at employee-owned companies work harder and pay more attention to quality and the firm's financial performance than do workers at nonemployee-owned companies. The survey also found that more than half the workers surveyed said they were willing to trade their next wage increase for a shared ownership in their firms. People almost unanimously would choose an otherwise similar product from an employee-owned company than one from a nonemployee-owned company. This was the most comprehensive public opinion poll ever conducted on employee ownership.[14]

The author's own experience, consisting of observations of several hundred ESOP companies, would tend to confirm these results, as does the Rosen, Klein, and Young book, *Employee Ownership in America: The Equity Solution,* cited earlier in this chapter.

---

[14] The Bureau of National Affairs, "Employee Ownership Plans: How 8,000 Companies and 8,000,000 Employees Invest in Their Futures," A BNA Special Report, 1987.

SPECIAL FIDUCIARY LIABILITY RULES UNDER ERISA FOR ESOPs

Introduction

The primary purpose of a stock bonus plan (the ancestor and major building block of an employee stock ownership plan) is "to give employee-participants an interest in the ownership and growth of the employer's business" (Revenue Ruling 69-65). This distinction is critical to interpreting the fiduciary responsibility provisions of ERISA. ERISA Section 404(a)(1) requires that fiduciaries act for the "exclusive purpose of providing benefits to participants," and serving as a "prudent man acting in a like capacity . . . would . . . in the conduct of an enterprise of a *like character* and with *like aims*."

The purpose of ESOP financing is the use of corporate credit to acquire ownership of employer stock for participants, and also to finance the capital requirements of the employer corporation. Revenue Ruling 79-122 properly recognizes the ESOP "as a technique of corporate finance." The prudent man and exclusive purpose requirements of ERISA Section 404(a)(1) and the exclusive benefit rule of Code Section 401(a) must be analyzed and interpreted with the understanding that the ESOP is a technique of corporate finance.

As long as an ESOP prudently acquires and holds company stock as the benefit to be provided to employees, ERISA's Sections 404(a)(2) and 407(b)(1) (which specifically permit an ESOP to be wholly invested in employer stock) are satisfied. Also, under Revenue Ruling 69-494, the exclusive benefit rule generally is satisfied if the purchase price does not exceed the fair market value *and,* if the prudent man standard also is complied with. Section 803(h) of the Tax Reform Act of 1976 makes it clear that Congress intended for ESOPs to be used under ERISA as a technique of corporate finance. Code Section 4975(d)(3) and ERISA Section 408(b)(3) provide for prohibited transaction exemptions, which are available only to an ESOP and are not applicable to conventional stock bonus or profit-sharing plans.

The legislative history of the Tax Reform Act of 1986, including statements by a number of senators on the floor of the Senate, indicate Congress' clear intention that ESOPs are a technique of corporate finance.[15] No other qualified plans may incur debt to be used to finance

---

[15] Congressional Record, June 19, 1986 pp. S7901-S7912 and S. Rep. No. 313, 99th Cong., 2nd Sess. p. 677 (1986).

corporate capital requirements or may be used as a vehicle for debt financing transactions involving parties in interest.

Internal Revenue Code

The Exclusive Benefit Rule

Treasury Regulation 1.401-1(b)(5) provides, "No specific limitations are provided in Code Section 401(a) with respect to investments which may be made by the trustees of a trust qualifying under Code Section 401(a). Generally, the contributions may be used by the trustees to purchase any investments permitted by the trust agreement to the extent allowed by local law." This exclusive benefit rule allowed the IRS to permit the trustees of tax-qualified trusts to invest in the stock of the employer maintaining the plan with the proviso that:[16]

1. The investment had to be permissible under the trust agreement.
2. The investment had to be permissible under local law.
3. The investment had to be for the "primary purpose" of benefiting the employer's employees.
4. The trustee had to notify the district director of the IRS of the investment so a determination could be made as to whether the requirements were met.

The third requirement, the "primary purpose" rule, was liberally construed to mean that the investment in company stock had to be for the primary purpose of benefiting employees. This meant that other people or groups, such as the employer maintaining the plan, or a key shareholder, also could derive a benefit. Revenue Ruling 69-494 also restated the requirements for compliance with the exclusive benefit rule when a qualified employees' trust invests funds in employer securities. The concern, of course, was that other people could derive a benefit only if the cost of the employer's stock or securities did not exceed its fair market value at the time of purchase. A fair return commensurate with the prevailing rate had to be provided. Sufficient liquidity was also to be maintained to pay benefits in accord with the terms of the plan. Furthermore, the safeguards and diversity a prudent investor would adhere to were also to be present. Criteria were established by the IRS in the ruling for permissible investments based on the purpose of the plan. Congress, while drafting ERISA, was aware of the position taken by the IRS, and this position is still a

---

[16] Rev. Rul. 69-494, 1969-2 C.B. 88.

reference for post-ERISA interpretation. Notably, a fiduciary who meets the prudent man rule contained in ERISA Section 404(a)(1) will be deemed to have satisfied the exclusive benefit rule contained in IRC Section 401(a).[17]

The Prudent Man Rule

Post-ERISA interpretations are less liberal. However, the fiduciary rules outlined in ERISA Section 404(a) are complied with, then the exclusive benefit rule of IRC Section 401(a) is deemed to be satisfied. The prudent man rule, as indicated above, has to be interpreted in light of the nature and purpose of the plan, and in particular, the characteristics of the plan as communicated to participating employees. However, satisfaction of the conditions contained in Revenue Ruling 69-494 does *not* mean that the prudent man rule has been satisfied. The prudent man rule would appear to be controlling. It will be some time before the courts have resolved exactly what the prudent man rule means. The IRS and DOL appear to prefer to leave the resolution on a case-by-case basis.

The Department of Labor's final regulation pertaining to the investment of plan assets under ERISA's "prudence" requirement does not specifically address the issue of an ESOP's investments in company stock under the prudence rule. The final regulation, however, does refer to the role of a particular investment "in furthering the purposes of the plan." The Department of Labor's (DOL) preamble to the regulation states that an "investment reasonably designed . . . to further the purposes of the plan . . . should not be deemed to be imprudent merely because the investment, standing alone, would have, for example, a relatively high degree of risk." The application of this standard to ESOP investments is not entirely clear; thus ESOP fiduciaries must act very carefully. In addition, the DOL states, "the prudence rule does not require that every plan investment produce current income under all circumstances." There appears to be an implicit recognition of the special purposes of an ESOP as an employee benefit plan and that proper investments in employer securities should comply with ERISA's prudence requirement. Further, since the ESOP regulations do not provide a mechanical test for determining compliance with this definitional requirement of an ESOP, the IRS and DOL have apparently determined that "designed to invest primarily" is a subjective standard relating to the purpose of an ESOP as an employee benefit plan and means just that. (For reference see DOL Opinion Letter 83-6.)

---

[17] See H. R. Rep. No. 93-1280, 93d Cong., 2d Sess., 302 (1974).

Fiduciary Rules

The general fiduciary rules of ERISA are applicable to ESOPs. These rules are discussed beginning on page 559. However, neither ERISA nor its legislative history gives any indication about how the general fiduciary rules are to be applied to ESOPs. Although ESOPs are exempt from the diversification requirements, and specific transactions involving ESOPs are exempt from the prohibited transaction rules, the general fiduciary responsibility provisions of ERISA for trustees and other fiduciaries are to act prudently, in the sole interests of participants and beneficiaries, and for the exclusive purpose of providing them benefits and defraying reasonable administrative expenses. The ESOP must operate for the exclusive (or at least primary) benefit of employees and their beneficiaries. These are important considerations in deciding whether an ESOP is appropriate as a tax-qualified employee pension benefit plan and not simply as a financing vehicle for a company.

Employee Pension Benefit Plan

ERISA Section 3(2) defines the key aspects of all employee pension benefit plans, including ESOPs. The key ingredients of the definition include "retirement income" and a "deferral of income." The nature, purpose, and characteristics of a particular plan are relevant, but so is the degree of risk Congress decided that employees could and should assume. ESOPs are recognized as different from other types of pension plans, and are permitted to purchase and hold employer securities, while other plans may not. However, it is important to note that ESOP administration and management are subject to both the provisions containing the fiduciary standards and the prohibited transaction restrictions. Each and every aspect of an ESOP transaction must be analyzed in terms of ERISA Section 404 and Sections 406 through 408. While a fiduciary must abide by the plan and the trust documents, these documents must be otherwise consistent with the duties of fiduciaries, and these duties override plan documents. The primary pupose of an ESOP as an employee benefit plan is to provide participants with an equity interest in the employer, with retirement benefits being provided through employer stock. The primary responsibility of the fiduciaries would not be to maximize retirement benefits through investments in assets other than employer stock, but rather to maximize the benefits attributable to investing "primarily" in employer securities.[18]

---

[18] ERISA Act Section 407(d)(6)(A) and Congressional Record, June 19, 1986, pp. S7904 and 7905, and DOL Advisory Opinion Letter 83-006A (January 24, 1983).

ERISA Fiduciary Rules

Exclusive Purpose Rule

This rule has been discussed earlier in this section. It is contained in ERISA Section 404(a)(1)(A), and is directed at making sure the plan is operated for the benefit of employees. It has a direct impact on ESOP loans and purchases and sales of employer securities. Such self-dealing is subject to special scrutiny by the regulatory agencies. ESOP fiduciaries are urged to "scrupulously exercise their discretion" in approving the nature, purpose, and the like of transactions with the ESOP.

Prudent Man Rule

ERISA Section 404(a)(1)(B) states the prudent man rule. It is a comparative rule and is to be viewed with reference to the "special nature and purpose of employee benefit plans."[19] Further, the relative riskiness of a specific investment does not make such investment, per se, prudent or imprudent. Accordingly, it would appear that a prudent ESOP fiduciary, subject to fiduciary duties under ERISA Section 404(a)(1), is one who prudently acquires, holds, and distributes employer stock for the benefit of participants (and their beneficiaries), and who prudently uses debt financing where appropriate, in a manner consistent with the plan documents and the provisions of Title I of ERISA.

Diversification Rule

ERISA Section 404(a)(1)(C) states the diversification rule and ERISA Section 404(a)(2) specifically provides that an eligible individual account plan is not subject to the general diversification requirements of 404(a)(1)(C), but only to the extent the plan invests in "qualifying" employer securities or employer real property.

One other important exception to this diversification rule: The diversification rule and related aspects of the prudent man rule are not violated by the acquisition or retention of the employer's stock—provided the acquisition and retention is consistent with ERISA Section 407. ERISA Section 407 contains an exception from the normal 10 percent limitation with respect to employer securities, so long as the ESOP explicitly provides for such acquisition and holding. ERISA Section 404(a)(2) does not seem to permit the holding of employer securities, if such holding would *otherwise* be considered not for the exclusive benefit of the employees. And so we have a "facts and circumstances" test, and the agencies retain

---

[19] See H. R. Rep. No. 93-1280, 93d Cong., 2d Sess., 302 (1974).

for themselves the advantage of the "hindsight rule"—being able to look at a transaction or series of events with the clear piety of absolute knowledge and history. To the extent the ESOP does diversify its investment in assets to hold assets other than employer stock, it is subject to the ERISA investment diversification requirement of ERISA Sections 404(a)(1)(C).

Document Rule

ERISA Section 404(a)(1)(D) states the "document rule." The significance of this rule is that it changes the pre-ERISA rules. Prior to ERISA, the trustee was required to carry out the intent of the trustor as specified in the trust agreement. With the advent of the document rule, ERISA now is controlling the conduct of ESOP fiduciaries, and the plan document(s) now can only authorize conduct that is consistent with ERISA. An ESOP fiduciary is in the interesting position of having to disregard the plan and trust agreement if compliance with those documents would be inconsistent with ERISA.

Prohibited Transactions and Special Exemptions and Exceptions

Fortunately for employers and shareholders, ERISA contains statutory exemptions from many of the restrictions that would otherwise prohibit ESOP transactions. ERISA's Sections 406 through 408 contain the prohibited transaction restrictions and the related exemptions. These restrictions apply independently of the fiduciary standards. Violation of any of the fiduciary standards or of the prohibited transaction restrictions by a fiduciary may result in civil penalties and personal liability. ERISA Section 409 provides that a fiduciary in breach will be personally responsible for any losses to the ESOP as a result of his or her breach, and profits have to be restored.

An ESOP is not subject to the prohibition on acquiring and retaining an investment in qualifying employer securities that exceeds 10 percent of the fair market value of its assets. ESOPs are exempt, with limitations, from the diversification requirement.

An ESOP also may purchase stock from (or sell stock to) the employer, a major shareholder, or any other party in interest without violating the prohibited transaction rules, provided the transaction is for adequate consideration and no commission is charged to the plan.

An ESOP may leverage its stock purchases, if the interest rate is reasonable, if the loan is primarily for the benefit of plan participants and their beneficiaries, and if certain other stringent requirements are met.[20]

---

[20] Sec. 408(b)(3) of ERISA and Sec. 4975(d)(3) of the IRC Code.

The only collateral acceptable for such loans is the stock purchased with the loan proceeds.

The ESOP loan documents must specifically provide that all the foregoing relating conditions be met, and that:

1. The loan will be repaid only from employer contributions made to enable the trustee to repay debt, earnings attributable to contributions, earnings on unallocated shares, and dividends on stock acquired with the loan proceeds or the proceeds of another exempt loan.
2. The lender's recourse on the note against the trust must be limited to the stock used as collateral, and the contributions and other amounts described in (1) above.
3. Each year, as the loan is repaid, the stock is allocated to the accounts of active participants as payments are made under the loan, according to the prescribed formulas.
4. The loan must be for a fixed term, and satisfy certain requirements in the event of default, including that a party in interest lender may not accelerate payments in the event of default, and the loan must not be payable on demand of the lender except in the case of default.[21]

Special Fiduciary Problems

Securities Exchange Act of 1934

The 1934 Securities Exchange Act relates to the rules regarding transactions in securities normally conducted on national securities exchanges and in the over-the-counter markets. It contains both registration and antifraud provisions. The act's registration and antifraud provisions are beyond the scope of this chapter. Since the rules in regard to all qualified plans (including employee stock ownership plans) are in a state of change, the current securities aspects should be carefully checked prior to engaging in transactions with the ESOP. For example, on February 19, 1981, the Securities and Exchange Commission (SEC) eliminated Rule 10b-6 for all employee benefit plans. Previously this rule on trading by persons interested in a distribution of securities required that ESOPs (and other employee benefit plans) stick to a strict set of criteria. In another example, the SEC exempted a qualified plan from the SEC requirement of the 5 percent beneficial owner disclosure rule in company proxy statements.

[21] Labor Regs. Sec. 2550.408 b-3(m); Treas. Reg. Sec. 54.4975-7(b)(13).

The SEC reasoned that the true beneficial owners of the stock are the plan participants when there is full voting pass-through, and when the plan documents and participants control the disposition of the stock.

National Bank Act

The Glass-Steagall Act relates to nationally or federally chartered banks and the activities engaged in by these entities. This act permits banks to act as trustees, and places the responsibility for this exercise of fiduciary responsibility squarely on the bank's board of directors. Assets held must be reviewed immediately, and then periodically. However, the SEC in its 1934 Securities Exchange Act, has provided that "inside" information, which can be easily compiled by the commercial side of the bank, should not be used by the trust department to violate the 1934 act. The comptroller of the currency has specified that written policies and procedures must preclude the trust department from using any material inside information of which it may become aware to make recommendations or decisions to sell or purchase securities for the account of pension and welfare plans. Employers maintaining these plans should be aware of these policies and discuss them with their trustees to prevent any surprises.

Blue-Sky Laws

Various states have laws and rules relating to transactions of employer securities. These laws generally require disclosure of the transactions and can be extremely complicated. Normally, there are exemptions for transactions with an ESOP, but there are exceptions, and care should be exercised that the applicable state laws are complied with.

Tender Offers

In recent years corporations subject to tender offers have established an ESOP after the tender offer is made, or used a previously established ESOP to secure loans to purchase additional employer securities in an effort to defeat the tender offer. This allows for more employer securities to be in "friendly" hands. The tender offer area is complicated and fraught with potential problems for an ESOP that borrows and/or purchases stock in an effort to defeat the tender offer. The IRS could argue that neither the loan nor the subsequent purchase of stock was for the exclusive benefit of participants and beneficiaries. This situation is further complicated if the trustees purchase employer securities at a premium price. If the tender offer is successful, the ESOP will generally be a minority shareholder in a debt-ridden corporation, and if the tender offer is unsuccessful, the ESOP will own stock for which the trustees paid too much. If these transactions violate the exclusive benefit rule:

- The trust could lose its tax-exempt status,
- Any contributions to the ESOP could be nondeductible,
- The earnings of the trust could become taxable, and
- Any partial interest exclusion under IRC Section 133 could be lost.
- Any borrowing by the ESOP that is not primarily for the benefit of the participants is a prohibited transaction that subjects disqualified persons to excise taxes.

Even the decision on how shares are to be tendered became subject to special consideration. For a more detailed analysis, see the most recent "BNA Tax Management Portfolio on ESOPs" (354–4th) by Jared Kaplan, Gregory K. Brown, and Ronald L. Ludwig (p. 28).

Procedural Prudence and Leveraged Buyouts

Procedural prudence requires that independent ESOP fiduciaries be represented by independent financial and legal counsel and that the interests of the ESOP and the participants and beneficiaries be fairly represented in meaningful negotiations. The ultimate responsibility for the decisions made by an ESOP fiduciary rests with the fiduciary. Procedural prudence must be strictly observed. The DOL advisory letters in the Blue Bell, Inc. ESOP transaction provide meaningful guidance.[22]

SUMMARY

Each of the series of laws mentioned earlier has some relevance to ESOPs. These laws highlight the importance of carefully considering the structure of an ESOP in terms of the relationships created and contemplated among the employer (and the officers and directors), the trustee, the shareholders, the public, and the participants. Responsibilities should be carefully discussed and allocated—at the outset. Once determined, careful monitoring and documentation of the ESOP's administration is mandatory for a smooth-running and trouble-free plan.

---

[22] *See* letter dated September 12, 1983 from Mr. Charles M. Williamson, Assistant Administrator for Enforcement, Pension and Welfare Benefit Programs to Gareth W. Cook, Esq., Vinson & Elkins, Houston, Texas regarding Raymond International, Inc., and letter dated November 23, 1984 from Mr. Norman P. Goldberg, Counsel for Fiduciary Litigation, Plan Benefits Security Division, to Charles R. Smith, Esq., Kirkpatrick, Lockhart, Johnson & Hutchison, Pittsburgh, Pennsylvania regarding Blue Bell, Inc.

CHAPTER 30

ESOPS (continued)

*Robert W. Smiley, Jr.**

PLAN DESIGN CONSIDERATIONS

Issues Inherent in All Qualified Plans as Applied to ESOPs[1]

Coverage

The requirements of Section 410 of the Internal Revenue Code (IRC or Code), which impose the age and service conditions for eligibility to participate, are applicable to ESOPs. However, most ESOPs, in practice, are more liberal. This is partially because employers adopting ESOPs have expressed a desire to permit employees to participate in a "piece of the action," and also to provide the maximum compensation base for purposes of assuring that contributions to the ESOP are sufficiently large to make the loan payments and are deductible under Section 404 of the Code. Many ESOPs do not have minimum age requirements. They may provide for a single, retroactive entry date. However, certain individual limitations on these generally liberal plan provisions may be important.

---

* This chapter has been reviewed by Gregory K. Brown, a partner in the Chicago law firm of Keck, Mahin & Cate. Mr. Brown specializes in employee benefits and executive compensation and has spoken and written extensively about employee benefit plans, particularly employee stock ownership plans. He received his J.D. from the University of Illinois at Urbana-Champaign in 1975 and a B.S. in Economics from the University of Kentucky in May 1973.

[1] See, generally, Ronald S. Rizzo, *Specific Drafting and Other Problems of ESOPs* (New York: Practising Law Institute, 1979) and Kaplan, Brown, and Ludwig, "BNA Tax Management Portfolio on ESOPs" (354-4th), 1987.

The rules that apply to all qualified plans for the inclusion or exclusion of particular groups or classes of employees are applicable to ESOPs and are covered elsewhere in the *Handbook*. Two different ESOPs may be established for purposes of satisfying the antidiscrimination and coverage tests if the proportion of employer securities to the total plan assets is substantially the same in each ESOP, and if either the securities held by each ESOP are the same class or the ratio of each class of employer securities to all classes of employer securities in each ESOP is substantially the same.[2]

The regulations on ESOPs[3] specifically prohibit a plan designated as an ESOP after November 1, 1977, from being integrated, directly or indirectly, with contributions or benefits under Social Security. These regulations are *excise* tax regulations; therefore, integrating the plan would not disqualify it. However, there would be a prohibited transaction if the plan engaged in a loan or another extension of credit to a disqualified person, and therefore an excise tax would be due.

Break-in-Service Rules

The two groups of break-in-service rules that are important for solving ESOP design and drafting problems are the eligibility break-in-service rules and the vesting break-in-service rules. Under these rules, an employee may have a one-year break in service if he or she fails to complete more than 500 hours of service in the relevant computation period. These rules are identical for ESOPs as for other qualified plans. These rules are covered in detail in other chapters of this book and apply to ESOPs the same as to other qualified plans.

Under the regulations, if any portion of a participant's account is forfeited, employer securities that have been acquired with the proceeds of an exempt loan may be forfeited only after other assets have been forfeited. For example, if a participant's account reflects both company stock acquired with the proceeds of an exempt loan and other investments, the participant's forfeiture(s) first must come from the other investments—if the amount forfeited is greater than the other investments available, then some of the company stock may be forfeited. If the distribution is to be deferred, say, until some specified age and/or actual retirement, the ESOP must generally provide for separate accounts for prebreak and postbreak service.

Most ESOPs do not have a "repayment" provision under the cash-

---

[2] Treasury Reg. Sec. 54.4975-11(e)(2).

[3] Treasury Reg. Sec. 54.4975-11(a)(7)(ii).

out and buy-back rules of the Employee Retirement Income Security Act (ERISA). Any such repayment may be a problem under the Securities Act of 1933 and relevant state securities laws. The repaid amount is voluntary on the part of the employee, and, therefore, none of the exemptions discussed later would be available, since employee "contributions" are being used to acquire employer securities. If state securities laws permit, an alternative is to establish a separate account vesting schedule or to provide that any repayments will not be used to purchase employer stock.[4]

Reemployment Problems

It is possible for a plan to require that a former participant who is reemployed after a one-year break in service meet the eligibility requirements of the plan again. However, once the eligibility requirements are again satisfied, participation is retroactive at least to the reemployment date; if overlapping plan years are involved, allocations and distributions already may have been made, making reallocation impossible.

Additionally, some care should be taken in utilizing the complex set of rules that relate to crediting and disregarding service for eligibility purposes.[5] When designing this section of the plan, and when designing the vesting computation period, several well-thought-out and well-presented examples can go a long way in educating the plan sponsor on just what the provisions mean. ESOPs traditionally have been for larger companies, and larger companies generally rehire employees on a more regular basis than smaller companies.

Section 415 Considerations

As a condition of tax qualification, a defined contribution plan must provide that the annual addition to the account(s) of a participant for a limitation year may not exceed the lesser of a stated dollar amount or 25 percent of the participant's compensation. This annual addition includes both contributions to all defined contribution plans of the sponsor in which the employee is a participant, forfeitures allocated to his or her account, and, if participant contributions are permitted (or required), the participant's own contributions for limitation years commencing on or after January 1, 1987, and the *employee's* aftertax contributions in excess of 6 percent of such compensation for limitation years commencing before January 1, 1987. However, no more than one-half of the participant's total contribu-

---

[4] Treasury Reg. Sec. 1.411(a)-7(d)(5)(iii).

[5] Labor Reg. Sec. 2530.202-2(b)(2).

tions for the years prior to January 1, 1987, have to be included in the calculation. Dividends paid on employer securities that are used to repay ESOP debt are not counted as annual additions.[6]

Code Section, 415(c)(6) increases the dollar amount of the annual addition to certain ESOPs. The limitation is increased to an amount equal to the sum of (1) the regular maximum dollar annual addition for the year, and (2) the lesser of the regular maximum annual dollar addition or the amount of employer securities contributed to the plan for the year, or purchased with cash contributed to the ESOP or released from a suspense account by reason of loan repayments. This special "doubling" is available only if the "one-third rule" is not violated. The one-third rule provides that no more than one-third of the employer's contributions for a limitation year be allocated to the accounts of participants who are highly compensated employees within the meaning of IRC Section 414(q).

In addition, if the immediately preceding conditions are met, Section 415(c)(6)(C) of the Code excludes employer contributions used to pay loan interest and also excludes forfeitures of leveraged employer securities from the annual additions limitations in the case of ESOPs that are established under 4975(e)(7) of the Code. When securities are released from the suspense account provided for the holding of the "unpaid-for securities," the contributions (but not dividends) used by the ESOP to pay the loan are treated as annual additions to participants' accounts, not the value of the securities released from the suspense account, which could conceivably be much greater (or much less).

If the special one-third rule is violated, then the forfeitures of leveraged employer securities are included in the computation of the annual addition at fair market value. Forfeitures of other than leveraged employer securities, for purposes of the annual addition, are always valued at fair market value on the date of reallocation even if the one-third rule exception described above is inapplicable. Several potential problems arise because of this treatment of the forfeitures. First, accurate and timely valuations are critical so as to permit a proper and timely allocation. Second, in the event of an audit, if the employer securities that were forfeited and reallocated to participants' accounts in a plan year were undervalued, the plan could be disqualified if the additional value, as determined by the IRS, increased any participant's annual addition beyond the permissible maximum amount. Third, since most loans require

---

[6] U.S. Senate, Committee on Finance, *Report to Accompany H.R. 3838,* 99th Cong., 2nd sess., May 29, 1986, Rept. 99-313, p. 682.

fixed payment dates, timely valuations are necessary to know whether the plan is qualified by the time the employer's contribution is due, because of forfeitures being revalued. The forfeiture suspense accounts, which are permitted by the final Code Section 415 regulations, require limiting employer contributions first—so, with forfeitures high enough, an ESOP may end up in default on the loan, since large enough contributions can't be made on a timely enough basis to amortize the loan repayment on schedule.

The Economic Recovery Tax Act of 1981 (ERTA) resolved this problem to a certain extent by amendments to both Section 415 (the allocation limits) and Section 404 (the deductibility limits) of the Code. After ERTA, an employer contributing to a leveraged ESOP may contribute and deduct an amount up to 25 percent of covered participants' compensation for purposes of principal reduction. Additional contributions used to service interest due on the ESOP loan are deductible in any amount. The Tax Reform Act of 1986 (TRA '86) also permits a corporate deduction for dividends on leveraged shares if used to repay principal and/or interest on any loan used to acquire those shares, provided the dividends are reasonable.

At the same time, the allocation limits (Section 415) were modified to eliminate from consideration as annual additions employer contributions used to make interest payments on an ESOP loan and reallocated forfeitures of ESOP stock originally purchased with an exempt loan.

These amendments partially resolved the obvious difficulty arising when three equally inflexible requirements (i.e., debt service, deduction limits, and allocation limits) are applied on different, sometimes unrelated, bases to the same transaction. For a particular company, therefore, the deductible and allocable contribution will set the practical limit for the amount of an ESOP loan after giving consideration to deductible dividends.

When designing the ESOP, the other plans of the employer have to be taken into account. The other plan(s) might be drafted to provide for a reduction in benefits under the other plans before reducing benefits under the ESOP. This would help to minimize the Code Section 415 problems and, at the same time, maximize the allocations to the ESOP participants. The favorite order of priority appears to be to first refund participants' contributions under all plans to the extent they are included in the excess annual additions; if more of a reduction is required, then place the excess forfeitures in a forfeiture suspense account or reduce or reallocate them in the *other* defined contribution plans. Furthermore, under the combined benefit limits of IRC Section 415(e), a related defined benefit plan might provide for first reducing the accrued benefits under the defined benefit plan.

Reversion of Employer's Contributions

As a qualified plan, an ESOP must provide that no part of the plan's assets are to be used for or diverted to purposes other than the primary benefit of participants. In an ESOP, there are unallocated shares and allocated shares (disregarding the forefeiture suspense account). The nonreversion provision applies both to the allocated and to the unallocated securities. If the unallocated employer securities are pledged as collateral for a loan on which a default occurs, they may be taken out of the trust in a foreclosure, provided the value of the securities taken does not exceed the amount of the loan default.

Employer contributions may be returned if made under a good faith mistake of fact (but not a mistake of law) or if deductions are disallowed and those contributions were conditioned on deductibility, if that condition is specifically stated in the plan document.

However, employer contributions can be conditioned only on initial qualification and not on continued plan qualification, according to Revenue Ruling 77-200 and the Revenue Act of 1987. That ruling also made clear that a permissible reversion will not be treated as a forfeiture in violation of Section 411(a) of the Code, even if an adjustment is made to participants' accounts that are partially or wholly nonforfeitable. If this is done, participants' accounts should be adjusted by first withdrawing assets other than employer securities. Also, leveraged ESOPs may not be able to take advantage of the reversion provisions conditioned on deductibility if they are subsequently determined to be nondeductible. It would be hard to establish that an employer who is making a contribution subject to the requirements of a fixed payment loan that satisfies the loan agreement but exceeds the deductible limits under Code Section 404 has made a "good faith mistake" in determining the deductibility of the contributions. Note also the nondeductible excise provisions of IRC Section 4972 for nondeductible contributions.

In Revenue Ruling 80-145, the IRS addressed the definition of "compensation" for computing the deduction limitation under Code Section 404(a)(3) and 404(a)(7). The IRS held that the deduction limits are based on total compensation, even in a situation where the plan defines compensation (for allocation purposes) as excluding certain items (such as limiting compensation to basic pay). Some ESOP companies may increase their deductible ESOP contributions by properly applying these guidelines. However, no deductions are permitted for the amount of contributions that cause the Section 415 limits to be exceeded.

Issues Unique to an ESOP

Leveraging

While leveraging has its positive aspects, some potential negatives exist that should be considered. Further, there will be an immediate dilution of existing shareholders' interests if the company issues new shares, or shares not previously outstanding, to the ESOP; this may, however, be offset by the other benefits, and a careful analysis should be done.

A leveraged ESOP also commits the employer to make contributions at least sufficient to amortize debt. This "commitment" disadvantage is offset in most cases by increased employee morale.

Dividends on a large block of stock purchased all at once can be a substantial cash drain over a long time. Further, a contraction in business conditions, and consequently fewer employees, could be construed as a termination or a partial termination of the plan resulting in full vesting for affected participants. Shares then distributed would be subject to the put option requirements (to be discussed in subsequent sections of this chapter) and may have to be purchased with nondeductible dollars, causing an additional and often untimely cash drain. If the covered compensation for deduction (and/or allocation) purposes drops below the threshold amount for making required payments on ESOP debt, or if the one-third rule is violated, then the ESOP may not be able to make its required payments on the ESOP note.

Allocations to Employees' Accounts

Suspense Account. An ESOP is required to contain specific provisions governing annual accounting for employer securities purchased with the proceeds of an exempt loan. The ESOP must provide for a suspense account to which the securities acquired with the proceeds of an exempt loan must first be credited, even if the securities are not pledged as collateral for the loan. Also, all ESOPs must provide for the release of the securities and their allocation to participants' accounts as payments of principal or payments of principal and interest are made with respect to the loan. Further, if the income from the securities is to be used to repay the loan, both the ESOP and the loan agreement must provide for that. Otherwise, any income must be allocated to participants' accounts and would not be available to amortize the loan. The provisions relating to the release of the shares from the suspense account for allocation to employees' accounts should be contained in the loan documents.[7]

The release of shares from the suspense account may be done in two ways. Under the first method of release permitted by the regulations, the number of securities released each year is equal to the number of securities held in the suspense account immediately before release—multiplied by a fraction, the numerator of which is the amount of principal and interest payments for the year, and the denominator of which is the sum of the numerator plus the amount of future principal and interest payments to be made during the remaining term of the loan, including the current year. The number of future years must be definite and cannot take into account any possible extensions or renewal periods. If the interest rate is variable, the interest is computed, for purposes of the fraction, by using the interest rate applicable at the end of the plan year in which the fraction is applied.

The second method is based on releasing securities based on the payment of principal alone. When a loan is amortized over a period of years, the interest portion of the payment is higher in the early years than in the late years. Many lenders would prefer that the shares be released based *only* on principal payments, so they stay secured. The regulations require that the securities be released from the suspense account of the ESOP in the same manner that the loan agreement provides. This second method gives some leeway for negotiation with lenders. The only other restrictions on this second method provide that the release based solely on principal payments must be part of a loan that cannot exceed 10 years (including extensions and renewals), and the annual payments of principal and interest under the loan may not be cumulatively less rapid than level annual payments of principal and interest. In computing amounts of principal under this method, interest is disregarded only to the extent it would be disregarded under standard loan amortization tables.[8] Apparently the agencies are concerned that the terms of the loan might provide greater interest payments during each year of the loan than would be permitted under standard loan amortization tables.

The unrealized appreciation or depreciation on the suspense account securities is not allocated to the participants' accounts. Shares are allocated at cost, then the value is extended to show a dollar amount. Employees who become participants in an ESOP after securities have been pur-

---

[7] Treas. Reg. Secs. 54.4975-11(c), 54.4975-7(b)(8); Labor Reg. Sec. 2550.408b-3(h).

[8] Treas. Reg. Sec. 54.4975-7(b)(1)(ii); Labor Reg. Sec. 2550.408b-3(h)(2).

chased and credited to the suspense account, but prior to these securities being released, will share in the unrealized appreciation or depreciation that occurred prior to their participation and will realize that appreciation or depreciation on distribution. The reverse is also true, in that employees who were participants when the shares were credited to the suspense account will not share in the unrealized gains or losses if they are not participants when the securities are released.

The forfeiture provisions must be so drafted as to require that a participant forfeit other plan assets before a forfeiture of employer securities may occur. When more than one class of employer securities has been allocated to the participant's account, forfeitures must reduce each class of security proportionately.[9]

Dividends. Dividends from the securities purchased with the proceeds of an exempt loan, to the extent not utilized to repay the loan, would be allocated entirely to participants' accounts once the shares were allocated. Alternatively, the dividends may be currently distributed to participants or held in the participants' accounts. Allocations to each participant's account and to the suspense account would be made in proportion to the shares held in the respective accounts. Dividends on unallocated shares could either be used to pay down debt (both principal and interest), or allocated to participants' accounts.

Allocation of Cost Basis of Shares

Because of the suspense account requirement, Code Section 415, and the requirement that employer securities that are acquired with the proceeds of an exempt loan be allocated to participants' accounts in terms of share units rather than in monetary terms,[10] most ESOP allocation sections contain two accounts for each participant. The first account is the "company stock account," which contains employer securities; and the other is the "other investments account," which is maintained to account for the participant's share of plan assets other than employer securities. The regulations also provide that amounts contributed to an ESOP must be allocated as provided under Sections 1.401-1(b)(1)(ii) and 1.401-1(b)(1)(iii) of the regulations. These sections relate to the requirement for a definite predetermined formula for allocating contributions among participants. Further, acquisition of employer stock must be accounted for, as provided under 1.402(a)-1(b)(2)(ii) of the regulations. This section refers to

[9] Treas. Reg. Sec. 54.4975-11(d)(4).

[10] Treas. Reg. Sec. 54.4975-11(d)(2).

the determination of the cost basis of the securities of the employer and sets forth four methods to treat cost basis. Cost basis is used primarily to determine the net unrealized appreciation in employer securities on distribution. The plan document need not contain whichever cost basis rule is adopted, although the chosen rule should be reflected in trustee or plan administrator's permanent plan records.

Public Policy Problems

The ESOP is clearly a long-range plan. This requires, of course, a healthy legislative environment. While plans that permit and encourage employee ownership have been around for decades, the tax benefits are fairly recent, and a rather important consideration is their ongoing effectiveness. While some practitioners are of the opinion that there are "tax expenditures," which means that any of the taxpayers' money not going to the government and that taxpayers get to keep is a tax expenditure (since the government doesn't take it), this author is not of that school. However, it is important to realize that many purported policymakers have this view, and they ask questions like, "Who will pay the taxes saved or deferred by the establishment of ESOPs?" and "How is this claim on the federal treasury made by ESOPs to be reconciled with other claims?" It is stated congressional policy to support ESOPs. Over 17 pieces of legislation since 1974 indicate this support in an unmistakable way.

Other questions, however, are more pertinent and deserve thoughtful consideration. For example, "Do ESOPs result in employees having too many eggs in one basket?" When employees' retirement income and their salaries are both dependent on the financial position of their employer, what will result over the long run? Care should be taken to examine when and if other plans should be implemented to help spread the retirement risk.

Voting Rights

All ESOPs must satisfy the requirements of Code Section 409(e) with respect to voting rights on employer securities. A stock bonus plan that is not an ESOP is subject to these requirements for shares acquired after December 31, 1986, only if *no* class of the employer's securities is publicly traded. A stock bonus plan of a closely held company must provide that each participant is entitled to exercise any and all voting rights in the employer's securities allocated to his or her account with respect to corporate matters that involve the voting of shares for or against corporate mergers, consolidations, sales of all or substantially all of the corporation's assets, recapitalization, reclassifications, liquidations, and dissolutions, or such similar matters as the secretary of the treasury may prescribe by regulation, if (1) the plan is maintained by an employer whose stock is not publicly traded, and (2) if, after acquiring securities of the employer, more than 10 percent of the plan's assets are invested in securities of the employer as required by Code Section 401(a)(22). Voting requirements for ESOPs other than stock bonus are treated elsewhere in this chapter and Chapter 29.

After December 31, 1986, Code Section 401(a)(22) eliminates the pass-through voting requirement for ESOPs maintained by certain newspapers, and Code Section 409(1)(4) also permits such newspapers to acquire nonvoting common stock in certain instances after December 31, 1986. This passing through of voting rights requirements for closely held companies extends not only to ESOPs but to any eligible individual account plan that invests more than 10 percent of its assets in the plan sponsor's stock, other than a profit sharing plan.

The voting requirements of Code Section 409(e) apply only to shares of employer stock allocated to participants' accounts and to the extent that shares are not allocated or have been acquired with the proceeds of an exempt loan and not yet released from the suspense account; voting rights may be exercised by designated fiduciaries at their own discretion except when the little used "one person, one vote" rule of Code Section 409(e)(5) is used.

An ESOP or TRASOP of a publicly traded employer whose securities are of a type generally required to be registered under the Securities Exchange Act of 1934 must pass through voting rights on all matters for all allocated shares, even nonvested shares. These provisions would appear to apply only to shares of employer securities acquired after December 31, 1979, for ESOPs other than TRASOPs.

When the employer has a class of securities that is required to be registered under Section 12 of the Securities Exchange Act of 1934, Code Section 409(e)(2) requires that participants and beneficiaries be entitled to direct the manner in which securities of the employer (not just "employer securities") allocated to their accounts are to be voted on all matters.

On or after October 22, 1986, an ESOP may permit each participant to have one vote with respect to each issue he or she is entitled to direct the trustee to vote, without regard to the actual number of shares allocated to his or her account. The trustee may vote the shares held in the plan in the proportions so directed by the participants.[11] An ESOP can be restructured with respect to its pass-through voting requirements whether or not the company has registration type securities, so that the ESOP may

---

[11] Code Section 409(e)(5).

provide each participant with one vote as long as the trustee votes the shares held by the ESOP in proportion to the votes of all participants. Therefore the trustee must give up all voting discretion on unallocated shares in order to use this voting method. Under prior law, voting pass-through on a one person, one vote basis was only permitted with respect to issues for which the law did not require voting pass-through.

Since the block of securities held in the ESOP may constitute a controlling interest, how voting rights are to be handled is very important now and in the future! Further, it can be argued that passing through voting rights is strong evidence that the ESOP is being operated for the primary benefit of plan participants, absent other clear evidence. When some participants do not vote their shares when voting pass-through is required by law, the IRS regulations regarding TRASOPs issued in 1979 indicate that such shares are not to be voted. This would treat a participant's failure to vote as an abstention. No similar rule expressly exists under Code Section 409 or 4975 or the regulations or interpretations thereunder.

When voting pass-through is required by law but not all of the shares held by the ESOP have been allocated to participants, the unallocated shares are voted in the manner prescribed by the ESOP document. The ESOP document may provide that the unallocated shares will be voted in the same proportion as participants vote allocated shares. In most cases, however, any unallocated shares are voted by the ESOP administrative committee or ESOP trustees and must be voted in the best interests of participants and beneficiaries. If the ESOP trustee is a bank or other institution, the trustee usually votes unallocated shares as directed by a committee appointed by the company. Only in extreme and unusual circumstances, when the trustee knows (or should know) that the voting instructions given to it are clearly improper (perhaps because of coercion or misinformation) and violate ERISA, may the trustee exercise its own judgment regarding the voting of such shares.

When voting pass-through is not required by law, the shares usually are voted in the same manner as unallocated shares. Voting rights may be provided to participants in excess of what is required by law, from full pass-through on all allocated shares on all issues requiring a shareholder vote to limiting the vote to certain specific issues (such as the election of one or more corporate directors, or limiting the vote to vested shares only). The procedures to be followed to solicit voting instructions should be established so as to permit participants to vote without any improper interference. Generally, participants will be sent the same shareholder meeting notice and any proxy solicitation materials that are sent to all other shareholders. The disclosure requirements for shareholder meetings are generally done in accordance with applicable state corporate laws and corporate by-laws (and SEC rules when a company is publicly traded). The proxy solicitation card or form instructs the ESOP trustee how to vote the shares and will generally be tabulated by the company on instructions given to or by the ESOP trustee.

ERTA limited the voting pass-through requirement by adding the phrase "(other than a profit-sharing plan)" to Code Section 401(a)(22). This gave birth to the profit-sharing stock ownership plan, which is not required to pass through voting rights at all. The other problems associated with this type of plan, though, are distinct in many ways from employee stock ownership plans and will not be treated here.

Rights and Restrictions on Employer Securities

General Rule. The general rule is that employer securities held by a qualified plan must have "unrestricted" marketability.[12] This rule was further modified by T.I.R. 1413's prohibition on a mandatory "call" option exercisable by the employer within a specified time. The regulations provide that employer securities acquired with the proceeds of an exempt loan may not be subject to a "put, call, or other option, or buyout, or similar arrangement," except that restrictions required under federal and state laws are permitted.[13] Since this applies only to securities purchased with the proceeds of an exempt loan, a violation of this provision will result in a prohibited transaction, not plan disqualification. However, since Revenue Ruling 57-372 continues to apply, a violation of this provision would also result in plan disqualification if the violation takes the form of a buy-sell, call option, or other market-restricting arrangement.

Right of First Refusal. The regulations permit a customary right of first refusal to attach to certain securities. First, the securities must not be publicly traded at the time the right may be exercised. Second, the right of first refusal may be only in favor of the employer, the ESOP, or both, in any order. Third, the right must not be in favor of shareholders *other* than the ESOP. Last, the right of first refusal must lapse no later than 14 days after written notice of the offer to purchase has been given to the party holding the right.

Further, the payment terms and purchase price must not be less favorable to the seller than the *greater* of (1) the purchase price and other

[12] Rev. Rul. 57-372 1957-2, C.B. 256, modified by Rev. Rul. 69-65 1969-1 C.B. 114.

[13] Treas. Reg. Sec. 54.4975-7(b)(4); Labor Reg. Sec. 2550.408(b)-3(d).

terms offered by the buyer (other than the sponsor or the ESOP, who has in good faith made an offer to purchase), or (2) the value of the security determined on the most recent valuation date under the ESOP.[14]

If the seller of employer securities is a disqualified person and the ESOP is buying, a special valuation date applies. The purchase price is determined on the date of the proposed transaction. A disqualified person is a person described in 4975(e)(2) of the Code. The key difference between a party in interest and a disqualified person is that, while ERISA only says all employees are parties in interest, both the Code and ERISA describe disqualified persons as officers, directors, 10 percent or more shareholders, and employees earning 10 percent or more of the yearly wages of an employer. Therefore, most employees receiving in-service distributions will not be disqualified persons even though they are parties in interest. Figure 30–1 and accompanying explanation illustrate the relationships prepared for properly identifying the parties.

Buy-Sell Agreements. An ESOP is not permitted to enter into agreements obligating it to acquire securities from a shareholder at an indefinite time in the future that is determined on the happening of an event—including certain events like the death of a shareholder.[15]

An ESOP also is not permitted to be obligated under put option arrangements.[16] Ostensibly the purpose of these prohibitions is to eliminate the possibility that plan fiduciaries may be required to act imprudently in the future, at the time of purchase.

Even agreements spelling out that the transaction will take place at fair market value and for adequate consideration at the time the obligation becomes due will not be acceptable, since the purchase (for all of the reasons outlined in this chapter) may not be an acceptable transaction.

Option arrangements, however, are permissible. An ESOP may enter into an agreement that would provide the ESOP with an option to purchase employer securities from a shareholder at some definite or indefinite date in the future. This type of arrangement clearly is in the interest of both the ESOP and the participants, since it provides a place to purchase employer securities and gives the fiduciaries a chance to determine the prudence of the exercise of the option. Careful drafting would require that the ESOP trust provisions specifically permit such agreements, but not require that they be entered into.

---

[14] Treas. Reg. Secs. 54.4975-7(b)9, 54.4975-11(d)(5); Labor Reg. Sec. 2550.408b-3(1).

[15] Treas. Reg. Sec. 54.4975-11(a)(4)(ii).

[16] Treas. Reg. Sec. 54.4975-7(b)(10); Labor Reg. Sec. 2550.408b-3(j).

FIGURE 30–1 Parties In Interest under ERISA and Disqualified Persons under the IRC

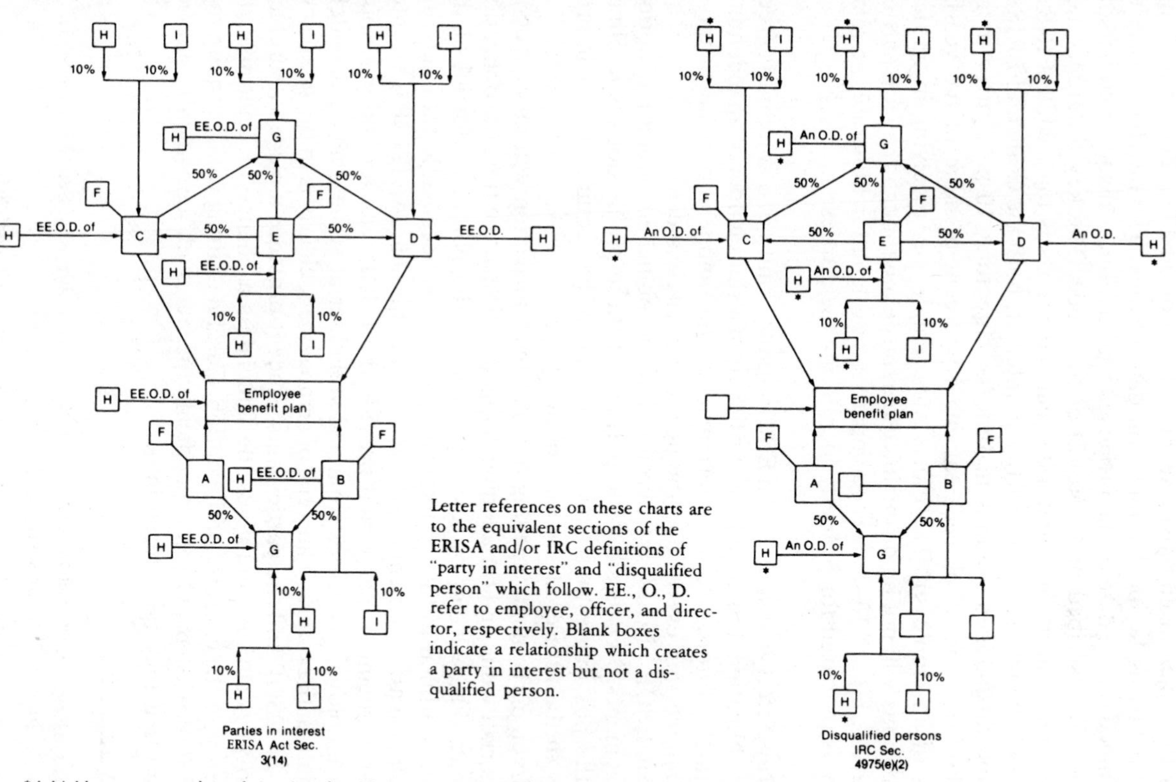

Letter references on these charts are to the equivalent sections of the ERISA and/or IRC definitions of "party in interest" and "disqualified person" which follow. EE., O., D. refer to employee, officer, and director, respectively. Blank boxes indicate a relationship which creates a party in interest but not a disqualified person.

*A highly compensated employee (earning 10 percent or more of the yearly wages of an employer).

Source: Prepared by Olney R. Fortier, former deputy assistant regional administrator for Pension Welfare Benefit Programs (U.S. Dept. of Labor).

FIGURE 30–1 (*continued*)

Act Sec *3(14)*	*IRC* *4975(e)(2)*
The term *party in interest* means, to an employee benefit plan:	Disqualified person—for purposes of this section, the term *disqualified person* means a person who is:
(A) Any fiduciary (including, but not limited to, any administrator, officer, trustee, or custodian), counsel, or employee of such benefit plan.	(A) A fiduciary.
(B) A person providing services to such plan.	(B) A person providing services to the plan.
(C) An employer, any of whose employees are covered by such plan.	(C) An employer any of whose employees are covered by the plan.
(D) An employee organization, any of whose members are covered by such plan.	(D) An employee organization, any of whose members are covered by the plan.
(E) An owner, direct or indirect, of 50 percent or more of:	(E) An owner, direct or indirect, of 50 percent or more of:
(1) The combined voting power of all classes of stock entitled to vote or the total value of shares of all classes of stock of a corporation,	(1) The combined voting power of all classes of stock entitled to vote or the total value of shares of all classes of stock of a corporation,
(2) The capital interest or the profits interest of a partnership,	(2) The capital interest or the profits interest of a partnership,
(3) The beneficial interest of a trust or unincorporated enterprise,	(3) The beneficial interest of a trust or unincorporated enterprise,
which is an employer or an employee organization described in subparagraph (C) or (D);	which is an employer or an employee organization described in subparagraph (C) or (D);
(F) A relative (as defined in paragraph (15)) of any individual described in subparagraph (A), (B), (C), or (E);	(F) A member of the family (as defined in paragraph (6)) of any individual described in subparagraph (A), (B), (C), or (E).
(G) A corporation, partnership, or trust or estate of which (or in which) 50 percent or more of:	(G) A corporation, partnership, or trust or estate of which (or in which) 50 percent or more of:
(1) The combined voting power of all classes of stock entitled to vote or the total value of shares of all classes of stock of such corporation,	(1) The combined voting power of all classes of stock entitled to vote or the total value of shares of all classes of stock of such corporation,

FIGURE 30–1 *(continued)*

Act Sec
3(14)

(2) The capital interest or profits interest of such partnership,

(3) The beneficial interest of such trust or estate, is owned directly or indirectly, or held by persons described in subparagraph (A), (B), (C), (D), or (E);

(H) An employee (EE.), officer (O.), director (D.) (or an individual having powers or responsibilities similar to those of officers or directors), or a 10 percent or more shareholder directly or indirectly, of a person described in subparagraph (B), (C), (D), (E), or (G), or of the employee benefit plan; or

(I) A 10 percent or more (directly or indirectly in capital or profits) partner or joint venturer of a person described in subparagraph (B), (C), (D), (E), or (G).

The secretary, after consultation and coordination with the Secretary of the Treasury, may by regulation prescribe a percentage lower than 50 percent for subparagraph (E) and (G) and lower than 10 percent for subparagraph (H) or (I). The Secretary may prescribe regulations for determining the ownership (direct or indirect) of profits and beneficial interests, and the manner in which indirect stockholdings are taken into account.

Act Sec
3(15)

The term "relative" means a spouse, ancestor, lineal descendant, or spouse of a lineal descendant.

IRC
4975(e)(2)

(2) The capital interest or profits interest of such partnership,

(3) The beneficial interest of such trust or estate, is owned directly or indirectly, or held by persons described in subparagraph (A), (B), (C), (D), or (E).

(H) An officer, director (or an individual having powers or responsibilities similar to those of officers or directors), a 10 percent or more shareholder, or a highly compensated employee (earning 10 percent or more of the yearly wages of an employer) of a person described in subparagraph (C), (D), (E), or (G).

(I) A 10 percent or more (in capital or profits) partner or joint venturer of a person described in subparagraph (C), (D), (E), or (G).

The secretary, after consultation and coordination with the Secretary of Labor or his delegate, may by regulation prescribe a percentage lower than 50 percent for subparagraphs (E) and (G) and lower than 10 percent for subparagraphs (H) and (I).

IRC
4975(e)(6)

For purposes of Paragraph (2)(F), the family of any individual shall include his or her spouse, ancestor, lineal descendant, and any spouse of a lineal descendant.

FIGURE 30–1 (*concluded*)

IRC
267(C)

Constructive ownership of stock.—For purposes of determining the ownership of stock under 4975(e)(2)(E)(i) and (G)(i), and for purposes of determining the ownership of profits and beneficial interests under 4975(e)(2)(E)(ii) and (iii), (G)(ii) and (iii), and (I) 267(c), as modified by 4975(e)(4), (5), and (6), provides that:

(1) Stock owned, directly or indirectly, by or for a corporation, partnership, estate, or trust shall be considered as being owned proportionately by or for its shareholders, partners, or beneficiaries;

(2) An individual shall be considered as owning the stock owned, directly or indirectly, by or for his family;

(3) An individual owning (otherwise than by the application of paragraph (2)) any stock in a corporation shall be considered as owning the stock owned, directly or indirectly, by or for his partner; provided, however, that this section (3) does not apply with respect to the ownership of profits or beneficial interests for purposes of 4975(e)(2)(E)(ii) and (iii), (G)(ii) and (iii) and (I);

(4) The family of an individual shall include only spouse, ancestor, lineal descendent, and any spouse of a lineal descendant; and

(5) Stock constructively owned by a person by reason of the application of paragraph (1) shall, for the purpose of applying paragraph (1), (2), or (3), be treated as actually owned by such person, but stock constructively owned by an individual by reason of the application of paragraph (2) or (3) shall not be treated as owned by him for the purpose of again applying either of such paragraphs in order to make another the constructive owner of such stock.

Put Options. One key question, which has always troubled nearly everyone concerned with ESOPs, is "What good is stock without a market?" Part of the answer has been set forth in regulations[17] and modified by statute.[18]

The Revenue Act of 1978 provides that participants or beneficiaries receiving a distribution of employer stock from a leveraged ESOP (or TRASOP) generally must be given a put option for the stock (1) if the employer securities are not readily tradable on an established market, and (2) if a participant who is entitled to a distribution from the plan has a right to require that the employer repurchase employer securities under a fair valuation formula.

As finally codified by The Revenue Act of 1978 and its legislative history as well as TRA '86, the put option must give the following benefits:

1. The trustee of the participant's individual retirement account must be able to exercise the same option.
2. The participant must have at least 60 days after receipt of the stock to require that the employer repurchase the stock at its fair market value[19] and make payment within 30 days, if the shares were distributed as part of an installment distribution.
3. The ESOP *may* elect to take the employer's role and repurchase the stock in lieu of the employer.
4. The participant must have an additional 60-day period in which to exercise the put option in the following plan year.[20]
5. At the option of the party buying back the stock, the stock may be bought back on an installment basis over a period not to exceed five years, provided the seller is given a promissory note that will accelerate (all become due at once) if the buyer defaults on any installment payment. The installment note must have adequate security and carry a reasonable interest rate. If the shares were distributed as part of a lump-sum distribution, payment for the shares must begin within 30 days on a schedule at least as rapid as substantially equal annual payments over a period not exceeding five years.

---

[17] Treas. Reg. Sec. 54.4975-7(b)(10); Labor Reg. Sec. 2550.408b-3(j).

[18] Revenue Act of 1978, Sec. 17(n).

[19] Economic Recovery Tax Act, Section 336.

[20] Ibid.

The legal obligation to repurchase shares is applicable under both a leveraged ESOP and a tax credit ESOP where the employer's securities are not readily tradable on an established market, if the shares were acquired by such ESOP after September 30, 1976. This put option requirement also applies to employer securities acquired after December 31, 1979 by unleveraged ESOPs qualified under Code Section 4975(e)(7). Under an ordinary stock bonus plan, the employer is legally obligated to repurchase its securities distributed to participants, but only if such securities were acquired after December 31, 1986.

A put option is always required on distributed stock that was acquired with the proceeds of an exempt loan and that is not publicly traded, even if the plan is subsequently changed from an ESOP. After ERTA, this does not apply in the case of a bank that is prohibited from purchasing its own stock if participants are given the right to receive benefits in cash thereby eliminating the need for the put option. Also, if it is known at the time the exempt loan is made that honoring the put option would cause the employer to violate federal or state law, the put option must permit the securities to be put to a third party having substantial net worth at the time the loan is made and whose net worth is reasonably expected to remain substantial. Very few individuals would, or could, accept the obligations of a perpetual putee. Also, the substituted putee rule was clearly not intended to cover situations in which the employer may be temporarily prevented from honoring the option, such as in the situation when the employer sponsor has no retained earnings from which to purchase securities (a requirement of many states). Not even publicly traded companies that are exempt from the rules can afford to ignore them. Sometimes public companies are acquired and are no longer public. Sometimes trading is suspended in certain securities, or perhaps the company goes "private," or fails to meet the continuing rules of the exchange(s) on which it is traded. In any case in which the employer securities are no longer publicly traded (i.e., readily tradable on an established market), the put option rule becomes effective.

Payments under put options also may not be restricted by loan agreements, other arrangements, or by the terms of the employer's bylaws or articles of incorporation, except to the extent necessary to comply with state laws.[21]

The ESOP will very likely lose its attractiveness as an employee benefit plan if terminating employees and their beneficiaries are liable for taxes on shares for which there is no market. Also, this lack of market-

---

[21] Treas. Reg. Sec. 54.4975-7(b)(12)(v); Labor Reg. Sec. 2550.408b-3(1)(5).

ability is a factor in determining the value of the shares and, without a put option, there will be a lower valuation of the securities. The company may wish to give discretionary put options, which do not have to conform in any respect to the rules applicable to mandatory put options.[22] If the discretionary put options are granted in a manner that is not uniform and nondiscriminatory, prohibited plan discrimination may result. This can be eliminated if the discretionary put options are for a fixed number of securities for each and every party receiving a distribution.

Valuation. For nonpublicly traded employer stock acquired after December 31 1986, all determinations of fair market value in connection with an ESOP must be based on an independent appraisal.[23] IRS regulations will establish standards for determining what constitutes an independent appraisal. The final regulations require that a valuation be made in good faith on the basis of *all* relevant factors affecting the value of securities.[24]

Conversions and Mergers Involving ESOPs

Conversions to an ESOP. The conversion of an existing plan's investments in general assets that have been accumulated for the purpose of providing retirement benefits into an ESOP should only be undertaken with extreme caution. Fiduciaries should document carefully why the conversion was prudent. Normally, it is only when the fortunes of the company and the value of the stock decline during the period following conversion that the fiduciaries are called on to explain. The board of directors authorizing the conversion would be acting as a fiduciary in connection with the adoption of the amendment.

Under proper circumstances, existing pension and profit-sharing plans may be converted (by amendment) into ESOPs. Once the requirements of prudence and the exclusive benefit rule under ERISA can be satisfied, existing assets of such converted plans may be used to acquire employer securities. Almost all the rules discussed earlier in this chapter come into play. The shares may be purchased from existing shareholders, the employer corporation, and/or the public market.

---

[22] Treas. Reg. Sec. 54.4975-11(a)(7)(i); Labor Reg. Sec. 2550.407d-6(a)(6).

[23] IRC Section 401(a)(28).

[24] Treas. Reg. Sec. 54.4975-11(d)(5). See also *Donovan* v. *Cunningham* 716 F2d 1455 (5th Circuit, 1983), Cert. denied, June 18, 1984.

Further, contribution credit carry-overs attributable to the existing plan under Code Sections 404(a)(3)(A) are available for use under the ESOP, provided the ESOP is similar to the preexisting trust within the meaning of the second sentence of Code Section 404(a)(3)(A), which means a stock bonus or a profit-sharing plan. No credit carry-over is permissible if the profit-sharing or stock bonus plan is converted into a money purchase pension plan, or vice versa.[25] Conversion of a money purchase pension plan into an ESOP may result in 100 percent vesting if the new ESOP does not constitute a comparable plan. For taxable years beginning after December 31, 1986, the ability to deduct up to 25 percent of participants' compensation (instead of the normal 15 percent of compensation) for contributions to a stock bonus or profit-sharing plan is eliminated to the extent that the increased deduction results from prior years' contributions being below 15 percent of compensation. The unused deduction carry-forwards that accumulated for taxable years beginning prior to January 1, 1987 are preserved and may be used after 1986 to increase the deduction limit to 25 percent of participants' compensation.

Conversion of a defined benefit pension plan into an ESOP is to be treated as a termination of the plan for purposes of Title IV of ERISA, and therefore will require 100 percent vesting of participants' actuarially determined benefits. Other types of plans, such as thrift and savings plans, also may be converted.

For any conversion, the provisions of such plans with respect to permissible investments are indeed critical. Since vested employee accounts are being used to purchase qualifying employer securities, the plan provisions almost universally require substantial amendments. Prior plans may be converted to an ESOP just to preserve the old vesting schedules or the provisions that are "grandfathered."[26]

Potential fiduciary liability for plan conversions may exist. Further information is available by reading the following decisions: (1) Usery v. Penn, 426 F. Supp. 830 (W.D. Okla. 1976), *aff'd sub nom.* Eaves v. Penn, 587 F.2d 453 (10th Cir. 1978); (2) Marshall v. Whatley, No. 77 Civ. 04-A (E.D. Va. Apr. 18, 1977); and (3) Baker v. Smith, No. 80 Civ. 3067 (E.D. Penn. Aug. 6, 1980).

A number of labor issues may have to be considered, including the existence of any collective bargaining agreements.

---

[25] Rev. Proc. 76-11 Sec. 4.

[26] T.I.R. 1413, para. T-9.

Pension Reversion Excise Tax Exception for ESOPs. If plan assets remain after a qualified plan has been terminated and all of its accrued benefits distributed, those assets may revert to the employer sponsoring the plan. To discourage employers from utilizing this reversion mechanism, Code Section 4980 imposes a 10 percent excise tax on such reversions.

However, Code Section 4980(c)(3) provides an exception for the direct transfer of all or a portion of such reversion to an ESOP if the following requirements are met. First, within 90 days of the transfer (which period may be extended by the IRS), the ESOP must use the transferred amount to purchase employer securities or to repay loans used to purchase such securities. The securities so acquired must be held by the plan until they are distributed to participants in accordance with plan provisions. Second, any portion of the transfer which is not allocated to participants' accounts in the year of transfer must be credited to a suspense account and allocated no less rapidly than ratably over a period not exceeding seven years. When allocated to participants' accounts, such amounts must be treated as employer contributions, except that, for purposes of Code Section 415, the annual additions attributable to an allocation may not exceed the value of the securities at the time they were first credited to the suspense account. An employer may not make additional contributions to the ESOP until the amount allocated to the suspense account has been distributed. Finally, the transfer of the reversion to the ESOP avoids the excise tax only if at least half of the active participants in the defined benefit plan from which the assets reverted are also participants in the ESOP (as of the close of the first plan year for which an allocation of securities is required).

The special provision for transfers to ESOPs applies to amounts transferred after March 31, 1985 and before January 1, 1989, or amounts transferred after December 31, 1988, pursuant to a termination which occurs after March 31, 1985 and before January 1, 1989.

Note that the IRS, as discussed in the Conference Report for TRA '86 at p. II–483, is studying plan-to-plan asset transfers in light of the exclusive benefit rule and other qualification requirements and circumstances which may result in income tax consequences to the employer.

The Revenue Act of 1987 changed the timing of pension plan terminations and the reversion of excess plan assets. The reversion change provides that no defined benefit plan provision for reversion (or increasing the amount that may revert) made after December 22, 1988, will be effective before the end of the fifth calendar year following its adoption, thus possibly restricting the ability to recover excess assets under amended plans. This change affects ESOPs contemplating rollovers of excess assets (to avoid the 10 percent excise tax), where defined benefit plan amendments will be required. Such amendments must be made during the 12-month window to avoid the five-year delay.

Mergers into an ESOP. Each qualified plan, as a condition of qualification, must provide that, in the case of merger or consolidation with or transfer of assets or liabilities to any other plan after September 2, 1974, each participant must receive a benefit immediately after the merger, consolidation, or transfer, determined as if the plan being transferred were then terminated; that is, no less than the benefit the participant would have been entitled to receive before the merger, consolidation, or transfer determined as if the plan into which the transfer occurs had then terminated.[27] This will be referred to as the ''transfer rules.'' The rules are extremely complicated and generally beyond the scope of this chapter. However, a few of the more essential rules are stated below.

If two or more defined contribution plans are merged or consolidated, the transfer rules will be met if all of the following conditions are met:

1. The sum of the account balances in the plans equals the fair market value of the assets of the surviving plan on the date of the merger or consolidation.
2. The assets of each plan are combined to form the assets of the plan as merged.
3. The participants' balances in the plans that survive right after the merger are equal to the sum of the participants' account balances (individually determined) in the plans just before the merger.

A defined benefit plan being merged into an existing ESOP is considered as being, first, converted to a defined contribution plan, and then, once converted it is considered as merged.[28] The Pension Benefit Guaranty Corporation (PBGC) requires the plan administrator to allow each participant to elect in writing either to receive the value of the participants' accrued benefits in the form provided under the plan or to have plan assets equal in value payable as an annuity transferred to an individual account under the ESOP.[29] This election probably constitutes a sale within the meaning of Section 2(3) of the Securities Act of 1933 and would require compliance unless some exception from registration is available.

---

[27] IRC Secs. 401(a)(12), 414(1).

[28] Treas. Reg. Sec. 1.414(1)-1(i).

[29] P.B.G.C. Opinion 76-30 (March 8, 1976); P.B.G.C. Opinion 76-12 (January 27, 1976).

Conversions from an ESOP. If the conversion out of an ESOP is accomplished by plan merger, consolidation, or transfer of assets, the transfer rules would apply and there would be no particular problems. If the plan merger, consolidation, or transfer of assets out of an ESOP is into another type of defined contribution plan, it will not necessarily trigger a termination within the meaning of the vesting requirements of Code Section 411(d)(3).

The conversion out of an ESOP also will not in itself relieve the employer from the put option requirements. However, the put option rule applies only when employer securities are distributed; and enough securities of the employer could be converted to other assets to permit distributions in other assets, or future contributions may supply enough cash for many years. Outstanding loans are a problem on the conversion out of an ESOP. If the balance of the loan cannot be repaid prior to conversion, ESOP fiduciaries have three options: (1) defer the conversion until the loan is paid off, (2) seek a specific exemption from the prohibited transaction rules of ERISA Section 408(a) and Code Section 4975(c)(2), or (3) proceed with the conversion risk and incur the penalties imposed with respect to prohibited transactions. There is a further risk that plan fiduciaries may be held liable for any losses incurred by the plan as a result of their violation of the prohibited transaction provisions of ERISA Section 409(a), and they may be removed by a court. The same fiduciary considerations applicable to converting *to* an ESOP are applicable in converting *from* one.

Last, converting to any other kind of plan but an eligible individual account plan gives rise to an absolute 10 percent limitation of ERISA Section 407 on the holding of employer securities.

Types of Employer Securities

With the changes brought about by the Technical Corrections Act of 1979, the definition of "qualifying employer securities" in Code Section 4975(e)(8) incorporates by reference the definition of employer securities that is applicable for Code Section 415(c)(6) and Code Section 409(1). This definition includes only the following:

1. Common stock readily tradable on an established securities market.
2. If there is no readily tradable common stock, common stock having a combination of voting power and dividend rights at least equal to the classes of common stock having the greatest voting power and the greatest dividend rights.

3. Preferred stock convertible (at any time) into common stock meeting one of the above definitions.

This definition of employer securities is now applicable to stock acquired by a statutory ESOP after December 31, 1979, but may be limited to stock acquired pursuant to the "ESOP loan exemption." Note that any kind of capital stock may be contributed or purchased on a nonleveraged basis, if the plan is a stock bonus plan that is not an ESOP or an ESOP that is otherwise primarily invested in qualifying employer securities.

Types of Distributions—Cash versus Stock

General. Until the changes brought about by the Revenue Act of 1978, the Technical Corrections Act of 1979, and the Miscellaneous Revenue Act of 1980, the regulations for ESOPs required that the portion of an ESOP consisting of a stock bonus plan must provide for benefits to be distributable only in stock of the employer.[30] This provision restated the requirements applicable to stock bonus plans set forth in Treasury Regulation Sections 1.401-1(a)(2)(iii) and 1.401-1(b)(1)(iii).

The Revenue Act of 1978 provided that a leveraged employee stock ownership plan could distribute cash in lieu of employer securities so long as the participant could demand that his or her distribution be made in employer securities.

The Technical Corrections Act of 1979 provided that the cash distribution option available to an ESOP under Code Section 4975(e)(7) and 409A(h), which is now 409(h), be made effective with respect to distributions of benefits after December 31, 1978.

The Miscellaneous Revenue Act of 1980 added Code Section 401(a)(23), which permits any qualified stock bonus plan, not just an ESOP or TRASOP, to make distributions of benefits in either cash or stock after December 31, 1980, so long as the participant or beneficiary has the right to demand distributions in the form of employer stock. ERTA further modified this to provide that mandatory cash distributions could occur if the articles or bylaws of the corporation restrict ownership of substantially all the company's stock to current employees and an employees' trust. Code Section 401(a)(23) cross-references IRC Section 409(h), which outlines the distribution provisions for TRASOPs. This put option under 401(a)(23) will be required only if the stock bonus plan (other

---

[30] Treas. Reg. Sec. 54.4975-11(f)(1).

than an ESOP or TRASOP) includes a cash distribution option and will be the same as that required for ESOPs and TRASOPs under Code Section 409A(h) [new Code Section 409(h)].

Special Distribution Requirements. TRA '86 imposes new requirements on the timing of distributions from an ESOP. These requirements apply to distributions attributable to employer stock acquired by the ESOP after December 31, 1986.

Unless a participant otherwise elects, the distribution of his or her ESOP benefits must begin no later than the last day of the plan year following the plan year of normal retirement age, disability, or death, or of the fifth plan year following the plan year in which his or her employment terminates for other reasons. However, there are two exceptions to this rule: (1) distribution is not required if the participant resumes employment before the distribution date; (2) any distribution attributable to employer stock acquired with the proceeds of an ESOP loan may, except in the case of such normal retirement, death, or disability, be postponed until the close of the plan year in which that ESOP loan is fully repaid.

Generally, unless a participant otherwise elects, distribution of ESOP benefits must be made at least as rapidly as substantially equal, annual installments over a period not exceeding five years. However, for participants whose benefits exceed $500,000 in value, the distribution period may be extended (up to an additional five years) by one year for each $100,000 (or fraction thereof) by which the value of benefits exceeds $500,000.

Subject to these and other qualified plan non-discrimination requirements, an ESOP may retain discretion in determining the timing and form of distributions without regard to the restrictions on discretionary distribution options generally applicable to qualified plans under the Retirement Equity Act of 1984 (REA).

Early Distribution Excise Tax Exception. TRA '86 imposes a 10 percent excise tax on taxable distributions (after 1986) from a qualified plan to a participant prior to age 59½, unless the distribution occurs as the result of the participant's death, disability, or terminated employment after age 55 under the plan, or is rolled over into an IRA. This excise tax will not generally apply to any ESOP distributions prior to 1990. In addition, cash dividends on employer stock that are passed through to ESOP participants are not subject to this excise tax even after 1990.

Which Distribution Is Best? A nearly universal participant question is, "Which distribution type is best—cash or stock?" The answer depends on the tax picture of the employee, the interplay of the "lump-sum distribution" rules under the Code, and Code Sections 402(e)(4)(D) and its regulations, which provide that the taxable amount of a lump-sum distribution does not include net unrealized appreciation on the employer's securities distributed to a participant. Net unrealized appreciation is the excess of the fair market value of the employer securities at the time of distribution from a plan over the trust's adjusted basis in the securities. The net unrealized appreciation on the date of distribution is taxed as a long-term capital gain when the securities are subsequently disposed of. Any additional appreciation is either short- or long-term capital gain, depending on how long the stock is held by the distributee.[31]

To determine which distribution is most advantageous, calculate the total tax from lump-sum treatment with each of the various possibilities. Surprisingly, in many large distributions, taking stock clearly results in a lower tax, both currently and subsequently. TRA '86 eliminates the preferential tax treatment for capital gains after December 31, 1986. However, it permits an ESOP distributee to elect to include any appreciation in value of employer stock while in the ESOP (net unrealized appreciation) as part of the taxable amount eligible for special income tax averaging available for certain lump-sum distributions.

Rollovers. Rollovers are very flexible for ESOPs. The stock may be distributed, then sold, and the proceeds contributed to an individual retirement account (IRA), provided the proceeds are contributed within the statutory 60-day period. Alternatively, partial rollovers are permitted, and of course, if the stock is acceptable to an IRA custodian or trustee, the stock can go right into the IRA. No tax is due by participants or beneficiaries if these special IRA rules are followed. The disadvantage of an IRA, however, is that the various options available by carefully calculating the tax effect of stock and cash in a lump-sum distribution are not available if the distribution stays in an IRA until distributions start. If a distribution is rolled over into an IRA, the benefit of the lump-sum and capital gains provisions of the Code are not available. The distributions from the IRA are taxed at earned ordinary income tax rates, and the special averaging and capital gains rates are lost forever. The only exception is when the amount rolled over is subsequently rolled over into another qualified plan or IAR.

---

[31] Rev. Rul. 81-122 1981-1 C.B..

Deduction of Employer Dividend Payments. The last sentence of Section 803(h) of the Tax Reform Act of 1976 reflects the intent of Congress to permit the employer to structure an ESOP "to distribute income on employer securities currently." The regulations provide that an ESOP will not fail to meet[32] the qualification requirements of Code Section 401(a) merely because the ESOP provides for the current payment of income with respect to employer securities.

DEFRA and TRA '86 made substantial and meaningful changes to the tax treatment of dividends on employer stock.

1. *Cash dividends paid to participants and beneficiaries.* Code Section 404(k) permits a deduction to a corporation for the amount of dividends paid in cash by such corporation with respect to stock of the corporation if:

1. Such stock is held on the record date of the dividend by a tax-credit ESOP or an ESOP that meets the requirements of Section 4975(e)(7) of the Code and regulations issued thereunder and is maintained by such corporation or a controlled group member thereof; and
2. In accordance with the ESOP provisions, one of the following occurs:
   a. The dividend is paid in cash directly to the participants and beneficiaries in the plan before the close of the employer's taxable year.
   b. The dividend is paid in cash to the ESOP before the close of the employer's taxable year and is distributed to the participants and beneficiaries in the ESOP not later than 90 days after the close of the plan year.

The temporary regulations issued under Section 404(k) expressly provide that the dividend deduction is available with respect to qualifying employer securities within the meaning of Subsection 409(l) of such corporation held by an ESOP and also is available with respect to other employer stock of the corporation (not just qualifying employer securities). However, such dividends must be immediately distributed under the terms of the plan and all of the applicable qualification and distribution rules. The deduction is allowed even if plan participants may elect to receive or not to receive payment of dividends. The Temporary Regulations (1.404(k)) clearly indicate that a deductible dividend under Section 404(k) is a taxable plan distribution even though an employee has unre-

[32] Treas. Reg. Secs. 54.4975-11(a)(8)(iii), 54.4975-11(f)(3).

covered employee contributions or basis in the plan. This is confirmed by provisions added by the Tax Reform Act of 1986 in Section 72(e)(5). Further, under Code Section 411(a)(11)(ii)(C), the distributions of dividends in excess of $3,500 are not subject to the general rule requiring participant consent.

2. *Dividends applied to loan payments.* The Tax Reform Act of 1986 expands the deduction for dividends by permitting a corporation to deduct the amount of cash dividends paid on employer stock held by an ESOP (both allocated and unallocated shares) to the extent that the dividends are used by the ESOP to make payments (of principal and interest) on the ESOP loan used to acquire those shares. Code Section 404(k)(2) significantly enhances the ability to finance ESOP transactions on a pretax basis. The deduction, which applies for taxable years commencing after October 22, 1986, is allowed for the taxable year of the corporation in which the dividends are so applied.[33]

As noted above, the statute makes no distinction between allocated and unallocated shares for purposes of the deduction of dividends applied to ESOP loan payments.

It appears that cash dividends paid on both allocated and unallocated ESOP shares should be able to be used to make deductible ESOP loan payments without violating the requirements of Section 4975, and it is expected that treasury regulations and other technical guidelines will reflect this fact.

Finally, dividends used to repay an ESOP loan will not be considered an annual addition for Section 415 purposes and will not be considered for purposes of determining an employer's deduction under Section 404.[34]

3. *Miscellaneous matters.* Section 404(k) dividends are treated as taxable income rather than a nontaxable return of basis, in the case of a contributory ESOP. No partial dividend exclusion on dividends paid in cash to participants and beneficiaries is permitted to the participants, and all such dividends will constitute ordinary income to the participants or recipients. Withholding is *not* required with respect to such dividend payment, nor are FICA or FUTA taxes withheld on these amounts.

Furthermore, in the case of a leveraged ESOP, the deduction appears to apply to cash dividends paid to participants and beneficiaries with respect to unallocated shares held in a suspense account, not just shares allocated to participants' accounts, although the statute does not ex-

---

[33] Tax Reform Act of 1986, Section 1173(c)(1).

[34] U.S. Senate Committee on Finance, 99th Congress, 2nd Session, *Report to Accompany H.R. 3838,* Rept. 99-313, p. 682.

pressly address the issue. However, the author perceives that the Senate Finance Committee Report takes a contrary position.[35]

In drafting an ESOP plan document, consideration should be given to whether the distribution of cash dividends will be automatic or whether it will be subject to the periodic choice of the ESOP fiduciaries, the ESOP participants, or even the board of directors of the employer corporation. In either case the dividend payout could be restricted to vested shares only. If the board of directors makes the choice, rather than the trustees, such choice may be justified on the grounds that it generates a corporate deduction that concurrently benefits the ESOP participants and beneficiaries.

One question not answered in the statute or in its legislative history is the following: Can an employee make a voluntary contribution of cash or employer stock to the ESOP and thereby create the deduction for the employer on dividends paid on such stock? Under Rev. Rul. 80-350, 1980-2 C.B. 133, an employee may make aftertax voluntary contributions to a tax-qualified retirement plan such as an ESOP in an amount not exceeding 10 percent of his or her aggregate compensation since he or she commenced participation in the plan. While nothing in the statute or the legislative history would preclude this, it is not inconceivable that the Internal Revenue Service could take the position that such a voluntary contribution by an employee is outside the purposes of the statute and, therefore, creates a windfall deduction to an employer with respect to the stock contributed by the employee. Since, however, the statute contains no restrictions concerning the source of the stock contribution, such a position by the Service would be of highly questionable validity unless it can prove a tax evasion scheme. Other issues which should be considered include: whether the voluntary contributions in kind are prohibited transactions for which there may be no exemption, including the valuation issues of an in-kind contribution from a party-in-interest; whether the voluntary contributions reduce the employer contributions or the allocation of employer contributions because of the reduction in the Code Section 415 annual additions; and whether the nondiscrimination test of Code Section 401(m) is violated because of the voluntary contributions being skewed in favor of the highly compensated.

Finally, Code Section 404(k) provides that the deduction for ESOP dividends may be disallowed if the Service determines that such dividend constitutes in substance an "evasion" of taxation. The statute says

---

[35] U.S. Senate Committee on Finance, *Report to Accompany H.R. 3838,* Rept. 99-313, (May 29, 1986) p. 1,033.

"avoidance," yet the legislative history suggests that "evasion" was the intended standard.

Stock Purchase by an ESOP. When a taxpayer sells shares of stock, he or she recognizes gain to the extent of the excess over the taxpayer's adjusted basis in the stock. When the stock is redeemed by the issuing corporation, the transaction is considered a distribution by the corporation, with respect to its stock, and will be taxable as a capital gain (or loss) only if the requirements of Code Section 302(b) are satisfied. Otherwise, it is a dividend to the shareholder and taxed twice—once at the corporate level and then again at the shareholder level.

The ESOP is clearly a separate legal entity, and so under normal circumstances the sale by a shareholder to an ESOP would be taxed as a sale or exchange at capital gains rates, too. However, the IRS may view certain transactions as a redemption by the sponsoring employer and hence subject to dividend treatment.

Revenue Procedure 87-22 sets forth operating rules with respect to the issuance of an advance ruling of the IRS: that the proposed sale of the employer's stock by a shareholder to a related employee plan is a sale or exchange, rather than a corporate distribution taxable under Code Section 301. The revenue procedure only provides a safe harbor, and failure to meet its tests will not be an automatic application of Code Section 301 to the sale of stock to a qualified plan. These guidelines do not, as a matter of law, precisely define the only situations in which the sale of stock to a plan will avoid treatment as a corporate distribution of property under Code Section 301. In the absence of such a ruling, the tax ramifications of such a sale will be subject to examination on audit.

A favorable ruling under Revenue Procedure 87-22 will be issued if three conditions are met:

1. The combined beneficial interests of the selling shareholder and all related persons in the plan on the date of the sale cannot exceed 20 percent of the total plan beneficial interests. This requirement will *not* be satisfied if *any* one of the following occurs:
   a. The combined covered compensation of the selling shareholder and related persons on the date of the sale exceeds 20 percent of the total compensation of all participants under the plan.
   b. The total account balances (vested and nonvested) of the selling shareholder and related persons under the plan on the date of the sale exceeds 20 percent of the account balances of all plan participants.
   c. The total interest (vested and nonvested) of the selling shareholder in any separately managed fund or account within the

plan on the date of the sale exceeds 20 percent of the total net assets in that fund or account.

In determining whether the interest of the selling shareholder and related persons in any fund exceeds 20 percent of the net assets of that fund, there may be excluded from consideration any separately managed fund or account of a plan that at no time may be invested in the employer's securities.[36] For purposes of these tests, "related person(s)" includes the spouse, parents, grandparents, children, and grandchildren of the selling shareholder.

2. The second requirement for a private letter ruling is that the restrictions on the disposition of the employer's stock held and distributed by the employee plan can be no more onerous than the disposition restrictions on at least a majority of the shares of the employer's securities held by other shareholders. Certain rights of first refusal that comply with the provisions of the ESOP regulations are acceptable restrictions that can apply to employer securities held or distributed by an ESOP.
3. The third requirement is that there be no intention, plan, or understanding on the part of the employer to redeem from the plan any of the stock being purchased by the plan from the selling shareholder.

A private letter ruling should always be requested in those situations in which doubt exists.

Tax-Deferred Sale of Stock to ESOP. For taxable years beginning after July 18, 1984, DEFRA added Code Section 1042, which permits a shareholder of a closely held corporation to sell employer stock to an ESOP and defer the taxation of gain to the extent that he or she purchases securities of other corporations. The sale must otherwise qualify for long-term capital gains treatment and the shares must not have been received by the seller from a qualified employee plan (such as an ESOP) or pursuant to an employee incentive program; e.g. by exercising a stock option. The replacement securities must be purchased within the 15-month period that begins 3 months before and ends 12 months after the sale of employer stock to the ESOP. The replacement securities must be securities of corporations whose passive investment income does not exceed 25 percent of gross receipts and other technical rules. After the sale the ESOP must own at least 30 percent of outstanding employer stock, and an excise tax is imposed on the employer for certain dispositions of the stock by the

---

[36] Rev. Proc. 87-22, I.R.B. 1987-20,11.

ESOP within three years after the sale. The stock that is purchased by the ESOP generally may not be allocated to the seller, members of his or her family, or any shareholder who owns more than 25 percent of any class of employer stock. Chapter 29, pp. 545 and 546, covers this in more detail.

ADDITIONAL ESOP CONSIDERATIONS

SEC Aspects

1933 Securities Act

On February 1, 1980, the Securities and Exchange Commission issued Release No. 33-6188 on the application of the 1933 Securities Act to employee plans. The purpose of the release was to provide guidance to the public and to assist employers and plan participants in complying with the '33 act. The release discusses circumstances under which interests in plans and related entities may be subject to the requirements of the '33 act. The release also provides an analysis of the criteria to be used to determine when an offer or sale of a security will occur, discusses the various exemptions from the act's registration provisions, discusses the act's application to the various types of securities transactions in which plans may engage, as well as resales of securities participants acquire through the operation of the plan, and further describes the methods of registration of securities under the act.

The interests of employees in a plan are securities only when the employees voluntarily participate in and contribute to the plan. Employee interests in plans that are not both voluntary and contributory are not securities and are not subject to the act, according to the release. While the release is lengthy and is intended to provide guidance, the release does point out that it should not be viewed as an all-inclusive treatment of the subject and that the SEC staff will continue to provide interpretive advice and assistance on request, as will the courts.

Another release (Release No. 33-6281), issued January 22, 1981, further clarifies the SEC's position on the application of the 1933 Securities Act to employee benefit plans, as well as describes developments under the act after the 1980 release was issued. Both releases are invaluable to an understanding of the issues involved.

Whether the ESOP has an independent bank trustee is another factor affecting the impact of the securities laws on the ESOP. Employer securities purchased by an independent trustee may be sold by an ESOP or distributed to and resold by participants who are not deemed affiliates of the employer without registration under the '33 Act. Shares purchased on the open market by an employer-controlled ESOP must be registered prior to resale by plan participants, and such securities are subject to very limited resale privileges until they are registered.

Securities Exchange Act of 1934

The Securities Exchange Act of 1934 is designed to regulate the trading markets for publicly held securities. Among other things, it requires issuers of such securities, subject to certain exemptions, to make continuing disclosures concerning their affairs through 1934 act registration statements, shareholder reports, proxy statements, and periodic and other reports filed with or submitted to the SEC. It also imposes reporting and other obligations on large holders of publicly traded equity securities, including ESOPs, and provides for margin regulation of securities transactions.

The compliance requirements are beyond the scope of this chapter. However, the 1934 act raises at least three significant issues with respect to the operation of an ESOP:

1. Under what circumstances is an ESOP required to comply with the shareholder reporting provisions of Sections 13(d) and 16(a) of the 1934 act?
2. Are purchases and sales of employer stock subject to the short-swing profit recovery provisions of Section 16(b) of the 1934 act?
3. Are borrowings by the ESOP to acquire employer stock subject to the margin requirements adopted by the Federal Reserve Board under the 1934 act?

These questions should be answered for each ESOP that is established by a publicly traded company.

Other Reporting and Disclosure Rules

There are additional reporting and disclosure rules that should be looked at:

1. Section 15(d) provides that if a registration statement pursuant to the 1933 act has to be filed with respect to certain stock-related qualified plans, then the registrant must file "such supplementary and periodic information documents and reports as may be required pursuant to Section 13 of this title."

2. Section 16(a) Reporting-Rule 16a-8(a)(2) provides that the "vested beneficial interests in a trust" must be reported by officers and directors and beneficial owners of more than 10 percent of any class of equity security, and they must report periodically on changes of ownership. The rules are exceedingly complex, and several exemptions may be available.

3. Antifraud rules: The 1934 act's antifraud rules apply to both initial sales as well as to subsequent sales. Section 10 of the 1934 act prohibits the use of manipulative and deceptive devices in the trading of securities. Certain fraudulent and deceptive practices are a crime. Various other rules require an issuer and its affiliate(s) to follow certain procedures in the repurchase of its stock, which might apply to the ESOP's trustee. Another section provides that a person who relies on a false or misleading statement contained in a document filed with the SEC may recover for reliance on such a statement. Other rules require insiders to disgorge profits made under certain circumstances. There are many unanswered questions under these rules. For example: Does a company have a duty to disclose material nonpublic information regarding the company? Does the employer or the ESOP have a duty to disclose "complete" information to a participant if it is known that the participant will immediately resell the employer securities in the public market?

Accounting Considerations[37]

ESOPs must address some difficult accounting issues, both from the employer's point of view in preparing the financial statements, and in the trust accounting and participant accounting areas.

Employer Accounting Considerations

In 1976 the American Institute of Certified Public Accountants (AICPA) issued a statement of position on accounting issues relating to ESOPs (SOP 76-3) and the accounting guidance outlined in that statement of position is considered preferable by the Financial Accounting Standards Board as well as the Securities and Exchange Commission according to a footnote to SFAS No. 32.[38]

The statement of position recommended the following accounting treatment:

---

[37] This section has been reviewed and substantially updated by Rebecca J. Miller, a partner in the Rochester Minnesota Office of the accounting firm of McGladrey, Hendrickson & Pullen. A portion of this material which originally appeared in Richard Reichler, ed., *Employee Stock Ownership Plans: Problems & Potentials,* was written by Norman N. Strauss, Copyright 1977, 1978, Law Journal Seminars-Press. Reprinted by permission of the publisher.

[38] American Institute of Certified Public Accountants, Accounting Standards Division, "Statement of Position on Accounting Practices for Certain Employee Stock Ownership Plans," issued December 20, 1976.

- The debt of the ESOP should be recorded as a liability in the employer's financial statements when the debt is guaranteed by the employer, or when the employer commits itself to make future contributions to the ESOP that are sufficient to service the debt.
- The offsetting debit to the liability recorded by the employer should be accounted for as a reduciton of shareholders' equity. Because no real expansion of equity has occurred, the increase in capital stock resulting from the issuance of shares to the ESOP is offset by the debit to equity (the equity contra account), set up when the loan is recorded. If new shares are not issued by the company, and the ESOP purchases shares from existing shareholders, the accounting treatment with respect to establishing the equity contra account is the same.
- Each year the amount contributed to the plan to reduce the loan balance should be charged to compensation expense. The portion of the contribution representing interest on the borrowing should be separately identified and charged to interest expense. Both the liability and the equity contra account should be reduced symmetrically as the loan is amortized.
- All shares held by an ESOP should be treated as outstanding shares in the earnings-per-share computation.

When the ESOP acquires shares already outstanding on a leveraged basis, the existing shareholders' equity section of the employer's balance sheet will be reduced, and increases in equity will be recorded as the debt is satisfied. A separate line-item deduction in the stockholders' equity section is preferable. In the event the ESOP acquires newly issued shares of stock on a leveraged basis, the existing shareholders' equity section of the employer's balance sheet will not decline as the effect of establishing the equity section contra account will be offset by the increase in equity resulting from the issuance of additional shares. The "Example of Accounting Treatment" at the end of this chapter illustrates the accounting treatment.

As the ESOP makes its payments, the corresponding liability on the balance sheet should be reduced, and the stockholders' equity section also adjusted. The accounts should move symmetrically.[39]

When reporting dividends per share, the dividends should be charged to retained earnings, just as dividends paid to any other shareholder. Dividends are *not* compensation expense, even if they are passed through to participants, and are instead merely a charge against retained earnings. Dividends paid on common stock of the employer may be invested in

---

[39] AICPA Statement of Position, para. 8.

additional stock of the employer. Such dividends do not give rise to income and should increase treasury stock in jurisdictions where this is permitted, rather than reduce retained earnings. Furthermore, pursuant to the Tax Reform Act of 1986, a tax deduction for the ESOP's sponsoring corporation can be obtained for dividends (on allocated and unallocated shares) paid in cash within 90 days to participants, or dividends can be used to repay an ESOP loan (leveraged ESOP). For financial reporting purposes these dividends are not generally classified as compensation expense. They remain dividends chargeable to retained earnings. However, any tax benefit realized can be credited to the current tax provision.[40]

The earnings-per-share questions are clearly resolved. The AICPA asserts "that all shares held by an ESOP should be treated as outstanding shares in the determination of earnings per share.[41]

When an ESOP receives a contribution in excess of the allowable deduction limitation, such excess is usually treated as a timing difference by the employer in determining the provision for income tax, since excess contributions made in one year can generally be carried over to ensuing years.

The accounting treatment for excess contributions to ESOPs has been settled by FASB's Emerging Issues Task Force.[42] This issue was raised by the provision in TRA '86 allowing an employer to make a tax-free transfer of a defined benefit plan reversion to an ESOP. This position varies somewhat from the traditional reporting of leveraged ESOPs. In general, the position follows the "Treasury Stock" method:[43]

- A contra equity account is created for the shares purchased with the excess contribution (reversion).
- As shares are allocated, the contra equity account is relieved for the cost of the shares. Compensation expense is charged for the *fair market* value of the shares. Any difference is applied to paid-in-capital.
- Dividends on these shares are accounted for as traditional dividends with one exception where dividends on unallocated shares are distributed to participants, they are treated as compensation expense.
- Only allocated shares are used in calculating earnings per share.

---

[40] Footnote to SFAS No. 96, para. 75, 141.

[41] AICPA Statement of Position, para. 11.

[42] *EITF Opinion 86-27*.

[43] *APB Opinion No. 25*.

Note: These rules only apply to an excess contribution. Also certain elements will be modified (i.e., the number of shares outstanding for earnings per share calculations) if the excess contribution is used to pay a pre-existing ESOP loan.

The financial statement reclassification into interest expense and compensation expense will not affect the deduction of the contribution(s) for tax purposes. Also, the possible impact of the ESOP financial statement accounting techniques on a future business combination accounting as a pooling of interests or purchase may be a consideration.

Any additional investment tax credit allowed for TRASOP contributions should be recorded as a reduction of the income tax expense in the year the contribution to the ESOP is charged as an expense. The recognition should conform to the general rule for any investment credit; that the credit will be utilized with reasonable certainty or is a reality.[44] This treatment applies regardless of the manner in which the employer normally accounts for investment tax credits in the financial statements (i.e. the "flow-through" or amortization method).

The footnotes should be as complete and descriptive as possible, and must at the barest minimum, include a description of the plan, including the purpose, any formula for contributions, how the trust assets are held, its effective date, and how employer stock has been (or will be) purchased. The current qualified status of the plan, dates of determination letters from the IRS, and a complete description of the loan also should be listed.

ESOP Accounting Considerations

The primary objective of a defined contribution plan's financial statements is to provide information about (a) plan resources and how the stewardship responsibility for those resources has been discharged, (b) the results of transactions and events that affect the information about those resources, and (c) other factors necessary for users to understand the information provided.

The financial statements of a defined contribution plan should include:

a. a statement that includes information regarding net assets available for benefits of the plan as of the financial statement date.
b. a statement that includes information regarding the changes during the period in net assets available for benefits of the plan.

---

[44] *APB Opinion No. 16.*

The accrual basis of accounting should be used in preparing information regarding net assets available for plan benefits and related changes. The accrual basis requires that purchases and sales of securities be recorded on a trade-date basis. If the settlement date is after the financial statement date, however, and (a) the fair market value of the securities purchased or sold just before the financial statement date does not change significantly from the trade date to the financial statement date and (b) the purchases or sales do not significantly affect the composition of the plan's assets available for benefits, accounting on a settlement-date basis for such sales and purchases is acceptable.[45] The information should be presented in such reasonable detail as necessary to identify the plan's net assets available for benefits and related changes. The trust must also account for the cost basis of the shares of stock held by the trust for purposes of calculating net unrealized appreciation in the accounts of participants receiving employer securities on distribution.[46]

The cost-basis accounting for shares is actually done by the participant record-keeping system. Each year the trustee is informed about the cost basis of the shares distributed to participants and beneficiaries during the year, so the trust's cost basis can be adjusted in the shares yet held by the trustee.

ESOP Administration and Manuals for Record-Keeping Rules

It is strongly suggested that written manuals be adopted to provide continuity in administration in the event of personnel turnover and, perhaps more important, to document the many discretionary decisions of the sponsoring company to insure "uniform and nondiscriminatory" application. This latter function conceivably would forestall potential litigation in the event of a participant's dissatisfaction with a particular policy. Manuals that would be advisable include: a brief plan interpretation, with examples covering the salient provisions; an accounting procedures manual, which specifies the various choices about methods discussed in this section; a distribution procedures manual, which reflects the company's policies on timing and method of distributions; and a general administration manual, designed to include all of the documentation required to be available to and for participants. Other manuals may be useful and should

---

[45] ERISA Section 103(b)(3)(A).

[46] Treas. Reg. Sec. 1.402(a)(1)-(b)(2).

be designed for individual cases.

One disadvantage of these types of manuals is that a policy once formally documented becomes potentially enforceable. Briefly, whatever a manual documents must be what is done.

Repurchase Liability

The ESOP repurchase liability[47] has not been given much attention. Basically, it arises because the employer contributes cash or stock and the stock has to be bought back, usually at an increased price. And, the employer must buy it back—for cash. Since ESOPs are relatively new, the cash needed to repurchase company stock from departed employees and their beneficiaries has not yet created a problem for most companies. But there is a clear risk it will, unless a company properly plans for it. It is this author's opinion that, potentially, this is the most serious difficulty the ESOP will experience. Since the repurchase liability affects the value of company stock, the balance sheet and income statement, the number of shareholders, and employee morale, it should be forecasted and planned for.

The first step in facing this potential problem is to develop a projection of future cash requirements. A computer model specifically suited for this purpose is particularly advantageous, since without one it is almost impossible to see how the plan operates under different assumptions, and how the company's income, cash flow, and balance sheet are affected. The final step is to analyze the various funding methods to determine which would work best in a particular situation. It is conceivable that the repurchase liability could consume more cash than the company could contribute in a given year, since the entire contribution may be used to make repurchases. All the more reason to plan!

The repurchase liability is alleviated by varying distributions over time, varying the size of the contribution, varying the stock and cash contributions mix, properly timing stock repurchases, and carefully planning for the proper use of dividends on employer securities and of the income on other assets. Other solutions include going public, private placements, being acquired, or the creative use of corporate-owned life insurance.

---

[47] Robert W. Smiley, Jr., "How to Plan for an ESOP's Repurchase Liability," Prentice-Hall's *Pension and Profit Sharing Service,* (Englewood Cliffs, N.J.: Prentice-Hall, 1987), pp. 1,215–29.

The employee's diversification right is a new concept added by TRA '86. It allows employees an elective diversification of their ESOP account balances as to securities acquired after December 31, 1986. This election is extended to any employee who is age 55 or older and has 10 years of plan participation in the ESOP. Elections for the first five years may cover up to 25 percent of an employee's account balance (less the portion diversified); the election in the final year may cover up to 50 percent of his or her account balance (less any prior portion diversified).

Companies should not be discouraged from adopting or continuing an ESOP because of the "unknown" repurchase liability, nor should a company adopt an ESOP without ample consideration of the potential repurchase liability. Instead, careful advance planning, ongoing review, good communications, increased productivity, and increased company profits, as well as continued flexibility and encouragement from Congress and the government agencies, should solve almost every problem created by the repurchase liability—but not without planning for it today. The repurchase liability plan must be implemented properly, carefully maintained, and revised as often as necessary to reflect the real world.

ESOP Exception to Net Operating Loss Limitations

TRA '86 imposes new limitations on the utilization of a corporation's net operating loss (and certain other tax credit) carry-forwards following a more than 50 percent change in ownership within prescribed periods of time. However, if any transaction(s) results in an ESOP's ownership of at least 50 percent of the common equity of the corporation, these limitations generally won't apply.

Floor-Offset Arrangements

Some employers maintain "floor-offset" arrangements that combine defined benefit and defined contribution plan features. Under such arrangements, a participant's accrued benefit under the defined benefit portion of the arrangement is reduced by the benefit provided to such participant under the defined contribution portion of the arrangement. The defined contribution portion of the arrangement is an eligible individual account plan and all, or substantially all, of the participant's individual accounts may be invested in employer securities. Such an arrangement offers the employee the opportunity to realize greater retirement benefits than the defined benefit portion could alone provide due to employer stock appreciation but has the potential downside risk to employees that a sudden change in the employer's fortunes (e.g., insolvency) could adversely affect benefit security. Where an employer has an existing defined benefit plan and uses an ESOP to buy out a current shareholder(s), the use of a floor-offset arrangement for prospective accruals can preserve employees' pension expectations.

Although the Internal Revenue Service has ruled in Revenue Ruling 76-259 that floor-offset arrangements may meet the qualification requirements of the Internal Revenue Code, the Department of Labor has not ruled that the individual account portions of these arrangements qualify for the eligible individual account exemption from the 10 percent limitation on acquisitions of qualifying employer securities.

The Department of Labor has, for a long time, felt that both plans should be subject to the 10 percent limit. The Revenue Act of 1987 modifies ERISA to add ERISA Sections 407(d)(3)(C) and 407(d)(9), which provide that, in a floor-offset arrangement, both plans are subject to the 10 percent limit. Thus, the assets in both plans are combined and the 10 percent limit is determined by reference to those combined assets. Presumably, the employer securities could be held in either of the plans.

The amendment applies to arrangements established after December 17, 1987. The 1987 act, thus, does not deal with whether these floor-offset arrangements were previously acceptable; although, an inference is created that any arrangement set up before 1987 can continue, whereas any arrangement established after December 17, 1987 would be subject to this more restrictive interpretation.

ESOPs and Plan Disqualification

If an employee stock ownership plan is ruled not to meet the requirements of either Code Section 401(a) or Code Section 4975(e)(7), a variety of problems result. First, any sales to such a plan will not qualify for the tax-free rollover treatment provided under Code Section 1042, since that section requires that the sales be made to an employee stock ownership plan within the meaning of Code Section 4975(e)(7).

Moreover, any loan by a lender to an ESOP will not qualify for the partial interest exclusion provided in Code Section 133 because that section requires that the plan be an employee stock ownership plan within the meaning of Code Section 4975(e)(7). While the lender will lose the ability to get the partial interest exclusion, properly drafted yield protection language in the loan documentation will ultimately shift that burden to the employer.

Disqualification will also have a negative effect on both the employer and its employees. Plan contributions will no longer be deductible under Code Section 404 (with its special limitations for ESOPs) but may be deductible under the ordinary and necessary provisions of Code Section

162. For the employees, disqualification will mean that the value of their vested account balances will be immediately taxable to them as ordinary income and all earnings of the ESOP will be subject to tax, thereby diminishing the account balances of the employees.

401(k) Plans and ESOPs

Most 401(k) plans maintained by employers are profit-sharing plans. However, a 401(k) plan may also be a stock bonus plan. Thus, the salary reduction contributions made by participants and employer matching contributions may be invested in employer stock. In that case, all of the requirements relating to stock bonus plans would apply to the 401(k) stock bonus plan. Particular care and attention should be given to applicable federal and state securities law provisions since, if the participant's salary reduction contributions are allowed to be invested in employer stock, plan registration and related disclosure may be required.

Wage Concession ESOPs

While several notable employee stock ownership plans, including the ones established by Weirton Steel, Eastern Airlines, and Continental Airlines, have involved wage concessions in exchange for the shared equity provided by an ESOP, such ESOPs are the exception rather than the rule. In fact, according to surveys conducted by the National Center for Employee Ownership, over 95 percent of the ESOPs established in the United States to date have not involved wage concessions or contributions by employees.

COMPARISON OF ESOPs WITH OTHER TYPES OF EMPLOYEE STOCK OWNERSHIP ARRANGEMENTS

General

Stock ownership arrangements have been around for a long time. Sears Roebuck & Co. has had a profit-sharing plan invested primarily in employer securities since July 1916. The Procter & Gamble Co. had a plan prior to 1900 where employees shared ownership. When the Revenue Act of 1921 was enacted, certain types of stock bonus trusts and profit-sharing trusts were granted tax exemptions. Many of the qualified deferred compensation plans are currently permitted to invest and hold employer securities.

Other Defined Contribution Plans

Defined contribution plans generally can give the feeling of meaningful employee ownership. The account balances of the participants reflect, like a mutual fund, how much gain or loss there is for the year. The ESOP is unique among employee stock ownership arrangements. First, it generally involves a broad base of employees and is operated within the purview of qualified deferred compensation plans, giving it considerable flexibility. Second, it permits financing acquisitions of employer securities through borrowing, by using the credit of the employer. Third, the initial purchase of stock on a leveraged basis generally means the employer is permanently committed to an ESOP-type plan, at least for the period of the loan repayment. From the employee's point of view, it's very hard for an employer to "back out" of a plan once the stock has been acquired by the trust. Other qualified plans cannot leverage to acquire the employer's stock by using the credit of the employer.

However, sometimes a non-ESOP eligible individual account plan may serve many of the same purposes as an ESOP, without some of the obvious disadvantages such as put options, specific allocation of shares, required distributions in employer securities, and the like. The eligible individual account plan, however, can help an employer add to its capital by means of contributions in employer securities or by cash contributions that purchase newly issued (or treasury) stock. Employees also share in

FIGURE 30–2
ESOP Tax Shield

	Without ESOP	*With ESOP*
Operating pretax income	1000	1000
ESOP contribution	–0–	500
Pretax income	1000	500
Income taxes	400	200
Net income	600	300
Equity		
Start of year	5000	5000
Add: Ret'd earnings	600	300
Add: ESOP stock purchase	–0–	500
	5600	5800

Source: Benefit Capital, Inc., Los Angeles, California.

FIGURE 30–3
Benefit of Tax Savings

Value of transaction	20.0	8.0	4.0	2.0
Payroll	2.0	2.0	2.0	2.0
Ratio (%)	1000	400	200	100
ESOP contribution	.5	.5	.5	.5
Tax savings on ESOP contribution (40%)	.2	.2	.2	.2
ESOP tax savings for 5 years pay this percent of value	5%	12.5%	25%	50%

Source: Benefit Capital, Inc., Los Angeles, California.

the economic benefits of corporate success in a visible way. All of these plans must face the repurchase liability problem eventually, however.

Other Stock Plans of an Employer

There are many other ways in which stock ownership opportunities are granted to executives and other selected employees. These include incentive stock plans under Code Section 422A, nonqualified stock option plans, stock appreciation rights plans, performance share plans, phantom stock plans, restricted stock plans, key employee stock plans, employee stock purchase plans under Code Section 423, stock *gifts* by the employer, stock sales to employees by the employer or by shareholders, and so on. Most of these are aimed at a limited group of employees, and since the context is so different, it is difficult to make comparisons. The qualified stock purchase plan under Code Section 423, while directed to a broad-based group, is substantially different from an ESOP, in that the contribution required of the employee is a major part of the acquisition cost. An ESOP's stock acquisition costs are, in most instances, borne solely by the employer! Compare this to the ESOP tax benefits shown in Figures 30–2 and 30–3.

CONCLUSION

Several million Americans are covered by ESOPs, with millions more being included in ESOPs every year. Employee stock ownership plans involve a complex array of business, legal, tax, accounting, and investment banking questions which are best handled by those with experience in employee ownership. While these include the basic questions any employer asks such as, "Do we want it?" "What will it do for us?" "How do we get out of it if something happens?" and "What do our employees get and when?" There are also many additional questions which require expertise in the ESOP area to answer fully. The legal questions include all the qualification questions under Code Section 401, the distribution, eligibility, and vesting sections, the fiduciary and prohibited transaction questions under ERISA, the accounting and financial questions, securities and corporate law questions, alternative financing questions, and myriad more. Congress has continually sought to encourage employers to share the fruits of capital and labor through profit participation and a "piece of the action." The ESOP is the latest, most popular, and by far the most practical, and in many ways, least expensive approach to providing employees with a piece of the company in which they work, on a tax-favored and creditor-proof basis. Over 8,000 companies are enjoying the many benefits of employee ownership. ESOPs continue to be the most popular benefit plan available today.

BIBLIOGRAPHY

"Assessing Employee Stock Ownership Plans (ESOPs)." Research Institute of America, Inc., Staff Recommendations, December 3, 1979.

Blasi, Joseph Raphael. *Employee Ownership Through ESOPs: Implications for the Public Corporation*. New York: Pergamon Press, 1987.

Bonaccorso, Matthew J.; Sheridan M. Cranmer; David G. Greenhut; Daphne T. Hoffman; and Neil Isbrandtsen. "Survey of Employee Stock Ownership Plans: Analysis and Evaluation of Current Experience." Master's thesis, University of California at Los Angeles, 1977.

"Broadening the Ownership of New Capital: ESOPs and Other Alternatives." A Staff Study prepared for the use of the Joint Economic Committee, 94th Congress, 2nd Session, June 17, 1976.

Chow, Andrew; Thomas Cunningham; Michael Horstein; and Jerrald Zweibel. "Repurchase Liability for ESOPs and Other Employee Stock Ownership Plans." Master's thesis, University of California at Los Angeles, 1979.

Conte, Michael, and Arnold S. Tannenbaum. *Employee Ownership*. Report to the Economic Development Administration, U.S. Department of Commerce. University of Michigan, Institute for Social Research, June 15, 1977.

Curtis, John E., Jr., and Anna Jeans. "ESOPs: A Decade of Congressional Encouragement." *Tax Management Compensation Planning* 12, 377 (December 1984).

Drucker, Peter F. *The Unseen Revolution*. New York: Harper & Row, 1976.

Epstein, Stanley A. "Employee Relations Considerations in Establishing ESOPs." *Employee Relations Law Journal* 3 (Autumn 1977), pp. 266–80.

ESOP Association of America. *ESOP Survey 1987*. Washington, D.C.

ESOP Association of America. National Employee Stock Ownership Conference Proceedings (Washington, D.C., 1980 through 1988). Washington, D.C.: ESOP Association of America, 1980–1988.

Ewing, David W. and Pamela M. Banks. "When Employees Run the Company: An Interview with Leamon J. Bennet." *Harvard Business Review,* January–February 1979, pp. 75–90.

Frisch, Robert. *The Magic of ESOPs and LBOs*. Rockville Centre, N.Y.: Farnsworth Publishing Company, 1985.

Kaplan, Jared. "Legal Considerations for ESOP Loans." Commercial Lending Review 2 (Winter 1986–1987): 20–24.

Kaplan, Jared, and Mark Bogart. "TRA Favors ESOPs." *The Tax Times,* Oct. 1986, p. 1.

Kaplan, Jared, and Gregory K. Brown. "Uses of Leveraged ESOPs in Corporate Transactions." *New York Law Journal,* Sept. 16, 1985.

Kaplan, Jared, Gregory K. Brown, and Ronald L. Ludwig. *BNA Tax Management Portfolio on ESOPs*. Washington, D.C.: Tax Management, Inc., 1987.

Keeling, J. Michael. "ESOPs and TRA '86: The Political Record in the *Congressional Record*." *Compensation and Benefits Management* 4 (1987): 43.

Kelso, Louis O., and Mortimer J. Adler. *The Capitalist Manifesto*. New York: Random House, 1958. Reprint ed., Westport, Conn.: Greenwood Press, 1975.

———. *The New Capitalists*. New York: Random House, 1961. Reprint ed., Westport, Conn.: Greenwood Press, 1975.

Kelso, Louis O., and Patricia Hetter. *Two-Factor Theory: The Economics of Reality*. New York: Random House, 1967.

Kelso, Louis O., and Patricia Hetter Kelso. *Democracy and Economic Power: Extending the ESOP Revolution*. Cambridge, Mass.: Ballinger Publishing Company, 1986.

Kurland, Norman G. "Beyond ESOP, Steps toward Tax Justice. Part 1." *Tax Executive,* April 1977.

———. "Beyond ESOP: Steps toward Tax Justice. Part II." *Tax Executive,* July 1977.

Latta, Geoffrey W. *Profit Sharing, Employee Stock Ownership, Savings, and Asset Formation Plans in the Western World*. Philadelphia: University of Pennsylvania, 1979.

Law Journal Seminars-Press. *ESOPs in Financial Transactions*. New York: Law Journal Seminars-Press, 1987.

Lee, M. Mark. *ESOPs in the 1980s*. New York: American Management Association, 1985.

Lewis, Stuart, "ESOP Provisions in the 1984 TRA." 13 *Tax Management Compensation Planning Journal,* 17 (Jan. 1985).

Ludwig, Ronald L. "Employee Stock Ownership Plans after ERISA." *Employee Relations Law Journal* 1 (Winter 1976).

Ludwig, Ronald L., and Jeffrey R. Gates. "The Final ESOP Regulations—A Return to Certainty." Prentice-Hall's *Pension and Profit Sharing Service,* Englewood Cliffs, N.J.: Prentice-Hall, March 23, 1978, pp. 1,237–54.

Lurie, Alvin D. *ESOPs Made Easy*. Jacksonville, Fla.: Corbel, 1985.

Mattingly, William, and Zarina O'Hagin. "Into the Future—ESOPs after 1986." 64 *Taxes* 699, Nov. 1986.

_______. "Planning for ESOPs under the Tax Reform Act of 1986." 63 *Taxes* 323, May 1985.

Maldonado, Kirk F. "Employee Stock Ownership Plans." In *Employee Benefits Handbook,* edited by Jeffrey D. Mamorsky. Boston: Warren, Gorham & Lamont, 1987.

_______. "Employee Stock Ownership Plans Under the Tax Reform Act of 1987." *Tax Management Memorandum* 28 (1987): 15–26.

_______. "Why Banks are Turning to ESOPs." Journal of Bank Taxation 1 (1987): 43–45 and 63.

Midkiff, Robert R., and Luis Granados. "Choosing an ESOP Trustee." *Journal of American Society of CLU and ChFC,* November 1987.

Miller, Marilyn V. "The Ins and Outs of ESOP Administration." *Financial Planner* 10 (January 1981), pp. 28 through 32.

Miller, Rebecca J. *ESOPs—Practical Applications*. New York: American Institute of Certified Public Accountants, 1988.

National Center for Employee Ownership. *An Employee Buyout Handbook*. Oakland, Calif.

National Center for Employee Ownership. *The Employee Ownership Casebook*. Oakland, Calif.

National Center for Employee Ownership. *Employee Ownership: A Union Handbook*. Oakland, Calif.

Olson, Deborah Groban. "Some Union Experiences with Issues Raised by Worker Ownership in the U.S.: ESOPs, TRASOPs, Co-ops, Stock Plans and Board Representation." *Wisconsin Law Review,* December 1982.

Practising Law Institute. *Tax Strategies for Leveraged Buyouts and Other Corporate Acquisitions and Restructurings*. New York: Practising Law Institute, 1987 (Course Handbook #261).

Prentice-Hall Law and Business. *Employee Stock Ownership Plans . . . New Techniques, Special Features and Enhanced Incentives Under the Tax Reform Act of 1986*. Clifton, N.J.: Prentice-Hall, 1987.

Quarrey, Michael; Joseph Blasi; and Corey Rosen. *Taking Stock: Employee Ownership at Work*. Cambridge, Mass.: Ballinger Publishing Company, 1986.

Reichler, Richard. "Deficit Reduction Act Makes Significant Changes to Rules Governing ESOPs." 62 Journal of Tax. 70, February 1985.

_______. *Employee Stock Ownership Plans: Problems and Potentials*. New York: Law Journal Press, 1978.

Reilly, Robert. "Owners of Closely Held Corporations Can Reap Special Benefits From ESOPs." 36 Tax. for Accts. 362, June 1986.

"The Role of the Federal Government and Employee Ownership of Business." Committee Print, Select Committee on Small Business, United States Senate, 96th Congress, 1st Session, March 20, 1979.

Rosen, Corey M.; Katherine J. Klein; and Karen M. Young. *Employee Owner-*

ship in America: The Equity Solution. Lexington Mass.: Lexington Books, 1986.

Rosen, Corey, and Michael Quarrey. "How Well is Employee Ownership Working?" *Harvard Business Review,* September–October 1987, pp. 126–32.

Schuchert, Joseph. "The Art of the ESOP Leveraged Buyout." In *Leveraged Buyouts,* edited by Stephen C. Diamond. Homewood, Ill.: Dow Jones–Irwin, 1985.

Smiley, Robert W., Jr. "How to Plan for an ESOP's Repurchase Liability." Prentice Hall's *Pension and Profit Sharing Service*. Englewood Cliffs, N.J.: Prentice-Hall, February 27, 1987, pp. 1,215–29.

Smiley, Robert W., Jr. and Ronald J. Gilbert, eds. *Employee Stock Ownership Plans*. Larchmont, N.Y.: Prentice Hall/Rosenfeld Emanuel, 1988.

Speiser, Stuart M. *A Piece of the Action*. New York: Van Nostrand Reinhold, 1977.

U.S. Congress Joint Economic Committee. *Employee Stock Ownership Plans (ESOPs)*. Hearings before the Joint Economic Committee, 94th Cong., 1st sess., Part 1, December 11, 1975; Part 2, December 12, 1975. Washington, D.C.: U.S. Government Printing Office, 1976.

U.S. General Accounting Office. *Employee Stock Ownership Plans: Benefits and Costs of ESOP Tax Incentives for Broadening Stock Ownership*. (GAO/PEMD97-8) Washington, D.C., February 1986.

U.S. General Accounting Office, Comptroller General. *Employee Stock Ownership Plans: Who Benefits Most in Closely-Held Companies?* (HRD-80-88), Washington, D.C., June 20, 1980.

Wassner, Neil A. "ESOPs, Can They Work for Your Corporation?" *Pension World,* June 1977.

Wells, Colin A. "The Role of Key-Man Life Insurance in an ESOP." *Financial Planner* 10 (January 1981), pp. 34 through 36.

Zukin, James H. "Capital Stock Valuations for Employee Stock Ownership Plan (ESOP) Purposes." Conference Proceedings. Los Angeles: Employee Stock Ownership Council of America, 1978.

EXAMPLE OF ACCOUNTING TREATMENT*

To illustrate the accounting required for a leveraged plan, consider the following example. At the beginning of 1987 Company B needs $10 million in order to modernize one of its production facilities. It has established a tax-qualified ESOP trust in order to finance the capital improvements.

* The author gratefully acknowledges the help of Kevin B. Reilly of Arthur Young, New York, for this example, as well as his general review of this section.

EXHIBIT I

COMPANY B
Balance Sheet Prior to ESOP Transaction
January 1, 1987
(in thousands)

Cash	$ 15,000	Accounts payable	$ 30,000
Inventory	30,000		
Receivables	15,000	Bank debt (12%)	10,000
	60,000		40,000
		Stockholders' equity	
Fixed assets	45,000	Common stock, $10 par	10,000
Other assets	5,000	Paid-in capital	25,000
		Retained earnings	35,000
			70,000
Total assets	$110,000	Total liabilities and stockholders' equity	$110,000

The trust will borrow $10 million from a bank, and will use the proceeds to acquire 200,000 shares of Company B common stock at $50 per share. The loan will bear interest at the rate of 10 percent, and will be repaid in $1 million installments over the next 10 years. Company B has issued a formal guarantee to make sufficient annual contributions to the trust for the trust to service the loan. The balance sheet of Company B just prior to the transaction is illustrated in Exhibit I. Note that Company B has 1 million shares outstanding. The following journal entry would be necessary to record the formation of the trust:

Debit cash	$10,000,000	
Debit equity contra account		
Unearned compensation	10,000,000	
Credit guaranteed bank indebtedness		$10,000,000
Credit common stock		2,000,000
Credit paid-in capital		8,000,000
To record the sale of 200,000 shares to the ESOP and the concurrent guarantee of the plan's bank indebtedness.		

The Company B balance sheet immediately after the transaction reflecting the above adjustments, is illustrated in Exhibit II.

EXHIBIT II

COMPANY B
Balance Sheet Subsequent to ESOP Transaction
(in thousands)

Cash	$ 25,000	Accounts payable	$ 30,000
Inventory	30,000		
Receivables	15,000	Bank debt (12%)	10,000
	70,000	Guarantee of ESOP Debt (10%)	10,000
			50,000
		Stockholders' equity	
Fixed assets	45,000	Common stock, $10 par	12,000
Other assets	5,000	Paid-in capital	33,000
		Retained earnings	35,000
			80,000
		Unearned compensation related to ESOP	(10,000)
			70,000
Total assets	$120,000	Total liabilities and stockholders' equity	$120,000

During 1987, Company B would contribute $2 million to the trust in order to provide for payment of interest ($1 million) and principal ($1 million). These contributions would be reflected in the 1987 results of operations through increased interest expense and a $1 million charge to ESOP contribution expense. The 1987 Company B income statement is presented in Exhibit III. It should be noted that after the creation of the ESOP trust, Company B will have increased the number of outstanding common shares used in the earnings per share computation from 1 million to 1.2 million, even though the bulk of the new shares are yet to be allocated to the plan participants.

As the Company's guarantee of the ESOP indebtedness is reduced by the $1 million principal contribution, the related unearned compensation account should also be reduced by $1 million in accordance with the SOP 76-3 guidelines. Note that the $1 million contribution charge to expense results in an after-tax decrement to stockholders' equity of $0.6 million ($1 million expense less the related $0.4 million tax benefit). Offsetting this charge is the $1 million reduction in the equity contra account. In total, the operation of the ESOP has resulted in a net increase in stock-

EXHIBIT III

COMPANY B
Income Statement 1987
(in thousands)

Sales	$100,000
Cost of sales	70,000
	30,000
Selling, general and other expenses	12,800
ESOP contribution expense	1,000
Interest expense	2,200
Income before taxes	14,000
Provision for taxes	(5,600)
Net income	$ 8,400
Earnings per share	$7.00

holders' equity of $0.4 million during the first year. This illustrates an important point with respect to leveraged ESOP accounting. Over time, a sponsor company's net worth will rise by the tax benefits received from the ESOP contributions. Assuming Company B continues to have a 40 percent effective tax rate during the 10-year term of the ESOP loan, net worth will have increased by $4 million at the end of the 10th year.

The journal entry necessary to record the year's ESOP related transactions before taxes would be as follows:

Debit ESOP contribution expense	$1,000,000	
Debit interest expense	$1,000,000	
Debit guarantee of ESOP bank debt	$1,000,000	
Credit cash		$2,000,000
Credit unearned compensation		$1,000,000
To record the ESOP contribution for 1987.		

The Company B balance sheet at the end of 1987 is illustrated in Exhibit IV.

With respect to leveraged ESOP accounting, two points require emphasis:

- Although the cash flow and tax benefits associated with leveraged plans are substantial, decreases in reported net income will result from (1) an increase in expenses attributable to the yearly contributions and (2) an

EXHIBIT IV

COMPANY B
Balance Sheet One Year subsequent to ESOP Transaction
December 31, 1987
(in thousands)

Cash	$ 17,000	Accounts payable	$ 28,600
Inventory	30,000		
Receivables	20,000	Bank debt (12%)	10,000
	67,000	Guaranteed bank debt (10%)	9,000
			47,600
		Stockholders' equity	
Fixed assets	55,000	Common stock, $10 par	12,000
Other assets	5,000	Paid-in capital	33,000
		Retained earnings	43,400
			88,400
		Unearned compensation related to ESOP	(9,000)
			79,400
Total assets	$127,000	Total liabilities and stockholders' equity	$127,000

increase in the number of shares used to calculate the company's earnings per share figures. Accordingly, a leveraged ESOP takes on characteristics of both debt and equity when measuring net income and related per-share data.

• Companies often inquire about the possibility of setting-up a leveraged plan without having to record the debt on their books. It is important to remember that even if no formal guarantee is issued with respect to the ESOP debt, SOP 76-3 guidelines require plan sponsors to record the liability on their books if they are "committed" to service the debt. Our experiences in this area show that companies rarely adopt leveraged ESOPs without having to record some portion of the attendant plan liability on the balance sheet.

CHAPTER 31

INDIVIDUAL RETIREMENT ARRANGEMENTS (IRAs) AND SIMPLIFIED EMPLOYEE PENSION (SEP) PLANS*

William H. Rabel
Ernest L. Martin

At the beginning of the 1970s, substantial numbers of American workers were covered by private pension plans. One important sector of the labor force, however, still was not receiving the benefits of a federal income-tax policy that had fostered the growth of qualified plans. This sector, comprised of employees of companies without pension plans, was forced to rely on accumulated aftertax savings to provide for future retirement income. Furthermore, unlike those covered by qualified plans, individuals in this sector were required to pay income taxes on the annual earnings of their aftertax retirement savings.[1] Thus, such individuals found it doubly difficult to accumulate funds for their future retirement.

In 1974, Congress enacted the Employee Retirement Income Security Act (ERISA), which profoundly affected the pension field. This act, as modified by subsequent legislation,[2] provided in part that an individual

---

* The authors wish to acknowledge the assistance of Dan. J. Fitzgerrell, Director, Pension Operations, the Principal Financial Group, while retaining sole responsibility for any errors or omissions.

[1] Tax-exempt investments, of course, would be an exception to this rule.

[2] The Economic Recovery Tax Act of 1981 made many substantial changes in rules regarding IRAs, as has the Tax Reform Act of 1986.

could make an annual tax-deductible contribution of 100 percent of personal service compensation up to $2,000 to an Individual Retirement Arrangement (IRA). Benefits were also made available to spouses, as described below. The funds in the account accumulate on a tax-free basis until the individual retires and begins to receive distributions. Provided distributions begin within the authorized age period, withdrawals are taxed as ordinary income in the year that they are received. Since 1979, employers have been allowed to set up simplified employee pension (SEP) plans for their employees. These plans use IRAs as a funding instrument and are subject to certain special requirements.

ELIGIBILITY

Initially, IRAs were created for the employee aged 70½ years or below who was not an active participant in a qualified employer-sponsored plan. Today, workers in this age range who are covered by a qualified plan can still make tax deductible contributions to an IRA, but only if earnings fall below certain amounts, as described later in this chapter.

From 1981 through 1986, the eligibility requirements were broader and included anyone under age 70½ receiving personal service compensation, without regard to the amount of such compensation. During this period, which also coincided with a relatively high level of interest rates and inflation, many Americans set up IRAs. Many of them later became particularly confused by the income-related constraints on contributions built into the Tax Reform Act of 1986 (TRA '86).

DEDUCTIBLE CONTRIBUTIONS

The population that could make tax-deductible contributions to an IRA was narrowed by income limitations built into TRA '86. Congress felt that the act's lower tax rates fostered a reasonable level of aftertax savings for those who were interested.

Individuals under age 70½ who are not covered by a qualified employer plan (defined below) may annually make deductible contributions up to $2,000 or 100 percent of compensation, whichever is less. For the purpose of determining the maximum annual contribution an eligible individual can make to an IRA, compensation is held to include any payment received for rendering personal service, such as salaries, wages, commissions, tips, fees, and bonuses. Since 1984, it has also included all taxable alimony and separate maintenance payments received under a decree of divorce. Investment income and capital gains may not be included in the calculation of compensation for IRA contribution purposes. Moreover, although a community property state regards one half of a spouse's income as belonging to the other spouse, the nonworking spouse may not count this amount for purposes of determining compensation.

The deductibility of contributions for individuals who are active participants in a retirement plan maintained by their employers, or for married couples filing jointly where either spouse is covered by a qualified plan, is summarized in Table 31–1.

Workers who are covered by an employer plan who have an adjusted gross income of $25,000 or less ($40,000 if married and filing jointly) receive the full deduction for contributions up to $2,000.

For individuals earning $25,000–$35,000 ($40,000–$50,000 for couples filing jointly), deductions will be reduced proportionately as income increases within the $10,000 spread that is shown. Thus, if an unmarried individual earns $26,000, his or her deductible contributions will decrease by $200 to $1,800 ($26,000 − $25,000 = $1,000; $1,000 = 10 percent of $10,000; 10 percent of $2,000 = $200). Workers covered by a qualified plan and whose adjusted gross income exceeds $35,000 ($50,000 for married couples filing jointly) do not receive a tax deduction for contributions.

Married people filing separately will have proportionate reductions in their IRA deductions between zero and $10,000 of income. Such a person earning $4,000 would be able to deduct up to $1,200 (40 percent of $2,000 = $800; $2,000 − $800 = $1,200).

Contributions may be attributed to a calendar year if they are made by the April 15 deadline for filing a tax return in the subsequent year. This provision prevents the taxpayer from having to guess what his or her earnings will be before the end of the tax year.

An *employer maintained retirement plan* is defined as: one that receives favorable tax treatment under Internal Revenue Code Section

TABLE 31–1
Deductibility of IRA Contributions for Taxpayers Covered by a Qualified Plan

Taxpayer Status	*Maximum Adjusted Gross Income for Fully Deductible Contribution*	*Phaseout Range*
Single	$25,000	$25,001–$35,000
Married/joint	40,000	40,001–$50,000
Married/separate	0	1–$10,000

401(a); an annuity qualified under 403(a); a simplified employee pension; a plan of the United States Government (or any political subdivision or government agency or instrumentality); a plan qualified under 501(c)(18); or a tax-sheltered annuity under 403(b). An *active participant* in a *defined contribution qualified plan* generally is one for whom any contribution is made or forfeiture reallocated during the year, or for whom any contribution is required to be made, whether actually made or not. In a *defined benefit plan,* an active participant is one who is not excluded under the plan's eligibility requirements at any time during the plan year ending with or within the individual's taxable year.

A working spouse with an IRA can set up a separate IRA (called a spousal IRA) for a spouse who is not working, or who earns little and elects to be treated as not earning compensation for the year. The maximum combined contribution to the two accounts is limited to the lesser of $2,250 or 100 percent of personal service compensation. To receive a deduction for the spousal contribution, the husband and wife must file a joint tax return. Contributions may be split in any way as long as no more than $2,000 is paid into either account. If a nonworking spouse begins to work, the spousal account then becomes a regular account and the spouse may contribute to it 100 percent of compensation up to $2,000 for that year. Contributions to spousal accounts must cease by the year the elder spouse reaches age 70½. However, if the younger spouse continues to be eligible otherwise, he or she may establish a new IRA and contribute to it until the year in which he or she reaches age 70½.

A divorced spouse with a spousal IRA (or one separated under a decree of separate maintenance) can continue to make deductible contributions to the spousal IRA. The contributions are limited to the lesser of $1,125 or the sum of the spouse's compensation and taxable alimony. Also, the spousal IRA must have been established for at least five years prior to the calendar year of the divorce, and the ex-spouse must have made contributions in at least three of the previous five years.

The tax penalty for contributions in excess of the allowable amount for a year is 6 percent of the excess. This tax penalty is cumulative from year to year, inasmuch as it applies not only to any excess that is not removed from the account, but also to income earned on the excess as well. The penalty is not tax deductible.

The penalty for excess contributions may be avoided under any one of three conditions. First, the amount of excess contributions and any earnings on them may be withdrawn before the individual's federal income tax return is filed for the year when the excess contribution is made. Earnings on the excess contributions must be treated as taxable income for the year the contribution was made. Second, excess contributions made in a preceding year subsequently may be applied to years when an employee's contributions are less than the maximum permitted. Third, if the excess contribution is made based on erroneous information supplied by a financial institution, and accepted in good faith, the excess may be withdrawn at any time.

As discussed in greater detail below, IRAs may be funded through trust or custodial agreements, or through an annuity contract sold by life insurance companies.[3] In order for a contract to qualify under the tax code, it must meet several stipulations. First, the contract must not be transferable. Second, premiums must not be fixed and must have a ceiling of $2,000. Third, policy dividends must be applied to the next year's premium or used to purchase additional benefits. And, finally, the entire interest of the owner must be nonforfeitable.

NONDEDUCTIBLE CONTRIBUTIONS

Individuals may make nondeductible contributions to an IRA, irrespective of their income. The limit on contributions is 100 percent of earnings, up to $2,000 (or $2,250 where contributions are made to a spousal IRA). These limits also apply to all contributions if both deductible and nondeductible contributions are made. Earnings accumulate tax free until they are withdrawn, at which time they are treated as normal IRA retirement benefits. That portion of withdrawals representing nondeductible contributions are, of course, not taxed on withdrawal, since they were made with aftertax dollars.

It may be in the taxpayer's interest to treat deductible IRA contributions as nondeductible under certain circumstances; this is permissible under the law. For example, a tax deduction would not be of value in a year when the individual has no taxable income, even though he or she received personal service compensation.

The taxpayer must report nondeductible contributions for the year when they are made. In addition, the following information must also be reported: (1) any distributions from an IRA; (2) the amount by which (*a*) total nondeductible contributions for all preceding years exceeds (*b*) the total distributions from IRAs that were excludable from gross income for

---

[3] Prior to November 6, 1978, endowment contracts could be purchased to fund IRAs. However, this is no longer permitted. Although some IRAs funded by endowments undoubtedly remain in force, they will not be discussed in this chapter except to note that the cost of insurance is not deductible.

such years; (3) the total balance of all IRA's owned by an individual as of the close of the calendar year in which the tax year ends; and (4) such other information as required by the secretary of the treasury.

Excess contributions are subject to a 6 percent excise tax. If the amount of the contribution is overstated, the taxpayer is subject to a $100 penalty.

Because nondeductible contributions trigger burdensome reporting requirements, some experts recommend that such savings be funneled into an annuity rather than an IRA. Annuities share the advantage of tax-deferral on earnings until the payment period, and there are no limitations on contributions.

ROLLOVERS

The law permits a tax-free transfer of assets from one IRA to another. These so-called rollovers also are permitted from the following types of plans into an IRA: (1) pension and profit-sharing plans qualifying under Section 401(a) of the Internal Revenue Code, (2) tax-deferred annuities meeting the requirements of Section 403(b), and (3) bond-purchase plans that are no longer offered but may still be in effect after having been started under now-repealed Section 405 of the Internal Revenue Code. Also, proceeds received as a distribution from a qualified plan, because of the death of a spouse, can be rolled over tax free into an IRA. Rollovers provide an element of flexibility that fosters investment, administrative, and other benefits arising from consolidation.

Every IRA-to-IRA rollover must meet two important requirements, in addition to several other less important ones. First, an individual is limited to only one tax-free rollover per IRA in any one year. However, it is worth noting that it is possible to make a direct transfer of funds from one funding agency to another without being considered to have made a rollover subject to the one-year restriction. Second, the rollover must take place within 60 days after the distribution is made. Any funds withdrawn but not rolled over are treated as a premature distribution, as described below. However, TRA '86 extends the period for deposits that are frozen in a financially distressed financial institution until 10 days after funds become available. Either whole or partial rollovers may be made, and the owner must notify the funding agency that a rollover is being effected. Funds from a regular IRA may not be rolled over into a qualified plan, although the reverse is not true.

Three tests must be met when an individual is rolling over money or other property from a plan qualified under Section 401(a) into an IRA. First, only employer contributions or deductible qualified voluntary employee contributions (discontinued under TRA '86) may be rolled over. If nondeductible employee contributions are rolled over, they shall be treated as excess contributions and subjected to the penalties discussed above. Second, the rollover must be completed within 60 days. Third, the distribution must be made because the employee is separated from service, has reached age 59½, or has died or become disabled, or because the plan has been terminated. Unlike IRA-to-IRA rollovers, there is no limit of one transfer per year.

Under certain circumstances partial rollovers are permitted from employer plans. The amount rolled over must consist of at least 50 percent of the balance, and must be due to separation from service, disability, or a person's being the beneficiary of a death benefit when a spouse dies. However, unlike other partial distributions, death benefits rolled over into an IRA may not subsequently be rolled over into a qualified plan.

Whether a partial or a total rollover of assets has been made from a qualified corporate or Keogh plan into an IRA, assets may then be rolled over again into the qualified plan of a subsequent employer; however, such a "rerollover" is allowable only if it is permitted by the subsequent employer's plan and if the assets of the IRA consist solely of the assets from the first qualified plan and earnings on those assets. The individual should not contribute to an IRA that is set up as a conduit between two qualified plans. Rather, to keep from losing favorable tax treatment, he or she should set up a second IRA for his or her contributions.

Rollover amounts may not be deposited in a spouse's IRA except when resulting from the taxpayer's death.

Assets rolled over into an IRA from a tax-sheltered annuity can be rerolled over into another tax-sheltered annuity.

FUNDING AGENCIES AND INVESTMENTS

Individuals have a large degree of freedom in the way they allocate their contributions in any particular year among the various financial institutions that offer IRAs. In addition, the amount allocated to any given institution need not remain fixed—the entire contribution may go to one plan in one year, and then be shifted to another plan the next year.

Among the financial institutions offering IRAs are commercial banks, savings and loan institutions, brokerage firms, mutual fund management companies, credit unions, life insurance companies, and companies that offer a broad variety of financial services. Accounts may be so arranged that the owner may make all investment decisions, or such decisions may be turned over completely to a financial institution.

Self-Directed Accounts

Where the individual decides to make all investment decisions, a self-directed retirement trust is set up. A corporate trustee is selected to take charge of all assets and to ensure that the activities of the account conform to the rules of the law. In some cases, the corporate trustee is directly connected with the financial institution through which the IRA is marketed. Alternatively, the services of a single independent trustee may be marketed by one or more brokerages or other financial services firms or both. These firms link up with a trustee in the belief they can serve their clientele more effectively by staying in their particular field, and by recommending another organization to provide services that clients need. Such an arrangement is not devoid of benefits for the firm recommending the trustee. Investments of the trust may bring to it brokerage or underwriting fees, or both. The trust also engenders a certain amount of goodwill, which may enhance other business relationships between the trustee and the firm that markets its services.

Normally, the trustee charges the grantor (contributor to the IRA) three types of fees. The first is an acceptance fee, a flat charge to cover the expense of setting up the trust. For example, such a fee might be $35 for the grantor and $5 for a spousal account. The second fee is an annual charge expressed as a percentage of the assets in the trust, subject to a minimum amount. For example, a fee might be .0015 of the first $100,000 and .0010 of any amount over that, subject to a minimum charge of $35 for the grantor's account and $5 for the spousal account. Finally, charges may be levied for services, such as certain processing activities, statements, returned checks, disbursements, terminations, and the like.

Self-directed trusts have provided great investment latitude since IRAs first were introduced, and, as a matter of practice, grantors have invested in all types of assets, including securities, commodities, debt instruments, real property, and personal property. However, after 1981, grantors have had less flexibility. Assets in an IRA may no longer be invested in collectibles, including works of art, rugs, antiques, metals, gems, stamps, alcoholic beverages, or other items of tangible personal property specified by the IRS. TRA '86 provided some relief to "gold bugs" and "hard money" advocates by permitting investments in legal tender gold and silver coins minted by the U.S Treasury.

Single-Institution Trust or Custodial Accounts

Many persons setting up an IRA do not want to actively manage the assets in the account. Instead, they prefer to invest them with a particular financial institution such as a bank, a broker, or a savings and loan institution. The customer chooses from among the investment options offered by the institution—for example, various types of accounts, certificates of deposit, and investment funds—according to his or her belief as to what will offer the greatest rate of return in the long run.

In response to the desire by customers for a single-institution approach, financial institutions of all types have developed trust or custodial accounts. While some technical distinctions exist between the trust and custodial approaches, from the purchaser's standpoint these differences are inconsequential in terms of cost or service.[4] For purposes of simplicity, and to help distinguish them from self-directed trusts, all such accounts will be called "custodial accounts." The institution with which funds are invested will be called the "custodian." However, this simplification of terms should not be construed as implying that all institutions are equally attractive—the customer should shop carefully for an IRA just as for any other product.

Just as there is a wide variety of financial institutions offering single-institution accounts, there is a wide variety of charges. Many deposit institutions, such as banks and savings and loan institutions, do not assess a direct charge for setting up an IRA. They operate under the philosophy that this is a way to attract funds, and that costs will be covered by the margin between the rate of interest earned by the institution and what is credited to the IRA. Other institutions levy charges that are similar to those employed with self-directed trusts. Also, some investments, such as mutual funds and annuities may contain a specific sales load, in addition to certain ongoing charges for managing the assets in the portfolio.

Insured Plans

Traditionally, premiums for annuity contracts were commingled with other funds accumulated over various periods. They were invested in the general account of the life insurance company, which guarantees a mini-

---

[4] Institutions providing these accounts may adopt model forms provided by the Treasury Department (No. 5305 for trusts and No. 5305A for custodial accounts), or request a letter of opinion concerning the acceptability of their own prototype master form. Many institutions have chosen the latter approach.

mum rate of return and assumes the full investment risk. Because interest rates were comparatively stable for most of the 20th century, consumer savings were not considered "hot money," which moved rapidly among investment alternatives seeking the highest rate of return. Insurers made long-term investments and remained competitive in the market for savings as well as for protection.

The traditional practice of commingling funds received in different periods works very well in a stable financial environment. However, in periods of rising inflation, policies designed as savings vehicles find it difficult to compete favorably, because rates of return on new investments rise more rapidly than the rates of return on the entire portfolio. The reverse holds true in the case of deflation, of course, but savers throughout the world have grown cynical about the possibility prices will stabilize, much less decline, in the foreseeable future. Therefore, instead of settling for a long-run rate of return, they have demanded products reflecting current market rates of return, and financial institutions, including life insurance companies, have responded.

Life insurance company annuity products that were developed for the IRA market offer a wide range of investment options and guarantees. Most still offer a minimum rate of return over the life of the contract, in which case the insurer must balance maturities in the portfolio to be able to meet guarantees and, at the same time, stay competitive with other financial institutions offering current market rates. Some contracts (e.g., some of those invested in equities) offer no investment guarantees at all, thus shifting the investment risk to the policyowner. Premiums from such contracts are invested to gain a rate of return that is competitive in the market the insurer wishes to penetrate, and the policyowners may be offered a variety of investment portfolios from which to choose. Often the policy provides that new premiums and existing funds may be shifted from one portfolio to another. In effect, an annuity policy that does not guarantee a rate of return can be compared to a mutual fund that offers a guaranteed annuity option at a given date.

Typically, three types of charges are associated with insured IRAs.[5] First are those that vary as a percentage of the premium. The most prominent of these is the sales charge, designed to cover the agent's commission. It is worth noting that many companies now market annuities having no sales load. A second charge, a fixed amount per annum, is designed to

---

[5] Those IRAs still extant which are funded by policies containing an element of life insurance protection (e.g., endowment contracts) also contain a charge for the mortality risk.

cover the expenses of putting the policy on the company's books and maintaining the policy. The final type of charge is designed to cover the cost of investing funds. It is expressed as a percentage of the assets, subject to a minimum amount.

BENEFITS

Benefits distributed from an IRA are subject to penalties if they begin earlier than age 59½ (with the exception of death or disability), or later than April 1 of the calendar year following the year in which the owner attains age 70½ (hereinafter referred to as age 70½). Benefits must begin after the latter date whether the owner has actually retired or not. All distributions, except those representing nondeductible contributions, are taxable as ordinary income in the year they are received. The form the benefits take varies somewhat with the type of financial institution through which they are funded.

The individual's interst in an IRA may be distributed in a lump sum or, alternatively, may be paid over (a) the individual's remaining lifetime; (b) the lives of the individual and designated beneficiary; (c) a period not extending beyond the life expectancy of the individual; or (d) a period not extending beyond the joint life expectancy of the individual and designated beneficiary.

If the individual's designated beneficiary is other than the spouse, then the amount of the periodic distribution must meet the following test: The present value of the distributions projected to be made to the participant, while living, must be more than 50% of the present value of the benefits projected to be made to the participant and the designated beneficiary. The purpose of this rule is to insure that the plan exists to benefit the worker, rather than the worker's beneficiary.

Trust or Custodial Accounts

The options for distributing benefits are identical for both self-directed and single-institution IRAs. The first approach is the single-sum distribution, whereby the account owner receives all contributions and the interest earned on them in one payment. However, a single-sum distribution may have unfavorable consequences for the individual's tax liability and postretirement financial security. Because of the progressive nature of income tax rates, a single distribution of any size could subject the depositor to a much higher tax bill than would result from a series of smaller distributions.

In most cases, it is advisable for the individual to at least begin with the second approach, the period certain option, which allows the distribution of benefits to be made in a series of payments. These disbursements may be spread out over a period that may not exceed the distribution timing described above. If the depositor chooses, the payments may be received over a shorter time. The limitation on the distribution period, when coupled with the requirement that the depositor begin to receive distributions not later than age 70½, in effect prevents a depositor from using an IRA as a mere tax shelter for investments, rather than as a means of providing for retirement income.

If the depositor dies *after* distribution from the account has begun, the balance of the account must be distributed to the beneficiary at least as rapidly as the rate that the depositor had selected. With three exceptions, if the depositor dies *before* distribution has started, the balance must be distributed within five years of the depositor's death. The first exception is that a beneficiary may elect to take payments in substantially equal installments for a period of up to his or her life expectancy. In this case, payments must begin within one year after the depositor's death. The second and third exceptions relate to surviving spouses who are beneficiaries. In such a case the spouse may elect not to receive the benefits until the date when the depositor would have reached age 70½. (If the surviving spouse dies in the meantime, payments to a subsequent beneficiary are treated as though the spouse were the depositor.) Or under the third exception, the surviving spouse can treat the balance as his or her own IRA, subject to the regular IRA distribution requirements.

Typically, custodians make several payment intervals available for election by depositors—including monthly, quarterly, semiannually, or annually—thus accommodating the budgetary needs of most retired persons.

Usually one associates retirement benefits with the concept of a lifelong pension. However, only a life insurance company can offer payments for a lifetime, through the mechanism of a life annuity contract. Such lifetime payments cannot be offered by a bank, a savings and loan institution, or any other thrift institution. Indeed, under the life expectancy distribution option of a custodial account, it would not be at all unusual for an individual to outlive the life expectancy established for an IRA account and thus to exhaust the funds. After all, life expectancy is only an average figure. To provide life income annuity options to their depositors, some custodians have established arrangements with one or more life insurance companies, under which immediate life annuities may be purchased by depositors at retirement, using custodial account funds. This arrangement allows a depositor to avoid tax complications by utilizing the rollover provisions described previously. While such an annuity purchase does not provide the depositor with a guarantee of annuity rates during the period when contributions to an IRA are being made, as an insured plan would have, this limitation may possibly be offset by the increased investment flexibility provided during the accumulation period by the noninsured IRA.

Insured Plans

The individual annuity contracts issued by insurers to fund IRAs provide that at retirement (normally between ages 59½ and 70½) a policyowner can select one of the settlement options guaranteed in the contract. No option need be selected prior to that time. Because of established minimum distribution requirements under the Internal Revenue Code (IRC), described above, policyowners may not select an interest-only option. However, both the period certain and the life income annuity options are made available.

The maximum length of time over which a distribution under an insured IRA can be stretched was described at the beginning of this section, and is the same as it is for custodial IRAs. When a policyowner selects a period certain distribution, it is permissible to make early withdrawals. It is advisable for the depositor who selects a period certain guarantee to designate a beneficiary.

A life income annuity may be so designed that all payments cease at the death of one or more annuitants, or it may pay until death but guarantee a minimum number of payments. In practice, most persons who choose a life income option also elect at least a minimum period certain. The prospect of giving up the full purchase price of an annuity when death occurs immediately after payments begin is a risk that most annuitants are unwilling to take. Of course, the longer the minimum guarantee period of a life income annuity, the more expensive the annuity.

Any assets remaining after the death of the depositor or the death of the second annuitant in the event of a joint and last survivor annuity, either before or after benefits have started, are subject to the same rules that apply to custodial IRAs.

No trustee or custodian is required for insured plans, since the policy is endorsed to conform with IRS requirements.

U.S. Retirement Bonds

In the past, some individuals preferred to have their IRA funds invested in United States government securities over any other investment. To facilitate IRA investments in government obligations, the Treasury created a special series of bonds issued in denominations of $50, $100, and $500. Although the bonds are no longer sold, some are still outstanding. They may be kept until retirement age or redeemed early and rolled over into an IRA.

The interest on these bonds is compounded semiannually and the rate is determined by the Treasury. The bonds were designed to conform with the requirements and restrictions applicable to IRAs. The payment of interest stops when the holder reaches age 70½, and at this time the bond is considered to be redeemed for tax purposes even if redemption has not taken place.

TAXATION OF IRA RETIREMENT BENEFITS

Providing the amount of the retirement benefit meets minimum requirements, it is taxed as ordinary income in the year received (subject to penalties on excess distributions described later in this chapter), irrespective of the funding mechanism. This taxation policy applies to sums received under life income options, as well as under periods certain. One rationale underlying the tax policy is that, since contributions are tax deductible when made, they are regarded as a deferred wage that therefore should be subject to taxation at some point. Of course, there is no tax on nondeductible contributions.

Five or ten year forward averaging provisions on lump sum distributions are not available for IRA distributions.

DISABILITY BENEFITS

A worker who becomes disabled before age 59½ may withdraw all or part of the funds in an IRA without incurring a penalty in the form of an excise tax. Under Regulation 172-17(f), a person is considered to be disabled if "unable to engage in any substantial gainful activity by reason of any medically determinable physical or mental impairment which can be expected to result in death or to be of long or continued duration."

Distributions of contributions and investment income to a disabled person less than 59½ years of age are taxed as they would be at normal retirement age under an IRA. It should be noted, however, that some funding agencies charge a "back-end load" for premature withdrawals, even if the individual is disabled.

PENALTIES FOR PREMATURE DISTRIBUTION OR BORROWING

Under TRA '86, any withdrawal of funds from a tax-favored retirement plan prior to age 59½ may result in a penalty tax of 10 percent of the amount withdrawn over and above the ordinary income tax on the distribution.

This general rule has exceptions when applied to IRAs, however. Distributions may be made (1) where the taxpayer is disabled or (2) to a beneficiary or estate of a taxpayer. Furthermore, if nondeductible contributions are made to an IRA, a certain proportion of any distributions will be attributed to those contributions and therefore that portion will not be subject to taxation. The amount excluded is the proportion that nondeductible contribution bears to the total value of the amount at the year's end plus any distributions made during the year.

An example will clarify the rule. Assume that an individual age 45 withdraws $4,000 from an IRA, and that he or she had never made nondeductible contributions to an IRA. The taxpayer will have to pay income tax on the $4,000 plus an excise tax of $400.

Assume further that the individual had made nondeductible contributions of $6,000 over several years, and at the end of the taxable year the value of the IRA was $20,000 after the $4,000 withdrawal. Taxes would be payable on only $3,000 of the $4,000 distribution, because $1,000 would be attributable to nondeductible contributions:

$$\$4{,}000 \times \left(\frac{\$6{,}000}{\$20{,}000 + \$4{,}000}\right) = \$1{,}000 \text{ excluded}$$

Note that there are some special rules that apply to IRAs: (1) all IRAs are treated as a single contract, (2) all distributions within a single year are treated as one distribution, and (3) the value of the IRA is calculated as of the end of the calendar year with or within which the tax year ends.

While the IRA owner may transfer the account to a spouse pursuant to a divorce decree and not trigger a tax penalty, any other assignment is treated as a constructive distribution of the assigned amount. Thus, if any portion of an IRA is pledged as collateral for a loan, that portion is treated as a distribution and is subject to both ordinary income tax and the tax penalty for the year in which the pledge was made.

A depositor who borrows from an IRA is considered to have received the entire interest in the account. Thus, the fair market value of the entire account is taxed as ordinary income and the account loses its tax-exempt status.

PENALTY FOR INSUFFICIENT DISTRIBUTION

The depositor of an IRA incurs a nondeductible penalty if distributions are not begun by April 1 of the year following attainment of age 70½, or if individual distributions are less than the amounts described earlier under the section on benefits. The penalty is a tax of 50 percent on the difference between the amount that should have been distributed and the amount that was distributed. Thus, if the distribution for a year should have been $600 and was actually only $400, the penalty would be $100 (50 percent of $600 − $400).

PENALTY FOR EXCESS DISTRIBUTION

Excess distributions made from qualified retirement plans, tax-sheltered annuities, and IRAs are subject to a 15 percent excise tax. The person receiving the distributions must pay the tax, which may be reduced by any payment of the 10 percent excise tax on early withdrawal (if any take place).

A distribution of more than $112,500 (as adjusted for price increases after TRA '86 went into effect) is regarded as being excessive. Certain distributions are exempt, however, namely: (1) distributions made on the death of the account owner; (2) distributions under a qualified domestic relations order (e.g., to a former spouse) if the distribution is includable in the recipient's income; (3) distributions attributable to nondeductible contributions; and (4) rollover distributions.

If an individual receives a lump-sum distribution, the $112,500 (or the index amount) is increased by a multiple of five (e.g., $112,500 × 5 = $562,500). Transition rules provide certain grandfathering privileges for individuals who elect to have the rules apply before January 1, 1989.

Postdeath distributions from retirement plans are subject to an additional estate tax of 15 percent of the retiree's "excess retirement accumulation" in lieu of the 15 percent tax on excess distribution. This amount is computed by subtracting (1) the present value of $112,500 (as indexed) over the period of the deceased retiree's life expectancy immediately prior to death, from (2) the value of the decedent's interest in all qualified employer plans. The estate tax on the excess retirement accumulation may not be offset by any credits (such as the unified credit). A reasonable rate of interest, in accordance with rules prescribed by the secretary of the treasury, must be used in computing present value.

SIMPLIFIED EMPLOYEE PENSION PLANS

A simplified employee pension plan (SEP) is an arrangement under which an employer contributes to an IRA that is set up for each covered employee.[6] First authorized in 1979, SEPs simplify the administration and reduce the paperwork associated with many other types of pension plans; for this reason, they are especially attractive to smaller employers. In particular, SEPs reduce the paperwork normally required for H.R. 10 or corporate plans covering common-law employees.

NONELECTIVE SEP

There are two types of SEPs. One is compulsory, or nonelective, in that all eligible employees are included. The other is elective, in that employees may choose to participate through a salary reduction plan (sometimes called a SARSEP, for salary reduction SEP), or may choose not to participate and receive their full salaries. The elective plan is a form of "cash or deferred compensation" (CODA) plan, like the familiar 401(k) plan. Throughout this section it will be assumed that a SEP is nonelective unless specified otherwise.

For a SEP to qualify for favorable tax treatment, an employer must make contributions for all eligible employees. An employee must be eligible who is at least 21 years of age, received at least $300 (indexed for inflation) of compensation for service during the calendar year, and worked for the employer during three of the preceding five years. These rules also may extend to employee groups controlled by the employer, even though such groups technically are employed by a separate firm (such as a wholly owned subsidiary), if exclusion of such group would result in discrimination in favor of the prohibited group. Two exceptions to these general rules are: (1) members of a collective bargaining unit that engaged in good faith bargaining of retirement benefits and (2) certain nonresident aliens.

---

[6] IRS Form 5305 is being used widely as a prototype.

Contributions on behalf of employees are excludable from their income as follows: 15 percent of total employee compensation up to $200,000, or $30,000 of contribution, whichever is less. Both the $200,000 base and $30,000 limit will be indexed for inflation. In addition, an employee covered by a SEP may treat the SEP as an IRA and make deductible or nondeductible contributions under IRA rules.

Employer contributions to a SEP must be made for all eligible employees in a manner that does not discriminate in favor of any "highly compensated" employees sometimes called "prohibited classes," as defined by IRS Code section 414(q). Among the highly compensated are those earning more than $75,000 per year in general, or $50,000 if within the top-paid group of employees. Discrimination is automatically deemed to exist if contributions do not represent a uniform percentage of each eligible employee's total compensation and favor the prohibited group. Unionized employees and aliens usually are excluded from the process of determining whether a plan is discriminatory.

The integration of pension plans with Social Security is an important cost-control measure for the employer. Rules generally applicable to qualified defined contribution plans permit a limited difference between the contribution percentage that is applied to salary below and above the Social Security wage base.

Some of the requirements typically associated with pension plans also apply to SEPs. For example, the plan must be in writing, it must set forth the eligibility requirements, and it must specify the ways in which contributions are computed. However, SEPs are somewhat unusual in that all rights to contributions are 100 percent vested in the employee immediately, and an employee may freely withdraw funds, subject to the penalties described above for withdrawing funds from an IRA. Most employers would consider these vesting provisions to be a disadvantage.

ELECTIVE SEP

Under an elective SARSEP the employee has the option of receiving his or her full salary, or deferring receipt of as much as $7,000 (indexed for inflation) per annum under a CODA. Elective deferrals under a SARSEP are treated as wages for employment tax purposes, just as under a 401(k) or a tax-sheltered annuity plan.

A SARSEP may be installed only if at least 50 percent of employees contribute, and only if the employer had 25 or fewer employees during the previous year. A nondiscrimination test limits the average amount deferred as a percentage of compensation for highly compensated employees. The percentage they may defer individually can be no more than 125 percent of the average deferral percentage of all other eligible employees.

THE SCOPE OF IRAs AND RECENT TRENDS

A notion of the scope of IRAs in the United States can be derived from Table 31–2, which shows recent data concerning IRA and Keogh assets combined, by market shares by financial institution, as reprinted from the October 1986 *Employee Benefit Notes* of the Employee Benefit Research Institute (EBRI).

From June 1985 to June 1986, IRA and Keogh accounts grew by 35.3 percent, or $70.1 billion. In the most recent two years reflected on the chart, the growth of IRA and Keogh assets has almost matched the total of the assets for 1984. Some notion of the number of individuals participating in IRA accounts can be derived from U.S. Internal Revenue Service data, which reveals that more than 15.4 million taxpayers claimed

TABLE 31–2
Total IRA and Keogh Assets, and Market Shares by Financial Institution
(June 30, 1986, June 30, 1985, and June 30, 1984, Dollars in Billions)

	June 1986		*June 1985**		*June 1984*	
Financial Institution	*Asset Amount*	*Percent of Market*	*Asset Amount*	*Percent of Market*	*Asset Amount*	*Percent of Market*
Commercial banks	$ 70.1	26.1%	$ 55.9	28.1%	$ 40.1	28.8%
Savings and loans	54.1	20.1	44.8	22.6	33.7	24.2
Mutual savings banks	13.6	5.1	12.8	6.4	9.4	6.8
Mutual funds	55.0†	20.5	32.4	16.3	19.2	13.8
Credit unions‡	18.5†	6.9	12.3	6.2	7.7	5.5
Life insurance companies§	20.3	7.6	15.9	8.0	12.1	8.7
Stock brokerage SDAs‡	37.1†	13.8	24.5	12.3	16.9	12.1
Total assets‖	$268.7	100.0%	$198.6	100.0%	$139.1	100.0%

* Revised figures.
† As of April 1986.
‡ Represents IRAs only.
§ As of prior year-end, December 31.
‖ Components may not add to totals due to rounding.

Source: EBRI tabulations of data collected from the Federal Reserve Board *Weekly Statistical Release,* the Federal Home Loan Bank Board, the National Council of Savings Institutes, the Investment Company Institute, the Credit Union National Association, the American Council of Life Insurance, and the *IRA Reporter.*

deductions for IRA contributions for tax year 1984.[7] An EBRI estimate is that there were 17.3 million taxpayers claiming a total of $40.8 billion in deductible IRA contributions in 1985.

A recent estimate is that there were 24.4 million IRA holders by the end of the 1985 tax year.[8]

The change in market shares by financial institution reflects a shift by account owners in favor of higher investment return. Mutual funds and self-directed brokerage accounts recorded gains in market share, while life insurance companies and all other types of financial institutions except credit unions registered declines. The October 1987 stock market crash notwithstanding, the trend is expected to continue as long as stocks continue to provide a higher long-run return than interest-bearing accounts.

The impact of the Tax Reform Act of 1986 on IRA investment patterns cannot yet be accurately assessed. Many projections are pessimistic. They point out that the lowering of tax rates has made the tax savings stemming from deductible IRA contributions much less attractive. Other factors cited as favoring a declining rate of participation include the new penalties on early withdrawals and the stiff nondiscrimination rules affecting employer-sponsored qualified plans.

The tightening of eligibility requirements for making deductible contributions to IRAs is expected to have some negative impact on IRA participation. The Employee Benefit Research Institute has studied data from 1985 tax returns and concluded that 17.8 million of the 24.4 million individuals who held IRAs during that tax year were covered by employer-sponsored pension plans. However, EBRI points out that of the 24.4 million individuals, 17.8 million would still have been allowed to make fully deductible IRA contributions had the 1986 Tax Reform Act been in effect in 1985; another 2.9 million would have been able to make partial deductible contributions, while 3.7 million would have been eligible to make only nondeductible IRA contributions.[9] The *IRA Reporter* estimates that deductible contributions to IRAs will decline between 47 percent and 56 percent for the 1987 tax year; however, the overall impact of the tightening of eligibility to make deductible contributions will be mitigated somewhat by an increase in rollover contributions and by both contributions to the new SEPs allowed by the 1986 act and an increase in nondeductible contributions. Under the best-case scenario, total 1987

---

[7] *1987 Pension Facts,* American Council of Life Insurance.

[8] *Employee Benefit Notes* 7, no. 10, October 1986, Employee Benefit Research Institute.

[9] *Employer Benefit Notes* 7, no. 10, October 1986, pp. 2–3.

contributions are estimated to be $2.5 billion lower than they would have been under the old law; in the worst case, the estimate is a decline of $13 billion.[10]

A poll of IRA users conducted by the Synergistics Research Corporation of Atlanta tends to support the argument that there will likely be an increase in the amount of nondeductible contributions; of those IRA users who were rendered ineligible to make deductible contributions by the 1986 act, 64 percent stated that they would make nondeductible contributions anyway.

For all taxpayers, however, the Tax Reform Act of 1986 retains the advantage of tax deferral for investment return on IRAs. The extent to which this feature counterbalances some of the more negative IRA provisions in the 1986 act in the minds of future retirees will largely determine many IRA participation patterns and trends in the next few years.

---

[10] *IRA Reporter* 5, no. 15, August 8, 1986, Protean Financial Corporation, Cleveland, Ohio.

CHAPTER 32

TAX–DEFERRED ANNUITIES

Mark R. Greene

Tax-deferred annuities (TDAs) are annuities available to certain eligible groups of employees on such a basis that they provide special exemptions from current federal and usually state income taxes. TDAs offer a way to create or supplement retirement income on a basis whereby taxes on current savings by the employee (or by the employer on behalf of the employee) are deferred until such time as the annuity begins, presumably at retirement. TDAs had their origin in the 1942 tax code, which provided that charitable organizations could make contributions to an annuity for their employees without having the employee pay current income tax on the benefits. The 1958 revisions in the federal income tax code (Section 403(b) refined the provisions for these annuities and established a 20 percent limitation on the amounts that could be used for this purpose. TDAs frequently are referred to as "403(b)" annuities, although subsequent legislation in 1974 under the Employee Retirement Income Security Act (ERISA) made further changes so that, strictly speaking, the distributions from a 403(b) account need not be in the form of a life annuity, but may be in a lump sum or in installments of any size or duration. The Tax Reform Act of 1986 placed further limitations on these plans.

HOW TDAs WORK

A typical procedure in establishing a TDA savings program is as follows. The eligible employer wishing to authorize a TDA program draws up an agreement with participating employees to reduce the employee's salary by the amount the employee wishes to contribute, subject to specified limits. (The employer also can make a contribution without a corresponding salary reduction.) The employer actually makes the purchase of the TDA through payroll deduction on behalf of the employee, who becomes the legal owner. The employee can name the beneficiary in case of death. The employer does not report the contribution to the U.S. Internal Revenue Service (IRS) and does not withhold taxes; the employee does not show the amount of the salary reduction as income for current federal income or Social Security tax purposes. Only when funds are distributed are they subject to federal income taxation.

The TDA is purchased from a custodian such as a life insurer or a mutual fund authorized to set up TDA accounts. The most common investment media include fixed annuities, variable annuities, and mutual funds.

Requirements

Tax-deferred annuities must meet certain requirements:

1. The employee must be "eligible" and work for an eligible employer (see below).
2. The annuity must be nonforfeitable and be purchased by the employer.
3. The premium must not exceed certain limits (see below).
4. There may not be more than one salary reduction agreement per year (Reg. 1.403(b)-1(b)(3)).
5. The TDA must be "nontransferable." This means that the owner may not sell, assign, discount, or pledge it as collateral for a loan.

Eligible Organizations

In general, organizations that are eligible include those mentioned in IRS Code 501(c)(3) or in a public school system. Eligible groups are those employees of religious, charitable, educational, scientific, and literary organizations, which are all chartered on a nonprofit basis. One must be an employee of such a group, not an independent contractor (Rev. Ruling 70-136 CB 1970-1, 12 and 73-607). Part-time employees are eligible, but the maximum allowable contribution is reduced in proportion to the time worked. A state, county, or city itself is not eligible; so, for example, a hospital operated directly by a city or county cannot qualify (Rev. Rul. 60-384), although a state university may qualify, as do public schools.

Advantages of Tax-Sheltered Savings

It generally is appreciated that saving under a program exempt from current income taxation can be advantageous to the saver. The extent to which more wealth may be accumulated under a tax shelter than with a taxable investment is greater than commonly realized. A major benefit of tax shelter is the interest earned on funds that would otherwise be payable in federal income taxes and state income taxes over a long period of years. In the example shown in Table 32–1, not only is the current amount saved exempt from income taxes but the interest and other investment returns on this saving also are exempt until the time received. The example assumes a combined federal and state tax bracket of 34 percent[1] that would otherwise be levied on a savings program of $1,000 a year. It also is assumed that long-term interest return of 8 percent is achievable each year. As of 1987, 8 percent was a reasonable figure to use as an estimate of an average available investment return over a period of years.

In reviewing Table 32–1, if one saves $1,000 a year for 20 years under tax shelter, the retirement fund is 2.04 times what would be available under an investment program fully taxable during the accumulation period. Even if the individual is in a higher tax bracket after retirement than before, the larger retirement income will make it extremely advantageous to have saved under tax shelter. In most cases, however, the taxpayer will be in a lower bracket after retirement than before. This is because much retirement income currently is totally or partially exempt from income tax, such as Social Security income. Other sources of income may cease, such as from employment, putting the individual in a lower tax bracket.

Conditions for Successful Use of TDAs

There are six conditions that should be considered if the TDA is to be used successfully. These are:

1. The income tax bracket of the investor following retirement will be such that total taxes paid on the TDA will not be more than would have been the case had income taxes been paid on the funds saved during the accumulation period. As demonstrated by Table 32–1, the investor's tax bracket actually can be higher after retirement than before, and a benefit will still accrue because of the compounding of interest on the "tax-free

---

[1] In 1987, a joint return showing over $29,500 of taxable income was taxed at 28 percent for federal taxes. In most states, state income tax of another 6 percent or higher would also be applied, bringing combined tax rates to 34 percent in most areas.

TABLE 32–1
Illustrative Results of a Tax-Sheltered Savings Program versus a Program Subject to Current Taxation

Assumptions:		
Marginal tax rate (federal and state tax brackets combined)	34 percent	
Average annual interest return, after management fees	8 percent	
Period of savings	20 years	
No current sales loading		

	Plan 1 (without tax shelter)	*Plan 2 (with tax shelter)*
1. Annual savings, before taxes	$ 1,000	$ 1,000
2. Current taxes	340	0
3. Available for savings	660	1,000
4. *a.* Accumulation of $1 a year for 20 years at 8 percent	—	45.76
b. Accumulation* of $1 at 5.28 percent	34.06	—
5. Value of accumulation (3) × (4)	$22,480	$45,760
6. Ratio of retirement fund under Plan 2 to that of Plan 1	2.04	
If money is withdrawn, taxes must be paid on Plan 2. This results in the following:		
7. Taxes due on withdrawal		
a. Plan 1	0	
b. Plan 2 (applying the 34 percent rate)		$15,558
8. Aftertax accumulation	$22,480	$30,202
9. Ratio of aftertax fund, Plan 2 to that of Plan 1, if funds are withdrawn	1.34	

* After taxes of 34 percent, an 8 percent yield is reduced to 5.28 percent.

loan'' by the government of current income taxes that would otherwise have been due during the accumulation period.

For example, if the investor purchases a straight life annuity with the accumulation funds shown in Table 32–1, a monthly life income of approximately $202 might be obtained, of which about $176 could be received tax-free under the ''annuity rule'' of the IRS under Plan 1. A fully taxable $412 would be received under Plan 2.[2] Thus, if the investor's income is taxed less than 42.7 percent after retirement, the net income after income taxes in retirement would be greater under Plan 2 than under Plan 1. For example, if taxes are 34 percent, the investor receives $272 after taxes ($412 − .34(412)) under Plan 2. This is 55 percent greater than the $176 received under Plan 1. In 1988, the maximum federal income tax bracket is 28 percent. Thus, most individuals correctly assume they will gain a tax advantage by delaying the imposition of income taxes on funds earmarked for savings.

2. It is assumed that capital losses will not be incurred in the TDA media, and that total investment return will be as high or higher than would be the case in taxable media. Inasmuch as media used for both taxable and tax deferred savings plans are usually similar, this assumption is justified in most cases.

3. It is assumed that, in emergencies, permission can be received to withdraw funds set aside in TDAs, if necessary, before retirement age or age 59½, and that income taxes or any withdrawal charges or penalties that must be paid on such withdrawals are not so high as to destroy the advantages of tax deferral up to that point. (The Tax Reform Act of 1986 subjects TDAs to a 10 percent penalty for early withdrawal.) Ordinarily, funds invested in TDAs are available to the employee before reaching age 59½, in cases of financial hardship, or in case of separation from the employer's service.

4. It is assumed that the TDA will be sufficiently liquid to allow withdrawal of the funds, if necessary, as discussed in condition (3).

5. It is assumed that loading and management fees charged on TDAs will not be so high as to destroy the economic advantages of the TDA compared to other investments (see discussion below).

6. It is assumed that savings made in TDAs will be regular and systematic, so as to gain the advantages of dollar cost averaging over a specified time.

---

[2] Assumes an annuity paying monthly life income of $9 for each $1,000 of available funds, for a male age 65. Under the "annuity rule," that portion of an annuity representing return of principal (the taxpayer's cost) on which income taxes have been previously paid may be excluded from annuity income. The exclusion ratio is *Taxpayer's cost ÷ Expected return*. In the current example, using 15 years as a life expectancy, the exclusion ratio would be:

$$\frac{22{,}480}{\$202 \times 12 \times 15} = \frac{22{,}480}{\$36{,}360} = 61.8\%$$

Thus, .618 × 202, or $125, may be received tax-free, and $77 is taxed. Under the Tax Reform Act of 1986, once the taxpayer's cost has been recovered, all payments are subject to tax. Assuming a 34 percent tax bracket, taxes amount to $26, leaving $176 as spendable income.

Loading and Expense Charges

Costs of acquiring TDAs, and continuing expenses of maintaining them, should not be ignored in the decision to utilize TDAs. Two general types of charges are made: (1) sales charges, or loading charges, applicable to each deposit made to purchase a TDA; and (2) overhead or continuing fees levied on the assets comprising the TDA fund each year. For convenience, the first charge may be termed a *deposit charge* and the second an *asset charge*.

Deposit Charges

Sales charges for acquiring TDAs depend on the type of media utilized. Not all media make explicit charges for sales commissions, since in some cases, the issuers of TDAs do not employ sales personnel, preferring instead to distribute their products by other means. Any marketing expense is absorbed by the particular medium as a part of general management expense. When sales charges are made, the amount usually ranges from 3 percent to 8 percent of the deposits made, although in some cases a TDA funded by an individually sold life insurance contract or endowment may carry a sales commission amounting to 50 percent or more of the first year's premium. In cases where mutual funds are utilized for funding TDAs, the loading is either zero for "no-load" funds or 8.5 percent, graded downward as the size of the deposit or the size of the accumulating fund increases for "load" funds. Thus, if the saver deposits $100, a sales commission of say $8 may be deducted first, and $92 is the actual amount invested in the TDA fund.

Asset Charges

Asset charges are levied to cover the continuing expenses of managing the TDA account. The size of these charges varies from about 0.5 percent to 1.5 percent of assets each year, although they may exceed this amount in some cases. Asset charges are earmarked for three general purposes: general overhead, investment advisory service, and mortality or annuity guarantees. Investment advisory fees cover the costs of buying and selling securities in a managed portfolio comprising the fund in which the TDA accounts are invested. The mortality charge is for guaranteeing that future annuity rates will not exceed a given level, and that, in case of death, at least the minimum amount invested will be returned to the estate of the owner, even if the amount in the owner's account is less than the total invested, a situation which might occur if the TDA is invested in common stocks that have gone down in value subsequent to the time the deposits were made.

A typical breakdown for these types of charges might be 0.15 percent for general overhead and administration, 0.85 percent for annuity or mortality guarantees, and 0.5 percent for investment advisory services.

Not all types of TDAs contain annuity or mortality guarantees. For example, TDAs funded by mutual funds offer no such guarantees and make charges only for general management and investment advisory fees. TDAs issued by life insurers contain annuity or mortality guarantees.

Importance of Deposit and Asset Charges

Loading and expense charges can amount to a sizable sum, particularly over a period of years. For example, consider a case in which the saver in a TDA variable annuity is putting aside \$100 a month on which a 6 percent deposit and a 1 percent asset charge are being made. First, consider the relative cost of the 6 percent loading. Assume that the interest return credited to the TDA is 7 percent annually. The TDA value stemming from the initial deposit will be \$100.58 at the end of the first year: (100 − \$6)1.07 = \$100.58. At the end of the second year, the \$100.58 will have grown to \$107.62: (100.58)1.07 = 107.62. At the end of the third year, the \$107.62 will have grown to \$115.15, and so on. By the 10th year, the account value will have grown to \$184.91, and by the 20th year to \$363.74. The initial charge of \$6 represents only about 3.2 percent of the

TABLE 32–2
Asset Charges on TDAs

Year	*Cumulative Value of \$100 at 7 Percent*	*Asset Charge of 1 Percent*
1	\$107.00	\$ 1.07
2	114.49	1.14
3	122.50	1.22
4	131.08	1.31
5	140.26	1.40
6	150.07	1.50
7	160.58	1.60
8	171.82	1.72
9	183.85	1.84
10	196.72	1.97
		\$14.77

Total, as a percent of original \$100 = 14.77 percent
Percent of 10-year value = 7.51 percent

savings fund of the 10th year and only 1.6 percent of the fund as of the 20th year. The longer one keeps the TDA, the lower the relative size of the deposit charge when compared to the original investment.

The asset charge made by TDA media is a much more significant item than the deposit charge. This is so because the percentage figure applied to the savings fund is cumulative in nature. For example, assume $100 is saved, to which a 1 percent asset charge is applied to cover the costs of investment service, administration, and annuity rate and mortality guarantees. Table 32–2 shows what these charges amount to.

Note that the cumulative sum of all the asset charges for continuing expenses amounts to nearly 15 percent of the original amount saved, compared to 6 percent typically charged for the deposit charge. Thus, even a modest-appearing asset charge may amount to over 2½ times the initial typical deposit charge after 10 years.

Comparing Charges

Frequently, the question is asked, "Don't all media charge about the same fees for TDAs?" The answer is, "Decidedly not." In one comparison of 26 insurers, a wide range of charges was discovered.[3] A way to compare the effect of the differences in charges may be described as follows:

Step 1. Calculate how much one would have in a simple savings account at some assumed rate of interest, say 7 percent, by saving $100 a month for periods up to 20 years.

Step 2. Calculate how much one would have in the account balance of a given TDA applying the insurer's stated deposit charges and asset charges, under the assumption that an identical amount, $100, is invested in the TDA for identical periods.

Step 3. Subtract the amount obtained in Step 2 from the amount obtained in Step 1. The difference represents the cost of dealing with the insurance company as compared to dealing with a medium not making explicit deposit or asset charges.

Step 4. Calculate the ratio of the amount determined in Step 3 by the amount determined in Step 2. This may be called the administrative cost ratio (ACR). The ACR can be expressed as a percentage. It reveals what

---

[3] Mark R. Greene and Paul Copeland, "Factors in Selecting Tax Deferred Annuities," *CLU Journal*, October 1975, pp. 34–46.

it costs, as a percentage of one's TDA account balance, to deal with an insurer. One is then in a position to compare the "administrative costs," as defined, among several insurers.

To illustrate the above steps, assume that one saves $100 in a savings institution at 7 percent interest compounded annually. The account balance at the end of one year is $107 (Step 1). If one purchased a TDA from an insurer with a 6 percent deposit charge and a 1 percent asset charge, the account balance at the end of one year would be approximately $99.57, if the insurer also credits 7 percent to the account (Step 2). The difference between these amounts is $7.43 (Step 3). The $7.43 represents the cost of dealing with the insurer, when compared to the savings institution. The administrative cost ratio would be calculated at $7.43/$99.57, or about 7.46 percent.

The above method is illustrated as it applies to an actual case in Table 32–3. After this first year, the ACR is 6.1 percent, but it rises steadily to 24.7 percent after 20 years. In dollars, the total administrative charge amounted to $5,765.69 after 20 years, which was comprised of $1,200 in deposit charges and $4,565.96 in asset charges. Asset charges were 3.8 times the deposit charges, in this example. Note, if the saver had saved $100 monthly in an alternative income tax–free plan, the accumulated sum of $46,735.11 (col. 2) would have been in the account balance, compared to $37,235.18 (col. 8) in the variable annuity plan.

How did the 26 insurers compare when the above four steps were applied to each company's TDA contracts, using amounts stated in the prospectus to represent deposit and asset charges? The following were the ranges of charges. Over a 10-year period: 11.1 percent to 28.1 percent. Over a 20-year period: 13.2 percent to 45.7 percent. These findings mean that for the highest cost insurer, over a 20-year period, the saver would have paid an amount for administration and other costs equal to 45.7 percent of the actual account balance in the TDA. The lowest cost insurer, over the same period, would have charged only 13.2 percent. Stated another way, the ACR represents a sum that could have been credited to the saver's account over 20 years in a bank or a savings and loan association had the saver not wanted to pay for the various services of the insurance company in connection with the TDA policy. Essentially, most insurers offer the same package of services, but the fees charged vary greatly.

In terms of dollars, the study results showed that, for the insurer with the lowest administrative cost ratio, the saver would have had an account balance of $41,031 at the end of 20 years. For the insurer with the highest administrative cost ratio, the saver's account balance would have been only $31,865, a difference of nearly $10,000. The difference is truly signifi-

TABLE 32–3 Calculation of Administrative Cost Ratio for a Variable Annuity

			Asset Charge‡						
Year	(1) Cumulative Deposit	(2) Compound Deposit*	(3) Deposit Charge† Cumulative	(4) Administrative Charge Cumulative	(5) Guaranty Cumulative	(6) Advisory Cumulative	(7) Total Charges Cumulative	(8) Account Balance	(9) Administrative Cost Ratio§
1	$ 1,200	$ 1,239.72	$ 60	$ .94	$ 5.32	$ 2.76	$ 69.02	$ 1,168.51	.061
2	2,400	2,555.91	120	3.67	20.79	10.76	155.22	2,391.34	.069
3	3,600	3,953.28	180	8.27	46.87	24.26	259.40	3,671.02	.077
4	4,800	5,436.83	240	14.83	84.05	43.51	382.39	5,010.20	.085
5	6,000	7,011.89	300	23.45	132.86	68.77	525.08	6,411.63	.094
6	7,200	8,684.09	360	34.21	192.83	100.34	688.38	7,878.22	.102
7	8,400	10,459.43	420	47.21	267.54	138.49	873.24	9,412.98	.111
8	9,600	12,344.27	480	62.57	354.56	183.54	1,080.67	11,019.10	.120
9	10,800	14,345.36	540	80.39	455.52	235.80	1,311.71	12,699.89	.130
10	12,000	16,469.87	600	100.78	571.08	295.62	1,567.47	14,458.82	.139
11	13,200	18,725.42	660	123.86	701.90	363.33	1,849.10	16,299.52	.149
12	14,400	21,120.09	720	149.77	848.69	439.32	2,157.79	18,225.80	.159
13	15,600	23,662.46	780	178.63	1,012.21	523.97	2,494.80	20,241.63	.169
14	16,800	26,361.13	840	210.57	1,193.22	617.67	2,861.46	22,351.17	.179
15	18,000	29,227.28	900	245.74	1,392.54	720.85	3,259.13	24,558.79	.190
16	19,200	32,269.68	960	284.30	1,611.03	833.94	3,689.27	26,869.04	.201
17	20,400	35,499.73	1,020	326.39	1,849.56	957.42	4,153.38	29,286.69	.212
18	21,600	38,929.00	1,080	372.19	2,109.08	1,091.76	4,653.03	31,816.74	.224
19	22,800	45,569.78	1,140	421.86	2,390.56	1,237.47	5,189.89	34,464.42	.235
20	24,000	46,435.11	1,200	475.59	2,695.02	1,395.07	5,765.69	37,235.18	.247

* Compounded at the rate of 6 percent monthly, without charges.
† Equal to 5 percent of each deposit.
‡ Equal to 0.15, 0.85, and 0.44 percent, respectively, of the account balance applied monthly.
§ Col (2) minus Col (8) divided by Col (8).

cant, particularly when one is receiving about the same package of services from these insurers.

Now, how can the average buyer of a TDA use these findings to make more effective purchases of a TDA? It usually is not practical for the buyer to repeat the study outlined above personally. However, the buyer armed with the above analytical findings can compare three or four TDA contracts. The buyer can ask many pertinent questions of each salesperson about the various costs of the TDA under consideration. The buyer can obtain some guidance in the matter from the following short table.

*Annual Asset Charge**	*Approximate 20-year Administrative Cost Ratio Associated with Asset Charge (assuming 6 percent interest compounded monthly)*
0.5%	11.6%
1.0	21.8
1.5	30.3

* The numbers are rounded off from actual results of the author's study conducted in 1975, cited above.

By examining the above guidelines, one can make a better and more easily understood estimate of the importance of the costs charged by insurers for both deposit and asset charges. If the prospectus says there is an asset charge of 0.5 percent, for example, one knows that, over a 20-year period, the dollars in the savings fund will be reduced by about 11.6 percent by the insurer's fees. If the asset charge is 1.0 percent, the savings fund will be reduced by about 21.8 percent by these fees, and so on. In terms of dollars, the fees are approximately as follows, when applied to a savings program of $100 monthly for 20 years:

Annual Asset Charge	*Dollars Saved at 6 percent without Insurer Fees*	*Approximate TDA Account Balance*	*Difference*
0.5%	$46,435	$41,598	$ 4,837
1.0	46,435	38,109	8,326
1.5	46,435	35,630	10,805

Thus, if the insurer makes an asset charge of 1 percent, over a 20-year period the saver will be paying about $8,326 for insurer services in addition to deposit charges above what would be paid if one saved the same amount in a savings and loan association or a bank at 6 percent compound interest.

MEDIA FOR FUNDING TDAs

In general, three types of funding media are employed for TDAs: fixed and variable annuity contracts, and mutual fund shares. Only life insurers issue fixed and variable annuities; mutual fund shares are sold by investment companies, by life insurers affiliated with mutual funds, and by investment brokerage firms affiliated both with life insurers and investment companies. Life insurers, through "separate accounts," also offer TDAs invested in a diversified portfolio of common stocks, an arrangement very similar to a mutual fund, except that the separate account is controlled by the life insurer.

Fixed-Dollar Annuities

Fixed-dollar annuities provide participants with lifetime annuity payments, guaranteed in dollar amount. Contributions applied to fixed annuities accumulate at a guaranteed minimum rate of interest (usually between 4 and 6 percent) with the possibility of higher actual rates being applied. At retirement, annuity payments are guaranteed each month for life, and each payment is a guaranteed fixed-dollar amount. The contract can be surrendered for its cash-surrender value at any time before the annuity begins. Funds are invested mainly in "fixed-dollar" securities such as bonds, mortgages, and other investments permitted for life insurers under state law.

Variable Annuities

Variable annuities provide participants with lifetime annuity payments, the amounts of which are designed to reflect changes in the cost of living. Variable annuities were first offered in 1952 by the College Retirement Equities Fund (CREF).[4] Contributions applied to variable annuities are

---

[4] The College Retirement Equities Fund is a companion organization to the Teachers Insurance and Annuity Association (TIAA), a life insurer organized to serve college personnel.

invested principally in a broad spectrum of carefully selected common stocks. In recent years, variable annuities have been invested in money market or bond investments. These allow participants to experience the risk and possible reward of more active investing similar to a mutual fund. Following retirement, annuity payments will be made during the life of the participant; the amount of the payments, however, will vary with the investment performance of the fund. The principal investment objective is to maintain growth of capital sufficient to offset any decline in value of the dollar. Like the fixed annuity, the variable annuity (except for CREF) may be "cashed in" before retirement, subject to specific conditions discussed later.

As of 1985, some 58 life insurers were offering variable annuities in the United States through 186 different types of investment portfolios. Assets in these separate accounts exceeded $11 billion, up from $1.8 billion in 1975.[5]

Variable versus Fixed Annuities

Variable annuities may be contrasted with fixed annuities in the following way: In fixed annuities, the retiree receives a guaranteed retirement income for life in dollars, the value of which is expected to fluctuate with the changing value of the dollar. Most economists expect the value of the dollar to decline, in the long run, because of inflation. In variable annuities, however, the retiree receives a guaranteed number of annuity units for life (similar to mutual fund shares), the value of which will fluctuate according to the plan's underlying portfolio of investments. Most studies reveal a long-run correspondence between consumer prices and stock market prices, but the correlation is not perfect and there may be periods of several years (e.g., the 1970s) in which stock market prices and consumer prices move in opposite directions. Nevertheless, the conceptual framework of variable annuities is based on the assumption that whatever risk is taken by the annuitant will be rewarded by longer term gains and by protection against an ever-declining value of a fixed number of dollars, which characterize a fixed annuity in times of inflation.

In both fixed and variable annuities, the retiree is given some retirement income for life. Thus, even if the retiree outlives the normal life expectancy by many years, an income will be assured. Thus, these instru-

---

[5] *Wiesenberger Investment Companies Service, 1986 Edition*. (New York, N.Y.: Warren, Gorham & Lamont, 1986). p. 807.

ments protect the retiree from the longevity risk (i.e., the risk of outliving a retirement income).

It is sometimes stated that in variable annuities the retiree takes the investment risk, while in fixed annuities the insurer takes the investment risk. While it is true that with fixed annuities the retiree is guaranteed a fixed number of dollars, there is no assurance that these dollars will have sufficient purchasing power over a period of years. For example, an income of $10,000 annually for a male age 65 will decline over a 15-year normal longevity to about $6,400 in real purchasing power if the inflation rate is a constant 3 percent. Thus, the retiree must accept financial risk whether depending either on a fixed or variable annuity. One might even argue the risk is greater with a fixed annuity, since it is likely that inflation will continue to cause a certain loss to the fixed annuity recipient.

Mutual Funds

Many mutual funds have qualified as vehicles for Sec. 403(b) savings plans under which the TDA is issued. The saver simply designates a fund that is qualified for such a plan to be the media to receive the TDA contributions. The funds are accumulated in the mutual fund under tax deferral, and may be distributed either as a lump sum or in fixed installments, depending on the wishes of the retiree. If funds are kept in the mutual fund shares, no charges usually are made to cover mortality or annuity rate guarantees, inasmuch as there are no such guarantees as long as funds are kept in the mutual fund itself.

A mutual fund may have an arrangement with a life insurer, under which the funds also may be employed to purchase either a fixed or variable annuity at or before retirement. If funds are invested by the life insurer in a separate account, the arrangement essentially is that of a variable annuity, discussed above.

One advantage of utilizing mutual funds as investment vehicles for TDAs is the investment flexibility many of these plans afford to the saver. The mutual fund management arrangement may offer the saver a choice of several funds from which to choose during the accumulation period. The saver may switch investments among these funds, according to current economic conditions, without charge, without tax consequences, and without undue delay. For example, if the saver wishes to take advantage of currently high interest rates, the money could be switched into a money market fund. If the saver believes the stock market will rise, the money could be moved into a fund invested in the type of stock portfolio that is expected to rise in the future. In such arrangements, the saver bears all the investment risk. Investments may be allocated among several of the available funds at one time, subject only to a stated minimum dollar amount such as $500, which can be transferred at any one time.

Load versus No-Load Funds

The TDA investor may choose between mutual funds that charge a "loading," usually between 3 percent and 8.5 percent of the amount deposited, and a "no-load," in which there is no deposit charge or other sales charge due when funds are invested. From some perspectives, a typical investor should prefer, other things being equal, a no-load mutual fund for long-term investment purposes. Unless the investor believes the investment potential of a load fund is superior to the potential of a no-load fund, the investor would prefer the no-load fund because in this way the full unreduced deposit will "go to work" for the investor. Various studies have been made of the relative performance of load versus no-load funds and, in general, little difference in average performance over a period of years has been observed. In any event, it is obvious that if a mutual fund has a similar portfolio of investments, the net investment performance for the investor will be superior in a no-load fund than in a load fund.

Group versus Individual Contracts

Some TDAs are issued only through master group contracts in a manner similar to the issuance of group life insurance to employees of a common employer. Other TDAs are sold individually on an individual contract basis and purchased through payroll deduction facilities of the employer. Although the technical arrangements for issuing both group and individual TDAs are similar, their contracts may differ somewhat in their terms and in the loading fees applicable. In general, group contracts are more favorable to the investor than individual contracts.

LIFE INSURANCE

A life insurance element may be included in a TDA so long as the protection is "incidental" [i.e., if the amount does not exceed 100 times the monthly retirement benefit or cash accumulation, Reg. 1.403(b)-(c)(3)]. However, the contract must not cover the employee's family or it will be disqualified (Rev. Rul. 69-146). If life insurance is included, its pure insurance value is subject to current taxation.

The Treasury Department has ruled that a modified endowment policy containing an annuity rider in which life insurance was incidental could be considered an annuity contract for purposes of a TDA. A disability waiver-of-premium provision, or a disability income provision, are considered incidental insurance and subject to tax in the employee's gross income—their value may not be excluded for purposes of a TDA.

MAXIMUM CONTRIBUTION LIMIT

Congress has placed certain maximum limits on contributions to TDAs. In general, the annual limit is 20 percent of "includable" compensation, which is defined as taxable pay left over after deducting the TDA contribution and other contributions to employer-paid, tax-deferred pension programs in all prior years. Thus, a new employee with a gross salary of $12,000 could contribute as much as $2,000 to a TDA if the employer had made no other tax-deferred contribution. In this case, includable compensation would be $10,000 ($12,000 − $2,000). The $2,000 represents 20 percent of includable compensation.

Under the terms of the Tax Reform Act of 1986, an employee may not elect to defer salary of more than $9,500 annually. The $9,500 limit includes excludable amounts contributed by the employee to other tax-shelter plans such as Simplified Employee Pensions (SEPs) and Section 401(k) plans arranged by the employer. The $9,500 limit is not subject to additional contributions by the employer. Thus, an employer can contribute an amount to supplement the $9,500, but the total must still fall beneath the 20 percent limitation noted above. Also, total contributions may not exceed $30,000 in any one year. Excess contributions are subject to a 10 percent excise tax.

Catch-Up Contributions

In addition to the exclusion allowance limitation discussed above, there are three "catch-up" exceptions to the limitation on contributions applicable to TDAs. These provisions permit greater than normal exclusions to allow eligible persons to make up for past years in which no contribution or small contributions were made, even though they could have been made under the law. The exceptions apply only to specified employees.

An employee with 15 years of service in a qualified organization may increase contributions above the $9,500 limit by the lesser of three amounts: (1) $3,000, (2) $15,000 less any prior catch-up contributions, and (3) the excess of $5,000 times prior years of service over prior salary reductions. Specified employees of qualified educational organizations, hospitals, home health service agencies, health and welfare service agencies, churches, and certain church organizations are eligible for catch-up contributions. Total contributions in any one year are subject to the $30,000 overall limit.

Antidiscrimination Rules

Before 1988 there were no coverage or nondiscrimination requirements. A 403(b) plan could benefit a single employee and there were no requirements that all participants be treated the same. After 1988, a 403(b) plan was subject to the same coverage requirements as other tax-qualified retirement plans. Employer contributions to such plans may not favor highly compensated employees. If salary reductions are permitted any employee, then all employees must be given the same option, with specified exceptions, such as plans maintained by churches and part-time student employees.

The new antidiscrimination requirements are many and complex. To give a few examples, without attempting a complete analysis of the new rules, we shall describe the coverage tests: To meet the new requirements, 403(b) plans must cover the lesser of 50 employees, or 40 percent of all employees. Thus, a college with 200 workers must cover at least 50 employees. In meeting this coverage test, students working fewer than 20 hours a week and unionized workers may usually be excluded from the eligible group, provided these do not meet the plan's minimum age and service requirements. However, the plan must cover 70 percent of all nonhighly paid workers, as defined. The percentage of nonhighly paid workers must constitute 70 percent or more of the percentage of highly paid workers covered. Thus, if 50 percent of the highly paid workers participate, 35 percent of the nonhighly paid workers must be covered. The plan must also meet a "fair cross-section" test, under which the average percentage of compensation contributed on behalf of the lower paid workers must equal at least 70 percent of the average benefit for the highly paid.

To illustrate the above rules, consider the case of the college with 200 workers. Assume that 20 are highly paid and half of these elect the TDA plan, contributing 15 percent of their pay. Assume further that 50 of the lower paid workers also elect coverage, contributing 10 percent of their pay. Is the plan discriminatory as to coverage? Yes, because the percentage of highly paid workers in the plan is 50 percent and the percentage of lower paid workers in the plan is 33⅓ percent, and to meet the 70 percent requirement, 35 percent of the lower paid workers must elect coverage (70 percent of 50 percent is 35 percent). Furthermore, the amount of the contribution of the lower paid workers, 10 percent, is only two thirds of the 15 percent benefit for the higher paid workers, not 70 percent as required to meet the fair cross-section test.

To meet the antidiscrimination coverage test, the college will have to increase the participation of eligible lower paid workers, and increase their contribution percentage, or reduce that of the higher paid workers.

Tax Status on Distribution

An employee with a TDA not only is exempt from current federal income and Social Security taxes on contributions and corresponding investment returns on these contributions, but, in addition, obtains certain tax advantages on death, disability, or retirement. Tax rules are complex and change constantly. This discussion is generalized, reflecting rules of the Tax Reform Act of 1986.

When Distributions May Be Taken

Distributions may be taken without penalty from a TDA on death, disability, and reaching age 59½.[6]

Employees may also remove funds from TDAs before age 59½ without penalty if the distribution meets certain other requirements:

1. The distribution is made to an employee who reaches age 55, separates from service, and meets the early retirement provisions of the plan.
2. The distribution is made for medical expenses to the extent they are deductible under the Internal Revenue Code.
3. The distribution is made in substantially equal payments over the life expectancy of the participant or the joint lives of the participant and his or her beneficiary after separation from service.
4. The distribution is made pursuant to a qualified domestic relations court order.

When these conditions are met, the proceeds are taxed according to the rules stated below. Thus, in case of lump-sum withdrawals, no penalty is levied other than that cash is reportable as ordinary income in the year it was received. In most cases, capital gains treatment is not available, but the taxpayer may, under specified conditions, use the rules of income averaging back over five or 10 years, if desired.[7]

A 10 percent penalty applies to all distributions from a TDA that do not meet the above requirements or conditions. The penalty is made to

---

[6] This rule applies after December 31, 1978 (P.L. 95-600, Par. 154, IRC Code 413(b)(7).

[7] See IRS, Announcement 87-2, Internal Revenue Bulletin 1987-2 January 12, 1987.

discourage the use of retirement plans as short-term savings vehicles while still encouraging their use for traditional pension goals.[8]

Loans

An employee may also remove funds by borrowing from an insured TDA plan without penalties or taxes if certain requirements are met:

1. The loan may not exceed $50,000 or one half of the accrued account value.
2. The loan must be repaid on a level amortization basis within five years unless it is made to acquire the principal residence of the employee. New 1986 tax requirements prohibit an employee from indefinitely renewing TDA loans by a provisions that limits such loans to the smaller of $50,000 or the highest outstanding balance during the previous year. Thus, if a $50,000 loan had been paid down to $10,000 at the beginning of the fifth year, the maximum permitted loan made at the beginning of the sixth year would be $10,000.

The Tax Reform Act of 1986 further discourages TDA loans by eliminating the deductibility of interest paid by consumers on debts, other than for home mortgage loans.

A 15 percent excise tax is imposed on all retirement distributions from all sources above a specific statutory amount in a calendar year. "Retirement distributions" means funds from qualified pension, profit-sharing and qualified annuity plans (including 403(b) plans), custodial accounts, or IRAs. In general, the maximum statutory amount in 1987 is $150,000. Not all distributions are taken into account for purposes of determining whether or not the 15 percent excise tax applies. For example, distributions from rollovers, excess employee contributions, nondeductible contributions, and certain other lump-sum distributions are not included in the $150,000.

Taxation of Annuities

TDA income received under an insured annuity plan is taxed as ordinary income when received, if the TDA was purchased with funds on which the employee paid no prior tax.

---

[8] Under transition rules, persons who have reached age 50 by January 1, 1986 may elect to use 5- or 10-year averaging provisions. They may also elect to apply the old capital gains rules (applicable to pre-1974 contributions). Only one election is available to an individual, and if made, it eliminates the ability to elect five-year averaging and capital gains treatment after age 59½. (Act Sec 1122(a) amending Code Sec. 402(e)(1) and e(4)(B).)

If the employee has made prior contributions with income on which tax has already been paid, a portion of each annuity payment will be treated as a recovery of employee contributions. The portion of each payment so treated is not taxable, and the remainder of the payment is taxable. Regulations determine the untaxed portion by applying the "exclusion ratio" to the total annuity. The exclusion ratio is defined as:

$$\text{Exclusion Ratio} = \frac{\text{Employee contributions}}{\text{Employee life expectancy} \times \text{Annuity}}$$

To illustrate, assume that Max has contributed $50,000 toward an annuity of $5,000 annually. Max is 65 and has a life expectancy of 15 years. The exclusion ratio would be $50,000/15 × $5,000, or two thirds. Max would report the difference, one third of his $5,000 annuity, as taxable. He would pay current income taxes on $1,666.66.

Life expectancy numbers recognized by the IRS may be determined from tables found in IRS Publication 575, "Pension and Annuity Income," available free at IRS offices.

Formerly, the excludable portion of an annuity could continue to be exempt from taxes even if the employee outlived his or her life expectancy. After 1986 this rule no longer applies. Once the employee has recovered the tax-free contributions, the full annuity is subject to income tax. If the employee dies before recovering the tax-free contributions, the unrecovered balance may be deducted on the annuitant's final tax return.

Taxation of Investment Company Distribution

If the TDA has been invested in mutual fund shares, the value of these shares is taxed as ordinary income when received. If paid in installments, the funds must be paid out over a period not exceeding the life expectancy of the employee (or joint life expectancy of the employee and spouse) or 30 years, whichever is less (Rev. Rul. 73-239 and 74-325).

Tax-Free Rollovers

Present law permits a tax-free rollover of a lump-sum distribution from a 403(b) annuity to another 403(b) TDA plan or to an IRA. Furthermore, a distribution from a 403(b) plan that is rolled over to an IRA may later be rolled over to another 403(b) plan. There is a prohibition, however, against distributing such funds later on, that is, rolling them over to an employer-qualified pension plan, even if it is first transferred to an IRA. Rolling over a TDA into an IRA may give certain investment flexibility that is not possible under a 403(b) plan.

Partial distributions also qualify for tax-free rollovers if certain conditions are met. The partial distribution must amount to at least 50 percent of the account balance, and the distribution must be due to the death or disability of the employee, or on account of the employee's separation from the employer's service.

Taxation of Death Benefits

In general, if an employee covered by a TDA dies, the beneficiary has the same income tax status as the employee had the employee received the proceeds of the TDA as an income during retirement. However, if the TDA has been financed by a retirement income policy or by another type of an insured annuity with a pure life insurance element, that part of the proceeds representing a pure insurance element escapes income taxation to the beneficiary. Only the cash value portion of the payment would be taxed in the manner indicated above.

Estate Taxation

In general, amounts attributable to employee contributions are subject to estate taxation. Amounts attributable to employer contributions, if any, are also subject to estate taxation.

Before passage of the Tax Reform Act of 1984 (TEFRA), up to $100,000 contributed by an employer was excludable from the taxable estate of the employee. This exemption was eliminated by TEFRA for persons dying after 1984. Transitional rules protected the exemption for benefits in pay status in 1983.

Gift Taxation

In all but favored institutions, such as state universities, irrevocable designation of a beneficiary amounts to a gift, which is subject to gift tax. Employees of favored institutions, however, escape such gift taxes, even if they make an irrevocable gift of their TDA to a beneficiary.

Effect of State Premium Taxes

As of 1985, five states levied a state premium tax of amounts ranging from 0.5 percent to 2.25 percent on annuity considerations received by insurance companies. The tax may be imposed either at the time of purchase of the contract or at the annuity commencement date, when the fund balance is actually committed to the purchase of the annuity agreement. All states have a premium tax on insurance contracts, but most have eliminated the state premium tax as applied to annuity considerations. Obviously, if the TDA investor resides in a state with such a tax, the advantages of the tax shelter are somewhat reduced. For example, if a saver has accumulated, say, $50,000 in a mutual fund for the purchase of an annuity, and actually purchases this annuity from an insurer, a state premium tax ranging from $250 to $1,250 must be paid by the insurer at the time of purchase, thus reducing the amount available to provide annuity payments.[9] The amount of the annuity reduction would be proportional to the amount of the tax.

The existence of state premium taxes favors the use of mutual funds as TDA media in states where these taxes exist, inasmuch as premium taxes apply only to insurance premiums, not to mutual fund savings.

Comparisons of TDAs in the Marketplace

There are many bases on which the investor in a TDA may make comparisons among agencies offering TDAs. Among the more important selection factors are:

1. Investment returns earned by funding agencies on funds committed to them.
2. Annuity rates offered to the annuitant.
3. Expenses charged for management, mortality and annuity rate guarantees, and for investment advisory services, if any.
4. Flexibility of investment media among agencies—opportunity to move funds from one type of media to another without difficulty or undue expense.
5. Extent and quality of service to the annuitant.

It is obvious that agencies with the greatest investment returns, the lowest expenses, and the largest annuity rates will be in a position to offer the highest annuities to the investor. Reference to the importance of expenses has been made earlier in this chapter. Studies of variations that occur in investment returns and annuity rates are discussed below. It should be noted that the ability of, and cost to, the investor to move funds from one type of investment to another may be a very important selection factor in the uncertain investment climate that characterizes the economy in any one period. As noted above, the superiority of agencies offering "families" of mutual funds or variable annuities with different investment objectives is apparent when it comes to judging this factor.

---

[9] States requiring a tax on 403(b) annuities in 1985 were: Alabama, 1 percent; California, 0.5 percent; District of Columbia, 2 percent; Georgia, 2.25 percent; and West Virginia, 1 percent. See Commerce Clearing House, Inc., *State Tax Handbook* (Chicago, Ill.: Commerce Clearing House 1985).

The extent and quality of service to the investor is difficult to compare in any quantitative sense because of the subjective nature of this factor. It is undoubtedly a significant factor, however, because of the complexity of TDAs, the ever-changing nature of the tax regulations, and the need for continuous study of and contact with the investment scene. TDA buyers should consider the number of states in which the agency servicing the TDA is operating, the number and quality of sales or service personnel, and the quality of service available from the research department of the agency. The last factor is important, inasmuch as the knowledge disseminated to sales and service personnel will be only as good or as current as the knowledge produced by those supplying it to these personnel.

Two recent studies of the important factors of annuity rates, interest returns, and annuity rents have been made that will illustrate some of the variations occurring in the marketplace among TDAs.

These studies reveal substantial differences among various agencies offering TDAs in the marketplace. The general conclusion of these studies is that it will be worthwhile for the potential investor in a TDA to make careful comparisons among funding agencies and their products at the time a long-term savings program is started, giving due consideration to the selection factors of greatest concern to the investor.

Rosenbloom Study

Rosenbloom (see Bibliography at the end of this chapter) studied fixed-dollar TDA offerings among 24 large life insurers in 1976 with regard to annuity rates and benefits (both current rates and guaranteed). Insurers were ranked both for guaranteed benefits and current benefits, according to a composite analysis of the factors. The study also revealed these rankings separately, according to the three selection factors.

Some of the findings of the Rosenbloom study were: (1) Insurers ranking high on some factors did not rank as high on others. For example, one insurer ranked first on offering the best annuity rates, but ranked 10th on expenses and 4th on current interest rates. (2) Insurers ranking high for short durations did not always rank as high on longer durations. For example, an insurer ranking second on accumulations of funds produced under current interest rates paid, ranked eighth on 30-year accumulations produced by its interest rate schedule. (3) However, it was fairly easy to pinpoint insurers that ranked fairly low on several of the selection factors and those that ranked fairly high on several selection factors. This finding suggests that the potential TDA investor would find it relatively easy to isolate the best four or five insurers for most of the important selection factors.

The following short table reveals the ranges and averages of three different selection factors for the 24 insurers in the Rosenbloom study:

	Monthly Life Annuity*	Annuity Rate†	Average Interest Rate‡
Average	$423.78	$8.36	6.68%
Highest	500.57	9.10	7.78
Lowest	360.96	7.32	5.24
Ratio, highest to lowest	1.39	1.24	1.48

* Payable on a 10-year certain basis, male age 65, for a contribution of $100 monthly for 20 years, if the insurer continues to earn current interest rates.
† An average over seven years of the fixed-dollar current annuity rates payable to males and females as a monthly life income per $1,000 of cash investment, 10 years certain.
‡ Average current interest rates paid by the insurers over the period 1970–76.

From the above tabulation, it is easy to see that an annuitant would have obtained 39 percent greater monthly life income from the insurer that ranked highest in this factor than from the insurer that ranked lowest. Similarly, an average annuity rate from the highest ranking insurer was 24 percent greater than from the insurer ranking lowest in this study. Average interest rates available from the top-ranking insurer were 48 percent greater than from the insurer ranking lowest in average interest rates paid.

Greene, Tenney, Neter Study

In a comparison of 42 life insurers and their TDA fixed annuities in 1975, Greene, Tenney, and Neter (see Bibliography at the end of this chapter) had findings similar to those of Rosenbloom. Wide variations existed concerning annuity rents (income) and rates (interest), on a guaranteed as well as on a current basis. Among the major findings were: (1) Variability seemed to stem more from variations in investment performance of insurers than from variations in mortality or expense experience. (2) Large insurers generally did not offer, on the average, higher annuity rents than smaller insurers. (3) Stock insurers offered slightly higher rents than mutuals. (4) Insurers offering higher annuity rates also tended to offer above-average investment performance. (5) There was practically no correlation between guaranteed and current annuity rates (i.e., one should not expect an insurer with a high (low) guaranteed annuity rate necessarily to have a high (low) current annuity rate). (6) There appear to be profitable opportunities for "switching" (i.e., saving funds in one insurer with a relatively high current investment return, and then at retirement, switching on a tax-free basis the accumulated funds to an insurer with a relatively high annuity rate). The reason for this is the substantial variation that exists among insurers on annuity rates and investment returns, particularly over longer periods. The charges for withdrawing funds and reinvesting them elsewhere should be considered.

Variations in Mutual Funds

It is well known that large variations also occur in the performance of mutual funds invested in common stocks, particularly over a long period of years. When using these media as a device to fund the TDA plan, the investor should consider the investment objectives and past investment performance of the particular funds that offer 403(b) annuities. Fortunately, several readily available services (Wiesenberger, Standard & Poor's, Moody's, and the like) are available that make continuous comparisons of fund performance. Obviously, it is to the advantage of the saver to select those funds with the best long-term performance and those offering opportunities for switching money among funds with differing investment objectives.

Market Acceptance of TDAs

Aggregate data are not available showing the extent to which TDAs are being utilized in the marketplace. However, a study by Mark Dorfman (see Bibliography) provides some evidence on the matter. Three thousand eligible faculty members of 13 different institutions of higher education in Ohio were surveyed, developing 1,753 usable replies—a response rate of 60 percent. It was discovered that about half of the respondents were currently purchasing TDAs. The use of TDAs varied directly with age and income. When nonusers of TDAs were asked reasons for their nonparticipation in the program, dominant reasons given were: "Could earn more on other investments" (31.2 percent); "Saw no tax advantage in program" (27.2 percent); "Program not sufficiently flexible" (22.1 percent); "Do not currently save" (22 percent); "Procrastination" (18.7 percent); and "Insufficient information to make decision" (18.2 percent). For participants in TDA programs, "reduction of current taxable income" was given as the most important reason by 60 percent of the respondents. Another 32.6 percent of the users gave as a reason that it provided an "automatic savings program."

Dorfman's study indicates the advantages of TDAs are not fully appreciated by all, and shows the need for further educational efforts to expand the use of this potentially valuable retirement media.

BIBLIOGRAPHY

Caplin, M. M. "Taxing Tax-Deferred Annuities: A Critique of 1978 Carter Proposal." *Taxes,* June 1978.

Colley, G. M. "Deferred Annuities as Tax Shelters." *CA Magazine: for Professional Accountants and Financial Managers,* October 1978, pp. 90–94.

Conant, Roger R. "Inflation and the Variable Annuity—Revisited." *CLU Journal,* October 1976, pp. 12–18.

Dorfman, Mark. "The Use and Nonuse of Tax Deferred Annuities." Paper given at the 1981 meeting of the Western Risk and Insurance Association, San Diego, Calif.

Greene, M. R., and J. Paul Copeland. "Factors in Selecting Tax-Deferred Annuities." *CLU Journal,* October 1975, pp. 34–46.

Greene, M. R.; John Neter; and Lester I. Tenney. "Annuity Rents and Rates—Guaranteed vs. Current." *The Journal of Risk and Insurance,* September 1977, pp. 383–401.

Greene, M. R. "A Note on Loading Charges for Variable Annuities." *The Journal of Risk and Insurance,* September 1973, pp. 474–78.

Healy, Richard C., Jr. "An Economic Analysis of Tax-Sheltered Annuities for Employees of Non-Profit Institutions." *Journal of Insurance Issues and Practices,* January 1981, pp. 43–50.

Morehart, Thomas B., and Gary L. Trennepohl. "Evaluating the Tax-Sheltered Annuity vs. the Taxed Investment." *CLU Journal,* January 1979, pp. 23–31.

Pusker, H. C. "Tax Deferred Annuities since ERISA." *Taxes,* November 1978.

R. & R. Service of America, Inc. "Tax-deferred Annuity Plans," Sec. 17-235-17-253.

Rosenbloom, Jerry S. "Fixed Dollar Tax Deferred Annuities—An Evaluation." *The Journal of Risk and Insurance,* December 1978, pp. 611–33.

Stoeber, Edward A. "A Review of Tax Sheltered Annuity Plans." *CLU Journal,* April 1978, pp. 37–52.

Todd, Jerry D. "Reevaluation of Tax-Sheltered Annuity Cost and Performance Measurement Techniques." *The Journal of Risk and Insurance,* December 1978, pp. 575–92.

CHAPTER 33

EXECUTIVE RETIREMENT BENEFIT PLANS

David L. Hewitt
Garry N. Teesdale

Special executive retirement benefits often are needed in addition to an organization's broadly based employee retirement plan. Many reasons exist for such arrangements. One is that executives themselves may have special needs. Another is that qualified plans must be nondiscriminatory, and a purpose of executive plans is to discriminate in favor of an executive or group of executives on a practical and economical basis. Also, the basic company plans often have built-in limits that prevent giving equal recognition to the highest pay levels.

This chapter discusses executive retirement benefits in the following order:

Why executive retirement benefits.
Total planning context.
Supplemental retirement plans.
Deferred compensation agreements.
Legal, accounting, and related background considerations.
Summary.

WHY EXECUTIVE RETIREMENT BENEFITS

Special Needs of Executives

Executives, particularly top executives, differ from the remaining work force of a company. They often have unique abilities and have an impact so great that extraordinary efforts are made to attract them and recognize their achievements. For an officer who joins the company in middle or late career, this may necessitate the promise of full career-equivalent retirement benefits. It also may necessitate the promise of benefits to replace those given up when leaving the prior employer.

For an executive being recruited, or one who is otherwise in a "high risk" situation, it is often appropriate to provide pension guarantees in case he or she is terminated prematurely. Changes in corporate direction often result in the unscheduled change of the top executive team. Further, many executive jobs involve such pressure that "burnout" can be a problem, and it may be mutually advantageous to the company and the individual to make available unreduced retirement benefits at a younger age than can be offered to the entire work force.

The compensation of top executives is high enough so that they may seek to postpone the receipt and taxation of a part of current earnings. At the same time, the company may wish to postpone a part of their compensation and make it depend on their meeting stated conditions, such as continued employment, availability to consult after retirement, or noncompetition after retirement. Also, a significant part of an executive's compensation may be geared to the operating success of the company and be payable in addition to salary.

Limits of Basic Plans

The limits on recognizing the earnings of top executives in basic retirement plans include restrictions on: the *types of pay* counted (perhaps base pay only, excluding bonus or incentives); the *amounts of pay* counted (limited by the Tax Reform Act of 1986)[1]; and the level of contributions or benefits that may be provided (including the Employee Retirement Income Security Act (ERISA) limits)[2].

Social Security reflects income only up to the maximum wage base, and its benefit formula is weighted in favor of lower paid employees. As a result, it can provide only a small fraction of an executive's retirement

---

[1] IRC Section 401(a)17, added by the Tax Reform Act of 1986, limits the amount of compensation includable for purposes of determining benefits or contributions to $200,000, indexed for inflation. The limit itself becomes effective in 1989, at which time indexing begins.

[2] IRC Section 415 states the ERISA limits on benefits or contributions for individuals under qualified plans. The benefit limit is $90,000 annually and the contribution limit is $30,000 annually. Under the IRC Section 415(d) as amended by the Tax Reform Act of 1986, the defined benefit limit is indexed for inflation beginning in 1988; the contribution limit is indexed when the benefit limit reaches $120,000.

income. Companywide plans usually are integrated with Social Security to make up part of this difference. However, Social Security benefits are fully indexed for inflation, while plan benefits are only partly adjusted for inflation, if at all, and usually on an occasional, ad hoc basis, at best. This means the combined pension from a plan and Social Security has better inflation-proofing for the lower paid worker than for the top executive, because Social Security represents a higher percentage of the lower paid worker's total retirement income.

TOTAL PLANNING CONTEXT

Executive retirement planning is part of a total picture that also includes salary, short-term and long-term incentives, and other qualified and non-qualified benefits. These interact, and all should be planned on an integrated basis to achieve an optimum result.

Therefore, several steps are appropriate in designing the executive retirement plan. First, consider the effects of any existing or contemplated long-term incentive arrangements or capital accumulation arrangements that may also provide for the executive's retirement needs. These include, for example, stock options, stock appreciation rights, phantom stock, stock bonuses, performance units or shares, and restricted stock and cash accumulation plans.

Second, take whatever reasonable steps are available to provide for the needs of the executive within the qualified plan. The tax and funding advantages of a qualified plan should be enjoyed to the maximum extent, within the framework of company policy for employees generally. Such measures include:

1. Recognizing the executive's service and earnings as fully as possible in computing plan benefits—for example, by removing nonstatutory upper limits on credited earnings and counting some or all of current bonus or incentive payments. The extent to which this meets other objectives of the organization, of course, must be considered. Some organizations may prefer to base retirement income only on salary, and to regard bonuses and incentive payments as extras, on the basis of which executives should make their own provision for added retirement income. This typically will not be the case, however, where companies have carefully established the mix of compensation tied to strategic design objectives. This also must coordinate with the organization's policies on the plan's recognition of bonuses, overtime, and the like for employees below the select executive level.

2. Integrating the qualified plan with Social Security to the fullest extent. This permits the plan to focus on the part of pay in excess of the Social Security wage base—to slant its formula in favor of the higher paid worker—within allowable limits.

3. Introducing other design features into the qualified plan, which can provide for executive needs. Depending on the company, its population distribution of executives and other employees, and its objectives, such features might include: (*a*) an unreduced benefit for early retirees with long service;[3] (*b*) a benefit formula that gives more than proportional credit for persons hired within, say, 20 years of the normal retirement age; or (*c*) provisions that permit optimum coordination of executive plan benefits with the qualified plan.

4. Adding a cash or deferred plan and advising the executive to make maximum use of salary reduction contributions up to the limit of $7,000 (indexed for inflation beginning in 1988).[4] Since such amounts are excluded from gross income when contributed, and since the investment earnings are also tax-exempt until drawn out as benefits, they can accumulate to much higher levels than if taxed at the outset and during each year of their income accumulation. The percent of compensation that high-paid employees may defer is limited by a rule that relates it to the percent that low-paid workers actually defer.[5]

SUPPLEMENTAL RETIREMENT PLANS

Supplemental retirement plans usually are adopted for one of the following reasons:

1. To restore to the executive any benefits lost under qualified plans because of maximum provisions.
2. To provide full benefits for short-service executives.
3. To provide more generous benefits for executives than for the rest of the work force.
4. To provide unreduced benefits at an earlier age.

---

[3] IRC Section 415(b), amended by the Tax Reform Act of 1986, reduces the $90,000 defined benefit limit in the same manner as Social Security benefits are reduced for retirement at or after age 62 and by the full actuarial reduction for retirement before age 62.

[4] IRC Section 402(g).

[5] IRC Section 401(k)(3).

They can cover either select groups of executives—all above a stated level—or specifically designated individuals. Supplemental plans, like qualified plans, take either the defined benefit or the defined contribution form.

Defined Benefit

If the benefit is defined, it may be a flat-dollar amount, an indexed-dollar amount, or a percent of some part of earnings with or without service weighting and with or without indexing. It may be offset by the basic pension plan, by the value of specified incentives, by the value of deferred compensation contracts, by Social Security, or by benefits paid by a previous employer. Payment may be for life or for a specified period.

A typical formula might provide 2 percent of final average earnings per year of service, including credit for predecessor company service, usually to a combined maximum of 25 or 30 years, less basic plan benefits from both the current and former company and primary Social Security. A variation might provide 4 percent per year, to a maximum of 15 years, less company plans. Other companies simply guarantee a stipulated percentage—usually 50 percent to 75 percent—less current and predecessor company benefits. The formula usually applies to total annual compensation (base salary and annual incentives).

In addition, such guarantees could either reproduce the company's basic survivorship benefit formula or increase it.[6] The ancillary benefits are either similar to those of the company's basic plans or more generous. The plan also may include options to convert from one form of annuity (such as single-life) to another form (such as joint-life) or to earlier or later retirement. The basis of converting from one form of benefit to another may be actuarially equivalent or may be subsidized or penalized by the employer. The plan's obligations following retirement may be unconditional or be conditioned on the executive's meeting requirements for length of service, noncompetition after retirement, or availability to consult after retirement. Conversely, the obligation may be limited specifically to those cases where the executive is terminated without cause or becomes disabled. In other words, within the limits of reasonableness, the plan may be designed to meet whatever simple or complex objectives the parties seek.

---

[6] IRC Sections 401(a)(11) and 417 require that the benefit provided under the basic plan to a surviving spouse be 50 to 100 percent of the employee's benefit, making a supplemental survivor's benefit desirable.

When the purpose is to provide unreduced benefits at an age lower than the qualified plan's normal retirement age, the employer has the choice of (1) paying a lifetime supplement, which restores the basic plan's early retirement reduction, or (2) paying a temporary full benefit up to normal retirement age and deferring the executive's qualified plan benefit until the normal age.

Defined Contribution

If contributions are to be defined, the first step is to spell out how. They may be related to the individual's earnings, to his or her performance, to the company performance, and so on. They even can be stated-dollar amounts. The so-called contribution cannot be a transfer of assets to an entity insulated from the employer's creditors. In fact, it is usually represented only by a bookkeeping entry. There is no typical pattern for such defined contribution: Each plan is designed to meet its own set of objectives. Frequently, a dollar amount or percent of pay is stipulated.

The second step is to determine a basis of "investment" growth. One approach is to hold specified assets earmarked for the purpose of defining such growth and meeting the benefit obligation when due. Another approach is to make hypothetical investments to determine the growth. An alternative is to define the growth by reference to the employer's earnings, a specified fixed or variable interest rate, or a specified index of investment yield or asset fluctuation, or of wage or living cost fluctuation. Many companies use the prime rate or the rate available to them for short-term borrowing.

As with defined benefit–type plans, other decisions include the commencement, timing, and duration of payments, the options to be offered, and the conditions for continuing payment. Lifetime payments to the executive or to specified dependents can be arranged by purchase of a life insurance contract (with the employer as beneficial owner).[7] Unlike a qualified defined contribution plan, lifetime payments also can be offered with the employer directly assuming the longevity risk.

A defined contribution arrangement can slide over into the defined benefit area, depending on what added promises are made, and how closely benefits are limited to the specific growth of the agreed "contributions."

---

[7] Prior to the Tax Reform Act of 1986, annuity contracts were attractive vehicles for supplemental retirement plans. IRC Section 72(u), added by the Tax Reform Act of 1986, made annuities unattractive by annually taxing the increase in the value of the annuity to the employer-owner.

Comparative Merits of Defined Benefit and Defined Contribution Approaches

The relative merits of defined benefits versus defined contributions are not the same for a single executive, a group of executives, or a qualified plan. For a single executive, or several executives with similar age and service characteristics, defined benefits and defined contributions are simply different approaches. The defined benefit may be a more direct way of achieving the goal of retirement security. The defined contribution may be a more appropriate way of gearing the level of retirement security to the events that determine the amount of contribution and the rate of accumulation. The main differences between the two approaches parallel those between qualified pension and profit-sharing plans—that is, the risk or reward of investment performance lies with the employer in defined benefit plans, and with the executive in defined contribution plans; and vesting tends to be more rapid under defined contribution plans.

For a group of executives with varied age and service characteristics, there is a further consideration. If the goal is to provide a given level of retirement security, the defined benefit approach may be the more convenient way of achieving it. If the goal is to reward group performance, the defined contribution approach, with contribution levels based on results, may be best. Note, however, the level of contribution needed to produce the same deferred benefits increases dramatically with the age at which it is set aside. Therefore, if the goal is both retirement security and reward for group performance, a more suitable approach may be a defined contribution plan under which the total contribution reflects the business performance of the organization, but the allocation to each individual is actuarially weighted for current age and, perhaps, also adjusted for length of past service.[8]

DEFERRED COMPENSATION AGREEMENTS

A deferred compensation agreement focuses primarily on the aspect of earnings deferral, and secondarily on the aspect of retirement income. The emphasis is more on the idea of an individual arrangement than of a

[8] Note that such a combined approach is not permitted under a qualified profit-sharing plan (except in the unlikely circumstance that the allocations as a percent of individual earnings will be as favorable to the low-paid as to the high-paid employee—Revenue Ruling 57-77).

plan perhaps covering more than one executive (although deferral for individuals may be done under the umbrella of a master agreement). While supplemental retirement plans (discussed in the preceding section) provide clear added benefits, a deferred compensation agreement delays receipt of specific income and places it in some peril.

Tax Purposes of Deferral

Traditionally, the idea behind deferred compensation agreements was to postpone income and thereby achieve a lower tax bracket. Marginal income tax rates were steeply graduated in the 1940s through the 1960s relative to compensation levels, and interest earnings and inflation had not reached the high rates prevailing in the late 1970s. It often was desirable for the executive to defer the receipt and taxation of a part of pay until retirement, when his or her total income would be lower, as this would frequently result in significantly lower tax rates.

However, events in the late 1970s and the 1980s changed this relationship. High inflation and interest rates in the late 1970s required the crediting of substantial earnings to amounts deferred to keep the executive "whole." Although inflation and interest rates have significantly declined in the 1980s, the need to credit earnings on deferred amounts continues. Beginning in 1982 the maximum federal income tax rate was reduced to 50 percent; as a result many executives' taxes would not decrease after retirement.[9] The impact of taxes on compensation planning is further lowered beginning in 1987 with the maximum tax rate reduced to 38.5 percent and in 1988 and thereafter to 28 percent, although many believe that marginal rates may increase in future years, resulting in the taxation of deferred amounts at higher rates than in effect when earned.[10] From a tax-planning viewpoint, it may be better to tax income when earned, pay the tax, and invest the net amount.

Nontax Purposes of Deferral

While tax planning continues to be a prominent consideration, the other objectives for deferral have grown in relative importance. The principal purpose of deferred compensation since 1981 has been to provide execu-

---

[9] IRC Section 1, amended by the Economic Recovery Tax Act of 1981.

[10] IRC Section 1, amended by The Tax Reform Act of 1986. Beginning in 1988 the maximum marginal rate of tax may be 33 percent, due to the five percent surtax imposed to phase out the 15 percent bracket and personal exemptions.

tives with pre-tax growth of amounts deferred. Additional goals are: to postpone or spread out the receipt of income beyond the executive's prime working life; to even out the effect of bonuses; to bind the executive to the organization for an extended period, by making receipt of the agreed amounts conditional on loyalty, availability, and the like; or simply to provide additional retirement income.

Substance of Agreement

Much of the earlier discussion of defined contribution supplemental retirement plans applies equally to deferred compensation agreements. This includes, first, the definition of what compensation will be deferred; and second, the rules determining appreciation and earnings on such sums. Usually, particularly if the deferral is voluntary, there will be a defined formula for earnings growth. Occasionally, there may be circumstances where no provision is made for growth—where the obligation is simply to pay the stated amounts at a specified future time. Also applicable are the comments on earmarked assets, and on the choices as to benefit options under supplemental retirement plans.

The degree to which the contract limits the executive's rights to the deferred benefits (making them conditional on his or her availability to consult, or on refraining from competition with the company), and the degree to which the employer adds to the executive's rights (through inflation guarantees, commitments to provide added payments to dependents, and so on) are matters of mutual agreement between the parties.

Drafting the Agreement

A deferred compensation agreement should be embodied in a written contract, specifically authorized or ratified by the corporation's directors. Drawing it up is a work of infinite care. The document must be drafted to accomplish the various nontax objectives that are being sought, and also to anticipate other pertinent circumstances that may arise—death, sickness, business changes, and so on. At the same time, it should protect the executive from incurring any tax liability until the deferred amounts actually are received. Finally, the agreement should be so structured that the employer is entitled to a tax deduction when the payments are made.

If the deferral is elected by the employee in lieu of income that could be taken currently, the IRS has indicated the following measures will protect the employee from constructive receipt in advance of actual payment: (1) the election to defer must be irrevocable, (2) the election should be made before the services for which the income is payable are performed, and (3) the period of deferral should be specific.[11] Measures short of these standards may suffice but leave the taxpayer vulnerable to challenge by the IRS.

LEGAL, ACCOUNTING, AND RELATED BACKGROUND CONSIDERATIONS

The application of federal law to executive retirement plans, as contrasted to qualified plans, has an important impact on their design. These considerations are discussed below.

Prohibitive Conditions for Funding

If an executive retirement plan is formally funded, it must satisfy ERISA's benefit and fiduciary requirements—including those concerning reporting, disclosure, vesting, accrual, joint and survivor annuity, other intricate benefit standards, merger and transfer rules, funding standards, fiduciary rules, prohibited transaction rules, and bonding.[12] But the plan still is not tax-qualified unless it is broadened to provide nondiscriminatory benefits for rank-and-file employees, in which case it is no longer an executive plan. The formal funding of executive retirement benefits has rarely been a worthwhile option because of the twin burdens of ERISA requirements and nonqualified tax status. Formal funding means placing plan assets beyond the reach of the employer and its creditors, usually by means of a trust. (See the discussion below of the income tax problems of nonqualified, funded benefits.)

Because executive benefits usually are unfunded, they depend on the future solvency of the company. This is a disadvantage to the executive; at the same time the availability of the assets for corporate uses can be an advantage to the company.

Other ERISA and Tax Law Distinctions

To be exempt from ERISA's benefit and fiduciary rules, an executive retirement plan must be maintained "primarily for . . . a select group of management or highly compensated employees"—as well as being un-

---

[11] Revenue Ruling 60-31.

[12] ERISA Title I, "Protection of Employee Benefit Rights," covers all retirement plans except as specifically exempted by Sections 4, 201, 301(a), and 401(a). The exemptions for executive plans are contingent on their unfunded status.

funded.[13] It can then discriminate in benefits and coverage to whatever extent is needed to meet its specific objectives.

ERISA, along with its benefit and contribution limits on qualified plans,[14] also defines a class of nonqualified "excess benefit plans," whose purpose is to pay benefits or contributions above those limits.[15] Excess benefit plans are particular examples of the executive retirement plans discussed in this chapter.

ERISA requires only minimal reporting and disclosure of unfunded executive retirement programs,[16] and none for those that are excess benefit plans.[17] Further, it omits such plans from its termination insurance program and from its federally imposed employer liability on plan termination.[18]

Normal Taxation and Deductibility of Benefits

Unfunded deferred executive benefits are deducted as business costs by the employer when they are paid to the executive (or assets representing their value are transferred to his or her unrestricted ownership).[19] The executive also reports the benefits as income at that time, with the following exception: If he or she is considered to have current access to the benefits, because the deferral is subject to cancellation by him or her without substantial penalty, the benefits can be deemed "constructively received" and taxable at the time he or she first has such access.[20] (This differs from qualified plans, where the availability of unpaid benefits is not a taxable event.)

A principal goal of executive retirement planning is to give some assurance that benefits will be paid—often including informal earmarking of assets—but not so much assurance that the executive currently is taxed for the value of the amounts being deferred. (See the discussion below regarding informal funding and security devices.)

---

[13] ERISA Sections 201(2), 301(a)(3), and 401(a)(1).

[14] See footnote 2, this chapter.

[15] ERISA Section 3(36).

[16] Department of Labor Regulations 2520.104-23.

[17] ERISA Section 4(b)(5).

[18] ERISA Section 4021(b)(6).

[19] Federal Tax Regulations 1.404(a)-12(b)(2).

[20] Federal Tax Regulations 1.451-2; Revenue Ruling 60-31.

Reasonableness

Executive retirement benefits must represent reasonable rewards for service to be deductible by the employer as business expenses. (This also is true of qualified plans.)[21]

Taxation of Survivor Benefits

The value of survivor benefits under a nonqualified executive retirement plan, like that provided by a qualified plan, generally is included in the executive's gross estate for federal tax purposes.[22] If the beneficiary is the executive's spouse, an unlimited marital deduction is available regardless of whether the plan is qualified or nonqualified.[23] Also, the sum of gifts and bequests to beneficiaries other than spouses is tax-free up to $600,000.[24] Such amounts are subject to income tax (except to the extent they qualify for any part of the allowable exclusion—up to $5,000 in total—of employer-provided death benefits).[25] The estate tax attributed to survivor benefits is deductible in computing the income tax thereon.[26]

Taxation and Deductibility of Nonqualified Funded Benefits

The income tax problems of a nonqualified, formally funded executive retirement plan have existed for many years. The executive is taxed on the plan's assets as soon as they become either nonforfeitable or transferable, even though *benefits* are deferred. The executive thus can be required to pay taxes on monies to which he or she does not yet have access.[27] The employer deducts its contributions when they become nonforfeitable to the executive, provided a separate account is maintained for each participant.[28] Executive plans are seldom formally funded because of these problems combined with the ERISA requirements.

---

[21] Federal Tax Regulations 1.162-7.

[22] IRC Section 2039.

[23] IRC Section 2056.

[24] IRC Sections 2001 and 2010.

[25] IRC Section 101(b).

[26] IRC Section 691(c).

[27] IRC Sections 402(b), as amended by the Tax Reform Act of 1986, and 83.

[28] IRC Section 404(a)(5).

The investment earnings of nonqualified trusts are taxable, subject to most of the same rules as those applying to individuals.

Informal Funding and Security Devices

In recent years, the portion of a top executive's retirement benefit provided through unfunded, nonqualified arrangements has become significant. Accordingly, a significant portion of an executive's retirement income is dependent on the future solvency of the company and its ability and willingness to pay accrued benefits.

The risks that supplemental retirement benefits will not be paid when due tend to flow from one of three circumstances: (1) that current management or future management (such as after a corporate takeover) will not honor the agreements; (2) that the company will have insufficient liquidity to pay obligations; or (3) that the company may become bankrupt. The importance of these circumstances will vary.

In order to better secure the payment of benefits, companies have experimented with a wide range of internal and external quasi-funding and security devices. While none of these provides the assurances that formal funding provides, each can satisfy specific objectives and provide some degree of protection under particular circumstances. As is generally the case, if assets are held and informally earmarked to provide the source of future benefits, the company receives no deduction for the "contribution." Furthermore, it must pay tax on any investment earnings (unless the investment is tax-exempt). However, if the earmarked assets consist of stock in other companies, 80 percent of the dividend income is exempt from tax.[29]

Two commonly used techniques include the use of "rabbi trusts" and corporate-owned life insurance. A rabbi trust can be useful to prevent corporate management from dishonoring agreements to pay retirement benefits. Under the arrangement, a company creates an irrevocable trust for the benefit of participating executives. Since the trust is irrevocable, it places the assets beyond the reach of current or future management, but specifically within the reach of the company's creditors in the event of bankruptcy or insolvency.

Corporate-owned life insurance, on the other hand, is a common method of informally setting aside or earmarking assets to provide liquid funds that can be used to pay executive retirement benefits, but provides

---

[29] IRC Section 243, as amended by The Tax Reform Act of 1986.

no security value since the company is both the policy owner and beneficiary, to avoid constructive receipt issues.

If an insurance contract is purchased on the life of the executive to back up the supplemental retirement plan, it must be carried as an asset of the corporation and be payable to the corporation. Premiums may not be deducted from the corporation's taxable income. However, the investment earnings of the contract are not currently taxable to the corporation (although the insurer may have to pay tax on them, and this may be reflected in the dividends or premiums); nor are policy dividends or death benefits taxable when received by the employer.[30] However, if the policy matures other than by death, is cashed in, or produces annuity payments, the value in excess of the net premiums paid is taxed to the employer as ordinary income.[31]

Generally, if insurance has a place as an earmarked asset, it is for small companies with substantial survivorship promises or other needs for liquidity on the executive's death. The use of insurance also has been attractive to other companies due to favorable tax leveraging, although the advantages have been greatly reduced by The Tax Reform Act of 1986.[32]

The use of corporate-owned life insurance to fund executive retirement benefits should be viewed as a corporate investment. There is significant downside risk to this investment and alternative investment mechanisms should be evaluated as part of the decision to purchase insurance. The evaluation must include consideration of all pertinent factors including opportunities or the need to utilize assets within the company's own operations, other available investment returns, time horizons, risk factors, and others.

Federal Insurance Contributions Act (FICA) Tax

Benefits under executive plans are subject to FICA at the later of the time when (1) the services are performed, or (2) there is no longer a substantial risk of forfeiture.[33] Under prior law, nonqualified benefits often escaped

---

[30] IRC Sections 264 and 101.

[31] IRC Section 72.

[32] IRC Section 264(a)(4), added by the Tax Reform Act of 1986, makes life insurance less attractive to small companies. Interest on loans in excess of $50,000 from company-owned policies is not deductible, making borrowing to pay premiums infeasible.

[33] IRC Section 3121(v)(2), added by the Social Security Amendments of 1983.

taxation entirely, under one of several loosely defined exemptions for payments made on account of retirement.

For deferred compensation payments that become nonforfeitable during active employment, this change will have little practical effect, since most executives earn more than the Social Security wage base. However, if nonqualified benefits become nonforfeitable at retirement, the consequences will vary. If the retired executive has no other income subject to FICA, his or her nonqualified plan payments will be taxed. On the other hand, if there is earned income during retirement that is greater than the taxable wage base, the nonqualified plan payments will not produce any additional FICA liability.

FICA Self-Employment Tax

If the deferred benefits are tied to the performance of future services—for example, a substantial consulting requirement—the executive may run the risk of being declared self-employed, and therefore be liable for the FICA self-employment tax at the time the payments are received.[34]

Earnings Test

The Social Security earnings test for receipt of benefits does not apply to amounts earned by an employee before retirement, even though paid on a deferred basis after retirement. However, if the deferred benefits are tied to the performance of postretirement services, some portion of the payments may count toward the earnings test. The result would be to cancel $1 of Social Security benefits for each $2 of earnings in excess of specified amounts paid before age 70 (starting in 1990 the penalty will be reduced to $1 of Social Security benefit for every $3 of excess earnings for those age 65 through 69). The $1-for-$2 trade-off will remain in effect for anyone less than 65. Starting in the year 2000, the foregoing references to age 65 will gradually rise, reaching 67 in the year 2027.[35]

---

[34] FICA tax on self-employment income is levied under IRC Section 1401. To determine whether an individual is retired, or whether he or she has performed substantial services in self-employment, the Social Security Administration considers several factors, which are outlined in Social Security Regulation 404.446.

[35] Social Security Act Section 203(f) and 216, added by the Social Security Amendments of 1983.

Accounting and SEC Disclosure

Accounting principles require that the cost of deferred benefits, net of estimated deferred tax deductions, be recognized as a current expense over the executive's active employment. The value of benefits accrued or amounts contributed as well as the value of accumulated benefits to date must be disclosed. The same standards apply whether the benefits are funded or unfunded.[36] The fact that such costs must be recognized as current expenses during the executive's service, even though payment will not be made until a future time, must be considered at the outset, as it can influence the initial decision to adopt a plan.

The Securities and Exchange Commission (SEC) requires the clear disclosure of executive compensation and retirement arrangements.[37] Aside from the disclosure requirements, there are no significant securities law issues in connection with the usual forms of unfunded executive retirement benefits. However, if employee contributions are permitted and are treated as invested in securities of the employer, deferred compensation could turn into a security requiring registration.

Shareholder-Employees in Closely Held Corporations

When the executives of a corporation also are its directors and principal shareholders, a deferred compensation agreement with them may lose some of its credibility. If the corporation has the financial ability to pay the deferred amounts currently, the IRS might assert that the doctrine of constructive receipt applies. Where deferred compensation arrangements are provided, in addition to basic pay, for the shareholder-employees of a closely held corporation, the question of reasonableness is certain to receive closer IRS scrutiny.[38]

However, situations exist when such a company would be justified in deferring a part of compensation and making it conditional on the long-term performance of the corporation. If the corporation then performed exceedingly well over a period of years, the ultimate payment of the

---

[36] *Financial Accounting Standards Board Statement No. 87,* Employers' Accounting for Pensions (December 1985).

[37] Standard Instructions for Filing Forms under Securities Act of 1933; Securities Exchange Act of 1934 and Energy Policy and Conservation Act of 1975—Regulation S-K, 17 CFR Section 229.10 et seq.

[38] Federal Tax Regulations 1.162-7.

deferred amounts might be justified as a reasonable reward for good management, even if payment of the same amounts on a current basis might have been found to be unreasonable.

Even then, however, the corporation might have interim problems in satisfying the IRS that any reserves being booked for payment of the deferred amounts should not be taxed as accumulated earnings.[39]

Therefore, in a closely held corporation, the deferrals for a major shareholder may better be handled through share accruals or expansion of ownership (with buy-back agreements if necessary).

Employees of Tax-Exempt Organizations

Special rules apply to executive plans of tax-exempt organizations such as hospitals, colleges and universities, and trade associations. Voluntary deferrals of compensation are limited to $7,500 per year and must be distributed in accordance with rules similar to those applying to qualified plans.[40] The $7,500 ceiling is reduced dollar for dollar by contributions to tax-sheltered annuities and cash or deferred arrangements.[41] For 1987 and 1988, distribution of deferred amounts must begin on April 1 of the year following the later of (1) the year in which the executive retires or (2) the year in which the executive reaches age 70½.[42] Beginning in 1989, distribution must begin by April 1 of the year after attaining age 70½, whether or not the executive has retired.[43] If distribution begins before the executive's death, two thirds of the amount deferred must be distributed over his or her life expectancy. If distribution begins after the executive's death, deferred amounts must be paid over no more than the surviving spouse's life expectancy, or 15 years for a beneficiary other than a spouse.

If compensation is deferred in a manner that does not comply with the foregoing rules, it will be taxed in the year earned unless subject to a substantial risk of forfeiture.[44] The IRS has interpreted this rule to apply not only to voluntary deferrals of compensation by the executive but to all forms of deferral, including nonqualified retirement benefits paid for

---

[39] IRC Sections 531-537.

[40] IRC Section 457.

[41] IRC Section 457(c).

[42] IRC Section 401(a)(9).

[43] IRC Section 401(a)(9), as amended by the Tax Reform Act of 1986.

[44] IRC Section 457(f). Under IRC Section 83 property is subject to a substantial risk of forfeiture if it cannot be sold or transferred and is forfeited on termination of employment.

solely by a tax-exempt employer.[45] As deferred compensation from tax-exempt entities is not usually forfeitable, the Internal Revenue Service's position precludes virtually all nonqualified deferred retirement benefits for their executives.[46] The IRS is expected to affirm this position in regulations, although business and professional groups have questioned the validity of its position on this matter.

SUMMARY

An executive retirement plan can add to the executive's benefits, bringing them up to or above those offered the general work force. It can provide unreduced early retirement, full pension after short periods of service, extra protection for dependents, deferral of current earnings, and guarantees of income beyond working life. Since it is free of the requirements for qualified plans, it can be drawn up to meet the particular needs of the individual executive or of a select group of executives. Aside from providing added benefits for the executive, it also can impose added obligations. Plan design is concerned with avoiding the tax pitfalls of nonqualified plans, rather than enjoying the tax advantages of qualified plans.

---

[45] Notice 87-13, Q&A 27, (January 26, 1987).

[46] Deferral arrangements entered into before August 17, 1986 are exempt from the rule. Notice 87-13, Q&A 28, (January 26, 1987).

CHAPTER 34

LOOKING THROUGH BOTH ENDS OF THE TELESCOPE: A PERSPECTIVE ON PENSION PLANS AND INFLATION

Lloyd S. Kaye
Eric P. Lofgren

PENSION ADEQUACY ISSUES

Just a few years ago the most publicized debate in pension-planning circles was the issue of indexation: the responsibility for a pension plan to maintain, after retirement, the purchasing power of pension payments. This is a critical aspect of the overall pension adequacy issue which is the essence of sound pension planning. The debate rose to a storm as inflation hit double digits, leading companies to make ad hoc adjustments of unprecedented size to retirees' pensions. Yet the storm quickly subsided in the mid 1980s as inflation declined to 3 percent or less.

The need for pension indexation should be analyzed within the perspective of long-range pension concepts, not simply in response to immediate demands and notions of equity. The best beginning point is not with the question of ''should we index?''; rather, it is worthwhile to begin an analysis of pension plans and inflation with a brief review of how ideas on effective pension planning have evolved over the last generation. To put this another way, the issue of pension indexation is more than just experimenting with percentages and numbers. It requires a philosophy; and that may depend on whether one is looking through the long- or short-range end of the telescope.

Career Average or Final Average?

During the 1950s and the 1960s, the most significant debate over pension adequacy was whether it was advisable for an employer's pension plan to have the pension benefit formula based on "career average" pay, measured over the employee's entire career, or on "final average" pay measured over a limited period, such as the 5 or 10 years immediately preceding retirement.

The great majority of pension plans were once based on career average pay. For example, for each year of credited service, an employee would receive credit for 1 percent of compensation recognized for that particular year. If the plan continued on this basis throughout an employee's career and retirement occurred after 30 years of service, then 30 percent of the employee's average pay throughout his or her entire career would be payable as the pension.

It is obvious that this would be far from perfectly adequate. Even if there had been no inflation over that 30-year period, the amount of the pension would be adequate only if the pay level remained fairly constant. A typical employee would receive merit increases, so that in order to reflect an attained pay level fairly close to retirement, it would be necessary to "update" pension credits periodically to bring prior pension credits into line with the current pay level.

Supporters of the career average concept pointed to its inherent conservatism and the continued control by the employer to assume new updating liabilities only when and to the extent they would be financially affordable. In contrast, those in favor of the final average pay approach maintained that the assurance of an adequate pension is paramount and that the employee should be able to rely absolutely on having his or her pension based on average pay over a limited period close to retirement.

In practice, there might be little difference between a final average pay plan and a career average plan which was periodically updated to make prior pension credits adequate in terms of current pay levels. Even the modest rates of inflation which prevailed through the mid-1960s, combined with merit increases, made it necessary for financially stable, conscientious employers to operate their career average plans as if they were final average pay plans by use of updatings every three to five years. As more and more companies came to appreciate the blurring of the distinction in practice, a major trend developed during the 1960s from the career average to the final average concept.

Inflation was at the heart of this movement, even though many companies did not fully appreciate their own motivation. Increases in worker productivity during the 1950s and 1960s generated increases in pay which were clearly merit increases in the sense that they were substantially in excess of the rate of inflation, which ranged between 2 and 3 percent over that period. However, even in times when there is only a 2 or 3 percent rate of inflation, this can accumulate to a very substantial difference after 10 or 15 years, eroding the real value of pension benefits by as much as a third. Thus, simply because of inflationary pressures, pay scales went up regardless of merit. Adoption of the final average pay concept committed companies to pay for the increased pension which derived from inflationary increases in current wages. The economics of the 1970s cautioned many companies and slowed or stopped the final average pay trend. An element that tended to dampen the enthusiasm for assuming final average pay commitments was the shock of sharper inflation at a rate not experienced within the working lifetimes of most employees. Careful analysts of the final average pay trend came to realize that in that type of plan the employer commits to paying for the inflation up to the point of retirement. In effect then, a final average pay plan is a form of guaranteed indexation.

The last several years have demonstrated that even guaranteed indexation through a final average pay plan does not mean assurance of pension adequacy to the employee. An employee who retires at age 65 after 30 years of service will be relying on that pension for life. If a joint and survivor option is in effect, so will the surviving spouse. Thus, the postretirement period for measuring pension adequacy can be as long as the working career of a long-service employee. Many employers who adopted final average pay plans had been lulled into the secure feeling that nothing more had to be done after that. It is now apparent that improvement during retirement years is essential if the same standard of adequacy which existed at the time of retirement is to be maintained thereafter.

By viewing the matter in this perspective, it is possible to identify the following issues and questions:

If the amount of the pension was adequate at the point of retirement, then it is axiomatic that the employer has underwritten the cost of inflation over the employee's working career. To what extent should the employer be responsible to continue to pay for inflation thereafter?

Is there a moral obligation? Should Congress compel indexation?

Is there a difference in the nature of a financial commitment to pay for inflation over the employee's working career, as compared to the commitment to pay for inflation in the future?

Social Security benefits are indexed with the consumer price index (CPI). To what extent should this be taken into account in future planning? Is it a model for private plans? Is the CPI a proper index, and if not, what is?

What is the potential cost impact for maintaining the purchasing power of pensions?

The New Mobility

Paradoxically, as employers have committed to final average pay plans, many employees will receive, in effect, career average benefits as a result of frequent job switching. For example, if an employee changes employers at ages 35, 45, and 55, pension accruals at retirement will be based on five or ten years final average pay calculated at 35 from the first employer for service prior to that age, on five or ten year final average pay calculated at age 45 from the second employer for the next decade of service, and so on. If the employee switches companies more frequently, he or she may never become vested, and receive nothing at all. Concern about this dilemma has led to faster mandated vesting twice in the past decade. But, faster vesting is only a partial step, only guaranteeing an inadequate career average pension. For the same reasons that career average updates (or a final average pay formula) are necessary for continuing employees, they are equally necessary to the job-hopping employee. But in practice, preretirement inflation updates rarely occur for terminated participants, for whom employers feel little responsibility. Further, making these adjustments would be certain to undermine one of the traditional tenets of private pension philosophy: retention of employees. Indexation of deferred pensions is equivalent to portability, which tends to encourage further mobility. Here we have a situation of private and governmental perspectives clearly at odds. If more and more employees exercise mobility, the private pension system will be viewed by government as failing a significant portion of the population, eventually requiring further government benefits.

Indexation, then, is a two-pronged problem, regarding postretirement inflation protection for everyone, and preretirement protection for a mobile workforce. Issues and questions about the employer's responsibility for inflation protection and the need or not for Congressional action extend to the mobile active workforce, and are not confined to retirees.

The Indexation Dilemma

The cost commitment for guaranteeing indexation up to the point of retirement for continuing active employees is a similar commitment to that of postretirement indexation. Periodic, discretionary pension indexing has been the prevailing pattern among employers. Persistent repetitions assume the character of the "updatings" which have been common among career average plans for active employees. Just as those updatings blur the distinction between career average and final average pay plans, so may updatings for pensioners blur the distinction between discretionary and automatic pension indexing.

One of the often heard comments by career average plan enthusiasts is that a final average pay plan formula is like signing a blank check because it makes the employer a financial hostage to future wage scales. It seems obvious that this is an overstatement, in the sense that the employer retains an important element of financial control because the amount of that check is budgetable.

The reason is that an important aspect of actuarial planning includes an assumption as to the best estimate of increases in salaries, so the employer begins to pay for the future pension immediately by assuming pay will go up. If the increase in assumed salary proves inadequate because pay increases faster than estimated in the actuarial assumption, periodic monitoring of the adequacy of that assumption facilitates suitable measurement and adjustment. In essence, the employer can always measure the cost commitment and see an appropriate ratio between payroll and pension plan contribution. Thus, up to the point of retirement, there has always been a controlled logical progression.

Similar logic applies after the point of retirement as well. A specified level of indexation could be guaranteed and the liability prefunded by including that commitment as part of the plan's actuarial assumptions. Since inflation and salary increases have a strong statistical correlation, the employer is still able to measure the cost commitment and see a relatively stable ratio between payroll and contributions. In particular, this is virtually assured if the guaranteed level of indexation is tied to changes in the company's wages, instead of to nationwide CPI changes. Over the long term, inflation rates and wages have moved in tandem.

There is one reason that the trend from career average pay plans to final average pay plans has not been accompanied by a trend from ad hoc to guaranteed pension updates. There is a huge short-term impact on employer costs. When a private pension plan indexes pensions, two additional costs are assumed: first, more cash is necessary to take account of immediately increased payout rates; second, larger reserves must be accumulated to fund future increases on a sound basis. A rule of thumb is that for every 1 percent of annual increase, reserves should be strengthened by at least 6 percent and perhaps as much as 10 percent. If one assumes, somewhat pessimistically, a long-range increase in the cost of living of 10 percent per year, a doubling of pension costs could be produced. An employer whose pension contributions are now 10 percent of payroll might pay 20 percent.

However, if the employer makes pension adjustments on an ad hoc basis, it will bear the same cost as if the same adjustments are made on a guaranteed basis. Only the incidence of cost is affected, not its absolute level over the lifetime of a plan.

Indexation of deferred pensions for terminated participants, on the other hand, would represent a true increase in cost, since few employers make any such adjustments on an ad hoc basis. Add to this most employers' lack of feeling of responsibility for terminated employees, and the fact that inflation protection for deferred pensions would negate one of the primary rationales of private pension plans, and it is clear that such indexation will not occur voluntarily.

If Social Security Can Do It, Why Not Private Plans?

Congress has decreed that Social Security benefits will be adjusted with the consumer price index. Why not private pension plans? What is the problem?

On a superficial level, it seems as if the Social Security system is far more effective than the private system, but as a conclusion, it ignores fundamental economics. Indexation, which looks like a solution for retired employees, is, in an important sense, part of the problem. Social Security benefits are financed by payroll taxes, and to the extent Social Security fully compensates retired employees for inflation, it takes away money from the working portion of the population. As humane as this may be, it cannot be a long-range solution. If private industry cannot afford to subsidize inflation for retired employees, then government cannot do so by siphoning taxes simply because it has the legislative and administrative mechanism to do so. Those revenues are generated by the private sector. The Social Security system is a conduit, not a creator of wealth.

The most serious crisis for the Social Security system has not yet arrived. As the ratio of active to retired workers decreases, the burden on workers to support the nonworking population will increase. In the early years of the 21st century, when the post-World War II baby-boom generation begins to reach age 65, there is a serious question whether the present structure of Social Security can remain intact, much less be liberalized. To commit a public system to subsidize inflation for nonworking people by exacting increased taxes from a gradually shrinking segment of the population—its productive workers—is a questionable long-range solution.

It is an economic mirage to assume a public system is better than a private system because the public mechanism can guarantee a portion of the population against inflation. The issue of indexation of retiree benefits must properly be dealt with, but this can only be done in an orderly economy and simply will not work unless inflation remains under control.

THE INDEXATION STANDARD

The consumer price index is the fundamental measure of the dollar's purchasing power. How valuable a standard is it, particularly when used as a measure of pension adequacy?

It is easy to criticize the CPI. Few ad hoc pension adjustments are based on the full CPI, since it is not a measure of price changes for the elderly. Further, the CPI was intended to measure price changes in a stable economy. The degree of changes experienced recently warrants a new look at how inflation is measured for different purposes. This is a critical problem. Failure to come up with a rational solution could create such conflicts—between different economic groups and the almost infinite subgroups (such as those based on generation, income level, occupation, geography, and so on)—as to create serious societal problems.

The essential challenge is to determine what is really happening to spending patterns and living costs. The CPI is based on charting a market basket established on the basis of goods and services purchased several years in the past. It is important to know what is a current market basket; but even before this, it is vital to know how and why spending patterns change and—this is fundamentally crucial—keep up-to-date on a 12-month moving average.

What is needed is a pragmatic sampling technique which will result in a vital index of living costs rather than just a measure of price increases. How have people and families been spending their money? A cross-section of people in different areas and financial circumstances could indicate through checks and credit card expenditures what they have spent on the different components of living. By utilizing sampling techniques, with cancelled checks and credit card receipts as evidence of expenditures, an exact CPI could be developed for any group segmented by income, age, geography, family situation, and so on.

For example, both common sense and personal experience would indicate that as prices of certain goods and services rise dramatically, shifts occur almost by automatic reaction. At times less steak, more chicken. At other times less chicken, more steak. Similarly less driving, more walking or public transportation; less expensive vacations; more do-it-yourself repairs; more bargain hunting for clothing, etc. What would be produced is an ongoing picture of what is really happening based on actual spending patterns.

The expected conclusion would be that increases in living costs are significantly less if measured in terms of what people actually spend, as contrasted with a price index of selected goods and services, the components of which change much more slowly. Critics of this approach may say that what is happening is a reduction in living standards. After all, a family that forgoes a vacation and buys less clothing is not living as well as previously.

The key issue here is that indexation, as now conceived, is price-oriented: it asks what is required to make everyone "whole." By concentrating on expenditures rather than prices, the emphasis could be changed to analyzing differences in buying and spending habits as people adjust.

It is almost impossible to keep social groups whole against a fixed standard in the face of major economic dislocation. The development of this new approach and technique tends to share more equitably a decline in living standards made necessary by such dislocations. If society wishes to overcompensate a particular group, such as the aged, it would not be the result of an index with questionable validity. Rather, careful analysis and discussion would produce that decision.

The Close-Up Look

So much for long-range philosophy. A look through the close-up end of the telescope would concentrate on the challenge to improve benefits for retirees in some fashion and make plans for those who will retire in the next several years. Planning through models is important if a satisfactory solution is to be devised.

The key points would be these:

1. The comparative amounts of Social Security dollars between the year of retirement and the year of plan improvement is a vital element. If the objective is to maintain purchasing power in terms of income replacement ratios at the time of retirement, the amount of Social Security increases must be considered. Across-the-board, uniform percentage increases have a tendency to do what any nonintegrated pension plan does: either overcompensate the lower-paid or undercompensate the higher-paid.

2. It is worthwhile to think through the indexing standard to be used. One standard worth considering is to treat retired people on no higher a standard than active employees. (This was one of the disparities in Social Security increases which have granted higher nontaxable raises to retired people as compared to the taxable pay increases for active workers.) Thus, the pay a retired worker would be getting had he or she remained employed would be projected. If pay increases have been 8 or 10 percent per year, that rate of increase would be added to the retired worker's last rate of pay and if the plan's pension objective were 60 percent of that pay, including Social Security, the appropriate adjustment could be made readily in recognition of the projected pay and current Social Security benefits. However, benefits would be limited to increase by no more than the change in prices since retirement.

It may be considered more appropriate to distinguish between the portion of active pay increases attributable to inflation compared to merit. This means that instead of hypothetically projecting a retiree's pay rate at 10 percent, a rate of 6 or 8 percent might be suitable.

What is recommended, then, for a concept of indexation for retirees is an integrated program, recognizing current Social Security payments based on the employer's recognition of living cost increases as evidenced by the inflation element of actual pay increases. Once these elements are in place, the employer will have an appropriate planning model. How much pensions are improved will then depend on how much additional liability the employer wishes to assume.

Having said this, it is appropriate to return to the initial theme: a private employer who agrees to underwrite a significant portion of inflation over an extended period is taking on an onerous burden.

PLANNING AHEAD

The consternation generated over the last several years by inflationary erosion of pension adequacy warrants a new look at pension planning. Some longer-range planning may be in order.

The recent proliferation of salary reduction contributions to 401(k) plans supports expansion of the concept that employees can be encouraged and assisted to start their own retirement planning. Further, the Tax Reform Act of 1986 now permits a defined benefit plan to maintain an arrangement under which employer and employee contributions can be used to provide cost-of-living increases. Helping employees to put aside money for their own supplemental security can serve the best interests of the employer as well as employees. Employee savings and accumulation may be the best way to modify the employer's long-range responsibilities as the employees would be investing currently for their own inflation hedge after retirement.

Capital accumulation through savings and thrift plans is not a scientific approach to the general problem of pension adequacy, including the issue of the post-retirement inflation spectre. A typical pension plan is a so-called defined benefit plan. The plan sponsor defines the amount of the pension benefit an employee would receive and assumes the financial burden to provide that benefit. In contrast, a defined contribution plan provides benefits based on the impact of investment performance on the contributions made by and for employees. In essence, a defined contribution plan merely accumulates capital; and the adequacy of that capital accumulation to provide security in long-range pension terms may be uncertain.

There are surely drawbacks to the capital accumulation approach in assuring adequacy for employees. The dependence on successful investment is critical in that a defined contribution program is based on career average pay. A contribution of, say, 5 percent of current pay may not mean much in terms of final average pay of a typical long-service employee. It is not really subject to updating, as a career average pension credit can be updated.

Yet, despite these obvious drawbacks, the concept of capital accumulation as an adjunct to a pension plan may represent an employer's best planning device. It has a major advantage in avoiding new unfunded liabilities and costs by the employer. Further, it invites the employee to participate and save, recognizing that inflation and the quest for security is a mutual problem. A failure of employers to act is an invitation to the government to act. Significantly, the first steps towards indexation in both Canada and the United Kingdom occurred not for pensioners but for terminated employees, for whom employers are unwilling to index voluntarily.

In essence, the employer's message to employees is: "Within our financial capacity, we will provide an adequate pension at the point of retirement. If you are concerned about inflation protection after that, a major part of satisfying that burden will depend on your willingness to start savings now."

The ultimate capital accumulation, whatever its dimension, could be used by retired employees as a counterinflationary pool in as flexible a manner as desired. The employer's future responsibility may be thereby eliminated or lessened. The time to plan ahead, as ever, is as soon as practicable—before an emergency or government intervention precludes long-range planning.

CHAPTER 35

RETIREMENT PREPARATION

Edmund W. Fitzpatrick

INTRODUCTION

After decades of slow growth, the number and scope of retirement preparation programs began to increase dramatically in the mid-1970s.[1] Some of the reasons for this phenomenon are:

- The occurrence of double-digit inflation in the late 1970s and early 1980s, causing an increased concern over the effects of inflation on retirement purchasing power.
- Federal legislation affecting private pensions and eliminating mandatory retirement.
- Improved pension systems that enable more people to retire early.
- Increasing complexity of the law taxing and otherwise affecting benefit plan distributions.
- Recognition that the population and work force are aging and the political, economic, and employment implications of this.

Each of these factors represents a long-term trend likely to continue. Since this suggests continued growth of retirement preparation programs, a brief review of the trends seems warranted.

---

[1] Retirement preparation goes by many names, such as retirement education, retirement counseling, preretirement planning, and life planning.

FACTORS AFFECTING GROWTH OF RETIREMENT PREPARATION PROGRAMS

An Aging Population

In 1980, the population age 55 and over was about 45 million and represented about 20 percent of the population (see Table 35–1). By the year 2030, this group is expected to number 83 million and, barring a new baby boom, will constitute about 31 percent of the population.

Indeed, unless there is a new baby boom the population age 65 and over in the year 2030 will represent about one in five persons (see Table 35–2). This age shift of the population has enormous implications for business and industry.

Increased Life Expectancy

Contributing to the aging of the population are significant increases in life expectancy. In fact, the fastest growing segment of the population is the age 75 and over segment. Longer life expectancies, of course, mean spending more years in retirement. If a man 62 and his wife 59 retire this year, he will likely live another 17 years, until about age 79, and she will likely live another 23 years, until about age 82. In reality, chances are that both will live even longer, since traditionally we have underestimated average life expectancies and must continuously revise them upward.

TABLE 35–1
Projection of Population Age 55 and Over

Year	*Persons Age 55 and Over (millions)*
1980	45
1990	49
2000	54
2010	66
2020	79
2030	83

Source: U.S. Bureau of the Census.

TABLE 35–2
Growth in the "Over 65" Population

	Persons Age 65 and Over
1900	1 in 25
Today	1 in 10
2030	1 in 5

Source: U.S. Bureau of the Census.

Early Retirement

The trend toward early retirement began decades ago and is continuing. In 1981, almost three of four employees (70 percent) were retiring early—that is, before age 65—and the great majority of this group retired at age 62 or before. Since this generally coincides with benefit eligibility under private and public pension systems (most notably Social Security), it reinforces the notion that the great majority of employees will retire as soon as they think they can afford it.

The growth of benefit plans that continue coverage into the retirement years—such as health insurance and life insurance continuation plans—and the growth of 401(k) plans may permit more employees to retire early rather than stay on for economic reasons.

Economic Trends

The inflation rate rises and falls with economic cycles, but the trend toward early retirement has continued virtually unaffected. Employees become more concerned with retirement finances when the inflation rate rises, as when it reached double-digit levels a few years back. Nevertheless, employees still retire early, good times or bad, and even though they may have doubts and fears about how well they are prepared financially.

Federal Legislation

Trends in private pension plans have been toward encouraging early retirement. This has caused concern at the federal level over the projected costs of financing Social Security benefits when people retire earlier and live longer. As a consequence, federal legislation has reduced the role of Social Security benefits as an incentive for early retirement. The 1983 amendments to the Social Security program will gradually raise the normal retirement age to 67 and reduce the level of benefits to those who retire earlier. Additional changes have been proposed that would further reduce early retirement incentives in both public and private plans. It is too early to know the extent to which existing and proposed legislation might affect retirement patterns.[2]

---

[2] United States General Accounting Office, *Retirement Before Age 65: Trends, Costs, and National Issues* (Washington, D.C.; USGAO, July 1986).

ONE RATIONALE FOR RETIREMENT PREPARATION PROGRAMS

A national survey found that 81 percent of current employees and 84 percent of retirees feel their standard of living during retirement should be about the same as before retirement.[3] The reality is that the average income of persons over 65 has been increasing relative to the rest of the population, but at present the average income of this group is only about two thirds of the national average.[4] The growing account balances in 401(k) and similar plans suggest that future retirees will cause the relative income of this 65+ group to continue to improve.

An important advantage of retirement preparation programs is they can encourage and show employees how to use savings and investment vehicles, including 401(k) plans, to accumulate assets for retirement. They can also demonstrate the importance of continuing investment management during the retirement years to counter inflation and maintain retirement purchasing power. Thus, retirement preparation programs can help to strengthen the "third leg" of the "three-legged stool" of retirement income—Social Security, private pension, and personal savings.

HOW PERSONNEL DIRECTORS SEE IT

Personnel directors and other human resource professionals generally believe a need exists for retirement preparation programs and that companies will be paying more attention to this matter in the future. In a survey conducted at an annual conference of the American Society of Personnel Administrators, 92 percent of the 1,500 survey respondents agreed that "preretirement counseling programs will receive increased emphasis" in the next five years.[5] Later in the same year, a survey of *Fortune* 1,000 company personnel directors obtained identical results (Table 35–3).

---

[3] Louis Harris and Associates, 1979 Study of American Attitudes Toward Pensions and Retirement, Commissioned by Johnson & Higgins (New York: Louis Harris and Associates, 1979), p. iv.

[4] Yung-Ping Chen, "Economic Status of the Aging," chapter in the *Handbook of Aging and the Social Sciences,* Robert H. Binstock and Ethel Shanas, editors (New York: Van Nostrand Reinhold Company, 1986).

[5] Harold L. Schneider, "Personnel Managers Look to the '80s," *The Personnel Administrator,* November 1979, p. 48.

Content Coverage

Retirement preparation programs may be classified as narrow, medium, or comprehensive in terms of topic coverage. A *narrow program* may concern only the financial and legal aspects of retirement. A *medium program* is likely to include three or four topics, such as finances, legal aspects, health, and leisure. A *comprehensive program* often will include seven to nine topics—the four just mentioned plus new careers, interpersonal relations, living arrangements, and lifestyle planning.

Among large companies with retirement preparation programs, about 85 percent of the programs fall into the medium or comprehensive categories. Indeed, the trend is toward comprehensive programs.[9]

Of course, how well a topic actually is covered can vary immensely from program to program. Financial planning, for example, may be dealt with in two hours in one program and in nine hours in another. In one program, a topic may be dealt with superficially, while in another it may be treated in some depth.

Here are some typical topics for retirement preparation programs:

Lifestyle planning.
Psychological adjustments.
Company and union benefits.
Financial planning.
Social Security.
Leisure time.
Interpersonal relations.
New careers.
Living arrangements.
Staying healthy.
Community services.

Use of Computer-Generated Personal Financial Reports

One of the most vexing concerns of many employees considering retirement is the long-term adequacy of their retirement income, since they realize they could live twenty or thirty years after they retire. Some firms, as part of a retirement preparation program are providing employees access to computer-generated personal financial analyses or comprehensive

---

[9] *Retirement Preparation,* p. 32.

TABLE 35–4
Corporate Goals for Retirement Preparation Programs, as Cited by Personnel Directors

	Frequency Selected by Personnel Directors (percent)
Improve relations with employees	91*
Reinforce morale/productivity	83
Fulfill social responsibilities	68
Enhance corporate image	53
Recruit and retain dependable employees	39
Induce early retirement among nonproductive employees	31
Protect funds in pension plans	29
Keep pace with competitors	22
Improve relations with unions	12
Comply with ERISA	8

* Many gave more than one goal.

Source: *Retirement Preparation: Growing Corporate Involvement,* p. 16.

and for retiree communications programs and the extent to which such programs are contributing to realizing corporate goals. His or her functions may include acquainting divisions with new developments and helping them to design, implement, and improve their retirement preparation and retiree communications programs.

Target Groups for Programs

Many companies face a backlog of employees when they begin to offer a retirement preparation program. Although an employer may invite all employees over age 50 or 55 to attend, the great majority of those accepted may be employees who have announced the date of their retirement or who are close to or past the average age of retirement in the company. When the backlog is reduced, all employees who have reached the eligibility age will be given a more equal opportunity to attend.

Employees generally are encouraged to have their spouses attend the program with them. The extent of spouse participation will vary, depending on the efforts made by the employer to encourage their attendance, the convenience of the time and location of the program, and the nature of the program.

TABLE 35–3
Developments in Retirement Planning Expected by *Fortune* 1,000 Personnel Directors (December 1979)

	Frequency (percent)
Companies will be more committed to retirement planning	92
More emphasis on retirement planning	87
Retirement planning will be started earlier in career	79

Source: *Retirement Preparation: Growing Corporate Involvement* (New York: Research & Forecasts, 1979), p. 21.

INDEPENDENT PLANNING BY EMPLOYEES

Employees apparently do relatively little advanced retirement planning of their own. This does not mean employees do not want to plan or are unaware of the need to plan. A survey of employees over age 40 from seven large companies found the following:[6]

> That 6 in 10 had made no plans for retirement and only 1 in 10 had made any definite plans.
>
> Of the employees, 70 percent said they wanted to attend a retirement counseling program; 15 percent said they did not want to; and 15 percent refused to answer.
>
> Over two thirds expect to run into money problems in retirement, while only one in four expects to have a health problem.
>
> Retirement preparation programs, they said, should be conducted in the early evening (56 percent), on weekends (13 percent), or late evening (7 percent). Only one in four (24 percent) said they should be conducted during the day, which coincided with work hours.

[6] Edmund W. Fitzpatrick, "An Industry Consortium Approach to Retirement Planning—New Program," *Aging and Work* 1, no. 3 (Summer 1978), pp. 184–88.

EXTENT OF PROGRAM USAGE

Generally, two factors are present before a company is likely to have its own retirement preparation program: (1) an "adequate" pension plan, and (2) enough employees retiring each year to justify a program. Consequently, in-house retirement preparation programs tend to be concentrated among large companies with good retirement benefits.

A survey of *Fortune* 1,000 companies in late 1979 found that two thirds of the companies responding either had a retirement preparation program or were "working on one."[7] A little more than one third had a program in place, and 85 percent of such programs had five or more topics. In a study conducted three years earlier, only one sixth of the large companies responding had a retirement preparation program in place, and only 48 percent of such programs had five or more topics.[8]

An organization may not have an in-house retirement preparation program but, instead, may make arrangements to send its employees to a program offered by an outside source, such as a community college. The extent that small, medium, and large organizations are using such outside programs is not known. However, the proliferation of outside sources suggests that the number of companies using them is growing.

CHARACTERISTICS OF PROGRAMS

Corporate Goals

Essentially, a retirement preparation program is a method of helping employees and their families plan for retirement. However, the main corporate goals of retirement preparation programs, according to personnel directors, are to improve employee relations, morale, and productivity (see Table 35–4).

Reflecting the strength of their commitment, a growing number of large corporations have created a new position of "manager of retirement and retiree relations." This person, who may report to a vice president, has corporate-wide responsibility for the quality of retirement preparation

---

[7] *Retirement Preparation: Growing Corporate Involvement* (New York: Research & Forecasts, 1980), p. 20.

[8] J. Roger O'Meara, *Retirement: Reward or Rejection?* (New York: The Conference Board, 1977), p. 37.

personal financial plans from outside sources. The types of analyses and reports available range from focused analyses, such as a comparison of an employee's plan annuity and distribution alternatives, to broad analyses, such as a long-term comprehensive personal financial plan.

Most of the reports include some amount of educational material. For example, a report may first provide a helpful general introduction to the principles of personal finance, investments, and related matters and then provide a relatively detailed analysis and projection of the employee's own financial situation, including the employee's pension and other retirement benefits.

While such financial reports can be very helpful to employees in terms of their peace of mind, helping them to identify and choose beneficial alternatives, and maintaining retirement financial independence, an employer needs to be cautious about recommending sources of such reports or otherwise implying an endorsement. There are questions of objectivity, quality, suitability, and other matters that need to be considered and resolved before a report should become associated with a company's retirement preparation program.

Who Conducts the Program

An organization's retirement preparation program may be conducted by (*a*) its own staff, (*b*) outside consultants, or (*c*) a combination of the two.

Large organizations generally prefer to use in-house staff to conduct their programs, though they may use outside experts in specific subject areas if they are not available within the organization. One major new "packaged" retirement preparation program is designed to be used without subject-matter experts; the expertise is built into the materials.

A not uncommon approach is for a firm to hire a consultant to serve as "program coordinator." This person generally has experience in organizing and presenting retirement preparation programs that rely on a speaker or resource person for each subject covered. The difficulty frequently encountered is finding knowledgeable, up-to-date experts who also are good communicators, will stick to the objectives of the program, and will be there as scheduled. Some firms hire a consultant to provide the materials and to personally conduct the complete program, except for the presentation and discussion of company benefits.

College- and university-based retirement preparation programs may draw upon experts from among their own faculties, which may include gerontologists, psychologists, legal and medical specialists, and others. Additionally, they may draw upon experts from the local community, much as the "program coordinator" does.

Number and Length of Sessions

The time devoted to a retirement preparation topic in a group program may vary from one hour to three hours or more. Two hours per topic probably is typical, except for the financial topic(s), which may be allocated more time. In general, the total length of a program in terms of hours usually is related to the number of topics covered.

Scheduling Sessions

Several formats for scheduling program sessions are being used. Some of the most common are discussed below.

One Session per Week. One two-hour session per week for six to eight weeks is most common. Typically, one topic is dealt with each session, except that financial planning might be allotted two or even three sessions.

Back-to-Back Topics. The one topic per week format is practical when there are large concentrations of employees and few commuting problems. If employees are at a number of locations in the city, topics may be presented in back-to-back sessions to reduce the number of meetings and the travel required. For example, two two-hour sessions may be combined to form a four-hour meeting, which may be held on Tuesdays and Thursdays for two weeks.

All-Day Programs. All-day programs of one, two, or three days may be used when employees are dispersed over a wide area and are brought in to attend a group program. Other companies simply prefer the full-day format over other formats.

In the case of dispersed employees, they and their spouses may be transported to a hotel, where the company will conduct the program. A company without dispersed employees may run its program either entirely on work time or on part work time and part personal time, such as on a Friday and a Saturday, or from 3:00 in the afternoon until 9:00 in the evening on two weekdays.

Inviting Employees

It generally is agreed that all employees of a given age within a region, plant, or division should be invited at the same time. Even a hint of selective invitations will generate suspicion regarding management's purpose in offering the program. Attendance should not be made compulsory. If employees don't wish to attend, it is better to learn why and to correct the problem. Surveys show that up to 85 percent of employees over age 40 want to attend such programs.[10]

In some cases, an initial reluctance exists among employees to attend, since they harbor concern that attendance could somehow jeopardize promotions and better job assignments. One way to combat these concerns is by giving much publicity to the program and its pilot presentations. Notices on bulletin boards, articles in company publications, and supportive statements by top management are helpful.

Some organizations enlist the aid of employees who enjoy much trust among their peers. These employees are encouraged to attend the pilot programs and to ask associates to join them. Also, publicizing the fact that specific supervisory and management personnel will attend the programs can help to dispel fears employees have about attending.

Employees are invited by notices on bulletin boards, articles in company publications, and by personal letters that go to the home. Letters to the home should be addressed to Mr. and Mrs. if the employee is married. In any case, the employee often is encouraged to bring any other person with whom he or she plans to retire. This is particularly important for single persons, who may retire (and share expenses) with a sister, brother, other relative, or friend. The chances are the single person will not bring another person, but much goodwill is generated by the sincere offer from the company. For the targeted employees (e.g., age 50 or 55 and over), a series of several invitational letters should be considered to ensure that a large percentage of these employees attend.

ESTABLISHING A PROGRAM

Basic Planning Questions

In establishing a retirement preparation program, a number of questions need to be answered:

1. What are the objectives of the program, and how will its success be measured?
2. Is top management committed to the program?

---

[10] Fitzpatrick, "An Industry Consortium's Approach to Retirement Planning," p. 187.

3. How much money can be devoted to the program? Over what time?
4. How many employees can be expected to attend the program? Who are they and where are they located? How many spouses will probably attend?
5. Are the company's retirement benefits adequate? Above average?
6. Are competitors offering retirement preparation programs? If so, what are the programs like?
7. What is the state of employee relations? Is there a problem that needs resolution before offering the program?
8. How concentrated or dispersed are the employees, and how will the program be made available to them?
9. Is the public relations value of the program important locally or nationally?
10. Is there a need to promote better understanding of company benefits, especially retirement benefits, among employees?

Program Design Considerations

The design of a retirement preparation program determines its effectiveness. There are four considerations.

1. In view of company characteristics, objectives, and the distribution of employees, what type of program or programs are feasible and will achieve the objectives? What trade-offs are necessary? What will be the measures of success?

2. Who should conduct the program? Central or division staffs? Consultants? Should there be a "traveling team" that conducts the program? Should employees be sent to programs conducted by community colleges or other organizations? Are subject-matter experts available (assuming they are needed) at proposed program locations?

3. Should the company purchase a commercially available package or develop its own? If purchased, should it be customized and by how much? (The development of professional quality retirement counseling materials involves a commitment of time, money, and specialized expertise that most companies do not have, or which is often more profitably focused on the company's main business. Consequently, the tendency is for companies to purchase packaged programs and then to customize them.)

4. What should be the nature of program follow-up activities? Should there be periodic updates through written communications and through refresher meetings? Should there be encouragement for the formation of employee planning or investment clubs? What about postretirement communications? Should there be a formal postretirement program?

Selecting Program Materials

Materials employed in a retirement counseling program should be designed to maximize the probability of success. Here are some aspects to consider:

1. Are the materials compatible with company philosophy and with the basic values of the employees who will attend the program?

2. Do the materials support the specific objectives for the program in each area? The personal finances area? Health area? Other areas?

3. Is the content presented efficiently and at the appropriate level, given the target employees? Or is it shallow and vague with too much jargon, or too technical?

4. What is the visual impact of the materials? Impressive in appearance to imply importance? Easy to read and use? Is the print large enough?

5. With regard to audiovisual materials, are the visuals (photographs and artwork) pleasant, and do the people look somewhat younger than the target employees (this is important)? Is the narrator's style, tone, and pronunciation suitable for the employees? How easily can the audiovisual materials be used? What equipment is required? Who will set up and operate it?

6. Are skill-building exercises provided for employees? Checklists for planning? Games, simulations, small group exercises, individual exercises, other aids? Are they merely entertaining or do they have a clearly identifiable objective?

7. How is the seminar or workshop designed? What will participants actually *do* in it—be active or passive? Is there a balance among lectures, audiovisual materials, small group activities, group discussion, and individual work? What qualifications or training are required of the seminar/workshop leaders?

Conducting the Pilot Program

An important objective of a pilot program is to give other people in the organization an opportunity to make recommendations and take part in making the final decision on the program. A pilot program generally will become the final program because the organization already has tooled up to present it and has gained experience in doing so. If a manager skips the pilot and makes the final decision independently, those who did not have an opportunity to make recommendations could be a source of continuing criticism, which ultimately dooms the program.

Even though an organization may plan to have its own staff regularly conduct its retirement counseling programs, it may decide to involve an experienced outside consultant to co-conduct the pilot and thereby maximize the likelihood that the pilot will be successful.

The location of the pilot is important. It should be convenient to those expected to attend. Room size and shape must be appropriate for the number attending and for the desired seating arrangements; effective room temperature control is necessary; dimming the lights and covering the windows must be possible if audiovisual presentations are to be used; and it should be free from outside noises; and have adequate electrical outlets. It may be important to have eating and sleeping accommodations close by.

Prior to conducting the pilot, there should be a detailed plan for its evaluation, complete with forms and procedures for how the data will be captured and analyzed and how the results will be used. Care must be exercised in how and when data are obtained from employees participating in the pilot program. Employees need to wear the "participant" hat and not the "evaluator" hat. In the program, they must concentrate on being a participant—and on their retirement concerns, needs, and objectives, or the evaluation will not have validity.

Postretirement Programs

Postretirement programs also are increasing in number and variety. Generally, they are aimed at updating former employees on benefits changes that may affect them, keeping them informed about company activities, and providing other information that may be of interest or help. A company may accomplish this through a special newsletter to retirees or by sending retirees the regular employee publication, which may include a section about and for retirees. Some companies hold annual affairs in large cities to which all retirees in the area are invited. Others send a person on tour from area to area to hold "update" meetings with groups of retirees. And some companies purchase subscriptions for all their retirees to a retirement-oriented newsletter or magazine.

BENEFITS OF RETIREMENT PREPARATION PROGRAMS

Benefits for the Employee

A well-designed retirement preparation program can have important benefits for employees and their spouses. Here are some of the major ones:[11]

1. Recognition that they have the responsibility for ensuring their own financial security and happiness in retirement (i.e., the company and union may help, but the ultimate responsibility is the employee's).
2. Better realization of the degree of control and options they have regarding future finances, health, personal relationships, and the like.
3. Knowing when retirement is financially possible for them—or what they must do to make it so.
4. Opportunity to articulate and discuss fears they and others may harbor about retirement.
5. Opportunity to specifically define one or more lifestyles they would find enjoyable and affordable, so they can look forward to concrete and positive alternatives.
6. Identification of problems that could arise during their own retirement, which they have an opportunity to solve before retirement.

Benefits for the Employer

The employer that provides an effective retirement preparation program for employees also benefits. In fact, the employer may find the returns are considerably greater than the investment. Here are the major benefits the employer may enjoy:[12]

1. General performance levels of employees may improve; when employees believe their employer cares about them, they in return care more about the quality of their work.
2. The productivity of specific employees may improve, since they

---

[11] Edmund W. Fitzpatrick, "Retirement Counseling: A Necessity for the 1980's," *Textbook for Employee Benefit Plan Trustees, Administrators, and Advisors,* Proceedings of the 1979 Annual Educational Conference, vol. 21 (Brookfield, Wis.: International Foundation of Employee Benefit Plans, 1980), pp. 295–301.

[12] Ibid.

will be able to make an informed retirement decision, rather than be afflicted by indecision and perhaps hang on beyond the time when they wish to retire.

3. Employees gain a better appreciation of the value of the employee benefits provided.
4. Employers can fulfill a social responsibility to loyal employees who helped the company prosper over the years.
5. It can help the employer maintain a leadership role in the employee benefits area.
6. It can result in positive feedback from retirees to present employees.
7. It can help to build and maintain a positive image in the community.

Postretirement Benefits

While the "preretirement" benefits of retirement preparation programs seem clear, the "postretirement" benefits require further research. Longitudinal studies examining the postretirement benefits either have been flawed or have pointed to weaknesses in the retirement preparation programs that were used. One study concluded that ". . . no retirement preparation program that involves a small, one-shot investment in time and effort is likely to have a long-term effect on personal adjustment and life satisfaction."[13] This argues for intensive and comprehensive programs, with periodic refreshers or updates and postretirement communications.

Some of the most intensive and comprehensive retirement preparation programs are very new. When employees who have attended these programs reach retirement, the postretirement effects may be significant in several areas, including the area of retirement finances.

PROGRAM EVALUATION

In general, retirement preparation programs are not being subjected to formal evaluations based on measurable objectives. Most rely upon asking participants if they like the speakers, the content, the method of conducting, and so on. These findings are important—but concern the

[13] Francis D. Glamser, "The Impact of Preretirement Programs on the Retirement Experience," *Journal of Gerontology* 36, no. 2 (March 1981), p. 249.

process not the results. Employees typically are so grateful for retirement preparation programs that almost any program, regardless of quality, will be given a high rating using such an evaluation approach.

One hindrance to the use of more scientific evaluation procedures is the newness of the programs and the fact they are still evolving. It is not practical to invest in longitudinal studies, which may involve years, before an organization is satisfied that it has arrived at the "best" feasible program and has standardized the use of it.

Most existing longitudinal studies are seriously flawed, so caution must be exercised in considering their conclusions.[14] However, as more organizations get their programs in place and "fine-tune" them, there are likely to be a growing number of useful longitudinal studies based on experimental design methodology.

Another appropriate evaluation methodology is based on defining measurable human performance objectives.[15] This assumes that the basic rationale for a retirement preparation program is to cause people to plan and thereby prevent certain problems or unfulfilled expectations when they retire. If human performance objectives are prepared for each topic or module in the program, effectiveness can be determined by measuring the degree to which participants achieve those objectives at the conclusion of the program. A human performance objective, as used in this approach, needs to be both measurable and observable—as an example, "the participant will be able to identify his tax bracket and compute aftertax earnings from a given investment." "Pre-post" assessments may be used to determine not only achievement but also the "learning gain" produced by the program.

The measurable objectives evaluation approach makes possible evaluation/revision cycles capable of producing successively more powerful versions of a module or complete program. A program development activity employing this evaluation approach can produce a statistically validated program—one that can be expected to produce similar results each time it is used.

Figure 35–1 illustrates the use of this approach for evaluating a retirement financial planning workshop in which the human performance objectives took the form of 14 measurable and observable financial planning tasks. The effectiveness of the workshop was determined by (*a*) the per-

---

[14] Glamser, *The Impact of Preretirement Programs,* pp. 244–50.

[15] Edmund W. Fitzpatrick, "Evaluating a New Retirement Planning Program—Results with Hourly Workers." *Aging and Work,* Spring 1979, (Washington, D.C.: National Council on the Aging), pp. 87–94.

FIGURE 35–1
Short-Range Effect of Personal Financial Planning Module: Change in Percentage of White-Collar Clerical Employees Taking Specified Financial Planning Actions as a Result of Workshop

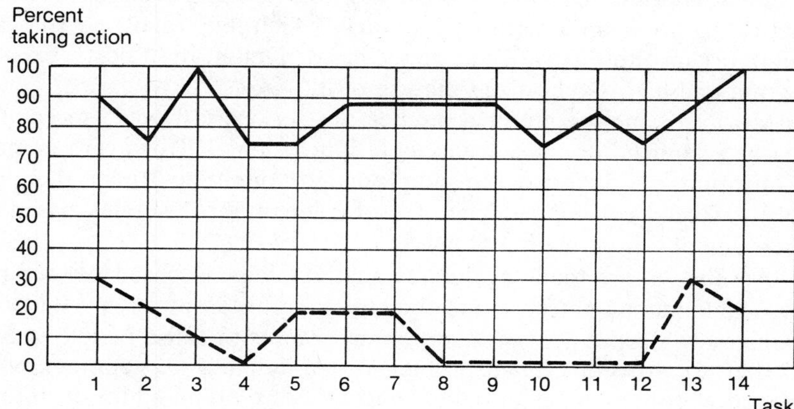

—Percent who had taken action prior to work shop.

—Percent who had taken action by end of work shop.

Financial Planning Tasks

1. Gathered and listed your important financial papers.
2. Discussed retirement finances in detail with your spouse or someone else.
3. Developed an estimate of your retirement expenses.
4. Developed a realistic, fact-based estimate of your future retirement income.
5. Determined what survivor's benefits you or your spouse (or other person) would get if either one of you died.
6. Figured the approximate amount of the nest egg you will have or will need at the time of your retirement.
7. Identified your own major financial assets and projected how they will grow in value between now and retirement.
8. Determined how much purchasing power your pension will lose in your retirement if inflation continues.
9. Figured how much money you would need in a fund to protect your pension from the effects of inflation.
10. Drawn your own Retirement Income Profile.
11. Obtained useful information for you to get more out of your savings and investments.
12. Used basic measures (e.g., growth versus income, risk versus return) in evaluating savings and investment alternatives.
13. Selected one or more investments for further investigation.
14. Made a plan to improve your own approach to saving and investing.

Source: Edmund W. Fitzpatrick, *Administrator's Guide: A Component of the Industry Consortium Retirement Planning Program* (Washington, D.C.: NCOA, 1980), p. 12.

cent of the participants who actually performed each of the tasks by the end of the workshop, and (*b*) the *gain* in the percent performing each task, based on a comparison of preworkshop achievement with post-workshop achievement.

A retirement preparation program is a vehicle for communicating information and influencing human behavior. Whether its objectives are achieved depends on the skill with which the vehicle is used. A person lacking musical talent and training may blow sour notes on a trumpet, but it is the fault of the player, not the horn. As with retirement preparation programs, the quality of the output depends upon the quality of the input. The talent and monetary and physical resources being devoted to these programs are improving, compared to past years, and we can expect improved results.

CONCLUSION

Trends in our society suggest that retirement preparation programs will continue to grow. Recent and expected future federal legislation affecting Social Security and private plans may make retirement planning decisions increasingly more complex for employees who may wish to retire early. Retirement preparation programs can communicate this need to employees and identify fruitful savings and investment alternatives.

A realization exists that a satisfying retirement depends on more than financial security. ''Free time'' can be a blessing or a curse, depending on what is done with it. Retirement preparation programs, by helping individuals and couples explore aspects of life that may have been long ignored, can open new doors to life enrichment and happiness in the later years. Perhaps the greatest ultimate impact of these programs will be in these more personal areas. And this is important to a society with a large older-person population.[16]

---

[16] For an annotated bibliography on retirement planning, see John N. Migliaccio and Peter C. Cairo, ''Preparation for Retirement: A Selective Bibliography, 1974–1980,'' *Aging and Work* 4, no. 1 (Winter 1980), pp. 31–33.

CHAPTER 36

ACCOUNTING AND REPORTING BY EMPLOYEE BENEFIT PLANS

Bradley J. Allen

INTRODUCTION

Since the enactment of Employee Retirement Income Security Act of 1974 (ERISA), there has been a more pronounced focus on plan sponsors' financial management of assets held in trust for the benefit of plan participants. As a result, the role of plan financial statements has increased in importance, causing the Financial Accounting Standards Board (FASB) to address the needs of the users of the plan financial statements and the objectives of those statements.

The most important objective of the plan financial statements is to assist the user in assessing the ability of the plan to pay benefits when due. Who is the user? Obviously, the plan is for the benefit of the participants and the ability of the plan to pay benefits when due is of critical importance to the participant. However, "the 'typical' plan participant would be uninterested in or unable to properly assimilate the information presented in plan financial statements and thus would be confused and possibly misled."[1] The FASB concluded that, even if some participants might need to be educated regarding the plan financial statements, those financial statements should nonetheless focus on their needs. Thus, the pri-

[1] Statement of Financial Accounting Standards No. 35, Paragraph 48.

mary users are deemed to be the participants, or those who advise or represent them.

This chapter will explain the financial reporting and accounting requirements of employee benefit plans. Employers' accounting for these plans are discussed in Chapter 37.

FINANCIAL STATEMENT REQUIREMENTS

ERISA requires many different reports be prepared and filed with the Internal Revenue Service (IRS) and furnished to participants, beneficiaries, the Department of Labor (DOL) and others. ERISA requires that most plans file an annual report with the IRS, which provides a copy to the DOL.

While it is ERISA that requires the plans to file an annual report, IRS and DOL regulations specify the filing requirements for plan financial statements. Principally, the requirements are that each plan must file an annual report containing IRS Form 5500 plus certain attachments. The attachments include, among other things, financial statements, notes thereto, supporting schedules, and an accountant's report. Pursuant to DOL regulations, the following plans are not required to file financial statements:

- Small plans (fewer than 100 participants at the beginning of the plan year).
- Insured plans funded exclusively through allocated insurance contracts and whose benefits are fully guaranteed by the insurance carrier.
- Unfunded plans.

DOL regulations generally provide that a plan required to file an annual report has the option of either reporting the information prescribed by "Section 103 of the Act, or in accordance with a limited exemption or alternative method of compliance (LEAM)."[2] The LEAM permits plans to fulfill annual reporting requirements by filing an annual report containing IRS Form 5500 (including required schedules), financial statements and notes, separate financial schedules, and an accountant's report. Since the rules for filing under the LEAM are more definitive, most plans now elect that method. In contrast to plans filing under the Act, the LEAM does not require the financial statements to be prepared in accordance

[2] ERISA, Section 2520.103–1.

with generally accepted accounting principles (GAAP). However, the LEAM regulations require disclosure of variations from GAAP.

Prior to 1980, there were no published guidelines on the application of GAAP to employee benefit plans. Consequently, there was great diversity in the accounting principles adopted and the methods of disclosure used in plan financial statements.

For example, where one plan may have reported its assets at their cost basis, another plan may have adjusted the cost basis of the assets to reflect market appreciation or depreciation.

In March, 1980 the FASB issued Statement of Financial Accounting Standards (SFAS) No. 35, *Accounting and Reporting by Defined Benefit Pension Plans*. Since SFAS No. 35 only addressed defined benefit plans, the American Institute of Certified Public Accountants (AICPA), when they issued their *Audit and Accounting Guide: Audits of Employee Benefit Plans* (the Guide) in 1983, incorporated accounting and reporting guidelines for defined contribution and health and welfare plans.

The remainder of this section is devoted to a discussion of the accounting records needed by and the generally accepted accounting principles applicable to defined benefit, defined contribution, and health and welfare employee benefit plans.

ACCOUNTING RECORDS

As with any entity, certain records are necessary in order to produce information necessary for effective management of the entity and for preparing financial statements of the entity. Records for employee benefit plans are no exception, but usually are maintained at a number of locations, e.g., the employer, trustee, administrator, etc. Depending on the plan, typical records include (but are not limited to):

- Investment asset records—Such records should include a portfolio listing of all investments and investment transactions.
- Participant records—Demographic records are needed to determine eligibility for participation and benefit payments.
- Contribution records—Records of contributions received and due are particularly important for plans having more than one contributor.
- Claim records—Records of claims for health and welfare plans are not only important for establishing claims history, but also for determining when benefit limits have been reached.

- Distribution records—These records, including entitlement, commencement data, forfeitures, terminations, etc. are necessary to support all distributions from the plan.
- Separate participants' accounts—Defined contribution plans require separate accounts to be maintained for each participant reflecting his or her share of the net assets of the plan.

EMPLOYEE BENEFIT PLAN FINANCIAL STATEMENTS

Introduction

The general requirements for financial statements prescribed by the FASB and AICPA for defined benefit, defined contribution, and health and welfare plans are similar in many aspects. This section of the chapter dealing with plan financial statements will be organized into a discussion of the general requirements equally applicable to all types of plans followed by some of the particular requirements applicable to the specific type of plan. Sample financial statements of a defined benefit pension plan are included in the Appendix.

Overview of General Requirements

SFAS No. 35 requires that every plan issuing financial statements is to present a statement of net assets available for plan benefits as of the end of the plan year, a statement of changes in net assets for the year then ended and the related notes to the financial statements.

Plans filing under ERISA must present the financial statements in comparative form, i.e., statements for the current year must be presented alongside statements for the previous year. Plans filing under the LEAM may present a statement of net assets available for plan benefits for two years while presenting the statement of changes in net assets available for plan benefits for one year.

The financial statements must also be presented using the accrual basis of accounting whereby financial recognition is given to an event when it occurs, regardless of whether cash was paid or received. The accrual basis also contemplates that, generally, purchases and sales of securities must be recognized on a "trade-date" basis as opposed to a "settlement-date" basis. Under ERISA, the cash basis method is acceptable.

Statement of Net Assets Available for Plan Benefits

The statement of net assets available for plan benefits shall present information regarding net assets in such reasonable detail as is necessary to identify the plan's resources available to pay plan benefits.

Plan resources typically include investments, and contributions receivable cash and operating assets, less any liabilities of the plan.

Investments

Since investments are usually a pension plan's largest asset, their valuation is particularly important. All plan investments except contracts with insurance companies, which are discussed below, are required to be stated at fair value as of the date of the financial statements.

Determining Fair Value

The fair value of an investment is the amount a pension plan could realistically expect to receive in a transaction between a willing buyer and a willing seller. Fair value is often difficult to determine because of the nature of the investment. For securities traded on an active market, the determination is relatively easy—fair value is the quoted market price. For securities for which there is no quoted market price, the determination of fair value becomes more difficult. Securities of closely held companies or investments in real estate generally will not have an active market. In these cases, market price must be determined using alternative means, such as discounted cash flow or valuations performed by independent experts.

Contracts with Insurance Companies

Contracts with insurance companies must be presented in the same manner required by ERISA. The presentation will generally depend on whether the payment to the insurance company is allocated to purchase insurance or annuities for the individual participants or whether the payments are accumulated in an unallocated fund to be used to pay retirement benefits. These are referred to as ''allocated'' and ''unallocated'' arrangements, respectively.

Allocated funding arrangements include contracts in which the insurer has a legally enforceable obligation to make the benefit payments. The obligations of the plan have been removed to the insurer and the investment in the allocated insurance contract should be excluded from plan assets. Conversely, unallocated funding instruments apply to any arrangement under which contributions are held in an undivided fund until they are used to make retirement benefits.

Unallocated funds are, therefore, included in plan assets. Examples of allocated contracts include individual insurance or annuity contracts, group permanent insurance contracts or conventional deferred group annuity contracts. Unallocated arrangements include deposit administration contracts and immediate participation guarantee contracts.

With respect to determining the value of the insurance contracts, generally accepted accounting principles require that the contracts be measured in the same manner as required by ERISA. The instructions to Form 5500 call for investments in separate accounts to be carried at fair value, but permit other insurance contracts to be valued at either fair value or amounts determined by the insurance company. Contract value is almost universally used to value insurance contracts because insurance companies generally do not report fair value.

Commingled and Master Trust Funds

Common or commingled trust funds, pooled separate accounts of insurance companies, and master trust funds generally contain the assets of two or more plans that are pooled for investment purposes. Common or commingled funds and insurance company pooled separate accounts generally contain plans sponsored by two or more employers. Master trusts hold the assets of plans sponsored by a single employer or by members of a controlled group. In a common or commingled fund or pooled separate account, the plan generally requires units of participation in the fund. The value of these investments is based on the unit value of the funds, but must be stated at fair value.

The accounting and reporting requirements for master trusts present certain additional considerations. Plans generally have two options as to how they account for such investments:

- A plan may present its interest in the Master Trust as one line, i.e., "Investment in master trust," or
- A plan may present its allocable share of each master trust line item.

While either method is acceptable under GAAP, the "one-line" method is required by IRS Form 5500. Plans that use the one-line method should also disclose their percentage interest in the master trust. Summarized financial information of the master trust should be presented in a footnote along with the information mentioned above regarding the method of determining fair value and general types of investments.

Disclosure

Disclosure must be provided, usually in the footnotes, of whether fair value was measured using quoted market prices in an active market, or otherwise determined. Contracts with insurance companies, as noted, are presented in the same manner required by ERISA. The method of valuation of insurance contracts must be disclosed. Detail of the investments must be provided either on the face of the statement of net assets available for plan benefits or in a footnote. Investments must be segregated, where material, by general types, such as corporate stocks, bonds, etc. In addition, individual investments representing 5 percent or more of net assets available for plan benefits must be separately disclosed.

Receivables

Receivables must be stated separately, if material, for the following:

- Employer contributions.
- Participant contributions.
- Amounts due from brokers for securities sold.
- Accrued interest and dividends.
- Other.

Contributions receivable may only include amounts due as of the reporting date. Participant contributions receivable, generally, are those amounts withheld from participants' pay and not yet remitted to the plan. Employer contributions can be evidenced by the following:

1. A legal or contractual obligation.
2. A formal commitment evidenced by:
   a. A resolution by the employer's governing body.
   b. A consistent pattern of making payments after the plan's year-end pursuant to an established funding policy.
   c. A deduction for federal income taxes by the employer.
   d. The employer's recognition of a liability (however, recognition of a liability by the employer in and of itself may not be sufficient to justify recording a receivable).

Advance employer contributions that relate to future years but are made to obtain a current tax deduction should be deferred on the plan's financial statements and described in a footnote. Conversely, if a deficiency in the plan's funding standard account exists at year-end, consideration should be given to establishing a receivable from the employer.

All of the foregoing should be tempered by the need to establish an appropriate allowance for estimated uncollectible receivables and, if material, disclose such allowance. For example, assume an employer has a contractual obligation to make a contribution to the plan. If the employer is a financially troubled company there may be some uncertainty that the full amount of the contribution will be received. In this situation, the amount of the contribution receivable should be reduced by the amount estimated to be uncollectible and this fact should be disclosed in the footnotes.

Other Assets

Typically, most plans do not have significant assets other than investments and contributions receivable. However, other types of assets that may exist are residual cash that has not yet been invested and operating assets, such as a building or equipment.

Cash and cash equivalents are recorded at face value, but should be segregated between interest-bearing and noninterest-bearing deposits.

GAAP requires that operating assets be recorded at cost less depreciation and amortization. ERISA requires these assets be recorded at fair value. This should rarely present a significant difference.

Liabilities

Liabilities, e.g., for the purchase of investments, should be stated at the amount owed by the plan.

Statement of Changes in Net Assets Available for Plan Benefits

The effects of significant changes in net assets available for plan benefits must be disclosed. At a minimum, this should include:

- The net appreciation or depreciation in fair value for each significant class of investment, segregated between investments whose fair values have been measured by quoted market prices and those whose fair values have been otherwise determined. The net appreciation or depreciation includes realized gains or losses from sales of investments and unrealized gains or losses from market appreciation or depreciation. Separate disclosure of realized gains or losses is not required by GAAP, but is required for IRS Form 5500.

- Investment income, exclusive of amount included in net appreciation of investments.
- Contributions from employer(s), participants and others.
- Benefits paid to participants.
- Payments to insurance companies to purchase contracts that are excluded from plan assets.
- Administrative expenses.

Additional Financial Statement Disclosures

Disclosure of the plan's accounting policies should include a description of the methods and significant assumptions used to determine the fair value of investments and the reported value of contracts with insurance companies. The accounting policy footnote should also disclose any variances from GAAP. This could be an important disclosure since the LEAM does not require plans to follow GAAP. Plans deciding only to comply with the LEAM may have significant variations from GAAP.

The notes to financial statements shall include the following additional information:

1. Description of the plan.
   a. A brief, general description of the plan agreement, including, but not limited to, vesting, benefit, and allocation provisions. Reference to a plan agreement or a description thereof may be made in lieu of this disclosure provided that the information is otherwise published and made available.
   b. A description of significant plan amendments adopted during the year.
   c. A brief general description of (1) the priority order of participants' claims to the assets of the plan upon plan termination and (2) benefits guaranteed by the Pension Benefit Guaranty Corporation (PBGC).
2. Funding Policy:
   a. A description of the funding policy and any changes in the funding policy during the year.
   b. A description, in general terms and in layman's language, of how contributions are determined.
   c. For contributory plans, the method of determining participants' contributions.
   d. For plans subject to ERISA, whether or not the minimum funding requirements have been met.
   e. The amount of significant administrative costs borne by the employer, if any.

3. The policy regarding the purchase of contracts with insurance companies that are excluded from plan assets.
4. The tax status of the plan if a favorable determination letter has not been obtained is required by GAAP. DOL regulations require disclosure of whether or not a tax ruling or determination letter has been obtained.
5. Significant real estate or other transactions in which the plan and any of the following parties participated:
   a. Sponsor
   b. Employer(s)
   c. Employee organizations
6. Unusual or infrequent events or transactions occurring before issuance of the financial statements.

Supplemental Schedules

In addition to the requirements of SFAS No. 35 and the Guide, ERISA and DOL regulations specify separate schedules of:

- Investment assets (one schedule of assets held at the plan year-end and another showing plan assets acquired or disposed of during the plan year) showing both cost and fair value or sales proceeds.
- Transactions with parties in interest.
- Loans on fixed income obligations in default or uncollectible.
- Leases in default or uncollectible.
- Reportable transactions.

DEFINED BENEFIT PLANS

A defined benefit plan is one that promises to pay participants' benefits that are determinable based on such factors as age, years of service, and compensation.

In addition to the general financial statement requirements, defined benefit plans must also disclose information regarding the actuarial present value of accumulated plan benefits (PVAB) as of either the beginning or end of the plan year and changes in the PVAB from year-to-year.

It is important to understand that the PVAB will generally not be the same amount as the actuarially determined liability pursuant to the cost method in the plan. This actuarial liability represents the present value of the estimated benefits that will be payable to participants upon retirement. The PVAB represents only those benefits that have accumulated as of a specific date as opposed to estimated benefits at retirement. There is no requirement that the assumptions used to calculate the PVAB (e.g. discount rates, investment rates, etc.) be the same as for the actuarial liability. Consequently, significant differences could exist.

Statement of Accumulated Plan Benefits

Information regarding the PVAB may be presented in the financial statements (on the same page as the statement of net assets available for plan benefits or as a separate statement) or in the footnotes, and must be segmented into the following categories:

Vested benefits of participants currently receiving benefits (including benefits due and payable as of the benefit information date).

Other vested benefits.

Nonvested benefits.

A description of the method and significant assumptions (for example, assumed rate of return, inflation rates, and retirement ages) used to determine the PVAB must be disclosed in the footnotes. The benefit information should exclude benefits to be paid by insurance companies pursuant to contracts that are excluded from plan assets.

Note that SFAS No. 35 requires a statement of net assets available for plan benefits only as of the end of the plan year. However, when the accumulated benefit information is presented as of the beginning of the plan year, then a statement of net assets available for plan benefits must be included as of the preceding plan year end. The reason is to give the reader the ability to make a comparison between plan assets available to pay benefits with the related accumulated benefits as of the same date. If the plan assets are as of the end of the year and the benefit information is as of the beginning of the year such comparability does not exist. By including plan assets as of the preceding year end, there is now comparability with the beginning of year benefit information. For plans complying with ERISA, this will not pose any problems because, as mentioned, ERISA requires comparative financial statements.

Statement of Changes in Accumulated Plan Benefits

The information regarding changes in the PVAB from the preceding to the current benefit information dates can be presented as a separate financial statement or in the footnotes, and either in a narrative or reconciliation format. The effects of any changes in accumulated plan benefits should be accounted for in the year of the change, not by restating amounts previously reported.

If significant, either individually or in the aggregate, the effects of certain factors affecting the change in the PVAB from the preceding to the current benefit information dates shall be identified. Minimum disclosure shall include the following:

Plan amendments.

Changes in the nature of the plan (for example, a plan spin-off or merger).

Changes in actuarial assumptions.

Any significant changes in methods or assumptions shall be described in the footnotes.

The significant effects of other factors may also be identified, including, for example, benefits accumulated (including actuarial gains or losses), the increase (for interest) as a result of the decrease in the discount period, benefits paid, etc.

If the minimum required information is presented in other than a reconciliation format, the PVAB as of the preceding benefit information date shall also be presented.

DEFINED CONTRIBUTION PLANS

A defined contribution plan is one that provides individual accounts for each participant's benefits based on amounts contributed to the participants' accounts, investment experience and, if applicable, forfeitures allocated to the account.

The additional key financial statement issue to address is the allocation of the plan assets to the participants' accounts. Required financial statement disclosures include:

- Amount of unallocated assets.
- The basis used to allocate asset values to participants' accounts when that basis differs from the one used to record assets in the financial statements.
- Amount of net assets and changes in net assets allocated to separate investment funds, if the plan provides for separate investment programs.
- The number of units of participation and net asset value per unit, if applicable.

- Amounts allocated to participants who have withdrawn from the plan.

Some defined contribution plans, such as employee stock-purchase plans, are required to register and report to the Securities and Exchange Commission (SEC). The form and content of the financial statements that must be filed with the SEC are prescribed in Regulation S-X.

The general requirements are included in Articles 1, 2, 3, and 4 of the Regulation S-X. Article 6A of Regulation S-X includes the specific requirements applicable to employee stock purchase, savings, and similar plans.

Article 6A requires that plans present their net assets available for plan benefits in statements of financial condition for the two most recent years. Items to be disclosed in this statement include:

Plan Assets:

1. Investments in securities of participating employer(s), stated separately for each employer.
2. Investments in securities of unaffiliated issuers, segregated between U.S. Government obligations, and other. Other securities must be segregated between marketable securities and other.
3. Investments other than securities.
4. Dividends and interest receivable.
5. Cash.
6. Other assets, stating separately amounts due from participating employers, directors, officers or principal shareholders, trustees, or managers of the plan, and other.

Liabilities and Plan Equity:

7. Liabilities, stating separately any payables to employers, employees, and other.
8. Reserves and other credits.
9. Plan equity (this is equivalent to the net assets available for plan benefits).

In addition, statements of income and changes in plan equity are required for the three most recent years. These statements must include:

1. Net investment income, stating separately:
   a. Income, stating separately cash dividends, interest and other. Income from investments in or indebtedness of participating employers shall be segregated.

  b. Expenses.
  c. Net investment income.
2. Realized gain or loss on investments, stating separately gains or losses from investments in securities of participating employer(s), other investments in securities and other investments.
3. Unrealized appreciation or depreciation of investments. In addition, in a footnote, the unrealized appreciation or depreciation as of the beginning and end of the period must be disclosed.
4. Contributions and deposits, separated between employer(s) and employees.
5. Withdrawals, lapses, and forfeitures, stating separately the balances of the employees' accounts, the amounts disbursed in settlement of the accounts, and the disposition of the remaining balance.
6. Plan equity at the beginning of the period and plan equity at the end of the period.

In addition, Article 6A requires certain schedules to be filed if the information is not readily apparent from the financial statements. These are:

Schedule I:	Investments.
Schedule II:	Allocation of plan assets and liabilities to investment programs.
Schedule III:	Allocation of plan income and changes in plan equity to investment programs.

The form and content of these schedules are specified in Rule 6A–05.

HEALTH AND WELFARE PLANS

Employee health and welfare plans are those plans providing benefits such as medical, dental, scholarship, etc. to employees of a single employer or group of employers. Such benefits may be provided by the plan or transferred to an insurance company. Whether a premium paid to an insurance company represents a deposit (i.e. an investment) or a transfer of risk will depend upon the exact nature of the contract.

Payment of a premium where the risk is transferred to the insurance company represents a reduction in the net assets of the plan. Premiums paid that represent deposits should be reflected as plan assets until such time as the deposit will be refunded or applied against claims.

In an insured plan, claims reported, and incurred but not reported will be paid by the insurance company. Such claims should not appear in the plan's financial statements. Self-insured plans should report those amounts. The footnotes should describe the significant assumptions and changes in assumptions used to determine such liabilities.

Certain group insurance contracts provide for experience rating adjustments that could result in a refund (premiums exceed claims) or deficit (claims exceed premiums). If the amount of a refund can be reasonably estimated, then a receivable should be recorded. If the amount of a deficit can be reasonably estimated and if it will be applied against future premiums, then a payable should be recorded. If a payable for a deficit is not recorded because one of the two conditions has not been met, disclosure should be made.

Some plans provide for payment of insurance benefits for a period of time subsequent to the financial statement date for participants who have accumulated a certain number of eligibility credits. Such credits will permit payment of benefits during times of unemployment. Such credits represent a liability of the plan as they have arisen from prior employee service. The liability should be calculated as follows:

- Insured plans—current insurance premium rates should be applied to the accumulated credits.
- Self-insured plans—the average cost per person of the benefits should be applied to the accumulated credits.

APPENDIX TO CHAPTER 36

SAMPLE COMPANY
PENSION PLAN

Statements of Net Assets Available for Plan Benefits and of Accumulated Plan Benefits

December 31, 19X2 and 19X1

Net assets available for plan benefits	*19X2*	*19X1*
Any Insurance Company		
Immediate participation guarantee contract, at contract value	$2,278,000	$1,934,000
U.S. Government Securities, at fair value	250,000	150,000
Employer contribution receivable	41,000	141,000
Total net assets available for plan benefits	$2,569,000	$2,225,000

Accumulated Plan Benefits	*January 1, 19X2*
Actuarial present value of accumulated plan benefits:	
Vested benefits:	
Participants currently receiving payments	$1,980,000
Other participants	177,000
	2,157,000
Nonvested benefits	264,000
Total actuarial present value of accumulated plan benefits	$2,421,000

Statement of Changes in Net Assets Available for Plan Benefits

For the Years Ended December 31, 19X2 and 19X1

	19X2	*19X1*
Additions:		
Contributions from employer	$ 183,000	$ 141,000
Net appreciation of U.S. Government Securities	20,000	10,000
Interest income	250,000	201,000
	453,000	352,000
Deductions:		
Benefits paid	101,000	80,000
Administrative expenses	8,000	8,000
	109,000	88,000
Net additions	344,000	264,000
Net assets available for plan benefits, beginning of year	2,225,000	1,961,000
Net assets available for plan benefits, end of year	$2,569,000	$2,225,000

NOTES TO FINANCIAL STATEMENTS

General Description of the Plan

The Sample Company Pension Plan (Plan) is a noncontributory defined benefit plan which covers all employees of Sample Company who have at least one year of service. Participants should refer to the Plan agreement for more complete information regarding benefit, vesting, and termination provisions.

Summary of Significant Accounting Policies

The underlying assets of the Immediate Participation Guarantee Contract (Contract) are invested in the unallocated general assets of an insurance company. The Contract is valued at fair value as determined by the insurance company. The Contract provides, among other matters, that the investment account is to be credited with the contributions received during the contract period plus its share of the insurance company's actual investment income. Annuities purchased in prior years to provide benefits are excluded from Plan assets.

Sample Company makes contributions, as are necessary, on an actuarial basis, to provide the Plan with assets sufficient to meet the benefits to be paid to Plan members. Contributions by Sample Company are designed to fund the Plan's normal cost on a current basis and to amortize the Plan's prior service cost (plus interest) over a period of twenty years. For the years ended December 31, 19X2 and 19X1, Sample Company has met the minimum funding requirements.

While Sample Company has not expressed any intent to discontinue its contributions, it is free to do so at any time, subject to penalties set forth in the Employee Retirement Income Security Act of 1974 (ERISA). In the event such discontinuance should result in the termination of the Plan, its net assets generally will not be available on a pro rata basis to provide a particular participant's benefits. Whether a particular participant's accumulated Plan benefits will be paid depends on both the priority of those benefits and the level of benefits guaranteed by the Pension Benefit Guarantee Corporation (PBGC) at that time. Some benefits may be fully or partially provided for by the then existing assets and the PBGC guaranty while other benefits may not be provided for at all.

Significant Actuarial Information

Accumulated plan benefits are those future periodic payments, including lump-sum distributions, that are attributable under the Plan's provisions to the service employees have rendered. Accumulated plan benefits include benefits expected to be paid to (a) retired or terminated employees or their beneficiaries, (b) beneficiaries of employees who have died, and

(c) present employees or their beneficiaries. Benefits under the Plan are based on employees' compensation during their last full 60 months of service. The accumulated plan benefits as of January 1, 19X2 for active employees are based on their service rendered and history of compensation as of December 31, 19X1.

Benefits payable under all circumstances (retirement, death, disability and termination of employment) are included to the extent they are deemed attributable to employee service rendered to the valuation date. Benefits to be provided via annuity contracts excluded from Plan assets are excluded from accumulated plan benefits.

The actuarial present value of accumulated plan benefits is that amount that results from applying actuarial assumptions to adjust the accumulated plan benefits to reflect the time value of money (through discounts for interest) and the probability of payment (by means of decrements such as for death, disability, withdrawal or retirement) between the valuation date and the expected date of payment. The significant assumptions used in the actuarial valuation and/or the computation of the present value of accumulated plan benefits as of January 1, 19X2 are as follows:

Actuarial cost methods:

Funding purposes	—Entry age normal.
Accumulated benefits	—Projected unit credit.
Assumed rate of return on investments	—7.5 percent per annum compounded annually.
Mortality basis	—1971 Group Annuity Table.
Expenses	—4.0 percent of estimated plan costs.
Assumed retirement age	—Normal, attained age 65; Early, attained age 55.
Salary increase assumption	—6.5 percent increase each year until retirement.
Social Security projection	—Benefits expected to be available at retirement based on a 6.0 percent increase in the Social Security average earnings and a 5.5 percent increase in the Consumer Price Index.
Asset valuation method	—Fixed income assets are valued on a contract basis.
Withdrawal rates	—Table 6 from the Actuary's Pension Handbook.

The total actuarial present value of accumulated plan benefits as of January 1, 19X1 was $2,075,000. In September 19X1, the Plan was amended to increase benefit levels. The effect of the changes was to increase the actuarial present value of accumulated plan benefits by approximately $285,000 as of January 1, 19X2.

Tax Status

The United States Treasury Department has advised the plan trustees that the Plan constitutes a qualified trust under Section 401(a) of the Internal Revenue Code and is, therefore, exempt from federal income taxes under provisions of Section 501(a).

CHAPTER 37

ACCOUNTING FOR EMPLOYERS' PENSION COSTS*

William E. Decker
Ronald J. Murray

INTRODUCTION

Pension accounting has evolved over the years in response to the increasing importance of information about pensions (because of the significant increase in the number and size of pension plans) and the changes in both the legal environment (i.e., the enactment of the Employee Retirement Income Security Act—ERISA) and the economic environment (i.e., higher inflation and interest rates). The Financial Accounting Standards Board (FASB) believes that the current pension accounting standards contained in *Statement of Financial Accounting Standards (SFAS) No. 87, Employers' Accounting for Pensions,* and *No. 88, Employers' Accounting for Settlements and Curtailments of Defined Benefit Pension Plans and for Termination Benefits,* issued in December 1985, represent an important step toward a more meaningful and useful approach to pension accounting. The FASB also points out, however, in an appendix to *SFAS No. 87,* that these standards are not likely to be the final step in the evolution of accounting for pensions.

In *SFAS No. 87,* the FASB expresses the view that it would be conceptually appropriate and preferable to recognize a net pension liability or asset measured as the difference between the projected benefit obligation and plan assets, either with no delay in the recognition of gains

---

* Steinberg, Richard M., ed., *Pensions: A Financial Reporting and Compliance Guide,* 3d ed. (New York: John Wiley & Sons, 1988). Reprinted by permission of John Wiley & Sons.

and losses, or perhaps with gains and losses reported currently in comprehensive income but not in earnings. Under this approach, if there were no delay in the recognition of gains and losses, pension cost would be the difference between what the FASB considers to be the conceptually appropriate balance sheet amounts at the beginning and end of any period. However, the FASB decided that this approach would represent too great a change from past practice to be viable at this time. Therefore, the statement allows for gains and losses, the cost of plan amendments that give credit for past service, and the effects of adopting *SFAS No. 87* to be recognized in pension cost over future periods. Many of the complex aspects of *SFAS No. 87* result from the provisions developed to accomplish the delayed recognition of these off-balance-sheet amounts.

This chapter deals primarily with the pension accounting standards contained in *SFAS Nos. 87* and *88*.

HISTORICAL BACKGROUND

Statements of the American Institute of Certified Public Accountants (AICPA)

The AICPA's first pronouncement on accounting for pension plan costs was issued by the Committee on Accounting Procedure, in *Accounting Research Bulletin (ARB) No. 36, Pension Plans: Accounting for Annuity Costs Based on Past Services,* published in 1948. In this bulletin the committee expressed the belief that costs of annuities based on past service were generally incurred in contemplation of present and future services, not necessarily of the individual affected, but of the organization as a whole. Thus, the AICPA took the position that such costs should be allocated to current and future services and not charged to retained earnings. It did not, however, specify how pension costs should be recognized in the accounts.

In 1956, *ARB No. 47, Accounting for Costs of Pension Plans,* was issued. In this bulletin the committee specified how past service cost should be accounted for and also recognized the concept of vested benefits. The bulletin reflected the AICPA's preference for full accrual of pension costs over the remaining service lives of employees covered by a plan, generally on the basis of actuarial calculations. However, it regarded as acceptable ("for the present") minimum accruals whereby "the accounts and financial statements should reflect the accruals which equal the present worth, actuarially calculated, of pension commitments to employees to the extent that pension rights have vested in the employees. . . ." The committee stated that these accruals should not necessarily depend on funding arrangements, or on strict legal interpretations of a plan, and suggested that past service cost should be charged off over a reasonable period on a systematic and rational basis that would not distort the operating results of any one year.

Divergent accounting practices nevertheless continued. In 1958, several companies that had previously accrued the full amount of current service costs (which coincided with contributions to the funds) either eliminated or drastically reduced pension costs charged to income. The supporters of these actions justified them on the grounds that funds provided in the past were sufficient to afford reasonable assurance that pension payments could be continued, and were more than sufficient to meet the company's obligation for the then-vested rights of employees. Thus, they believed that the minimum requirements of *ARB No. 47* were satisfied.

Against this background, the Accounting Principles Board (APB), which succeeded the Committee on Accounting Procedure, decided that the subject needed further study and authorized an accounting research study. This study, published in 1965, detailed the accounting complexities of pension plans. In 1966, after lengthy consideration, the APB promulgated its *Opinion No. 8, Accounting for the Cost of Pension Plans,* primarily to eliminate inappropriate fluctuations in the amount of annual provisions for pension costs.

APB Opinion No. 8

APB Opinion No. 8 provided that, effective for fiscal periods beginning after December 31, 1966, the provision for pension cost be based on an actuarial cost method that gave effect, in a consistent manner, to pension benefits, pension fund earnings, investment gains or losses (including unrealized gains and losses), and other assumptions regarding future events, and resulted in a systematic and rational allocation of the total cost of pensions.

Limits on the annual provision for pension cost were narrowed when *APB Opinion No. 8:*

- Required the minimum annual provision for pension cost to be the sum of (1) normal cost, (2) interest on unfunded prior service cost, and (3) a provision for vested benefits, if applicable.
- Required that actuarial gains and losses and unrealized appreciation and depreciation be recognized in the computation of the annual provision for pension cost in a consistent manner that reflected the long-range nature of pension cost and avoided giving undue weight to short-term market fluctuations.

- Eliminated pay-as-you-go and terminal funding as acceptable methods of computing the annual provision for pension cost, except in the rare instances in which their application did not result in amounts differing materially from those obtained by the application of acceptable actuarial cost methods.

The APB concluded that all employees who could reasonably be expected to receive benefits under a pension plan should be included in the pension cost determination. It also concluded that any change made in the method of accounting for pension cost should not be applied retroactively. The opinion set forth disclosure requirements for accounting method changes, as well as for other pertinent pension cost data.

APB Opinion No. 8 applied "both to written plans and to plans whose existence may be implied from a well-defined, although perhaps unwritten, company policy." If a company had been providing its retired employees with benefits that could be determined or estimated in advance, there was generally a presumption that a pension plan existed within the meaning contemplated by the opinion.

FASB Statement No. 36

The FASB, which replaced the APB, issued *SFAS No. 36, Disclosure of Pension Information,* in May 1980, amending the disclosure requirements of *APB Opinion No. 8*. This statement, which was effective for fiscal periods beginning after December 15, 1979, addressed the lack of comparable disclosures in employers' financial statements concerning the financial status of their pension plans, and prescribed new disclosures to help correct this deficiency. It did not, however, modify any of the other provisions of *APB Opinion No. 8*.

FASB Statement No. 87

After several more years of deliberating the complex and controversial issues related to pension accounting, the FASB issued *SFAS No. 87, Employers' Accounting for Pensions,* in December 1985. This statement supersedes *APB Opinion No. 8, SFAS No. 36,* and *FASB Interpretation No. 3, Accounting for the Cost of Pension Plans Subject to the Employee Retirement Income Act of 1974*.

SFAS No. 87 establishes financial reporting and accounting standards for an employer that offers pension benefits to its employees. Such benefits are ordinarily periodic pension payments to retired employees, but may also include lump-sum payments and other types of benefits (such as death and disability benefits) provided through a pension plan. The provisions of *SFAS No. 87* apply to *any* arrangement that is similar in substance to a pension plan, regardless of the form or means of financing.[1]

While the new rules apply to all pension plans, they have the most significant impact on defined benefit plans. *SFAS No. 87:*

- Requires that a single attribution (or actuarial cost) method be used to calculate pension cost and obligations.[2]
- Provides specific guidance on how to select (actuarial) assumptions.
- Requires amortization of (actuarial) gains and losses in excess of a prescribed amount.
- Limits the acceptable methods and time periods for amortizing prior service cost.
- Requires that a transition amount be computed when *SFAS No. 87* is adopted and that it be amortized to expense on a straight-line basis over future periods.
- Specifies that an employer's balance sheet reflect a liability for any unfunded accumulated pension benefits (without considering salary progression), generally offset by an intangible asset.
- Requires that a significant amount of additional pension information be disclosed in a company's financial statements.

Figure 37–1 highlights some of the key terms used in *SFAS No. 87*. A comparison of accounting standards under *APB Opinion No. 8* and *SFAS No. 87* is provided in Figure 37–2.

The pension cost and disclosure provisions of *SFAS No. 87* are generally applicable for fiscal years beginning after December 15, 1986. The requirement to reflect an additional balance sheet liability for unfunded accumulated benefits is not effective until 1989. Sponsors of foreign plans and nonpublic companies with small plans have until 1989 to apply all the new rules. Earlier application is encouraged but restatement of prior years' financial statements is not permitted.

---

[1] *SFAS No. 87* does not apply to a plan that provides only life and/or health insurance benefits to retirees. Employers also are not required to apply *SFAS No. 87* to a plan that provides postemployment health care benefits, although they are permitted to do so. The FASB is addressing the accounting for postemployment benefits other than pensions as a separate project. A final pronouncement is expected to be released in 1989.

[2] *SFAS No. 87* avoids using the adjective *actuarial* whenever possible and introduces terminology that is different from that used previously. In certain instances, the term *actuarial* is included parenthetically as an aid in the transition to the revised language.

FIGURE 37–1
Glossary of Terms

Accumulated benefit obligation (ABO) The actuarial present value of benefits as of a specified date, determined according to the terms of a pension plan and based on employees' compensation and service to that date (salary progression is not considered in making this computation).

Actuarial gains and losses Same as gains or losses.

Adjusted plan assets The fair value of plan assets plus previously recognized unfunded accrued pension cost or less previously recognized prepaid pension cost on the employer's balance sheet.

Benefit approaches A group of basic approaches for allocating or attributing benefits or the cost of benefits to service periods (heretofore referred to as actuarial methods). These approaches assign a unit of retirement benefit to each year of credited service. The actuarial present value of that unit of benefit is computed separately and determines the cost assigned to that year. The projected unit credit method and the unit credit method are benefit approaches.

Career average pay plan A pension plan that provides benefits based on a benefit formula using the amount of compensation over an employee's entire service life.

Corridor approach A method of accounting for amortization of gains and losses whereby an employer amortizes only the portion of the accumulated net gain or loss that exceeds a prescribed limit—10 percent of the greater of the market-related value of plan assets or the projected benefit obligation.

Cost approaches A group of basic approaches for allocating or attributing benefits or the cost of benefits to service periods (heretofore referred to as actuarial methods). These approaches assign pension cost to periods so that the same amount of cost or the same percentage of compensation is allocated to each period. The entry age normal, attained age normal, individual level premium, and aggregate methods are cost approaches.

Curtailment An event that significantly reduces the expected years of future service of present employees or eliminates for a significant number of employees the accrual of defined benefits for some or all of their future services.

Defined benefit pension plan A pension plan that specifies a determinable pension benefit, usually based on factors such as age, years of service, and compensation. Under *SFAS No. 87* any plan that is not a defined contribution pension plan is considered a defined benefit pension plan.

Defined contribution pension plan A pension plan that provides an individual account for each participant and specifies how contributions to the individual's account are to be determined instead of specifying the amount of benefits the individual is to receive. Under a defined contribution pension plan, the benefits

FIGURE 37–1 (*continued*)

a participant will receive depend solely on the amount contributed to the participant's account, plus any income, expense, gains or losses, and forfeitures of other participants' benefits that may be allocated to such participant's account.

Discount rate The assumed interest rate at which the pension obligation could be effectively settled or eliminated, used to adjust for the time value of money between a specified date and the expected dates of payment. This rate is also referred to as the settlement rate.

Earnings rate The average long-term rate of return expected to be earned on pension fund assets.

Final pay plan A pension plan that provides retirement benefits based on a benefit formula using the amount of employee compensation over a specified period near the end of the employee's service life.

Flat benefit plan A pension plan that provides retirement benefits based on a fixed amount for each year of employee service.

Gains or losses Changes in the value of either the projected benefit obligation or plan assets resulting from experience different from that assumed and from changes in assumptions.

Market-related asset value Either the fair market value of an asset or a calculated value derived by systematic and rational adjustments to fair market value over a period of not more than five years.

Multiemployer plan A pension plan to which two or more unrelated employers contribute, usually pursuant to one or more collective bargaining agreements.

Participating annuity contract An annuity contract that provides for the purchaser to participate in the investment performance and possibly other experience, both favorable and unfavorable (e.g., mortality), of the insurance company.

Prior service cost The cost of retroactive benefits granted in a plan amendment (or a new plan).

Projected benefit obligation (PBO) The actuarial present value of all benefits attributed to employee service up to a specific date, based on the terms of the plan. A salary progression factor is included for final pay and career average pay plans.

Projected unit credit method A benefit/years-of-service actuarial approach that is generally required to be used for final pay and career average pay plans. Under this method, an equal portion of the total estimated benefit (including a salary progression factor) is attributed to each year of service. The cost of that benefit is then computed, with appropriate consideration to reflect the time value of money (discounting) and the probability of payment (e.g., mortality and turnover). Accordingly, this method results in progressively higher benefit costs each successive year for each participant, since the probability of survival to normal retirement increases and the discount period decreases.

Salary progression A projection of the assumed rate of salaries to

FIGURE 37–1 (*concluded*)

be earned in future years based on all components of future compensation levels (i.e., merit, productivity, and inflation).

Service cost The portion of benefits attributed to employee service for the period.

Settlement rate See Discount rate.

Settlement A transaction that is an irrevocable action, relieves the employer (or the plan) of primary responsibility for a pension benefit obligation, and eliminates significant risks related to the obligation and the assets used to effect the settlement.

Transition amount The difference between the projected benefit obligation and the fair value of adjusted plan assets at the date *SFAS No. 87* is adopted. If the projected benefit obligation exceeds adjusted plan assets, there is an unrecognized net obligation and loss (or transition debit). Conversely, if adjusted plan assets exceed the projected benefit obligation, there is an unrecognized net asset and gain (or transition credit).

Unit credit method An accumulated benefits approach that is generally required to be used for flat benefit plans. Under this method, benefits earned to date are based on the plan formula and on employees' history of pay, service, and other factors.

Volatility Changes in pension cost from period to period.

FIGURE 37–2
Principal Provisions in *SFAS No. 87,* Employers' Accounting for Pensions, Compared with *APB Opinion No. 8*

Issue	*APB Opinion No. 8*	*SFAS No. 87*
Balance sheet recognition	A liability (or asset) is recognized equal to cumulative pension cost based on an acceptable actuarial method less amounts funded. Plan assets are not recognized as employer's assets. In accounting for plan changes (prior service cost), an accounting liability is not immediately recognized.	A base liability (or asset) is recognized equal to cumulative pension cost less amounts funded. An additional liability for unfunded accumulated benefits (without salary progression) is required to be recorded and generally offset by an intangible asset.
Attribution approach (actuarial cost method)	Measurement is based on a number of actuarial cost methods that achieve systematic and rational allocation of pension cost.	Use of a single actuarial cost method is required: for final pay and career average pay plans, the projected-unit-credit method (with salary

FIGURE 37–2 (*continued*)

Issue	*APB Opinion No. 8*	*SFAS No. 87*
		progression); for flat benefit plans, the accumulated benefits (unit credit) method.
Actuarial assumptions	Authoritative pronouncements do not provide any guidance on selecting actuarial assumptions for use in measuring pension cost. Often, the reasonableness of assumptions is based on an overall assessment, not evaluated for each individual item (an "implicit" approach).	Use of explicit assumptions is required—each significant assumption used must reflect the best estimate solely with respect to that individual assumption.
	A reasonably conservative interest (discount) rate is generally used to determine pension cost. The assumed rate is generally the average rate of earnings that can be expected on the funds invested or to be invested to provide for future benefits. The rate generally is changed moderately and relatively infrequently.	Employers are required to use two interest rates to compute pension cost components: (1) an assumed discount rate based on the rate at which the pension obligation could effectively be settled or eliminated for service and interest cost components; and (2) an estimated average long-term earnings rate on plan assets (earnings rate) for the return-on-assets component. The discount rate used to compute pension cost is based on long-term rates existing at the beginning of the year. The earnings rate is based on current returns on plan assets and returns expected to be available for reinvestment.
	Salary progression assumptions are based on the employer's experience.	In determining the salary progression assumption, all components of salary progression are to be considered. An inflation assumption consistent with the inflation component of the discount and earnings rates must be used.

FIGURE 37–2 (*continued*)

Issue	*APB Opinion No. 8*	*SFAS No. 87*
Amortization of prior service cost	Except in certain circumstances, prior service cost amortization is not required for accounting purposes; only interest on the unamortized balance need be included in pension cost. In practice, most companies use a mortgage-type method that provides a level amount of amortization of the sum of prior service cost (principal) and interest, over an amortization period of 20 to 30 years.	Principal and interest are separated, with interest on the projected benefit obligation considered a component of pension cost. The principal is to be amortized using an accelerated method that results in a declining pattern of amortization over the future service period of employees active at the date of the amendment who are expected to receive benefits under the plan (or any faster method).
Actuarial gains and losses	Actuarial gains and losses are amortized using any systematic and rational manner (i.e., spread or averaged over a period of 10 to 20 years).	Consistent use of any systematic and rational method is still allowed as long as it results in amortization greater than the minimum amount calculated based on the "corridor approach" (i.e., a company only amortizes the portion of accumulated gains and losses that exceeds a prescribed limit).
Transition and effective date	*APB Opinion No. 8* required prospective transition accounting, in which changes to the opinion's accounting standards are treated as if they resulted from a plan amendment as of the date of the *Opinion*.	A prospective approach is required, with the entire transition amount (the difference between adjusted plan assets—the fair value of plan assets adjusted for any pension liability or asset on the sponsor's balance sheet—and the projected benefit obligation at the transition date) amortized on a straight-line basis over the average remaining service lives of employees expected to receive benefits (or 15 years if the average remaining service period is less than 15 years).

FIGURE 37–2 (*continued*)

Issue	*APB Opinion No. 8*	*SFAS No. 87*
		Except for foreign plans and small plans of nonpublic companies, expense provisions of the new standard are to be applied for years beginning after December 15, 1986, but balance sheet changes and all foreign and small-plan requirements are not required until 1989. Earlier application is encouraged.
Measurement dates	A specific measurement date is not specified in authoritative pronouncements. Some companies perform actuarial valuations every two or three years.	Plan assets and liabilities must be measured as of a date not more than three months before year-end. An actuarial valuation is not required as of the measurement date; the information can be prepared as of an earlier date and reconciled forward to the measurement date. Pension cost is generally based on beginning-of-the-year data and amortization.
Companies with more than one plan	If the assets in any of the plans can ultimately be used to pay benefits of another plan, such plans are treated as one plan when pension cost is being determined. Otherwise, each plan is accounted for separately. The disclosures required by *SFAS No. 36* are generally reported in total for all plans.	Pension cost, liabilities, and assets are to be computed on a plan-by-plan basis. Unless an employer clearly has a right to use assets of one plan to pay benefits of another, the liability for unfunded accumulated benefits required to be recognized cannot be reduced or eliminated because of another plan that has assets in excess of its accumulated benefit obligation. In addition, disclosures may be aggregated, except that overfunded and underfunded plans may not be combined and foreign plans may not be combined with U.S. plans unless the foreign plans use similar economic assumptions.

FIGURE 37–2 (*concluded*)

Issue	*APB Opinion No. 8*	*SFAS No. 87*
Defined contribution plans	The contribution applicable to a particular year is generally the pension cost for that year.	The accounting is, in substance, the same as practice under *APB Opinion No. 8*. Definitions of defined benefit and defined contribution are clarified.
Multiemployer plans	Pension cost is recognized as employer contributions are required under the terms of the plan.	The accounting is the same as practice under *APB Opinion No. 8*.
Business combinations—single-employer plans	A liability is recognized in the purchase price allocation for the greater of accrued pension cost based on the acquiring company's accounting policies or unfunded vested benefits related to the acquired company's defined benefit pension plan. Authoritative pronouncements do not specify whether an asset should be reflected in the purchase price allocation in an overfunded situation.	The acquiring company is required to recognize an acquisition asset or liability equal to the difference between the acquiree's projected benefit obligation (including salary progression) and the fair value of plan assets.
Business combinations—multi-employer plans	Authoritative pronouncements do not specify whether the withdrawal liability related to multiemployer plans of the acquired company should be included as an acquisition liability by the acquiring company.	The acquiring company is required to recognize an acquisition liability for the acquiree's multiemployer plan withdrawal liability only in situations in which withdrawal is probable.
Pension plans funded through contracts with insurance companies	Generally, the amount of net premiums paid is charged to expense. Dividends are recognized in the year credited, and termination credits are spread or averaged like actuarial gains and losses.	If an employer effectively transfers the primary obligation for payment of benefits to an insurance company, the premium paid is an appropriate measure of pension cost for the benefits covered by the insurance contract. Insurance contracts not substantively equivalent to the purchase of annuities must be accounted for as investments.

FASB Statement No. 88

In conjunction with *SFAS No. 87,* the FASB also issued *SFAS No. 88, Employers' Accounting for Settlements and Curtailments of Defined Benefit Pension Plans and for Termination Benefits*. This statement defines an event (a settlement) that requires, among other things, immediate recognition of previously unrecognized gains and losses and another event (a curtailment) that requires immediate recognition of previously unrecognized prior service cost. Companies are required to adopt both *SFAS Nos. 87* and *88* simultaneously.

FASB Staff Special Reports

The FASB does not attempt to anticipate all of the implementation questions that may arise in connection with a particular accounting pronouncement, nor to provide answers to those questions when the pronouncement is issued. Accordingly, many implementation issues are addressed orally by the FASB staff. Because of the unusually high number of questions raised and the inherent complexities of pension accounting, in January 1988 two members of the FASB staff published two special reports, one entitled *A Guide to Implementation of Statement 87 on Employers' Accounting for Pensions* in December 1986, and the other entitled *A Guide to Implementation of Statement 88 on Employers' Accounting for Settlements and Curtailments of Defined Benefit Pension Plans and for Termination Benefits*. The special reports contain the FASB staff members' views on a wide range of issues relating to the implementation of *SFAS Nos. 87 and 88*.

The publications clearly state that the opinions expressed are those of its authors and should not be considered the official positions of the FASB. However, the authors believe that the SEC staff takes the view that companies subject to SEC reporting requirements should be prepared to justify any significant deviations from the guidance set forth in the special reports.

DEFINED BENEFIT PENSION PLANS: ANNUAL PROVISION FOR PENSION COST

Under *SFAS No. 87,* pension cost may be more volatile (i.e., pension cost may change by a significant amount from year to year) than it was under the provisions of *APB Opinion No. 8*. This increased volatility is likely to result from:

- Changing from a discount rate based on the expected long-term earnings on plan assets (a rate that fluctuated infrequently and moderately) to discount (settlement) rate assumptions based on point-in-time interest rates.
- Changing from a method of amortizing prior service cost that provided a level amount of prior service cost and interest to a method that generally accelerates amortization over a shorter period.

SFAS No. 87 allows companies some latitude in the mechanics of applying the standards, the objective being to control pension cost volatility to some extent. Whether this objective will be achieved is still an open question. Under the rules set forth in the statement:

- Some forms of smoothed asset values are allowed, and asset gains and losses not reflected in these values need not be amortized.
- Only the portion of accumulated gains and losses that exceeds a prescribed amount is required to be amortized.

Components of Pension Cost

Under *SFAS No. 87,* an employer is required to select a consistent date on which to measure plan assets and obligations (and thus determine pension cost) from year to year. This ''measurement date'' is defined as either the employer's year-end or a date not more than three months before the year-end date. The FASB staff's special report, *A Guide to Implementation of Statement 87 on Employers' Accounting for Pensions,* indicates that:

- Although the pension obligation (and thus pension cost) must be based on census data and actuarial assumptions as of the measurement date, a full actuarial valuation is not required if a company is satisfied that the amount of the pension obligation determined by rolling forward data based on a valuation prior to the measurement date is substantially the same as the amount that would be determined by an actuarial valuation as of that date.
- If an employer remeasures plan asssets and obligations or performs a full actuarial valuation as of an interim date other than the established measurement date, pension cost for the period prior to the remeasurement should not be restated. However, pension cost for the remainder of the year should be based on the revised measurements.

SFAS No. 87 requires that an employer's pension cost consist of several components, computed as follows:

- Service cost—The increase in the projected benefit obligation attributable to employee service for the period calculated using the beginning-of-the-year discount rate and the required cost method.[3]
- Interest cost—The increase in the projected benefit obligation attributable to the accrual of interest on the beginning-of-the-year balance of the obligation calculated using the beginning-of-the-year discount rate. Anticipated changes in the projected benefit obligation for employee services rendered and benefit payments made during the year should be considered in determining interest cost.
- Return on plan assets—The expected earnings on plan assets calculated using the earnings rate and the market-related value of plan assets (both at the beginning of the year) taking into consideration anticipated contributions and benefit payments made during the year. Although paragraph 20 of *SFAS No. 87* specifies the "actual" return on plan assets as a component of pension cost, paragraph 34(a) states that the difference between the actual and expected return on plan assets must be accounted for as part of the gain or loss component of pension cost. The net result of these paragraphs is that the expected return on plan assets is used to calculate pension cost for the period.

  The market-related value of plan assets is defined as fair value or a calculated value that recognizes changes in fair value in a systematic or rational manner over not more than five years. Employers may use different methods of calculating the market-related value for different classes of assets (for example, an employer might use fair value for bonds and a five-year moving average value for equities), provided that the methodologies are applied consistently from year to year. The use of a market-related value other than fair value may reduce pension cost volatility somewhat, since the expected return component would be based on a smoothed asset value.
- Prior service cost—The amortization of prior service cost resulting from plan amendments.
- Gains and losses—The amortization of the beginning-of-the-year net gain or loss.

---

[3] The projected benefit obligation is the actuarial present value as of a specified date of all benefits attributed by the pension benefit formula to employee service rendered prior to that date. It is measured using assumptions regarding future compensation levels if the pension benefit formula is based on those future compensation levels (e.g., final pay or career average pay plans).

- Transition amount—The amortization of the transition amount.

An illustrative example of the manner in which pension cost is to be calculated is included in Figure 37–3 beginning on page 748.

Attribution Method

SFAS No. 87 requires companies to use a single attribution method based on the plan's terms to determine pension cost (a benefits approach). For final pay and career average pay plans, this is equivalent to the projected unit credit method. For flat benefit plans, the unit credit method is required. Companies may not use cost approaches (e.g., entry age normal or aggregate method) for accounting purposes, although they may do so for funding purposes.

Substantive Commitments

Paragraph 41 of *SFAS No. 87* states that in some situations, a history of regular amendments that improve benefits in flat benefit or career average plans (in addition to other evidence) may indicate that a company has a present commitment to make future amendments and that the substance of the plan is to provide benefits greater than the benefits defined by its written terms. In these situations, the "substantive commitment" is required to be taken into consideration in determining pension cost and obligations.

This provision has created confusion with respect to what constitutes a substantive commitment. The FASB staff's special report indicates that determining whether a substantive commitment exists requires careful consideration of the facts and circumstances surrounding the pension plan and points out that the company's past actions, including communications to employees, may embody a commitment to have a benefit formula that provides benefits beyond those specified by the written terms of the plan. The special report also indicates, however, that it is not the intent of paragraph 41 to permit the anticipation of an individual plan amendment (i.e., one that is not part of a series).

In the authors' experience, many companies have concluded that they do not have a substantive commitment to make future plan amendments. Consequently, they do not include the cost of anticipated amendments in the calculation of pension cost and obligations until they have been contractually agreed to. However, some companies have concluded that they have such a commitment and make their pension calculations accordingly; in these cases, paragraph 41 requires footnote disclosure of the existence and nature of the commitment.

Selecting Assumptions

Explicit Assumptions

SFAS No. 87 requires that each significant assumption reflect the best estimate solely with respect to that individual assumption (referred to as an explicit approach).

Two Interest Rates

Under *SFAS No. 87,* companies are required to select two interest rates: (1) an assumed discount (or settlement) rate based on the rate at which the pension obligation could be effectively settled or eliminated and (2) an expected long-term rate of return on plan assets (earnings rate).

The discount rate is used to measure the projected, accumulated, and vested benefit obligations and the service and interest cost components of pension cost. *SFAS No. 87* allows a certain degree of latitude in selecting this rate. In this connection, paragraph 44 states:

> Assumed discount rates shall reflect the rates at which the pension benefits could be effectively settled. It is appropriate in estimating those rates to look to available information about rates implicit in current prices of annuity contracts that could be used to effect settlement of the obligation (including information about available annuity rates currently published by the Pension Benefit Guaranty Corporation). In making those estimates, employers may also look to rates of return on high-quality fixed-income investments currently available and expected to be available during the period to maturity of the pension benefits.

This rather broad guidance has given rise to a number of questions with respect to the appropriate methodology for determining the discount rate. The FASB staff's special report indicates that selecting the discount rate is not a mechanical process based on a standard formula. It states that the primary objective of selecting the discount rate is to select the *best* estimate of the interest rates inherent in the price at which the pension obligation could be settled, given the pension plan's particular facts and circumstances and current market conditions, and that the methodology used in the selection process is subordinate to that primary objective.

The following specific guidance on selecting the discount rate is provided:

- A methodology for determining the discount rate, once selected, should be followed consistently. If the facts and circumstances surrounding the pension plan do not change from year to year, it would be inappropriate to change the methodology, particularly if the intent in changing it is to avoid a change in the discount rate.
- A change in facts and circumstances may, however, warrant the use of a different approach for determining the discount rate. This

change in methodology—which, in the author's view, would occur infrequently—would be a change in accounting estimate, not a change in accounting method.

- The discount rate should be reevaluated each year to determine whether it reflects current market conditions. The discount rate is *expected* to change as interest rates generally decline or rise.
- It would be inappropriate to use a range of rates (e.g., from PBGC rates at one end to high-quality bond rates at the other) and;
  —Arbitrarily select any rate within the range, or
  —Use the same rate each year provided it falls within the range.
- If the pension plan has a "dedicated" bond portfolio, that yield should not be used as the discount rate, since it is the current rates of return on those investments (not historical rates of return as of the dedication date) that are relevant.

Based on the foregoing, it is apparent that the authors of the special report expect pension cost to be more volatile under *SFAS No. 87* and that any attempt to manage the discount rate to avoid such volatility would be inappropriate. While there is some latitude regarding the methodology that a particular company may select to determine the discount rate, it is clear that whatever approach is selected should be followed consistently (unless circumstances change).

The earnings rate is used in connection with the market-related value of plan assets to compute the return-on-assets component of pension cost. Consistent with previous practice, *SFAS No. 87* indicates that in estimating the earnings rate, consideration should be given to current returns being earned and returns expected to be available for reinvestment.

Salary Progression Rate

In determining the salary progression assumption under *SFAS No. 87*, employers are required to consider all salary increase components (merit, productivity, promotion, and inflation). The statement indicates that all assumptions must be consistent to the extent that each reflects expectations of the same future economic conditions, such as rates of inflation. For example, if an employer uses a 5 percent inflation factor for purposes of determining the earnings rate, that same factor should be used to determine the inflation component of the salary progression rate.

Amortization of Prior Service Cost

Historically, the costs related to plan changes—or new plans—that give credit for past service have been recognized over future periods, using a variety of acceptable methods that generally produced a level amount representing the sum of prior service cost and interest on the unamortized balance. *SFAS No. 87* prescribes a method of amortization that separates these two elements and uses an accelerated method to amortize the prior service cost, generally over fewer years. As a result, prior service cost will generally be amortized to expense at a faster rate than under previous practice, which may contribute to the volatility of pension cost.

Amortization Period

SFAS No. 87 requires that pension cost include amortization of prior service cost, generally over the future service period of employees active as of the date of amendment who are expected to receive benefits under the plan. The FASB staff's special report indicates that once an amortization period has been established, it may be revised only if a curtailment (as defined in *SFAS No. 88*) occurs or if events indicate that (1) the period benefited is shorter than originally estimated or (2) the future economic benefits of the plan amendment have been impaired. The special report also indicates that the amortization period would not necessarily be revised because of ordinary variances in the expected future service period of employees.

Amortization Method

SFAS No. 87 requires prior service cost and the related interest on the unrecognized amount to be accounted for separately. The interest component of pension cost includes the interest on the unamortized prior service cost, while the principal is amortized to expense using an accelerated method that results in a declining amortization pattern. This method assigns an equal amount of prior service cost to each future period of service of each employee active at the date of the plan amendment who is expected to receive benefits under the plan. In other words, the method (similar to sum-of-the-years' digits) is based on the relationship between the total expected employee years of service and the service years expected to expire in a period.

The statement, however, also indicates that methods that result in amortization that is more rapid than the method described above can be used—including straight-line amortization over the average remaining service period of employees expected to receive benefits.

Using the amortization method set forth in *SFAS No. 87* results in accelerated principal amortization of prior service cost. If an alternative method (such as straight-line) is selected, the amortization period must be reduced to no more than the average remaining service period to achieve the more rapid amortization called for by the statement. In either case, it appears that under *SFAS No. 87,* prior service cost will generally be amortized to expense at a faster rate than under previous practice.

Some employers have expressed the view that immediate recognition of prior service cost resulting from *all* plan amendments (present and future) is an acceptable alternative amortization method. The special report indicates that immediate recognition is appropriate only if, after assessing the facts and circumstances surrounding the particular plan amendment, the employer does not expect to realize any future economic benefits from that plan amendment. Accordingly, an employer may not adopt an accounting policy to immediately recognize prior service cost, since such a policy would preclude the employer from making this assessment for future plan amendments *as they occur*.

Plans with a History of Regular Amendments

The statement also indicates that a shorter amortization period for certain plans may be warranted. Paragraph 27 of *SFAS No. 87* states that if a company has a history of regular plan amendments (e.g., when flat benefit plans are amended with each renegotiation of a union contract), that practice, along with other evidence, may indicate a shortening of the period during which the company expects economic benefits from each amendment. When a situation of this nature is deemed to exist, amortization is required over the period benefited. In its deliberations, the Board considered, and rejected, recommendations that the final statement specify that the "period benefited" (and thus the prior service cost amortization period) is the period between contract renegotiations.

The language in paragraph 27 has created confusion with respect to what constitutes a history of regular plan amendments and what amortization period should be used if such a situation exists. While it addresses these issues, the special report provides little additional guidance, essentially indicating that the assessment of whether such a situation exists and, if so, what amortization period should be used is fact specific. It therefore appears that the appropriate amortization period in a situation of this nature is not necessarily the contract period. The authors are aware of a number of companies that, based on an assessment of the particular facts and circumstances involved, have been able to support an amortization period in such a situation that is longer than the contract period but not longer than the future service period of active employees expected to receive benefits under the plan.

Gains and Losses

SFAS No. 87 defines gains and losses as changes in either the projected benefit obligation or plan assets resulting from experience different from that assumed and from changes in assumptions, and requires that all gains and losses, including those arising from changes in the discount rate, be accounted for on a combined basis. Companies are permitted to apply consistently any systematic and rational amortization method, as long as it results in the amortization of the net gain or loss in an amount greater than the minimum based on the so-called corridor approach. The FASB staff's special report indicates that companies may immediately recognize gains and losses provided that (1) this approach is applied consistently, (2) the method is applied to *both* gains and losses (on plan assets *and* obligations), and (3) the method used is disclosed.

Under the corridor approach, only the portion of the net gain or loss that exceeds a prescribed amount (10 percent of the greater of the market-related value of plan assets or the projected benefit obligation) must be amortized. The excess is required to be amortized on a straight-line basis over the average remaining service period of active employees expected to receive benefits. Asset gains and losses not yet reflected in the market-related value of plan assets (the difference between the fair value and the market-related value of plan assets) are not, however, required to be included in the computation.

Controlling Volatility

As noted above, the FASB developed the corridor approach and the market-related value of plan assets concept in an attempt to reduce the volatility of pension cost as follows:

- First, only the asset gains or losses reflected in the market-related value of plan assets must be considered for amortization (as little as 20 percent per year).
- Second, all gains and losses may be offset; amortization is required only if the net gain or loss is in excess of the corridor.
- Third, the excess may be spread over the average remaining service period of active employees expected to receive benefits.

Balance Sheet Recognition

Under previous accounting rules, a pension liability was recorded only if the employer's contributions to the plan were less than cumulative pension cost determined under an acceptable actuarial cost method. Conversely, a pension asset was recorded only if the contributions were more than the recorded cost. While *SFAS No. 87* retains those practices, it also requires that an additional liability be recognized when the unfunded accumulated benefit obligation (the excess of the accumulated benefit obligation over the fair value of plan assets) exceeds the balance sheet liability for accrued pension cost.[4] Under this approach, when an additional liability is recorded, an intangible asset is also recognized to the extent that unamortized prior service cost and/or an unamortized transition debit (discussed in the following section) exists. If the additional liability exceeds the total of these two items, the excess is recorded as a separate component (i.e., a reduction) of stockholders' equity. Under no circumstances does the recording of the additional liability affect earnings.

For companies with more than one plan, liability recognition is determined on a plan-by-plan basis. For example, unless an employer clearly has a right to use the assets of one plan to pay the benefits of another, the excess assets of an overfunded plan cannot offset the additional liability for unfunded accumulated benefits of another plan sponsored by the same company. Thus, as a general rule, companies that previously disclosed plan assets in excess of accumulated benefits are now required to recognize a liability under *SFAS No. 87* if they sponsor any underfunded plans.

SFAS No. 87 does not allow companies with overfunded plans to reflect an asset on their balance sheet.

Transition

SFAS No. 87 requires a company to compute a "transition amount" as of the measurement date for the beginning of the year of adoption equal to the difference between:

- The projected benefit obligation, which includes a salary progression factor and is computed using the attribution method and the assumption guidance set forth in *SFAS No. 87.*
- Adjusted plan assets, which are the fair value of plan assets plus the pension liability or less the pension asset on the employer's balance sheet at the measurement date.

If the projected benefit obligation exceeds adjusted plan assets, a transition debit exists; if adjusted plan assets exceed the projected benefit obligation, a transition credit exists. In either case, the transition amount (which is not recorded in the financial statements) must be amortized on a straight-line basis over the average remaining service period of active employees expected to receive benefits under the plan except that (1) the

---

[4] The accumulated benefit obligation is the actuarial present value as of a specified date of all benefits attributed by the pension benefit formula to employee service rendered prior to that date, based on *current* compensation levels. The accumulated benefit obligation differs from the projected benefit obligation in that it does *not* consider future compensation levels.

employer may elect to use a 15-year period if this average remaining period is less than 15 years and (2) if all or almost all of the plan's participants are inactive, the employer must use the average remaining life expectancy of the inactive participants.

Illustrative Example of the Pension Cost Calculation

Figure 37–3 provides an illustrative example of the pension cost calculation for a company with a single defined benefit pension plan.

FIGURE 37–3
Illustrative Example of the Pension Cost Calculation

XYZ Company has a defined benefit pension plan covering substantially all employees. The company decided to adopt *SFAS No. 87,* including the balance sheet requirements, as of January 1, 1987.

Plan Data and Key (Actuarial) Assumptions

Benefit formula	Career average	
Accounting policies		
Amortization of gains and losses	Corridor approach	
Amortization of transition amount	Average future service period of employees	
Market-related value of plan assets	Equal to fair value	
	1987	*1988*
Assumed discount rate	11.5%	10%
Assumed salary progression rate	6	6
Assumed earnings rate	11	9
	1987	*1988*
Plan assets and obligations (as of beginning of year)		
Vested benefit obligation (VBO)	$ 8,500,000	$11,700,000
Accumulated benefit obligation (ABO)	10,000,000	13,800,000
Projected benefit obligation (PBO)	11,500,000	14,653,000
Fair value of plan assets	12,000,000	15,000,000
Prepaid pension cost as of January 1, 1987	$ 1,000,000	
For the year ended December 31, 1987		
Service cost	$ 300,000	
Benefit payments made	360,000*	
Contributions made	500,000†	
Actual return on plan assets	2,860,000	

FIGURE 37–3 (*continued*)

XYZ Company's pension cost for the year ended December 31, 1987 (the year *SFAS No. 87* was adopted) was $338,215, computed as follows:

Service cost		$ 300,000
Interest cost‡		
PBO at 1/1/87	$11,500,000	
Discount rate at 1/1/87	× 11½%	1,322,500
Expected return on plan assets		
Market-related value at 1/1/87	12,000,000	
Earnings rate at 1/1/87	× 11%	(1,320,000)
Amortization of prior service cost		—§
Amortization of gains and losses		—‖
Amortization of transition amount		
Fair value of plan assets at 1/1/87	12,000,000	
Less prepaid pension cost at 1/1/87	(1,000,000)	
Less PBO at 1/1/87	(11,500,000)	
Transition debit	500,000	
Average future service period of employees at 1/1/87	÷ 14 years	35,715
Pension cost for the year ended December 31, 1987		$ 338,215

The company's additional liability at December 31, 1987 was $0, computed as follows:

Fair value of plan assets at 12/31/87		$15,000,000
Less prepaid pension cost at 12/31/87		
Prepaid pension cost at 1/1/87	$ 1,000,000	
Contribution on 12/31/87	500,000	
Pension cost for the year ended 12/31/87	(338,215)	(1,161,785)
Less ABO at 12/31/87		(13,800,000)
		$ 38,215
Amount of additional liability		$ 0#

* Benefits payments are made ratably during the year.

† Contributions are made on December 31.

‡ The calculation of the interest cost component should take into consideration anticipated benefit payments; however, they were not considered for purposes of this illustrative example.

§ There were no plan amendments in 1987.

‖ The corridor approach requires amortization of the beginning-of-the-year unrecognized net gain or loss. At January 1, 1987, this amount was $0.

Since adjusted plan assets exceed the ABO at December 31, 1987, no additional liability is required to be recorded. Note that *SFAS No. 87* does not permit companies to record a pension asset in a situation of this nature.

DEFINED CONTRIBUTION PENSION PLANS

SFAS No. 87 states that the approximate periodic cost of a defined contribution plan is measured by the required contribution amount determined using the plan formula, since, in a defined contribution plan, the pension benefits that participants will receive depend only on the amount contributed to the participants' accounts, the returns earned on investments of these contributions, and forfeitures of other participants' benefits that may be reallocated. If a plan requires contributions to continue after participants retire or terminate, the cost of these benefits also should be accrued during the participants' service period.

When a plan has both a formula for plan contributions and a scale for plan benefits, a careful analysis is required to determine whether the substance of the plan is to provide a defined contribution or a defined benefit. If the plan history indicates that the scale of benefits is adjusted to reflect the amount actually contributed, as a general rule the plan should be treated as a defined contribution plan. If, however, a company's liability for pension benefits is not limited by the amount of the pension fund or if the plan history indicates (and/or the current employer policy contemplates) the maintenance of benefit levels regardless of the amount of defined contribution or legal limitation of the employer's liability for such benefits, as a general rule the plan should be treated as a defined benefit plan. The accounting and disclosure requirements should be determined in accordance with the applicable provisions of *SFAS No. 87*.

MULTIEMPLOYER PENSION PLANS

Under *SFAS No. 87*, a multiemployer plan is a pension plan to which two or more unrelated employers contribute, usually pursuant to one or more collective bargaining agreements. A characteristic of multiemployer plans is that assets contributed by one participating employer may be used to provide benefits to employees of other participating employers, since assets contributed by an employer are not segregated in a separate account or restricted to provide benefits only to employees of that employer.

SFAS No. 87 states that an employer participating in a multiemployer plan should recognize as pension cost the required contribution for the period and recognize as a liability any contributions due and unpaid. In other words, even though a multiemployer plan may be a defined benefit plan, the employer can account for its participation as though it were a defined contribution plan.

DISCLOSURE

SFAS No. 87 requires the disclosure of a significant amount of information by all sponsors of defined benefit plans, including descriptive information about plan provisions, funding policy, plan assets, and employee groups covered; the components of pension cost; the interest rate and salary progression assumptions; and a reconciliation of the projected benefit obligation to the asset or liability recorded on the company's balance sheet. Disclosures regarding defined contribution and multiemployer plans are also required. Figure 37–4 summarizes these disclosure requirements.

The reconciliation of the projected benefit obligation to the balance sheet amounts recorded by sponsors of defined benefit plans provides users of financial statements with information that is consistent with the FASB's theoretical preference regarding the asset or liability that should be recorded—the difference between the projected benefit obligation and the fair value of plan assets. The remaining items in the reconciliation reflect the delayed recognition of prior service cost, gains and losses, and the transition amount allowed under *SFAS No. 87*. Companies may not aggregate plans with pension assets (i.e., plan assets in excess of accumulated benefits) with plans that have pension liabilities (i.e., accumulated benefits in excess of plan assets) for purposes of complying with this disclosure requirement. Furthermore, companies may not aggregate foreign and domestic plans for purposes of this disclosure requirement unless the foreign plans use similar assumptions.

Figure 37–5 provides an illustrative example of the financial statement disclosures of the XYZ Company (based on the same hypothetical facts used in the illustrative example in Figure 37–3). The format presented and the wording of the footnote are consistent with Illustration 6 in *SFAS No. 87*.

FUNDING AND PLAN ADMINISTRATION

As previously noted, prior to *SFAS No. 87* a substantial number of companies funded the amount of pension cost that was accrued for financial statement purposes. *SFAS No. 87* makes this impossible for many compa-

FIGURE 37–4
Required Pension Disclosures Under *SFAS No. 87*

Defined Benefit Plans

A description of the plan, including employee groups covered, type of benefit formula, funding policy, types of assets held, and significant non-benefit liabilities, as well as the nature and effect of significant matters affecting comparability of information for all periods presented.

Net pension cost for the period, showing separately service cost, interest cost, actual return on plan assets for the period, and the net total of other components.

A schedule reconciling the funded status of the plan with amounts reported in the employer's balance sheet, showing separately:

1. The fair value of plan assets.
2. The projected benefit obligation, identifying:
   a. The accumulated benefit obligation.
   b. The vested benefit obligation.
3. The amount of unrecognized prior service cost.
4. The amount of unrecognized net gain or loss (including asset gains and losses not yet reflected in the market-related value of assets).
5. The balance of the unrecognized transition amount.
6. The amount of any additional liability recognized.
7. The amount of net pension asset or liability recognized in the balance sheet (the net result of combining the preceding six items).

The weighted-average assumed discount and earnings' rates and the salary progression rate used.

The amounts and types of securities of the employer and related parties included in plan assets and the amount of annual benefits of employees and retirees covered by annuity contracts issued by the employer and related parties.

A description of any alternative methods used to amortize prior service cost and gains or losses and the existence and nature of commitments beyond the written terms of the plan.

Defined Contribution Plans

A description of the plan, including employee groups covered, the basis for determining contributions, and the nature and effects of significant matters affecting comparability of information for all periods presented.

The amount of cost recognized during the period.

Multiemployer Plans

A general description of the multiemployer plan, including employee groups covered, the type of benefits (defined benefit or defined contribution), and the nature and effect of significant matters affecting comparability of information for all periods presented.

The amount of cost recognized during the period.

If withdrawal from a multiemployer plan is reasonably possible, the amount (if reasonably estimable) of obligation the employer would have on withdrawal from the plan. If the amount is not reasonably estimable, disclose the best reasonably available general information about the extent of the obligation the employer would have on withdrawal from the plan.

FIGURE 37–5
Illustrative Example of Financial Statement Disclosures

NOTE P: The company has a defined benefit pension plan covering substantially all of its employees. The benefits are based on years of service and the employee's average compensation during employment. The company's funding policy is to contribute annually the maximum amount that can be deducted for federal income tax purposes. Contributions are intended to provide not only for benefits attributed to service to date but also for those expected to be earned in the future.

The following table sets forth the plan's funded status and amounts recognized in the company's statement of financial position at December 31, 1987 (in thousands):

Actuarial present value of benefit obligations:	
Accumulated benefit obligation, including vested benefits of $11,700	$13,800
Projected benefit obligation for service rendered to date	($14,653)
Plan assets at fair value, primarily listed stocks and U.S. bonds	15,000
Plan assets in excess of projected benefit obligation	347
Unrecognized net loss from past experience different from that assumed and effects of changes in assumptions	351*
Unrecognized net transition debit at January 1, 1987, being recognized over 14 years	464
Prepaid pension cost included in other assets	$ 1,162

Net pension cost for 1987 included the following components (in thousands):

Service cost—benefits earned during the period	$ 300
Interest cost on the projected benefit obligation	1,322
Actual return on plan assets	(2,860)
Net amortization and deferral	1,576†
Net pension cost	$ 338

The weighted average discount rate and rate of increase in future compensation levels used in determining the actuarial present value of the projected benefit obligation were 10 percent and 6 percent, respectively. The expected long-term rate of return on assets was 11 percent.

* The sum of (1) a loss ($1,891) equal to the difference between the expected PBO at 12/31/87 ($11,500 + 300 + 1,322 − 360) and the actual PBO at 12/31/87 ($14,653) and (2) a gain ($1,540) equal to the difference between the actual return on plan assets ($2,860) and the expected return on plan assets ($1,320).

† The sum of (1) the reversal of the deferred gain for the period ($1,540) that should not be reflected in pension cost but that is required to be included in the actual return on plan assets and (2) the amortization of the transition debit ($36).

nies, because in many cases pension cost determined pursuant to *SFAS No. 87* is greater than the maximum deductible amount permitted under the Internal Revenue Code or less than the minimum required contribution under ERISA. Many companies are therefore considering modifications to their funding policy in an attempt to attain some level of consistency with the methodology under *SFAS No. 87*.

This consistency may, however, be difficult to achieve. Certainly, companies that have used a different actuarial cost method from the one required by the statement may switch to the new method for funding purposes as well. However, the new methods and periods for amortizing prior service cost and gains and losses, and certain other requirements of the statement, are not permissible for purposes of computing the maximum allowable income tax deduction. Furthermore, actuarial assumptions would likely be different because the discount rate assumption required by *SFAS No. 87* may be too high to use for funding purposes. Accordingly, many companies are finding it necessary to perform separate actuarial calculations for funding and accounting purposes.

Moreover, companies are being confronted with another problem:

- If funding levels are reduced to reflect lower pension cost, appropriate explanations and communications may be needed to explain the reduced funding levels to plan participants and other interested parties.
- If funding levels are not reduced even though pension cost is lower, management may be required to explain the difference between these levels and the reduced pension cost, as well as the potentially large assets that would be included on the company's balance sheet based on the excess of amounts funded over amounts expensed, to stockholders, the board of directors, plan participants, and other interested parties.

ACCOUNTING FOR SETTLEMENTS AND CURTAILMENTS OF DEFINED BENEFIT PLANS AND TERMINATION BENEFITS

SFAS No. 88 defines an event (a settlement) that requires, among other things, immediate recognition of previously unrecognized gains and losses but no accelerated recognition of prior service cost, and another event (a curtailment) that requires immediate recognition of previously unrecognized prior service cost, but no accelerated recognition of previously unrecognized gains and losses. The new rules on accounting for settlements represent a substantial change to practice under *APB Opinion No. 8*. Immediate gain or loss recognition is now required in many cases in which gains or losses have previously been spread over 10 to 20 years.

SFAS No. 88 also requires all companies to accelerate the recognition of prior service cost when it is probable a curtailment will occur, thus providing more consistent accounting among companies for the same types of transactions. Past practice was varied and subjective; some companies immediately recognized some amount of expense in situations of this nature, while others continued to use their normal deferral practice.

Accounting for Settlements

SFAS No. 88 defines a settlement as a transaction that:

- Is an irrevocable action.
- Relieves the employer (or the plan) of primary responsibility for a pension benefit obligation.
- Eliminates significant risks related to the obligation and the assets used to effect the settlement.

The statement indicates that purchasing annuity contracts or making lump-sum cash payments to plan participants in exchange for their rights to receive specified pension benefits constitutes a settlement, since all three criteria are met. However, a decision to invest in a portfolio of high-quality, fixed-income securities with principal and interest payment dates similar to the estimated payment dates of benefits does not constitute a settlement, since such a decision (1) may be reversed, (2) does not relieve the employer of primary responsibility for the obligation, and (3) does not eliminate mortality risk.

SFAS No. 88 requires that companies accelerate the recognition of previously unrecognized gains and losses when a settlement occurs, since the possibility of future gains or losses related to the obligation and to the assets used to effect the transaction is eliminated in such a situation. Specifically, the new rules require companies to immediately recognize a percentage of (1) the previously unrecognized net gain or loss, (2) the gain or loss arising from the settlement (i.e., the difference between the expected value of the pension obligation and plan assets and their actual (remeasured) value at the time of the settlement), and (3) the unamortized transition credit (as defined on page 747) based on the percentage of the projected benefit obligation eliminated by the settlement. The amortization of prior service cost and/or transition debit (if any) is not, however, accelerated unless a curtailment also takes place, since the benefits derived from the future services of employees (which is one of the bases for delayed recognition of prior service cost) have not been affected by the settlement. Figure 37–6 illustrates how a settlement gain would be calculated.

Under the new rules, whenever a defined benefit plan in the United States is terminated (and a settlement occurs) and a replacement defined benefit plan is established, the gain (or loss in rare cases) recognized is to be determined not by the amount of assets that revert to the company, but by the settlement computation discussed in the preceding paragraph.

FIGURE 37–6
Illustrative Example of a Settlement Gain Calculation

ABC Company sponsors a final pay defined benefit pension plan. On July 15, 1987, the plan settled its accumulated benefit obligation through the purchase of nonparticipating annuity contracts for $18 million. In order to determine the settlement gain of $5,148,000, the company remeasured its plan assets and obligations as of the settlement date, July 15, 1987.

Revaluation (in thousands):

	Expected Values at 7/15/87	*Revaluation**	*Actual Values at 7/15/87*
Accumulated benefit obligation (ABO)	($16,000)	($2,000)	($18,000)
Projected benefit obligation (PBO)	($23,700)	($3,600)	$(27,300)
Fair value of plan assets	31,300	2,700	34,000
Funded status	7,600	(900)	6,700
Unamortized transition (credit)	(8,700)		(8,700)
Unrecognized net loss	–0–	900	900
(Accrued) pension cost	($ 1,100)	$ –0–	($ 1,100)

The settlement gain is calculated as follows (in thousands):

Maximum gain		
Unrecognized net gain/loss before the revaluation	$ –0–	
Loss arising from the settlement	900	
Unamortized transition credit	(8,700)	$7,800
Percentage of the PBO settled		
ABO after the revaluation	$18,000	
PBO after the revaluation	÷27,300	× 66%
Settlement gain		$5,148

* The revaluation is necessary in this situation because the discount rate at 7/15/87 (9 percent) is lower than the assumed discount rate (10 percent) at 1/1/87, and the actual return on plan assets is greater than the expected return.

SFAS No. 88 provides that the difference between the recognized gain (or loss) and the reverted assets is to be accounted for as an asset or liability on the company's balance sheet. In theory this asset or liability will be eliminated by differences between funding and expense over future years.

SFAS No. 88 further specifies that routine annuity purchases (for retiring employees, for example) result in a settlement. However, employers may elect to adopt a consistently applied policy of not recognizing a gain or loss if the cost of all settlements in a year is less than or equal to the sum of the service cost and the interest cost components of pension cost for the year.

Figure 37–7 discusses how settlement accounting would be applied in some common situations.

FIGURE 37–7
Settlement Accounting in Common Situations

SETTLEMENT ACCOUNTING—ANALYSIS OF SPECIFIC SITUATIONS

A Defined Benefit Plan Is Terminated and Replaced with a Defined Contribution Plan

This type of transaction is both a curtailment (because pension benefits cease to accumulate) and a settlement (because annuities are purchased to eliminate the obligation). As a result, the unrecognized prior service cost, the unrecognized net gain or loss, and the remaining transition amount are recognized immediately, with the amount of the gain generally being equal to the excess assets that revert to the company. This treatment is consistent with practice under *APB Opinion No. 8, Accounting for the Cost of Pension Plans,* except that under *SFAS No. 88* the gain generally should not be extraordinary.

A Defined Benefit Plan Is Terminated and Replaced with Another Defined Benefit Plan

Since employees continue to earn benefits under the successor plan, this transaction is not considered a curtailment and unrecognized prior service cost continues to be amortized as before the termination. It is considered to be a settlement, however, since annuities must be purchased under IRS/Department of Labor/PBGC guidelines. The gain is to be computed as follows:

- Flat benefit plans: Because 100 percent of the PBO (before termination) is settled by purchasing annuities—salary progression is not considered in actuarial calculations for flat benefit plans—the entire unrecognized gain (including any gain or loss arising directly from the annuity purchase and any remaining unamortized transition credit) is recognized immediately.

FIGURE 37–7 (*concluded*)

- Final pay or career average plans: Because to the best of our knowledge insurance companies do not sell annuities for the salary progression component of the PBO, it is impossible to settle 100 percent of the PBO for such plans. Pro rata recognition is required when less than 100 percent of the PBO is settled. The immediate gain or loss recognized is computed as follows:

  Recognized amount = Percentage reduction of the PBO × Maximum gain or loss

  The maximum gain or loss equals the unrecognized net gain or loss (including asset gains and losses not yet reflected in the market-related value of plan assets as discussed in paragraphs 30 and 31 of *SFAS No. 87*) plus or minus the gain or loss first measured at the time of the annuity purchase plus any remaining unamortized transition credit (see paragraph 77 of *SFAS No. 87*).

Annuities Are Purchased without Plan Termination or Asset Reversion

Under the new rules, if a company purchases annuities in order to settle all or part of the vested benefits portion of the PBO, a pro rata portion of the maximum gain or loss is recognized immediately. It is, therefore, not necessary to terminate the plan and recover the assets in order to recognize a gain. Thus, companies in an overfunded situation can trigger gain recognition by purchasing annuities at any particular time.

Under *APB Opinion No. 8,* purchasing annuities does not result in immediate gain recognition unless it is done in conjunction with some other unusual event (e.g., a plant closing).

The Pension Obligation Is Settled Using Participating Annuity Contracts

SFAS No. 88 describes some contracts with insurance companies (referred to as participating annuities) that allow a company or the plan to receive dividends if the insurance company has favorable experience. *SFAS No. 88* indicates that if the substance of a participating annuity contract is such that the employer remains subject to all or most of the risks and rewards associated with the benefit obligation covered or the assets transferred to the insurance company, the purchase of the contract does not constitute a settlement. In interpreting this provision, however, the prevailing view appears to be that if an employer transfers the risks associated with the benefit obligation and plan assets but retains some potential rewards, the transaction should be considered a settlement.

If a participating annuity contract does constitute a settlement of the pension benefit obligation, then a gain can be recognized. Although the wording in *SFAS No. 88* is somewhat complex, the gain is generally measured by reducing the amount to be recognized by the cost of the participation feature. (While footnote 3 states that the gain or loss first measured at the time of the annuity purchase is computed by excluding the cost of the participating feature, paragraph 10 states that the maximum gain must be reduced by the cost of the participating feature. These two provisions normally cancel each other.)

Accounting for Curtailments

SFAS No. 88 defines a curtailment as an event that significantly reduces the expected years of future service of present employees or eliminates for a significant number of employees the accrual of defined benefits for some or all of their future services. Curtailments include:

- Termination of employees' service earlier than had been expected, which may or may not involve closing a facility or discontinuing a segment of a business.
- Termination or suspension of a plan so that employees do not earn additional defined benefits for future services.

When it is probable a curtailment will occur *and* its impact (dollar effect) can be reasonably estimated, an employer is required to compute a net gain or loss that includes accelerated recognition of previously unrecognized prior service cost. Unless an employer also settles the pension obligation, accelerated recognition of previously unrecognized gains or losses is not permitted, since the employer has not been relieved of the primary responsibility for the pension obligation and remains subject to the risks associated with it as well as the related plan assets. If the result of this computation is a net loss, an employer must recognize the amount involved immediately. However, if the result is a net gain, an employer may recognize this amount only when realized (i.e., when the related employees terminate or the plan suspension or amendment is adopted). *SFAS No. 88* sets forth the specific computational requirements to be followed when determining the net gain or loss in a curtailment situation. In very basic terms, the net gain or loss represents the sum of the following two items:

- A loss computed as the portion of unrecognized prior service cost that relates to years of service no longer expected to be rendered.
- A gain or loss computed as the net change in the projected benefit obligation resulting from the event. If the net change is a gain, it must first be offset against any existing unrecognized net loss. If the net change is a loss, it must first be offset against any existing unrecognized net gain.

For purposes of these computations, any remaining unamortized transition credit is considered to be an unrecognized net gain; any remaining transition debit is considered to be an unrecognized prior service cost.

Termination Benefits

The accounting provisions of *SFAS No. 88* dealing with the benefits given to terminated employees supersede *SFAS No. 74, Accounting for Special Termination Benefits Paid to Employees*. However, *SFAS No. 88* does incorporate the rules set forth in *SFAS No. 74* for "special termination benefits." In situations of this nature, an employer is required to recognize a liability and a loss when the employees accept the offer and the amount can be reasonably estimated.

SFAS No. 88 goes beyond *SFAS No. 74,* however, and addresses "contractual termination benefits" provided by the existing terms of a plan but payable only if a specified event (such as a plant closing) occurs. *SFAS No. 88* specifies that an employer that provides such benefits should recognize a liability and a loss when it is probable that employees will be entitled to benefits and the amount can be reasonably estimated.

A situation involving termination benefits would generally also involve a curtailment that must be accounted for under *SFAS No. 88*.

Recognition, Classification, and Disclosure

SFAS No. 88 contains the following provisions regarding financial statement recognition, classification, and disclosure:

- A description of the event and the amount of gain or loss resulting from settlement, curtailment, or termination benefits are required to be disclosed.
- Extraordinary item treatment is not permitted unless the requirements of *APB Opinion No. 30, Reporting the Results of Operations—Reporting the Effects of Disposal of a Segment of a Business, and Extraordinary, Unusual, and Infrequently Occurring Events and Transactions,* are met (i.e., the event must be both unusual and infrequent). However, Appendix A (paragraph 48) of *SFAS No. 88* indicates that the gains or losses resulting from settlement, curtailment, or termination benefits generally do not result from the type of unusual and infrequent event required by *APB Opinion No. 30* to be reported as an extraordinary item. The authors agree with this interpretation.
- The effect of a settlement and/or curtailment and/or the offer of termination benefits directly related to a disposal of a segment of a business is required to be recognized as part of the gain or loss associated with the disposal, not as part of pension cost. The gain

or loss on disposal of a segment of a business is computed and recognized in accordance with *APB Opinion No. 30.*

- Unless the settlement or curtailment or the offer of termination benefits is directly related to a disposal of a segment (see the preceding paragraph), the recognition criteria of each event must be followed, even if a single management decision results in recognizing gains or losses in different reporting periods. A settlement gain or loss is recognized when the transaction is completed; a curtailment loss is recognized when it is probable a curtailment will occur and the amount can be estimated; a curtailment gain is recognized when realized; a special termination benefits loss is recognized when the employees accept the offer; and a contractual termination benefits loss is recognized when it is probable that employees will be entitled to benefits and the amount can be estimated. Therefore, a situation could arise in which a plan is terminated and a curtailment loss and the loss relating to contractual termination benefits granted to the employees are recognized in one period (when it is probable that the events will occur and the amounts can be estimated), the loss relating to special termination benefits offered in the same period is recognized in a later period (when the offer is accepted), and the gain on settlement is recognized in still another later period (when the annuities are purchased).

Special Transition Rules

SFAS No. 88 requires special transition rules for a termination/reversion transaction (e.g., when a defined benefit plan is terminated and a replacement defined benefit plan is established, with the excess assets reverting back to the employer) that occurred prior to the adoption of *SFAS Nos. 87* and *88*. The major effect of the special transition rules is that companies that have completed a termination/reversion transaction with the purchase of annuities before adopting the new rules are required to record a catch-up adjustment when *SFAS No. 87* is adopted. Historically, employers that have completed termination/reversion transactions and established replacement defined benefit pension plans have deferred the gain on the transaction. This gain, equal to the amount withdrawn from the plan, was amortized in subsequent periods. *SFAS No. 88* requires that employers recognize a gain as the cumulative effect of a change in accounting principles equal to the lesser of:

- The unamortized amount related to the termination/reversion.
- Any transition credit for the plan (or the successor plan) existing at the date *SFAS No. 87* is adopted.

EMPLOYEE STOCK OWNERSHIP PLANS

Employee stock ownership plans (ESOPs) are a type of defined contribution plan and are not a new phenomenon. Before 1976, the accounting for costs associated with an employee stock ownership plan was not well defined. *APB Opinion No. 8* discussed defined contribution plans in general. Although other pronouncements discussed stock option plans, stock purchase plans, and stock appreciation rights, none directly discussed the accounting problems peculiar to ESOPs.[5] After the FASB's initial decision to decline consideration of the subject, the Accounting Standards Division of the AICPA issued a *Statement of Position* (*SOP 76-3*), *Accounting Practices for Certain Employee Stock Ownership Plans*. This *SOP* represents the most significant effort of the profession to define appropriate accounting by the employer for costs incurred in connection with an ESOP.

To illustrate the provisions of *SOP 76-3*, it is helpful to present a hypothetical set of facts that might apply to a typical ESOP. These assumptions provide a common frame of reference as the basis for subsequent discussion of ESOP-related accounting and reporting issues. The fact pattern is as follows:

- A company forms a qualified ESOP (i.e., conforming to the applicable provisions of the Internal Revenue Code).
- The ESOP borrows money from an unrelated financial institution. The company is a party to the loan agreement and commits itself to make future contributions to the ESOP sufficient in amount to meet the debt service requirements. The commitment is frequently accompanied by a formal guarantee of the loan.
- The ESOP uses the loan proceeds to buy common stock of the company from present stockholders and from the company.
- The debt is collateralized by the company stock owned by the ESOP and is repaid in annual installments of principal plus interest.

SOP 76-3 states that when either the ESOP's debt is guaranteed by the employer or the employer is committed to make future contributions to the ESOP sufficient to cover the debt service requirements, the debt should be recorded in the employer's financial statements. The employer

---

[5] Chapter 13B of *Accounting Research Bulletin No. 43, Compensation Involved in Stock Option and Stock Purchase Plans, APB Opinion No. 25, Accounting for Stock Issued to Employees,* and *FASB Interpretation No. 28, Accounting for Stock Appreciation Rights and Other Variable Stock Option or Award Plans, an interpretation of APB Opinions No. 15 and 25.*

should record a liability because, in substance, the debt is the employer's debt; the employer has every intention, and is legally obligated, to make the contributions required for repayment of the loan. The *SOP* requires the recording of a liability regardless of whether the funds received from the ESOP are used to finance additional working capital (or fund other company needs) or to buy back its own shares. In addition, the *SOP* requires that the related interest rate and other relevant terms of the debt be disclosed in the financial statements.

In reaching its conclusion, the Accounting Standards Division of the AICPA rejected the view that while the employer should record a liability when the ESOP purchases previously unissued shares, it should not record a liability when the ESOP purchases shares that are already outstanding, since the purchase of outstanding shares is a transaction solely between two stockholders, and thus the employer has neither received cash proceeds of a sale nor bought back its own shares. That premise is incorrect, since the employer, by guaranteeing the loan or committing to make future contributions, becomes a party to the transaction.

With respect to the offsetting debit to the recorded liability, the *SOP* requires that the debit be presented as a reduction of stockholders' equity, rather than as a deferred charge. The following premises underlie this conclusion:

- When the company issues previously unissued shares to the ESOP, no real increase in equity capital results. Another event (i.e., repayment of the debt) must occur to trigger an expansion of equity capital. An analogy may be drawn to paragraph 14 of *APB Opinion No. 25,* which states that "if stock is issued to a plan before some or all of the services are performed, part of the consideration recorded for stock issued is unearned compensation and should be shown as a separate reduction of shareholders' equity."
- When the ESOP acquires shares from existing stockholders, a contraction of equity may be deemed to occur. Only when the related debt is liquidated can those shares acquired by the ESOP be considered outstanding.

The division rejected the view that the ESOP's purchase of already outstanding shares has no effect on the number of shares legally or substantively outstanding, such that the offsetting debit to the recorded liability should be recorded not as a reduction of stockholders' equity but rather as a deferred charge representing future employee services.

In a related issue, the *SOP* indicates that the recorded liability and offsetting charge to stockholders' equity should be reduced symmetrically as the ESOP liquidates the debt. This accounting treatment is consistent with the overall premise of the *SOP* that the employer's liability is in substance a debt to the lender and, consequently, the liability is reduced not when funds are transferred to the ESOP through contributions, but rather when funds are transmitted by the ESOP to the lender.

Measuring Compensation Expense

Prior to the issuance of *SOP 76-3,* some accountants held the view that compensation expense should be recognized based on the fair market value of shares allocated to individual employees at the time such allocations are made (see paragraph 10 of *APB Opinion No. 25*). A similar but slightly different approach calls for recognition of compensation expense as employees' rights to the shares vest. These treatments are based on the view that the period of allocation or vesting is the period in which the employee performs the services that "earn" the compensation. It was argued that this approach is consistent with paragraph 14 of *APB Opinion No. 25,* which states, "if stock is issued in a plan before some or all of the services are performed . . . the unearned compensation should be accounted for as an expense of the period or periods in which the employee performs services."

The *SOP* refutes these arguments in recommending that compensation expense should be measured by the amount contributed or committed to be contributed by the employer to an ESOP for a given year. The rationale supporting this accounting treatment is that such contributions are the proper measure of expense inasmuch as they represent expense irrevocably incurred regardless of whether the ESOP uses the funds to reduce the debt guaranteed by the employer. This treatment is consistent with accounting practice for discretionary contributions to profit-sharing plans.

The statement also provides that the portion of the contribution that in substance represents funding of the interest due on the recorded debt should be reported as interest expense in the income statement. In the fact pattern previously presented (in which the employer is committed to make contributions to the ESOP in amounts sufficient to cover debt service requirements), that portion of contributions representing principal liquidation would be identified and charged to compensation expense, while the interest element would be charged to interest expense. It should be noted, however, that "a significant minority within the division" believes that the entire amount contributed to the ESOP should be reported as compensation expense.

Earnings per Share and Dividends

The potential impact on earnings per share after an ESOP has acquired the employer's stock is a significant concern of management. This issue received considerable attention from the division and represents one of the few areas in which *SOP 76-3* includes the expression of a minority viewpoint.

The majority view in the *SOP* reflects a conservative position resulting in maximum dilution of earnings per share. Specifically, the division states that all shares held by an ESOP, whether acquired from the employer or from existing stockholders, should be treated as outstanding shares in the determination of earnings per share. In stating its conclusion, the division placed emphasis on the fact that an ESOP is a legal entity holding shares issued by the employer. Similarly, the *SOP* provides that dividends declared on shares held by an ESOP should be charged to retained earnings.

The minority viewpoint expressed in the *SOP* considers shares acquired by an ESOP from the employer as outstanding only to the extent that they become constructively unencumbered by repayments of debt principal. Consistent with this position, the minority believes that dividends on such shares should be charged to retained earnings only to the extent that the shares are constructively unencumbered. Any balance remaining would be reported as additional compensation expense. The minority apparently did not take exception to the majority's treatment for computing earnings per share or recording dividend payments when the ESOP acquires outstanding shares.[6]

Excess Contributions to a Defined Contribution Plan or ESOP

The FASB's Emerging Issues Task Force (EITF) in Issue 86-27, "Measurement of Excess Contributions to a Defined Contribution Plan," addressed the issue of accounting for a transaction in which an employer terminates a defined benefit plan and contributes the withdrawn assets to a defined contribution plan or ESOP. In such situations the amount contributed is generally in excess of the employer's required (or maximum) annual contribution to the plan, and is therefore maintained in a suspense account pending allocation to plan participants. Because the assets in excess of the required contribution are not allocated to individual partici-

---

[6] In stating its position, the minority points out that "when trust debt proceeds are transferred to the employer corporation, a transaction of a predominantly financing nature has occurred." It appears that the minority position refers only to a case in which the ESOP acquired shares from the employer rather than from existing stockholders.

pants' accounts, and the risks and rewards of ownership of the assets are retained by the employer, the EITF concluded that the excess contribution should not be accounted for as expense until the assets contributed to the plan are allocated to plan participants. Accordingly, it concluded that the employer should report the portion of the unallocated assets of the plan that consists of employer common stock as treasury stock in the financial statements. In addition, the EITF concluded that unallocated shares of the employer's common stock should not be considered outstanding for purposes of the earnings-per-share computation.

OTHER ISSUES

Business Combinations

For a single employer defined benefit pension plan, *SFAS No. 87* requires that in a business combination accounted for under the purchase method prescribed in *APB Opinion No. 16, Business Combinations,* the acquiring company recognize a liability (or asset) if the acquired company has a projected benefit obligation in excess of (or less than) fair value of plan assets. For purposes of this calculation, the projected benefit obligation and the fair value of plan assets at the date of the acquisition should reflect current interest rates and assumptions and the effects of intended plan restructuring. For a multiemployer plan, *SFAS No. 87* states that the estimated withdrawal liability should be recorded only when it is probable that the acquiring company will withdraw from the plan.

The pension asset or liability thus recorded eliminates any previously unrecognized gain or loss, unrecognized prior service cost, and transition debit or credit. To the extent that the pension asset or liability is considered in determining the level of funding, the difference between the acquirer's net pension cost and contributions will reduce the liability or asset recognized at the date of acquisition.

Rate-regulated Enterprises

SFAS Nos. 87 and *88* do not include special provisions relating to employer subject to certain types of regulation. In this connection, paragraph 210 of *SFAS No. 87* states:

> For rate-regulated enterprises, *FASB Statement No. 71, Accounting for the Effects of Certain Types of Regulation,* may require that the difference between net periodic pension cost as defined in this *Statement* and amounts of pension cost considered for rate-making purposes be recognized as an asset [if the criteria in paragraph 9 of *SFAS No. 71* are met] or a liability [if

the situation is as described in paragraph 11(b) of *SFAS No. 71*] created by the actions of the regulator. Those actions of the regulator change the timing of recognition of net pension cost as an expense; they do not otherwise affect the requirements of this *Statement*.

Paragraph 9 of *SFAS No. 71* states:

> Rate actions of a regulator can provide reasonable assurance of the existence of an asset. An enterprise shall capitalize all or part of an incurred cost that would otherwise be charged to expense if both of the following criteria are met:
>
> a. It is probable that future revenue in an amount at least equal to the capitalized cost will result from inclusion of that cost in allowable costs for rate-making purposes.
> b. Based on available evidence, the future revenue will be provided to permit recovery of the previously incurred cost rather than to provide for expected levels of similar future costs. If the revenue will be provided through an automatic rate-adjustment clause, this criterion requires that the regulator's intent clearly be to permit recovery of the previously incurred cost.

Paragraph 11(b) of *SFAS No. 71* states:

> Rate actions of a regulator can impose a liability on a regulated enterprise. Such liabilities are usually obligations to the enterprise's customers. The following are the usual ways in which liabilities can be imposed and the resulting accounting:
>
> b. A regulator can provide current rates intended to recover costs that are expected to be incurred in the future with the understanding that if those costs are not incurred future rates will be reduced by corresponding amounts. If current rates are intended to recover such costs and the regulator requires the enterprise to remain accountable for any amounts charged pursuant to such rates and not yet expended for the intended purpose, the enterprise shall not recognize as revenues amounts charged pursuant to such rates. Those amounts shall be recognized as liabilities and taken to income only when the associated costs are incurred.

The FASB staff's special report indicates that continued use of different methods of determining pension cost for rate-making purposes and financial accounting purposes would result in either the criteria in paragraph 9 of *SFAS No. 71* being met or the situation described in paragraph 11(b) of *SFAS No. 71*. However, the special report also indicates that the criteria in paragraph 9 of *SFAS No. 71* would *not* be met, and an asset due to the actions of the regulator would not be required to be recorded, if:

> (a) it is probable that the regulator soon will accept a change for rate-making purposes so that pension cost is determined in accordance with

> *Statement 87* and (b) it is not probable that the regulator will provide revenue to recover the excess cost that results from the use of *Statement 87* for financial reporting purposes during the period between the date that the employer adopts *Statement 87* and the rate case implementing the change.

Similarly, the special report indicates that the situation would not be as described in paragraph 11(b) of *SFAS No. 71*, and a liability due to the actions of the regulator would not be required to be recorded, if it is probable that:

> (a) the regulator soon will accept a change for rate-making purposes so that pension cost is determined in accordance with *Statement 87*, (b) the regulator will not hold the employer responsible for the costs that were intended to be recovered by the current rates and that have been deferred by the change in method, and (c) the regulator will provide revenue to recover those same costs when they are eventually recognized under the method required by *Statement 87*.

State and Local Governments

In September 1986, the Governmental Accounting Standards Board (GASB) issued its *Statement No. 4, Applicability of FASB Statement No. 87, "Employers' Accounting for Pensions," to State and Local Governmental Employers*. Paragraph 10 of *GASB Statement No. 4* states:

> State and local governmental employers, including proprietary and similar trust funds, should not change their accounting and reporting of pension activities as a result of the issuance of *FASB Statement No. 87*.

The statement also indicates, however, that employers may change to any attribution (actuarial cost) method, provided the method (1) is in conformity with *APB Opinion No. 8*, National Council on Government Accounting *(NCGA) Statement 1, Governmental Accounting and Financial Reporting Principles*, and *NCGA Statement 6, Pension Accounting and Financial Reporting: Public Employee Retirement Systems and State and Local Government Employers*, and (2) is considered preferable for purposes of making an accounting change in accordance with *APB Opinion No. 20, Accounting Changes*.

Government Contracts

Some companies perform work for the U.S. federal government under contracts that are subject to price adjustment pursuant to the rules of the Cost Accounting Standards Board (CASB). Certain of the standards issued by the CASB have provisions that are at variance with *SFAS Nos. 87* and *88*. For example:

- *SFAS No. 87* prescribes specific methodologies for determining pension cost and emphasizes that pension cost is *not* necessarily determined by the amount the employer deides to contribute to the plan. For cost accounting purposes the CASB rules limit the pension provision to amounts the employer is legally "compelled" to fund (e.g., under ERISA) or to amounts actually funded up to the amount of the provision for financial accounting purposes.
- *SFAS No. 87* requires employers to amortize (actuarial) gains and losses over the expected future service period of employees using the corridor approach. CASB rules generally require these gains and losses to be amortized over a 15-year period.

The above examples represent only two of the existing variances. Auditors engaged in an examination of financial statements of a company subject to CASB standards should be aware of these and other differences that may exist between *SFAS Nos. 87* and *88* and the CASB standards. Auditors should also be aware that adjustments may be needed when financial statements prepared in accordance with generally accepted accounting principles are to be used for CASB purposes, as such differences may affect the company's position in the determination or redetermination of prices under its government contracts.

Plan Compliance with ERISA

SFAS No. 87 requires companies to compute pension cost in accordance with the plan's requirements. If the plan is not in compliance with ERISA, the provision for pension cost may be based on plan provisions that do not comply with ERISA. This may result in a loss contingency that may need to be reflected in the financial statements, depending on the likelihood of incurring and reasonably estimating the amount of a liability. In this connection, the guidance in *SFAS No. 5, Accounting for Contingencies,* although not directly applicable, may be helpful. To illustrate, if a plan instrument does not conform to ERISA's participation requirements, the provision for pension cost would be computed excluding certain legally eligible participants, and the pension accrual will be inadequate. Thus, a determination would need to be made as to the likelihood (as defined by *SFAS No. 5*) that a liability will be incurred for the additional benefits, and for any fines and penalties that may be imposed for lack of compliance.[7]

---

[7] ERISA specifies that certain penalties are levied against the plan or against the plan administrator. However, the employer may ultimately become liable for such penalties even if it is not the plan administrator.

CHAPTER 38

FUNDING RETIREMENT PLANS—INVESTMENT OBJECTIVES

Eugene B. Burroughs

The successful funding of the future pension benefit payment promise through investment operations is made possible through the exercise of prudence, the application of time-proven principles, the dedication of people conducting themselves in a professional manner, and the resultant efficacy of the adopted policy and practices. The growth in real asset value over time through successful investment funding activities will require fewer contributions and will allow greater potential for enhancing retirement benefit payments.

Representatives of sponsors of employee benefit plans play a significant role in the benefit payments funding process, for if they collectively address the asset management part of their responsibilities in an objective, professional manner, they may find their stewardship producing the major portion of the benefit payments stream from the pension plan. The power of compounding interest, earnings reinvested, rents redeployed, and realized capital appreciation are powerful elements in the wealth enhancement process. To the degree the supervising fiduciaries are successful in systematically adding value over time from investment operations, less of a need exists to increase employer, or employee, contributions to the plan.

It, therefore, behooves the supervising group to endeavor through knowledge and insight into the workings of the financial markets to propitiously allocate plan assets. Unfortunately, many plan sponsors miss their opportunities to add value to the plan by:

The frequent hiring of "winning" managers and firing of "losing" managers.

Excessive turnover in the portfolio.

Inordinate emphasis on stock-picking activities as opposed to the more productive asset allocation decisions.

Assuming unrealizable return expectations based upon the most recent market experience and ignoring the long-term risk/return relationships in the securities markets.

Since asset stewardship activities so significantly impact the net bottom line, choosing among funding vehicles is extremely important. With $12,838.4 billion (12/31/85) of investable capital in the world, there are many roads to value enhancement. The following discussion of funding pensions through asset management activities provides the elements basic to the process. The discussion is necessarily limited to investing alternatives. The important point of this discussion is to grasp the principles and process to achieve a plan's funding goals through investment operations.

The discussion includes:

1. *Four elements fundamental to successful investing* employee benefit plan monies.
2. Attributes of the *prudent fiduciary.*
3. Characteristics of the *three favored classes of investments.*
4. Identification of appropriate *investment objectives.*
5. Evaluation and selection of the *investment facility.*
6. Development and documentation of *investment policy.*
7. Exercising the option to engage in *strategic asset deployment* activities.
8. *Monitoring, reevaluation, and modification* of policy and strategy.

FOUR ELEMENTS FUNDAMENTAL TO SUCCESSFUL INVESTING

Before proceeding with the discussion of investment planning as it relates to achieving funding objectives, it is necessary to review four principles fundamental to the investment process:

1. The level of risk assumed by a fund determines the level of return achieved. (Figure 38–1)
2. Returns normally attributed to variable assets (common stock,

FIGURE 38–1

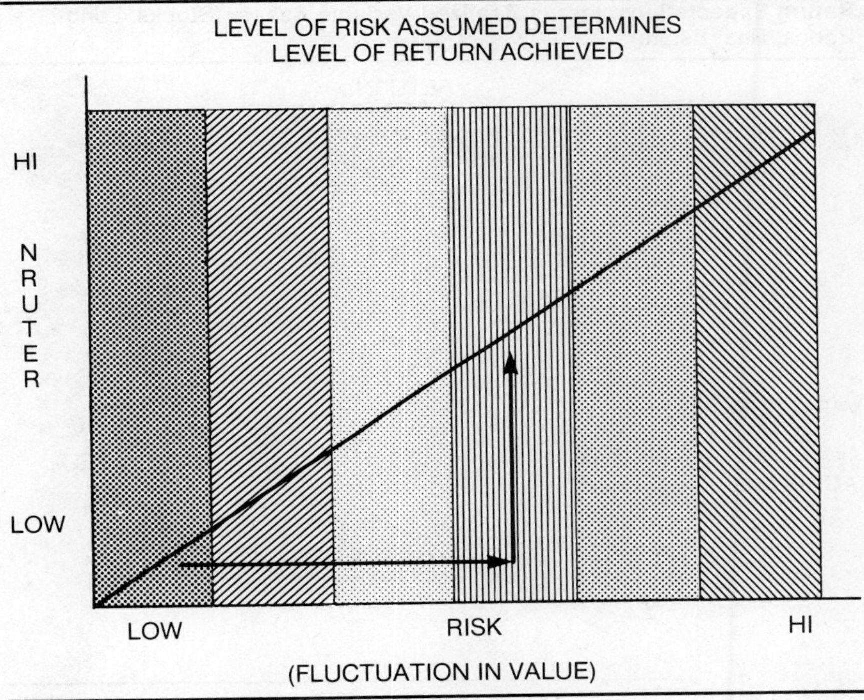

long duration bonds, and real estate) are assured only as the holding period is extended. (Figure 38–2)

3. The time permitted to lapse before converting an investment position to cash determines the level of return.
4. Market studies have confirmed the orderliness that exists between risk and reward in the financial markets. (Figure 38–3)

THE PRUDENT FIDUCIARY

Since successful investment programs are a product of human judgment, it is also important to consider briefly the attributes of a prudent fiduciary. ERISA, Sec. 404(a)(1)(B), stipulates that a fiduciary shall discharge his or her duties with respect to a plan solely in the interest of the participants and beneficiaries, and "with the care, skill, prudence, and diligence under the circumstances then prevailing that a prudent man acting in a like

FIGURE 38–2
Return Expectations versus Realized Variable Assets (Stocks, Long Bonds, Real Estate)

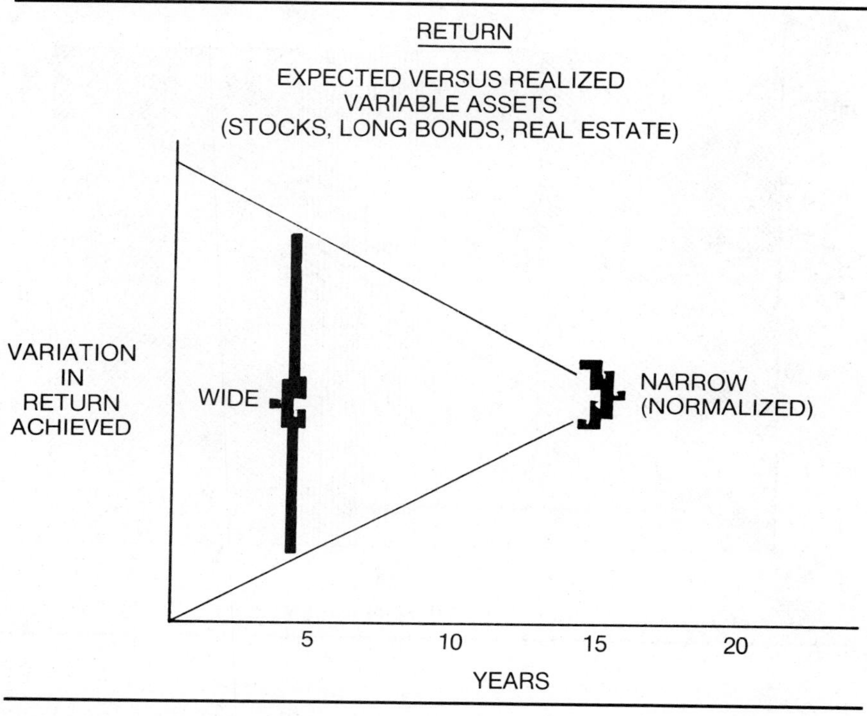

capacity and familiar with such matters would use in the conduct of an enterprise of a like character and with like aims."

To qualify, in retrospect, as prudent, fiduciaries of plans must have conducted themselves as prudent experts, having set up an administrative approach to facilitate the decision-making process, considered internal factors of the fund, hired and listened to investment experts and qualified legal counsel, obtained independent studies when advisable, considered the financial variables of the prospective course of action, and set up an arm's-length mechanism to negotiate with any parties-in-interest. Such a documented sequence of activities probably should be sufficient to stand the test of prudence required by the law.

In any technically demanding investment course of action, there should be an effective blending of the judgment of those who are charged

FIGURE 38–3
Orderliness in Financial Markets (Types of Mutual Funds)

ORDERLINESS IN FINANCIAL MARKETS

Types of Mutual Funds

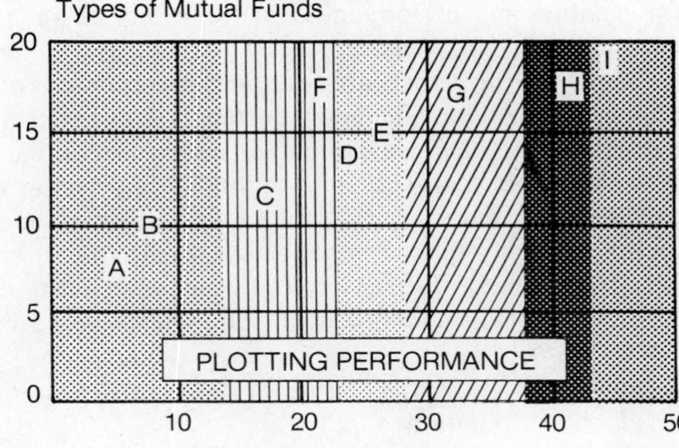

REWARD
Compound Annual Return for Ten Year Period Ended June 30

RISK
Maximum Fluctuation, in Percentage Points, Between Best and Worst Quarters Over the Past Ten Years

CATEGORIES OF FUNDS

A	91 Day U.S. Treasury Bills (Short Term Instruments)
B	Money Market Funds (Short Term Fixed Income Pool)
C	Fixed Income Funds (More than 75% in Fixed Income Assets)
D	Balanced Funds (Conserves Principal; Mix of Stocks and Bonds)
E	Growth and Income Funds (Stock Mix Aimed for Short and Long Term)
F	Equity Income Funds (Mostly Stocks with High Current Value)
G	Growth Funds (Stocks with Higher Growth than Market Average)
H	Capital Appreciation Funds (Diverse Means to Build Capital)
I	Small Company Growth Funds

Source: Lipper Advisory Services, Inc., Milwaukee.

to be the overseers of a trust fund, with the opinions of the experts who provide the counsel and research in support of a defensible conclusion. If done properly, this team approach will most likely be judged sufficient to support a sound decision. There also should be a careful preservation of the lines of demarcation among cofiduciaries. Plans go afoul with the counsel of too few. Sufficient counsel increases the likelihood of success. This is not a carte blanche vote in favor of multimanagement investment systems but recognition that just as the diversification requirement calls for balance in assembling the components of the portfolio, prudence calls for balance and effectiveness in the selection of people and how they perform their varied assignments.

There is no substitute for the fiduciary's exercise of informed and reasoned judgment. The fiduciary must pursue each alternative until he or she gets to the heart of the matter, examining all the facts available prior to making the decision. In addition to performing resourceful due diligence, there appears to be unanimous agreement among legal counselors on the necessity for the preparation of resourceful documentation on the part of all fiduciaries party to the process.

Put succinctly, the "prudent" fiduciary possesses the following characteristics:

1. Determination.
2. Knowledge, leading to insightful decisions.
3. Organization.
4. Openmindedness.
5. Objectivity.
6. Maintaining realistic expectations.
7. Patience.

There are myriad investment vehicles available as funding vehicles; insured, noninsured; pooled separate accounts; aggregated pools of individual securities; privately placed and publicly traded. The characteristics of the investment medium chosen should be conducive to the attainment of the investment objectives sought. To recognize which vehicles are most appropriate, a fiduciary needs to understand the differing characteristics of the various classes of investments.

CHARACTERISTICS OF THE THREE FAVORED CLASSES OF INVESTMENTS

To understand why fiduciaries choose to blend equity and fixed income securities in portfolios, the characteristics of common stock, fixed income securities and real estate are reviewed. In order of preference, common stock is the preferred investment medium, with bonds, cash equivalents and real estate vehicles following.

Common Stock

The characteristic that most attracts the employee benefit plan investor to common stock is its ability to add real value to a portfolio. According to SEI Evaluation Service, the S & P 500 has achieved +7.4 percent per year in real return over the past ten years (through 12/31/86). If, during this time, a plan manager was able to constructively exploit this class of investment, the fund was able to compete effectively with, and substantially outdistance inflation's impact on portfolio values. Since one of the long-range goals for many employee benefit plans is to pay benefits in inflation-adjusted dollars, then the choice of common stock as the preferred asset class has proven to be a productive funding facility.

The driving forces behind stock prices are earnings, return on equity, and the issuing firm's dividend policy. Increased earnings influence the company's board of directors to increase dividend payouts, which in turn influences stock analysts to pay a higher price for the shares. As demand for the shares increase, at some point the stock becomes fully valued, or overvalued, which should lead the investment manager to take the plan's profits and reinvest the proceeds in a stock that is still passing through the undervalued part of its pricing cycle. Such portfolio management should produce the historical 6 percent real return expected from common stock ownership. The astute manager picks up additional return from his or her superior information processing ability.

The rewards of stock ownership, resulting from a combination of an increasing dividend stream and appreciation in the value of the shares can be unlimited. These rewards accrue from investors' willingness to pay a higher multiple for the increased earnings and the ability of the firm to "manage its store" successfully. The increases in the price/earnings (p/e) multiple and dividend payout stream flow in part from the firm's ability to capitalize on its research and development activity. This in turn fosters consumer acceptance of its products or services and eventually leads to increased sales. If costs are efficiently controlled, increasing sales should lead to growing earning power, profitable reinvestment opportunities for the earnings, and ultimately increased confidence shown by the investment community in the firm's ability to manage its affairs successfully in the future. Investors, reflecting their increased confidence in the future fortunes of the firm, will increase their activity in accumulating the stock, which in turn will bid up the price/earnings multiple. Thus, the p/e multiple becomes a measure of the attractiveness of a particular security versus all other available securities as determined by the investing public.

Even though common stock as a class has proven to be an attractive funding facility, plan sponsors need to identify stock managers who have developed and can apply superior selection techniques. Unless the manager can consistently buy stock with a present price at or below its intrinsic value, the sponsor may have to forsake active management and resort to dollar cost averaging into a passively managed index fund. The sponsor in turn must exercise patience while longer-term investment trends overcome the shorter-term cyclical influences in the determination of share value. Actively managing a portfolio of common stock can achieve superior results, but the results do not come automatically. It takes a combination of superior stock selection, successful market timing, or both, all of which result from superior forecasting ability. Charles Ellis of Greenwich Research Associates sums it up well when he says that the "keys to successful common stock management are: (1) adopt a policy (style) and apply it consistently; (2) strive for excellence in a few areas; (3) concentrate on when to sell; and (4) maintain modest expectations."

Many plan sponsors have adopted passive stock management (a style of management that seeks to attain average risk-adjusted performance) because the hurdle rate required from active management is so high. To justify its use, the return from active management must exceed the return from a comparable market index plus a recoupment return for the higher relative transaction costs. Plan sponsors are also adopting passive strategies to implement asset redeployment moves to complement their existing active managers and as a temporary parking place for equity-destined monies while undertaking a management search.

Common stock has evolved over time to become the favored investment medium of the funds because it offers the possibility of providing the most attractive real rate of return. However, before that possibility becomes a reality, a plan sponsor has two options. The sponsor can find a manager who can recognize change early, select those stocks whose emerging positive attributes will be discovered by other analysts, and pays attention to the price paid for stocks as a class, and for his or her stocks in particular. Or, in the absence of finding such a manager, the sponsor can participate in a passively supervised stock portfolio for that portion of total portfolio dedicated to long-term common stock ownership.

Fixed Income Securities

Fixed income securities have traditionally been the bellwether asset in employee benefit plan portfolios. However, with the turbulence created in interest rates several years ago by unanticipated and volatile inflation rates, confidence has been shaken in the traditionally passive approach to bond management. Because of the resultant concern for volatility, bond managers have developed a number of strategies and products to more effectively compete with the challenging environment.

There are many alternatives to choose from in the fixed income area. Within the money market area alone, one can choose from a broad spectrum of securities. The advent of money market deposit accounts and short-term investment fund (STIF) accounts offered by the banks in the deregulation environment, has increased both the options and relative yields for monies limited to short-term maturities. For a plan willing to embrace a higher degree of credit risk, Eurodollar CD's, corporate master notes and repurchase agreements are available. CARS (Consumer Auto Receivables), CATS (Certificates of Accrual on Treasury Securities), and TIGRS (Treasury Investment Growth Receipts) are examples of the many new fixed income products available in the bond markets.

With the proliferation of products has come an increase in the number of ways of increasing wealth in a portfolio through the use of fixed income securities. Whether a plan's supervising fiduciaries accomplish their goals through a high or low turnover approach, there is no substitute for the adoption of and adherence to a reasoned, disciplined, strategy. To the degree possible, a plan should exploit its longer-term planning horizon and forsake the extreme comfort of money market instruments by extending the duration of its fixed income portfolio. Here again there are a number of alternatives and strategies—active/active, passive/active, passive/passive. You can make active bets on interest rate movements while also engaging in sector swaps, etc.; you can forgo (or limit) your interest rate anticipation moves while still actively trading the portfolio with arbitrage moves; or you can immunize or dedicate the portfolio and forgo shorter-term upside potential (or limit downside risk) through a wholly passive approach. These strategies can be implemented using governments, corporates and utilities, or the more recent market entrants—mortgage-backed securities and derivative instruments. The newest entrant is the "accounts receivable backed bond," which securitizes credit card and automobile purchases.

Why would a fiduciary include bonds as a part of a plan's funding mechanism? First, the plan (the lender) has a preferred claim on the income and assets of the issuer (the borrower). The lender has a contractual right to the return of stated principal and a contractual right to receive the periodic stated interest payments. From this right springs a plan's expectation of receiving and cultivating an income stream. It is the periodic reinvestment of this income stream that permits a plan to exploit the principle of the "power of compounding interest." In just 20 years, $100 growing at 7 percent (i.e., 4 percent inflation + 3 percent "rent" for loaning money) results in an accumulation of $386. The tax-exempt status of the plan increases all the more the efficacy of compounding interest.

The success of a bond investment depends upon whether the financial accumulation from ownership compares favorably to the original expectations at purchase. If a plan's objective is to produce a real rate of return, the income stream from the bond should exceed the loss due to inflation in purchasing power of the principal. Unfortunately, this is only one of the risks faced in bond investment. Others are credit (default) risk (if the issuer goes bankrupt), interest rate risk (if bonds must be sold below the price paid), call risk (if the issuer calls in the bond in a lower interest rate environment), and reinvestment risk (if comparable, creditworthy bonds are paying a lower rate of interest when principal or coupons are being reinvested).

Bond risk can be controlled. Besides the use of interest rate futures (not in the scope of this discussion), there are many portfolio management techniques that can provide comfort to the plan sponsor. Inflation risk can be reduced by buying bonds only when the real spread (interest rates minus probable inflation) is at a historical premium. Correctly assessing when a premium spread is available takes a combination of astute historical perspective, forecasting ability, and luck! The phenomenon of lagging return premiums probably exists because bond buyers, having previously erred in their forecasting of inflation's rise, demand high rates long after inflation has subsided in intensity. (Although inflation peaked in March 1980, wider than usual spreads have been available for quite some time now.) Credit risk can be controlled through the exercise of superior credit analysis and adequate quality threshold guidelines. Interest rate risk can be reduced by keeping maturities short, dollar-cost-averaging purchases, and adopting the various immunization and dedication strategies.

Partitioning out the retired lives and purchasing bonds dedicated to meet these benefit payments as they fall due has become a popular planning technique. In some cases, the potential this technique offers for withdrawal liabilities reduction (or elimination) to the multiemployer plans has been sufficient to justify the trustees' implementing such a risk-reduction strategy. Single-sponsor plans also have chosen such techniques to control the fluctuation in plan surplus, or the rate at which contributions are required. To manage call risk, one must simply "read the fine print." Reinvestment risk can be eliminated by purchasing zero coupon bonds or laddering the bond maturities.

Real Estate

A third, but less popular, funding facility is the fee ownership of real properties. The class of equity real estate is added to a portfolio within the context of a pension plan's objectives to (a) exploit its long-term time horizon, (b) defend against the possibility that higher inflationary periods may reappear (repeat of the 1976–81 environment), (c) add a third asset class that offers the potential to produce real rates of return in all price environments, and (d) because of its noncovariance characteristics when combined with stocks and bonds in a portfolio.

Like common stock, equity real estate has the potential to add significant real value over time. Its hybrid nature of being both financial (leases) and tangible (bricks and mortar) in character enables its owner to hedge effectively against either a low or high inflation scenario. Overage rents, net net leases, expense escalation clauses, equity equivalent loans, etc., all result in the investor being assured that his or her principal will stay competitive with inflation. The hybrid nature of convertible participating mortgages enables the pension fund sponsor to hedge against an unknown future.

Successful real estate investing requires attention to location, product, and management. Therefore, a fund must retain a real estate manager with a resourceful research staff. Since real estate is a relatively inefficient market, a real estate management organization should, by processing information in an effective manner, ultimately acquire those properties whose configurations of attributes will assure relatively high demand. Building on a firm base of research capability, the manager(s) must have developed a strategic approach compatible with the plan and have demonstrated the ability to acquire properties astutely through analytical talent and negotiating skills. An underrated resource of a manager is his or her property (asset) management capability, whether developed in-house or successfully retained and monitored. It also is important to determine that the principals of the firm have formed a team that enjoys industry peer group respect. It takes time and effort to develop marketing packages for complex properties. Those management teams who (a) have attracted a sufficient client base to provide continuing cash flow availability, (b) have available the diverse disciplines to evaluate a deal effectively, and (c) can quickly respond to the offer to capitalize on a market opportunity, will be afforded priority in being shown the more desirable properties.

Other caveats that must be considered are: (1) the properties acquired must be well conceived, well located, and well managed; (2) the sponsor must be willing to undergo "income only" years in anticipation of the slower emerging capital appreciation years; (3) the manager must purchase the properties using the current effective rents as the basis for determination of value; (4) a plan just beginning in real estate may be well advised to dollar-cost-average into the market over several years; and (5) if a plan is going into open-ended funds that use net asset valuations supported by yearly appraisals of the portfolio properties, due diligence should be performed by the plan sponsor to assure that the net asset valuation currently used reflects the realities of the current marketplace. One would not want to place new dollars indirectly into real estate assets at inflated valuations resulting from a lagging recognition of deteriorating portfolio values.

Asset Allocation

Although collectively the classes of common stock, bonds, and equity real estate represent the preponderance of allocations in employee benefit plan portfolios, other vehicles used in the funding process include guaranteed investment contracts, mortgages, venture capital, and oil and gas investments. To protect a fund's future valuations from being overly vulnerable to the fortunes of any one class, supervising fiduciaries construct diversified portfolios. An employee benefit plan portfolio's value is the sum of its component parts. If the plan is to reach its ultimate performance objectives, these component parts must, each in its own way, make a contribution to the whole fund. No class of assets exists in isolation. Such an orderly blending of related units is not happenstance, but must be carefully orchestrated to produce a harmonious conclusion. Thus, a cardinal rule in plan investing is "diversify, diversify, diversify."

Someone, or some group, usually serves in the role of "investment coordinator" for a plan. The following list describes the coordinator's duties and responsibilities.

1. Lead the plan's professional team in the identification of the investment and noninvestment constraints of the plan and the subsequent development of the appropriate portfolio performance objectives, policies, and strategies.
2. Continually examine and evaluate all acceptable investment alternatives, and recognize and value the strengths that each team member can bring to the task.
3. Watch for early warning signs of weaknesses evidenced by people, policies, or practices of the program, and fosters the reasonable expectations of investment performance, recognizing the inherent limitations in the investment management process.
4. Recognize the importance of establishing an appropriate risk posture for the fund predicated on a thorough examination of the risk/reward trade-offs.
5. Set targets in ranges rather than in absolutes.
6. Recognize and be responsive to change, being knowledgeable in techniques on the cutting edge of contemporary investment management.

7. Respect the opinions of gray-haired peers, realizing that to ignore the past may cause the fund to repeat it.
8. Foster a spirit of meaningful review, evaluation, and modification of previous policy decisions.

Since numerous studies have confirmed that the single most significant decision in terms of its potential to add value to the portfolio is the asset allocation decision, it is important that the plan's portfolio be effectively supervised in the aggregate. Because one is always dealing with an uncertain future, portfolios must be broadly diversified, thus hedged against the possibilities of higher inflation, continuing stable inflation, or the onset of deflation. Having diversified the bulk of the portfolio's assets, strategic moves can be made from cycle to cycle with a smaller portion of the assets in the quest to achieve rates of return above the rates of return the longer-term policy portfolio produces. Any strategic moves made will be the result of an assessment of changes in the general prices within the economy, the profits of the companies in which assets are invested and, ultimately, the valuation of the asset classes themselves, both now and projected into the future. All this activity is for the purpose of tilting the portfolio toward investment success. Producing real gains in value is the ultimate goal in the asset management portion of the funding process since such gains will be used to replace the lost wages of the deserving retirees and to pay benefits to the beneficiaries of the plans.

The extent to which one permits flexibility in asset allocation and asset shift activities depends upon the volatility constraint that logically evolves from the investment objectives and goals adopted by the benefit plan's representatives. Before a discussion can proceed to conclusion on what would appear to be the "best" allocation of the assets from time to time, a constraints analysis must be performed. Such analysis coordinates the portfolio-building activities of the investment manager with the objectives and goals as perceived and articulated by the plan sponsor.

The place to begin in the asset allocation process is with the plan sponsor representative(s). As previously mentioned, this could be the investment coordinator. An ideal plan sponsor representative:

1. Has researched and properly analyzed the demographics of the plan.
2. Can speak for the intentions of the principals of the contributing source as to their attitudes toward funding and risk taking policies.
3. Understands the risk/reward dimensions of the investment markets.
4. Has thorough knowledge, insight, and experience, and is emotionally capable of handling investment fluctuations without abandoning the adopted long-term policy.

Asset allocation decisions are policy and strategy decisions which are separate and distinct from objective setting. Objective setting has to do with the sponsor targeting a desired result, or range of results. The characteristics of the plan are the driving force in objective setting. Policy and strategy are implementation phases which evolve logically in the quest to attain the objectives. Thus, the ideal fiduciary sets out initially to articulate, as succinctly as possible, the appropriate objectives for the investment program and then adopts the appropriate policy and strategy methodology.

IDENTIFICATION OF APPROPRIATE INVESTMENT OBJECTIVES

One should also be careful not to confuse *portfolio guideline setting* with *setting investment objectives*. Guidelines are adopted to facilitate the attainment of the objectives and, thus, form the building blocks of policy and strategy. Not only do some fiduciaries confuse objective setting and adopting portfolio guidelines but they adopt guidelines which impede the attainment of their stated objectives!

Investment objective setting by employee benefit plan representatives is a delicate balancing act. The supervising fiduciaries find their loyalties pulled in different directions resulting from the natural tendencies that exist among the economic players in the process. These understandable tendencies create tensions among fiduciaries when adopting policy. The contributing sponsor wants to pay the highest level of benefits for the least cost. The participant wants the assurance that the pension promise will be fulfilled at a level competitive to an acceptable cost-of-living standard. The regulators want "prudent management," resulting in principal protection and growth in assets to assure that private plans in the aggregate will fulfill the socially redeeming goal of providing financial security during retirement. The plans' fiduciaries themselves often have their own agendas; in addition to embracing worthy and constructive goals they often desire personal fulfillment and respect from their peer group, reelection to office, promotion in a job, etc. Since it is impossible to satisfy all these conflicting aspirations and influences simultaneously, investment objective setting in many instances becomes a process of negotiation and compromise. The goals of the various constituencies are weighted according to importance and, in the process, policy and strategy evolve. To the extent that the process can remain professionally objective the probability increases that the objectives ultimately adopted will be the most appropriate given the long-term needs of the plan.

Investment objectives should be set in tandem with the overall funding policy of the plan. Conservative funding, i.e., accelerated reduction in the unfunded liabilities, can be accompanied by an aggressive investment posture. Conversely, a sponsor who chooses to fund the liabilities as minimally as possible out of current resources, may be obligated to the participants to manage those fewer assets which have been accumulated in a conservative manner. However, sponsors' attitude toward risk may very well reverse these relationships. In any event, an important principle to apply in objective setting is funding coordination.

What are some of the specific elements in objective setting? Foremost, the objectives adopted should be in conformance with the plan's documents and with the fiduciary standards of ERISA and related regulations. Also, an objective fundamental to all plans is that cash be available to make benefit payments in a timely manner. No investment course of action is complete until cash has been returned to the fund. To facilitate the setting of this objective, the consulting actuary should develop a financial profile of the fund which projects the immediate, short-term, and long-term cash flow requirements. In such an analysis the present value of assets, investment return expectations, anticipated contributions, and liabilities are considered and the fiscal integrity of the sponsoring entity is projected.

After the cash-flow needs are identified and targeted, the planning process turns to risk/reward considerations. To what degree can the fund sustain volatility in values in the quest for higher returns? How important is it to the sponsors that the future flow of contributions be stabilized and controlled? Is there a limit on the level of contributions that can be expected? Must principal value be preserved or enhanced? Does it seem wise, in the case of a plan with a relatively young work force, to place added importance on seeking growth in value in *real* terms? Conversely, in the case of a mature plan, should the manager seek cash flow from income-producing investments to augment dwindling contributions? How willing is the control group to exercise patience and accept short-term disappointment as a "contrarian investor" in the search for long-term positive results? The answers to these questions become the portfolio constraints. The aggregation of constraints influence policy and strategy decisions, including asset allocation. Portfolio guidelines; beta, quality, diversification, etc. also emanate from the constraints analysis.

Part and parcel with establishing the investment return objectives is the selection of the performance measurement period and the comparative benchmarks to be used in the monitoring process. The performance objectives can be set in nominal terms, or *real* terms; several performance objectives can be adopted for the same fund. For instance, it may be deemed appropriate to compare the aggregate portfolio on a *real* basis, i.e., comparing the total return to a cost-of-living index while also comparing segments of the fund to referenced benchmarks on a nominal basis, i.e., comparing the growth stock component to an index of growth stock portfolios, and comparing the bond component to the Shearson Lehman Government Corporate Bond Index. A set of performance objectives, both nominal and real, spanning differing time frames, may be more insightful to the stewards of the fund than relying on a single measurement statistic.

Very few sponsors still express their performance objectives using a single absolute number. Since most fiduciaries are aware that the investment earnings assumption used by the actuary for planning purposes is an inappropriate performance target (it should follow not lead the investment experience), any other single absolute number chosen is even more of an arbitrary target. An 8 percent absolute target return would seem reasonable and attainable in a disinflationary environment; it would be less meaningful and attainable in higher inflation periods. More funds seem to be favoring the adoption of relative return objectives; returns relative to the CPI, returns relative to chosen referenced benchmarks, etc. The acceptance of relative return objectives recognizes the inherent environmental limitations that exist in the management of institutional portfolios.

Producing a real rate of return can be a formidable, and rewarding, task for an employee benefit plan. There is obviously no single way to accomplish this quest, but careful attention to detail and skillful consideration of many alternatives just may add sufficient basis points to a fund's bottom line to enable it to compete effectively with the problem of purchasing power erosion. Certainly, with a modicum of success from the management process, real value may very well be added to the plan's portfolio if the responsible fiduciaries:

- Assume responsibility for allocating the portfolio's assets in the aggregate.
- Develop a resourceful information system resulting in group conviction as to which direction the general prices in the nation are heading.
- Understand historically the attractiveness of various investment media in different price environments.
- Consistently diversify a majority of the portfolio to hedge against the occurrence of general price level extremes in either direction.
- Preserve flexibility in the management of a minority of the portfolio to exploit the evolving price environment scenario.

The following objectives excerpted from a plan's investment policy statement are an example of the use of relative *and* real rate of return objectives:

> The long-term investment objective of the Trust is to produce a total rate of return of three percent (3 percent) in excess of the rate of inflation as measured by the Department of Labor, Bureau of Labor Statistics Consumer Price Index, All Cities Average, 1967 = 100. Since the duration, direction, and intensity of inflation cycles vary from cycle to cycle, it is recognized that the return experienced by the Trust over any one cycle may vary from this objective; but it is deemed reasonable to expect a three percent (3 percent) real rate of return over succeeding cycles. A complementary investment objective of the Trust is that the total rate of return achieved by the Trust competes favorably, when compared over comparable periods, to other trust funds having similar objectives and constraints and using similar investment media.

Other examples of portfolio performance objectives, stated or implied, include the following:

1. To achieve the rate of return of a published index, including income, plus x percent.
2. To achieve the rate of return of a special benchmark index reflecting a chosen risk-reward preference.
3. To achieve performance comparability to other accounts having similar objectives.
4. To achieve a minimum of x percent.
5. To preserve portfolio value sufficient to eliminate the potential for withdrawal liability (Taft-Hartley funds).
6. To achieve total return sufficient to stabilize contributions at x percent of payroll.
7. To maintain a specified level of plan surplus.

Performance objectives expressed in risk-adjusted returns are preferred. Returns expressed in risk-adjusted terms are the most precise in objective setting since they take into account volatility as well as return. Unfortunately risk-adjusted return analysis has not been broadly practiced and, thus, statistics are not readily available for comparative purposes.

Someone said that the application of portfolio management operations is both an art and a science. Engineering the portfolio to attain the stated objectives would seem to be more scientific in nature, particularly since the advent of computer technology to assist in modeling and portfolio control activities. The fact finding and related analysis so vital to the objective-setting process also requires resourceful analytical activities.

The "artful" part of the process would seem, in the present environment, to be at the plan sponsor level. The supervising fiduciaries must examine the facts, balance what appear to be opposing agendas of the various constituencies, fend off any potentially inhibiting subjective influences, objectively adopt the most appropriate set of investment objectives, and, carefully articulate them to the managers of the assets. Choosing appropriate objectives points the manager of the assets in the proper direction in the quest to assist in fulfilling the benefit payment promise.

EVALUATION AND SELECTION OF THE INVESTMENT FACILITY

Having identified the appropriate investment objectives, the supervising group can next turn to evaluating and selecting the investment facility. If the sponsor decides to passively invest, then an organization is sought that can administratively replicate the return of the chosen benchmark portfolios. If, however, the sponsor chooses value-added management, the structure of the organization is not nearly as important as is its demonstrated ability to add value to the portfolio. Success in investment decision making is indifferent to either the structure of the organization, or its size and location. Whether the firm is organized as a bank, insurance company, mutual fund organization, or independent counsel firm, the keys to success are its people and program. To the degree any one of these four organizational classes becomes more successful in attracting, compensating, and motivating the best and brightest professionals, then this group as a class should eventually produce superior performance.

To be successful, an investment management firm should possess the following characteristics: It should have an approach to investing that has proven successful in the past. It should consistently apply that approach and articulate it clearly. The firm should have highly intelligent, insightful, well-trained, experienced people and motivate them with performance incentives. It should cultivate an environment conducive to creativity and innovation. It should target investment management activities to attain the client's objectives and goals. It should have resourceful quantitative support systems. It should maintain high internal quality control systems in the delivery of investment services and communicate effectively with the client's representatives.

Funding the benefit payment promise through asset-enhancement activities requires a systematic planning and execution process. Having identified the objectives and with the manager in place, the supervising fiduciaries, together with a consultant can, if desired, address themselves collectively to finalizing an investment policy statement. Before proceeding with a discussion of the elements of a written policy statement let us review the relevant issues covered thus far.

DEVELOPMENT AND DOCUMENTATION OF INVESTMENT POLICY

To produce a cohesive, well-organized, investment policy statement, fiduciaries of an employee benefit plan, assisted by the plan's legal counsel, actuary, administrator, investment manager, and other consultants (as deemed appropriate) must identify, debate, and define the relevant issues and identify the investment objectives that will complement and augment the overall funding process.

The policy development process includes the identification and analysis of various internal compelling forces:

- Characteristics of the plan's sponsors that produce a certain attitude toward risk taking.
- Trends within the sponsors' industries.
- The current funding level of the plan's obligations.
- The cash-flow projection from a financial profile analysis.

Thus, the sponsors' attitude toward risk, the industry and company trends, the plan's status (underfunding, full funding, or overfunding), and the prospective cash-flow needs all impact investment policy choices because they impact funding requirements. Funding policies necessarily influence investment policies since the return from investments over the life of the plan plays such an important part in the benefit payment delivery process.

After examining the internal plan factors, and other noninvestment criteria embraced by the group, one can move next to the external factors, an examination of the capital markets themselves. Risk and reward trade-offs are considered. Will the fiduciaries be satisfied with achieving the markets' rates of return, or do they want to attempt to achieve returns, with the accompanying volatility, above the markets' returns? This decision has an impact on the investment management structure adopted. The range of choices includes:

1. Using only accounts that replicate the markets' returns (*passive* approach.
2. Using accounts that replicate the return of a chosen referenced (benchmark) portfolio (*passive-plus* approach).

3. Using accounts that are supervised within the discretion of the investment management organization (*active* approach).
4. Using a weighted combination of the above (*passive/active* approach).

As mentioned previously, a supervising group's *attitude* toward risk will affect the degree of flexibility in policy. Is the group willing to achieve slower growth in value in exchange for less volatile returns, or does it seek faster growth in value accompanied by higher volatility? The former would constrain the system to include, at the riskiest level, balanced growth and income stocks and real estate vehicles; the latter would permit moving out further on the risk spectrum and include the use of growth and capital appreciation stocks and small company growth stocks.

How much management risk is the group willing to embrace? The answer to this question indicates how much of the portfolio can be deployed to value-adding active managers. Fiduciaries desiring to eliminate investment management risk completely have to content themselves with the markets' rates of return and suffer the accompanying short-term volatility. The group in reality trades off investment manager vulnerability for market vulnerability. It accepts prices set by the masses, versus the assessment of value by a professional.

Part and parcel of finalizing the investment policy statement is an articulation of the investment performance objectives, as previously reviewed. Choices of objectives are influenced by the somewhat conflicting goals to preserve principal value, produce current income, enhance principal value, preserve purchasing power, produce capital gains and enhance purchasing power. To the degree one emphasizes the performance objective of value enhancement over value preservation, one must be willing to move out on the risk/reward spectrum. The wider the range of alternatives granted the investment managers, the less control the supervising group maintains over portfolio values. Objectives to preserve and enhance principal value, produce current income, and preserve purchasing power would most probably encourage the use of money market accounts, fixed-income accounts, equity income accounts, and real estate accounts. Performance objectives to enhance purchasing power and produce capital gains would most probably encourage the use of real estate accounts, balanced (stocks & bonds) accounts, growth and income accounts, growth stock accounts, capital appreciation accounts, and small company growth stocks accounts, and even venture capital.

Once the objectives are articulated a decision must be made whether to adopt a *fixed* asset mix, a *flexible* posture, or some *combination* of both. A fixed posture is constrained to accept the long-term risk/reward trade-offs in the markets. A flexible posture assumes that a management system can periodically exploit the occasional undervaluations that exist and do it consistently enough to add value over and above that which a passive fixed policy would have achieved. Because of the difficulty in correctly and consistently timing the markets, many funds prefer a combination of the two approaches. An example would be the decision to allocate 80 percent of the assets to be fully invested at all times, weighted among the classes in accordance with long-term historical returns and attendant volatility, and then to grant discretion to an investment manager to strategically redeploy the remaining 20 percent of the fund based upon an assessment of the short-term cyclical pricing outlook.

If the supervising group has the confidence in its manager to grant the use of either a flexible policy or a fixed/flexible posture, it needs to adopt procedures that can be accomplished in a timely enough fashion to opportunistically exploit market turns. In most cases, boards and committees function poorly with such time constraints. This is the reason that the majority of funds embracing such a market approach use an in-house coordinator, an investment consultant and/or an investment manager(s), or some combination of these professionals. Timely market awareness to capitalize on market turns is generally only available through a full-time information gathering and analysis process. Thus supervising fidiuciaries who attempt cyclical redeployment activities must realize they are competing with highly trained professionals who work full time in their search for value. And, for all their effort and expertise, the record reveals that a majority of the professionals attempting to fortuitously time the markets fail to add value to the portfolios. Part-time fiduciaries, to be successful in this highly competitive game, must either be unusually prescient or lucky, or both.

Prior to implementing any strategic portfolio moves permitted within the plan's overall policy constraints, a methodology must be adopted to assess the levels of investment risk. Financial (business) risk, market (interest rate) risk, inflation (purchasing power) risk, political (confiscation) risk, and social change risk should be evaluated. Within the context of such an analysis, an assessment is next made whether a class or subclass of investments is undervalued, fully valued, or overvalued. If sufficient belief in the evaluation system exists, the supervising group may comfortably grant full discretion to the professional(s) to implement such periodic asset shifts. The degree to which discretion is granted is influenced by the willingness of the group to embrace timing risk, confidence of the group in the manager to whom full discretion is delegated, and the previous experience of the fiduciaries in asset shift activities.

Needless to say, those boards or committees who have seen portfolio values squandered from poor timing decisions generally are inclined to constrain such activities in the future. Also, it is better to learn from observation, or through published studies, than from a disappointing first-hand experience.

Even when an employee benefit fund permits strategic asset mix shifts, it generally permits only a small shift at any one time. Portfolio repositioning phased in over time profits from the principle of time diversification. Significant asset shifts implemented all at once place at risk the long-term value enhancement objective of most funds. Contrarianism is wonderful when it's right, but the opportunity costs (or real losses) can be very expensive if proven wrong.

Both the approach to policy adoption and the approach to strategy implementation should be systematic. A step-by-step "seek and search" mission should coalesce into both policy decisions, which enable the fund to attain its long-term investment objective, and strategic decisions that add value over time above that which the policy alone would have achieved. Resourceful documentation accumulated during the dialogue when policy and strategy constraints were considered can be very helpful when finalizing the investment policy statement.

In investing, the way one approaches the process is just as important as the choice of the vehicles themselves. Thus, the policy statement becomes the necessary road map to successful funding. The absence of a cohesive written statement results in an investment context composed of a loose aggregation of ideas, which usually results in a fuzzy understanding of the objectives. The investment manager may be seeking objectives incompatible with the needs of the plan, or the investment vehicles selected for the plan may be inappropriate, given its needs. If a policy is not in writing, it cannot be mutually understood, and the absence of understanding between the supervising groups and professionals is the most significant cause of poor investment results.

The investment policy statement becomes the overall "game plan" from which all substrategies and implementation of those strategies evolve. Investment decisions will then be in concert with the needs of the plan, and the group's stewardship role will have been fulfilled as the "management of risk" directives have been effectively articulated. Cohesive investment policy fosters good understanding among all participants in the process. Lines of demarcation are carefully drawn, permitting appropriate accountability and adjustments in the review, reevaluation, and modification process. Diverse areas—the requirements of ERISA, fiduciary liability, acceptable performance, diversification, the discretion delegated to managers, and attitudes toward social investing—need to be addressed. Without the development of policy and its subsequent reduction to a written statement, the plan, like a ship without a rudder, may flounder in a dynamic economic environment.

Such an empirical process is an on-going effort. The policy and evolving strategies of the plan must respond to its dynamic political, social, and economic environment. The policy statement for the plan in the aggregate then becomes the stepping stone for the individual policy statements for the separate investment managers.

Reducing a plan's investment policy to a written statement provides legal protection, improves communication, and supplies instructions to investment managers. The statement prepared for the fund in the aggregate generally includes at least the following elements:

1. Background information on the fund.
2. Identification of fiduciaries.
3. Organizational structure.
4. Cash-flow requirements.
5. Lines of authority and delegation.
6. Diversification of the portfolio.
7. Active/passive strategies.
8. Definition of assets.
9. Performance objectives.
10. Guidelines.
11. Brokerage.
12. Voting of proxies.
13. Trusteeship/custodianship.

The statement related to each investment manager would include background information; future fund and cash-flow projection; investment objectives; policies related to the voting of proxies; portfolio guidelines; reporting requirements; and review, evaluation, and modification methods.

Monitoring, reevaluation, and modification of the investment funding process is an unending task because of the dynamic spheres of influence affecting policy selection. Characteristics of the plan sponsor change, plan demographics change, markets change, and investing facilities change. Thus an ongoing ability to effectively monitor and modify, if necessary, is important to long-term success. Independent performance measurement services assist in objective evaluation. Plan liability studies assist in achieving objective-setting precision. Analysis of expected rates of return helps in portfolio-tilting activities. The exercise of patience on the part of the plan fiduciaries is important to assure that counterproductive changes do not unnecessarily squander portfolio values.

Quality control in management procedures is important to attain maximum productiveness from the accumulated assets. In summary, the ultimate result of this procedural quest for successful funding techniques through successful stewardship of accumulated assets is to adopt an appropriate long-term investment policy, and, if so inclined, to periodically implement successful investment strategy moves permitted within the overall policy constraints.

The investment funding process begins with those fiduciaries charged with the stewardship responsibility. Determined to ask the right questions, and resourcefully armed with knowledge of basic investment principles, the fiduciaries can add significant value to a plan's portfolio. With such determination, knowledge and insight, the supervising fiduciaries need to examine the internal factors to adopt investment objectives appropriate to the plan's requirements. They must next examine the long-term historical risk/reward characteristics of the various investment classes. Then, with the objectives in mind, and with an awareness of which classes and subclasses of securities can best facilitate the attainment of those objectives, they can next turn to the selection of the funding vehicles. The most appropriate investment management structure is identified, evaluated, and selected. Part and parcel with the adoption of these policy decisions is the asset-mix policy decision—whether it will over time be fixed, flexible, or a combination of both.

If an element of flexibility is permitted in the asset-mix policy, then there must be an adoption of an additional set of procedures that provide the context within which strategy moves are implemented. It is in the strategy area that most groups supervising employee benefit plans choose to retain either an in-house coordinator or an independent investment consultant, and/or to engage investment manager(s). And finally, the monitoring, reevaluation, and modification process must be accomplished with thoroughness and insight.

CHAPTER 39

COSTING AND FUNDING RETIREMENT BENEFITS

Donald S. Grubbs, Jr.

INTRODUCTION

Funding retirement benefits includes setting aside contributions, investing them in a funding medium, and making benefit payments from the amounts set aside. It involves administrative and accounting functions and important tax considerations.

This chapter discusses funding retirement programs that are qualified plans under the Internal Revenue Code. Special considerations, not discussed here, apply to plans covering employees of governments and of churches.

FUNDING MEDIA

The funding medium is the vehicle which contains the plan's assets and from which the benefits are paid. All pension plan assets must be held by one or more trusts, custodial accounts, annuity or insurance contracts.[1]

---

[1] Employee Retirement Income Security Act of 1974 (ERISA) sec. 403; Internal Revenue Code of 1986 (IRC) sec. 401(a),(f), 403(a), 404(a)(2).

Trusts and Their Investments

Trusts are used as the investment medium for about two thirds of all pension assets. A trust is a legal entity under which a trustee holds assets for the benefit of another. Trusts are governed by state law. However, the Internal Revenue Service deems a trust to exist even before it has a corpus (assets), even though most state laws require a corpus for a trust to exist.[2] A trust agreement is entered into between the employer or other plan sponsor and the trustee.

The trust instrument states the purpose of the trust and defines the authority and the responsibilities of the trustee. It includes provisions for terminating the trust or replacing the trustee. A trust must provide that plan assets be used for the exclusive benefit of participants and beneficiaries.[3]

Trustees

Generally, trustees may be either individuals or institutions with trust powers, such as banks or trust companies. A bank usually is designated as trustee. Some large plans divide plan assets among two or more banks serving as trustees.

Some plans have a board of trustees consisting of a group of individuals. Collectively bargained multiemployer plans usually follow this approach. In such a case, the board of trustees usually enters a second trust agreement with a bank, delegating responsibility for holding and investing plan assets. Sometimes the trustee is a single individual, but many individuals hesitate to assume the fiduciary responsibilities of trustees.

The duties of trustees differ from plan to plan. In every case the trustee must hold the plan assets and account for them. Some trustees have complete responsibility for determining investment policy and making every investment decision. Under other trust agreements the trustee is required to follow investment decisions made by the employer or a separate investment manager. For many plans the trustee's authority lies between these two extremes; for example, the trustee may make individual investments in accordance with investment policies or limitations established by the employer, an investment manager, or trust agreement.

Trustees usually pay the plan's benefits to participants and often assume other administrative responsibilities. Sometimes the trustee is designated plan administrator, with the full responsibility for administer-

---

[2] Rev. Rul. 57-419, 1957-2 CB 264.

[3] IRC sec. 401(a)(2).

ing the plan. The trustee is a fiduciary of the plan and subject to ERISA's fiduciary responsibilities.

Trust Investments

Many banks maintain one or more collective trust funds to pool the assets of a number of plans for investment purposes. These commingled trusts are very similar to mutual funds. They may provide more diversification and better investment management and may reduce investment expense, particularly for small plans, compared to a trust investing in individual securities. Many banks have several separate commingled funds for particular types of investments; e.g., common stocks or bonds. For the same reasons some trusts invest in commingled funds, others invest in mutual funds as an intermediary. Most larger trusts acquire individual securities rather than use commingled funds or mutual funds.

Many trusts invest only in securities listed on a major stock exchange to assure marketability, avoid valuation problems, and reduce fiduciary problems. Common stocks and corporate bonds are the most common investments. Trusts also often invest in preferred stocks, certificates of deposit, commercial or government notes, government bonds, mortgages, and real estate. Occasionally, they invest in art, precious metals, and other collectibles, but this is, in effect, prohibited if individuals direct the investment of their own accounts in a defined contribution plan.

A plan may invest in securities of the employer only if they are "qualifying employer securities." A qualifying employer security is a security of the employer which is either a stock or a marketable security which meets several criteria of ERISA. A defined benefit plan generally may not invest more than 10 percent of its assets in securities of the employer, but stock bonus plans, profit-sharing plans, and some money purchase pension plans are not so limited.

Insured Plans

Approximately one third of pension plan assets are held by insurance companies. Many different kinds of contracts are used. These include group contracts covering a group of participants and individual contracts for each participant.

Annuity contracts and insurance contracts are used, and both generally provide annuity income after retirement. Life insurance contracts generally guarantee to pay death benefits which exceed the reserve for the individual participant while annuity contracts generally do not. The extent to which the contracts guarantee the payment of benefits or the employer's costs varies greatly between contract types.

Deposit Administration (DA) Group Annuity Contract

A deposit administration (DA) contract has a deposit fund into which all contributions to the plan are deposited. For defined benefit plans the fund is not allocated among participants. The insurance company credits the fund with interest at a guaranteed rate and may assess the fund with a stipulated expense charge. When a participant becomes eligible for a pension, a withdrawal is made from the deposit fund to purchase an annuity. Sometimes lump-sum distributions, disability payments, or other benefits are paid directly from the deposit fund without the purchase of an annuity.

The DA contract specifies the guaranteed rate of interest to be credited to the deposit fund, the expense charge to be subtracted from the deposit fund, and the rates which will be used to purchase annuities when individuals retire. There generally is no expense charge for larger plans. The insurer guarantees payment of the pensions after annuities have been purchased but does not guarantee the deposit fund will be sufficient to purchase the annuities.

The guaranteed interest rates and annuity purchase rates generally are quite conservative. When actual experience is more favorable than the guaranteed assumptions, the difference may be recognized by adding dividends or experience credits to the deposit fund. Consulting, administrative, and actuarial services for the plan may be provided by the insurance company, independent consultants, or the employer.

If the contract is discontinued, it may allow the employer either to apply the balance of the deposit fund to purchase annuities or to transfer it to a trust or another insurance company. If the fund is transferred in a lump sum, the insurance company may deduct a surrender charge or a market value adjustment or alternatively, the insurer may require that the transfer be made in installments over a period of years.

The assets of the deposit fund represent a contractual obligation of the insurer, but do not represent any particular assets of the insurer. The insurer invests the monies received as part of the total assets of the insurance company, usually primarily in bonds and mortgages. The insurer usually reflects the investment earnings of its entire portfolio in determining the amount of interest to credit in determining dividends or experience credits. In determining the interest to credit, most insurers use the "investment year" or "new money" method, which determines the rate of investment earnings on investments made by the insurance company in each year that deposits were added to the deposit fund.

Many deposit administration contracts provide that part or all of the employer contributions to the plan may be invested in separate accounts rather than the deposit fund. Separate accounts operate similarly to mutual funds and are invested in common stocks or other forms of investment. The employer may direct transfers from the deposit account into the separate account. As in a mutual fund, deposits to the fund are converted to units by dividing by the current unit value of the separate account. The unit value equals the total market value of the fund divided by the number of units held by all of the contracts that invest in the separate account. Withdrawals also are based upon the current unit value. Many insurance companies maintain separate accounts for common stocks, bonds, mortgages, and other classes of investment.

Immediate Participation Guarantee (IPG) Contract

An immediate participation guarantee (IPG) contract, like a deposit administration contract, has a deposit account into which employer contributions are paid. The insurance company generally agrees to credit to the deposit account the actual rate of investment earnings it earns on its general portfolio using the investment-year method, and to deduct an allocation of expenses for the particular contract based upon accounting records for that contract. Pensions are paid from the deposit account monthly as they become due, rather than by purchasing an annuity. Thus the contract immediately participates in its actual experience for mortality, expenses, and investment income. Annuity purchase rates are guaranteed under the contract, but annuities are not usually purchased unless the contract is discontinued. Some companies use an accounting device which appears to purchase annuities, but ordinarily no annuities are actually purchased. Some insurers call such contracts "pension administration" or "investment only" contracts, rather than IPG contracts. Separate accounts generally are used with IPG contracts, just as they are used with DA contracts.

Guaranteed Investment Contract (GIC)

A guaranteed investment contract (GIC) guarantees the rate of interest to be credited to the deposit account for a limited period, usually 5 to 10 years. Most GICs guarantee that the full principal will be paid out with no surrender charge or adjustment at the end of that period. It may provide only for an initial deposit or may provide for continuing deposits during its lifetime. It may allow benefits to be paid from the deposit account during that period. These characteristics can be particularly valuable for a thrift plan or a regular profit-sharing plan where the entire fund balance is allocated to individual participants; many participants want a guarantee of principal and interest.

The GIC may include all the plan's assets, or it may be only one of several investments held by the plan's trust. At the end of the guarantee period, the entire balance of the GIC will be paid out to the trust or other funding medium of the plan, or it may be left on deposit and a new guarantee period established. The GIC may have annuity purchase options, but in practice annuities usually are not purchased.

Group Deferred Annuity Contracts

A deferred annuity contract is one under which the insurance company promises to pay a monthly annuity beginning at a future date. Under a group deferred annuity contract, the employer purchases a deferred annuity for each participant each year to fund the amount of pension earned in that year. The insurance company guarantees payment of the pension purchased to date, beginning at the normal retirement date, or payment of a reduced pension beginning at an early retirement date.

For example, assume a pension plan provides a pension at age 65 equal to $10 monthly for each year of participation in the plan. Each year the employer pays a premium for each participant to purchase a deferred annuity of $10 monthly to begin at age 65. Premium rates are based on the participant's age and sex. Since a small deferred annuity is purchased and guaranteed each year, by the time a participant reaches age 65 his or her entire pension will be purchased.

Before deposit administration contracts became popular, group deferred annuities were the most common type of group annuity. In recent years, however, very few new deferred annuity contracts have been issued, except to purchase annuities under terminated plans. Most plans which formerly used deferred annuities have changed to other methods of funding pensions earned after the date of change, but large amounts of deferred annuities purchased before the change remain in force.

Individual Level Premium Annuities

Under some plans, usually small plans, an individual level premium annuity contract is purchased to fund the projected pension of each participant. The insurance company deducts an expense charge from each premium and accumulates the balance at a guaranteed rate of interest. At retirement the balance of the account is converted into a monthly annuity, applying guaranteed purchase rates. The insurance company actually may use interest credits and annuity purchase rates more favorable than the conservative rates guaranteed in the contract.

The annual premium is the level annual amount determined so that the accumulation at normal retirement age is sufficient to purchase the promised pension. If the participant receives a salary increase which causes the originally projected pension to increase, a second level premium annuity is purchased to fund the increase. Further salary increases may require purchase of a third, fourth, etc.

Upon termination of employment before retirement, the accumulated balance (cash value) of each policy is available to provide a benefit for the employee if he or she is vested or a credit for the employer if the employee is not vested. Upon death before retirement, the death benefit usually equals the greater of the cash value or the sum of the premiums paid.

Individual Retirement Income Insurance Contracts

An individual retirement income insurance contract (sometimes called "income endowment") is similar to an individual level premium annuity, except the death benefit equals the greater of the cash value or 100 times the projected monthly pension. The retirement income contract also has level annual premiums, but these must be larger than under the level annual premium annuity to provide the larger death benefit.

Split-Funded Plans—Individual Life Insurance and an Auxiliary Fund

Many plans are funded by a combination of individual life insurance policies plus an auxiliary fund (often called "side fund"). The type of policy used is most frequently an ordinary life ("whole life") policy or a universal life policy. In many defined benefit plans, the amount of life insurance equals 100 times the projected pension, as in the retirement income contracts. The life insurance contract builds up a cash value sufficient to provide part of the pension. Deposits are made to the auxiliary fund to provide the balance. The auxiliary fund may be held by the insurance company or may be in a trust.

At retirement, two alternatives are available to provide a pension. Some plans surrender the insurance contract at retirement, deposit the cash value in the trust, and pay pensions monthly out of the trust. Other plans make a transfer from the trust to the insurance company at the time of retirement; the amount transferred is the amount required, together with the policy cash value, to purchase an annuity from the insurer to guarantee payment of the pension.

Many plans originally funded with retirement income insurance contracts have been converted to a split-funded basis to reduce the cost of funding the plan and to allow part of the plan's assets to be invested in common stocks. In turn, many split-funded plans have been converted to fund the pensions with a trust or group annuity contract and to provide the death benefits outside the pension plan under group term insurance in order to reduce the employer's cost.

When death benefits are funded with individual insurance under a qualified plan, the employee has current taxable income equal to the cost of insurance (called "P.S. 58" cost). Instead, if insurance is funded with group term insurance, the cost of providing the first $50,000 of insurance paid by employer contributions is tax-free to the employee, and the cost of insurance on amounts over $50,000 is computed on a less expensive basis than under individual contracts. Thus, employees pay less income tax if death benefits are funded with group term insurance. But death benefits provided by insurance contracts under pension plans generally are excluded from estate tax, which may be an advantage for participants with large enough estates to pay estate tax.

Group Permanent Contracts

Group permanent insurance contracts are designed to preserve the characteristics of individual insurance contracts while achieving some of the economy of group insurance. Whole life, universal life, and other types of contracts are available. All participants are covered under a single contract which has cash values, death benefits, and other characteristics similar to a collection of individual contracts. Because the group contract pays lower commissions and has lower administrative expense than individual contracts, the premiums are lower. Such contracts are termed "permanent" insurance to distinguish them from group term insurance.

FACTORS AFFECTING FUNDING

Many factors affect an employer's decision regarding how much to contribute to the pension plan. Different considerations affect different plans.

Type of Plan

The type of plan and its provisions often completely or partially determine the amount of employer contribution. A thrift plan, for example, may require the employer to match employee contributions up to 6 percent of pay. A profit-sharing plan may require the employer to contribute 20 percent of profits but not more than 15 percent of pay. A money purchase pension plan may require contributions of 10 percent of pay. Such plans leave no discretion in the amount of contribution. But most profit-sharing plans provide the employer complete discretion in determining what to contribute, if anything, and most defined benefit pension plans allow substantial discretion in determining how much to contribute each year.

Laws and Regulations

Minimum funding requirements under the Employee Retirement Income Security Act of 1974 (ERISA) set an absolute minimum on the contributions for most pension plans. These are described later.

If the employer is a taxpayer, it is subject to limits on the amount of pension contribution that may be claimed as a deduction for income tax purposes. Employers are subject to a 10 percent excise tax on any contributions greater than can be deducted currently.[4] An employer may want to contribute more in a year when it is in a higher tax bracket and less in a year when it is in a low tax bracket or has no taxable income at all.

Other governmental requirements affect the amount of contributions of some employers. Federal Procurement Regulations and Defense Acquisition Regulations control pension costs assessed under federal contracts. The Department of Housing and Urban Development has rules applicable to reimbursement of pension costs for local housing authorities. Public utilities commissions regulate the amount of pension contributions which may be recognized for rate-making purposes by utilities.

Collective Bargaining

Collective bargaining agreements affect the funding of many plans. Some collective bargaining agreements set the amount of employer contributions specifically in cents per hour, as a percent of pay, or as, for example, cents per ton of coal produced. Many other collective bargaining agreements, however, specify what benefits the plan provides, but do not specify the amount of employer contributions.

Funding Media

Under most plans funded with group annuity contracts or with trusts, the funding medium does not usually limit the amount of contributions. Under a traditional deposit administration group annuity contract, the deposit fund must be sufficient to purchase annuities for individuals currently retiring. Usually, the deposit fund is far more than sufficient for this purpose, so this requirement has no impact. But occasionally the deposit fund is not sufficient, particularly if a number of employees with large

---

[4] IRC sec. 4972.

pensions retire shortly after the plan is established; this may require additional employer contributions to purchase annuities. To solve this problem, deposit administration contracts often are modified to allow annuities to be purchased in installments after retirement.

Accounting

Generally accepted accounting principles (GAAP) establish the charge for pension expense in the employer's profit and loss statement. This does not directly control the amount actually contributed, but some employers prefer the amount contributed to equal the charge to expense.

Financial Considerations

An employer often considers its cash position in determining the amount of contribution to the plan. Cash shortages may stem from lack of profits or from a need to reinvest earnings in the business or to reduce indebtedness. Reducing pension contributions helps solve cash shortages. But an employer in a strong cash position may want to increase its pension contributions, since an additional dollar paid this year reduces the required contributions in future years and earns tax-free income in the pension trust. For an employer with lots of cash, larger pension contributions may help in avoiding the accumulated earnings tax on accumulated earnings in excess of the greater of $250,000 or the amount required for the reasonable needs of the business.[5] Larger contributions also reduce the cash available for dividends.

Interest rates often are considered. Increasing the pension contributions may require increased borrowing by the employer or may prevent reducing debts. The rate of interest on debt may be compared with the rate of investment earnings of the pension fund, but taxes also should be considered. Similarly, an employer with no indebtedness may consider how much could be earned by additional investments in the business, using amounts that would otherwise be contributed to the pension fund.

Employers may establish a funding policy based on many other considerations. Most employers want the plan to be soundly funded to assure the plan actually will be able to pay promised benefits. Some employers want pension costs to be stable as a percent of pay over future years. The

---

[5] IRC sec. 531–537.

employer may decide to fund the unfunded liabilities over a fixed period, such as 20 years. Future trends in pension costs may be projected, based upon projected increases or decreases in the number of future participants, changes in work pattern histories, investment earnings, future salary increases, anticipated plan amendments, or possible plan termination or merger.

Statutory Requirement for Funding Policy

ERISA requires every employee benefit plan to "provide a procedure for establishing and carrying out a funding policy and method."[6] Many plan documents merely state the employer will contribute to the trust each year the minimum amount required by ERISA's minimum funding standards and such additional amounts as the employer determines in its discretion. This retains the maximum discretion to change the funding policy without a plan amendment.

ACTUARIAL COSTS

Fundamental concepts of actuarial science are used in the costing of retirement benefits. The following illustrate the factors involved in the actuarial costing of such benefits.

Probability

When rolling an honest die, the probability of getting a 3 is 1/6 (or .16667). This statement does not tell us what the outcome of the next roll will be, but it does tell us something about the average experience that might be expected if many dice were rolled.

Mortality tables show the probability of dying at each particular age of life. This probability is determined by examining the experience of many thousands of lives. For example, according to one mortality table the probability of death at age 30 is .000991. This means if there were 1 million men age 30, it might be expected that 991 of them would die before reaching age 31. It does not tell us which ones might die and which ones might live, and hence tells us nothing about the expected lifetime of any one individual. But it does give us information about the average experiences to be expected in a large group of persons age 30.

---

[6] ERISA sec. 402(b)(1).

Interest Discount

If someone deposits $100.00 in a savings account at 5 percent interest, one year later it will grow to $105.00 (1.05 × $100.00). If the individual leaves the funds on deposit for a second year they will grow to $110.25 (1.05 × 105.00). Thus, if an individual wants to obtain $110.25 two years from now (assuming 5 percent interest), $100.00 must be deposited today. The $100.00 is the "present value" of $110.25 payable two years from now.

Viewed another way, the present value of an amount payable two years from now is .907029 times that amount (determined by dividing $100.00 by $110.25). At 5 percent interest, .907029 is the present value factor, or interest discount factor, for two years. To know the present value of any amount due two years from now (assuming 5 percent interest), simply multiply it by .907029.

There is a discount factor for any number of years. Of course, these factors vary with the interest rate. Sample discount factors for zero years to five years are shown in Table 39–1 at 5 percent interest and 6 percent interest.

Present Value of Future Amounts

Suppose a person agreed that two years from now 600 dice would be rolled, and the person must pay $1.00 for each 3 that resulted. Further suppose that he or she wanted to know the present value, the amount that could be set aside in a savings account today, which would be expected to be sufficient, together with interest, to pay the amounts when they become due. The total expected payments are $100.00 (1/6 × 600 × $1.00). Assuming 5 percent interest, the present value of that is $90.70 (the 2-year

TABLE 39–1
Sample Discount Factors

Number of Years	Interest Discount Factor	
	5 Percent	*6 Percent*
0	1.000000	1.000000
1	.952381	.943396
2	.907029	.889996
3	.863838	.839619
4	.822702	.792094
5	.783526	.747258

discount factor or .907029 × $100.00). Thus, if a deposit of $90.70 is made today it would grow to $100.00 two years from now, which would be sufficient to make the expected payments if exactly one sixth of the 600 dice turned up a 3. Thus, $90.70 is called the present value of the expected future payments. Of course, it might turn out to be more or less than needed, if the account earned more or less than the 5 percent assumed or if more or less than exactly one sixth of the dice turned up a 3. The present value of any future event is the number of exposures (600 dice) times the probability of occurrence (1/6) times the amount of payment on each occurrence ($1.00) times the interest discount factor (.907029).

Suppose, in addition to the obligation related to the 600 dice to be rolled two years from now, the individual had an obligation to pay $3.00 for each head that results from flipping 1,000 coins five years from now. The present value of the coin-flipping could be determined similarly to that for the dice-throwing. Then the two present values for dice-rolling and coin-flipping could be added to get the total present value of both obligations combined. Similarly, total present value can be determined for the combination of many possible future events, each with its own exposure, probability of occurrence, amount of payment, and time of occurrence.

Actuarial Cost Methods

Underlying actuarial concepts of pension funding are the actuarial cost methods which establish the level of pension contributions needed to fund promised pension benefits.

When a pension plan is first established, it may give past service credit to provide benefits related to employment before the effective date. Employees then covered under the plan will work for various amounts of time in the future. When employees terminate employment, some of them will be eligible to receive benefits, either beginning immediately or deferred into the future. After pension benefits begin, they usually continue for the retiree's lifetime, and sometimes payments are made after death to beneficiaries.

Actuarial cost methods are merely methods for assigning the cost of the benefit payments to particular years. Ultimately, the cost of a pension plan equals the sum of all the benefits and expenses paid from the plan, less any employee contributions and less the plan's investment return. If the employer contributes an additional dollar in any year, that dollar together with the interest it earns reduces the amount the employer needs to contribute in future years. Actuarial cost methods do not affect these ultimate costs, except as indirectly they may influence the amount of investment income by influencing the size of the fund or the timing of contributions.

To the extent any insurance or annuity contracts guarantee the costs of the plan, the employer's cost equals the premiums paid to the insurance company reduced by any dividends or credits, rather than the plan's own experience of benefits and expenses paid and investment return.

Basic Categories of Actuarial Cost Methods

All actuarial cost methods for pensions fall into three categories: current disbursement, terminal funding, and advance funding. All are in current use, although the advance funding is more commonly used and is required for plans subject to ERISA's minimum funding requirements.

Under the current disbursement method, also called "pay-as-you-go," each year the employer contributes the current year's benefit payments. This is not really an actuarial cost method at all. However, actuarial techniques can be used to project payments in future years, which may assist those responsible for the plan's operation. If a plan is funded precisely under the current disbursement method, the plan will have no assets whatsoever available to pay future benefits; next month's benefits will depend on next month's contributions.

Under terminal funding, as under current disbursement, no cost is recognized for a participant while he or she continues employment. The entire cost of the participant's future benefits is recognized, however, at the moment the participant retires and benefits begin. If a participant terminates and is entitled to a deferred pension beginning at a later date, the cost of the pension may be recognized either at the time of termination of employment or at the time payments begin, under two variations of the terminal funding method. If a plan is funded on the terminal funding method, the assets are expected to be sufficient to pay all the future benefits for those already retired (and terminated vested, if they also have been funded); no assets would be available to provide benefits for those not yet retired.

An advance funding actuarial cost method is one that spreads the cost of a participant's pension over a working lifetime. It recognizes the cost of a worker's pension as a cost of employment. If all the costs attributable to the past have been funded, the plan assets usually are larger than under the terminal funding method and thus usually expected to be sufficient to provide all future benefits for those already retired and terminated and to have some additional assets available to provide benefits for those still employed. Advance funding usually results in more rapid funding than terminal funding, but that is not always the case.

Except as otherwise noted herein, all actuarial cost methods are assumed to be advance funding methods.

Present Value of Future Benefits

For any group of individuals, the present value of their future benefits is the amount expected to be sufficient to pay those future benefits. If the present value of the future benefits were invested in a fund today, it would be sufficient, together with the investment income, to pay all such future benefits as they become due; no additional contributions would be needed, but the fund would be exactly exhausted when the last individual dies.

A participant or beneficiary may become eligible to receive future benefits if he or she retires (before or after normal retirement date), becomes disabled, dies, or otherwise terminates employment. The present value of future benefits is determined by the same principles as described earlier.

Consider a new employee just hired at age 25 under a pension plan which provides normal retirement benefits at age 65, assuming all payments are made annually at the beginning of the year. The present value of the single payment the participant may receive at age 65 is determined by multiplying the number of exposures (one person) times the probability of occurrence (the probability he or she will not die or terminate employment before age 65 and will then retire) times the amount of payment (the annual pension) times the interest discount factor (for 40 years from age 25 to 65). The present value of the payments to be received at 66, and each later age, could be similarly calculated; in each case the probability would need to consider not only the employee's chance of receiving the first payment but of continuing to survive to receive subsequent payments, and the interest discount factor would be smaller as the years become more distant. By adding the present value of each future normal retirement payment, the present value of all normal retirement payments can be determined. By similar techniques the present value of the payments that may be paid for this worker in the event of early retirement, disability, death, or vested termination can be determined. Adding these all together, the present value of all future benefits which may become payable to the individual or his or her beneficiary is ascertained.

For this individual, the present value may be meaningless. He or she may quit before becoming vested and never receive a cent. Or the employee may collect a pension until age 99, with costs greater than anticipated. But if the plan has a large number of participants, the sum of their present values will accurately reflect the amount needed to pay all future benefits, *if* the assumptions are correct concerning the various probabilities, the interest rate, and the amount of each future payment that might become payable. This concept is key to all actuarial cost methods.

Components of Present Value of Future Benefits

Actuarial cost methods generally divide the present value of future benefits into two portions, the part attributable to the past and the part attributable to the future. The part attributable to the past is called the "accrued liability." It also has sometimes been called "past service liability," "prior service liability," "actuarial liability," "supplemental present value," etc. The part of the present value of future benefits attributable to the future is called the present value of future normal costs. This present value of future normal costs is the portion of the present value expected to be paid in the future by "normal costs," the cost attributable to each of the future years.

If the same assumptions are used, all actuarial cost methods have the same present value of future benefits (although under one of the methods it is not required to calculate the present value of future benefits). The methods differ in how they divide this present value between the accrued liability and the present value of future normal costs. Obviously, a method which produces a larger accrued liability has a smaller present value of future normal costs, and vice versa. Under some methods, when a plan is first established no accrued liability exists at all, even though benefits are actually credited for past service; in this case, the present value of future normal costs equals the entire present value of future benefits.

Except when a plan is first established, it usually will have assets equal to part of the accrued liability. Any excess of the total accrued liability over the assets is the "unfunded accrued liability" sometimes called the "unfunded past service liability."[7]

If the assets exactly equal the accrued liability, there is no unfunded accrued liability, and the plan is "fully funded." Under some actuarial cost methods, the assets always exactly equal the accrued liability and there never is an unfunded liability.

Each actuarial method determines the normal cost for the current year.[8] The normal cost usually is calculated for the year beginning on the valuation date, but under one method it is sometimes calculated for the year ending on the valuation date. The normal cost may be calculated in dollars or it may be calculated as a percent of payroll, cost per employee,

---

[7] ERISA sec. 3(30), 302(b)(2)(B), IRC sec. 412(b)(2)(B).

[8] ERISA sec. 3(28).

per hour, per shift, etc. If not originally expressed in dollars, it is converted to dollars by multiplying by the actual or expected payroll, number of employees, hours, shifts, etc. The normal cost for the coming year is, of course, part of the present value of future normal costs.

Gain or Loss

As part of the actuarial valuation, the actuary can calculate what the present unfunded liability would have been expected to be currently, if the experience since the date of the last actuarial valuation had exactly followed the actuarial assumptions. This expected unfunded liability can then be compared with the actual unfunded liability calculated in the current valuation. The difference between the expected unfunded liability and the actual unfunded liability is the gain or loss since the last valuation. This gain or loss shows the extent to which the actual experience was better or worse than would have been expected by the actuarial assumptions.

Under some actuarial cost methods, called "spread-gain" methods, the actual unfunded liability is assumed to equal the expected unfunded liability and thus there is no gain or loss. Under these methods deviations between expected and actual experience are spread over the future working lifetimes of participants as increases or decreases in the normal cost.

SUMMARY OF VALUATION RESULTS

Under every actuarial cost method, the valuation produces the following results:

1. Normal cost for the current year.
2. Accrued liability.
3. Assets.
4. Unfunded accrued liability (the accrued liability less the assets, assumed $0 under one method).
5. Gain or loss (assumed $0 under spread-gain methods).

ACTUARIAL COST METHODS

Statutory Requirements for Actuarial Cost Methods

ERISA states, "The term *advance funding actuarial cost method* or *actuarial cost method* means a recognized actuarial technique utilized for establishing the amount and incidence of the annual actuarial cost of pension plan benefits and expenses. Acceptable actuarial cost methods shall include the accrued benefit cost method (unit credit method), the entry age normal cost method, the individual level premium cost method, the aggregate cost method, the attained age normal cost method, and the frozen liability cost method. The terminal funding cost method and the current funding (pay-as-you-go) cost method are not acceptable actuarial cost methods. The Secretary of the Treasury shall issue regulations to further define acceptable actuarial cost methods."[9] Under the statute, the Internal Revenue Service may recognize other methods as "acceptable" for determining ERISA's minimum funding requirements. They have so far recognized one additional method, the shortfall method. The same actuarial cost method and the same assumptions must be used for determining deductible limits as are used for minimum funding purposes.[10] The actuarial cost method and actuarial assumptions must be reasonable in the aggregate and must offer the actuary's best estimate of anticipated experience under the plan.[11]

Classification of Actuarial Cost Methods

There are a variety of ways in which actuarial cost methods may be classified. Only advance funding methods are considered in the following classifications.

Methods may be divided between (*a*) those which allocate the *benefits* of the plan to particular plan years and then determine the actuarial present value associated with the benefits assigned, and (*b*) methods which allocate the actuarial present *value* of all future benefits to particular plan years without allocating the benefits themselves. Those methods that allocate the benefits to particular plan years may be further divided between those that allocate the benefits according to the plan's provisions describing the accrued benefit and those that allocate the projected benefits as a level dollar benefit for each year of service.

A second way of classifying actuarial cost methods is between accrued benefit methods and projected benefit methods. An accrued benefit method is based upon the amount of benefit earned to date, while a projected benefit method is instead based upon the projected amounts of benefits expected to be paid from the plan upon retirement or other termination of employment. This is similar to the first classification above, since all *accrued* benefit methods allocate the *benefits* to particular years

---

[9] ERISA sec. 3(31).

[10] IRC sec. 404(a)(1)(A).

[11] ERISA sec. 302(c)(3), IRC sec. 412(c)(3).

while *projected* benefit methods generally allocate the actuarial present *value* to particular years.

A third way of classifying divides actuarial cost methods between those which directly determine the actuarial gain or loss and those which do not. Actuarial cost methods which do not directly determine the actuarial gain or loss have the effect of automatically spreading the gain or loss over the future working lifetimes of all active participants as part of the normal cost; such methods are called spread-gain methods.

A fourth way of classifying divides actuarial cost methods between individual methods and aggregate methods. Under an individual method, the normal cost and the accrued liability may be calculated for each individual participant; the normal cost and the accrued liability for the entire plan are the sums of these respective items for all of the participants. Under an aggregate method, the costs are determined for the group as a whole in such a way that they cannot be determined separately for individuals.

A fifth way of classifying is between methods which result in an initial accrued liability when the plan is established or amended (usually related to past service benefits or plan amendments which increase accrued benefits) and those which do not. If a method does not produce an initial accrued liability, the cost of all benefits (including past service benefits) must be funded through normal costs.

A sixth way of classifying is between methods which use an entry age basis and those which use an attained age basis. Under an attained age basis, the normal cost is determined on the basis of the participants' current attained ages, without reference to their ages at entry. Under an entry age basis, age at entry is a key element in determining normal cost.

A seventh way of classifying is between open group methods and closed group methods. A closed group method considers only the group of present plan participants, while an open group method considers employees expected to be hired in the future as well.[12] Except as otherwise specifically noted, this chapter only considers closed group methods. All six methods listed in ERISA are closed group methods.

The above classifications are each presented as dichotomies. Actually a number of methods exist which combine elements of the dichotomies.

---

[12] For a discussion of an open group method, see Donald R. Fleischer, "The Forecast Valuation Method for Pension Plans," *Transactions* 27 (1975), pp. 93–154, Society of Actuaries.

Accrued Benefit Cost Method

The plan document usually defines the "accrued benefit," the annual amount of benefit earned to date which is payable at normal retirement age. If a participant is 100 percent vested, his vested benefit equals his accrued benefit.[13]

The accrued benefit cost method, also called "unit credit cost method," defines the accrued liability as the present value of the plan's accrued benefits. The normal cost equals the present value of the benefit accrued during the current year. If a plan is funded with a group deferred annuity contract, a small deferred annuity is purchased each year to fund the amount of benefit assumed for each participant in that year, automatically using the accrued benefit cost method.

The traditional accrued benefit cost method is based upon the accrued benefit defined in the plan. This does not recognize future salary increases. If a plan's benefits are based upon final average pay, salary increases will cause the benefit credited for past years to increase from year to year as salaries increase, causing liabilities to increase and creating actuarial losses. For this reason, the IRS will not allow a final average pay plan to use the traditional accrued benefit cost method.

A modified accrued benefit cost method may be used for final average pay plans and other plans. Under this method, the projected benefit at normal retirement age is first calculated based upon projected service to normal retirement age and future salary increases. A modified accrued benefit is then calculated, equal to the projected benefit multiplied by the ratio of the participant's actual years of service to date to his or her projected years of service at normal retirement age. This modified accrued benefit cost method, sometimes called the "projected unit credit" method, does not have the problems of increasing liabilities and actuarial losses because of salary increases which are part of the traditional method.

Entry Age Normal Cost Method

The entry age normal cost method is a type of projected benefit cost method. This means the cost is based upon the projected amount of pension expected to be payable at retirement, rather than the accrued benefit earned to date.

---

[13] ERISA sec. 3(23), 204, IRC sec. 411(b).

The entry age normal cost equals the level annual amount of contribution (level in dollars or as a percent of pay) from an employee's date of hire (or other entry age) to retirement date calculated as sufficient to fund the projected benefit. The accrued liability equals the present value of all future benefits for retired and present employees and their beneficiaries, less the portion of that value expected to be funded by future normal costs.

Under the entry age normal cost method, unlike the accrued benefit cost method, the normal cost of each individual is expected to remain level each year. For plans with benefits not related to pay, the normal cost is calculated to remain level in dollars, while for a plan with benefits expressed as a percentage of pay the normal cost is calculated to remain level as a percentage of pay. The average normal cost for the entire group can also usually be expected to remain fairly level per employee or as a percentage of pay, even if the average attained age increases, unless there is a change in the average *entry* age.

Under the entry age normal cost method, when the plan is first established an initial accrued liability exists that equals the accumulation of the normal costs for members for years prior to the effective date. Similarly, if an amendment increases benefits, there is an increase in the accrued liability which equals the accumulation of prior normal costs for the increase in projected benefits.

Individual Level Premium Cost Method

The individual level premium cost method determines the level annual cost to fund each participant's projected pension from the date participation begins to normal retirement date. When participation begins, the plan has no accrued liability, even if the participant has substantial benefits credited for past service. Usually no salary increase assumption is used in projecting the benefit at retirement. If a participant's projected benefit increases during a year, this increase in the projected benefit will be separately funded by an additional level annual cost from the participant's then attained age to normal retirement age. If the plan is amended increasing benefits, the increase in the projected benefit for each individual is funded by a level premium from his or her then attained age to retirement age, with no immediate increase in the accrued liability.

Under the individual level premium cost method, the accrued liability for each individual equals the present value of future benefits less the present value of future normal costs. The accrued liability for the entire plan, less the plan assets, equals the unfunded accrued liability.

An allowable variation of this method is sometimes called the "individual aggregate method." Under this variation, the normal cost for the first year is the same as previously described. To determine the normal cost in subsequent years, it is first necessary to allocate the plan's assets. The assets attributable to retired or terminated vested employees are assumed to equal the present value of their benefits; those assets attributable to retired and terminated employees are subtracted from the total actual assets to determine the portion of the actual assets attributable to active employees. Several methods are used to allocate assets among active employees. Each individual's allocated assets are subtracted from the present value of future benefits to obtain the remaining unfunded cost of his benefits. This unfunded cost is spread as a level premium (level in dollars or as a percentage of pay) from attained age to the participant's retirement age.

Aggregate Cost Method

The aggregate cost method is another projected benefit cost method. Under this method, there is no unfunded liability. The accrued liability is, in effect, assumed to equal the assets. Thus, all costs are funded through the future normal costs, determined as a level percent of pay (or level in dollars) during the future working lifetimes of all current employees from their current attained ages.

The excess of the present value of future benefits over the value of any plan assets is the portion of that present value which must be funded by normal costs in the future. This excess is the present value of future normal costs. The actuary then determines the present value of all future compensation for all employees. By dividing the present value of future normal costs by the present value of future compensation, the actuary determines the ratio of future normal costs to future compensation. The actuary multiplies this ratio by the current year's compensation to determine the current year's normal cost. A similar procedure is used to determine the normal cost per employee, rather than as a percent of compensation, if benefits are not related to compensation.

Costs are determined in the aggregate and cannot be determined individually. Thus, the normal cost is calculated as a percentage of the total payroll, or a cost per employee for the entire group. The aggregate cost method automatically spreads gains and losses through the future normal costs and has no separately identifiable gains or losses.

Attained Age Normal Cost Method

The attained age normal method is a combination of the unit credit cost method and either the aggregate cost method or the individual level premium cost method. The accrued liability at the plan's effective date is calculated using the accrued benefit cost method. The cost of the excess of the projected benefit over the accrued benefit on the effective date is funded by level costs over the future working lifetimes of participants, using either the individual level premium cost method or the aggregate cost method. Both individual and aggregate variations have long been recognized as the attained age normal cost method, but some use the name only to apply to one or the other variation.

If the individual variation is used, each individual's original past service benefit is valued every year using the unit credit cost method to determine the accrued liability. The difference between the employee's total projected benefit and this frozen past service benefit is valued as under the individual level premium cost method, without spreading gains. This method funds any increase in projected benefits because of salary increases from the then attained age to retirement age.

If the aggregate variation is chosen after the first year, the frozen initial liability technique, described below, is used. In that event, gains and losses are spread over the future working lifetimes of employees.

Frozen Initial Liability Cost Method

ERISA lists the frozen initial liability method. Many actuaries do not regard this as an actuarial cost method at all but rather a method for spreading gains under other methods. This latter group might describe a method as "entry age normal cost method with frozen initial liability" or "attained age normal cost method with frozen liability." But this difference of viewpoint does not reflect an actual difference in how the method operates.

The frozen initial liability method is not a method for determining the plan's initial accrued liability. The entry age normal cost method usually is used to determine the initial accrued liability and the first year's normal cost, but sometimes the attained age normal cost method is used instead. In subsequent years the unfunded liability is "frozen" and does not reflect actuarial gains and losses. This method has no gain or loss. What would be a gain or loss is spread over the future working lifetimes of all participants through increases or decreases in future normal costs.

To accomplish this, the unfunded accrued liability on the valuation date is set equal to the expected unfunded liability; i.e., what the unfunded liability would be if the actuarial assumptions had been exactly realized during the prior year. This unfunded liability plus the plan assets equals the total accrued liability. The excess of the present value of all future benefits over the accrued liability is the portion of that present value which must be funded by future normal costs and is designated as the present value of future normal costs. From this present value of future normal costs, the current year's normal cost is determined in the same manner as for the aggregate cost method.

Shortfall Method

The shortfall method was created to solve a problem created by ERISA's minimum funding requirements. It applies only to collectively bargained plans. The shortfall method is not really an actuarial cost method but a way of adapting other actuarial methods to ERISA's funding requirements.[14]

Retired and Terminated Participants and Beneficiaries

Under the traditional accrued benefit cost method, the accrued liability equals the value of accrued benefits. This is true for retired participants, terminated participants with vested rights, and beneficiaries of deceased participants, as well as for active employees.

This same approach is used for retired and terminated members and beneficiaries under all actuarial cost methods which determine the accrued liability on an individual basis. Thus, the accrued liability for retired and terminated members and beneficiaries is the same under the entry age normal cost method as under the accrued benefit cost method.

For aggregate methods, this same value for retired and terminated members and beneficiaries is part of the present value of future benefits.

Table 39–2 summarizes the actuarial cost methods.

Actuarial Assumptions

Purpose of Assumptions

Determining the present value of future benefits is basic to all actuarial cost methods. The present value of any future benefit is the amount of the future benefit times the probability it will be paid, discounted to present value at interest. For example, a plan may provide a disability benefit equal to 50 percent of pay to workers who become disabled after 15 years of service. The amount of future benefits depends upon the probability each worker will survive in the group to become eligible; i.e., that he or she will not die, retire, become disabled, or otherwise terminate employment before becoming eligible for such benefits. The amount of future benefits also depends upon the probabilities of becoming disabled, as well

---

[14] Treasury Reg. 1.412(c)(1)-2.

TABLE 39–2
Summary of Actuarial Cost Methods (excluding shortfall)

	Accrued Benefit or Projected Benefit	*Calculates Gain or Loss*	*Individual or Aggregate*	*Initial Accrued Liability*	*Age Used for Computation of Normal Cost*
1. Accrued benefit cost	Accrued	Yes	Individual	Yes	Attained
2. Entry age normal cost					
a. Individual ages	Projected	Yes	Individual	Yes	Entry
b. Average entry age	Projected	Yes	Aggregate	Yes	Entry (average)
3. Individual level premium					
a. No-spread	Projected	Yes	Individual	No	Attained
b. Spread-gain	Projected	No	Individual	No	Attained
4. Aggregate cost	Projected	No	Aggregate	No	Attained
5. Attained age normal					
a. Individual	Mixed	Yes	Individual	Yes	Attained
b. Aggregate	Mixed	No	Aggregate	Yes	Attained
6. Frozen initial liability	Projected	No	Aggregate	Yes	Attained

Note: For a more detailed presentation of actuarial cost methods, see C. L. Trowbridge and C. E. Farr, *The Theory and Practice of Pension Funding* (Homewood, Ill.: Richard D. Irwin, 1976); and B. N. Berin, *The Fundamentals of Pension Mathematics* (New York: Wm. M. Mercer-Meidinger-Hansen, Inc., 1978).

as the period of disability before either death or recovery. It also depends on future salary increases. Actuarial assumptions are used to predict these matters.

The present value of future benefits is calculated using an interest discount. It may not be apparent why an assumption concerning the assets is used to determine the present value of future benefits. The present value of a future benefit is the amount of assets which could be invested today, so that the assets plus the interest they would earn would be sufficient to provide the expected benefits in the future. The interest to be earned is key to deciding what amount of present assets are needed.

The actuarial valuation allocates the present value of benefits to various periods of the past and future. Frequently, that allocation is made in proportion to periods of employment or to compensation. For example, actuarial assumptions are used to estimate those periods of employment or amount of compensation. Thus, the selection of the assumptions affects the allocation of present values between periods of the past and future.

Long-Range Nature

For an employee now age 25, the actuarial assumptions are used to estimate whether he or she may become eligible for a pension 40 years in the future, what the employee's salary will be after 40 years, how long the employee will live to receive a pension, and what the fund will earn over the entire period.

Thus, the actuarial assumptions are extremely long-range in nature. The more distant any event is, the less likely it can be predicted correctly. Mortality rates for next year are fairly predictable (barring a war), but mortality rates 50 years hence depend upon events that cannot possibly be predicted such as remarkable medical discoveries or a disastrous deterioration of the environment. Assumptions other than mortality are even less predictable for long periods. The experience of last year, or expected experience of next year, is relevant to the process of establishing assumptions only to the extent that it may indicate long-term trends.

Most experts will not even conjecture for such long periods. When economists talk of long-range projections, they often mean five years. Yet such long-range assumptions are essential to actuarial valuations. The actuary, faced with this difficult task, usually assumes the future will be generally similar to the present, often with some element of conservatism (conservative in the direction of producing higher costs).

ERISA Requirements for Assumptions

ERISA requires the actuary to use "actuarial assumptions and methods which, in the aggregate, are reasonable expectations and which, in combination, offer the actuary's best estimate of anticipated experience under the plan."[15] The statutory language provides more questions than answers. What is the meaning of "reasonable"? How can the assumptions

---

[15] ERISA sec. 302(c)(3), IRC sec. 412(c)(3).

be reasonably related to the plan's experience when the large majority of plans are so small their experience is not statistically valid? Is the "best estimate" one that has a 50 percent chance of being on the high side and a 50 percent chance of being on the low side (in which case the "best estimate" requirement would tend to weaken the funding of pensions)? If not, what does "best estimate" mean? What should the probability be that the estimated costs are less than sufficient to fund the plan in the long run? Detailed discussion of the individual assumptions may be found in the actuarial literature.[16]

In addition to the above requirements which apply to all of the actuarial assumptions in the aggregate, additional requirements apply to the interest assumption.

Asset Valuation Methods

Under some actuarial cost methods, the value of plan assets affects the unfunded liability, which must be funded by amortization payments. Under other actuarial cost methods, the value of plan assets affects the normal cost. Under either approach, the method used to determine the value of plan assets determines the required employer contributions for a particular year and the fluctuation in contributions from year to year.

Some plans use the market value of assets for the actuarial valuation. It is argued this is the real value of the plan's assets and therefore makes the valuation more realistic. The disadvantage of this method is that fluctuations in market value may result in substantial fluctuation in the required employer contributions from year to year, which is generally undesirable.

Some plans use cost or book value of assets for the actuarial valuation. This can avoid the problems of fluctuation in plan costs. However, if the asset value used differs substantially from market value, it may present an unrealistic picture of the true costs and liabilities.

A variety of actuarial methods of asset valuation are used to avoid these problems. Some plans use the cost or book value so long as it lies within a stated corridor around market value; e.g., not less than 80 percent or more than 120 percent of market value. Some plans use a formula or method to gradually recognize asset appreciation; e.g., five-year-aver-

---

[16] Study notes of the Society of Actuaries and articles and discussions in numerous volumes of the *Transactions* and *Record* of the Society of Actuaries, and the *Proceedings* of the Conference of Actuaries in Public Practice.

age market value. A wide variety of methods are used to gradually recognize appreciation but avoid extreme asset value fluctuation. ERISA requires plans to use "any reasonable actuarial method of valuation which takes into account fair market value and which is permitted under regulations." Regulations require the asset value used either be between 80 percent and 120 percent of market value or between 85 percent and 115 percent of the average market value for a period of five years or less. A plan is permitted to elect to value bonds and other evidences of indebtedness separately using amortized cost, but few plans have done so.

CHAPTER 40

COSTING AND FUNDING RETIREMENT BENEFITS (continued)

Donald S. Grubbs, Jr.

MINIMUM FUNDING REQUIREMENTS

General Requirements

The Employee Retirement Income Security Act of 1974 (ERISA) established minimum funding requirements to provide greater assurance that pension plans will be able to pay the promised benefits.

Applicability

The minimum funding requirements appear twice in ERISA in duplicate language, in Title I and Title II.[1] The Internal Revenue Service issues regulations that apply to both Title I and Title II.

Under Title II the minimum funding requirements apply to almost all qualified pension plans (excluding profit-sharing and stock bonus plans) except government plans, church plans, and "insurance contract plans."

Under Title I, the minimum funding requirements apply to nonqualified plans as well as qualified plans. The exemptions described above for Title II also apply under Title I along with a few other exemptions. Plans exempt from the funding requirements include "a plan which is unfunded

---

[1] ERISA sec. 301-306, IRC sec. 412.

and is maintained by an employer primarily for the purpose of providing deferred compensation for a select group of management or highly compensated employees'' and ''excess benefit plans.'' The broad definition of ''pension plan'' under ERISA makes the funding requirements apply to many deferred compensation arrangements, previously unfunded plans, and other arrangements not previously thought of as pension plans.

Basic Requirements

Employers are required to contribute at least the normal cost plus amounts calculated to amortize any unfunded liabilities over a period of years. The required amortization period ranges from 15 years to 40 years depending on when it arose and its source. Additional requirements apply to certain plans with a low level of funding. If contributions in any year exceed the minimum required, the excess reduces the minimum required in subsequent years.

Penalties and Enforcement

If contributions are less than required, the shortfall is an ''accumulated funding deficiency.'' If an accumulated funding deficiency exists at the end of the plan year, a 5 percent excise tax is assessed on the deficiency. If the funding deficiency is not corrected within 90 days after the IRS mails a notice of deficiency, an additional tax is imposed equal to 100 percent of any uncorrected deficiency. In addition to paying these nondeductible taxes, the employer must also correct the accumulated funding deficiency itself. These taxes apply only to qualified plans. Whether or not the plan is qualified, the Secretary of Labor, participants, beneficiaries, and fiduciaries may bring civil actions to enforce the minimum funding requirements.

Funding Standard Account

A ''funding standard account'' is an accounting device used to keep track of the funding requirements. Amounts which increase the funding obligation for the year are charges to the funding standard account. This includes the normal cost and annual payments needed to amortize any unfunded liabilities. Amounts that decrease the employer's obligation are credits to the funding standard account. This includes employer contributions and annual amounts that may be used to amortize any decrease in the unfunded liability.

If the credits exceed the charges for a year, the excess is carried over as a credit balance to decrease the contributions required for the following year. Similarly, if the credits are less than the charges, the resulting accumulated funding deficiency is carried forward to increase the contributions required in the following year.

Reporting

For defined benefit pension plans, the plan administrator must engage an enrolled actuary "on behalf of all plan participants." Satisfaction of the minimum funding requirements is demonstrated on Schedule B "Actuarial Information," which must be certified by an enrolled actuary and attached to Form 5500. For defined contribution pension plans, satisfaction of the requirements is shown on Form 5500 itself.

Full Funding Limitation

No employer is required or allowed to contribute more than the amount needed to fully fund the accrued liability. This full funding limitation may reduce or eliminate the minimum contribution otherwise required. Special rules govern the determination of the amounts of assets and liabilities for this purpose.

Alternative Minimum Funding Requirement

Some plans are allowed to use the alternative minimum funding standard to determine their minimum funding requirement. If a plan uses the alternative miminum funding standard, it must nonetheless also maintain records for the regular funding standard account. A plan may not use the alternative minimum funding standard unless it uses the entry age normal cost method under its regular funding standard account. If an alternative minimum funding standard account is maintained, it is charged with (1) the lesser of the normal cost under the actuarial cost method used under the plan or the normal cost determined under the unit credit cost method, (2) the excess, if any, of the present value of accrued benefits over the fair market value of assets, and (3) any credit balance in the account as of the beginning of the year. The alternative minimum funding standard account is credited with employer contributions for the year.

The alternative minimum funding requirement is based upon a plan discontinuance concept. It is not a sound basis for funding an ongoing plan. Very few plans use this alternative.

Extension of Amortization Period

Another form of relief from the minimum funding requirement is an extension of the amortization periods. The Internal Revenue Service may extend the time required to amortize any unfunded liability by up to 10 years. Extending an amortization period reduces slightly the required employer contribution. No employer is known to have applied for such an extension.

Waiver

The Internal Revenue Service may grant a waiver of part or all of the minimum funding requirement. A waiver will be approved only if the employer faces "substantial business hardship" and if failure to approve the waiver would be "adverse to the interests of plan participants in the aggregate."

Multiemployer Plan Requirements

ERISA contained slightly different funding requirements for collectively bargained multiemployer plans than for other plans. The Multiemployer Pension Plans Amendment Act of 1980 (MEPPA) made further changes for multiemployer plans. The most significant difference is that an employer that withdraws from a multiemployer plan may be assessed "withdrawal liability," requiring significant contributions after the withdrawal.

TAX DEDUCTION OF EMPLOYER CONTRIBUTIONS

Purposes

Like most other business expenses, contributions to qualified pension plans must be deducted as ordinary and necessary business expenses. In addition, Section 404 of the Internal Revenue Code sets maximum limits on the amount that may be deducted in each year. Section 404 reflects two concerns of Congress.

First, Congress wanted to encourage employers to establish qualified plans for their employees. Congress also wanted to encourage employers to soundly fund the plans to assure promised benefits would be paid. Thus Congress wanted to allow tax deductions for the amounts needed to soundly fund the plans.

Second, Congress wanted to limit the deduction for a particular year to expense attributable to that year. This would prevent an employer from prepaying future expenses to evade taxes. But it is not clear how much of the payments for past service costs and actuarial gains and losses should be considered attributable to a particular year.

Timing of Deductible Contributions

To be deductible, contributions to pension and profit-sharing plans for a year must be paid no later than the tax filing date for the year, including extensions. No deduction may be claimed for the contribution of a promissory note of the employer, even if secured.

If the employer contributes more than the deductible limit for a year, the excess is carried over to be deducted in future years, subject to the 15 percent deductible limit in future years. However, a 10 percent excise tax is assessed on any contributions which exceed the maximum deductible amount for the year.[2]

Maximum Deductible Limit for Pension Plans

Section 404 has three alternative ways to determine the maximum limit on deductible employer contributions. Usually, the maximum deductible limit equals the normal cost plus the amount needed to amortize any past service liability over 10 years. If a plan has no unfunded liability, its deductible limit does not include a past service amount.

The amount of past service cost to be amortized is called a "10-year amortization base." For a new plan, the 10-year amortization base equals the initial unfunded accrued liability base. If the unfunded accrued liability is changed by a plan amendment, change in the actuarial method or assumptions, or actuarial gains or losses, the amount of change in the unfunded accrued liability becomes an additional 10-year amortization base. The old base continues until it is fully amortized. Any event which increases the unfunded liability creates a new positive base. Any event which decreases the unfunded liability creates a new negative base. A plan may have many bases.

The amount required to amortize each 10-year amortization base over 10 years is the "limit adjustment." Each 10-year amortization base has its own limit adjustment. The limit adjustment is positive if its base is positive and negative if its base is negative. All of a plan's limit adjustments are added to determine the plan's maximum deductible limit for past service contributions. Detailed regulations provide rules for determining the amount of bases and limit adjustments.[3]

---

[2] IRC sec. 4972.

[3] Treasury Reg. sec. 1.404(a).

The second method of determining the maximum deductible limit is the individual aggregate method. The maximum deductible limit for each participant is the amount necessary to provide the remaining unfunded cost of the projected benefit distributed as a level amount, or a level percentage of compensation, over the participant's remaining future service. But if the remaining unfunded cost for any three individuals exceeds 50 percent of the unfunded cost for the entire plan, then the unfunded cost for each such individual must be distributed over at least five years.

The third alternative for determining the deductible limit equals the amount required to satisfy the plan's minimum funding requirement. The full funding limitation determined under the minimum funding requirements is an overriding maximum limit on the amount that may be deducted for a year.

Maximum Deductible Limits for Profit-Sharing and Stock Bonus Plans

The maximum deductible limit for a profit-sharing plan or stock bonus plan is 15 percent of the compensation paid or accrued for all participants during the tax year. The limitation is on the aggregate contributions for all participants, not the contribution for each. Thus, more than 15 percent may be contributed and deducted for a particular participant if the aggregate limit is not exceeded.

Maximum Deductible for Combined Plans

If an employer maintains more than one profit-sharing or stock bonus plan, they are treated as a single plan for purposes of determining the deductible limit. If an employer maintains both a defined benefit plan and a defined contribution plan which have one or more participants in common, there is an additional limitation on deductible contributions. Deductible contributions to the combined plans are limited to 25 percent of compensation of all of the participants in either plan or, if greater, the pension plan contribution required by the minimum funding requirements. This is so even though an employer that has no defined contribution plan may deduct more than 25 percent of pay under a defined benefit plan. If contributions to combined defined benefit and defined contribution plans exceed the combined 25 percent limit, they may be carried over for deduction in a later year, but the 10 percent excise tax on nondeductible contributions applies.

DEDUCTION OF EMPLOYEE CONTRIBUTIONS

Some plans require employees to contribute to the plan as a condition for participation or for receiving certain employer-provided benefits. Some plans allow employees to make voluntary contributions to increase the benefits otherwise provided under the plan. Neither mandatory nor voluntary employee contributions are deductible by employees.

Under a 401(k) plan an employee may elect to defer receipt of part of his or her compensation and have the employer contribute it to the plan. Subject to limits, the amount deferred is excluded from the employee's taxable income and is treated as an employer contribution.

ACCOUNTING FOR PENSION PLAN LIABILITIES AND COSTS

There are two parts to pension plan accounting, accounting for the plan itself and accounting for the employer.

Accounting for the Plan

Form 5500 or a related form must be filed each year with the Internal Revenue Service. Form 5500 includes a statement of plan assets and liabilities, a statement of income and expenses, and certain other financial information. For plans with 100 or more participants the plan administrator is required to engage an independent qualified public accountant. A statement from the accountant, prepared in accordance with generally accepted accounting principles, must be attached to Form 5500. *Statement of Financial Accounting Standards No. 35* of the Financial Accounting Standards Board (FASB) established generally accepted accounting principles for pension plans.

For defined benefit plans with 100 or more participants Schedule B of Form 5500 requires reporting the value of accrued benefits. This same item is required in accounting statements under *Statement No. 35*. It ordinarily bears no relation to the plan's funding, is misleading as an indication of funding for an ongoing plan, and does not purport to represent the plan's liabilities if the plan were discontinued.

Both Form 5500 and *Statement No. 35* also require a statement of assets and liabilities (other than actuarial liabilities), a statement of changes in fund balances, and additional information.

Accounting for the Employer

An employer's accounting for a defined contribution plan usually is simple. Contributions paid for the employer's fiscal year are treated as an expense. An employer's accounting for a defined benefit plan is more complex. It requires certain disclosures in addition to determining the charge to expense and possible balance sheet entries.

For a defined benefit plan an employer's charge to expense for pension cost is the subject of *Statements No. 87* and *No. 88* of the Financial Accounting Standards Board (FASB). *Statement No. 87* requires the profit and loss statement to include a charge for pension expense that represents the pension cost properly attributable to the current year, regardless of the amount contributed for the year.

The employer's pension expense is the "net periodic pension cost." It must be determined using the projected unit credit cost method.

The net periodic pension cost consists of six components:

1. Service cost.
2. Interest cost.
3. Actual return on plan assets.
4. Amortization of any prior service cost.
5. Gain or loss (including the effect of changes in actuarial assumptions).
6. Amortization of unrecognized obligation at the date of initial application of *Statement 87*.

The service cost is the plan's normal cost. The interest cost equals one year's interest at the valuation interest rate (called the "discount rate") on the plan's accrued liability (which is called the "projected benefit obligation"). The "actual return on plan assets," which reduces the net periodic pension cost, equals the investment income earned plus realized and unrealized appreciation and depreciation of the fair value of plan assets. The initial projected benefit obligation for a new plan, or the increase in the projected benefit obligation resulting from a plan amendment, generally must be amortized over the expected future period of service of participants expected to receive benefits; this forms the annual amortization of any prior service cost. In order to smooth fluctuations in pension cost from year to year, *Statement 87* includes rules for delaying and spreading the recognition of actuarial gains and losses, so that only a portion of the gain or loss is included in the net periodic pension cost for any year. However, any difference between the actual return on plan assets and the expected return on plan assets in the year is recognized currently, immediately offsetting any investment return greater or smaller than expected. The difference between the projected benefit obligation and the fair value of plan assets on the effective date of *Statement 87,* adjusted for an accrued or prepaid pension cost at that date, is the plan's unrecognized net obligation or asset at that date. This amount is to be amortized over the expected future period of service of participants expected to receive benefits, although the employer may elect to use a 15-year amortization period if that is longer.

Negative components of the net periodic pension cost may exceed positive components, resulting in a negative net periodic pension cost.

Differences between the net periodic pension cost and the amount of contribution to the plan result in a balance sheet asset or liability for prepaid or accrued pension cost. In addition, any excess of the value of accrued benefits (called the "accumulated benefit obligation") over the fair value of plan assets will require recognition on the balance sheet as a liability. In this case an offsetting intangible asset is usually allowed on the balance sheet.

Statement 87 also requires certain disclosures in the employer's financial statements. *Statement 88* contains accounting rules related to termination or curtailment of plans, purchase of annuities, and payment of lump-sum distributions under plans.

Relationship of Accounting and Funding

Accounting for the pension plan itself and accounting for the employer do not directly control the plan's funding. However, there may be an important indirect effect, since the manner in which accountants report funding influences some employers' decisions concerning funding.

CHAPTER 41

TAX TREATMENT OF QUALIFIED PLAN DISTRIBUTIONS AFTER THE TAX REFORM ACT OF 1986

John M. Bernard
*Clifford J. Schoner**

INTRODUCTION

The Tax Reform Act of 1986 (TRA) made numerous changes in the taxation of amounts received from plans qualified under section 401(a) of the Internal Revenue Code of 1986 (Code). In general, these changes reflect a congressional desire to discourage use of qualified plans to accumulate capital rather than to provide retirement income. This policy is particularly apparent in the way the TRA restricts or penalizes payments that begin before age 59½, or after age 70½, while continuing the tax preference for benefits payable on a lifetime basis during what are commonly considered retirement years. With these aspects of the TRA as an organizing principle, this article will survey the changes made by the TRA in the treatment of amounts received from qualified plans.[1]

---

* The authors express their appreciation to our colleague, Lawrence J. Kramer, for his helpful comments and suggestions on this chapter.

[1] This article reflects the law as in effect and interpreted by the government through May 1, 1988. Interpretations of the TRA subsequent to that date are not reflected herein.

AMOUNTS RECEIVED FROM QUALIFIED PLANS DURING EMPLOYMENT

Limiting access to amounts held in qualified plans during employment is a major theme of the TRA. The TRA discourages access to these amounts by fundamentally changing the way income is computed for in-service withdrawals, by imposing a 10 percent additional tax on the taxable portion of most distributions before age 59½, by reducing the availability and attractiveness of loans and by drastically restricting the scope of hardship withdrawals under plans described in section 401(k). As the more detailed discussion that follows demonstrates, however, reducing the availability of the money does not reduce the complexity of the rules.

Basis Recovery Rules

Prior to the TRA, an interest in a qualified plan was almost always treated as a single contract for the purposes of applying the basis recovery rules of section 72.[2] Thus, any amount withdrawn before the annuity starting date was treated first as a nontaxable return of the participant's basis in the plan.[3] A participant's basis in a qualified plan generally reflects amounts held by the plan on which the participant has already paid federal income tax (*e.g.*, primarily aftertax contributions, but also P.S. 58 costs, repayments of taxable loans, and employer contributions made during a period when the plan was not qualified). Thus, in a profit-sharing plan with aftertax contributions or in a thrift plan (even a plan in which contributions attributable to each year were accounted for separately), any amount withdrawn from the plan before separation from service (and thus before the annuity starting date) would have been nontaxable to the extent of any unwithdrawn participant aftertax contributions.[4]

Sheltered by this rule, a participant could make aftertax contributions throughout his period of participation, withdrawing nontaxable money from time to time and leaving the earnings on such contributions behind for further tax-deferred accumulation. This feature contributed

---

[2] *E.g.* PLR 7951156, PLR 8125071, PLR 8639065; Treas. Reg. §1.72–2(a)(3). However, at an earlier time, the government took a position that sometimes resulted in a conclusion that a single plan consisted of multiple contracts. Treas. Reg. §1.72–2(a)(3)(iv), Ex. (3). More recent PLRs, including those cited above, appear to reflect a modification of the IRS' position.

[3] Internal Revenue Code of 1954, §72(e); Treas. Reg. §1.72–1(d).

[4] *Id.*

greatly to the popularity of aftertax thrift plans which operated as tax-free investment funds with the added bonus of an employer matching contribution.[5]

After the TRA, however, the general rule is that amounts received before the annuity starting date from a qualified plan will be treated as partially taxable.[6] For qualified plans that did not permit in-service withdrawals of aftertax contributions on May 5, 1986, the new rule is effective for preannuity starting date payments made after July 1, 1986.[7] For qualified plans that did permit such in-service withdrawals on May 5, 1986, the new rule is effective for preannuity starting date payments made after December 31, 1986.[8] However, participants in qualified plans that did permit in-service withdrawals of aftertax contributions on May 5, 1986 benefit from a grandfathering provision that permits them to make non-taxable withdrawals under the pre-TRA rules until they exhaust their basis in the qualified plan as of December 31, 1986.[9]

Preannuity starting date distributions from a qualified plan subject to the TRA are treated as returning to a participant a pro rata portion of his basis in the qualified plan.[10] The portion of a distribution which is to be treated as a nontaxable return of the employee's basis in the qualified plan is calculated by multiplying the distribution by the ratio of the participant's basis in the qualified plan to the vested portion of the participant's interest in the qualified plan.[11] The remainder of the distribution is taxable income to the participant.[12]

---

[5] Prior to the Tax Reform Act of 1984, the favorable tax treatment given preannuity starting date withdrawals was available even if no employer contributions were being made to the qualified plan. A plan of this type permitted a participant to enjoy tax-deferred earnings on his aftertax contributions and still have virtually unfettered access to his aftertax contributions on a tax-free basis. The Tax Reform Act of 1984 legislated against these plans by adding section 72(e)(7), which treats the first amounts withdrawn before the annuity starting date as a return of earnings when 85 percent or more of contributions to the qualified plan during a "representative period" are aftertax contributions. This prevents such qualified plans from being used to provide tax-deferred savings accounts. Section 72(e)(7) is unaffected by the TRA. Internal Revenue Code of 1986 (hereinafter cited as "IRC") §72(e)(7). A proposed technical correction would repeal §72(e)(7). S. 2238; H.R. 4333, 100th Cong., 2d Sess., §111A(b) (1988) (hereinafter cited as "Proposed Technical Corrections Act of 1988").

[6] IRC §72(e)(8)(A); IRC §72(e)(2)(B).

[7] TRA §1122(h)(2)(C).

[8] TRA §1122(h)(1).

[9] IRC §72(e)(8)(D).

[10] IRC §72(e)(2)(B).

[11] IRC §72(e)(8)(B); Internal Revenue Service Advance Notice 87–13, I.R.B. No. 87–4, p. 14 (hereinafter cited "Notice 87–13"), Q&A–11. The participant's basis in the qualified plan

In a significant departure from prior law, the TRA permits defined contribution and certain defined benefit plans to categorize the portion of a participant's interest in the qualified plan attributable to aftertax contributions and earnings thereon as a separate contract for section 72 purposes.[13] A qualified plan that can take advantage of the ability to create a separate contract for amounts attributable to aftertax contributions provides a significant tax benefit to its participants. Preannuity starting date

---

and the value of the vested portion of the total account balance or accrued benefit generally are to be determined as of the date of distribution. As an alternative, the taxpayer's basis in the qualified plan may be determined as of December 31 of the calendar year immediately preceding the year of distribution and the total value of the vested account balance may be determined as of the last valuation date in that preceding calendar year if this date is used on a reasonable and consistent basis for all preannuity starting date distributions. Instead of being based on the vested account balance as of the last valuation date in the preceding calendar year, the value of the account balance may be determined as of any valuation date during the preceding calendar year which is not more than one hundred days before the end of such calendar year. If the vested account balance is valued other than on the date of distribution, the value of the account balance as of the valuation date in the preceding calendar year must be reduced by the value of any distribution after the valuation date but before the end of the preceding calendar year, increased by the value of any contributions or forfeitures between the valuation date and the end of the preceding calendar year and also increased by the value of any portion of the account balance which became vested after the valuation date but before the end of the preceding calendar year. Although these complicated rules are to be used uniformly, the qualified plan is not required to contain provisions identifying the method and valuation dates. *See* Notice 87–13, Q&A–12.

The value of the total account balance in a defined contribution plan generally is the fair market value of the assets attributable to such account including, for example, net unrealized appreciation on employer securities not included in the distribution. If a distribution includes employer securities with a net unrealized appreciation not currently taxable, the value of the vested portion of the account balance is reduced by the amount of the net unrealized appreciation for the purpose of determining how much of the remainder of the distribution is to be treated as a return of the participant's basis in the qualified plan.

In the case of a defined benefit plan, the present value of the vested portion of the accrued benefit is treated as the vested portion of the account balance. Present value is determined with reference to the factors set forth in the qualified plan for calculating single sum distributions. Notice 87–13, Q&A–11.

[12] IRC §72(e)(8)(B). Apparently to prevent circumvention of the new TRA basis proration rules, rollovers of partial distributions are now limited to instances in which a separation from service has occurred. IRC §402(a)(5)(D). *See* text at fns. 89 through 97 *infra*. This prevents a participant from receiving a distribution during employment and rolling over all but the portion of such distribution that represents a return of his basis.

[13] IRC §72(e)(9). A defined benefit plan is to be treated as a defined contribution plan for purposes of applying section 72(e)(9) to the extent that a separate account is maintained for employee contributions to which is credited actual earnings and losses. Crediting employee contributions with a specified rate of earnings will not be sufficient to create a separate account. Notice 87–13, Q&A–14. Except for plans permitting unmatched voluntary contri-

distributions from this contract can be prorated with respect to the ratio of the participant's basis in this contract to the separate account balance attributable to such contract.[14] In most instances a preannuity starting date distribution from this separate contract will return a higher proportion of nontaxable amounts to a participant than a distribution prorated with respect to a qualified plan as a whole.

To be given effect as a separate contract, employee contributions and earnings thereon must be accounted for on an acceptable basis by the qualified plan and the plan document (or plan procedure) must either specify the contract from which each distribution is deemed made or permit the participant to select the contract from which the distribution is made.[15]

A qualified plan maintains adequate separate accounts if a separate record of aftertax contributions (and earnings) is kept and the allocation of earnings, gains, losses, and other credits between this account and the remainder of the interests in the qualified plan is done on a reasonable and consistent basis.[16] Most defined contribution plans that permit aftertax contributions will already maintain adequate separate accounts; however, a qualified plan that has not met the accounting requirement may begin to maintain acceptable records prospectively at any time.[17]

The discretion to treat aftertax contributions and earnings thereon as a separate contract on a prospective basis gives rise to a planning opportunity for qualified plans that provided for aftertax contributions before December 31, 1986 and that continue to provide for such contributions after that date. According to the Internal Revenue Service, these plans can treat post-1986 aftertax contributions and earnings thereon as a separate contract for section 72 purposes, thereby allocating pre-1987 aftertax contributions and earnings on such contributions (including earnings actu-

---

butions allocated to a separate account, most employee-contributory defined benefit plans will probably not involve an adequate separate accounting for employee contributions. When the separate accounting requirement is not met, a nonannuity distribution will be nontaxable to the extent calculated on the basis of the participant's entire interest in the plan.

[14] IRC §72(e)(9). The participant's basis in the qualified plan is not necessarily allocable in its entirety to the separate contract created for aftertax contributions and earnings thereon. Basis attributable to PS-58 costs or repayment of a taxable loan, for example, are allocated to the contract under the qualified plan to which such costs or repayments relate. Notice 87–13, Q&A–16.

[15] Notice 87–13, Q&A–14.

[16] Id.

[17] Id.

ally occurring after 1986) to the plan's other contract. Under this approach, preannuity starting date distributions will first be offset by the pre-1987 grandfathered employee aftertax contributions[18] (if the qualified plan making the distribution qualifies)[19] and then be prorated by looking solely to post-1986 aftertax contributions and earnings thereon.[20]

In effect, the Internal Revenue Service has granted qualified plans the opportunity to give their participants a fresh start in calculating the aftertax contributions and earnings that will make up the separate contract. This fresh start will be particularly beneficial to participants in qualified plans that permitted preannuity starting date distributions before December 31, 1986. Because of frequent withdrawals, it is not unusual for participants in such plans to have earnings on pre-1987 aftertax contributions far in excess of the unwithdrawn amount of aftertax contributions. The ability to ignore the impact of pre-1987 earnings in calculating the taxable portion of withdrawals from post-1986 employee contributions will minimize taxability in such instances. Moreover, the operation of the grandfather rule will result in the participant's earnings on pre-1987 aftertax contributions continuing to compound on a tax-deferred basis even after all of the pre-1987 aftertax contributions have been withdrawn.

The impact of the TRA's rules can be illustrated by comparing the tax consequences of a participant's in-service withdrawal from a profit-sharing plan in 1990 to those that would have arisen if prior law had continued to apply. Since the participant's tax consequences depend in part on the features of the profit-sharing plan, this illustration also highlights the somewhat surprising fact that participants with identical profit-sharing plan account balances can have different tax consequences (depending on the recordkeeping procedures applied) when making in-service withdrawals.

For purposes of the illustration, assume that X Company established a profit-sharing plan in 1975. The profit-sharing plan is funded with company contributions and voluntary aftertax employee contributions of up to 10 percent of compensation. On December 31, 1986 A's company account has a value of $20,000 and, his separate voluntary account consists of $10,000 of contributions and $5,000 of earnings thereon. On De-

---

[18] IRC §72(e)(8)(D).

[19] *See* text at fn. 9, *supra*.

[20] Notice 87–13, Q&A–15. A qualified plan can also begin treating aftertax contributions and earnings thereon as a separate contract on a prospective basis at any time, regardless of when it began complying with the recordkeeping requirements necessary to create the separate contract. Notice 87–13, Q&A–14.

cember 31, 1989 A's company account has a value of $32,000. His voluntary account has a value of $31,000 consisting of $10,000 of pre-1987 contributions, $11,000 of earnings on these contributions, $7,000 of post-1986 voluntary contributions and $3,000 of earnings on these contributions. A's accounts are fully vested and he has made no withdrawals from the plan since December 31, 1986. A wishes to make a withdrawal of $12,000 on January 1, 1990 while employed, and the profit-sharing plan specifies that withdrawals (after use of the grandfathered amount, if applicable) are first charged against the contract maintained for aftertax contributions and earnings thereon, if any, and then against the other contract maintained under the profit-sharing plan.

	Distribution	
Alternatives	*Nontaxable*	*Taxable*
1. Pre-TRA	12,000	0
2. Post-TRA, plan is treated as single contract and grandfather rule not applicable.	3,238[21]	8,762
3. Post-TRA, plan is treated as single contract and grandfather rule applies.	10,264[22]	1,736
4. Post-TRA, plan is treated as two contracts (all aftertax contributions and earnings allocated to one contract), grandfather rule not applicable.	6,581[23]	5,419
5. Post-TRA, plan is treated as two contracts (post-1986 aftertax contributions and earnings allocated to one contract), grandfather rule not applicable.	7,377[24]	4,623
6. Post-TRA, plan is treated as two contracts (all aftertax contributions and earnings allocated to one contract), grandfather rule applicable.	10,667[25]	1,333
7. Post-TRA, plan is treated as two contracts (post-1986 aftertax contributions and earnings allocated to one contract), grandfather rule applicable.	11,400[26]	600

[21] $\$12{,}000 \times \frac{\$17{,}000}{\$63{,}000}$

[22] $10,000 grandfathered plus $\$2{,}000 \times \frac{\$7{,}000}{\$53{,}000}$

[23] $\$12{,}000 \times \frac{\$17{,}000}{\$31{,}000}$

In addition to the results above, even under a plan established in 1987, there are a number of alternatives.[27]

Ten Percent Additional Tax on Early Distributions

In addition to distributed amounts no longer being treated simply as nontaxable to the extent not in excess of basis, a further impediment to distributions before the annuity starting date is the 10 percent additional

---

24 $7,000 nontaxable out of the post-1986 aftertax contract, plus $377 derived by the following:

$$\$2{,}000 \times \frac{\$10{,}000}{\$53{,}000}$$

25 $10,000 grandfathered plus $2,000 × $\frac{\$7{,}000}{\$21{,}000}$

26 $10,000 grandfathered plus $2,000 × $\frac{\$7{,}000}{\$10{,}000}$

27 Assume that an employer establishes a class year savings plan that is treated as one contract under section 72. The plan accounts for employee contributions (and earnings) separately from employer contributions (and earnings) on a class year basis. The employee contributions and related earnings are such as may be treated as a separate section 72(e)(9) contract. The participant makes the following contributions and receives the following employer matching contributions for the first three class years as follows:

Class Year	Employee Contributions	Earnings	Employer Contributions	Earnings	Total
1987	$1,000	$ 750	$ 500	$375	$2,625
1988	1,000	500	500	250	2,250
1989	1,000	250	500	125	1,875
Totals	$3,000	$1,500	$1,500	$750	$6,750

On January 1, 1990 the participant receives a distribution of $2,625. If the plan treats this distribution as a complete distribution of the 1987 class year balance, $1,750 will be treated as coming from the separate section 72(e)(9) contract and $875 will be treated as coming from the remaining contract. On these facts, the $1,750 employee contributory withdrawal is treated as nontaxable to the extent of $3,000 over $4,500 or $1,166.67. The remaining $583.33 of the $1,750 portion of the distribution is included in the participant's income. The entire $875 from the employer contribution contract is fully taxable.

If, however, the plan treats the entire $2,625 distribution as coming from the separate section 72(e)(9) contract (even though the amount of the distribution is determined by reference to the 1987 class year balance) the full $2,625 is subject to proration on the basis of $3,000 of employee aftertax contributions divided by a $4,500 employee contributory account. Thus, $1,750 of that distribution will be nontaxable with the remaining $875 being included in income as a result of the proration. In this latter instance, because of the plan

tax on the taxable portion of early distributions.[28] Consistent with the congressional desire to have qualified plans used as vehicles to provide retirement income, the major category of distributions excepted from the 10 percent additional tax are those that have retirement-type attributes. Another category of distributions (*e.g.* those needed for unusually heavy medical expenses) have also been excluded from the tax for no purpose other than a congressional determination to grant such distributions favored status.

The age and status of the participant are two of the major criteria used by the TRA to exempt retirement-type distributions from the 10 percent additional tax. Thus, distributions (whether before or after the annuity starting date) from a qualified plan to a person who has attained age 59½ are not subject to the 10 percent additional tax.[29] Similarly, the 10 percent additional tax does not apply to payments on account of an employee's death or disability of a severe and anticipated long-term nature.[30]

---

recordkeeping method, the entire distribution was deemed subject to proration on the basis of the separate contract derived from employee contributions.

If, as a third alternative, the plan treated the entire $2,625 as coming from the portion of the plan comprising employer contributions, the full amount of the distribution could be taxable. Notice 87–13, Q&A–14, Ex. 2.

While tax consequences do not have to follow the manner in which the amount of the distribution is calculated (*i.e.* a distribution of $2,625 in the above example can be treated as entirely out of the separate section 72(e)(9) contract), plan recordkeeping may become excessively complicated if the plans and tax consequences do not correspond.

[28] The 10 percent tax applies to distributions from qualified plans, tax sheltered annuities and individual retirement accounts (but not to section 457 plans) after December 31, 1986. Two types of distributions are exempted from the 10 percent tax. First, distributions which are being made to an employee who, as of March 1, 1986, had both separated from service with the employer maintaining the qualified plan commenced receiving benefits and elected in writing a specific distribution schedule for the payments he is receiving from the qualified plan are exempted from the 10 percent tax. A change in the distribution schedule subjects subsequent payments to the 10 percent tax. TRA §1123(e)(3). Secondly, under a transition rule distributions for which the employee elects special treatment are viewed as if received by the employee when he separated from service in 1986, and thus are exempt from the 10 percent tax. TRA §1124(a).

[29] IRC §72(t)(2)(A)(i).

[30] IRC §72(t)(2)(A)(ii) and (iii). An individual is considered disabled under this provision:

> "if he is unable to engage in any substantial gainful activity by reason of any medically determinable physical or mental impairment which can be expected to result in death or to be of long-continued and indefinite duration." IRC §72(m)(7).

Even a disability of a sort sufficient to result in payments under many long-term disability plans might not be sufficient to exempt corresponding distributions from a qualified plan from the 10 percent additional tax.

Age and status are combined in the exception from the additional tax granted for distributions after separation from service "on account of early retirement *under the plan* after attainment of age 55" (emphasis supplied).[31] The Internal Revenue Service has been somewhat lenient in its interpretation of this requirement, taking the position that the distribution need not necessarily have occurred as a result of "retirement" as defined in the plan, provided that the separation occurs during or after the calendar year in which the employee attained age 55.[32] The 10 percent tax will apply, however, to an employee who separates from service before the calendar year in which he attains age 55 with benefits not commencing after age 55 (but before age 59½).[33]

The other factor identified by the statute as indicative of a retirement-type distribution is a payout duration tied to life or life expectancy. Thus, any payment, even one commencing before age 55, is exempt from the additional tax if it is part of a series of substantially equal periodic payments (at least annual in frequency) for the life or life expectancy of the employee or for the joint lives or joint life expectancies of the employee and his designated beneficiary.[34]

So as to avoid manipulation, if substantially equal payments begin for life or a period measured with respect to life expectancy, and the series is modified (other than because of death or disability) before the employee attains age 59½ or after the employee attains 59½, but before five full years of payments have been made, the 10 percent tax is triggered in the year in which the modification occurs.[35] The 10 percent tax, plus interest, is then owed on all payments previously received.[36]

Although not having any retirement-type attributes, the TRA exception for distributions to an employee to the extent of the deduction allowable under section 213 for medical expenses[37] is relatively easy to understand from a policy perspective. Limiting this exclusion to an amount equal to the portion of an employee's deductible medical expenses that exceed 7.5 percent of his adjusted gross income appears consistent with the congressional policy underlying section 213. Further, not conditioning

---

[31] IRC §72(t)(2)(v).

[32] Notice 87–13, Q&A–20.

[33] H.R. Rept. 99–841, 99th Cong., 2d Sess., p. II–457 (hereinafter cited as "Conference Report").

[34] IRC §72(t)(2)(A)(iv); Proposed Technical Corrections Act of 1988 §111A(c).

[35] IRC §72(t)(4)(A).

[36] IRC §72(t)(4)(B).

[37] IRC §72(t)(2)(B).

the exception on the employee's actually claiming the deduction on an itemized return ensures its uniform availability.

Payments under qualified domestic relations orders are also exempt from the 10 percent additional tax.[38] This exemption encourages the use of QDROs and is consistent with the congressional policy behind their creation in the Retirement Equity Act.

Certain distributions from employee stock ownership plans (ESOPs) are also excepted from the additional tax.[39] Distributions exempted from the 10 percent additional tax include dividends distributed to participants under section 404(k)[40] as well as any distributions made before January 1, 1990 from an ESOP:

> . . . to the extent that, on average, a majority of assets in the plan have been invested in employer securities . . . for the 5-plan-year period preceding the plan year in which distribution is made.[41]

The distribution must have been "attributable to assets" which have "been invested in employer securities" that satisfy the applicable requirements of sections 409 and 401(a)(28) "at all times" during the five preceding plan years.[42]

Beyond a congressional predisposition to encourage the use of ESOPs, it is difficult to perceive any reason for ESOPs to be singled out for preferential treatment. If this exception is intended to facilitate distributions from terminated PAYSOPs and TRASOPs, the application to ongoing plans may not be appropriate. On the other hand, if the goal is to facilitate accelerated distributions under the revised ESOP rules,[43] the elimination of the ESOP exception in 1990 does not appear sensible.

The Internal Revenue Service has interpreted the conditions of the exception from the 10 percent tax to apply with respect to an ESOP that has been in existence for less than five full plan years if the investment requirements have been met during the entire period of the plan's existence.[44] If benefits have been in existence for less than five full plan years, the full period of the existence of the benefits will be treated as the five-plan year period for determining whether the distribution qualifies. Bene-

---

[38] IRC §72(t)(2)(D).

[39] IRC §72(t)(2)(C).

[40] IRC §72(t)(2)(A)(vi).

[41] IRC §72(t)(2)(C)(i).

[42] IRC §72(t)(2)(C)(ii), Proposed Technical Corrections Act of 1988, §111a(c).

[43] IRC §409(o)(1).

[44] Notice 87–13, Q&A–21.

fits from a non-ESOP transferred to a newly formed ESOP will be treated as having been in existence prior to the establishment of the ESOP and thus must have met the full five-plan-year investment requirement, including the period prior to transfer to the ESOP. Distributions from a tax credit ESOP (PAYSOP or TRASOP) will qualify for the exception if the investment period requirements have been met. There is a 2 percent *de minimis* exception for cash-type assets included in an ESOP.[45]

If some plan assets have met the five-year investment requirement but others have not, the distribution will be treated as first consisting of employer securities invested for the requisite period, then as being attributable to employer securities invested for less than the requisite period and thirdly, as attributable to benefits never invested in employer securities.[46]

Although numerous types of distributions are exempted from the 10 percent additional tax, most in-service distributions are not of these types. Thus, the 10 percent additional tax is best viewed as a penalty designed to discourage in-service withdrawals. It is open to question whether the 10 percent additional tax when combined with reduced tax rates for many employees will act as an effective deterrent.

Loans

Loans have long been a popular means of providing participants in qualified plans with access to plan assets during employment. The tax-free use of the funds borrowed, combined with an interest deduction for federal income tax purposes and often the crediting of the interest payment to the debtor participant's own account balance in a defined contribution plan, made loans very attractive to participants. Loan provisions have been particularly useful in encouraging employees to participate in section 401(k) plans notwithstanding the in-service withdrawal restrictions applicable to such plans.

The availability of loans was first curtailed by the Tax Equity and Fiscal Responsibility Act of 1982 (TEFRA).[47] For the most part, the TRA refines the limitations introduced by TEFRA.

The maximum amount that can be borrowed from all employer plans without the borrower being deemed to have received a taxable distribution is limited to the lesser of $50,000 or one half of the present value of the participant's nonforfeitable account (or $10,000 if greater). The

---

[45] *Id.*

[46] *Id.*

[47] P.L. 97–248, §236(a).

$50,000 figure, however, now must be reduced not only by any other outstanding loans from plans of the employer (applying subsections 414(b), (c), and (m))[48] but also by the excess, if any, of the highest outstanding loan balance during the one-year period before the date on which a loan was made over the outstanding balance of loans from the plan on the date on which such loan was made.[49] Thus, an employee who borrowed $25,000 on January 1, 1988 and who repays $5,000 of the balance by August 1, 1988 cannot borrow on August 2, 1988 more than $25,000, *i.e.* $50,000 reduced by the $20,000 outstanding balance on that date and reduced as well by the $5,000 excess of $25,000, the highest outstanding balance during the preceding one-year period, over the $20,000 outstanding balance.

Whereas under TEFRA the term of any loan used to "acquire, construct, reconstruct, or substantially rehabilitate" any dwelling unit to be a principal residence of the participant or a member of the participant's family could have extended for more than five years, only loans used to "acquire" a dwelling which is to be the "principal residence of the participant" can now be for a period longer than five years.[50] From a policy perspective it seems that the construction of a new residence should come within the definition of "acquire"; the wording of the TRA, however, seems to indicate a contrary conclusion.

Moreover, all loans must be amortized on a substantially level basis requiring payments no less frequently than quarterly.[51] This rule eliminates balloon loans, and combined with the offsets to the $50,000 maximum, prevents the maintenance of a large permanent loan balance.

The new loan provisions are effective as to any loan "made, renewed, renegotiated, modified, or extended after December 31, 1986."[52] It can be expected that the Internal Revenue Service will apply the transition rules stringently. Thus, it would not be surprising for a post-1986 pledge of real estate in connection with a pre-1987 loan being deemed "renegotiated" at the time of the pledge.

One additional area in which the TRA imposes restrictions beyond the conceptual limitations originally imposed on loans by TEFRA involves the loss of the interest deduction in connection with loan repayments. All employees with loans outstanding from qualified plans will be

---

[48] IRC §72(p)(2)(D).

[49] IRC §72(p)(2)(A).

[50] IRC §72(p)(2)(B)(ii).

[51] IRC §72(p)(2)(C).

[52] TRA §1134(e).

subject to the general phaseout of the interest deduction for consumer interest.[53] Given the administrative complexities of structuring plan loans to qualify as loans secured by the participant's residence, it is anticipated that relatively few borrowers from qualified plans will be able to base their interest deduction on any other grounds. Thus, one of the incentives for borrowing from a qualified plan will be diminished significantly starting in 1987 and will vanish by 1991.

Persons who are key employees, as defined in section 416(i), or who seek to secure their repayment obligation with an account balance in a section 401(k) plan fare particularly poorly under the TRA. For these persons, no interest deduction is available. Interest for which no deduction is allowed does *not* create any basis in the participant's account.[54]

While plan loans still remain permissible, the combination of level amortization, the stricter limitation of loans to a five-year period, the offsets to the $50,000 loan ceiling, and the limited availability of the interest deduction act to curtail the attractiveness of such loans. This further limits preretirement access to qualified plan assets.

Hardship Withdrawals

Effective for plan years commencing after December 31, 1988, in-service withdrawals of amounts contributed pursuant to the participant's election to a qualified plan under section 401(k) are curtailed. Combined with the new restrictions on loans from qualified plans, the restrictions on hardship withdrawals severely limit access to amounts held by section 401(k) plans during employment.

Specifically, the TRA limits hardship withdrawals from a section 401(k) plan to a participant's elective contributions.[55] With earnings on elective contributions, including pre-1989 earnings, excluded from withdrawal upon hardship, the utility of the cash or deferred plan as a device to accumulate capital for use during employment is further impaired, especially for long-term participants.

Although the rule is not entirely clear from the statute, it appears that qualified nonelective contributions and earnings thereon which meet the section 401(k) requirements of full vesting and nonwithdrawability prior

---

[53] IRC §163(h)(6); §163(d)(6).

[54] IRC §72(p)(3). See Conference Report, p. II–465.

[55] IRC §401(k)(2)(b)(i)(VI) made effective January 1, 1989 by TRA §1116(f)(1). See Conference Report, p. II–389.

to age 59½ are not withdrawable even in the event of hardship, if such contributions are used to satisfy the actual deferral percentage test of section 401(k).[56]

MINIMUM DISTRIBUTION REQUIREMENTS

The TRA refines the minimum distribution requirements initially applied to qualified plans by TEFRA. These requirements, along with the incidental death benefits rule, seek to ensure that qualified plans provide participants with retirement income, rather than serve merely to delay federal income tax or to transfer wealth upon death.[57] The refinements made by the TRA correct an administrative problem that hampered enforcement of the provision and create a sanction for noncompliance (apart from disqualification of the qualified plan) that participants can reasonably expect the Internal Revenue Service will impose when circumstances warrant. A sensible result of these refinements is that identical minimum distribution requirements will apply to all tax-favored retirement income vehicles (*e.g.*, qualified plans, tax-sheltered annuities, IRAs, and section 457 plans).[58]

Required Beginning Date

Prior to January 1, 1989, distributions from a qualified plan are required to begin by April 1 of the calendar year following the calendar year in which a participant (other than a 5 percent owner) attains age 70½ or retires, whichever is later. Distributions to a 5 percent owner must begin after he attains age 70½, regardless of his continued employment.[59]

The Congress apparently believed that a required beginning date defined with reference to a participant's separation from service was unsatisfactory because a potential for abuse is inherent in such a standard. Thus, although the legislative history speaks of the administrative difficulty associated with determining whether a separation from service has

---

[56] Conference Report, p. II–389.

[57] H.R. Rept. No. 99–426, 99th Cong., 1st Sess., p. 726 (hereinafter cited as "House Report"); S. Report. No. 99–313, 99th Cong., 2d Sess., p. 605 (hereinafter cited as "Senate Report"); Joint Committee on Taxation, General Explanation of the Revenue Provisions of the Deficit Reduction Act of 1984, p. 868.

[58] TRA §1121(b); IRC §401(a)(9).

[59] IRC §401(a)(9)(C).

occurred, the example used to illustrate this difficulty concerns a participant who postpones his required beginning date, even though ceasing regular employment, by continuing to perform work under a consulting agreement.[60] Similarly, mention is made of an individual who is not a 5 percent owner, but nonetheless controls the employer and thus the date of his separation from service. Since this individual is said to be no different from the owner of an IRA, there is no reason for not requiring that his distribution begin after age 70½, regardless of his employment status.[61]

In response to those perceived abuses and in an effort to standardize to the extent possible the minimum distribution requirements applicable to tax-favored retirement income vehicles, the TRA provides that effective January 1, 1989, distributions from qualified plans must begin by the April 1 following the calendar year in which the participant attains age 70½.[62] Persons who attained age 70½ before January 1, 1988 are in general grandfathered so that they need not commence receiving distributions until their separation from service.[63] However, as under the pre-TRA rule, a person who is a 5 percent owner at any time during the five plan years beginning with the plan year that ends within the calendar year in which such person attains age 66½ must begin to receive distributions from a qualified plan no later than the April 1 following the calendar year in which he attains age 70½.[64]

Fifty Percent Excise Tax

Not only must distributions from qualified plans begin on time, but they must also proceed at a prescribed rate. Otherwise, the recipient (or nonrecipient in the case of nonpayment) will be subject to a nondeductible excise tax equal to 50 percent of the amount by which the minimum required distribution for the calendar year exceeds the amount actually distributed from the qualified plan.[65]

The minimum required distribution is not defined in the Code. Instead the Secretary of the Treasury is granted authority to define the term

---

[60] House Report, p. 725.

[61] Senate Report, p. 604.

[62] IRC §401(a)(9)(C); TRA §1121(d)(1).

[63] TRA §1121(d)(4)(B)(i). Under proposed technical corrections, an employee who has attained age 70½ prior to 1989 but has not retired, would be considered to have attained age 70½ in 1989 and would be required to begin receiving distributions by April 1, 1990. Proposed Technical Corrections Act of 1988, §111a(a).

[64] TRA §1121(d)(4)(B)(ii).

[65] IRC §4974(a).

in regulations.[66] According to proposed Treasury regulations,[67] the annual minimum required distribution for a participant who does not designate a beneficiary will be measured with reference to the payments that the participant would have received during a calendar year from the qualified plan if his benefit had been payable from the required beginning date in the form of a single life annuity for his life expectancy. A participant who has designated a beneficiary will also have an annual minimum required distribution measured with reference to a life annuity payable from the required beginning date for the joint lives of the participant and beneficiary. The annual amount payable from this annuity will be calculated on the assumption that the survivor benefit is not more than 100 percent of the periodic amount payable to the participant, or less to the extent necessary to satisfy the incidental death benefits rule.[68]

Although the excise tax provides the Internal Revenue Service with a sanction that can be imposed on the recipient of the offending distribution, the qualified plan must nevertheless be required to provide expressly that all distributions will satisfy the minimum distribution rules.[69] The excise tax is technically in addition to, and not in lieu of the sanction of disqualification. However, it is likely that in all but the most abusive of situations the excise tax will be the only sanction. Nevertheless, nothing in the minimum distribution rules suggests that disqualification is no longer a sanction available to the Internal Revenue Service. Conversely, approval of an improper form of distribution by the Internal Revenue Service in connection with the issuance of a favorable determination letter will not exempt such distribution from the excise tax.[70]

Most common forms of distribution now allowed by qualified plans will comply with the new minimum distribution rules. The statute also gives the Internal Revenue Service discretionary authority to waive the excise tax due in case of reasonable error when corrective action is taken to rectify the short fall.[71] Given the highly technical nature of these requirements, the Internal Revenue Service may exercise this discretionary authority to exempt distributions from the excise tax whenever a taxpayer can show that a good faith attempt at compliance was made.

---

[66] IRC §4974(b).

[67] IRS Proposed Regulations §1.401(a)(9)–1, Q&A–F-3.

[68] Conference Report p. II–451.

[69] House Report, pp. 726–27.

[70] Conference Report, p. II–451.

[71] IRC §4974(d). Presumably, under some circumstances reliance on an Internal Revenue Service determination letter might prove to be a good faith error. *See* text at fn. 70, *supra*.

Section 242(b)(2) Elections

The TRA continues to except from the new rules any distributions made in accordance with a form of benefit designation made before January 1, 1984 under section 242(b)(2) of TEFRA.[72] Proper designations made in accordance with this section will be given effect and will not be subject to the 50 percent excise tax.

RETIREMENT DISTRIBUTIONS

As part of the overall trend of the TRA to encourage the use of qualified plans as devices to provide retirement income, the favorable income averaging and capital gains treatment associated with the receipt of lump-sum distributions from qualified plans upon separation from service, disability or death, prior to attainment of age 59½, have been deleted from the Code[73] for distributions after December 31, 1986[74] for all but a class of grandfathered taxpayers.[75] The legislative history points out that the Congress's policy of encouraging retirement income is better served by rollovers of amounts received in such circumstances to IRAs.[76] The continued availability of income averaging and capital gains treatment under these circumstances encouraged the preretirement use of amounts accumulated in tax-favored retirement vehicles.

Lump-Sum Distributions

The TRA did not change the Code's description of a lump-sum distribution.[77] The major change made by the TRA is to limit the availability of favorable income averaging and capital gains treatment to lump-sum distributions made with respect to a participant who had attained age 59½.[78] Further, the TRA only permits one income averaging and/or capital gain election to be made with respect to a participant.[79]

---

[72] TRA §1121(d)(4)(A).

[73] IRC §402(e)(4)(B).

[74] TRA §1122(h)(1).

[75] TRA §1122(h)(3)(C).

[76] Senate Report, pp. 608, 609.

[77] IRC §402(e)(4)(A).

[78] IRC §402(e)(4)(B).

[79] *Id.*

Income Averaging

Except to the extent modified indirectly by the new rate structure under the TRA, the income-averaging calculation will generally be carried out as under prior law, merely with the substitution of 5 years for 10 years.[80] Since the 10-year averaging period was originally selected because it was thought to approximate the life expectancy over which a person age 65 would have received the lump-sum distribution,[81] the switch to a 5-year averaging period appears to be motivated by revenue concerns. In light of the new tax rates, however, 5-year averaging may not produce a greater tax than 10-year averaging under pre-TRA rules.

Although the new income-averaging provisions apply to distributions received after December 31, 1986, a grandfather rule covers any individual who attained age 50 before January 1, 1986.[82] Such an individual can elect to apply the 1986 rules for determining the eligibility of a lump-sum distribution for income-averaging treatment and the 1986 tax rates to any distribution received from a qualified plan.[83] This means that a person who attained age 50, for example, in 1984, could elect that a lump-sum distribution received from a qualified plan when he or she attained age 56 in 1990 be evaluated (for purposes of eligibility for income averaging treatment) under the 1986 rules. If this distribution is received, for example, on account of separation from service, the fact that the individual had not attained age 59½ at the time of the distribution would not be enough to prevent the distribution from being a lump-sum distribution entitled to income-averaging treatment. Although no election is necessary to take advantage of the grandfather rule prior to the receipt of a distribution, an election under the grandfather rule will eliminate any further opportunity to elect five-year income averaging, even as to a participant who has not attained age 59½ at the time the grandfather rule becomes applicable to a distribution.[84]

The age 50 requirement of the grandfather rule relates to the age of

---

[80] IRC §402(e)(1)(B). See IRS Form 4972 for 1987 for the IRS interpretation of the new income averaging rules.

[81] H.R. Rept. No. 93-779, 93d Cong. 2d Sess. 148–49 (1974).

[82] TRA §1122(h)(3).

[83] TRA §1122(h)(3)(A).

[84] TRA §1122(h)(3)(C) and (h)(5). Similarly, an election under the grandfather rule eliminates any further opportunity to elect grandfathering treatment with respect to any other distribution from a qualified plan.

the employee who receives the benefit.[85] Thus, an individual, trust, or estate that receives a postdeath lump-sum distribution on behalf of an employee who had attained age 50 on January 1, 1986 is permitted to make one election with respect to the employee to use income averaging on the lump-sum distribution. An individual who makes an income averaging election on an amount he receives as a beneficiary does not lose his opportunity to make an income-averaging election with respect to a single lump-sum distribution made on his behalf.

Capital Gains

The long-term capital gain treatment available with respect to the portion of a lump-sum distribution attributable to pre-1974 participation is phased out by the TRA for distributions received after December 31, 1986 over a six-year period as described in the following schedule:

Year	*Percentage Treated as[86] Capital Gain*
1987	100
1988	95
1989	75
1990	50
1991	25
1992	0

Although there was initially some confusion on this point, it is fairly clear that the percentage of a distribution characterized as a long-term capital gain is subject to tax at the normal income tax rates established by the TRA, without applying the 60 percent long-term capital gains deduction that was a feature of the pre-TRA Code. Thus, the advantage of the phaseout lies in the opportunity to offset pre-1987 capital losses against the post-1986 capital gains preserved by the phaseout.

Support for this reading comes from the TRA's silence about the applicable tax rate in the capital gain phaseout rule and the failure to mention expressly the 60 percent long-term capital gains deduction (especially because a specific tax rate is mentioned in connection with the grandfather rule discussed below) which is otherwise repealed by the

---

[85] Staff of the Joint Committee on Taxation, *General Explanation of the Tax Reform Act of 1986,* (May 4, 1987) p. 722 (hereinafter cited "Blue Book").

[86] TRA §1122(h)(4).

TRA for tax years beginning after December 31, 1986. Additionally, applying the 60 percent long-term capital gains deduction would produce the anomalous result of a lower tax rate for amounts subject to the phaseout (*i.e.*, 40 percent of 28 percent = 11.2 percent) than amounts subject to the grandfather rule discussed below.

Under the grandfather rule, individuals who have attained age 50 before January 1, 1986 may elect to apply the 1986 rules for determining the eligibility of a lump-sum distribution for capital gains treatment to a distribution from a qualified plan and to have the portion of a resulting lump-sum distribution attributable to pre-1974 participation taxed at a flat 20 percent rate.[87] This 20 percent rate, the maximum effective tax rate applicable to long term capital gains under the pre-TRA Code, will apply even to an individual for whom capital gains in 1986 would have been taxed at an effective tax rate lower than 20 percent. As with the grandfather rule for income averaging, no election is necessary to take advantage of the grandfather rule prior to the receipt of a distribution, and an election under the grandfather rule will eliminate any further opportunity to elect five-year income averaging, even as to a participant who has not attained age 59½ at the time the grandfather rule becomes applicable to a distribution.[88]

Revised Treatment for Rollovers of Partial Distributions

As under prior law, an employee who takes advantage of the rule permitting a rollover of a partial distribution will forego the right to report a subsequent distribution from the same plan (or any plan aggregated with such plan under section 402(e)(4)(C)) on an income-averaging basis.[89] However, the TRA amends the Code to limit the opportunity to rollover a partial distribution to situations involving a separation from service, death or disability.[90] Prior law permitted an in-service rollover of a partial distribution.[91] An IRA is still the only acceptable recipient of a partial rollover.[92]

---

[87] TRA §1122(h)(3)(B)(ii).

[88] TRA §1122(h)(3)(C). Similarly, an election under the grandfather rule eliminates any further opportunity to elect grandfathering treatment with respect to any other distribution from a qualified plan.

[89] IRC §402(a)(5)(D)(iii).

[90] IRC §402(a)(5)(D)(i); IRC §402(e)(4)(A).

[91] §402(a)(5)(D)(i) of the Internal Revenue Code of 1954.

[92] IRC §402(a)(5)(D)(ii).

Effective for distributions made after December 31, 1986, a partial distribution eligible to be rolled over without being included in current income is defined as a distribution:

1. from a trust which is part of a qualified plan;
2. that represents payment within one taxable year of the recipient of at least 50 percent of the balance to the credit of the employee, applying section 402(e)(4)(C); and
3. which is payable on account of the employee's death, on account of the employee's separation from service, or after the employee has become disabled (within the meaning of section 72(m)(7)).[93]

Satisfaction of these requirements is determined with reference to the normal lump-sum distribution rules, with certain modifications. Only 50 percent (rather than 100 percent) of the balance to the credit of the employee must be distributed from the qualified plan. Since there is no tax involved, there is no need to make a lump-sum election under section 402(e)(4)(B). Whether or not the participant is a self-employed person or a common law employee, suffering a disability (within the meaning of section 72(m)(7)) gives the right to rollover a partial distribution. The partial distribution cannot be rolled over merely because it is paid after age 59½.[94]

Notice 87–13 makes clear that the aggregation rules of section 402(e)(4)(C) are applicable to partial rollovers.[95] Although Notice 87–13 does not refer to other subsections of section 402(e)(4), it appears that the Internal Revenue Service intends the nonapplication of community property laws[96] to apply. The five-year minimum service period does not apply.[97]

Net Unrealized Appreciation

Perhaps as part of the overall statutory structure which favors the acquisition of employer securities by qualified plans, the rules with respect to unrealized appreciation in employer securities are left intact by the TRA.

---

[93] Notice 87–13, Q&A–19. A distribution made by an ESOP to satisfy the diversification requirements of section 401(a)(28) is treated as satisfying these requirements. IRC §402(a)(5)(D).

[94] *Id.*

[95] A proposed technical correction would repeal the application of aggregation rules for this purpose.

[96] IRC §402(e)(4)(G).

[97] IRC §402(e)(4)(H); Blue Book p 725.

Thus, recognition of all unrealized appreciation in employer securities will be deferred if such securities are part of a lump-sum distribution.[98] There is no requirement that the lump-sum distribution be received after the recipient attains age 59½ or any limitation on the number of times a person can benefit from the rule applicable to unrealized appreciation of employer securities received as part of a lump-sum distribution.[99]

Unrealized appreciation in employer securities that are part of a lump-sum distribution received after December 31, 1986 may be recognized at the time of the distribution, however, if the taxpayer elects such recognition pursuant to regulations to be promulgated.[100] This TRA change probably results from the elimination of special treatment for capital gains so that a distributee in many instances may well be better off reporting the full market value of employer securities as part of a lump-sum distribution.

Potential Future Vesting

The TRA resolves a technical issue created by the fact that participants in qualified plans who receive distributions at separation from service when they are less than fully vested retain a contingent right to increase their vested interest upon subsequent reemployment. A question existed before the TRA about the impact, if any, of this future vesting on any income averaging, capital gains, or rollover treatment obtained for the previous distribution. The TRA answers this question, retroactive to the effective date of the Retirement Equity Act of 1984 provision being amended by the TRA, but the answer depends on how the previous distribution was taxed.[101]

If the previous distribution benefitted from income averaging or capital gains treatment, an increase in the recipient's vested interest in the benefit accrued prior to his separation from service because of his reemployment will trigger a recapture of the tax benefit resulting from such treatment.[102] The amount of the recapture presumably will be the difference between the tax that would have been payable if the previous distribution had not benefitted from income averaging or capital gains treatment and the tax actually paid on such distribution. The details of the

---

98 IRC §402(e)(4)(J).

99 IRC §402(e)(4)(J).

100 IRC §402(e)(4)(J).

101 IRC §402(e)(6).

102 IRC §402(e)(6)(B).

recapture are left to regulations. For purposes of determining whether an election of income averaging or capital gains treatment has been made with respect to the employee, the election made for the previous distribution is ignored when the tax benefit associated with that election is the subject of recapture.[103]

Qualified plans typically condition an employee's right to increase his vested interest in the benefit accrued prior to separation from service upon the employee repaying the full amount of the prior distribution to the qualified plan. Although not required by the Code, consideration should be given to notifying the employee that such a repayment could generate tax liability. With the TRA accelerated vesting rules[104] and the five-year minimum participation period for lump-sum distributions, the issue of potential future vesting will become less significant in 1989.

If the previous distribution has been the subject of a rollover, an increase in the person's vested interest in the benefit accrued prior to his separation from service because of reemployment will deprive the employee of the tax benefits associated with income averaging treatment for any subsequent distribution from the qualified plan.[105] However, the employee can elect income averaging treatment for a distribution received from another qualified plan, so long as that plan was not aggregrated with the plan from which the original distribution was made, under section 402(e)(4)(C). Further, if the rollover has been made in connection with a distribution received without the participant's consent (*e.g.,* $3,500 or less), income averaging treatment would be available for any subsequent distribution received from the qualified plan.[106]

Basis Recovery Rules

Under pre-TRA law if under an annuity form of benefit, the projected payments within the first three years after the annuity starting date were equal to or in excess of the employee's unrecovered basis in the qualified plan, payments in the form of an annuity would be nontaxable until an amount equal to the unrecovered basis was received by the employee.[107] The "three-year recovery rule," which was a popular way of receiving distributions under qualified plans that provided for aftertax contribu-

---

[103] *Id.*

[104] *See* IRC §411(a)(2).

[105] IRC §402(a)(6)(G).

[106] IRC §402(a)(6)(G)(ii).

[107] Internal Revenue Code of 1954, §72(d)(1).

tions, was repealed retroactively by the TRA with respect to any individual whose annuity starting date was after July 1, 1986.[108]

Since the three-year recovery rule has been repealed, each payment received in an annuity form will be at least partially taxable. The nontaxable portion of each payment will be determined with reference to the ratio of the employee's unrecovered basis in the qualified plan to the total expected payments the recipient is to receive from the qualified plan.[109] Correcting an apparent oversight under prior law, the TRA limits the nontaxable amount that can be recovered to the precise amount of the employee's unrecovered basis.[110] If annuity payments terminate, on the other hand, before the employee's unrecovered basis has been fully recovered (as a result of the death of the employee and any annuitant prior to the end of the anticipated payment period) the unrecovered basis is allowed as a deduction to the last surviving annuitant for the last year of his life.[111] When payments are made to a beneficiary or estate of the annuitant by the qualified plan in the form of a refund of consideration paid by the employee, the deduction is allowed to the beneficiary or estate.[112] Any deduction under these provisions is treated as if arising out of a trade or business conducted by the taxpayer for purposes of the net operating loss deduction under section 172.[113]

RESTRICTIONS UPON LARGE BENEFIT PAYMENTS

The TRA tightens the restrictions imposed by section 415 upon benefits payable from defined benefit plans and the annual additions allocable under defined contribution plans. Because the section 415 restrictions can be avoided when an individual works for multiple employers and because section 415 ignores amounts accumulated by the individual for retirement in other tax-favored retirement income vehicles, the TRA introduces the concept of a 15 percent excise tax on the individual for "excess retire-

---

[108] TRA §1122(c)(1); TRA §1122(h)(2)(A).

[109] IRC §72(b)(1).

[110] IRC §72(b)(2).

[111] IRC §72(b)(3)(A). The old law did "rough justice" by giving a break to recipients who outlived their life expectancies and overtaxing those who failed to survive their full life expectancies.

[112] IRC §72(b)(3)(B).

[113] IRC §72(b)(3)(C).

ment distributions'' received during his lifetime[114] and on the individual's estate for ''excess retirement accumulations'' remaining in tax-favored retirement income vehicles at his death.[115] Distributions from or amounts accumulated under qualified plans subject to section 401(a), annuity plans subject to section 403(a), tax-deferred annuities, custodial accounts or retirement income accounts subject to section 403(b), individual retirement arrangements under section 408 or plans that once satisfied these qualification requirements are subject to the excise tax provision.[116]

Excess Retirement Distributions

With the exception of a complicated grandfather clause, the mechanics of the penalty tax payable on excess retirement distributions are straightforward. All distributions, with certain stated exceptions, from the tax-favored retirement income vehicles listed above received by or with respect to a taxpayer during a calendar year are aggregated by the taxpayer and subjected to the penalty tax to the extent in excess of a threshold.[117] Certain distributions are excluded from consideration:

1. Any distributions received by a taxpayer with respect to a deceased person.
2. Any distribution made with respect to the taxpayer to an alternate payee pursuant to a qualified domestic relations order which are includable in the alternate payee's income.
3. The portion of any distribution to a taxpayer that represents a return of an employee's basis in the tax-favored retirement income vehicle.
4. The portion of any distribution rolled over to another tax-favored retirement income vehicle without tax.[118]
5. Any health coverage or distribution of medical benefits under section 401(h) to the extent includable under sections 104, 105 or 106.[118]

---

114 IRC §4981A(c). *See* House Report, p. 740.

115 IRC §4981A(d). *See* House Report, p. 740.

116 IRC §4981A(e).

117 IRC §4981A(c)(1).

118 IRC §4981A(c)(2); Temporary Regulations §54.4981A–IT, Q&A a-4.

The general rule is that the 15 percent excise tax is imposed on distributions received by or made with respect to the taxpayer during the calendar year to the extent in excess of $112,500. The $112,500 figure is adjusted in the same manner and to the same extent as under section 415(d).[119] Net unrealized appreciation in employer securities, even if not taxable, appears subject to the 15 percent excise tax.

Although the rule is somewhat confusingly worded in the statute, any employee who does not make the special grandfathering election discussed below, as well as any employee for whom the grandfathering election would not be relevant, will actually benefit from a threshold amount excluded from tax equal to the greater of $150,000 (without adjustment) or $112,500 (with adjustment).[120]

A lump-sum distribution for which an income-averaging election is made under section 402(e)(4)(B) (or an election to apply capital gains treatment) is subject to a separately calculated excise tax to the extent in excess of a separate threshold; the tax will be imposed only to the extent the distribution exceeds five times the limitation applicable to other distributions.[121] Thus, the limitation for a lump-sum before the excise tax will apply is the greater of $750,000 (under the grandfather clause) or $562,500 adjusted. The amount of the excise tax due on excess distributions, whether or not qualifying for the special rule applicable to a lump-sum distribution for which an income averaging election is made, is 15 percent.[122]

An individual can be liable for both the 10 percent penalty tax imposed on early distributions and the 15 percent excise tax imposed on excess retirement distributions. In these circumstances, however, the taxpayer is permitted to offset the 10 percent penalty tax against the 15 percent excise tax, to the extent both taxes are assessed on the same distributions.[123]

A grandfather rule applies if the accrued benefit of an employee under the tax-favored retirement income vehicles in which he participates exceeded $562,500 as of August 1, 1986.[124] If the employee elects grandfather treatment on his federal income tax ending before January 1, 1980,

---

[119] IRC §4981A(c)(1). The $112,500 figure has increased to $117,529 in 1988.

[120] IRC §4981A(c)(5)(C); Internal Revenue Service Advance Announcement 87–2, I.R.B. No. 87–2, p. 17, Q&A–B(3).

[121] IRC §4981A(c)(4).

[122] IRC §4981A(a).

[123] IRC §4981A(b).

[124] IRC §4981A(c)(5).

the 15 percent excise tax will be imposed on the amount by which the annual distributions exceed the greater of $112,500 adjusted as described above, or the amount deemed to be attributable to the grandfathered accrued benefit, as determined in accordance with regulations.[125] If the distribution qualified for income averaging under section 402(e)(4)(B), the amount exempt from the excise tax will be the greater of $562,500, as adjusted, or the amount determined to be attributable to the grandfathered accrued benefit.[126]

In the case of tax-favored retirement income vehicles that maintain separate accounts (*e.g.*, defined contribution plans), the accrued benefit as of August 1, 1986 will be equal to the account balance as of that date. Tax-favored retirement income vehicles that provide a stated benefit for life commencing at sometime in the future (*e.g.*, defined benefit plans) are to use the accrued benefit (presumably on a present value basis) that would be payable if the employee separated from service on August 1, 1986.[127] Apparently the accrued benefit as of August 1, 1986, whether forfeitable or nonforfeitable, counts for purposes of determining an individual's eligibility for the grandfather rule.

Excess Retirement Accumulation

The mechanics of the 15 percent excise tax imposed on an estate on excess retirement accumulations are complex. Generally, the excise tax is imposed on the excess of the "value" of a decedent's interests in tax-favored retirement income vehicles over the present value of a single life annuity that provides for equal annual payments, commencing on the decedent's date of death for the life of an individual the same age as the decedent equal to the limitation in effect for excess retirement distributions in the year of death.[128] The respective values are to be measured either as of the date of the decedent's death or the alternate valuation date under section 2032,[129] using interest rate and other assumptions to be prescribed in regulations.[130]

The value of the decedent's interest in tax-favored retirement income vehicles does not include the portion thereof that is subject to a quali-

---

[125] IRC §4981A(c)(5); IRS Temporary Regulations §54.4918A–IT, Q&A, b-4 and b-14.

[126] IRC §4981A(c)(5)(A); IRS Temporary Regulations §54.4981A–IT, Q&A c-1.

[127] Conference Report, p. II–477.

[128] IRS Temporary Regulations §54.4981A–IT, Q&A d-7.

[129] IRC §4981A(d)(3)(A).

[130] IRC §4981A(d)(3)(B).

fied domestic relations order in favor of the decedent's spouse or former spouse, that represent the decedent's basis in the tax-favored retirement income vehicles that is attributable to life insurance proceeds payable by reason of the decedent's death excludible from income under section 101(a) of the Code, and that represents the decedent's interest in a tax-favored retirement vehicle by reason of the death of another individual.

If a decedent has made the grandfather election with respect to his annuity distribution, the excise tax on excess retirement accumulations is imposed on the excess of the "value" of the decedent's interest in the tax-favored retirement income vehicles over the greater of the present value of a single life annuity as described above or the amount deemed to be the unrecovered portion of his grandfathered accrued benefit, as determined under regulations.[131]

An estate can be liable for the 15 percent excise tax, even if the estate will not otherwise pay an estate tax. Neither the unified credit[132] nor, since the tax is imposed without taking into account the amount of the taxable estate, the marital deduction or the charitable deduction can be used to reduce or eliminate the 15 percent excise tax. The penalty tax is payable by the estate, regardless of who benefits from the excess retirement accumulation, and the estate has no separate right under section 4981A of the Code to seek reimbursement of the tax from persons that the decedent has designated as the beneficiaries of the tax-favored retirement income vehicles that gave rise to the excise tax. However, the decedent's will or the state apportionment law may provide that the estate is entitled to such reimbursement. Once amounts are subjected to the estate tax subsequent payments received by beneficiaries are not again subject to the excise tax as received.[133]

Effective Dates

The provisions relating to the penalty tax on excess retirement distributions are generally applicable with respect to distributions after December

---

[131] IRS Temporary Regulations §54.4981A–IT, Q&A d-4.

[132] IRC §4981A(d)(2).

[133] Conference Report, p. II–471.

[134] TRA §1133(c)(1).

[135] Conference Report, p. II–477.

[136] TRA §1133(c)(2).

31, 1986.[134] However, distributions after August 1, 1986 but before January 1, 1987 may reduce the grandfathered amount.[135]

The excise tax on excess retirement accumulations applies to the estates of individuals dying after December 31, 1986.[136]

Distributions from (and presumably accumulations under) qualified plans subject to section 401(a), annuity plans subject to section 403(a), and any tax-deferred annuity, custodial account or retirement income account subject to section 403(b) are exempted from the 15 percent excise tax, if such arrangements are terminated before January 1, 1987 and distributions from such arrangements occur before January 1, 1988.[137]

CONCLUSION

The changes made by the TRA to the Code to discourage the use of qualified plans as devices to accumulate capital rather than to provide retirement income radically alter the pre-TRA rules and, together with the grandfather rules, complicate tax planning for qualified plan distributions. This article can only present a preliminary picture of what these changes mean. The reader of this article might keep in mind the recent statement of an attorney for the Joint Committee on Taxation to the effect that people "should not assume that a provision [of the TRA] intentionally gives the result you end up with."[138]

---

[137] TRA §1133(c)(3).

[138] P–H Pension and Profit Sharing Bulletin 7 (January 28, 1987) p. 1, quoting Mary Levontin.

CHAPTER 42

PRINCIPLES OF ADMINISTRATION

Edward E. Mack, Jr.
Mary A. Carroll

To an average participant, the complex issues of plan design, costing, and funding seem mysterious and perhaps irrelevant—problems for the decision makers in the executive suite or on the board of trustees to ponder. The participant's questions are more practical: Am I covered? How do I file a claim? How much of my claim will be paid? How long will I have to wait for payment? Just what does this plan do for me? Answering these questions—and establishing systems to ensure these questions *can* be answered promptly, accurately, efficiently, and in ways that help the participant understand his or her benefits—is the central objective of benefit plan administration.

"Administration," as discussed in this chapter, is not necessarily the work of an "administrator" as defined by ERISA:

(i) the person specifically so designated by the terms of the instrument under which the plan is operated;
(ii) if an administrator is not so designated, the plan sponsor; or
(iii) in the case of a plan for which an administrator is not designated and a plan sponsor cannot be identified, such other person as the Secretary may by regulation prescribe (Section 3, 353(16)(A)).

The administrator, under this definition, would typically hold discretionary authority and responsibility under the plan and serve in a fiduciary capacity. Throughout this chapter, however, "administration" is viewed as the *implementation* of decisions—on plan design, costing, funding, and any other discretionary issues—made by the plan sponsor or other plan fiduciaries.

Administration includes all the activities that translate elaborate proposals, complicated cash-flow analyses, and labyrinthine contract language into the daily operating reality which is the participants' only point of contact with the plan. In many cases, participants will evaluate their plan largely, if not entirely, on the basis of their satisfaction (or dissatisfaction) with its day-to-day administration. Thus, it is essential the plan sponsor pay at least as much attention to the *administration* of its benefit plans as to their structure and funding.

Administrative functions may be performed by employees of the plan sponsor (the personnel or benefits department of a corporation, for example, or the salaried administrator(s) of a jointly administered Taft-Hartley fund), or by firms which specialize in this field (contract or third-party administrators, banks, benefit consultants, insurance brokers, or insurance companies). All administrative functions may be performed by a single entity, or there may be a number of groups involved.

No matter what structure is selected, those who manage the administration of a benefit plan must be prepared to perform certain basic functions: to determine participants' eligibility for coverage; communicate the nature and impact of plan provisions to participants and their families, plan advisers, and government agencies; adjudicate claims for benefits; and maintain the accounting and data processing systems which enable them to perform these functions.

DETERMINATION OF ELIGIBILITY

Determining who is eligible for the plan is the first requirement, and a number of plan provisions interact to affect eligibility. If a health plan, for example, does not require employee contributions, all employees within the eligible class(es) are covered; if employees contribute to the cost of coverage, their election of the benefit and payment of the required contribution must be verified. Health programs frequently delay the effective date of coverage until the employee is actively at work (or until a dependent ceases to be confined in a hospital or at home under the care of a doctor); if such a provision applies, eligibility cannot be verified without determining whether the individual has satisfied this requirement. Many employers impose an eligibility waiting period of 1 to 3 months (and may impose an even longer waiting period, such as 6 to 12 months, for certain benefits); the administrator must establish systems to ensure that new employees' protection becomes effective after the applicable waiting period. A retirement plan participant's ultimate benefit may rise or fall depending on the accuracy of the administrator's eligibility records.

Care must be taken when nonretirement coverage terminates—for an employee, a dependent, a class of employees, or the entire covered group—since claims incurred before termination are a liability of the plan, while those incurred after the termination date should generally be denied. With many plans extending coverage after termination—voluntarily, or under federal or state mandate—the administrator's eligibility determination function becomes even more complex.

The plan administrator also generally is responsible for determining individuals' eligibility for special plan provisions, such as conversion privileges or waiver of premium. A pension or profit-sharing plan administrator generally is responsible for maintaining the records which permit determination of participants' years of service for vesting and benefit accrual purposes as well as the applicability of other plan provisions.

Special Problems

Employers frequently assign responsibility for eligibility verification to their personnel departments. Large firms with multiple locations may need one or more employees at each plant or office to maintain accurate eligibility records, together with a home office staff to coordinate the eligibility provisions of various plans and assist in resolving questions and disputes. Within a smaller company, eligibility determination may be only one of the several responsibilities of a personnel or administration department employee.

For most plans—and especially for multiple and multiemployer benefit plans—a second eligibility verification will be made by the insurance company or third-party administrator which handles claims for the plan. This function is particularly important in the administration of multiemployer plans in industries (like construction) where participants change employers frequently. If no single employer can certify an individual has worked enough hours, days, or weeks to earn eligibility for plan benefits, it is vital that the administrative office maintain comprehensive and accurate data on participants' service with all contributing employers.

COMMUNICATIONS

Effective communication of plan benefits to participants and their families is essential if the plan is to achieve its objectives. In establishing a program of benefits, most employers hope to attract and retain productive employees and maintain good morale; if the program is poorly communicated, however, it is likely to be unappreciated and even ignored until a claim arises, and may lower, rather than improve, employee morale when a claim must be denied or reduced. This *internal* need for benefit communication is matched by an *external* mandate: under the Employee Retirement Income Security Act of 1974 (ERISA), all benefit plans subject to this legislation must be communicated "in language calculated to be understood by the average plan participant." The passage of ERISA has stimulated a major investment in improved communication techniques by large employers, benefit consultants, brokers, and insurers; since 1974, benefit communications has been a "growth industry."

Communicating with Participants and Their Families

ERISA established minimum standards for benefit plan communications with participants in specific documents like the summary plan description and summary annual report. Larger companies frequently supplement these plan documents with employee meetings, multimedia presentations, and other printed material designed to gain for benefit plans the visibility that their place in the expense budget demands; they feel employee understanding is essential to their plans' effective operation. These formal modes of communication, however, are probably less important to plan participants than their direct contact—on the telephone and through correspondence—with the people who administer the plan. The administrative office answers participants' questions about their eligibility and the plan's benefits, assists them in filing claims and appealing claim denials, and explains how specific payments were calculated. The skill and empathy of the administrative staff in handling these communications may have more impact on participants' sense of security and satisfaction with their benefits than glossy brochures and films and slide-shows.

Communicating with Health Care Providers

In underwriting coverage and processing claims, an administrator often needs to communicate directly with hospitals and other health care providers. The most frequent contact of this type is undoubtedly verification of benefits calls or letters from hospitals, which seek to ascertain what portion of the participant's charges will be paid by the plan. Accuracy in confirming benefits is particularly vital in certain parts of the country where carrier-provider agreements may require a plan to pay provider charges when coverage is erroneously confirmed.

In addition to benefit confirmations, an administrator's communications with providers frequently include requests for additional information about participants' medical histories and about specific charges, audits of large or complicated claims, and direct payment of assigned benefits. A plan sponsor's cost containment or case management programs can produce a near-adversary relationship—for example, when a provider's recommendation is questioned. In all these areas, an administrative staff which thoroughly understands providers' operations and concerns is likely to provide more effective service to plan participants.

Communicating with Other Plan Advisers and Government Agencies

The administrator's control of plan data establishes an important information flow from the administrative office to the various professionals who provide services to the plan, as well as to the plan sponsor. Actuaries, brokers, and consultants need detailed information on participation, losses, expenses, and trends to evaluate the plan's status from time to time. As a surrogate for both the plan sponsor and, in insured plans, the insurance company, the administrator must provide sponsor and carrier with frequent reports comprehensive enough to convince these entities that the functions they have delegated are being performed properly. The administrator must provide the plan's (or company's) attorney with details of any situation which may produce legal action against the plan or its sponsor, and frequently works with counsel in analyzing the impact of federal and state legislation. Auditors, too, must depend upon the cooperation of the administrator in performing their examination of the plan's financial condition.

Finally, most benefit plans are required to file reports with a variety of government agencies. As statutory requirements change, in such areas, for example, as nondiscrimination and vesting, administrative systems must be revised to capture and summarize effectively the statistics needed to demonstrate the plan's compliance with the new standards.

Although most of the administrator's communications with the plan sponsor, professional advisers, and government agencies are invisible to participants, they are essential to effective functioning of the plan, and are an important part of the administrator's overall responsibilities.

Special Problems

Large employers can take advantage of economies of scale and centralization in developing sophisticated benefit communication programs; jointly administered plans frequently supplement required plan documents with articles in union publications and presentations at union meetings. Effective communications may be most difficult for multiple employer plans: association-sponsored programs and multiple employer trusts with minimal communications budgets and covering primarily small employers. For such plans particularly, the quality of participants' day-to-day contact with the administrative office is likely to be central to their satisfaction with the plan. And at the heart of that contact are participants' claims for benefits.

PROCESSING OF CLAIMS

Some types of employee benefit plans—for example, group term life insurance or a retirement program covering younger workers—can operate successfully for years without ever paying a claim: their value lies in their *promise* to pay, and participants understand that there may be no current claims activity. Most employees judge their benefit program, however, by those portions which *pay* rather than promise to pay: by its handling of the medical, dental, and disability claims they submit from time to time. However effective an administrator's functioning in other areas may be, its claim processing must satisfy participants' expectations if the program is to achieve the sponsor's objectives.

In reviewing claims, the administrator has obligations to many masters. The demands of the plan sponsor, insurer, provider, and participant compete for the administrator's attention and may produce different treatment of specific claims. The administrator must generally rely on the plan document (and the insurance contract, if the plan is insured), together with any deviations adopted by the plan sponsor (and agreed upon with the carrier, where appropriate) in resolving doubtful situations. At the same time, the administrative staff must be diplomatic and empathetic in working with participants and health care providers. The administrator is a "middleman," balancing the desire of participants and providers for speedy, complete payment against the plan's requirement—of vital interest to the sponsor (and insurer)—that claims be investigated carefully and adjudicated in accordance with all relevant plan provisions. In the conflict between speed and accuracy, the administrative office must opt for accuracy, working hard meanwhile to help participants understand why investigative delay is necessary. An administrator able to handle effectively these multiple demands on its claim operation has a head start toward success in other areas of administration as well.

Retirement Plans

In pension plans, once the administrator has reviewed the participant's eligibility for benefits and determined the benefit payable based on work history and plan provisions, payments are generally issued automatically. Even here, however, it is essential the administrative office establish checking procedures to prevent issuance of benefit payments to deceased or ineligible individuals. In addition, a defined benefit plan's sponsor may provide for an automatic or *ad hoc* adjustment in benefits for current retirees; when this occurs, the administrator must apply the adjustment accurately and consistently.

Health Protection

Medical claims are probably the most difficult to adjudicate because of the number of factors involved in determining the availability and amount of benefits for submitted charges. The administrative staff must examine whether the claimant is a covered individual, what benefits are in force, when the claimant's coverage became effective, and whether any special restrictions or exclusions apply. It must analyze the availability of other coverage—under government programs, including Medicare, workers' compensation, or occupational disability laws, or other insurance programs—and the effect, if any, of such duplicate coverage on the plan's liability for the charges submitted. In reviewing specific charges, the administrator's claim specialists must make sure that the expenses themselves are eligible for payment under the plan and that they were incurred at a time when the relevant coverage was in force for the individual. The plan document must be reviewed for any exclusions or limitations which may apply; "preexisting condition" provisions require special care at this point in claim adjudication. Proper investigation of medical claims is complex and often time-consuming: the examiner must carefully compare the claim submitted to eligibility records and to the plan document and may seek additional required information from other administrative records, from providers, and from the claimant before a single calculation can be made. This attention to detail is essential, however, to make sure only legitimate claims are paid under the plan.

Once an examiner has verified that the submitted expenses are *eligible* for benefits under the plan, he or she must apply all relevant plan provisions to determine the *amount* which should be paid. Unless first-dollar benefits are available for these charges, the file must be checked for possible satisfaction of the plan's deductible and coinsurance provisions. If the plan includes "first-dollar" coverage or internal limits for particular types of treatment, the applicability of these provisions to the submitted charges must be reviewed. If the plan's benefits are provided on a "usual, reasonable, and customary" basis, the administrative office must compare the charges submitted with the appropriate statistical data. Whether benefits are scheduled or unscheduled, the examiner should analyze each claim to be sure that the claimant's treatment, including the duration of any hospital confinement, is consistent with the diagnosis indicated, perhaps recommending an audit of the provider's billing if there appear to be serious discrepancies.

Life and Accidental Death and Dismemberment (AD&D) Coverage

In some respects, death claims would seem to be the least complicated claims to adjust, since the occurrence of the covered event can be easily verified by reviewing certified death certificates, newspaper obituaries and other documents. Although life and accidental death plan provisions may affect the availability of benefits for a particular claimant, and the deceased participant's file must be reviewed to ascertain the proper beneficiary, most death claims can be processed straightforwardly. It is in this area of claim administration, however, that insurance companies have been most reluctant to delegate responsibility, generally insisting that, even if an outside administrator reviews the submission and file and prepares the payment authorization, the draft itself must be issued by the carrier. The relatively large dollar amounts payable for death claims, the complexity of probate law, and the special legal problems involved in adjusting AD&D claims are the major reasons offered in support of maintaining insurer control of these claim payments.

Loss of Income Protection

Disability income claims also are frequently a source of concern for the plan sponsor and/or insurer. The loss itself is difficult to prove (or disprove), the plan's potential liability may be quite large, and the combined disability benefits available under employment-related, Social Security, and other plans may be sufficient to discourage claimants from returning to work. Therefore, careful investigation is essential when a claim is first submitted, recertification of disability by the claimant's physician is frequently required, and carriers providing long-term disability benefits often review claims on a regular schedule, using service bureau investigators or their own employees to confirm the continued qualification of the claimant for plan benefits.

Special Problems

Self-administration of employee benefit plans may be attractive to large employers because it appears to give the corporate staff more direct control over plan costs and services; however, many companies prefer to retain an outside administrator (or to have claims processed by insurance company employees) to direct employee dissatisfaction with claim denials away from the company and toward a third party. Multiemployer plans frequently employ a staff of salaried administrators, including experienced claim examiners; other jointly-administered plans delegate claim administration to a third-party administrator or an insurance carrier. In both corporate and Taft-Hartley plans, claim administration may sometimes be subject to internal pressures (from a key manager in a corporate plan or a trustee in a jointly administered plan) to handle some claims more favorably than would be justified by the plan's provisions. While the plan sponsor may intend for some provisions to be enforced less rigidly than others, the administrator must use extreme care in making exceptions to the provisions of the legal document which governs the plan's operations.

A significant problem in processing claims for multiple employer plans (whose participants are, for the most part, employees of smaller employers) is that, with no one on the employer's staff who is really qualified to assist employees, many claims are incomplete or otherwise unacceptable when first submitted. Claim examiners for these plans must be especially patient in explaining to participants the reasons for various requirements. A similar problem may exist in the administration of some industrywide Taft-Hartley funds; here, too, participants may not have ready access to advice in submitting claims (although union trustees and business agents may be able to provide some assistance).

Because ERISA defines in considerable detail participants' rights when their claims are denied, controls are needed to ensure that the administrator's benefit explanations, response time, and appeals procedures meet or exceed the law's minimum standards.

ACCOUNTING FOR PLAN FUNDS

In essence, an employee benefit plan is simply a flow of funds: dollars flow in from the employer (and the employees if the plan is contributory), earn interest while they are held, and then flow out again to pay benefits to participants and providers, and to cover the plan's expenses. To control this flow, the administrator must establish accounting systems adequate to ensure the plan's monies are being used properly. Larger plans, particularly those which are funded through a trust, generally maintain accounting systems parallel to those of other economic entities: the plan sponsor and/or trustee(s) regularly review financial statements for the plan; the administrative office must maintain the general and subsidiary ledgers which are the basis for these statements, must control accounts payable and receivable and cash receipts and disbursements, and may be involved in tax reporting for the plan, its participants, and providers to whom benefits have been paid. If the plan is insured, the carrier frequently requires detailed premium breakdowns from the administrator, who is sometimes also involved in claim-accounting functions and in commission accounting on plans marketed through a network of insurance agents or brokers.

Special Problems

In some respects, administrative accounting systems for large corporate benefit plans are fairly simple, since plan funds generally come from a single source. Even here, however, benefit expenses are likely to be charged to the corporation's profit centers on some equitable basis, and accounting systems must be established to handle this allocation. More complicated systems are required to control the billing and collection process for the hundreds of smaller firms which participate in multiple employer or multiemployer plans, or for companies which maintain a dozen or more *different* benefit plans for various classes of salaried and hourly employees.

DATA PROCESSING

There are few areas of plan administration which cannot benefit from the application of flexible, thoughtfully designed data processing systems. While a very small benefit plan can perhaps be handled effectively with manual systems, most larger life, health, disability, and retirement plans can provide faster, more efficient service to participants and more accurate information for the plan sponsor, advisers, and insurers if the administrative office can rely on an appropriate level of computer support.

In designing data processing systems for benefit plan administration, administrative managers and systems analysts often work together to establish the system's parameters, define the database and reporting requirements and backup and retention criteria, and analyze methods of developing or converting data to build the system's master files. This approach has the advantage of matching the administrator's knowledge of the details of the plan's benefit provisions and limitations, rate structure, and other variables with the systems analyst's expertise in solving information-handling problems through computer hardware and software.

Special Problems

The objectives of the plan sponsor generally determine which aspect of the administrative operation is likely to be automated first. In an industry-wide Taft-Hartley welfare or pension plan, eligibility record keeping may be high on the list because of the errors and expense which result from manual tracking of participants' relatively frequent shifts from one employer to another. Large employers may be most interested in establishing a database which permits effective cost control and analysis of health care cost trends. Insurance carriers also are likely to be vitally concerned with information of this type. Because of the number of firms involved, multiple employer plans generally require substantial computer support in the billing and collection process. The volume of paper generated in processing claims—and the impact of normal human error on benefit calculation—encourages administrators of all types of plans to develop or purchase software to allow computer adjudication of many types of claims. For most employee benefit plans, more information and more efficient systems are almost always better; the only significant restriction on the value of more sophisticated reports and analyses and more automated operations is the investment required to produce them.

SUMMARY

Though employee benefit plans existed before World War II, they have had a significant impact on the American economy and the American public only during the past 40 years. Their administration, like their benefit structure, funding, and other areas, has changed substantially during this period, and this pattern seems likely to accelerate in the coming decade. However much benefit plans may change, however, it seems clear that cost-efficient administration which meets employee needs and achieves the objectives of the plan sponsor will continue to be a vital element of effective plans.

CHAPTER 43

DEVELOPING PLAN SPECIFICATIONS

David R. Klock
Sharon S. Graham

Every few years, an organization may wish to reevaluate its group insurance program and to test the marketplace by obtaining bids on its benefit program. The process provides an opportunity to review how well the program meets benefit objectives. This reevaluation process typically consists of the following steps:

1. Determine if the program should be rebid.
2. Review plan design.
3. Select appropriate financing techniques.
4. Draft specifications for either negotiated placement or competitive bid.
5. Undertake prebid screening.
6. Analyze bids and select insurer or other carrier.
7. Complete final negotiations with selected carrier.
8. Implement new program.

Before proceeding, one very important caveat should be emphasized. The entire selection process should be conducted at the highest professional level. Too frequently, group insurers perceive the selection process as very political, with apparent advantage going to friends and relations. As one publication recently reported,

> Insurance companies should never be selected based on the basis of friendship, old school ties, or other subjective means. In these days, the

> insurance broker represents an important business relationship. Treat him as a professional and expect and demand that he act like one.[1]

Many excellent insurers will not submit bids if nonprofessional conditions exist between them and the client.

This chapter focuses on the first five steps in the reevaluation process. Steps six and seven are covered in the next chapter. Plan implementation is covered in Chapter 44.

WHY REBID?

Some employers (especially government units) believe that frequent bidding of their group insurance plans results in the lowest possible cost outlay. This contention generally is a misconception. Organizations that too often enter the employee benefits marketplace face the risk of being considered unstable or capricious consumers who frequently seek bids and/or change carriers. Insurers, knowing an account is unlikely to prove profitable unless it remains with the insurer for several years and thus allows the insurer to recover certain front-end costs associated with the installation of a group insurance plan, may shy away from an organization with this reputation. The organization soon discovers that the number of cost-competitive insurers or other service organizations willing to bid for its business declines dramatically.

This does not imply that the rebidding of an employee benefits package is seldom advisable. There are several excellent reasons why organizations may wish to enter the reevaluation process. The following discussion covers the most important considerations in this decision.

Irreconcilable Management Dissatisfaction

The executives of a firm occasionally become disenchanted or frustrated with their insurance agent/broker/consultant and/or with their insurance company. A thorough investigation of the reasons for the dissatisfaction should be conducted prior to any decision to rebid the coverage. Corrective actions and/or repair of poor communication lines may be a viable alternative. If, however, the credibility of the current insurer or adviser is beyond repair, rebidding will undoubtedly prove necessary.

---

[1] Bernard M. Brown and Charles F. Moody, Jr., "Insurance Bidding and Specifications," *Risk Management Reports* 5, no. 5, p. 14.

Legal Requirements

Many government entities are required by law or by administrative resolution to rebid their insurance programs periodically. However, many experts believe a change in the regulations may be appropriate if rebidding is required more frequently than once every five to seven years. Brown and Moody summarize this viewpoint when they state:

> In our opinion, this situation [frequent rebidding] has created a belief among underwriters that municipalities tend to look only at short-term cost considerations and will move to another underwriter or broker without the slightest hesitation. Of course, the cost of coverage is very important and is a major factor in selecting an insurance program; but equally important is scope of coverage, service, and availability of acceptable markets. This practice of frequent rebidding has undoubtedly diminished the general market capacity available to municipalities. In our opinion, municipalities and other governmental entities, as a general rule, should not rebid more frequently than once every six years. This might be shortened, under certain circumstances. . . . However, the general principle remains that governmental entities should take a much longer term view of the implications of their insurance program decisions than they have in the past.[2]

The same guidelines apply to nongovernmental employers. Frequent rebidding should be avoided.

Underwriting Cycle

Many insurance markets undergo underwriting cycles, with periods of very restrained markets and conservative pricing/underwriting decisions followed by more aggressive and very competitive pricing/underwriting decisions. Employee benefit managers or risk managers occasionally try to take advantage of a perceived period of lower costs and/or expanded underwriting capacity by rebidding their insurance programs.

Adviser Recommendations

The agent/broker/consultant is responsible for maintaining a high level of knowledge regarding the availability and relative competitiveness of alternative insurance carriers. When an organization has confidence in its adviser, his or her advice should be given serious consideration. If this

---

[2] Ibid., p. 8.

confidence is lacking, a reevaluation of the relationship with the adviser is in order. The employer should, however, be both skeptical of and interested in the advice of commissioned advisers not currently handling the account. These advisers have a potential financial interest in rebidding the coverage.

Substantial Change in the Organization

Mergers, acquisitions, or rapid growth may mean that the nature of the organization has changed dramatically since the current group coverage was obtained. Such changes often result in a need for changes in plan design and can necessitate a level of service or expertise unavailable from the current insurer or service organization. This problem will be especially evident if the employer has developed significant foreign operations with many overseas employees because international employee benefits management often requires unique skills and products.

Nonrenewal or Significant Change in Conditions or Cost

An organization clearly has no choice but to rebid if its current plan is canceled. Alternatively, rebidding may be needed if the current insurer has given notice that renewed coverage will be altered significantly so that a serious diminution of benefits will occur almost certainly resulting in reduced employee morale. A renewal price increase that the employer perceives to greatly exceed general market costs likewise should trigger a rebidding of the program.

Inadequate Service

The most important reason for changing insurance carriers (or advisers) is proof of an inadequate level of service. The key areas of service can be divided into the following categories: timeliness, quality and expertise in cost reduction analysis, review of all financing alternatives (e.g., self-funding), and claims handling.

Significant Time since Last Market Test

A periodic market test of the relative competitiveness of the current insurance program is recommended regardless of current service levels. Experts seem to hold that an appropriate rebidding cycle is once every five to seven years.

REVIEWING PLAN DESIGN

Prior to writing bid specifications, the organization and its agent/broker/consultant should review carefully the current plan design. Benefit programs often evolve in a piecemeal and haphazard fashion, with little or no consistent input for personnel goals, long-term cash flow constraints, and employee equity. The bidding process provides an excellent opportunity to seriously evaluate plan design in light of other critical and evolving corporate goals. A set of suggested questions to be answered would include:

1. What is the employer's attitude toward group insurance? For example, are group insurance benefits viewed as traditional compensation for work provided, an incentive to increase employee productivity, and/or a benevolent reward?
2. How should the responsibility for economic security be shared by the employer and individual employees?
3. What effect should seniority, salary, or position have on the level of benefits?
4. What is the firm's present cash flow available for employee benefits, and what are the probabilities of future cash flows at various levels?
5. How important is ''income leveling''?
6. What are the quantity and quality of the corporate staff who will be responsible for handling the details of a group insurance program?
7. Should an agent, broker, or consultant be used?
8. Does the firm have subsidiaries with unique benefit planning problems?
9. Is company management concerned enough about unionization or about attracting key employees to affect employee benefit design by type of employee?
10. How should changes (increases) in employee benefits be ranked with other changes (increases) in the total employee compensation package?
11. Should flexibility be built into the program to recognize the differences in needs and desires among employees?
12. How much attention should be given to the attitudes of employees when making changes?
13. Is the proposed plan design consistent with cost control standards concerning plan objectives, eligibility, preexisting conditions, utilization of outpatient and home health care, second

opinions on surgery, out-of-pocket and copay provisions, and preventive care in lieu of larger claims stemming from neglect?
14. How will the contributions of the employee benefit plan to the employer's benefit plan objectives be measured? How often?[3]
15. Does the plan meet nondiscrimination tests?
16. What competitive pressures exist from the industry and/or region.

In addition to addressing these questions, the benefit planners will also wish to carefully review experience data to detect any areas where changes in the current benefits package might result in significant cost reductions and/or benefit improvements with little or no additional premium outlay or compromise in personnel goals. This in-depth statistical analysis of plan experience may lead, for example, to changes in the existing plan deductibles and/or the addition of new deductibles. Effective use of deductibles may reduce excessive utilization of certain medical services by creating a financial disincentive. Redesign of plan deductibles based on actual plan experience could help create one source of funds to be used for the expansion of benefits in more critical areas of potential catastrophic loss.

The effectiveness of the foregoing plan design analysis is dependent on both the quality of the loss data provided in periodic claims reports and the level of technical service provided by the outside adviser or by the insurer. If a satisfactory level of data or statistical assistance is not currently provided, this poor service emphasizes the need to rebid the coverage. New bid specifications should clearly communicate a request for periodic loss data analysis.

FINANCING TECHNIQUES

During the past several decades, numerous alternatives to the traditional methods of financing group employee benefits have been developed. These alternatives to a pure insurance arrangement include experience-rated plans, monthly experience arrangements, retrospective premium agreements, minimum premium plans, administrative services only (ASO) programs, and various types of self-administered and/or self-

[3] For further discussion of this topic, see David R. Klock and Bruce Palmer, "Group Insurance and the Role of the Professional Life Underwriter," *CLU Journal* 33, no. 3 (July 1979), pp. 44–53.

funded plans. Other chapters of this handbook have covered these alternatives in considerable detail.

Prior to developing its bidding strategy, the organization (with help from its agent/broker/consultant) must decide on the financing or cash flow method most compatible with its circumstances. The selection of certain financing alternatives will significantly influence the type of information solicited from bidders.

SPECIFICATIONS: NEGOTIATED PLACEMENT OR COMPETITIVE BID

There are at least three methods of entry into the employee benefits marketplace:

1. Negotiated placement with a single insurer or service organization.
2. Competitive bidding, with a public announcement that all qualified insurance companies may obtain bid specifications and submit proposals.
3. Closed bidding, with only invited insurers allowed to submit bids.

Negotiated placement is appropriate if the employer, on advice from a qualified adviser, is convinced it has identified an insurer that is very competitive in the class of group business to be purchased. By developing and maintaining strong rapport and communication with a few highly competitive insurers in each line of group coverage, a firm can often obtain underwriting or pricing concessions that may not be possible in a more open bid process. Personal contacts and commitment can be very important in periods when the underwriting cycle is to the employer's disadvantage. However, it is often possible to obtain many of these financial gains through a multistaged bidding process that eliminates "nonqualified" bidders. The bidding process does not preclude personal contact and negotiations.

Open competitive bidding typically is used only when required by law. For example, many government entities advertise the bidding of group insurance. In theory, an open competitive bid system creates the widest possible market survey. It can, however, significantly increase the cost of the bidding process as a result of the added cost associated with reviewing very weak or poorly presented proposals. Without some prescreening, the employer or its consultant may be forced to analyze numerous noncompetitive bids. Furthermore, many qualified bidders will not play in an open field due to possible misunderstanding and/or communication failures.

With a closed or limited bidding process, the employer and/or the agent/broker/consultant will prescreen potential bidders. Only "qualified" bidders will be allowed to obtain detailed bid specifications and to submit a proposal. Since bids will be received from only a limited number of insurers, the employer retains the flexibility to negotiate the final contract. If a change of coverage or of financing techniques is desired by the employer, this can be accomplished in the final negotiation stage rather than in an expensive rebidding process. Most corporate employers and a growing number of public employers use some form of closed negotiated bidding.

Negotiated Placement

The negotiated placement method of purchasing group coverage is also referred to as the "interview method" because it consists of a series of preliminary interviews during which the list of several potential service organizations is narrowed to the one that will be provided with detailed census information and will be the only insurer or other service organization to submit a price quotation.

Negotiated placement typically consists of several steps. First, after informing the current insurer of a decision to consider a plan change, the employer or its agent/broker/consultant prescreens several insurers (including the current one). These insurers should be recommended by the adviser and/or by such reliable sources of information as other risk managers or employee benefit managers. Prescreening considerations include the financial solvency of the insurer, its service facilities, its reputation regarding cost, and the quality of its sales, administrative, and claims staff. Prescreening is described in more detail in a later section of this chapter.

Second, the decision makers will select a few insurers or service organizations (perhaps four to six) from those that have been prescreened and provide these organizations with general information about the employer, its current group insurance program, and any changes it would like to see in the new plan. Each of these companies should be requested to prepare a brief report on the general approach, philosophy, and structure of its proposed group insurance program. The purpose of this step is to determine if the risk management philosophy of the proposed insurer or other service organization is compatible with that of the employer and if the organization has the expertise and capacity to handle the employer's unique needs.

Third, the suggestions of the alternative insurers will be evaluated to select the one company with which the final details of the group insurance plan will be negotiated. This company alone will be provided with detailed loss, financial, and employee data. Furthermore, only this one insurer or service organization will submit a detailed bid on the desired group plan.

Finally, after receiving this bid, the employer will negotiate any necessary changes with the help of the agent/broker/consultant. Success at this point depends heavily on the competence of the adviser. If an organization wishes to use the negotiated placement method but lacks confidence in the technical skills of its adviser, an obvious preliminary step would be the selection of a new adviser. This process is similar to that for selecting an insurer. Should an organization believe it will be incapable of selecting a highly qualified adviser, the organization will have an additional reason to prefer the bidding procedure for selecting an insurer or service organization.

BID SPECIFICATIONS

Assuming an organization wishes to use a multiple-insurer bidding process (either open or closed) rather than a negotiated placement with one insurer or other service organization, specifications must be designed and distributed to all qualified bidders. The specifications must deal with the role of any adviser, the coverage desired, and the financing method to be used. Bid specifications must also provide detailed underwriting data (e.g., employee census and paid losses).

The organization could provide several insurers with broad guidelines as to the type of coverage and then request proposals from these insurers. In fact, this is frequently what happens. The requests are often made verbally, and the specifications are so broad that different insurers propose significantly different benefit designs. The resulting proposals seldom furnish detailed information on the fixed and variable retention charges and interest credits. *The solution to the potential problem of incomparable proposals is to write clear specifications and to include a format for the itemization of all cost factors.*

Specifications should consist of the following parts:

1. Cover letter.
2. Plan experience data.
3. Description of desired coverage.
4. Census data.
5. Questionnaire and bid forms.

Cover Letter

A cover letter, which serves as an invitation to bid, should accompany the specifications. A primary purpose of this letter is to motivate the competitive insurers to bid. Responding to a bid request requires time and expenditure by an insurer. Each insurer needs some assurance that the process will be fair and that the corporation requesting the bid is a desirable client. The major elements of the cover letter include:

1. Name.
2. A description of the employer's principal operations.
3. If the organization has operations in more than one location, a complete listing of all locations should be provided.
4. Collective bargaining status. Indication should be made if any groups of employees will not be covered under the proposed plan.
5. Name of the employee or consultant to whom the proposal should be submitted. This person should be capable of answering technical and nontechnical questions. If a consultant has been retained and is available to answer questions, this fact should be indicated in the cover letter or the bid specifications.
6. Date and place for proposal submission. Insurers should be given at least 30 days to prepare their proposals.
7. Anticipated effective date of the new plan.

Plan Experience

Most competitive insurers are unlikely to prepare a bid unless a reasonable amount of information for at least the last three (preferably five) years is provided.

The following types of historical information should be furnished:

1. *A complete description of the benefits in effect during each period for which claims data are furnished.* This description is essential in helping the actuaries detect if changes in rates or claims resulted from a change in the benefit plan or from adverse experience. If copies of the plan document are unavailable, any booklets containing descriptions of pertinent benefits and plan provisions will usually be adequate.

2. *Detailed information on all claims.* If the firm does not maintain its own computerized database on losses, an alternative source of information on claims charged to the account may be the insurer's year-end financial accounting reports to the group. This report should contain a breakdown of both paid claims and changes in claim reserves. Data on the following deductions from premiums are also desirable: (*a*) changes in reserves other than those for incurred-but-not-paid claims, (*b*) any losses carried forward from prior years, (*c*) pooling charges, (*d*) conversion charges on death benefit coverage, (*e*) charges for waiver of premium claims, (*f*) retention charges for commissions, risk, and other expenses, and (*g*) balances in the various reserve accounts as of the end of the policy year. Any interest credited on the various categories of reserves and refunds should be clearly depicted.

3. *Pooling levels should be provided in the specifications.* If insurers use different pooling levels, the bids will not be strictly comparable. A breakdown of claims experiences between employee and dependent claims is also desirable. While this report is not always furnished as a part of the insurer's annual financial statement, most carriers will make it available when requested by the group.

4. *Average number of persons insured during each period.* Premium statements for most insurers show the number of persons insured for the premium payment period. If the average number of persons insured cannot be obtained in this way, the information can be documented from employment records.

The organization is likely to have some unique characteristics that should be explained to the bidding insurers. For example, large claims that heavily influenced the claims experience for a particular year should be documented. A listing of each large claim (over $10,000 or $25,000) with a brief description of the nature of the claim should be provided in the loss data section of the bid specifications. A special rate stabilization reserve will allow an existing insurer to offer a lower premium for the next premium paying period than is true for new insurers. The balance in this reserve should be obtained and furnished to all bidders. Currently disabled employees and other facts that might influence the rates quoted by an insurer should be furnished to all insurers.

Description of Desired Coverages

As noted earlier, specifications for desired coverages should be drawn up only after a very careful design of a plan that will meet the objectives of the group. The design should reflect a compromise among employer needs, employee desires, and the need for cost controls.

Detailed descriptions of all desired coverages should be provided to each insurer from whom bids are requested. If any "special" benefits are desired, they should be requested as "alternatives" so that they will not discourage insurers from bidding.

Sample specifications for group insurance coverages appear in Appendix A to this chapter.

Census Data

To prepare their bids, insurers need underwriting data about the people to be insured. This information typically is called an employee census report and includes distributions of employees by age, sex, geographical location, salary bracket, and dependent status. A listing by occupational class also may be helpful if many widely diverse occupations are represented and disability coverages are provided.

Census data ideally should be supplied in a grid format. While a printout of personnel data is acceptable to most insurers, its use does not encourage bidding because of the extra time the insurer will have to spend in organizing the personnel data.

Questionnaire and Bid Forms

Bids will be easier to compare if the responding insurers are required to use the same format. The bid form should be designed to provide both an itemization of rates by type of coverage (life, employee health, dependent health, dental coverage, and any other benefits) and an exhibit detailing all the fixed and variable costs of the proposed retentions. The bid form also is an excellent tool to solicit insurer responses to questions about claims payment, services facilities locations, interest rates on reserves, and similar concerns. These questions can be valuable if later disagreements arise between the insurer and group since they provide a written record of the promises of the insurer.

A sample bid form appears in Appendix B to this chapter. Note that the questions in this appendix are only illustrative. Questions to be included in actual specifications vary with each situation.

PRESCREEN BIDDERS

To preclude the need to analyze proposals from insurers or other service organizations not qualified to serve the specific needs of an employer, a prescreening procedure often is advisable. This can be accomplished through the use of a prebid questionnaire and/or in a prebid conference.

Prebid Questionnaire

Appendix C to this chapter contains two sample questionnaires that could be used to evaluate the qualifications of either an agent/broker/consultant or an insurer. The use of a prescreening device of this kind allows an employer to gain the advantages of both an open and a closed bidding process. A notice to bid insurance can be provided to all interested purveyors of group insurance products. A government entity might even go one step further and issue a press release giving notice of a desire to rebid an insurance program. Any letter or public notice would indicate that all respondents would be provided not with bid specifications but with a prebid application or questionnaire. Only those purveyors who "pass" this initial evaluation would be provided with the detailed bid specifications and invited either to proceed directly with bid preparation or to first attend a prebid conference.

Prebid Conference

The prebid conference is designed to accomplish three important goals: (1) clarify any uncertainties about the specifications and the bidding forms, (2) motivate the selected insurance companies to submit bids, and (3) encourage creativity in bids.

Too frequently employers forget that in the bidding process they are marketing risks. Unless the insurance company representatives are convinced the potential new client will be profitable, they may decide not to bid. Thus, one goal of the prebid conference is to stimulate the enthusiasm of the agent/broker/consultant and insurer for the employer. The conference must be conducted in a very positive manner. As one expert says, "Present the package, 'warts' and all, in as appealing a manner as possible, but consistent with the facts."

It is important to encourage all bidders to be imaginative and creative because an adviser or insurer can conceivably make suggestions that would significantly improve the quality of the group plan. Many group insurance purveyors have decades of experience that can be used to the employer's advantage. All "creative" alternative bids should be submitted in addition to the bid requested in the detailed specifications.

Finally, it is essential to assure all bidders of the confidentiality of their bids and to ask that they maintain confidentiality of all data provided in the bid specifications.

APPENDIX A: Sample Group Insurance Specifications—Life and Health Insurance Benefits

THE PRESENT PLAN OF GROUP LIFE AND HEALTH INSURANCE

The employer has had its group life and health insurance plan underwritten by ABC Insurance Company under Group Policy 1234-A since January 1, 1975. Employees are provided $10,000 of life insurance and $10,000 of accidental death and dismemberment insurance. The health insurance consists of a comprehensive major medical plan. The principal provisions of the plan are set forth in detail in a group insurance certificate related to Group Policy 1234-A, issued by ABC Insurance Company.

The principal features of the plan are summarized in Table 43A–1.

TABLE 43A–1
Brief Summary of Existing Group Life and Health Plan

Life insurance	$10,000
Accidental death and dismemberment	$10,000
Comprehensive major medical	
Maximum benefit	Unlimited*
Deductible	$200 per person; $600 per family
Copay provisions	80 percent–20 percent of first $4,000; 100 percent thereafter
Hospital expenses	Paid according to normal copay provisions; based on average semiprivate room charge
Surgical expenses	Paid according to normal copay provisions; based on usual and customary fees

TABLE 43A–1 (*continued*)

Supplementary accident benefit	100 percent of first $100 of covered expenses; balance paid according to normal copay provisions
Maternity	Covered as any other illness.
Premium arrangements	Premiums for insurance for employees are fully paid by the employer. Premiums for insurance for dependents are deducted from the paychecks of the employees. Premium classifications for dependents include (1) children only, (2) spouse only, and (3) spouse and children.

* If your company does not write maximum benefits without limit, a $1 million maximum, or higher, will be considered.

POOLING LEVEL

Please pool all life and health claims at the level of $10,000 per claim per year.

OPTIONAL GROUP LIFE INSURANCE AND ACCIDENTAL DEATH AND DISMEMBERMENT INSURANCE

The employer will also consider an arrangement under which employees may obtain an additional $10,000 of group life insurance and $10,000 of group accidental death and dismemberment insurance. Premiums will be borne entirely by employees who choose this additional insurance.

APPENDIX B: Questionnaire and Bid Forms

Please complete this questionnaire and return it with your proposal. If you answer the questions on a separate sheet, please include the questions together with your answers.

Company ______________________________

Address

____

____

Company service
representative ______________________________

Address ______________________________

____

Telephone ______________________________

Nearest claims paying office that will supervise the payment of claims

____

Manager ______________________________

Address ______________________________

____

Telephone ______________________________

Questions Related to Life Insurance, Accidental Death and Dismemberment Insurance, and Health Insurance

1. Please explain the services the employer may expect from the insurance agent who will receive a commission on this business (if none, so state).

2. To what licensed agent do you propose to pay a commission on this business?

   Name:

   Address:

   Telephone:

3. All items quoted shall be in compliance with these specifications. If you are taking exception, indicate those exceptions on company letterhead and attach to this proposal.

Questions Related to Group Health Insurance

4. For what period of time will the premium rates you quote be guaranteed?
5. Please briefly describe the basis on which your company determines health insurance reserves.
6. In the event of termination of the contract with the employer, either on or off the anniversary date, are all unused reserves returned to the policyholder? If so, when are they returned? If not, explain how these reserves are treated.
7. If incurred claims plus your retention and any other charges result in a deficit at the end of a policy year, how would this deficit be treated in the following year?
8. What rate of interest will be credited on reserves that are held for incurred-but-unpaid claims?
9. What would be the approximate dollar change in your retention:
   a. If the ratio of incurred claims to premiums increased by 10 percent?
   b. If the ratio of incurred claims to premiums decreased by 10 percent?
10. Do the figures for paid claims or incurred claims in your retention exhibit include any allowance for administrative expense, actuarial expense, overhead expense, or other expense? If so, please explain.
11. Will your contract provide unlimited indemnity under the major medical coverage? If not, please state your maximum limit.
12. Will your company provide financial experience data in the same format as that indicated in the retention exhibits? If not, please attach a form illustrating the type of report of financial results you propose to make each year.

13. What information will you provide to the employer related to health losses paid under the contract?
14. Please explain how a change from the present insurer will be made without depriving any employees of benefits.
15. Please describe, as you think appropriate, your method of handling claims.
16. If your claims-handling procedure does not require the employer to participate in verification of claims and in additional processing of claims, please explain how these matters are handled.
17. Please describe the administrative and accounting procedures the employer must adopt to administer the plan if your company is selected as the carrier.
18. With respect to the anniversary date, when does renewal underwriting take place? When do rate changes (if any) become effective? How much advance notice is given?

Questions Related to Group Life Insurance and Group Accidental Death and Dismemberment Insurance

19. Please describe briefly the basis on which your company determines group life insurance reserves.
20. Please describe briefly the basis on which your company determines group accidental death and dismemberment insurance reserves.
21. In the event of termination of the contract, either on or off the anniversary date, are all unused reserves returned to the policyholder? If so, when are they returned? If not, explain how these reserves are treated.
22. If incurred claims plus your retention and any other charges result in a deficit at the end of a policy year, how would this deficit be treated in the following year?
23. What rate of interest will be credited on any group life insurance reserves and group accidental death and dismemberment insurance reserves that are held by the carrier?
24. Do the figures for paid claims or incurred claims in your retention exhibit include any allowance for administrative expense, actuarial expense, overhead expense, or other expense? If so, please explain.

25. Will your company provide financial experience data in the same format as that indicated in the retention exhibits? If not, please attach a form illustrating the type of report of financial results you propose to make each year.
26. What information will you provide to the employer related to life insurance losses and to accidental death and dismemberment insurance losses paid under the contract?
27. Please explain how a change from the present carrier will be made without depriving any employees of benefits.
28. Please answer the following questions with regard to the optional life insurance and accidental death and dismemberment insurance.
    a. What would be the monthly premium rates in the following age and sex classifications for the optional group life insurance and accidental death and dismemberment insurance? (If you prefer not to quote rates at this time, please indicate how the rates would be determined.)

Age	*Male*	*Female*
30 and under	______	______
31–35	______	______
36–40	______	______
41–45	______	______
46–50	______	______
51–55	______	______
56–60	______	______
61–65	______	______
66–70	______	______

    b. What percentage participation do you require to put the optional insurance into effect?
    c. What other conditions, if any, would you require before placing the optional insurance into effect?
29. With respect to the anniversary date, when does renewal underwriting take place? When do rate changes (if any) become effective? How much advance notice is given?

INSTRUCTIONS FOR COMPLETING RETENTION EXHIBITS*

Retention exhibits are to be completed on the following basis:

1. The number and the amount of paid claims for each of the three years following a change in the contract or the carrier are to be shown on the retention exhibits.
2. Your figures for paid claims and for incurred claims on the retention exhibits should not include any allowance for administrative costs, actuarial costs, or any costs other than the claims. These costs should be included in Item 9 (Expense charges).
3. The entire amount your company plans to pay licensed agents, other than your company's regular employees, should be shown in Item 9.

---

* For illustrative purposes only one exhibit has been included.

Summary of Monthly Premiums—Present Plan (Life and AD&D at $10,000)

Name of Proposing Carrier: ______________________

	Number of Employees (as of 6/1/88)	*Volume*	*Quoted (per person) Monthly Premium*	*Monthly Premium*
Life insurance	962			
AD&D	959			
Employee health insurance	954			
Spouse only health insurance	76			
Child(ren) health insurance	111			
Spouse and child(ren) health insurance	101			
Employee Medicare	16			
Dependent Medicare	9			
			Total Monthly Premium	
			Total Annual Premium	

APPENDIX C: Sample Prebid Questionnaires

Insurance Agent/Brokerage House/Consultant Qualifying Questionnaire

Date ________

A. Name of Firm ____________________
Address ____________________
____________ Zip ____________ Phone ____________
Date Established ____________

Name and residence address of principals, their experience, and professional qualifications. Attach a detailed resume that should as a minimum include the following information:

Number of employee benefit accounts and premium levels
Approximate percentage of accounts by type of insurance

Number of licensed agents ________

Premium volume: ____ Under $500,000
____ $501,000–$1,000,000
____ $1,001,000–$1,500,000
____ $1,501,000–$2,500,000
____ Over $2,500,000

Companies licensed by agent and brokerage houses utilized:

	As Agent	*As Broker*
Group Life		
1. ________	________	________
2. ________	________	________
3. ________	________	________
Group Health		
1. ________	________	________
2. ________	________	________
3. ________	________	________
Group Disability		
1. ________	________	________
2. ________	________	________
3. ________	________	________

Other

1. ____________________ ____________ ____________

2. ____________________ ____________ ____________

3. ____________________ ____________ ____________

Special services available (e.g., loss analysis, claims service, etc.)

In House	*Company or Outside*
____________________	____________________
____________________	____________________
____________________	____________________
____________________	____________________

If your firm is selected to handle part or all of the group insurance program, who would be responsible for account?

Principal ____________________________________

Alternate ____________________________________

Clients—Name and approximate annual premium of two (2) largest accounts most similar in each category:

____

____

B. Would you be willing to handle part or all of our program on a fee basis, rather than for a commission? On this basis, the services to be performed would be outlined for the particular category of insurance such as:

____

____

____

Company writing errors and omission coverage for you:

____

Limits: ____________________ Deductible: ____________________

Retention Exhibit—Based on Present Health Insurance Benefits

	First Year	Second Year	Third Year
1. Paid premiums			
2. Pooled premiums			
3. Paid claims	$600,000†	$750,000	$750,000
4. Number of paid claims	1,600†	2,100	2,100
5. Pooled claims			
6. Claim reserve, beginning			
7. Claim reserve, ending			
8. Incurred claims: (3) − (5) − (6) + (7)			
9. Expense charges			
a. Agents' commissions			
b. State premium taxes			
c. Other charges			
d. Credit for interest on reserves*			
Total: (*a*) + (*b*) + (*c*) − (*d*)			
10. Total of Item 9 (Expense charges) as percentage of Item 1 (Paid premiums)			
11. Credit (or debit) carried over from previous year			
12. Credit (or debit) carried over to following year: (1) − (2) − (8) − (9) ± (11)			

* Include interest on credit carried over from previous year (Item 11).

† ABC Insurance Company, the present carrier, will be asked to assume that 2,100 claims will be paid amounting to $750,000 in the first year, since it will be responsible for claims incurred before a change in the contract is made.

Insurance Company Qualifying Questionnaire

PLEASE NOTE: It is the intention of XYZ Company to rebid this group insurance program no sooner than five (5) years. In the past, we have remained with an insurance company for an average of eight (8) years. Our goal is to establish and maintain a long-term professional relationship.

Date ________

A. Name of Insurance Company ______________________________

Address ______________________________

__________ Zip __________ Phone __________

B. Please provide copies of the following:
   1. Best's financial rating report for last three years.
   2. Offices that will handle the group claims.
   3. Name of the individual in your company who will be responsible for the account in the event your firm is selected to handle the group insurance program.

C. Briefly describe the annual services you can provide in the following areas:
   1. Claims reporting and analysis.
   2. Cost control.
   3. Evaluation of financing alternatives (e.g., ASO).
   4. Evaluation of plan specifications.

D. With regard to your current operations, briefly summarize your premium volume and number of accounts in group life, health, and disability insurance.

   What percentage of this business is in the same state as XYZ Company?

   (Optional) Provide a list of at least two (2) of your current clients who are in the same size class as XYZ Company.

E. Would you be willing to allow a qualified representative of XYZ Company to negotiate directly with the internal underwriter assigned to this case?

F. Provide any other information relative to the firm that might be pertinent to selection:

____

____

____

____

____

____

____

____

G. (Optional) References qualified to judge your ability to provide service and insurance expertise:

____

____

____

____

____

____

CHAPTER 44

AN ANALYTICAL FRAMEWORK FOR THE REVIEW OF INSURANCE BIDS

David R. Klock
Phyllis A. Klock
Joseph Casey

In the previous chapter, the process of preparing bid specifications was reviewed. In this chapter, the analysis of group insurance bids and the selection of an appropriate insurance carrier and/or service organization is analyzed. This critical process consists of the following steps:

1. Confirm that all bidders meet minimum requirements and eliminate any nonqualifiers.
2. Evaluate the financial implications of each bid (quantitative factors).
3. Review the policy specifications, claims-handling procedures, and loss control services provided by each bidding organization (qualitative factors).
4. Select the best purveyor(s) and negotiate the final details of the group insurance plan.
5. Present your findings and recommendations to the appropriate decision-making body (generally superior officers, executive committee, or board of directors).

MINIMUM REQUIREMENTS

Employers seeking group insurance coverage often require that all bidders meet important minimum requirements, with no exceptions made for nonqualifiers. For example, the employer may require that bidding insurance companies have at least an "A" rating from Best's. Other minimum requirements may be that a qualified local agent or salaried representative is available on a regular basis at all employer locations to service the group and/or that the insurer maintain a full-time claims staff within a specified distance from the employer. Specified minimum requirements typically depend on the size and nature of the employer. For example, a very large corporate employer with a full-time risk management and/or employee benefits professional staff may not perceive the need for a local servicing agent, whereas a local or regional government employer may require all bidders to be domestic insurers and all servicing agents to maintain offices in the same community as the government seat.

FINANCIAL IMPLICATIONS

Assuming that bidders comply with the plan specifications, financial or cash flow implications typically will be the critical variable in selecting among proposed carriers. This analysis often is the subject of considerable confusion because employers do not understand the mathematics and resulting cash flow implications of group insurance proposals and because not all insurers use consistent terminology and methodology in presenting their proposed financial bids.

The confusion may easily result in the selection of an inappropriate bid by an employer who lacks a professional staff capable of fully understanding the financial implications of each bid. Accordingly, an employer without the appropriate internal staff is generally well advised to retain an experienced broker/consultant to review the financial implications of the bids.

Financial analysis of proposed group insurance programs is often considerably more complex than one might initially suspect. If, for example, the proposal under review contemplates an experienced or retrospective rated program, an analyst would be misled by a simple comparison of the standard premium paid at the beginning of the plan year (or monthly). Numerous other critical variables affect the ultimate cash flow cost of such a plan.

The true cost of a group plan can be depicted as follows:

$$\text{Cost} = \text{Claims} + \text{Retention} - \text{Interest return}$$

Claims are further broken into paid claims and reserves for future payments. A thorough analysis of the retention exhibit should allow the risk manager/employee benefits manager or the broker/consultant to determine which bidders have presented the best financial proposal for the employer.

ANALYSIS OF RETENTION

Proposed retention factors are the major financial criteria that should be used to distinguish among bids. The term *retention* refers to that portion of the insurance premium kept by the insurer to cover expenses, pooling charges, risk charges, and/or profit. The part of the retention factor designed to realize a profit for the insurer is typically not an identifiable factor in the retention exhibit but is built into many of the other factors, especially the risk charge. Mutual insurance companies will not have a profit factor as such but will include a contribution to surplus in their risk charge.

Careful analysis of the retention exhibit requires a comparison of the dollars that alternative insurance companies seek to "retain" for their own use through their various charges and those funds that they will credit to the employer in the form of reserves, refunds, and/or investment returns on any premiums paid in advance.

In reviewing alternative retention exhibits, the risk manager/employee benefits manager or the broker/consultant should determine if any inconsistencies are present in the claims expense factors. If all insurers used the assumed claims provided in the bid specifications, the claims expense factor in the various proposals should be comparable. If, on the other hand, insurers were left on their own to estimate incurred claims and claims adjustment costs, significant variations could be expected. Comparable retention illustrations demand that claims assumptions be as close as possible to the specified level, but experience has proven that some bidders use different claims assumptions than those provided in the bid specifications. If such is the case, the "nonconforming" bids must first be adjusted to a claims level consistent with all other bids. If this adjustment is not feasible, the employer may wish to return the bid to the insurer with a request to make the necessary adjustments or to reject the bid from further consideration.

The risk manager/employee benefits manager or the broker/consultant should determine that all bidders have complied with specifications regarding premium quotations. Some insurers will quote abnormally high premiums to produce unusually high dividends or refunds that can then be credited with interest. Such a practice can result in an understatement of the insurer's retention because interest credited to a dividend or refund remains with the insurer and is used to reduce retentions. If this potential distortion is suspected, the bidding insurer should be requested to separately specify the interest credited to dividends.

Bids must be checked to assure that insurers have consistently included expenses associated with claims processing in their retentions. Accounting practices relative to the treatment of claims payment expenses vary among insurers. Some insurers add these expenses to paid or incurred claims, while others combine claims payment expenses with the administrative expenses in the retention. The bid of an insurer that has assumed claims payment expenses to be part of the specified incurred claims will understate their retention. If such a problem is detected, the employer should request the insurer to provide the specific claims payment expense figures in order to adjust the retention illustration.

The manner in which bidding insurers have treated pooling charges should likewise be checked for consistency. Pooling charges are essentially a retention item, because none of the pooling charges will be returned to the employer in the form of either dividends or retrospective rate credits. If the request for bids did not specify that pooling charges be itemized, some bidding insurance companies might have included these charges as a part of paid or incurred claims. The retentions of such a carrier would thus be significantly understated.

Premium taxes are another item that should be illustrated on a common basis. Unless specific instructions were included in the request for bids, some insurers might have depicted premium taxes on the basis of gross premiums, while other underwriters could have illustrated them as premiums minus anticipated dividends or other rate credits. These potential sources of retention exhibit distortion require adjustments on a case-by-case basis.

In summary, consistent retention illustrations can form the basis for determining the premium dollars that will be returned to the organization and the amount that will remain with the insurance company. This analysis must review not simply the absolute dollar amounts but the timing of the cash flows as well. Thus, it is very important that each bidder provide very specific information on the elements of fixed and variable costs in their bid.

BID–COST MATRIX

Table 44–1 provides an illustration of a quantitative analysis of group insurance bids. This type of analysis is commonly referred to as a bid-cost matrix. Section I of the matrix summarizes the basic assumptions the companies were requested to use in preparing their bids. Assumed claims levels have been provided in the bid specifications in order to increase the likelihood that the cost figures provided by the various insurance companies will be determined on a consistent basis.

Section II outlines the monthly rates quoted by each of five bidders. Premium bids for each line of coverage are separated into pooled and nonpooled premiums. This information is needed to provide details for the stop-loss provision. Section III provides both the retention factors quoted by each insurance company and the basis or method used by these bidders in calculating this factor.

Section IV gives the variable cost and the fixed cost for each bid based on the assumed claims and premium data appearing in Sections II and III. Most importantly, this section provides the critical "claims/cost ratio." Typically, the higher this ratio, the better the bid. On this basis, bids 1 and 5 appear to be the most attractive.

Section V responds to a question often asked by the ultimate decision body (CEO, board of directors, etc.): "What if assumed claims varied from the levels assumed in Section I?" Based on claims ranging from 70 percent to 130 percent of those used in Section I, total costs are calculated for each bid. In addition to summarizing the range of possible costs, Section V also provides the risk manager/employee benefits manager with the maximum costs for each bid and the level of claims where the maximum cost is obtained. If feasible, the risk manager/employee benefits manager is well advised to include this data in the cost matrix provided to executive management.

QUALITATIVE FACTORS

In the previous section, the detailed financial or cash flow aspects of the premium bids provided by each insurance company were reviewed. While this analysis is extremely important, several reasons exist why a satisfactory analysis of bids must include far more than a consideration of financial aspects. Premiums and retention factors are guaranteed for only a short period of time (usually 12 to 18 months at best). Furthermore, as discussed in Chapter 43, a change of companies after only one or two years is generally undesirable, although not always unconscionable. The

TABLE 44–1

ABC & Associates Group Insurance Bid Comparison Annual Cost

SECTION I

Life insurance in force	$37,500,000	Employee health claims	$390,000
AD&D insurance in force	37,500,000	Dependent health claims	350,000
Monthly covered payroll	2,083,333	Employee life claims	10,000
Covered employees*	800		
Covered dependent units*	650	Total claims	$750,000

SECTION II

Quote No.	*1*	*2*	*3*	*4*	*5*
Company	*Longwood Life*	*Orlando Life*	*Sanford Life*	*Deland Life*	*Oviedo Life*
Monthly rates (as quoted by purveyors)					
Pooled Premium					
Life rate†	$ .275	$ .56	$ .322	$ .28	$ .1995
AD&D rate†	.055	.062	.06	.0598	.07
LTD‡	.325	.581	.434	.55	.495
Employee health§	1.40	1.00	1.10	1.10	1.92
Dependent health§	2.05	2.00	1.95	1.65	1.92
Nonpooled premium (aggregate stop loss)					
Life rate	$ .28	$ 0‖	$ .44	$ .40	$ .39
Employee health	36.25	40.00	50.00	42.27	35.00
Dependent health	52.37	51.50	72.25	52.65	39.50

SECTION III

Retention based on					
Claims			.055	.07	
Employees		6.00			5.25
Aggregate	.065				

SECTION IV					
Cost					
Pooled Premium					
Life	$123,750	$252,000	$144,900	$126,000	$89,775
AD&D	24,750	27,900	27,000	26,910	31,500
LTD	81,250	145,250	108,500	137,500	123,750
Employee health	13,440	9,600	10,560	10,560	18,432
Dependent health	15,990	15,600	15,210	12,870	14,976
Total fixed cost	$259,180	$450,350	$306,170	$313,840	$278,433
Claims cost	$750,000	$740,000‖	$750,000	$750,000	$750,000
Retention	57,362	57,600	41,250	52,500	50,400
Total variable cost	$807,362	$797,600	$791,250	$802,500	$800,400
Total cost	$1,066,542	$1,236,050	$1,097,420	$1,116,340	$1,078,833
Claims/cost ratio	0.70	0.59	0.68	0.67	0.70
SECTION V					
Cost at other claims levels:					
70 percent	$841,542	$1,025,950	$872,420	$891,340	$853,833
80 percent	916,542	1,099,950	947,420	966,340	928,833
90 percent	991,542	1,173,950	1,022,420	1,041,340	1,003,833
110 percent	1,141,542	1,236,050	1,172,420	1,191,340	1,098,033
120 percent	1,141,666	1,236,050	1,247,420	1,266,340	1,098,033
130 percent	1,141,666	1,236,050	1,322,420	1,310,302	1,098,033
Maximum Cost	$1,141,666	$1,236,050	$1,547,720	$1,310,302	$1,098,033

* Employee and dependent units eligible for Medicare supplements are excluded from consideration.

† Life and AD&D rates are quoted per $1,000 face amount.

‡ LTD rates are quoted per $100 of monthly benefit.

§ Employee and dependent health rates are quoted per unit.

‖ Included in pooled premium.

employer and its broker/consultant must carefully consider the most important qualitative factors associated with the alternative bids and choose an insurer that has a verified reputation for the desired quality of service. The selection of an insurer with a questionable service capability or contract specifications typically is a mistake. Minor differences in retention charges do not justify acceptance if day-to-day difficulties concerning administration and claims service are to be expected.

The first step in analyzing the qualitative aspects of the bids is to verify that all proposals have complied with the minimum coverage provisions outlined in the bid specifications. A valid bid comparison is possible only if all proposals are consistent for both the type of program proposed (e.g., a comprehensive major medical plan or a basic hospital-surgical plan with a supplementary major medical) and such basic coverage elements as limits on the maximum lifetime benefits, deductible levels, copay provisions, maximum employee out-of-pocket amounts, and scheduled versus "reasonable and customary" coverage of medical expenses.

When applicable, the question of the length of any rate guarantees must be addressed. Differences among the bids often arise on the issue of both initial and renewal guarantees of premiums and retention factors.

The risk manager/employee benefits manager or the broker/consultant should carefully review any descriptive literature provided with the bids. Listing of definitions, covered expenses, exclusions, and limitations may reveal significant benefit differences. Variations sometimes exist, for example, in the definitions of the terms *hospital* and *physician*. Some plans may include coverage for second surgical opinions, home health care, ambulatory surgical facilities, nursing home care, hospitalization in a "progressive care unit," well-baby care, treatment of mental illness, and/or treatment of alcoholism and drug-related illnesses. Other plans may provide exceptional rehabilitation benefits. A review of the conversion provisions and of the provisions of any Medicare supplement included in the programs is also in order. For example, the analyst should know if a "carve-out" or a "coordination" approach is being utilized in the Medicare supplement.

In reviewing the qualitative areas of plan coverage, the risk manager/employee benefits manager should attempt to minimize the aggregate inconvenience for employees and should be conscious that the demographics and financial needs of the employee group will be important to the acceptance of any change in the group insurance plan. For example, if many of the employees reside in rural areas and receive their primary care from medical professionals other than M.D.s (e.g., D.O.s, chiropractors, and/or nurse practitioners), any restrictions on benefits for services provided by these medical professionals would be likely to create significant employee discontent. The best analytical decisions concerning the cost of alternative bids can be in error if the decision process fails to consider the cost of extensive employee dissatisfaction with a proposed change.

The risk manager/employee benefits manager or the broker/consultant should attempt to predict whether the various insurance companies will render a satisfactory level of claims and administrative service. Some questions that might be asked here include:

1. What is the average projected turnaround time for claims payments?
2. Are local claims facilities available? If not, will the insurer provide a toll-free telephone number or accept collect calls on claims inquiries?
3. What will be the extent of employer involvement in the verification or other processing of claims? Will this require the employer to hire or train additional staff?
4. What administrative and/or accounting procedures must the employer adopt to facilitate such matters as premium collections, enrollments, and terminations?
5. How satisfied with programs underwritten by the carrier in question are other employers with similar demographic characteristics?

Finally, the risk manager/employee benefits manager or the broker/consultant will want to evaluate the potential flexibility with which the alternative insurers could respond to major changes in the employer organization and/or to employer desires to consider alternative financial arrangements at some point in the future. This analysis is particularly relevant if, for example, the employer's five-year goals include acquisitions, mergers, or a major plant relocation. Alternatively, the employer might have determined that an ASO contract or a self-insurance arrangement did not suit its current needs but may wish to consider these alternatives in two to three years. The employer may place a high value on an ability to effectively respond to changes such as these without undergoing the potential disruption of a change in insurance carrier.

NEGOTIATING WITH CARRIER

Based on the analysis of the financial and qualitative implications of alternative bids, the company manager charged with responsibility for group insurance will select that carrier most compatible with the needs of employer and employees alike. In many situations, this company manager draws solely on his or her own skills and experience in making the selection, and guidance from outside the company is not sought. In other situations, the decision is aided by technical advice from a qualified broker/consultant. Regardless of the manner in which this preliminary selection is reached, two final steps usually are required: (1) detailed negotiation with the selected underwriter and (2) presentation of the recommendations to the appropriate decision-making body, be it the CEO, an executive committee, or the board of directors (as is common in many smaller- or medium-sized companies). The sequence of these steps may vary. Some risk managers/employee benefits managers prefer to obtain a consensus on the selection of a particular insurance company prior to initiating final negotiations with the underwriter; others attempt to wrest all available concessions from the carrier before presenting their findings for a final decision.

This section deals with the final negotiation process, and the final discussion considers the critical ingredients of an effective presentation to the ultimate decision makers. The importance of the final negotiation process rests on two assumptions. First, the cost and provisions of a group insurance program are in fact negotiable. Armed with knowledge of the very complex technical aspects of a group program, a competent broker/consultant or risk manager/employee benefits manager can win concessions from the insurance company that will benefit the corporation and its employees. Second, specific areas in the bid of the selected insurer may not be as competitive as those found in other bids. If these discrepancies are pointed out to the underwriter, he or she may be willing to reevaluate and improve this particular portion of the bid. This process takes on added importance if the insurance company with the "lowest" bid is not that selected by the risk manager/employee benefits manager and the broker/consultant. The "lowest" bidder may not be chosen for a variety of reasons relating to service considerations or to long-term costs not immediately evident in the bids. If this selection is going to "pass muster" with the CEO, the executive committee, or the board, all possible cost and coverage concessions must be obtained from this carrier.

The first step in the negotiating process is to select the proper "players." The decision as to whether the risk manager/employee benefits manager or the broker/consultant will handle direct negotiations with the underwriter is often a difficult one. Allowing the broker/consultant to take the lead in this area often proves more efficient. The broker/consultant is usually more familiar with the behavioral aspects of negotiations with specific underwriters; he or she may also have more leverage with the carrier. Should a decision be reached that the broker/consultant will primarily handle the negotiations, the risk manager/employee benefits manager should clearly understand the areas to be negotiated and should be prepared to use his or her influence with the insurer when and if called on by the broker/consultant.

Whomever is chosen, the negotiator must be familiar with the terminology used by the particular insurance company. Most home office underwriters converse in terms that may be unique to their company. In fact, many of the common group insurance terms (like *retro*) have different meanings depending on the insurer in question. An ability to speak the appropriate lingo is crucial if one is seeking financial concessions from an insurer. This simple but important step can reduce significant confusion.

The negotiator(s) for the employer must develop a strategy for quickly directing the attention of home office underwriters to the items where profit and/or excess interest may be hidden and thus where concessions may be obtained. This strategy often involves a list of very probing questions that go beyond the routine areas such as reducing premium margins, releasing incurred but not reported reserves, or negotiating commission levels.

Peter B. O'Brien, president of Johnson & Higgins of Colorado, has provided an excellent list of 10 very specific questions to use as the basis for final negotiations with a group insurance underwriter.[1]

1. Why should a C&R (conservation and review) charge be levied against our account when we have a 10-year service plaque hanging on the wall?
2. Why is your computer programmed to ''load'' our triangle chart when the results are supposed to represent our actual claims runout?
3. Why can't our ''risk charge'' be scaled based on our loss ratio rather than on a flat percentage of our premium?
4. Why, after years of consistency in policy language for disability payments, is there a wide inconsistency in percentage of face value claim charges?
5. Why can't we be presented with our state premium tax bill and eliminate the tax escrow account?
6. Why have you been lenient with customers whose premiums are delinquent by a few months while we are charged prevailing interest rates when late by only one month?
7. Why can't our pooling ''point'' and ''factor'' be adjusted to re-

[1] Peter B. O'Brien, ''Negotiating Lower Costs for Group Insurance Plans,'' *Risk Management,* December 1978, pp. 34–38.

flect our class of business and experience, rather than using overall company tables and rates that haven't been updated in years?
8. We hear lots of talk about severely escalating health care trend factors, but where is the offsetting, advance credit, life deflation factor?
9. Why does a financial accounting have to occur every 12 months? Can't we have custom rates and retention factors to coincide with our collective bargaining periods?
10. Can't we define paid claims as money that has actually been withdrawn from your account rather than amounts on claims forms?

The foregoing questions are illustrative only. Some of these questions obviously may not be relevant in certain cases, while other questions of similar detail and nature may be more appropriate for other groups. The point is that the use of very specific questions significantly enhances the ability of negotiators for the employer to obtain all valid concessions. The underwriter should be allowed sufficient time (usually several weeks) to evaluate the case and to either agree to the requests or to propose alternative adjustments. The impact of the underwriter's decisions must, of course, be evaluated prior to a presentation to the appropriate decision makers.

PRESENTATION TO DECISION MAKERS

The risk manager/employee benefits manager typically will be required to make a presentation on the group insurance reevaluation process to a top-management decision maker or committee. This presentation has taken on increased importance in recent years as high-level executives have become more attentive to cost savings that can be realized in the employee benefits area. Rapid escalation of the costs of employee benefits (and especially of group insurance) means group insurance decisions no longer constitute a relatively minor decision. This phenomenon is compounded by increased volatility in the cost of money. Executives have become very conscious of the need to optimize the management of scarce and very costly cash flows. CEOs and other high-level executives have decided to periodically review and influence group insurance decisions in the hopes of more effectively managing required cash flows.

The following outline suggests the critical item that should be communicated during the presentation to top management:

1. State the objectives that dictated and influenced the decision to remarket the group insurance program. What financial and/or employee benefit goals were to be achieved by the rebidding process?
2. Identify any weaknesses in the current group insurance contract or carrier and specify the steps in the bidding process that are aimed at avoiding these same weaknesses in any new program or insurance company.
3. Identify any restrictions imposed by top management on the use of certain alternative financial arrangements with an insurance company (e.g., self-insurance was or was not to be considered) and on the use of specific carriers, agents, or broker/consultants.
4. Identify the markets (insurance companies or self-funding service organizations) that have been approached, the responses received, and the bids that were considered qualified and responsive to the needs of the employer. The decision makers will want to know that a thorough market test was conducted and that all qualified and competitive insurers had an opportunity to provide bids. If the decision makers perceive that the market test was less than complete, they may require a reexamination of other alternative purveyors.
5. Present the bid matrix (see Table 44–1), and outline the strengths and weaknesses of the individual bids.
6. Present the specific recommendation and the supporting logic.
7. Try to anticipate potential questions and deal with them in the presentation. For example, it was noted earlier that the decision makers are likely to ask why the bid specifications stipulated a specific level of claims be assumed in the preparation of the bids and how alternative loss assumptions would have affected the bid matrix.

CHAPTER 45

IMPLEMENTING AND REVIEWING EMPLOYEE BENEFIT PLANS

Joseph D. Young

THE IMPLEMENTING PROCESS

The process of implementing new benefits and amendments to existing employee benefit plans contains five essential steps, which are: (1) approval of top management (including board of directors); (2) development of plan specifications for bidding (where appropriate) and analysis of proposals; (3) legal document preparation, including government filing requirements; (4) preparation and distribution of announcement and enrollment materials; (5) development of administration procedures and manuals. The order in which these steps are taken may vary depending upon each organization's makeup and style. No matter what the order, each of these steps needs to be addressed during the implementation process.

Approval of Top Management

Once the organization's employee benefit reviewer(s) have adopted recommendations for new plans and amendments, final approval by top management, (unless the committee reviewer has been given the authority to move ahead) is necessary. In many companies today (since ERISA), a committee appointed by the board of directors is charged with the responsibility of ensuring that all benefit plans and proposals comply with

ERISA and subsequent benefit laws. In some cases, the committee is named Plan Administrator as defined by ERISA—in other cases such committees merely serve to oversee the benefits function on behalf of the board to assure compliance. When such committee(s) exist, new plans and amendments should, of course, be presented to them as part of the implementation process. This may not be a distinctly separate step, depending on the organization—in some cases all levels of management may be parties to the review process so that when alternatives are adopted the next step in the implementation process can be taken. This may be the point at which board resolutions are prepared for adoption. The drafting of such resolutions is, of course, a task assigned to legal counsel and may not be done until all plan documents are drafted.

Development of Plan Specifications

In a situation where the new benefits are to be put out for bid by insurance carriers or other providers of services, it is critical that very precise plan specifications be drafted. This is an area where competent, impartial consulting help is invaluable. This is also the point at which the benefit manager must be assured that the consultant has "no stake" in the choice of carriers or providers. This is sometimes difficult to assess if the consultant's firm is one which accepts commissions from carriers as a part of its compensation. In such cases, even though a consultant is objective, the question always seems to be in the back of one's mind as to "how objective?" Of course, there are many excellent consulting firms which work strictly on a fee basis. This approach, at least, eliminates the question of financial motivation in the selection process.

Contract and underwriting provisions for insured plans including group insurance and pension plans can vary subtly from carrier to carrier—so too can the reserving and rating techniques used. Thus, the specifications drafted and presented to the various bidders should be as inclusive of all items of contractual concern as possible. This approach also helps to ensure that all bidders respond to the same questions—those which you the buyer deem to be important and not only those which they the sellers wish to emphasize.

Once specifications are completed and the bidders are selected, they should all be sent the same data, mailed at the same time, and with the same deadline for reply. To assure that none of the bidders is placed at a disadvantage, it is wise to contact them beforehand to (1) determine that they are truly interested in submitting a bid; (2) ascertain exactly who in their company should be the recipient of the specifications; and (3) be sure that they know and understand your "ground rules." To avoid giving one or more bidders an unfair advantage, it should be clearly stated and adhered to that the bids received after the deadline will not be considered.

Analysis of the proposals once received also is a critical point. It can be as complex and as interesting as the preparation of the specifications. It is important to make certain you verify for yourself the promises made in proposals. For example, one company decided to change from a conventional group insurance arrangement to self-funding, and also sought to enter into an administrative services only (ASO) contract with one of the bidding carriers. More than a half-dozen carriers including two of the prepaid medical provider organizations were asked to submit proposals. Since the employer company already had decided to self-fund the medical program, the real issues were quality and cost of administrative and claims services. Each carrier was allowed to present its proposal in writing and to also meet face to face with the benefit staff, the consultant, and other internal decision makers. Subsequent to these meetings but before a final decision was made, the benefit manager and selected staff members also visited the site of each carrier's claims processing unit. These visits were key in establishing the priority of choices based on the claims service to be provided. It can be very revealing to visit the site where the work will be done, to see and talk to the people, and to see the equipment used and the atmosphere in which your company's claims work will be handled. In this case, after the visit, one of the carriers withdrew its bid because it felt the disorganized atmosphere viewed during the tour of its claims facility simply refuted the position it took in its proposal in promising quality claims service. The point is when you are buying a service, you should see first-hand how the service commitments will be met. This is especially critical because employees' perceptions about benefit plans can be affected by the quality of claims service they receive.

Because the relationship with a group insurance carrier (whether fully insured or an administrative services only arrangement) is so much a part of the very framework of personnel relationships, the design and implementation of these benefits is concerned with a myriad of human relationships. Hence, the atmosphere created by the carrier's staff of personnel who deals with the employer's plan is very important. There must be a commitment and a spirit of true service to the employer and its employees. The old line of a dogmatic and legalistic approach by carriers and others who administer employee benefits is simply not acceptable, and during this phase of implementation these concerns must be addressed by the employer. It has been proven that a benefit plan with lesser benefit levels but quality-level, employee-oriented claims service receives higher regard by employees than does one which pays higher levels of benefits with poor service, long delays, and incorrect benefit determinations.

Legal Document Preparation

When the time arrives to prepare legal documents, the early involvement of legal counsel as a member of the review committee is essential. Even if the company uses outside counsel for drafting these documents, the time spent in the review process by the inside legal counsel should make the document preparation go much smoother. Working with a clear set of benefit objectives should be most helpful to legal counsel in preparing plan instruments, trust agreements, and enrollment forms as necessary to implement new plans or provisions.

Pension Plans

If a group insurance or pension contract is involved, the insurance company prepares the plan document; even so, the employer's legal counsel should review the provisions of the instrument. Even though the insurance company has plan documents preprinted with the provisions having been predetermined, the employer's attorney(s) must review these forms and determine how appropriate they are for the plan design intended.

In a situation where the new plan or provisions do not involve an insurance carrier, the employer's attorney may have the assignment of drafting the plan documents alone. While the attorney has the drafting responsibility, the remaining professionals on the employer's team (i.e., the consultant and the actuary) should also provide input and review of the documents before they are finally adopted. This approach helps to ensure that the many administrative complexities imposed by ERISA and other regulations are addressed prior to full implementation.

Other legal documents may include (1) board and/or stockholders' resolutions, (2) trust agreements, and (3) employee enrollment forms. In the case of enrollment forms, even though they must meet legal requirements and so on, their design should be coordinated with other announcements and communications styles.

Self-Funded Health and Welfare Plans

The review process may very well result in a commitment to self-fund all or a portion of a welfare plan. While this decision can be a design and a funding issue, it also is an administration and an implementation issue.

Implementing a self-funded plan requires that the employer perform many responsibilities which might otherwise be done by a carrier. These include but are not limited to:

1. Drafting the plan, including a claims review process.
2. Drafting the trust document and related trust operational procedures.
3. Drafting employees' enrollment and informational and procedural forms, manuals, and documents.
4. Establishing a separate checking account from which claims will be paid.
5. Arranging for stop-loss protection (if appropriate).
6. Developing Summary Plan Descriptions.

Much of the new-found employer responsibility is legal in nature—thus the involvement of legal staff representatives in the review process pays dividends at the time of implementation.

Filing with Government Agencies

The regulatory environment of employee benefit plans was discussed in Chapter 3. There are, however, certain aspects of these regulatory requirements which must be addressed during the implementation phase to ensure timely compliance. The areas to be addressed are (1) obtaining an advance determination letter from the IRS for pension plan changes; (2) filing of a Summary of Material Modification in cases where an existing plan is being changed significantly; (3) in the case of certain capital accumulation plans adopted by public corporations, the Securities and Exchange Commission (SEC) has certain requirements regarding registration which should be addressed in the implementation process. The major portion of the regulatory reporting requirements dictate timing which substantially follows the implementation step. Even so, benefit planners and their legal counsel must be aware of those requirements which must be met early in the implementation phase.

Announcement and Enrollment Materials

An important step in the implementation of new benefit plans or changes is the preparation of (1) announcement pieces or letters to employees and managers; (2) administrative guidelines and manuals for supervisors and managers; (3) the enrollment materials and procedure. The actual design of these items and a plan for disseminating them are projects for which help should be obtained from communications specialists (especially in large organizations); but getting it done is an item for the implementation phase.

In most organizations, new benefit plans are announced in a letter from either the president or the top personnel executive. Regardless of who signs the letter, the organization should recognize that as the first news to employees of the new plan or improvements the letter must be drafted carefully. This is the stage where the best communications experts the organization has should be used to obtain the proper mileage out of this announcement.

It often is advisable to prepare and send confidential advance notification to managers and supervisors about what is coming. This gives them the opportunity to be "in the know" about these matters and also gives them time to prepare for the initial questions employees will ask after receiving the announcement letter.

If supervisors and managers are to be involved in the enrollment process, the confidential advance notice is more critical, and also clearly defined procedures should be provided to them in advance of the enrollment date.

Enrollment materials (i.e., descriptive literature and cards which include payroll deduction authorizations) are necessary, and good design calls for a plan that ties all of these items together to look like a "family" of literature. In addition to the need for enrollment materials to be well designed from an aesthetic point of view, there must be a view towards their use in the administration of the plan once implemented. Thus, the enrollment materials design should be done in conjunction with representatives from the staff of day-to-day administrators. This includes the payroll and accounting departments since they must also provide some administrative services once the plan is installed. It is amazing how much more effectively new plans can be implemented and later administered if all interested parties are given the opportunity to be a part of the planning and design of forms, procedures and manuals, etc., during the implementation phase. When all concerned are included early on, it becomes "our plan or program" and all have a stake in it.

Record-Keeping and Reporting

The subject of record-keeping and reporting is discussed in Chapter 42 on administration. It is important that implementation is done with an eye and concern toward record-keeping and reporting requirements. Consideration must be given to the electronic data processing requirements such as (1) the data base needed; (2) the system's input requirements; and (3) the reports to be generated. Many of these concerns and the related elements may already be a part of the current data processing system, and at this point the need may be only to ensure that necessary reports can be formatted and reviewed when needed. Facing these issues during the implementation process will make the subsequent administration and reporting processes much simpler. It also should assist in developing the information needed to perform future reviews of the benefit package.

REVIEWING EMPLOYEE BENEFIT PLANS

Establishing Objectives

An organization's overall philosophy about employee benefits and where they fit in the total compensation program should be established as an initial step before new benefit plans or changes in plans are implemented. An effective benefits package is part of the total compensation program which should be designed to meet specified objectives of the employer and also help to meet the needs and desires of employees. These objectives are not always as compatible as would be desired; hence, a need exists for the company's management to step back from the present benefit plans, rethink existing policy, and establish a posture for the future. Through this approach, a benefit program can emerge that implements the company's philosophy or objectives, rather than one that is a hodgepodge because it is merely a reaction to recommendations which come either from inside or outside the organization.

Management Review Committee

From the organization's viewpoint, one very effective way to review benefit plans, develop philosophy, and establish objectives is to appoint a committee of senior managers with the benefits manager as the lead person or chairperson. The size of the committee is optional but should include representatives from various areas of the organization. An example of one such committee would include (1) the controller, (2) the personnel executive, (3) the marketing executive, (4) the manufacturing executive, (5) the legal counsel, and (6) the benefits manager. Essentially, the committee makeup should be representative of the total organization without making it too cumbersome. The objective is to obtain individuals who have broad backgrounds and responsibilities so that a diversity of attitudes can be represented. This committee should be able to perform an in-depth study of the current program and develop a company philosophy themselves or to present it to top management for adoption.

If the company uses an outside benefits consultant, this process usually is more effective if the consultant is included in the meetings and used as a resource for the committee. The consultant can be helpful in supplying an outside perspective along with knowledge of what is being done by other organizations and generally what can be done. The consultant also can provide data on current trends in benefits, the status of legislation and proposed regulations, etc. Considering the proliferation of regulations and legislation in this area, it can be vital to the process.

Review Considerations

In its discussion of benefit goals and objectives, the committee should give consideration to some of the following issues and questions:

1. The organization's attitude toward its employees—its role as an employer. Are there social responsibilities to be considered?
2. What should be the relationship of benefits to direct compensation?
3. The organization's attitudes regarding retirement, survivor benefits, health care protection, etc.
4. Attitudes regarding forms and levels of survivor and retirement benefits.
5. To what extent is retirement security the responsibility of the company? The government? The individual employee?
6. In establishing benefit levels, should recognition be given to:
   a. Variations in length of service?
   b. Variations in pay level?
   c. Variations in levels of responsibility?
7. Which of the following is to be considered in determining the level of retirement income? Base salary? Bonuses? Overtime? Sales incentive? Other?
8. How important is competitive practice? In the industry? In the geographic location? In other industries?
9. Generally, how comprehensive should the benefits program be?

Certainly there are other issues and questions which the committee should address in this process. The idea is to achieve consensus on the issues addressed from which written benefit objectives can be prepared.

Analyzing Current Plans

Once the management review committee has completed the organization's statement of benefit objectives and it is adopted by top management, the committee should begin to determine to what extent the existing plans meet these objectives.

Some of the useful tools available to use in the analysis include:

1. Surveys conducted by the benefits staff, the consulting firm, and other

organizations, such as The Conference Board, Chamber of Commerce of the United States, and others.

2. Comparative analysis (available from your group insurance carrier) of claims versus charges made for medical plans—also, the carrier(s) can and should provide analysis of how your plan benefits compare to the usual customary and reasonable (UCR) charges by geographic location, and essentially show the effectiveness of the current health care package.
3. Many benefit consulting firms today have their own very sophisticated benefits measurement tools which are helpful in this process. Some popular benefits measurement programs are:
   a. Benefits Index.
   b. Benefit Value Comparison.
   c. Benval.
4. Projected pension benefits payable from the current pension and capital accumulation plans.

Employee Sensing

During the review process, modern day management committees and benefits managers like to include in their consideration the views and perceptions employees have about their benefits. These views are best obtained by means of employee sensing. The sensing process has considerable value to the organization when its communications program is being developed; hence, internal communications specialists should be helpful in developing the sensing format. The sensing can be done formally with professionally drafted questionnaires, using third-party interviewers or by conducting meetings with employee groups or individuals in open guided discussions. It also can be achieved on a much less formal basis by asking employees to return postcards with indications of their benefit concerns and views. If formal sensing is to be done, consideration should be given to including spouses in the process. Retirement and survivor benefits affect spouses directly, and their input can be important. Also, the health care plans often are utilized more frequently by dependents than by employees, so that their views and perceptions should be significant when it comes to plan design or amendments.

The sensing must be done in such a way that employees understand management wants their views but that final decisions regarding benefits must necessarily be made by management. A key point in the sensing process is to avoid raising employees' expectations that some new benefit or changes are forthcoming.

Having measured the effectiveness of current plans compared to stated objectives, and having received input from employees and spouses, the review process should now be giving shape and direction to what needs to be done in the future. Moreover, the committee or benefits reviewer(s) should be able to establish priorities for benefit changes; i.e., immediate versus intermediate and long-term needs.

During the sensing process it may be discovered that employee's perceptions and management's benefit objectives are not totally compatible. If this is the case, the benefit planners need to address how to achieve compatibility. This may require that management's objectives be adjusted, or it may indicate a need to improve the communications process to better educate and inform employees.

Developing Alternative Plans or Amendments

Assuming that portions of the company's current benefit program are not consistent with its newly developed objectives, the next step in the review process is to develop detailed descriptions of suggested revisions or of new plans and the pros and cons of each. This is a point where the professionals (i.e., consultant, actuary, and attorney) will be helpful in developing alternatives by reflecting on prior experience, what other employers are doing and the latest trends, and by acting as a sounding board regarding the choices. The actuary (who may also be the consultant) can provide cost information and also act as a sounding board regarding cost/benefit trade-offs of the choices. The attorney simply provides legal direction, keeping in mind the many laws and regulations which affect employee benefits, and thus keeps the design choices on legally "safe" grounds. Together the professionals should perform not as decision makers but as a team to provide as much knowledge and information as possible so that the most intelligent and appropriate decisions can be made for the organization and its employees.

The final product of the committee or benefits reviewer(s) is a list of recommended alternative plans or amendments to existing plans with suggested time frames for implementation and related costs of each change. There may also be recommendations on the benefits communication process for the future. At this point the committee has developed a program of objectives and specific plans and amendments to be considered for adoption to meet those objectives. The next step is to implement these plans and objectives.

CHAPTER 46

COMMUNICATION AND DISCLOSURE OF EMPLOYEE BENEFIT PLANS

Thomas Martinez
Robert V. Nally

REASONS FOR THE COMMUNICATION OF EMPLOYEE BENEFITS

The communication and disclosure of employee benefits to plan participants and their beneficiaries, in addition to fulfilling the reporting requirements of the federal law, is essential to the efficient operation of any benefit plan. The reasons for this can be categorized into two broad groupings: the legal requirements and the managerial requirements.

Legal Requirements

The Internal Revenue Code (IRC) has required from the very beginning of qualified pension or profit-sharing plans that such plans be in writing and communicated by appropriate means to covered individuals. Thus, for such retirement plans to receive the desired favorable tax treatment, communication is essential. Moreover, the Employee Retirement Income Security Act (ERISA) and other federal enactments have specific reporting and disclosure requirements covering private employee pension and welfare plans. All types of qualified pension and profit-sharing plans are subject to the disclosure requirements regardless of the number of participants in the plan. Some nonqualified retirement plans also are subject to the reporting and disclosure requirements. Additionally, certain welfare plans providing such benefits as life insurance, medical expense, disability income, and other employee benefits are subject to reporting and disclosure requirements.

The reporting and disclosure regulations provide for three categories of information. First, certain documents must be filed with the appropriate government agencies at required times and made available to employees. Second, certain information must be distributed automatically to plan participants under each plan and to beneficiaries receiving benefits under each plan. Third, certain specified information must be given to plan participants on written request and/or made available for examination at the principal office of the plan administrator and at other locations convenient for participants. These three categories of information cover five general groups of activities: (1) annual plan maintenance, (2) ongoing plan maintenance, (3) the installation of a new plan, (4) revisions in an existing plan, and (5) the termination of a plan. Moreover, the requirements differ for the various types of employee benefit plans.

The annual plan maintenance activities that must be reported and/or disclosed include reporting the financial activity of a plan for the current year and payment of plan termination insurance premiums to the federal government. They also cover providing employees with a summary of the financial activities of the plan for the year and providing terminated vested employees with a status report on their individual benefits under a pension plan.

The ongoing maintenance activities subject to the reporting and disclosure requirements basically cover situations and activities related to individual participants and employee requests for information. The federal government generally need not be notified of these matters. The only ongoing maintenance activity requiring notification of the federal government is when there is a reportable event; that is, a change in a covered retirement plan or its activities that might lead to a termination of the plan by the Pension Benefit Guaranty Corporation (PBGC).

New plan activities involve three major tasks. All participants must be furnished with a summary description of the plan. Application must be made to the Internal Revenue Service (IRS) for favorable tax qualification of a plan. Also, participants under some plans must be notified in advance of qualification that application has been made for such status.

Revised plan activities cover cases of the merger, consolidation, or transfer of the assets of an existing plan. Where applicable, these actions require the filing of a new application for tax-qualified status and notification of participants in advance of the application. Also, any material modification that occurs in a plan is classified as a revised plan activity.

TABLE 46–1

Document Summary of Reporting and Disclosure Requirements

Item	To Plan Participants				To Government	
	Given Automatically	*Given on Written Request**	*Made Available for Review†*	*When*	*To Be Filed with*	*When*
1. Summary plan description.	X			Within *90 days* after employees become participants, or beneficiaries start receiving benefits. Within *120 days* after a new plan becomes subject to ERISA. New complete summary at least every *10 years*.	Secretary of labor.	Within *120 days* after a new plan becomes subject to ERISA. New complete summary at least every *10 years*.
2. Plan documents (any instrument under which the plan is operated).		X	X	Within *10 days* after request to review; *30 days* after request for personal copies.	Secretary of labor.	"Any document relating to an employee benefit plan" at secretary of labor's request only.
3. Summary of material modification.	X			Within *210 days* after end of plan year in which modification is made.	Secretary of labor.	Within *210 days* after end of plan year in which modification is made.
4. Annual report (Form 5500).‡		X	X	As soon as report is filed with Internal Revenue Service.	Internal Revenue Service.	Within *7 months* after the end of the plan year (plus any applicable extensions for income tax filing).
5. Summary annual report.	X			Within *2 months* after deadline for filing annual report.		
6. Benefits statement for terminating vested employees.§	X			Within *180 days* after end of plan year in which termination occurs.		
7. Personal pension benefits statement.§		X (not more than once a year)		By the later of *60 days* after request *or 120 days* after end of prior plan year.		

8. Written explanation of claims denial.	X			Within *90 days* (*180* in special circumstances), whenever a claim is denied, in whole or in part.		
9. Plan termination report (Form 5310).		X	X	After report is filed with the IRS.	Internal Revenue Service.	At least *30 days* prior to plan termination, if determination of qualified status is required.
10. Joint and survivor notification.	X			Timing requirements vary depending on early retirement and survivor benefit provisions of the plan.		
11. Notification of intent to terminate a plan.	X			At least *10 days* prior to the proposed plan termination date. This notification should be delivered to the union representative where employees are represented by a union, or may be posted in prominent locations where they are not. (This is simply a notification that the statutory notice [*right*] has been filed with the PBGC.)	Pension Benefit Guaranty Corporation.	At least *10 days* prior to the proposed date of termination. Contents and attachments are specified by regulation.
12. Notice to interested parties.	X			Between *7 and 24 days* before application for determination of a plan's qualified status is made to the IRS.		

* Material must be supplied within 30 days of written request; a reasonable charge may be made for all requested material.
† Material must be made available for examination within 10 days of a verbal request.
‡ For applicable plans, Form 5500C is due every three years and Registration Statement R for the two intervening years.
§ As of date of publication, final regulations had not yet been adopted.

Source: Allen, Melone, Rosenbloom and Van Derhei, *Pension Planning,* 6th ed. (Homewood, Ill., Richard D. Irwin, Inc., 1988), pp. 380–381.

Plan termination actions of covered retirement plans must be supported by notice to the PBGC of the intention to terminate a plan, advance notice to the participants of this intention, and an application to the IRS for determination of the matter. A terminal report also is required.

Table 46–1 sets forth a summary of certain information that must be disclosed to the government, participants, and beneficiaries. It also indicates the dates by which such information must be disclosed and whether it must be automatically disclosed, given on written request, or made available for review. There are many more specific and detailed items included in the reporting and disclosure regulations. Table 46–1 merely covers those topics that are of more general concern. The overall reportable matters and procedures change from time to time, making a permanent list of such things impossible. However, current and complete brochures on these matters typically are made available on an annual basis by various public accounting firms and employee benefits consulting organizations. The disclosure requirements are enforceable against noncomplying individuals by injunctive civil action, and violations also are subject to fine and/or imprisonment. In addition, a failure to comply with the communications-oriented requirements could ultimately result in a loss of the special tax treatment afforded a plan. Thus, communication of employee benefits is essential for an employer to retain the favorable federal income tax status of such plans and avoid legal penalties.

Managerial Requirements

Even if plans did not receive favorable tax treatment on meeting disclosure and other criteria, the basic managerial reasons for the communication of employee benefits still would exist. Modern management thinking fosters the use of employee benefits as an effective means of competing in labor markets for the attraction and retention of qualified personnel. Benefit plans also are viewed as tools for building and maintaining high morale within a work force and for meeting the social and ethical responsibilities of employers within the employment relationship. These managerial reasons for instituting employee benefit plans can be met only if the relevant people are made aware of their existence. Benefit plans must be communicated and administered in a manner consistent with and supportive of the personnel policy goals that the benefits are designed to help accomplish. Benefit plans cannot motivate a person if the individual does not know of the existence of the plans or how they affect him or her individually. An employee cannot be influenced to remain with a specific employer, to be more productive, or to view an employer in a favorable light by the presence of benefits that have not been communicated properly. Moreover, an employee cannot use a benefit plan as it is fully intended (e.g., cost containment features in a medical plan or the use of a capital accumulation plan) if he or she is not acquainted with the nature and purposes of such plan provisions. When viewed in this context, the communication of employee benefits is an essential factor in the whole array of activities commonly termed "good management practice."

RESPONSIBILITY FOR COMMUNICATING EMPLOYEE BENEFITS

Realistically, the responsibility for communicating employee benefits is shared throughout the management hierarchy of an organization. Top management, the employee benefits manager, and line managers all have roles to play.

Top Management

Top management ultimately is responsible for employee benefit communications since it has the basic authority for setting all organizational policies and plans. The term *top management* has different connotations depending on the size of an organization. In small organizations, there is usually little or no differentiation of top, middle, and first-line management people. There is just one level of management. However, as organizations grow in size, they tend to acquire several middle and upper levels of management, each with varying degrees and types of authority and responsibility. Moreover, the management positions are structured to function in a coordinated manner, with each contributing to the fulfillment of the total management process.

In large corporate organizations, the responsibility for recommending policies and establishing and implementing plans and procedures is typically delegated to upper-level division and department heads. In addition, all line and staff managers of an organization are expected to administer their departments in a manner that is consistent and supportive of overall organizational policymaking and planning. For example, a vice president of marketing should run his or her division in a manner that accomplishes the marketing objectives of the firm and also includes appropriate consideration of the financial, production, personnel, and employee benefits policies established by top management. For employee benefits matters, the described planning and implementation responsibilities typically are placed with the person who serves as the vice president of personnel or as the employee benefits manager.

Employee Benefits Manager

An employee benefits manager engages in many activities in recommending and implementing employee benefits policies. The basic organizational responsibility for the communication of employee benefits to participants and their beneficiaries typically is vested in the individual who has this role or title in a firm. This situation exists regardless of whether a plan is self-funded and/or administered, insurance-funded and/or administered, or trusteed or structured under some other type of arrangement. Supporting services, including communications support activities and materials, usually are provided to the sponsoring employer by a third-party administrator of a plan. However, the overall responsibilities of an employee benefits manager may not be diminished under such arrangements. Indeed, the presence of an insured or trusteed plan could increase the workload of the employee benefits manager, because the efforts of the third-party administrator must be monitored, evaluated, and coordinated with the firm's employee benefit program.

One of the employee benefits manager's major concerns is to make certain that the employees understand the coverages, operation, and value of the benefits package. Although many easily comprehend the nature of the benefits extended, there may be employees who need to have these matters explained with greater care.

Attractive and readable posters, standard forms, pamphlets, brochures, and other written materials should be prepared. Perhaps the development of audio and visual materials might be necessary. The planning and conducting of meetings with groups of employees also may be required. Additionally, staff and line personnel must be trained to conduct meetings and deal with employees individually about employee benefits matters. The actual communication of employee benefits information to employees and others occurs in many ways at both specified and unspecified times. The efforts of the employee benefits manager, other personnel department people, and line people all are involved.

Line Management

Contemporary management theory emphasizes that the process of personnel management is spread throughout an organization. All managers are viewed as personnel managers because they are vitally connected with directing and motivating human resources. Their job effectiveness is dependent on the quality of the performance of the employees over whom they exercise authority.

Line managers of sales, manufacturing, and other departments usually play a substantial role in recruiting, selecting, evaluating, training, developing, and disciplining employees. Because of their close daily contact line, managers often are initially approached by employees with personal and employment-related problems and questions. In carrying out these activities, all managers can be viewed as employee benefits managers as well as personnel managers. Each of these activities involves a real or potential employee benefit communication event. Line managers must be equipped to give accurate employee benefit information. At a minimum, a line supervisor should be able to direct an inquiring employee to the office within the firm where assistance or advice can be obtained. Also, when a line manager makes a decision or takes any action involving an employee, the implications concerning a change in the benefits status of an employee should be considered. Disciplinary transfers, suspensions, layoffs, and terminations all typically involve employee changes with respect to the entitlement or loss of benefits. Any such actions taken imprudently could be counterproductive.

Employee Benefit Communication Events

Many occasions exist in the working career of each employee that can be classified as employee benefit communications events. There are incidents in the life span of an organization that also involve such events. Several of these bear particular mention.

As part of the recruitment process, it is advisable to notify potential and active job applicants of the general nature of the total employee benefit package of the firm. Competition among employers for qualified people is an ever-present economic factor, and prospective employees usually are quite aware of the important role of employee benefits in the total compensation package of a firm. The presence of a fine benefits program could be the ultimate factor in attracting superior job applicants and maintaining their interest in the firm. At the selection and placement stages more specific employee benefit information should be given to employment candidates. This will reinforce the commitment of the employer and help to increase positive attitudes in the candidates. The recruitment, selection, and placement processes typically are conducted through the interaction of personnel department staff and line people. Thus, both should be advised concerning their benefit communication functions and supplied with supporting brochures and other materials through the employee benefits office.

In the orientation process, new employees usually receive a tremendous quantity of information about their jobs, the products or services produced by the firm, and the organization itself. The employee benefits manager and his or her staff typically play the primary role in the orientation process of explaining the employee benefits program of the organization. Effective communications are essential at this point to aid in establishing lasting positive attitudes and keeping productive and mobile employees in the organization. In such a case, employees should understand the program fully from the very earliest point in their employment relationship.

An organization also should schedule employee benefits communication events rather than merely react to or deal with them as they occur. It is necessary to keep established employees informed of their benefits as a matter of legal and managerial responsibility. This can be accomplished by the employee benefits manager through the use of a continuous schedule for contacting employees at definitely set time intervals. Attractive and creative written communications can be sent to employees directly, placed in their pay envelopes, or displayed on bulletin boards. Meetings and seminars with groups of employees involving written and oral messages integrated with audio and visual materials often are useful.

Most employee communications events are generated by employees themselves. Whenever an employee has some question or misunderstanding regarding benefit entitlements, has a claim processed, or meets some difficulty in the administration of a claim, this requires an immediate managerial response. The lines of communication between the employee benefits department and employees should be kept open continuously. This is essential to give proper attention to any benefits questions or problems that employees may have.

It has been noted that employee status changes. Events such as suspensions and layoffs have benefit effects that should be considered before making any decisions in these areas. As a corollary to this policy, the formal communications network of a firm should be geared to generate an awareness among employees of any loss, decrease, or freeze of benefits that accompany a layoff, demotion, suspension, leave of absence, or termination. Likewise, increases or adjustments in benefits that take place in conjunction with transfers and promotions should be understood. When an event involving a change in the employment status of an individual takes place, the person should be counseled specifically about the benefit aspects as an additional measure of insurance. In connection with this, financial counseling programs and preretirement counseling sessions can play significant roles.

The general operating posture of a firm may be revised periodically.

For example, product lines are changed or broadened, geographic relocations or expansions occur, and other types of return on investment-oriented decisions take place. These actions sometimes are facilitated through modifications of the existing structure of a firm. This could mean a change in the basic method of departmentalization, an increased emphasis on centralization, the entire sale of a firm as a subsidiary to a competitor or a conglomerate, a merger arrangement, or a consolidation. These types of incidents typically cause concern among employees regarding their employment status and existing employee benefit programs. A firm should take steps at the time of such events to acquaint its employees with the nature and purpose of the organizational realignment and its impact on them personally. Whenever a merger or consolidation is carried out, some revisions of existing employee benefit plans invariably are necessary to dovetail existing plans with those of the new partner firm. Aside from the legal disclosure requirements that might apply in such circumstances, there is a need to acquaint employees with any benefit adjustments made. Moreover, sound management practice requires that existing benefits programs should seldom be downgraded or reduced at these times.

THE COMMUNICATION PROCESS

The communication process includes a sequence of several steps, regardless of whether the form of communication is the spoken or written word or some other method. It begins with the formation of an idea and its placement into a message form. The message then is transmitted and received by the person or persons for whom it is intended. Understanding the content of the message and appropriate action by the receiver then follows. The final step consists of the transmission of feedback by the receiver to the sender of the message.

Steps of the Communication Process

A complete sequence of the steps in the communication process is set forth below. Each of the steps—idea, message formation, transmission, receipt, understanding, action, and feedback—is discussed separately.

Idea

This step provides the content of a specific communication or message when the sender creates an idea or chooses a fact to communicate. An individual must have some fact, feeling, or concept to convey before the communication process moves forward. The first step is crucial because further steps are superfluous without a solid content message. Moreover, a poor message cannot be improved by trimmings such as glossy paper or a bigger loudspeaker.

Message Formation

The sender organizes an idea into a series of symbols that transmit the idea to those with whom communication is desired. The selected symbols may be words, gestures, pictures, scientific formulas, graphs, and so on. After the message is organized for rationality and coherence, the appropriate media to be used are selected. Therefore this step is related to the media used as well as to intended receivers. For example, a letter usually is worded differently from a brochure, and both are different from a face-to-face conversation. Moreover, the media selected must be capable of transmitting a message to the intended receivers. Thus, the written word usually is used for employee benefit messages because of their nature and content. However, in other situations this would be totally inefficient. For example, hand signals are used to communicate with a crane operator because the spoken word or other media are inappropriate due to distance, noise, and other physical factors.

Transmission

The message is transmitted over or through the medium selected in the preceding step. A specific channel is chosen to perform this step, and appropriate timing also is important. For example, a channel may be used to bypass a particular group, or a message may be delayed because the sender feels this is not the best time for it to be sent. The sender also tries to keep the communication channel free of interferences so that the message can reach the receiver and hold his or her attention. For example, in interviewing a beneficiary regarding a complex claim, distraction is undesirable.

Receipt

In this step, the initiative in the communication process shifts to the receiver. He or she must be ready and capable of receiving the message. If it is oral, the receiver must be a good listener; if written, the receiver must be a good reader; if in some symbolic language, the receiver must be knowledgeable and observant in the appropriate area. If the receiver does not function well, the message is lost.

Understanding

The receiver takes meaning from the symbols used by the sender. An effective and cooperative receiver tries diligently to capture the meaning intended in the message by the sender. Nevertheless, the meaning the receiver takes will not be exactly the same as the one sent. This happens because the perceptions of the sender and receiver invariably differ to some extent. Thus, the sender of a message should be aware that some degree of distortion or lack of comprehension by the receiver usually is inevitable. This can be ultimately overcome by devoting careful attention to the formation of the message and through the use of repetition and message follow-up techniques.

Action

On the basis of the message, the receiver acts or responds in some way. For example, he or she may verbally respond to the sender by writing a memo to the sender requesting further information; the receiver may store the information contained in the message for the future or may engage in other activities in response to a request or command, such as forming a group to openly discuss the proposals at issue.

Feedback

It is desirable to give feedback to the sender to establish two-way communication. One-way communication processes unfortunately do not include this step. The purpose of feedback is to provide the sender with information about his or her message that clarifies whether it was understood or put into effect. In some cases, the action step of the process includes the element of feedback. For example, when the beneficiaries of an employee benefit plan are sent notices of claims procedure changes, their degree of compliance in response to the message is an action step that can be observed as a form of feedback.

EFFECTIVE AND INEFFECTIVE COMMUNICATIONS

An effective communication takes place when a common understanding exists between the sender and receiver of a message. However, as indicated, this goal is not always achieved because of one or more of several interrelated factors. Sometimes individuals unintentionally send out messages, barriers can exist within the communications process itself, and all messages do not fully reflect the thoughts of the senders. Additionally, the receiver can be an impediment to an effective communication because of a low level of literacy, a suspicious nature regarding management-sponsored benefits programs, or general indifference.

Many unintended messages are transmitted for innumerable reasons.

For example, the receiver of a message may delay in responding to a request for information because of a heavy workload. The sender of the request, who does not know of the circumstances, interprets the delay as disinterest or hostility. Thus, a message has been communicated by each person, but only one was intended. The same result can occur because of body language or voice inflections unconsciously used by the sender.

The communication process does not always function in a complementary environment. When this is the case, the existing barrier makes effective communications difficult. Noise usually is the most annoying barrier to effective communications because of its distracting characteristic. Organizational distance, another barrier, occurs when a message must be transmitted through several people before ultimately reaching the receiver. The presence of message competition also operates as a barrier to effective communication. This exists when the receiver is bombarded by many related messages at the same time. If there is little indication of the relative importance of each message, the receiver may become confused.

A message should be constructed carefully to reflect the thoughts of the sender. The language selected must be understood by the receiver. For example, employee benefits-oriented terms such as *coinsurance, deductible,* or *third-party payee* are not universally understood, and thus great care must be exercised in using them. The language of a message also should not antagonize the receiver. Words such as *minorities, unisex,* or *welfare* can produce negative feelings that impede understanding. Slang, jargon, and buzzwords can be effective; however, such terms tend to be fashionable for brief periods of time and thus should be avoided in written communications that are intended for use over an extended period.

Messages often can be too long or too brief. Excessively long messages lose reader interest and comprehension. Conversely, the receiver may make abstractions or inferences not intended by the sender if the message is too brief.

The sender and receiver of a message must be in tune for effective communications to take place. Unfortunately, the receiver sometimes presents a problem because his or her perceptions may differ from the sender's. Thus, when the sender refers to holding down costs, the receiver may interpret this as a directive to deny benefit claims accepted in the past. As another example, any message that involves a change of existing conditions may be met with resistance by the receiver. This includes such matters as changes in existing benefit policies, programs, or operating procedures. Also, the status of the sender can be important to the receiver. Communications from the employee benefits manager of a large organization may carry greater impact than those of the support staff in the benefits department.

FORMS OF COMMUNICATION

Communications typically are classified as written, oral, or action messages. Written communications consist of many types, from handbooks, booklets, bulletins, memos, letters, and standard forms to posters, cartoons, films, prepared tapes, and pictures. Oral communications, on the other hand, generally consist of the spoken word in a speech, an order, a comment, or a discussion. Actions also are recognized as communication forms, regardless of whether the action exists independently or occurs in consort with a written or oral communication. Thus, such things as laughter, a smile, a handshake, silence, and personal mannerisms significantly communicate some kind of message.

Written Communications

The primary focus in this chapter is on the written form of communication because federal laws concerning employee benefits require the use of such communications in specific instances. Moreover, the basic principles of effective writing also apply to the development and transmission of oral messages.

Written communications provide a permanent record of a transmitted message. Accordingly, written messages usually are constructed with greater care and have a higher degree of formality than oral messages. A written message can be read carefully and reread by the receiver to gain a fuller understanding of the content. Thus, when a message is lengthy or detailed, the written form often is used because oral communication would not be as effective. In addition, when a message must be transmitted through several people to the ultimate receiver, the written form is selected to avoid change or dilution of its content.

The federal regulations concerning the written communication of employee benefit matters provide that required information must be written in a manner calculated to be understood by the average plan participant. Also, it must be sufficiently accurate and comprehensive to inform participants and beneficiaries of their rights and obligations under a plan. Generally, plan sponsors do not encounter any great difficulty in complying with these broadly stated legal guidelines. However, to obtain the improved morale and productivity that can flow from an effective employee benefits communication system, preparers of written communications must understand the nature and steps of the writing process and some basic writing principles.

The Writing Process

The first consideration in developing written materials is the nature of the readership. The technical, educational, and literacy levels of anyone who will receive the message must be ascertained, along with the language, social, and economic background of the reader. In writing, this is called knowing the audience. As one should not write down to or patronize an audience, one should always consider how an idea can be best expressed in writing to all who will read the message. Clarity, the precision of the words chosen, is of paramount importance for readers to understand a communication's major facets. Once this is accepted, the writing process can begin with its four fundamental steps, namely, prewriting, writing or drafting, revising, and final editing and proofing.

Prewriting. Before writing the first word of the first draft, there are preliminary considerations. A writer must gather the necessary data, review it, and order it in a fashion that will be clear and logical for the readers. The writer then shapes the focus, reconsiders the audience at hand, and finally settles on the length of the communication. At this time the writer should reflect on what will be written and for whom it will be written.

Writing or Drafting. The next step is to compose the initial or rough draft. A writer need not be troubled with general correctness at this juncture because the central function is to elucidate the position being taken, express the ideas, and unravel what may seem to be ambiguous, sophisticated material. After this run-through to test the length of the communication, the accuracy of its concepts, and its clarity, the writer may return to the draft to check for its stylistic flow. This is the time to work on those principles of style that add a sense of unity and fluidity to the thought. The basic reason for multiple drafts is to avoid rushing through the total composition process at one sitting. It is advisable to allow a first draft to rest, to age, as it were, so that ideas have time to reassemble, solidify in time, and perhaps be reshuffled to include fresh points of view, more solidly supportive detail and clarifying concepts not previously incorporated.

Revising. The revision process is important because by this time writers have completed their thought processes, included most of their purposeful detail, and arrived at useful conclusions. Since writing is a recursive act—that is, writers throughout the writing process always return to previous thoughts to review their logic, reread previous sentences to readjust their flow, or seek a fresher word to replace a stale one—some of this activity is an ongoing process as one pushes to complete a first draft. Yet this revision segment is reserved for writers to assess seriously how clearly and focused their ideas have been expressed, to check the logical arrangement of paragraphs and the transitions between them, to measure the variety of the length and pattern of sentences, and to judge the effectiveness of word choice. This, then, leads to what can be loosely called "the final draft." However, in truth there may not be such a thing as a final draft, since a writer can always find a better word, delete wordiness that has crept in seemingly from nowhere, reposition a runaway sentence more precisely, or eliminate a detail that suddenly has become irrelevant.

Final Editing or Proofreading. This last part of the writing process allows for fixing spelling, "ironing out" the typos, correcting punctuation and other mechanical gremlins, and deleting infelicitous phrases. It is necessary to proofread your final draft in order to eliminate anything that might reflect adversely on your carefulness. When a memo or communication, no matter how trivial, is sent under a writer's signature, that person is responsible for every thought, word, and structure. The more errors left undetected, the more that person's work will be considered careless. If little care is taken with obvious writing difficulties that can be easily corrected, how much can that person be depended on to *carefully* deliver or administer the material represented in the communication? Do not create a negative impression by not following through with a thorough proofreading of the final draft.

Finally, writers can relax when they realize that the act of composing is a continuous process, rather than an activity that stops completely with the distribution of the written communication. What has been overlooked or ungracefully expressed can be improved in the future. Also, the revising and subsequent editing or proofreading process allows writers the luxury of time to evaluate and correct both the real and imagined imperfections in their current drafts.

Overall Approach and Tone

Writers should take the middle road between high formality, and low informality. An overly formal approach may be read as too pompous and officious, while an informal presentation may appear too casual, hurried, and ill-formed. Both extremes produce negative responses from readers.

The predominant impression sought should be one of careful, honest thoroughness to allow readers to judge the reasonableness of a communication's proposition.

Some Writing Principles

Additions to the steps outlined in the writing process undoubtedly will lead to more effective communications. Also, some specific guides should be followed to improve the efficiency of written communications. Among these are the "10-20-30 formula" for paragraphs, sentences, and word choice, and the "U-shaped curve" concept. Simply stated, the 10-20-30 formula is a rule of thumb that aids a writer in sustaining reader interest. When the writer limits paragraphs to an average of 10 sentences, sentence length to 20 words, and the number of polysyllabic words to 30 percent of the total words in the entire composition, reader interest does not diminish, and more effective written communication results.

It is most important not to lose the interest of readers or receivers of messages. Initially, within the first paragraph of a written communication, the reader's attention is high. It is at the top or the peak of a U-shaped curve. Unfortunately, this interest wavers as one reads other paragraphs, and it drops to the bottom part of the U—the "valley of disinterest." Toward the conclusion of a communication, the typical pattern of attention moves upward to a second peak of the U, although this second peak is not as high as the initial peak. Thus, it seems to follow that when written communications are received, readers are compelled to read the first paragraph. The reader is highly motivated at first, particularly when the message may have singular significance for him or her. Nevertheless, interest tends to decrease as the message continues, especially when the receiver finds the message so common that it can be filed away for another day. However, curiosity could move that reader to push ahead to the concluding paragraphs to see if there may be some content more personally pertinent than that contained in earlier paragraphs. Thus, a writer should mold a written communication so that the full body of the message is contained in the early paragraphs. The meat of the message must be presented early and in a manner sufficiently viable to hold the reader's interest and not be casually dismissed.

There also is an "effort-reward ratio" theory associated with the effectiveness of written communication. The reader typically asks, "How much reward is there for the effort I expend over this reading?" More selfishly stated, the reader asks: "What will this memo do for me?" or "What will it not do for me?" If the first paragraph does not elicit interest for the overall message, the reader quickly dips into the valley of disinterest by skimming over the rest of the material. The earlier a written message can relay a sense of importance for the reader, the longer it will be read and the less disinterest there will be. A writer must strive to keep readers as constantly at the peak of interest as possible or else ineffective communication may result.

To the 10-20-30 formula can be added the "three Ss." Writing should be short, simple, and sincere. Brevity induces recipients to read the message totally. Simplicity and clarity enable readers to understand the transmitted ideas, and sincerity is the intangible that might convince them to accept the content of a message. Too little information may lead the reader to feel that the company is merely paying lip service to the idea of benefits, a point that can undermine the sincerity of effort behind the company's intentions.

Most people quickly tire of reading long, drawn-out communications. Conversely, they fully appreciate deriving the most information from the fewest words. Brevity is more than "the soul of wit;" it is the investment that pays ample dividends. A reader more frequently reads through something short and specific than something wordy and tedious. Too much in a paragraph tends to bore, confuse, or turn readers against the topic at hand.

A writing can be made visually appealing and immediately informative by headlining significant sections. Centering some major headings may be even more inviting. This provides the reader with an opportunity to read a skeletal outline of a proposal and then return to each segment separately. Readers do not have to pore over each paragraph to find the topic thought. Instead, they can scan the entire message, look for substantive matter, and be directed to what catches their interest.

Samples of Effective Benefits Communications

Several samples and accompanying explanations are included to show applications of the preceding thoughts. The numbers in brackets after each sentence in each figure represent, *first,* the number of words in the sentence, and *second,* the number of polysyllabic words used in the sentence to see how they both correspond to the 10-20-30 formula.

Example 1. The first example consists of an introductory section of a memorandum regarding an employee benefit package:

TO: Current and Future Employees of XYZ Company

FROM: Employee Benefits Management Committee

SUBJECT: Employee Benefits Package

> The management committee in charge of the Employee Benefit Package is presenting its plan to everyone currently employed and to all prospective employees [23 words, 11 polysyllabic words]. The introductory outline of the full package and the breakdown of each item should serve to acquaint you with the general provisions of each benefit [25,8]. If you have any questions about the following, Mr. B_______ from the Personnel Office will gladly discuss specific areas of the plan with you [24,7].

This memo clearly introduces its purpose. The approach is solicitous; the beginning suggests that there was a group meeting to discuss the welfare of the employees, the second sentence guides the reader to what the memo includes, and the last sentence opens the door for oral, personal communication if for some reason the written message is misunderstood. As for attention span, there would seem to be no time for disinterest, because by the time the reader might possibly begin to stray, the introductory pleasantries stop and the actual package is presented.

Example 2. The second example consists of an outline of the benefits package made available by an employer. The outline is taken from the employee handbook of the sponsoring employer:

> EMPLOYEE BENEFITS PACKAGE
>
> Every employee with the XYZ Company at least six months is eligible for the benefits listed below: [16,6].
>
> A. Major Medical Insurance Coverage
> B. Accident Insurance Coverage
> C. Life Insurance Coverage
> D. Disability Income
> E. Supplemental Unemployment Benefits
> F. Scholarship Services
> G. Prepaid Legal Services
>
> Each of the above benefits is explained briefly in the following sections [12,5].

Visually, the above captures the reader because there is no word clutter. If readers were turned off by the earlier introductory material, they can be brought to another peak of interest by looking through the seven offerings and selecting as many benefits as are appealing: two, three, five, or one. Therefore, the memo automatically directs readers to a high peak of interest and sustains that level as they locate the areas to investigate further. If sections A through G above are kept relatively short, there should be no time to allow for a fall into that valley of disinterest. Note that the number of words per sentence and the number of polysyllabic words corresponds neatly to the 10-20-30 formula.

Example 3. The third example consists of a section in the employee handbook explaining the nature of one of the employee benefits provided:

MAJOR MEDICAL INSURANCE COVERAGE ELIGIBILITY

All employees with the company at least six months are eligible for medical benefits as outlined by the participating program the employee chooses [23,10]. The company offers a choice of the following plans [9,3]:

A. Blue Cross/Blue Shield, Plan B.
B. Great River Valley Health Plan.
C. The Priority Health Maintenance Plan.

Each of the above is described in separate brochures available from the Personnel Office [14,7].

Cost

The company will underwrite the cost of whatever plan an employee chooses, provided that employee meets the requirements of the plan [21,8]. Dependent coverage is also available, but that cost must be paid by the employee [14,4]. Although the costs of some plans may vary, the company will pay the employee's fee regardless of the differential [19,6].

Exclusions

The only exclusions in medical coverage for employees and their families will be those imposed by the medical plan itself [20,9]. The company will not exclude any one of its employees from choosing one of its medical plans [17,5].

The above example demonstrates the principles outlined previously, and it shows the flexibility it gives management in citing its medical offerings. Under a heading such as ''Eligibility,'' management may choose to introduce a brief summary of each plan or merely list the three. Each succinct paragraph forces readers to cover main points as they glance quickly at the benefits that interest them most.

The longest section is the first with its three sentences and list of three plans, but the spacing serves a good purpose because readers can easily follow what is being offered. Since everything is spelled out clearly, there are no traps. The eight sentences average 17 words each, well within the 10-20-30 prescribed formula; although approximately 35 percent of the words are polysyllabic, any layperson can understand the language without resorting to a dictionary.

The sample is *short* and *simple,* but there is a note of erudition; nothing in the sample talks down or up to the reader. The tone is easy, direct, neither supercilious nor superior. It promotes its benefits honestly and adds *sincerity* by listing a number of alternatives, by informing an employee where specific material is available, and by insisting that the company excludes no one from its medical plans.

Oral Communications

Oral communications take place in many different ways. They involve face-to-face discussions or verbal orders between two or more people, the use of telephones, speeches, meetings, the employment of public address systems, and other uses of the spoken word. Generally, oral communications are transmitted faster than written communications. Also, under some circumstances, oral communication can provide a greater basis for achieving common understanding by the participants than that allowable through written communication. This ability to gain a higher degree of common understanding varies with the form of oral communication used. For example, face-to-face communications between two people or within small groups typically have this quality to a greater extent than telephone conversations and speeches. Face-to-face communication gives each participant the immediate opportunity to observe the body language of the other, ask questions, and eliminate misunderstanding.

The seven-step communication process—idea, message formation, transmission, receipt, understanding, action, and feedback—applies to oral as well as written communications. Thus, the sender of an oral message should know him- or herself and the audience, understand the potential barriers to an effective communication, formulate the message in a thoughtful and articulate manner, as well as select and use an appropriate medium to transmit the message. The action and feedback steps then can be used to appraise the receipt and understanding of the message by the receiver or audience.

Oral communications also are subject to the same guides or principles as written communications. That is, oral messages should be constructed in accordance with the 10-20-30 formula, the U-shaped curve or valley of disinterest concept, the effect-reward ratio theory, and the admonition of the three Ss to keep messages short, simple, and sincere.

There are some additional factors concerning oral communication that should be noted. Oral communications are more effective when there is verbal interaction between the participants. A speaker can use gestures, facial expressions, and other types of body language to enhance the process. The level of the speaker's voice, the use of pauses, the rate of speaking, enunciation, and other vocal characteristics play an important role in speech communication. Moreover, as is the case with written communications, visual materials such as pamphlets, graphs, charts, diagrams, posters, and slides can improve the quality of oral communications immensely.

CHAPTER 47

QUALIFIED RETIREMENT PLANS FOR SMALL BUSINESS: CHOICE OF PLAN

Harry V. Lamon, Jr.
James A. Clark

INTRODUCTION

Adoption of a qualified retirement plan is one of the major tax benefits that may be obtained by a small-business organization. Such a plan permits current income tax deductions by the small business, a deferral of income tax until receipt by the participants, tax-exempt earnings during the existence of the trust, exemption of the trust from the claims of most creditors of both the participants and the small business, and the availability of favorable treatment under the income tax rules on the payment of benefits from the plan. Although most of these tax advantages may be obtained by the *unincorporated* business under what is commonly referred to as an H.R. 10 plan, several distinctions remain between corporate plans and H.R. 10 plans despite Congress' attempt in the Tax Equity and Fiscal Responsibility Act of 1982 (TEFRA) to achieve parity between corporate and H.R. 10 plans.

First, this chapter will review the various types of qualified plans that are available to, and generally used by, small businesses and describe those factors that aid in choosing a particular type of qualified retirement plan. Second, the discussion will focus on the *top-heavy plan* concept that was inaugurated in TEFRA and the concept's effect on plan choice. Finally, Section 401(k) *cash or deferred arrangements* will be discussed separately because of their large potential for use by small businesses. The specific TEFRA and Tax Reform Act of 1986 (TRA '86) changes that effect approximate parity between corporate plans and H.R. 10 plans are discussed in Chapter 48.

GENERAL CONSIDERATION IN PLAN CHOICE—TYPES OF PLAN

Once the decision to establish a qualified retirement plan is made by the small business, care should be taken to assure that the plan is designed to meet its goals. The decisions regarding the type and design of the qualified retirement plan to be established are almost as crucial as the decision to adopt any plan at all.

Of course, a portion of the income received from any small business must be used to pay overhead (including rent, insurance, etc.), another portion must be used to provide direct compensation to the employees, and only the remainder may be used to provide fringe benefits and qualified retirement plan benefits. Thus, probably the most important aspect of choosing the appropriate qualified retirement plan is determining the amount of contributions that can be made on an annual, recurring basis to the plan. If the income of the small business is entirely exhausted through the payment of overhead expenses and the payment of direct compensation to the employees, funds will obviously not be available to make contributions to any plan. On the other hand, if the employer elects to reduce the amount of direct compensation or is able to economize in other ways, funds will be available for the qualified plan.

The choice of qualified retirement plans is probably easiest in a small business with one shareholder and probably most difficult in a small business with more than one but fewer than 10 shareholders, particularly where there is wide divergence in the ages of the various shareholders. The authors' experience is that generally the older shareholders have seen the "handwriting on the wall" and desire to create as much in the form of retirement benefits as their income will allow, while the younger employee-shareholders may prefer to defer little or nothing.

The establishment of a qualified retirement plan should not proceed without seeking the advice of attorneys, accountants, and consultants. Even if the shareholders desire to adopt one of the many available master or prototype plans, the assistance of an attorney and accountant should be sought prior to the adoption of the plan. After carefully reviewing the various needs and desires of the small business, in conjunction with the practical and legal ramifications of the various types of plans that are available, these advisers can greatly assist in designing the most appropriate plan for the small business.

The following discussion is not intended to provide exhaustive treatment of all aspects of qualified retirement plans; rather, the discussion merely focuses on those aspects that are particularly applicable to small business so that the owners of the small business and their advisers will not overlook them in designing the qualified retirement plan.

Regular Profit-Sharing Plans

A profit-sharing plan is typically the first type of qualified retirement plan that an employer should consider. Profit-sharing plans are among the many types of defined contribution plans. The common characteristic of all defined contribution plans is that they provide individual accounts for each participant, although all plan assets are normally commingled for investment purposes. A participant's retirement benefit under a defined contribution plan is based solely on the amount in the participant's account.[1] This arrangement provides a certain measure of security for the employer maintaining the plan because, unlike a defined benefit plan, a defined contribution plan does not promise any specific level of benefits; therefore, if the plan suffers poor investment experience, the employer will not be called on to underwrite the unanticipated shortfall in funds necessary to provide guaranteed benefits. A necessary corollary is that participants in a defined contribution plan bear the burden of poor investment experience and reap the benefit of favorable investment experience.

As the result of a change introduced by TRA '86, profit-sharing plan contributions no longer must be made using the current or accumulated profits of the small business. Since contributions may be totally discretionary on the part of the board of directors, partners, or proprietor, a profit-sharing plan is among the most flexible of tax-favored employee benefits. For example, a plan could require mandatory contributions equal to 5 percent of the participant's compensation but not in excess of current profits. For purposes of determining the amount of current or accumulated profits out of which such contribution is to be made, the plan could define profits in any manner desirable to the business owners. If a small business has profits as determined under generally accepted ac-

---

[1] IRC § 414(i).

counting principles, for example, contributions could be made even if there are no current or accumulated profits from a tax standpoint.[2]

Amounts that are contributed to a profit-sharing plan are allocated to each participant based on the percentage of the total compensation of all participants that his or her individual compensation represents. However, if the profit-sharing plan is integrated with Social Security, as discussed later in this chapter, then the allocation pertaining to the portion of a participant's compensation that is not in excess of the Social Security wage base may be reduced when allocating employer contributions to the participant's individual account.

Amounts that are allocated to participant accounts are held by the trustee of the plan, and the earnings and losses arising from plan investments are allocated on an annual basis to the accounts of the participants. As noted, no guaranteed retirement benefit exists under a profit-sharing plan because a retiring participant is entitled to receive only the amount in his or her account, which may be more or less than the total of the contributions actually made to the account, depending on the investments made by the trustee.

A participant's account balance also may change due to forfeitures. A forfeiture is the unvested portion of a participant's account that is forfeited by the participant on his or her early termination of employment. Forfeitures are reallocated among the remaining participants, thus increasing the accounts of those participants who continue their employment with the small business.

The allocation of forfeitures usually is based on the current compensation levels of the remaining participants in the year in which forfeiture occurs. Allocation of forfeitures may be based on other factors, such as the account balances of all remaining participants; however, if this results in highly compensated employees receiving forfeitures that are a larger percentage of current compensation than is the case with rank and file employees, then the plan will lose its qualified status.[3] To prevent possible disqualification, forfeitures in profit-sharing plans should not be allocated on any basis other than current compensation.

Section 404(a)(3) of the Internal Revenue Code limits deductible contributions to a profit-sharing plan to 15 percent of the compensation of all

---

[2] Rev. Rul. 80-252, 1980-2 C.B. 130; Rev. Rul. 66-174, 1966-1 C.B. 81.

[3] Rev. Rul. 81-10, 1981-1 C.B. 172. For years beginning after 1988, the nondiscrimination rules, as set out in IRC § 401(a)(4), prohibit discrimination in favor of "highly compensated employees" as defined in IRC § 414(q). See below.

plan participants. If a contribution of more than 15 percent is made during a given year, then the amount of the excess may be deducted in the next subsequent year(s) to the extent that the *total* profit-sharing deduction for any such subsequent year does not exceed 15 percent of the compensation of all plan participants for the given year.[4]

In addition to this annual aggregate contribution limitation, Section 415(c) of the Code limits annual additions to the account of each participant, a concept discussed further later in this chapter.

The authors feel that profit-sharing plans certainly should be *considered* by any small business, primarily because profit-sharing plans allow the amount of contributions to be based entirely on the profitability of the business and/or the discretion of the owners. For example, profit-sharing plans may be very useful for owners of new small businesses who desire to implement some type of qualified retirement plan but are unsure of exactly how successful the small business will be—many small businesses experience wide fluctuations in income from year to year. Although the contributions to a profit-sharing plan may be discretionary, employers should be aware that plan contributions must be substantial and recurring.[5] In order to meet this test, the general opinion is that contributions must be made at least once every three years. In any event, however, the failure to make contributions because of insufficient profits will not disqualify the plan.[6]

The allocation of unintegrated profit-sharing plan contributions for a small business with four employees where the contribution equals 15 percent of compensation is illustrated in the following chart:

Participant	*Compensation*	*Contribution Allocation*
Shareholder	$175,900.00	$26,385.00
Staff employee	12,000.00	1,800.00
Staff employee	10,000.00	1,500.00
Staff employee	8,000.00	1,200.00
Total	$205,900.00	$30,885.00

[4] In the case of an existing profit-sharing plan, where any pre-1987 contribution was less than 15 percent of the participant's compensation during the relevant period, the unused contribution amount may be carried forward so as to increase the deduction limit for years after 1986 up to a maximum deduction of 25 percent in any one year. IRC § 404(a)(3).

[5] Treas. Regs. § 1.401-1(b)(2).

[6] See *Sherwood Swan & Co.*, 42 T.C. 299 (1964); Rev. Rul. 80-146, 1980-1 C.B. 90.

As the chart illustrates, although the shareholder receives the largest contribution, the contribution is based on the same percentage of compensation (15 percent) as that granted to the staff employees. As explained later in this chapter, however, TEFRA's top-heavy rules limit the flexible allocation of contributions in defined contribution plans such that a minimum contribution must be made on behalf of nonkey employees (generally nonowners and nonexecutive employees) equal to 3 percent of their compensation or, if lesser, the highest percentage contribution made on behalf of any key employee (generally an owner-employee, executive employee, or officer).

An employer may alter this pro rata allocation by integrating its contributions to a profit-sharing plan with the Social Security taxes that the corporation must pay. Generally, if a profit-sharing plan is integrated with Social Security benefits, contributions will be allocated *first*, to those participants whose compensation is in excess of the Social Security wage base, in an amount up to 5.7 percent of such excess, with a corresponding allocation to *all* participants so that 5.7 percent (or lesser excess allocation) is not greater than twice the contribution percentage with respect to compensation that is below the Social Security wage base; and *second*, to all participants as their compensation relates to total compensation. If the profit-sharing plan discussed above was integrated with Social Security benefits using the 1987 Social Security wage base of $43,300 and the same $30,885 contribution was made, then the maximum integration allocation would be as follows:

Participant	*Compensation*	*Contribution Allocation*
Shareholder	$175,900.00	$27,486.24
Staff employee	12,000.00	1,359.50
Staff employee	10,000.00	1,132.92
Staff employee	8,000.00	906.34
Total		$30,885.00

Obviously, an integrated profit-sharing plan provides a larger allocation for the shareholder. However, an important factor that should be considered before integrating a profit-sharing plan is that the integrated portion of an account may not be distributed prior to retirement, death, or other separation from service.[7] In contrast, a nonintegrated profit-sharing

[7] Rev. Rul. 71-446, § 15.03, 1971-2 C.B. 187.

plan may provide for distributions to participants during their employment after a period of deferral of as little as two years, the attainment of a stated age, or the prior occurrence of some event demonstrating financial need. (However, a 10 percent excise tax may apply on an early distribution, as discussed in Chapter 48.) Finally, as discussed below, TEFRA severely restricts the integration of top-heavy profit-sharing plans, top-heavy plans being those plans in which a disproportionate amount of contributions are made on behalf of officers, owners, and executive employees.

Profit-Sharing Thrift Plans

Mandatory and/or voluntary employee contributions may be a feature of any profit-sharing plan. Aggregate voluntary employee contributions may not exceed 10 percent of the compensation paid to an employee during his or her participation in the plan.[8] As a general rule, for any year, mandatory employee contributions (the minimum contribution required as a prerequisite for participation or as a condition for increased employer contributions) may not exceed 6 percent of the amount of compensation paid to the employee for the year in question; however, the Internal Revenue Service refuses to treat the 6 percent rule as a "safe harbor" from a possible challenge of discrimination in operation.[9]

Where employee contributions to a profit-sharing plan are required as a condition of participation, such a plan often is called a *contributory plan*. For example, a contributory plan might require employees to contribute 6 percent of their compensation before they are entitled to share in the employer contribution. Where the level of employer contributions is based on the amount or rate of employee contributions, such a plan is commonly referred to as a *thrift* or *savings plan*. An example of a *thrift plan* is where an employer matches 50 percent of an employee's contribution, up to a maximum of 5 percent of pay.

Thrift plans have several attractive features. First, employee contributions are normally made through payroll deductions and an employee receives no company contributions unless he or she has authorized payroll deductions. Second, the company contribution is not tied to current profits; rather, the company usually contributes a fixed dollar amount for each dollar contributed by the employee. Historically, thrift plans have

---

[8] Rev. Rul. 80-350, 1980-2 C.B. 133.

[9] Rev. Rul. 80-307, 1980-2 C.B. 136.

generally received an enthusiastic employee response, which is somewhat unusual since a regular profit-sharing plan normally provides the same type of benefits without the requirement of employee contributions. However, cash or deferred arrangements (CODAs) are increasingly becoming much more popular with employees (see the discussion later in this chapter).

As a general rule, thrift plans offer the same benefits as other profit-sharing plans to a small business. However, thrift plans serve an additional need in those small businesses in which shareholders have divergent retirement objectives, since the amount that is deferred is directly related to each shareholders' own voluntary contributions and may be adjusted annually. As a *caveat,* however, if a thrift plan is adopted and the compensation of those employees who do not contribute to the thrift plan is adjusted upward by the employer, then the plan may be a *de facto* CODA, as discussed later in this chapter, which is only qualified if certain additional requirements are met pursuant to Section 401(k) of the Code.

A disadvantage of thrift plans is that employee contributions that are matched by employer contributions are not eligible for treatment as deductible employee contributions.[10] One alternative that may be used to allow employees to make before-tax thrift contributions would be to convert a thrift plan to a CODA with the employer matching the amounts that employees elect to contribute to the plan under the cash or deferred provision.

After 1986, thrift plans are subject to an additional qualification requirement: the *contribution percentage test* that applies to matching and employee contributions. This test, which closely resembles the nondiscrimination test for CODAs, is discussed in detail later in this chapter.

Pension Plans

Pension plans, as opposed to profit-sharing plans, must provide definitely determinable benefits. Pension plan contributions are mandatory, irrespective of corporate profits, in an amount necessary to fund the benefits provided by the plan. Further, in the case of defined benefit pension plans, forfeitures may *not* be used to increase the benefits of the individual participants but must reduce the annual employer contributions under such plans.[11]

---

[10] IRC § 219(e).

[11] See Treas. Reg. §1.401-1(a)(2)(i) and § 1.401-1(b)(1)(i); IRC § 401(a)(8).

Defined Benefit Pension Plans

As a general rule, defined benefit pension plans apply a greater share of the employer contributions for the benefit of older employees than for younger employees.[12] This result occurs because the defined benefit plan rules fix the amount of the retirement benefit, not the amount of the annual contribution that will produce the benefit. Where both individuals are to ultimately receive the same level of retirement benefit, the portion of each annual contribution that is required to fund the benefit of the older employee is larger than the amount required to fund the benefit of the younger employee, since there are fewer years in which to contribute the assets necessary to produce the older employee's benefit level. In contrast, the defined contribution plan rules fix the maximum amount of the annual *contribution* on behalf of each employee but do not limit the amount of the ultimate benefit. Thus, employers may produce a larger retirement benefit for younger employees than for older employees in a defined contribution plan because younger employees have more years in which to receive employer contributions before retirement. Thus, defined benefit pension plans are often very useful in a small business where older employees desire to defer a substantial amount of current income until retirement.

If an employee has not been a participant in the defined benefit plan for at least 10 years as of his or her date of retirement, then the maximum pension benefit that may be provided under Section 415(b) of the Code (the lesser of 100 percent of annual compensation use or $90,000 per year) must be reduced by 10 percent for each year of participation less than 10.[13] A technique that is often available to increase the size of the maximum deductible pension plan contribution, particularly for senior employees, is to use a benefit formula that gives credit for service with the employer prior to the effective date of the plan; however, a limitation exists on the rate at which past service costs may be funded. If the unfunded cost of past and current service benefits attributable to any three individuals is more than 50 percent of the unfunded cost of past and current service benefits of all participants covered by the pension plan,

---

[12] In Rev. Rul. 74-142, 1974-1 C.B. 95, a professional corporation established a pension plan providing a retirement benefit of 60 percent of average compensation for each participant. There were only two participants under the plan, a 60-year-old professional and a 52-year-old staff employee. Because of the differences in ages and compensation, 90 percent of the contributions were applied to fund the benefits for the older professional. Yet, the Service ruled that the plan was qualified and did not discriminate in favor of the older professional. See also *Ryan School Retirement Trust*, 24 T.C. 127 (1955).

[13] IRC § 415(b)(5).

then the cost attributable to such three individuals may not be funded over fewer than five years.[14] However, it is not necessary in such instances to have the benefits fully funded as of such individual's normal retirement date.

Although the ability to defer large amounts of compensation through deductible contributions to defined benefit pension plans may work well in some small businesses, it may create problems in others. For example, once the older employee has retired, the younger employees will be required to continue funding benefits under the existing plan or to terminate the plan. A problem inherently exists if an older employee in a small business was credited with a sufficient amount of past service at the time the plan was established, and this past service credit is not fully funded by the date on which the older employee retires. In this case, the remaining younger employees will find their corporation making contributions to fund the pension of a person who no longer performs services for the corporation, and the temptation to terminate the plan may be overwhelming. Since a majority of the contributions of the employer to a defined benefit plan fund the retirement benefits of those employees closest to retirement, defined benefit pension plans work well in larger corporations where a sufficient number of employees exists at various age levels such that a level method of funding benefits over a number of years also exists. On the other hand, in a small corporation with one younger employee and one older employee, the majority of the employer contributions will be used to fund the benefit of the older employee, thus leaving the younger employee after the retirement of the older employee with a virtually unfunded benefit and many years of plan funding ahead. These aspects of defined benefit pension plans must be understood and must be carefully applied to a particular small-business setting as part of the initial plan design.

The annual contributions required under a defined benefit pension plan must be determined actuarially and based on factors such as the ages of the participants, the earnings of the trust fund, and inflation. Consequently, the administration of a defined benefit pension plan is normally more costly than that of a profit-sharing plan or a money purchase pension plan.

Except for those defined benefit plans that at no time cover more than 25 active professional participants and that are maintained by employers whose principal businesses are providing services, defined benefit plans

---

[14] IRC § 404(a)(1)(A)(ii). More rapid funding may be allowed under the minimum funding standard. IRC § 404(a)(1)(A)(i).

generally are subject to the Pension Benefit Guaranty Provisions of Title IV of the Employee Retirement Income Security Act (ERISA). The Pension Benefit Guaranty Corporation (PBGC), which administers these provisions of Title IV, acts as an insurer of the pension benefits of plans that are not exempted from its protection.

One commonly used exception to PBGC coverage applies to professional service providers, including employers whose principal business is the performance of professional services and who are owned or controlled by physicians, dentists, chiropractors, osteopaths, optometrists, other licensed practitioners of the healing arts, attorneys, public accountants, public engineers, architects, drafters, actuaries, psychologists, social or physical scientists, and performing artists.[15] However, the PBGC, in a series of opinion letters, has taken the position that the professional service provider exception does not apply to opticians, food brokers, artists, designers, real estate brokers, individuals in advertising and public relations, foresters, and river boat pilots.[16] The rationale of the PBGC in these opinion letters is that these occupational groups are outside the scope of the exception because the occupations involved do not require a prolonged course of specialized intellectual instruction and are not predominantly intellectual in character.

The PBGC exception is valuable to employers because pension plans that are subject to Title IV must pay annual premiums to the PBGC of $8.50 per participant per year. For this purpose, the term *participant* includes all actual participants plus former participants or their beneficiaries who are currently receiving or who have a future right to receive plan benefits.

There are also other important restrictions that apply to defined benefit plans including, for example, the so-called 5717 limitations. The 5717 limitations, which are contained in Treasury Regulations Section 1.401-4(c), restrict the benefits that may be paid to the 25 highest paid employees at the time the plan is established or at the time that plan benefits are increased substantially. The 5717 limitations may have a substantial impact on pension plans of a small business; they generally are effective if a lump-sum distribution is payable with respect to a participant within 10 years after the plan either is established or amended to increase benefits substantially or if the plan either is terminated within its first 10 years or within 10 years of an amendment that substantially increases benefits.

---

[15] Employee Retirement Income Security Act of 1974, Pub. L. No. 93-406, § 4021(c)(2)(B), 818 stat. 829 (1974).

[16] PBGC Opinion Letters 80-9 through 80-15.

Further, if the plan is underfunded within the first 10 years, these limitations may apply beyond 10 years.

The following is a discussion of the several types of defined benefit plans that are available.

Fixed Benefit Plans

Fixed benefit plans generally define a participant's ultimate retirement benefit in terms of a specified percentage of a participant's average monthly compensation for the 3 or 5 highest paid consecutive years of service during the participant's last 10 years of service. However, the participant's entitlement to the benefit generally is phased in over a period of time. For example, if a participant has completed 15 or more years of service by retirement age, then the participant might be entitled at normal retirement age to an annuity for life equal to 25 percent of his or her average monthly compensation for the highest 5 consecutive years of service out of his or her last 10 years of service. If the participant has completed fewer than 15 years of service by normal retirement age, the annuity determined under the immediately preceding sentence might be reduced by one fifteenth for each year of service less than 15 that the participant has then completed. As a *caveat,* however, to the extent that a plan is top-heavy, as discussed later in this chapter, the nonkey employees (nonowners and nonexecutives) must accrue a benefit at least equal to 2 percent of their compensation for each year of service.[17] Thus, top-heavy fixed benefit plans may be unable to offer this advantageous phase-in period.

A fixed benefit plan can be particularly advantageous in a small business where a limited number of employees are in their mid-to-late forties or early fifties and intend to work at least 10 more years. For example, assume that a company has the following employees:

Employee	*Age*	*Years of Service*	*Salary*
Older shareholder	55	20	$100,000
Younger shareholder	30	5	30,000
Staff employee	30	5	10,000

Assume further that the normal retirement benefit formula is 25 percent of a participant's average monthly compensation for the highest 5 consecu-

[17] IRC § 416(c)(1).

tive years of service during the participant's last 10 years of service. Finally, ignoring interest considerations and salary increases, assume that a total of $500,000 will be needed to fund the older shareholder's benefit at age 65, $150,000 will be needed to fund the younger shareholder's benefit at age 65, and $50,000 ultimately will be needed to fund the staff employee's benefit at age 65. Based on these assumptions, $500,000 must be funded over 10 years for the older shareholder; hence, the contribution on behalf of that employee must be $50,000 or 50 percent of his or her annual compensation during each of his or her final 10 years. In contrast, $50,000 must be funded over 35 years for the staff employee, producing an annual contribution of under $1,500, or less than 15 percent of the staff employee's annual compensation.

If an interest assumption is added to this example, the disparity in the contribution levels, expressed as a percentage of compensation, required to fund the older versus the younger shareholder's benefit becomes even more pronounced, since the contributions made on behalf of the younger shareholder will have a much longer period of time to compound interest; hence, even smaller contributions would be needed to fund the younger shareholder's benefit. To illustrate, a dollar invested at an 8 percent return for 10 years will be worth $2.16, while a dollar invested at an 8 percent return for 35 years will be worth $14.79. Admittedly, this example does not conform to accepted actuarial practice; however, it illustrates that a disproportionate percentage of the employer contributions in a fixed benefit plan will be allocated to the older shareholder who is approaching normal retirement date.

Unit Benefit Plans

Unit benefit plans usually define a participant's pension amount by reference to an annually adjusted formula that takes into account both years of service and compensation. As before, top-heavy plans subject to the minimum benefit rules for non-key employees will face greater restrictions than the following discussion indicates.

1. Career Average Unit Benefit Plans. Under this type of plan, each participant is credited with a benefit for each year of service based on the participant's compensation for that particular year of service. For example, assume that a participant who is age 55 when first employed is entitled to a benefit equal to 1 percent of his or her compensation for each year of service. If such participant earns the compensation shown in the first column of the following table, his or her annual benefit accrual and annual pension benefit will be as listed in the second column.

Year	Compensation	Benefit
1	$ 50,000	$ 500
2	55,000	550
3	60,000	600
4	65,000	650
5	70,000	700
6	80,000	800
7	85,000	850
8	90,000	900
9	95,000	950
10	100,000	1,000
Annual pension equals:		$7,500

2. Final Average Unit Benefit Plans. Under this type of plan, each participant is credited with benefits for each year of service, and these benefits are based on a participant's average compensation for a particular period of time, generally the highest 5 consecutive years out of the last 10 years. For example, assume that a benefit formula provides 1 percent for each year of service multiplied by a participant's highest 5 consecutive years of service out of the last 10 years. Assume further that the participant was age 55 when initially employed and worked 10 years and that his or her compensation is as shown in the career average unit benefit plan example above. The average compensation for the highest 5 consecutive years of service out of the last 10 years of service is $90,000. Since this employee has completed 10 years of service he or she will be entitled to an annual pension of 10 percent of $90,000, or $9,000.

A unit benefit plan will principally be advantageous when the shareholders either have, or are expected to have, many years of service. A career average unit benefit plan, as opposed to a final average benefit plan, will serve to avoid both a large unfunded liability and accelerated funding during later years in the event of substantial salary increases, since benefits under a career average plan are determined each year based on each year's income. Of course, as a result, the benefits under a career average unit benefit plan are not likely to keep pace with inflation.

3. Flat Benefit Plans. Benefits under a flat benefit plan are not dependent on a participant's compensation. Under a pure flat benefit plan, the participant will be entitled to a flat monthly pension at normal retirement, such as $200, irrespective of his or her length of service or compensation. Alternatively, the monthly pension at normal retirement may be defined in terms of a specified dollar amount per year of service, for example, $20 multiplied by the participant's years of service. Flat benefit plans usually are adopted only in collectively bargained plans between labor and management.

Choosing between Defined Benefit Pension Plans

In the small-business setting, a fixed benefit plan with a final average formula is usually considered to be the most appropriate type of defined benefit plan. Normally, after careful consideration of personal savings, investments, and anticipated Social Security benefits, an employer will be able to determine the percentage of the employee's income that must be continued after retirement through qualified plan benefits in order to provide adequate retirement security. Since the objective of the small-business owner is the continuation during retirement of that standard of living attained immediately prior to retirement, a final average pay formula usually will be selected. The plan's actuary will make assumptions regarding the anticipated impact of inflation on salaries and, using these assumptions, calculte the level of funding necessary to provide a benefit that anticipates future salary levels. Of course, if several shareholders or owners are involved, a collective decision must be made regarding the benefit level as a percentage of income.

Usually a flat benefit plan approach is completely out of the question for a small-business employer since it fails to take compensation levels into account. A unit benefit plan is a plausible alternative; however, in many cases the owners or controlling shareholders will be uncertain as to how long they will remain in service with the small business, and, in many cases, age differences among the shareholders will result in a wide divergence of opinions as to the ideal level of benefits based on a percentage of salary if this approach is used. For example, older shareholders with shorter periods of total service will want higher unit benefits levels (i.e., 7 to 10 percent per year of service) so as to accrue higher levels of benefits. Younger shareholders, however, who expect to retire with higher total years of service can obtain high levels of benefits using more moderate unit benefit levels (i.e., 2 to 3 percent per year of service).

As previously discussed, defined benefit plans and, in particular, fixed benefit plans that require only a 10- to 15-year minimum period of service for full benefits create a greater funding obligation for the older participants. Acknowledging this fact, the compensation package of older and younger employees may be adjusted equitably after adoption of the qualified pension plan so that the current compensation of younger employees will be reduced as a result of the plan to a lesser extent than the compensation of the older employees. This kind of adjustment can be responsive to the financial realities and the desires of the employees since the younger employees generally want almost all their compensation paid currently while older employees are more cognizant of their retirement needs and, therefore, are more willing to relinquish current compensation to provide for retirement security. In addition, the younger employees often are faced with the personal expenses associated with starting a home and family that the older employees have already experienced. If the younger employees desire to shelter more current compensation than the amount required to fund their defined benefits, adopting a defined contribution plan in addition to the defined benefit plan should be considered. Furthermore, the defined contribution plan may be drafted in such a manner that the older employees are excluded from participation.[18]

Target Benefit Pension Plans

A target benefit plan is technically a defined contribution plan but functionally it operates as a hybrid of a defined contribution plan and a defined benefit plan.[19] Under a target benefit plan, benefits are defined by using formulas similar to those that are incorporated in defined benefit plans. As in the case of defined benefit plans, employer contributions are determined actuarially. However, as with defined contribution plans, the contributions and the earnings and losses thereon are allocated to the individual accounts of the plan participants, and actual pensions are based on the amounts in the respective individual accounts as of retirement. Thus, a target benefit plan is simply a pension plan that sets a "target" benefit that ultimately may or may not be funded by the amount in an individual participant's account. The employer only has an obligation to make the contribution required by the plan formula; the employer has no obligation to make sufficient contributions to produce the actual benefit targeted. The targeted benefit provided under the plan is not a promise to the participant of a fixed benefit since the ultimate benefit that will be paid is simply that amount that is actually in the participant's account.

Four factors should be considered before a small employer adopts a target benefit plan: (1) the PBGC provisions of Title IV of ERISA do not apply to target benefit plans; (2) the 5717 limitations do not apply to target benefit plans; (3) determining whether a target benefit plan discriminates

---

[18] See *James E. Thompson, Jr.*, 74 T.C. 873 (1980).

[19] Rev. Rul. 76-464, 1976-2 C.B. 115.

in favor of the highly compensated employees is sometimes difficult and the resulting need for actuarial allocations may prove quite costly; and (4) the annual addition limitations that apply to target benefit plans are those that apply to defined contribution plans, a significant consideration since the dollar amount limitations were reduced drastically by TEFRA, as noted later in this chapter, and may be significantly less than the contribution that could otherwise be made in a regular defined benefit plan.

Money Purchase Pension Plans

A money purchase pension plan contains a formula that determines the amount of employer contributions to the plan. The amount of contributions is not subject to the employer's discretion and may not be made a function of profits. Amounts contributed to the plan are allocated to participant accounts and no guaranteed benefits exist. Consequently, on retirement, the participant will be entitled only to the benefit that can be purchased with the "money" in his or her account; hence, the term *money purchase*.

Money purchase pension plans typically provide for a contribution based on a stated percentage of a participant's annual compensation. The contribution required under such plans may be integrated with Social Security benefits, subject, of course, to the top-heavy limitations, if applicable. Under the integration formula generally permissible in money purchase pension plans, a maximum differential of 5.7 percent may exist as to contributions on wages below and above the Social Security wage base, provided that the contribution percentage above the wage base does not exceed twice the contribution percentage below the wage base. For example, the employer may contribute 2.85 percent of a participant's compensation below the wage base and 5.7 percent of compensation above the wage base (differential is twice [2 × 2.85 = 5.7] and is less than 5.7 percent [5.7 − 2.85 = 2.85]); or 5.7 percent of compensation below the wage base and 11.4 percent of compensation above the wage base (differential is twice and equal to 5.7 percent); or 7 percent of compensation below the wage base and 12.7 percent above the wage base (differential is less than twice and 5.7 percent). The following table illustrates a fully integrated money purchase pension plan that has a contribution formula of 5.7 percent of compensation up to the Social Security wage base of $43,300 for 1987 plus 11.4 percent of all compensation in excess of that wage base. This table should be compared with the table illustrating the integrated profit-sharing plan presented earlier in this chapter in the "Regular Profit-Sharing Plan" section.

Participant	Compensation	Contribution Allocation
Shareholder	$175,900.00	$17,584.50
Staff employee	12,000.00	684.00
Staff employee	10,000.00	570.00
Staff employee	8,000.00	456.00
Total		$19,294.50

The comparison reveals that the shareholder who is more highly compensated receives 89.0 percent of the total contribution to the integrated profit-sharing plan, yet receives 91.1 percent of the total contribution to the integrated money purchase plan. The staff employee having the least amount of compensation, on the other hand, receives 2.9 percent of the total contribution to the integrated profit-sharing plan, yet only 2.3 percent of the total contribution to the integrated money purchase plan. This differential is not inherent in the comparison of the two types of plans. Rather, it shows that the effect of integration decreases slightly as the size of the total contribution increases.

In considering the adoption of a money purchase pension plan, the employer should note four facts. First, contributions to a money purchase plan are mandatory and are in proportion to compensation. The allocation is similar to the allocation under a profit-sharing plan and stands in contrast to the possibility of disproportionately higher contributions on behalf of higher/paid employees under fixed benefit plans, unit benefit plans, and target benefit plans. Second, neither the PBGC provisions of Title IV of ERISA nor the 5717 limitations apply.[20] Third, a money purchase pension plan is a defined contribution plan for purposes of the annual addition limitation under Section 415 of the Code. Finally, unlike a defined benefit plan for which forfeitures must be applied to reduce future employer contributions, after TRA '86, money purchase forfeitures may be allocated to the accounts of participants.

Combinations of Plans

Defined Contribution Plans

As noted, target benefit plans, money purchase pension plans, and profit-sharing plans are all classified as *defined contribution plans* because benefits are determined by the participant's individual account balance. Under

[20] ERISA, § 4021(b)(1).

Section 415 of the Code, the annual additions that are made to all such plans maintained by one employer on behalf of any participant must be aggregated. The aggregate maximum annual addition must not exceed the lesser of (1) 25 percent of the participant's compensation for the year or (2) $30,000 or, if greater, one quarter of the dollar limitation for defined benefit plans, as discussed later in this chapter.

A combination of defined contribution plans, each requiring contributions of less than the Section 415 limit, often provides an excellent method of maximizing benefits while also maximizing flexibility. For example, if only a profit-sharing plan is maintained, the maximum deductible contribution is limited to 15 percent of compensation paid during the year. Therefore, while the profit-sharing plan provides flexibility, the contribution ceiling under Code Section 415 cannot be fully utilized. On the other hand, an employer could adopt only a money purchase plan having a contribution formula that itself requires the maximum contribution allowed by Section 415; however, the full contribution to the plan will always be required, even in "lean" years, since money purchase plan contributions are mandatory. If, in a given year, the small business experiences cash flow problems and is unable to make the required contribution, a nondeductible excise tax equal to 5 percent of the deficiency will be imposed under Section 4971 of the Code. Moreover, if a timely correction of the deficiency is not made, an additional nondeductible excise tax equal to 100 percent of the deficiency will be imposed. However, exemptions to the funding requirements may be granted by the IRS in situations involving unforeseen business hardships.

To escape these restrictions on single plans, a small business may adopt a money purchase plan requiring the contribution of that part of the total benefit that the employer feels reasonably certain could be paid even in cash-lean years, in tandem with a totally discretionary profit-sharing plan. This combination ameliorates the inflexible funding requirement created by exclusive use of a money purchase plan, yet it avoids the bar on making a full "25 percent of compensation" employer contribution that arises with the exclusive use of a profit-sharing plan. Also, in this scheme, the money purchase plan may be fully integrated so that the employer always will receive the full benefit of integration even for those years in which substantial contributions are not made to the profit-sharing plan.

Defined Benefit and Defined Contribution Plans

If a small-business employer wants to defer more than the 25 percent of compensation or the $30,000 limit applicable to defined contribution plans, then the only alternative is to adopt either a defined benefit plan or a combination of plans that includes both a defined benefit plan and a defined contribution plan.

Any combination of defined benefit and defined contribution plans is subject to a complex mathematical limitation imposed by Code Section 415(e). Basically, an employer is prevented by this subsection from adopting *both* (1) a defined contribution plan or plans providing the *maximum contribution,* that is, 25 percent of compensation or $30,000 and (2) a defined benefit plan or plans providing the *maximum benefit,* that is, $90,000 or 100 percent of the participant's average compensation for his or her high three years.[21] Instead, as the percentage of the defined contribution maximum that is provided by the defined contribution plans increases, the percentage of the defined benefit maximum that may be provided by the defined benefit plans decreases. Prior to TEFRA, this limitation was embodied in the so-called 1.4 Rule; after TEFRA, this limitation is embodied in a "1.0 Rule."[22]

The calculation of these rules is complex; however, the following example illustrates the old 1.4 Rule and the new 1.0 Rule.

Step 1. Assume Employee A is in his first year of service. He earns $60,000; participates in defined benefit and defined contribution plans; prefers to defer $7,500 of income, or 12.5 percent of his compensation, using the defined contribution plan; and wants to defer the maximum amount allowed under a defined benefit plan.

Step 2: Under the Old 1.4 Rule. The old and new rules are based on defined benefit and defined contribution fractions. One of the two fractions is computed first, using certain assumptions about the amount of contributions to that type of plan; thereafter, application of the appropriate "rule" produces the other fraction, from which the permitted amount of contribution to the other type of plan may be calculated. Given the assumptions above, the defined contribution fraction in this case is:

$$\frac{\$\ 7{,}500 \text{ (contribution to defined contribution plan)}}{\$15{,}000 \text{ (maximum according to § 415(c)(1) as amended)}} = .50$$

The 1.4 test: 1.4 − .5 = .90

The defined benefit fraction can equal 0.90.

The calculation of the fraction is:

---

[21] IRC §§ 415(b), 415(c).

[22] IRC §§ 415(e), 416(h).

$$\frac{\$\ X\ \text{(anticipated benefit that employee may fund)}}{\$60{,}000\ \text{(maximum anticipated benefit if employer maintains only a defined benefit plan)}} = .90$$

$$X = \$60{,}000 \times .9 = \$54{,}000$$

Step 3: Conclusion under 1.4 Rule. The employee can fund an anticipated benefit of $54,000 per year using the defined benefit plan.

Step 4: Under the New 1.0 Rule. The defined contribution fraction denominator is the *lesser* of:

a. 1.25 (assuming the plan is not top-heavy) multiplied by $30,000 (the IRC § 415(c)(1)(A) limitation for the year) *or* $37,500; or
b. 1.4 multiplied by $15,000 (the IRC § 415(c)(1)(B) limitation) *or* $21,000.

The fraction is thus:

$$\frac{\$\ 7{,}500\ \text{(amount of contribution to plan)}}{\$21{,}000\ \text{(the maximum amount according to new section 415(c))}} = .357$$

The 1.0 test: 1.0 − .357 = .643.

The defined benefit fraction can equal .643.

The defined benefit fraction denominator is the *lesser* of:

a. 1.25 (since not a top-heavy plan) multiplied by $90,000 (the dollar limitation in effect for the year for defined benefit plans) *or* $112,500; or
b. 1.4 multiplied by $60,000 (the IRC § 415(c)(1)(B) limitation) *or* $84,000.

The calculation of the fraction is thus:

$$\frac{\$\ X\ \text{(anticipated benefit that employee may fund)}}{\$84{,}000\ \text{(maximum anticipated benefit if employer maintains only a defined benefit plan)}} = .643$$

$$X = .643 \times \$84{,}000 = \$54{,}000$$

Step 5: Conclusion under New 1.0 Rule. The employee can fund an anticipated benefit of $54,000 per year using the defined benefit plan.

Clearly, the new 1.0 Rule imposed by TEFRA produces no change from the old 1.4 Rule in the amount of compensation that an employee who earns $60,000 per year may defer. However, the small-business owner's income may be far in excess of $60,000, in which case a substantial difference exists between the old 1.4 Rule and the new 1.0 Rule. Algebraic examination reveals that the new rule severely restricts the ability of an employee or owner/employee earning more than $80,357.14 to defer income using a combination of defined benefit and defined contribution plans. Moreover, as explained later in this chapter, certain top-heavy plans are subject to a more restrictive version of the 1.0 Rule and employees and owner/employees who participate in those plans will be adversely affected if they individually earn more than $64,285.71.

Notwithstanding the 1.0 Rule, if a combination involves a defined benefit plan and one or more money purchase or profit-sharing plans, TRA '86 imposes a further limitation for tax years commencing after 1986. The deductible contributions under the combined plans may not exceed the *greater* of (1) 25 percent of the compensation paid to the plan participants during the year, or (2) the employer contributions required to satisfy the minimum funding standards that are applicable to the defined benefit plan alone. Hence, if a defined benefit plan and a defined contribution plan are maintained by an employer, and if the annual contribution required under the defined benefit plan is equal to 20 percent of the compensation paid to the participants during the year, the deductible contribution for the defined contribution plan will be limited to only 5 percent of the compensation paid to the participants during the year, regardless of such plan's contribution formula. However, any contribution that is not deductible for a given year as the result of this rule may be carried forward and deducted in a subsequent year to the extent that the total contribution deducted in such subsequent period does not exceed 25 percent of participant compensation for that year. However, a 10 percent excise tax will apply each year until the excess contribution has been removed or "used up."

Simplified Pension Plans

The Revenue Act of 1978 established the Simplified Employee Pension (SEP) for years beginning after 1978. Effectively, a SEP is not a qualified plan; rather, it is a plan for contributing to a group of individual retirement accounts (SEP–IRAs).[23] The primary advantage of a SEP is simplicity; it is not subject to most of the government reporting and disclosure requirements that apply to other qualified retirement plans. Generally, SEP ad-

[23] IRC § 408(k).

ministration consists only of filing a single form, Form 5305SEP, with the IRS annually.

A SEP generally must cover every employee who is at least age 21, has performed any service for the employer maintaining the plan during at least three of the immediately preceding five calendar years and has received at least $300 in compensation from the employer for the year. Contributions must be fully vested when made. Only the first $200,000 of a given employee's compensation may be taken into account under the plan, and employer contributions to the SEPs must bear a uniform relationship to the total compensation of each participant. Further, if compensation in excess of $100,000 is taken into account, all eligible SEP participants must receive contributions of not less than 7.5 percent of their compensation.

Effective for tax years beginning after 1986, TRA '86 allows employers with 25 or fewer employees to establish SEPs on a salary reduction basis. Under such an approach, an employee may elect to have the employer make payments to the SEP on his or her behalf (not currently taxable) or to pay such amounts to them in cash (taxable as current income). A salary reduction SEP will be qualified only if at least 50 percent of employees elect to have SEP contributions and the "deferral percentage" for *each* highly compensated employee does not exceed 125 percent of the average "deferral percentage" for employees who are not highly compensated employees. (The terms *deferral percentage* and *highly compensated employees* are described in detail in the next two sections of this chapter).

SPECIFIC QUALIFICATION ASPECTS RELEVANT TO SMALL–BUSINESS EMPLOYERS

Eligibility and Minimum Participation Standards

Section 410 of the Code sets forth the minimum participation standards imposed on all qualified retirement plans. In order to obtain qualified status, a plan may not, as a condition of participation, require that an employee complete a period of service extending beyond the later of reaching age 21 or completing one year of service. Part-time employees working fewer than 1,000 hours during any given year may be indefinitely excluded, even if they are older than 21. Currently, where a plan provides immediate full vesting for all participants, employees may be excluded until they have completed three years of service. (CODAs may only require one year of service). However, for plan years commencing after 1988, TRA '86 reduces the maximum service requirement to two years of service under such circumstances.

A plan must provide that an employee who has satisfied the age and service requirements will participate in the plan no later than the earlier of (1) the first day of the first plan year beginning after the date on which the employee satisfied the requirements, or (2) the date six months after the date on which the employee satisfied the requirements.[24] However, in the interest of simplicity, qualified retirement plans adopted by a small business should provide that participation begins after the completion of one year of service and attainment of age 21 and that participation is retroactive to the first day of the first plan year in which the later of these two requirements is met. Under tax law, for plan years commencing prior to 1989, a defined benefit plan or a target benefit plan may exclude employees who are within five years of normal retirement age when they begin employment.[25] The maximum age provision has been repealed by TRA '86 and, for plan years commencing after 1988, no maximum age exclusion is permitted regardless of plan type.[26] However, recent cases and rulings under the Age Discrimination in Employment Act (ADEA) and the Omnibus Budget Reconciliation Act (OBRA) appear to make use of a maximum age *currently* unlawful.[27]

Code Section 410(b), which specifies minimum eligibility standards for qualified plans, has been substantially amended by TRA '86. Under pre–TRA '86 law, which remains in effect through 1988, a plan must benefit 70 percent or more of all employees or 80 percent or more of the employees who are eligible to benefit if at least 70 percent of all employees are so eligible. A plan that fails to meet one of the two "percentage tests" may qualify as long as the eligibility classifications established by the employer are found by the secretary of the treasury not to be discriminatory in favor of employees who are officers, shareholders, or highly compensated. Normally this classification test is met where the plan covers a reasonable cross-section of employees in all compensation ranges.[28]

Effective for plan years commencing after 1988, the rules of Code

---

[24] IRC § 410(a)(4).

[25] Former IRC § 410(a)(2); Treas. Reg. § 1.410(a)-4(a)(1).

[26] IRC § 410(a)(2).

[27] 29 C.F.R. § 860.120(f)(1)(iv)(A).

[28] *Federal Land Bank Association of Asheville, North Carolina*, 74 T.C. 1106 (1980) (in which a thrift plan in which only 2 of 23 employees participated was held to cover a nondiscriminatory classification).

Section 410(b) are substantially changed by TRA '86. To be qualified, a plan must satisfy one of the following tests:

1. Seventy percent of employees who are not highly compensated employees must be covered by the plan (percentage test).
2. The percentage of employees who are not highly compensated employees covered by the plan must be at least 70 percent of the percentage of highly compensated employees who are covered (ratio test).
3. The plan must have an eligibility classification that does not discriminate in favor of highly compensated employees *and* the average benefit (expressed as a percentage of pay) provided to employees other than highly compensated employees must equal at least 70 percent of the average benefit provided to highly compensated employees.

The term *highly compensated employees* includes employees who, during the year in question or the preceding year (1) were 5 percent owners of the business; (2) earned more than $75,000 or more than $50,000 *and* were among the top 20 percent of employees by pay; *or* (3) were officers of the corporation receiving compensation greater than $45,000 per year.

The minimum eligibility requirements usually do not present a problem for a small business unless groups of related or affiliated small businesses are involved. If there are several such small businesses involved, then an insufficient number of employees may be eligible to participate in each business plan or plans, since Code Sections 414(b), 414(c), and 414(m) provide that all employees of all corporations and partnerships that are members of a controlled or affiliated group are treated as if employed by a single employer.

A major problem in the controlled group context is posed by the definition of a brother-sister controlled group of corporations that is contained in Code Section 1563. Section 414 incorporates this definition for certain qualified plan purposes. The term *brother-sister controlled group of corporations* generally means two or more organizations conducting trades or businesses: (1) if the same five or fewer persons own, singularly or in combination, a controlling interest in each organization; and (2) if, taking into account the ownership of each such person only to the extent such ownership is identical with respect to each such organization, such persons are in effective control of each corporation. The term *controlling interest* means ownership of 80 percent of the total combined voting power of all classes of stock entitled to vote or at least 80 percent of the total value of shares of all classes of stock. The term *effective control* means ownership of stock possessing more than 50 percent of the total combined voting power of all classes of stock entitled to vote or 50 percent of the total value of shares of all classes of stock of such corporation.

In *U.S.* v. *Vogel Fertilizer Co.* [455 U.S. 16, 70 L. Ed. 2d 792, 102 S Ct. 821 (1982)], the U.S. Supreme Court held that for purposes of computing the 80 percent controlling interest, only persons who owned an interest in each tested corporation should be taken into account—a holding that vastly restricts the Service's ability to amalgamate employees of several corporate employers for eligibility test purposes. The following two examples illustrate the interaction of the 50 percent test and the 80 percent test and the restrictive effect of *Vogel.*

Example 1. Mr. A owns 90 percent of corporation X and 55 percent of corporation Y. Ms. B, who is unrelated to Mr. A, owns 10 percent of corporation X and 45 percent of corporation Y.

	80 Percent Controlling Interest Test		*50 Percent Identical Ownership Test*	
	Corporation X	*Corporation Y*	*Corporation X*	*Corporation Y*
Mr. A	90	55	55	55
Ms. B	10	45	10	10
	100	100	65	65

In example one, Mr. A and Ms. B together own 100 percent of both corporations; therefore, the 80 percent controlling interest test is satisfied. Mr. A's identical ownership interest in corporations X and Y is 55 percent, since he owns at least 55 percent of each corporation. Ms. B's identical ownership of corporations X and Y is 10 percent, since she owns at least 10 percent of each corporation. Since the sum of the identical ownership of Mr. A and Ms. B exceeds 50 percent, the 50 percent identical ownership test is met. Since both tests are met, corporations X and Y are brother-sister controlled corporations.

Example 2. Assume the same facts as in example 1 except that Mr. A owns 100 percent of corporation X.

	80 Percent Controlling Interest Test		*50 Percent Identical Ownership Test*	
	Corporation X	*Corporation Y*	*Corporation X*	*Corporation Y*
Mr. A	100	55	55	55
Ms. B	0	45	0	45
	100	100	55	100

At first blush it might appear that both the 80 percent controlling interest test and the 50 percent identical ownership test are satisfied; however, under *Vogel,* Ms. B cannot be taken into account for purposes of applying the 80 percent controlling interest test, because she does not have an interest in each corporation that is being tested under the 80 percent test. As a result, the 80 percent controlling interest test is not satisfied in example 2 and the two corporations are not part of a brother-sister controlled group.

If two or more entities constitute either a controlled group of corporations or trades or businesses under common control, as defined in Code Section 414(b) and (c), respectively, then the rules of Section 401 (qualification standards), Section 410 (participation), Section 411 (vesting), and Section 415 (limitations on benefits and contributions) are applied to all members of the controlled group as if all of the employees worked for the employer adopting the plan. (For purposes of Section 415 limits, the 80 percent ownership requirement for a controlled group is reduced to 50 percent.) The rules under Section 404 (deductions) and Section 412 (funding) generally are applied only with respect to members of the controlled group who adopt the same plan.[29]

As noted, special rules exists under Section 414(m) of the Code that relate to affiliated groups of service corporations; however, these are discussed in Chapter 49.

Vesting and Benefits Accrual

Subject to Section 416 of the Code, which, as discussed later in this chapter, establishes special rules for so-called top-heavy plans, Section 411 of ERISA provides the minimum vesting standards. Prior to 1989, when the vesting rules of TRA '86 are effective, these sections generally authorize the adoption of three types of vesting schedules, two of which have been widely used. The first is so-called *10-year cliff vesting.* A cliff vesting schedule requires full vesting for a participant with at least 10 years of service, but no vesting for a participant with fewer than 10 years of service. The second common pre–TRA '86 statutory vesting schedule is the so-called *5-15–year vesting schedule.* A 5-15–year vesting schedule calls for at least 25 percent vesting after 5 years of service, an additional 5 percent for each of the next 5 years, and 10 percent every year thereafter so that the participant will be 100 percent vested after 15 years of service. The third pre–TRA '86 statutory vesting schedule, known as *the rule of*

[29] G.C.M. 39208, Dec. 28, 1983.

45, generally requires 50 percent vesting when a participant completes at least 5 years of service *and* the sum of his or her age and service equals or exceeds 45, with an additional 10 percent for each year thereafter until 100 percent vested.

Notwithstanding these statutory vesting schedules, the Service has required that professional corporations use the so-called *4-40 vesting schedule* unless it can be shown that the turnover rate of highly paid employees is not appreciably lower than the turnover rate among the rank and file employees.[30] The 4-40 vesting schedule calls for vesting as described below:

Years of Service	*Nonforfeitable Percentage*
1	0
2	0
3	0
4	40
5	45
6	50
7	60
8	70
9	80
10	90
11	100

During 1980, the Service made a concerted attempt to enforce vesting schedules that are significantly more restrictive than the 4-40 schedule. Specifically, it tried to enforce a three-year vesting schedule for closely held and professional corporations where the owners typically do not terminate their employment. There is, however, specific authority in the legislative history of ERISA that vesting at a rate more rapid than the 4-40 rate is not required, notwithstanding a substantial turnover rate among staff employees, unless there is actual misuse in operation of vesting to deny participants' accrued benefits.[31]

Effective for plan years commencing after 1988, TRA '86 replaces the three statutory vesting schedules just described (10-year cliff vesting, 5–15 vesting, and rule of 45) with two more restrictive schedules. The first of

---

[30] See Rev. Proc. 75-40, 1975-2 C.B. 571, as modified by Rev. Proc. 76-11, 1976-1 C.B. 550.

[31] House Committee on Ways and Means, Brief Summary of the Provisions of H.R. 12481, 93 Cong., 2nd. sess. 3 (February 5, 1974).

these, *five-year cliff vesting,* requires that a participant be 100 percent vested on his or her completion of five years of service. The second schedule is *3-7–year graded vesting*. The 3-7–year graded schedule requires that participants be 20 percent vested after completing three years of service and receive an additional 20 percent for each year thereafter until 100 percent vested after seven years of service.

The vesting schedule is obviously an inducement to employees to continue employment until they are fully vested. If a participant's employment is terminated before he or she is fully vested, benefits that are forfeited either will be distributed to the advantage of the other participants under the plan or will serve to reduce the employer contributions. Forfeitures may be substantial if the employee turnover rate is high.

Assuming that the accelerated vesting schedules applicable to top-heavy plans are not applicable, the authors feel that the 3-7–year graded vesting schedule is appropriate and should be adopted for most small businesses, unless a shorter vesting schedule is desired. The 3-7–year graded schedule should provide a sufficient deferral period during the first three years of employment to eliminate short-term employees from the vesting rules, and the schedule should provide vesting that will induce employees to remain with the employer for at least four years of employment.

Past Service

Past service with former employers may be used for determining eligibility to participate in a qualified retirement plan, for benefit accrual, and for vesting of benefits. At one time, the Service maintained that past service as a self-employed individual (partner or sole proprietor) could not be counted for purposes of a plan adopted by a corporate successor of the unincorporated business. The Service was unsuccessful with this position in litigation,[32] and it now acknowledges that a corporate qualified plan may include service with a prior partnership or as a sole proprietor for purposes of participation, vesting, and benefit accrual.[33]

Until 1980, the Service had maintained that, if past service credit was given for purposes of benefit accrual in a defined benefit plan, then the plan provisions giving past service credit had to prohibit "duplication of benefits," the crediting of benefits under two plans simultaneously.[34] In

---

[32] *Farley Funeral Home,* 62 T.C. 150 (1974).

[33] Tech. Advice Memo. 7742003.

[34] See Rev. Rul. 62-139, 1962-2 C.B. 123, Rev. Rul. 72-531, 1972-2 C.B. 221.

Rev. Rul. 80-349,[35] the Service reversed its position on prevention of "duplication of benefits"; however, the ruling implies that where duplication of benefits does exist it may result in discrimination, thereby disqualifying the plan.

The Service also takes the position that the use of prior service for purposes of eligibility, vesting, and benefit accrual is subject to the nondiscrimination rules. Using prior service may disqualify a plan where no staff employees received past service credit for their service with a former employer, or possibly where none of the existing staff employees were employed with the former employer.[36] Consequently, the authors generally do not recommend that past service credit be granted for service with predecessor employers unless there are also staff employees who were employed by the predecessor organization.

Integration with Social Security Benefits

In computing contributions to a qualified retirement plan, the Service generally permits an employer in a nontop-heavy plan to take into consideration its contributions to the Social Security system. For example, in 1987 an employer will pay a Social Security tax equal to 7.20 percent of the first $43,300 of compensation paid for each employee. Since Social Security taxes theoretically are used to fund an employee's government-sponsored retirement benefit, a somewhat lower contribution or benefit may be provided under a qualified plan with respect to a participant's compensation below the Social Security wage base. This concept of taking into account Social Security taxes when computing contributions or benefits under a qualified plan is known as "integration." Although TRA '86 reduces the cost-saving effect of integration, the authors feel that small businesses should always consider adopting integrated plans and should not hesitate to do so where a desirable cost-savings can be achieved.[37]

The rules governing Social Security integration are provided under Code Sections 401(a)(5) and 401(1), Treasury Regulations Section 1.401-3(e), and Revenue Ruling 71-446.[38] Profit-sharing plans and money purchase pension plans are generally integrated with the Social Security

---

[35] 1980-2 C.B. 132.

[36] *See* Rev. Rul. 69-409, 1969-2 C.B. 98.

[37] For a complete discussion of integration, see para. 19.056 et. seq. of Prentice-Hall *Federal Taxes*.

[38] 1971-2 C.B. 187.

wage base using an integration factor equal to the Old-Age, Survivors, and Disability Insurance (OASDI) contribution rate, which is 5.7 for 1987. Thus, in both a money purchase pension plan and in a profit-sharing plan, the account of each participant may be credited with a contribution equal to 5.7 percent of the compensation earned by the participant during the plan year that was in excess of the Social Security wage base. Any contribution in excess of the amount allocated under the preceding sentence is then allocated to the accounts of all participants in an amount equal to a uniform percentage of all compensation earned.

Effective for plan years beginning after 1988, TRA '86 adds another requirement to integrated money purchase and profit-sharing plans. Such plans will then only be integrated properly where, in addition to the rule described above, the contribution rate below the wage base is at least 50 percent of the contribution rate above the wage base.[39]

A defined benefit pension plan is properly integrated with Social Security if the benefits provided by the plan, when added to the benefits provided by the employer-financed portion of Social Security, result in a combined benefit that is a uniform percentage of the compensation paid by the employer to each participant in the plan. Basically, there are three types of integrated defined benefit plans: excess plans, step-rate plans, and offset plans.

Excess Plans

An excess plan pays a benefit based solely on an employee's compensation in excess of a certain amount, referred to as the plan's *integration level*. The plan provides proportionately greater benefits to higher paid participants since a greater proportion of their compensation will exceed the integration level. For example, if participant A's compensation is $10,000 and participant B's compensation is $20,000, a nonintegrated defined benefit plan could provide a benefit to B that is no greater than twice the benefit provided to A. However, if the plan is integrated at an integration level of $8,000, then only $2,000 of A's compensation and $12,000 of B's compensation is taken into account in computing the benefits and, therefore, the plan can provide a benefit to B that is up to 6 times greater than the benefit provided to A. In this example, if A's compensation had been less than the $8,000 integration level, A would not accrue any benefit.

The *maximum integration level* for an individual is determined by averaging the Social Security wage bases in effect during the individual's

---

[39] IRC § 401(1) as amended by TRA '86 § 1111.

working career. Since the Social Security wage base has increased over past years, and will no doubt continue to increase in the future, a plan's integration level may be drafted to automatically increase with the Social Security wage base.

Once a permissible integration level has been determined, the second critical variable to be determined is the *integration rate*. The integration rate is the retirement benefit provided by the plan, expressed as a percentage of compensation, that is in excess of the integration level. The range of permissible integration rates will depend on whether the plan is a *fixed benefit* plan or a *unit benefit* plan.

In an integrated fixed benefit plan, the benefit is normally expressed as a fixed percentage of the excess of the final average compensation over the integration level. For example, assume that a plan provided a defined benefit equal to (1) the excess of average compensation for the last five years of participation over $8,000 (2) multiplied by 25 percent. This integrated benefit represents an *integration level* of $8,000 and an *integration rate* of 25 percent. The greatest *integration rate* permitted for a fixed benefit plan that provides no benefit other than a life annuity at age 65 is 37.5 percent. (As described later in this section, however, TRA '86 imposes further limits in this regard after 1988). If a participant has fewer than 15 years of service with the employer maintaining the plan, this 37.5 rate may be phased in no more rapidly than 2.5 percent per year. Thus, for example, if a participant retires with only eight years of service with the employer, the greatest integration rate that may be used for the participant will be eight times 2.5 percent or 20 percent.

A participant's compensation with respect to which a fixed benefit plan's integrated benefit is determined normally must be averaged over a period of at least five consecutive years. This is to prevent the creation of a large integrated benefit based on only one or two years' compensation.[40]

As explained earlier in this chapter, a *unit benefit plan* provides a unit of benefit for each year of service. An integrated unit benefit excess plan provides a unit of benefit equal to the excess of compensation over the plan's integration level multiplied by the plan's integration rate. Thus, for example, if the benefit equaled (1) the average compensation in the last five years of service in excess of $8,000 (2) multiplied by .5 percent (3) multiplied by the years of service, then the *integration level* would be $8,000 and the *integration rate* would be .5 percent. The maximum permissible integration rate is 1.0 percent for final average unit benefit plans providing solely a straight life annuity at age 65 (except as explained later

---

[40] IRC § 401(a)(5)(D).

in this section). Such a plan may use an integration level determined in the same manner as for fixed benefit plans. The maximum permissible integration rate for a career average unit benefit plan is 1.4 percent and the integration level for such a plan may not exceed the Social Security wage base in each year for which benefits are accrued. Thus, for *each* year of service, a participant may earn a benefit equal to 1.4 percent of the excess of compensation earned in that year over the Social Security wage base in effect for that year.

If a plan provides benefits other than a straight-life annuity beginning at age 65, then the integration rate for either fixed benefit or unit benefit plans must be reduced. This reduction will be required, for example, if there is a preretirement death benefit, if early retirement before age 65 is permitted, or if the retirement benefit is other than a single-life annuity. These reduction factors are rather complex; however, the important fact for an individual contemplating adoption of an integrated plan to bear in mind is that, in order to add benefits other than an annuity for life beginning at age 65, the maximum permitted *integration rate* will normally decrease.

The *excess plan* integration rules just described for both *fixed benefit* and *unit benefit* plans are further complicated by TRA '86. Effective for plan years commencing after 1988, the benefit rate below the wage base may not be less than 50 percent of the benefit rate above the wage base. Further, the maximum excess benefit percentage may not exceed .75 percent multiplied by the participant's total years of service taken into account under the plan, up to 35 years. Thus, for example, a participant who retires with 24 years of service, could receive a maximum *excess only* benefit of 18 percent (24 years of service × .75 percent) of compensation over the relevant integration level and, in such case, would have to receive an additional benefit equal to 9 percent (50 percent × 18 percent excess benefits) of compensation below such integration level.

Step-Rate Plans

A fixed benefit or unit benefit plan that provides an *integrated* benefit based on compensation in excess of the plan's integration level may, *in addition,* provide a nonintegrated benefit for compensation above *or* below the integration level. Such plans are referred to as step-rate plans, and can be thought of as a combination of an integrated excess plan and a nonintegrated plan. For example, a fixed benefit plan could provide, as a sole benefit, a straight-life annuity beginning at age 65 of 30 percent of a participant's final five years average pay up to $8,000 plus 67.5 percent (56.25 percent after 1988) of his or her final five years average pay in excess of $8,000, provided he or she retired with at least 35 years of service. This formula is acceptable since it provides the same benefit as an integrated excess plan paying 37.5 percent (26.25 percent after 1988) of compensation in excess of $8,000 *plus* a nonintegrated plan paying 30 percent of total compensation.

Offset Plans

An offset plan establishes a defined benefit under which no participant and no part of a participant's compensation is excluded because of a minimum compensation level. However, the benefit so determined is then reduced or "offset" by a percentage of the participant's Social Security benefit. For example, a fixed benefit offset plan could provide a benefit equal to (1) 25 percent of a participant's final five years' average pay (2) *minus* one half of the participant's OASDI pension. The maximum permitted percentage offset for a plan that provides only a straight-life annuity at age 65 is an offset of 83⅓ percent of the participant's Social Security benefit. As with excess plans, when the offset plan benefits provided are other than a straight-life annuity beginning at age 65, the maximum permissible percentage offset must be reduced.

Effective for plan years beginning after 1988, TRA '86 further restricts the degree to which defined benefits may be offset by Social Security benefits. Generally, Social Security offsets may not reduce a benefit by more than 50 percent of the amount of the benefit that would have otherwise accrued under the plan. Further, the maximum offset allowance percentage may not exceed .75 percent multiplied by the participant's years of service taken into account under the plan, up to 35 years.

Payment of Benefits

Benefits normally become payable under qualified retirement plans on retirement, the termination of employment prior to retirement, disability, or death. The vesting schedule established under the plan generally will apply only to benefits payable on termination of employment prior to the normal retirement dates. On death, disability, or attainment of normal retirement age, participants must be fully vested. In drafting qualified retirement plans for a small business, questions often arise with regard to when benefits should be paid to employees who terminate employment prior to reaching normal retirement age. Some retirement plans provide, and some advisers recommend, that qualified retirement plans actually be *retirement* plans and that benefits should be postponed until actual retirement. Under this arrangement, an employee who terminates participation at age 30 must wait until either the normal or early retirement date established under the plan before benefits are received. Those employers who utilize this approach maintain that it prevents employees who leave the business from immediately receiving their benefits and using them to fund a competing business.

Although providing retirement benefits for participants and prohibiting competition by departing employees are important, the authors feel that benefit payments usually should be made to terminating participants as soon after termination as possible. If the payment of benefits is held until retirement age, terminated employees will remain participants under the plan and must be furnished with annual reports and other documents required under the reporting and disclosure regulations. Paying vested benefits to terminated participants also should eliminate the proliferation of partially vested participants that will normally occur over the years as turnover occurs in a small business.

Following the passage of ERISA, various rules have been enacted with regard to providing survivorship annuities to married participants under qualified retirement plans so as to protect them from premature loss of retirement benefits due to death. The most recent of such rules were included in the Retirement Equity Act of 1984 (REA). Generally, a plan will only be qualified if it provides married participants with *both* (1) a *qualified joint and survivor annuity,* as the normal form of retirement benefit, and (2) a *qualified preretirement survivor annuity,* in the event of the participant's death prior to benefit commencement. However, these rules do not generally apply to profit-sharing plans if the participants thereunder cannot elect benefits in the form of a *life annuity*.

A life annuity means an annuity that requires the survival of an annuitant thereunder as one of the conditions for payment. For example, an annuity that makes payments for the duration of the participant's life, and an annuity that makes payments until the earlier of 10 payments or the participant's death both constitute life annuities and would invoke the qualified joint and survivor annuity and qualified preretirement survivor annuity requirements in a profit-sharing plan. However, an annuity for a period of 30 years certain is not a life annuity and would not cause the joint and survivor provisions to apply to the plan.[41]

While the annuity rules provide protection to participants and their spouses, they can be very burdensome on plan administrators. Since, in practice, the authors have found most small businesses have overlooked the notice and election requirements of the joint and survivor annuity regulations, they generally recommend that profit-sharing plans of small business not include an annuity option. While this approach avoids the qualified annuity requirements, the authors feel that employees will not be

---

[41] IRC § 401(a)(11) and Treas. Reg. § 1.401(a)-11.

prejudiced since they are still in a position to obtain an annuity, if one is desired, by rolling over a lump-sum distribution of their account into an individual retirement account or an individual retirement annuity as permitted under Section 402(a)(5) of the Code. If a rollover is made, the participant will not be taxed on the initial distribution of funds from the plan prior to the rollover but, instead, will only be taxed on subsequent distributions from the individual retirement account or annuity.

Code Section 417(b) defines a qualified joint and survivor annuity as an annuity that is the actuarial equivalent of a single-life annuity for the participant, makes payments for the participant's life, and also pays a survivor's benefit for the life of the spouse (if the spouse survives the participant) that is at least 50 percent of the primary annuity payment. Where required, a qualified joint and survivor annuity *must* be the normal form of benefit paid under a plan unless *both* the participant and the participant's spouse elect otherwise in writing.

A qualified preretirement survivor annuity is designed to protect the surviving spouse of a participant who dies prior to retiring. Upon the preretirement death of a participant, the surviving spouse must receive lifetime annuity payments that are at least equal to the survivor benefits that he or she would have received had the participant commenced the receipt of plan benefits in the form of a qualified joint and survivor annuity one day prior to dying. As with the qualified joint and survivor annuity, a qualified preretirement survivor annuity *must* be provided unless the participant and the spouse elect otherwise in writing.

TOP–HEAVY RULES

One of the most radical changes to pension law that was invoked by TEFRA was the creation of the top-heavy plan concept. TEFRA Section 240 added Section 416 to the Code, effective for years beginning after December 31, 1983. Code Section 416(a) states that a trust is not a qualified trust if it is a part of a top-heavy plan unless the plan meets certain additional requirements, as discussed below. Before the top-heavy rules can be understood, however, several key terms that are applicable to top-heavy plans must be defined.

Top-Heavy Terminology

Key Employee

Key employee means a plan participant who at anytime during *a current plan year or the last four immediately preceding plan years* was: (1) an officer with compensation in excess of $45,000, (2) one of the 10 employees holding the largest ownership interest in the employer, (3) a 5 percent owner of the employer, or (4) a 1 percent owner of the employer receiving annual compensation of more than $150,000 from the employer.[42] Unlike the $45,000 level for officers, the $150,000 compensation figure for 1 percent owners is not adjusted for cost-of-living increases.[43] Treasury Regulations issued under Section 416 also provide that, for example, if 20 people have equal ownership of all of a corporation's stock, then all 20 are key employees because all are holders of the "largest interest in the employer."[44]

Employees
Not surprisingly, self-employed individuals, as defined in Code Section 401(c)(1), are treated as employees—an implicit "price" for the establishment of parity between corporate and noncorporate plans—and the earned income of self-employed individuals constitutes their "compensation" for purposes of computing their status as key employees.[45] Moreover, the terms *employee* and *key employee* include the beneficiaries of such persons.[46]

Officers
The number of employees who are treated as officers is limited to the lesser of: (1) 50 or (2) the greater of 3 employees or 10 percent of all employees.[47] The Conference Report on TEFRA states that if an employer has more officers than are required to be counted as key employees, then only those officers with the highest compensation are to be considered in applying the top-heavy rules.[48] The Conference Report relies on prior authority to define *officer*.[49] Thus, although all of the facts and circumstances are to be considered in determining whether a particular employee is an officer, several key facts that must be considered are:

---

[42] IRC § 416(i)(1)(A).

[43] Ibid.

[44] Treas. Reg. § 1.416-1, T-12.

[45] IRC § 416(i)(3).

[46] IRC § 416(i)(5); Treas. Reg. § 1.416-1, T-12.

[47] IRC § 416(i)(1).

[48] S. REP. NO. 530, 97th Cong., 2nd. sess. 626 (1982). See Treas. Reg. § 1.416-1, T-14.

[49] S. REP. NO. 530, 97th Cong., 2nd. Sess. 626, n. 1 (1982) (Citing Rev. Rul. 80-314, 1980-2 C.B. 152).

the source of the employee's authority; the term of service; the nature and extent of his or her duties; and whether the employee is characterized fairly as an administrative executive engaged in regular and continued service.[50] For years beginning after February 28, 1985, noncorporate business organizations may have officers.[51]

Ownership

Ownership, for purposes of Code Section 416, is defined specifically and in a complex fashion. If the employer is a corporation, ownership, for purposes of the 1 percent owner and 5 percent owner rules, means (1) ownership of either 1 percent or 5 percent of the stock of the corporation or (2) ownership of stock possessing more than 1 percent or 5 percent of the total combined voting power of all stock of the corporation. If the employer is not a corporation, ownership means possession of 1 percent or 5 percent of the capital or profits interest of the employer.[52] The constructive ownership rules of Code Section 318 generally apply in determining the ownership percentage of corporate employees. The "from entity" rules of Section 318 are altered, however, such that if 5 percent of a corporation's stock is owned by a potential key employee (instead of 50 percent as usual) then the proportionate share of the corporation's holdings of the plan employer's stock is attributed to the employer.[53] The Conference Report and Code require the secretary of the treasury to issue regulations that define *constructive ownership* as it pertains to *noncorporate employers,* and that are based on principles similar to the Code Section 318 regulations.[54] While Code Section 318 rules are used in determining ownership by employees, the Section 414 aggregation rules are not used in calculating ownership.[55]

Determination Date

Determination date means the last day of the preceding plan year or the last day of the first plan year.[56]

---

[50] Treas. Reg. § 1.416-1, T-13.

[51] Treas. Reg. § 1.416-1, T-15.

[52] IRC § 416(i)(1)(B).

[53] IRC § 416(i)(1)(B)(iii)(I).

[54] IRC § 416(i)(1)(B)(iii)(II); S. REP. NO. 530, 97th Cong., 2nd. sess. 626 (1982).

[55] IRC § 416(i)(1)(C).

[56] IRC § 416(g)(4)(C).

What Is a Top-Heavy Plan?

A defined benefit plan is a top-heavy plan if "the present value of the cumulative accrued benefits under the plan for key employees exceeds 60 percent of the present value of the cumulative accrued benefits under the plan for all employees" on the determination date.[57] The "present value" aspect of the calculation means that the benefits are treated as if they were accrued in a defined contribution plan.[58] A defined contribution plan is a top-heavy plan if "the aggregate of the accounts of key employees under the plan exceeds 60 percent of the aggregate of the accounts of all employees under such plan" on the determination date.[59] Treasury Regulations state that only accrued benefits attributable to deductible employee contributions are excluded from the computation of accrued benefits.[60]

A plan is also top-heavy if it is part of a top-heavy group. First, the proper grouping of plans must be determined. Two types of plans *must* be aggregated (mandatory aggregation): plans in which any of the employer's key employees participate and plans that are grouped by the employer to meet the coverage and discrimination tests of Code Sections 401(a)(4) and 410(b).[61] As discussed in Chapter 49, the Conference Report states that the top-heavy group rule applies to affiliated service groups, as well as the other Section 414 groups of related employees that were discussed earlier.[62]

The employer also *may* aggregate plans with a top-heavy group (permissive aggregation) in an attempt to destroy the top-heavy group classification as long as the new aggregated group satisfies the coverage and nondiscrimination requirements.[63] A group of plans is a top-heavy group if the sum of "the present value of the cumulative accrued benefits for key employees under all defined benefit plans included in such group" and "the aggregate of the accounts of key employees under all defined contri-

---

[57] IRC § 416(g)(1)(A)(i).

[58] See Treas. Reg. § 1.416-1, T-25 for a discussion of how the present value of accrued benefits is determined for a defined benefit plan.

[59] IRC § 416(g)(1)(A)(ii). See Treas. Reg. § 1.416-1, T-24, for a discussion of how the present value of accrued benefits is determined for a defined contribution plan.

[60] Treas. Reg. § 1.416-1, T-28.

[61] IRC § 416(g)(2)(A)(i); Treas. Reg. § 1.416-1, T-1, T-6.

[62] S. REP. NO. 530, 97th Cong., 2nd Sess. 625 (1982).

[63] IRC § 416(g)(2)(A)(ii); S. REP. NO. 530, 97th Cong., 2nd Sess. 625 (1982); Treas. Reg. § 1.416-1, T-7.

bution plans included in such group'' exceeds 60 percent of the same sum computed for all employees.[64]

Impact of Top-Heavy Rules

The consequences of being a top-heavy plan are severe. Aside from the 1.0 Rule discussed earlier, several restrictions exist on top-heavy plans.

First, only $200,000 of an employee's annual compensation during top-heavy years may be considered in computing plan benefits or contributions. Originally, the $200,000 limit was to be subject to a cost-of-living adjustment beginning in 1986.[65] However, effective for years beginning after 1988, TRA '86 requires all plans (top-heavy or otherwise) to disregard compensation in excess of $200,000 and, correspondingly, repeals this aspect of the top-heavy rules.

Second, a top-heavy plan must vest accrued benefits derived from employer contributions according to one of two vesting schedules.[66]

1. *Three-year cliff vesting,* in which the benefits of an employee who has three years of service are 100 percent vested.
2. *Six-year graded vesting* according to the following chart:

Years of Service	*Nonforfeitable Percent*
2	20%
3	40
4	60
5	80
6 or more	100

Again, however, the accelerated vesting schedules that TRA '86 imposes for plan years commencing after 1988 make this top-heavy rule of dubious significance for most plans.

Third, a top-heavy defined benefit plan must provide an annual retirement benefit derived from employer contributions to nonkey employees that at least equals the lesser of (1) 2 percent of the participant's average compensation per year of service or (2) 20 percent, multiplied by the

---

[64] IRC § 416(g)(2)(B).

[65] Former IRC § 416(d).

[66] See IRC § 416(b).

employee's average annual compensation during his or her highest consecutive five years.[67] Social Security benefits originating from an employer's contribution to the Social Security system *cannot* be integrated to reduce the minimum benefit.[68]

For defined contribution plans, the employer must contribute on behalf of nonkey employees at least the smaller of (1) 3 percent of the employee's compensation or (2) the highest percentage contribution made on behalf of any key employee.[69] As before, Social Security benefits arising from employer contributions to the Social Security system *cannot* be used to reduce the minimum contribution.[70]

The rule that allows minimum contributions on behalf of nonkey employees merely to equal the highest percentage contribution on behalf of any key employee (instead of requiring such contributions to equal at least 3 percent) obviously creates the potential for abuse in the case of employers sponsoring two or more plans. To prevent this abuse, Code Section 416 requires use of the 3 percent rule if the defined contribution plan enables a defined benefit plan that is required to be included in a top-heavy group to meet the coverage and antidiscrimination rules of Code Sections 401(a)(4) and 410. Moreover, all defined contribution plans that are required to be included in a top-heavy group are treated as one plan.[71]

If an employer provides both a defined benefit and defined contribution plan to an employee, then the employee is not entitled to both minimum benefits.[72]

Finally, as noted earlier, if a small business maintains a defined contribution plan and a defined benefit plan, the new 1.0 Rule is applicable.[73] The required mathematical changes in the 1.0 Rule formula generally mean that the maximum contribution and benefits for employees earning over $64,285.71 annually be severely reduced.

Depending on the circumstances, the consequences of having a plan characterized as top-heavy may be harsh and quite expensive. Accordingly, care must be taken to avoid top-heavy status whenever possible and, when not possible, to react in the most advantageous manner.

---

[67] IRC § 416(c)(1); Treas. Reg. § 1.416-1, M-2 through M-6.

[68] IRC § 416(e); Treas. Reg. § 1.416-1, M-11.

[69] IRC § 416(c)(2); Treas. Reg. § 1.416-1, M-7 through M-10.

[70] IRC § 416(e); Treas. Reg. §1.416-1, M-11.

[71] IRC § 416(c)(2)(B)(ii).

[72] Treas. Reg. § 1.416-1, M-8.

[73] IRC § 416(h)(i).

SECTION 401(k) CASH–DEFERRED/SALARY REDUCTION PLANS

In a survey of major U.S. companies by Hewitt & Associates, two thirds of the 150 companies surveyed stated that they intended to provide, probably would provide, or favored providing a cash-deferred/salary reduction plan for the benefit of their employees.[74] These plans are sanctioned by Section 401(k) of the Internal Revenue Code as interpreted by several regulations. Any employer who is considering adopting a Section 401(k) plan should understand the basic elements of such a plan and the restrictions on employer and employee contributions to such a plan.

Basic Elements of a Cash-Deferred/Salary Reduction Plan

A Section 401(k) plan is distinguished by a cash or deferred option. The proposed regulations for that Section allow two types of cash or deferred options.[75]

Salary Reduction Agreement Plans

The proposed regulations specifically allow a Section 401(k) plan to be in the form of a salary reduction agreement between an eligible employee and the employer. Under a salary reduction agreement plan, a contribution is made by the employer to the employee's account only if the employee elects to reduce his or her compensation or to forgo an increase in his or her compensation equal to the contribution.[76] A salary reduction agreement plan may provide for contributions by the employer and the employee other than those subject to the salary reduction agreement.

Election Plans

The proposed regulations also authorize a plan under which an eligible employee elects either to have his or her employer contribute an amount to the plan or to have the employer pay that amount to the employee in cash.[77] Again, the plan may provide for contributions by both the employer and the employee other than those subject to the election.

---

[74] 390 Pens. Rep. (BNA) 621 (1982).

[75] Prop. Reg. § 1.401(k)-1(a).

[76] Prop. Reg. § 1.401(k)-1(a)(1).

[77] Ibid.

The proposed regulations limit the cash or deferred option to profit-sharing or stock bonus plans.[78] Of course, the plan and the trust that implements the plan must meet the general requirements of the Code for tax-favored treatment under Sections 401(a) and 501(a) of the Code.

Discrimination Restrictions on Contributions to Cash-Deferred/Salary Reduction Plans

The Code generally discourages discrimination between lower paid employees and other employees by imposing several coverage and discrimination requirements on *all* qualified retirement plans. If a cash-deferred plan consists only of *elective contributions,* then the plan satisfies the coverage and discrimination requirements imposed by the Code if the plan either satisfies the general discrimination requirements imposed by Code Section 410(b)(1) and Code Section 401(a)(4) *or* satisfies the special cash or deferred discrimination rules discussed below. Effective in 1987, TRA '86 restricts the annual amount of a participant's *elective contribution* to $7,000. If a plan consists of both *elective contributions* and *nonelective contributions,* then the plan may satisfy the coverage and discrimination requirement if the nonelective portion of the plan satisfies the general requirements of Code Section 410(b)(1) and Code Section 401(a)(4) and if the combined elective and nonelective portions of the plan satisfy the special cash or deferred discrimination rules discussed below.[79] *Nonelective contributions* are those that are not subject to the cash or deferred election.

The General Coverage Requirement of Section 401(b)(1)
As noted earlier, this Section provides that a plan will qualify for favorable tax treatment only if one of the percentage tests specified therein is met. Also noted above, TRA '86 has imposed new, more rigorous tests that will come into effect in 1989.

The Nondiscrimination Requirement of Section 401(a)(4)
Prior to 1989, this Section provides that a retirement plan will qualify for favorable tax treatment only if the contributions or benefits provided thereunder do not discriminate in favor of officers, shareholders, or highly compensated individuals. Effective in 1989, this test is applied in terms of *highly compensated employees,* as defined in Code Section 414(q).

---

[78] Ibid.

[79] Prop. Reg. § 1.401(k)-1(b)(2)(iii).

Special Cash or Deferred Discrimination Rules

In a cash-deferred/salary reduction plan, special discrimination rules apply. However, before these rules can be understood, the following terms must be defined.

Actual deferral percentage. The actual deferral percentage of any employee is the amount of employer contributions paid under the plan on behalf of that employee during a plan year divided by the employee's compensation for such period. The actual deferral percentage for either the group of highly compensated employees or for a group of other employees is the average of those separately determined ratios.[80]

Highly compensated employee. A highly compensated employee is defined in Code Section 414(q) and generally includes (1) 5 percent owners, (2) employees earning more than $75,000, or more than $50,000 and are among the top 20 percent of employees by pay, or (3) officers of the corporation who receive compensation in excess of $45,000 per year.

There are two actual deferral percentage tests under Code Section 401(k), *either* of which must be met for a cash or deferred plan to meet the special nondiscrimination rules.

1. The actual deferral percentage for the group of highly compensated employees is not more than the actual deferred percentage for *all* other eligible employees multiplied by 1.25.
2. The actual deferral percentage for the group of highly compensated employees is not more than the actual deferred percentage for all other eligible employees multiplied by 2.0 *and* does not exceed such other actual deferred percentage by more than 2 percentage points.[81]

If the cash or deferred plan does not meet either test for a given year, the plan will be disqualified unless the excess contributions for the highly compensated employees are distributed prior to the close of the following plan year or are treated as nondeductible employee contributions.[82]

---

[80] IRC § 401(k)(3)(B).

[81] IRC § 401(k)(3)(A)(ii).

[82] IRC § 401(k)(8).

Example of a Cash-Deferred/Salary Reduction Plan that Satisfies the Special Cash or Deferred Discrimination Rules

Assume that X Corporation has six employees who are all eligible to participate in the X Corporation cash-deferred/salary reduction plan. The employees earn the following compensation:

Employee	*Compensation*	*Shareholder*	*Officer*
A	$100,000	50%	Yes
B	100,000	50	Yes
C	50,000	–0–	No
D	50,000	–0–	No
E	50,000	–0–	No
F	50,000	–0–	No

Employees A and B are highly compensated employees while employees C, D, E, and F are not. Assume further that X Corporation, *as a nonelective employer contribution,* contributes 2 percent of each employee's compensation to the plan. That is, each employee receives the following nonelective employer contributions:

Employee	*Compensation*	*Nonelective Employer Contribution*	*Percentage of Compensation*
Highly compensated employees			
A	$100,000	$2,000	2%
B	100,000	2,000	2
Other eligible employees			
C	50,000	1,000	2
D	50,000	1,000	2
E	50,000	1,000	2
F	50,000	1,000	2

Now assume that employee C enters into a salary reduction agreement with X Corporation by which she elects to contribute $1,000 to the plan from her compensation. Employee D also chooses to reduce his salary by $1,000 and makes a $1,000 contribution to the plan. As to the employees who are not highly compensated employees, the chart below illustrates the actual deferral percentage for such lower paid group. As noted, the actual deferral percentage for the group of lower paid employees is the average of the ratios, calculated separately for each employee in such group, of the amount of employer contributions paid under the plan on behalf of each such employee to the employee's compensation for such plan year.

Lower Paid Employees	*Compen-sation*	*Nonelective Employer Contribution*	*Elective Contribution*	*Deferral Percentage*
C	$50,000	$1,000	$1,000	4%
D	50,000	1,000	1,000	4
E	50,000	1,000	–0–	2
F	50,000	1,000	–0–	2
Average of all lower paid employees' deferral percentages	—	—	—	3%

In this example, the actual deferral percentage for the lower paid group of employees equals 3 percent. As noted above, the 1.25 Test allows the highly compensated employees, as a group, to defer 125 percent of the actual deferral percentage of the other eligible employees. Under this test, employees A and B, as a group, can defer 3.75 percent of their compensation. Under the 2.0 Test, employees A and B may defer 200 percent of the actual deferral percentage for the lower paid employees as long as the difference is not more than two percentage points. In this example, therefore, the highly compensated employees may defer 5 percent of their compensation, since 3 percent times 2.0 is 6.0 percent and 5 percent is within two percentage points of 3 percent.

Finally, assume that employee B does not wish to make an elective contribution to the plan by way of a salary reduction agreement. Employee A, on the other hand, wishes to make the maximum elective contribution. As the following chart reveals, employee A can defer 6 percent of his salary as an elective contribution in addition to the 2 percent nonelective employer contribution.

Higher Paid Employees	*Compen-sation*	*Nonelective Employer Contribution*	*Elective Contribution*	*Deferral Percentage*
A	$100,000	$2,000(2%)	$6,000(6%)	8%
B	100,000	2,000	–0–	2
Average of all highly compensated employees' deferral percentages	—	—	—	5%

A final factor that does not appear in the above example but that limits contributions to a cash-deferred plan is the general limitation on employer contributions to profit-sharing plans imposed by Code Section 404. As noted, that Section provides that an employer may not deduct employer contributions to a stock bonus or profit-sharing plan that are in excess of 15 percent of the participant's total compensation. Obviously, few employers will allow employees to direct employer contributions to profit-sharing plans that the employer cannot deduct.

Cash-deferred/salary reduction plans offer an attractive alternative for those employers who are considering the adoption of new retirement plans or the revision of existing profit-sharing or stock bonus plans. At the same time, all cash or deferred arrangements are restricted by Code Section 401(k) and the proposed regulations; therefore, a cash or deferred arrangement should only be adopted after careful thought and study.

CHAPTER 48

QUALIFIED RETIREMENT PLANS FOR SMALL BUSINESS: ADMINISTRATIVE ISSUES

Harry V. Lamon, Jr.
James A. Clark

GENERAL ADMINISTRATION OF THE PLAN

Employees are often too busy to handle their own personal financial affairs and, as a result, the administrative aspects of the qualified retirement plans adopted by small businesses are often overlooked. It is important that qualified retirement plans be administered properly because, if they are not, it is possible that such plans may become "discriminatory in operation" and be disqualified by the Internal Revenue Service.

Once a qualified retirement plan is established, someone should be assigned the responsibility of dealing with the attorney, the accountant, the trustee, and the investment manager (if all of these exist). Also, in establishing the plan, some consideration should be given to who will perform the technical administrative functions of the plan, such as filing annual reports and making annual allocations. Under defined benefit pension plans, these functions are almost always performed by the actuary, since an actuarial analysis is necessary to compute the benefit annually. The normal fees for actuaries for most small businesses' defined benefit plans range from $1,000 to $3,000 per annum, depending on the number of employees and the complexity of the plan.

Most problems arise, however, under defined contribution plans where it is not necessary to have an actuary. In many such cases, the plan trustee is a local bank that will offer administrative services. However, not all banks seek out small-business plans because such plans often have total assets that are not within the scope of the bank's overall employee benefit market. Moreover, not all plan sponsors and participants desire to have a bank act as trustee and invest plan funds due to the generally conservative nature of most banks. Many brokerage houses, life insurance companies, and retirement plan consulting firms offer administrative services for defined contribution plans. Further, some accounting firms will assist a small business in its annual administrative function; but most accounting firms will do so only if there are fewer than 10 employees, due to the complexity of the allocations when more than 10 employees are involved. The administrative services for defined contribution plans sponsored by small businesses should normally run between $500 and $1,500 per year per plan, depending on the number of participants and the activity in the plan.

The fees for administering qualified retirement plans on an annual basis may be paid either by the trust or by the business. The authors generally recommend that such fees be paid by the business, as they are deductible by the corporation. Further, payment of such fees by the plans reduces the funds that will eventually be available to pay retirement benefits.

The authors also generally recommend that the corporation, and not one of the shareholders or employees, be designated as the plan administrator. To designate an individual as the plan administrator requires obtaining a separate employer identification number (EIN) from the Internal Revenue Service for the individual and formally changing plan administrators if the individual leaves the corporation. In addition, an individual who serves as plan administrator may be subject to suits by disgruntled participants.

REPORTING AND DISCLOSURE REQUIREMENTS OF ERISA

The following are the reporting and disclosure requirements for qualified retirement plans.[1]

---

[1] Prentice-Hall *Pension Reporter* ¶16021, et seq.

Summary Plan Description

A summary plan description, prepared in a manner calculated to be understood by the average plan participant, must be provided to participants and beneficiaries within 120 days after the plan is adopted. A copy must also be filed with the Department of Labor within that 120-day period. Further, a summary description of material modifications to the plan must be furnished to participants and beneficiaries within 210 days after the end of the plan year in which such modifications occur. The summary plan description must be provided to new employees within 90 days after they become participants.

The required contents of the summary plan description are described in Labor Regulations § 2520.102-3 and include a general statement of the benefits provided under the plan and the manner in which the plan operates.

Participant's Benefit Statements on Request

On the written request of a participant or beneficiary, the plan administrator must supply, without charge to the participant or beneficiary, a statement based on the latest available information of his or her total accrued benefit, and either the percentage of accrued benefits that are nonforfeitable or the date on which benefits will become nonforfeitable.[2] The plan administrator is not required to provide more than one such benefit statement during any 12-month period.[3]

Furnishing Other Documents Relating to the Plan

The plan administrator must make available for inspection by participants and beneficiaries copies of the plan document and trust agreement, copies of any collective bargaining agreement or contract under which the plan was established or is maintained, a copy of the latest annual report filed with the Service, and a copy of the latest summary plan description.[4] No charge may be made for exercising the right to inspect these documents. If the participant or beneficiary requests copies of these documents, copies must be provided. A reasonable charge not in excess of the actual cost of reproducing the documents may be required, but no charge may be

---

[2] ERISA § 105(a).

[3] ERISA § 105(b).

[4] ERISA § 104(b)(2).

made for the postage or handling involved in providing requested documents.[5] Not later than nine months after the close of a plan year, the plan administrator must furnish each participant and each beneficiary receiving benefits with a "summary annual report" that summarizes the annual report that was sent to the Service. The format for this report is prescribed in Labor Regulations § 2520.104b-10.

ADOPTION OF PLANS AND ADOPTION OF AMENDMENTS

A qualified retirement plan may be established or amended at any time prior to the close of the employer's taxable year, with such plan or plan amendment effective retroactive to the first day of the employer's taxable year. For example, assume a calendar-year employer adopted a qualified defined benefit plan on December 31, 1987, with an effective date of January 1, 1987. The employer could contribute and deduct for 1987 the amount necessary to pay the normal cost for the entire 1987 plan year plus an amount necessary to amortize the cost of past service credit (if any) provided for in the plan. The contribution and deduction could be made at any time prior to the date for filing the 1987 tax returns, including extensions.

An employer who adopts or amends a qualified plan is permitted to file a request that the Service make a determination that the provisions of the plan as adopted or as amended satisfy the requirements of the Internal Revenue Code for qualification; such a request is allowed during the "remedial amendment period." The significance of filing the determination request during the remedial amendment period is that if a request is filed during that period and the Service determines that changes are necessary to cause the plan to be qualified, then the necessary changes may be adopted *retroactively* to the effective date of the plan (or the effective date of a plan amendment) so that the plan will be qualified from its initial effective date (or the effective date of an amendment).[6] If a request for a determination is filed after the close of the remedial amendment period and the Service discovers deficiencies in the plan, retroactive cure of the deficiencies may not be possible. Where the plan year corresponds to the employer's taxable year, the remedial amendment period for initial qualification or for a plan amendment will extend until the date for filing the

[5] Labor Regulations § 2520.104b-30.

[6] Treas. Regs. § 1.401(b)-1.

employer's tax return (including extensions) for the first taxable year of the employer in which the plan or the amendment is effective. The remedial amendment period may be extended at the discretion of the Service, but the Service does not extend the period where failure to timely file a determination letter request was due merely to oversight.

It should be remembered that the period for adopting a qualified retirement plan by an employer ends with the last day of the first taxable year of the employer for which the plan is effective. Although contributions may be made after the end of the employer's taxable year and may be deducted for the year to which they apply, the plan itself may not be adopted retroactive to a taxable year that ended prior to the date of adoption. In *Engineered Timber Sales,*[7] the Tax Court held that no deductions would be permitted for the first taxable year for which a plan was made effective where the employer had adopted a trust agreement and the employer's board of directors had passed a resolution to adopt the plan prior to the expiration of the employer's first taxable year for which the plan was to be effective, but no enforceable plan was drafted until the following taxable year of the employer.

A plan that satisfies all the requirements of the Code for qualification and that receives a favorable determination letter is not assured of *permanent* qualification. Two distinct classes of events could occur that would disqualify the plan. First, the plan might become disqualified *in operation*. As an example, the plan administrator might improperly exclude some rank and file employees, despite the plan's express eligibility requirements, and thereby cause the plan to discriminate.[8] Second, the legal requirements applicable to qualified plans might change—for example, by issuance of new or modified Treasury Regulations, by enactment of a new law, or by a new revenue ruling.[9] Generally, when there is a change in applicable law, a plan will remain qualified if the plan is amended not later than the close of the plan year following the plan year in which the change in law occurred, and if the amendment is made effective as of the first day of the plan year following the plan year in which the change in law occurred. It is therefore critical that plan administrators, or their counsel, keep abreast of changes in the laws applicable to qualified plans so that timely plan amendments may be adopted.

---

[7] 74 T.C. 808 (1980).

[8] *Myron* v. *U.S.*, 550 F.2d 1145 (9th Cir. 1977).

[9] *Wisconsin Nipple & Fabricating Co.* v. *Commissioner,* 67 T.C. 490 (1976), aff'd. 581 F.2d 1235 (7th Cir. 1978).

LOANS TO PARTICIPANTS

A loan from a qualified retirement plan to a participant of that plan is a prohibited transaction under Section 406(a)(1)(B) of the Employee Retirement Income Security Act (ERISA) and Section 4975(c)(1)(B) of the Code. However, Section 408(b)(1) of ERISA and Section 4975(d)(1) of the Code provide an exemption from the prohibited transaction rules where the following requirements are met:

1. Loans are made to all participants and beneficiaries on a reasonably equivalent basis.
2. Loans are not made available to highly compensated employees, officers, or shareholders in an amount greater than the amount made available to other employees.
3. Loans are made in accordance with specific provisions regarding such loans set forth in the plan.
4. Loans bear a reasonable rate of interest.
5. Loans are adequately secured.

The second requirement—no disproportionate amounts of loans to highly compensated individuals—will not be violated merely because the plan permits all plan participants to borrow the same percentage of their vested accrued benefits even though officers, shareholders, and highly compensated employees may, as a group, have larger vested accrued benefits than rank and file employees.

As a caveat, while Congress purported to establish parity between corporate and noncorporate plans in the Tax Equity and Fiscal Responsibility Act (TEFRA), loans to owner-employees of proprietorships and partnerships continue to be prohibited transactions after TEFRA.

Further, a direct or indirect loan from *any* qualified plan to a participant or beneficiary is treated as a distribution and, thereby, is taxable unless the loan falls within an exception specified in Code Section 72(p). A loan falls within the exception and is not treated as a distribution only if it meets all three of the following requirements:

1. The loan must be repaid within five years.
2. The aggregate balance of all loans from the plan made to the borrower-participant does not exceed the lesser of (*a*) $50,000 reduced by the highest outstanding balance of such loans during the preceding one-year period or (*b*) one half of the present value of the nonforfeitable accrued benefit of the employee in the plan (but not less than $10,000).

3. The loan requires substantially level amortization (with payments made at least quarterly) over its term.

The five-year limitation does not apply if the loan is applied toward acquiring any house, apartment, condominium, or mobile home (not used on a transient basis) that is used or is to be used within a reasonable time as the principal residence of the participant.

This provision severely restricts the availability of plan loans to participants and their beneficiaries; however, plan loans remain an invaluable advantage of qualified retirement plans. Fortunately, that a loan is treated as a taxable distribution will not disqualify the plan.

As the funds in an existing qualified retirement plan accumulate, the participants often desire to borrow those funds so that they can, in effect, "pay interest to themselves." Thus, availability of loans from qualified retirement plans is useful in times of inflation. Although plan loan interest is no longer deductible by the participant after the Tax Reform Act of 1986 (TRA '86), the authors believe that, as long as the loans are made within the exemption provided in Section 408(b)(1) of ERISA, they can still serve as an attractive source of financing or emergency funds to plan participants. Loans cannot, however, be made either directly or indirectly to the business without obtaining a specific exemption from the Department of Labor.

The authors feel that loans can be made to participants if the following criteria are met:

1. Either the plan or an administrative committee sets forth the specific reasons for loans, such as medical emergencies, second mortgages, college costs, and so on, and such standards are adhered to for high-paid and low-paid employees alike.

2. The interest rates and other terms set by the plan are equivalent to rates and terms that would be applied by local banks on similar loans.

3. The loan must be represented by a bona fide promissory note.

4. Loans should generally be made only to the extent of the vested account balance or accrued benefit of the participant, with the vested account balance acting as security. If loans in excess of the vested account balance of the participant are made, the plan should obtain sufficient additional security, such as listed stocks, bonds, or a second mortgage. Any security taken by the plan should be segregated from the assets of the employees and held by the trustee.

5. Loans should be made in a consistent, businesslike manner, and loan applications should be executed by the participant desiring to borrow.

6. Loans made by a participant should be earmarked as investments of that participant's account so that, if that participant does default on the loan, only that participant and not the other participants will suffer.

7. Although the commercially available interest rate should be charged on the loans, care should be taken that state usury laws are not violated.

8. Loans from defined benefit plans should be made only to the extent of the borrower-participant's vested accrued benefit.

A rather subtle problem may arise in the case of loans from a pension plan (defined benefit or money purchase plan). One of the characteristics of qualified pension plans is that such plans may not make distributions to participants prior to separation from service or attainment of normal retirement age. A *loan* from a pension plan does not violate this distribution limitation since bona fide loans are not plan distributions. A problem may arise, however, if the security for a loan from a pension plan is the vested accrued benefit of the participant. If the participant defaults on the plan loan and the only assets out of which collection may be made are the participant's vested accrued benefit, the satisfaction of the loan by reduction of the participant's accrued benefit could constitute a premature distribution that would disqualify the plan. A similar problem could arise in the case of loans from integrated profit-sharing plans, since distributions from integrated profit-sharing plans are proscribed prior to separation from service or attainment of normal retirement age. To avoid the premature distribution problem, the authors suggest that pension and integrated profit-sharing plans that provide for loans to participants require adequate security for such loans *other than* the participant's accrued benefit. Loans from a cash or deferred salary reduction plan also should not be secured only by the account balance since a foreclosure of any loan by resort to the funds in an account may constitute an in-service distribution to a participant and, thereby, disqualify the plan under Section 401(k).

BONDING REQUIREMENTS OF ERISA

Section 412 of ERISA requires that every fiduciary and every person who handles funds or other property of a qualified retirement plan must be bonded and that the bond shall be not less than 10 percent of the amount of the funds handled. While such bonds (ERISA bonds) are inexpensive and can be obtained as a rider to the general fidelity insurance of the business, they are often overlooked. Further, questions arise with regard to who "handles" funds and what are the "funds" handled. For these reasons, it is prudent to require that all trustees or members of a plan administrative committee be bonded and that the bond be in the amount of 10 percent of the funds in the plan.

INVESTMENTS

ERISA does not require any specific type of investment to be maintained by any type of qualified retirement plan. However, Section 404 of ERISA requires that fiduciaries exercise the care, skill, prudence, and diligence that a "prudent man acting in a like capacity and familiar with such matters" would use and also requires that fiduciaries diversify investments unless it is clearly prudent not to do so. These standards can normally be met by investments that are generally available, such as listed stocks and bonds. However, since a qualified trust is tax-exempt, the authors feel that an effort should be made to maximize the annual income under the trust in order to take advantage of the compounding effect that the tax-exempt status provides. Obviously, tax shelters and other investments with tax-favored status provide very little benefit to a tax-exempt trust, and as such, they should generally be avoided.

Often, employers desire to leverage the ability of their qualified retirement plans to purchase various assets such as real estate. Where the assets are purchased within a qualified retirement plan, and either funds are borrowed to acquire those assets or the assets are purchased through the use of purchase money indebtedness, the income generated from the sale of those assets will be partially taxable to the trust as if it were a regular taxable entity. This rule also applies to margin accounts.[10] There are, however, certain exceptions with regard to the purchase of real estate if the property is purchased from the owner and the owner takes back a second mortgage.

Many qualified retirement plans of small businesses will have assets of less than $500,000. Such plans may be unable to obtain the services of a registered investment adviser to handle investments. Consequently, the management of fund assets will fall to the trustee, be it a bank or the employers themselves. If employers are the trustees of the plan, they should take steps to insure that all assets held by the plan are segregated

---

[10] *Elliot Knitwear Profit Sharing Plan,* 614 F.2d 347 (3rd Cir. 1980) aff'g. 71 T.C. 765 (1970); Sections 511-514 of the Code; investment in partnerships (even as a limited partner) may also generate unrelated business taxable income, see Rev. Rul. 79-222, 1979-2 C.B. 236, Treas. Regs. §1.514(c)-1(a)(2) example (4).

from their personal assets and from the assets of the business. Also, as trustees, the employers will be responsible for the investments of the plan.

Since most employers either do not have the time or are not adept at investing large sums of money, the investment of assets of a qualified retirement plan of many small businesses falls to a stock broker or to an investment company. If a local stock broker is employed, it should be recognized that he or she will generally not be considered a fiduciary unless he or she exercises discretionary control or authority over the fund or renders investment advice for a fee. Most stock brokers have disclaimers that eliminate them from the fiduciary responsibility rules of ERISA. Further, many qualified retirement plans of small businesses are invested in "guaranteed investment contracts" with insurance companies. While these contracts appear to offer a good annual return, employers should be fully aware of the implications of investing in such contracts, since they usually involve some type of termination discount or some type of extended payout on termination.

Very often, the investment ideas of the plan shareholders will differ from the ideas of the plan trustee. It is possible to provide in a qualified retirement plan that the participants will have the ability to earmark (direct the investment of) their accounts. Under an earmarking arrangement, the participant will have the authority to direct the trustee with regard to the vested balance of his or her account.

There are limitations on earmarking. First, earmarking exists only in defined contribution plans and is not available with respect to defined benefit plan assets derived from employer contributions, although defined benefit plans that permit voluntary employee contributions may permit employees to earmark their voluntary employee contribution accounts. Further, if a participant does earmark the investment of his or her account, the fiduciary will be relieved of liability for a loss by reason of the participant's control.[11]

Finally, it should be recognized that participants may not direct the investment of their accounts into items that are used personally, since such use would constitute a prohibited transaction and would result in the imposition of excise taxes under Section 4975 of the Code. Furthermore, Code Section 408(m) provides that the acquisition by an individually directed account under a qualified pension or profit-sharing plan of any collectible will be treated as a distribution from the account in an amount equal to the cost of the collectible. Collectibles are defined to mean any

---

[11] ERISA § 404(c).

work of art, any rug or antique, any metal or gem, any stamp or coin, any alcoholic beverage, or any other tangible personal property specified by the secretary of the treasury. This provision "grandfathers" collectibles that were already held by accounts as of December 31, 1981 and does not apply to collectibles acquired by the plan's trustee as plan assets not earmarked to the account of any participant. In addition, it may be possible to use aftertax voluntary employee contributions to make earmarked investments in collectibles, since the "deemed distribution" of an employee contribution does not give rise to gross income. Overall, it would probably be wise to await regulations in this area.

Some investment managers feel that the type of investment a plan makes should vary with the type of plan; that is, that a defined benefit pension plan with a definite fixed benefit that must be reached should be invested in interest-bearing bonds, preferred stocks, and blue chip stocks. On the other hand, they feel that since there is no definite retirement benefit provided under profit-sharing and money purchase plans, funds from such plans may be invested in higher risk assets. While the character of investments may vary from defined benefit to defined contribution plans, security of principal is an essential element to any investment strategy under any qualified retirement plan.

Following ERISA, it was felt that corporate trustees should be employed in order to minimize the risk of a suit against the individual employer acting as trustee. However, in the period following ERISA, although there have been a number of suits under ERISA, there have been few suits against employees who have acted as trustees under their qualified retirement plans. For this reason, shareholder/employees should feel free to act as trustees of the qualified retirement plans established by their corporations. If shareholder/employees do choose to serve as trustees, to serve as plan administrators, or to perform other services for the plan, they normally must do so without pay other than reimbursement of expenses properly and actually incurred, since Section 408(c)(2) of ERISA prohibits persons who already receive full-time pay from an employer from receiving compensation from the plan other than expense reimbursement. Care should be taken, however, to assure that the investment of the plan's assets, particularly the amounts credited to the accounts of the staff employees, be done in a conservative manner.

Whether an employee of the business or a bank acts as trustee, the rights and duties of the trustee must be prescribed either in the plan itself or in a separate trust document. Although many plans and trust agreements are unified in a single document, the authors recommend establishing both a plan and a separate trust agreement. In this manner, the plan need only be executed by the corporation, whereas the trust agreement must be executed by the corporation and the trustee. Consequently, if the corporation decides to amend the plan, it need only pass a board resolution and sign the amendment; the signature of the trustee is not necessary.

MASTER PLANS VERSUS INDIVIDUALLY DESIGNED PLANS

A number of banks, brokerage houses, and insurance companies offer preapproved master or prototype plans that can be adopted by a small business. These plans have received a master determination letter and can be adopted by the small business without the necessity of seeking further Service approval. Such plans are typically adopted by the completion of an adoption agreement under which a number of alternatives can be selected, such as participation rules and vesting schedules.

Master plans appear to offer an attractive alternative to employers because they can be executed with very little assistance from the attorney and accountant of the business and, consequently, with a minimum fee. Employers should be aware, however, that most master plans are offered by entities that are selling a service. Banks, brokerage houses, and insurance companies all sell investment products and/or services and may charge administrative fees. Master plans also have the following drawbacks:

1. Master plans usually offer less flexibility than individually designed plans since the employer can only choose among the terms contained in the adoption agreement.

2. Master plans may contain hidden problems. The terms of the master plan may be generally acceptable to the Service but may, in the particular situation of the small business, be unacceptable. Although the representatives of the company offering the master plan will be knowledgeable about the plan, the authors have found that they typically do not scrupulously review the plan in light of the particular situation of the small business. This is particularly true in situations where provisions in the master plan may eventually produce discrimination in operation.

3. Once a master plan is adopted, it may be difficult to terminate that plan and transfer assets to a successor trustee. Most master plans contain a provision stating that the assets may only be transferred to a plan that has received a determination letter from the Service. Consequently, if the employer desires to terminate the master plan arrangement and transfer the funds to an individually designed plan, the delay in obtaining the determination letter (usually six to eight months) will delay the transfer of the funds.

4. Master plans may have hidden administrative costs that must be borne by the plan or the employer. This is particularly true with the so-called deposit administration plans maintained by insurance companies.

5. The fees of the attorney and accountant for the small business will probably not be insubstantial if they are requested to review and comment on the master plan proposed. Problems often are identified on a review of a master plan because master plans are not tailor-made to deal with the individual needs of any specific business. Where the attorney of the small business is called on to review and interpret provisions of master plans, the time required and, therefore, the fees charged are often significantly greater than if the attorney had drafted an individually designed plan for the corporation. This occurs because it is much easier for the attorney to work with plans with which he or she is familiar than to undertake a complete examination of new plans.

6. Master plans often restrict investment alternatives to the products offered by the sponsors of such plans. Thus, trustees may not be able to take advantage of other investment opportunities that may arise.

Employers should realize that some organizations offer plans that appear to be master or prototype plans but that are, in fact, individually designed plans. The authors are aware of a number of insurance companies that engage in this practice and, in fact, draft individually designed retirement plans for small businesses. Employers encountering this arrangement should carefully assess the potential problems that may arise in adopting an individually designed plan drafted by someone other than the employer's attorney. There is a greater possibility that problems will arise under such a plan than under a master or prototype plan. Further, drafting such plans and the accompanying trust agreements is generally considered by the American Bar Association to be unauthorized practicing of law.[12]

Because qualified retirement plans are such an important tax benefit, in most instances, employers should consider adopting individually designed plans that have been coordinated by their attorney and accountant. By adopting individually designed plans, the small business can assure that the plan initially meets its needs and objectives and creates no latent problems. Moreover, as the law governing qualified plans changes in the future, the attorney and accountant will be on hand to make appropriate amendments.

---

[12] "Final Opinion on Employee Benefit Planning" issued by the Committee on Unauthorized Practice of Law dated October 17, 1977.

PROHIBITED TRANSACTIONS

Section 406 of ERISA and parallel provisions of Section 4975 of the Code prohibit employee benefit plans from engaging in certain types of transactions. The provisions of Section 4975 of the Code only apply to qualified *retirement* plans, while the provisions of Section 406 of ERISA apply to both *retirement* plans (whether or not "qualified" under the Code) and *welfare* plans (such as medical, accident, or layoff benefit plans). Violations of the prohibited transaction provisions of the Code can result in the imposition of a nondeductible excise tax equal to 5 percent of the "amount involved" in the transaction for each year that the transaction continues. An additional excise tax of 100 percent of the amount involved is imposed if correction is not made on notice by the Service. A fiduciary who permits a prohibited transaction to which Section 406 of ERISA applies may be held personally liable under Section 409 of ERISA for any loss to the plan resulting from the transaction.

Transactions that constitute prohibited transactions are absolutely forbidden, regardless of the financial or economic soundness of the transaction and regardless of whether the transaction offers the plan a more attractive financial opportunity than is available elsewhere. Generally, the defenses of good faith, innocence, and reasonable lack of knowledge that a transaction is prohibited will not prevent imposition of the excise tax under Code Section 4975; however, violation of Section 406 of ERISA can be avoided with these defenses.

The specific transactions prohibited are certain transactions between plans and "parties in interest." ERISA Section 3(14) enumerates a rather broad class of persons who constitute parties in interest with respect to a plan. Parties in interest include all plan fiduciaries, including the plan administrator, trustee, or custodian of plan assets, any person who provides services to a plan, the employer whose employees are covered by the plan, a relative (spouse, ancestor, lineal descendant, or spouse of a lineal descendant) of any of the foregoing individuals, and any employee, officer, director, or 10 percent (direct or indirect) shareholder of the employer who maintains the plan.

A prohibited transaction will occur if there is a direct or indirect:

1. Sale, exchange, or leasing of any property between a plan and a party in interest.
2. Lending of money or other extension of credit between a plan and a party in interest.
3. Furnishing of any goods, services, or facilities between a plan and a party in interest.

4. Transfer of any plan assets to or use of any plan assets by or for the benefit of a party in interest.
5. Acquisition of securities of the employer under certain circumstances or in excess of certain maximum amounts.

In addition, certain dealings by fiduciaries will constitute prohibited transactions. Specifically, a fiduciary is prohibited from dealing with assets of the plan for his or her own personal gain, representing any person in a transaction involving the plan in which the party represented has interests adverse to the plan, and receiving a kickback from any person in connection with a transaction involving assets of the plan.

Section 4975 of the Code and Section 408(b) of ERISA contain a number of "statutory exemptions" from the prohibited transaction provisions. For example, the statutory exemption dealing with loans to participants has been discussed. Other statutory exemptions include exemptions:

1. To provide reasonable services necessary to establish or operate the plan.
2. To permit bank trustees to invest plan assets in savings accounts and pooled investment accounts of the bank and to provide ancillary banking services to the plan.
3. To permit fiduciaries to receive reasonable compensation for services (unless they are full-time employees of the employer).
4. To permit fiduciaries who are plan participants to receive plan benefits as they become payable.

In addition to the statutory exemptions, Section 408(a) of ERISA and Section 4975(c)(2) of the Code permit administrative exemptions from the prohibited transaction rules to be granted. Administrative exemptions may be granted in favor of a particular transaction (an individual exemption) or a class of transactions (class exemptions). Individual exemptions apply only to the specific transaction for which the exemption was granted and will not authorize an identical transaction engaged in by different parties. Class exemptions generally exempt any present, certain past, or any future transaction that satisfies the requirements of the exemption.

Requests for prohibited transaction exemptions are filed with the Department of Labor. It normally takes from four to six months for an exemption request to be finally resolved, and nearly 90 percent of the requests for exemptions are *denied*. In order to obtain an administrative exemption, a plan must complete a rather tedious application in which it must be demonstrated that the exemption, if granted, would be: (1) administratively feasible, (2) in the interest of the plan, its participants and beneficiaries, and (3) protective of the rights of participants and beneficiaries of the plan. Chances for approval are increased if the applicant can show that, due to the independent safeguards, the transaction provides a "no lose" opportunity for larger financial benefit to the plan than other available investment alternatives. Until recently, the Department of Labor was very reluctant to grant exemptions that authorized continuing transactions between the plan and parties in interest, (e.g., loans and leases). However, the Department of Labor has recently granted a number of such continuing transaction exemptions, including several that have permitted improved real property to be contributed to a plan and leased back to the employer.[13]

CONTRIBUTIONS

The determination of the deductibility of contributions to a qualified retirement plan is generally made pursuant to Section 404 of the Code. The amounts that may be deducted as contributions to a qualified pension plan (defined benefit or money purchase) are determined under Section 404(a)(1).

An employer may deduct its contribution to a pension plan (defined benefit or money purchase) to the extent the contribution was necessary to pay the normal cost of plan benefits plus any amount necessary to amortize past service liabilities. The normal cost of a defined benefit plan must be calculated by the plan's actuary. The normal cost of a money purchase plan is determined by the plan's contribution formula; for example, 10 percent of participants' compensation. Generally, past service liabilities are created by plan amendments that increase the rate at which benefits accrue for prior service and by plan provisions that grant past service benefits on establishment of the plan. Past service liabilities attributable to all participants may be amortized over as many as 30 years or as few as 10 years. Alternatively, past service liabilities may be amortized over the remaining future service of each employee; but, if over 50 percent of plan costs are attributable to three or fewer individuals, past service liabilities attributable to those three or fewer individuals may not be amortized over fewer than five years.

Effective for tax years beginning after 1986, TRA '86 imposed an overall limit on the total amount of the annual deduction that may be

---

[13] Prohibited Transaction Exemptions 80-78, 80-86, 80-97, and 81-1.

taken for contributions made to a combination of defined benefit and defined contribution plans. Generally, the total deductible amount may not exceed 25 percent of the plan participants' annual compensation. However, if the defined benefit plan contribution required by the minimum funding standards exceeds such 25 percent, the greater amount may be deducted.[14]

The deductibility of contributions to profit-sharing plans is determined under Section 404(a)(3), which sets a basic deduction limit for profit-sharing contributions of 15 percent of the compensation otherwise paid or accrued during the taxable year to all beneficiaries of the plan. If an employer contributes an amount in excess of the deduction limits for a particular year, the excess payment is deductible in succeeding years. However, effective for taxable years beginning after 1986, nondeductible contributions are subject to an annual 10 percent excise tax until the excess is eliminated. If a pre-1987 contribution made to a profit-sharing plan is less than 15 percent of the annual total compensation for the period the contribution is made, the difference between the amount actually contributed and the 15 percent limitation may be carried forward so as to increase the deductible amount in a succeeding taxable year to the extent that the total deduction in any later year does not exceed 25 percent of compensation.[15]

If amounts are deductible under both pension plans and profit-sharing plans, the employer may first deduct the entire amount deductible with respect to the pension plans. If the amount deductible on account of the pension plans is less than 25 percent of the participants' compensation for the plan year, the employer can make up the difference by making additional contributions to profit-sharing plans. If the employer's contribution to the pension plans equals or exceeds 25 percent of the participants' compensation for the plan year, then obviously no amount may be deducted for the profit-sharing plans. Contributions must also satisfy the applicable contribution and benefit limitations of Section 415 of the Code.

Corporate contributions to qualified retirement plans are considered general business expenses. Consequently, in order for an employer to obtain a deduction for such expenses under Section 404, the expenses

---

[14] I.R.C. § 404(a)(7).

[15] I.R.C. § 404(a)(3)(A). In one case, however, where the employer made "advance contributions" to a profit-sharing plan to enable the plan to make an investment, the Tax Court found the advance to constitute a loan, and the plan was held to have debt-financed, unrelated business income as a result of the investment. *Marprowear Profit Sharing Trust* v. *Commissioner,* 74 T.C. 1086 (1980).

must be ordinary and necessary under Section 162 of the Code. In determining whether deductions to qualified retirement plans are ordinary and necessary, the question of reasonable compensation must be considered. When determining reasonable compensation for an employee, all benefits are taken into account, including contributions under qualified retirement plans. Consequently, if the reasonableness of the compensation to the employer is challenged, a challenge may also be made to the qualified retirement plan. If the compensation is found to be unreasonable, a portion of the deduction for contributions may be disallowed or the Service may attempt to disqualify the plan. If discrimination results from contributions attributable to unreasonable compensation, a defined contribution plan may avoid disqualification by permitting the reallocation to other employees of any contribution determined to be unreasonable.[16]

The reasonable compensation requirement may be a particular problem where the first year of the small business is a short fiscal year during which large contributions are made. This may be especially true if large amounts of income are held over from the preincorporation period and paid during the first year of incorporation in order to permit large contributions to the qualified plans.[17]

Under Section 404 of the Code, deductions are generally allowed for the tax year in which they are made. However, under ERISA, Section 404(a)(6) of the Code was amended to permit a deduction for a particular year to be taken where the contribution for that year is made on or before the filing deadline of the federal income tax return (plus extensions thereof). In order to obtain a deduction under Section 404(a)(6) of the Code, the contribution for a year must be (i) paid to the plan on or before the due date for filing the federal income tax return (plus extensions, if any), (ii) allocated on the books of the plan in the same manner as they would have been allocated if they had been actually contributed on the last day of the plan year, and (iii) deducted on the federal income tax return.[18]

The initial contributions to a qualified retirement plan may also be made during the grace period. That is, although it is absolutely necessary to adopt the plan prior to the end of the fiscal year of the employer, no contribution to that plan need be made (even though the trust may be a

---

[16] Rev. Rul. 67-341, 1967-2 C.B. 156.

[17] *Angelo J. Bianchi,* 66 T.C. 324 (1976), aff'd. 553 F.2d 93 (2d Cir. 1977). *Anthony LaMaestro,* 72 T.C. 377 (1979), *Robert A. Young,* 650 F.2d 1085 (9th Cir. 1981).

[18] Rev. Rul. 76-28, 1976-1 C.B. 106.

"dry trust" under local law) until the time for filing the corporation's federal income tax return.[19] However, the authors recommend that, on the establishment of a qualified plan, the trust of that plan be funded with a $100 contribution even though the remainder of the contribution will be made at a later date.

Nondeductible Voluntary Employee Contributions

Qualified retirement plans may permit nondeductible voluntary employee contributions of up to 10 percent of an employee's compensation.[20] This 10 percent limit is a maximum limitation for all plans, so that if 10 percent is contributed under a profit-sharing plan, nothing may be contributed under a money purchase pension plan.[21] However, the 10 percent voluntary contribution is cumulative so that the contribution may be made equal to 10 percent of the employee's aggregate compensation for all years that he or she has been a participant.[22] Furthermore, the 10 percent limitation is not reduced or affected by amounts rolled over or directly transferred from another qualified plan.

Nondeductible voluntary employee contributions are also subject to the annual addition limitations under Section 415 of the Code. Thus, if the employer contribution for a given year places an employee near or at his or her Section 415 limit, little or no amount may be contributed as a voluntary employee contribution, regardless of the 10 percent rule.

The ability of an employee to make voluntary employee contributions to a qualified retirement plan is an excellent benefit that creates for the employee the ability to defer income taxes on the earnings in the voluntary account. Although voluntary employee contributions must be made with aftertax dollars, the earnings on the amounts contributed voluntarily by the employee remain tax-exempt until withdrawn. Consequently, the employee may take advantage of the compounding effect of tax-exempt earnings through the use of voluntary employee contributions. Voluntary employee contributions are particularly useful for deferring income until later years when it will be needed for expenses such as college education for children.

---

[19] Rev. Rul. 57-419, 1957-2 C.B. 264.

[20] Rev. Rul. 80-350, 1980-2 C.B. 133; Rev. Rul. 59-185, 1959-1 C.B. 86.

[21] Rev. Rul. 69-627, 1969-2 C.B. 92.

[22] Rev. Rul. 69-217, 1969-1 C.B. 115, as clarified by Rev. Rul. 74-385, 1974-2 C.B. 130.

Deductible Voluntary Employee Contributions

Effective January 1, 1982, Section 311(a) of the Economic Recovery Tax Act of 1981 (ERTA) amended Code Section 219 to permit participants in a plan qualified under Code Sections 401(a), 403(a), or 408(k) to make voluntary deductible employee contributions (DECs) equal to the lesser of $2,000 or 100 percent of compensation. However, Section 1101(b) of TRA '86 repealed the deduction for DECs, effective for tax years beginning after 1986.

ANNUAL ADDITION LIMITATION

Section 415 of the Code provides limitations on the annual benefits that may be provided under qualified retirement plans. Under Section 415(b)(1), the employer may not fund a defined benefit plan benefit that is greater than the lesser of $90,000 or 100 percent of the participant's average compensation for his or her highest three consecutive calendar years.

With respect to defined contribution plans, the annual addition made on behalf of a participant may not exceed the lesser of $30,000 or 25 percent of the participant's compensation. For purposes of determining the annual addition, the following allocations are considered: (1) the employer contributions, (2) the employee contributions (voluntary and mandatory), and (3) any forfeitures allocated to the participant's account.

QUALIFYING PLANS WITH THE INTERNAL REVENUE SERVICE

Although obtaining a determination letter with regard to a retirement plan is not a prerequisite for having a "qualified" plan, obtaining a determination letter does permit the sponsoring employer to receive advance determination of the qualified status of the plan. For this reason, the authors feel that all plans that are intended to be qualified plans should be filed with the district director of the local Service office for qualification. If plans are filed for determination during the remedial amendment period discussed above and qualified status is not received, either the plans may be amended retroactively to permit qualified status or the contributions may be returned to the employer. Further, the authors believe that all amendments to a plan or trust document, other than ministerial amendments like the change of the trustee or the change in the name of the plan, should be filed with the Service for continued qualification.

The receipt of a determination letter from the district director does not, however, give carte blanche as to a plan's qualified status. The determination letter merely states that, on the facts and law that exist as of the date of letter's issuance, the plan in *form* meets the qualification rules. Further changes in the facts relating to the employer and the employees and changes in the rules and regulations of the Service may later disqualify the plan. In *Wisconsin Nipple & Fabricating Corporation* v. *Commissioner,*[23] the court upheld the Commissioner's retroactive revocation of determination letters (issued in 1960 and 1962) where a later revenue ruling (issued in 1971) indicated that the plan discriminated in favor of a prohibited group. In arriving at this result, the seventh circuit clearly placed responsibility on the taxpayer for "keeping abreast of current developments in the law to be assured that the plan is still in compliance." For this reason, the authors feel that sponsoring employers should continue to monitor the status of their retirement plans with their professional advisers to assure that they remain qualified.

Rev. Proc. 80-30, Sec. 2.15.[24] states that "a favorable determination letter on the qualification of a pension, annuity, profit-sharing, stock bonus, or bond purchase plan, and the exempt status of a related trust, if any, is not required as a condition for obtaining the benefits pertaining to the plan or trust."

DISCRIMINATION IN OPERATION

Obviously, qualified retirement plans may be disqualified if they fail to meet the specific statutory requirements provided under Section 401, *et seq.*, of the Code such as the minimum participation rules, vesting rules, and so on. However, it is possible for qualified retirement plans to be disqualified due to the manner in which they have been operated, even though determination letters have been issued on those plans.

In addition to the specific statutory requirements for qualified plans, Section 401 also contains several rather vague prohibitions. For example, under Section 401(a)(2), a plan must be used for the "exclusive benefit" of participants and their beneficiaries. Further, under Section 401(a)(4), a plan may not discriminate in favor of highly compensated employees

---

[23] *Wisconsin Nipple & Fabricating Co.* v. *Commissioner,* 67 T.C. 490 (1976), aff'd 581 F.2d 1235 (7th Cir. 1978).

[24] 1980-1 C.B. 685.

(defined in Chapter 47). Treasury Regulations § 1.401-1(b)(3) provides a general overview of what may constitute impermissible discrimination:

> The plan must benefit the employees in general, although it need not provide benefits for all of the employees. Among the employees to be benefited may be persons who are officers and shareholders. However, a plan is not for the exclusive benefit of employees in general if, by any device whatever, it discriminates either in eligibility requirements, contributions, or benefits in favor of employees who are officers, shareholders, . . . or highly compensated employees.

Those situations in which a qualified retirement plan is diverted to the use of the highly compensated employees of the small business are often apparent from the plan's terms (for example, a plan that permits loans of plan funds only to such employees). However, even if the terms of a plan in *form* comply with the statutory requirements, it is possible that in *operation* the benefits and contributions provisions may discriminate in favor of highly compensated employees, even though there is no intention that they do so. It is difficult to anticipate when discrimination in operation may occur, but the following are a few examples.

Erroneous Administration of Plan Provisions

In several cases, the participation provisions of qualified retirement plans were inadvertently not followed, leading to disqualification of the plans due to discrimination in operation. In *Myron* v. *U.S.*,[25] five eligible employees were excluded from coverage for two consecutive years, and the company's contributions were allocated only to the account of the corporation's sole shareholder. The lower court found that the exclusion was inadvertent but, nevertheless, concluded this innocent error justified disqualification. In affirming, the seventh circuit court of appeals agreed that even an inadvertent failure in coverage could be a proper basis for denying qualification.[26]

Several cases of erroneous administration of plan provisions specifically involve small businesses. In *Allen Ludden,*[27] a pre-ERISA case, Allen Ludden and Betty White, the famous actor and actress, formed a corporation, Albets, that adopted a money purchase pension plan and a profit-sharing plan for the benefit of the corporation's employees. The

[25] *Myron* v. *U.S.*, 550 F.2d 1145 (9th Cir. 1977).

[26] Also see *Ma-Tran Corp.*, 70 T.C. 158 (1978).

[27] 68 T.C. 826 (1977), aff'g. 620 F.2d 700 (9th Cir. 1980).

plans, as written, met the requirements for qualification, and determination letters were issued by the Service. Through a bookkeeping error, the only staff employee of Albets, a production secretary, was inadvertently excluded from participation in the plan even though she met the plan's participation requirements. The Service argued, and the court held, that the exclusion of the production secretary constituted discrimination in favor of highly compensated officers in violation of (pre-1986 Code) Sections 401(a)(3)(B) and 401(a)(4) of the Code and meant that the plan had failed to meet the minimum coverage provisions of (pre-1986 Code) Section 401(a)(3)(A).

In *Forsyth Emergency Services, P.A.,*[28] a professional corporation was engaged in emergency medical services and operated the emergency room facilities at Forsyth Memorial Hospital in Winston-Salem, North Carolina. The corporation was owned by three physicians who adopted a money purchase pension plan. They received a determination letter from the Service. During 1972 and 1973, certain nonprofessional employees of the corporation were inadvertently omitted from coverage under the retirement plan. However, in August of 1975, after this fact was brought to the corporation's attention by the Service, additional contributions were made so that allocations could be made for these nonprofessional employees for the years in which they were excluded. The exclusion of the nonprofessional employees resulted from a misreading of the plan by the professional adviser to the corporation.

The court held that the plan did not meet the eligibility requirements for coverage and that the plan discriminated in operation. The court further held that discrimination in operation could not be cured by retroactively funding contributions accrued but unallocated to the nonprofessional employees, even if such retroactive allocation was made voluntarily by the corporation. The court noted that, because the plan covered primarily professional employees, the plan did not cover a cross-section of all employees. In examining the question of whether a retroactive cure for discrimination was available, the court stated that it found no support in the Code, the Regulations, or the case law that would permit retroactive correction.

Cases like *Ludden* and *Forsyth* are dramatic examples of the problems that can occur due to the inadvertent errors of employers, even where they seek the advice of their professional advisers. The Service has, in some situations, relented from its position in *Ludden* and *Forsyth.* In Private Letter Ruling No. 7949001 a corporation was permitted to

---

[28] 68 T.C. 881 (1977).

reallocate contributions to its money purchase pension plan and profit-sharing plan so that the plans would qualify under Section 401 of the Code. The corporation adopted a prototype plan in 1973 and made contributions in 1973, 1974, and 1975. On audit, the Service held that the eligibility requirements of the plan were not followed and that one part-time employee was erroneously included while three full-time employees were excluded from coverage. The Service ruled that the entity sponsoring the prototype plan was in error, not the corporation. Since the mistake was one of fact and not one of law, and since no distributions had been made from the plan, the corporation would be allowed to restructure the plan to meet the coverage requirements.

In 1980, the Service promulgated Document 6651, "IRS Employee Plans Restoration Guidelines." Under these guidelines, retroactive relief is available for a variety of plan deficiencies. In the case of plans that are discriminatory, restoration may be accomplished by increasing benefits to defined benefit plans or making supplemental contributions to defined contribution plans. Such corrections will reinstate the qualified status of the plan but will not restore qualified plan status treatment of employer contributions made during the plan's discriminatory period. As a result, contributions to defined benefit plans during open tax years in which there was discrimination will normally be disallowed, and contributions to defined contribution plans during open years in which there was discrimination will be deductible only when an amount attributable to the contribution is includable in the gross income of participants.[29]

Improper Exclusion of Employees

If the plan sponsor expressly attempts to categorize employees as independent contractors or employees of third-party organizations, the plan may discriminate in favor of the highly compensated employees by denying participation to staff employees.

Withdrawals from Qualified Plans

A profit-sharing plan may permit participants to withdraw all or part of their vested benefits provided that the underlying contributions have been allocated to their accounts for at least two years.[30] However, if withdrawals are subject to the approval of a plan administrative committee

---

[29] IRC § 404(a)(5).

[30] Rev. Rul. 71-295, 1971-2 C.B. 184.

and withdrawals are permitted only by highly compensated employees, then the plan discriminates in favor of the prohibited group and will be disqualified.[31]

Voluntary Waivers of Participation

Due to the often divergent needs of employees, some employers consider placing a provision in qualified retirement plans that permits employees to "opt out" of the plan. There appears to be little for the employer to lose by placing such a provision in a plan. However, several problems do exist. First, persons who voluntarily waive their participation are taken into account under the minimum participation tests. Therefore, if the number of persons opting out is substantial, such a provision may create coverage problems. Also, any opting out provision should be disclosed in the summary plan description. Moreover, if the plan is administered so that only highly paid individuals are permitted to opt out and if their compensation is correspondingly increased, then the plan may be considered a *de facto* cash or deferred profit-sharing plan. There is, however, no general prohibition against permitting highly paid employees to opt out of the plan as long as their compensation is not otherwise increased. Most district directors do not view the opting out of highly paid employees as a disqualifying event.

On the other hand, if lower paid employees opt out of the plan, the plan may be found to discriminate against them.[32]

Defining Compensation

Although most qualified retirement plans provide benefits based on the compensation listed in the employee's W-2 (the basic compensation), the term *compensation* would normally include both contractual and voluntary bonuses paid to the employees. Such a definition normally should not cause problems. However, if the shareholders normally receive substantial bonuses and the staff employees receive small or no bonuses, the plan

---

[31] Rev. Rul. 57-587, 1957-2 C.B. 270.

[32] Rev. Rul. 80-351, 1980-2 C.B. 152, Rev. Rul. 73-340, 1973-2 C.B. 134. Also, in *Richard F. Olmo,* 38 T.C.M. 112 (1979), pension and profit-sharing plans established by a professional corporation wholly owned by two dentists failed to qualify. The plan discriminated in favor of the prohibited group because, for the years in issue, the only participants in the plan were the two dentists. Of the two other employees who met the plan's minimum service requirements, one did not meet the minimum age requirement and the other had voluntarily waived her right to participate pursuant to provisions in the plan.

may be considered discriminatory if bonuses are used to figure contributions.[33]

Employee Turnover

During the pendency of a qualified retirement plan, if the staff employees of the corporation regularly terminate their service or are fired prior to their benefits becoming vested, the plan may be considered to have a discriminatory vesting schedule. Prior to TRA '86, this result was more likely where the schedule was less favorable than the 4-40 schedule.[34] Arguably, however, employee turnover may pose less of a threat to plan qualification after 1988 when the accelerated vesting schedules of TRA '86 take effect.

Further, the use of so-called last-day rules in qualified retirement plans may prove discriminatory if, due to the turnover statistics of the employer, they generally have been applied only against staff personnel. Last day rules provide that an employee will not be entitled to receive an allocation of employer contributions for the particular plan year of a defined contribution plan unless he or she is employed at the end of that plan year. Since it is generally staff personnel and not highly compensated employees who terminate during a plan year, the rules in operation only apply to staff personnel. Last-day rules should be eliminated from plans established by small businesses in order to avoid this potential discrimination in operation.[35]

Tax Consequences of Disqualification

If a plan is disqualified because it discriminates in operation, the following tax consequences will occur:

1. The trust will lose its tax-exempt status under Section 501(a), making the trust income taxable to the trust.

2. Section 402(b) will govern the taxability of employer contributions to the beneficiaries of the trust. Generally, contributions will be included in the employees' income under Section 83 to the extent they have a vested right to such benefits. Employer contributions that are taxable to the employee are considered part of current compensation; thus, the withholding of taxes by the employer is required.

---

[33] *Perry Epstein,* 70 T.C. 439 (1978).

[34] Rev. Proc. 76-11, 1976-1, C.B. 550.

[35] Ibid

3. The contributions of the employer will be deductible only to the extent that such amounts are includable in the participant's income and only if separate accounts are maintained to record the interest of each participant.[36] As a result, deduction of employer contributions to non-qualified defined contribution plans will be delayed for the period of years necessary for employer contributions to vest, and employer contributions to nonqualified defined benefit plans will simply not be deductible. Because of the possible loss of the deduction, the authors recommend that plans incorporate provisions requiring employer contributions to revert to the employer within one year of the disallowance of a deduction under Code Section 404.[37]

INSURANCE

Qualified retirement plans may insure the lives of the participants. There are a number of advantages in maintaining insurance in a qualified plan.

1. First, the possibility of an immediate and substantial benefit is secured without the necessity of relying on plan investments.
2. Second, life insurance purchased by a qualified retirement plan is purchased with tax-deductible dollars.
3. Finally, the proceeds of the life insurance policy are received income tax–free by the trust or other designated beneficiary. The "at risk" portion of the proceeds is the excess of the face value of the policy over its cash surrender value immediately prior to death.

There are also disadvantages in maintaining insurance in a qualified plan.

1. First, whole life insurance historically provides a low-yield investment for the trust. However, with the development in recent years of new insurance products such as universal life that pay close to market rates on the investment component, this may no longer be the general trend.
2. Second, adequate death benefits may be provided outside a qualified retirement plan through the use of other types of insurance such as split-dollar arrangements and group term insurance.

---

[36] IRC § 404(a)(5).

[37] ERISA § 403(c)(2)(C) permitting this type of reversion.

3. Third, the payment of life insurance premiums by the trust will reduce the amount of cash available to pay retirement benefits.
4. Finally, the cost of term life insurance protection (the P.S. 58[38] cost) is currently taxed to the employee.

Since the purpose of a qualified retirement plan is to provide *retirement benefits,* life insurance protection may be provided only if it is "incidental."[39] As a result, specific limitations are placed on the amount of life insurance that may be maintained in each type of qualified plan.

Profit-Sharing Plans

A profit-sharing plan is a plan that is primarily established to provide deferred distribution of benefits.[40] As previously mentioned, profit-sharing plan funds may generally be distributed only after the funds have been accumulated for a fixed number of years, which is at least two years.[41] A distribution of funds before that time may cause a profit-sharing plan to lose its qualified status.

Applying this general rule to the purchase of life insurance, premiums

---

[38] The P.S. 58 rate, one-year premium cost for $1,000 of life insurance protection:

Age	*Cost*	*Age*	*Cost*	*Age*	*Cost*	*Age*	*Cost*
15	$1.27	31	$2.57	46	$ 6.78	61	$22.53
16	1.38	32	2.70	47	7.32	62	24.50
17	1.48	33	2.86	48	7.89	63	26.63
18	1.52	34	3.02	49	8.53	64	28.98
19	1.56	35	3.21	50	9.22	65	31.51
20	1.61	36	3.41	51	9.97	66	34.28
21	1.67	37	3.63	52	10.79	67	37.31
22	1.73	38	3.87	53	11.69	68	40.59
23	1.79	39	4.14	54	12.67	69	44.17
24	1.86	40	4.42	55	13.74	70	48.06
25	1.93	41	4.73	56	14.91	71	52.29
26	2.02	42	5.07	57	16.18	72	56.89
27	2.11	43	5.44	58	17.56	73	61.89
28	2.20	44	5.85	59	19.08	74	67.33
29	2.31	45	6.30	60	20.73	75	73.23
30	2.43						

These rates are published in Rev. Rul. 57-747, 1955-2 C.B. 228; Rev. Rul. 66-110, 1966-1 C.B. 12.

[39] Treas. Reg. §1.401-1(b).

[40] Ibid.

[41] Rev. Rul. 54-231, 1954-1 C.B. 150.

for life insurance in a profit-sharing plan may be paid using funds that have been accumulated for two or more years without causing disqualification of the plan.[42] On the other hand, insurance premiums that are paid out of funds that have not been accumulated for at least two years normally are considered to be distributions to the employee. An exception exists if the purchase of insurance with funds that have not been accumulated for two years is *incidental* to the plan's primary purpose of providing deferred benefits. The purchase will be deemed incidental if certain requirements are met.

1. Where ordinary (whole life) insurance is purchased, the aggregate life insurance premiums for each participant must be less than one half the aggregate contributions allocated to that participant at any particular time, without regard to trust earnings and capital gains and losses. Moreover, the plan must require the trustee either to convert the entire value of the life insurance policy at or before the employee's retirement into cash, or to provide periodic income so that no portion of such value may be used to continue life insurance protection beyond retirement.[43]

2. In the case of term insurance, the aggregate life insurance premiums for each participant must not exceed 25 percent of the total amount of funds allocated to the participant's account.[44] The limitations on the purchase of life insurance protection do not apply to voluntary employee contributions.[45]

Notwithstanding that it is permissible for qualified profit-sharing plans to maintain life insurance on the lives of the employees, the authors generally recommend that profit-sharing plans not be used as life insurance vehicles. It is possible that in certain years a profit-sharing plan may not be funded, and thus the plan may not have sufficient funds to pay the premiums without causing the incidental limits to be exceeded.

Defined Benefit Pension Plans

A defined benefit pension plan funded with life insurance will be deemed to provide an incidental (and hence permissible) preretirement death benefit if either of two sets of requirements is met.

---

[42] Rev. Rul. 54-231, 1953-1 C.B. 150.

[43] Rev. Rul. 73-501, 1973-2 C.B. 127; Rev. Rul. 69-421, 69-2 C.B. 59; Rev. Rul. 54-51, 1954-1 C.B. 147, as amplified by Rev. Rul. 57-213, 1957-1 C.B. 157, and Rev. Rul. 60-84, 1960-1 C.B. 159.

[44] Rev. Rul. 61-164, 1961-2 C.B. 99; Rev. Rul. 66-143, 1966-1 C.B. 79; Rev. Rul. 70-611, 1970-2 C.B. 89; and Rev. Rul. 73-510, 1973-2 C.B. 386.

[45] Rev. Rul. 69-408, 1969-2 C.B. 58.

1. The purchase of insurance will be incidental if less than 50 percent of the employer contributions credited to each participant's account is used to purchase ordinary life insurance policies on the participant's life, even if the death benefit consists of both the face amount of the policies and the amount of other contributions credited to the participant's retirement benefit.

2. The purchase will also be incidental if the death benefit is funded by ordinary life insurance providing 100 times a participant's anticipated monthly normal retirement benefit, and if the preretirement death benefit does not exceed the greater of: (*a*) the proceeds of the 100 times life insurance policy or (*b*) the reserve under the 100 times life insurance policy plus the participant's account in the auxiliary fund.[46]

A defined benefit pension plan will not qualify if all of the employer's contributions are used for the purchase of ordinary life insurance policies on the lives of the participants.[47]

A postretirement death benefit is considered incidental if it does not exceed 50 percent of the base salary in the year before retirement and it costs less than 10 percent of the total cost of funding other pension plan benefits.[48]

Money Purchase Pension Plans

A money purchase pension plan may provide incidental preretirement death benefits that meet either the tests for profit-sharing plans or defined benefit pension plans.[49]

Tax Treatment

Employer contributions made to a qualified retirement plan that are used to pay insurance premiums are deductible to the employer, as are other contributions. However, the cost of the insurance provided under a qualified plan is treated as a current distribution to the participant and must be included in the participant's income for the year in which the premium is paid. The result is the same without regard to the type of policy purchased. The employee is taxed on the cost of the insurance protection if

---

[46] Rev. Rul. 74-307, 1974-2 C.B. 126, clarifying Rev. Rul. 68-453, 1968-2 C.B. 163 and Rev. Rul. 73-501, 1973-2 C.B. 127.

[47] Rev. Rul. 61-164, 1961-2 C.B. 99, and Rev. Rul. 54-67, 1954-1 C.B. 149.

[48] Rev. Rul. 60-59, 1960-1 C.B. 154.

[49] Rev. Rul. 74-307, 1974-2 C.B. 126, and Rev. Rul. 69-421, 1969-2 C.B. 59.

either the proceeds are payable to his or her estate or his or her designated beneficiary, or if the proceeds are payable to the trustee of the plan where the trustee is required by the terms of the plan to pay all proceeds over to the beneficiary of the participant. A participant is not taxed on the purchase of "key man" insurance by a qualified retirement plan where the proceeds of the insurance are payable into the general assets of the plan.

The amount of current taxable income to the participant is measured by the pure insurance protection under Regulations §1.72-16. The rates to be used are the one-year term rates established under Rev. Rul. 55-747 or the so-called P.S. 58 rates.[50] However, if the insurance company's rates for individual one-year term policies available to all standard risk customers is lower than the P.S. 58 rates, the lower rates may be used.[51]

Where group term life insurance is provided under a qualified retirement plan, the cost of the entire amount of protection is taxable to the employee and no part is exempt.[52] It is important to note that the P.S. 58 costs that have been taxed to the employee for life insurance protection may be recovered tax-free from the benefits received under the policy.[53] Tax-free recovery of the P.S. 58 costs will be available only if the benefits are ultimately received from the insurance contract with respect to which the P.S. 58 costs were included in gross income. If, however, the life insurance policy is surrendered and the proceeds are used to purchase an annuity or the proceeds are distributed in cash, tax-free recovery of the P.S. 58 basis will be forfeited.[54]

OTHER ISSUES

One significant result of the passage of TEFRA was the establishment of approximate parity between corporate plans and noncorporate or H.R. 10 plans. Prior to TEFRA, qualified plans maintained by corporations offered significant advantages over qualified plans maintained by partnerships and proprietorships. These advantages were so great that many practitioners advised small businesses to incorporate in order to obtain the more favorable tax treatment afforded to corporate plans. TEFRA largely eliminated the advantages of corporate plans such that a small

---

[50] 1955-2 C.B. 228.

[51] Rev. Rul. 66-110, 1966-1 C.B. 12.

[52] IRC § 72 and 79(b)(3).

[53] Treas. Reg. §1.72-1(b).

[54] Private Letter Rulings 7830082 and 7902083, and Rev. Rul. 67-336, 1967-2 C.B. 66.

business probably should not be incorporated if the only advantage of incorporation is the availability of a qualified *corporate* plan.

Nevertheless, several differences between corporate and noncorporate plans remain. First, the aggregation rules applicable to entities controlled by an owner-employee (a significant partner or a sole proprietor) are more inclusive than the aggregation rules applicable to related corporations.[55] Second, no deductions are allowed for qualified plan contributions on behalf of self-employed individuals to the extent that the contributions are allocable to the purchase of life, accident, health, or other insurance.[56] Third, self-employed participants may *not* elect forward averaging for distributions "on account of" separation from service except when the separation from service is caused by disability.[57] Fourth, a Treasury Regulation issued under pre-TEFRA law, which may or may not be rescinded, prohibits forfeitures in defined contribution plans from being allocated to the accounts of self-employed individuals.[58]

While these differences are not the only differences between qualified corporate and noncorporate plans, they illustrate the relatively minor nature of the current discrimination against noncorporate plans. Assuming, however, that the small-business owner wishes to incorporate, whether for the purpose of obtaining these advantages or for other purposes, the small employer's existing H.R. 10 plan or plans must be dealt with in some fashion.

DISPOSITION OF H.R. 10 PLANS ON INCORPORATION

Freezing the H.R. 10 Plan

Many tax advisers recommend that, upon an employer's incorporation, its existing H.R. 10 plan be "frozen"; that is, no further contributions will be made to the plan, and benefits of participants are either distributed in a lump sum or held for distribution under the normal distribution provisions of the plan. As a caveat, Code Section 72(t), as enacted by TRA '86, imposes a 10 percent penalty tax on certain distributions to employees who are under age 59½. The distribution method may be elected by

---

[55] IRC § 401(d)(1)(2).

[56] IRC § 404(a)(8)(C).

[57] IRC § 402(e)(4)(A).

[58] Treas. Reg. §1.401-11(b)(3).

participants in a one-time irrevocable election offered for an election period that expires prior to the date on which distributions may be made under the election. Earnings on amounts that are not distributed will continue to compound tax-free, and the frozen plan will simply constitute another deferred compensation benefit that will be payable at a later date. Generally, savings and loan institutions, as opposed to banks, offer lower minimum fees and, consequently, employers should consider transferring frozen H.R. 10 plans to savings and loan institutions.

Termination of Plans and Distribution to Participants

If the H.R. 10 plan participant is over 59½, he or she may generally receive a distribution of funds on plan termination without incurring a penalty. However, if the employee is under age 59½ and a distribution is made, the 10 percent penalty tax on the premature distribution will generally be assessed under Section 72(t)(5) of the Code unless the distribution, reduced by any amounts contributed by the employee, is rolled over within 60 days into an individual retirement account or individual retirement annuity.

A termination distribution that is rolled over will not be subject to the 10 percent excise tax imposed as a result of a premature distribution since Section 72(t)(5) of the Code only imposes the tax on amounts that are included in gross income. Given a rollover of the entire H.R. 10 distribution less employee contributions, no amount is included in gross income. It should be noted, however, that a distribution from an H.R. 10 plan on behalf of a participant who is a 5 percent owner may not be rolled over into another H.R. 10 plan or corporate qualified plan either directly[59] or through a conduit IRA.[60] The IRS has approved a direct transfer from the trustee of one H.R. 10 plan to the trustee of another H.R. 10 plan or to the trustee of a corporate plan.[61]

Termination of Plan and Transfer of H.R. 10 Funds to Qualified Retirement Plans of the New Small Business

The assets of an existing H.R. 10 plan may be transferred from the trustee of the H.R. 10 plan directly to the trustee of the successor corporate qualified retirement plan without creating a premature distribution, as

[59] IRC § 402(a)(5)(F)(ii).

[60] IRC § 408(d)(3)(A).

[61] See Private Letter Ruling 7733009.

long as the special requirements of H.R. 10 plans for the owner-employees are observed and as long as the assets do not pass through the hands of participants. In Rev. Rul. 71-541,[62] the Service approved the transfer of H.R. 10 plan assets to a profit-sharing plan of a successor corporation since the profit-sharing plan provided that (1) the trustee would always be a bank; (2) separate accounts would be maintained for funds transferred on behalf of each owner-employee; (3) no payment of benefits would be made from the separate accounts on or before the owner-employee reached age 59½ or became disabled; and (4) distribution from the owner-employee's account had to begin prior to the end of the taxable year in which he or she attained age 70½. As noted, however, TEFRA and TRA '86 eliminated many of the distinctions between H.R. 10 plans and corporate plans, some of which are provisions of Rev. Rul. 71-541. Thus, while Rev. Rul. 71-541 has not been withdrawn, these restrictions should no longer apply to plan-to-plan transfers.

---

[62] 1971-2 C.B. 209

CHAPTER 49

QUALIFIED RETIREMENT PLANS FOR SMALL BUSINESS: TAX CONSIDERATIONS

HARRY V. LAMON, JR.
JAMES A. CLARK

INCOME AND ESTATE TAX CONSEQUENCES OF DISTRIBUTIONS ON TERMINATION

Qualified retirement plans are normally established because of the tax advantages that they offer at the time they are adopted: the corporation is able to deduct contributions currently, and participants can defer inclusion of the contributions in their gross incomes until amounts are distributed or made available under the plan. However, the employer should not overlook the important and unique tax opportunities that are available on the ultimate distribution of benefits. This section will deal with the unique tax aspects of benefits received on termination of participation in a qualified retirement plan. The tax treatment of certain preretirement benefits, such as life insurance, preretirement profit-sharing plan distributions, and loan provisions has been dealt with previously and will not be repeated here.

Plan provisions govern the various forms in which plan benefits may be paid to participants and beneficiaries. In an individually designed plan the employer may assure that the benefit provisions are drafted in such a manner as to be consistent with the tax planning and business needs of the company. For example, while certain valuable tax advantages are available only if a participant's accrued benefit is paid as a lump-sum distribution, employers often decide to limit the circumstances under which lump sums are paid so as to prevent a departing employee from using a lump-sum payment as a financial springboard for setting up a competing business.

The initial step in determining which forms of benefit distribution are to be included in a plan is to consider the various benefit options that are theoretically available. If the participant's vested accrued benefit (i.e., the vested amount in the participant's profit-sharing or money purchase account, or the present value of the participant's vested defined benefit) does not exceed $3,500, the plan may be drafted so as to give the plan administrator the option to involuntarily "cash out" the participant on his or her termination by paying the participant the lump-sum value of the vested accrued benefit.[1]

In most situations, the retiring employee will have a choice that includes: (1) receiving the benefit as a lump-sum distribution, (2) receiving payments for a fixed number of years certain, or (3) receiving payments in the form of an annuity measured by the participant's expected lifetime (a life annuity) or the combined lifetime of the participant and some other person such as the spouse or designated beneficiary of the participant (a joint and survivor annuity). It is quite common for profit-sharing plans and stock bonus plans to eliminate the life annuity option so that the plan will be able to avoid compliance with the burdensome joint and survivor annuity rules. However, all plans that are subject to the minimum funding standards of Code Section 412 (money purchase and defined benefit plans) must make a qualified joint and survivor annuity the normal form of benefit.

Once the employer determines the options that are available, he or she should consider the following issues as they apply to each alternative:

1. What are the immediate income tax consequences of this form of distribution?
2. What are the long-term income tax consequences of this form of distribution?
3. What are the estate tax consequences of this form of distribution?
4. Is this form of distribution coordinated with the employee's personal retirement planning?

---

[1] IRC § 411(a)(7)(B)(i).

Consequences of Lump-Sum Distributions

A lump-sum distribution, in general terms, is a distribution of the balance of a participant's account under a plan (and in certain cases several plans maintained by an employer must be aggregated) within one taxable year of the recipient, which distribution is made as a result of the participant's death, disability, or separation from service or after the employee attains age 59½. Complexities and potential pitfalls for the unwary abound in the area of lump-sum distributions, and professional advice should normally be sought in advance if this alternative is considered. If a lump sum is received, the employee is faced with the critical decision of determining whether to "roll the distribution over" into an individual retirement plan or to retain the distribution and elect to have it taxed under the special five-year averaging rule of Section 402(e) of the Code.

Tax Consequences of Five-Year Averaging

A recipient of a lump-sum distribution will be taxed under five-year averaging only if this method of taxation is elected.[2] An election to use five-year averaging is made by filing Form 4972 with the recipient's income tax return. This election can be made or revoked at any time during the period in which the income tax return for the year of receipt of the distribution can be amended; that is, within three years of the filing deadline. Five-year averaging may be elected only once with respect to a participant and may only be elected if the participant whose accrued benefit is distributed was an active participant in the plan, including certain predecessor plans, for at least five years.[3]

In general, the amount of tax imposed on a lump-sum distribution will be five times the amount of tax that would be imposed under Section 1(c) of the Code if an unmarried individual received 1/5th of the lump sum as his or her only income during the taxable year and if the zero bracket amount or standard deduction did not apply to the individual.[4] The tax may be further reduced by a minimum distribution allowance under Section 402(e)(1)(c) of the Code. (See Chapter 47 for a discussion of the grandfather provisions of TRA '86 that may make 10-year averaging and/

---

[2] IRC § 402(e)(4)(B).

[3] IRC § 402(e)(4)(H) and Private Letter Rulings 8002078 and 8027025, with respect to using service in a predecessor plan to satisfy the five-year requirement.

[4] IRC § 402(e)(1)(B).

or capital gains treatment available, as under pre-1987 tax law, to certain electing recipients of lump-sum distributions.) Table 49–1 indicates the amount of tax that would be imposed in 1987 on a lump-sum distribution of various amounts, as well as the percentage of the distribution that would be paid to satisfy the tax imposed:

TABLE 49–1
Tax Imposed on Lump-Sum Distributions, 1987

Amount of Lump Sum	*Tax Imposed*	*Percentage of Distribution Required to Pay Income Taxes*
$ 20,000	$ 1,500	7.50%
100,000	16,398	16.40
250,000	60,110	24.04
500,000	140,000	28.00
1,000,000	280,000	28.00

Table 49–1 indicates that, if the amount of the distribution is small, the five-year averaging election will create a very attractive tax rate. On the other hand, as the size of the lump-sum increases, the advantage of continued deferral of tax by way of a rollover to an individual retirement account will in many cases outweigh the benefit of an immediate "reduced" tax under the five-year averaging formula. Persons contemplating the use of five-year averaging should consider not only the immediate tax impact but also the long-term tax consequences. First, once the distribution is received, earnings generated by the distribution are exposed to immediate taxation. Also, where made on account of a participant's death, a lump sum is included in the individual's gross estate for estate tax purposes. Finally, lump-sum recipients might be tempted to increase current expenditures for unneeded or luxury items, so that a large portion of the lump sum might not be available to provide for future retirement security.

Rollover of Lump Sums

The alternative to electing five-year averaging of a lump-sum distribution is rolling over all or any part of the lump sum into an individual retirement account or individual retirement annuity (IRA). An amount may be rolled over *no later than* 60 days after receipt of a lump-sum distribution.[5] Therefore, one should plan in advance and identify the specific vehicle to be used for the rollover prior to receipt of the distribution. If a recipient changes his or her mind after completing a rollover, the rollover may be revoked with a minimum financial penalty if action to revoke is taken prior to the time for filing an income tax return, including extensions, for the taxable year in which the lump sum was received.[6] However, generally if the recipient is younger than 59½ in the year of receipt of a revoked IRA rollover, the 10 percent penalty on early distributions will apply to the rollover that is returned. In addition, the financial institution that maintains the IRA may impose interest or administrative cost penalties for early revocation. Once the IRA is revoked, the recipient may elect five-year averaging of the distribution.

Rollover of a lump sum is available even if the participant whose accrued benefit is distributed was not an active participant in the plan for five years or any other minimum period. Furthermore, a rollover may be accomplished even if the recipient has previously elected five-year averaging after age 59½. The entire amount received in a lump-sum distribution need not be rolled over,[7] and any amounts not rolled over will be subject to tax at ordinary income rates. A recipient cannot elect five-year averaging with respect to a portion of a lump sum that is not rolled over.

The amount of a lump sum that represents employee contributions may not be rolled over but will be retained by the recipient tax-free.[8] Income attributable to employee contributions may, however, be rolled over.[9] If the distribution includes property other than cash, the recipient either must roll over the identical property distributed, or he or she must sell the property distributed during the period of up to 60 days between receipt of a lump sum and its rollover and roll over the proceeds of sale.[10] No gain or loss will be recognized on such sales to the extent the proceeds are rolled over. A rollover is available not only to a participant who receives a lump sum, but also to the spouse of a participant who receives a lump sum on account of the participant's death.[11]

The immediate tax consequence of a rollover is that taxation of benefits is deferred with respect to the amount rolled over until such amount is

[5] IRC § 402(a)(5)(C).

[6] IRC § 408(d)(4) and Private Letter Rulings 8044031 and 8045026.

[7] IRC § 402(a)(5)(A)(ii).

[8] IRC § 402(a)(5)(B).

[9] Private Letter Ruling 8037034.

[10] IRC §§ 402(a)(5)(A)(ii) and 402(a)(6)(D).

[11] IRC § 402(a)(7).

actually received from the IRA. Distributions from the IRA may begin at any time after the year in which the owner of the IRA reaches age 59½. An earlier distribution would result in a 10 percent excise tax under Section 72(t) of the Code. Once age 59½ is attained and prior to reaching age 70½, distributions from the IRA are up to the discretion of the owner. Furthermore, there is no "constructive receipt" from an IRA. Thus, the owner can have the ability to demand all or any part of the IRA at any time without fear of being taxed before the money is actually received.[12] Amounts actually distributed from an IRA are taxed as ordinary income. One cannot receive a lump sum from an IRA and elect five-year averaging on the amount received; therefore, in most cases the decision to use an IRA will foreclose use of five-year averaging.

Once age 70½ is attained, or beginning with the year of the rollover if in that year the owner is older than 70-½,[13] the owner of an IRA must have an amount distributed from the IRA that is a certain fraction of the balance in the IRA at the beginning of the year. Failure to receive the minimum required distribution results in an excise tax under Section 4974 of the Code equal to 50 percent of the amount by which the required distribution exceeds the actual distribution. The fraction of the beginning year's balance in the IRA that must be distributed has a numerator equal to one and a denominator equal to the life expectancy of the owner, or combined expectancies of the owner and his or her spouse, as of the owner's 70th birthday *minus* the number of calendar years that have commenced after the owner attained age 70½.[14] The single life expectancy of a male age 70 is currently 12.1 years and of a female age 70 is 15 years. The joint life expectancy of a husband and wife who are both age 70 is 18.3 years.[15] Rather than receiving payments for a period certain, an annuity for the life of the participants or joint lives of a participant and his or her spouse may be purchased at age 70½. This option might be attractive to an individual who is relying on a rollover IRA as the principal source of retirement income.

TEFRA added a new level of complexity to the use of rollover IRAs. Specifically, effective for individuals dying after December 31, 1983, an

---

[12] Private Letter Rulings 8008170, 8015093, and 8038101.

[13] Private Letter Ruling 8044059.

[14] Treas. Regs. § 1.408-2(b)(6).

[15] A deferred payment over 18.3 years may be very attractive because, under the formula of Treas. Regs. §1.408-2(b)(6), the required annual distribution during the first 10 years will normally not even be equal to the interest earned on the IRA. This permits continued deferral of all the principal and some of the interest until future years.

individual's entire interest in an IRA must be distributed within five years of his or her death or, if applicable, the death of his or her surviving spouse, if distributions over a term certain have not commenced before the death of the individual for whose benefit the account was maintained.[16]

Summarizing the key characteristics of using a rollover IRA, this alternative will create no initial income taxation since neither the rollover nor the return of employee contributions are subject to tax. In the long term, the IRA alternative may be used to defer taxation of benefits distributed from a qualified plan; however, since voluntary employee contributions cannot be rolled over, use of the IRA rollover forecloses further deferral of income earned on voluntary employee contributions. The use of a rollover IRA will undoubtedly increase the likelihood that the participant will retain his or her plan benefits to provide retirement income, rather than use the distribution for current expenditures, as might be the case where five-year averaging is utilized with a lump-sum distribution.

Receipt of Periodic Retirement Benefits from the Qualified Corporate Plan

Rather than receiving a lump-sum distribution, a participant could elect to receive a distribution over a fixed number of years from the qualified corporate plan. One advantage of this alternative is that payments may commence prior to age 59½ without giving rise to the 10 percent penalty on early distributions. However, the manner of distribution elected by a participant must provide for the payment of his or her entire interest under the plan over his or her life, or over the joint life expectancies of the participant and his or her designated beneficiary. As discussed below, failure to receive periodic payments that meet this requirement can give rise to a 50 percent penalty.

Receipt of installment benefits directly from the corporate plan provides greater flexibility in the timing of payments than receipt from an IRA. Also, the doctrine of "constructive receipt" does not apply to qualified retirement plans. Therefore, a participant will not be subject to income tax on amounts made available to him or her until such amounts are actually distributed.

If an employee has a large amount of voluntary contributions, he or she might prefer electing installment payments from the plan rather than receiving and rolling over a lump sum. This is because employee contribu-

---

[16] IRC § 401(a)(9).

tions may not be rolled over, and therefore, earnings attributable to employee contributions would lose their tax shelter under the rollover alternative. By contrast, these contributions would remain tax-sheltered if benefits were distributed in installments from the plan.

Distributions from a qualified corporate plan after the death of the participant, including amounts attributable to employee contributions, are included in the participant's gross estate. However, where the participant's spouse is the designated beneficiary, or receives the proceeds through the participant's estate, the distribution will qualify for the unlimited marital deduction under Code Section 2056(a). Also, to reduce the income tax payable on the death benefit, the spouse could elect five-year averaging on a lump-sum distribution. Alternatively, the spouse of the participant may be given a lump-sum distribution that could be rolled over into an IRA by the spouse.[17]

In summary, a participant may prefer receiving deferred benefits directly from a corporate plan, particularly if the participant has a large amount of voluntary employee contributions. This alternative permits continued deferral of income taxation of accrued benefits and of earnings on accrued benefits including earnings on employee contributions. This alternative might be best suited for a corporation that has only one shareholder since, after the shareholder participant retires, the plan could be frozen. Freezing the plan would minimize the opportunity for later events to disqualify the plan, alter the investment strategy, or modify the administration in a manner that would be to the detriment of the retired shareholder.

Minimum Payout Rules

As alluded to above, effective for years beginning after 1988, TRA '86 imposes minimum distribution rules on *all* qualified plans including IRAs and annuity plans. Generally, the rules require that distribution of a participant's benefit must commence by the April 1 following the year in which the participant attains age 70½.[18]

The minimum distribution amount is generally the participant's entire interest in the plan. However, where distribution is in the form of periodic payments, the minimum periodic payment amount must be sufficient to distribute the participant's entire interest under the plan over his or her life expectancy or the joint life expectancies of the participant and his or

---

[17] IRC § 402(a)(7).

[18] IRC § 401(a)(9)(c).

her designated beneficiary.[19] Where the amount distributed during a year is less than the maximum periodic payment, the *recipient* is liable for an excise tax equal to 50 percent of the amount by which the minimum required payout exceeds the amount actually distributed.[20]

TRA '86 provides a transitional rule that excludes certain participants from the minimum distribution requirements. To be so exempted, a participant must *not* be a 5 percent owner and must have attained age 70½ by January 1, 1988. Such individuals may defer the commencement of benefits until they actually retire under the plan.[21]

Excise Tax on Large Benefits

TRA '86 also imposes a 15 percent excise tax on benefits that exceed certain distribution limits. Generally, the annual limit is equal to $150,000 and includes distributions from *all* plans in which an individual participates, including IRAs. The recipient of an excess distribution is liable for the excise tax.[22] Where a distribution qualifies as a lump-sum distribution, the limit is increased to $562,500.

For purposes of determining whether a distribution exceeds the limits, amounts that are attributable to employee contributions or rollovers are *not* taken into account. Further, TRA '86 offers transitional relief with respect to benefits that were accrued prior to August 1, 1986.

AFFILIATED SERVICE GROUPS

Section 414(m) of the Code requires that all related entities that constitute an "affiliated service group" must be treated as a single employer for purposes of determining whether a qualified retirement plan maintained by any member of the affiliated service group satisfies a number of the qualification requirements, including the nondiscrimination provisions, minimum participation rules, vesting rules, and Code Section 415 limitations. The applicability of Code Section 414(m) is specifically limited to "service organizations"—entities that have as their principal business the performance of services—and to other entities that regularly perform services for or in connection with *service* organizations. Because the

---

[19] IRC § 4974(b).

[20] IRC § 4974(a).

[21] TRA '86 § 1121(d)(4).

[22] IRC § 4981.

focus of Code Section 414(m) is service organizations, the principal target of Code Section 414(m) is professional corporations. Therefore, the discussion that follows will examine the impact of Code Section 414(m) in the context of professional corporations, although it should be kept in mind that any "service organization" is within the purview of Code Section 414(m).

Under Code Section 414(m), partnerships of professional or other service corporations may not discriminate in favor of the shareholder/professionals in providing qualified retirement plans. To enable the reader to better understand the reasoning behind the complex affiliated service group rules, what follows is an examination of the state of the relevant law prior to the enactment of the affiliated service group rules in 1980, an analysis of Code Section 414(m), and a recommendation with regard to what action should be taken while final regulations under that Section are pending.

Revenue Ruling 68-370—The IRS States Its Position

Until December 28, 1980, the rules that governed employee participation in the qualified retirement plans of partnerships of professional corporations were clearly stated by the Service. Through Rev. Rul. 68-370,[23] (now obsolete) the Service ruled that a corporation that participated in a joint venture would be required to take employees of the joint venture into account in determining whether the corporation's profit-sharing plan met the requirements of Section 401(a). The Service viewed the joint venture of the two corporations as a partnership that, while not itself a taxable entity, was nonetheless the aggregate of the constituent partners. Therefore, the establishment of the requisite employment relationship between the partnership and the common-law employees of the partnership also established such relationship between each corporate partner and such employees for purposes of Section 401.

The important effect of this conclusion was to attribute to each corporate partner the common-law employment relationship that existed between the partnership and the individual employees. Thus, since the employees of the joint venture were considered employees of the corporate partners, the Service held that such employees, and a pro rata share of the compensation paid to them, must be taken into account by each corporate partner in determining whether the qualified plan of each corporate part-

---

[23] 1968-2 C.B. 174.

ner met the coverage and nondiscrimination requirements set forth in Section 401(a).

Packard/Burnetta Cases—The Tax Court Approves the Service Position

In *Ronald C. Packard*,[24] three dentists, practicing in a partnership, formed a service corporation to which all nonprofessional employees were transferred. The service corporation owned the office building in which the partnership was located and provided bookkeeping and general staff services and facilities to the partnership and to other dentists not in the partnership.

The Tax Court held that the profit-sharing plan adopted by the partnership (which covered only the dentists-partners) was qualified. The court reached this decision after determining that: (1) the service corporation was formed for a bona fide business purpose and was not a subterfuge and (2) the service personnel were directed and controlled by and therefore, by the familiar common-law test, were employees of the service corporation as opposed to the partnership. The court emphasized the following factors:

1. The service corporation marketed a complete package of services incidental to the practice of dentistry and sold this complete service not only to the partnership but also to three independent dentists.
2. The fee paid to the service corporation was not limited to a percentage of wages and expenses but rather was a percentage of gross billings with respect to subscribers.
3. The relationship between the service corporation and the subscribers was formalized in a written lease and management contract.
4. The partnership and the other subscribers were entitled to specify only the results to be accomplished by the service personnel while the service corporation maintained the right to control, hire, and fire service personnel.

It should be noted that *Packard* involved tax years prior to the enactment of Section 414(b) and (c) of the Code. If the *Packard* situation arose today, the likely and proper result would be that, under Section 414(c),

---

[24] 63 T.C. 621 (1975).

the service employees would be treated as employed by the dental partnership, since the three dentists were in a single partnership and had the requisite degree of control in both the partnership and the service corporation.

The Tax Court again used the common-law employee attribution test in *Edward L. Burnetta, O.D., P.A.*[25] In that case, an opthalmologist and an optometrist formed separate professional corporations and adopted qualified retirement plans. Subsequently, they contracted with a service corporation, owned by the accountant for the professional corporations, to provide service personnel. As originally conceived, the service corporation was to be responsible for the selection, hiring, training, and supervision of all service personnel for a number of unrelated professional corporations. In practice, however, the selection, hiring, training, and supervision of the service personnel were maintained by the respective professional corporations. Thus, the Tax Court held that the service personnel were employees of the professional corporations for whom they worked and, consequently, the qualified retirement plans did not meet the coverage requirements of Section 401(a)(3)(A) (pre-ERISA).

The Tax Court distinguished the *Packard* decision on the basis that in *Packard* the taxpayers were able to establish under the common-law employee test that control over the service personnel in fact rested in the service corporation, not in the partnership. If Sections 414(b) and (c) had been in existence, their strict application to this case, without consideration of the common-law employee test espoused under Rev. Rul. 68-370, would have resulted in the opposite conclusion.

The *Kiddie* Case—Pre-ERISA

In the pre-ERISA case of *Thomas Kiddie, M.D., Inc.*,[26] the Tax Court, discussing partnership law instead of the common-law employee/employer rules, thoroughly confused the area of employee participation in qualified plans of professional partnerships. Dr. Kiddie's professional corporation provided pathological services to a hospital. In 1972, the corporation created a partnership with another professional service corporation to provide pathological services, with each corporation owning 50 percent of the partnership. The staff employees of Dr. Kiddie's corpo-

---

[25] 68 T.C. 387 (1977), government appeal dismissed *nolle pros*. (10th Cir. 1978).

[26] 69 T.C. 1055 (1978).

ration then became employees of the partnership, and Dr. Kiddie's corporation adopted a qualified pension plan.

The court held that the staff employees were employees of the partnership and were properly excluded from Dr. Kiddie's pension plan. The court, holding that the Section 707(b) "greater than 50 percent test" should apply for purposes of Section 401(a)(3), refused to attribute the partnership's employees to Dr. Kiddie's corporation because it owned only 50 percent of the partnership and therefore did not control the partnership. Whether Dr. Kiddie's corporation controlled the partnership's employees and, thus, was their employer, was not examined by the Tax Court.

The IRS Position after *Kiddie*

The Service refused to follow *Kiddie* and continued to follow Rev. Rul. 68-370. For instance, in Letter Ruling 7834059, three professional corporations each held a one-third interest in the capital and profits of a law partnership with six full-time employees. One of the professional corporations proposed the adoption of a profit-sharing plan. The Service ruled that this corporation could adopt a profit-sharing plan, complying with the coverage and nondiscrimination requirements of Section 401(a), even if the other two corporations and the partnership did not adopt such a plan. Further, the employees of the partnership would be considered the full-time employees of the professional corporation and would participate in the profit-sharing plan to the extent of one third of their compensation received from the partnership. If the professional corporations included the six employees of the partnership as participants in their qualified retirement plans, if any, to the extent of one third of their compensation received from the partnership, then the participation and nondiscrimination requirements of Section 401(a) of the Code would be satisfied. The Service then stated:

> It is our conclusion that the conclusion stated in Rev. Rul. 68-370 has not been affected by the enactment of the Employee Retirement Income Security Act of 1974 [ERISA] and that it still may be relied upon for authority that the employees of a partnership or joint venture are considered employees of each member or partner for purposes of testing for coverage and nondiscrimination in contributions or benefits. We believe that Sections 414(b) and (c) do not establish exclusive rules for aggregation of employees for these purposes. It is our belief that Congress in enacting ERISA did not seek to erode the established rules of the Internal Revenue Service pertaining to such matters, but rather sought to extend the coverage and nondiscrimination requirements of the Code with respect to affiliated business

entities regardless of whether any employee of a member of the control group performs services for another member of the control group.[27]

The *Garland* Case—Post-ERISA

An approach similar to that taken by the Service in Letter Ruling 7834059 was rejected by the Tax Court in its unfortunate opinion in *Lloyd M. Garland, M.D., F.A.C.S., P.A.*[28] Petitioner, a professional medical corporation, formed a partnership with a physician, and each partner owned a 50 percent interest in the partnership. The professional corporation adopted a pension plan that did not cover the common-law employees of the partnership. Dr. Garland felt that his professional corporation was not required by either Section 414(b) or Section 414(c) to cover the partnership's employees under the plan. Nevertheless, the Service determined that the plan did not qualify under Section 401(a) because it did not comply with the antidiscrimination provisions of Sections 401(a)(4) and 410(b)(1).

The Tax Court held, directly contrary to the position stated in Letter Ruling 7834059, that Sections 414(b) and 414(c) *are the exclusive* means for determining whether the employees of affiliated entities should be aggregated for purposes of applying the antidiscrimination provisions. Further, the Tax Court held that, since the professional corporation did not control the partnership's employees, they were properly excluded from participation in the plan. The reasoning in *Kiddie* was followed, totally ignoring the logic and desirability of using the common-law employee test as used in Rev. Rul. 68-370 as an alternative means of compliance with the antidiscrimination provisions.

Effects of Section 414(m)

Section 414(m), which was enacted in 1980, provides rules for the aggregation of employees of certain separate organizations for purposes of applying qualification tests to various employee benefit plans. It is an emphatic response to the absurd results that have received judicial approval in *Kiddie* and *Garland,* but applies *only* to service organizations.[29]

For purposes of determining the qualified status of a member's pension plan under Section 414(m), all employees of members of an "affili-

---

27 The Service took the same position in Letter Ruling 7902086 and Letter Ruling 7905020.

28 73 T.C. 5 (1979).

29 A complete text of Section 414(m) is given in the appendix to this chapter.

ated service group'' are treated as employed by a single employer. An affiliated service group consists of a service organization and one or more other organizations, service or otherwise, that are related in their ownership. The broad definition of organization includes a corporation, partnership, or ''other organization.'' Section 414(m)(2) defines an affiliated service group as follows:

> (2) AFFILIATED SERVICE GROUP—For purposes of this subsection, the term ''affiliated service group'' means a group consisting of a service organization (hereinafter in this paragraph referred to as the ''first organization'') and one or more of the following:
>
> (A) any service organization which
>
> (i) is a shareholder or partner in the first organization, and
>
> (ii) regularly performs services for the first organization or is regularly associated with the first organization in performing services for third persons, and
>
> (B) any other organization if—
>
> (i) a significant portion of the business of such organization is the performance of services (for the first organization, for organizations described in subparagraph (A), or for both) of a type historically performed in such service field by employees, and
>
> (ii) 10 percent or more of the interests in such organization is held by persons who are highly compensated employees, (within the meaning of section 414(q)) of the first organization described in subparagraph (A).

In Rev. Rul. 81-105,[30] the Service provided an explanation of Section 414(m) and illustrated the application of the affiliated service group classification by way of three examples. Rev. Rul. 81-105 ruled that it obsoletes Rev. Rul. 68-370, so that entities that must be treated as a single employer under Section 414(m) may not satisfy the minimum coverage and nondiscrimination requirements by providing a full benefit to one entity of the affiliated service group and providing a partial benefit to the rank and file employees in affiliated entities.

In Rev. Proc. 81-12,[31] the Service provided a procedure under which plan sponsors may request a ruling from the national office of the IRS as to whether two or more entities are part of an affiliated service group, and may request a determination letter from the key district director as to whether plans maintained by members of an affiliated service group satisfy the qualification requirements. It is important that plan sponsors who believe they may be part of an affiliated service group make a specific

---

[30] 181-1 C.B. 256.

[31] 181-1 C.B. 652.

request for the determination when submitting plans for qualification, since a determination letter will not apply to the Section 414(m) issue unless the determination letter request raises this issue. The Service has revised Item 10 of Forms 5300 and 5301 to permit plan sponsors to indicate whether they are, or believe they are, a part of an affiliated service group.

In the typical affiliated service group situation, a corporate partner that is a member of a partnership of professional corporations establishes a plan covering only the individual who is the sole shareholder and sole employee of the professional corporation. As a result of the required aggregation of Section 414(m), the plan, when considered alone, fails to satisfy the minimum participation and nondiscrimination requirements for qualification.

Prior to TRA '86, it was necessary for the corporate partnership to establish a qualified plan that benefits the staff employees employed by the partnership, in order that the professional corporations could establish retirement plans that were "comparable" to the partnership's plan. In Rev. Rul. 81-202,[32] the Service provided a comprehensive set of rules for testing the comparability of contributions and benefits provided by qualified pension and profit-sharing plans. These rules permitted plans that were required to be aggregated under Sections 414(b), (c), or (m) to provide either comparable contributions *or* comparable benefits and thereby satisfy the nondiscrimination tests of Section 401(a)(4) and the minimum participation tests of Section 410(b)(1).

Commencing after 1988, the new minimum participation rules under Section 401(a)(26), that were introduced by TRA '86, will eliminate the use of comparable plans in most affiliated service group settings. As an affiliated service group will be treated as a single employer for purposes of Section 401(a)(26), the requirement that *each* plan include the lesser of (a) 50 employees of the employer, or (b) 40 percent of the employees of the employer will effectively force small affiliated service groups to adopt single plans covering all members.

Reallocation of Income

In its attempts to recharacterize transactions and arrangements for tax purposes, the Service may use statutory provisions in addition to the basic "substance over form" theory. Two sections are particularly useful to the service: Code Section 482 and Code Section 269A.

---

[32] 1981-2, C.B. 93.

Section 482 permits the Service to allocate income and deductions among taxpayers in order to clearly reflect their income. For example, in order for a partnership of professional corporations to achieve favorable results, it is necessary that the professional corporations be taxed on their distributive shares of partnership income and that the shareholder-employees of the professional corporations be taxable only on the compensation paid to them by their respective professional corporations. Section 482 may be utilized by the Service in an effort to reallocate income away from the professional corporation and to its shareholder-employee on the theory that the distributive share of partnership income was earned by the shareholder.

The Service may take the position that it is the professional shareholder-employees and not the professional corporations who are, in fact, the members of the partnership because it is their personal efforts that actually create the partnership income. If such a position were to prevail, all professional income would be attributable to the individual shareholder-employees as opposed to the professional corporations. Also, in a one-person service corporation, the service may take the position that the corporation's income is actually the shareholder's personal income.

The Service has, over the years, had varying degrees of success in reallocating income under Section 482 between a sole shareholder and his or her corporation. For instance, in *Borge* v. *Commissioner,*[33] the taxpayer was deemed, for purposes of Section 482, to own or to control two businesses (an entertainment business and a poultry business) and a portion of the entertainment compensation paid to his corporation was reallocated to him personally. The reallocation was predicated on the finding that the taxpayer merely assigned a portion of his entertainment income to his corporation and the corporation did nothing to earn or assist in earning that income. In the case of *Richard Rubin,*[34] the controlling shareholder had corporation A enter into a management contract with corporation B, whereby the controlling shareholder, as an employee of corporation A, would provide management services for corporation B. The controlling shareholder carried on a separate trade or business of rendering managerial services and thus fell within the purview of Section 482, and income was reallocated from corporation A to the shareholder.

In *Silvano Achiro,*[35] the Tax Court refused to sustain the Commis-

---

[33] 26 T.C.M. 816 (1967), aff'd 405 F.2d 673 (2d Cir. 1968), cert. denied sub nom. *Danica Enter., Inc.* v. *Commissioner,* 395 U.S. 933 (1969).

[34] 51 T.C. 251 (1968), reversed and remanded, 429 F.2d 650 (2d Cir. 1970), on remand 56 T.C. 1155 (1971), aff'd per curiam 460 F.2d 1216 (2d Cir. 1972).

[35] 77 T.C. 881 (1981).

sioner's asserted 100 percent reallocation of income under Code Section 482 from a management corporation to the controlling shareholders of the management corporation where the management corporation was established for the purposes of entering into management contracts with two other operating corporations that were controlled by the shareholders of the management corporation, and where the terms of the management contracts and the terms of the shareholders' employment contracts with their management corporation were arm's-length. The management corporation's taxable income was nominal since over 90 percent of the management fees that it received were paid out for salary and pension contributions. The Tax Court held that for purposes of determining whether the shareholders' compensation was an arm's-length rate of pay or whether it was subject to reallocation under Code Section 482, qualified plan contributions will be taken into account. The Tax Court rejected the Commissioner's position that incorporations motivated by a desire to obtain the benefits of corporate qualified plans was improper. Specifically, the Tax Court stated:

> The keynote in respondent's present position under Sections 482, 269, and 61 is his contention that incorporation for the principal purpose of taking advantage of corporate pension and profit-sharing plans amounts to an evasion or avoidance of income taxes, an unclear reflection of income, and/or an assignment of income. We disagree. Of course, a mere corporate skeleton, standing alone and without any flesh on its bones, will not suffice to provide its shareholder-employees with corporate retirement benefits. See *Roubik* v. *Commissioner,* 53 T.C. 365, 382 (1969) (Tannenwald, J., concurring). Once incorporated, the personal service business must be run as a corporation. Its shareholder-employees must recognize, respect, and treat their personal service corporation as a corporation. The corporation must accept the disadvantages as well as advantages of incorporation. Once a corporation is formed and all organizational and operational requirements are met it should be recognized for tax purposes regardless of the fact that it was formed to take advantage of the richer corporate retirement plans.

In *Keller* v. *Commissioner,*[36] the Tax Court similarly rejected the Commissioner's challenge under Code Sections 482, 269, and 61 of a one-person professional corporation formed by a pathologist and used to replace the pathologist as a partner with other doctors. The Tax Court noted that: (1) the doctor's professional corporation was properly formed, (2) the corporation had entered into an arm's-length employment contract with the doctor (taking into account both cash compensation and qualified

[36] 77 T.C. 1014 (1981).

plan contributions), (3) the corporation was substituted as partner with the consent of all other partners, (4) the corporation maintained a bank account in its own name, and (5) the corporation used its own name on its office door and all stationery. Under these circumstances the Tax Court held that reallocation of income under Code Section 482 between the corporation and the doctor was improper because the total compensation, both cash and qualified plan contributions, was "essentially equivalent to that which he would have received absent incorporation." A portion of the corporation's first year's income was reallocated to Dr. Kelley for personal services he performed in his individual capacity before his corporation was submitted as partners. A strong dissent was written by six Tax Court judges. The Tax Court has followed the *Keller* line of reasoning in *Garbini Electric, Inc.*,[37] and *Pacella*.[38] In *Edwin C. Davis*,[39] the Service was unsuccessful in attempting to allocate income under Code Section 482 from X-ray and physical therapy corporations to an orthopedic surgeon who set them up and then gave the stock to his children.

The possibility that the professional corporation may not be recognized for tax purposes under the *Roubik* rationale or that income may be allocated either away from the professional corporation partners or among them in a different fashion under Section 482 represents a formidable, but not insurmountable, obstacle to the operation of a partnership of professional corporations. Certainly the Tax Court's decisions in *Silvano Achivo* and *Keller* provided a good deal of reassurance to tax planners. The determination of whether to apply the *Roubik* rationale or Section 482 is essentially a factual one, and proper adherence to both the form and substance of rendering professional services as a corporate partner in a professional partnership should minimize the risk in this area. At the very least, the parties should take steps to insure that the professional corporations are the actual earners of the income. The professional corporations should enter into employment agreements with the professional employees and should, in fact, retain and exercise control over the professionals' employment. The professional employees should be prohibited from entering into contracts in their individual names, and all contracts should be in the names of the professional corporations or the partnership. Also, the professional corporations must hold themselves out to the public as rendering professional services by insuring that all statements, letterheads, office signs, business cards, telephone listings, building directories, and

---

[37] 43 T.C.M. 919 (1982).

[38] 78 T.C. 604 (1982).

[39] 64 T.C. 1034 (1975).

similar business practices reflect the status of the professional corporations. A written partnership agreement should be made and consideration should be given to placing all leases, insurance policies, and other contractual agreements in the name of the professional partnership. Also, the professional partnership should hold itself out to the public as such and should also hold itself out to the Service as a partnership by obtaining an employer identification number as a partnership, by making employer tax deposits for its common-law employees, and by filing partnership income tax returns.

If, in fact, the Service prevails in disregarding a corporate entity, the professional corporation's qualified retirement plan will probably be disqualified and the employees of the corporations will lose the other employee benefits, such as group term life insurance, health and medical reimbursement plans, and so on. However, if income is reallocated under Section 482, it is possible that the corporations' qualified retirement plans would not be disqualified, but plan contributions could be disallowed as deductions since the corporations would not be considered as having income and would pay no compensation.

The Service also may use new Code Section 269A to reallocate income, deductions, and other tax items between a corporation and its shareholder or shareholders. Code Section 269A provides that, if substantially all of the services of a personal service corporation are performed for on or behalf of one other corporation, partnership, or other entity and if the principal purpose for forming or availing of the corporation is the avoidance or evasion of federal income tax, then the Service may allocate all income, deductions, credits, exclusions, and other allowances between such personal service corporation and its employee-owners. The report of the Conference Committee on TEFRA states that "[t]he conferees intend that the provisions [of Section 269A] overturn the results reached in cases like *Keller* v. *Commissioner* where the Corporation served no meaningful business purpose other than to secure tax benefits which will not otherwise be available."[40] The Conference Committee's reference to *Keller* implies that Section 269A only is applicable to partnerships of professional corporations, since *Keller* concerned a partnership of professional corporations formed for the purpose of maximizing the tax benefits available on incorporation. Nonetheless, by its terms, Section 269A is applicable to any small-business corporation that performs substantially all of its services for one customer, client, or patient. Obvi-

[40] CONF. REP. NO. 97-530, 97th Cong. 2nd. sess. 634 (1982).

ously, Section 269A may be applicable to most hospital-based physicians who operate in corporate form.

While those service providers who now operate in corporate form may have incorporated for nontax reasons, for example, the availability of corporate limited liability, service providers who adopted and continue to maintain qualified retirement plans and who receive other corporate tax benefits may find the Service only too willing to read Section 269A broadly.

APPENDIX: A COMPLETE TEXT OF SECTION 414(m)

(m) EMPLOYEES OF AN AFFILIATED SERVICE GROUP.

(1) IN GENERAL—For purposes of the employee benefit requirements listed in paragraph (4), except to the extent otherwise provided in regulations, all employees of the members of an affiliated service group shall be treated as employed by a single employer.

(2) AFFILIATED SERVICE GROUP—For purposes of this subsection, the term "affiliated service group" means a group consisting of a service organization (hereinafter in this paragraph referred to as the "first organization") and one or more of the following:

(A) any service organization which
- (i) is a shareholder or partner in the first organization, and
- (ii) regularly performs services for the first organization or is regularly associated with the first organization in performing services for third persons, and

(B) any other organization if—
- (i) a significant portion of the business of such organization is the performance of services (for the first organization, for organizations described in subparagraph (A), or for both) of a type historically performed in such service field by employees, and
- (ii) 10 percent or more of the interests in such organization is held by persons who are highly compensated employees (within the meaning of section 414(q)) of the first organization or an organization described in subparagraph (A).

(3) SERVICE ORGANIZATIONS—For purposes of this subsection, the term "service organization" means an organization the principal business of which is the performance of services.

(4) EMPLOYEE BENEFIT REQUIREMENTS—For purposes of this subsection, the employee benefit requirements listed in this paragraph are—

(A) paragraphs (3), (4), (7), and (16) of section 401(a),

(B) sections 408(k), 410, 411, 415, and 416

(C) section 105(h), and

(D) section 125.

(5) CERTAIN ORGANIZATIONS PERFORMING MANAGEMENT FUNCTIONS—For purposes of this subsection, the term "affiliated service group" also includes a group consisting of—

(A) an organization the principal business of which is the performing, on a regular and continuing basis, management functions for 1 organization (or for 1 organization and other organizations related to such organization), and

(B) the organization (and related organizations) for which such functions are so performed by the organization described in subparagraph (A).

For purposes of this paragraph, the term "related organizations" has the same meaning as the term "related persons" when used in section 144(a)(3).

(6) OTHER DEFINITIONS—For purposes of this subsection—

(A) ORGANIZATION DEFINED—The term "organization" means a corporation, partnership, or other organization.

(B) OWNERSHIP—In determining ownership, the principles of section 318(a) shall apply.

CHAPTER 50

WELFARE BENEFITS FOR RETIREES

Richard Ostuw

Almost all large companies provide life insurance and health care benefits for their retired employees. Because most of the U.S. work force is employed by small- to medium-sized companies, however, only a minority of workers is currently eligible for postretirement welfare benefits.

Many employers began providing postretirement benefits when their retiree populations were small and their costs were low. Costs have grown tremendously since then. As a result, companies are paying close attention to their retiree benefit programs and are attempting to ensure that they meet specific objectives, including the following:

- Protecting retirees against the cost of unbudgetable medical expenses and providing a modest life insurance benefit to cover burial expenses.
- Promoting cost-effective use of medical care and discouraging the use of unnecessary care.
- Ensuring that employer contributions make the program competitive with that of other employers and that the employee contributions are affordable.

In the following pages we will review current practice with respect to retiree benefits, focusing primarily on medical benefits.

LIFE INSURANCE

In general, retirees' death benefit needs are less than those of active employees, and are met to some extent by survivor income benefits under the pension plan or by significant savings or profit-sharing balances at retirement. Many employers also provide some form of retiree life insurance.

Benefit Design

Life insurance for active employees typically takes the form of a basic employer-paid benefit amount that can be supplemented with optional employee-paid insurance. For retirees, the life insurance benefit is usually a flat dollar amount—generally in the range of $3,000 to $20,000—that the employer may update from time to time for new retirees. Ad hoc increases for current retirees are unusual. Another common approach, particularly for salaried employees, is to express the postretirement life insurance schedule as a percentage of the employee's final preretirement life insurance amount or final preretirement salary. Some employers reduce the benefit amount during retirement. They might, for example, reduce life insurance of two times salary for active employees by 20 percent per year during retirement to an ultimate level of 20 percent of the preretirement benefit—i.e., 40 percent of final pay. Such a benefit may also have a modest postretirement coverage maximum of perhaps $20,000.

Cost

Growth in the size of the retiree population—exacerbated in many companies by downsizing—has increased the cost of postretirement benefits substantially. More and more employers who once provided coverage on a pay-as-you-go basis now believe they should recognize the cost of these benefits on a pension-style expensing basis.

On such an advance expensing basis, the cost of postretirement life insurance is typically about .5 percent or less of the active employee payroll. In those companies that provide significant postretirement life insurance (such as two times pay without reduction), however, the advance expensing cost can approach 2 percent of payroll.

HEALTH BENEFITS

Few employers provided medical coverage to retirees before 1965 because the cost of doing so was prohibitive. When Medicare became effective in 1966, however, companies realized they could supplement Medicare coverage for their retirees at a modest cost. Over the years, the share of medical expenses covered by Medicare has diminished—although Medicare is still the primary payer for retirees—and the benefits provided by these employers have become more and more liberal. Thus, what was once low-cost postretirement medical coverage has become enormously expensive.

Benefit Design

Retirees usually receive the same medical benefits as active employees until they reach age 65 and become eligible for Medicare. At that point, their employer-provided benefits are coordinated with Medicare in one of two ways:

- The employer plan continues to provide the same benefits, but those benefits are offset by Medicare payments.
- Plan coverage is limited to expenses that are not paid by Medicare. This Medicare fill-in approach is often called MediGap or MediFill coverage.

Under the Medicare fill-in approach, the employer plan might pay all or part of the following hospital expenses for its retirees:

- The first level of expenses for each hospital admission, i.e., the Medicare Part A deductible ($540 in 1988).
- The Medicare copayment amounts beginning on the 61st day of hospitalization ($135 in 1988).
- Copayment amounts during the lifetime reserve days ($270 in 1988).
- The cost of hospital care extending beyond the period covered by Medicare.

Similarly, the employer plan may pay all or part of the expenses for physician and other nonhospital services not reimbursed by Medicare Part B. It may also cover all or part of the expenses commonly excluded by both parts of Medicare, such as prescription drugs and private nursing. Few plans cover custodial care in a nursing home.

We can use the Medicare Part A deductible to illustrate two methods of updating retiree medical coverage. Under one approach, the employer plan defines covered expense as the Medicare Part A deductible. When the Part A deductible amount increases, the employer plan automatically fills the gap. Under the other approach, the employer specifies a coverage amount (such as $500) and increases that amount only by plan amendment. The latter approach gives the employer the ability to control the impact of inflation and Medicare changes on its plan and its costs.

Liberal Medicare fill-in plans virtually eliminate out-of-pocket medical expenses for retirees; more restrictive plans may provide only modest benefits. For example, some plans do not cover hospital stays beyond the Medicare limit, physicians' fees not fully covered by Medicare, and prescription drugs and nursing care.

By its terms, Medicare appears to reimburse 80 percent of physician's fees after a modest deductible ($75 in 1988). In actual practice, however, the reimbursement level is much lower—closer to 50 percent—because of Medicare's low level of allowed charges. Most employer plans define "reasonable and customary" physician fees as those charged by about 90 percent of physicians in the area—the 90th percentile. Medicare's reasonable and customary fees were set at a lower level and are increased on the basis of general price increases (the overall Consumer Price Index). Because physicians' fees have risen significantly faster than overall prices, Medicare fee limits have fallen further and further behind actual doctors' fees.

Eligibility

In the typical retiree benefit program, eligibility rules for postretirement health care and life insurance benefits follow the employer's pension plan definition of retirement. The most common such definition is termination of employment after attainment of age 55 and 10 years of active service. An employee hired at age 40, for example, first becomes eligible for retirement at age 55; a person hired at age 50 becomes eligible at age 60. Many plans impose no minimum service requirement for employees who terminate employment at or after age 65.

Employees may also be eligible for retirement after 30 years of service regardless of age, or upon attaining a specified number of years of age plus service. The "Rule of 80," for example, would be satisfied by any combination of age and service that equals or exceeds 80. This approach is common for both unionized and salaried employees in industries with a strong union presence. These eligibility rules are very liberal, considering the value of lifetime medical benefits and the potentially short working careers of some covered retirees. Few employers impose more restrictive eligibility requirements, however. For one thing, they are concerned about meeting employee needs. For another, many of them have not yet recognized the true cost of providing these benefits.

Nearly all retiree medical plans extend coverage to the spouses and children of retirees as those relationships are defined in the active employee plan. Some plans are more restrictive, however, and may, for example, exclude the spouses of marriages that occur after employees retire.

Employee Contributions

According to TPF&C's Employee Benefit Information Center, the prevalence of contributory plans for retiree medical coverage among large employers is approximately as follows:

	Percentage of Plans Requiring Employee Contributions	
	Until Age 65	*Age 65 and Later*
Employee coverage	55%	45%
Dependent coverage	70	55

In general, it is more common for employers to require contributions from retirees than from active employees. Post-age-65 retiree contributions cover a greater portion of total plan cost than do contributions by pre-65 retirees or active employees. Employee-pay-all coverage is rare for active employees, for example, but not for retirees over 65.

Employee contributions may represent a percentage of plan cost or a flat dollar amount as summarized below:

Percentage of Cost

Under this approach, often used for post-65 coverage, retirees are required to contribute a specified percentage of the expected plan cost for the coming year—usually 20 percent to 33 percent but sometimes as much as 100 percent. If a plan required a 25 percent employee contribution and plan costs were expected to be $80 per month per covered person, for example, retirees would have to contribute $20 per month.

Dollar Amounts

It is more usual for employers to require specified dollar contributions. Although such an approach may reflect a cost-sharing policy, the underlying percentage of plan cost is generally not disclosed to employees or retirees. Employers using this approach usually update dollar amounts every three to five years. Nonetheless, updates generally have failed to keep pace with increases in plan costs. Employers often procrastinate in making changes that employees will view as benefit reductions. Further, planning for and implementing such updates is very time consuming.

The percentage approach is becoming more popular because it allows employers to update contribution amounts without creating the perception of a benefit take-away. This is especially important in view of recent court decisions limiting employers' ability to reduce retiree benefits.

Employee contributions are generally payable by deduction from the employee's pension check, although in some companies retirees send a monthly check to the employer. Coverage is terminated if payment is not made on a timely basis.

Medical Plan Design Elements

Medical plan design elements are the same for retirees and active employees. There are key differences between the two groups, however. For example:

- Age differences make retiree medical costs substantially higher than those of active employees. The average annual cost per person for retirees under age 65 is commonly about two times the average cost for active employees. Both the frequency and intensity of health care increase with age.
- Certain health conditions are more common among the elderly, such as hearing impairments and the need for implants.
- Elderly individuals require more time to recover from serious medical conditions and are therefore much more likely to need institutional care after a hospital discharge. Depending on the situation, that care may include extensive medical attention or may be largely custodial.
- Medicare assumes the bulk of the cost of hospital and physician services after age 65. The relative share of employer plan costs by type of expense for retirees over 65 thus differs from the cost share for active employees.

Covered Services

As with active employee plans, retiree medical plans generally cover a wide range of care and treatment, including hospital care, surgery, doctors' visits, therapy, and prescription drugs. Typically excluded from coverage are routine physical examinations, hearing and vision care, cosmetic surgery, and experimental procedures.

New developments in technology will have a substantial impact on medical costs for retirees. How the plan defines experimental procedures and how the administrator updates the rules will have significant consequences.

Benefit Levels

During the 1980s, many employers changed from "basic plus major medical" programs to comprehensive plans for both active employees and retirees. The two types of coverage are summarized below:

Basic Plus Major Medical. Basic benefits provide 100 percent reimbursement of covered expenses for certain types of services. Examples might include:

- Hospital inpatient services for up to 180 days.
- Surgery.
- Diagnostic X-ray and laboratory procedures.
- Emergency treatment for an accident.

The major medical component supplements basic benefits but reimburses less than the full expense—usually 80 percent of the expense in excess of an annual deductible of $100 per person.

Comprehensive. The typical plan pays 80 percent of expenses for all services, with an annual deductible of perhaps $100 per person, until the individual incurs out-of-pocket expenses of a specified amount—perhaps $1,000 in a year (taking into account the 20 percent coinsurance and the deductible). The plan pays 100 percent of expenses thereafter.

Employers have shifted to comprehensive programs for a number of reasons, including the following:

- Medical costs almost doubled between 1982 and 1984. Many companies that were unable or unwilling to absorb the full increase changed to a comprehensive program to reduce plan costs.
- Basic/major medical programs provide no financial incentives for patients to avoid costly in-hospital treatment and, in fact, often provide an incentive to use inpatient care rather than less expensive outpatient care. The change to a comprehensive plan redefines the reimbursement basis to establish financial incentives for using medical care more efficiently.
- Relatively low-cost services such as laboratory work and treatment for accidents add up to a significant portion of basic/major medical plan costs. Comprehensive plans shift these low-cost items to the employee through application of the annual deductible.

The following table illustrates the cost impact of a switch from a basic/major medical plan to a comprehensive medical plan for the active employee group and for retirees under age 65.

Annual Plan Cost for Employee Coverage	*Active Employees*	*Retirees Under 65*
Basic/major medical	$1,000	$2,000
Comprehensive	800	1,700
Cost reduction		
Amount	$200	$300
Percentage	20%	15%

Although the dollar amount of savings is larger for the retiree group, the reduction represents a smaller percentage of plan costs. The difference is due largely to the greater frequency of high-cost cases among retirees. The following examples show how the reimbursement percentage varies by level of expense for a plan with a $100 deductible, 80 percent reimbursement and a $1,000 out-of-pocket limit:

	Expense A	*Expense B*	*Expense C*
Charge	$100	$1,000	$10,000
Benefit	0	720	9,000
Reimbursement	0%	72%	90%

Utilization Review

In addition to or in lieu of the change to comprehensive coverage, many employers have established utilization review programs or incentive arrangements to minimize the use of unneeded medical care. Such provisions can be summarized as follows:

- *Reimbursement differences*. The plan pays a higher level of reimbursement (such as 100 percent instead of 80 percent) for types or locations of services presumed to be more cost-efficient, including preadmission testing and outpatient surgery. The benefit differential may apply only in certain circumstances—for specific surgical procedures identified by the employer, for example.
- *Review requirements*. The plan pays a higher reimbursement when there is a pretreatment review such as a second surgical opinion or hospital preadmission review.

The goal of these incentives is to reduce the use—and cost—of unnecessary care or to substitute less costly forms of care. To achieve these savings, a plan will incur some added cost in the form of administration expenses and more liberal benefits for selected services. For active employees and retirees who are not eligible for Medicare, the employer will experience a net cost reduction. There may be a net cost increase to the employer for retirees covered by Medicare. This is because the employer pays administration expenses and the cost of benefit increases while Medicare enjoys most of the savings from reduced in-hospital care or surgery.

Defined Dollar Benefit Approach

Under a traditional retiree medical plan, the employer "promises" to provide a stated level of benefits (with the possibility of changes in the benefit provisions). The key element is the *benefits level*. Under a new approach, the key element is the *dollar amount* the employer will pay toward the cost of the benefits. The employer contribution is the defined dollar benefit (DDB). Here is an illustration of how the DDB approach might work:

- The employer offers a medical plan with benefit features comparable to those offered to active employees.
- The employer contributes up to $100 per month per person for coverage until age 65 and $50 per month thereafter. The retiree must pay the balance of the plan cost. The employer contribution is available only as a subsidy toward the cost of the medical plan.
- The employer updates benefit features from time to time and will consider ad hoc increases in the defined dollar benefit.

The defined dollar benefit approach has these advantages:

- The employer has full control over future increases in its benefit costs because it determines the amount and timing of any increases in its contributions. (Employee concern about benefit adequacy and competition may create pressure for ad hoc increases, however.)
- Benefit features can be updated more easily than in traditional programs. This is because the employer's promise involves its contribution—not the benefits themselves—and any reduction in the benefit level will directly reduce employee contributions.
- Because benefit costs are communicated, employees will better understand the substantial value of the benefits they receive.
- The approach facilitates service-related benefit coverage, which is discussed below. In the above illustration, for example, the $100 and $50 employer contribution amounts could be prorated for service of less than 25 years.

- Retirees can be offered choices in how to apply their defined dollar benefit.

Service Recognition

The cost of retiree medical benefits is prompting more and more employers to tie employee contributions to service. Employee contributions might vary with service as follows:

Years of Service	*Retiree Contribution As Percentage of Plan Cost*
10–14	70%
15–19	55
20–24	40
25–29	25
30+	10

In this example, the employer contribution is approximately 3 percent of the plan cost for each year of employee service.

It is also possible to vary the benefit level by length of service, although this approach is generally more difficult to administer than one that uses variable employee contributions.

FINANCING

The three key considerations in financing retiree benefits are expense recognition, level of cost, and the funding vehicle.

Expense Recognition

Nearly all employers recognize the cost of retiree welfare benefits on a pay-as-you-go basis. In a sense, this is an historical accident. When employers began providing these benefits, they believed they were making a year-by-year commitment rather than a lifetime promise. They did not consider postretirement benefits to be a form of deferred compensation earned during an employee's working career. This was in sharp contrast to prevailing views applicable to postretirement income benefits, i.e., pension plans. Court decisions (which we will discuss below) and studies conducted by the accounting profession have now prompted many employers to change their views.

The Financial Accounting Standards Board (FASB) has been considering the issue of how retiree welfare benefits should be expensed for a number of years. The key question is this: Should companies be required to recognize the expense of postretirement welfare benefits during the working careers of employees and charge such amounts against current earnings? As a first step, FASB Statement 81 requires the disclosure of the amount expensed for these benefits and the basis for expensing. Pay-as-you-go cost recognition is still permitted.

Most observers expect that the FASB will ultimately require a pension-type expensing approach for medical benefits on the ground that such benefits represent a form of deferred compensation whose cost should be charged against earnings during the period when employees are productive.

Cost

On a pay-as-you-go basis, retiree medical plan costs are typically about $2,000 per year per person until age 65 and $600 per year thereafter. Overall, the average cost per employee (including dependents) is usually something more than $1,000 per year. (The cost for individual employers may be significantly higher or lower.) The present value of these costs depends on employee age at retirement and, of course, on the assumptions for the interest discount rate, mortality rates and inflation. Representative amounts are as follows:

Age at Retirement	*Present Value of Medical Benefits (per employee)*
55	$75,000
60	50,000
65	25,000

Roughly 60 percent of the cost is attributable to retired employees and 40 percent to their dependents. By comparison, the cost is commonly split 50–50 between active employees and their dependents, reflecting the larger average family size of these employees. Relatively few retirees have children who are still eligible under the medical plan.

Pay-as-you-go costs will rise in the future as a result of:

- Price increases measured by the Consumer Price Index (CPI).
- The introduction of new medical technology and new procedures.
- Changes in the frequency or utilization of health care or in the mix of services.
- Cost shifting by Medicare.

The health care share of the gross national product (GNP) was approximately 10.5 percent from 1982 through 1986. Continued growth of national medical care costs at the pace we have witnessed in the last ten years would result in an unaffordable level of costs. Society will not allow the health care share of the GNP to reach 25 percent.

Nonetheless, employers will experience substantial cost increases if Medicare fails to maintain its share of health care costs. The following example shows the impact of overall medical cost increases of 8 percent per year and Medicare benefit increases of 7 percent on annual per person costs.

	Year 1	*Year 2*	*Year 3*
Medical expense	$3,000	$3,240	$3,499
Gross plan benefit (80%)	2,400	2,592	2,799
Medicare benefit	1,900	2,033	2,175
Net plan benefit			
Amount	500	559	624
Percent of expense	16.7%	17.3%	17.8%
Average annual increase			
Medical expense	—	8.0%	8.0%
Medicare	—	7.0%	7.0%
Net benefit	—	11.8%	11.6%

The 1 percent "slippage" in Medicare benefits adds almost another 4 percent to employer plan costs on top of the 8 percent increase in medical expenses. This is equivalent to a plan liberalization from 16.7 percent benefit reimbursment to 17.8 percent in only two years and is largely beyond the control of the employer.

Expensing annual retiree benefit costs on a pension-type basis during the working years of employees has these results for representative groups of employees:

	Cost as Percent of Payroll
Normal cost	1–3%
Amortization of unrecognized past service cost	3–5
Total Expense	4–8

Funding

Several funding alternatives are available to employers who want to recognize the cost of retiree benefits on a pension-type basis. These include:

- *Book reserve*. The employer accrues the cost on its financial statement and retains the assets within the organization.
- *Voluntary Employees' Beneficiary Association (VEBA)* under §501(c)(9) of the Internal Revenue Code. The employer contributes funds to an independent trust from which benefits are subsequently paid. The Deficit Reduction Act of 1984 (DEFRA) severely restricts the use of VEBAs for retiree health plans by limiting the amount of tax-deductible contributions to such trusts and subjecting the investment income to the Unrelated Business Income Tax. Neither of these problems applies to prefunding of retiree life insurance or to the welfare plans of a not-for-profit organization.
- *Pension plans*. A special account for medical benefits may be maintained as part of a pension plan under Section 401(h) of the Internal Revenue Code. Within limits, contributions to the account are deductible when made and investment income is exempt from tax even after DEFRA.
- *Insurance contracts*. Insurance contracts can be used in either of two ways to prefund retiree welfare benefits. Assets can be accumulated in an insurance continuation fund for subsequent payment of pay-as-you-go costs. Paid-up insurance may also be used. Under the latter approach, a one-time premium is paid to fund benefits for the lifetime of the retirees. These insurance approaches may be used for either life or medical insurance, but are much more common for the former.
- *Union funds*. Under many multiple-employer union-negotiated plans, contributions are made to a Taft-Hartley fund. The fund is responsible for the benefits to retirees.

Legal Issues

Employee communication materials often describe current postretirement welfare benefits and include a statement reserving the employer's right to modify or terminate the overall benefit plan. Many employers, however, fail to communicate their right to reduce benefits or fail to reserve this right consistently, omitting it in certain editions of the summary plan description or in such ancillary vehicles as employee newsletters or preretirement counseling materials.

Employer attempts to reduce or eliminate medical benefits for current retirees have resulted in significant litigation. (It is interesting to note that no case has involved the issue of whether such actions improperly infringed on the rights of active employees.) Following is a summary of several representative cases:

- In *U.A.W.* v. *Yardman,* the employer attempted to terminate medical coverage for retirees. A federal appeals court held that the employer was obligated to continue the benefits because it had promised coverage to retirees. Once an individual achieved the *status* of retiree, the benefits could be discontinued only if the individual no longer held that status. Thus, the employer was obligated to continue lifetime coverage for retirees.
- In *Eardman* v. *Bethlehem Steel,* the employer attempted to reduce the level of benefits and increase the level of required contributions by retirees. A federal district court ruled that, in effect, the employer had given up its right to make such changes by omitting the required language in written communications and by making oral promises to retirees at exit interviews. The company and its retirees subsequently reached a compromise whereby benefit reductions and increased contributions were implemented but the company promised not to attempt such changes again.
- In the case of *In Re White Farm Equipment,* a federal district court went further than the above cases. It concluded that benefits were vested and could not be reduced or eliminated regardless of any statements by the employer. On appeal, however, this reasoning was not accepted and the case was returned to the lower court for review on its merits.

In another situation, LTV terminated its retiree welfare benefits when it filed for protection under Chapter 11 of the bankruptcy laws. It restored the benefits under great pressure from Congress and others. Congress then legislated a mandatory continuation of coverage for an interim period—during which Congress will presumably develop a permanent solution.

These cases have been widely reported and have received a great deal of attention. Many other employers have made changes in their medical benefits for current retirees, usually concurrent with and similar to changes in their active employee plans, but these actions have not been reported by the press because there has been no litigation.

At this time, neither the employers' ability to modify retiree benefits nor the employees' rights under the plans are fully defined. Further litigation—and perhaps legislation—will probably help clarify the situation.

CHAPTER 51

PLAN TERMINATION INSURANCE FOR SINGLE–EMPLOYER PENSION PLANS*

Jack L. VanDerhei

The Pension Benefit Guaranty Corporation (PBGC) is a federal government agency created under Title IV of the Employee Retirement Income Security Act (ERISA). In general, the purposes of the PBGC are to encourage the continuation and maintenance of voluntary private pension plans for the benefit of their participants, provide for the timely and uninterrupted payment of pension benefits to the participants and beneficiaries under all insured plans, and minimize over the long run the premiums charged for the insurance coverage. The PBGC administers two insurance programs: one for single-employer and one for multiemployer pension plans. This chapter deals exclusively with single-employer plans.

COVERAGE

The PBGC's single-employer plan termination insurance provisions apply to virtually all defined benefit pension plans. The following material examines the specific plans covered and then describes the types of pension benefits protected by this insurance program.

---

* Parts of this chapter are based on material that appeared in Everett T. Allen, Jr.; Joseph J. Melone; Jerry S. Rosenbloom; and Jack L. VanDerhei, *Pension Planning,* 6th ed. (Homewood, Ill.: Richard D. Irwin, 1988). Subsequent to the time this chapter was written, the Omnibus Budget Reconciliation Act of 1987 substantially modified the plan termination insurance program for single-employer pension plans. The implications of these changes are summarized in the appendix.

Plans Covered

Subject to specific exceptions, ERISA Section 4021(a) requires mandatory coverage of employee pension benefit plans that either affect interstate commerce (and, in the case of nonqualified plans, have for five years met the standards for qualified plans) or that are qualified under the Internal Revenue Code. Thirteen types of plans are specifically excluded from coverage:

1. Individual account plans (e.g., money purchase pension plans).
2. Governmental plans.
3. Certain church plans, unless an election has been made to have the provisions apply.
4. Certain plans established and maintained by a society, order, or association if no part of the contributions to or under the plan is made by employers of participants in the plan.
5. Plans that do not provide for employer contributions.
6. Unfunded plans that are maintained by an employer primarily for the purpose of providing deferred compensation for a select group of management or highly compensated employees.
7. Plans that are established and maintained outside of the United States primarily for the benefit of individuals substantially all of whom are nonresident aliens.
8. Plans that are maintained by an employer solely for the purpose of providing benefits for certain employees in excess of the limitation on contributions and benefits imposed by Section 415.[1]
9. Plans established and maintained exclusively for substantial owners.[2]
10. Plans of an international organization that are exempt from taxation under the International Organizations Immunities Act.
11. Plans that are maintained solely for the purpose of complying with applicable worker's compensation laws or unemployment compensation or disability insurance laws.

---

[1] See Chapter 47 for a discussion of the Section 415 limits.

[2] A substantial owner is defined as any individual who:

1. Owns the entire interest in an unincorporated trade or business.
2. Is a partner with more than 10 percent of the capital or profits interest.
3. Is a stockholder with more than 10 percent of the value of voting stock, or more than 10 percent of all classes of stock.

Any individual who was a substantial owner within 60 months preceding the termination must be treated as a substantial owner.

12. Defined benefit plans, to the extent that they are treated as individual account plans under ERISA Section 3(35)B.
13. Plans established and maintained by a professional service employer that does not (at any time after the enactment of ERISA) have more than 25 active participants in the plan.

For purposes of the last category, a professional service employer means any proprietorship, partnership, corporation, or other association or organization owned or controlled by professional individuals or by executors or administrators of professional individuals, the principal business of which is the performance of professional services. Professional individuals include, but are not limited to, physicians, dentists, chiropractors, osteopaths, optometrists, other licensed practitioners of the healing arts, attorneys-at-law, public accountants, public engineers, architects, drafters, actuaries, psychologists, social or physical scientists, and performing artists.

Guaranteed Benefits

Even though a plan is covered by the PBGC's single-employer plan termination insurance, there is no assurance that all accrued pension benefits will be paid after the plan's termination. The individual participant (or beneficiary) must first meet three prerequisites before the benefit is guaranteed by the PBGC. Assuming the prerequisites are met, the individual may still be subject to specific limitations on the amount of the benefit covered. Both of these issues are examined in this section.

Prerequisites for PBGC Guarantees

Subject to various limits described below, the PBGC guarantees the payment of all nonforfeitable benefits that qualify as a pension benefit other than those accelerated by plan termination. A benefit that becomes nonforfeitable solely because of plan termination is not subject to ERISA benefit guarantees; however, a benefit won't fail to satisfy the PBGC requirements merely because a participant is required to submit a written application, retire, or complete a mandatory waiting period as a condition for receiving pension payments.

There are two additional exceptions to the general rule on forfeitability. First, guaranteed benefits paid to surviving beneficiaries are not deemed to be forfeitable for purposes of the PBGC guarantee merely because the plan provides for termination of benefit payment should the beneficiary remarry or attain a specific age. Second, disability benefits will not be deemed forfeitable solely because they end on a participant's recovery.

For a payment to qualify as a pension benefit, it must be payable as an annuity or as one or more payments related to an annuity. Further, the benefit must be payable either to a participant who permanently leaves or has left covered employment or to a surviving beneficiary. It is also necessary for the pension benefit payment to provide a substantially level income to the recipient, although the leveling could be accomplished in conjunction with social security payments. Under certain circumstances, the PBGC will also guarantee annuities payable for total disability[3] and benefits payable in a single installment.[4]

The final requirement for protection under the PBGC guarantee is that the participant or beneficiary be entitled to the benefit. This prerequisite is satisfied if any of the following conditions apply:

1. The benefit was in pay status on the date of plan termination.
2. The benefit payable at normal retirement age is an optional benefit under the plan and the participant elected the optional form of payment before the plan termination date.
3. The participant is actually eligible to receive benefits and could have received them before the plan terminated.
4. The benefit would be payable on the participant's retirement absent a contrary election.
5. The PBGC determines the participant is entitled to the benefit based on the particular circumstances.

Limitations on Insurance Coverage

Although a participant's or beneficiary's pension is insured by the PBGC without regard to the degree of funding by the plan sponsor prior to the termination, there are certain safeguards in the system to protect the PBGC against the possibility that a sponsor on the verge of bankruptcy will provide a generous increase in plan benefits. Instead of immediately phasing in insurance coverage for benefit liberalizations, the PBGC increases coverage at the rate of 20 percent per year.[5] However, the period of existence of a successor plan is added to the period of existence of the predecessor plan for purposes of the phase-in rule if substantially the same employees are covered and substantially the same benefits are provided.

---

[3] PBGC Regulation Section 2613.7.

[4] The benefit will not be paid in a single installment, but the PBGC will guarantee the alternative benefit, if any, in the plan that provides for the payment of equal periodic installments for the life of the recipient. PBGC Regulation Section 2613.8.

[5] In the case of a substantial owner, the guarantee of benefit payable is phased in over a 30-year period. This is subject to alternative phase-in formulas depending on whether or not participants have experienced a benefit increase and any change in plan provisions that advance a participant's or beneficiary's entitlement to benefits (e.g., liberalized vesting).

Even though all the preceding conditions are satisfied and any benefit increases have been fully phased in over a five-year period, it is possible that a participant or beneficiary may have his or her pension benefit reduced if the plan is terminated. This is due to the fact that the PBGC limits the insured amount to the actuarial equivalent of a straight life annuity payable monthly at age 65 equal to the lesser of:

1. A participant's average monthly income during the highest paid five consecutive years.
2. A specific dollar amount per month ($1,789 in 1986).

The average monthly income is determined without regard to temporary absences from participation and the specified dollar amount is indexed to reflect changes in the Social Security benefit base.

TERMINATIONS

During the first 10 years of the PBGC's existence, the insured event for single-employer plan termination insurance was simply the termination of the defined benefit pension plan. This event is generally within the control of the sponsor and, coupled with the fact that the sponsor's liability to the PBGC was at that time limited to 30 percent of its net worth, several underfunded plans were terminated even though the sponsor continued in existence and in some cases even attempted to establish a new pension plan immediately after the original plan was terminated. As the financial condition of the PBGC continued to deteriorate in the first half of the 1980s, several attempts were made to legislatively amend the definition of the insured event. The Single Employer Pension Plan Amendments Act of 1986 (SEPPAA) radically changed these provisions in an attempt to preserve the financial integrity of the system. The following section describes the new circumstances under which the single-employer plan termination insurance applies.

Types of Termination

A plan termination can be voluntary or involuntary. However, the PBGC will not proceed with a voluntary termination of a plan if it would violate the terms and conditions of an existing collective bargaining agreement.[6]

---

[6] It should be noted that this will not limit the PBGC's authority to proceed with an involuntary termination as described later in this chapter.

Voluntary Plan Termination

A single-employer plan may be terminated voluntarily only in a standard termination or a distress termination.

Standard Termination. A single-employer plan may terminate under a standard termination if, *inter alia,* the plan is sufficient for benefit commitments (determined as of the termination date) when the final distribution of assets occurs. Benefit commitments are defined as all benefits provided by the plan with respect to the participant or beneficiary that are guaranteed, would be guaranteed if not for the exceptions in the PBGC's insurance coverage (e.g., amounts in excess of the maximum guaranteed amount), or constitute either plant-closing benefits or early retirement supplements or subsidies. Determination of a benefit commitment is made irrespective of whether any such benefits are guaranteed, as long as the participant or beneficiary has satisfied all of the conditions required under the provisions of the plan to establish entitlement to the benefits, except for the submission of a formal application, retirement, completion of a required waiting period, or designation of a beneficiary.

Provided the PBGC has not issued a notice of noncompliance and the plan is sufficient for benefit commitments when the final distribution occurs, the plan administrator must distribute the plan's assets in accordance with the requirements for allocation of assets under ERISA Section 4044 (described later in this chapter).

Distress Termination. For a single-employer plan to terminate under a distress termination, the plan administrator must provide the PBGC with certification by an enrolled actuary of:

1. The amount (as of the proposed termination date) of the current value of the assets of the plan.
2. The actuarial present value of the benefit commitments under the plan.
3. Whether the plan is sufficient for benefit commitments.
4. The actuarial present value of guaranteed benefits.
5. Whether the plan is sufficient for guaranteed benefits.

After receiving this information, the PBGC must then determine whether the necessary distress criteria have been satisfied. Basically, these criteria are met if each person who is a contributing sponsor or a substantial member[7] of the sponsor's controlled group satisfies any of the following:

---

[7] The term *substantial member of a controlled group* means a person whose assets comprise 5 percent or more of the total assets of the controlled group as a whole.

1. Liquidation in bankruptcy or insolvency proceedings.
2. Reorganization in bankruptcy or insolvency proceedings.
3. Termination is required to enable payment of debts while staying in business or to avoid unreasonably burdensome pension costs caused by a declining work force.

If the PBGC determines that the requirements for a distress termination are met, it will determine (1) that the plan is sufficient for *guaranteed benefits* or that it is unable to make such determination on the basis of the available information, and (2) that the plan is sufficient for *benefit commitments* or that it is unable to make such determination on the basis of the available information. The plan administrator will be notified of the decision and one of the following types of terminations will be carried out:

1. In any case in which the PBGC determines that the plan is sufficient for *benefit commitments,* the plan administrator must distribute the plan's assets in the same manner as described for a standard termination.
2. In any case in which the PBGC determines that the plan is sufficient for *guaranteed benefits,* but unable to determine that the plan is sufficient for *benefit commitments,* the plan administrator must distribute the plan's assets in the same manner as described for a standard termination. In addition, the PBGC will establish a separate Section 4049 trust[8] for the plan.
3. In any case in which the PBGC is unable to determine that the plan is sufficient for guaranteed benefits, it will commence proceedings as though an involuntary termination (described later in this chapter) was taking place and set up a Section 4049 trust for the plan.

The plan administrator must meet certain requirements during the interim period from the time the PBGC is notified to the time a sufficiency determination is made. Essentially the administrator must:

1. Refrain from distributing assets or taking any other actions to carry out the proposed termination.

---

[8] A Section 4049 trust is used exclusively for receiving liability payments from the persons who were contributing sponsors of the terminated plan and members of their controlled groups, making distributions to the persons who were participants and beneficiaries under the terminated plan, and defraying the reasonable administrative expenses of the trust. Additional details of Section 4049 trusts are provided later in this chapter.

2. Pay benefits attributable to employer contributions, other than death benefits, only in the form of an annuity.
3. Not use plan assets to purchase irrevocable commitments to provide benefits from an insurer.
4. Continue to pay all benefit commitments under the plan, but, commencing on the proposed termination date, limit the payment of benefit under the plan to those benefits guaranteed by the PBGC or to which assets are required to be allocated under Section 4044.

The changing or amending of a plan from a defined benefit plan to a defined contribution plan is considered as a voluntary termination for insurance purposes. Therefore, unless the requirements for a standard termination or a distress termination are met, such conversions are not allowed.

Involuntary Plan Termination

The PBGC may institute termination proceedings in a U.S. district court in the jurisdiction where the employer does business if it finds at least one of the following:

1. The plan does not comply with the minimum funding standards of the Internal Revenue Code.
2. The plan is unable to pay benefits when due.
3. Within the preceding 24 months, and for a reason other than death, a distribution of $10,000 or more has been made to a participant who is the substantial owner of the sponsoring firm, and that following the distribution there are unfunded liabilities.
4. The eventual loss to the PBGC for the plan may be expected to increase unreasonably if the plan is not terminated.

Moreover, the PBGC is required to institute proceedings to terminate a single-employer plan whenever it determines that the plan does not have assets available to pay benefits that are currently due under the terms of the plan. The PBGC may decide not to seek involuntary termination even if one of the conditions for action has occurred if it deems that it would be in the best interest of those involved not to force termination of the plan.

Reportable Events

Certain events indicating possible danger of plan termination must be reported to the PBGC. Notification must be made within 30 days after the plan administrator knows or has reason to know that a reportable event has occurred. A reportable event takes place when:[9]

1. The IRS issues notice that a plan has become disqualified for tax purposes.
2. The Department of Labor determines the plan is not in compliance with Title I of ERISA.
3. An amendment of the plan is adopted that decreases the benefit payable with respect to any participant.
4. The number of active participants is less than 80 percent of the number of such participants at the beginning of the plan year, or is less than 75 percent of the number of such participants at the beginning of the previous plan year.
5. The IRS determines that there has been a termination or partial termination of the plan.
6. The plan fails to meet the minimum funding standards.
7. The plan is unable to pay benefits when due.
8. There is a distribution under the plan to a participant who is a substantial owner providing:
   a. Such distribution has a value of $10,000 or more.
   b. Such distribution is not made by reason of the death of the participant.
   c. Immediately after the distribution, the plan has nonforfeitable benefits that are not funded.
9. A plan merges, consolidates, or transfers its assets.
10. An alternative method of compliance is prescribed by the Department of Labor.

In addition, a reportable event takes place when any other event occurs that the PBGC determines may be indicative of a need to terminate the plan.

Allocation of Assets

Plan assets must be allocated to the benefit categories applicable on plan termination under ERISA Section 4044. Section 4044 prevents employers from establishing new benefit levels, terminating plans, and allocating existing plan assets to such benefits resulting in the subordination of insured to uninsured benefits. In order of descending priority, the categories are as follows:

---

[9] See PBGC Regulation Section 2615 for amplification of the requirements.

1. Participant's accrued benefits derived from voluntary employee contributions.
2. Participant's accrued benefits attributable to mandatory employee contributions.
3. Annuity benefits that were or could have been in pay status before the beginning of the three-year period ending on the date of plan termination.
4. In general, all other guaranteed basic benefits that do not exceed the guarantee limits.[10]
5. All other uninsured vested benefits.
6. All other benefits under a plan.

Subclasses can be established within priority categories 3–6; however, they may only be based on service, age, or existence of disability. Assets allocated to noninsured benefits must be reallocated if the initial allocation results in prohibited discrimination to highly compensated employees.

Reversion of Residual Assets to the Employer

In general, the funds in a qualified pension plan may not be used for purposes other than the exclusive benefit of employees or their beneficiaries prior to the termination of the plan and the satisfaction of all liabilities. However, with the exception of pension plan assets attributable to employee contributions, employers may recapture any residual assets of a terminated single-employer defined benefit pension plan if the following conditions are satisfied:

1. All liabilities of the plan to participants and their beneficiaries have been satisfied.
2. The distribution does not contravene any provision of law.
3. The plan provides for such a distribution in these circumstances.

Residual assets are equal to the plan funds remaining after satisfaction of all liabilities.[11]

The Tax Reform Act of 1986 imposed a tax of 10 percent of the amount of employer reversions from a qualified plan. The tax will not be

---

[10] This determination is made without regard to aggregate benefit limitations for individuals who are participants in more than one plan and phase-in limitations applicable to substantial owners.

[11] ERISA Section 4044(d). The allocation of residual assets attributable to employee contributions is described in PBGC Reg. Sections 2618.31–2.

imposed on certain amounts distributed to or on behalf of an employee (or the employee's beneficiaries). An exception to the tax also exists for certain reversions transferred from a qualified plan to an employee stock ownership plan (ESOP) prior to January 1, 1989.

The PBGC, Treasury Department, and the Department of Labor have issued the following joint implementation guidelines on asset reversions:

1. An employer may not recover any surplus assets until it has fully vested all participants' benefits and has purchased and distributed annuity contracts.
2. If employees are offered lump-sum payments in lieu of future pensions, the amount of the lump-sum distribution must fairly reflect the value of the pension to the individual.
3. An employer that terminates a sufficiently funded defined benefit pension plan may establish a new defined benefit plan covering the same group of employees, granting past service credit for the period during which an employee was covered by the terminated plan. This is known as a termination/reestablishment and the successor plan is exempt from the five-year phase-in of benefit guarantees that applies to newly established plans.
4. Spinoff/terminations[12] will not be recognized and any attempt to recover surplus assets will be treated as a diversion of assets for a purpose other than the exclusive benefit of employees and beneficiaries unless the employees receive timely notice of the event and the following conditions are satisfied:
   a. The benefits of all employees must be fully vested and nonforfeitable as of the date of the termination. This also applies to the benefits covered by the ongoing plan.
   b. All accrued benefits must be provided for by the purchase of annuity contracts.
5. In the case of a spinoff/termination and a termination/reestablishment, attempts to recover surplus assets will be treated as a diversion of assets for a purpose other than the exclusive benefit of employees and beneficiaries unless the funding methods for the

[12] Under a spinoff/termination, the active participants (and their liabilities) are spun off from the original defined benefit plan. Assets are then transferred from the original plan to the new plan in an amount at least equal to the active participants' liabilities. The original plan, which at this point covers only retired and terminated employees, is then terminated and annuities are used to satisfy the plan's obligations.

ongoing plans are to be changed by modifying the amortization bases.[13]

6. An employer may not engage in either a termination/reestablishment or spinoff/termination transaction involving reversion of assets any earlier than 15 years following such transaction.

Recapture of Certain Payments

ERISA Section 4045 permits recapture of all or part of any distribution made to a participant within three years of plan termination. This prevents the use of lump-sum or other preferential distributions to evade limitations on guaranteed benefits. The PBGC may recover all payments to a participant in excess of $10,000 made during any consecutive 12-month period within three years before termination, or, if greater, recapture the amount of any distribution in excess of the amount the participant would have received as a monthly benefit under a life annuity beginning at age 65 (provided the recapture is made during the same 12-month period).

Three exceptions to the general recapture rules exist. First, distributions made on account of death or disability are not subject to recapture. Second, if the recipient died within three years of termination, the payments are exempt, even if not paid on account of death. Finally, the PBGC can waive recapture of payments if it would result in hardship.

Date of Termination

For purposes of Title IV of ERISA, the termination date of a single-employer plan is one of the following:

1. In the case of a plan termination in a standard termination, the termination date proposed in the notice of intent to terminate.
2. In the case of a plan terminated in a distress termination, the date established by the plan administrator and agreed to by the PBGC.
3. In the case of an involuntary termination, the date established by the PBGC and agreed to by the plan administrator.
4. In the case of distress or involuntary termination in any case in which no agreement is reached between the plan administrator and the PBGC, the date established by the court.

---

[13] The modification must be in accordance with IRC Section 412(b)(4) (see Chapter 40 for a discussion of the minimum funding standards). Details of the modification are provided in PBGC News Rel. 84-23.

LIABILITY OF PLAN SPONSOR ON PLAN TERMINATION[14]

During the legislative process leading up to the enactment of ERISA, concern was expressed that in the absence of appropriate safeguards under an insurance system, an employer might establish or amend a plan to provide substantial benefits with the realization that its funding may be inadequate to pay the benefits called for. Such an employer might, it was argued, rely on the insurance as the backup that enables it to be more generous in promised pension benefits to meet labor demand than would be the case if it knew that the benefits would have to be paid for entirely out of the assets of the employer. On the other hand, it was clear that the imposition of heavy obligations on employers would discourage provisions for adequate pension plans.

To deal with these competing considerations, it was determined to impose on the employer a *limited* liability to reimburse the insurance system for a portion of the payment that must be made by the PBGC in satisfaction of its obligation if the employer's plan fails. Unfortunately, the limited liability was much smaller than the amount of unfunded benefits for many sponsors and several plans in this category were terminated to take advantage of this so-called pension put.

SEPPAA substantially modified the computation of the sponsor's liability on termination. Now, in any case in which a single-employer plan is terminated in a distress termination or an involuntary termination is instituted by the PBGC, any person who is, on the termination date, a contributing sponsor of the plan or a member of such a contributing sponsor's controlled group will incur a liability under Section 4062 of ERISA. This liability consists of three components:

1. The liability to the PBGC.
2. The liability to the Section 4049 trust.
3. The liability to the Section 4042 trustee.

Although special rules pertain to the case in which it is discovered that the plan is unable to pay guaranteed benefits after the authorized commencement of termination,[15] the following section defines the rules

---

[14] Special rules exist for determining the liability of substantial employers for *withdrawal* from single-employer plans under multiple controlled groups (ERISA Section 4063) and the liability on *termination* of single-employer plans under multiple controlled groups (ERISA Section 4064).

[15] ERISA Sections 4062(b)(1)(B) and 4062(c)(1)(B).

generally applying to the three components of the sponsor's liability and the required means of payment.

Liability to the PBGC

The liability to the PBGC consists of the sum of two components:

1. The lesser of:
   a. The total amount of unfunded guaranteed benefits of all participants and employees under the plan.
   b. Thirty percent of the collective net worth of the sponsor and the controlled group members.
2. The excess (if any) of:
   a. Seventy-five percent of the total amount of unfunded guaranteed benefits of all participants and beneficiaries under the plan, over
   b. Thirty percent of the collective net worth of the sponsor and the controlled group members.

In addition, interest is calculated from the termination date.

The liability to the PBGC is generally due as of the termination date. However, payment of the excess (if any) of 75 percent of the total amount of unfunded guaranteed benefits of all participants and beneficiaries under the plan over 30 percent of the collective net worth of the sponsor and the controlled group members will be made under commercially reasonable terms prescribed by the PBGC. Any terms prescribed by the PBGC for this excess amount must provide for deferral of 50 percent of any amount of liability otherwise payable for any year if a person subject to the liability demonstrates that no person subject to the liability has any individual pre-tax profits for the fiscal year ending in the year. The PBGC and any person liable for payment may also agree to alternative arrangements for the satisfaction of the liability.

Liability to the Section 4049 Trust

In any case in which there is an outstanding amount of benefit commitment[16] under a plan terminated under a distress termination or an involuntary termination, a contributing sponsor to the plan or a member of such a

---

[16] The outstanding amount of benefit commitment is defined as the excess of the actuarial present value of the benefit commitments to a participant or beneficiary under the plan, over the actuarial present value of the benefits of the participant or beneficiary that are guaranteed or to which assets of the plan are required to be allocated under ERISA Section 4044.

contributing sponsor's controlled group will be subject to liability to a Section 4049 trust. The liability consists of the lesser of:

1. Seventy-five percent of the total outstanding amount of benefit commitments under the plan.
2. Fifteen percent of the actuarial present value of all benefit commitments under the plan.

Payment of a liability to a Section 4049 trust must be made for liability payment years under commercially reasonable terms prescribed by the fiduciary designated by the PBGC. However, in any case in which the amount of liability is less than $100,000,[17] the payment requirements may be satisfied by payment of the liability (plus interest) over 10 liability payment years in equal annual installments. The terms for payment of liability also must provide for deferral of 75 percent of any amount of liability otherwise payable for any liability payment year if it is demonstrated to the PBGC that no person subject to such liability has any individual pre-tax profits for the fiscal year ending in that year. The amount of liability deferred is payable only after payment in full of any deferred amount of liability to the PBGC in connection with the termination of the same plan.

Liability to the Section 4042 Trustee

The liability to a Section 4042 trustee for the sponsoring employer and each member of its controlled group consists of the outstanding balance (accumulated with interest from the termination date) of:

1. The accumulated funding deficiency of the plan, modified to include the amount of any increase that would result if all pending applications for waiver of the minimum funding standard account and for extension of the amortization period were denied and if no additional contributions were made.
2. The amount of waived funding deficiencies.
3. The amount of decreases in the minimum funding standard account.

PBGC PREMIUMS

Although Congress corrected several of the major design flaws in the single-employer plan termination insurance system with the passage of SEPPAA, there were still lingering doubts concerning the equity of the

---

[17] The PBGC may increase this dollar amount by regulation.

premium structure. Therefore, Congress mandated that the PBGC prepare a study on several issues relating to the premium structure. The study was released in April 1987 and concluded, *inter alia,* that:[18]

1. In its present form, the single-employer insurance program rewards troubled firms for draining assets from their pension plans, thus rendering the costs of the program essentially uncontrollable.
2. The program reforms enacted in 1986 forestalled some potential problems but did not eliminate the perverse incentives that currently exist.

On the basis of these findings, the PBGC recommended that:[19]

1. Premiums for the single-employer pension insurance program be assessed on a basis that relates premiums to costs.
2. Premiums be set at a level that can reasonably be anticipated to amortize in real terms the program's current deficit over a period of no more than 30 years and fully fund future claims as they are incurred.
3. The Congress establish a system for adjusting premium schedules automatically, within specified limits, to reflect the program's experience.

To accomplish these objectives, the PBGC proposed a variable-rate premium structure that includes:[20]

1. A flat-rate participant charge, equal to the current rate and indexed to increases in wages, to be paid by all plans.
2. An additional funding charge based on the difference between a specified funding target and the value of plan assets, to be paid by all plans with 100 or more participants that do not have sufficient assets to meet the funding target.
3. A cap on how much any plan could pay per participant, which would be increased more rapidly than the wage index and thus would be phased out very gradually.
4. An additional charge for plans that had recently obtained minimum funding waivers or failed to meet minimum contribution requirements; the additional charge would be higher where plan

---

[18] Pension Benefit Guaranty Corporation, *SEPPAA PREMIUM STUDY REPORT:* A Report Requested by the Congress of the United States (Washington, D.C., 1987), p. 7.

[19] Ibid., p. 8.

[20] Ibid., p. 55.

underfunding would significantly increase as a result of plant shutdown or layoffs.

5. Automatic adjustment of the funding charge at specific intervals, to reflect differences between the insurance programs' actual and projected financial condition.
6. Placement of the liability for premiums on the plan sponsor and members of its controlled group.

At the time this chapter was prepared, it was too early to tell exactly how this proposal might be implemented, if at all. However, the specific parameters recommended by the PBGC include a funding charge of $6.00 per $1,000 of exposure. Instead of applying this additional premium rate component to the unfunded guaranteed benefits of the plan, it would be applied to the "funding target insufficiency." This figure is determined by subtracting the value of the plan's assets from 125 percent of the present value of its vested benefits. Although this figure does not represent perfectly the potential exposure of the plan to the PBGC, the present value of its vested benefits is a reasonable proxy for the guaranteed benefits and is readily available from the plan's Form 5500. The logic behind multiplying this figure by 125 percent (instead of 100 percent) may be more difficult to understand; however, it should be noted that a plan that is 100 percent funded still constitutes a potential exposure to the PBGC if the market value of its assets suddenly decrease. Of course, this investment risk may be eliminated by purchasing annuities for the accrued benefits and the PBGC recognizes this in its proposal by disregarding these liabilities from the funding charge.[21]

The final aspect of this implementation involves the standardization of the reported liabilities to the PBGC closeout interest rate. Due to the fact that most "underfunded" plans could eliminate the funding charge by choosing an interest assumption that was sufficiently large, there is a need to provide a common basis for assessing this component of a plan's total premium to the PBGC. It was proposed that large plans (more than 5,000 participants) be required to conduct a second valuation using the PBGC closeout interest rate, while smaller plans could use conversion tables developed by the PBGC. Details of the conversion for smaller plans were not available at the time this chapter was prepared; however, it will be interesting to observe how the PBGC handles the problem of vastly differ-

---

[21] In addition, if an employer gave the PBGC a security interest in assets equal to the amount of plan underfunding plus a cushion, plan benefits would be exempt from the funding charge.

ent liability durations for plans on the opposite ends of the demographic spectrum.[22]

Even though more than 40 percent of the premium that would have been generated in 1987 (had the proposed system been in place) would have been attributable to plans with a pre-participant premium in excess of $100, the PBGC proposal caps the sum of the flat-rate premium and funding charge at $100 per participant. However, this cap would be indexed to 150 percent of the wage growth and its impact would eventually be phased out.

The proposed premium structure also includes an automatic adjustment mechanism. The adjustment would apply to the funding rate charge and has three principal components:

1. A revision of projected annual net claims based on the average of the most recent three years' actual net claims, adjusted to current dollars.
2. Amortization of the difference between the actual and projected deficit.
3. Changes in the premium bases (number of participants and funding target insufficiency).

The remaining portion of this chapter deals with the current provisions of the PBGC single-employer plan termination insurance premiums.

Premium Rates

The current premium structure for single-employer plans is $8.50 per plan participant per year. The PBGC has the authority to revise rate and base schedules whenever a revision is deemed necessary, although it must submit proposals and reasons to both the House and the Senate.

---

[22] See D. Don Ezra and Keith P. Ambachtsheer, "Pension Funds: Rich or Poor?" *Financial Analysts Journal,* 1985, pp. 43–56, for a calculation of the duration of the plan obligation, given the average age of the active members, the average assumed retirement age, the average age for the pensioners, the proportion of the obligations attributable to actives and pensioners, the investment return, and the salary assumptions used. An alternative transformation process, based exclusively on Form 5500 information, is used in Francois P. Joanette, "Managing Corporate Pension Funds—A Study of the Determinants of Funding and Assets Allocation Decision," unpublished manuscript (University of Pennsylvania, Philadelphia, Pennsylvania). The adjustment factor in his model is derived from a dynamic model of pension funding presented by Newton L. Bowers, James C. Hickman, and Cecil H. Nesbitt, "Introduction to the Dynamics of Pension Funding," *Transactions of the Society of Actuaries,* 1976, pp. 177–204.

Payment of Premiums

For plan years beginning on or after January 1, 1986, the premium is due on the last day of the seventh month following the close of the prior plan year if the plan has fewer than 500 participants for the plan year. If the plan has 500 or more participants, the premium is due on the last day of the second month following the close of the prior plan year. For any year other than the first two plan years, the number of participants is determined as of the last day of the second preceding plan year. Special rules are used to determine the number of participants for new plans[23] and the number of participants on the first day of the first plan year is used as the premium base in the second plan year. Special rules are also used if there is a change in the plan year.[24]

If a premium is paid after the filing due date, the plan is subject to both a late payment penalty and an interest charge. The late payment charge is the greater of:

1. Five percent per month up to 100 percent of unpaid premium.
2. The lesser of $25 or 100 percent of the unpaid premium.

The interest charge is imposed at the same rate the IRS uses for late payment of income taxes. The late payment penalty (but not the interest charge) will not be assessed in whole or in part if a waiver is received from the PBGC.[25]

It is important to note that the PBGC has no authority to end basic benefit guarantees because an administrator fails to live up to its premium payment obligations.

---

[23] PBGC regulation Section 2610.3(a)(7).

[24] PBGC regulation Section 2610.3(a)(8).

[25] See PBGC Regulation Section 2610.9 for specific requirements.

APPENDIX
THE IMPACT OF THE OMNIBUS BUDGET RECONCILIATION ACT OF 1987 ON PLAN TERMINATION INSURANCE FOR SINGLE-EMPLOYER PLANS

PLAN TERMINATIONS

Limitations on Employer Reversions Upon Plan Termination

Restrictions on Reversions Pursuant to Recently Amended Plans. In determining the extent to which a plan provides for the distribution of plan assets to the employer for purposes of ERISA Section 4044(d), any such provision (and any amendment increasing the amount which may be distributed to the employer) will not be treated as effective before the end of the fifth calendar year following the adoption date. Special rules apply to plans that have been in effect for fewer than five years and to assets received as a result of plan transfers or mergers. The term "employer" includes any member of the controlled group[26] of which the employer is a member.

In the case of plans which, as of December 17, 1987, have no provisions relating to the distribution of plan assets to the employer for purposes of ERISA Section 4044(d), this new rule will apply only with respect to plan amendments adopted after December 17, 1988.

Distribution of Assets Attributable to Employee Contributions. If any assets of the plan attributable to employee contributions remain after satisfaction of all liabilities described in ERISA Section 4044(a), such remaining assets must be equitably distributed to the participants who made those contributions (or their beneficiaries) before any distribution from a plan under Section 4044(d). The portion (P) of the remaining assets attributable to employee contributions is:

$$P = \text{MARKET VALUE}_{TRA} \times (PV_{MC}/PV_{AB})$$

where:

$\text{MARKET VALUE}_{TRA}$ = the market value of the total remaining assets,

[26] The term "controlled group" means any group treated as a single employer under IRC Sections 414 (b), (c), (m) or (o).

PV_{MC} = the present value of all portions of the accrued benefits with respect to participants which are derived from participants' mandatory contributions, and

PV_{AB} = the present value of all benefits with respect to which assets are allocated under ERISA Section 4044(a)(2)-(6) (i.e., benefits attributable to voluntary employee contributions are excluded from this calculation).

A person will be treated as a participant with respect to the termination if at least a portion of his or her nonforfeitable benefit consisted of mandatory contributions and, as of the termination date, he or she was either a participant in the plan or an individual who received a distribution from the plan (during the three-year period ending with the termination date) equal to his or her entire nonforfeitable benefit. The distribution either may be in a single sum or in the form of an irrevocable commitment purchased from an insurer.

Effective Date. These new rules apply to terminations in which the notice of intent to terminate is provided after December 17, 1987 and terminations with respect to which proceedings are instituted by the PBGC after that date.

Employer Liability and Distributions to Participants

Section 4049 Trusts. This concept has been entirely repealed.

Employer Liability to the PBGC. The employer liability to the PBGC is increased to the total amount of the unfunded benefit liabilities to all participants and beneficiaries under the plan, together with interest calculated from the termination date. However, the lien that may be assessed is limited to 30 percent of the collective net worth of the employer and all related employers.

PBGC Payments to Participants and Beneficiaries. In addition to the guaranteed benefits, the PBGC will pay an additional amount equal to the outstanding amount of benefit liabilities[27] under the plan (including

---

[27] The outstanding amount of benefit liabilities is equal to the excess (if any) of the value of the plan's benefit liabilities over the value of the benefit liabilities which would be determined by only taking into account benefits which are guaranteed under ERISA Section 4022 or to which assets of the plan are allocated under ERISA Section 4044.

interest) times the applicable recovery ratio. The term *recovery ratio* means the average ratio with respect to prior plan terminations (defined as terminations for which the notice of intent to terminate was received after December 31, 1987) of:

> the value of the recovery of the PBGC in connection with such prior terminations, divided by
> the amount of unfunded benefit liabilities under such plans as of the termination date.[28]

Effective Date. These new rules apply to terminations in which the notice of intent to terminate is provided after December 17, 1987 and terminations with respect to which proceedings are instituted by the PBGC after that date.

Standards for Termination

Standard Terminations. Standard termination procedures are now available only when assets are sufficient to meet benefit liabilities.

Distress Terminations. The criteria for a distress termination must now be met by all members of a controlled group (previously, only substantial members were required to meet the criteria).

In order for a sponsor to qualify for a distress termination based on reorganization in bankruptcy, the court must approve the termination and determine that, unless the plan is terminated, such person will be unable to pay all its debts pursuant to a plan or reorganization and will be unable to continue in business outside the Chapter 11 reorganization process. However, the act did clarify that a plan may qualify for the distress termination proceedings where a petition for bankruptcy reorganization has been converted to a petition for liquidation.

Finally, to qualify under the reorganization distress test, employers must submit to the PBGC any request for the approval of the plan termination by the bankruptcy (or other appropriate) court.

---

[28] Special rules apply in the case of a terminated plan with outstanding benefit liabilities in excess of $20,000,000.

INCREASE IN PREMIUM RATES

Determination of Additional Premium

The flat-rate per-participant premium is increased to $16, and an additional premium is charged equal to $6 per $1,000 of unfunded vested benefits, with a maximum additional per-participant premium of $34. For purposes of determining the value of vested benefits, the interest rate is equal to 80 percent of the yield per annum on 30-year Treasury securities for the month period preceding the plan year.

In addition, if an employer made the maximum deductible contributions to the plan for one or more of the five plan years preceding the first plan year beginning after December 31, 1987, the cap on the additional premium is reduced by $3 for each plan year for which such contributions were made. This special rule only applies for the first five plan years the premium is in effect.

Liability for Premium Payments

The obligation to pay is now placed on the "designated payors," who in the case of a single-employer plan is either the contributing plan sponsor or plan administrator. If that employer is a member of a controlled group of companies, however, each member of that group is jointly and severally liable for the premium payments.

Deposit of Premiums into Separate Revolving Fund

The additional premiums collected under the amendment are credited to a separate revolving fund that cannot be used to pay PBGC administrative expenses or benefits in pre-1988 terminations unless all other PBGC assets are depleted.

Effective Date

The provisions above generally apply to plan years beginning after December 31, 1987.

CHAPTER 52

NONPROFIT ASSOCIATION SPONSORED INSURANCE PLANS

Gary K. Stone

INTRODUCTION

The potential market for association insurance is enormous, with membership in the millions. For example, the American Automobile Association has 26,191,000 members, the American Association of Retired Persons has 22 million members, and the YMCA includes 14 million members. The smallest listed association in the top 100 ranked by membership has 250,000 members.[1] This chapter will concentrate on the nonprofit associations and their sponsorship of insurance plans. The number of nonprofit organizations registered in this country in 1985 was over 857,000.[2] Not all sponsor insurance programs, but this number gives one an idea of the market potential. A survey sponsored by *Association Management* concluded that about 65 percent of the trade associations, 56 percent of individual membership societies, and 52 percent of federations sponsor some type of insurance program.[3]

The most prevalent type of employee benefit coverage sponsored is major medical, with 67 percent of the associations sponsoring a plan. Hospitalization (66 percent), group life (55 percent), and disability income

---

[1] "Association Management's Top 100," *Association Management,* April 1987, p. 34.

[2] *Dimensions of the Independent Sector, A Statistical Profile,* 2nd ed. (Washington, D.C.: Independent Sector, 1986), p. 17.

[3] "Tracking Trends in Insurance," *Association Management,* November 1984, p. 104.

(54 percent) are next in line in terms of sponsorship.[4] Property and liability insurance is not as often found, but workers' compensation is sponsored by 49 percent of the associations, professional liability by 35 percent, and general liability by 35 percent. Directors and officers insurance is only sponsored by 19 percent of all associations.

The market penetration is an important criteria as to whether the program is in fact a membership benefit. The American Society of Association Executives (ASAE) survey indicated that 30–33 percent was common for the medical and life coverage. An interesting finding of the survey was that 42 percent of the membership was participating in the professional liability programs and 37 percent in the directors and officers liability programs.[5] This may be attributed to the fact that the coverage is expensive and difficult to find individually. The problem recently for associations is to find an insurance carrier willing to provide the coverage.

The actual participation of any association program will depend on many factors, including the type of membership, the competitiveness of the insurance in the location of the member, and overall economic conditions. It may well be that low participation, for example, 5–15 percent, may still be providing valuable service to members. If an association is providing insurance not otherwise available or at a cost that saves the member money, then a service is being provided to that member even if not all members might benefit. Retention of membership is important and this may well be the key to keeping members.

New products are being introduced in the association market. Universal life, 401 (k) plans, HMOs, nursing home protection, business overhead insurance, kidnap and ransom protection, and catastrophic or excess major medical coverage are but a few of the newer products found in association plans. The future for association insurance products appears excellent, with much potential to be realized both by associations and the membership.

ADVANTAGES AND DISADVANTAGES OF ASSOCIATION GROUP INSURANCE

An association can gain a number of potential benefits from endorsing an insurance plan. Insurance can be a definite member benefit as well as a source of income to the association itself. Typical advantages of sponsoring insurance include:

---

[4] Ibid.

[5] Ibid.

1. Providing income to the association.
2. Providing insurance to members at group rates.
3. Acquiring and retaining members for the association.
4. Providing a type of insurance not generally available in the open market.
5. Providing a ready-made product for the membership that can save them time and expense of development.

Associations often endorse insurance because it can provide a valuable source of income. They may receive commission income, refunds when plans have good experience, reimbursement for expenses and administrative costs, and even direct profits. Some associations have even formed their own captive or cooperative forms of insurance organizations. The income from these may be taxable as unrelated business income, but it is not unusual to have subsidiaries designed specifically for profit-making activities. Income, whether taxable or not, is usually welcomed by associations.

The membership of many associations is made up of small firms and individuals. In such cases, they may not be in a position to effectively bargain for insurance coverage and rates. Association group insurance can be less costly for members and the policies themselves may be broader, including specialized coverage designed for the association. The effect of a sponsored program is to give members group rates and group coverages in situations in which they are unable to obtain it themselves.

Insurance can increase or retain membership for the association. A constant problem for associations is membership retention and new membership. An association's income often depends on membership dues. This means that new members and membership retention are critical. A well-designed insurance package can help in this role. A good example is a default bond program that is endorsed by the American Society of Travel Agents (ASTA). The airlines require all travel agents that sell airline tickets to be bonded against bankruptcy. This is to protect the airlines for tickets that have been sold but for which the airlines have not yet collected the money from the travel agent. The market rate for these bonds is in the \$25–\$30 per \$1,000 of bond amount. The endorsed program has a rate of \$8.80 per \$1,000 of bond amount (1987). Many firms join to take advantage of the bond rate. It can be a sizable cost savings, because the bond amount can be as high as \$70,000 (1988).

Certain types of insurance such as professional liability, general liability, and surety bonding are difficult to obtain for an individual, but may be available on a mass basis. A few examples of associations that have endorsed such programs would be the ASTA bond program, and professional liability programs of the American Society of Association Executives and the Institute of Electrical and Electronics Engineers. Associations are also moving into the more exotic types of endorsed programs such as kidnap and ransom insurance and nursing home coverage. These programs are often not even sold in the individual market.

Programs such as IRAs, pension and profit-sharing plans, and thrift plans may be readily available to members, but the cost of developing and administering such programs is prohibitive. Master or prototype plans developed for an association can save time and expense for the members. They can join a plan that is already up and running for a low cost.

DISADVANTAGES OF ENDORSED PROGRAMS

Association insurance has several potential problems that must be considered. The program may not be competitive from a rate and benefit standpoint, it may leave the members without needed protection if canceled, and can cause a backlash when rates or benefits have to be adjusted. For example, assume that a plan is found to contain an inequity in its health rates. The common rate being used favors certain ages or geographic regions of the country. The plan provides a subsidy to certain members, and those in the lower ages and low-cost areas that are subsidizing the plan are dropping out. To correct these problems the plan can go to geographic and age rating. The older age members and those in the high-cost regions of the country would have their rates increased substantially. Reactions to these kinds of changes may be serious, depending on the demographics of the association. Blame may be levied on the association whether or not the plan changes can be well documented. Constant monitoring is needed to prevent this type of problem.

Another problem is the service of the insurance company. Improper billing, slow claim payment, inadequate claim payment, or any dissatisfaction with the product can result in the association being blamed. The fact that the name of the association is on the product may result in a negative reaction from the membership. The endorsement that was supposed to support and create membership can actually do the opposite. Corrective measures such as switching insurance carriers or administrators must be carefully studied. These steps themselves may result in delays in claims settlement and record-keeping until the new carrier or administrator is up and running.

ORGANIZATIONAL CONTROL

The ultimate control over any sponsored insurance program usually rests with the board of directors of the association. A few have given up control to external trustees or administrators, but this is not common. The typical organizational structure is to have an internal staff liaison or committee oversee the programs and report to the board of directors for final decision purposes.

The following structure is typical and it is in use by the American Society of Travel Agents. This association has a membership of over 23,000 with a staff of approximately 80 employees. The board of directors has a committee specifically designated as the bonding and insurance committee. This committee is comprised of 6–10 active travel agents, a staff liaison, and an outside insurance consultant. One of the members of the committee is designated as the chairperson of the committee. This chairperson is usually a member of the board of directors. The chairperson and staff liaison review all insurance matters and set the agenda for committee meetings. The meetings are held 3–4 times per year, depending on the need. The committee decides coverage and other insurance issues and makes recommendations to the board. The committee chairperson will bring to the board those decisions that must be made at that level. The ultimate decision on critical matters is in the hands of the board of directors.

A form of organizational structure that has been used by associations to monitor and control insurance plans is the trust arrangement. A trust is a property interest held by a person(s) called a trustee(s) for the benefit of others. This can work well in sponsored insurance plans and is found extensively in health insurance and life insurance, and in the pension area. A specialized form of trust is the Section 501 (c)(9) trust or, as it is commonly referred to, the voluntary employees beneficiary association (VEBA). A VEBA has the advantage of permitting contributions on a tax-deductible basis, with investment income to the trust not taxed, and appreciation of trust assets being tax-free. A nonprofit association can use this form of trust to protect itself against excess accumulation of unrelated income. The requirements for qualification under Section 501 (c)(9) are as follows:

1. It must be an employees' association.
2. Membership in the plan must be voluntary from the employees' standpoint.
3. Earnings must not benefit any private individual or private shareholder.

4. The trust must be designed to pay life, sickness, accident, or other insurance benefits to the members, their dependents, or their beneficiaries.[6]

An IRS regulation issued in 1981 had serious implications for the use of the VEBA for regional and national associations. Part of the regulation centered on the definition of an employee association. It said in essence that the participating employers must be engaged in the same line of business and be in the *same geographic area*.[7] The effect of this regulation was to make national, regional, and even statewide association trusts of this type taxable. The Water Quality Association Employees' Benefit Corp. sought in court a refund of taxes paid under the new regulation because of the unreasonable restrictions imposed. Initially, they lost, but on appeal, the Seventh Circuit Court of Appeals reversed the district court decision and held that the geographic limitation was invalid.[8] This decision is not binding on the IRS for all associations and it will take time for new regulations to be developed. Hopefully for associations, they will be able to regain their tax-exempt status and obtain a refund of taxes paid during the period of taxability.

In summary, the administrative control of association sponsored insurance plans usually rests internally with a staff liaison, or an insurance committee and a staff liaison. The day-to-day administration of the plans can be carried out by the staff liaison. Most associations rely on board of director action on major decisions. Another mechanism for control is the use of a trust. The trust can work in conjunction with the insurance committee or staff liaison, or it may be a separate trust run by trustees outside of the control of the association itself. One form of control that is usually not desirable is to have a broker or insurance agent act as administrator, with complete control over the workings of the plan. This dual role of broker and administrator can create a conflict of interest. It is usually preferable to have complete control exercised by the association or a group of trustees from the association.

---

[6] Jerry S. Rosenbloom, *The Handbook of Employee Benefits* (Homewood, Ill.: Dow Jones-Irwin, 1984), p. 97.

[7] See Treas. Reg. §1.501(c)(9)-2(a)(1); 46 Fed. Reg. 1719, 1721 (1981)

[8] *Water Quality Association Employees' Benefit Corp.* v. *U.S.*, 795 F. 2d 1303 (7th Cir. 1986).

PROGRAM CHARACTERISTICS

Rating of Association Insurance Plans

The rating of association plans is similar to the rating that would be used in any employee benefit plan. It depends on the type of insurance being sold, the numbers covered, and the expected losses. Rating factors include age in life plans, compensation in disability protection plans, and age and geographic location in medical and major medical plans; dental plans often use a per participant cost. Tables 52–1, 52–2, and 52–3 show partial schedules of premiums associated with an association plan.[9] Table

TABLE 52–1
Geographic Insurance Areas

State	*Zip Code*	*Area*	*State*	*Zip Code*	*Area*
Alabama	350–355	2	California	900–902	6
	900–902	6		903	5
	903	5		.	
	.	.		.	
	.	.		.	
	.	.		951–961	6
	951–961	6			
	356	3			
	357–358	2			
	.	.			
	.	.			
	.	.	Puerto Rico	006–009	1
	006–009	1			
	.	.			
	.	.			
	.	.			
	367–369	2			

[9] The rates are from programs endorsed by the American Society of Travel Agents Group Insurance Trust for the year 1987.

TABLE 52–2
Rates for Basic Medical Plan Benefits
(Employee Coverage Only)

	Geographic Area			
Age	*1*	*2*	. . .	*6*
<25	$ 50.45	$ 53.46		$ 69.00
25–29	60.54	64.14		82.80
30–34	69.18	73.30		94.63
.	.	.		.
.	.	.		.
.	.	.		.
65+	139.10	147.37		190.26

52–1 shows how ZIP code groupings in each state are broken down into geographic areas. Table 52–2 shows basic medical and dental plan rates, and Table 52–3 shows life insurance plan rates.

One precaution should be taken when setting and determining the rates to be used. It is important that geographic rating be used when a plan covers a wide geographic area. Furthermore, age rating is essential if the coverage will apply to different age groups in forms of insurance in which age is relevant to the loss situation. Using a common rate for all participants may sound attractive to an association, but it could lead to the

TABLE 52–3
Life Insurance Rates per $1,000

Age	*Rate per Month*
<30	$ .23
30–34	.25
35–39	.30
.	
.	
.	
65–69	3.25

eventual collapse of the plan. Hospital and doctors' charges vary extensively by geographic area. Also, as one gets older, medical expenses tend to increase. A common rate for all tends to invite adverse selection. The plan may be quickly populated with members from the high-cost states (California, New York, Connecticut) and the elderly. The young and those from the lower cost medical areas will find cheaper insurance in other plans. The result may be a plan for the residual or poor risks.

Underwriting of Association Plans

Underwriting of association plans takes the form of minimum eligibility standards for plan participation plus policy restrictions. Eligibility requirements commonly will depend on being a member of the association, the type of insurance being sold, the number of participants (i.e., single person versus employer and employees), and the loss characteristics of the particular risk. Underwriting must be done with care to prevent the plan from being populated with the bad risks.

Individual underwriting will be the norm for endorsed property and liability programs. Homeowner, auto, business insurance, and especially errors and omissions insurance will require individual applications. The loss experience and characteristics relevant to that person will be reviewed to determine if the risk is acceptable. A person unable to obtain insurance individually may also find out that he or she is unacceptable in an endorsed association plan. The primary advantage of the program may be a cost advantage, and not ease of underwriting.

Life and health underwriting rarely requires a physical examination, but often includes medical underwriting in the application. This will take the form of statements about medical history and current health problems. Any questionable area may be followed up with additional requests for information prior to the sale. Underwriting often is supplemented through policy provisions. Preexisting conditions clauses, exclusions for losses from mental or alcohol related problems, or self-inflicted injuries would be typical of clauses used to reduce adverse selection. In other words, the clauses normally found in all health and life plans will be found in association endorsed plans. Restricting the amounts of insurance is common in association plans. For example, a plan may permit up to a certain amount of life insurance to be purchased (e.g., $30,000), but if a firm has over 10 employees the amount may be higher (e.g., up to $75,000). In summary, medical underwriting, policy provisions, and restricted amounts of coverage can all be found in the underwriting of association plans.

The size of the group applying for insurance will influence the degree of underwriting needed. As the number in a group increases, the closer the underwriting resembles that found in a true group situation. Guaranteed issue with few medical requirements will be found when a firm reaches a minimum size such as 10 or 15 employees. In addition, most plans require minimum numbers, minimum percentage participation, and restricted definition of eligible participants. The following requirements are typical:

1. To insure all new employees who are eligible, as of the first day of the month following their employment date, and to pay 100 percent of the cost of employee basic insurance for all eligible employees of the firm.
2. To insure 75 percent of all eligible employees in the insurance plan.
3. To require evidence of insurance in groups of six or fewer employees; (For a group of seven or more employees, no evidence of insurability is required.)
4. To enroll only full-time employees including principals, partners, and officers who are employed 30 or more hours per week.
5. To enroll all eligible employees within 60 days of initial employment date, otherwise full medical underwriting will be required.
6. To make payroll deductions when necessary in order for all employees to cover their eligible dependents.[10]

Most plans permit employees that have duplicate coverage to be excluded in the definition of an eligible employee. This can occur when both the husband and wife are employed and each has health benefits that cover dependents.

Association plans are carefully underwritten to prevent adverse selection. Underwriting is needed to preserve the financial viability of the plan and to make it a true membership benefit. Members may complain when they have been refused coverage. They may have the attitude that they are entitled to protection because they are a member of a particular association. It is far easier to handle this problem than the alternative situation where rates and claims have gotten out of control and the plan collapses.

---

[10] The American Institute of Architects Benefit Insurance Trust, participation agreement, dated 10/86.

MARKETING ASSOCIATION INSURANCE PLANS

One of the most important functions in an association insurance plan is the marketing to the membership. Failure to properly market results in poor membership penetration and, in turn, poor overall results for the association. The administrator should make a careful market analysis of the association before extensive marketing is done. What works for one group may be completely ineffective for another. The three primary methods of marketing are mail solicitation, telephone marketing, and direct contact by representatives of the administrator. No single method of marketing is best for all plans.

A two-step direct mail solicitation is common. The first step involves a letter or postcard introduction to the plan. A second step involves additional information or possibly a rate quote being sent to those expressing interest. Members can write in or return an enclosed postcard and detailed information will be delivered, either by mail or by a representative of the plan. It is expensive to send the options and various brochures to every member of an association. This two-step approach allows the plan to concentrate on those most interested. The same procedures can be followed by using telemarketing as a first step, with detailed information sent to those interested.

A popular contact point for plan representatives and association members is at local, state, and national meetings of the association. This can be beneficial to effective marketing provided the plan representative has direct access to members, such as being a speaker or on a panel discussion. In most cases, the primary marketing is not done at such meetings. Members attend meetings for professional advancement and may devote little time to such things as insurance. Few plans would rely on meeting attendance as the primary marketing technique. Meeting attendance combined with a form of direct mail or telemarketing is more likely to be used.

Some plans use an insurance agency force to sell directly to the members in their own locality. For some groups, this is the preferred approach and it may be the most effective. The association should be aware that the use of an insurance agency force will have the effect of increasing the cost to the members. An agent must receive a reasonable commission to make it worthwhile. This can increase the gross premium charged by 5–10 percent. The association has to determine if this increase in cost is justified. It is important to determine if the increase in cost will be offset by increased participation or if the cost will be prohibitive and make the product unsalable. Each association must take into consideration its own unique circumstances before deciding to use an insurance agency force.

Advertising is an important aspect of the marketing. An association should attempt to keep complete control over all of the materials that are used to solicit members concerning the plan. Insurance companies or the administrator may not be aware of the political or practical implications of the advertising. It may be offensive or contrary to some goals of the association. This can easily happen inadvertently because the insurer is not involved in the day-to-day work of the association. Such problems can usually be avoided if the association requires all materials to have prior approval before being used. This should be written into the contract with the administrator and the insurance company.

There is no single preferred technique to market an association insurance plan. The preferred method may be one form or another or a combination of all approaches. Knowing the membership is key to determining the best overall marketing strategy.

FUNDING ALTERNATIVES

There are many ways to fund association insurance plans. The key to the available alternatives depends on whether the association owns the rights to the plan or is just providing an endorsement to an externally controlled plan. This section will assume that the association owns the rights to the plan and can control its funding. The alternatives to be discussed will be:

1. Nonexperience rated insurance plans.
2. Experience rated insurance plans.
3. Self-insurance and captive insurance companies.

Nonexperience Rated Insurance Plans

The nonexperience rated plans are typically used by small associations. The number of members covered is not large enough to be given full statistical credibility. Data from a particular association will be pooled with data from other accounts in order to develop needed statistics.

Losses of an association will go into the pool and future rates and/or refunds will be reflected in the overall pool losses. What is important is the loss history of the entire pooled account and not the experience of any one piece of business within the pool. Losses of any one association may not be representative of the pool losses. If the overall losses are low and the pool reflects a surplus, a rate decrease or a refund is in order. Of course, the reverse will also be true.

Experience Rated Insurance Plans

Experience rating occurs when the plan is large and the loss results have statistical reliability. This means the rates can be predicated on the losses. The size of the membership of a plan will dictate the degree of reliability that can be placed on the association's losses. The larger plans will be 100 percent experience rated and rates and refunds can be developed solely from that account's experience. In some medium-sized association plans, it is possible that 100 percent reliance cannot be placed on the plan losses. In such cases, a combination of experience rating and conventional non-experience rating will apply.

Table 52–4 is an example of how an experience rated account might work. It is assumed that the association is large enough to be fully experience rated. A multitude of formulas can be used and one should realize that this is a typical formula but certainly not the only one available. The ABC Association account will be reviewed as of the end of the year (19XX). All of the numbers will be calculated on an annual basis. The administrative expenses, commissions, marketing expenses, and so on have been negotiated and are noted as percentages of gross premiums in the formula itself.

TABLE 52–4
Experience Account of the ABC Association For the Year 19XX

A.	Premiums collected	$6,900,000	
B.	Unearned premium reserve (beginning)	760,000	
C.	Unearned premium reserve (ending)	778,000	
D.	Earned premiums ([A] + [B] minus [C])		$6,882,000
E.	Paid claims	5,400,000	
F.	Claim reserve (beginning)	1,725,000	
G.	Claim reserve (ending)	1,814,000	
H.	Incurred claims ([E] + [G] minus [F])		$5,489,000
I.	Commissions and fees	241,500 (3.5%)	
J.	Profit and expenses	655,500 (9.5%)	
K.	Marketing expenses	138,000 (2.0%)	
L.	Retention charges		1,035,000
M.	Gain or (loss) ([D] minus [H] + [L])		$ 358,000

In Table 52–4, the account indicated a positive balance of $358,000 for the year. This amount can be refunded to the association, used to lower future rates, used to supplement a contingency reserve, or to improve benefits. Should a loss have been incurred, the insurer would have to carry the loss forward and try to recover it in a future time period. No doubt a rate increase would be forthcoming.

It is not unusual for an association to have a special account designed to prevent abnormal rate fluctuations within a given time period. This account may be referred to as a stabilization reserve or contingency reserve. Positive balances in the account can be used to offset or partially offset future rate increases. What in effect happens is that the insurance company may forgo a rate increase or accept a smaller increase than desired if it has the right to offset excess losses against this reserve. For example, assume that the ABC Association has such an account. Table 52–5 shows what might be typical of an actual situation.

TABLE 52–5
Premium Stabilization Account—ABC Association

M. Gain or (loss)	$358,000	
N. Reserve (end of the previous year)	814,000	
O. Reserve (beginning of the year)		$1,172,000
P. Interest earned on reserve		73,260
Q. Reserve (end of the year) ([O] + [P])		$1,245,260
R. Adjustment to the reserve		—
S. Year-end reserve		$1,245,260

The insurance company would credit the fund with the gain for the year (19XX). The beginning reserve will earn interest during the year at a rate negotiated with the association. Should the insurance company determine that a rate increase is in order, the insurer may agree to a smaller rate increase than desired if future losses can be offset against the reserve. This reserve can serve as a temporary cushion for rate increases or as a fund to be used for marketing, and so on. Care must be taken, however, so that the fund is not depleted because of inadequate rates. The result can be a very high rate increase when the fund no longer covers the losses. It would be sounder to have rates increase as needed, with this reserve being used only for short-term problems. Members react very negatively when rates jump excessively.

There are a number of arrangements that an association can reach with an insurance company on funding. There are forms of flexible funding, premium-delay mechanisms, cost plus plans, and others that can fit the needs of a particular association. Chapter 22 of this book discusses in detail the various funding alternatives that could be used.

Self-Insurance and Captive Insurance Companies

Self-funding can be done in a number of ways. It can use a taxable trust, tax-exempt trusts, a self-fund without a trust arrangement, or even form a captive insurance company.

Often in self-funding the association uses some form of administrative services contract and/or stop-loss insurance to back up the plan. With an administrative services only contract, the plan uses 100 percent of the experience of the association, but has an outside administrator perform certain duties. The duties might be claim settlement, actuarial services, or any other administrative functions the association desires to have performed. Rarely will an association desire to administer a plan itself, so heavy reliance is placed on outside help.

Stop-loss insurance is also common. This amounts to a backup insurance or reinsurance plan should losses be higher than projected. Stop-loss insurance may be in the form of protection on aggregate losses for the year, or on individual claims. The potential cost of claims from Acquired Immune Deficiency Syndrome (AIDS) has spurred interest in individual stop-loss insurance. It is not unusual for AIDS losses from a single incident to run to many hundreds of thousands of dollars. Stop-loss insurance plus special underwriting may be needed to protect the association plan from catastrophic losses. Individual stop-loss insurance above $10,000 or $20,000 per loss has been common over the years, but insurance companies have been raising the levels and the premiums for the protection. Amounts in the $50,000 to $100,000 range are now common.

Many plans combine administrative services contracts and stop-loss insurance. This can provide the advantages normally associated with self-insurance with the security permitted under insured plans. The combination of services and insurance that is needed by any particular association requires a detailed study of the size of the plan and membership characteristics.

The ultimate in self-insurance is to form a captive insurance company. This can be done by setting it up under the laws of a state or forming an offshore captive. A captive is a major undertaking and should be done only after a careful feasibility study is completed. There are definite advantages of owning your own insurance company, but they must be weighed against the major capital outlay and the possibility of a venture that could fail. The form of the captive organization can be a stock company or a cooperative form such as a mutual or a reciprocal.

SELECTION OF AN ADMINISTRATOR (BROKER)

The selection of the proper administrator is critical to the long-term success of the program. The administrator must have the ability to market the plan, service the membership, make recommendations for rate and coverage change, and must know the membership. Many association plans fail to meet expectations because the administrator either does not have the ability to handle the account or becomes complacent over time and fails to meet the demands of the marketplace. In this section, the terms *administrator* and *insurance broker* will be used interchangeably. It is possible that the administrator could be the insurance company. In this case, a broker would not be used but the association would deal directly with the insurer. For simplicity, the assumption will be made that the administrator and broker are one and the same.

The type and size of the firm to be the administrator will depend on the association itself. A national or international association cannot rely on a small local brokerage firm to have the skill needed to market and service the members. Conversely, a large brokerage firm may not have the financial incentive to provide adequate service to a small regional, state, or local association.

In negotiating with an administrator, it is important to set forth the specifics of the agreement. The need for a detailed contract is obvious. The association must know how much it will cost to run the program, how it will be marketed, what are the obligations of the association, how long the contract will be in force, legal obligations of each party, relationship of the broker to the members, compensation of the broker, and record ownership. The following is a suggested list of factors that should be considered in a contract with the administrator (broker).

1. The length of the contract should be clearly specified. It is common for a contract to run for three to five years or longer. The rationale for the multiple-year contract is that the first year or two after a plan goes in force are high-expense years. The extensive marketing and promotion expenses cannot be recovered in a shorter time period. Few administrators will be willing to provide the heavy outlay of funds needed to market the program in the early years if they have no assurance that the association will continue the program.

2. The duties of the administrator should be spelled out. This would include marketing and promotions, negotiations with insurance companies, administrative duties (premium collections, record-keeping, etc.), noncommingling of premiums with brokers funds, reporting of activities to the association, and how claims will be settled. It is important to know what can be expected from the administrator.

3. The compensation should be stated. The compensation of the broker is normally in the form of a commission paid by the insurance company. The association should be aware of the amount and its form, and make sure that the broker does not have a claim for reimbursement from the association. The form of marketing will have an impact on the broker compensation. The use of agents to market the product directly to members may increase the cost by 5–10 percent. This increase has to be reconciled with the advantages of this type of marketing. The association should require that any compensation agreement between the broker and insurer be disclosed as well as any other contract that materially affects the cost of the association plan.

4. The broker should be required to make certain legal representations to the association with respect to their legal authority. An association might logically require a certification that the broker:

a. Is legally licensed under the law.
b. Will not alter the program without permission.
c. Has the legal power to be an administrator.
d. Is not under any legal or other suit that would restrict the ability to administer the program.

5. The association will appoint the broker as the exclusive broker for the program. This will usually be required to prevent the association from becoming a competitor. There is nothing wrong with this provision provided that specific grounds for termination of the broker are stated should the association be unhappy with the appointment.

6. It is important to determine the ownership of the records of association plans and the form and time period that pertinent records should be kept. The records should be the exclusive property of the association and all records, tapes, software, and so on should be returned at the end of the contract. It should be stated that the broker has no right to use any list or record of the association after the contract has terminated. Failure to get this point clearly in the contract can result in difficulty in providing a smooth transition to another broker should it become necessary.

7. Any compensation going to the association should be stated. It may be a based on a percentage of premiums or a flat fee. It should be determined if it is to be based on earned or billed premiums, and how often it will be paid.

8. Confidentiality of information provided by the association and the members must be maintained. The contract should indicate that the broker must respect the confidential nature of the information. Closely related is a restriction imposed for using the association name or symbol in any manner not consistent with the terms of the contract. All uses of the name must have approval of the association.

9. A noncompetition provision can be included to preclude the broker from going into direct competition with the association on termination of the contract. A one- or two-year time period is not unusual.

10. An important clause is a hold-harmless provision. The association does not want to become legally responsible for errors of the administrator. It is possible that members or others may sue the association because of some negligent act or omission of the broker. This provision should state that the responsibility for payment and legal fees belongs to the broker. The broker might be required to provide evidence of minimum amounts of errors and omissions insurance and general liability insurance. The hold-harmless clause should, however, not have any dollar limit with respect to the potential liability imposed on the broker, irrespective of whether or not insurance may exist. It is possible and probably desirable that the hold-harmless and insurance clauses be separate provisions and not connected in the contract.

11. A definite mechanism for contract termination should be included. The length of the contract is to be stated and also the conditions under which a premature termination could take place. The reference here is to termination should a default in the contract terms occur, if one of the parties is insolvent, or if the association no longer desires to provide insurance to the members. On termination, the transition of records to the association or to a new broker must be orderly and should be so stated.

12. There are many other points that may be in the contract. Examples would be provisions for notification of the parties, the state law that would apply to disputes, nonwaiver of contract provisions unless in writing by both parties, arbitration provisions, and a statement that the broker is an independent party and not an employee of the association.

It is important for the association to have legal counsel in arranging the contracts. The contracts are technical and care has to be exercised to protect the interests of the association and the members. The intent of providing the insurance is to provide a membership benefit. The last thing that should happen is for the association to become legally or financially entangled in problems created by the insurance sale.

SELECTION OF AN INSURANCE COMPANY

The insurance company selection will usually be done by the administrator in conjunction with the association. The broker will normally be working with one or more companies and will make recommendations. It is important to have an insurance company that is reputable, financially sound, and able to handle the account in an accurate and efficient manner. A high financial rating such as an A+ Bests rating is important when endorsing a company. Another factor in company selection is to make sure that the company has not taken any political or nonpolitical positions that are in opposition to the goals of the association. This may sound trivial but not doing so may, in fact, cause a serious problem for the success of the program.

The contract between the association and the insurer has to be designed with the same care that was exercised with the administrator's contract. Details with respect to claim settlement, reserves, credited interest, and so on must be spelled out clearly. The following are suggested minimum areas of concern that must be addressed:

1. Details of the insurance coverage should be provided including the rating system that will be used. The association should be in a position to approve or reject any coverage change.

2. If the plan is to be experience rated, the specifics of the formula should be provided. The association should know the extent to which its experience will be considered and all charges and credits involved should be disclosed. Particularly critical is the retention charge of the insurer. This is the amount charged to run the plan. It includes company profits, taxes, marketing charges, administrative fees, pooling charges, claims, and administration fees. The higher the retention amount, the higher the cost of the product.

3. The method of calculation of the reserves needs to be disclosed. Reserves include premium reserves, claim reserves, premium stabilization reserves, and other miscellaneous contingency reserves. It is important to know how the reserve is developed, the interest rate (if any) that is being credited, and the ownership of the reserves on plan termination. The workings of the reserves have a definite impact on the ultimate cost of the plan.

4. Claim settlement is important and it should be clearly indicated who will pay the claims. Will the insurance company or the administrator be paying claims? Claim settlement is the way members judge the plan. Slow or inefficient payment will result in complaints and loss of plan participants. The larger brokerage firms are often allowed to settle claims for the insurer. The association must know the party responsible for claim settlement.

5. The premium collection can be done by the administrator, the insurance company, or the association itself. The association will normally not want to be involved in administrative detail and so the insurer or the administrator will probably be responsible for these functions. The association must know how float income is handled. This is the interest earned from the time of premium payment to the time of claim payment. A premium delay arrangement may allow the association to invest the paid premiums for additional income prior to forwarding to the insurance carrier. Often, however, with the premium delay situations, the carrier will make a charge against the experience rating formula for this right. Whatever the situation, the association should be aware of the details.

6. The contract should specify which reports are to be provided. They may be on a weekly, monthly, quarterly, or annual basis depending on the needs and desires of the association. One has to be able to keep track of the developing trends. The type of records needed would be, at a minimum, the premiums paid and earned, claims paid and incurred, participants in the plan, attrition of members, new members, geographic location of participants, and any factor affecting the experience rating formulas. The association could require any information that it believes useful for its purposes. Most large brokers and insurance companies have prototype reports that are used by associations. It is possible that the information desired is normally provided without any special request by the association. The frequency of reports depends on the desires of the association. Monthly, quarterly, or semiannually are common, although weekly reports may be needed in certain circumstances.

It is not possible to provide all the details that might be included in a contract or agreement with the insurer. What is important is that when taken together—the administrator's contract and the insurer's contract—the association has all the needed information and has protected itself legally to the extent possible. Again it should be emphasized that competent legal help is an essential element in reaching a contractual arrangement to provide insurance coverage to the membership.

THE FUTURE FOR ASSOCIATION INSURANCE

The future for association insurance should continue to be bright. Programs designed specifically for the needs of an association have extensive appeal. This can take the form of insurance that is difficult to purchase, for example, errors and omissions insurance, or special coverage within the insurance that caters to the membership. Association insurance also should continue to be popular with small employer-employee groups. Competitive rates and coverage are difficult for the small groups to purchase. An association plan may allow the advantages of a large group to the small groups or individuals because of the overall numbers of insured risks in the association plan. The fastest growing type of company in recent years has been the firm with fewer than 100 employees, and about one third of these has fewer than 20 employees.[11]

The success of the plan depends on the membership perceiving the endorsed insurance as a benefit. This requires the association to provide insurance desired by the membership, and to make sure the underwriting is flexible enough so that the majority of the membership can qualify. The key to success is similar to other insurance products. The product will be successful if it is a product in demand, is competitively priced, is prompt in claim payment and other services, and is properly marketed.

---

[11] Jeffrey D. Miller, "The Future of Small Group Health," *Best's Review—Life and Health Edition* 87 (September 1986), pp. 28.

CHAPTER 53

PUBLIC EMPLOYEE PENSION PLANS*

Dan M. McGill

Pension plans operated for the employees of state and local governments are distinctive and diverse. As a group, they antedate the plans adopted by business firms to provide for the orderly and humane retirement of their employees. The first public employee retirement system was established in 1857, covering the police force of New York City. During the next half century, many other municipal employee retirement systems were brought into existence, including several whose coverage was confined to teachers. In 1911, Massachusetts established the first retirement system at the state level, the system covering the general employees of the state. Since then plans at all levels of government have proliferated until today the vast majority of all state and local government employees participate in a staff retirement system of some kind.

State and local government retirement systems function in an environment that has been well described by Thomas Bleakney in the Prologue to his book, *Retirement Systems for Public Employees*.[1] This environment gives rise to some unique problems and renders less tractable other problems commonly encountered by pension plans generally. Creatures of the political process, public employee retirement systems do not lend themselves well to the traditional constraints and disciplines that

---

* This material first appeared in Howard E. Winklevoss and Dan M. McGill, *Public Pension Plans* (Homewood, Ill.: Dow Jones-Irwin, 1979). It is reproduced herein with written permission of the publisher.

[1] Thomas P. Bleakney, *Retirement Systems for Public Employees* (Homewood, Ill.: Richard D. Irwin, 1972), pp. 1–9.

shape the structure and reinforce the foundation of pension plans in the private sector. They present challenges in plan design, funding, and financial disclosure.

The boundaries of the public retirement system universe have not been firmly established. Several years ago the Pension Task Force of the House of Representatives Subcommittee on Labor Standards identified nearly 7,000 pension plans of state and local government subdivisions and estimated that there may be 10 to 15 percent more unaccounted for, presumably small in size. Over 1,400 plans have been located in the Commonwealth of Pennsylvania alone. About 75 percent of the total universe of plans are found in 10 states, including in descending order Pennsylvania, Minnesota, Illinois, Oklahoma, and Colorado. The systems range in size from the New York State Employees' Retirement System, with more than 400,000 participants, to arrangements at the township or borough level covering fewer than five employees. Nearly 75 percent of the plans have fewer than 100 active members. At the other extreme, there are 131 known plans with 10,000 or more active members, and these plans are believed to account for approximately 85 percent of the total active membership of all state and local government pension plans.

State and local government retirement systems cover about 15 million full-time and part-time employees, 40 percent of the coverage of plans in the private sector. Employer and employee contributions to the plan amount to about $38 billion per year, with benefit disbursements running around $20 billion annually. The plans hold assets of more than $500 billion, as compared to roughly $1.5 trillion held by private sector plans.

A profile of the retirement systems operated by states, municipalities, counties, townships, boroughs, school districts, and other public authorities is presented in this chapter. The systems or plans are examined from the standpoint of several pertinent characteristics: (1) classes of employees covered, (2) level of plan administration, (3) legal form, (4) exposure to collective bargaining, (5) legal commitment of the plan sponsor, (6) Social Security coverage, and (7) source of contributions.

CLASSES OF EMPLOYEES COVERED

Some plans cover all types of employees of the jurisdictions involved, sometimes with different benefit formulas and other pertinent plan provisions. In the great majority of jurisdictions, however, there are separate plans for different categories of employees, reflecting varying conditions of employment, jockeying for preferential pension treatment, political clout, and other indigenous influences.

Public school teachers frequently have their own pension plan, especially when the plan operates at the state level and covers all teachers in the state. There is a variety of arrangements for the faculty and staff of institutions of higher learning. They may have their own plan, they may participate in the plan for elementary and secondary school teachers, or they may be members of a general retirement system for all employees. The faculty and staff of many state colleges and universities participate in the individual annuity contract agreement made available by the Teachers Insurance and Annuity Association (TIAA) and its sister institution, College Retirement Equities Fund (CREF), both chartered under special laws of the New York State Legislature.

In almost every jurisdiction, police and firefighters have their own plans, usually one for police officers and another for firefighters. In a few instances, these two classes of employees are combined for pension purposes and placed in their own distinctive plan. These plans are characterized by relatively generous age and service requirements for retirement, as well as other attractive features. They typically permit retirement with one half of final average salary at age 50 or 55 after 20 or 30 years of service. Some provide half-pay after 20 or 25 years of service, irrespective of attained age. Such favorable retirement terms have been justified as necessary to maintain an energetic force to carry out the hazardous and physically demanding duties of these two occupations.

Other groups that often have their own pension plans are judges and legislators. Even when they do not have their own plan, they are almost certain to receive preferential treatment under the general plan in which they participate. It is common for judges to receive a pension of two thirds to three fourths of their salary at retirement with only 10 to 15 years of service. Retirement with such a benefit may be permitted as early as age 60 or at any age after 20 to 30 years of service. Under some plans for the judiciary, benefits for retired individuals are linked to the compensation of active members, being expressed as a percentage of the salary currently associated with the position occupied by the pensioner before his or her retirement. This practice, called recomputation, has been used in the federal military retirement system (but not since 1958) and in many plans for police and firefighters, and not only protects the purchasing power of the pension benefits but gives retired persons a share in the productivity gains of the economy (as reflected in the salaries of their successors). With Social Security, most judges receive greater aftertax income in retirement than they enjoyed while on the bench. They generally contribute to their retirement systems at a higher rate than other employees. It has been considered sound public policy to place members of the judiciary in a position where they have no concern over their future economic security, freeing their minds for their judicial duties and minimizing their susceptibility to bribery and other forms of improper financial rewards.

Legislators are less likely than judges to have their own pension plan, but they are almost certain to receive preferential treatment. This preferential treatment may take the form of higher annual benefit accruals, a lower retirement age, shorter required period of service, earlier vesting, or all of these. In one state, legislators, who are also covered by Social Security, accrue a pension benefit equal to 7.5 percent of their final average salary for each year of service and may retire at age 50 with full, unreduced benefits. At the expense of an actuarial reduction, they may begin receiving their pension at any age after only six years of legislative service. Legislators who have voted more generous benefits to themselves than to rank-and-file employees have generally defended their action on the grounds that they are underpaid and are entitled to higher pensions to redress the inequity. It is less obtrusive to increase their pensions than to increase their pay. It is generally agreed that earlier vesting is justified for legislators (and members of city councils) because of their uncertain and frequently short tenure.

Perhaps the most common type of public employee retirement system is that for the general employees of the governmental unit—all employees other than teachers, police, firefighters, and other special groups who have their own plan. This plan is frequently known by the acronym PERS (Public Employment Retirement System). It tends to be the largest retirement system for a given governmental subdivision, especially if it includes the public school teachers, as it may. In many jurisdictions the teacher retirement system and the retirement system for general employees are about the same size.

LEVEL OF PLAN ADMINISTRATION

As might be expected, the great majority (80 percent according to the findings of the Pension Task Force) of public employee retirement systems are administered at the city, county, or township level. This is due in large part to the fact that plans for police or firefighters account for two thirds of the entire universe of public plans, and these tend to be local in character and sponsorship.

All states operate retirement systems for their own employees, and some operate them for employees of their political subdivisions. Most states operate at least two plans, one for public school teachers and another for all other state employees. There may be separate plans for the judiciary, state police, guards at correctional institutions, and other special groups. Some states permit the employees of their political subdivisions to participate in the appropriate state plans. In some cases, participation by local government employees is voluntary (in the sense that the local government entities elect to have their employees participate in a state-wide plan rather than operating their own plans), whereas in other cases participation is mandatory. Some states operate state-wide plans for employees of their political subdivisions in which local government employees are not commingled with state employees. Participation by the local units may be either voluntary or mandatory. It is worthy of noting that in 21 states teachers, who are typically local employees, participate in a state-wide retirement system covering state employees as well as teachers. In other states, public school teachers participate in a state-wide plan for teachers only. Except for large cities, public school teachers tend to participate in state-wide plans of some sort. In Hawaii, all state employees and all employees of the state's political subdivisions participate in a single retirement system operated by the state. This is the only state in which all public employees are covered by a consolidated system. Massachusetts has a single pension law for all new employees (since 1945) that provides a uniform set of benefits and retirement conditions for all state and local government employees, with the exception of security personnel and others in hazardous occupations, but the law is administered through 101 separate systems.

There is a trend toward merging the plans of numerous and frequently small political subdivisions into state-wide plans, either on a voluntary or mandatory basis. There are many advantages to consolidation: (1) administrative economies; (2) the potential for better investment performance through greater diversification, improved cash flow, and employment of more sophisticated investment managers; (3) pooling of mortality risk; (4) elimination of competition among systems for plan improvements; (5) protection of benefit accruals of employees who move from one locality to another; (6) sounder benefit design because of the legislature's freedom to concentrate its attention on fewer systems; and (7) improved services to plan members and their beneficiaries because of a large and more professional staff.[2]

There are some potential disadvantages in consolidation. There is clearly some loss of flexibility: a uniform plan may not accommodate local circumstances and needs. There is also the possibility that, in an effort to

---

[2] Bleakney, *Retirement Systems,* p. 20.

make the consolidated plan attractive to all groups, the plan designers will make the benefits and other substantive features too generous. There may be a tendency to build in the most appealing features of all the plans to be merged into the state-wide plan. Unless safeguards are applied, the consolidated system may attract only those groups whose benefit expectations have a greater actuarial value than their anticipated contributions. This threat can be dealt with through making participation mandatory or by adapting contributions to the population characteristics of the participating units. A final disadvantage is diminished ability to experiment and to seek answers from a diversity of approaches to problems.

Bleakney concludes that the biggest obstacle to consolidation is political, the reluctance of local authorities to relinquish any of their influence and the resistance of the administrative staffs of existing systems. "Combining two or more systems into one results in fewer titles, fewer boards and fewer persons bearing the trappings of office, minimal as they may be."[3] There may also be opposition from the local employee groups unless the consolidated plan holds out the promise of more generous benefits and other features.

LEGAL FORM

One of the distinctive features of state and local government retirement systems is that their terms and provisions are promulgated in the form of a legislative enactment of some type. The terms of a retirement system for state employees are invariably contained in a law enacted by the state legislature and, of course, approved by the governor. States that provide a state-administered system for the employees of local government units, on an optional or mandatory basis, also embody the terms of such a plan in a conventionally enacted law. The plan, as contained in the law, may permit some discretion by the local jurisdictions as to benefit levels, normal retirement age, employee contribution rate, and other critical features. The legislated plan would be duly adopted by the city council, county commission, or other legislative body of the local unit, with whatever variations might be desired and permitted. In a sense, this arrangement permits separate "plans" within a central or consolidated "system."

States that do not operate a central system or systems for local government employees still have something to say about the types of pension

[3] Ibid., p. 23.

plans that may be adopted by their subdivisions, except for municipalities that have been granted home rule. A state with this policy enacts a law that outlines the essential features of a pension plan that can legally be adopted by municipalities and other local subdivisions, the provisions being keyed to the size of the unit. Again, the law may permit variations within prescribed limits. In these states, the pension plan actually adopted by the local unit may be contained in an ordinance or other legislative document. Retirement systems instituted by municipalities with home-rule charters will be evidenced by duly adopted ordinances.

Several of the largest cities established municipal pension plans before the state in which they are located established retirement systems for its own employees or enacted broad pension guidelines for its political subdivisions. Some of these pioneer systems continue to function under the exclusive authority of the sponsoring municipality, especially when the latter has a home-rule charter. In many jurisdictions these plans have been brought under the control of the state legislature in one way or the other. Several of the New York City pension plans predate the statewide plans established by the legislature. Despite this and the fact that New York City has home rule in a broad sense, the state legislature reserves to itself the right to make changes in the New York City retirement systems, with two limited exceptions. However, the state constitution requires the city to consent to changes in three of its major pension plans, unless the legislature acts by general law applicable to a broad class of municipalities.

In 22 states there are pension commissions or oversight committees that evaluate all proposals for amending retirement systems subject to the state legislature and make recommendations to the legislature. These bodies vary greatly as to their structure, the scope of their functions, their authority, their independence, and overall effectiveness.[4]

EXPOSURE TO COLLECTIVE BARGAINING

The Inland Steel decision of 1949[5] declared pensions to be a bargainable issue, and since that time bargaining over pension has become standard (indeed, required) practice in those segments of the private economy

---

[4] See Robert Tilove, *Public Employee Pensions Funds* (New York: Columbia University Press, 1976), pp. 257–59, and Suzanne Taylor, *Public Employee Retirement Systems* (ILR Press, New York School of Industrial and Labor Relations 1986), pp. 72–74, for a critique of pension commissions.

[5] *Inland Steel Company* v. *National Labor Relations Board,* 170 F. 2d 247, 251 (1949). Certiorari denied by the Supreme Court, 336 U.S. 960 (1949).

subject to collective bargaining. Many states have recognized the right of public employees to bargain collectively, and in those states they bargain vigorously over wages and other conditions of employment. Yet it is the exception for public employee unions to bargain over pensions.

The explanation of this anomaly is the statutory foundation of public employee retirement systems. There is an inherent conflict over the right of the legislature to legislate and the right of organized employees to bargain collectively.

A municipality with home rule could presumably negotiate pension demands to a definitive conclusion, assuming that its negotiator has the authority to commit the municipality's legislative body. Moreover, a public authority might have enough autonomy to negotiate its own pension arrangements. In all other cases, however, it would be necessary for the legislature to approve any pension bargain that might be negotiated between a political subdivision and a public employee union. In practical effect, the pension pact would be nothing more than a recommendation to the legislature that it amend the pension law or laws in a particular manner. If the legislature refused to do so, the bargain would be of no effect. The only recourse of the union would be to take its case to the legislature and the governor. In the light of this political reality, most collective bargaining units have apparently concluded that they might as well go to the legislature in the first place, where in the past they have had considerable success.

The conflict between New York City and the New York State legislature in the early 1970s over negotiated pension increases, which for fiscal reasons the legislature refused to approve, led to strikes and ultimately to the amending of the Taylor Law on public employee collective bargaining to eliminate pensions as an item of bargaining. The Permanent Pension Commission was directed to develop some form of "coalition bargaining" by the various unions involved as a substitute for conventional bargaining and in an effort to avoid conflicting union demands.

Given the statutory foundation of public employee pension plans, the only way that collective bargaining over pensions could be meaningful would be for the state, through its constitution or appropriate legislation, to commit itself to implement any pension agreements reached by the collective bargaining parties. The Commonwealth of Pennsylvania has come close to making such a commitment. Since 1966 its constitution has authorized the General Assembly to enact laws that would make it mandatory for the General Assembly to take such legislative action as might be necessary to implement a collective bargaining agreement between police and firefighters and their public employers. Pursuant to this constitutional authority, the General Assembly enacted a law which states that if the appropriate law-making body does not approve a collective bargaining agreement (on any subject) negotiated by police and firefighters or if the bargaining reaches an impasse, the issues are to be submitted to a three-member board of arbitration. The decision of the arbitration boards is final and binding, with no recourse to the courts. Moreover, if the issue involves legislation, the decision constitutes a mandate to the appropriate lawmaking body (of the Commonwealth or a political subdivision) to enact the required legislation. In a separate law, the General Assembly has provided that for public employees generally a binding arbitration decision that would have to be implemented through legislative, as opposed to administrative, action shall be considered advisory only. The disparity in treatment of general employees and uniformed employees is another example of the political influence wielded by the latter group.

Collective bargaining over pensions could be made effective, of course, by removing the statutory foundation of public employee retirement systems. This would leave the parties free to arrive at their own pension arrangements, just as they do for wages and salaries and other conditions of employment. This would open up the possibility of plan changes with each new labor contract and more "leapfrogging" (seeking benefits superior to other groups) of pension benefits than has occurred heretofore. The various state legislatures have thus far shown no disposition to relinquish their control over the retirement systems of their political subdivisions. In view of the fiscal plight of many municipalities and the growing realization, hastened by the New York City experience, of the threat to municipal solvency posed by unwise pension expansion, it is doubtful that state legislators in the near future will be willing to grant autonomy to local government units over their retirement systems.

There is a broader question of whether pension benefits in the public sector should be subject to collective bargaining, even subject to state legislature surveillance. A pension plan is a highly technical arrangement, the terms of which with their actuarial overtones do not lend themselves well to the pressure and compromises of collective bargaining. More important, pension promises are deferred obligations that need not be funded immediately. In a budget crisis (or at any other time) it is all too easy for the incumbent public officials to relieve the pressure for higher salaries by granting pension increases that will become a charge against future budgets, the responsibility of subsequent administrations. To harried public officials it looks like a painless way to win points with public employees and their families. Unfortunately, the costs have to be met eventually, but a different generation of taxpayers will have to pay them.

It should be recognized, of course, that the same pressures and forces are at work whether or not the public employees engage in formal collective bargaining. Employees will always be seeking plan liberalizations, and public officials, who themselves may be participants in the same plan, will always be tempted to substitute deferred obligations for current ones. Public employees are adept at lobbying for their objectives at all levels of authority and can be expected to continue to pursue what they consider to be legitimate goals.

LEGAL COMMITMENT OF THE PLAN SPONSOR

There are two aspects to this question. The first is whether the sponsoring governmental unit undertakes to provide a stipulated set of benefits, as articulated in a benefit formula, to employees who meet certain age and service requirements, or whether it merely undertakes to contribute to the retirement system on behalf of each participating employee on a scale specified in the governing law or document. Plans set up under the first concept are known as *defined benefit* plans. Plans operated under the second concept are referred to as *defined contribution* plans. While many of the early plans were established on the defined contribution basis, with the sponsoring agency and the participating employees contributing at the same rate (a specified percentage of the employee's salary), the overwhelming majority of plans today observe the defined benefit principle.

The second type of commitment is concerned with the right of the sponsoring agency to change the terms of the pension bargain. It is well settled for private sector plans that, except for termination of employment before the vesting requirements have been satisfied, pension benefit rights *already accrued* cannot be rescinded, altered, or diminished without the consent of the individuals involved. This is in accordance with the concept that an accrued pension right is legally enforceable under the principles of contract law, in contrast to the older view that pensions, especially those granted by a public body, were gratuities and not enforceable at law. Unfortunately, the contract theory of benefit entitlement is not as firmly anchored in the public sector as in the private sector. In fact, the case law of the majority of states and the federal government continues to apply the gratuity theory to public sector pension plans. This theory holds that the benefits of a public pension plan are gifts of the governmental sponsor, which entity is free to confer, modify, or deny as long as it avoids arbitrary action.[6] For the participants this is an unfortunate state of

[6] For a comprehensive analysis of participants' rights under public employee retirement systems, see Robert W. Kalman and Michael T. Leibig, *The Public Pension Crisis: Myth, Reality, Reform* (Washington, D.C.: American Federation of State, County, and Municipal Employees, 1979), chap. 5.

affairs which should be remedied as promptly as possible by legislation if necessary. For the purpose at hand, however, the primary legal question is whether the term of a pension plan can be changed in such a manner as to adversely affect the accrual of pension benefits *in the future* by persons already in the plan.

By statute, judicial decision, or constitutional provision, a number of states have declared that pension rights under a public employee retirement system are contractual obligations of the system that cannot be diminished or impaired in respect of present members *now or in the future*. New York, Florida, and Illinois have constitutional provisions to that effect. For example, Article 5, Section 7 of the New York State Constitution provides that "membership in any pension or retirement system of the state or of a civil division thereof shall be a contractual relationship, the benefits of which shall not be diminished or impaired." This provision was adopted by the Constitutional Convention of 1938 out of concern fostered by the recent Great Depression that benefits might be cut as an economy measure. It has been construed to mean that for each individual participant the benefits in a system's law at the time that he or she first becomes a member may not in any way be diminished, not only in regard to benefit accruals based on past years of service but also with respect to future years of service. In practice the guarantee of nondiminution has the same effect as if the permanent provisions of the retirement plans were embodied in the Constitution itself.

Massachusetts has stated in its retirement statute that the rights created thereunder are contractual obligations, not subject to reduction. The courts in several states have held that pension expectations are implicit contractual obligations, the terms of which cannot be changed with respect to present members. The Supreme Court of California has ruled that the terms of a retirement plan cannot be changed with respect to present members unless the change is necessary to preserve the integrity of the system or is accompanied by comparable new advantages to the members. Pennsylvania permits an adverse change only when it bears "some reasonable relation to enhancing the actuarial soundness of the retirement system." On the other hand, a 1969 survey found that in 35 states benefit accruals based on prospective service could be legally reduced, even for present members.[7] Even without constitutional, statutory, or judicial con-

---

[7] Report of the Governor's Committee to Study the State Employees' Retirement System, New York State, Albany, 1969.

straints, however, state legislatures and local councils have been extremely reluctant to reduce benefits promised to persons already in the system.[8]

SOCIAL SECURITY COVERAGE

In the beginning, employees of state and local governments were excluded from Social Security coverage because of concern that the taxation of state and local government entities by the federal government might be unconstitutional. In 1950 the Social Security Act was amended to permit states to elect Social Security coverage for such of their employees as were not already under a retirement system, and, at the option of the employing unit, the employees of all their subdivisions, thus waiving their immunity from federal taxation in their capacity as employer. In 1954 the act was further amended to permit election of coverage for employees already participating in a staff retirement system, but such an election was to be effective only if a majority of the members voted in favor of the coverage. Coverage was to be automatic for all public employees not holding membership in a retirement system on the effective date of the election and for those entering an existing retirement system thereafter. Except in specified states, members of a police retirement system do not have the privilege of electing Social Security coverage. This restriction was sought by police and the persons who administer their retirement systems.

About 70 percent of all full-time employees of state and local governments are covered by Social Security, and 70 percent of this group are also participating in an employer-sponsored staff retirement system. About 93 percent of all public school teachers are covered by Social Security.

The section of the Social Security Act that permitted states and their political subdivisions to elect coverage under the act also permitted them to revoke their election and terminate coverage of their employees. After five years of participation in the Social Security system, a state or local government unit could terminate its affiliation by giving notice to the

---

[8] For a more detailed discussion of contractual guarantees, see Tilove, *Public Employee Pension Funds,* pp. 253–56 and 304–7.

Social Security Administration of its intention two years in advance of the effective date.[9] No referendum of the affected employees was required.

Under this authority, a number of governmental units, mostly small and concentrated in the states of California, Texas, and Louisiana, withdrew from the Social Security system in a desire to avoid Social Security employer payroll taxes and in the belief that Social Security benefits could be duplicated at less cost through a staff retirement system.[10] New York City filed a notice of intent to withdraw from the system but revoked it before the proposed date of withdrawal. After revoking one notice of intention to withdraw from the Social Security system, the state of Alaska filed another notice and eventually withdrew, its action being binding on all governmental units in the state. Recognizing that employees of disaffiliated agencies continue to be entitled to some protection and some benefits under the Social Security program and desiring to protect the program against further loss of much-needed revenue from disaffiliations, Congress included a provision in the Social Security Amendments Act of 1983 removing the right of state and local government units to withdraw from the system thereafter. The provision was made applicable to governmental agencies that had already filed a notice of intention to withdraw. The applicability of the provision to pending withdrawals has been upheld in several judicial challenges.

In the Budget Reconciliation Act of 1986, Congress amended the Social Security Act to require all persons thereafter becoming an employee of a state or local government agency not participating in Social Security, whether by original choice or withdrawal, to be covered under the HI segment of the program and to be subject to the employer and employee payroll taxes allocable to that portion of the overall program. Knowledgeable observers believe that eventually new "hires" of all state and local government entities will be made subject to coverage under all components of the Social Security system.

By their collective choice, policemen continue to be excluded from all portions of the Social Security program.

---

[9] A local government unit can terminate its affiliation only with the approval of its own state authorities.

[10] On this latter point, the interested reader should consult Actuarial Note No. 95, published by the Social Security Administration in April 1978. This study shows that, except for unusual circumstances, the present value of Social Security benefits to be "gained" in the future exceed the present value of the combined employer and employee payroll taxes to be paid in the future. The results of this comparison are highly sensitive to the underlying assumptions, especially the interest assumption.

SOURCE OF CONTRIBUTION

State and local retirement systems have traditionally been supported by contributions from both the employing agencies and the participating employees. Employee contributions have been required to provide a steady source of income to the plan, independent of the whims of the legislature or other financing agency and the state of the public coffers, and to dampen employee demands for plan liberalizations.

The Pension Task Force found that about 75 percent of the plans that it surveyed require employee contributions. A substantial number of other plans permit voluntary contributions by employees. In the aggregate and for all the state and local government plans surveyed, employee contributions accounted for about one third of total contributions. Contributions of the employing agencies generally come out of general revenues. In some jurisdictions they are drawn from special earmarked taxes or levies.[11] Some small plans are financed on a pay-as-you-go basis through public subscriptions from an annual appeal.

---

[11] For example, in one state the plan for firefighters is financed out of taxes levied on fire insurance premiums paid to out-of-state companies.

CHAPTER 54

INTERNATIONAL BENEFITS

Arthur C. Folli

The administration of international benefits has become increasingly important as the number of multinational corporations with substantial numbers of employees overseas has increased. There are some 500 large U.S. multinational firms with foreign operations that generate earnings important to their worldwide financial results. In the petroleum industry, for example, as much as half of the consolidated operating earnings of the parent company may be generated by foreign sources. Some large banking institutions headquartered in New York report proportionately larger earnings from foreign sources than from operations in the United States.

As a result, international operations have warranted careful management attention. From the viewpoint of employee benefits, this includes attention to the analysis, design, and administration of employee benefit programs that make up a significant portion of compensation cost overseas.

BENEFIT PLAN DESIGN AND OBJECTIVES

The design of benefit programs for foreign affiliates must take into account the business and social situation prevailing in the country. No two countries are alike, and local regulations, tax laws, customs, and competitive practice vary. For example, the practice in many countries in Europe of paying lifetime retirement annuities contrasts with the practice in the Far East where, because of local custom and favorable tax treatment, retirement programs often are designed to provide lump-sum benefits.

Two additional factors can influence plan design. One is the rate of inflation, and the other is the role of foreign governments in providing benefits to employees.

The international benefit environment differs from the benefit environment in the United States, and as a result, benefit programs acceptable in the United States may not be acceptable in foreign areas; however, the objectives of international benefit administration will nevertheless be the same:

1. To provide benefit programs to address the risks of retirement, death, sickness, disability, and termination.
2. To assure that the programs are competitive.
3. To design programs that are cost effective.
4. To establish benefit programs responsive to the company's business and staffing objectives.

The attraction and retention of qualified local national employees is a challenge since there may be some reluctance on the part of local nationals to work for a multinational company with "foreign" stockholders. Local nationals, other things being equal, generally prefer to work for a local company as opposed to a subsidiary, affiliate, or branch of a multinational. So the challenge to the compensation and benefits specialist advising on programs for foreign affiliates of the multinational may be greater as compared with servicing a company competing in a market with other local companies.

The material that follows deals with many of the major factors that are important considerations in the planning and administration of international benefits such as inflation, benefit plan design elements, financing, and plan evaluation methods. Inflation is addressed first because (1) it provides a quick flavor of the overall economic conditions in the country and (2) it affects benefit plan entitlements and plan costs.

INFLATION

Table 54–1 shows the inflation rates in countries located in various parts of the world. The worldwide average annual rate of inflation over the five-year period 1981–85 has been approximately 13 percent.

Singapore, West Germany, Malaysia, and Switzerland have experienced moderate rates of inflation. However, countries such as the Phillippines, Egypt, Italy, and Greece have experienced double-digit inflation. There have been very high rates of inflation in Mexico, Brazil, Israel, and Turkey. A high rate of inflation has a considerable impact, over time, on

TABLE 54–1
Inflation Rates (percent)

	1981	*1982*	*1983*	*1984*	*1985*	*Five-Year Average*
Saudi Arabia	2.7	1.1	−0.6	−1.2	−3.3	−0.3
Japan	4.9	2.6	1.9	2.3	2.0	2.7
Singapore	8.3	3.9	1.2	2.6	0.5	3.3
West Germany	6.3	5.3	3.3	2.4	2.2	3.9
Netherlands	6.7	5.9	2.8	3.3	2.2	4.2
Switzerland	6.5	5.7	3.0	2.9	3.4	4.3
Malaysia	9.7	5.8	3.7	3.9	.3	4.7
United States	10.4	6.1	3.2	4.3	3.6	5.5
Belgium	7.6	8.7	7.7	6.3	4.9	7.0
United Kingdom	11.9	8.6	4.6	5.0	6.1	7.2
Canada	12.4	10.8	5.8	4.3	4.0	7.5
Australia	9.7	11.1	10.1	4.0	6.7	8.3
France	13.4	11.8	9.6	7.4	5.8	9.6
Indonesia	12.2	9.5	11.8	10.5	4.7	9.7
South Africa	15.2	14.7	12.3	11.7	16.2	14.0
Egypt	10.4	14.8	16.1	17.1	13.3	14.3
Italy	17.8	16.5	14.7	10.8	9.2	13.8
Nigeria	20.8	7.7	23.2	39.6	5.5	19.4
Greece	24.5	21.0	20.2	18.4	19.3	20.7
Philippines	13.1	10.2	10.0	50.3	23.1	21.3
Columbia	27.5	24.5	19.8	16.1	24.0	22.4
Turkey	36.6	30.8	32.9	48.4	45.0	38.7
Mexico	27.9	58.9	101.8	65.5	57.7	62.4
Brazil	105.6	98.0	142.0	196.7	227.0	153.9
Israel	116.8	120.4	145.4	373.8	304.6	212.2
Worldwide Average	14.1	12.2	12.5	13.7	13.7	13.2

Source: International Monetary Fund, International Financial Statistics, Washington, D.C., April 1987.

plan costs and on the real value of benefits received by employees from company-provided benefit programs.

Pension Plan Design

Pension plans generally are defined benefit plans. The benefit at retirement is determined by a formula. There are three major types of pension programs: final average pay (FAP) plans, career average (CAP) plans, and lump-sum plans based on multiples of pay determined by service.

A typical final average pay pension plan might have the following formula: 1.5 percent × years of service × FAP-3. The multiple 1.5 percent is applied to the years of service. FAP-3 would be the average earnings over the three years prior to retirement. If an individual earned $25,000 in the last year of service and $23,000 and $21,000 in the other two years, the final average earnings over the three years would be $23,000. The annual benefit using the above formula would be $10,350, assuming 30 years of service. This would be the gross benefit before taking into account any benefits attributable to governmental social security programs. It is common practice in many countries to integrate, with the private plan, benefits provided through social security schemes or legally required termination indemnities. If the pension formula were FAP-1 instead of FAP-3 in the above example, the benefit entitlement would be $11,250, or almost 9 percent higher.

In the case of high inflation, a pension program based on an FAP-3 or FAP-5 formula often does not provide sufficient replacement income for the prospective retiree. Concern about the erosion in purchasing power caused by price inflation has resulted in a trend to higher multiple final average pay pension plans or final average pay plans based on salaries in the years or months closest to the retirement date. Generally, pension plans are designed to provide between 50 and 80 percent replacement income, after taking into consideration taxes and governmental benefits. The higher replacement ratio might be appropriate for lower salaried employees, whereas lower replacement ratios could be considered for individuals in higher salary brackets.

Career average plans, which provide benefits taking into account total earnings while employed as contrasted to final average earnings, also have been used overseas. However, during periods of high inflation and rapidly rising wages, the career average plan does not provide sufficient replacement income for employees. These programs have often been replaced by final average pay plans.

Lump-sum pension plans are common in the Far East, particularly in Hong Kong, Japan, and the Philippines. This plan design is generally used because of favorable tax laws, which tend to encourage lump-sum payments, or because of local custom. The lump-sum benefit is calculated as a multiple of final pay or the actuarial equivalent of the lifetime annuity option that also may be permitted under the plan.

It is common in European countries to provide widows'/spouses' and orphans' benefits within the pension plan. Typically, the widow's benefit is one half of the employee's entitlement. Single orphan coverage is provided when one parent survives; double orphan benefits, usually twice the single orphan benefit, may be provided when there is no surviving parent.

Also, disability and death benefits often are incorporated within the pension program, in contrast to the usual practice in the United States where such benefits may be provided through separately insured programs. Vesting, the guaranteed right to a benefit after a specified period of service, may not specifically be provided in foreign plans unless required by local laws.

Retirement programs may be noncontributory or contributory. In countries such as the United Kingdom, South Africa, Australia, New Zealand, and Canada, employee contributions are treated favorably as a deduction against taxable earnings under local income tax laws, and as a result, contributory programs are not unusual.

As mentioned previously, governments, in providing benefits through legislated programs, can have an important impact on plan design. Many governments, either through social security or labor legislation, provide retirement and survivor benefits. As a result, there may be less need for supplementary private company-provided benefit programs, except to meet special needs of employees.

Besides governmental influences, it is not unusual in countries in continental Europe to have the participation of works councils in benefit plan matters as part of the codetermination process. These councils include blue-collar as well as white-collar representatives and can influence the employee benefit program.

Savings Plan and Provident Funds

Savings plans are defined contribution plans. The benefit at retirement or termination is based on the sum of the annual contributions made to the plan by the employer and/or employee and the accrued earnings and/or capital appreciation at the time of settlement. Employees often have a choice of investments including fixed income securities, government bonds, company stock, and so on. Employee savings plans, although currently not in common use overseas, may be included in benefit plan design in countries such as Canada, Nigeria, Mexico, and Germany. These plans supplement the benefits available from the primary retirement plan.

Provident funds are similar to savings plans and are prevalent in the Far East; for example, Thailand, the Philippines, Singapore, and Malaysia. These funds, which provide lump-sum benefits at retirement or termination, also are based on the defined contribution principle, and employees as well as employers may contribute to the fund. The investment vehicle generally is restricted and often is limited to interest-bearing accounts such as bank deposits, government bonds, or a combination.

Use of a savings plan to provide retirement benefits, as contrasted with a defined benefit plan based on final average pay, provides more control on company costs. The company contribution is a fixed amount and the benefit is generally paid as a lump sum; as a result, pension supplements to take into account increases in pensioners cost of living are not paid. The liability under a final pay plan is less controllable because final pay generally increases each year and pension supplements are common; this can result in liabilities often double the originally assumed amounts.

Health Coverage

Medical care for active employees, dependents, and retirees commonly is provided through governmental programs in international areas. For example, in the United Kingdom this is accomplished through the National Health Service; in West Germany, Australia, Canada, France, Japan, and some countries in South America, medical coverage is provided through the social security system or through other programs sponsored by the government.

Some governmental health programs are more comprehensive than others. To the extent these plans lack desired health coverage or lead to delays in obtaining treatment, multinationals as well as local companies have adopted private medical programs to supplement or provide health care alternatives to governmental programs.

FINANCING THE PLAN

Unlike in the United States, where the Employee Retirement Income Security Act (ERISA) prescribed limited procedures to be followed for funding benefit programs, legislation overseas may permit many different approaches. The financing mechanisms include:

- Funded plans administered through trustees.
- Insured programs.
- Multinational pooling arrangements.
- Book reserved plans or self-insured plans.
- Pay-as-you-go programs.
- A combination of the above; that is, split-funding.

Pension plans in countries such as the United Kingdom, South Africa, Canada, Australia, the Philippines, and New Zealand typically are funded through trusts and the assets managed by professional investment advisers. In Norway, Denmark, Finland, Belgium, the Netherlands, and Barbados, retirement plans typically are insured. In these cases, the plan costs generally are deductible for tax purposes.

Pooling arrangements can be used to provide a means of lowering benefit cost by spreading the risk. This results in administrative savings, lower reserve requirements, better investment returns, and reduced reinsurance costs. Many large insurance companies pool pension, medical, death, and disability benefit risks of multinational corporations covered by contracts with local insurers in various foreign countries.

It is not necessary, in some countries, to have funded or insured plans in order to obtain tax benefits. For example, in Germany, Austria, Japan, and Mexico, retirement plans may be book reserved, and full or partial tax benefits may be obtained under the law.

The book reserve defines on the balance sheet the liability the company has undertaken for providing pensions for employees at retirement. This method may provide less security to the employee as compared with funding, since no specific assets are set aside to support the pension promise. However, the book reserve procedure has worked satisfactorily in foreign countries and enables the company to retain the cash for investment in the business, which reduces the cost of borrowing funds. Also, there are advantages to this funding method during periods of high inflation when better incremental returns may be available on investments in the business as compared with investments in securities, particularly if availability of local capital becomes restricted or costly.

Although book reserved, some countries may require a company guarantee that benefits will be paid when due. For example, in West Germany, the law requires that vested benefits or benefits in the course of payment be insured against the company's insolvency through a special insurance organization (PSV). The premium paid by the company is based on a percentage of the reserve.

The choice of the financing method for benefit programs must take into account cash flow requirements, local law, investment earnings, and the tax liability, to the company as well as to the employee, on annual plan contributions and annual plan earnings. When there is high inflation, the challenge to investment managers of trusteed plans to maintain satisfactory rates of return is great. In some countries such as Brazil, investments can be made in indexed securities. In other countries in Latin America, pension benefits may be handled on a pay-as-you-go basis, in which case liabilities normally are not accrued.

Each foreign country has different requirements to "qualify" benefit programs for purposes of obtaining corporate tax deductions as well as to assure the nontaxability of current benefit accruals to the employee.

EVALUATION OF FOREIGN BENEFIT PROGRAMS

To insure that the benefit programs designed are cost effective and responsive to the needs of the employees, the programs should be evaluated carefully, taking into account the company's objectives. A well-structured benefit program, as a part of the total compensation approach, will assist in attracting, motivating, and retaining qualified personnel.

Short- and long-range planning programs should be developed by the overseas affiliate and the multinational working together to establish a framework within which to evaluate the appropriate levels of employee benefits. One method used to evaluate compensation and benefit programs is to establish a target-ranking objective for the affiliate with respect to the local market. For example, the company objective might be to maintain a position in the middle of competition as a desired ranking for its benefit programs. Therefore, the acceptability of an employee benefit scheme would be judged on how the benefit plan meets this criterion.

Determination of the desired ranking position would depend on the needs and objectives of the company; that is, (1) whether the company is well established in the market, (2) whether the company is seeking to attract employees to foster future growth, and (3) the financial resources of the company. A ranking position in the upper quartile for compensation and benefits vis-à-vis the competitive market may be necessary in cases where the company is not well established or is seeking rapid growth in a competitive labor market. On the other hand, a less ambitious ranking may be more desirable when a new operation is started to control costs; it is far easier to improve benefit programs than to reduce them.

Once a target-ranking objective is established, the ranking analysis can be made by determining the value of various employee benefit programs and developing "strawman" comparisons that rank the company's plan with the competitive community. Each competitive plan, as well as the company's present plan and alternatives, can be evaluated in terms of the benefit the employee would receive. Table 54–2 is a sample of a strawman comparison.

Although this table shows data for one salary and service level, a composite could be developed to show the ranking for the typical or average retiree. It is important, however, to determine relative rankings for various salary and service levels to assure that equitable treatment is provided both at the low end and high end of the salary and service ranges. The percentages shown for the retirement benefit take into account the value of the total retirement income received by the employee as a percentage of his or her final average pay. Total retirement income would include the company-provided pension as well as governmental

TABLE 54–2
Strawman Comparisons

Company XYZ versus competitive community total retirement income (including social security) at age 65 as percent of employee's final three-year average salary.

Service = 30 years
Final average salary = LC65,000
LC = Local currency

Ranking	*Company*	*Percent of Final Average Salary*
1	A	75.1%
2	B	74.0
3	C	72.8
4	D	71.5
5	E	70.8
6	XYZ	70.1
7	F	69.1
8	G	68.5
9	H	67.5
10	I	67.2
Average (excluding XYZ)		70.7%

social security or other legislated benefits. The table deals with the basic retirement benefit only. It does not cover other benefits that may be provided in the plan, such as death protection for widows and orphans, and so on, nor does it cover benefit entitlements from thrift plans, if any. For these important items, separate strawman analyses can be prepared.

Another method of evaluating benefit plan programs and alternatives is the relative value method. This method ties into one bundle, on a present value basis, the total value of benefits provided under the pension, savings, life insurance, disability, and health programs. The relative value method permits comparison of the entire employee benefit package versus the competitive community or versus an alternative mix of benefit programs and is an extremely valuable measurement tool.

In addition, the relative value method can be useful in comparing the benefit program with other types of company investments and in measuring the extent of the company's commitment. For example, the investment cost of constructing a paint factory can be readily measured. The factory might cost $25 million to build, and a present value could be developed for the investment after taking into account any corporate tax savings from depreciation. In this case, the financial outlay and company commitment and risk are relatively clear.

Development of a comparable measurement for benefit plan programs or plan improvements is more complex. Using actuarial assumptions, the present value of projected benefits for pension plans can be calculated. This liability is an estimated measurement of the company's long-term financial commitment. On the other hand, welfare plans, such as medical and life insurance programs, are often established on a one-year term cost basis. A present value of future costs can nevertheless also be developed in this case assuming an ongoing program since, for all practical purposes, the welfare plan probably will be renewed from year to year. Although the annual cost of a welfare plan benefit might be, for example, $500,000, on an equivalent liability basis the actuarial present value of future costs could be many millions of dollars. Adoption of the welfare plan could involve a more serious financial obligation that is not readily apparent when the program is evaluated on the basis of annual cost alone.

The present value approach affords a reasonable measurement of the company's financial commitment. Its use can point out the need for greater care in the evaluation and design of benefit plan programs. Although construction of the paint factory involves a large financial commitment, the pension or welfare plan change could involve a commitment as large or larger. Also, with the benefit program there may be less flexibility for adjusting the commitment in the future, particularly where unions or

TABLE 54–3
Comparison of Compounded Costs—6 Percent Program versus 5.5 Percent Program

Year	*Annual Cost of a 6 Percent Program*	*Annual Cost of a 5.5 Percent Program*	*Difference in Annual Cost*	*Ratio: Current Year versus 1st-Year Costs*	*Difference as Percentage of 6 Percent Program*
	(A)	*(B)*	*(C)*	*(D)*	*(E)*
0	100	100			
1	106	105.5	0.5		0.5%
2	112.4	111.3	1.1	2.2	1.0
3	119.1	117.4	1.7	3.4	1.4
4	126.2	123.9	2.3	4.6	1.8
5	133.8	130.7	3.1	6.2	2.3

works councils are involved. This contrasts with the options available for modifications in manufacturing capacity, equipment, or processes.

Benefit programs such as retirement plans are a form of deferred compensation. As a result, it is important that compensation programs, which establish base salary to which benefit programs are related, take into account the effect on such costs that compound over time. For example, a compensation and benefits program that may have been designed to produce a cost of 6 percent, per year (adopted instead of a more conservative 5.5 percent program) would cost considerably more than the apparent 0.5 percent delta by the fifth year, as shown in Table 54–3.

As can be seen, the difference in annual cost (Column C) increases sixfold, from 0.5 to 3.1, in five years. Expressed as a percent of total payroll cost, the added cost increases from about 0.5 percent of payroll in the first year to 2.3 percent of payroll by the fifth year (Column E). If the annual payroll is $500 million and includes 0.5 percent of excess, approximately 2.3 percent or $11.5 million in additional cost in the fifth year could have been avoided by a more conservatively developed compensation/benefit scheme. (This does not take into account that over the five years, this hypothetical company "overspent" by over $40 million, draining cash flow more than necessary.)

This cost continues to grow as an integral part of base pay. If this hypothetical company had designed the additional 0.5 percent in the form of an annual performance bonus, (or welfare plan benefit such as health care) and not as a part of base pay, the five-year cost would have been only about $15 million and the "rollover" effect on benefit costs would have been minimized. Since benefit policy interrelates with compensation policy, these factors need to be considered in evaluating the total cost of program changes.

U.S. TAX DEDUCTION—FOREIGN PENSION PLANS

Legislation enacted in the United States in 1980 (P.L. 96-603) makes available to U.S. multinational corporations certain U.S. tax advantages for pension plans of foreign branches and subsidiaries, provided the foreign plans meet the requirements of foreign law and applicable U.S. laws. Whereas in the United States a pension plan must be qualified under ERISA to obtain tax benefits, P.L. 96-603 imposes less stringent requirements on foreign plans. Tax deductions may be sought for contributions made to qualified branch book reserved plans and branch funded plans, and foreign tax credits utilized for subsidiary reserve plans. The treatment for each class of plan differs under the legislation. Tax benefits were previously possible only for contributions made to subsidiary funded plans and branch funded plans qualified under ERISA.

Qualified reserve plans are plans for which a balance sheet liability is established. Additions to the reserve may be deductible under P.L. 96-603, Section 404A, under the following provisions:

- Plan accruals must be for the benefit of the employees, with little risk of forfeiture.
- Accruals or additions to the book reserve must be tax deductible under the foreign law.
- Accruals must be computed by the unit credit method or other method prescribed by the U.S. IRS with no salary increase assumption.
- Only vested employees can be included in the valuation.
- Cost-of-living adjustments can be assumed in the valuation only if they are part of the accrued benefit entitlement.
- Adjustments to the reserve due to experience gains or losses, plan improvements, changes in actuarial assumptions, and so on must be amortized over a 10-year period.
- A special interest rate must be used based on a corridor of 80 percent and 120 percent of the average long-term corporate bond rate over the past 15 years in the foreign country.

Qualified funded plans must meet the following requirements:

- The plan must be maintained for the exclusive benefit of the employees and beneficiaries.
- The annual contribution to the fund must be tax deductible under the foreign law and must meet limitations provided under U.S. law.
- Contributions must be made to a trust fund or its equivalent such as an insurance company for the purchase of a retirement annuity or directly to a plan participant.
- The valuation of the fund assets is subject to limitations prescribed under U.S. law.

In both cases, 90 percent or more of the amounts paid into or accrued for the year under the plan must be attributable to the services performed by nonresident aliens whose compensation is not subject to U.S. federal income tax. P.L. 96-603 will result in U.S. tax savings for U.S. companies doing business overseas, particularly for branch and subsidiary plans that are book reserved and meet the requirements of the law. Of course, in the case of foreign subsidiaries, the extent of any U.S. tax savings depends on whether the subsidiary is in a dividend-paying position; if there are no dividends, there would not be any current savings possible under P.L. 96-603.

OTHER LEGISLATION AFFECTING PLAN DESIGN

From time to time, various foreign countries may adopt legislation freezing wages and prices, including the level of benefits. Canada adopted a wage/price freeze between 1972 and 1979. Norway did this in 1979 and Belgium in 1981. When a foreign country imposes a freeze on wages, the freeze also may apply to benefit plan changes, although the practice has been to exempt pensioners.

Some foreign countries have ERISA-type legislation, antidiscrimination legislation, and organizations comparable to the Pension Benefit Guaranty Corporation (PBGC) in the United States. The Pension Benefits Act in Canada establishes standards for vesting of pensions, plan solvency, investments, and disclosure. There is similar legislation in other countries, for example, Norway and West Germany. West Germany requires a company guarantee on benefits similar in some respects to the PBGC. These rules and regulations have an influence on foreign benefit plan design. Also, antidiscrimination legislation has been enacted in some foreign countries, for example, Australia and New Zealand.

PENSION SUPPLEMENTATION

The high level of inflation in many countries has brought about an appreciable erosion in the purchasing power of the annuitant's pension. The speed at which this erosion occurs depends on the rate of inflation. For example, a pension worth LC100 at retirement would be worth only LC50 in approximately 10 years, assuming a 7 percent inflation rate. At a 10 percent inflation rate, the pension would be worth LC50 in about seven years. At 13 or 14 percent inflation rates, which have existed in some countries (see Table 54–1), the value of the pension would be halved in approximately five years. As a result, there has been pressure from retirees for pension supplements to offset the effects of price inflation on their annuities.

Most companies have followed an ad hoc approach to pension supplementation where this is permitted under local law. Practices vary, from providing pension supplements to take into account the full amount of the advance in consumer prices, to a portion or percentage of the full amount. A regular program of fully protecting a pensioner against the erosion in purchasing power, tantamount to automatic indexing, would be expensive to the plan. If directly indexed to the movement in the consumer price index (CPI), the cost could be prohibitive, at even average rates of inflation, with almost no control over the ultimate plan liability.

Since the spending patterns of the retired population differ from those of active employees, the usual price index or CPI applicable to the average wage earner may not be representative of the effect of inflation on pensioners. Also, a significant part of the pensioner's income—governmental social insurance payments—often is indexed. The trend in average wages can also be used as a measurement, since it establishes the rate at which wages of active employees have increased; this rate of increase in the wage index, if lower than the rate of change in the CPI, can indicate a possible upper control of pensioner adjustments. In some countries, a separate CPI may be developed for the retired group.

Some countries require automatic indexing of pensions. In Brazil, pensions are subject to annual increases based on an index acceptable to the government. In West Germany, there is legislation requiring that private pensions be reviewed every three years and an additional allowance paid to pensioners to restore the purchasing power eroded by inflation. This is tantamount to indexing, although West Germany has experienced lower inflation rates as compared with rates prevalent in many other parts of the world.

COUNTRY BENEFIT PROFILES

The following are brief profiles of the different benefit environments existing in some large countries where multinational companies have major operations: Canada, Mexico, Nigeria, Japan, and the United Kingdom. Canada is included because of its proximity to and similarity with the United States, Mexico as an area of the world where private benefit programs are developing, Nigeria as representative of a large African country, Japan representing the Far East, and the United Kingdom as a country with a long history of government and private benefit programs.

Canada

Governmental pensions are paid to annuitants primarily under two programs. The first program, the Old Age Security Act, provides to every Canadian who meets the residency test at age 65 a flat rate pension that is indexed quarterly to protect the purchasing power of the original pension.

The second program, the Canada Pension Plan (CPP), provides an additional earnings-related benefit. (There is a separate earnings-related benefit provided under the Quebec plan in lieu of the CPP. Under Canada's constitution, the provinces have primary jurisdiction over pensions and health insurance, and Quebec chose to set up its own plan (QPP) with benefits similar to the CPP.) The CPP benefit amounts to 25 percent of final three-year average covered earnings up to a ceiling that changes each year. The benefits under this program, including survivor and disability benefits, are indexed annually, which enhances their value in an economy where inflation has averaged about 7.5 percent in the past five years. Unlike the flat rate pension, which is financed from general revenues, both employers and employees contribute to the compulsory earnings-related pension program (either the CPP or QPP). The benefits under both programs are taxable; however, employee contributions under CPP are tax deductible. An additional program, the Federal Guaranteed Income Supplement, provides additional income on a needs basis. These pensions are payable from age 65 and are also indexed with the CPI.

Medical benefits are provided in Canada for all residents regardless of age through hospital and medical programs administered by the 10 provinces. Three provinces currently require contributions from plan participants, while the remainder do not. The health plans are subsidized by the federal government. Dental coverage is included in provincial plans only to a limited extent or not at all, so some companies provide dental benefits through privately insured programs. Also, programs for vision care and drugs often are privately insured.

Private pension plans in Canada, which may be integrated, within limits, with governmental programs, must meet the requirements of the federal Canadian income tax laws as well as provincial rules and regulations to obtain tax advantages. Employee contributions to registered private pension plans are deductible, and therefore employee contributions are common. Spousal benefits are payable, although long-term disability benefits are commonly provided through insured plans.

The Registered Retirement Savings Plan (RRSP) permits tax-sheltered employee contributions. The amount of tax-favored contributions will vary and depend on whether or not the employee is a member of a pension plan. Higher tax-sheltered contributions are permitted if the employee is not a member of a pension plan. In the end result, the RRSP is not unlike the individual retirement accounts (IRAs) utilized in the United States.

Mexico

The Mexican government has legislated benefits through enactment of various labor laws that have lessened the need for private pension programs. The current principal provisions under the law are:

1. Cesantia: This is a basic termination indemnity equal to three-months' pay plus 20-days' pay for each year of service. The benefit is payable on all terminations except death or termination for cause. The payment is taxable to the employee.
2. Antiguedad: This benefit is equal to 12-days' pay for each year of service. It is payable at retirement, death, disability, or termination (voluntary or involuntary, with or without cause). There is a cap (currently twice the legal minimum wage) on the earnings on which the calculation is made (unlike Cesantia for which there is no earnings limit for calculation purposes). The payment is taxable to the employee.

In both cases, the payments (lump sums) are made by the employer and are deductible for corporate tax purposes. Most employers book reserve the liability under the Antiguedad although the liability can be prefunded to obtain a current tax deduction. No deduction may be taken on a book reserve or trust fund for the Cesantia, however. Some companies have considered adoption of pension plans to approximate the Cesantia benefit, which would permit current tax deductions. The pension payment, which would be offset against the Cesantia payment, would generally not be taxable to the employee.

There are also old age, invalidity (disability), medical, and death benefits provided under the Social Insurance System, which maintains its own hospitals, clinics, and physicians. This program is financed by employee and employer contributions and governmental subsidies. Normal retirement age is 65 for males and females.

Privately insured group life, disability, and medical programs supplement the governmental benefits. Insurance premiums, however, are not tax deductible if loans, based on policy cash values, were obtained. Tax-effective programs are desirable in view of the high tax rates. Inflation and interest rates have been high, which tends to focus the employee's attention on direct compensation; the government has been regarded as the supplier of benefits.

There is compulsory profit sharing in Mexico of 8 percent of before-tax profits for all employees except senior management.

Legislation enacted in 1978 included favorable tax treatment for employer and employee contributions to savings funds. These savings funds, in which participants vest immediately, permit employees to withdraw the employee and employer contributions and accrued earnings annually, tax-free. The maximum that can be contributed to these savings plans is 13 percent of base pay up to 10 times the minimum wage.

Nigeria

In the social security pension fund program under which most employees are required to be covered, a lump sum equal to the employee and employer contributions plus accrued interest is paid to the employee at age 55. It also may be payable after one year of unemployment or in the case of invalidity. The survivor's benefit is equal to the benefit to which the employee would have been entitled. Pension benefits are taxable. The program is administered under the National Provident Fund.

Retirement ages in Nigeria generally are lower than the retirement ages prevailing in most non-African countries. Early retirement under some plans may start at age 45 on a discounted basis; normal retirement age generally is 55 for males and females.

In addition to benefits provided through social insurance, life insurance and disability provisions may be incorporated within private retirement plans or provided separately through insured plans. Because of wide swings in rates of inflation, pension programs provided by multinationals, which are commonly funded plans, are often final average pay plans integrated with governmental benefits. Some plans may provide for full or partial commutation. Other plans provide simple gratuities at retirement based on final earnings and service.

Savings plans have been adopted by private companies in Nigeria to take advantage of favorable tax treatment on employee and employer contributions. Some companies adopt provident funds similar to employee savings plans.

Medical benefits, particularly for subsidiaries of multinational firms, typically are provided through company clinics or on a contractual basis. Free medical care is available to residents through public dispensaries and hospitals.

Insurance premiums and pension contributions are deductible for tax purposes; current maximum is N2,000.

Japan

The government pension system implemented in 1986 consists of two programs, the Welfare Pension Scheme (WPS) for employees and the National Pension Scheme (NPS) for the self-employed. The Welfare Pension Scheme provides a benefit that includes a flat amount related to participation and an earnings-related component based on career average. The national pension is the basic pension, which includes a flat amount related to participation under the NPS and the flat amount component from the WPS. The basic pension is fully indexed based on the CPI. Earnings-related contributions are shared equally between the employer and employee. The government subsidizes one third of the total cost of the basic pension.

The National Pension Scheme also covers individuals not covered by any other pension program. Monthly old age as well as survivor and disability benefits are provided. Benefits are generally paid at age 65 and are taxable. Under WPS, early retirement is possible at age 60 for males and age 55 for females, although the retirement age for females will be raised gradually (by the year 2000) to age 60, the same as for males.

Health coverage is provided through the national health insurance system, which may be supplemented through private health insurance societies. Certain items, such as cosmetic surgery, special dental work, and hospital expense above ward facilities (e.g., private room charges), normally are excluded from coverage provided under the national health insurance system.

Private company-provided retirement plans generally are lump-sum retirement/termination plans, although annuity plans are becoming more acceptable. These supplement the governmental social insurance. The lump-sum or annuity benefits vary with service and salary, and in this case, there often is no provision for direct integration with statutory benefits. Book reserve plans are tax deductible up to about 50 percent of the termination benefit. If the plan is funded either through a trust or insurance company and is qualified under Japanese law, the annual plan contributions may be fully deductible. Death and disability benefits are normally included in private pension plans and paid as lump sums.

Group life insurance also may be arranged through private carriers to supplement social insurance death benefits.

United Kingdom

The British social security system, in one form or another, dates back many years. As a result, it has evolved into a sophisticated system incorporating automatic indexing of benefits and options for employers.

The social security system consists of two parts: (1) a flat rate amount and (2) an earnings-related amount. Coverage under social security generally is universal. Companies have been permitted to "contract out" of social security; that is, to provide, through a privately funded plan, the earnings-related benefit portion. In return, employer and employee contributions to social security are reduced. Many multinationals have considered this option in the expectation that the earnings-related benefit can be funded through private plans at lesser cost. The decision to contract out is not irrevocable.

The social insurance benefits, which are taxable, include old age, sickness, disability, and survivor benefits. Normal retirement ages for social security and most private pension plans are 65 for males and 60 for females.

Private pension plans in the United Kingdom are often final average pay plans that reflect the influence of relatively high inflation rates (ranging up to 18 percent in the past 10 years). The final average pay calculation may be based on the average of the last five-, three-, or in some cases one-year's pay. Employee contributions to pension plans and retirement annuity premiums are deductible for local tax purposes and, as a result, many pension plans are contributory. The benefit may be paid as a life annuity or commuted in part subject to a legislated maximum. In addition to benefits provided under social insurance, death and disability benefits generally are included within private retirement plans. This is also true for widows' and orphans' benefits subject to prescribed limits.

Comprehensive medical and dental coverage is provided through the National Health Service (NHS). Patients pay a portion of the cost for such items as dental treatment, prescriptions, eyeglasses, and so on. Children, new mothers, and certain low-income persons are exempt from fees. Some companies provide separately insured medical coverage through private plans as a supplement or alternative to NHS. Employer contributions to private plans are considered taxable benefits to the employee.

BENEFIT PROGRAMS FOR THIRD–COUNTRY NATIONALS (TCNs)

The development of employee benefits programs for foreign nationals (TCNs) assigned to posts outside of their home countries presents special problems. Normally, the benefit programs for expatriates are based on the benefits prevailing in the home-country affiliate. However, in some cases, the full home-country benefit package may not be available. For example, the U.K. National Health Service covers employees for medical expenses incurred only in the United Kingdom, although continued coverage under the home-country retirement plan may be possible. Therefore, the TCN benefit plan program may have to be augmented either by providing medical coverage under host country plans or by providing coverage through other sources. If, because of legal restrictions, the expatriate is not able to continue participating in home-country social security for accruing old age benefits, or if there are tax disadvantages to maintaining pension coverage under the home-country plan, other alternatives may have to be developed. Some multinationals have adopted the international expatriate concept in which the employee is not related to the home country for benefit plan purposes but is covered under a separate "worldwide" package. Either concept—the home-country or international expatriate approach—can be used. However, there may be advantages to the home-country approach from the viewpoint of benefit plan continuity if the expatriate is expected to return to the home country in the future for assignment or retirement.

Relating the TCN benefits to the host country can result in dissimilar benefit treatment as the TCN is reassigned to other posts. Nevertheless, this approach may be desirable in some cases to assure the availability of local tax deductions. The additional application of a worldwide or "umbrella" plan for such TCNs can provide a guaranteed minimum level of benefits regardless of the post or posts to which the employee may be assigned.

A number of bilateral agreements have been entered into between countries to avoid dual coverage and the double withholding of social security taxes on expatriates; that is, payment of host-country as well as home-country social security taxes. The United States has concluded bilateral agreements with Italy, West Germany, Switzerland, Belgium, Canada, Norway, the United Kingdom, and Sweden; a number of other agreements are pending. These agreements can result in significant savings to multinational companies with expatriates assigned overseas since contributions, on their behalf, to foreign security plans will no longer be required. The duplicate expenditure, in most cases, did not result in any benefit to the expatriate; that is, the assignment of the expatriate to the foreign country often was not of sufficient duration to qualify for benefits under local law.

The agreements generally deal with old age, survivors, and disability insurance programs of the countries involved, but not with health insurance or other social programs. In some cases, credits that may be accrued under the social security programs of both countries may be taken into account to determine eligibility for partial benefits under the home-country and/or foreign plans.

SUMMARY

Each foreign country has different cultures, laws, governmental benefit programs, and business climates; inflation rates range from low to very high. Local environments and employee expectations and preferences vary. These factors have an impact on the types of benefits developed and should be considered in the design of benefit plan programs for the multinational.

It probably is neither possible nor desirable to adopt a standard employee benefit program for all countries. What may be acceptable or suitable in one area may not be acceptable in another; it may be too expensive or not responsive to the needs of the employees and families for whom the benefit plans are designed.

The programs should be competitive, in order to attract and retain qualified employees, and cost effective. New benefit plan packages, and improvements to current programs, should be evaluated carefully to provide optimum levels of benefits at costs within the company and employee resources.

There should be reasonable stability to employee benefit program design. Frequent changes, particularly in retirement programs, are generally not desirable. Employees are entitled to some stability in terms of expectations and benefits should not fluctuate widely depending on the date selected for retirement. Of equal importance, the programs obligate the company to future liabilities that the company should be aware of before pension or other benefit plan improvements are made.

A wide range of methods is permitted under foreign law for financing employee benefit programs. Plans may be funded through trustees or insurance companies, book reserved, administered on a pay-as-you-go basis, or split-funded. The choice often depends on the degree of tax deductibility under local laws of annual plan contributions or accruals to the company and, as appropriate, to the employee as well.

Many foreign countries have been at the benefits business for a long time. Germany, under Bismarck, was the first to introduce social security plans. The United Kingdom was among the first to introduce a comprehensive national health system; and survivors benefits for widows and orphans have a long history. The indexing of social security benefits overseas, based on changes in the consumer price index, also has a long history.

International benefits is a complex area. There are many different customs, laws, bilateral agreements between countries, and other regulations that must be taken into account in plan design. And it is a growing area as foreign source earnings have represented a significant proportion of a multinational's consolidated worldwide corporate earnings. As a result, the design and administration of international benefit programs warrants careful management review.

CHAPTER 55

THE FUTURE OF EMPLOYEE BENEFIT PLANS

Dallas L. Salisbury

Predicting the future is a game of chance in which the normal laws of probability do not hold. The passage of time allows numerous unexpected events to intervene, and this has been the rule rather than the exception with employee benefits.

The field of employee benefits will be increasingly dynamic and challenging during the 90s. The greatest rewards will go to those who carefully anticipate and plan. This chapter attempts to lay a base for that purpose.

PRE-ERISA PREDICTIONS ABOUT EMPLOYEE BENEFIT PLANS (1970)

In 1970 experts made predictions concerning the future of employee benefits. The predictions were based upon specific beliefs regarding (*a*) the economy of the 1970s and (*b*) expected population change.

The economy of the 70s was expected to be strong. Median incomes were expected to rise substantially: they did. Inflation was expected to drop from the abnormally high rate of 4 percent: it has. The makeup of the work force (male–female) was expected to remain fairly constant: it didn't. The population over age 65 was expected to approach 23 million: it did. The average workweek was expected to move to 35 hours per week or less: it didn't.

Based upon these economic and population predictions the seers specified future benefit trends. They predicted that:

- The 70s would see dramatic increases in income replacement, reaching an average of 75 percent of final earnings (for many it did, and it's moving this way).
- The 70s would see a movement towards encouraging early retirement with the average moving to age 55 (it moved down to the 61–62 range for all individuals; to 58 for large employers).
- The 70s would see plans move toward shorter vesting periods and earlier participation (it happened).
- The 70s would see dramatic growth of, and pressure for, survivor benefits (it happened).
- The 70s would see liberalization of eligibility rules for disability benefits (it happened).
- The 70s would mark the beginning of active and competitive portfolio management (it happened).

The seers of 1970 were surprisingly accurate.

Many things are known now about the 70s and 80s. Inflation reached its highest historical point for the United States and then came back down. Median income rose dramatically, but then slowed. The over-65 population continues to grow, and the proportion of women in the work force grew dramatically.

These economic and population trends of the 70s and 80s are still with us. They will help to shape what occurs in the 90s as they did in the 70s and 80s. They are relevant to a number of factors which will determine the future of benefit programs.

SOCIAL SECURITY

In 1980, on the 45th anniversary of Social Security, William Driver, then commissioner of the Social Security Administration, made bold predictions about its future. "Social security will not go bankrupt," he said. "Its benefits will continue to be the basic source of retirement income upon which people rely." The Social Security Act Amendments of 1983 brought renewed stability to the retirement portion of the program.

Predicting the future of Social Security or the stability of the entire employee benefit system has never been an easy task, but Social Security was in severe financial trouble. The Medicare portion still faces the potential of bankruptcy by the year 2000.

For the plan sponsor, the participant, and the taxpayer, the stability of Social Security has far-reaching implications. The prospects for stability are affected by numerous factors, but the level of inflation, the size and makeup of the work force, and the selected age for retirement are particularly important.

There is no easy solution to Social Security's financial problems. The importance of Social Security to all elements of benefit programs and current employee compensation cannot be overstated. Should Social Security continue to absorb an ever-growing share of our nation's resources, it *will* limit the expansion of other benefit programs and take-home pay. Incremental change is likely to remain the rule. This will cause the cost of the program to go steadily upward and the resources available for other benefits to shrink.

THE EMPLOYEE'S DECISION TO RETIRE

The retirement decision is crucial for retirement income programs: it determines the amount of money required by the programs. The difference between paying benefits for 20 years versus 10 years is much greater than a doubling. Future trends, therefore, are extremely important.

What motivates a person to leave a job? What are the factors considered by an individual who has worked for 30 or 40 years and has the opportunity to decide whether to continue working or to retire? The worker must examine all sources of income, from Social Security, savings, and pensions. To the extent that the income from these sources promises to be inadequate, the worker is likely to delay retirement.

During the 90s actions are likely to be taken which will encourage later retirement. Such changes for Social Security might include relaxing the earnings test, raising the age of eligibility for initial benefits to 68 or 70, and adjusting the level of indexing.

Private plan changes are also possible. Changes in the tax status of benefit program contributions and benefits could alter the future pattern of benefit receipt. Government could require private plans to raise normal retirement age (with mandatory retirement eliminated, workers may want to work longer) to match Social Security.

But what are the effects of a mandatory retirement age change? Studies indicate that few older workers previously subject to mandatory retirement chose to remain on the job just because the mandatory age had been lifted to 70. The effects on firms if the worker *does* remain past the previous age limit will in large part determine whether the outlawing of mandatory retirement will encourage later retirement. This unknown will have large work force implications in the 90s and beyond.

High inflation does seem to cause persons to delay retirement. The worker may anticipate that wages will rise with prices, especially if the older worker expects several years of inflation. The worker can also anticipate that higher wages will result in higher pension benefits, so that a delay in retirement will pay off. A return of high inflation would affect retirement patterns.

Other factors affecting retirement trends are health, education, personnel policies, and changes in negotiating employee benefit plans. On the whole, health has improved, and further improvements could increase the proportion of older workers in the labor force. Were the result to increase the length of retirement rather than work, the implications for plan financing would be extremely adverse.

Older workers may desire to reduce their hours of work gradually or shift to less arduous tasks while remaining employed. Whether or not unions continue to press for subsidized early retirement features will have an effect on future retirement patterns.

The consequences of retirement age are great for all benefit programs in terms of the period of coverage, the cost of coverage, and the mix of programs. Benefit professionals should watch developing trends carefully.

DEMOGRAPHIC CHANGE

The makeup of both the retired and working populations affects all public and private benefit programs. The 70s saw the World War II baby boom entering the work force for the first time. The 80s saw this group in its 40s and possibly focusing for the first time on long-term security issues.

While the Social Security program is sound today, we must consider the prospects for the years beyond 2010 when this group will retire. Payroll tax rates could rise to between 25 percent and 64 percent to finance the present program, dependent upon economic performance and population behavior. Should rates go this high numerous other benefit programs could find themselves crowded out.

The 90s will be the period during which the nation begins to seriously focus upon the implications of the baby boom. The implications, however, go well beyond the age mix of the population.

- Due to longer life expectancies the cost of providing health care and retirement income support to current retirees is higher than expected and rising. This will continue to be the case for future retiree groups.
- Changing family relationships are having, and will continue to have, a major effect on the stability and future development of benefit programs. The number of families headed by a woman is increasing, as is woman's labor force participation.

These changes will lead to greater flexibility in benefit design. The traditional model—working husband, housewife, children—around which benefit programs have been designed in the past, now represents less than 15 percent of households.

The productive work force will continue to shrink as a proportion of the total population, increasing the proportion of each worker's income that will be needed to support the young, the old, and the infirm. As the consequences of this change become more clearly understood, decision makers will be forced to make policy changes. While this began in the 80s, it is not likely to have its full effect until the 90s.

ECONOMIC CHANGE

The strength of the economy during the 90s will be a principal determinant of the future of employee benefits. A low-growth, high-unemployment, high-inflation economy like that of the 70s would carry with it very negative consequences. A brief look at those years allows one to understand why.

Inflation was a persistent problem during the 70s, averaging 7.4 percent per year and topping 14 percent in 1979. Social Security and many other public benefit programs are indexed to inflation. The 14.3 percent July 1980 adjustment, attributable to 1979 inflation, increased Social Security costs by over 16 billion dollars per year. The July 1981 increase added approximately 17 billion dollars to annual program costs. The nation would have difficulty affording such a trend through the 80s.

For private pension plans a fixed pension would lose 66 percent of its value over 10 years, and 90 percent over 20 years, at 12 percent inflation: a rate which was exceeded in the 1979–80 period.

The only real solution for retirees is the end of inflation. The same is true for active workers. Renewed inflation would jeopardize both Social Security *and* private pensions. The fact that one system is indexed and the other is not does not represent a statement of success and failure. Over the long term society cannot afford the luxury of full indexing if initial benefit levels are maintained.

GOVERNMENT REGULATION

The 70s and 80s saw a marked increase in the scope of government regulation of employee benefits—both pension and welfare programs. The movement in this area was part of a broad general expansion of the government's role in numerous areas of the economy. Many of the changes adopted were not preceded by detailed analysis of costs, benefits, or secondary consequences. Experience with the changes indicates that many carried undesired and unexpected results.

Regulatory thrusts which never succeeded were also prominent. Such was the case of government run national health insurance and comprehensive health care cost containment.

During the 90s it is unlikely that these initiatives will be enacted into law. In addition, it is likely that regulation imposed by ERISA will be adjusted and in some cases removed.

- Reporting and disclosure requirements are likely to be reduced in cases where no apparent gain resulted from the requirement.
- Adjustments to the program of the Pension Benefit Guaranty Corporation are likely to continue as more experience with the program is gathered.
- Emphasis is likely to be given to making all benefit components work better together—including emphasis on integration of retirement benefit programs, disability benefit programs, and health benefit programs.
- Greater equity is likely to be sought for various benefit programs in terms of tax treatment, particularly retirement programs. This is likely to include maximizing flexibility of program design so that the maximum number of people are accommodated while introducing portability and limiting preretirement distributions.
- Continued attention will be given to improving the quality and cost effectiveness of health care, with special emphasis on provision for the needy and assuring that retirement, health, and income promises are kept, once made.
- Welfare reform will continue to be discussed, with reforms likely to place increased emphasis on state and local governments. In addition, the Supplemental Security Income program is likely to be expanded as a vehicle for income delivery.

The overall role of government as direct provider is not likely to *expand* significantly in the 90s. It will, however, continue to be a very active actor and will continue to impose new requirements. Knowledge of the regulatory environment will become no less necessary, in spite of the Reagan administration's emphasis on fairer regulation. The 90s will provide an excellent opportunity for study, review, and refinement, with the public and private sector increasingly working together as partners rather than adversaries.

EMPLOYEE BENEFIT TRENDS

The period ahead will be one of challenge and change for employee benefits. Their major role in the total compensation package will be recognized, even if the characterization of "fringe benefits" persists. The combined effects of economic, political, and population changes will not and cannot be ignored. The dynamics of change are already in progress, with much of the 90s likely to be reinforcing.

During the late 1970s a number of study groups were appointed to look at the future of components of the employee benefits world including the National Commission on Social Security (NCSS), the President's Commission on Pension Policy (PCPP), the National Commission for an Agenda for the 80s, the Minimum Wage Study Commission (MWSC), and the White House Conference On the Aging.

These groups produced well over 100 recommendations on how to "improve" employee benefit programs. The recommendations most likely to be adopted relate to incentives to encourage retirement income savings and capital formation: they deal with recognized economic problems. In other areas action is not as likely. For example, the keystone recommendation of the PCPP was for creation of a mandatory private pension system. The NCSS recommended strongly *against* such a system. Further, such a requirement would appear to be contrary to the increasing strong spirit of deregulation present in the country.[1]

The private sector also exhibited increasing concern in the late 1970s with creation of organizations such as the Employee Benefit Research Institute (EBRI) in Washington, D.C., and development of programs such as Certified Employee Benefit Specialist (CEBS) training. Both give recognition to the growing importance of employee benefits to national and organizational policy and management.

There are already trends for the 1990s taking form which are likely to reinforce the concern noted above. They include:

- The management of employee benefits is increasingly recognized as an important and vital business function. As such, the function will be given increasing prominence within organizations and increasing responsibility. Employee benefits will become more of a career

---

[1] Much of the research by MWSC is applicable to the mandatory private pension proposal since it would require a payroll expense. Discussion of the PCPP recommendations can be found in "Toward a National Retirement Income Policy: Priorities for the Eighties?" *Labor Law Journal,* May 1981, and *Retirement Income Opportunities in an Aging America: Program Coverage and Benefit Entitlement,* Employee Benefit Research Institute, 1981.

area, rather than a stop along the management training schedule. This should lead to increasingly responsible management of benefit programs to the advantage of employers and employees.

- Efficiency in the financing of benefit programs will be increasingly emphasized. Cost management will be the watchword. Some of these changes may be the result of legislative activity. Cutbacks in federal government expenditures will lead to "cost shifting" to other levels of government and employers, and to greater consumer choice and the development of classes of medical care. (In addition, emphasis on better health and wellness is likely to increase.)
- Efficiency in benefit design will be increasingly emphasized in an effort to eliminate and prevent overlap and to provide participants with the particular benefits they need. Depending on economic developments, this could include benefit cutbacks during the 90s. Flexible compensation and benefits will expand as cost pressures close in and as the makeup of the work force continues to change. A continuing emphasis on employee productivity will speed this trend.
- Continued expansion of dental plans, vision care plans, group legal plans, and other benefits, which realized substantial growth during the 70s and 80s will be experienced. The more broadly flexible compensation is adopted, the greater the speed with which extension of those benefits will occur.
- Relatively new employee benefits, such as long-term care insurance, group auto and group homeowners, will be offered, and preretirement counseling and financial counseling will expand as employee benefits.
- The trend toward providing supplemental defined contribution plans will continue. Such plans provide a means of better accommodating relatively short-service workers. Defined benefit plans will continue to provide the base level of retirement income above social security.
- Advances in computers and their voice simulation capabilities will lead to more understanding of programs by participants, will enhance communications, and make flexible compensation an option for the smallest employers.
- Continuation of employee benefits into retirement will be more and more common, as will part-time or contract employment of annuitants. These changes will be a natural addition to a growing emphasis on preretirement counseling and the effects of the Age Discrimination in Employment Act. Employers have increasing incentives to make retirement attractive. Retirees have now been recognized

as both a growing market and as a growing political force. Both their relative numbers and life expectancies are increasing, and the market is beginning to respond. Further, flexible compensation and benefit programs make it easier to accommodate the needs of retirees by balancing pre- and postretirement benefits.

- Employers will recognize the liability associated with retiree health and life benefits and move to (1) prefund them and (2) redesign them with cost-management in mind.

Beyond these developments we are likely to see increasing recognition of the advantages of private sector benefit provisions. The most striking advantage of providing benefits through the private sector is flexibility: the ability to adjust quickly to changing employee desires. Flexible benefit programs, whether formally structured or not, are likely to become much more common during the 90s to accommodate changes in the work force. These programs allow the employee to select the particular benefits desired. For two-earner families—now nearly 60 percent of all households—this is particularly attractive. In addition, such an approach could help achieve the goals of efficiency in financing and benefit design.

The public and private sectors will see increasing advantages in cooperation, coordination, and nonduplication. Regulatory and legislative initiatives are likely to be consistent with such recognition.

CONCLUSION

The vast majority of public and private sector workers now enjoy protection for health care. Through government programs such protection is available to nonworkers as well. And, means will develop to assure access to protection to all individuals.

Social Security now promises a floor of income protection to most workers while nonworkers have access to Supplemental Security Income, in-kind benefits, unemployment compensation, workers' compensation, disability income, and other programs.

Supplementing these programs are an array of private income security programs. Private pensions, for example, are now participated in by over 64 percent of all steady full-time workers over age 25. Over 85 percent of those working for large employers have pensions. A quarter of present retirees now receive private pension income, and the percentage continues to grow. Public pensions provide coverage and benefits to many more workers. Of present 22-year-old workers, over 70 percent are likely to retire with an employer-provided pension benefit.

Employers are also providing a wide array of additional programs discussed in this book. They help to meet the needs of tens of millions of persons. They help to maintain morale, ensure family security, and maintain employee health.

Taken together, employee benefit programs provide a blanket of protection against numerous risks. For the most part they deliver with reliability, effectiveness, and efficiency. They are an integral part of our social structure, and they will continue to be.

INDEX

B

F

G

J–K

L

T

U

V

W